AMERICA INTERPRETED

A CONCISE HISTORY WITH READINGS

AMERICA INTERPRETED

A CONCISE HISTORY WITH READINGS

RANDALL B. WOODS
WILLARD B. GATEWOOD

UNIVERSITY OF ARKANSAS

Harcourt Brace College Publishers

Fort Worth   Philadelphia   San Diego   New York   Orlando   Austin   San Antonio
Toronto   Montreal   London   Sydney   Tokyo

PUBLISHER	Christopher P. Klein
SENIOR ACQUISITIONS EDITOR	David Tatom
PRODUCT MANAGER	Steven K. Drummond
DEVELOPMENTAL EDITOR	Sarah Helyar Smith
SENIOR PROJECT EDITOR	Laura J. Hanna
ART DIRECTOR	Candice Johnson Clifford
PRODUCTION MANAGER	Melinda Esco

Cover image: J.C. Wild, *Cincinnati: The Public Landing*, 1835. Cincinnati Historical Society. Detail on spine.

ISBN: 0-15-508293-0
Library of Congress Catalog Number: 97-70873

Address for orders:
Harcourt Brace College Publishers
6277 Sea Harbor Drive
Orlando, FL 32887-6777
1-800-782-4479

Address for editorial correspondence:
Harcourt Brace College Publishers
301 Commerce Street, Suite 3700
Fort Worth, TX 76102

Web site address: http://www.hbcollege.com

Harcourt Brace & Company will provide complimentary instructional aids and supplements or supplement packages to those adopters qualified under our adoption policy. Please contact your sales representative for more information. If as an adopter or potential user you receive supplements you do not need, please return them to your sales representative or send them to: Attn: Returns Department, Troy Warehouse, 465 South Lincoln Drive, Troy, MO 63379.

Printed in the United States of America

7 8 9 0 1 2 3 4 5 6   039   9 8 7 6 5 4 3 2 1

To our wives,

RHODA LANNEN WOODS
and
LU BROWN GATEWOOD

PREFACE

About the Book

America Interpreted, in two volumes, combines concise text with interpretive readings to provide a balanced, yet brief, survey of United States history.

The idea for this work originated several years ago as we searched in vain for a brief textbook and an accompanying reader that complemented and illuminated each other. There are, of course, abundant textbooks and readers, but they are separate and distinct entities. Aside from the expense involved in acquiring two books, students often fail to detect the relationship between assignments in the textbook and in the reader. Without a narrative text to play upon, selections in readers often make little sense to students. To avoid this discontinuity and to reduce costs, we decided to pair in each chapter a concise, engaging narrative text with a compelling article that both supports and builds upon the text. This combined format enables students to relate interpretation to narrative and exposes them to historical analysis in a meaningful way. Readers of *America Interpreted* will cover the factual information as they learn how historians abstract meaning from the past.

There are also stylistic advantages to this approach. Because each new chapter begins with a smooth, articulate transition from the previous chapter, and the text leads the reader into each article by explaining how the selection author came to interpret a given event, the reader can easily proceed from one chapter to the next. Volumes I and II constitute a seamless whole that may be read from start to finish without interruption.

The concise text focuses on events, personalities, and movements that have proved enduring ingredients of the college introductory course in American history. Volume I, up to 1877, addresses the roles of commerce and religion in the development of the colonies; the forces and circumstances leading to the American Revolution; the contours of republicanism; the origins and development of slavery; the evolution of political parties and the two-party system; Manifest Destiny and continental expansion; and the events leading up to and through the Civil War and Reconstruction. Volume II, after 1865, addresses Reconstruction; the impact of industrialization; the American West; prosperity and depression; reform efforts; the rise and decline of liberalism; and the transformation of America's relationship to the international community. At the same time, the narrative incorporates significant aspects of the new social history—gender, everyday life, the role of non-elite groups, and especially

African and Native Americans—that have been the subject of some of the best historical writing during the recent past. We describe and analyze the forces that have contributed to both conflict and continuity in American society.

In selecting articles to be included in *America Interpreted*, we chose significant contributions in intellectual, diplomatic, political, economic, military, social, and cultural history that address themes in the narrative text. The interpretive readings focus on women; African Americans; Native Americans; economic, social, and political institutions; diplomatic policies; reform movements; the marketplace; everyday life; and military affairs. The authors of these selections range from mature, prize-winning scholars to young historians on the cutting edge of their discipline. A wide variety of ideological perspectives are represented, and each of the articles is both provocative and gracefully written.

Although we did not use region as a basic organizing principle, both the text and the readings deal extensively with regional development and distinctiveness. From colonial New England to the slave-holding South to the pre-industrial Midwest to the moving frontier, we describe and analyze the social, cultural, economic, and political makeup of the communities that constituted America. Using a broad range of data from personality sketches to sociological findings, we show how one nation has emerged from many peoples.

The book is organized chronologically and topically. We avoid chronological overlap as much as possible, but to maintain continuity we frequently found it necessary to follow a topic across time.

Pedagogy

In recognition of the enormous resources on the internet becoming available to students of history, we provide a master list of **websites** that are of high quality, extensive in scope, easily accessible, and reliable. Applicable to both volumes of *America Interpreted*, the list is located just before the first chapter in each volume.

To help students synthesize information and learn to draw their own interpretations, the end of each chapter provides **questions for classroom discussion and study** and an extensive list of **recommended readings**. Throughout the text, pictures, tables, figures, and maps bring life and depth to events and concepts.

Instructor's Materials

The **Instructor's Resource Manual,** which covers both Volumes I and II, was carefully prepared by Dr. Thomas DeBlack (Arkansas Tech University) and Dr. Randy Finley (DeKalb College). It consists of two parts: an instructor's manual with test bank, and a multimedia guide. The *instructor's manual* portion of part one contains for each chapter a summary, lecture suggestions, a list of people and terms, a chronology of events covered, and maps with exercises to help students hone their geography skills and reinforce spatially what they have learned. The *test bank* portion of part one contains for each chapter 25–30 multiple-choice items covering both the text and the article, short-answer, and essay questions. The multiple-choice items are balanced by levels of difficulty and by their factual/analytical focus. Answers are provided for each item.

The *multimedia guide* of part two, sorted by chapter, contains a detailed, annotated list of websites; as well as lists of laser discs, videos, films, and transparencies available from commercial and educational organizations.

Acknowledgments

We wish to thank those colleagues who reviewed the many drafts of the manuscript and provided invaluable suggestions. These persons include Frank Alduino, *Anne Arundel Community College*; Janet Allured, *McNeese State University*; Edward H. Beardsley, *University of South Carolina, Columbia*; Jay Coughtry, *University of Nevada, Las Vegas*; Thomas DeBlack, *Arkansas Tech University*; Randy Finley, *DeKalb College*; Julia Greene, *University of Colorado, Boulder*; David E. Hamilton, *University of Kentucky*; Theresa Kaminski, *University of Wisconsin, Stevens Point*; Gail Murray, *Rhodes College*; Carolyn Shapiro, *Grand Valley State University*; David Strauss, *Kalamazoo College*; and Mark Summers, *University of Kentucky*.

We are indebted to numerous other individuals for assistance in bringing this project to fruition. We owe a very special debt of gratitude to Sarah Helyar Smith and Laura J. Hanna, our editors whose skills are equaled only by their patience and graciousness. We relied heavily upon our research assistants, Lori Bogle, April Brown, and Thomas Olmstead. We profited enormously from the counsel provided by our faculty colleagues at the University of Arkansas: Professors James S. Chase, David Sloan, and Jeannie Whayne. In the typing and retyping of the manuscript we depended upon the expertise of Jeanie Wyant, Suzanne Smith, Kimberly Chenault, and Yolanda Amos; we are profoundly grateful for their assistance. Our wives, Rhoda Woods and Lu Gatewood, were constant sources of support and encouragement and are in large measure responsible for the completion of this work.

Randall B. Woods
Willard B. Gatewood

WEB SITES

The following web sites from public, private, educational, and commercial sources are helpful both as broad resources in themselves and as springboards to additional sites. (See the detailed web site list for specific eras or topics in the Instructor's Resource Manual that accompanies this textbook.) Each of these sites has been carefully evaluated, but note that web sites are constantly evolving. You may wish to add, revise, or delete some web sites from this list as additional resources become available. Use these web site addresses exactly as they appear here.

http://lcweb2.loc.gov/ammem/ammemhome.html

Library of Congress American memory digital files; primary source and archival collections of American culture and history. See, e.g., the Library of Congress Prints and Photo Division for Civil War daguerreotypes; and the list and status of future collections.

http://lcweb.loc.gov/spcoll/spclhome.html

Library of Congress special collections; see, e.g., the Lewis & Clark map collection.

http://www.msstate.edu/Archives/History/USA/usa.html

Extensive historical text archive housed at Mississippi State University from early colonial period to present; springboard to sources from other web sites. See, e.g., the nineteenth-century collections.

http://www.thehistorynet.com

Covers American and world history, articles from journals, other resources; from the National Historical Society and Cowles Enthusiast Media

gopher://wiretap.spies.com/11/Gov

Selected federal documents from American history, 1621 to present; international documents

http://www.whitehouse.gov/WH/glimpse/top.html

White House history, presidents, first ladies, and first families

http://www.ipl.org/ref/POTUS

Internet public library reference on presidents of the United States

http://elections.eb.com

Encyclopedia Brittanica's articles on all presidential elections to the present; presidents, vice presidents, documents, data, links to related sites

http://grid.let.rug.nl/~welling/usa/presidents/addresses.html

Presidential inaugural addresses, speeches, and documents from the Revolution to Reconstruction

http://earlyamerica.com

Historic documents from eighteenth-century America; see, e.g., the Keigwin & Mathews Collection of maps, newspapers, and other documents; articles from the *Early American Review.*

http://www.civil-war.net
http://ils.unc.edu/civilwar/civilwar.html

Civil War letters, diaries, photos, battles, documents

http://www.cr.nps.gov/abpp/battles/Contents.html

Civil War summaries of the National Park Service's American Battlefield Protection Program; battle summaries by campaign or by state

http://squash.la.psu.edu/~plarson/smuseum/homepage.html

Museum of Slavery in the Atlantic

http://www.worldwar1.com

Extensive resources on World War I

http://www.bunt.com/~mconrad.links.htm
http://www.lib.muohio.edu/~skimmel/wwii/index.html

Extensive resources on World War II; links to other sites

http://ac.acusd.edu/history/20th/coldwar0.html

Cold War policies, 1945–1991, by year; extensive listings, links to other sites

BRIEF CONTENTS

http://www.ksc.nasa.gov/history/history.html

NASA and the space program

http://www.nara.gov/nara/jfk/jfk.html

President Kennedy assassination records collection of the National Archives and Records Administration

CONTENTS

CHAPTER THREE

CULTURE AND SOCIETY IN COLONIAL AMERICA   76

CHAPTER FOUR

THE AMERICAN REVOLUTION   111

CHAPTER FIVE

THE SEARCH FOR A REPUBLICAN ORDER:
From the Articles of Confederation to the Constitution   167

CHAPTER   SIX

THE NEW REPUBLIC, 1788–1815   201

CHAPTER SEVEN

CHAPTER EIGHT

REORDERING AMERICAN SOCIETY AND CULTURE, 1825–1850   299

CHAPTER NINE

WESTWARD EXPANSION AND THE WAR WITH MEXICO   350

CHAPTER TEN

"THE PECULIAR INSTITUTION":
Slavery and Society in the Antebellum South   382

CHAPTER FOURTEEN

THE INDUSTRIAL REVOLUTION   564

CHAPTER SEVENTEEN

PROGRESSIVISM: The Many Faces of Reform   649

CHAPTER EIGHTEEN

CHAPTER NINETEEN

THE "NEW ERA": 1919–1932   719

C H A P T E R   T W E N T Y

ROOSEVELT'S NEW DEAL   746

CHAPTER TWENTY-ONE

FROM ISOLATIONISM TO GLOBALISM:
The United States and World War II   782

CHAPTER TWENTY-TWO

THE ORIGINS OF THE COLD WAR   833

CHAPTER TWENTY-SEVEN

CHAPTER TWENTY-NINE

SEARCH FOR IDENTITY:
American Politics and Society from Ford to Reagan   1059

CHAPTER   THIRTY

AMERICA INTERPRETED

A CONCISE HISTORY WITH READINGS

CHAPTER ONE

DISCOVERY AND DISASTER:
The Old World Meets the New

During the late sixteenth century and early seventeenth century Europeans, prompted by economics, religion, and statecraft, decided to venture forth upon the high seas and explore the unknown regions that lay beyond the western horizon. In hopes of finding a more direct, less complicated route to the Orient, they encountered instead a huge land mass teeming with strange animal and plant life peopled by individuals they deemed to be uncivilized. The Europeans came by and large to exploit, which they did, but the Americas shaped and even determined the future of those who explored and settled. Out of this intense, fascinating, and often violent encounter emerged nations and peoples that were genetic, cultural, and political blends of European, African, and Native American societies. Out of that mixture, in turn, came communities that were absolutely unique. Two hundred and fifty years after Columbus' voyage, thirteen of those communities, nestled along the east coast of North America, would join together to form the United States.

THE COLUMBIAN DISCOVERY OF AMERICA

By Thursday, October 9, 1492, the tiny Spanish fleet had been at sea for weeks. The three ships, the *Nina*, the *Pinta*, and the *Santa Maria*, were sailing westward across the Atlantic venturing where they believed no European had ever gone before. For several days there had been grumblings and mutinous talk among the crews of all three ships. The admiral of the fleet, Christopher Columbus (Cristobál Colón), conferred with his captains, and they agreed to continue on westward for three more days. On Saturday, October 11, according to the ship's log, there came "floating by the vessel a green rush." Men aboard the *Pinta* fished "a reed and a stick" out of the ocean. Throughout the day the wind blew a gale and the flotilla made a record run of seventy-eight miles. That evening the admiral stood on the sterncastle of the *Santa Maria* and delivered an inspirational talk. Noting "the comfort of the signs of better things to come," he ordered the ships to carry on at full sail through the night despite the high seas.

At two o'clock on the morning of October 12 the lookout aboard the *Pinta*, a seaman named Rodrigo de Triana, spotted a "white sand cliff" gleaming in the moonlight and shouted, "Tierra!, Tierra!" Because Columbus rightly feared reefs and breakers, he ordered the ships to lower sail and lay off shore until dawn. The following morning, the Spaniards found passage through the western reef of a tiny island in the Bahamas and dropped anchor. There on the sandy beach, records the chronicle, "presently they saw naked people, and the Admiral went ashore in the armed ship's boat with the royal standard displayed." Columbus believed that the island upon which he landed—to be named San Salvador—was part of the archipelago that included Japan. He computed the distance by using Italian explorer Marco Polo's overestimates of distances on his overland travels to the Orient plus his own overestimate of the distance Japan was from the Asian mainland (1,500 miles), along with the Egyptian astronomer Ptolemy's underestimate of the size of the world. Thus did Columbus believe that his three thousand mile journey had brought him to the "Indies," when in fact Japan was some 10,600 miles from Europe. Because of this error, the original human inhabitants of the Americas would forever be known to Europeans as "Indians." Perhaps it was poetic justice that the New World took its name not from Columbus but from Amerigo Vespucci, a Florentine travel writer who made four voyages across the Atlantic from 1497 through 1505.

PRE-COLUMBIAN AMERICA

The notion that Columbus "discovered" America ignores the fact, of course, that the Western Hemisphere had been continuously inhabited by human beings for thousands of years. At the time of the first European contact, the Western Hemisphere included more than two thousand distinct ethnic groups speaking nearly five hundred languages. Though Columbus and his successors used one name to refer to the natives they encountered, the inhabitants of the Americas, of course, lived in dozens of distinct communities, each with a separate name. The indigenous peoples of the northern plains referred to themselves as Lakota, meaning "allies," while the inhabitants of the Southwest called themselves Dine, meaning "the people." Now familiar tribal names were usually assigned by Europeans. The terms Apache and Sioux meant "enemy" and were used by those living adjacent to these tribes.

FIGURE 1-1
The Indian Settlement of America

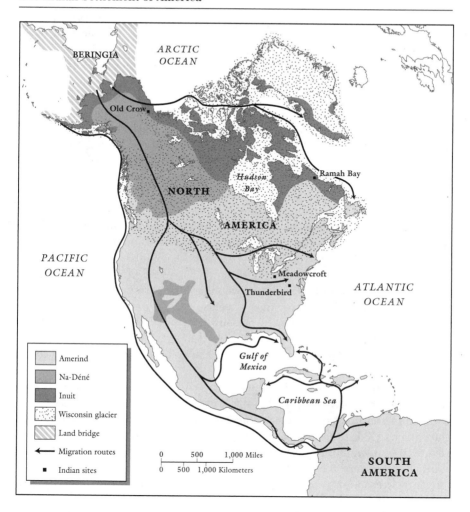

According to the best archaeological data, indigenous Americans were descended from the inhabitants of northeastern Asia (see Figure 1–1). They crossed over a huge land bridge linking the far northwest with Asia some twenty-five thousand years ago during the Pleistocene era. During that epoch much of northern North America was covered with glaciers, and sea levels were as much as 300 feet below current shore lines. Beringia, corresponding to the present-day Bering Straits, was a 750-mile wide neck of temperate land inhabited by mammoths, mastodons, bison, reindeer, and horses. Ancient man pursued this game across the land bridge and through corridors in the ice or by sea along the west coast of North America. South of the glaciers in the Great Plains they encountered another perfect environment for large mammals. Ancient Asian-American hunter-gatherers depended on these herds to provide them with hides for clothing, bones for tools and weapons, and meat for food.

Tools excavated from the earliest settlements were crude choppers or scrapers, but around twelve thousand years ago Native Americans developed a much more advanced weapons system, so-called *Clovis points* (named for the present-day city in New Mexico where they were first found). These sharply pointed, three- to six-inch fluted stones made deadly spears. Clovis bands, evidence of which has been found from present-day New Mexico to Montana and across America to Nova Scotia, consisted of from thirty to fifty individuals who interbred with each other and occasionally took members of other groups as mates. They returned to the same hunting grounds each year and hunted clearly defined geographical areas.

Between ten and fifteen thousand years ago the Pleistocene era came to an end as the huge glaciers melted. The seas rose, inundating coastlines and creating rich fishing banks. Melting glaciers spawned hundreds of rivers and lakes, which enriched the land and diversified the game of North America. The continent came to include all six general classes of global climate: frozen tundra, subarctic forests, temperate woodlands, deserts, arid grasslands, and tropical jungles. Observing the river systems, weather patterns, vegetation, and soil types, geographers divided the present-day United States into seven distinct regions: Northeast, Southwest, South, Northwest, Great Basin, Great Plains, and California. These regions shaped the lives and cultures of the Indian peoples who inhabited them.

The melting of the glaciers spelled the end of dozens of species of large mammals who thrived in a glacial environment. Native Americans had to depend increasingly on smaller game such as deer and bison. Weapons technology changed to accommodate this new type of game. Spears and arrows featured smaller, more delicate but deadlier points, called *Folsom* after the New Mexico site where they were first discovered. Archaeologists also uncovered stone tools used for grinding cereals and processing other vegetables. By 9000 B.C., then, diet had begun to vary among the Indians of the Great Plains. The end of the Pleistocene era prompted new adaptations in other regions: hunting and gathering along the humid eastern seaboard, subsistence foraging in the arid Great Basin, and fishing along the northwest coast.

CULTURES OF THE ARID SOUTHWEST

In the huge basin surrounded by mountains that comprises the present-day states of Utah and Nevada a distinctive desert culture developed. This one-time gigantic inland sea was arid and hostile to life forms while at the same time stunningly beautiful, consisting as it did of yawning canyons and majestic mesas. Small bands of nomads gathered roots, harvested prickly pear, and hunted small game in one season; moved to the tops of mesas to collect pinon nuts, berries, and seeds in another; and fished in mountain streams in another. They lived in caves and stone enclosures. The harsh climate and prevailing religious beliefs created a strong sense of community and a deemphasis on excessive personal accumulation. Men and women from different tribes intermarried, creating ties and gradually a sense of shared identity. Decisions were made through negotiation and consensus.

EASTERN WOODLANDS

During this period the whole of eastern North America was one gigantic forest, hardwoods to the north and southern pine to the south. The denizens of these woodlands (archaeologists use the term *Archaic peoples* to refer to native North Americans who lived from c. 8000 B.C. to 1500 B.C.) lived off a wide variety of smaller mammals, fish, and wild plants. They utilized bone, shell, copper, horn, ivory, and leather to fashion tools, weapons, utensils, and ornaments. Over time, trade networks developed linking villages, markets, ideas, and religious beliefs. Human burials became more elaborate during the Archaic era as native Americans began burying their dead with their personal possessions. Extensive, complex burial mounds remain the most visible testimony to these ancient peoples. Archaic Americans did not as a rule make distinctions based on rank, class, or political power. Gender roles were another matter, however. Men fished and hunted; women harvested and prepared wild plants. Both men and women made tools and weapons, but in general, the male's duties entailed travel, whereas the female's activities kept the women close to the settlement where they bore and raised children.

THE DIVERSIFICATION OF NATIVE AMERICAN CULTURES

By 1500 B.C. the inhabitants of North America were in transition. New, more complex mores and institutions emerged from Archaic cultures. In the Northeast, Southeast, and Southwest, agriculture paved the way for populous trading centers and the beginning of settled life. Plant cultivation had originated in the highlands of central Mexico about 7000 B.C. Maize in particular flourished, and by 1500 B.C. it had adapted to a wide range of American climates. Societies fully committed to farming were able to support as many as one hundred people per square mile, whereas foraging and hunting societies required nearly one hundred times that area to feed the same number of people. Agriculture spawned settled communities which in turn facilitated cultural complexity.

Higher population density led Native Americans to group themselves into clans, and they in turn associated themselves in tribes which demonstrated ethnic, linguistic, and cultural identity. Chiefs—individuals respected for their deeds and longevity—led during times of war and presided over councils of

Native Americans, ca. 1500, fishing and planting in their natural habitat as depicted by early European settlers.

elders who made decisions for the tribe. Crimes committed by individuals against individuals of another clan were usually avenged by the entire membership of the victim's clan against the entire membership of the offender's extended family. Native Americans invariably considered land to be the common property of the people, to be hunted and farmed collectively.

Religion, not surprisingly, grew out of life's two basic activities: hunting and fishing. The hunting tradition exalted the relationship between man and animal. Tribes frequently paid homage to a master animal such as the sacred bear. Male adolescents usually endured a rite of passage involving exposure to the elements, fasting, self-inflicted wounds, and hallucination. Tribal members evidencing deep spirituality, that is, sensitivity to the realm in which animal and man intersected, became shamen—"medicine" men or women. In the farming tradition, tribes worshipped the elements and seasons. These religions usually featured organized cults with permanent priesthoods. The more complex societies were characterized by a war–sacrifice–cannibalism cycle that glorified violence and the consumption of a foe's flesh.

THE ANCIENT ONES

Agriculture and thus tribal civilization moved northward from Central and South America very slowly. Around 2000 B.C. rainfall had increased in the Southwest, augmenting food sources and raising population density. Cultivated plants from Mexico began to appear during this time in what is now New Mexico, Arizona, and Utah. Among the most notable of the cultures growing out of the agricultural revolution were the Anasazi (a Navajo term meaning "ancient ones"). Between 600 and 1200 A.D. these ancestors of the modern Pueblo Indians expanded over a wide area and became the most powerful people in the region. Living originally in round houses with walls of stone slabs or clay plaster, and domed roofs of logs and mud, the Anasazi eventually carved complex dwellings out of caves high in the canyons of the Southwest. In Chaco Canyon in present-day northwestern New Mexico, a cluster of twelve villages forged a powerful confederation numbering about fifteen thousand people. A system of roads radiated out of the canyon to satellite pueblos situated as far as sixty-five miles away. A drought began dispersing the Anasazi around 1500 A.D., but their descendents, the Pueblo, Zuni, and Hopi, continue to inhabit the Southwest (see Figure 1–2).

SOCIETIES OF THE MISSISSIPPI

Effective maize cultivation spread gradually into the Great Plains and the trans-Mississippi east from the Southwest. As a result, outside the land of the Pueblos (a Spanish word meaning "village"), social life remained relatively undeveloped. Indeed, societies in the modern sense were scarce. There were exceptions. Native Americans occupying the Ohio and lower Mississippi River Valleys participated in a mound-building culture. Complex earthen mounds acted as fortresses in time of war and as burial sites for the elite. The Mississippian settlement at Cahokia, near present-day East St. Louis, Illinois, comprised some forty thousand inhabitants in 1100 A.D. Cahokia was the religious and trading center for villages all over Central and Northeastern North America. While Cahokia flourished, some five thousand persons had concentrated in a single settlement at what is now Poverty Point on the Mississippi River in present-day Louisiana. That community was flanked by two large mounds and surrounded by eight concentric embankments which were used for solar observations and religious practices. For three centuries Poverty Point imported crystal, obsidian, copper, and quartz and redistributed them to nearby communities.

EASTERN WOODLAND CULTURES

Squash, maize, and bean culture reached the Southeastern portions of North America around 1000 A.D. The rich soil there coupled with sophisticated

FIGURE 1-2
Early Indian Societies

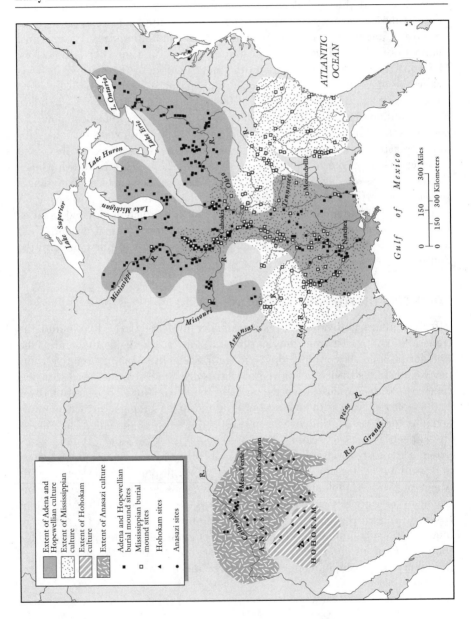

farming techniques resulted in some of the densest populations in pre-Columbian North America, including the Cherokees, Choctaws, and Creeks. In the northeastern woodlands, the Iroquois came closest to duplicating the great nation-states of South America, the Aztec and Inca.

According to legend, the Iroquois Confederacy, which included the Mohawks, the Oneidas, the Onondagas, the Cayugas, and the Senecas, was formed in the late 1500s by Deganawidah and Hiawatha. At the center of Iroquois society was the longhouse, a wooden structure twenty-five feet wide and up to four hundred feet long. Each contained three to five fireplaces around which extended families, all related through the maternal bloodline, gathered. Female members of the tribe raised squash, sunflowers, corn, and other crops that supported up to fifty longhouses. These communities were surrounded by log palisades.

The peoples who inhabited upstate New York eventually coalesced into the five nations that Hiawatha formed into the Iroquois confederation. Apparently, persistent warfare for control of territory was responsible for the alliance. The Iroquois Confederacy outlawed warfare among members and established regulated gift giving as a substitute for conflict and revenge. The nations or chiefdoms celebrated together and presented a common front to outsiders, but they remained essentially independent of one another. On the eastern flank of the association, the Mohawks would come to specialize as traders with the Europeans while the Senecas to the west became fur suppliers.

NATIVE AMERICANS ON THE EVE OF EUROPEAN CONTACT

For the most part, however, Native Americans at the time of Columbus' arrival in 1492 lived in small, scattered villages; they were hunter-gatherers who farmed. Members of a tribe might congregate periodically for feasts, religious rituals, or for protection from rival tribes, but there were few permanent settlements. In contrast to Europeans, who sought aggressively to manipulate nature for their comfort and profit, Indians treaded lightly on the land. They based their lives on the life-cycles of the plants and animals. Native Americans revered the physical world and attributed spiritual properties to the sun, earth, sky, and water as well as to animals. The Indians' respect for the environment was as much a matter of necessity as choice, however. Inhabitants of the Northeast set massive forest fires to establish open areas better suited to hunting deer and wild game. This explained the open, park-like environment that confronted and astounded Europeans who arrived in the early seventeenth century. Most obviously, Indians did not obtrude on nature because there were too few of them to do so. At the time of Columbus' arrival, no more than ten million persons inhabited the deserts of the Southwest, the plains of central North America, and the great forests of the Northeast. In addition, the shock of

European "discovery" would descend upon them with a force that far exceeded any act of war or natural disaster that they had hitherto experienced.

EXPLORATIONS TO THE NEW WORLD

PRE-COLUMBIAN EXPLORERS

Christopher Columbus was certainly not the first explorer to reach the Americas. According to legend and folklore an Irish monk, St. Brendan, journeyed to North America in the sixth century, and seaborn explorers from Polynesia and East Asia reached the coast of what is now British Columbia around the same time. More based in fact were the Scandinavian expeditions of the Norsemen, who settled Iceland in 874 and Greenland in 986. Around 1000 A.D. Leif Ericson probably sighted Labrador and Newfoundland, and possibly sailed as far as Cape Cod. It is almost certain that continental Europeans had not heard of the explorations of the Norsemen. Charts of the Atlantic and beyond simply did not exist. Europeans faced in the opposite direction toward the eastern Mediterranean, the Middle East, and beyond. It was this concern, ironically, that was ultimately to provide the motive for Columbus' voyages.

MOTIVATIONS TO EXPLORE

The Spice Trade

By the fifteenth century trade with the Orient—or the Indies, as Asia was called in Europe—in such exotic products as spices, chinaware, carpets, perfumes, and silk—was extensive and extremely profitable. Initially, the Italian city-states dominated this commerce because of their strategic location athwart the main trading routes between West and East. In the fourteenth century the nation-states of Western Europe—Spain, Portugal, England, and France—began taking shape, and they grew increasingly dissatisfied with the existing trade pattern. Having to rely on the Italians was expensive and strategically unwise. Thus did the governments of the Western European states begin to look for a direct route to the East.

The Age of Discovery

The Age of Discovery, which stretched from the fifteenth through the eighteenth centuries, was, then, the product of economic imperatives and the resulting rivalry between nations. These processes and conditions determined the timing, extent, and nature of European contact with the New World. During the Renaissance—approximately 1300 A.D. through 1650 A.D.—three developments of great importance occurred.

Emergence of Nation-States   From the thirteenth through the fifteenth centuries, the feudal lords that ruled Europe in loose associations tied together by shifting, temporary obligations gave way to the *new monarchs*, kings with the money and military might sufficient to enforce their will through law and taxes on fixed geographical areas. Portugal emerged as a nation-state in the thirteenth and fourteenth centuries; Spain, England, and France in the fifteenth.

According to the economic theory of mercantilism that prevailed at the time, all nations were engaged in a constant struggle for survival with each other. The wealth of the world, defined primarily in terms of silver and gold and secondarily in terms of raw materials—food, fiber, timber, minerals—was fixed. The object of foreign trade was to acquire as much of the world's wealth as possible either directly through colonization or indirectly by supplying at an exorbitant price the essentials of life to one's competitors. Thus did the governments of the early nation-states encourage their citizens to venture out into the unexplored corners of the world.

The Reformation   The Protestant Reformation, which began with Martin Luther's dissent from Catholic doctrine in 1519, also served as an important impetus to the Age of Exploration. Luther and other dissenters insisted that individual Christians could communicate with God through prayer and scripture, called for greater participation of laypersons in religious services, and in general argued for a less dominating role in the church for the pope and priests. The Catholic church launched the Counter-Reformation, and a number of dissenters sought refuge in the New World. Catholicism took a very dim view of commerce and business—the taking of interest was for centuries viewed by the church as a sin—while Protestantism looked with favor on these activities.

Among the most active and influential of the Protestant reformers was the French-born Swiss theologian, John Calvin. Calvinism involved the doctrine of predestination; that is, one's salvation was determined before birth. Notification of salvation came through divine revelation during the believer's lifetime. But lest this emphasis lead to a life of irresponsible behavior, Calvinist divines emphasized that only those who led lives of thrift, industry, sobriety, and social responsibility could possibly have been singled out by God. This in turn led to the notion that one's material well-being, one's level of prosperity, was an outward symbol of an inner state of grace.

Technological Advances   More prosaic but just as important in stimulating European exploration were technical innovations in sailing and navigation. During the 1400s most European sea trade was conducted in galleys, but these low-beamed, oar-driven vessels were unsuitable for transoceanic voyages. By the end of the century sails had taken over. Ships used in early voyages of discovery were square-rigged, or a combination of square- and lateen-rigged. Square-rigged ships had the advantage of the sail area being broken up into manageable parts. Their disadvantage was that they were not as maneuverable as lateen-rigged vessels. A combination of the two was thought to be the best compromise. Ship hulls became heavy and broad-beamed for stability, and they were raised at each end to create "castles" for purposes of waging war.

By the end of the fifteenth century navigators, relearning knowledge gleaned by Arab astronomers and astrologers, had devised several methods for finding latitude, thus enabling voyagers to locate their positions relative to land masses. Astrolabes and, subsequently, quadrants measured the angle between a chosen star and the horizon. Ships had carried compasses since at least 1300: They had evolved from magnetized needles on chips of wood floating in bowls of water to a pivoted needle swinging above a compass marked with the four cardinal "winds" and the now familiar thirty-two points.

PORTUGAL LEADS THE WAY

Of the four Atlantic-bordering European nations, Portugal was the early leader in venturing out onto the open seas. Its pioneering status was due to early unification, geographical position, and vision of such figures as Prince Henry the Navigator, a clearheaded man who dispelled legends about dragons and boiling oceans. The fifth son of John I of Portugal, born in 1394, Henry devoted his life to the advancement of nautical science, geography, astronomy, cartography, and Portuguese commerce. His dream and that of the Portuguese monarchy was to Christianize middle Africa and then establish commercial and religious beachheads in Asia, activities that would both halt the spread of Islam, which had by then penetrated both Spain and the Balkans, and enrich the mother country.

SPANISH DISCOVERIES

Portugal was too small and poor to maintain its preeminence, however. It soon was eclipsed by Spain and in 1580 was absorbed by that country. In 1492 Columbus claimed the entire New World for Spain, and two years later, Pope Alexander VI promulgated the Demarcation Line of 1494, also known as the Treaty of Tordesillas, which established a north-south boundary bisecting the Atlantic, giving the Old World for purposes of colonization to Portugal and the New to Spain. A miscalculation cut off the eastern shoulder of South America, thus ensuring that Brazil would belong to Portugal. Columbus himself explored much of the Caribbean during his four voyages conducted between 1492 and 1504. He died two years later, but within a generation Spanish adventurers had taken possession of most of the Caribbean basin.

A second wave of exploration was stimulated by rumors of an incredibly wealthy city, the capital of the highly complex Aztec civilization, deep in the interior of what is now Mexico. Between 1519 and 1521 the brutal conquistador Hernando Cortés, in search of gold and silver, destroyed the Aztec empire, killing, torturing, terrorizing, and eventually enslaving the Native Americans whom he encountered. In succeeding years Alvar Núñez Cabeza de Vaca explored the northern edge of the Gulf of Mexico. Between 1539 and 1541

*Francisco Pizarro, conquistadores, and a Catholic
priest seek to convert an Indian chieftain to Christianity
through torture.*

Hernando de Soto trekked through the Southeast and discovered the Mississippi River. In 1542 Francisco Vásquez de Coronado, in search of El Dorado, one of the names given to the mythical city of gold and silver that helped inspire Spanish exploration, reached into the Southwest making contact with Indian villages as far north as the present-day states of Colorado and Kansas.

A final, third wave of exploration led by Francisco Pizarro—a man who was illiterate and as unscrupulous as Cortés—established Spanish rule in Peru, Ecuador, Chile, and northern Argentina, and in the process destroyed the ancient civilization of the Incas.

THE SPANISH EMPIRE

Spanish rule in the Americas was hierarchical, exploitive, and rigid. Thousands of colonial officials reported to the Council of the Indies and regulated every aspect of the economic and social life of the colony. Spain's rulers viewed their New World possessions solely as producers of wealth, and in their determination to extract every last escudo they ravaged the human and material resources of the Americas.

Five principal groups constituted the population of Spain's New World empire. Sitting atop the colonial social structure were imperial officeholders—viceroys, judges, church officials, and governors. Recruited in Spain and expecting to return there, they never developed any sense of independence from Madrid or commitment to their respective colonies. American-born leaders of Spanish descent, or creoles, were more firmly rooted in the New World, but they constituted only 1.25 percent of the population. Mestizos, people of mixed European and Indian ancestry, constituted a lower middle class of small farmers and shopkeepers. African Americans were imported as slaves and brutally exploited; culturally important, they remained politically insignificant. Finally, by far the most numerous population were Native Americans, mostly Aztecs and Incas. Though members of sophisticated civilizations, the Indians were for the most part viewed by their European conquerors as savages and heathens. Native Americans were used as a mass labor force, the plight of whose members was only somewhat less onerous if they converted to Catholicism.

Not only were the indigenous residents of the Americas denied political rights and enmeshed in a system of permanent debt servitude called peonage, they also were devastated by smallpox, cholera, and other Old World bacteria and viruses. The natives of pre-Columbian America were free of epidemic diseases and consequently free of the antibodies needed to fight them. A shipload of colonists arriving in Hispaniola in 1516 introduced smallpox to the native population. By 1520 the disease had spread to Mexico and thence through trade routes to the Aztec and Inca populations to the south. In 1524 smallpox devastated the Incas of Peru, softening up the population for Spanish conquest eight years later. Measles arrived in 1531, the bubonic plague in 1545, and influenza in 1559. According to recently compiled statistics the population of New Spain declined from twenty-five million at the time of the conquest to around one million at the beginning of the seventeenth century.

Ironically, at the same time the Europeans were introducing bacteria and viruses that undermined the physical well-being of Native Americans, the indigenous culture was supplying Spain and its neighbors with nutrients that sustained life. Centuries of geographic isolation had produced different evolutionary patterns; as a result, the flora and fauna of the Western and Eastern Hemispheres were strikingly different. Europeans encountered a wealth of new food crops—many of them cultivated by Native Americans—and exported them to Europe. Beans, squash, potatoes, and maize (corn) so enriched the diet of Europeans that the continent experienced a major population explosion as a result of the age of exploration.

Meanwhile, the riches accruing to metropolitan Spain were being squandered by inept rulers such as Philip II who expelled the Jews and Moors from his population, thus depriving that country of its merchants and middle class. Gradually, Spain lost ground to its principal colonial rivals, England and France, its decline culminating with the defeat in 1588 of the Spanish Armada in the stormy seas of the English Channel.

ORIGINS OF ENGLISH COLONIALISM

England's entrance into the colonial enterprise was far less dramatic, decisive, and profitable than Spain's, although the British Empire proved in the end to be far more powerful and enduring. The first Englishman to assert a claim to North America was John Cabot who, under the reign of Henry VII (1485–1509), discovered and began the exploration of Labrador, Nova Scotia, and Newfoundland. Upon his death, Cabot's son, Sebastian, continued into the interior and encountered the Hudson Bay area during the years 1508–1509.

Henry VIII (1509–1547) proved to be far more interested in consolidating his power at home and in Europe than in settling the New World. While Henry was busy creating the Anglican church and dividing his countrymen between Catholics and Protestants, British fishermen exploited the rich grounds off Newfoundland and Nova Scotia. Beyond erecting a few shacks for wintering and drying fish, however, the English established no permanent presence. Then in the middle of the sixteenth century a series of dramatic events, economic and diplomatic, turned England's attention westward.

British prosperity during the first half of the sixteenth century was based on the growing, weaving, and sale of wool—primarily to Europe through the market at Antwerp in the Netherlands. More and more of England's land was converted to pasture for sheep, and the bulk of its capital was invested in machinery and labor for producing cloth. In 1551 the market, glutted with raw fiber, collapsed; woolen exports fell by 35 percent. Merchants and financiers began looking for other markets and trade routes and for new investment opportunities. The New World beckoned.

At the same time, Britain's traditionally pro-Spanish foreign policy began to change. Throughout Henry VIII's reign England's preoccupation had been its rivalry with France. In this confrontation, friendship with Spain had been helpful. But in 1558 Queen Elizabeth ascended the throne. She was more and more inclined toward Protestantism, and that predeliction increasingly dominated British foreign policy. In Europe, the English supported the Huguenots—French Protestants who engaged in intermittent rebellion against the crown—and the equally rebellious Protestants in the Netherlands who were struggling against Spanish rule. Elizabeth did not feel strong enough to take on the Spanish Empire directly, but she encouraged her countrymen to raid Spanish shipping and ports in the Caribbean and on the Spanish mainland. John Hawkins and Sir Francis Drake, two of the Queen's favorites, proved spectacularly successful.

THE ADVENT OF THE CHARTER COMPANIES

By the middle of the sixteenth century, enterprising English businessmen were seeking and obtaining charters from the crown for trading monopolies with overseas areas. These organizations, from the Guinea Company established in 1555 to the East India Company founded in 1600, were joint stock operations, efficient machines for the establishment and exploitation of distant points. This type of concern was initiated by the Dutch but perfected by the English. In the early stages of colonization, in West Africa and India, for example, merchants engaged in a common line of trade with a distant place were anxious to protect their ships at sea and their goods once they had reached their destination. To achieve this end businessmen and financiers associated in voluntary companies that might last for one voyage or several. As trade expanded, the advantages of continuity and control became clear. Only a permanent company, for instance, could erect buildings overseas to store and protect goods. Only a body with the power to make rules could control the activities of the colonists. Both ends could be accomplished by obtaining a charter from the crown which granted the company a monopoly on trade with the designated area, empowered the members of the company to make laws, and provided for perpetual succession. In the joint stock variation that typified British colonial operations in North America, members or "freemen" acquired shares by putting up money or material, or by going to the colony as planters. The members met regularly in general court to conduct their affairs; selectmen managed the enterprise between court meetings.

PROPAGANDISTS FOR EMPIRE

During the last quarter of the sixteenth century, interest in westward expansion took root in the British popular mind. In 1576 Sir Humphrey Gilbert published an essay called "Discourse of a Discovery of a New Passage to Cataia" (roughly, China) in which he "proved" that America was an island cut off from Asia. North America, Gilbert correctly observed, had no Asiatic animals nor any "Tartars." He deduced the existence of a Northwest Passage (from accounts of Hudson's Bay) that would allow mariners to traverse the New World by sea and reach the Orient. In 1578 Gilbert sought and obtained from the crown a charter for establishing a colony in New England or Nova Scotia. The enterprise was a disastrous failure, no Northwest Passage was ever found, and Sir Humphrey drowned in 1583 when his ship, the *Squirrel*, sank on the way home from yet another attempt to establish a colony in the New World.

Equally unsuccessful was Sir Walter Raleigh who tried in 1585 and 1587 to establish colonies on Roanoke Island adjacent to the coast of North Carolina. The first group of colonists returned to England after a year, and members of the second had mysteriously vanished by the time a relief expedition arrived in 1590. Though the settlement was quite intact, no Europeans were to be found. This last expedition, however, was responsible for the first American-born child of English parents, Virginia Dare.

The most effective propagandist for colonizing America was Richard Hakluyt, a cousin of Sir Humphrey Gilbert. He told the British people of the world beyond the sea in *Principal Navigations, Voyages, and Discoveries of the English Nation* published in 1589. This and other pieces, including *Discourse Concerning Western Planting* (1584), expounded on the various justifications for colonizing: It was England's duty to Christianize the heathens who occupied the virgin lands of the New World; North America would make an excellent base

Anglorum in Virginiam aduentus.   II.

A map drawn by early English explorers, ca. 1600, depicting Sir Walter Raleigh's colony on Roanoke Island.

for attacking Spanish possessions; colonies would provide England with raw materials it would otherwise have to buy from Spain, and they would constitute new markets for British manufactured products; finally, settlements in America would provide outlets for England's "surplus" population, making available opportunities especially for those worthy but unfortunate men who then "pestered" the nation's prisons and who "for small robberies are daily hanged."

And, in fact, the rigid class structure, injustices, squalor, and disease that characterized London and other British towns in the sixteenth century made Britons dream of a better place. Sir Thomas More published *Utopia* in 1516, and by the latter part of the century it was being widely read by would-be colonizers. Utopia was a fictional island set in the northern sea with temperate climate. Everyone was honestly employed and no one exploited or overworked. Cities were separated by at least a day's journey and were surrounded by extensive pastoral settings. City workers and farmers labored six hours a day and changed places every six months. Cities consisted of wide streets and three-story fireproof houses with gardens. Democracy prevailed and education was free and compulsory. Utopians cultivated virtue but not to the point of denying the pleasures of life. This early English dream underlay efforts at colonization—the creation of an ideal society. It was therefore not surprising that as Humphrey Gilbert's ship sank, he was last seen on the quarterdeck joyfully reading to his men from More's *Utopia*.

In the following passage from his book, Conquest of Paradise, *Kirkpatrick Sale provides a fiercely revisionist view of Christopher Columbus and his first encounter with the New World. Columbus comes across as a typical fifteenth-century European, uninterested in nature, culturally provincial, and, above all, avaricious. Columbus and his fellows looked at the Americas, with their flora and fauna, primarily as sources of wealth, as resources for personal and national exploitation. Native Americans, in Sale's account, come across as inhabitants of an Edenic world free of conflict and perfectly attuned to nature.*

1492–93
Kirkpatrick Sale

Admiral Colón [Cristobál Colón, i.e., Christopher Columbus] spent a total of ninety-six days exploring the lands he encountered on the far side of the Ocean Sea—four rather small coralline islands in the Bahamian chain and two substantial coastlines of what he finally acknowledged were larger islands—every one of which he "took possession of" in the name of his Sovereigns.

The first he named San Salvador, no doubt as much in thanksgiving for its welcome presence after more than a month at sea as for the Son of God whom it honored; the second he called Santa María de la Concepcíon, after the Virgin whose name his flagship bore; and the third and fourth he called Fernandina and Isabela, for his patrons, honoring Aragon before Castile for reasons never explained (possibly protocol, possibly in recognition of the chief sources of backing for the voyage). . . .

It was not that the islands were in need of names, mind you, nor indeed that Colón was ignorant of the names the native peoples had already given them, for he frequently used those original names before endowing them with his own. Rather, the process of bestowing new names went along with "taking possession of" those parts of the world he deemed suitable for Spanish ownership, showing the royal

from Kirkpatrick Sale, *The Conquest of Paradise: Christopher Columbus and the Columbian Legacy* (New York: Alfred A. Knopf, 1990) pp. 92–122.

banners, erecting various crosses and pronouncing certain oaths and pledges. If this was presumption, it had an honored heritage: it was Adam who was charged by his Creator with the task of naming "every living creature," including the product of his own rib, in the course of establishing "dominion over" them. . . .

This business of naming and "possessing" foreign islands was by no means casual. The Admiral took it very seriously, pointing out that "it was my wish to bypass no island without taking possession" (October 15) and that "in all regions [I] always left a cross standing" (November 16) as a mark of Christian dominance. . . .

But consider the implications of this act and the questions it raises again about what was in the Sovereigns' minds, what in Colón's. Why would the Admiral assume that these territories were in some way *un*possessed—even by those clearly inhabiting them—and thus available for Spain to claim? Why would he not think twice about the possibility that some considerable potentate—the Grand Khan of China, for example, whom he later acknowledged (November 6) "must be" the ruler of Española—might descend upon him at any moment with a greater military force than his three vessels commanded and punish him for his territorial presumption? Why would he make the ceremony of possession his very first act on shore, even before meeting the inhabitants or exploring the environs, or finding out if anybody there objected to being thus possessed—particularly if they actually owned the great treasures he hoped would be there? No European would have imagined that anyone—three small boatloads of Indians, say—could come up to a European shore or island and "take possession" of it, nor would a European imagine marching up to some part of North Africa or the Middle East and claiming sovereignty there with impunity. Why were these lands thought to be different?

Could there be any reason for the Admiral to assume he had reached "unclaimed" shores, new lands that lay far from the domains of any of the potentates of the East? Can that really have been in his mind—or can it all be explained as simple Eurocentrism, or Euro-superiority, mixed with cupidity and naiveté?

In any case, it is quite curious how casually and calmly the Admiral took to this task of possession, so much so that he gave only the most meager description of the initial ceremony on San Salvador. . . . We are left only with the image of a party of fully dressed and armored Europeans standing there on the white sand in the blazing morning heat while Escobedo, with his parchment and inkpot and quill, painstakingly writes down the Admiral's oaths. . . .

Once safely "possessed," San Salvador was open for inspection. Now the Admiral turned his attention for the first time to the "naked people" staring at him on the beach—he did not automatically give them a name, interestingly enough, and it would be another six days before he decided what he might call them—and tried to win their favor with his trinkets.

> They all go around as naked as their mothers bore them; and also the women, although I didn't see more than one really young girl. All that I saw were young people [*mancebos*], none of them more than 30 years old. They are very well built, with very handsome bodies and very good faces; their hair [is] coarse, almost like the silk of a horse's tail, and short. They wear their hair over their eyebrows, except for a little in the back that they wear long and never cut. Some of them paint themselves black (and they are of the color of the Canary Islanders, neither black nor

white), and some paint themselves white, and some red, and some with what they find. And some paint their faces, and some of them the whole body, and some the eyes only, and some of them only the nose.

It may fairly be called the birth of American anthropology.

A crude anthropology, of course, as superficial as Colón's descriptions always were when his interest was limited, but simple and straightforward enough, with none of the fable and fantasy that characterized many earlier (and even some later) accounts of new-found peoples. There was no pretense to objectivity, or any sense that these people might be representatives of a culture equal to, or in any way a model for, Europe's. Colón immediately presumed the inferiority of the natives, not merely because (a sure enough sign) they were naked, but because (his society could have no surer measure) they seemed so technologically backward. "It appeared to me that these people were very poor in everything," he wrote on that first day, and, worse still, "they have no iron." And they went on to prove their inferiority to the Admiral by being ignorant of even such a basic artifact of European life as a sword: "They bear no arms, nor are they acquainted with them," he wrote, "for I showed them swords and they grasped them by the blade and cut themselves through ignorance." Thus did European arms spill the first drops of native blood on the sands of the New World, accompanied not with a gasp of compassion but with a smirk of superiority.

Then, just six sentences further on, Colón clarified what this inferiority meant in his eyes:

> They ought to be good servants and of good intelligence [*ingenio*]. . . . I believe that they would easily be made Christians, because it seemed to me that they had no religion. Our Lord pleasing, I will carry off six of them at my departure to Your Highnesses, in order that they may learn to speak.

No clothes, no arms, no possessions, no iron, and now no religion—not even speech: hence they were fit to be servants, and captives. It may fairly be called the birth of American slavery. . . .

To be sure, Colón knew nothing about these people he encountered and considered enslaving, and he was hardly trained to find out very much, even if he was moved to care. But they were in fact members of an extensive, populous, and successful people whom Europe, using its own peculiar taxonomy, subsequently called "Taino" (or "Taíno"), their own word for "good" or "noble," and their response when asked who they were. They were related distantly by both language and culture to the Arawak people of the South American mainland, but it is misleading (and needlessly imprecise) to call them Arawaks, as historians are wont to do, when the term "Taino" better establishes their ethnic and historical distinctiveness. They had migrated to the islands from the mainland at about the time of the birth of Christ, occupying the three large islands we now call the Greater Antilles and arriving at Guanahani (Colón's San Salvador) and the end of the Bahamian chain probably sometime around A.D. 900. There they displaced an earlier people, the Guanahacabibes (sometimes called Guanahatabeys), who by the time of the European discovery occupied only the western third of Cuba and possibly remote corners of Española; and there, probably in the early fifteenth century, they eventually confronted another people moving up the islands from the mainland, the Caribs, whose culture eventually occupied a dozen small islands of what are called the Lesser Antilles.

The Tainos were not nearly so backward as Colón assumed from their lack of dress. (It might be said that it was the Europeans, who generally kept clothed head to foot during the day despite temperatures regularly in the eighties, who were the more unsophisticated in garmenture—especially since the Tainos, as Colón later noted, also used their body paint to prevent sunburn.) Indeed, they had achieved a means of living in a balanced and fruitful harmony with their natural surroundings that any society might well have envied. They had, to begin with, a not unsophisticated technology that made exact use of their available resources, two parts of which were so impressive that they were picked up and adopted by the European invaders: canoa (canoes) that were carved and fire-burned from large silk-cotton trees, "all in one piece, and wonderfully made" (October 13), some of which were capable of carrying up to 150 passengers; and hamaca (hammocks) that were "like nets of cotton" (October 17) and may have been a staple item of trade with Indian tribes as far away as the Florida mainland. Their houses were not only spacious and clean—as the Europeans noted with surprise and appreciation, used as they were to the generally crowded and slovenly hovels and huts of south European peasantry—but more apropos, remarkably resistant to hurricanes; the circular walls were made of strong cane poles set deep and close together ("as close as the fingers of a hand," Colón noted), the conical roofs of branches and vines tightly interwoven on a frame of smaller poles and covered with heavy palm leaves. Their artifacts and jewelry, with the exception of a few gold trinkets and ornaments, were based largely on renewable materials, including bracelets and necklaces of coral, shells, bone, and stone, embroidered cotton belts, woven baskets, carved statues and chairs, wooden and shell utensils, and pottery of variously intricate decoration depending on period and place.

Perhaps the most sophisticated, and most carefully integrated, part of their technology was their agricultural system, extraordinarily productive and perfectly adapted to the conditions of the island environment. It was based primarily on fields of knee-high mounds, called conucos, planted with yuca (sometimes called manioc), batata (sweet potato), and various squashes and beans grown all together in multicrop harmony: the root crops were excellent in resisting erosion and producing minerals and potash, the leaf crops effective in providing shade and moisture, and the mound configurations largely resistant to erosion and flooding and adaptable to almost all topographic conditions including steep hillsides. Not only was the conuco system environmentally appropriate—"conuco agriculture seems to have provided an exceptionally ecologically well-balanced and protective form of land use," according to David Watts's recent and authoritative West Indies—but it was also highly productive, surpassing in yields anything known in Europe at the time, with labor that amounted to hardly more than two or three hours a week, and in continuous yearlong harvest. . . .

In their arts of government the Tainos seem to have achieved a parallel sort of harmony. Most villages were small (ten to fifteen families) and autonomous, although many apparently recognized loose allegiances with neighboring villages, and they were governed by a hereditary official called a *kaseke* (*cacique,* in the Spanish form), something of a cross between an arbiter and a prolocutor, supported by advisers and elders. So little a part did violence play in their system that they seem, remarkably, to have been a society without war (at least we know of no war music or signals or artifacts, and no evidence of intertribal combats) and even without overt conflict (Las Casas reports that no Spaniard ever saw two Tainos fighting). And here we come to what was obviously the Tainos' outstanding cultural achievement, a proficiency in the social arts that led those who first met them to comment unfailingly on their friendliness, their warmth, their openness, and above all—so striking to those of an acquisitive culture—their generosity.

"They are the best people in the world and above all the gentlest," Colón recorded in his *Journal* (December 16), and from first to last he was astonished at their kindness:

> They became so much our friends that it was a marvel. . . . They traded and gave everything they had, with good will [October 12].
>
> I sent the ship's boat ashore for water, and they very willingly showed my people where the water was, and they themselves carried the full barrels to the boat, and took great delight in pleasing us [October 16].
>
> They are very gentle and without knowledge of what is evil; nor do they murder or steal [November 12].
>
> Your Highnesses may believe that in all the world there can be no better or gentler people . . . for neither better people nor land can there be. . . . All the people show the most singular loving behavior and they speak pleasantly [December 24].
>
> I assure Your Highnesses that I believe that in all the world there is no better people nor better country. They love their neighbors as themselves, and they have the sweetest talk in the world, and are gentle and always laughing [December 25].

Even if one allows for some exaggeration—Colón was clearly trying to convince Ferdinand and Isabella that his Indians could be easily conquered and converted, should that be the Sovereigns' wish—it is obvious that the Tainos exhibited a manner of social discourse that quite impressed the rough Europeans. But that was not high among the traits of "civilized" nations, as Colón and Europe understood it, and it counted for little in the Admiral's assessment of these people. However struck he was with such behavior, he would not have thought that it was the mark of a benign and harmonious society, or that from it another culture might learn. For him it was something like the wondrous behavior of children, the naive guilelessness of prelapsarian creatures who knew no better how to bargain and chaffer and cheat than they did to dress themselves: "For a lace-point they gave good pieces of gold the size of two fingers" (January 6), and "They even took pieces of the broken hoops of the wine casks and, like beasts *[como besti],* gave what they had" (Santangel Letter). Like beasts; such innocence was not human.

It is to be regretted that the Admiral, unable to see past their nakedness, as it were, knew not the real virtues of the people he confronted. For the Tainos' lives were in many ways as idyllic as their surroundings, into which they fit with such skill and comfort. They were well fed and well housed, without poverty or serious disease. They enjoyed considerable leisure, given over to dancing, singing, ballgames, and sex, and expressed themselves artistically in basketry, woodworking, pottery, and jewelry. They lived in general harmony and peace, without greed or covetousness or theft. In short, as Sauer says, "the tropical idyll of the accounts of Columbus and Peter Martyr was largely true." . . .

It is perhaps only natural that Colón should devote his initial attention to the handsome, naked, naive islanders, but it does seem peculiar that he pays almost no attention, especially in the early days, to the spectacular scenery around them. Here he was, in the middle of an old-growth tropical forest the likes of which he could not have imagined before, its trees reaching sixty or seventy feet into the sky, more varieties than he knew how to count much less name, exhibiting a lushness that stood in sharp contrast to the sparse and denuded lands he had known in the Mediterranean, hearing a melodious multiplicity of bird songs and parrot calls—why was it not an occasion of wonder, excitement, and the sheer joy at nature in its full, arrogant abundance? But there is not a word of that: he actually said nothing about the physical surroundings on the first day. . . .

Eventually Colón succumbed to the islands' natural charms as he sailed on—how could he not?—and began to wax warmly about how "these islands are very green and fertile and the air very sweet" (October 15), with "trees which were more beautiful to see than any other thing that has ever been seen" (October 17) and "so good and sweet a smell of flowers or trees from the land" (October 19). But his descriptions are curiously vapid and vague, the language opaque and lifeless. . . .

You begin to see the Admiral's problem: he cares little about the features of nature, at least the ones he doesn't use for sailing, and even when he admires them he has little experience in assessing them and less acquaintance with a vocabulary to describe them. . . .

Such was his ignorance—a failing he repeatedly bemoaned ("I don't recognize them, which gives me great grief," October 19)—that when he did stop to examine a species he often had no idea what he was looking at. "I saw many trees very different from ours," he wrote on October 16, "and many of them have branches of many kinds, and all on one trunk, and one twig is of one kind and another of another, and so different that it is the greatest wonder in the world how much diversity there is of one kind from the other. That is to say, one branch has leaves like a cane, and another like mastic, and thus on one tree five or six kinds, and all so different." There is no such tree in existence, much less "many of them," and never was: why would anyone imagine, or so contrive, such a thing to be? . . .

This all seems a little sad, revealing a man rather lost in a world that he cannot come to know, a man with a "geographic and naturalistic knowledge that doesn't turn out to be very deep or nearly complete," and "a limited imagination and a capacity for comparisons conditioned by a not very broad geographic culture," in the words of Gaetano Ferro, a Columbus scholar and professor of geography at the University of Genoa. One could not of course have expected that an adventurer and sailor of this era would also be a naturalist, or necessarily even have some genuine interest in or curiosity about the natural world, but it is a disappointment nonetheless that the Discoverer of the New World turns out to be quite so simple, quite so inexperienced, in the ways of discovering his environment. . . .

MONDAY, 15 OCTOBER: And so I departed when it was about 10 o'clock with the wind southeast shifting to the south, to go to the other island, which is very big, and where all those men that I am taking from San Salvador make signs that there is a lot of gold and that they wear it in bracelets on their arms and their legs and their ears and their noses and their chests. . . . I do not wish to delay but to discover and go to many islands to find gold. And since the people make signs that they wear it on their arms and their legs, and it is gold because I showed them some pieces that I have, I cannot fail with Our Lord's help to find out where it comes from.

One measure that Colón could make, and did so frequently, was the utilitarian: if he was not up to describing natural beauty or distinguishing trees, he was a master at determining the potential use and value of all that he saw, even when (as so often) he was deluding himself. Nature for him was all one form of treasure or another, whether aloes, mastic, spices, cinnamon, nutmeg, dyes, or medicines, or gold and silver and pearls—it hardly mattered as long as it could be sold in Europe. "Columbus's attitude to nature," says the Italian scholar Antonello Gerbi in his authoritative study *Nature in the New World,* "is strictly subordinated to his ambitions," ambitions largely of riches; or, as the Spanish scholar Ramón Iglesia has put it somewhat more starkly, Colón was nothing more than "a businessman" describing resources for potential markets. . . .

But the treasure that Colón wanted most of all—and kept convincing himself he was on the verge of discovering—was gold. Following the Admiral on his three rather cursory days on San Salvador and then on his fruitless rounds of one Bahamian island after another, one feels it was nothing less than an obsession. There were 16 references to gold, some of them lengthy, in the two weeks he spent on these first islands, another 13 during his coasting of Cuba, and finally no fewer than 46 during his scant five weeks on Española. (The word *oro* is used in these references 23 times in the outislands, 19 times along Cuba, and 98 times in Española.) It was the one constant of his *Journal,* the one recurrent goal, and on some days he seemed hardly able to get it out of his mind.

The fixation was evident from the start. On his second day, tiring of the gifts of cotton and parrots and "other trifles" the Tainos lavished on him, he "worked hard to know if there was any gold," and finally noticed that "some of them wore a little piece" in their noses; in the next breath he somehow understood the islanders to say that to the south "there was a king there who had great vessels of it and possessed a lot." Never mind that for the next eight weeks he did not find more than scattered tiny bits of gold jewelry ("so little it amounts to nothing at all," October 22), he interpreted every sign, every conversation in tongues he knew not, as telling him that on the next island "there is a lot of gold . . . there is a mine of gold. . . ."

One might even say the Admiral was driven by this quest, and at times he was even apologetic about it: "There may be many things that I don't know, for I do not wish to delay but to discover and go to many islands to find gold" (October 15); "I will not delay here any longer . . . [or] go to the town . . . so as not to delay much, since I see that there's no mine of gold here" (October 23). . . .

The Admiral then ordered that there should be no trading with those who came out to the ships in their canoes with cotton skeins and "other little things," in order that "they might surmise that the Admiral wanted nothing but gold" (November 11). Still no treasures appeared. Hearing tales of people who "gather gold on the beach by candles at night" (November 12), Colón headed off on a long journey to the southeast, but as he went along not only was there no gold to be found, there were not even any people: all fled their villages at the first sight of the three white men's ships. Frustration mounted still further.

By the middle of December, after two full months of exploring the islands, Colón had found no more than the smallest traces of gold, nothing more than a few grains worn as decorations, and he seemed on the verge of despair: "The breezes were like April in Castile," he reported on December 13, grasping at atmospheric straws, "the nightingale and other little birds were singing as in that month in Spain. . . . They saw many mastic trees and aloes and cotton trees," he went on, but—one feels it was painful to record—"gold they found not.". . .

Even the golden trinkets and little pieces Colón did find, given to him freely by the obliging Tainos if he did no more than admire them, were never enough in themselves: each one in his eyes betokened vast mines and hoards of gold somewhere else, *beyond,* in the river farther east, in the interior, on the next island, around the next promontory. Gold, there must be gold here, there *had* to be—and when, at one point, the Tainos saw how joyous the Admiral became with their little gifts of gold ("they rejoiced much to see the Admiral merry"), they reassured him that farther inland "there was a great quantity of gold. . . and told him that there he would find as much as he might want" (December 26).

Alas, they had no idea, and it would be a few years before they found out, that there was in truth no such quantity.

SUNDAY, 21 OCTOBER: I sought here to fill up all the containers on the ships with water . . . and afterwards I will depart for another very large island that I believe must be Cipango according to the description of these Indians whom I carry. . . . But in any case I am determined to go to the mainland and to the city of Quisay [Quinsay] and to present Your Highnesses' letters to the Grand Khan, and to ask for a reply and come home with it.

It was on October 17, after nearly a week in the islands, that Colón first declared that he was somewhere in "the Indies" (all earlier references being clearly Las Casas's words), and not until October 21 did he put forth the idea that he was somewhere in the vicinity of the Grand Khan. It was patent by then that he was not actually in Marco Polo's Orient of marble and gold nor in the fabled islands of monsters and treasures, but he must have been genuinely perplexed as to where he really was. Under the circumstances he no doubt figured that a vague unspecified "the Indies" would do for his crew, and his journal.

But it did present something of a dilemma. How was he going to justify this expensive voyage to the Spanish court and the financiers who had put up the money, some of it personally to him, if there was nothing here of the "Pearls, Precious Stones, Gold, Silver," etc., he was sent to find?

His first thought was that he might be in the vicinity of the Grand Khan, that one of these large islands, in fact, was part of the Chinese mainland, and so twice he sent missions inland to make contact with what he hoped would be the court of Quinsay. The reports back not only were negative but must have convinced him that such an idea was fanciful, for after no more than a week he gave up the search for the Chinese ruler—the last reference is on November 1—and soon merely suggested that the cities of the Grand Khan "doubtless will be discovered" (November 12).

His next thought was that if he wasn't on the mainland he must be among the thousands of outislands in the China Sea—"all these islands of India," he decided on November 12—and that it would be simplicity itself on the *next* voyage to visit the court of the Khan, for "from here to *tierra firme* [the mainland] was a journey of ten days" (October 28). All very well and good, but what then had that left him for *this* voyage? No king, no palace, no great cities—and no gold—*but* the Admiral finally perceived now that these islands were not nearly so poor as they seemed to be at first, and in fact held hidden wealth, hidden possibilities for Spanish grandeur. The Admiral thus began to discover "a thousand kinds of fruit . . . and all should be very profitable" (November 4), trees "that he recognized . . . to be mastic" (November 5), a "very fine" cotton tree that "gives fruit the year round" (November 6), "tremendous quantity of mastic . . . a great quantity of cotton . . . an endless quantity of aloes" (November 12), not to mention magnificent harbors, lofty hills, "immense riches and precious stones and spiceries" (November 14), and of course, just over the next hill, gold mines of great munificence. After a month in the islands, in fact, Colón made but one more glancing reference to the Grand Khan and did not mention China or its ruler again, even dropping the use of "Indies" entirely until the journey home. . . .

So much for the Grand Scheme. He had not reached Asia, if that's what he had sought, but only the route thereto "over there"; he had not found much treasure to speak of, only uncertain promises of it everywhere; and there was no mainland of any kind, eastern or southern, only a string of small, green islands. The rest of his life—with three more journeys and some seven years in these islands—would be spent trying to justify this strange, uncharacterizable discovery: to himself, to his Sovereigns, to his countrymen, to Europe.

MONDAY, 5 NOVEMBER: At dawn, he ordered the ship and the other vessels to be pulled out ashore [for cleaning and pitching], but not all at the same time, so that two should always remain in the place where they were for security; although he says that these people were very safe. . . . He says further that this harbor of Mares is among the better ones in the world and has the best breezes and the most gentle people, and because it has a cape of high rock, where a fortress could be built, so that if that trade became a rich and great thing, the merchants would all be protected there from other nations, and he says that Our Lord, in whose hands are all victories, leads the way to all things that will be done in His service.

One of the alternative possibilities for future Spanish glory in these none too promising islands suggested itself to Colón almost from the first. On his third day of exploration—a Sunday at that—he had set out to see "where there might be a fortress [built]" and in no time at all found a spit of land on which "there might be a fortress"—and from which "with fifty men they [the Tainos] could all be subjected and made to do all that one might wish" (October 14). Now, during the second leg of exploration along the north coast of Cuba, this grew into a full-blown fantasy of a colonial outpost, complete with a rich trade and merchants. . . .

Now there was no particular reason to go about constructing fortresses—"I don't see that it would be necessary, because these people are very unskilled in arms" (October 14)—but that was the way his architectural imagination, suffused with his vision of colonial destiny, seemed to work: a spit of land, a promontory, a protected harbor, and right away he saw a fort. Such was the deeply ingrained militarism of fifteenth-century Europe, in which fortresses represent edifices more essential to civilization even than churches or castles.

It may have been that Colón began his explorations with nothing more than an idea of establishing some sort of entrepôt in these islands, a fortress-protected trading post rather like the one the Portuguese had established, and Colón had perhaps visited, on the Gold Coast of Africa, at El Mina. But as he sailed along the coast of Cuba he seems to have contrived something even grander, not just a trading port but an outright colonial settlement, an outpost of empire where Spaniards would settle and prosper, living off the labor of the natives ("Command them to do what you will," December 16) and the trade of the Europeans. . . .

It may fairly be called the birth of European colonialism.

Here, for the first time that we know, are the outlines of the policy that not only Spain but other European countries would indeed adopt in the years to come, complete with conquest, religious conversion, city settlements, fortresses, exploitation, international trade, and exclusive domain. And that colonial policy would be very largely responsible for endowing those countries with the pelf, power, patronage, and prestige that allowed them to become the nation-states they did.

Again, one is at a loss to explain quite why Colón would so casually assume a right to the conquest and colonialization, even the displacement and enslavement, of these peaceful and inoffensive people 3,000 miles across the ocean. Except, of course, insofar as might, in European eyes, made that right, and after all "they bear no arms, and are all naked and of no skill in arms, and so very cowardly that a thousand would not stand against [aguardariá] three" (December 16). But assume it he did, and even Morison suggests that "every man in the fleet from servant boy to Admiral was convinced that no Christian need do a hand's turn of work in the Indies; and before them opened the delightful vision of growing rich by exploiting the labor of docile natives." The Admiral at least had no difficulty in seeing the Tainos in this light: "They are fit to be ordered about and made to work, to sow and do everything else that may be needed" (December 16); "nothing was lacking but to know the language and to give them orders, because all that they are ordered to do they will do without opposition" (December 21). . . .

SUNDAY, 9 DECEMBER: This day it rained and the weather was wintry as in
Castile in October. . . . The island is very big, and the Admiral says it would
not be surprising if it is two hundred leagues around. . . . This harbor at its
entrance is a thousand pasos wide, which is a quarter of a league. . . . Facing
it are some plains [vegas], the most beautiful in the world, and almost like the
lands of Castile; rather, these are better, for which he gave the name to the said
island la Ysla Española.

Rain and cold were no doubt fitting companions for the Admiral's mood, which
must have been dark indeed as he came to his sixth and (what would turn out to be)
last island, Española. For after two months of exploration, there was virtually
nothing to show for it, and the whole voyage was likely to be written off by the Sovereigns, and history, as a foolish and expensive profligacy. The Indians were singularly
uncooperative, most of them running away as soon as they saw the European ships
put in. The weather was rotten and the seas so high and winds so strong that Colón
dared not leave his harbor here for days on end. And to top it off, Martín Alonso
Pinzón had abruptly deserted the fleet two weeks before, with no explanation and
not so much as a by-your-leave, taking the *Pinta* off to the east as the Admiral was
sailing on a tack north of Cuba—and what if *he* were the one to find gold and pack
on sail to get back to Palos and win all the glory? Island plains, however beautiful—
one so lovely that Colón would name it, tellingly, Valle del Parayso—were surely
scant recompense.

The depleted fleet finally resumed its coasting after five days of this miserable
weather, putting into this harbor and that along the north coast of Colón's Ysla Española. And then, finally, on December 17, *gold,* or at least enough of it for a gold leaf
"as big as a hand" and some small pieces, and signs that there would be more, "and
the Admiral believed that he was very near the source, and that Our Lord would
show him where the gold came from." . . . So, at last, the justification for all the
hardship, all the peril, seemed to be at hand.

The Admiral was in a most expansive mood. "Your Highnesses may believe," he
wrote on December 24, "that in all the world there can be no better or gentler
people":

> Your Highnesses should take great joy because soon they will become Christians
> and be instructed in the good customs of your realms, for neither better people
> nor land can there be. . . . All are of the most singular loving behavior and speak
> pleasantly, not like the others [unspecified] who it seems when they speak are
> making threats; and they are of good stature, men and women, and not black. . . .
> And the houses and villages are so pretty *[hermosos]* and with government in all,
> such as a judge or lord, and all obey him so that it is a marvel. And all these lords
> are of few words and very attractive manners; and their commands are for the
> most part effected by signs of the hand, so soon understood that it is a marvel.

So expansive indeed, that he ordered that these people be entertained on board the
ships ("more than a thousand persons had come to the ship" by canoe, and "more
than five hundred came to the ship swimming for want of canoes") and after due
celebration he even decided that he would sail on that night to visit Guacanagarí,

just down the coast, and see what his promises of gold were all about. It was Christmas Eve.

The wind was light and the seas calm—as "in a porringer," the Admiral noted—and the clear skies above showed the crescent of a new moon low on the horizon, as the two ships, the *Niña* in the lead, made their way slowly along the coast. . . .

Not long after midnight, with the gromet at the helm and the Admiral asleep, the *Santa María* hit a coral reef a few miles from the shore and "went upon it so gently that it was hardly felt." The boy "gave tongue," the Admiral leapt from his bed, the sailors whose watch it was ran on deck. Colón gave orders for the longboat to carry an anchor astern to try to ease the ship off, but once set free of the flagship the sailors in the longboat unaccountably made for the *Niña,* sailing nearby—perhaps to alert it to the grounding and enlist its aid, or perhaps, so the Admiral says, "they cared for nothing but to flee to the caravel" (though if that was really the case he inexplicably did nothing thereafter to chastise or punish the deserters). In any case, the ship was quickly fixed firmly on the reef, her stern swung around so that the whole beam drove against the coral, and each wave lifted her up and down on the hard, sharp extrusions of the rock. Within hours "the planking opened" and she took in so much water that she was listing hopelessly into the surf. The Admiral ordered his flagship abandoned and watched in the light of the dawn as she began to break up and sink. . . .

There seemed to be nothing for it but to begin the colonial strategy immediately: there were something like sixty men or more with but a single small caravel at their disposal, so obviously some would have to be left behind and become the willy-nilly beachhead of the imperial project. Colón gave "orders to erect a tower and fortress, all very well done, and a great moat, not that I believe it to be necessary for these people. . . . But it is right that this tower should be built, and that it be as it should be, being so far from Your Highnesses, that they may recognize the skill *[insenio]* of Your Highnesses' people and what they can do, so that they may obey them with love and fear." There can be no irony in this, yet when Colón returned eleven months later the tragic nuance of those words would be all too clear: by then "these people" had certainly seen what the Spanish colonists could do.

In spite of what he recorded as "the anguish and pain which he had received and kept from the loss of the ship," Colón took considerable consolation from the prospect of establishing his new colony, which he named La Navidad in honor of the Day of Nativity on which its inadvertent founding took place. Naturally he thought he detected God's hand in all this—he "recognized that Our Lord had caused the ship to run aground there, in order that he might found a settlement there" (December 26)—and even declared that "it is the best place in all of the island to make a settlement" (January 6), despite the fact that it was a patently poor harbor, fully exposed to northern storms, perhaps as ill chosen a spot as could be found along that coast. Using the timber salvaged from the *Santa María,* and with the help of the willing Tainos, in a few days the Spaniards had constructed the essential buildings of the village. The first structure erected by Europe in the New World was a fortress. . . .

Originally, so he tells us (October 19), Colón had planned to return to Castile sometime in April, when, he presumably knew from his earlier travels, the North

Atlantic would be past its winter storm season. But now, after the wreck of the *Santa María* and with news that the *Pinta* was not far away, he apparently decided to sail back immediately. It was a risky decision and most unseamanlike—as he would soon discover, when he was blown off course and almost capsized by two fierce storms in February and March—that leads one to assume that the Admiral's need was dire. Yet all he ever said, a few days later, was that he intended to head back home "without detaining himself further," because "he had found that which he was seeking" (January 9) and intended "to come at full speed to carry the news" (January 8).

Strange locutions, those, and never explained: what, after all, *had* he found, and why exactly did he have to go at full speed, and why was he determined to set sail into the Atlantic in midwinter? There is a likely answer, but since it is never stated outright we are forced to tease it out from the few suggestions the *Journal* offers.

It was on the day that news came that Pinzón and the *Pinta* were farther down the coast of Española that the Admiral first decided to depart, and it was three days after he finally met up with Pinzón on January 6 that he spoke of having found "that which he was seeking." Could it be that on his detour *Pinzón had actually found* "the mines of gold" in the interior of Española, and had first conveyed that and then demonstrated it to the Admiral? Certainly he had put in at some harbor closer to the interior mountains of Española, where there were in fact gold nuggets to be found—Colón confirmed this on the Second Voyage—and where several of the rivers actually do wash gold dust down from the mountains—as Colón confirmed on January 8, when he explored one such river and called it Rio del Oro because its sand was "all full of gold, and of such quality that it is marvelous.". . .

And if so, might that not be the reason Colón wanted to get back to Castile in such unseemly, such unseamanly, haste, so that the crafty Pinzón might not go off by himself again and, supported by all his friends from Palos, claim to Castile that *he* was the one who really found all that was worth finding in the islands? And also the reason Colón never came right out and gave Pinzón due credit for his crucial discovery, instead burying it in such confusing prose that most historians to this day have concluded, quite wrongly, that there was scant gold on Española and Pinzón, the deserter, had no part in finding it anyway. . . .

Whatever the reasons for his haste, the Admiral certainly made his way along the remainder of the island's coast with great alacrity, and little more than a week after he met up with Pinzón, the two caravels were off on the homeward leg. Only one notable stop was made, at a narrow bay some 200 miles east of La Navidad, where a party Colón sent ashore discovered, for the first time, some Indians with bows and arrows.

The Admiral having given standing orders that his men should buy or barter away the weaponry of the Indians—they had done so on at least two previous occasions, presumably without causing enmity—these men in the longboat began to dicker with the bowmen with the plumes. After just two bows were sold, the Indians turned and ran back to the cover of the trees where they kept their remaining weapons and, so the sailors assumed, "prepared . . . to attack the Christians and capture them." When they came toward the Spaniards again brandishing ropes—almost certainly meaning to trade these rather than give up their precious bows—

the sailors panicked and, "being prepared as always the Admiral advised them to be," attacked the Indians with swords and halberds, gave one "a great slash on the buttocks" and shot another in the breast with a crossbow. The Tainos grabbed their fallen comrades and fled in fright, and the sailors would have chased them and "killed many of them" but for the pilot in charge of the party, who somehow "prevented it." It may fairly be called the first pitched battle between Europeans and Indians in the New World—the first display of the armed power, and the will to use it, of the white invaders.

And did the Admiral object to this, transgressing as it did his previous idea of trying to maintain good relations with the natives so as to make them willing trading partners, if not docile servants? Hardly at all: now, he said, "they would have fear of the Christians," and he celebrated the skirmish by naming the cape and the harbor de las Flechas—of the Arrows. . . .

WEDNESDAY, 16 JANUARY: He departed three hours before daybreak with the land breeze from the gulf which he called Golfo de las Flechas. . . . He . . . turned to the direct course for Spain northeast by east. . . . After losing sight of the cape that he named San Theramo on the Island Española, which was sixteen leagues to the west, he made twelve leagues to the east by north, accompanied by very fine weather.

Thus ended that most portentous event, the first encounter of the Old World with the New, though the representatives of neither one would have known to call it that, any more than they could have begun to imagine its consequences. The depleted fleet, now with about fifty crewmen and perhaps two dozen Taino captives, both ships taking on water, set their prows to the north and to the latitude where the Admiral believed he would find the westerlies that would take him back to Spain.

January was an especially fitting month for this crossing, for it is the month named for the god Janus, in ancient times the god of the doorway, and hence of beginnings, of both time and place, of which there has never been a more consequential example. It was after that same god that the first king of Italy was named, the great-grandson of Noah, so it is said . . . and the founder of Genoa.

Suggested Readings

General

Kenneth R. Andrews, *Trade, Plunder, and Settlement: Maritime Enterprise and the Genesis of the British Empire, 1480–1630* (1985).

Alfred Crosby, Jr., *The Columbian Exchange* (1972) and *Ecological Imperialism: The Biological Expansion of Europe, 900–1900* (1986).

W. J. Eccles, *France in America*, rev. ed. (1990).

Brian M. Fagan, *The Great Journey: The Peopling of Ancient America* (1987).

Stuart Fiedel, *The Prehistory of the Americas* (1987).

Alvin M. Josephy, Jr., *America in 1492: The World of the Indian Peoples Before the Arrival of Columbus* (1992).

Alice B. Kehoe, *North American Indians: A Comprehensive Account* (1992).

James Lang, *Conquest and Commerce: Spain and England in the Americas* (1975).

Samuel Eliot Morison, *The European Discovery of America: The Northern Voyages*, A.D. *500–1600* (1971) and *The Southern Voyages*, A.D. *1492–1616* (1974).

David J. Weber, *The Spanish Frontier in North America* (1992).

Pre-Columbian America

Larry D. Agenbroad, et al., eds. *Megafauna and Man* (1990).

William F. Keegan, ed., *Emergent Horticultural Economies of the Eastern Woodlands* (1987); James Phillips and James A. Brown, eds., *Archaic Hunters and Gatherers in the American Midwest* (1983); Howard S. Russell, *Indian New England Before the Mayflower* (1980); and Paul Shao, *The Origin of Ancient American Cultures* (1983).

Age of Exploration and Spanish Colonization

Charles Gibson, *Spain in America* (1966); Stephen Greenblatt, *Marvelous Possessions: The Wonder of the New World* (1991); Lyle N. McAlister, *Spain and Portugal in the New World, 1492–1700* (1984); Jerald T. Milanich, *Hernando de Soto and the Indians of Florida* (1993); and John J. TePaske, ed., *Three American Empires* (1967).

Origins of English Colonialism

T.H. Breen, *Puritans and Adventurers: Change and Persistence in Early America* (1980); Carl Bridenbaugh, *Vexed and Troubled Englishmen, 1590–1642: The Beginning of the American People* (1968); David Hackett Fischer, *Albion's Seed: Four British Folkways in America* (1989); Jack P. Greene, *Pursuits of Happiness: The Social Development of Early Modern British Colonies and the Formation of American Culture* (1988); and Keith Wrightson, *English Society, 1580–1680* (1982).

QUESTIONS FOR DISCUSSION

1. Describe the varied lifestyles of the indigenous peoples inhabiting the American continents prior to 1492.
2. Identify the economic, religious, and technological developments that prompted Europeans to explore the New World.
3. Assess the impact of the early European contact on Native Americans.
4. What claims did propagandists make to encourage Europeans to emigrate to the Americas? Were any of these valid?
5. Describe the political and economic structures employed by the Spanish in their New World colonies. Were they effective?
6. Using information from the selection by Kirkpatrick Sale, identify the motives that prompted Colón (Columbus) and his fellow explorers to seek a new world.
7. What are the characteristics that Sale attributes to the Native Americans?

THE FOUNDING
OF THE ENGLISH COLONIES

The British colonial enterprise was driven by different forces and was different in character from the Spanish experiment in imperialism. First, the conquistadores were generally the sons of poor farmers or working-class townspeople, many of them illiterate. They came to exploit, "drunk with a heroic and brutal dream," as one Spanish poet put it. By contrast, the early leaders of the English colonizing effort were West Country gentlemen, generally younger sons who were barred from inheriting property and interested in duplicating in the New World the secure, genteel pastoral existence that they had known as youths.

Second, unlike Spain, England possessed a mass of unemployed labor. The population of London had grown from sixty thousand in 1500 to two hundred thousand in 1600, and the countryside swarmed with migrant laborers. The notion of overpopulation in a nation of five million was absurd, but the wool market crash in 1551 together with the enclosure movement—the consolidation of small farms into large landed estates—and the mechanization of agriculture produced high unemployment and a sense of overpopulation.

Third, there was an abundance of capital to finance exploration and settlement. Raleigh, Gilbert, and the other West Country gentlemen soon gave way to the much richer London merchants. Their capital, combined with the advent of the joint-stock concept which allowed sale of shares to the public, served as the necessary financial bases of English colonization.

Finally, the crown played a rather passive role in the establishment of settlements in North America and the Caribbean. It established the rules and legal framework for colonization, provided the form of government, and imposed some supervision, but compared to the French and Spanish, the British monarchy exhibited little desire to exert direct control over colonies established by Englishmen. Governance no less than finance was to be exercised by the organizers of the companies and the settlers themselves.

THE VIRGINIA COLONY

JAMESTOWN

Between 1607 and 1681 England established, subdivided, or conquered settlements extending from the present-day states of Maine to Georgia. The settlements began in a variety of ways and sprang from diverse motives, but over time each developed essentially similar political if not social systems. Nowhere is this better illustrated than in the stories of Virginia, Maryland, and Massachusetts Bay.

In 1606 King James I chartered the Virginia Company of London, a joint-stock company formed for the quick enrichment of its owners and the glory of England. In December of that year the company dispatched three ships, the *Susan Constant*, the *Godspeed*, and the *Discovery*, tiny vessels crammed with 144 souls. Despite the frigid midwinter crossing and frequent illness, only one person died during the voyage, and he from a wild boar attack during an island stopover. When the expedition arrived in May, 104 settlers disembarked, and the ships with thirty-nine crew members aboard returned to England. Jamestown, situated some thirty miles up the James River in a strategically defensible place, was well populated with malaria-carrying mosquitoes. The Virginia Company was a private business venture established to exploit the natural resources of the New World, to search for a passage to the Indies, and to monopolize whatever local trade there might be.

The Starving Times

Life was initially miserable for the inhabitants of Jamestown. There was an acute labor shortage because the English believed that they, like the Spanish, would encounter and be able to exploit local communities of natives. The makeup of the new arrivals was revealing: the manifest of one of the vessels listed twenty-nine gentlemen, one preacher, four carpenters, twelve laborers, one surgeon, one blacksmith, one sailor, one barber, two bricklayers, one mason, one tailor, one drummer, and four boys. There was initially some political confusion. Though the company had had the wisdom to appoint a local council to manage affairs in Virginia (named for Elizabeth, the late Virgin Queen), that body was riven by jealousy and factionalism. Crucial questions concerning what crops should be planted, relations with the Indians, and further explorations went unanswered. These problems, coupled with the atrocious climate and disease rate, caused grave anxiety for the first five years of Jamestown's existence. The nadir came during the winter of 1609–1610, the "starving time" when, according to one chronicle, "so lamentable was our scarcity that we were constrained to eat dogs, cats, rats, snakes, toadstools, and horsehides; and one man, out of the misery that he endured, killing his wife, powdered her up to eat her, for which he was burned. . . . Many besides fed on the corpses of dead men."

The Tobacco Culture

In 1613 John Rolfe imported tobacco seed from the West Indies and began cultivating it in Virginia. Tobacco, an Arawak Indian word for the cigars they smoked, was introduced into England in the 1560s and proved to be immensely popular. The native weed found in North America was too raw and bitter for European palates, however, and for years the English bought Caribbean tobacco from the Spanish. The West Indian variety that Rolfe imported flourished. In 1616 Virginia exported twenty-five hundred pounds of the leaf to England and by 1618 fifty thousand pounds.

Tobacco cultivation was a labor-intensive operation, and the introduction of that crop only further accentuated Virginia's manpower shortage. Slaves were introduced in 1619 by Dutch traders, but they did not become numerous until much later in the century. During the first years of the colony the work force consisted largely of indentured servants who sold their labor for a given number of years—usually five to seven—to pay for their passage.

By the 1630s tobacco was determining the social structure of the colony as well as the prevailing economic pattern. The crop exhausted the soil; as the annual yield declined, the planters had to cultivate more land to make the same crop. At the same time, the European market became glutted and prices declined, forcing the planters to grow more each year to make the same amount of money. Small farmers could not compete; they either moved further west or went to work for the large landowners. Increasingly, large plantations became the dominating political and economic institutions in the colony. The early planters were a rough lot, caring little for the graces of life. They gambled, swore, drank, and brutalized the Indians. The Virginia of Thomas Jefferson and John Carroll came much later, not until the middle and latter stages of the eighteenth century. Yet, ironically, the gentility and erudition of Jefferson's generation were made possible in no small part by the rise of chattel slavery. The first generations of planters were too closely bound to the labor cycle for philosophy, music, and science.

The Spread of Democracy

The need to populate Virginia was the colony's most immediate and pressing need. Without planters, laborers, and consumers Jamestown would never return a profit to the stockholders. To this end in 1618 the Virginia Company introduced a decisive innovation. It offered a headright of fifty acres to every man, woman, and child who agreed to migrate to Virginia. Those who paid the passage received the land outright. Those who paid the passage of indentured servants received the land for themselves.

Those who oversaw Virginia anticipated that as soon as the landholders came to form a sizable group, they would expect to enjoy the rights of English citizens. Consequently, in 1618 the company ordered Governor George Yeardly to follow English common law and consult with a representative assembly. A year later adult male landholders met for the first time in a six-day session in Jamestown to make rules for their own conduct. The General Court's enactments still needed the approval of the governor and the advisory council appointed by the company, but this body was the foundation for the legislature, or House of Burgesses, that would in time govern the colony.

As Jamestown spawned other settlements, the selectmen were forced to make provision for local government. In 1619 the company divided the colony into counties in each of which courts were regularly summoned. There the influential men of the region met to provide for defense, to judge legal cases, and to make all necessary local regulations. Partially as a result of these reforms, 4,800 emigrants came to Virginia between 1619 and 1625, almost twice as many as had come between 1607 and 1619.

INDIAN-WHITE RELATIONS

The population of Virginia with Europeans resulted in its depopulation of Native Americans. The Algonquian confederation led by Powhatan at first had attempted to assimilate this new white "tribe," even adopting Governor John Smith as one of its members. Hunger and the ever-present need for land prompted the English to steal the Indians' corn and seize their hunting grounds, however, and the natives quickly became hostile. Low-level warfare continued from 1609 through 1614 with atrocities on both sides. In 1614 a truce was concluded and sealed by the marriage of John Rolfe to Pocahontas, daughter of the chief of the Chesapeake Algonquians. Land proved peace's undoing, however. By 1622 there were forty-six plantations on the James River. In that year, despairing of ever appeasing the Britons' land hunger, the Indians massacred 347 men, women, and children. The English responded with military reprisals that crescendoed into a campaign of genocide. After another massacre of colonists in 1644 and further reprisals, the natives capitulated and in 1645 retired to a reservation created for them by the colonists. By 1660 the Algonquians were a tiny minority in the land they had once ruled.

Despite the profitability of tobacco and limited democracy, Virginia brought small return to the stockholders of the Virginia Company. Fractured by internal disputes and virtually bankrupt, the enterprise lost its charter, and Virginia became a royal colony under James I in 1624. This would seem to have augured a more direct connection with London, but James died later that year, and his son, Charles I, was so preoccupied with internal difficulties that Virginia was left largely to go its own way.

IN SEARCH OF A CATHOLIC HAVEN

The collapse of the Virginia Company deeply affected the fortunes of one of its principal stockholders, Sir George Calvert, the first Lord Baltimore, and in the process produced a new chapter in the history of British colonization in North America. Though close to the king, Calvert was a Catholic and as such subject to discrimination in Protestant England. In search of an estate for himself and a haven for his co-religionists, he turned to the New World.

MARYLAND

During the 1620s Calvert's schemes for settling Newfoundland and Virginia came to nothing, but he remained interested in colonization. Because of his Catholicism, he decided that his project would succeed only in an area free from interference from old settlers who were predominantly Protestant. Calvert was willing to invest substantially in money and time to be able to control the political, economic, and religious life of the new community. Lord Baltimore died before his plans could come to fruition, but his son Cecelius Calvert secured a charter in 1632 for a proprietary province that became Maryland. The charter detached a substantial section of northern Virginia and bestowed it on Calvert as a palatinate, or large feudal barony. Thus did the younger Calvert not only acquire a huge tract of the New World as property, but gained almost absolute powers of government over his prospective colony as well. In 1634 Cecelius' brother, Leonard, took possession of the colony and became its first governor.

FUTILE FEUDALISM

Maryland, named after the Catholic Queen Henrietta Maria, was initially organized as a feudal fiefdom of the Calvert family. The proprietors were empowered to grant great estates, called baronies, to Catholic gentlemen who were to exercise complete governmental rights over their tenants. The estates were divided up into one or more manors upon which peasants could be settled who would toil for their sustenance and for the profit of their noble lord. The Lord Proprietor, in return, was entitled to call upon his vassals for military service and a variety of fees. The Calverts envisioned a thriving city, St. Mary's, which would be inhabited by free artisans and merchants who would also be obligated to Lord Baltimore. The Calverts expected to attract disgruntled English Catholics by the droves, but their dream went unrealized. In America neither law nor custom compelled obedience to feudal obligations. Prospective immigrants were unwilling to come to Maryland to be permanent peons and toil away on a manor when they could go to Virginia and become freeholders after a period of indentured servitude.

In 1632 the Calverts set up a recruiting office on the outskirts of London and advertised their enterprise if not their religion as widely as possible. Two hundred colonists arrived at the mouth of the Potomac in 1634 well equipped to survive their first winter. Land was distributed among the original colonists, six thousand acres to each head of household. But without peasants, the lords of the manor were able to work only tiny portions of their holdings. The manorial lords began selling off portions of their plantations.

So the Calvert family proved to be pragmatists; the need to attract settlers convinced them to alter the land system in ways that made it resemble Virginia's. The governor began granting smaller manors of one thousand to three thousand acres without feudal trappings, and in time he made headrights available. The Calverts even diluted the Catholic nature of their colony. In 1649 the English Civil War erupted, and Calvinist Puritan rebels beheaded the Anglican king, Charles I. In deference to the rising Puritan tide, the proprietor appointed a Protestant governor in 1648, and a year later an act of toleration assured freedom of religion to all Christians living in Maryland. Finally, in 1650 the assembly of freemen became a permanent body of elected representatives; it met separately from the council and initiated as well as approved legislation.

Thus, from unlikely feudal origins a political order developed in Maryland that depended upon a balance between three forces: the assembly which spoke for the mass of landholders, the council comprising the owners of the great estates, and the governor representing the proprietor. Except that in Virginia the governor spoke for the crown and in Maryland for the proprietor, the two Chesapeake colonies had developed essentially similar forms of government. That one had started as a trading company and the other as a Catholic barony was much less important than the conditions prevailing in America.

NEW ENGLAND

Religion of a very different sort played a dominant role in the founding of the New England colonies. It came in the form of two Protestant sects: the Pilgrims and the Puritans. And religion affected the political, economic, and social life of the region far more and far longer than it did in Virginia and Maryland.

THE PILGRIMS

An extreme, separatist variety of Puritans whose members came to be called Pilgrims flourished in a perpetually turbulent region of England known as East Anglia. As the sixteenth century drew to a close, the enclosure movement broke up scores of rural communities and consolidated tiny plots into great estates. At the same time, farmers and peasants were being driven off the land, the industrial revolution was either turning textile workers into cogs in a machine or throwing them out of work. Many of the oppressed and exploited met in tiny congregations, secret religious assemblies characterized by services stripped of all ritual. There was no hierarchy, no liturgy, no organization—only common zeal and aspiration.

For years the congregation of Scrooby under the leadership of Robert Browne had been persecuted by royal officials and condemned by the Anglican church. Between 1607 and 1609 they fled to the more congenial soil of the Netherlands where Calvinists held political power. For ten years these

*A domestic scene from early seventeenth-century
Plymouth Plantation. Early colonists lived very close to
the subsistence level.*

Protestant refugees lived in Holland where they toiled as humble craftsmen. As
their living standard continued to decline, as their children became assimilated
into Dutch society, and as God's true commonwealth failed to materialize, the
Puritans looked to the New World. In 1619 Sir Edward Sandys negotiated an
agreement with the Virginia Company to permit the Pilgrims to migrate to
America and live by themselves in a separate colony. The English government
agreed not to molest them.

Plymouth Plantation

Under the leadership of William Bradford, 101 passengers set sail for the New
World aboard the 180-ton *Mayflower*. Approximately eighty-seven of the 101
souls aboard were separatists or members of separatist families. Two children
were born during the voyage. Miraculously only one person died, but many
were sick with scurvy by the time the *Mayflower* arrived at Plymouth harbor on
November 11, 1620. Bradford and his companions knew where they were

because John Smith had earlier charted the region. The Pilgrims realized that they had touched land well north of the Virginia line, and thus their colony was without legal status. Forty-one men therefore drew up and signed an agreement which provided simply that the signatories would obey whatever rules the community devised. This, the Mayflower Compact, provided for rule by consent of the governed. The unauthorized government that subsequently evolved in Plymouth plantation was primitive. The freemen simply came together annually to choose a governor (William Bradford was elected thirty times) and assistants to help him. The electors, adult male church members, actually convened only on extraordinary occasions.

Plymouth began as a single covenanted community, a group of people bound together by a religious agreement, but as time passed and emigrants trickled in, Plymouth lost its singleness of purpose. By 1657 more than 1,360 colonists were living in eleven towns scattered throughout the colony. When in 1691 Massachusetts Bay Company to the north of Plymouth received its second charter, Plymouth was included within its boundaries.

THE PURITANS

The Puritans were dissenters within the Church of England. They believed that the Church of England that Henry VIII had established in the 1530s was only a political compromise between Catholicism and Protestant Calvinism. They wanted to purify Anglicanism. As Calvinists, the Puritans believed in predestination and the absolute sovereignty of God. Individuals were selected before birth for either heaven or hell. Notice of one's salvation came through an emotional experience, a direct revelation from God, which was described before other church members and certified by them. The salvation experience was certain to come to those who lived wholesome, productive, prayerful lives, the Calvinists believed. Good deeds and a productive life did not earn salvation but were a badge of that salvation. The Puritan church consisted not of all professed believers but only the chosen, although all members of the community were expected to be faithful and attend church. Puritans denounced hierarchy—the Anglican church like the Catholic was composed of various orders: bishops, priests, deacons, and laypeople—because it was not called for in scripture. In fact, for Calvinists priests and deacons were unnecessary. A chosen Puritan would know how God would want him or her to live and would not need to be told by a cleric. Puritans dressed somberly and lived a carefully controlled lifestyle not because they were opposed to sex, art, liquor, or gaiety in general but because life was short and had to be devoted to the essentials of eternity.

The New England Experiment

In 1629 the Massachusetts Bay Company was formed by John White, the Puritan minister of Dorchester. Originally Massachusetts Bay was a venture launched by Puritan gentlemen to make money and to rehabilitate England's swelling population of paupers. The elaborate charter bestowed by the crown granted to the company the power not only to settle and do business within the stated boundaries of New England, but also "to govern and rule all of His Majesty's subjects that reside within the limits of our plantation." Within weeks the company was able to dispatch five vessels bearing more than two hundred souls to settle on the shores of Cape Ann. Then during the spring and summer, Massachusetts Bay Company attracted new backers with a more dramatic purpose.

The Puritan Dilemma

In 1629 Charles I dissolved Parliament, and many Puritans despaired of seeing a political solution to their problems. Not only did the crown seem intent on quashing dissent, the Church of England continued to insist on the value of priests, bishops, and ritual as necessary mediators between God and man, and on a church that included all professed believers, not just the chosen. The Puritans who were not separatists had hoped against hope for the purification of the Church of England; its failure to meet Calvinist standards presented them with a considerable moral dilemma. As loyal subjects who acknowledged the authority of the civil government and who valued social order, they could not simply cut themselves off as the separatists had done and allow the rest of the world to be damned while they sought their own salvation. Yet neither could they acquiesce in the corruption of the church. Emigration to the New World seemed to offer a heaven-sent opportunity to move without a permanent withdrawal from society, to conduct their own affairs without renouncing allegiance to the crown. The experiment in holy living would save those Puritans who went and also provide a model of righteousness, a shining "city upon a hill," for those who stayed behind.

The leader of those who saw a new destiny for Massachusetts Bay and who succeeded in taking over the company in the summer of 1629 was John Winthrop. A pious, forty-one-year-old Puritan lawyer and landowner, he and his fellows were not prayerful recluses. They were powerful men of affairs, self-confident and accustomed to exercising authority. They wanted to seize and transform society, by persuasion if possible but by force if necessary. With either course impossible in England for the time being, they decided to found a righteous community that would be at the same time apart from and remain part of England. In August 1629 Winthrop and eleven of his fellows met in Cambridge, there deciding to transfer themselves and whatever supplies they could gather to New England. The directors agreed to transfer the Massachusetts Bay Company—charter and government—to America, and in October 1629 Winthrop was elected governor of Massachusetts. In the spring of 1630 the great Puritan migration began; between 1630 and 1643 two hundred vessels transferred 20,000 dissenting Englishmen and women to the bay colony.

Theocracy and the New England Town

The charter of the Massachusetts Bay Company had created a commercial operation; it made no provision for a civil government. The structure that emerged resembled a self-governing English town. Winthrop was governor while the company directors who had made the trip formed the council of magistrates (advisers to the governor). Most of the founders of Massachusetts Bay Company were distrustful of democracy, but rule by a tiny oligarchy seemed unfeasible as well. Winthrop and his fellows received an increasing number of petitions to extend the suffrage. They were sympathetic but apprehensive. The original leaders wanted to maintain strict control of the colony in order to sustain and further its religious purposes. But, if some flexibility were not shown, many settlers might move away and destroy the economic base of the colony.

When 109 settlers asked Governor Winthrop in 1630 to be made freemen, Winthrop agreed, but they were allowed only to vote for new magistrates or assistants when vacancies appeared. All real authority remained with the assistants who chose the governor and deputy governor and levied taxes. In 1634, however, the freemen discovered that the terms of the original charter vested legislative power in them and not the assistants, and they succeeded in constituting themselves into an assembly that assumed the lawmaking function, imposed taxes, and in effect acted as a third branch of government.

In time the Massachusetts General Court, the governing body of the colony, formally divided into two houses, one of assistants and one of representatives of the freemen. The number of assistants was small and qualifications were high. They were less stringent for the House of Deputies. Throughout this period, however, freemen were restricted to church members—the elect and the electorate were identical. The general populace was in awe enough of the church to assent. Not until 1662 in an agreement known as the Half-Way Covenant would Massachusetts open participation in civil affairs to adult non-Puritans who satisfied certain property requirements.

The original settlement in the Bay colony, Salem, situated on Cape Ann, spun off satellite communities to the south. Boston soon became the dominant town in Massachusetts and spawned other settlements around the bay. Within a decade a concentric ring of communities grew up twenty to thirty miles inland—Concord, Sudbury, and Haverhill, for example. Originally, all the freemen of Massachusetts had assembled annually to elect the governor and his assistants. But when settlement spread into the interior, the residents of distant towns found such a gathering inconvenient and secured the right to send representatives who could act for them in general court. By 1644 the House of Deputies had become a legislative body made up of representatives of the various towns. Beginning in 1636 congregations of Puritans broke away completely from Massachusetts and formed an independent cluster of towns along the Connecticut River. The colony of Connecticut formed its own government in 1639 and received a charter in 1662 (see Figure 2–1).

The New England town was the basic unit of government for the area's colonies, but it was more than a political entity. The meetinghouse was also the

FIGURE 2-1
Colonial and Indian Settlements in New England, 1640s

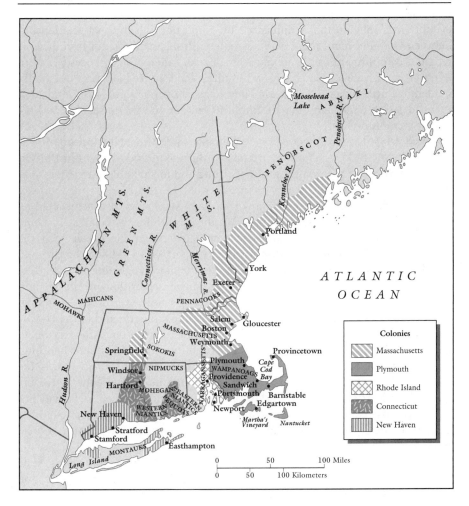

place of worship. Freemen assembled there to pray and bear witness as well as to elect representatives, levy local taxes, build roads, and provide for education. Indeed, New England resembled a theocracy. The town was both civil and religious in nature, providing support for the local minister and exacting obedience to the laws of the church as well as to the state.

Heresy and the Roots of Religious Freedom

Winthrop and the other leaders of Massachusetts Bay believed that godly behavior was the only alternative to chaos. They were convinced that their approach to religion was uniquely correct, and they were determined that no heresy or sin would flourish. Any deviation from orthodox belief, whether in religion, politics, or behavior, was sternly corrected. Those of other persuasions were expelled; the civil government was in effect the police arm of the church, with magistrates enforcing church rules, such as compulsory attendance. Inevitably in a religion that emphasized the importance of a direct relationship between God and man, there were dissenters. Problems arose not from lack of religious commitment but from an excess of zeal. Among the early settlers were a number of radical sectarians who threatened to reduce the essentially moderate Puritan world to chaos. They focused on points of belief and took them to an extreme, ignoring the implications for the wider secular and religious community.

Two who dissented were Roger Williams and Anne Hutchinson. Roger Williams came to Massachusetts in 1631 at the age of twenty-eight, a Puritan of deep spirituality and integrity, but of strong and unshakable convictions and a hot temper. He found deeply offensive what he regarded as the halfway reforms of the nonseparatist Puritans who had established Massachusetts Bay Colony. He publicly dissented from Winthrop and his associates on three grounds. First, Williams demanded a complete and public break with the polluted Church of England. Absolute purity—perfection—should be the goal of religion. Second, he criticized land grants for not recognizing the rights of Indians. And third, Williams called for complete separation of church and state. Civil officials, he insisted, should have power only over individuals' civil affairs and outward behavior, not over matters of conscience and faith. The intrusion of the secular on the religious corrupted the latter. After trying to convince Williams of the error of his ways, the Puritan fathers banished him. Williams went south to form the colony of Rhode Island. So great was the freedom of the individual among his disciples that no formal church was organized for four years. Finally in 1639, a congregation formed in Providence which Baptists claim as their first church. Religious toleration prevailed; other sects including Jews and Quakers were allowed to practice their faith, a most un-Puritan arrangement.

Just as important and perhaps more interesting than Williams was Anne Hutchinson. Brilliant, charismatic, Mrs. Hutchinson charged from her first arrival in Massachusetts Bay that the religious regime placed too much emphasis on community, ministerial authority, and scripture. For her all that mattered was "justification," the gift of divine grace by which a sinful person became one of God's elect. "Sanctifications"—that is, moral behavior, prayer, adherence to the teachings of the Bible—were secondary, even superfluous considerations. Hutchinson rejected the efficacy of good works even as a badge of salvation; that logic caused her ultimately to denounce all worldly discipline and responsibility. Tried for her heresy in a dramatic proceeding in 1637, she defended her faith with erudition. When, however, she admitted that her knowledge of God came from direct, divine revelation and was not subject to institutional, scriptural, or ministerial verification, she was excommunicated and banished. Expelled in 1638, she and her band of followers established themselves at Narragansett Bay.

THE MIDDLE COLONIES

NEW NETHERLAND

While the English were populating Chesapeake Bay and New England, the Dutch were establishing the province of New Netherland, or New York as the colony later came to be known. In 1624 the Dutch West India Company sent thirty Dutch and Walloon families to begin settlements on the upper Hudson River. Supplies, equipment, and two hundred additional families arrived in 1625 and the newcomers built a fort and village on Manhattan Island. This village became the town of New Amsterdam; it and the Hudson colonies of New Netherland attracted settlers and artisans from a variety of countries and from English Connecticut to the north. In 1629 the Dutch company authorized the creation of "patroonships" operated by proprietors, or patroons. New Netherland as a whole remained ill-organized, ill-managed, and disorderly. In 1647 a new director-general, Peter Stuyvesant, arrived and attempted to establish Reformed Calvinism as the state religion. He was a brutal, intemperate man. Stuyvesant's persecution of dissenters and intermittent but savage warfare with the local Indians further depopulated and weakened the colony. When, therefore, an English squadron arrived on the scene in 1664 to claim the town of New Amsterdam and its province for the British crown, it easily prevailed. Indeed, the mixed population looked to the British government with far more hope than ever they had the Dutch.

NEW JERSEY

To counterbalance the dangerously independent Puritan settlements in New England, Charles II granted New Netherland and additional territories northeast and southwest of the Hudson to his brother, James, the Duke of York. In turn the duke awarded the territory between the Hudson and the Delaware rivers, some five million acres, to Lord John Berkeley and Sir George Carteret. These two gentlemen proved to be cavalierly unconcerned with the governance and management of their domain. During the last half of the seventeenth century fourteen thousand Dutch, French Protestants (Huguenots), English, Scots, West Africans, and Irish settled in what became in 1702 the crown colony of New Jersey. Nearly all lived on single-family farms of fifty to 150 acres, and a variety of religious practices flourished—Quakers, Baptists, Anglicans, Presbyterians, Calvinists, and Dutch Reformed.

PENNSYLVANIA

Pennsylvania, fittingly enough, grew out of an amalgam of religious vision, a powerful personality, and local circumstance. One of the most extreme and persecuted religious sects of seventeenth-century England was the Quakers, so named because they frequently shook and trembled during their services. Life for these intensely religious people was a constant search for the "inner light" which they assumed existed within every human being. Their services were completely unstructured; participants sat in silence until the urge to bear witness overcame them. Quakers dismissed ritual, clergy, and any sort of formal procedure as superfluous. Advocates of absolute freedom of conscience, they were pacifists and political reformers. Indeed, it was the Quakers who would most vociferously and most earnestly oppose slavery. The Church of England and the crown considered the Quakers the most radical of all dissidents, persecuting them terribly. When members of the sect refused to attend Anglican services they were jailed and their property, including tools, machinery, and whole shops, was confiscated. Because an occupation was considered a divine calling, the practice of which was a Christian duty, these seizures were doubly oppressive.

The court of Charles II included one of England's most prominent Quakers, William Penn, the son of a famous naval officer who had converted in his early twenties. A deeply religious man, Penn, suffering personally for his own beliefs, struggled to gain some degree of protection for his coreligionists, most of whom were poor and disadvantaged. Politically, Penn was a radical aristocrat, believing that government existed to improve the condition of the masses and that the individual was entitled to protection from the arbitrary exercise of power. But he also believed that civil society ought to be ruled by its educated and well placed men. This philosophy of benign aristocracy would infuse Penn's New World vision.

For reasons that are unclear—perhaps to rid England of its gentle troublemakers; perhaps because the crown was deeply indebted to Penn's father—Charles II in 1681 bestowed on Penn the last remaining unassigned coastal and inland portion of North America claimed by the crown. The grant, totalling twenty-nine million acres, comprised the entire area between New York and Maryland. The colony was a commercial and social success, but from Penn's point of view a political disaster. A central "city of brotherly love"—Philadelphia—was established at an auspicious site at the confluence of the Delaware and Schuykill rivers. The climate was temperate, the soil fertile, and the social and political environment tolerant.

Dutch, French, English, West Indian, German, Swedish, and Finnish settlers flocked into the area, some twenty-one thousand by 1700. Under the plan of government Penn drew up—the charter from the crown gave him virtually a free hand—the governor and council, both appointed by the proprietor, would exercise executive, legislative, and judicial power. An assembly of landowners would have the authority only to approve or disapprove legislation. But as in the other colonies of North America, the economic, social, and political forces in behalf of greater democracy proved irresistible. In 1696 the house of representatives forced Penn to allow it to initiate legislation, and it challenged his title to undistributed land. In 1701 under a new Frame of Government, the council was completely eliminated from the legislative process, making Pennsylvania the only colony with a one-house (unicameral) legislature. All that remained for Penn and his family was title to the undistributed land and the right to appoint governors. Once again circumstance and local conditions had transformed the vision of a colonial founder, but in the end Pennsylvania proved none the worse for it.

THE SOUTHERN COLONIES

THE CAROLINAS

Although fifty thousand Europeans had established themselves along the Chesapeake Bay, the rivers of northern Virginia, central and southern New England, and the banks of the Hudson, huge tracts of coastline between Maryland and New England and south of Virginia to St. Augustine, the capital of Spanish Florida, went unexplored and unsettled. The development of the southern regions, the colonies that were to become North and South Carolina, was rooted in the turbulent political history of seventeenth-century England. Between 1642 and 1648 the English fought a major civil war, Charles I was beheaded, Charles II driven to exile in France, and the country subjected for ten years to the autocratic, Puritan rule of Oliver Cromwell. By 1660 England was exhausted, anxious for reconciliation and stability. Parliament welcomed back Charles II who declared religious freedom, amnesty for all, and the validity of all land titles. In 1663 he granted a charter to eight of his closest friends to all the land lying between Virginia and Florida.

The noble proprietors presided over the establishment of three settlements peopled by emigrants from England, enterprising colonists from Virginia and New England, and land-hungry West Indians driven out of the Caribbean islands by the plantation system. Two of the three settlements survived: an isolated community of Virginians around Albermarle Sound, out of which came the colony of North Carolina; and a more vigorous village at Oyster Point, the site of the present-day city of Charleston, South Carolina. In 1664 the settlement around Albermarle received its first governor and was authorized to elect representatives to a popular assembly. Northern Carolina prospered, and within fifteen years the settlement comprised some five thousand planters and small farmers.

Charles Town (Charleston), South Carolina, was located at the confluence of two rivers and had easy access to the sea. The West Indian planters were enterprising, experimental agriculturalists. Within a generation rice and indigo (a plant producing a deep blue dye important in textile manufacturing) plantations had been established. From the earliest days slavery was a basic fact of life for this labor-intensive plantation region. Africans, West Indian blacks, and Native Americans alike were captured, bought, and sold. The original proprietors developed an elaborate constitution which envisioned a world of manors and nobles. What in fact evolved was a system in which the proprietors retained estates for themselves but sold the rest of their property in large holdings or granted headrights to attract settlers. The standard three-branch pattern of government evolved with religious freedom prevailing from the outset.

GEORGIA

The last English colony established in North America was Georgia, founded in 1732 (see Figure 2–2). Parliament, which chartered Georgia, envisioned it as a haven for the thousands who were then wasting away in Britain's debtor prisons. Anticipating that the colony would earn immense profits exporting silk and wine, Parliament actually invested money in Georgia. The population grew slowly, however. Rules laid down by the British government for debtor immigration proved too stringent, and most of the early residents were German, Swiss, or Scots with a small contingent of Jews.

The most significant figure in Georgia's early life was James Oglethorpe, a powerful governor who dominated the board of trustees. Because a secondary consideration in the founding of Georgia was to create a barrier protecting the Carolinas from the Spanish to the south, Oglethorpe led an unsuccessful attack on St. Augustine in 1740 but then repelled a Spanish invading force two years later. This last battle effectively ended the threat of military conquest from the Spanish Floridas.

Oglethorpe opposed both hard liquor and slavery. He had the trustees issue decrees prohibiting the importation and distillation of liquor and persuaded Parliament to ban slavery from Georgia, the only colony to be so singled out. Oglethorpe insisted that bondage corrupted blacks and whites alike, and by exposing the colony to the constant threat of slave rebellion weakened its security. At Oglethorpe's insistence, the provincial government also restricted the size of landholdings and decreed that each estate be inhabited by at least one white male. The governor's objective was to ensure that Georgia's population continue to be made up of soldier-farmers who could guarantee the colony's security.

As was the case in the other English colonies, visions of the founders fell prey to environment and the profit motive. The only crop that proved profitable in Georgia was rice, and its cultivation required huge amounts of labor. In 1750 the ban on slavery was lifted. The trustees also eased restrictions on landholdings. As a result, the plantation system took hold in Georgia with a vengeance. During the twenty years between 1750 and 1770, Georgia's population grew from four thousand to twenty-three thousand, nearly half of this number being slaves.

PATTERNS OF COLONIAL GOVERNMENT

IMPERIAL TIES

At the provincial level social, economic, and demographic patterns in England and America produced a three-branch government in all but one of the

FIGURE 2-2
The Growth of Colonial Population, 1607-1760

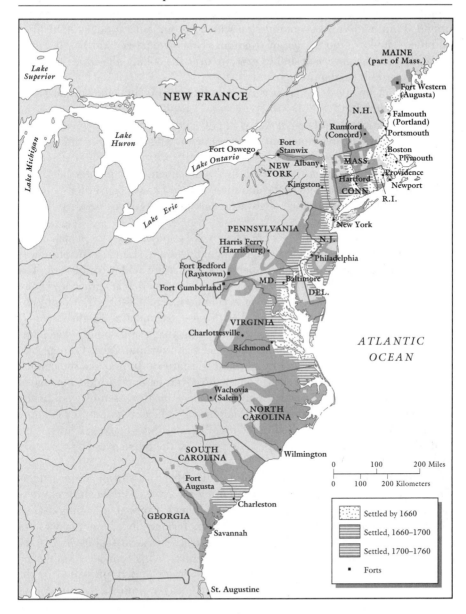

colonies. The governor of each colony was appointed by the king or proprietor, and performed a dual role, serving as a link to London and a personal representative of the king as well as the head of the colonial government. The crown provided him with a royal commission which set out general policy guidelines and then laid down more exact instructions. This royal patent was based on the principle that the governor should exercise over the colony all powers that the king exercised in England.

The council in each colony was composed of prominent colonists chosen by the Privy Council in London—the king's advisers—from a list made up by the colonial governors. Members served as an advisory cabinet to the governor but also performed all three functions of government. The council was the highest court of appeals and enjoyed legislative equality with the popular assembly except it could not initiate money bills. Councilmen were planters or businessmen of wealth and high social standing, but, in fact, the governor's cabinet was the least important branch of government, caught as it was between the executive and the assembly.

Representative assemblies were chosen by popular vote for which there were property and sometimes religious qualifications. Land ownership was diffused enough that a fairly high percentage of adult males could vote. The crown took the view that the colonial assemblies existed at its grace and were not a right. As early as the 1630s some colonists were insisting that representation in a legislative assembly was their legal entitlement as Englishmen; by the mid-1700s colonial democrats were arguing that the assembly was comparable to Parliament in England. Both the governor and Privy Council had power of veto over bills passed by colonial legislatures. In practice the council generally endorsed measures approved by the governor, and with the passage of time, that officer became increasingly dependent on the assembly, politically and financially. The government in London was reluctant to pay for colonial administration and hence relied on colonial legislatures to pass tax laws. This reality gave the assemblies considerable power of the purse over the governor, even over his salary.

The central feature of colonial political life, then, was the ongoing struggle for power between the governor, representing the crown and wealthy planters and businessmen, and the assemblies representing the property-owning middle class. A secondary tension was that between farmers living on the western frontier and the more established residents of the eastern seaboard. Distant from the seats of government and frequently living outside established townships, frontier farmers claimed that they were underrepresented in the colonial legislatures and as a result received meager protection from Native Americans, Spanish, and French; suffered from poor roads which in bad weather cut them off from market; and were denied adequate court facilities.

TOWN, COUNTY, AND PARISH

All of the North American colonies quickly developed systems of local government that were complex and fundamental. In the plantation areas of the

Chesapeake (Virginia and Maryland) and the Carolinas, the parish, consisting of members of the local Anglican church, was the smallest political unit. A vestry governed the congregation, cared for the poor, levied taxes, and exercised other civil functions. The county consisted of several parishes and was overseen by justices of the peace who were appointed by the governor from among the local planters. The justices of the peace met several times a year to administer justice, assess taxes, and order the building of roads. Their decrees were enforced by a sheriff who was appointed by the governor.

In New England, the town was the local political unit. Initially church members and later all property-owning men met to decide matters of local concern, secular and religious at first, and then just secular. These restricted franchises elected selectmen to administer the affairs of the town between meetings and choose representatives to the colonial legislature.

In the mid-Atlantic colonies a combination of the southern and northern systems prevailed. As was the case in Virginia and the Carolinas, counties were formed, but they were split into townships. This combination, of course, was the model employed as the United States expanded westward.

THE DOMINION OF NEW ENGLAND

In 1685 Charles II died, and his brother and successor, James II, immediately set about strengthening royal authority at home and in America. Disgusted at displays of independence by colonial assemblies and moved by complaints from Anglicans that they were being persecuted by Puritan authorities, James revoked the charters of New York, New Jersey, and the various New England colonies, combining them in 1686 into the Dominion of New England and placing them under control of a single royal authority, Governor Edmund Andros. The king's appointee duly ignored local authorities, attempted to supplant Puritan churches with the Church of England, and set about strictly enforcing various British maritime decrees.

Similar efforts to consolidate the royal authority in England alienated Parliament and led to open revolt. In 1688 James' enemies in and out of Parliament deposed him in what became known as the Glorious Revolution and put his daughter Mary, and son-in-law, William of Orange, on the throne. Meanwhile, in Boston, New York, and Maryland, Protestants rose up against royal authorities—Andros and his fellows were actually Catholics, the colonists charged—and overthrew them in 1689. The parent country did not fully reestablish its authority in these dependencies until 1691–1692 when Massachusetts, Maryland, and New York were made royal colonies.

SLAVERY

Though there was little intermarriage and assimilation between whites and natives in the North American colonies, these communities were both multicultural and multiracial. The tens of thousands of nonwhites who lived in various settlements from Georgia to Massachusetts Bay were nearly all of African descent and were trapped in a system of involuntary servitude. By the first quarter of the eighteenth century black slavery had become an economic and social mainstay of the southern and Chesapeake colonies and an important facet of life in colonial New England.

Slavery had existed since the dawn of civilization though it had not been primarily racial in character, being based instead on the fact of captivity. Egypt enslaved the semitic peoples of the Middle East as well as Ethiopians. Greeks and Romans held humans in bondage, but slavery in those societies did not mean the loss of humanity. The followers of Mohammed the Prophet who invaded Africa from the ninth through the thirteenth centuries contributed to the institutionalization of black slavery by seizing African women for their Arab harems and men for menial and military service. With the conversion of various African kings to Islam, the nation-states of that continent came to participate in the development of the international slave trade.

DEVELOPMENT OF THE EUROPEAN SLAVE TRADE

Europeans did not begin to trade in human beings until the fourteenth century. Portuguese explorers who visited the west coast of Africa brought back gold, olive oil, fruit, and human beings. Africans imported into Portugal were made lifetime servants. Their masters justified slavery on the grounds that it made possible the conversion of the heathen to Christianity and thus saved them from eternal damnation. Within a few short years the slave trade became an accepted part of European commerce, but Europeans never found a use for black slaves as a labor force. Commerce and industry, which characterized economic development on the continent during the 1400s and 1500s, did not require vast amounts of labor. In addition, an extensive peasantry already existed to till the soil. By the time of Prince Henry the Navigator in 1460, Portugal was importing a mere seven to eight hundred slaves a year. It would be the New World with its vast expanses and undeveloped resources that would provide Europeans with the opportunity to put slavery to use on a mass scale.

In 1517 Bishop Bartolomé de las Casas, a champion of Native Americans who hoped to limit their exploitation by Spanish colonists, suggested that African slaves be used as miners, construction workers, and tillers of the soil. With the acceptance of his proposal that every Spaniard be allowed to import twelve black slaves each, the slave trade boomed. Dutch, Portuguese, French, and English traders competed to ship Africans to South and Central America. By 1540 slave traders were importing ten thousand Africans into the West Indies each year.

Portugal pioneered the slave trade but was quickly eclipsed by other nations. The Portuguese crown left slaving in the hands of individuals, while its competitors granted monopolies to huge joint-stock companies which were immeasurably more efficient. Spain, which had overtaken Portugal by the fifteenth century, was prohibited by the Spanish Line of Demarcation from settling or trading with Africa. It was Spain's American colonies, however, that provided the greatest market for human beings. The Spanish turned to the companies and nationals of other countries, namely the Dutch, to provide them with slaves.

In 1621 the Dutch government chartered the Dutch West Indian Company and it immediately challenged the Portuguese claim to a monopoly on the African slave trade. At the same time they harvested human beings and sold them in America, the Dutch, highly skilled at trade and finance, greatly expanded the European market for sugar, engineering its transition from a luxury item to a staple. Thus did they vastly expand the market for the primary New World commodity manufactured by slaves. Following extensive wars with both Britain and France, however, the Dutch empire fell into decline at the end of the seventeenth century.

By the end of Henry VIII's reign in 1517, British slave traders had established contacts along the coast of Guinea and with Spanish plantations in Brazil. This lucrative carrying trade consisted initially of gold, spices, and ivory until in 1562 English naval commander and trader John Hawkins broke the fiction of Portuguese monopoly in Africa and Spanish monopoly in Central and South America when he carried slaves from Portuguese Africa to Spanish America. For a hundred years various individuals and corporations competed with each other for control of the African slave trade. Then in 1672 the British crown chartered the Royal African Company, and for the next half century this powerful enterprise dominated the English slave trade.

In the Anglo-Dutch Wars of the 1650s and 1660s, England replaced Holland as the dominant European power. Then in the War of the Spanish Succession, a conflict that lasted from 1702 through 1713, the British defeated the Spanish and French. As part of the Peace of Utrecht that ended the war, Spain ceded to the English the exclusive right to supply slaves to its American colonies.

At the same time the British were settling Virginia and Massachusetts, they were also establishing themselves in Bermuda and on several Caribbean islands: Providence, Barbados, St. Christopher, Nevis, Montserrat, and Antigua. When the Dutch introduced sugar cultivation into Barbados, that tiny island became the most valuable of England's colonies. Once the profitability of sugar had been demonstrated, the English expanded their Caribbean holdings, seizing the island of Jamaica from the Spanish in 1665 and making it over in the image of Barbados. With a vast navy and almost unlimited capital for investment, Britain set about satisfying the slave demands of the entire New World.

THE PROCESS OF ENSLAVEMENT

West African Society

Nearly all of the slaves harvested and imported into the Americas came from West Africa. Though Europeans viewed Africa as a huge grassland and tropical forest inhabited by heathens and savages, the areas they came in contact with consisted of centuries-old empires like Songhai and Mali and complex tribal systems including the Wolofs, Malinkes, Mandingoes, Ashantis, Ibos, and Bantus. The empires were century-old monarchies with hierarchical social and political systems and lucrative trading networks. Like many Native American societies, African tribes were clan-based. Clan leaders made decisions about war, planting time, and movement, and arbitrated legal disputes among individuals and families. The practice of polygamy or multiple marriage produced large, complex families, but women enjoyed some economic independence as tradeswomen and social status as parents. Africans practiced shifting cultivation due to the thinness of the soil, but by the time the first Europeans arrived, they had mastered iron and bronze casting which in turn spawned a wide variety of tools, weapons, and artistic work. Most West African tribes featured household slaves, and this familiarity with "unfree" labor made possible European-African collaboration in the construction of the burgeoning trans-Atlantic slave trade.

During the four centuries of the slave trade, from ten to twelve million human beings were transported from Africa to the Americas. Over 75 percent were imported during the peak period of 1701 to 1810 when each year tens of thousands of Africans were enslaved and sent to the sugar, cotton, rice, and indigo plantations of the New World. Approximately half went to serve the agricultural enterprises of the Dutch, French, and British islands in the Caribbean and a third to Portuguese Brazil. Ten percent went to Spanish America and only 5 percent, an estimated 596,000, were imported into the North American colonies. The demand in virtually all of the American colonies was for field hands, so virtually all of the newly enslaved were young, and two-thirds were male.

Harvesting

Those who designed the slave trade viewed Africans not really as human beings but as commodities to be valued just as gold or spices. Slaving enterprises built small settlements along the west coast of Africa that were simultaneously fortresses capable of fending off attack from rival slave-trading companies and facilities for the housing of the newly enslaved. Initially, European slave traders harvested human beings by trading cloth, weapons, pottery, and other items to local rulers for individuals captured in war. Soon, however, the demand for slaves far exceeded the number of those taken in intertribal conflict; in addition, once African chieftains learned that the European's concept of slavery differed dramatically from their own, they refused to cooperate. Soon the traders sent raiding parties into the interior to kidnap prospective slaves.

The forced removal of millions of human beings and the warfare involved ripped apart the social fabric of West Africa, sending tribes and kingdoms into social and economic decline. Once the healthiest young Africans were

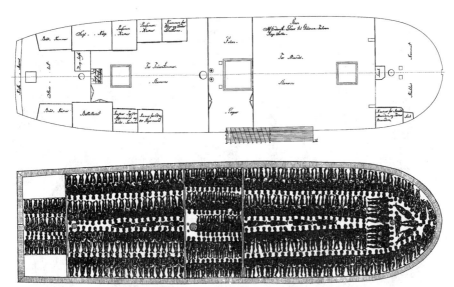

The "tight" packing technique portrayed in a diagram of a European slave ship.

harvested, they were stored at the coastal "factories" in preparation for the middle passage, as the trip across the Atlantic was called.

The Middle Passage

A philosophical difference between "tight packing" and "loose packing" divided the captains of slave ships. The loose packers argued that providing their human cargo with adequate living space, sufficient food, and some exercise ensured that a maximum number of Africans in the best possible condition arrived in the New World to be sold for the highest price. The tight packers, whose philosophy generally prevailed, insisted that the key to high profits was to cram the greatest number of slaves possible into their ships. Though the mortality rate would be high, more live bodies would arrive in America than under the more humane scheme. On a typical slave ship, then, hundreds of Africans would be crowded below decks onto specially constructed shelves. Chained together in twos, the slaves were forced to lie in a space eighteen inches wide and thirty-six inches high. Smallpox, dysentery, and a variety of other diseases wreaked havoc in these crowded, unsanitary conditions.

The harvesting process and the middle passage terrified the Africans. Many committed suicide by jumping overboard or starving themselves. Others rebelled. Fifty-five full-scale uprisings occurred on British and American ships between 1699 and 1845. Many of the captives believed that they were being

An antislavery depiction of an American slave auction—"not a pretty sight."

transported to a world inhabited by evil spirits, there to be eaten. Under these conditions only an estimated 40 percent of the cargoes of the slave ships reached their destination alive.

Distribution

Once the slave ships reached port in the Americas, two primary mechanisms were available for distribution. The favored method in the West Indies was the scramble market. Upon its arrival, the slaver would fire its cannons to alert prospective buyers and then erect an enclosure made of sails on deck. Plantation owners or their overseers would go on board for an uninhibited inspection. In North America, auction platforms were constructed in the main squares of major port cities. Slavers exhibited their merchandise to the curious and the avaricious. After spending two to three months in the hell of the middle passage, the chattel were usually in deplorable condition, "walking skeletons covered over with a piece of tanned leather," according to one observer. Nevertheless, virtually all Africans displayed on the block were sold to the highest bidder.

The slave trade, the "African holocaust," decimated the tribal societies of West Africa, killed millions of human beings, and condemned millions of others to a lifetime of servitude enforced with the gun and the whip. Given the brutality of enslavement—torn from their families, permanently exiled from their homeland, exposed to every kind of brutality including whipping, branding, castration, and rape—it is a wonder that as many Africans survived as did.

INSTITUTIONALIZATION OF NORTH AMERICAN SLAVERY

Slavery was slow to take hold in North America. In 1620 a Dutch slave ship calling at Jamestown traded twenty Africans for desperately needed provisions, but because the purchase price of slaves was approximately twice as high as the initial cost of indentured servants, and both groups exhibited the same short life expectancy, tobacco planters preferred indentured servants to do their labor. Undoubtedly there were slaves scattered throughout the North American colonies after 1620, but the first recorded instances of permanent bondage date from 1640. In that year an African named John Castor went to court to complain that his master, Anthony Johnson, had held him in bondage twice the allowable seven years. Johnson, a black indentured servant who had served out his term and become a landowner, claimed that he had received Castor as a lifetime bondsman and intended to hold him in that condition. The Virginia court found for the master. The Johnson-Castor incident was not that ironic for in the seventeenth century black skin was not automatically associated with slavery.

A variety of factors combined in the late seventeenth century that entrenched slavery in the southern and middle Atlantic colonies. As the colonies matured economically and socially, diet and health care improved, and both indentured servants and slaves lived longer. Increased longevity meant that there were more landowners requiring labor and that lifetime slaves became more economical compared to indentured servants. During this period, the Royal African Company began importing slaves directly into North America, thus greatly increasing the supply. Finally, the demand for tobacco in Europe grew dramatically; it and other labor-intensive crops such as rice and indigo expanded throughout the Chesapeake area and the southern colonies. Slavery was perceived to be not only profitable but in some areas economically essential.

Between 1660 and 1700 the colonial government of Virginia enacted decrees and passed a series of laws that institutionalized slavery, and in turn this body of laws, Virginia's "slave code," became a model for other colonies. In 1662 colonial officials ruled that the children of slave mothers inherited the status of their parent and in 1667 decreed that baptism did not exempt Africans from lifetime bondage. Over the next few years, Virginia's courts held that masters and overseers who punished their bondsmen unto death were not guilty of a felonious crime. Subsequent decisions permitted the mutilation or private execution of runaways.

Slavery in the Chesapeake

In the Chesapeake colonies the tobacco economy boomed during the eighteenth century as the European demand increased tenfold. Tobacco plantations proliferated along the coasts of Delaware, Maryland, Virginia, and North Carolina. But because the crop could be grown on small farms as well as on large plantations, tobacco constituted the economic mainstay in both the piedmont as well as the tidewater region. Tobacco cultivation had always been labor-intensive, and thus the Chesapeake area was prime for the development of a slave economy. As tobacco production increased in volume and area, the number of slaves grew correspondingly. Approximately eighty thousand Africans were imported into the upper South from 1700 to 1770; by 1750 one-half of upcountry households and as many as three-quarters of the tidewater households owned slaves.

Slavery in the Chesapeake area of North America differed in a remarkable way from slavery in the Caribbean. Importation into the West Indies was so heavy because the slave population could not reproduce itself, whereas a majority of the slaves living in the area stretching from Delaware to North Carolina were American-born. Life was much harsher on the Caribbean plantations, where masters preferred to work their slaves to death and then buy fresh ones. The tropical climate permitted year-round cultivation. In the Chesapeake the lower profit level for tobacco compared to sugar may have caused owners to be more careful with their property and to treat slaves better. A winter season gave bondsmen and bondswomen some respite. Finally, food was more varied and abundant in the Chesapeake than in the Caribbean.

Slavery in the Lower South

The lower South proved congenial to slavery from the beginning. By 1700 Africans constituted 40 percent of the nonnative population of South Carolina. As has been noted, in Georgia James Edward Oglethorpe and his fellow trustees abandoned their attempt to make the colony a refuge for poor English farmers and in 1752 permitted the importation of slaves. Early English settlers in South Carolina, the few who could survive outside Charleston, raised cattle with the help of West African slaves well trained for this pastoral activity in their native societies. But then in the 1720s rice cultivation and in the 1740s indigo production took hold in South Carolina. The growing seasons of the two crops complemented each other, and, like tobacco, both were labor-intensive. Enslavement of Native Americans was a common practice in South Carolina, but because they were dangerous as long as they lived in proximity to their homeland, most were shipped to the northern colonies or to the plantations of the Caribbean. Slavery in the lower South meant black slavery.

Thus did rice, indigo, and slavery spread together up and down the coasts of South Carolina and Georgia and gradually into the hinterland. Most slaves living in the lower South worked on large plantations in communities of fifty to seventy-five, their brutal dawn-to-dusk labor overseen by colonial plantation owners or African drivers. By 1770 black slaves constituted 60 percent of the settler populations of Georgia and South Carolina; along the coast, however, the concentration was much higher. By the time the importation of slaves into the United States ended in 1807, 100,000 Africans had passed in chains through the port of Charleston.

KEYSTONE OF THE BRITISH ECONOMY

By the eighteenth century slavery and the slave plantations of the South and the Caribbean had become one of the cornerstones of the British economy. These plantations accounted for 95 percent of American colonial exports to Great Britain. In addition, the slave trade itself was immensely profitable. Over the eighteenth century, profits on the traffic in human beings averaged 15 percent and on sugar, tobacco, rice, and indigo, 10 percent. According to one estimate, the slave economy generated 300 million pounds sterling of new wealth in England alone. The slave traffic and the transport of goods produced by slave labor accelerated the growth of the American and British merchant marines and the Royal Navy until they were the largest in the world. The capital from these enterprises helped found Britain's banks and insurance companies and the textile industry that was to become the mainstay of the English economy. As one contemporary said of Bristol, England: "There is not a brick in the city but what is cemented with the blood of a slave."

RED AND WHITE IN COLONIAL AMERICA

In some areas of British North America, English settlers traded with the natives and even formed military alliances with them. But frequently the object of these alliances was the expulsion or destruction of other tribes and their French and Spanish allies. Indeed, the 1500s and 1600s were punctuated by brutal, bloody encounters between European settlers and Indians as the colonists pushed inland from the coast.

KING PHILIP'S WAR

Compared to the Catholic Spanish and French, Puritan efforts to convert the Native Americans to Christianity were halfhearted. By 1675, Puritan missionaries had established some thirty satellite communities made up of Algonquian believers and called praying towns. The Indians resisted the efforts of missionaries to Anglicize them, however, and most praying Indians saw Christianity as just an appendage to their long-established religions. For the most part New Englanders viewed the Indians as savages and heathens who were beyond the pale, part of the chaotic and dangerous natural environment to be subdued. Though the rhythm of life for both Europeans and Indians was much the same—both were farmer-hunters who cultivated corn and other crops in the spring and fall, and hunted and fished in the summer and winter—there was little mutually beneficial commerce beyond some fur trading.

No confederation existed among the Indians of New England such as the one Powhatan had established in Virginia. Indeed, the Narragansett, Abenakis, Pawtucket, and Wampanoag not only warred with each other but sometimes among themselves. Like Puritan congregations, native villages were autonomous, with consensus leaders, or sachems, settling disputes, deciding economic questions, and negotiating with the colonists and with other tribes. This political and military decentralization proved to be a great boon to the colonists.

An uneasy peace prevailed during the forty years after the Pequot War of 1637; indeed, with the passage of time European-native relations grew increasingly tense. In cutting trees and unleashing livestock on the land, the colonists damaged the ecosystem in which the natives lived. Wind and erosion further damaged the forest, and deer and other wild game retreated into the interior. Most important, the colonists began pressuring the Indians to relinquish their land.

In 1675 authorities in Plymouth hanged three Wampanoags for killing a Christian Indian, prompting Metacomet, an English-educated sachem, to organize armed resistance. While fighting a running battle with the Puritan militia, Metacomet, or King Philip, as the English called him, organized a majority of the local Indians. Armed and trained as well as the Europeans, King Philip and his allies attacked fifty-two of New England's ninety towns, completely destroying twelve of them. Six hundred colonists were killed and thousands of cattle were slaughtered. In 1676, however, with the help of Iroquois allies and some Christianized natives, the Puritans put down the rebellion, killing King Philip and hundreds of his fellows and selling the sachem's family into bondage. Almost 40 percent of the natives living in the vicinity of the New England colonies died, and white attitudes toward Native Americans hardened even further.

NEW YORK AND THE IROQUOIS

Meanwhile in New York, Native Americans—the Iroquois, Mohicans, Hurons, and other tribes—far outnumbered the European colonists and could have crushed them anytime during the first fifty years of New Amsterdam–New York's existence. But incapable of confederation and seduced by the fur trade, they did not. Dutch and English traders played off one tribe against the other, in the process trapping out their hunting grounds. Only one tribe adapted and grew stronger. By the 1640s the Dutch had exhausted the Iroquois's territory of fur-bearing animals, but instead of bowing to the inevitable, that tribe, armed and encouraged by the Dutch, attacked the Hurons to the west and seized their rivers and forests. During the next half century, the Iroquois, having virtually decimated the Huron, presided over its confederation, which included the Oneida, Onondaga, Cayuga, Seneca, and Mohawk tribes, and dominated the area around the Great Lakes.

BACON'S REBELLION

The frontier farmers of the Chesapeake did not want anything from the Indians but their land. Pressure upon the Susquehannock who lived around the upper Potomac finally produced war. In retaliation for native resistance to European expansion and the inability of Jamestown to protect them, backcountry farmers led by Nathaniel Bacon launched a series of murderous raids in 1675 against the Susquehannock, killing men, women, and children. When the government of Virginia attempted to stop these unauthorized raids, Bacon and his followers marched on Jamestown. Governor William Berkeley fled and Bacon sacked the town. When its leader subsequently died of dysentery, Bacon's Rebellion collapsed. The following year the government of Virginia signed a treaty with the Susquehannock, but by then most members of the tribe had either died or fled.

ENSLAVEMENT AND WARFARE ON THE SOUTHERN FRONTIER

Indian-white relations were perhaps their most brutal on the southern frontier. During the 1670s Charleston merchants encouraged the Creeks, Chickasaws, Cherokees, and Yamasees to make war on each other and then to sell their captives into slavery. White slave traders grew immensely wealthy buying human beings for a pittance and then selling them in the northern colonies or the Caribbean. Fearful of the Spanish Catholics who ruled Florida to the south, Carolinians and Georgians persuaded their local Native American allies that the real threat to their independence came from the Spanish. As a result, by 1712 nearly twelve thousand mission Indians had been captured and sold, and thousands of others killed by Carolina colonists and their native allies. In 1712 white Carolinians attacked the Tuscaroras, a neighboring tribe they felt to be a potential menace, killing a thousand warriors and selling another thousand men, women, and children into slavery. Enraged by the slaving activities of the whites, a confederation of tribes led by the Yamasees rose up against the settlers in 1715. Had the Cherokees, dependent on English trading goods, not come to their aid, the colonists might well have been annihilated.

NEW FRANCE

Further contributing to the climate of violence in colonial America was a bitter rivalry between England and France that erupted into open warfare in 1689. The French were no less caught up in the exploration fever of the fifteenth and sixteenth centuries than the Spanish, Dutch, or English. In 1524 Giovanni da Verrazano, a Florentine navigator in the employ of the Dutch, set sail for the New World in hopes of discovering a northwest passage to Asia. He probed the coastline from Nova Scotia to North Carolina but, of course, found nothing.

The following year Jacques Cartier discovered the St. Lawrence River. In the years that followed, a handful of Frenchmen fished and traded along the coast. But then in 1608 Samuel de Champlain founded Quebec. He dreamed of exploring the network of rivers spreading out into the interior from Quebec and in the process leaving a trail of prosperous immigrants in his wake. The hundred or so explorers and traders who did come established excellent relations with the Algonquian and Huron, a nation of hunters and fishers then twenty-five thousand strong. The natives supplied the French, and through them Europe, with beaver, raccoon, and ermine. Nevertheless, a hundred years after Cartier's discovery of the St. Lawrence, New France (or what would become the eastern provinces of Canada) was nothing more than a *comptoir*, a warehouse for the skins of dead animals.

The shell that was New France began to fill up in 1630 when Louis XIII and his principal adviser, Cardinal Richelieu, decided that America could become the economic backbone of a new, more powerful France. The king granted a trade monopoly and huge tracts of land to the Company of the Hundred Associates which in turn settled several thousand farmers along the upper St. Lawrence. Accompanying the French farmers and traders were Catholic missionaries—members of the Society of Jesus, or Jesuits. Louis XIII and Richelieu were ardent supporters of the Counter-Reformation, the effort by the Catholic church to reform itself in the wake of the Reformation. In France the Counter-Reformation took the form of persecution of French Protestants—Huguenots—and abroad an effort to convert the heathen to Christianity.

The natives living around the Great Lakes found the French not uncongenial. The Jesuits were at first a nuisance and objects of derision, but their lack of interest in furs, land, and women together with their facility for language soon won them grudging acceptance. Because the French in general were interested in trade and not land, and because they were respectful of Indian customs, frequently intermarrying with native women, New France did not experience the bitter native-European conflicts that characterized British North America.

ANGLO-FRENCH RIVALRY

It was inevitable that English fur traders and their Indian allies in the Iroquois federation would clash with the French and their Native American clients. In 1670 the British government chartered the Hudson's Bay Company in order to challenge French dominance of the area around the Great Lakes. In 1689 England joined the Netherlands and several German states and went to war with France. While the War of the League of Augsburg raged in Europe, violence erupted between rival French and English traders on Hudson's Bay. In 1690 the French and Algonquians put to the torch settlements in Maine, New Hampshire, and New York and destroyed several Iroquois settlements. The English retaliated by attacking French settlements along the St. Lawrence but were unable to capture any. The conflict ended with the Treaty of Ryswick in 1697, but war would again erupt between the French and English only five years later.

As the first permanent English settlement in North America, Jamestown has re-ceived a great deal of attention from scholars. In examining the life and times of John Smith and other settlers during the first fifty years of Jamestown's existence, historians have discovered much about early colonial attitudes toward labor, social stratification, religion, gender roles, and Indian life and culture. In this se-lection from American Slavery, American Freedom, *Edmund S. Morgan looks into the possible causes for the "starving times" of 1609–1610. He declares ex-planations such as poor labor organization, diffusion of authority, and the aris-tocratic tendencies of the first settlers to be secondary and focuses instead on the Europeans' cultural, indeed, racial bias against the Indians.*

THE JAMESTOWN FIASCO

Edmund S. Morgan

The first wave of Englishmen reached Virginia at Cape Henry, the southern headland at the opening of Chesapeake Bay, on April 26, 1607. The same day their troubles began. The Indians of the Cape Henry region . . . when they found a party of twenty or thirty strangers walking about on their territory, drove them back to the ships they came on. It was not the last Indian victory, but it was no more effective than later ones. In spite of troubles, the English were there to stay. They spent until May 14 exploring Virginia's broad waters and then chose a site that fitted the formula Hakluyt had prescribed. The place which they named Jamestown, on the James (formerly Powhatan) River, was inland from the capes about sixty miles, ample distance for warning of a Spanish invasion by sea. It was situated on a peninsula, making it easily defensible by land; and the river was navigable by oceangoing ships for another seventy-five miles into the interior, thus giving access to other tribes in case the local Indians should prove as unfriendly as the Chesapeakes.

Captain Christopher Newport had landed the settlers in time to plant something for a harvest that year if they put their minds to it. After a week, in which they built a fort for protection, Newport and twenty-one others took a small boat and headed up the river on a diplomatic and reconnoitering mission, while the

from Edmund S. Morgan, *American Slavery, American Freedom: The Ordeal of Colonial Virginia* (New York: W.W. Norton, 1995) pp. 71–91.

settlers behind set about the crucial business of planting corn. Newport paused at various Indian villages along the way and assured the people, as best he could, of the friendship of the English and of his readiness to assist them against their enemies. Newport gathered correctly from his attempted conversations that one man, Powhatan, ruled the whole area above Jamestown, as far as the falls at the present site of Richmond. . . .

Skip over the first couple of years, when it was easy for Englishmen to make mistakes in the strange new world to which they had come, and look at Jamestown in the winter of 1609–10. It is three planting seasons since the colony began. The settlers have fallen into an uneasy truce with the Indians, punctuated by guerrilla raids on both sides, but they have had plenty of time in which they could have grown crops. They have obtained corn from the Indians and supplies from England. They have firearms. Game abounds in the woods; and Virginia's rivers are filled with sturgeon in the summer and covered with geese and ducks in the winter. There are five hundred people in the colony now. And they are starving. They scour the woods listlessly for nuts, roots, and berries. And they offer the only authentic examples of cannibalism witnessed in Virginia. One provident man chops up his wife and salts down the pieces. Others dig up graves to eat the corpses. By spring only sixty are left alive.

Another scene, a year later, in the spring of 1611. The settlers have been reinforced with more men and supplies from England. The preceding winter has not been as gruesome as the one before, thanks in part to corn obtained from the Indians. But the colony still is not growing its own corn. The governor, Lord De la Warr, weakened by the winter, has returned to England for his health. His replacement, Sir Thomas Dale, reaches Jamestown in May, a time when all hands could have been used in planting. Dale finds nothing planted except "some few seeds put into a private garden or two." And the people he finds at "their daily and usuall workes, bowling in the streetes."

It is evident that the settlers, failing to plant for themselves, depend heavily on the Indians for food. The Indians can finish them off at any time simply by leaving the area. And the Indians know it. One of them tells the English flatly that "we can plant any where . . . and we know that you cannot live if you want [i.e., lack] our harvest, and that reliefe we bring you." If the English drive out the Indians, they will starve.

With that in mind, we look back a year on a scene in the summer following the starving, cannibal winter. It is August, when corn is ripening. The governor has been negotiating with Powhatan about some runaway Englishmen he is thought to be harboring. Powhatan returns "noe other then prowde and disdaynefull Answers," and so the governor sends George Percy "to take Revendge upon the Paspeheans and Chiconamians [Chickahominies]," the tribes closest to Jamestown. Percy, the brother of the Earl of Northumberland and the perennial second in command at Jamestown, takes a group of soldiers up the James a few miles by boat and then marches inland three miles to the principal town of the Paspaheghs. They fall upon the town, kill fifteen or sixteen Indians, and capture the queen of the tribe and her children.

Percy then has his men burn the houses and "cutt downe their Corne groweinge about the Towne." He takes the queen and her children back to his boats and embarks for Jamestown, but his men "begin to murmur becawse the quene and her Children weare spared." Percy therefore obliges them by throwing the children overboard "and shoteinge owtt their Braynes in the water." Meanwhile he sends another party under Captain James Davis to attack another Indian town (presumably a Chickahominy town), where again they cut down the corn and burn the houses. Upon returning to Jamestown, Percy hears that the governor is displeased that the queen of the Paspaheghs has been spared. Davis wants to burn her, but Percy, "haveinge seene so mutche Bloodshedd that day," insists that she merely be put to the sword. So she is led away and stabbed.

Thus the English, unable or unwilling to feed themselves, continually demanding corn from the Indians, take pains to destroy both the Indians and their corn.

One final scene. It is the spring of 1612, and Governor Dale is supervising the building of a fort at Henrico, near the present site of Richmond. He pauses to deal with some of his men, Englishmen, who have committed a serious crime. In the words of George Percy, "Some he apointed to be hanged Some burned Some to be broken upon wheles, others to be staked and some to be shott to death." The reason for such extremities was the seriousness of the crime and the need to deter others from it: "all theis extreme and crewell tortures he used and inflicted upon them to terrify the reste for Attempting the Lyke." What, then, was the crime these men had committed? They had run away to live with the Indians and had been recaptured.

It is not easy to make sense out of the behavior displayed in these episodes. How to explain the suicidal impulse that led the hungry English to destroy the corn that might have fed them and to commit atrocities upon the people who grew it? And how to account for the seeming unwillingness or incapacity of the English to feed themselves? Although they had invaded Indian territory and quarreled with the owners, the difficulty of obtaining land was not great. The Indians were no match for English weapons. Moreover, since the Indians could afford to give up the land around Jamestown as well as Henrico without seriously endangering their own economy, they made no concerted effort to drive the English out. Although Indian attacks may have prevented the English from getting a crop into the ground in time for a harvest in the fall of 1607, the occasional Indian raids thereafter cannot explain the English failure to grow food in succeeding years. How, then, can we account for it?

The answer that comes first to mind is the poor organization and direction of the colony. The government prescribed by the charter placed full powers in a council appointed by the king, with a president elected by the other members. The president had virtually no authority of his own; and while the council lasted, the members spent most of their time bickering and intriguing against one another and especially against the one man who had the experience and the assurance to take command. The names of the councillors had been kept secret (even from themselves) in a locked box, until the ships carrying the first settlers arrived in Virginia. By that time a bumptious young man named John Smith had made himself unpopular with Captain Christopher Newport (in command until their arrival) and with most of the other gentlemen of consequence aboard. When they opened the box, they were appalled to find Smith's name on the list of councillors. But during the next two years Smith's confidence in himself and his willingness to act while others talked overcame most of the handicaps imposed by the feeble frame of government. It was Smith who kept the colony going during those years. But in doing so he dealt more decisively with the Indians than with his own quarreling countrymen, and he gave an initial turn to the colony's Indian relations that was not quite what the company had intended. . . .

When the supplies ran out in the first autumn, Smith succeeded in trading with the Indians for corn. Then, on an exploring expedition up the Chickahominy River, he was made a prisoner and brought before Powhatan. This was the point at which another fair princess, Pocahontas, stepped in to save his life—or so Smith later told it; and in spite of the skepticism engendered by the larger-than-life view of himself that Smith always affected, there seems to be no good reason to doubt him. In any case, he returned unharmed; and while he remained in Virginia (until the fall of 1609), he conducted most of the colony's relations both with Powhatan and with the tribes under Powhatan's dominion.

Smith took a keener interest in the Indians than anyone else in Virginia for a century to come. The astonishingly accurate map he made of the country shows the locations of the different tribes, and his writings give us most of the information we will ever have about them. But his interest in them was neither philanthropic nor philosophic. As he came to know them, he was convinced that they could be incorporated into the English settlement, but he scorned the notion that gentleness was the way to do it. . . .

Years later, as he reflected in England on the frustrations that continued to beset Virginia, he was sure he had been right, that the Spanish had shown the way to deal with Indians. The English should have learned the lesson of how the Spanish "forced the treacherous and rebellious Infidels to doe all manner of drudgery worke and slavery for them, themselves living like Souldiers upon the fruits of their labours." John Smith's idea of the proper role of the Virginia Indians in English Virginia was something close to slavery. Given the superiority of English arms, he had no doubt of his ability to conquer the lot of them with a handful of men, just as Cortez had conquered the much more populous and formidable Aztecs. Once conquered, they could forthwith be put to work for their conquerors.

Smith was not afraid of work himself; and in the absence of Indian slaves he bent his efforts as much toward getting work out of Englishmen as he did toward supplying their deficiencies from Indian larders. In these first years many Englishmen perceived that the Indians had a satisfactory way of living without much work, and they slipped away "to live Idle among the Salvages." Those who remained were so averse to any kind of labor, Smith reported, "that had they not beene forced nolens volens perforce to gather and prepare their victuall they would all have starved, and have eaten one another." While the governing council ruled, under the presidency of men of greater social prestige than Smith, he could make little headway against the jealousies and intrigues that greeted all his efforts to organize the people either for planting or for gathering food. But month by month other members of the council died or returned to England; and by the end of 1608 Smith was left in complete control. He divided the remaining settlers into work gangs and made them a little speech, in which he told them they could either work or starve. . . .

Had Smith been left in charge, it is not impossible that he would have achieved a society which, in one way or another, would have included the Indians. They might have had a role not much better than the Spanish assigned them, and they might have died as rapidly as the Arawaks from disease and overwork. But it is unlikely that the grisly scenes already described would have taken place (they all occurred after his departure). In spite of his eagerness to subdue the Indians, Smith was in continual contact and communication with them. He bullied and threatened and browbeat them, but we do not read of any atrocities committed upon them under his direction, nor did he feel obliged to hang, break, or burn any Englishman who went off to live with them. . . .

The members of the council who returned to England complained of Smith's overbearing ways, with Englishmen as well as Indians. So the company decided not to leave the colony in the hands of so pushy a young man. At the same time, however, they recognized that the conciliar form of government was ineffective, and that a firmer authority was necessary to put their lazy colonists to work. They accordingly asked, and were given, a new charter, in which the king relinquished his government of the colony. Henceforth the company would have full control and would rule through a governor who would exercise absolute powers in the colony. He would be assisted by a council, but their advice would not be binding on him. In fact, he would be as much a military commander as a governor, and the whole enterprise would take on a more military character.

For the next eight or nine years whatever evils befell the colony were not the result of any diffusion of authority except when the appointed governor was absent—as happened when the first governor, Lord De la Warr, delayed his departure from England and his deputy, Sir Thomas Gates, was shipwrecked en route at Bermuda. The starving winter of 1609–10 occurred during this interval; but Gates arrived in May, 1610, followed by De la Warr himself in June. Thereafter Virginia was firmly governed under a clear set of laws, drafted by Gates and by De la Warr's subsequent deputy, Sir Thomas Dale. The so-called *Lawes Divine, Morall and Martiall* were mostly martial, and they set the colonists to work with military discipline and no pretense of gentle government. They prescribed that the settlers be divided into work gangs, much as Smith had divided them, each of which would proceed to its assigned tasks at regular hours. At the beating of a drum, the master of each gang would set them to work and "not suffer any of his company to be negligent, and idle, or depart from his worke" until another beat of the drums allowed it. . . .

The *Laws* did not even contemplate that the Indians would become a part of the English settlement. Though the company had frowned on Smith's swashbuckling way with Indians, it was disenchanted with Powhatan and convinced that he and those under his dominion did need to be dealt with more sternly. Sir Thomas Gates was instructed to get some Indian children to bring up in the English manner, free of their parents' evil influence. And he was also told to subjugate the neighboring tribes, to make them pay tribute, and to seize the chiefs of any that refused. If he wanted to make friends with any Indians, they must be "those that are farthest from you and enemies unto those amonge whom you dwell." The company's new attitude was incorporated in several provisions of the *Laws*. When Indians came to Jamestown to trade or visit, they were to be placed under guard to prevent them from stealing anything; no inhabitant was to speak to them without the governor's permission; and the settlers were forbidden on pain of death to "runne away from the Colonie, to Powhathan, or any savage Werowance else whatsoever." The company's desire to bring the Indians into the community had given way to an effort to keep settlers and Indians apart.

In their relations to the Indians, as in their rule of the settlers, the new governing officers of the colony were ruthless. The guerrilla raids that the two races conducted against each other became increasingly hideous, especially on the part of the English. Indians coming to Jamestown with food were treated as spies. Gates had them seized and killed "for a Terrour to the Reste to cawse them to desiste from their subtell practyses.". . . . It is possible that the rank and file of settlers aggravated the bad relations with the Indians by unauthorized attacks, but unauthorized fraternization seems to have bothered the governors more. . . .

John Smith had not had his way in wishing to reduce the Indians to slavery, or something like it, on the Spanish model. But the policy of his successors, though perhaps not with company approval, made Virginia look far more like the Hispaniola of Las Casas than it did when Smith was in charge. And the company and the colony had few benefits to show for all the rigor. At the end of ten years, in spite of the military discipline of work gangs, the colonists were still not growing enough to feed themselves and were still begging, bullying, and buying corn from the Indians whose lands they scorched so deliberately. We cannot, it seems, blame the colony's failures on lax discipline and diffusion of authority. Failures continued and atrocities multiplied after authority was made absolute and concentrated in one man.

Another explanation, often advanced, for Virginia's early troubles, and especially for its failure to feed itself, is the collective organization of labor in the colony. All the settlers were expected to work together in a single community effort, to produce both their food and the exports that would make the company rich. Those who held shares would ultimately get part of the profits, but meanwhile the incentives of private enterprise were lacking. The work a man did bore no direct relation to his reward. The laggard would receive as large a share in the end as the man who worked hard.

The communal production of food seems to have been somewhat modified after the reorganization of 1609 by the assignment of small amounts of land to individuals for private gardens. It is not clear who received such allotments, perhaps only those who came at their own expense. Men who came at company expense may have been expected to continue working exclusively for the common stock until their seven-year terms expired. At any rate, in 1614, the year when the first shipment of company men concluded their service, Governor Dale apparently assigned private allotments to them and to other independent "farmers." Each man got three acres, or twelve acres if he had a family. He was responsible for growing his own food plus two and a half barrels of corn annually for the company as a supply for newcomers to tide them over the first year. And henceforth each "farmer" would work for the company only one month a year.

By this time Gates and Dale had succeeded in planting settlements at several points along the James as high up as Henrico, just below the falls. The many close-spaced tributary rivers and creeks made it possible to throw up a palisade between two of them to make a small fortified peninsula. Within the space thus enclosed by water on three sides and palisaded on the fourth, the settlers could build their houses, dig their gardens, and pasture their cattle. It was within these enclaves that Dale parceled out private allotments. Dignified by hopeful names like "Rochdale Hundred" or "Bermuda City," they were affirmations of an expectation that would linger for a century, that Virginia was about to become the site of thriving cities and towns. In point of fact, the new "cities" scarcely matched in size the tiny villages from which Powhatan's people threatened them. And the "farmers" who huddled together on the allotments assigned to them proved incapable of supporting themselves or the colony with adequate supplies of food. . . .

According to John Rolfe, a settler who had married John Smith's fair Pocahontas, the switch to private enterprise transformed the colony's food deficit instantly to a surplus: instead of the settlers seeking corn from the Indians, the Indians sought it from them. If so, the situation did not last long. Governor Samuel Argall, who took charge at the end of May, 1617, bought 600 bushels from the Indians that fall, "which did greatly relieve the whole Colonie." And when Governor George Yeardley relieved Argall in April, 1619, he found the colony "in a great scarcity for want of corn" and made immediate preparations to seek it from the Indians. If, then, the colony's failure to grow food arose from its communal organization of production, the failure was not overcome by the switch to private enterprise.

Still another explanation for the improvidence of Virginia's pioneers is one that John Smith often emphasized, namely, the character of the immigrants. They were certainly an odd assortment, for the most conspicuous group among them was an extraordinary number of gentlemen. Virginia, as a patriotic enterprise, had excited the imagination of England's nobility and gentry. The shareholders included 32 present or future earls, 4 countesses, and 3 viscounts (all members of the nobility) as well as hundreds of lesser gentlemen, some of them perhaps retainers of the larger men. Not all were content to risk only their money. Of the 105 settlers who started the colony, 36 could be classified as gentlemen. In the first "supply" of 120 additional settlers, 28 were gentlemen, and in the second supply of 70, again 28 were gentlemen. These numbers gave Virginia's population about six times as large a proportion of gentlemen as England had.

Gentlemen, by definition, had no manual skill, nor could they be expected to work at ordinary labor. They were supposed to be useful for "the force of knowledge, the exercise of counsell"; but to have ninety-odd wise men offering advice while a couple of hundred did the work was inauspicious, especially when the wise men included "many unruly gallants packed thether by their friends to escape il destinies" at home.

What was worse, the gentlemen were apparently accompanied by the personal attendants that gentlemen thought necessary to make life bearable even in England. The colony's laborers "were for most part footmen, and such as they that were Adventurers brought to attend them, or such as they could perswade to goe with them, that never did know what a dayes worke was." Smith complained that he could never get any real work from more than thirty out of two hundred, and he later argued that of all the people sent to Virginia, a hundred good laborers "would have done more than a thousand of those that went." Samuel Argall and John Rolfe also argued that while a few gentlemen would have been useful to serve as military leaders, "to have more to wait and play than worke, or more commanders and officers than industrious labourers was not so necessarie."

The company may actually have had little choice in allowing gentlemen and their servants to make so large a number of their settlers. The gentlemen were paying their own way, and the company perhaps could not afford to deny them. But even if unencumbered by these volunteers, the colony might have foundered on the kind of settlers that the company itself did want to send. What the company wanted for Virginia was a variety of craftsmen. Richard Hakluyt had made up a list for Walter Raleigh that suggests the degree of specialization contemplated in an infant settlement: Hakluyt wanted both carpenters and joiners, tallow chandlers and wax chandlers, bowstave preparers and bowyers, fletchers and arrowhead makers, men to rough-hew pikestaffs and other men to finish them. In 1610 and again in 1611 the Virginia Company published lists of the kind of workers it wanted. Some were for building, making tools, and other jobs needed to keep the settlers alive, but the purpose of staying alive would be to see just what Virginia was good for and then start sending the goods back to England. Everybody hoped for gold and silver and jewels, so the colony needed refiners and mineral men. But they might have to settle for iron, so send men with all the skills needed to smelt it. The silk grass that Hariot described might produce something like silk, and there were native mulberry trees for growing worms, so send silk dressers. Sturgeon swam in the rivers, so send men who knew how to make caviar. And so on. Since not all the needed skills for Virginia's potential products were to be found in England, the company sought them abroad: glassmakers from Italy, millwrights from Holland, pitch boilers from Poland, vine dressers and saltmakers from France. The settlers of Virginia were expected to create a more complex, more varied economy than England itself possessed. As an extension of England, the colony would impart its variety and health to the mother country.

If the company had succeeded in filling the early ships for Virginia with as great a variety of specialized craftsmen as it wanted, the results might conceivably have been worse than they were. We have already noticed the effect of specialization in England itself, where the division of labor had become a source not of efficiency but of idleness. In Virginia the effect was magnified. Among the skilled men who started the settlement in 1607 were four carpenters, two bricklayers, one mason (apparently a higher skill than bricklaying), a blacksmith, a tailor, and a barber. The first "supply" in 1608 had six tailors, two goldsmiths, two refiners, two apothecaries, a blacksmith, a gunner (i.e., gunsmith?), a cooper, a tobacco pipe maker, a jeweler, and a perfumer. There were doubtless others, and being skilled they expected to be paid and fed for doing the kind of work for which they had been hired. Some were obviously useful. But others may have found themselves without means to use their special talents. If they were conscientious, the jeweler may have spent some time looking for jewels, the goldsmiths for gold, the perfumer for something to make perfume with. But when the search proved futile, it did not follow that they should or would exercise their skilled hands at any other tasks. It was not suitable for a perfumer or a jeweler or a goldsmith to put his hand to the hoe. Rather, they could join the gentlemen in genteel loafing while a handful of ordinary laborers worked at the ordinary labor of growing and gathering food.

The laborers could be required to work at whatever they were told to; but they were, by all accounts, too few and too feeble. The company may have rounded them up as it did in 1609 when it appealed to the mayor of London to rid the city of its "swarme of unnecessary inmates" by sending to Virginia any who were destitute and lying in the streets. . . .

The company never considered the problem of staying alive in Virginia to be a serious one. And why should they have? England's swarming population had had ample experience in moving to new areas and staying alive. The people who drifted north and west into the pasture-farming areas got along, and the lands there were marginal, far poorer than those that awaited the settlers of tidewater Virginia. Though there may have been some farmers among the early settlers, no one for whom an occupation is given was listed as a husbandman or yeoman. And though thirty husbandmen were included in the 1611 list of men wanted, few came. As late as 1620 the colony reported "a great scarcity, or none at all" of "husbandmen truely bred," by which was meant farmers from the arable regions. In spite of the experience at Roanoke and in spite of the repeated starving times at Jamestown, the company simply did not envisage the provision of food as a serious problem. They sent some food supplies with every ship but never enough to last more than a few months. After that people should be able to do for themselves.

The colonists were apparently expected to live from the land like England's woodland and pasture people, who gave only small amounts of time to their small garden plots, cattle, and sheep and spent the rest in spinning, weaving, mining, handicrafts, and loafing. Virginians would spend their time on the more varied commodities of the New World. To enable them to live in this manner, the company sent cattle, swine, and sheep: and when Dale assigned them private plots of land, the plots were small, in keeping with the expectation that they would not spend much time at farming. The company never intended the colony to supply England with grain and did not even expect that agricultural products might be its principal exports. They did want to give sugar, silk, and wine a try, but most of the skills they sought showed an expectation of setting up extractive industries such as iron mining, smelting, saltmaking, pitch making, and glassmaking. The major part of the colonists' work time was supposed to be devoted to processing the promised riches of the land for export; and with the establishment of martial law the company had the means of seeing that they put their shoulders to the task. . . .

The predicament of those in charge is reflected in the hours of work they prescribed for the colonists, which contrast sharply with those specified in the English Statute of Artificers. There was no point in demanding dawn-to-dusk toil unless there was work worth doing. When John Smith demanded that men work or starve, how much work did he demand? By his own account, "4 hours each day was spent in worke, the rest in pastimes and merry exercise." The governors who took charge after the reorganization of 1609 were equally modest in their demands. William Strachey, who was present, described the work program under Gates and De la Warr in the summer of 1610:

> It is to be understood that such as labor are not yet so taxed but that easily they perform the same and ever by ten of the clock they have done their morning's work: at what time they have their allowances [of food] set out ready for them, and

until it be three of the clock again they take their own pleasure, and afterward, with the sunset, their day's labor is finished.

The Virginia Company offered much the same account of this period. According to a tract issued late in 1610, "the setled times of working (to effect all themselves, or the Adventurers neede desire) [require] no more pains then from six of clocke in the morning untill ten, and from two of the clocke in the afternoone till foure." The long lunch period described here was spelled out in the *Lawes Divine, Morall and Martiall*. If we calculate the total hours demanded of the work gangs between the various beatings of the drum, they come to roughly five to eight hours a day in summer and three to six hours in winter. And it is not to be supposed that these hours refer only to work done in the fields and that the men were expected to work at other tasks like building houses during the remainder of the day. The *Laws* indicate that at the appointed hours every laborer was to repair to his work "and every crafts man to his occupation, Smiths, Joyners, Carpenters, Brick makers, etc." Nor did military training occupy the time not spent in working. The *Laws* provided for different groups to train at different times and to be exempt from work during the training days. Although colonists and historians alike have condemned the *Laws* as harsh, and with reason, the working hours that the code prescribed sound astonishingly short to modern ears. They certainly fell way below those demanded at the time in English law; and they seem utterly irrational in a chronically starving community.

To have grown enough corn to feed the colony would have required only a fraction of the brief working time specified, yet it was not grown. Even in their free time men shunned the simple planting tasks that sufficed for the Indians. And the very fact that the Indians did grow corn may be one more reason why the colonists did not. For the Indians presented a challenge that Englishmen were not prepared to meet, a challenge to their image of themselves, to their self-esteem, to their conviction of their own superiority over foreigners, and especially over barbarous foreigners like the Irish and the Indians.

If you were a colonist, you knew that your technology was superior to the Indians'. You knew that you were civilized, and they were savages. It was evident in your firearms, your clothing, your housing, your government, your religion. The Indians were supposed to be overcome with admiration and to join you in extracting riches from the country. But your superior technology had proved insufficient to extract anything. The Indians, keeping to themselves, laughed at your superior methods and lived from the land more abundantly and with less labor than you did. They even furnished you with the food that you somehow did not get around to growing enough of yourselves. To be thus condescended to by heathen savages was intolerable. And when your own people started deserting in order to live with them, it was too much. If it came to that, the whole enterprise of Virginia would be over. So you killed the Indians, tortured them, burned their villages, burned their cornfields. It proved your superiority in spite of your failures. And you gave similar treatment to any of your own people who succumbed to the savage way of life. But you still did not grow much corn. That was not what you had come to Virginia for.

By the time the colony was ten years old and an almost total loss to the men who had invested their lives and fortunes in it, only one ray of hope had appeared. It had been known, from the Roanoke experience, that the Indians grew and smoked a kind of tobacco; and tobacco grown in the Spanish West Indies was already being imported into England, where it sold at eighteen shillings a pound. Virginia tobacco had proved, like everything else, a disappointment; but one of the settlers, John Rolfe, tried some seeds of the West Indian variety, and the result was much better. The colonists stopped bowling in the streets and planted tobacco in them—and everywhere else that they could find open land. In 1617, ten years after the first landing at Jamestown, they shipped their first cargo to England. It was not up to Spanish tobacco, but it sold at three shillings a pound. . . .

SUGGESTED READINGS

General

James Axtell, *The European and the Indian: Essays in the Ethnohistory of Colonial America* (1981).

Bernard Bailyn, *The Origins of American Politics* (1968).

Patricia Bonomi, *Under the Cope of Heaven: Religion, Society, and Politics in Colonial America* (1986).

Michael Craton, *Sinews of Empire: A Short History of British Slavery* (1974).

Richard S. Dunn and Mary Maples Dunn, eds., *The World of William Penn* (1986).

David W. Jordan, *Foundations of Representative Government in Maryland* (1988).

Winthrop D. Jordan, *White over Black: American Attitudes Toward the Negro, 1550–1812* (1968).

Allan Kulikoff, *Tobacco and Slaves: The Development of Southern Cultures in the Chesapeake: 1680–1800* (1986).

Edmund S. Morgan, *The Puritan Dilemma: The Story of John Winthrop* (1958) and *American Slavery, American Freedom* (1975).

Peter H. Wood, *Black Majority: Negroes in Colonial South Carolina from 1670 Through the Stono Rebellion* (1974).

Jamestown and the Virginia Colony

Philip Barbour, *The Jamestown Voyages Under the First Charter, 1606–1609* (1969); Helen C. Rountree, *The Powhatan Indians of Virginia* (1989); and Darrett B. Rutman and Anita H. Rutman, *A Place in Time: Middlesex County, Virginia, 1650–1750* (1984).

Creation of Maryland

Paul G.E. Clemens, *The Atlantic Economy and Colonial Maryland's Eastern Shore: From Tobacco to Grain* (1980); Gloria L. Main, *Tobacco Colony: Life in Early Maryland, 1650–1720* (1982); and David B. Quinn, ed., *Early Maryland in a Wider World* (1982).

Founding of the New England Colonies

Richard L. Bushman, *From Puritan to Yankee: Character and the Social Order in Connecticut, 1690–1765* (1967); David Cressy, *Coming Over: Migration and Communication Between England and New England in the Seventeenth Century* (1987); and William Cronon, *Changes in the Land: Indians, Colonists and the Ecology of New England* (1983).

Establishment of the Middle Colonies

Wesley F. Craven, *New Jersey and the English Colonization of North America* (1964); Michael Kammen, *Colonial New York, A History* (1975); and Gary B. Nash, *Quakers and Politics: Pennsylvania, 1681–1726* (1968).

Early History of the Southern Colonies

Harold E. Davis, *The Fledgling Province: Social and Cultural Life in Colonial Georgia, 1733–1776* (1976); and Robert Weir, *Colonial South Carolina* (1983).

Imperial Ties and Colonial Governance

Bruce C. Daniels, ed., *Town and Country: Essays on the Structure of Local Government in the American Colonies* (1978); Jack M. Sosin, *English America and the Revolution of 1688: Royal Administration and the Structure of Provincial Government* (1982); and S.S. Webb, *The Governors-General: The English Army and the Definition of Empire* (1979).

Relations Between Native Americans and White Settlers

James Axtell, *The Invasion Within: The Contest of Culture in Colonial North America* (1985); John Demos, *The Unredeemed Captive: A Family Story from Early America* (1994); Francis Jennings, *The Ambiguous Iroquois Empire: The Covenant Chain Confederation of Indian Tribes with English Colonies* (1984); Michael J. Publisi, *Puritans Besieged: The Legacy of King Philip's War in the Massachusetts Bay Colony* (1991); and Ian K. Steele, *Betrayals: Fort William Henry & the Massacre* (1990).

Slave Trade and the Establishment of Slavery

T.H. Breen and Stephen Innes, *'Myne Owne Ground': Race and Freedom on Virginia's Eastern Shore, 1640–1676* (1980); Richard S. Dunn, *Sugar and Slaves: The Rise of the Planter Class in the English West Indies, 1624–1713* (1972); and James A. Rawley, *The Transatlantic Slave Trade, A History* (1981).

QUESTIONS FOR DISCUSSION

1. Compare and contrast the British and French colonial systems.
2. Discuss the role of religion in shaping society and government in Maryland, Massachusetts Bay, and Plymouth Plantation.

3. Why were Roger Williams and Anne Hutchinson so threatening to the Puritans?

4. How did William Penn's vision of the ideal community become transformed by political, environmental, and demographic conditions?

5. Why was the Dominion of New England created? Did this entity advance the interests of the British crown? Explain.

6. Explain the emergence of chattel slavery. How did slavery in the Chesapeake region differ from slavery in the lower South?

7. The English colony at Jamestown very nearly failed. What factors did Edmund Morgan cite as contributing to Jamestown's difficulties?

CHAPTER THREE

CULTURE AND SOCIETY
IN COLONIAL AMERICA

CULTURAL DIVERSITY

IMMIGRATION PATTERNS

The 1600s bore witness to a remarkable transfer of human beings from the Old World to the New. Nearly 380,000 people immigrated to the West Indies and North America from Europe prior to 1700. According to historian Bernard Bailyn, the typical colonist from southern England was a young, single male who left his homeland because of perceived opportunity in the New World, not because of dissatisfaction with the political or economic situation in Great Britain. He most likely was an artisan of some type and settled in either Maryland or Virginia. Those coming from the north, including Scotland and northern Ireland, were by contrast usually members of a nuclear family, in their early thirties, farmers, and individuals deeply threatened by unemployment and/or political persecution. These immigrants were most likely to settle in New York, North Carolina, or Pennsylvania. Early settlers in New England were generally members of family groups originating in East Anglia or the West Country of Britain, especially Devon. Driven by visions of economic opportunity and religious freedom, the heads of household were artisans, farmers, and merchants, generally skilled and literate.

But these were archetypes. The North American colonies were amazingly diverse, complex mixtures of European cultures interacting with Native Americans and African slave communities. During the 1600s 150,000 English men, women, and children immigrated to America, but at the turn of the century that outpouring came to a sudden halt. The English Civil War and a

76

disastrous fire in London gave rise to fears in England of "underpopulation." For this reason, government officials began to discourage emigration. In New England, the Puritan authorities insisted that any newcomer from the British Isles adhere strictly to the Calvinist line.

Because government officials in England and in the colonies were committed to populating the New World, however, they began to encourage non-English immigration. In the 1680s William Penn received permission to recruit settlers in Holland, France, and from the German states situated adjacent to the Rhine River. Other colonies followed suit and sent recruiting agents to the continent and to Scotland and Ireland. Colonial governments passed naturalization laws in the early eighteenth century requiring only that immigrants accept Protestant Christianity and swear allegiance to the English crown. Those that did were endowed with all of the political and economic rights of English citizens. In 1740 Parliament passed a general naturalization law which forced even Puritan New England to accept foreign-born immigrants on easy terms. Tolerance had its limits, however. Naturalization remained virtually impossible for Catholics (except, of course, in Maryland) and for Jews.

Non-English immigration was particularly heavy from the German Rhineland and Scotland. Ravaged by warfare, the Rhineland states delivered one hundred thousand souls to the American wilderness by the 1770s, with the heaviest concentrations along the Hudson River in New York and the up-countries of Pennsylvania and North Carolina. Frustrated by religious discrimination and economic exploitation by the English, 250,000 Scottish and Northern Irish Protestants, most of them Presbyterians, flooded into the colonies during the first three-quarters of the eighteenth century. They tended to settle even further inland than the Germans and Dutch along the eastern edges of the Appalachian Mountains with a large pocket in piedmont North Carolina. Tens of thousands of Dutch settled in the Hudson River Valley and in upstate New York. By the time of the first census in 1790, America was just under 50 percent English, 15 percent Irish or Scottish, 7 percent German, and almost 25 percent African. This did not include hundreds of thousands of Native Americans.

DEMOGRAPHIC PATTERNS

The northern and southern portions of British North America grew at very different rates. The one hundred twenty thousand Europeans and twenty-five thousand slaves who arrived in the southern colonies during the eighteenth century were unable to sustain a natural population growth. Indeed, by 1700 the number of inhabitants had dwindled to just over one hundred thousand. In sharp contrast, the Middle Atlantic and New England colonies attracted some forty thousand people and a handful of slaves during the same period. But by the close of the century the survivors and their descendants numbered almost one hundred fifty thousand, including five thousand slaves. This rapid proliferation of the free labor portion of the British Empire was one of the most striking and unusual features of European overseas expansion. The growth differential between north and south was due to migration patterns, family structure, and health factors.

Maryland and Virginia attracted approximately six men for every woman. The ratio declined steadily but slowly. In addition, because most female immigrants into the Chesapeake colonies were indentured servants, they were not free to marry until they were well into their twenties. By contrast, men outnumbered women by only three to two in New England, and most women came as members of nuclear families.

In Virginia and Maryland because of disease and other factors the average life expectancy was a mere forty-five years. Women lived for an even shorter period, especially if they were exposed to malaria. In New England women married fairly late but had two or three more pregnancies than their southern counterparts, fewer died in childbirth, and they lost a relatively small number of their children to disease. It was not unusual for a resident of Salem or Concord, Massachusetts, to live into his or her eighties.

As a result of these factors, New England, New York, and New Jersey achieved natural growth within a generation. By contrast, the southern colonies took a hundred years—three to four generations—to become self-sustaining. Indeed, Virginia remained a colony dominated by immigrants until 1710 when native-born men finally grew into leadership.

THE MEANS OF SUPPORT

For the most part, English immigrants who ventured forth to the New World in the 1600s looked forward to economic stability. They viewed the world from the perspective of consumers and producers, anticipating that all of the goods necessary to a comfortable existence would pass through their communities. To ensure this result and to prevent uncertainty and dangerous economic fluctuations, the early colonists anticipated that their local governments would closely regulate production and consumption of goods, and trade in general. Entrepreneurs and officials struggled ceaselessly to regulate the market place, but the economies that emerged were characterized more by risk, opportunity, and innovation, rather than stability and predictability.

NEW ENGLAND AND THE ATLANTIC TRADE

Not surprisingly, the Puritans who founded the New England colonies looked forward to economic self-sufficiency. Commerce of any sort with the outside world brought the risk of corruption, they believed. With the active support of the government of Massachusetts, Puritan entrepreneurs sought to replicate the commodities supplied by English manufacturing, namely iron goods and cloth. The Saugus Iron Works, an ambitious and expensive enterprise spearheaded by John Winthrop, Jr., quickly collapsed in bankruptcy, however. Government appeals to the colonists to engage in spinning and weaving went unheeded. There was no free time for cottage industry; all were employed working the land. For a time New Englanders were able to exchange beaver, otter, and raccoon skins in England for the manufactured items they needed, but by the 1650s trappers had exhausted the supply.

In desperation Bay Colony merchants looked to trade and seaborne commerce for the solution to their problem. They found it. New England merchants and shipowners soon discovered that Catholic Spain and France and the Wine Islands of Madeira, the Azores, and the Canaries would take all of the fish that the Grand Banks, the extensive fishing grounds off the coast of Newfoundland and Nova Scotia, could produce. In addition, the Wine Islands and the West Indies needed timber, of which there was an abundance in New England, and horses. On their return voyages, Puritan ships carried sugar from the West Indies and wine from Madeira and the Canaries to all the ports of the Atlantic. This complex system of trade was frequently profitable, but also risky. No monopolies existed. The dozens of small merchant firms were highly competitive. Prices fluctuated wildly as island markets became glutted and then emptied. Participants had to accumulate a variety of goods and be prepared to sell, trade, or barter in a half dozen different ports on a single voyage. Yet this complex trading system supplied the New England colonies with essential goods and with endless opportunity for enterprising newcomers with a little capital and a lot of nerve.

THE IRON LAW OF TOBACCO

Tobacco's dominance of the mid-Atlantic and southern colonies continued throughout the late seventeenth and eighteenth centuries. The tobacco economy was simpler but just as unstable as the complex Atlantic trade that developed in New England. The primary problem was overproduction. From an annual output of 1.5 million pounds in the late 1630s, production grew to 38 million pounds in 1700. Operating on the erroneous assumption that the more crop they grew, the more money they would make, planters refused to tailor output to demand. Tobacco was popular in England, but not that popular. As the market became glutted, the bottom fell out of prices, first in the 1640s, then again in the 1660s and periodically thereafter. Of the 38 million pounds exported to England in 1700, 25 million pounds were reexported to the continent. Further affecting prices, French and Spanish authorities taxed tobacco from the American colonies and established monopolies to control its import and thereby its prices.

Chesapeake planters found themselves powerless and locked into perpetual debt by a system of purchase, transport, and marketing called consignment. Tobacco merchants would take a Chesapeake farmer's annual crop and agree to sell it in England. The merchant would then transport the tobacco, sell it for whatever he could get, keep a nice profit, and give what was left to the planter, which usually was not much. In addition, the consignment merchants furnished their agricultural clients in Maryland and Virginia with cloth, tools, furniture, and other items which they charged against the sale of the crop. The planters usually found themselves locked in a cycle of debt, expansion, overproduction, and more debt. In addition, the consignment system eliminated the need and opportunity for local manufacturers and merchants thereby ensuring that the production of finished goods and marketing of colonial goods were concentrated in England. As a consequence, the Chesapeake colonies remained largely rural. These conditions were characteristic of the rice and indigo economies of South Carolina and Georgia as well.

YEOMEN FARMERS

Though the Atlantic trade was the principal capital-creating activity for New England, tobacco for the Chesapeake colonies, and rice and indigo for the lower South, the vast majority of white male North Americans were subsistence farmers. They grew food crops and raised livestock for their own needs and for local barter. Most managed to produce a surplus which they sold for small sums, usually enough to pay taxes and purchase cloth, farm implements, and a few other manufactured goods. Rather than focusing on one crop, these independent agriculturalists diversified to take advantage of every marketing opportunity. Like the plantation-owning aristocracy, however, they concentrated on acquiring more land. Farm families had to practice crafts, such as weaving, carpentry, and blacksmithing.

ARTISANS AND CRAFTSMEN

Colonial cities were populated by unskilled day laborers and skilled craftsmen. In cities from Boston to Savannah, coopers, shipwrights, silversmiths, and iron workers plied their trade full-time. Atop the craft system sat master artisans who owned their own shops. In their employ were journeymen, skilled craftsmen who had not accumulated enough capital to open their own businesses; and apprentices, young men who worked for room, board, and a chance to learn the trade. In most cities skilled artisans formed guilds, self-governing associations which met for social purposes and to establish loose rules governing apprenticeship and other essential activities.

SOCIAL STRATIFICATION

The first wave of English settlers who came to America expected to duplicate the social structure that existed in the parent country, a system that had developed during the reign of Queen Elizabeth I who ruled during the late 1500s. Those who settled Jamestown viewed society as a tightly knit, interdependent whole, not a collection of individuals pursuing their separate interests,

Craftsmen made up an important element in the economic life and social structure of the colonial America. "Patrick Lyon at the Forge" by John Neagle, 1827.

interacting intermittently and haphazardly. They believed that the various components of society ought to complement each other, that they ought to harmonize. Elizabethan society was hierarchical with status deriving from birth, wealth, and behavioral traits such as dignity and confidence. Superiority was expected to demonstrate itself in all walks of life. Those with wealth would own property, exercise political power, evidence moral rectitude, and behave in a dignified manner. Conditions in America conspired to subvert the Elizabethan ideal, however.

In fact the social structure that had developed in the colonies by 1700 only roughly resembled that of England. English nobility did not migrate; their positions brought them privilege and wealth, so there was no incentive to live elsewhere. The unemployed and destitute did not have the means to migrate; only a relatively small number came as indentured servants, although some fifty thousand convicts were transported, chiefly to Georgia and Maryland. Most who made the journey westward across the Atlantic were artisans and small farmers, solid members of the working class.

The most important social determinant in the colonies in 1650 was land ownership, and the abundance of this commodity, especially in the southern colonies, produced a good deal of upward social mobility. An upper class developed in America which included planters, governors and council members, and merchants who had financed and led settlements but which also included migrants who had accumulated property and wealth after coming to the New World. In New England one could move up the social ladder by entering the ministry or by conducting a successful business enterprise.

The residents of colonial America did not automatically accord their leaders the respect they would have commanded in England. Though those who dominated the political and economic life of the colonies were successful in battling nature and the natives, they frequently did not possess the education, self-confidence, or social bearing that seventeenth-century Europeans associated with the aristocracy. The Puritans recognized that the Bible condoned both monarchy and aristocracy, but they believed that religion, specifically a salvation experience, ought to be the ultimate badge of social as well as moral worth. In addition, on farms in New England and the Chesapeake, and in the South, it was difficult to maintain social distance. Landowner and indentured servant had to labor side by side in the fields.

The social environment in colonial towns was even more fluid. Skilled craftsmen and small businessmen took advantage of new markets and emerging opportunities to enrich themselves. Many who succeeded did not hesitate to flaunt their wealth and mimic their social superiors, much to the disgust of traditionalists. It was common in the 1600s for colonial governments to issue decrees or pass laws limiting wages or forbidding certain kinds of dress for the working classes.

SLAVE COMMUNITIES

Life among enslaved Africans was characterized by brutally hard agricultural labor. To their masters, slaves were commodities to be exploited and not human beings to be nurtured. Slave codes prohibited the teaching of slaves to read and write and outlawed their conversion to Christianity. Masters assumed that literacy and notions of human equality and brotherhood in the Bible would render their chattel intractable and rebellious. The vast majority of Africans were field hands; even household workers tilled the soil part of the year. With the passage of time, however, larger plantations became more complex and slaves learned to be blacksmiths, weavers, tanners, and carpenters. Masters furnished newly acquired slaves with the rudest of clothing, but burlap and sackcloth were soon supplemented by hand-me-downs from the plantation house so that slave dress assumed a colorful, indiscriminate, patchwork

THE BROOMSTICK WEDDING.

"Look squar' at de broomstick !   All ready now ! one-two-three-jump ! "

Jumping the broomstick at a slave wedding in the antebellum South. Excluded from white churches, those in bondage had to devise their own ceremonies to celebrate birth, marriage, and death.

appearance. Shoes, ill-fitting and crude, were worn only in the winter. Food was simple but generally abundant—corn and pork—but over time this diet was supplemented by vegetables grown in tiny patches near the slave quarters and fish and game from the forest.

Christian marriage was not permitted for slaves, but the majority lived their lives as part of a nuclear family. Masters had the right to break up families, selling off husbands, wives, and children to different owners. Yet, the family was the basis of slave community life. Most men and women lived together in slave communities numbering ten or more; they made love, conceived, and then usually married in a ritual featuring the exchange of simple gifts. (Premarital sex was socially acceptable in many African societies, and if not acceptable, frequently engaged in by colonists both with each other and with slaves.) In the South the couple typically jumped over a broomstick together to announce their union to the community. During the first half of the eighteenth century, visitors to large plantations reported the prevalence of traditional nuclear families. Men on smaller plantations would frequently have to marry women on neighboring farms. Their children would remain with the mothers; the fathers would have to be content with visiting their wives and children at night and on holidays, always with the permission of their masters. Slave owners generally knew their chattel only by their first names, but married slaves were careful to take surnames to establish and maintain patterns of kinship. Only two of five adult male slaves took the names of their masters. Surnames frequently reflected parental residence either in Africa or America. Given names were both Anglo and African. Because the nuclear family was constantly threatened by separation, violence, and death, Africans encouraged extended kinship. Hence, children were encouraged to call adults to which they were unrelated "auntie" or "uncle" and other children "brother" or "sister."

AFRICAN-AMERICAN CULTURE

Christianity did not take root among African Americans until after the revival movement known as the Great Awakening swept the South in the 1760s, but slaves practiced varieties of religion they brought with them from Africa. Members of slave communities kept separate graveyards which they covered with shells or pottery as markers. It was commonly believed that the souls of the dead would return to Africa, so that death and burial were occasions for both sadness and joy. Indeed, the most important of the slave rituals was the burial ceremony. Staged at night to avoid detection by white authorities who generally opposed the preservation of African customs, the ritual featured ancestral songs and a counter-clockwise dance around the deceased that gradually increased in speed and intensity until it reached a joyful conclusion. For Africans, dance was a primary form of worship, a means for achieving union with ancestors and the gods.

Indeed, music and dance comprised the core of African-American slave culture. The black slaves' oft-commented-on facility for rhythm and melody was a natural outgrowth of a culture for which dance and music were primary forms of worship. Slaves celebrated European holidays and voting days because those were the periods during which they were allowed time to themselves. They recreated native African stringed instruments, such as the banjo, and eventually made them integral parts of southern culture. Slave quarter music featured rhythmic complexity and innovation, two additional gifts that Africans would bequeath to American music.

Out of necessity, slaves developed their own dialect, or patois. Black English was a mixture of traditional English and various African dialects. Such a language made it possible for first generation black slaves to communicate with their American-born brethren. It also had the added advantage of insulating the slave community somewhat from masters and overseers. Many a white complained about the fact that slaves employed a variety of English that they could not understand. The two most important dialects were Gullah and Geeche, named for two African tribes, the Golas and Gizzis, which supplied a significant portion of the black populations of Georgia and South Carolina.

A CLIMATE OF FEAR

The master-slave relationship was based on fear and violence. Some masters were kind and others sadistic, but even the most well-disposed whipped their slaves as a matter of course. A flogging of fifty to seventy-five lashes was considered almost routine. Slaves were disciplined with extra work, public humiliation, or solitary confinement, but the whip always lurked in the background as the ultimate coercive tool.

Slaves did not endure their suffering willingly. Resistance was commonplace. Bondsmen and -women broke tools, destroyed crops, malingered, and, most frequently, ran away. Indeed, despite harsh punishments including severe whipping and mutilation, tens of thousands of African slaves, most of them unattached males in their twenties, ran away. Some in the deep South fled to the Everglades and formed semipermanent communities called "maroons" (for the Spanish word *cimarron* meaning wild and untamed). In the upper South the Great Dismal Swamp between Virginia and North Carolina provided refuge. In 1771 the governor of Georgia warned that north of Savannah "a great number of fugitive Negroes had committed many robberies and insults," and dispatched a contingent of militia to destroy their camp. As slave communities grew in size and complexity, armed resistance to slaveholders increased. Between 1720 and 1740 in the lower South where slaves were in a majority, a number of small uprisings occurred. The most serious of these was the Stono Rebellion in South Carolina.

THE STONO REBELLION

In 1739 a group of twenty Angolans sacked the colonial armory at Stono Bridge. They armed themselves and marched southward toward Florida and freedom. Beating drums to attract other slaves, the original band soon increased their number to over one hundred. The rebels plundered several plantations and killed over thirty white colonists. The slaves stopped to celebrate their freedom with singing and dancing, thus allowing pursuing militia to catch up. In the battle that followed, the Stono rebels were destroyed.

Compared to Spanish America and the West Indies, North America produced relatively few slave revolts, however. Physical conditions were favorable enough that a flourishing native-born population emerged. In addition, the success of African Americans at nurturing families and communities and cultivating distinctive folkways and mores militated against armed revolution.

THE COLONIAL FRONTIER
AND THE CORROSION OF NATIVE AMERICA

THE BACKCOUNTRY

By the 1720s the line of settlement had moved westward across the first range of the Appalachians and into the interior. Though they dreamed of becoming commercial farmers these residents of the backcountry were, like their Indian neighbors, gatherers, hunters, and primitive agriculturalists. They raised Indian corn, hunted for meat and furs, and lived in log cabins, a type of architecture that originated with the settlers of New Sweden on the Delaware River. Backcountry society was egalitarian, violent, and basic. Proximity to nature, the difficulty of eking out a living, and the fact that most were squatters who had no legal title to their land blurred social distinctions. Most were Scottish or Irish, people for whom clan and ethnic violence was commonplace, and this coupled with constant friction with the Indians led to frequent bloodshed. These were a hard-drinking, hard-fighting, sexually uninhibited people whom those living along the coastal tidelands regarded as little better than barbarians. They were to be the cutting edge of American civilization as it spread across the continent, however.

INFLUENCE ON THE INDIANS

From the late seventeenth century and through the eighteenth century, Native Americans continued to be dramatically affected by contact with European colonists. Diseases imported by the English, Dutch, French, and Spanish wreaked havoc on those tribes that occupied a crescent stretching from Newfoundland into the lower South and westward across the Spanish borderlands into the current American Southwest. From an estimated high of seven to ten million in 1500, the Native American population, ravaged by influenza, measles, and smallpox, dwindled to one million by 1800. Tribes in the interior were, of course, less affected than those in frequent contact with the colonists on the periphery of the continent.

European contact introduced technological innovations among Native Americans, such as the use of firearms and, in some areas, the construction of log cabins. Perhaps the most important new tool appropriated by Native Americans was the horse. During the early 1700s Indians living on the edges of the Great Plains began capturing and taming wild horses, the descendents of animals imported by the Spanish conquistadors in the sixteenth century. With mounts, various nomadic tribes were able to roam much larger areas and hunt buffalo more efficiently. The Plains Indians, a network of tribes boasting a complex, nomadic culture, were indigenous but dramatically affected by European colonization.

The early eighteenth century also bore witness to massive Indian migrations from the Great Lakes and Appalachia into the interior. Thousands of Native Americans who lost their lands to colonists through treaties or battles moved westward, frequently coming into conflict with other tribes. Between 1720 and 1741, Pennsylvania, a colony with a reputation for fair dealing and respect for human rights, foisted a series of fraudulent treaties on the Delawares that in effect deprived them of their ancestral lands. The pattern would repeat itself hundreds of times until Native Americans found themselves, a century and a half later, decimated and confined to barren reservations west of the Mississippi.

COLONIAL RELIGION

Religion was important everywhere in colonial America; churches were the pre-eminent agencies of socialization and acculturation. The colonists were overwhelmingly Christian, but in sixteenth- and seventeenth-century Europe Christianity was in crisis. Colonists all assumed that some doctrines were orthodox and others heretical, but they disagreed as to which were which. They all believed that orthodoxy ought to be encouraged and that the state ought to be deeply involved in religious matters, as the church ought to be with the social and political order. Finally, immigrants from Europe expected simply to transplant and continue the religious communities they had experienced in their home countries. To their dismay, that proved impossible.

CORRUPTION OF THE ANGLICAN CHURCH

Those English persons who settled Virginia expected to reproduce exactly the Church of England; that they were unable to do so had more to do with economics than with heresy or reform. Anglican churches in the parent country were supported by income earned from land donated by wealthy parishioners. In 1618 the colonial government of Virginia set aside one hundred acres from each of the boroughs into which Virginia was divided for the support of the church. Unfortunately, because land ownership was universally desired and relatively easy to achieve, no one rented the church's land, and so it received no income. The second alternative, and the one adopted, was to provide support for the church and its minister through taxation. The Virginia Company ordered colonists to supplement their local church's rental income until the total reached £200 a year. This practice evolved into an annual subsidy voted by the vestry, the governing body of the parish.

Taxation worked in theory but not in practice. In England population density was such that taxation would generate the desired revenue at an affordable rate, but because Virginia's population was thin and unevenly distributed, taxation did not. For an Anglican minister to have effectively ministered to his flock, the numbers of parishioners would have been so small that support of clergy would have been prohibitively expensive. In fact, parishes were so large and the population so dispersed that meaningful community became impossible. To make matters worse, the Virginia House of Burgesses decreed in 1662 that ministers be paid £80 per year. But the prevailing currency in Virginia was tobacco, the price of which varied dramatically from year to year. As a result colonial priests lived in a continual state of economic insecurity.

The upshot was that Virginia was able to attract only the most poorly trained and undisciplined ministers. English clergy considered conditions in America to be intolerable. Clergy were completely dependent upon the vestry, the self-perpetuating governing body of the parish, and as a result, were usually underpaid and overworked. To make matters worse, the hierarchical structure, which was characteristic of the Church of England, collapsed in America. There were no local bishops; governors were empowered to appoint parish clergy for life from nominations submitted by vestries. But the parish governing bodies rarely submitted nominations, preferring to retain direct control themselves. Anglicanism became decentralized and to an extent secularized. Because ministers found it difficult to reach remote areas, laypersons often conducted services. Funerals, marriages, and baptisms were frequently private affairs devoid of the official church liturgy, vestments, and ordained ministers. What developed, then, was a kind of Anglican congregationalism with each parish going its own doctrinal and sacramental way. Anglican and Catholic communities in Maryland, which were legitimized in 1649 in the Calvert's Act Concerning Religion and lived thereafter in uneasy coexistence, endured the same decentralizing and secularizing forces.

NEW YORK AND THE DUTCH REFORMED CHURCH

The prevailing religion in New York was the Dutch Reformed Church established when the colony was New Netherlands. All sects were tolerated, including Jews and Quakers, on the condition that those other than Dutch Reformed practice in private and pay taxes to support the established church. A year after the English conquered the colony in 1664 a "local option" plan went into effect in which each community was to choose a Protestant denomination that would be supported with tax dollars. The Dutch Reformed Church continued to prevail, causing some tension with the English colonial government which viewed loyalty to the Dutch church and loyalty to the English crown as incompatible. As in other colonies, low pay and poor working conditions created a poorly trained and poorly motivated clergy, and wide dispersal of population contributed to improvisation and sometimes heresy in religious practice.

SECULARIZATION OF THE PURITAN COMMONWEALTH

Puritans in New England continued to be concerned with the creation of a Bible commonwealth. What distinguished the Puritans from other Protestants was their insistence that only the "chosen," those who had had a saving experience validated by the church, could become church members, and decentralization, the organization of church as a series of autonomous congregational units. Within three decades, the spiritual fervor and emotional commitment that had characterized John Winthrop's generation diminished, and church membership declined. Children of the saved were baptized but not allowed to become full-fledged church members. Meanwhile, nonchurch members who had originally found the structure and social security provided by the theocracy comforting, began to grow restive under the rule of a constantly shrinking minority.

To deal with the problem of declining church membership and an increasingly unpopular theocracy, a convention of ministers began meeting in 1657. In 1662 they came up with the Halfway Covenant. The children of those who had had a salvation experience could be baptized but not receive communion or vote. These halfway members had to take an oath to obey church/community rules and to raise their children as Christians. Within a generation, however, the distinction between full and halfway members began to blur. In the final analysis, the Halfway Covenant proved acceptable to neither group. It struck at the fundamental precept of Puritanism—that is, the church as a community of proven saints—and continued to make the unconverted feel like second-class citizens.

THE GREAT AWAKENING

By the second quarter of the eighteenth century, a century after the colonies were founded, the established denominations in America were failing to meet the religious needs of their congregations. Doctrinal divisions led to legalistic disputes, poorly trained clergy to undisciplined and uninspired congregations, and excessive lay ministry to secularization of church services. It was noteworthy that the most effective religious organization in America was the Society for the Propagation of the Gospel in Foreign Parts, originally established to bring Christianity to the Indians. Frustrated and spiritually undernourished, the colonists hungered for revival and renewal.

The stage was set for the Great Awakening. The early leader of this evangelical movement was the remarkable young minister of Northampton, Massachusetts, Jonathan Edwards. After graduating from Yale at the age of seventeen, Edwards devoted himself to the principal philosophical and theological problems of the age and eventually succeeded his grandfather as the chief cleric at Northampton in western Massachusetts. In 1734 and 1735 the young preacher delivered a series of carefully reasoned sermons emphasizing justification by faith rather than birth, scriptural knowledge, or church certification. The emphasis on the absolute sovereignty of God and depravity of man was there, as his "Sinners in the Hands of an Angry God" abundantly bore witness to, but God was merciful and would save all those who turned to Him. After suspending his listeners over the fiery pit in "Sinners," Edwards offered them rescue: "And now you have an extraordinary opportunity, a day wherein Christ has thrown the door of mercy wide open, and stands in the door calling and crying with a loud voice to poor sinners." Northampton was seized with religious fervor, and word of the revival swept through the Connecticut River Valley.

In 1740 the young, dynamic Methodist cleric, George Whitefield, arrived in New England following successful revivals in the southern and mid-Atlantic colonies. His impassioned, spirit-filled appeals inspired thousands who had for years been subjected to dry, scholarly sermons usually read to them from prepared texts. Edwards' and Whitefield's efforts sent shock waves through the Presbyterian and Dutch Reformed communities of the middle colonies, dividing them into conservative and evangelical wings. Their crusade split Anglican communities in the South, and inspired evangelical Baptists to proselytize among backcountry farmers.

The Great Awakening's impact on the English colonies in North America was long-lasting and far-reaching. It affected all regions and all social classes. The movement weakened time-encrusted, dogma-ridden established churches and clergy. The evangelicals cared little for established form and authority. Stimulation and satisfaction of the flock's spiritual longings were the only criteria for success. To challenge Yale and Harvard, the preeminent institutions for training clerics in New England, Presbyterian "New Lights" established the College of New Jersey, subsequently renamed Princeton, to teach a religion of the emotions as well as the mind.

The Awakening also threatened the traditional identification of churches with specific territorial boundaries. To the anger and dismay of traditional clergy, the evangelicals believed that their mission was to spread the word to the churched and unchurched alike in all regions. Splintering established religious communities, operating within and outside existing congregations, evangelical activists inadvertently destroyed institutionalized religion as the fundamental instrument of social organization at the local level.

Finally and most important, the Great Awakening accelerated the trend toward separation of church and state. The evangelicals, of course, claimed that they were the true orthodox Christians and that the established churches were the deviants. But given that close association between church and state represented the status quo, the New Lights came to believe that the very notion of an established church was false and an obstacle to an authentic, personal relationship with God.

COLONIAL FAMILIES

WOMEN'S ROLES

In colonial America the vast majority of women were farm wives who bore large numbers of children. Most women spent the entire period between puberty and menopause, if they did not die in the meantime, pregnant. They minded households and produced what was eaten and worn. They cooked, sewed, wove, raised vegetables, tended to fruit trees, churned butter, and raised bees. Their lives were characterized by mind-numbing routine. While men and boys could look forward to trips to taverns or mills and to hunting and fishing, women were tied to hearth and children year-round. A handful who carved out careers as midwives, herbalists, or tradeswomen managed to instill some variety in their lives.

Under English common law and colonial regulations, married women could not hold property, make contracts, or sue in court. Women could not vote. Upon marriage, females had to surrender all property to their husbands; only a handful of widows and spinsters were property owners. Until the end of the seventeenth century, divorce in colonial America was virtually impossible.

Only in church life did women approach equality with men. Puritans legitimized salvation experiences for women as well as men. "Women are creatures without which there is no comfortable living for man," wrote the Puritan minister John Cotton, but that was more a summary of the condition of Puritan women than it was a divine's assertion that the life of the soul knew no sex. The Puritan ideal of the virtuous woman was a chaste, submissive helpmate, who served God by serving her man. Outspoken females such as Anne Hutchinson fared badly. By 1700, however, women constituted a majority within the community of saints, and in some congregations membership enabled them to vote for ministerial candidates and pass on the validity of salvation experiences. The Quakers were distinguished by the power and status they accorded women members. Female Quakers could speak in meetings and act as missionaries.

It was not unusual for independent women in New England to be suspected of contributing to mishaps in the community and accused of witchcraft. During the last quarter of the eighteenth century, Puritan divines and popular writers wrote dozens of books and pamphlets recounting "wonders"—supernatural occurrences that disturbed the natural order of things, and witchcraft figured prominently in such accounts. Both men and women—wizards and witches—were believed capable of supernatural powers and susceptible to possession by Satan. But of the 344 persons charged with witchcraft during the period from 1620 to 1720, more than three-quarters were women. Typically, they were middle-aged and persons of power and status in the community. Many were publicly identified with a political or social faction; came from families suspected of having Anglican, Baptist, or Quaker sympathies; and were property owners. Most lived alone. The infamous Salem village episode of 1692 produced numerous accusations and twenty executions. Most of the victims were women.

Although New England villages were egalitarian communities with decision making shared equally by male heads of household, families in that region were predominately patriarchal and authoritarian. Quakers in New Jersey and Pennsylvania boasted families that were nuclear and long-lined, but they were not focused on original sin or the concept of predestination. Consequently, they were more likely to provide a warm and nurturing environment for their children. Family structure in the southern colonies differed dramatically in the southern climes. Early death, late marriage, and a shortage of females meant that very few males became grandfathers. Many never married; those who became engaged did so relatively late in life, and one of the spouses—usually the male—died within seven or eight years. Widows frequently remarried. As a result, southern families tended to be extended rather than nuclear, with children tied to uncles, aunts, and cousins as well as to parents.

An urban scene from colonial America—"High Street, from the Country Marketplace, Philadelphia," etching, ca. 1750-60.

DAILY LIFE

Housing

The physical world in which the colonists lived was small and close to nature. The early settlers spent a great deal of time dealing with their surroundings—the weather, disease, the soil, the natives. Even after 175 years of colonial experience, the line of settlement had barely crept inland from the coastline.

Most colonial houses were one-story or story-and-a-half wooden structures with typical English characteristics—an overhanging second story; steep, shingled roofs; leaded glass windows; a large central chimney, and timbered walls with clapboard for protection against the climate. Early residences were typically fastened together with wooden pegs, as was the furniture of the period. Except for the finer mansions that began to appear in the late seventeenth century, houses went unpainted, for paint was expensive. It was not uncommon for colonials to whitewash their clapboarded houses, using a lime-based material made from burnt oyster shells.

Food and Vices

Following the early "starving times" of the Jamestown colony, food was abundant in most areas and during most periods. The well-to-do enjoyed a good deal of variety; the working class did not, subsisting primarily on corn bread, hominy, and pork. Beef, pork, fish, and other game were readily available, especially in the South. Fresh vegetables and fruit were scarce except in season. A publication entitled *The Compleat Housewife* suggested the following as a winter meal for an obviously prosperous family: first course: giblet pie, gravy soup and chicken, and roast beef with horseradish and pickles; second course: a tansy [butter tasting herb] with orange; woodcocks on toast; rabbit with savory pudding; roast turkey; and, finally, butter apple pie. Beverages included tea, coffee, and chocolate, all of which were imported. Tea was more often consumed in towns and by the upper classes. Those of more humble means and rural dwellers substituted a native herb. Hard liquor was consumed in quart amounts everywhere. Tobacco was universally used as well—most smoked pipes or took snuff. The working classes dipped; sniffing a pinch up the nose was considered more genteel and thus was practiced by the upper classes.

Dress

Dress was a point of social class in sixteenth- and seventeenth-century America. This convention led to extravagant costumes among the aristocracy and to legislation against "excessive dress" by the "common people." Most well-to-do males possessed three suits of clothes: a durable, practical suit for work; a better outfit suited for going to market; and finery for church and social affairs. The affluent wore long frock coats, tight-fitting, knee-length trousers of brocade, velvet, or silk—and silk stockings and shoes with silver or gold buckles. Upper-class women dressed in silk, satin, muslin, and a fancy calico. The hoop skirt, featuring wasp waists made so by whalebone corsets, and high, feathered hats would be fashionable for much of the eighteenth and into the nineteenth centuries.

A GROWING SENSE OF PLACE

By 1700, then, some 250,000 people of European and African descent had clustered along a stretch of the Atlantic coast from present-day Maine to South Carolina. For the most part, these free and enslaved peoples—there were free blacks as well as chattels, living mostly in the larger towns—resided in the fertile river valleys where they could grow crops and avail themselves of water transportation. They still confronted a densely forested interior and lived close to nature, but towns and even cities had emerged with second and third generation native-born inhabitants living in them. These people did not think of themselves as American, but they had a sense of place that was strong and immediate.

African Americans were dispossessed and displaced, but they accommodated themselves as best they could, in the process preserving the folkways of their native regions and even infusing them into the dominant white culture. Native American tribes inhabiting the eastern coastal regions of North America, meanwhile, died of European disease, were killed in savage warfare with the newcomers, or moved west. The survivors attempted to form new relationships with the inland tribes and to adapt to a new physical environment, but their lives had been changed forever.

The Europeans who inhabited England's North American colonies were basically conservative people who saw change as threatening and who wished above all to control their local communities and prosper. This was not the stuff of which revolutions were made, but when the perception grew that the parent country was infringing on both of these rights, revolution would indeed come.

As Mary Beth Norton and others have pointed out, historians of American women long portrayed the colonial period as a kind of golden age in which females in Britain's North American colonies fared better than their contemporaries in England or their successors in the Victorian era. According to this view, the gender imbalance placed a premium on wives, particularly before 1700, and thus gave women power over their suitors and their mates. Because women performed economic functions crucial to the survival of the family and society in general, namely food processing and clothing production, they enjoyed status and power. Finally, the fluidity of the frontier enabled colonial women to participate in activities—running a business, for example—that in the future would be considered exclusively masculine. In the passage that follows, Margaret Ripley Wolfe acknowledges the accuracy of some of these contentions, but argues that American women living in the colonial South were caught up in a society that was relentlessly patriarchal and frequently demeaning and abusive.

IN THE BEGINNING
Margaret Ripley Wolfe

During the seventeenth and early eighteenth centuries the American South witnessed a fundamental social, political, economic, and environmental transformation.

from "In the Beginning" from Margaret Ripley Wolfe, *Daughters of Canaan: A Saga of Southern Women* (Lexington: The University Press of Kentucky, 1995), pp. 11–32.

European white males in the Chesapeake area and elsewhere in the southern colonies began the process of subduing the Native-American cultures that they encountered and imposing their will on this new land and its people. The dominant English as well as other ethnic groups carried with them to North America considerable cultural baggage which formed the basis of the New World that they subsequently created. As a creole society took shape on land that Europeans considered virgin, old familiar ideas about gender relations proved amazingly resilient.

Although transplanted Englishmen found it possible to adjust their views temporarily as circumstances warranted, they rarely deviated over the long haul from what they considered the tried and true. In the southern colonies, they relegated women—red, white, and black—to perhaps even more pronounced positions of inferiority. For Indian females, this meant a devaluation of the status they had enjoyed in their traditional societies; for whites the continuation and, in some instances, the exacerbation of circumstances that had affected them in Europe; and for blacks, transplanted to America against their will, seemingly endless servitude and degradation. Elaborate philosophical arguments buttressed these emerging circumstances and, perhaps for white women, ameliorated the harsher aspects of a patriarchal order, because opportunities abounded in the Chesapeake and also in the other southern colonies for white women as well as men to better themselves socially and economically. For these females the measure of their success usually rested on either the accidents of their births and who their fathers were or on the matrimonial arrangements they made or had made for them and the status of their husbands. This, however, was hardly the case for Native-American and African-American women.

What historians know of initial encounters between European men and Native-American women is almost all from the perspective of the conquerors. If some of their accounts are taken literally, notes the historian Theda Perdue even as she challenges them, then Spaniards subjected the women at their mercy to rape as well as other forms of violence and abuse, whereas the English found themselves besieged by native women and almost overwhelmed by their uninvited attentions. According to popular legend, the venerable Pocahontas rescued John Smith, married John Rolfe, and saved Jamestown; and if Smith is to be believed, on one occasion thirty naked young women, covered only partially by a few green leaves in front and behind, set upon him in his house. "These Nymphes more tormented him [than] ever," he complained in third person, "with crowding, pressing, and hanging about him, most tediously crying, Love you not me? Love you not me?"

The combination of forwardness and nakedness hardly rendered the native women physically unattractive. More than one European thought to mention not only their pretty bodies but also the fact that Indian women seemed to do all of the work. The historian Edmund S. Morgan has written: "Nearly any activity that could be designated as work at all was left to the women. They were the principal means of production in Indian Virginia." When a man took a wife, which meant the exchange of goods, he expected her to support him. "He could make canoes, weapons, and weirs without losing his dignity," Morgan explains, "but the only other labor he ordinarily engaged in was clearing fields for planting, and the method employed [girdling the trees and burning brush] made this less than arduous." When the next growing season came, however, "the women worked the ground between the trees, using a crooked stick as a hoe and planting corn, beans, squash, and melons all together in little hills." Superficially accurate though this statement may be, it fails to take into account the carefully defined gender roles and the relatively separate but nonetheless significant status of women in Native-American societies. It is true that women performed most of the labor, but they also had acknowledged title to the land they tilled, the houses they occupied, and the children they bore.

Captain Arthur Barlow[e], a participant in Sir Walter Raleigh's first expedition of 1584, had commented extensively and favorably on the wife of the Indian "king's" brother and the women around her, describing her as "very well favored, of mean stature, and very bashful." As for her dress, "she had on her back a long cloak of leather, with the fur side next to her body, and before her a piece of the same. About her forehead she had a band of white coral. . . . In her ears she had bracelets of pearl hanging down on her middle . . . and those were of the bigness of good peas." The "rest of her women of the better sort" wore copper pendants in their ears. Barlow also reported that the Indians were "of color yellowish, and their hair black for the most part, and yet we saw children that had very fine auburn and chestnut colored hair." The latter may have been the issue of native women and European sailors who had been shipwrecked on the coast several years earlier.

The females Barlow described appeared to be thoroughly clad, but such was not always the case. European men generally linked the absence of clothing with licentiousness, and the Christians found nakedness uncommonly arousing. The bare breasts and sometimes uncovered pudenda proved disconcerting enough; that Indian women plucked their pubic hair distracted white males even more. Native-American women as well as men sometimes also wore tattoos, and whites considered this an effort to enhance sexuality. The Europeans also scrutinized the relative sexual freedom and overall conduct of Indian women, condemning it on one hand but maximizing it to their advantage on the other and rarely if ever viewing native mores within their own social context. The bawdy sense of humor that some Indian women displayed, their directness in sexual matters, their seeming lack of modesty, as well as the occurrence of premarital relations, easy divorce, and the practice of sororal polygamy, contradicted European male notions of appropriate feminine conduct. The eighteenth-century English trader-author James Adair, a visitor among the Cherokees, remarked with disgust that they "have been a considerable while under petticoat-government, and allow their women full liberty to plant their brows with horns as oft as they please, without fear of punishment."

In some respects, however, the Indians were even more proscribed in their sexual conduct than were Europeans. Standards existed among the southeastern Indians relative to when, where, and with whom one might engage in sexual intercourse. Indeed, warriors preparing for or returning from battle, ball players readying for games, men on the winter hunts, and pregnant and menstruating women had to forgo pleasures of the flesh. Natives in the South, then, denied themselves for a greater portion of their lives than did their European counterparts. Taboos also existed against coupling in the agricultural fields, and rules regarding incest severely limited such possibilities. Among the Cherokees with their seven clans, for example, no one could marry into the clan of either parent, which meant that approximately one-third of all Cherokees were forbidden as partners.

What the European men found especially peculiar and grievous, however, in the American South, given the fact that they regarded women as property, was the relative independence of Indian women and the seeming lack of concern or control on the part of their male counterparts. From the European perspective it was the responsibility of an honorable man to protect the chastity of his wife and daughters. Native males sometimes not only tolerated but even encouraged sexual activity between visitors and women who "belonged" to the native men. Matrilocal residence patterns and matrilineal kinship proved equally baffling to the English as well as other Western Europeans. When marriage occurred among southern Indians, the male took up residence among his wife's relatives because all buildings, garden plots, and sections of the common fields belonged to her lineage. Children traced kinship through their female relatives, and when and if divorce occurred, children remained with their mothers. Thus, men had no claim to the property they occupied or the offspring they fathered.

By the early nineteenth century, southern Indians came to be known as the Five Civilized Tribes, in recognition of the alacrity with which they had adapted to transplanted European culture. Among other things, this meant a redefinition of gender roles. In the meantime the Spanish and French as well as the English accommodated themselves with Native-American women, sometimes even taking them as lifetime partners or "wives." "Sex," Theda Perdue has written, "was a kind of commodity to Europeans: they purchased it from prostitutes with money and from respectable women with marriage." Consequently, the fact that some Indian women bartered their favors could hardly have been too surprising to the Europeans. . . .

In practice, Englishmen during the age of exploration and colonization wasted little chivalry on women of any race, nor were their relations with the opposite sex particularly harmonious. In February 1585, for instance, Sir Francis Drake appeared off Cartagena, in South America, subsequently capturing it, burning the galleys that defended it, and liberating the slaves. When he finally left Cartagena in ashes on 10 April, he took with him three hundred Indians, most of them women, and two hundred Negroes, Turks, and Moors. It is doubtful that Drake took time to pay deference to the wishes of the native or Negro women. He then headed for the Florida channel and attacked the Spanish fort at St. Augustine; local Indians meanwhile began to burn the town. The Spanish women and children who had been evacuated to the interior to escape the English then faced the danger of an Indian attack. Apparently Drake's moves at Cartagena and in Florida were intended to solidify Anglo-Indian relations at the expense of the Spanish and additionally to reduce the threat that St. Augustine might pose to any future English settlement.

Later, in 1611, after Jamestown had been established but was still struggling against great odds, Sir Thomas Dale, its governor, sent George Percy to exact revenge on the Indians nearest Jamestown because he believed that Powhatan was harboring some runaway Englishmen. Percy and his men attacked the town, killed fifteen or sixteen Indians, and captured the "queen" of the tribe and her children.

Percy took them back to the boats and embarked for Jamestown. His men began to grumble because the woman and her children had been spared. Percy obligingly threw the children into the brink, "shoteinge owtt their Braynes in the water." Back in Jamestown, Percy learned that Dale was displeased that the woman had been spared. One suggestion was to burn her, but Percy, already "haveinge seene so mutche Bloodshedd that day," rejected the more heinous fiery method in favor of the sword. She was led away and stabbed. By the same token the Indians could hardly be described as lacking in grisly imagination. In one instance, native women used mussel shells to flay a live English captive.

If white women fared better at the hands of Englishmen in the Chesapeake than did the native women, it was only because they were so desperately needed to nurture and sustain the struggling Virginia colony. Proper Christian Englishmen, for the most part, could hardly expect to find suitable mates among heathens, a fact that virtually dictated the early presence of white women in the colonial South. Seagoing vessels during the colonial era sometimes carried in their holds crudely fashioned cheap iron as ballast, which a few centuries later would prove extremely valuable as architectural ornamentation. Almost from the beginning of colonization they likewise carried women—equally practical "iron lace," as the ballast came to be called in English-speaking Australia—to undergird households and support families. More to the point, Englishmen in Virginia placed intrinsic economic value on women as breeders and servants.

Although there were no females among the earliest arrivals at Jamestown in 1607, seventeen women had come to Roanoke Island, the ill-fated colony off the coast of North Carolina, in 1587 and ultimately had disappeared. Out of that experience, Virginia Dare, reputedly the first white English Christian child born in North America, won her place in American history. Governor John White recorded in his narrative that on "the 13th, Elenor, daughter of the Governor [the narrator's own daughter], and wife of Ananias Dare, one of the Assistants, was delivered of a daughter in Roanoke, and the same was christened there the Sunday following, and because this child was the first Christian born in Virginia, she was named Virginia."

With the initial failures of English colonial ventures, promoters seemed all the more determined to achieve success; and white women figured prominently in their plans. A member of His Majesty's Council of Virginia wrote: "When the Plantation grows to strength, then it is time to plant with women as well as with men; that the plantation may spread into generations, and not be ever pieced from without." It was his perspective and the masculine viewpoint in general that women had a dual role: to reproduce and to see to the comforts of men so that "their minds might be faster tyed to Virginia."

Even before 1619, when the Virginia Company of London became actively engaged in sending women to the new colony, females had made their way to Jamestown. The wife of Thomas Forrest and her maid, Anne Burras, arrived during the fall of 1608 in what was called the Second Supply. Some twenty women and children arrived the following August. In 1609 there were approximately one hundred women and four to five hundred men in Jamestown. These first women, just as the men, fell victims to sickness, hunger, and Indian massacres. Around 1610, when only about sixty men, women, and children remained, cannibalism entered the picture. An account exists of a man who ate his wife during the "Starving Time." The truth, according to a pamphlet published by the Council of Virginia, was that he hated his wife and had taken advantage of circumstances to kill her, attempting to conceal his crime by claiming that she had died of natural causes and that he had eaten parts of her body to sustain himself. A modern chronicler, Arthur Frederick Ide, quoting from colonial records, reports that the starving denizens of Jamestown devoured "those Hogges, Dogges & Horses that were then in the Collony, together with Rates, mice, snakes . . . [and] the flesh . . . of man, as well of our owne nation as of an Indian, digged by some out of his grave after he had laien buried three daies & wholly devoured." Preference was given to female flesh, however, because it was deemed "in the better state of bodie" than that of a male "which proves toughe and sinewy."

Those involved with the colony's development agreed that masculine comfort required the presence of women, which would serve to prevent men from returning to England. Sir Edwin Sandys, the company's treasurer, employed this justification when he recommended the sending of a hundred women to Virginia, with the share-holders to be reimbursed by planters who married them. In the spring of 1620 the company dispatched ninety maidens and fifty or so more in 1621–22. Apparently all of these had found husbands by 1622. A planter who married one of them incurred an obligation to the company of 120 pounds of his best tobacco. All the same, these early females had plenty of male attention. Some of them even stirred controversy by becoming engaged to several men at the same time, which forced the House of Burgesses to pass a law forbidding such practices. One disgruntled bachelor complained in 1623 of being unable to afford a woman servant and therefore being forced to pay an exorbitant price to have his washing done. Furthermore, because not enough women were available to attend to men who were sick, he claimed, many of the ailing departed the world in an unduly nasty condition. Nonetheless, even as he lamented the absence of enough females to make him and other males comfortable, he disparaged those already present, saying: "For all that I can find that the multitude of women doe is nothing but to devour the food of the land without dooing any dayes deed whereby any benefitt may arise either to the Company or countrey."

Despite the initial feeble efforts of the Virginia Company and the various forms that the importation of women took after Virginia became a royal colony, more males than females immigrated. This, coupled with natural attrition, so profoundly affected the colonists that women remained a scarcity throughout the seventeenth century. The company went to considerable lengths to cast the women whom they dispatched in the best possible light as suitable brides for male colonists. According to the historian David R. Ransome, writing in 1991, "fifty-seven young women . . . went out to Virginia in 1621 to become wives for the settlers." Daughters of artisans and gentry, two of whom were nieces of knights, they sailed aboard the *Marmaduke,* the *Warwick,* and the *Tiger.* Documents now available "testify to the women's social respectability and domestic skills." Just before departing for Virginia, most of these women had resided in London or nearby—this in keeping with circumstances of subsequent migration to America when that great English city served as a catch basin through which human elements of the British Isles drained.

These women may have departed for America willingly enough, but others were misled or in some other manner were sent on their way to Virginia and elsewhere under duress. Even the willing incurred obligations. According to the historian Suzanne Lebsock, the vast majority of women colonists were bound laborers. During the seventeenth century a relatively small number of black women from Africa or from Africa by way of the West Indies may also have fallen into this category of temporary servitude. According to some accounts, about 80 percent of all English colonists, females among them, came as indentured servants, owing four to seven years of labor to those who paid their passages.

How these individuals came to be procured and transported to Virginia and elsewhere has not been highlighted in the pages of American history. Expected to bring a "bride" price of 120 pounds of tobacco each and to become wives of planters, the 140 or more women of 1620–22, "tobacco maids" as they have sometimes been called, were not felons. Nonetheless, female convicts, most of whose offenses were relatively minor, were subsequently introduced into the Old Dominion and other colonies as well. During the 1650s, soldiers of the London garrison had reportedly even raided brothels, capturing more than four hundred women and dispatching them to Barbados as "breeders." In 1925, the historian Harold U. Faulkner wrote: "Probably more liberties have been taken with the truth as regards the history of Virginia than with that of any other of the colonies . . . The white population of Virginia instead of being composed of the best elements of English society, was composed to a considerable extent of the worst." Phrased differently, more colonists represented the lower social and economic strata of English society than the privileged upper echelon.

Later in the colonial era, during the eighteenth century, Sir Alexander Grant hit upon a scheme to populate proposed English settlements in East Florida; he turned to the Magdalen House in London. Sir Alexander served as vice-president of that charitable establishment, which was intended to rescue from disease and degradation the several thousand prostitutes who walked the streets of that great city. "'Tis true," he had to admit, they "are not virgins." All the same, he declared them "comly, good tempered, reformed penitents, whose youth & inadvertency plunged into misfortunes which brought them into sad sufferings." Around 1768, four of the redeemed made their way to Florida and then disappeared from the historical record.

English empire builders looked not only to the reproductive capacities of less fortunate white females but also to the work that might be squeezed from the inferior ranks of both sexes. For most of the seventeenth century in Maryland and Virginia, black slavery had not yet replaced demands for cheap white labor. As extensions of the English economy whose investors sought quick profits, Virginia and Maryland discovered a market for tobacco; and its production diminished the need for or interest in other mercantile activities. The two colonies quickly became a refuge or a dumping ground, depending on one's perspective, for the downtrodden men and women of the Old Country whom the privileged classes there considered dangerous and best disposed of elsewhere. They filled the void for what seemed at times to be the insatiable demands of the tobacco culture. The practice existed of "spiriting" or kidnapping young waifs, both male and female, and dispatching them to America. Some early planters in Virginia also ransomed white captives from the Indians in order to exact service from them.

The historian Edmund S. Morgan has documented early instances of the physical abuse of male and female servants in Virginia. Elizabeth Abbott, for example, died after a series of beatings at the hands of her masters and their other servants. "Whether physically abused or not," declared Morgan, "Englishmen [and English women] found servitude in Virginia more degrading than servitude in England . . . [where] the hiring of workers was dignified by laws and customs that gave a servant some control over his [or her] own life." A servant could not only be sold to another master against her will but might also be gambled away. "Virginians," according to Morgan, "dealt in servants the way Englishmen dealt in land or chattels."

Nonetheless, the historians Lois Green Carr and Lorena S. Walsh have pointed to the opportunities that existed for women in the raw environment of the Chesapeake even as they acknowledge the difficulties and pitfalls that awaited white female indentured servants. Untimely death, field work, sexual abuse, and bearing a bastard were definite possibilities, perhaps even likelihoods, in seventeenth-century Virginia and Maryland. All the same, according to Carr and Walsh, "until the 1660s, the expanding economy of Maryland and Virginia offered opportunities well beyond those available in England to men without capital and to the women who became their wives." If finding husbands were their objective, as indeed it was for many women, their chances were excellent. Carr and Walsh argue that "the woman who immigrated to Maryland, survived seasoning and service, and gained her freedom became a planter's wife." Because men so dramatically outnumbered women and because a female did not have to take into account the viewpoints of a father or brothers, "she had considerable liberty in making her choice," even though she might have longed for the presence of a male protector.

Despite the glowing accounts floated by promoters, women who survived the seasoning process of the seventeenth century had hardly happened upon a New-World version of the Garden of Eden. Theirs was a beleaguered existence, for they performed hard physical labor just to carry out "all the day-to-day, never-done tasks" that made life possible. In reconstructing the life of a typical white woman of the period in Virginia, Suzanne Lebsock found that this female was about twenty years old when she arrived as an indentured servant. If she survived servitude, she married almost immediately, bore a child every year or two, and probably buried at least two of her offspring as children. She herself might not live to see her children reach maturity. Probably her husband, older than she, succumbed seven years into the marriage; and her demise followed in a few years. Untimely deaths disrupted Virginia families: only one marriage in three lasted as long as ten years; half of the children who reached the age of nine had lost one or both of their parents. The first successful English colony in North America was "a land of widows, widowers, bachelors, and, above all, orphans."

Lorena S. Walsh, in her work focusing heavily on the early English experience in Maryland, points out that because "the typical former [white] servant woman" had not entered into marriage until after her indenture ended, probably in her mid-twenties, she bore a relatively small number of children, perhaps three or four on average. Relieving the debt of passage used up several years of her childbearing cycle. The next generation of females, however, daughters of women who formerly had been servants, tended to marry younger and give birth to more children. Whatever the vicissitudes that accompanied the marital state, matrimony seemed a prerequisite for an adult female who wanted to enhance her social and economic status and acquire a modicum of security. Otherwise she probably remained a servant or perhaps an unwelcome dependent in another woman's household.

"The prevailing legal and societal restrictions," according to Walsh, "did mean, however, that the nearly inevitable decision to marry had graver consequences for women than for men." Under common law the male exercised authority over his spouse and offspring; this extended to physical punishment for corrective purposes. A married woman, a feme covert, could not enter into contracts or retain control of property that she brought into the marriage unless she or a protective male relative had thought to negotiate a prenuptial agreement. Furthermore, she could not bestow gifts or execute her own will without her husband's consent. Assuming that no legal document existed to protect and enhance her economic position, she was expected to comply with her husband's judgment in the disposition of her property or any wealth they might accumulate together. An unfortunate choice of a mate therefore had profound consequences for a woman. Absolute divorces were unobtainable in either early Maryland or Virginia, and legal separations, not easily accomplished, hardly worked to the advantage of the female since the husband retained flexibility in his personal behavior and probably still had control of her property. If she resorted to desertion, she usually faced social ostracism. . . .

"Virginians may have believed in patriarchal authority with all their hearts, but conditions in the New World at times made enforcement difficult," Suzanne Lebsock notes. "The patriarchs simply did not live long enough." The chaos that death visited upon Chesapeake families may indeed have been an impediment, but ultimately it did not prevent the development of a well-entrenched patriarchy. Middling and gentry families had become "increasingly patriarchal in seventeenth-century England," and some English law bearing on this matter made its way to the American colonies. The historian Allan Kulikoff, in his unvarnished and masterful study of the tobacco culture of the Chesapeake, minces no words about the flux in which the colonists found themselves even as he carefully outlines the rise of the patriarchal family in this section of the American South: "No Chesapeake family could possibly attain the harmony and complete separation of tasks that the domestic patriarchal ideal demanded. Husbands and wives bickered, argued, and occasionally even separated . . . [and] from time to time . . . brought their difficulties to local or provincial courts." "Disagreements about the management or disposition of dower property were a major cause of legal separations and must have troubled many marriages that remained intact," Walsh notes.

Kulikoff is of the opinion that the circumstances of the times did not dictate the development of domestic patriarchies, a strong class system, or a slave society. "Chesapeake planters did not *have* to choose to form domestic patriarchies," he writes; such alternatives existed as "the relatively egalitarian family system of the seventeenth century." He assumes that the planters adopted this arrangement because they harbored preconceived notions about how best to organize domestic life. Peculiarities of the colonial Chesapeake experience certainly encouraged the fruition of these ideas. Not least among these characteristics were the climate and the fertility of the soil, which permitted and fostered the development of labor-intensive single-crop agriculture to which bound servitude and then the institution of slavery grafted easily.

Three factors hastened the development of the patriarchal order in the Chesapeake. First, the slave trade accelerated, which resolved the labor shortage and essentially eliminated the need for the white wives of slaveholders to work in the tobacco fields. Second, white immigration declined and natural increase kicked in to reduce the inequitable male-female sex ratio and the concomitant demand for teenaged brides. Finally, adult life expectancy increased and with that the longevity of marriages, which allowed clear patterns of authority within the household to emerge. By the early eighteenth century, Kulikoff observes, "tidewater gentlemen and their yeoman allies constructed a stable, conservative social order, characterized by inter-locking class, racial, and gender relations." "White women," he explains, "usually ac-quiesced in patriarchal family government because of the rights and privileges they enjoyed as planters' wives." Reciprocity was the order of the day as long as each free partner in the contractual arrangement lived up to obligations, and gentlemen gen-erally acquitted themselves in a manner that permitted them to tolerate and accom-modate their "perceived inferiors," be they women, black slaves, or white males of the lower classes. The development of slavery, of course, became the most critical element in the social formula of the Chesapeake. Slaves, whether females or males, had little say in the matter although "the ordinary tensions embedded within Chesapeake society provided subservient groups like slaves and women with means to challenge domination without seeking to overthrow the system itself."

The first black bond servants appeared in Virginia in 1619, but most of the sev-enteenth century seems to have passed before slavery became an intrinsic and rigidly fixed aspect of colonial life. Not until the late seventeenth or early eighteenth century did the demand for black slave labor replace the earlier reliance on in-dentured white servants. The circumstances under which blacks first labored in the seventeenth century remain somewhat nebulous. The historian Winthrop D. Jordan takes the position that "there is only one major historical certainty, and unfortu-nately it is the sort which historians find hardest to bear. There is simply not enough evidence to indicate with any certainty whether Negroes were treated like white servants or not." It is apparent that by about 1640 "*some* Negroes in both Virginia and Maryland were serving for life and some Negro children inheriting the same obligation." . . .

That "Mary a Negro Woman" arrived in Virginia around 1621 or 1622 is a matter of record. She managed to gain her freedom in some manner, and she married a free Negro man, Anthony, who worked with her on the same plantation. The family of Mary and Anthony, who appropriated the surname Johnson, included four children and eventually grandchildren as well. Whatever the explanation, they fared well economically; and the fluidity that initially characterized race relations seems to have worked to their advantage. Between 1662 and 1705, however, the House of Burgesses enacted a series of laws that defined slavery and delineated race relations in the colony. Although blacks themselves were not totally powerless to influence their masters and their circumstances, as the historian Eugene D. Genovese in *Roll, Jordan, Roll: The World the Slaves Made* has amply demonstrated, severe and fairly rigid proscriptions were put into place. "The typical black Virginia woman" by 1700, according to Lebsock, was "'chattel'—property—and as such she could be bought, sold, mortgaged, or swapped, or even gambled away in a card game." She would remain property for the duration of her natural life; so, too, her children for theirs—and they could be stripped from her any time, any place, at the pleasure of her master.

African-born slave women of the seventeenth century had fewer marriage possibilities than white indentured female servants of the Chesapeake. Among blacks as well as whites, males outnumbered females throughout the first century. Nonetheless, initially the black women may have been owned by masters who possessed few other blacks; and later, in the early eighteenth century, slavery came to be concentrated on the large, relatively isolated estates where blacks—men, women, and children—may not have numbered more than twenty or thirty. Restricted in their movement from one plantation to another, some first-generation females quite probably found no mates who were acceptable to them. They seem to have been slow to enter into "marriages" and have children; they averaged about three offspring, usually losing one in its infancy. Lorena S. Walsh identifies such causative factors as "isolation, a diversity of tribal origins and languages, chronic ill health, and extreme alienation" for these patterns. Creole black women, the daughters of the African-born, not unlike the white females, married earlier and produced more children—six to eight, perhaps half of whom did not live to maturity. On large estates it was easier for black women to find mates among the local slave population; women who were owned by smaller planters and farmers often had both to look elsewhere for a husband and to face the consequences of living alone and rearing children with only occasional visits from the husband and father. Walsh concedes that by the late eighteenth century, slave women tended to reside among their kinfolks, and most of them had found mates and produced children. The conjugal pair and the nuclear family emerged. Still, the decisions or whims of their masters might disrupt family relationships.

In retrospect it seems that slavery as it evolved in Virginia affected black females somewhat differently from males. Women were only about half as likely as men to be exported from Africa to America. In their native cultures, black women had farmed, their roles in agriculture resembling those of Indian counterparts in the American South. It may be that the Africans who acted as procurers for slave traders possessed some reluctance about upsetting this arrangement by which their societies subsisted. Women who were snatched from the land of their birth and dispatched to the New World experienced the horrible middle passage, which exacted a heavy toll of lives. They also faced the prospect of sexual exploitation while on board ship and in America as well. In Virginia the females labored in the fields just as the males did. The whip could be brought to bear on both sexes. Black females soon learned also that no legal protection existed for slave families. Although runaways included males and females, only about one in ten was a woman. Strong maternal bonds may have led women to express their resistance to slavery by more commonly resorting to such other means as slowing their pace of labor, destroying tools, feigning illness, setting fires, or, in the most extreme instances, attempting to poison their masters.

During most of the seventeenth and early eighteenth centuries, Tidewater Virginia and Maryland hardly represented an orderly, pristine English society. Instead the reality was a raw, chaotic society, convulsed by tensions associated with class, gender, and race. All the common human frailties manifested themselves. Female culprits slandered their own kind, gossiped about their neighbors, and fornicated with willing partners. Some unfortunate souls came in for charges of witchcraft in seventeenth-century Virginia, but apparently no one was executed. Premarital sex excited little attention; a third of the brides were already pregnant on their wedding day. Nonmarital sex that might produce a child to burden the community required public censure. Authorities meted out punishments of public whippings and fines; sometimes they forced offenders to appear before church congregations draped in white sheets and clutching white wands.

In a setting like seventeenth-century Virginia, where three races collided and interacted, miscegenation raised its head almost by default. For a while and in some instances, interracial fornicators simply faced the same types of punishments as any other couple. Even a 1662 act declaring that a child should be slave or free according to the status of its mother may not have been dictated entirely by racism. Mixed marriages also occurred, but in 1691 the assembly outlawed miscegenation in or out of wedlock. It called "for prevention of that abominable mixture and spurious issue which hereafter may encrease in this dominion, as well by negroes, mulattoes, and Indians intermarrying with English, or other white women, as by their unlawfull accompanying with one another." This act and the 1705 revision of it revealed more concern about illicit relations between white women and black men than intermarriage per se.

The relative scarcity of white women placed their affections at a premium, and white men fervently expected to be the recipients of their attentions. Given the existence of documented cases of mulatto children born to white women during the late seventeenth and early eighteenth centuries, black men surely succeeded sometimes in the quest for their sexual favors. As for black slave women who gave birth to mulatto children, it hardly mattered. Their offspring were neither legitimate nor illegitimate, and the variations in skin tones had no bearing on their enslavement. Apparently this legislation did not cast a pall over the earlier and much-vaunted relationship between Pocahontas and John Rolfe or their descendants. But she was an Indian woman, not a white one, and he was an English man. Similar laws also appeared in Maryland.

Female sexuality concerned colonial officialdom, for they valued the reproductive capacities of their women. In the case of black slaves, fecundity enhanced
wealth; and how fertilization transpired concerned the owners very little as long as
it generated healthy offspring. Patriarchs of the Old Dominion and her sister
southern colonies, however, fixated on the chastity of unmarried white women and
the fidelity of wives. Their code of honor permitted not a scintilla of doubt as to the
paternity of their heirs, which they zealously set about getting. Notwithstanding
the strict standards of virtue to which they held the females of their families,
predatory males roamed the highways and byways, partaking of sexual favors freely
given or forcibly taken where they found them. The wives, sisters, and daughters of
their peers were not necessarily off-limits, and Indian and black women, as well
as whites whom they considered their social inferiors, often represented easy
prey. . . .

Some gentlewomen proved as lusty and sensual as their male counterparts.
Whether creatures of passion or unenthusiastic but dutiful wives, the ladies of their
class as well as those lower in the social order lived up to their obligations as
"breeders" or died trying. "Large families . . . were the rule and the boast of rich
and poor," writes Julia Cherry Spruill. "A large part of the time, strength, and attention of women went into the bearing and rearing of large families." Colonists,
more than English kinsmen in the mother country, considered numerous children a
material advantage and therefore assets. Virginians, who definitely earned their reputation as "great breeders," did not have sole claim to the title. In 1708, for example,
a traveler remarked that most of the 250 families in South Carolina's Charles Town
had ten or twelve children. A North Carolina promoter credited that colony with
fostering fecundity even for women who moved there after many years of bar-
renness. It was not unusual for a couple to count in double digits the children of
their union alone; in second marriages, his and hers plus theirs raised the ante. The
risks of such profligacy ran high for women, and when a widower replaced the wife
he had buried, who may have succumbed to the rigors of pregnancy and childbirth,
his record of successful fertilization sometimes reached astonishingly high levels of
twenty or more. . . .

Examples of the vapid helpless female, so much a part of the mediamade
mythology associated with the "lady," could probably be found in the colonial South,
but strong, spirited women of all social ranks outnumbered them. Patriarchy in its
most extreme forms depended on uncompromising acquiescence, and not enough
women complied to allow the most dictatorial men unqualified rein on all fronts.
Mary Horsmanden Filmer Byrd represented a durable female and a classic case of
the far-ranging ties of kinship and influence that an elite colonial woman might pro-
mulgate. She married her cousin, Samuel Filmer, and moved to Virginia, where he
died in the "seasoning" process. The widow Mary quickly married William Byrd and
gave birth to William Byrd II. Robert Beverley and James Duke were her sons-in-law;
Thomas Chamberlayne, Charles and Landon Carter, and John Page were her
grandsons. Over the course of three generations, most of Virginia's first families
claimed Mary Horsmanden Filmer Byrd as an ancestress. Nor were her familial
connections confined to the Old Dominion. Frances Culpeper, Mary's first cousin,

successively married three colonial governors. Frances also counted William Penn and Nathaniel Bacon among her cousins; the latter led a rebellion in 1676 against her third husband, Sir William Berkeley. Similar convoluted genealogies existed in Virginia and other colonies, cutting across class lines and giving rise to the kinship ties that came to lace southern society.

Highborn women enjoyed influence by birth, and others who recognized feminine scarcity for the powerful bargaining chip that it was throughout much of the colonial era sometimes demonstrated a strong sense of self. In Maryland, Margaret Brent acted as executrix for a governor, averted a mutiny, and requested the right to vote, making her in all likelihood the first woman to do so in the English colonies. When the Maryland assembly refused her request (actually for two votes—one as executrix and one as her own person), she protested, but to no avail. She moved to Virginia during the early 1650s and spent the remainder of her life more quietly at a Westmoreland plantation aptly named Peace. Sarah Harrison of Surry County, Virginia, refused to take the vow of obedience when she and James Blair were married in 1687. After making three futile attempts, the minister gave up on "obey," acceded to her wishes, and went on with the ceremony. Women participated in Bacon's Rebellion, and one, Anne Cotton, may have written a history of it. This occurred at a time in the South when correspondence, labeled the "gentlest Art in Seventeenth-Century Virginia" by the eminent scholar Richard Beale Davis, afforded women virtually their only literary outlet. Lady Frances Berkeley, the wife of the governor, rallied support in England and returned to Virginia with a thousand regulars and the authorization to crush those who challenged her husband's authority. After he died, she married her third governor, who served North Carolina but took up residence at Green Spring, her home in Virginia. Because men generally deemed females inferior, they ranked women like these who participated actively or made their wishes and opinions known in public life as exceptional—honorary men of sorts, or "deputy husbands.". . .

It remains customary to wax nostalgic about the quaint housewifery skills of colonial women and their powers of procreation. Without wallowing in all of it, it must be recognized that the exigencies of existence required that their lot include a steady regimen of cooking, gardening, and food preservation as well as nursing the sick, manufacturing clothing, and tending animals—all of this intermixed with seemingly incessant childbearing. If they were still emotionally inclined and physically able to "kick up their heels" at social gatherings or express themselves artistically in their needlework, all the more credit is due them.

"Women's sphere was not a subject of controversy or reflection in pioneer America," Elisabeth Anthony Dexter observes in *Career Women of America, 1776–1840*. "Men ruled in church and state, and they furnished the great majority of workers in practically all callings outside the home." Still, during the colonial and early national eras in the South and indeed throughout the English-influenced North, females pursued "a surprising number of occupations" and met the challenges with which their times and circumstances confronted them. Women teachers, planters, tavern operators and innkeepers, printers, actors, and even preaching Quakeresses intermittently graced the social milieu of the colonial South.

Serving as helpmates to their husbands or carrying on as determined widows most often occasioned activities beyond the bounds of housewifery. Other feminine lives followed the course of quiet reflection as recorded in their diaries and letters, a few manifested themselves in somewhat more flamboyant and public fashion, but the great majority spent themselves in silent anonymity. . . .

A specific Anglo-Saxon male elite set the parameters of southern society and, in as much as they could do so, on the backs of others. The demands of carving a new society in the wilderness deprived these men of absolute authority, and the expanse of western land that awaited acquisitive newcomers denied them unlimited control. Non-English groups among them included the French Huguenots of South Carolina, the Germans in Georgia, the Swedes in early Delaware (where Quakery and slavery subsequently coexisted), and the fiery Scotch-Irish Presbyterians of the back country; all of these and more were interwoven into the English social fabric, rendering it a hybrid and strengthening it in the process. Still, the presence of other ethnic and racial groups, though real enough, posed no serious threat to English influence in the colonial South. With the patriarchy in place, the other Europeans who joined the English showed no serious inclinations toward abolishing black slavery, dismantling the class system, or elevating the status of women.

Suggested Readings

General

Virginia DeJohn Anderson, *New England's Generation: The Great Migration and the Formation of Society and Culture in the Seventeenth Century* (1991).

John Axtell, *The Invasion Within: The Contest of Cultures in Colonial North America* (1985).

Bernard Bailyn and Philip D. Morgan, eds., *Strangers Within the Realm* (1991).

David Hackett Fischer, *Albion's Seed: Four British Folkways in America* (1990).

David Galenson, *White Servitude in Colonial America* (1981).

Jack P. Greene, *Pursuits of Happiness: The Social Development of Early Modern British Colonies and the Formation of American Culture* (1986).

James A. Henretta and Gregory H. Nobles, *Evolution and Revolution: American Society, 1600–1820* (1987).

Christine Heyrman, *Commerce and Culture* (1984).

Lyle Koehler, *A Search for Power: The "Weaker Sex" in Seventeenth Century New England* (1980).

Jackson Turner Main, *The Social Structure of Revolutionary America* (1965).

Demography and Ethnic Diversity

Bernard Bailyn, *The Peopling of British North America: An Introduction* (1986); D.W. Meinig, *The Shaping of America: A Geographical Perspective on 500 Years of History, vol. 1, Atlantic America, 1492–1800* (1986); and Joel Williamson, *New People: Miscegenation and Mulattoes in the United States* (1980).

Economic Development

Edwin J. Perkins, *The Economy of Colonial America* (1980); Daniel H. Usner, Jr., *Indians, Settlers, and Slaves in a Frontier Exchange Economy: The Lower Mississippi Valley Before 1783* (1992); and Gary M. Walton and James F. Shepherd, *The Economic Rise of Early America* (1979).

Women in Colonial America

Carol F. Karlsen, *The Devil in the Shape of a Woman: Witchcraft in Colonial New England* (1987); Amy Scrager Lang, *Prophetic Women: Anne Hutchinson and the Problem of Dissent in the Literature of New England* (1987); Marylynn Salmon, *Women and the Law of Property in Early America* (1986); and Laurel T. Ulrich, *A Midwife's Tale: The Life of Martha Ballard, Based on Her Diary, 1785–1812* (1990).

Slavery

David Brion Davis, *The Problem of Slavery in Western Culture* (1966); Orlando Patterson, *Slavery and Social Death* (1982); and Peter Wood, *Black Majority: Negroes in Colonial South Carolina from 1670 through the Stono Rebellion* (1974).

Colonial Religion

Patricia U. Bonomi, *Under the Cope of Heaven: Religion, Society, and Politics in Colonial America* (1986); Charles L. Cohen, *God's Caress: The Psychology of Puritan Religious Experience* (1986); Alan Heimert and Perry Miller, eds., *The Great Awakening* (1967); and Harry S. Stout, *The New England Soul: Preaching and Religious Culture in Colonial New England* (1986).

Family Life

James Axtell, *The School Upon a Hill: Education and Society in Colonial New England* (1974); John Demos, *A Little Commonwealth: Family Life in Plymouth Colony* (1970); and Stephanie G. Wolf, *As Various As Their Land: The Everyday Lives of Eighteenth-Century Americans* (1994).

QUESTIONS FOR DISCUSSION

1. Describe the immigration and demographic patterns that characterized the settlement of the North American colonies.

2. Compare and contrast the experience of African immigrants and Native Americans during the first one hundred years of the colonial experience.

3. Analyze the impact of tobacco on the Chesapeake region. Compare its economy to that of New England and the deep South.

4. In what ways did the social structure of the colonies differ from that of England?

5. How did the "Great Awakening" affect colonial society?
6. How did family structure among white settlers vary from region to region?
7. After reading Margaret Ripley Wolfe's article do you believe that white women fared better in the southern or the northern colonies? Explain.

CHAPTER FOUR

THE AMERICAN REVOLUTION

In 1776 the thirteen American colonies declared their independence from Great Britain and then fought a successful war against the government of King George III to secure that independence. Literally and figuratively, the revolution was America's defining moment. The act of separation required the citizens of the new nation to decide upon a collective value system and to construct political and economic institutions that would reflect those values. It was during the revolutionary era that Americans made their commitment to individual liberty, democracy, constitutional government, and to the creation of a commonwealth dedicated to the welfare of all citizens.

As the revolution developed, Americans came to see themselves not only as the guardians of their own liberty and virtue but as a nation singled out by God or destiny to spread freedom throughout the world. America was the first modern nation to be founded on political and social principles, a necessity for a society as ethnically and culturally diverse as the thirteen colonies, but no less remarkable for that fact. Republicanism rather than blood, soil, and even language would be the ideology of the new country.

ENGLISH COLONIAL ADMINISTRATION

Colonial assemblies in America acquired as much power as they did during the seventeenth and eighteenth centuries in no small part because colonial administration in London was decentralized and inefficient. No separate office existed to supervise overseas affairs. The Board of Trade and Plantations was established in 1696, but it could only make recommendations to the Privy Council. In fact a number of agencies, including the Council, the Board, the Exchequer (treasury), and the Admiralty affected colonial policy, and for the most part none knew what the other was doing.

The system was further weakened by the character and ability of many of the officials London dispatched to America to run the colonies. Some were conscientious and farsighted, but most were political appointees chosen on the basis of whom they knew rather than their qualifications. To make matters worse, some customs officers, governors, and lieutenant-governors hired substitutes, a practice which further diluted quality and frequently made the poorly paid substitute vulnerable to bribery. Representative assemblies gained additional autonomy when in the early eighteenth century British Prime Minister Robert Walpole instituted a policy of "salutary neglect." Administration of colonial trade regulations was relaxed out of the belief that the resulting prosperity would enrich the colonists and enable them to purchase more goods from England.

MERCANTILISM

Nevertheless, in the minds of both the English people and their American brethren, the colonies existed for the benefit of the parent country. Under the mercantilist assumptions that prevailed during the seventeenth and eighteenth centuries, all nation-states were in constant competition with each other for the finite wealth of the world. Colonies were viewed as supplements to the parent country, assets which would free it from dependence on foreign powers. Ideally, colonies would render large quantities of silver and gold, but these precious metals were not to be found in England's North American dependencies. Nevertheless, the American colonies fit into the mercantilist system and served Britain's interests in three important ways: (1) the colonies acted as a source of raw materials allowing the exchequer to conserve silver and gold; (2) they constituted a market for English products providing employment for domestic workers and enriching the nation's merchants; and (3) finally, the exchange of colonial raw materials for English finished goods stimulated the merchant marine and added to the naval strength of England.

THE NAVIGATION AND MANUFACTURING ACTS

During the seventeenth and eighteenth centuries Parliament passed legislation designed to ensure that the American colonies benefitted Britain exclusively. These laws were of two types. In a series of Navigation Acts, London decreed that all ships engaged in imperial trade would have to be built, owned, and manned by British subjects. The English did not want their competitors, especially the Dutch, to profit from transporting goods to and from British ports. Certain "enumerated articles," including tobacco, indigo, rice, and cotton, produced in the colonies could be shipped only to England or other British ports. The Navigation Acts, in other words, permitted no direct trade with foreign nations thus giving England a monopoly on these goods and vastly increasing customs revenues. Finally, all non-English goods shipped to the colonies first must be sent to England, unloaded, and reloaded. Because they were taxed at every stage, foreign-made goods became prohibitively expensive, and the colonists had no choice but to buy British.

A second category of regulations, the Manufacturing Acts, prohibited the exportation of certain finished goods to England or to other colonies. These took the form of specific measures—the Hat Act, the Wool Act, and the Iron Act, for example. The object of these regulations was to discourage the production of finished goods that would compete with similar British products. The Navigation and Manufacturing Acts were designed to ensure that the mother country always enjoyed a favorable balance of trade—that is, that America furnished raw materials and acted as a market for British manufactured items and that wealth would flow across the Atlantic from west to east.

Though it seemed manifestly contrary to their interests, the colonists for a time acquiesced in the British system of trade. They did so for a number of reasons. Most men and women thought of themselves as English citizens and thus welcomed the strengthening of the parent country. But there were other, more concrete reasons. First, the principal colonial crops enjoyed monopoly status in the British market. Second, British manufactured items were the highest quality and least expensive in the world, and the colonists would probably have preferred them anyway. Third, colonial shipping enjoyed protection from the Royal Navy, the most powerful maritime force in the world, something the colonists could never have afforded themselves. And fourth, until the middle of the eighteenth century, well over 90 percent of those who had settled in the Americas were agriculturalists whose activities fit in with Britain's mercantilist objectives. Actually, after the policy of salutary neglect was implemented, the mercantile acts were not enforced, allowing colonial merchants and shippers to smuggle and to avoid paying customs duties. Finally, beginning in the late sixteenth century, New England traders reaped immense profits from the complex transatlantic trade network that developed in the seventeenth century. The Anglo-French rivalry which involved a struggle for control of the trans-Appalachian West coupled with an economic growth and political turmoil in the colonies, however, caused Britain's American dependencies to question the benefits of empire.

THE CLASH OF EMPIRES

Beginning in 1739 Britain fought three wars with various European coalitions, and the American colonists played an increasingly important role in each of them. Spanish efforts to control British smuggling in the Caribbean led to the War of Jenkins' Ear (so-called because Captain Robert Jenkins displayed to Parliament his ear which had been severed by the Spanish in punishment for smuggling). Most of the action took place in the southeastern colonies and in the Caribbean. A disastrous attack in 1740 on Cartagena, Colombia, by a force of thirty-five hundred American colonials ended in failure and led to the deaths of all but six hundred. The ineptness and insensitivity of those British officers in command of the operation left a bitter heritage in the colonies for years afterward. The War of the Austrian Succession (1740–1748) followed immediately. Britain in this case took up arms against France and its continental allies to prevent that nation from becoming the dominant force on the European continent. In the New World the focus of the struggle was the huge fortified city of Louisbourg on Cape Breton Island northeast of Nova Scotia. In April 1745 a force of four thousand New Englanders captured Louisbourg and then held it against French and Indian counterattack. To the fury of the northern colonies, London ended the war with a treaty that returned the hard-won fortress to France.

THE FRENCH AND INDIAN WAR

Far more important to Britain's relationship with its North American colonies was the French and Indian War which extended from 1754 through 1763. In this conflict North America was the principal theater of battle.

By the first quarter of the eighteenth century, English and French fishermen were competing with each other for control of the rich fishing grounds off the coast of Newfoundland and Nova Scotia. In the backwoods, trappers vied for the valuable furs and the friendship and support of the resident native tribes, the French allying with the Algonquians and the English with their rivals, the Iroquois. Both England and France looked upon their colonies as integral and exceedingly valuable parts of their national economies; colonial trade for each country made up nearly one-third of its entire foreign commerce, and the wealth of the influential merchant classes in both countries stemmed in no small part from colonial profits. Conflict was inevitable.

The relative position of the two great colonial powers was well defined by 1756. English colonies were clustered along the eastern seaboard, although the line of settlement had advanced well inland. Indeed, explorers and a few frontier farmers had penetrated into the Appalachian Mountains. New France extended in an L-shaped pattern from Quebec southwestward down the St. Lawrence River and across the Great Lakes, and from there down the Mississippi River to its mouth at New Orleans.

The French empire in North America seemed to be a giant roadblock to future generations of English men and women intent on settling the interior. And, in fact, the French and Indian War was touched off by a series of clashes between French soldiers and their native allies on the one hand and Virginians on the other. In 1754 the French military built a series of forts in the Ohio River Valley to consolidate control of the area. Virginia's original charter loosely described the northern and southern boundaries of the colony and then granted to the company and its stockholders all land between those borders from the Atlantic to the Mississippi which, of course, included much of the present-day state of Ohio. With a powerful group of land speculators—organized as the Ohio Company of Virginia—thoroughly aroused, Virginia sent a force under the command of twenty-two-year-old Major George Washington to dislodge the

French from Fort Duquesne. That expedition failed, as did a much larger force two years later under command of British General Edward Braddock. By then Britain and France were formally at war.

Despite the disparity in population—English colonials outnumbered their French counterparts by twenty-to-one—the French in America were better prepared for armed conflict. French military power rested in its army, the greatest on the European continent, while Britain relied more on the Royal Navy. The French boasted a larger military establishment in America, and their soldiers were better trained and better led. Braddock, for example, was an arrogant disciplinarian with little sympathy for or understanding of the colonials whom he had to lead. Also, France's native allies fought harder for the French cause than Britain's did for the British cause.

In view of these realities, Britain's best chance for victory was to fight a war of attrition, using its fleet to cut off the flow of supplies from France to Canada, while stockpiling resources and building up its military forces in the thirteen colonies. Instead, during the early years of the war, British army units and their colonial allies made repeated and usually disastrous attempts to break out of the iron ring the French had forged. Braddock, who himself was mortally wounded, suffered a thousand casualties in the futile attempt to take Fort Duquesne. A British effort to recapture Louisbourg was repulsed, and in 1757 the French overwhelmed Oswego on the eastern side of Lake Ontario and Fort William Henry on Lake George, capturing two thousand British troops in the process.

Finally, under the astute leadership of Prime Minister William Pitt, the British military machine began to function. He diverted French attention and forces by funnelling huge amounts of money and materiel to England's continental ally, Prussia. At Pitt's direction British officials in North America began cultivating the colonials, converting them into enthusiastic rather than reluctant allies. Promotion on merit rather than favoritism vastly improved the quality of the British officer corps. In 1758 combined British and colonial forces captured Louisbourg (for the second time in just over a decade) and Fort Duquesne. The iron ring was broken. The following year, Fort Niagara, which linked New France with the far west, fell to British forces. The stage was set for the final blow, the capture of Quebec, a fortress city situated on cliffs rising a hundred and fifty feet above the St. Lawrence. On September 12, 1759, thirty-two-year-old General James Wolfe led forty-five hundred men up the cliff along a partially hidden diagonal path. A furious battle ensued on the Plains of Abraham west of the city. Both Wolfe and the French commander, the Marquis de Montcalm, were killed, but Quebec surrendered on September 17. A year later Montreal fell, and for all intents and purposes the war was over.

THE TREATY OF PARIS AND THE SEEDS OF REVOLUTION

The Treaty of Paris signed in 1763 demonstrated in its various provisions just how decisively the French had been defeated. Britain gained control of all of

Figure 4-1
Territorial Outcome of the French and Indian War

New France including Nova Scotia and Canada, as well as undisputed possession of the area between the Appalachians and the Mississippi excluding New Orleans. (See Figure 4–1.) France retained the right to fish off the Grand Banks and was allowed to keep the islands of St. Pierre and Miquelon as fishing bases. In the Caribbean, Britain returned to France the islands of Guadeloupe and Martinique which had been captured during the war, but at the same time acquired East and West Florida from France's ally, Spain. France in turn was forced to relinquish to Spain a vast area west of the Mississippi and east of the Rocky Mountains.

Britain's decisive victory in the French and Indian War had profound and unforeseen consequences for its relationship with its North American colonies. It removed the checks on westward expansion and virtually ensured that British institutions and culture would cross the Appalachians. The French and Indian War laid the basis for the coming of the American Revolution. Indeed, it might be said that the Anglo-French conflict was a necessary prelude to revolution because not only did it create specific points of dispute—new debts and increased taxation, management of Indian territory, and different trade patterns—it also freed the colonists from the need for protection from the French. They could, ironically, assert their rights as they saw them with much more security.

In addition, the war served as something of a unifying force for the colonies. Anticipating a general struggle with the French, the British government summoned representatives to a conference at Albany, New York, in 1754. Benjamin Franklin and other colonial leaders proposed creating a union with a president-general appointed by the crown and representatives who would provide for the common defense. The Albany Plan came to nothing, but helped create a collective consciousness among Americans and established relationships that would serve as a basis for colonial resistance to British decrees and regulations a decade later.

A SEPARATE AMERICAN IDENTITY

Although the causes of the American Revolution were complex and had as much to do with social and cultural patterns in America as with Britain's efforts to regulate its empire more efficiently, a common philosophy or ideology bound together those wishing to separate from the parent country. Those favoring independence believed that they were struggling for self-government, that human beings were basically good and capable of governing themselves. Those opposed were convinced that the common man, uneducated and uncultured, was debased and venal, and had to be ruled for his (and her) own good by an enlightened aristocracy.

In fact, by the middle of the eighteenth century many Americans viewed themselves as a people apart. The self-image that emerged in England's North American settlements was a blend of various influences. Europeans attributed certain traits to the Indians—simplicity, savagery, innocence, and paganism— and believed that over time, Creoles—Europeans born in the New World—had taken on these traits. Recruiting literature depicted the colonies as societies in which land ownership was easily attained, prosperity was directly related to the sweat of one's brow, government hardly existed, and all beliefs and creeds were tolerated. Eighteenth-century Enlightenment thinkers, especially Voltaire and Montesquieu, held up America and Americans as the essence of civic virtue. They believed that all that was evil in human society could be traced to "artificial" institutions and processes—the church and religious dogma or the state and economic regulation. They hailed America as proof that free individuals could govern themselves and create a peaceful, enlightened society. Many Americans internalized these views.

By contrast, Great Britain seemed to its New World colonists a land increasingly corrupt. Colonial officials stationed in London and visitors to the parent country bemoaned the graft and corruption that characterized English electoral politics. The trend seemed to be toward less rather than more democracy and individual liberty. Instead of acting as selfless guardians of the public interest, the aristocracy seemed determined to manipulate the political and economic system for their own benefit. Mercantilism stifled individual initiative, and a rigid class structure prevented the emergence of a meritocracy. There emerged in America, then, a diffuse but strong feeling that the colonies were different and somehow superior—provincial but sound and vital, uncomplicated and undeveloped but prosperous. Most were more than willing to tolerate the imperial connection—despite the perniciousness of British politics and culture—as long as it permitted the colonies continuing economic opportunity, religious freedom, and local political control.

KING GEORGE III

In 1760 England crowned a new king, George III, the grandson of George II; he would preside over the momentous developments leading to revolution and independence. George III was the third monarch of the Hanoverian dynasty which had been recruited from Germany and installed in Britain in 1714. Unlike his two predecessors, who spoke little English and cared more for their native Hanover than their adopted land, George III was thoroughly British and determined to be king in deed as well as in name. He and supporters of royal authority—the Tories—maneuvered the Whigs—advocates of parliamentary power—out of control of the government which they had held since 1721. Neither the ravening tyrant pictured by Whig historians nor the bumbling, paranoid portrayed by members of other schools, George III was a strong-willed ruler who thought he was doing what was best for the empire. In 1763 George III named George Grenville to be his prime minister. Though he was William Pitt's brother-in-law, Grenville did not share Pitt's tolerant attitude toward the colonies which he believed should obey the law and share part of the cost of running the empire.

A SOCIETY IN TRANSITION

Population Explosion

The land which George III's government sought to discipline and more closely integrate into the empire was a diverse, complex, and turbulent society peopled by individuals unlikely to submit meekly to British efforts to regulate their lives. By the second quarter of the eighteenth century the thirteen North

American colonies were experiencing an explosive growth in population. At the beginning of the century the population of the American settlements had constituted one-twentieth of that of Britain and Ireland; by 1750 it comprised one-fifth. The doubling of the American population between 1750 and 1770, totalling now 2 million, created pressure on uses of the land and provoked a massive migration into the interior. Between 1760 and 1776, for example, 264 new towns were established in northern New England. Meanwhile, the plantation economies of the Chesapeake and lower South exhausted the soil and placed a premium on increased production. Established planters bought up contiguous lands, pushing small farmers into and across the Appalachians. Because the defeat of the French opened vast new tracts to English exploration and settlement, by the early 1760s frontiersmen like Daniel Boone were opening paths through western Kentucky into the Mississippi River Valley. Frontier farmers followed, establishing themselves along the Ohio River and the upper reaches of the Mississippi.

A Turbulent Frontier

Population growth and the massive movement of peoples had a destabilizing effect on British North America. Families, communities, and church congregations splintered. Colonial governments lost control over newly established frontier communities, and as a result, lawlessness and vagrancy often characterized life in the backcountry. In the Carolinas, frontier inhabitants formed vigilante organizations called "Regulators" to deal with thieves and murderers, but these self-appointed distributors of justice frequently looted and destroyed what they were pledged to protect. In Vermont, Ethan Allen's "Green Mountain Boys" made a living raiding settlements in northern New York. In 1763–1764 Scotch-Irish settlers in western Pennsylvania openly rebelled when their demands for greater representation in the colonial assembly went unheeded. Angry at the unwillingness of the government in Philadelphia to protect them and to help them despoil the Indians, these frontier dwellers under the leadership of the Paxton Boys killed natives who were under official government protection and marched on Philadelphia. Only intervention by Benjamin Franklin and a promise of greater representation kept them from sacking the city.

The loosening of social mores and disintegration of established authority opened the door to further violence between Indians and colonists and contributed to a vicious cycle of violence. Frontier traders and land speculators attempted to bribe local Native Americans with cloth, tools, weapons, and, most frequently, rum. Lied to, cheated, pushed off their land, the Indians retaliated with murderous raids on colonial settlements. In New York two thousand Senecas menaced the frontier; in the Ohio Valley, twelve thousand Delawares, Shawnees, and Hurons took up arms; and in the southern piedmont, twenty thousand Cherokees, Choctaws, and Creeks went on the warpath. After calling in vain on their colonial governments to defend them, frontiersmen took matters into their own hands, formed militias, and made war not only on armed, male adults, but also on defenseless women and children.

Economic Expansion

America in the mid-eighteenth century was characterized not only by mass migration and a violent, turbulent frontier, but also by economic expansion in every geographical area and among people of every social class. During the twenty years preceding the Treaty of 1763, the value of American exports to Great Britain doubled to nearly £1.5 million annually. Because neither Britain nor its West Indian colonies could feed themselves, the prices for North American foodstuffs soared. Between 1740 and 1765 the price of wheat increased 60 percent. Even tobacco prices went up. The vast majority of Americans continued to till the soil, but manufacturing was on the increase as well. In 1768 Pennsylvania alone bought eight thousand pairs of colonial-made shoes. Most New England communities boasted an assortment of workshops and mills. Shipowners and planters prospered but so did mechanics and small farmers. Living standards increased virtually everywhere among the colonial population.

Economic opportunity, mass migration, and the lawless climate on the frontier bred disrespect for established authority and contributed to the breakdown of traditional institutions. No longer dependent upon plantation owners, small farmers felt free to challenge the reigning political elite. Newly established communities rejected stolid and increasingly sterile Anglican and Congregationalist churches. Methodists, New Light Presbyterians, and Separate Baptists proliferated. It was in this fluid and skeptical atmosphere that the British parliament and crown attempted to reestablish imperial authority.

THE GROWING BREACH

DISALLOWANCE

During the period from 1763 through 1770 a series of specific disputes arose between Great Britain and its North American colonies, disputes that were both causes and symptoms of the growing breach between America and England. The first of these had to do with disallowance, the power of the British government to veto colonial laws. The Privy Council disallowed dozens of measures enacted by popular assemblies in all of the colonies, but one incident in Virginia became noteworthy on both sides of the Atlantic, signifying to some a flagrant abuse of power and to others its legitimate exercise. Between 1755 and 1763 crop failures in Virginia cut the supply of tobacco and raised its price severalfold. In 1755 the House of Burgesses passed measures setting at two pence per pound the official price of tobacco to be paid as compensation to public officials including Anglican ministers. Because this piece of colonial legislation cut the salaries of Anglican clerics by up to 300 percent, the powerful

Church of England (as well as merchant creditors) pressured the Privy Council into vetoing the "two-penny" acts. Meanwhile, in America local governments refused to pay in tobacco, and several ministers brought suit. The governments were represented in court by Patrick Henry, a young firebrand still in his twenties who went so far as to declare during the trial that the king had "degenerated into a Tyrant, and forfeits all rights to his subject's obedience." The jury found for the preachers but awarded damages of just one penny, an indirect and maddening challenge to the Privy Council and Anglican church.

ADMINISTRATION OF WESTERN LANDS

The most pressing problem confronting the British government following the French and Indian War was administration of the western lands, including the newly won territory west of the Appalachians and south of the Great Lakes. As we have seen, along with underrepresentation, a perennial complaint of back-country inhabitants was that colonial governments and the British military did not provide adequate protection from the Indians. Just months following the signing of the Treaty of Paris, an Ottawa chief named Pontiac led the largest Indian uprising in colonial history. A federation of tribes under his command destroyed all but three British forts west of the Appalachians and penetrated to the back country of Pennsylvania and Maryland. Before Pontiac was defeated, his warriors had killed more than two thousand settlers.

Soon after Pontiac's rebellion was crushed, the British government issued the Proclamation of 1763. That decree temporarily closed the trans-Appalachian west to settlement and provided for the establishment of a definite native-colonial boundary to be negotiated with the affected tribes. Western lands were to be opened gradually and settlement was to be closely supervised by British officials. Then in 1774 Parliament passed the Quebec Act, transferring the vast area between the Ohio and Mississippi to the province of Quebec and in the process legitimizing French law and Roman Catholicism in the territories. The Proclamation of 1763 cancelled the western land claims of colonies such as Virginia and offended those powerful interests which had speculated in western lands. The independent-minded inhabitants of the frontier who believed that British authorities were obligated to help them despoil the natives of their lands were angered as well. Finally, American Protestants denounced the Quebec Act as a vengeful effort to establish a Roman Catholic beachhead on the colonies' northwestern flank.

BRITISH MONETARY POLICY

Parliamentary restrictions on the issuance of paper money also contributed to the growing discontent in the colonies. The coinage of money was deemed a prerogative of the king and thus was prohibited in the colonies after the original Massachusetts charter was cancelled in 1684. By 1750 two forms of paper money existed in the colonies: bills of credit issued by colonial governments to pay merchant contractors, and notes issued by land banks that were secured by mortgages on land or other property. Some colonial governments had acted irresponsibly, overissuing in response to the demands of debtor groups or to finance military operations during the French and Indian War, but others, notably that of Pennsylvania, had operated a stable monetary system. Creditors in the colonies and in England pressured Parliament to suppress paper money.

In 1751 Parliament passed the Currency Act which prohibited the issuance of bills of exchange in New England and required the withdrawal of existing notes according to a fixed schedule. In 1764 Parliament extended that prohibition to the rest of the colonies. Some businesspeople and bankers, and virtually all debtors were offended, the former because they believed the Currency Acts to be part of an effort to prevent economic growth in the colonies, and the latter because they were convinced that creditors were trying to keep them from repaying their debts.

The Sugar Act

At the same time Parliament was working to keep the colonies from raising up economies that competed with rather than complemented that of the parent country, the British government began taxing their North American brethren for purposes of revenue rather than for regulation of commerce. The French and Indian War had been very expensive; by 1763 England's war debt totalled £137 million. The annual interest on that sum alone was £5 million, a staggering amount when compared with the total peacetime budget of £8 million a year.

In 1764 Parliament passed the Sugar Act which replaced the infrequently enforced Molasses Act of 1733. The Sugar Act reduced the high six pence a gallon duty on foreign molasses to three pence and subsequently one pence but provided for strict enforcement. The 1764 measure also imposed duties on foreign cloth, sugar, indigo, coffee, and wine imported into the colonies and eliminated refunds paid on foreign goods reexported from England to America. The Sugar Act was particularly resented in New England because of that region's dependence on the Atlantic trade. If sugar and molasses were too expensive to import, the rum industry and slave trade would break down. Merchants offended by the new parliamentary taxes organized an informal boycott of products taxed by the Sugar Act, including Madeira wine, a colonial favorite. In October of that year the New York assembly submitted a petition to Parliament which declared that "exemption from burden of ungranted involuntary taxes must be the grand principle of every free state."

The Stamp Act

Even more controversial than the Sugar Act was the Stamp Act of 1765. Designed as a revenue-raising measure, the law imposed a tax in the form of a stamp (an embossment or watermark) on a variety of important colonial products, including newspapers, legal documents, pamphlets—even decks of cards and dice. The tax affected virtually all Americans, and the inclusion of newspapers and tavern licenses irritated those who were most responsible for molding public opinion. A flood of newspaper articles and pamphlets expressed the colonists' bitter resentment. Encouraged by merchants, clergy, lawyers, and journalists, importers organized a boycott of English goods, and trade with the mother country fell off by £300,000 in the summer of 1765. Angry mobs, led by the Sons of Liberty, attacked collectors and burned down stamp offices. One of the most notorious acts of violence occurred in Massachusetts where two separate mobs wrecked the magnificent colonial mansion of Lieutenant Governor Thomas Hutchinson. A town meeting expressed regret, but not one of the miscreants was ever apprehended.

The Stamp Act galvanized the colonists into organized action. In the spring of 1765 the Virginia House of Burgesses adopted a series of resolutions proposed by Patrick Henry denouncing parliamentary taxation for revenue and declaring that the colonists could be taxed only by their own representatives. The Rhode Island assembly denounced the Stamp Act as "unconstitutional." In October thirty-seven delegates from nine colonies met in New York and drew up a set of petitions asking relief from this so-called internal tax. The Stamp Act Congress constituted a remarkable display of colonial unity and helped organize yet another boycott of English goods.

In the end, pressure from British merchants and financiers was responsible for the demise of the Stamp Act. The former were being gouged by the colonial boycott while the latter were worried about collecting the £4 million owed them by American planters and merchants. Following a long debate, Parliament decided that the Stamp Act was inexpedient because its enforcement would involve the use of armed force against fellow Englishmen. At the same time that it repealed the Stamp Act, the House of Commons defiantly passed the Declaratory Act, asserting Parliament's authority over the colonies "in all cases whatsoever."

When news of the repeal reached America, wild celebrations erupted. The New York assembly voted to fund an equestrian statue of George III. Colonials wanted reconciliation, but not at the cost of their relative autonomy within the empire. As passage of the Declaratory Act indicated, repeal of the Stamp Act signified only a lull while the British government decided on new methods designed to compel the colonists to assume their share of the cost of running the empire.

The Townshend Duties

In 1767 the British government decided that it would have to raise revenues in the colonies using the traditional method of levying duties on imported goods. At the suggestion of Chancellor of the Exchequer Charles Townshend, Parliament imposed special duties on such commonly used items as glass, tea, paint, and paper. An early advocate of the exercise of parliamentary authority of the colonies, Townshend was also responsible for the creation of the American Board of Customs which was headquartered in Boston and reported directly to the British Treasury. These officials, Townshend believed, would be immune to pressure and bribery.

Not surprisingly, New England merchants took the lead in organizing a colonial boycott of the items taxed. In 1770 the new British prime minister, Lord North, persuaded Parliament to revoke all of the Townshend duties except that on tea. By that date the tariffs on glass, lead, paint, and tea had brought in only £21,000 in tax monies, while the colonial boycott had cost British merchants an estimated £700,000.

The damage to English-colonial relations had been done, however. The Stamp Act and Townshend duties created a sense of unity and common purpose among the colonists; the various conferences and boycotts established inter-colonial lines of communication. These together with various resolutions invoking English common law and justifying resistance on constitutional grounds generated a sense of injustice and provoked political participation by even the most apathetic. John Dickinson, a distinguished Philadelphia lawyer, wrote the widely read *Letters from a Philadelphia Lawyer* which insisted that Parliament lacked the authority to levy taxes for revenue whether or not they were "external" or "internal." The Sons of Liberty encouraged the wearing of homespun cloth, and in New England the "Daughters of Liberty" held spinning bees to support the cause.

The Tyranny of Unrepresented Taxation

The American colonists were disturbed for a variety of reasons by England's efforts to raise revenue among them through taxation. They understood that taxation by a body in which they were not represented would inevitably lead to discrimination in favor of British taxpayers who were represented. Colonials realized that one of the objectives of the Sugar and Stamp Acts as well as the Townshend duties was to create monies with which Britain could pay its officials in America, thus relieving them of their dependence on popular assemblies. The colonial legislatures wanted to retain the sole right to raise and allocate tax monies within their respective colonies. Finally, the crown's subjects in America believed that if they gave up on their demand for "no taxation without representation," they would forfeit all their rights as English citizens.

Some Americans acknowledged Britain's right to tax them but objected to the methods that England used. Under the rules governing the customs commissioners, officials were entitled to one-third of the value of the ships and cargoes that they condemned. New England merchants believed that this provision was an open invitation to the commissioners to enrich themselves at the expense of American shipowners. In addition, the crown established three new admiralty courts in America to hear cases involving violation of the Navigation Acts and various revenue measures. These courts featured crown-appointed judges and no juries. Their decisions, the colonists believed, were bound to be arbitrary because the courts could not be held accountable by those they were judging. Finally, in 1767 Parliament authorized the use of general search warrants which allowed customs officials to enter any building at any time to search for evidence of smuggling.

The Boston Massacre, portrayed here, was used by separatists to whip up sentiment against Great Britain.

A Standing Army

In 1765 the British government announced that in order to economize—the maintenance of British forces in North America was costing the crown £400,000 annually—a majority of western military posts were being shut down and their troops transferred to the major colonial cities along the eastern seaboard. Under Parliament's Quartering Act passed in 1765, each colony was to be responsible for room and board for the troops stationed within its boundaries. When New York refused to provide for its resident redcoats, Parliament suspended its legislature.

The colonists believed that the concentration of troops in the population centers was meant to intimidate and force them to obey the new duties and maritime regulations. They were correct. With customs commissioners operating in fear of their lives and mob violence an almost weekly occurrence in Boston, Lord Hillsborough, secretary of state of the newly created American Department within the British government, ordered four thousand soldiers transferred from Ireland into Boston. Tensions mounted. On March 5, 1770, a contingent of redcoats intervened to protect a customs official from an irate mob. The soldiers fired into the crowd, killing five Bostonians, including Crispus Attucks, an unemployed black seaman. The local chapter of the Sons of Liberty dubbed the incident the "Boston Massacre." One of their leaders, Samuel Adams, a forty-six-year-old revolutionary with a deep hatred for the monarchy, skillfully propagandized against the British in his pamphlet, *Innocent Blood Crying to God From the Streets of Boston.*

The New Imperialism

Though tax collections were ten times their pre-1763 level, the new imperialism was counterproductive of British interests. Colonial nonimportation agreements did substantial damage to British exporters and shippers. Moreover, stringent trade regulations, the manufacturing acts, prohibitions on the issuance of currency, and taxation for revenue inhibited economic growth in the colonies and made it more difficult for the crown's subjects in America to make purchases in England. British leaders understood that in the end, maintenance of the colonial–parent country relationship with the colonies depended upon the goodwill of the colonists. Parliament, the North ministry, and British officials in America compromised, conciliated, advanced, and retreated. They were only postponing the inevitable, however.

THE ROOTS OF MASSIVE RESISTANCE

Despite the uproar over the Boston Massacre, an uneasy calm prevailed from 1770 through 1772. Trade had revived following a postwar depression, and in colonies distant from Massachusetts the massacre was quickly forgotten. In New England smuggling was still possible for the discreet, while the fishing industry and shipbuilding flourished. Then, suddenly, British-colonial relations deteriorated once again. In 1772 Rhode Islanders, outraged at what they perceived to be the arbitrary and heavy-handed enforcement of commercial regulations, boarded the *Gaspee,* a schooner in service to British customs, and sank it, wounding its captain in the process. The British government sent a royal commission to investigate and armed it with the power to extradite suspects directly to England for trial. Alarmed, the Virginia House of Burgesses called for the establishment of intercolonial committees of correspondence, and five colonies responded. It was Massachusetts, however, that continued to provide a revolutionary example to the rest of North America. In 1772 Bostonians led by the fiery Sam Adams published *The Votes and Proceedings* of their town meetings which indicted the British government for taxing the colonists without their consent, imposing a standing army, denying American colonists due process of law, and threatening to foist Anglican bishops on the colonies. The pamphlet was distributed to the colony's 260 towns and more than half indicated their support, a remarkable outpouring of popular sentiment.

THE BOSTON TEA PARTY

The crowning blows to British-colonial relations came in 1773 with passage of the Tea Act and the port of Boston's reaction to it. For 175 years the British East India Company had reaped huge profits from its monopoly on trade between India and the rest of the empire. By the 1770s, however, this once powerful enterprise had fallen on hard times. Tea glutted the English market, and bankruptcy stared the East India directors in the face. In 1773 Lord North came up with a plan that he believed would save the company and simultaneously please the American colonists. The Tea Act of 1773 granted to the East India Company the exclusive privilege of importing tea into England's New World colonies. Because the duty on tea imported to and reexported from England was removed, the price of leaves sold in America would drop dramatically even given the Townshend duty.

To North's astonishment, the colonists, at least the powerful merchant class, were enraged. Many businesses' shelves were already sagging with smuggled Dutch tea which would now be undersold. Moreover, the East India Company was given the power to choose the American retailers who could market their product, and early indications were that it would discriminate against concerns which had participated in anti-British boycotts. Finally, if the British government could set up monopolies for the importation of tea, why could it not do so for spices and other commodities? In a number of ports, mobs led by members of the local Sons of Liberty chapters merely prevented the tea from being landed or sold, but in Boston local patriots went a step further. On December 16, 1773, a hundred and fifty men, organized and probably led by Samuel Adams, and loosely disguised as "Mohawks," boarded three ships and dumped approximately £10,000 worth of tea into the harbor. Though the government of Massachusetts condemned this wanton destruction of private property, no real attempt was made to apprehend the culprits.

THE INTOLERABLE ACTS

The Boston Tea Party was an act of defiance so outrageous that even the most conciliatory member of Parliament was aroused. "We are now to establish our authority," Lord North told the House of Commons, "or give it up entirely." Parliament responded with a series of measures the colonists dubbed the Intolerable or Coercive Acts. The Port of Boston Act closed the harbor to further traffic until all of the dumped tea had been paid for. In the Massachusetts Government Act Parliament declared that the upper house of the General Court should henceforward be appointed rather than elected and placed severe restrictions on the holding of town meetings. A third measure provided that British officials accused of capital offenses while performing their duties in America should be tried in England or a colony other than the one in which they were charged. Finally, the Quartering Act authorized colonial governors to seize privately owned buildings to house British troops. To ensure that Massachusetts obeyed, the British government ordered General Thomas Gage and four regiments of soldiers to Boston, Gage to act as governor of the colony and the redcoats as a kind of palace guard.

THE FIRST CONTINENTAL CONGRESS

The response in America to the Intolerable Acts was, upon agreement of the committees of correspondence, to convene the First Continental Congress at Carpenter's Hall in Philadelphia on September 5, 1774. Fifty-five delegates from twelve of the colonies—only Georgia was unrepresented—attended, and young John Adams of Braintree, Massachusetts, observed of the colonists: "a collection of the greatest men upon this Continent in point of abilities, virtues, and fortunes." In an effort to coerce Britain into repealing its punitive legislation, the assemblage in Philadelphia formed the Continental Association, thus recognizing informal local authorities that had grown up apart from and in defiance of the established colonial governments. The association was to supervise and enforce economic sanctions that included complete nonimportation of British goods as of December 1, 1774, and if that did not work, complete non-exportation of colonial products to Britain as of September 10, 1775. At this point colonial leaders were still divided: "one-third Tories, another Whigs, and rest Mongrels," observed Adams.

It was at the First Continental Congress that the informal imperial debate between the parent country and American radicals came to a head. From the time of the Stamp Act Congress onward, the colonists insisted that it was their right as Englishmen to be taxed only by legislative bodies in which they were represented. Because they were not and could never be represented in Parliament, taxes imposed by the House of Commons were operable only if the colonists voluntarily chose to submit to them. British pamphleteers and political theorists responded with the concept of "virtual" representation. Only one out of six adult males in England voted compared to approximately two out of three in America. The disfranchised in England did not suffer injustice and discrimination, however, because each member of Parliament perceived himself as representing and speaking for all Englishmen. Colonial leaders responded that America was a society distinct and apart, both geographically and culturally, from England, and thus could never be "virtually" represented like the disfranchised citizens of Birmingham and Manchester (which, because redistricting did not keep up with population shifts, had no members in Parliament). From first to last, Americans clung to the concept of "actual" representation, insisting that the closer the connection between voters and their representatives, the better.

The First Continental Congress did not speak of independence—"We ask only for peace, liberty, and security" proclaimed one of their resolutions—but it did put forward a novel interpretation of the constitutional relationship between England and America. Delegates to the Philadelphia gathering took the position that Parliament had no authority over the colonies, that their connection with Britain was through the monarchy, and that they thus were willing to recognize the king's veto through the Privy Council over colonial legislation. Colonial legislatures were, the Congress insisted, sovereign within their borders, and Parliament was not an imperial legislature but had authority in England only. With a view to British public opinion, the delegates first declared the Navigation Acts illegal but then offered to obey them voluntarily. The Continental Congress did declare the Intolerable Acts null and void, however. Moreover it advised the people of Massachusetts to form their own local and provincial governments independent of royal authority, and the delegates urged colonists everywhere to arm themselves and form militias. This latter decree was to constitute the basis of mass, organized resistance when the break with Britain came.

THE BATTLES OF LEXINGTON
AND CONCORD AND OF BUNKER HILL

Massachusetts' determination to resist the Intolerable Acts and the Continental Congress' encouragement of that resistance set the stage for the first major military conflict between Britain and its rebellious colonies. During the spring of 1775 county militias in New England began to collect arms and ammunition and to hold training sessions. When Governor Thomas Gage in Boston learned of the existence of an arsenal of colonial arms in the village of Concord, he dispatched a detachment of seven hundred men to seize it.

As the soldiers marched through Lexington on April 19, several dozen minutemen, alerted the previous night by Paul Revere and William Dawes, waited silently on the village green. Who fired the first shot is unclear, but a flurry of gunfire left eight minutemen dead and ten wounded. The redcoats moved on to Concord and not finding any munitions, which the local militia had moved and rehidden, collected the contents of shops and homes in the village and burned them. The minutemen, who were gathering from nearby communities on a hill outside Concord, saw the smoke rising from the town and, fearful for their families, advanced on the British detachment holding the river bridge at the base of the hill. A skirmish broke out, causing the redcoats to retreat quickly to the village commons, and from there the entire British detachment turned back toward Boston. On the long march back to Boston, the British soldiers took repeated fire from colonials hiding behind trees and stone walls. This unorthodox tactic produced 273 English dead while the minutemen lost but 93 of their number.

During the weeks that followed, militias from Massachusetts and other New England colonies laid siege to the British garrison in Boston. In June Gage's men dislodged the colonials from a spur of Bunker Hill overlooking the city. The British soldiers assumed that their untrained adversaries would crumble under assault, but the colonials retreated only after turning back one frontal assault after another. British forces under the command of General William Howe suffered one thousand casualties.

These momentous events coincided and were in part the product of a political revolution in the colonies that had only partially to do with British-American relations. The Great Awakening had fractured traditional denominations and diminished respect for established clergy and authority in general. Increasing literacy among both men and women gave the common person a new sense of independence and self-confidence. In a number of colonies, merchants, lawyers, shipowners, and planters vied with each other in whipping up animosity against British maritime and taxation measures. Once involved in the political process, artisans, sailors, small farmers, and laborers were loath to exit. Various groups, particularly backcountry dwellers, debtors, ethnic groups, and religious minorities, came to feel that their interests were such that they could be represented only by members of their own group. In 1775 the governor of Georgia noted that the town of Savannah was then being run by a local committee consisting of "a Parcel of the Lowest People, chiefly carpenters, shoemakers, Blacksmiths etc. with a Jew at their head." These local committees as well as provincial committees of correspondence frequently entertained resolutions to expand the suffrage, make voting easier, and publish all legislative deliberations. Royal authorities in America and their colonial sympathizers could barely comprehend these democratizing forces, much less reconcile themselves to them.

CREATING A NATION

In May 1775 the Second Continental Congress assembled in Philadelphia. Its chief purpose was to legitimize the various colonial militias that had gathered at Boston and to prepare for further resistance. George Washington, a Virginia planter and veteran of the French and Indian War, was chosen commander in chief of the Continental Army. The delegates selected him because of his experience and because he was from the largest colony, Virginia, which New England wished to involve in the fighting. Washington took command almost immediately, wrote his wife, Martha, that he would be home by Christmas (an overly optimistic prediction, as it turned out); and he supervised a siege of Boston. This encirclement proved successful; in the spring of 1776 colonial artillery mounted in the hills overlooking the city forced General Gage to retire to Halifax, Nova Scotia.

The Second Continental Congress would sit in Philadelphia until near the end of the Revolutionary War. Though an ad hoc body chosen in different ways by various organized groups throughout the colonies, the congress assumed the attributes of a national government, raising an army, issuing money, opening relations with other countries, and concluding treaties. Congress had no power of compulsion; it had to depend on the goodwill and voluntary cooperation of the several colonies. In July Congress approved and submitted to George III the Olive Branch Petition which proclaimed the colonies' enduring allegiance to the crown and asked the king to break with his ministers whom the petition portrayed as agents of discord. At the same time, the delegates approved the Declaration of the Causes and Necessities of Taking Up Arms, an eloquent statement of the colonial position prepared largely by John Dickinson and Thomas Jefferson. On August 23, 1775, George III proclaimed the colonies in open rebellion and denounced the leaders of the insurrection as traitors. In December the crown declared all American shipping subject to seizure. Meanwhile, in May continental troops had captured Fort Ticonderoga at the head of Lake Champlain, while another force under Richard Montgomery and Benedict Arnold was badly defeated while trying to invade Canada.

Despite belligerent decrees and a rising level of hostilities, as of mid-1775 most members of the colonial aristocracy were conflicted about independence. They had no real concept of America as a separate identity; they thought of themselves as British and were proud of it. Many, including those sitting in Congress, regarded continued submission to British authority as intolerable, and yet they blanched at the idea of independence. Identity aside, the world was a dangerous place, especially for a community of 2.5 million souls widely dispersed across a portion of a huge and largely unexplored land mass. Moreover, many men and women of affairs were apprehensive over the increasingly powerful political role being played by artisans, small farmers, sailors, and the working class in general. Yet, the fact of independence was becoming more and more apparent. The continental army was a symbol of nationhood as was the Second Continental Congress. Virtually every American newspaper favored independence while radicals from all social classes and walks of life agitated for it. In the spring of 1776 Congress declared American ports open for trade with all the other nations of the world.

COMMON SENSE

Perhaps the most influential agitator for a complete break with the mother country was Thomas Paine. A former school teacher and excise tax collector, Paine had arrived in the colonies from England only in 1774. A superb propagandist, Paine published a pro-independence pamphlet entitled *Common Sense* in January 1776. Before the year was out, it had gone through twenty-five printings. *Common Sense* was aimed at the working class, devoid of literary references except to the Bible. A separate national existence, Paine wrote, would enable America to trade freely with all the world. No longer would Britain's former colonists be forced to fight in European wars that had little or no bearing on their interests. Paine analogized: "To know whether it be the interest of this continent to be Independent, we need only ask this simple question: Is it the interest of a man to be a boy all his life?" For the first time in anti-British literature, Paine's pamphlet ridiculed the concept of monarchy and called George III a "royal brute." The king no less than his ministers was responsible for the repression of America.

THE DECLARATION OF INDEPENDENCE

In the spring of 1776 several colonies instructed their delegations in Philadelphia to vote for separation from England if the issue arose. In June Virginian Richard Henry Lee moved a resolution of separation, and the Continental Congress appointed a five-member committee to work out the details and set forth the reasons for independence. The committee included Massachusetts lawyer John Adams, Virginia planter and philosopher Thomas Jefferson, and the Philadelphia inventor and man of affairs Benjamin Franklin. To Jefferson, the best literary stylist of the three, was given the task of writing up the committee's report. On July 2, 1776, Congress formally declared independence and on July 4 it adopted the report of Jefferson's committee, which was then signed by the members over a period of several weeks.

The Declaration of Independence was nothing more or less than an elegant piece of propaganda. It was aimed at the undecided in America and abroad, especially France where Enlightenment figures had long looked at America as the ideal society. Jefferson and his colleagues attempted to convince the wavering that there were certain times in the affairs of man when revolution was justified. They drew upon the thinking of natural rights philosophers such as John Locke who had written to legitimize the Glorious Revolution in England in 1688. Just like his predecessors, Jefferson asserted that in an original state of nature the strong tended to deny the weak basic rights such as life, liberty, and property. To provide for the common good and to end a state of anarchy, the members of society agreed to relinquish a part of their freedom, obey rules, and submit to a few who would govern. Power and wealth would come to those chosen to rule, but these advantages were incidental. The fundamental duty of governors was to protect the rights of their subjects. Indeed, the good of the commonweal was the fundamental objective of the social compact or agreement entered into by governors and governed. At the time Jefferson wrote, this natural rights philosophy was generally accepted so that he was able to refer to it as "self-evident." It was entirely fitting for citizens to alter their government and/or rulers when they violated the social contract. Thus, the bulk of the Declaration was a list of grievances designed to prove that George III and his ministers had done just that. The Declaration made it clear, however, that these specific abuses pointed to a greater threat—the intent of the British government to submit the American colonists to arbitrary rule.

BRITAIN AND AMERICA ON THE EVE OF WAR

Following adoption of the Declaration, the revolutionary war began in earnest. Initially, the two sides maneuvered warily, attempting to stockpile matériel and to build up their respective military machines in America. Britain enjoyed a number of advantages at the outset. The British Isles could claim 11 million inhabitants to America's 2.5 million. The Royal Navy was the largest and best in the world, while the British Army was experienced and well trained.

Approximately 20 percent of white male Americans were loyalists, individuals who believed that separation was no answer to imperial problems and who regarded defense of king and country a matter of personal honor. Eventually some twenty-one thousand loyalists fought with the British against their fellow Americans, and some of the most vicious combat of the revolution occurred between loyalists and Continentals. French Canadians, impressed by the Quebec Act, refused to make common cause with the American rebels. And, finally, many nonwhites sided with Great Britain. The Indian tribes to the west sensed that the crown was one of the few restraints on the insatiably land-hungry Anglo-Americans. During the war nearly twenty thousand slaves ran away to enlist in the Royal Army as laborers or soldiers.

Americans, of course, had the psychological advantage. To their minds they were fighting for freedom and independence and to defend their families and homesteads. Despite its smaller population, the former colonies proved more efficient than Britain in mobilizing manpower. Britain eventually fielded an army in America of 162,000, but this included loyalists and thirty thousand German mercenaries, or Hessians. Perhaps one-half of free males in America were enlisted into the Continental Army, some 220,000 souls. Although its formal navy was insignificant compared to Britain's, American privateers captured some two thousand British merchant vessels during the war, making it very difficult for London to supply its troops with munitions and food. Finally, America did not have to win outright; the Continental Army and Congress had merely to survive until British taxpayers wearied of paying the increasingly burdensome costs of war.

THE WAR

WASHINGTON AND THE CONTINENTAL ARMY

Still, things did not go well for Washington and his troops early in the conflict. The Americans could not simply rely on guerrilla warfare. Independence depended in no small part on Congress' ability to gain diplomatic recognition and aid from Britain's European enemies, especially France. To do that the Continental Army would have to demonstrate that it could fight and win pitched battles involving regular troops fighting in formation at close range.

The 16,600 men who constituted the first Continental Army were recruited from the New England militias that converged on Boston following the clashes at Lexington and Concord. Washington bemoaned the inexperience of his officers and the lack of discipline among his enlisted men. These first American soldiers sometimes left sentry duty before being properly relieved, were loath to use the latrine, and frequently took potshots at the enemy. Worse, they seemed to come and go as they pleased.

Indeed, after the first wave of enthusiasm filled the ranks of the regular army, enlistment became a problem. Most colonials much preferred to fight in their local militias, taking up arms only when the war intruded on their home territory. Enlistment in the regular army took men away from their farms; moreover, the life of a Continental was full of hard discipline, danger, and disease. In need of a regular army that could be trained over time and that could fight in long campaigns, Washington appealed to Congress. That body responded in September 1776 by setting the term of enlistment in the Continental Army at three years or for the duration of the war, and assigning each state a troop quota. Congress offered a signing bonus and one hundred acres of land to any man serving for the duration. Still, enlistment remained a problem throughout the war. The widespread preference for service in local militias persisted, and Americans were generally distrustful of standing armies.

Despite these problems, more than one hundred thousand men served in the Continental Army with an equal amount enlisting in local militias. At least five thousand of these were African Americans. The fighting in the Revolutionary War was brutal; musket and cannon fire killed and maimed, and battles frequently ended in hand-to-hand fighting. On more than one occasion the victorious troops from one side slaughtered their wounded opponents as they lay on the battlefield. Between 26,000 and 27,000 American soldiers died during the war, 6,000 from battle wounds, 10,000 from disease, and the rest as prisoners of war or missing in action. Civilian casualties were unusually low.

WOMEN AND THE WAR

Women played a prominent part in the Revolutionary War. It fell to the wives of soldiers to keep the home fires burning, to run the family farm or business, and to raise the children. Patriot women came together to sew clothes; make blankets; and gather food, lead, and bandages for the men at the battle front. In Philadelphia, a group of upper-class women formed the Ladies Association of Philadelphia, divided the city into districts, and went door-to-door collecting aid. Patriot women also organized aid societies to help the widows and orphans of soldiers killed in battle. The Daughters of Liberty joined enthusiastically in persecuting suspected loyalists. In Massachusetts a mob of some four hundred women descended upon a merchant believed to be hoarding coffee, the beverage of choice since the boycott of tea. The spouses of poor men were frequently unable to support themselves, and in desperation they followed the army. For half rations these "women of the army," as they were called at the time, cooked, sewed, and performed nursing duties. Among these camp followers, of course, were a number of prostitutes. Washington objected to the presence of women among his soldiers, but he could not outlaw them completely for fear of driving up the desertion rate.

THE LOYALISTS

The American Revolution was a civil war in that it pitted colonist against colonist as well as American against Briton. As many as half a million people remained loyal to England during the Revolution. Virtually all Anglican clergy were loyalists as well as a large number of lawyers who had worked with the British colonial administration. Members of ethnic minorities persecuted by the majority—Highland Scots and some Germans, for example—sided with the crown. Not surprisingly there was much sympathy for the British among Indians and slaves. Tenant farmers frequently allied with the redcoats against their patriot landlords. Loyalist sentiment was most widespread in the South and least prevalent in New England. Most who wanted to retain the imperial tie were apathetic, however. Active loyalists were subject to beatings, tar and feathering, and confiscation of their property. Still, during the Revolution as many as fifty thousand Americans fought for the crown, most as irregulars or in local loyalist militias. By war's end some eighty thousand of the king's loyal subjects had fled America for other parts of the empire.

THE STRUGGLE TO SURVIVE

Washington's strategy was to avoid exposing his untrained and poorly equipped soldiers to pitched battles against superior forces. As time passed and his army matured, he could harass the British, denying them victory and challenging them at places of his choosing. General William Howe, who replaced Gage as commander in chief of British forces in North America, hoped to crush the rebellion in its infancy by winning a decisive battle in Massachusetts. After Washington occupied Dorchester Heights overlooking Boston Harbor, however, Howe retreated with his five thousand men to Halifax, Nova Scotia, and the British realized that they would have to wage a long protracted war, capturing major rebel cities and defeating the colonials in a major battle.

Howe's first target was New York. He believed that if his army could take the city and link up with another force moving south from Canada, the British could isolate New England from the rest of the colonies. In the summer of 1776, 130 warships under Admiral Richard Howe (Earl Howe), William's brother, landed thirty-two thousand royal troops near New York Harbor. Within months this force compelled Washington to flee across the Delaware River from New Jersey into Pennsylvania. At the time he ferried his remaining troops across the river from Trenton, on December 7, 1776, Washington commanded some three thousand men, a mere fraction of the twenty-three thousand that had originally faced Howe at New York.

William Howe was given to fits of timidity and indecisiveness, a general who seemed to care more for minimizing casualties among his own men than finishing the enemy. Thus, instead of crossing the Delaware and finishing the Americans, the British commander pulled the bulk of his troops back to New York, leaving a thousand Hessians to garrison Trenton. Sensing that morale required a victory, Washington risked everything. On Christmas night, 1776, he led his soldiers back into New Jersey and won a decisive victory at Trenton. The Continentals had floated across the Delaware at night, winding their way through ice floes and caught the Hessians at dawn, drowsy from their

Christmas revelries. The American commander in chief followed Trenton with another triumph over the British at the village of Princeton. Stung by these audacious thrusts, Howe withdrew his troops to a perimeter around New York City. While Washington wintered in Morristown, New Jersey, Howe's troops proceeded to alienate the civilian population of New York. The arrogance of the redcoats who occupied buildings, seized property and lifestock, harassed and even raped young women drove many fence-sitters into the patriot camp.

With the return of warm weather in the spring of 1777, the Howe brothers broke camp, their sights set on Philadelphia, the rebel capital. To avoid a long march through the hostile New Jersey countryside, General Howe decided to assault Philadelphia from the sea. In July he set sail with an army of fifteen thousand. By the time the British landed on the Maryland coast south of Philadelphia, Washington had rushed down to meet them. The American commander had rebuilt his army to eleven thousand and had hoped for some time to train and equip it, but he could not afford to surrender the new nation's capital without a struggle. The Continental Army fought well at the battle of Brandywine Creek but was defeated. The British then maneuvered Washington's crippled force out of the way and occupied Philadelphia on September 26. Howe stationed the bulk of his troops at Germantown some five miles northwest of the capitol. A defiant Washington struck hard at Germantown, was repulsed, and finally retreated (see Figure 4–2).

THE FRANCO-AMERICAN ALLIANCE

While Washington's army attacked and retreated, the Continental Congress labored to draw France into the war on America's side. The outbreak of the American Revolution saw French distrust and dislike of the British at an all-time high. The Bourbon monarchy and French nationalists considered the Treaty of 1763, which ended the French and Indian War, to be unreasonable, humiliating, and proof that Britain intended to dominate the world. England was "an enemy at once grasping, ambitious, unjust, and perfidious," wrote Charles Gravier Comte de Vergennes, the French foreign minister in 1774. "The invariable and most cherished purpose in her politics has been, if not the destruction of France at least her overthrow, her humiliation, and her ruin. . . . It is our duty then to seize every possible opportunity to reduce the power and the greatness of England." Thus did Vergennes and his countrymen applaud America's decision to go to war for independence. Indeed, from January 1776 through October 1777 France and its Catholic ally, Spain, sent just under one-half million dollars in aid to the Americans. Included in this life-giving flow of supplies were 300,000 pounds of powder for cannon, 30,000 muskets, 3,000 tents, and 200 cannon. Yet France held back on formal recognition, knowing that diplomatic recognition would mean certain war with England.

In late 1776 Congress named three emissaries to France with the goal of obtaining diplomatic recognition and securing a formal alliance. Arthur Lee,

FIGURE 4-2

The Revolutionary War in the North, 1776-1778

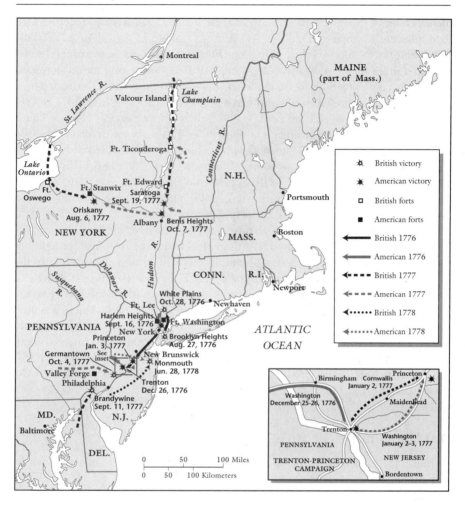

previously the agent of Massachusetts in London, and Silas Deane, a respected member of Congress from Connecticut, were already in Paris. The third, Benjamin Franklin, joined them in December. The famous Philadelphian, then seventy years of age, took Paris society by storm. His writings had been translated into dozens of languages, and his spectacular experiments with electricity had already captivated the imagination of the science-loving French. Donning the garb of a simple American agriculturalist, Franklin established himself at court and ensured that French aid continued to flow across the Atlantic. But the crown would go no further until the Continental Army won a significant battlefield victory.

SARATOGA

Again, to capture New York and thus isolate New England, General John "Gentleman Johnny" Burgoyne led some 9,500 British and Hessian troops together with two thousand women and children south from Quebec in the fall of 1777. This lumbering force succeeded in capturing Fort Ticonderoga, approximately one hundred miles north of Albany. The battle for Ticonderoga and an unsuccessful sortie into Vermont left his forces depleted, however. As the redcoats struggled over twisting, boulder-strewn roads and across yawning chasms spanned by rickety bridges, a contingent of Continentals and militia under General Horatio Gates waited for them below Saratoga. On September 19 the rebels descended on the redcoats from the surrounding woods, and a bloody battle ensued at Freeman's Farm. Benedict Arnold, a brave young officer who would later betray his country, led a number of the charges. The British retreated northward, but they could not escape. On October 17, 1777, Burgoyne's 5,800 remaining troops surrendered to an army of seventeen thousand Continentals under Gates.

News of the British defeat at Saratoga opened the door for Franklin and his colleagues in Paris. Emboldened by this evidence that the Revolution might actually succeed, France signed a treaty of friendship and alliance with the American representatives on February 6, 1778. France recognized American independence, and each nation guaranteed the territory of the other. The treaty stipulated that in case of war between England and France, America would have a free hand to conquer British Canada and Bermuda, and France would be entitled to seize the British West Indies. Neither nation was to conclude a truce or peace without the other's consent. France and Britain did indeed drift into war in June 1778. Spain initiated hostilities the following year, and the Dutch followed suit in 1780. England was isolated.

VALLEY FORGE

While representatives of the Continental Congress negotiated in Paris, Washington and his eleven thousand men spent the winter of 1777–1778 miserably encamped at Valley Forge, Pennsylvania. The ragged, starving troops lived twelve to a cabin while their officers pled in vain with Congress and the inhabitants of the surrounding countryside for food and clothing. The meager provisions that the Continentals did receive were frequently too rancid to eat and the garments too threadbare to give protection against the biting wind. Most of the men came from thinly populated rural areas and were unacquainted with the rudiments of community hygiene, and as a result dysentery and cholera ravaged the ranks of Washington's army. The tendency of the troops to ignore latrines became such a problem that officers ordered sentries to fire upon any soldier "easing himself elsewhere than at ye vaults." During that terrible winter twenty-five hundred men died of exposure and disease.

The reasons for the neglect of Washington's troops at Valley Forge were political and social. The Continental Congress lacked the money to purchase

General Washington and the Marquis de Lafayette at Valley Forge. The Continental Army's suffering during the winter of 1777-78 came to symbolize the heroism of those who struggled for independence.

supplies and the mechanism to distribute them. Merchants preferred to sell to the British who could pay rather than to the Continentals who could not. Most important, the social and ethnic makeup of the regular army had changed. Instead of farmers, artisans, small merchants—most of whom were heads of household—who first comprised the bulk of America's fighting force, the Continental Army by late 1777 consisted primarily of young, single, semiliterate males. They were unemployed laborers, vagrants, landless sons of farmers, slaves, recent immigrants, even British deserters. Most joined the army out of desperation; some had hired themselves out as substitutes. Middle- and upper-class Americans increasingly viewed them as rabble.

Nevertheless, the terrible winter at Valley Forge bound Washington's soldiers together. Warmer weather brought in new recruits, fresh food, and a Prussian soldier of fortune, General Friedrich von Steuben. A genius at training, motivation, and logistics, von Steuben turned the Continental Army into a modern fighting force within four months.

LAFAYETTE

In 1777, the Marquis de Lafayette, a young French nobleman, and a group of military officers whom he recruited to assist Americans in their struggle for independence landed in South Carolina. Commissioned a major general at the age of nineteen in the Revolutionary Army, he quickly became a trusted cohort of General George Washington who treated him as a favorite son. Lafayette reciprocated the affection and named his son for America's founding father. The marquis participated in military engagements from the Battle of Brandywine in 1777 to the final defeat of the British in the Battle of Yorktown in 1781. Unlike some of the pretentious Europeans given high military rank in the Revolutionary Army, Lafayette was extraordinarily popular with American officers; not the least of these were Colonels James Monroe and Alexander Hamilton and Captains John Marshall and Aaron Burr who were his comrades-in-arms.

MONMOUTH COURTHOUSE

In May 1778 Sir Henry Clinton replaced General Howe as British commander in chief. With France's entry into the war Britain was going to have to fight on a number of fronts rather than concentrate on America. As a consequence, Clinton received orders to retire northward from Philadelphia to New York. At dawn on June 18, 1778, Clinton's ten thousand men left for the overland march across New Jersey. Rejuvenated, the 13,500 soldiers of the Continental Army caught up with Clinton's force and fought it to a stalemate at Monmouth Courthouse. Under cover of night, the British slipped into New York City, while Washington encamped at White Plains to wait, in vain, for reinforcements sufficient to allow him to drive Clinton from the city.

THE SOUTHERN STRATEGY

Late in 1778 British strategists decided to focus their efforts on the colonies of the mainland South (see Figure 4–3). The Chesapeake and southern colonies were the main revenue earners for the empire, and they were more strategically located than the mid-Atlantic and New England colonies, being closer to the sugar islands of the Caribbean. The British believed that they could rely on pacification rather than pure force to control the area. They reasoned that loyalist sentiment was strong in the piedmont and that if they could establish footholds on the coast, the upcountry residents would rally to the crown and help them defeat the rebels. To this end Sir Henry Clinton, who had replaced William Howe, dispatched five thousand troops to the Caribbean and another three thousand to Florida.

In the fall of 1778, thirty-five hundred redcoats easily overwhelmed the colonial settlement at Savannah, and the British turned their sights on South Carolina. During the waning days of 1779 a large force under the command of Clinton himself landed on the Carolina coast and slowly made their way through the swamps until they reached the outskirts of Charleston to which they laid siege. By then spring and warm weather had set in. Sweltering in their wool uniforms and beset by malaria-bearing mosquitoes, the redcoats slowly advanced their trenches and barricades toward the city. From their stronghold

FIGURE 4-3
The War in the Lower South, 1778-1781

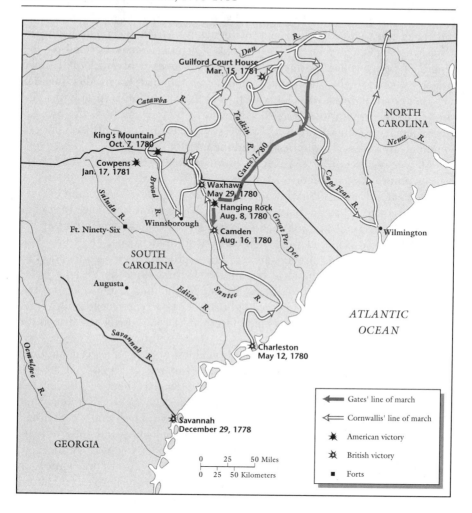

in the Citadel, some five thousand Continentals and South Carolina militia fought fiercely to defend the city. On May 12 Charleston surrendered. Clinton had hoped to pacify the area by treating rebel soldiers and civilian leaders leniently. This policy only succeeded in alienating the loyalists who had rallied to his cause, while his insistence that the rebels take a personal oath of loyalty to the crown ensured their continued alienation. Clinton then departed, leaving behind eighty-three hundred troops under the command of Charles, Lord Cornwallis.

The fall of Charleston revived loyalist sentiment in the backcountry. Supporters of the crown, for years hunted, tortured, hanged, and shot by rebel militia, rallied to the crown. Between 1780 and 1782 bloody civil war raged in the piedmont of the Carolinas, a conflict that pitted neighbor against neighbor and even brother against brother. Loyalist militia plundered rebel plantations and raped the wives and daughters of their adversaries. Insurgents whipped suspected loyalists and burned their farms. Criminal looters hovered on the fringes of both armies, posing as soldiers and stealing livestock and other property. Increasingly, the civilian population blamed Cornwallis for not restoring order and cast their lot with the rebels. New militias sprang up. The most famous, or notorious, was that headed by Francis Marion, the Swamp Fox, whose band of black and white raiders succeeded in cutting British lines of communication between Charleston and the interior.

All was not gloom for Cornwallis, however. In August of 1780 the Continentals, under the command of the aged General Horatio Gates, suffered a major defeat at Camden, South Carolina. The rout of Gates' troops and his unseemly departure from the battlefield caused Washington to replace him with the thirty-eight-year-old Nathaniel Greene. The new commander had at his disposal fourteen hundred ragged, hungry, dispirited troops. He decided to mold his strategy to his circumstances. Greene ordered his troops to stop harassing and plundering the local population, he pressured the Virginia legislature to provide for his troops, he encouraged local militia leaders like Marion, and he did the unthinkable—he divided his troops. Greene recognized that he could not defeat Cornwallis' combined forces; if he could divide the British divisions, however, he could conquer.

The British commander obliged, dispatching a force of eleven hundred redcoats under Lieutenant Colonel Banastre Tarleton to catch and subdue six hundred rebels under Greene's lieutenant, Daniel Morgan. Morgan led the British on an exhausting chase across western South Carolina, but was finally cornered at Cowpens, an open meadow bordering on a broad river. Tarleton attacked prematurely; his troops panicked and then retreated. Meanwhile, Cornwallis chased Greene, subsequently joined by Morgan, into North Carolina. At Guilford Courthouse the two sides joined in fierce battle. The British carried the day, but the costly battle of Guilford Courthouse convinced Cornwallis that he could not put down the rebellion in the Carolinas.

YORKTOWN

Discouraged, the British commander abandoned his pacification program and turned once again to a more conventional strategy. He decided that the war could still be won if the crown could win a decisive victory over the Continental Army; the site he chose for battle was the Chesapeake. In the summer of 1781 Cornwallis established a base at Yorktown, Virginia, from which he could expand westward through Virginia, cutting Greene's supply lines and isolating his bands of marauders and at the same time lure Washington into a decisive battle (see Figure 4–4).

FIGURE 4-4
The Yorktown Campaign, 1781

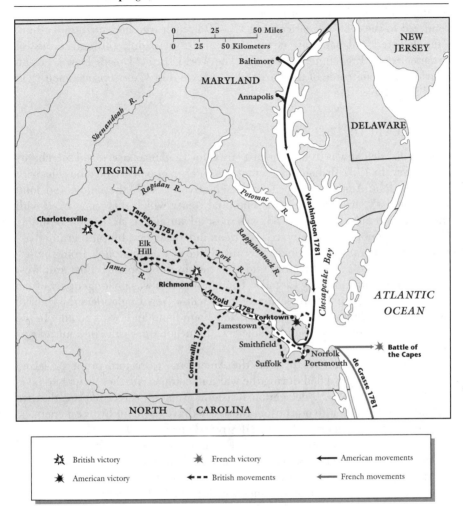

Meanwhile, the French had taken advantage of Britain's decision to shift troops from New England to the South to land a five thousand–man force under the Comte de Rochambeau in Rhode Island. By the summer of 1781 Rochambeau had joined forces with Washington. Upon hearing that the French Caribbean fleet was headed for the Chesapeake to take on Cornwallis' army, the American commander in chief decided to head south. Leaving a small force behind in White Plains to fool the British, Washington and his French compatriot moved quickly down the Virginia coast.

In late August the French fleet arrived from the West Indies, landed a large force near Yorktown, and sealed off Cornwallis from the sea. A contingent of

Continentals under the command of the Marquis de Lafayette moved up to join them while Washington and Rochambeau pressed down from the north. Following weeks of intermittent combat Cornwallis' six thousand–man force surrendered to the 8,800 Americans and 7,800 French who had surrounded him. The defeated redcoats lay down their arms, marching through ranks of Americans and Frenchmen who sang "The World Turned Upside Down." Upon hearing of the outcome of the Battle of Yorktown, Lord North proclaimed, "Oh God! It's all over."

THE TREATY OF 1783

Cornwallis' defeat was in fact the last straw for England's overtaxed merchants and gentry. In 1782 British representatives entered into peace negotiations with Franklin, John Adams, America's representative to the Netherlands, and John Jay, Congress' emissary to Spain. The final treaty which they concluded with the British on September 3, 1783, was most advantageous to the new republic. Great Britain not only recognized American independence, but also granted astonishingly liberal boundaries. The United States was to stretch from the Atlantic to the Mississippi River, bounded to the south by Spanish East and West Florida and to the north by Canada. Though America was no longer part of the British Empire, John Adams secured for his fellow New Englanders the right to fish the Grand Banks off the coasts of New Foundland and Nova Scotia. To the relief of British merchants and financiers, the negotiators validated all prewar debts.

British representatives pressed the Americans to restore property seized from loyalists who had fled during the war and compensate those who had been persecuted, but the U.S. delegation resisted. "Your ministers require that we should receive again into our bosom those who have been our bitterest enemies, and restore their property who have destroyed ours; and this while the wounds they have given us are still bleeding," Franklin complained. The most he and his colleagues would grant was a provision promising an end to persecution and recommending that the states restore property illegally seized.

Thus did thirteen British colonies which in 1763 were earnestly protesting their attachment to the mother country fight a successful revolution some twenty years later and through force of arms and shrewd diplomacy gain full independence and a generous peace. The new nation was diverse, pragmatic, proud, and briefly confident. It possessed a thriving agriculture and seaborne commerce and the beginnings of a manufacturing economy. Its population was vigorous, ambitious, and politically active. But, though possessed of the largest merchant marine in the world, America had almost no navy and would have to confront a hostile and dangerous world without the protection of the Royal Navy. Moreover, all of the problems—administration of western lands, creation of a stable currency, distribution of political power, establishment and management of an equitable tax system—that had plagued the British government now devolved upon Congress and the states.

At one level the American Revolution was a struggle between elites, a conflict to determine who would rule over the colonies and who would rule in the colonies. But it was also a comprehensive historical event which affected every region, social class, and occupational group. It changed the way Britain's former subjects thought about themselves and the world. In the essay that follows Alfred F. Young describes the impact of the Revolution on George Robert Twelves Hewes, a Boston shoemaker, a member of the "humble classes." In instilling a sense of self-worth and empowerment in Hewes and his fellow working-class Americans, the Revolution contributed to the democratization of America in fact as well as in name.

GEORGE ROBERT TWELVES HEWES (1742–1840): A BOSTON SHOEMAKER AND THE MEMORY OF THE AMERICAN REVOLUTION

Alfred F. Young

Late in 1762 or early in 1763, George Robert Twelves Hewes, a Boston shoemaker in the last year or so of his apprenticeship, repaired a shoe for John Hancock and delivered it to him at his uncle Thomas Hancock's store in Dock Square. Hancock was pleased and invited the young man to "come and see him on New Year's day, and bid him a happy New-Year," according to the custom of the day, a ritual of noblesse oblige on the part of the gentry. We know of the episode through Benjamin Bussey Thatcher, who interviewed Hewes and wrote it up for his *Memoir* of Hewes in 1835. On New Year's Day, as Thatcher tells the story, after some urging by his master,

> George washed his face, and put his best jacket on, and proceeded straightaway to the Hancock House (as it is still called). His heart was in his mouth, but assuming a cheerful courage, he knocked at the front door, and took his hat off. The servant came:
> "Is 'Squire Hancock at home, Sir?" enquired Hewes, making a bow.
> He was introduced directly to the *kitchen,* and requested to seat himself, while

from Alfred F. Young, "George Robert Twelves Hewes (1742–1840): A Boston Shoemaker and the Memory of the American Revolution," *The William and Mary Quarterly,* Vol. XXXVIII, No. 4 (October, 1981).

report should be made above stairs. The man came down directly, with a new varnish of civility suddenly spread over his face. He ushered him into the 'Squire's sitting-room, and left him to make his obeisance. Hancock remembered him, and addressed him kindly. George was anxious to get through, and he commenced a desperate speech—"as pretty a one," he says, "as he any way knew how,"—intended to announce the purpose of his visit, and to accomplish it, in the same breath.

"Very well, my lad," said the 'Squire—now take a chair, my lad."

He sat down, scared all the while (as he now confesses) "almost to death," while Hancock put his hand into his breeches-pocket and pulled out a crown-piece, which he placed softly in his hand, thanking him at the same time for his punctual attendance, and his compliments. He then invited his young friend to drink his health—called for wine—poured it out for him—and ticked glasses with him,—a feat in which Hewes, though he had never seen it performed before, having acquitted himself with a creditable dexterity, hastened to make his bow again, and secure his retreat, though not till the 'Squire had extorted a sort of half promise from him to come the next New-Year's—which, for a rarity, he never discharged.

The episode is a demonstration of what the eighteenth century called deference.

Another episode catches the point at which Hewes had arrived a decade and a half later. In 1778 or 1779, after one stint in the war on board a privateer and another in the militia, he was ready to ship out again, from Boston. As Thatcher tells the story: "Here he enlisted, or engaged to enlist, on board the Hancock, a twenty-gun ship, but not liking the manners of the Lieutenant very well, who ordered him one day in the streets to take his hat off to him—which he refused to do for any man,—he went aboard the 'Defence,' Captain Smedley, of Fairfield Connecticut." This, with a vengeance, is the casting off of deference.

What had happened in the intervening years? What had turned the young shoemaker tongue-tied in the face of his betters into the defiant person who would not take his hat off for any man? And why should stories like this have stayed in his memory sixty and seventy years later?

George Robert Twelves Hewes was born in Boston in 1742 and died in Richfield Springs, New York, in 1840. He participated in several of the principal political events of the American Revolution in Boston, among them the Massacre and the Tea Party, and during the war he served as a privateersman and militiaman. A shoemaker all his life, and intermittently or concurrently a fisherman, sailor, and farmer, he remained a poor man. He never made it, not before the war in Boston, not at sea, not after the war in Wrentham and Attleborough, Massachusetts, not in Otsego County, New York. He was a nobody who briefly became a somebody in the Revolution and, for a moment near the end of his life, a hero.

Hewes might have been unknown to posterity save for his longevity and a shift in the historical mood that rekindled the "spirit of '76." To Americans of the 1830s the Boston Tea Party had become a leading symbol of the Revolution, and Hewes lived long enough to be thought of as one of the last surviving participants, perhaps the very last. In 1833, when James Hawkes "discovered" him in the "obscurity" of upstate New York, Hewes was ninety-one but thought he was ninety-eight, a claim Hawkes accepted when he published the first memoir of Hewes that year. Thus in

1835 when Hewes was invited to Boston, people thought that this survivor of one of the greatest moments of the Revolution was approaching his one hundredth birthday and on "the verge of eternity," as a Fourth of July orator put it. He became a celebrity, the guest of honor on Independence Day, the subject of a second biography by Thatcher and of an oil portrait by Joseph Cole, which hangs today in Boston's Old State House.

To Thatcher, Hewes was one of the "humble classes" that made the success of the Revolution possible. How typical he was we can only suggest at this point in our limited knowledge of the "humble classes." Probably he was as representative a member of the "lower trades" of the cities and as much a rank-and-file participant in the political events and the war as historians have found. The two biographies, which come close to being oral histories (and give us clues to track down Hewes in other ways), provide an unusually rich cumulative record, over a very long period of time, of his thoughts, attitudes, and values. Consequently, we can answer, with varying degrees of satisfaction, a number of questions about one man of the "humble classes." About the "lower trades": why did a boy enter a craft with such bleak prospects as shoemaking? what was the life of an apprentice? what did it mean to be a shoemaker and a poor man in Boston? About the Revolution: what moved such a rank-and-file person to action? what action did he take? may we speak of his "ideology"? does the evidence of his loss of deference permit us to speak of change in his consciousness? About the war: how did a poor man, an older man, a man with a family exercise his patriotism? what choices did he make? About the results of the Revolution: how did the war affect him? to what extent did he achieve his life goals? why did he go west? what did it mean to be an aged veteran of the Revolution? What, in sum, after more than half a century had passed, was the meaning of the Revolution to someone still in the "humble classes"? . . .

In 1756, when Hewes was fourteen, he was apprenticed to a shoemaker. Why did a boy become a shoemaker in mid-eighteenth-century Boston? The town's shoemakers were generally poor and their prospects were worsening. From 1756 to 1775, eight out of thirteen shoemakers who died and left wills at probate did not even own their own homes. In 1790, shoemakers ranked thirty-eighth among forty-four occupations in mean tax assessments.

It was not a trade in which boys were eager to be apprentices. Few sons continued in their father's footsteps, as they did, for example, in prosperous trades like silversmithing or shipbuilding. Leatherworkers, after mariners, headed the list of artisans who got their apprentices from the orphans, illegitimate children, and boys put out to apprenticeship by Boston's Overseers of the Poor. In England, shoemaking was a trade with proud traditions, symbolized by St. Crispin's Day, a shoemakers' holiday, a trade with a reputation for producing poets, philosophers, and politicians, celebrated by Elizabethan playwrights as "the gentle craft." But there were few signs of a flourishing shoemaker culture in Boston before the Revolution. In children's lore shoemakers were proverbially poor, like the cobbler in a Boston chapbook who "labored hard and took a great deal of pains for a small livelihood." Shoemakers, moreover, were low in status. John Adams spoke of shoemaking as "too mean and dimi[nu]tive an Occupation" to hold a client of his who wanted to "rise in the World."

Where one ended up in life depended very much on where one started out. George was born under the sign of the Bulls Head and Horns on Water Street near the docks in the South End. His father—also named George—was a tallow chandler and erstwhile tanner. Hewes drew the connections between his class origins and his life chances as he began his narrative for Hawkes:

> My father, said he, was born in Wrentham in the state of Massachusetts, about twenty-eight miles from Boston. My grandfather having made no provision for his support, and being unable to give him an education, apprenticed him at Boston to learn a mechanical trade. . . .
>
> In my childhood, my advantages for education were very limited, much more so than children enjoy at the present time in my native state. My whole education which my opportunities permitted me to acquire, consisted only of a moderate knowledge of reading and writing; my father's circumstances being confined to such humble means as he was enabled to acquire by his mechanical employment, I was kept running of errands, and exposed of course to all the mischiefs to which children are liable in populous cities.

Hewes's family on his father's side was "no better off than what is called in New England *moderate,* and probably not as good." The American progenitor of the line seems to have come from Wales and was in Salisbury, near Newburyport, in 1677, doing what we do not know. Solomon Hewes, George Robert's grandfather, was born in Portsmouth, New Hampshire, in 1674, became a joiner, and moved with collateral members of his family to Wrentham, originally part of Dedham, near Rhode Island. There he became a landholder; most of his brothers were farmers; two became doctors, one of whom prospered in nearby Providence. His son—our George's father—was born in 1701. On the side of his mother, Abigail Seaver, Hewes's family was a shade different. They had lived for four generations in Roxbury, a small farming town immediately south of Boston across the neck. Abigail's ancestors seem to have been farmers, but one was a minister. Her father, Shubael, was a country cordwainer who owned a house, barn, and two acres. She was born in 1711 and married in 1728.

George Robert Twelves Hewes, born August 25, 1742, was the sixth of nine children, the fourth of seven sons. Five of the nine survived childhood—his three older brothers, Samuel, Shubael, and Solomon, and a younger brother, Daniel. He was named George after his father, Robert after a paternal uncle, and the unlikely Twelves, he thought, for his mother's great uncle, "whose Christian name was Twelve, for whom she appeared to have great admiration. Why he was called by that singular name I never knew." More likely, his mother was honoring her own mother, also Abigail, whose maiden name was Twelves.

The family heritage to George, it might be argued, was more genetic than economic. He inherited a chance to live long: the men in the Seaver line were all long-lived. And he inherited his size. He was unusually short—five feet, one inch. "I have never acquired the ordinary weight or size of other men," Hewes told Hawkes, who wrote that "his whole person is of a slight and slender texture." In old age he was known as "the little old man." Anatomy is not destiny, but Hewes's short size and long name helped shape his personality. It was a big name for a small boy to carry. He was the butt of endless teasing jibes—George Robert what?—that Thatcher turned into anecdotes the humor of which may have masked the pain Hewes may have felt.

"Moderate" as it was, Hewes had a sense of family. Wrentham, town of his grandfather and uncles, was a place he would be sent as a boy, a place of refuge in the war, and after the war his home. He would receive an inheritance three times in his life, each one a reminder of the importance or potential importance of relatives. And he was quite aware of any relative of status, like Dr. Joseph Warren, a distant kinsman on his mother's side.

His father's life in Boston had been an endless, futile struggle to succeed as a tanner. Capital was the problem. In 1729 he bought a one-third ownership in a tannery for £600 in bills of credit. Two years later, he sold half of his third to his brother Robert, who became a working partner. The two brothers turned to a rich merchant, Nathaniel Cunningham, who put up £3500 in return for half the profits. The investment was huge: pits, a yard, workshops, hides, bark, two horses, four slaves, journeymen. For a time the tannery flourished. Then there was a disastrous falling out with Cunningham: furious fights, a raid on the yards, debtors' jail twice for George, suits and countersuits that dragged on in the courts for years. The Hewes brothers saw themselves as "very laborious" artisans who "managed their trade with good skill," only to be ruined by a wealthy, arrogant merchant. To Cunningham, they were incompetent and defaulters. Several years before George Robert was born, his father had fallen back to "butchering, tallow chandlering, hog killing, soap boiling &c."

The family was not impoverished. George had a memory as a little boy of boarding a ship with his mother to buy a small slave girl "at the rate of two dollars a pound." And there was enough money to pay the fees for his early schooling. But beginning in 1748, when he was six, there was a series of family tragedies. In 1748 an infant brother, Joseph, died, followed later in the year by his sister Abigail, age thirteen, and brother Ebenezer, age two. In 1749 his father died suddenly of a stroke, leaving the family nothing it would seem, his estate tangled in debt and litigation. George's mother would have joined the more than one thousand widows in Boston, most of whom were on poor relief. Sometime before 1755 she died. In 1756 Grandfather Seaver died, leaving less than £15 to be divided among George and his four surviving brothers. Thus in 1756, at the age of fourteen, when boys were customarily put out to apprenticeship, George was an orphan, the ward of his uncle Robert, as was his brother Daniel, age twelve, each with a legacy of £2 17S. 4d. Uncle Robert, though warmly recollected by Hewes, could not do much to help him: a gluemaker, he was struggling to set up his own manufactory. Nor could George's three older brothers, whom he also remembered fondly. In 1756 they were all in the "lower" trades. Samuel, age twenty-six, and Solomon, twenty-two, were fishermen; Shubael, twenty-four, was a butcher.

The reason why George was put to shoemaking becomes clearer: no one in the family had the indenture fee to enable him to enter one of the more lucrative "higher" trades. Josiah Franklin, also a tallow chandler, could not make his son Benjamin a cutler because he lacked the fee. But in shoemaking the prospects were so poor that some masters would pay to get an apprentice. In addition, George was too small to enter trades that demanded brawn; he could hardly have become a ropewalk worker, a housewright, or a shipwright. Ebenezer McIntosh, the Boston shoemaker who led the annual Pope's Day festivities and the Stamp Act demonstrations, was a small man. The trade was a sort of dumping ground for poor boys who could not handle heavy work. Boston's Overseers of the Poor acted on this assumption in 1770; so did recruiting officers for the American navy forty years later. The same was true in Europe. Getting into a good trade required "connections"; the family connections were in the leather trades, through Uncle Robert, the gluemaker, or brother Shubael, the butcher. Finally, there was a family tradition. Grandfather Shubael had been a cordwainer, and on his death in 1756 there might even have been a prospect of acquiring his tools and lasts. In any case, the capital that would be needed to set up a shop of one's own was relatively small. And so the boy became a shoemaker—because he had very little choice.

Josiah Franklin had known how important it was to place a boy in a trade that was to his liking. Otherwise there was the threat that Benjamin made explicit: he would run away to sea. Hawkes saw the same thrust in Hewes's life: shoemaking "was never an occupation of his choice," he "being inclined to more active pursuits." George was the wrong boy to put in a sedentary trade that was not to his liking. He was what Bostonians called "saucy." . . . The memories of his childhood and youth that Thatcher elicited were almost all of defying authority—his mother, his teachers at dame school, his schoolmaster, his aunt, his shoemaker master, a farmer, a doctor.

Hewes spoke of his mother only as a figure who inflicted punishment for disobedience. The earliest incident he remembered could have happened only to a poor family living near the waterfront. When George was about six, Abigail Hewes sent him off to the nearby shipyards with a basket to gather chips for the fire. At the water's edge George put the basket aside, straddled some floating planks to watch the fish, fell in, and sank to the bottom. He was saved only when some ship carpenters saw the basket without the boy, "found him motionless on the bottom, hooked him out with a boat hook, and rolled him on a tar barrel until signs of life were discovered." His mother nursed him back to health. Then she flogged him.

The lesson did not take, nor did others in school. First there was a dame school with Miss Tinkum, wife of the town crier. He ran away. She put him in a dark closet. He dug his way out. The next day she put him in again. This time he discovered a jar of quince marmalade and devoured it. A new dame school with "mother McLeod" followed. Then school with "our famous Master Holyoke," which Hewes remembered as "little more than a series of escapes made or attempted from the reign of the birch."

Abigail Hewes must have been desperate to control George. She sent him back after one truancy with a note requesting Holyoke to give him a good whipping. Uncle Robert took pity and sent a substitute note. Abigail threatened, "If you run away again I shall go to school with you myself." When George was about ten, she took the final step: she sent him to Wrentham to live with one of his paternal uncles. Here, George recalled, "he spent several years of his boyhood . . . in the monotonous routine of his Uncle's farm." The only incident he recounted was of defying his aunt. His five-year-old cousin hit him in the face with a stick "without any provocation." George cursed the boy out, for which his aunt whipped him, and when she refused to do the same with her son, George undertook to "chastise" him himself. "I caught my cousin at the barn" and applied the rod. The aunt locked him up but his uncle let him go, responsive to his plea for "equal justice."

Thus when George entered his apprenticeship, if he was not quite the young whig his biographers made him out to be, he was not a youth who would suffer arbitrary authority easily. His master, Downing, had an irascible side and was willing to use a cowhide. Hewes lived in Downing's attic with a fellow apprentice, John Gilbert. All the incidents Hewes recalled from this period had two motifs: petty defiance and a quest for food. There was an escapade on a Saturday night when the two apprentices made off for Gilbert's house and bought a loaf of bread, a pound of butter, taken before the farmer, who was also justice of the peace and who laughed uproariously at Hewes's name and let him go. There was an incident with a doctor who inoculated Hewes and a fellow worker for smallpox and warned them to abstain from food. Sick, fearful of death, Hewes and his friend consumed a dish of venison in melted butter and a mug of flip—and lived to tell the tale.

These memories of youthful defiance and youthful hunger lingered on for seventy years: a loaf of bread and a pound of butter, a parcel of apples, a dish of venison. This shoemaker's apprentice could hardly have been well fed or treated with affection.

The proof is that Hewes tried to end his apprenticeship by the only way he saw possible: escape to the military. "After finding that my depressed condition would probably render it impracticable for me to acquire that education requisite for civil employments," he told Hawkes, "I had resolved to engage in the military service of my country, should an opportunity present." Late in the 1750s, possibly in 1760, as the fourth and last of England's great colonial wars with France ground on and his majesty's army recruiters beat their drums through Boston's streets, Hewes and Gilbert tried to enlist. Gilbert was accepted, but Hewes was not. Recruiting captains were under orders to "enlist no Roman-Catholic, nor any under five feet two inches high without their shoes." "I could not pass muster," Hewes told Hawkes, "because I was not tall enough." As Thatcher embroiders Hawkes's story, Hewes then "went to the shoe shop of several of his acquaintances and heightened his heels by several taps [;] then stuffing his stocking with paper and rags," he returned. The examining captain saw through the trick and rejected him again. Frustrated, humiliated, vowing he would never return to Downing, he took an even more desperate step: he went down to the wharf and tried to enlist on a British ship of war. "His brothers, however, soon heard of it and interfered," and, in Thatcher's words, "he was compelled to abandon that plan." Bostonians like Solomon and Samuel Hewes, who made their living on the waterfront, did not need long memories to remember the city's massive resistance to the impressment sweeps of 1747 and to know that the British navy would be, not escape, but another prison.

About this time, shoemaker Downing failed after fire swept his shop (possibly the great fire of 1760). This would have freed Hewes of his indenture, but he was not qualified to be a shoemaker until he had completed apprenticeship. As Hewes told it, he therefore apprenticed himself "for the remainder of his minority," that is, until he turned twenty-one, to Harry Rhoades, who paid him $40. In 1835 he could tell

Thatcher how much time he then had left to serve, down to the month and day. Of the rest of his "time" he had no bad memories.

Apprenticeship had a lighter side. Hewes's anecdotes give tantalizing glimpses into an embryonic apprentice culture in Boston to which other sources attest— glimpses of pranks played on masters, of revelry after curfew, of Training Day, when the militia displayed its maneuvers and there was drink, food, and "frolicking" on the Common. One may speculate that George also took part in the annual Pope's Day festival, November 5, when apprentices, servants, artisans in the lower trades, and young people of all classes took over the town, parading effigies of Pope, Devil, and Pretender, exacting tribute from the better sort, and engaging in a battle royal between North End and South End Pope's Day "companies."

Hewes's stories of his youth, strained as they are through Thatcher's conde-scension, hint at his winning a place for himself as the small schoolboy who got the better of his elders, the apprentice who defied his master, perhaps even a leader among his peers. There are also hints of the adult personality. Hewes was punished often, but if childhood punishment inured some to pain, it made Hewes reluctant to inflict pain on others. He developed a generous streak that led him to reach out to others in trouble. When Downing, a broken man, was on the verge of leaving for Nova Scotia to start anew, Hewes went down to his ship and gave him half of the $40 fee Rhoades had paid him. Downing broke into tears. The story smacks of the Good Samaritan, of the Methodist of the 1830s counting his good deeds; and yet the memory was so vivid, wrote Thatcher, that "his features light up even now with a gleam of rejoicing pride." Hewes spoke later of the "tender sympathies of my nature." He did not want to be, but he was a fit candidate for the "gentle craft" he was about to enter.

In Boston from 1763, when he entered his majority, until 1775, when he went off to war, Hewes never made a go of it as a shoemaker. He remembered these years more fondly than he had lived them. As Hawkes took down his story, shifting from the third to the first person:

> Hewes said he cheerfully submitted to the course of life to which his destinies di-rected.
>
> He built him a shop and pursued the private avocation of his trade for a consid-erable length of time, until on the application of his brother he was induced to go with him on two fishing voyages to the banks of New Foundland, which occupied his time for two years.
>
> After the conclusion of the French war . . . he continued at Boston, except the two years absence with his brother.
>
> During that period, said Hewes, when I was at the age of twenty-six, I married the daughter of Benjamin Sumner, of Boston. At the time of our intermarriage, the age of my wife was seventeen. We lived together very happily seventy years. She died at the age of eighty-seven.
>
> At the time when the British troops were first stationed at Boston, we had several children, the exact number I do not recollect. By our industry and mutual efforts we were improving our condition.

Thatcher added a few bits to this narrative, some illuminating. The "little shop was at the head of Griffin's Wharf," later the site of the Tea Party. Benjamin Sumner, "if we mistake not," was a "sexton of one of the principal churches in town." His wife was a "washer-woman" near the Mill Pond, assisted by her five daughters. Hewes courted one of the girls when he "used to go to the house regularly every Saturday night to pay Sally for the week's washing." The father was stern, the swain persistent, and after a couple of years George and Sally were married. "The business was good, and growing better," Thatcher wrote, "especially as it became more and more fashionable to encourage our own manufactures."

The reality was more harsh. What kind of shoemaker was Hewes? He had his own shop—this much is clear, but the rest is surmise. There were at that time in Boston about sixty to seventy shoemakers, most of whom seem to have catered to the local market. If Hewes was typical, he would have made shoes to order, "bespoke" work; this would have made him a cordwainer. And he would have repaired shoes; this would have made him a cobbler. Who were his customers? No business records survive. A shoemaker probably drew his customers from his immediate neighborhood. Located as he was near the waterfront and the ropewalks, Hewes might well have had customers of the "meaner" sort. In a ward inhabited by the "middling" sort he may also have drawn on them. When the British troops occupied Boston, he did some work for them. Nothing suggests that he catered to the "carriage trade."

Was his business "improving" or "growing better"? Probably it was never very good and grew worse. From his own words we know that he took off two years on fishing voyages with his brothers. He did not mention that during this period he lived for a short time in Roxbury. His prospects were thus not good enough to keep him in Boston. His marriage is another clue to his low fortune. Sally (or Sarah) Sumner's father was a sexton so poor that his wife and daughters had to take in washing. The couple was married by the Reverend Samuel Stillman of the First Baptist Church, which suggests that this was the church that Benjamin Sumner served. Though Stillman was respected, First Baptist was not "one of the principal churches in town," as Thatcher guessed, but one of the poorest and smallest, with a congregation heavy with laboring people, sailors, and blacks. Marriage, one of the few potential sources of capital for an aspiring tradesman, as Benjamin Franklin made clear in his autobiography, did not lift Hewes up.

Other sources fill in what Hewes forgot. He married in January 1768. In September 1770 he landed in debtors' prison. In 1767 he had contracted a debt of £6 8s. 3d. to Thomas Courtney, a merchant tailor, for "making a sappled coat & breeches of fine cloth." The shoemaker bought this extravagant outfit when he was courting. What other way was there to persuade Sally's parents that he had good prospects? Over the three years since, he had neither earned enough to pay the debt nor accumulated £9 property that might be confiscated to satisfy it. "For want of Goods or Estate of the within named George Robt Twelve Hewes, I have taken his bodey & committed him to his majesty's goal [sic] in Boston," wrote Constable Thomas Rice on the back of the writ. There may have been a touch of political vindictiveness in the action: Courtney was a rich tory later banished by the state. Who got Hewes out of jail? Perhaps his uncle Robert, perhaps a brother.

Once out of jail, Hewes stayed poor. The Boston tax records of 1771, the only ones that have survived for these years, show him living as a lodger in the house of Christopher Ranks, a watchmaker, in the old North End. He was not taxed for any property. In 1773 he and his family, which now included three children, were apparently living with his uncle Robert in the South End; at some time during these years before the war they also lived with a brother. After almost a decade on his own, Hewes could not afford his own place. In January 1774 he inadvertently summed up his condition and reputation in the course of a violent street encounter. Damned as "a rascal" and "a vagabond" who had no right to "speak to a gentleman in the street," Hewes retorted that he was neither "and though a poor man, in as good credit in town" as his well-to-do antagonist.

The economic odds were against a Boston shoemaker thriving these years. Even the movement "to encourage our manufactures" may have worked against him, contrary to Thatcher. The patriot boycott would have raised his hopes; the Boston town meeting of 1767 put men's and women's shoes on the list of items Bostonians were encouraged to buy from American craftsmen. But if this meant shoes made in Lynn—the manufacturing town ten miles to the north that produced 80,000 shoes in 1767 alone—it might well have put Hewes at a competitive disadvantage, certainly for the ladies' shoes for which Lynn already had a reputation. And if Hewes was caught up in the system whereby Lynn masters were already "putting out" shoes in Boston, he would have made even less. Whatever the reason, the early 1770s were hard times for shoemakers. Ebenezer McIntosh also landed in debtors' jail in 1770.

As a struggling shoemaker, what would have been Hewes's aspirations? He does not tell us in so many words, but "the course of his life," Hawkes was convinced, was marked "by habits of industry, integrity, temperance and economy"; in other words, he practiced the virtues set down by "another soap boiler and tallow chandler's son" (Thatcher's phrase for Benjamin Franklin). "From childhood," Hewes told Hawkes, "he has been accustomed to rise very early and expose himself to the morning air; that his father compelled him to do this from his infancy." ("Early to bed, Early to rise, makes a man healthy, wealthy and wise.") "I was often . . . admonished," said Hewes, "of the importance of faithfulness in executing the commands of my parents, or others who had a right to my services." Thatcher also reported that "he makes it a rule to rise from the table with an appetite, and another to partake of but a single dish at a meal." ("A Fat kitchen makes a lean will, as Poor Richard says.")

Poor Richard spoke to and for artisans at every level—masters, journeymen, and apprentices—whose goal was "independence" or "a competency" in their trade. What he advocated, we need remind ourselves, "was not unlimited acquisition but rather prosperity, which was the mid-point between the ruin of extravagance and the want of poverty. The living he envisaged was a decent middling wealth, which could only be attained through unremitting labor and self-control." Hewes's likely goal, then, was to keep his shop so that his shop would keep him.

But he could no more live by Poor Richard's precepts than could Franklin. "Industry" must have come hard. He was in an occupation "never of his choice." How could he "stick to his last" when he was "inclined towards more active pursuits"? "Avoid, above all else, debt," counselled Poor Richard, warning that "fond pride of dress is sure a very curse; E'er Fancy you consult, consult your purse." But Hewes surrendered to pride and as a consequence to the warden of the debtors' jail. "Economy"—that is, saving—produced no surplus. And so he would succumb, when war presented the opportunity, to the gamble for sudden wealth. He was as much the object as the exemplar of Poor Richard's advice, as indeed was Franklin himself.

If Hewes's memories softened such realities, in other ways his silences spoke. He said nothing about being part of any of Boston's traditional institutions—church, town meeting, or private associations. He was baptized in Old South, a Congregational church, and married by the minister of the First Baptist Church; there is no evidence that he took part in either. In his old age a convert to Methodism, a churchgoer, and Bible reader, he reminisced to neither biographer about the religion of youth.

Nor does he seem to have taken part in town government. He was not a taxpayer in 1771. He probably did not own enough property to qualify as a voter for either provincial offices (£40 sterling) or town offices (£20 sterling). Recollecting the political events of the Revolution, he did not speak of attending town meetings until they became what patriots called meetings of "the whole body of the people," without regard to property. The town had to fill some two hundred minor positions; it was customary to stick artisans with the menial jobs. Hewes's father was hogreeve and measurer of boards. Harry Rhoades held town offices. McIntosh was made a sealer of leather. Hewes was appointed to nothing.

He does not seem to have belonged to any associations. McIntosh was in a fire company. So was Hewes's brother Shubael. Hewes was not. Shubael and a handful of prosperous artisans became Masons. Hewes did not. It was not that he was a loner. There was simply not much for a poor artisan to belong to. There was no shoemakers' society or general society of mechanics. Shoemakers had a long tradition of taking ad hoc collective action, as did other Boston craftsmen, and Hewes may have participated in such occasional informal activities of the trade. Very likely he drilled in the militia with other artisans on Training Day (size would not have barred him). He seems to have known many artisans and recalled their names in describing events. So it is not hard to imagine him at a South End tavern enjoying a mug of flip with Adam Colson, leatherworker, or Patrick Carr, breechesmaker. Nor is it difficult to imagine him in the streets on November 5, in the South End Pope's Day company captained by McIntosh. After all what else was there in respectable Boston for him to belong to? All this is conjecture, but it is clear that, though he lived in Boston proper, he was not part of proper Boston—not until the events of the Revolution.

Between 1768 and 1775, the shoemaker became a citizen—an active participant in the events that led to the Revolution, an angry, assertive man who won recognition as a patriot. What explains the transformation? We have enough evidence to take stock of Hewes's role in three major events of the decade: the Massacre (1770), the Tea Party (1773), and the tarring and feathering of John Malcolm (1774).

Thatcher began the story of Hewes in the Revolution at the Stamp Act but based his account on other sources and even then claimed no more than that Hewes was a bystander at the famous effigy-hanging at the Liberty Tree, August 14, 1765, that launched Boston's protest. "The town's-people left their work—and Hewes, his hammer among the rest—to swell the multitude." The only episode for which Thatcher seems to have drawn on Hewes's personal recollection was the celebration of the repeal of the act in May 1766, at which Hewes remembered drinking from the pipe of madeira that John Hancock set out on the Common. "Such a day has not been seen in Boston before or since," wrote Thatcher.

It is possible that Thatcher's bias against mobs led him to draw a curtain over Hewes's role. It is reasonable to suppose that if Hewes was a member of the South End Pope's Day company, he followed McIntosh who was a major leader of the crowd actions of August 14 and 26, the massive processions of the united North and South End companies on November 1 and 5, and the forced resignation of stamp-master Andrew Oliver in December. But it is not likely; in fact, he may well have been off on fishing voyages in 1765. Perhaps the proof is negative: when Hewes told Hawkes the story of his role in the Revolution, he began not at the Stamp Act but at the Massacre, five years later. On the night of the Massacre, March 5, Hewes was in the thick of the action. What he tells us about what brought him to King Street, what brought others there, and what he did during and after this tumultuous event gives us the perspective of a man in the street.

The presence of British troops in Boston beginning in the summer of 1768—four thousand soldiers in a town of fewer than sixteen thousand inhabitants—touched Hewes personally. Anecdotes about soldiers flowed from him. He had seen them march off the transports at the Long Wharf; he had seen them every day occupying civilian buildings on Griffin's Wharf near his shop. He knew how irritating it was to be challenged by British sentries after curfew (his solution was to offer a swig of rum from the bottle he carried).

More important, he was personally cheated by a soldier. Sergeant Mark Burk ordered shoes allegedly for Captain Thomas Preston, picked them up, but never paid for them. Hewes complained to Preston, who made good and suggested he bring a complaint. A military hearing ensued, at which Hewes testified. The soldier, to Hewes's horror, was sentenced to three hundred fifty lashes. He "remarked to the court that if he had thought the fellow was to be punished so severely for such an offense, bad as he was, he would have said nothing about it." And he saw others victimized by soldiers. He witnessed an incident in which a soldier sneaked up behind a woman, felled her with his fist, and "stripped her of her bonnet, cardinal muff and tippet." He followed the man to his barracks, identified him (Hewes remembered him as Private Kilroy, who would appear later at the Massacre), and got him to give up the stolen goods, but decided this time not to press charges. Hewes was also keenly aware of grievances felt by the laboring men and youths who formed the bulk of the crowd—and the principal victims—at the Massacre. From Hawkes and Thatcher three causes can be pieced together.

First in time, and vividly recalled by Hewes, was the murder of eleven-year-old Christopher Seider on February 23, ten days before the Massacre. Seider was one of a large crowd of schoolboys and apprentices picketing the shop of Theophilus Lilly, a merchant violating the antiimport resolutions. Ebenezer Richardson, a paid customs informer, shot into the throng and killed Seider. Richardson would have been tarred and feathered, or worse, had not whig leaders intervened to hustle him off to jail. At Seider's funeral, only a week before the Massacre, five hundred boys marched two by two behind the coffin, followed by two thousand or more adults, "the largest [funeral] perhaps ever known in America," Thomas Hutchinson thought.

Second, Hewes emphasized the bitter fight two days before the Massacre between soldiers and workers at Gray's ropewalk down the block from Hewes's shop. Off-duty soldiers were allowed to moonlight, taking work from civilians. On Friday, March 3, when one of them asked for work at Gray's, a battle ensued between a few score soldiers and ropewalk workers joined by others in the maritime trades. The soldiers were beaten and sought revenge. Consequently, in Thatcher's words, "quite a number of soldiers, in a word, were determined to have a row on the night of the 5th."

Third, the precipitating events on the night of the Massacre, by Hewes's account, were an attempt by a barber's apprentice to collect an overdue bill from a British officer, the sentry's abuse of the boy, and the subsequent harassment of the sentry by a small band of boys that led to the calling of the guard commanded by Captain Preston. Thatcher found this hard to swallow—"a dun from a greasy barber's boy is rather an extraordinary explanation of the origin, or one of the occasions, of the massacre of the 5th of March"—but at the trial the lawyers did not. They battled over defining "boys" and over the age, size, and degree of aggressiveness of the numerous apprentices on the scene.

Hewes viewed the civilians as essentially defensive. On the evening of the Massacre he appeared early on the scene at King Street, attracted by the clamor over the apprentice. "I was soon on the ground among them," he said, as if it were only natural that he should turn out in defense of fellow townsmen against what was assumed to be the danger of aggressive action by soldiers. He was not part of a conspiracy; neither was he there out of curiosity. He was unarmed, carrying neither club nor stave as some others did. He saw snow, ice, and "missiles" thrown at the soldiers. When the main guard rushed out in support of the sentry, Private Kilroy dealt Hewes a blow on his shoulder with his gun. Preston ordered the townspeople to disperse. Hewes believed they had a legal basis to refuse: "they were in the king's highway, and had as good a right to be there" as Preston.

The five men killed were all workingmen. Hewes claimed to know four: Samuel Gray, a ropewalk worker; Samuel Maverick, age seventeen, an apprentice to an ivory turner; Patrick Carr, an apprentice to a leather breeches worker; and James Caldwell, second mate on a ship—all but Christopher Attucks. Caldwell, "who was shot in the back was standing by the side of Hewes, and the latter caught him in his arms as he fell," helped carry him to Dr. Thomas Young in Prison Lane, then ran to Caldwell's ship captain on Cold Lane.

More than horror was burned into Hewes's memory. He remembered the political confrontation that followed the slaughter, when thousands of angry townspeople faced hundreds of British troops massed with ready rifles. "The people,"

Hewes recounted, "then immediately chose a committee to report to the governor the result of Captain Preston's conduct, and to demand of him satisfaction." Actually the "people" did not choose a committee "immediately." In the dark hours after the Massacre a self-appointed group of patriot leaders met with officials and forced Hutchinson to commit Preston and the soldiers to jail. Hewes was remembering the town meeting the next day, so huge that it had to adjourn from Fanueil Hall, the traditional meeting place that held only twelve hundred, to Old South Church, which had room for five to six thousand. This meeting approved a committee to wait on the officials and then adjourned, but met again the same day, received and voted down an offer to remove one regiment, then accepted another to remove two. This was one of the meetings at which property bars were let down.

What Hewes did not recount, but what he had promptly put down in a deposition the next day, was how militant he was after the Massacre. At 1:00 A.M., like many other enraged Bostonians, he went home to arm himself. On his way back to the Town House with a cane he had a defiant exchange with Sergeant Chambers of the 29th Regiment and eight or nine soldiers, "all with very large clubs or cutlasses." A soldier, Dobson, "ask'd him how he far'd; he told him very badly to see his townsmen shot in such a manner, and asked him if he did not think it was a dreadful thing." Dobson swore "it was a fine thing" and "you shall see more of it." Chambers "seized and forced" the cane from Hewes, "saying I had no right to carry it. I told him I had as good a right to carry a cane as they had to carry clubs."

The Massacre had stirred Hewes to political action. He was one of ninety-nine Bostonians who gave depositions for the prosecution that were published by the town in a pamphlet. Undoubtedly, he marched in the great funeral procession for the victims that brought the city to a standstill. He attended the tempestuous trial of Ebenezer Richardson, Seider's slayer, which was linked politically with the Massacre. ("He remembers to this moment, even the precise words of the Judge's sentence," wrote Thatcher.) He seems to have attended the trial of the soldiers or Preston or both.

It was in this context that he remembered something for which there is no corroborating evidence, namely, testifying at Preston's trial on a crucial point. He told Hawkes:

> When Preston, their captain, was tried, I was called as one of the witnesses, on the part of the government, and testified, that I believed it was the same man, Captain Preston, that ordered his soldiers to make ready, who also ordered them to fire. Mr. John Adams, former president of the United States, was advocate for the prisoners, and denied the fact, that Captain Preston gave orders to his men to fire; and on his cross examination of me asked whether my position was such, that I could see the captain's lips in motion when the order to fire was given; to which I answered, that I could not.

Perhaps so: Hewes's account is particular and precise, and there are many lacunae in the record of the trial (we have no verbatim transcript) that modern editors have assiduously assembled. Perhaps not: Hewes may have "remembered" his brother Shubael on the stand at the trial of the soldiers (although Shubael was a defense witness) or his uncle Robert testifying at Richardson's trial. Or he may have given pre-trial testimony but was not called to the stand.

In one sense, it does not matter. What he was remembering was that he had become involved. He turned out because of a sense of kinship with "his townsmen" in danger; he stood his ground in defense of his "rights"; he was among the "people" who delegated a committee to act on their behalf; he took part in the legal process by giving a deposition, by attending the trials, and, as he remembered it, by testifying. In sum, he had become a citizen, a political man.

Four years later, at the Tea Party on the night of December 16, 1773, the citizen "volunteered" and became the kind of leader for whom most historians have never found a place. The Tea Party, unlike the Massacre, was organized by the radical whig leaders of Boston. They mapped the strategy, organized the public meetings, appointed the companies to guard the tea ships at Griffin's Wharf (among them Daniel Hewes, George's brother), and planned the official boarding parties. As in 1770, they converted the town meetings into meetings of "the whole body of the people," one of which Hutchinson found "consisted principally of the Lower ranks of the People & even Journeymen Tradesmen were brought in to increase the number & the Rabble were not excluded yet there were divers Gentlemen of Good Fortunes among them."

The boarding parties showed this same combination of "ranks." Hawkes wrote:

> On my inquiring of Hewes if he knew who first proposed the project of destroying the tea, to prevent its being landed, he replied that he did not; neither did he know who or what number were to volunteer their services for that purpose. But from the significant allusion of some persons in whom I had confidence, together with the knowledge I had of the spirit of those times, I had no doubt but that a sufficient number of associates would accompany me in that enterprise.

The recollection of Joshua Wyeth, a journeyman blacksmith, verified Hewes's story in explicit detail: "It was proposed that young men, not much known in town and not liable to be easily recognized should lead in the business." Wyeth believed that "most of the persons selected for the occasion were apprentices and journeymen, as was the case with myself, living with tory masters." Wyeth "had but a few hours warning of what was intended to be done." Those in the officially designated parties, about thirty men better known, appeared in well-prepared Indian disguises. As nobodies, the volunteers—anywhere from fifty to one hundred men—could get away with hastily improvised disguises. Hewes said he got himself up as an Indian and daubed his "face and hands with coal dust in the shop of blacksmith." In the streets "I fell in with many who were dressed, equipped and painted as I was, and who fell in with me and marched in order to the place of our destination."

At Griffin's Wharf the volunteers were orderly, self-disciplined, and ready to accept leadership.

> When we arrived at the wharf, there were three of our number who assumed an authority to direct our operations, to which we readily submitted. They divided us into three parties, for the purpose of boarding the three ships which contained the tea at the same time. The name of him who commanded the division to which I was

assigned was Leonard Pitt [Lendell Pitts]. The names of the other commanders I never knew. We were immediately ordered by the respective commanders to board all the ships at the same time, which we promptly obeyed.

But for Hewes there was something new: he was singled out of the rank and file and made an officer in the field.

The commander of the division to which I belonged, as soon as we were on board the ship, appointed me boatswain, and ordered me to go to the captain and demand of him the keys to the hatches and a dozen candles. I made the demand accordingly, and the captain promptly replied, and delivered the articles; but requested me at the same time to do no damage to the ship or rigging. We then were ordered by our commander to open the hatches, and take out all the chests of tea and throw them overboard, and we immediately proceeded to execute his orders; first cutting and splitting the chests with our tomahawks, so as thoroughly to expose them to the effects of the water. In about three hours from the time we went on board, we had thus broken and thrown overboard every tea chest to be found in the ship; while those in the other ships were disposing of the tea in the same way, at the same time. We were surrounded by British armed ships, but no attempt was made to resist us. We then quietly retired to our several places of residence, without having any conversation with each other, or taking any measures to discover who were our associates.

. . . As the Tea Party ended, Hewes was stirred to further action on his own initiative, just as he had been in the hours after the Massacre. While the crews were throwing the tea overboard, a few other men tried to smuggle off some of the tea scattered on the decks. "One Captain O'Connor whom I well knew," said Hewes, "came on board for that purpose, and when he supposed he was not noticed, filled his pockets, and also the lining of his coat. But I had detected him, and gave information to the captain of what he was doing. We were ordered to take him into custody, and just as he was stepping from the vessel, I seized him by the skirt of his coat, and in attempting to pull him back, I tore it off." They scuffled. O'Connor recognized him and "threatened to 'complain to the Governor.' 'You had better make your will first,' quoth Hewes, doubling his fist expressively," and O'Connor escaped, running the gauntlet of the crowd on the wharf. "The next day we nailed the skirt of his coat, which I had pulled off, to the whipping post in Charlestown, the place of his residence, with a label upon it," to shame O'Connor by "popular indignation."

A month later, at the third event for which we have full evidence, Hewes won public recognition for an act of courage that almost cost his life and precipitated the most publicized tarring and feathering of the Revolution. The incident that set it off would have been trivial at any other time. On Tuesday, January 25, 1774, at about two in the afternoon, the shoemaker was making his way back to his shop after his dinner. According to the very full account in the *Massachusetts Gazette,*

Mr. George-Robert-Twelves Hewes was coming along Fore-Street, near Captain Ridgway's, and found the redoubted John Malcolm, standing over a small boy, who was pushing a little sled before him, cursing, damning, threatening and shaking a very large cane with a very heavy ferril on it over his head. The boy at that time was perfectly quiet, notwithstanding which Malcolm continued his threats of striking him, which Mr. Hewes conceiving if he struck him with that weapon he must have killed him out-right, came up to him, and said to him, Mr. Malcolm I hope you are not going to strike this boy with that stick.

Malcolm had already acquired an odious reputation with patriots of the lower sort. A Bostonian, he had been a sea captain, an army officer, and recently an employee of the customs service. He was so strong a supporter of royal authority that he had traveled to North Carolina to fight the Regulators and boasted of having a horse shot out from under him. He had a fiery temper. As a customs informer he was known to have turned in a vessel to punish sailors for petty smuggling, a custom of the sea. In November 1773, near Portsmouth, New Hampshire, a crowd of thirty sailors had "genteely tarr'd and feather'd" him, as the *Boston Gazette* put it: they did the job over his clothes. Back in Boston he made "frequent complaints" to Hutchinson of "being hooted at in the streets" for this by "tradesmen"; and the lieutenant governor cautioned him, "being a passionate man," not to reply in kind.

The exchange between Malcolm and Hewes resonated with class as well as political differences:

> Malcolm returned, you are an impertinent rascal, it is none of your business. Mr. Hewes then asked him, what had the child done to him. Malcolm damned him and asked him if he was going to take his part? Mr. Hewes answered no further than this, that he thought it was a shame for him to strike the child with such a club as that, if he intended to strike him. Malcolm on that damned Mr. Hewes, called him a vagabond, and said he would let him know he should not speak to a gentleman in the street. Mr. Hewes returned to that, he was neither a rascal nor vagabond, and though a poor man was in as good credit in town as he was. Malcolm called him a liar, and said he was not, nor ever would be. Mr. Hewes retorted, be that as it will, I never was tarred nor feathered any how. On this Malcolm struck him, and wounded him deeply on the forehead, so that Mr. Hewes for some time lost his senses. Capt. Godfrey, then present, interposed, and after some altercation, Malcolm went home.

Hewes was rushed to Joseph Warren, the patriot doctor, his distant relative. Malcolm's cane had almost penetrated his skull. Thatcher found "the indentation as plainly perceptible as it was sixty years ago." So did Hawkes. Warren dressed the wound, and Hewes was able to make his way to a magistrate to swear out a warrant for Malcolm's arrest "which he carried to a constable named Justice Hale." Malcolm, meanwhile, had retreated to his house, where he responded in white heat to taunts about the half-way tarring and feathering in Portsmouth with "damn you let me see the man that dare do it better."

In the evening a crowd took Malcolm from his house and dragged him on a sled into King Street "amidst the huzzas of thousands." At this point "several gentlemen endeavoured to divert the populace from their intention." The ensuing dialogue laid bare the clash of conceptions of justice between the sailors and laboring people heading the action and Sons of Liberty leaders. The "gentlemen" argued that Malcolm was "open to the laws of the land which would undoubtedly award a reasonable satisfaction to the parties he had abused," that is, the child and Hewes. The answer was political. Malcolm "had been an old impudent and mischievious [sic] offender—he had joined in the murders at North Carolina—he had seized vessels on account of sailors having a bottle or two of gin on board—he had in other words behaved in the most capricious, insulting and daringly abusive manner." He could not be trusted to justice. "When they were told the law would have its course with him, they asked what course had the law taken with Preston or his soldiers, with Capt. Wilson or Richardson? And for their parts they had seen so much partiality to the soldiers and customhouse officers by the present Judges, that while things remained as they were, they would, on all such occasions, take satisfaction their own way, and let them take it off." The references were to Captain Preston who had been tried and found innocent of the Massacre, the soldiers who had been let off with token punishment, Captain John Wilson, who had been indicted for inciting slaves to murder their masters but never tried, and Ebenezer Richardson, who had been tried and found guilty of killing Seider, sentenced, and then pardoned by the crown.

The crowd won and proceeded to a ritualized tarring and feathering, the purpose of which was to punish Malcolm, force a recantation, and ostracize him.

> With these and such like arguments, together with a gentle crouding of persons not of their way of thinking out of the ring they proceeded to elevate Mr. Malcolm from his sled into a cart, and stripping him to buff and breeches, gave him a modern jacket [a coat of tar and feathers] and hied him away to liberty-tree, where they proposed to him to renounce his present commission, and swear that he would never hold another inconsistent with the liberties of his country; but this he obstinately refusing, they then carted him to the gallows, passed a rope round his neck, and threw the other end over the beam as if they intended to hang him: But this manoeuvre he set at defiance. They then basted him for some time with a rope's end, and threatened to cut his ears off, and on this he complied, and they then brought him home.

Hewes had precipitated an electrifying event. It was part of the upsurge of spontaneous action in the wake of the Tea Party that prompted the whig leaders to promote a "Committee for Tarring and Feathering" as an instrument of crowd control. The "Committee" made its appearance in broadsides signed by "Captain Joyce, Jun.," a sobriquet meant to invoke the bold cornet who had captured King Charles in 1647. The event was reported in the English newspapers, popularized in three or four satirical prints, and dramatized still further when Malcolm went to England, where he campaigned for a pension and ran for Parliament (without success) against John Wilkes, the leading champion of America. The event confirmed the British ministry in its punitive effort to bring rebellious Boston to heel. . . .

As he became active politically he may have had a growing awareness of his worth as a shoemaker. McIntosh was clearly the man of the year in 1765; indeed, whigs were no less fearful than loyalists that "the Captain General of the Liberty Tree" might become the Masaniello of Boston. After a shoemaker made the boot to hang in the Liberty Tree as an effigy of Lord Bute, "Jack Cobler" served notice that "whenever the Public Good requires my services, I shall be ready to distinguish myself." In 1772 "Crispin" began an anti-loyalist diatribe by saying, "I am a shoemaker, a citizen, a free man and a freeholder." The editor added a postscript justifying

"Crispin's performance" and explaining that "it should be known what common people, even *coblers* think and feel under the present administration." In city after city, "cobblers" were singled out for derision by conservatives for leaving their lasts to engage in the body politic. Hewes could not have been unaware of all this; he was part of it.

He may also have responded to the rising demand among artisans for support of American manufacturers, whether or not it brought him immediate benefit. He most certainly subscribed to the secularized Puritan ethic—self-denial, industry, frugality—that made artisans take to the nonimportation agreement with its crusade against foreign luxury and its vision of American manufactures. And he could easily have identified with the appeal of the Massachusetts Provincial Congress of 1774 that equated the political need "to encourage agriculture, manufacturers and economy so as to render this state as independent of every other state as the nature of our country will admit" with the "happiness of particular families" in being "independent."

But what ideas did Hewes articulate? He spoke of what he did but very little of what he thought. In the brief statement he offered Hawkes about why he went off to war in 1776, he expressed a commitment to general principles as they had been brought home to him by his experiences. "I was continually reflecting upon the unwarrantable sufferings inflicted on the citizens of Boston by the usurpation and tyranny of Great Britain, and my mind was excited with an unextinguishable desire to aid in chastising them." When Hawkes expressed a doubt "as to the correctness of his conduct in absenting himself from his family," Hewes "emphatically reiterated" the same phrases, adding to a "desire to aid in chastising them" the phrase "and securing our independence." This was clearly not an afterthought; it probably reflected the way many others moved toward the goal of Independence, not as a matter of original intent, but as a step made necessary when all other resorts failed. Ideology thus did not set George Hewes apart from Samuel Adams or John Hancock. The difference lies in what the Revolution did to him as a person. His experiences transformed him, giving him a sense of citizenship and personal worth. Adams and Hancock began with both; Hewes had to arrive there, and in arriving he cast off the constraints of deference.

The two incidents with which we introduced Hewes's life measure the distance he had come: from the young man tongue-tied in the presence of John Hancock to the man who would not take his hat off to the officer of the ship named *Hancock*. Did he cast off his deference to Hancock? Hewes's affirmation of his worth as a human being was a form of class consciousness. Implicit in the idea, "I am as good as any man regardless of rank or wealth," was the idea that any poor man might be as good as any rich man. This did not mean that all rich men were bad. On the contrary, in Boston, more than any other major colonial seaport, a majority of the merchants were part of the patriot coalition; "divers Gentelmen of Good Fortunes," as Hutchinson put it, were with the "Rabble." This blunted class consciousness. Boston's mechanics, unlike New York's or Philadelphia's, did not develop mechanic committees or a mechanic consciousness before the Revolution. Yet in Boston the rich were forced to defer to the people in order to obtain or retain their support.

Indeed, the entire public career of Hancock from 1765 on—distributing largesse, buying uniforms for Pope's Day marchers, building ships to employ artisans—can be understood as an exercise of this kind of deference, proving his civic virtue and patriotism.

This gives meaning to Hewes's tale of working beside Hancock at the Tea Party—"a curious reminiscence," Thatcher called it, "but we believe it a mistake."

> Mr. Hewes, however, positively affirms, as of his own observation, that *Samuel Adams and John Hancock were both actively engaged in the process of destruction.* Of the latter he speaks more particularly, being entirely confident that he was himself at one time engaged with him in the demolition of the same chest of tea. He recognized him not only by his *ruffles* making their appearance in the heat of the work, from under the disguise which pretty thoroughly covered him,—and by his figure, and gait;—but by his features, which neither his paint nor his loosened club of hair behind wholly concealed from a close view;—and by his voice also, for he exchanged with him an Indian *grunt,* and the expression *"me know you,"* which was a good deal used on that occasion for a countersign.

Thatcher was justifiably skeptical; it is very unlikely that Hancock was there. Participants swore themselves to secrecy; their identity was one of the best-kept secrets of the Revolution. In fact, in 1835 Thatcher published in an appendix the first list of those "more or less actively engaged" in the Tea Party as furnished by "an aged Bostonian," clearly not Hewes. Hancock was not named. More important, it was not part of the patriot plan for the well-known leaders to be present. When the all-day meeting that sanctioned the action adjourned, the leaders, including Hancock, stayed behind conspicuously in Old South. Still, there can be little question that Hewes was convinced at the time that Hancock was on the ship: some gentlemen were indeed present; it was reasonable to assume that Hancock, who had been so conspicuous on the tea issue, was there; Hewes knew what Hancock looked like; he was too insistent about details for his testimony to be dismissed as made up. And the way he recorded it in his mind at the time was the way he stored it in his memory.

Hewes in effect had brought Hancock down to his own level. The poor shoemaker had not toppled the wealthy merchant; he was no "leveller." But the rich and powerful—the men in "ruffles"—had become, in his revealing word, his "associates." John Hancock and George Hewes breaking open the same chest at the Tea Party remained for Hewes a symbol of a moment of equality. To the shoemaker, one suspects, this above all was what the Revolutionary events of Boston meant, as did the war that followed. . . .

Suggested Readings

General

David Ammerman, *In the Common Cause; American Response to the Coercive Acts of 1774* (1974).

Bernard Bailyn, *The Ideological Origins of the American Revolution* (1967).

John Brewer, *Party Ideology and Popular Politics at the Accession of George III* (1976).

Eric Foner, *Tom Paine and Revolutionary America* (1976).

Jack P. Greene, *Peripheries and Center: Constitutional Development in the Extended Politics of the British Empire and the United States, 1607–1788* (1986).

Francis Jennings, *Empire of Fortune: Crowns, Colonies, and Tribes in the Seven Years War in America* (1988).

Michael Kammen, *Empire and Interest; The American Colonies and the Politics of Mercantilism* (1970).

Pauline Maier, *From Resistance to Revolution: Colonial Radicals and the Development of American Opposition to Britain, 1765–1776* (1972).

Mary Beth Norton, *Liberty's Daughters; The Revolutionary Experience of American Women, 1750–1800* (1980).

Peter D.G. Thomas, *The Townshend Duties Crisis; The Second Phase of the American Revolution, 1767–1773* (1987).

Mercantilism

Eugene Genovese and Elizabeth Fox-Genovese, *Fruits of Merchant Capital* (1983); John J. McCusker and Russell R. Menard, *The Economy of British America, 1607–1787* (1985); and Jacob M. Price, *Capital and Credit in British Overseas Trade* (1980).

Wars for Empire

Fred Anderson, *A People's Army: Massachusetts Soldiers and Society in the Seven Years' War* (1984); Douglas E. Leach, *Arms for Empire: A Military History of the British Colonies in North America, 1607–1763* (1973); and Richard Middleton, *The Bells of Victory: The Pitt-Newcastle Ministry and the Conduct of the Seven Years' War, 1757–1762* (1985).

Emerging American Identity

Bernard Bailyn, *Voyagers to the West* (1986); Marc Egnal, *A Mighty Empire: The Origins of the American Revolution* (1988); and Ralph Ketchum, *From Colony to Country: The Revolution in American Thought, 1750–1820* (1974).

Precipitating Crises of the Revolution

T.H. Breen, *Tobacco Culture: The Mentality of the Great Tidewater Planters on the Eve of Revolution* (1985); Lawrence H. Gipson, *The Coming of the Revolution, 1763–1775* (1954); and John Shy, *Toward Lexington: The Role of the British Army in the Coming of the American Revolution* (1965).

Roots of Massive Resistance

Richard D. Brown, *Revolutionary Politics in Massachusetts: The Boston Committee of Correspondence and the Towns, 1772–1774* (1970); Edward Countryman, *A People in Revolution* (1981); and Gary B. Nash, *The Urban Crucible: Social Change, Political Consciousness, and the Origins of the American Revolution* (1979).

The War Itself

Edward Countryman, *The American Revolution* (1985); Lawrence D. Cress, *Citizens in Arms: The Army and the Militia in American Society to the War of 1812* (1982); and Charles Royster, *A Revolutionary People at War* (1979).

QUESTIONS FOR DISCUSSION

1. What role did the North American colonies play in the British mercantilist system? Analyze the consequences of "salutary neglect."
2. Discuss the impact of the French and Indian War on British–colonial relations.
3. Identify the changes in colonial demography and economy that contributed to heightened tensions between America and England.
4. How did colonists respond to the Stamp Act and other imperial taxes and penalties? Were they justified? Why or why not?
5. Explain the British response to the American demand of "no taxation without representation."
6. Describe the advantages and disadvantages of the Continental Army compared to the British army during the War of Independence. What were the decisive factors in the American victory?
7. How did the war change the life of George Robert Twelves Hewes? What does his experience say about the causes of the Revolutionary War?

CHAPTER FIVE

THE SEARCH FOR A REPUBLICAN ORDER:
From the Articles of Confederation to the Constitution

The American Revolution did not solve the problems that had led to it; it merely transferred finally and completely the responsibility for solving them from the eastern shore of the Atlantic to the western. Beginning in 1775 when it became apparent that there would be no sweet reconciliation between Great Britain and its erstwhile colonies, Americans produced a great body of thought and writing on political and constitutional theory. The citizens of the nation that was being born did not want to abandon what was best about the British governing system, but they were determined to erect a new nation based on liberty, equality, and opportunity rather than monarchy, hierarchy, privilege, and corruption. Americans were determined to erect republican forms of government. In the eighteenth century, republicanism was as radical an idea as Marxism was in the twentieth century or Christianity in the first century. It proposed to alter the entire basis upon which society was organized. That a people who had throughout their history responded to a utopian view of the future should embrace radicalism is, perhaps, not surprising.

REPUBLICANISM

Republicanism gained popularity in Europe during the Renaissance among those upwardly mobile groups, most notably the bourgeoisie, who were able to achieve some degree of status and wealth but were blocked by birth from the higher rungs of the social ladder and, more important, from the exercise of political power. These ideas were transported to seventeenth-century England by intellectuals such as John Milton and James Harrington. In countless pamphlets, sermons, memoirs, and political tracts English republicans decried the existing world of monarchical privilege, entrenched nobility, favoritism, bribery, monopoly, and corruption. The disaffected increasingly harked back to the days of ancient Greece and Rome in which independent, landowning citizens exercised political power directly or through their elected representatives. It was this vision that had led to the execution of Charles I in England and to the Cromwellian Commonwealth (1649–1653).

Republicanism was not suited in theory to large nations with mixed populations. The only examples of successful republics were Switzerland, the Netherlands, the Italian city-states, and ancient Greece and Rome. Conventional wisdom had it that republicanism in sprawling, populous states like England or France inevitably degenerated into dictatorship—Oliver Cromwell, for example. Unlike monarchies where civil order was enforced from above, republics had to depend on the voluntary actions of the people for cohesion, justice, due process, and collective action. Despite its size, however, America fancied itself uniquely suited to this radical political departure. Most Europeans had come to the New World to escape rigid social stratification, economic monopoly, hereditary privilege, and an established religion enforced by the state. Had not social order rooted in township and parish stood like a rock in the face of disintegrating royal authority and revolution?

The roots of American republicanism were public virtue, land ownership, and equality. Not surprisingly, Americans distrusted government. Much of the poverty, factionalism, and inequality that existed in the colonies, they believed, stemmed from the extension of British institutions and procedures into the New World. Appointed officials, maritime and tax decrees, and monopolies were all the products of an intrusive, oppressive state. That government which governed least, Americans reasoned, governed best. If representative democracy, voluntarism, and free, unregulated enterprise were to work, however, each citizen would have to demonstrate devotion to the community, indeed, would have to identify the welfare of the individual absolutely with the welfare of the body politic. Thus it was that in adopting constitutions, states such as Virginia, Massachusetts, and Pennsylvania referred to themselves as commonwealths.

For citizens of a republic to act virtuously they would have to be independent. The semifeudal nature of European monarchism with its titles, privileges, and influence peddling bred dependency and corruption. Crucial to civic independence, revolutionary ideologists believed, was land ownership. That was true to a degree in England, but whereas there ownership had been quite restricted, in America it was widespread. True, women, slaves, and indentured servants did not fall into this category and thus could legitimately be denied the vote, but most adult white males did. The independent yeoman farmer that typified American society was not a rustic provincial wallowing in the backwash of European society, but the ideal citizen, the keystone of a republican arch that Americans were certain would encompass the entire civilized world.

The most controversial but most important component of American republicanism was the notion of equality. European society was rooted in the very idea of inequality. Social order depended upon recognition of status based on birth, on inherited position and wealth. Survival depended upon one's acceptance of one's place in the social order. Americans believed in equality of opportunity if not condition. Men were born equal; they did not remain so, but their status was a reflection of their efforts and talents, not an abstraction or an accident of birth. Republicans like Thomas Jefferson envisioned an American aristocracy, but it would be a natural one based on merit. Unlike its European counterpart which was luxury-loving, venal, and money-grubbing, Jefferson's aristocracy would be virtuous, selfless, and public spirited. With this lofty vision in mind, Americans turned in 1776 to the concrete business of constitution making.

REVOLUTIONARY DEMOCRACY

In May 1776 the Second Continental Congress advised the various colonies to establish new governments "under the authority of the people." That advice was taken literally and reflected the popularization of politics that had taken place in the events leading up to the Revolution. The American Revolution was the product of a democratizing process and it in turn stimulated greater democracy. In cities, towns, and rural communities artisans, small farmers, and laborers—many of them without formal education—took their place in Sons of Liberty chapters and committees of correspondence alongside lawyers, merchants, and planters. By the mid-1770s a much greater proportion of the population was participating in public life than in England or in colonial America a decade before. The provincial assemblies passed legislation reflecting that fact. South Carolina, for example, required only that voters be white male adults to vote for representatives to the Continental Congress. By 1776 rebel assemblies included far more rural dwellers and backcountry farmers than they had in 1750.

The principal political distinction in colonial America had been between Tories—colonial administrators, Anglican clergy, and well-to-do lawyers, merchants, and planters—those who argued that colonial governments existed through the grace of the British government and were nothing more than instruments of that government, and Whigs, those who argued that colonial assemblies existed to represent local interests. Most Whigs were members of colonial elites struggling to advance their economic interests and safeguard their privileged positions. The Revolution effectively eliminated the Tories; they were replaced by the small farmers, mechanics, and laborers, the previously underrepresented debtors who lived in the backcountry or who comprised the urban working class. After 1776 the Whigs made up the conservative end of the political spectrum.

The philosophy of the popular majority was summed up in *The People the Best Governors*, a pamphlet published in Massachusetts in 1776. Because

individual citizens were in the best position to "know their wants and necessities, and therefore are best able to govern themselves," the fundamental unit
of government was the town or community meeting which should have the
power to raise a militia, levy taxes, control the local school and church, and
regulate the marketplace. State government existed only to coordinate action
by the communities. Conservatives recoiled at such "rantings," and warned of
the tyranny of the majority. The Revolution and the ardor for democracy that it
inspired placed them on the defensive, however.

STATE CONSTITUTIONS AND LEGISLATIVE SUPREMACY

By the end of 1776 New Jersey, North Carolina, Maryland, Pennsylvania, and
Delaware had adopted new constitutions. Rhode Island and Connecticut, with
corporate charters, were already republics, and they contented themselves with
eliminating all mention of royal authority. Georgia and New York, distracted by
the war, did not hammer out new charters until 1777. Massachusetts chose to
resurrect the charter which Britain had abolished following the Boston Tea
Party, and to use it as the basis for a new constitution.

It was unusual but, in retrospect, inevitable that Britain's erstwhile
colonies adopt written constitutions. In England constitution meant the collection of laws, institutions, and processes that had evolved over time.
Americans initially built on and appealed to English common law, but in the
events leading to the Revolution, they came to regard the very vagueness of un-
written constitutions as an invitation to tyranny. In addition, since the seventeenth century they had used their written charters as barriers to royal
authority. The delegates to the state constitutional conventions and/or the
colonial legislatures attempted to do nothing less than institutionalize the best
features of their colonial governments with the republican theories that crys-
talized during the Revolution. Overriding all other considerations, however,
was the desire of the framers to protect the liberties of the people from the
power of government.

Most states built on prior experience and continued with the customary
arrangement of a governor and bicameral legislature, with at least one house
elected by the people. All except Georgia, Pennsylvania, and the new state of
Vermont replaced colonial councils with senates (taken from Roman history).
Adult male property owners were entitled to vote for representatives to the
lower house, but property and other qualifications were required to vote for
senators. The older, wiser, wealthier, and presumably more conservative
senators would act as a check on the less efficient, more impetuous popular assemblies. There were a few radical innovations, however. Under the constitution that New Jersey adopted in 1776, women as well as men who met the
property requirement were allowed to vote.

In general the new state constitutions incorporated two significant innovations. First, they placed severe checks on the executive. In eleven states the
governor lost his veto over measures enacted by the legislature. In ten states,

the executive was limited to a single one-year term. In eight states, he was chosen by the legislature, and in the others, the legislature created an administrative council to assist the governor. The exclusive right of appointment traditionally exercised by the governor was to be shared with or checked by the senates and popular assemblies. Second, the state constitutions provided for independent judiciaries, that is, judges who were elected or appointed and who usually served for life. All of these developments meant a system of checks and balances instead of a parliamentary system in which executive and legislature were inextricably intertwined. The trend toward a weak executive would be unfortunate. Americans, it seemed, failed to recognize the implications of their own revolution. A democratically elected governor would be a far different creature than one appointed by a monarch.

Those powers taken from the executive were given for the most part to legislatures, even to the point of forming alliances and granting pardons. Recognizing the supremacy of the legislators, the framers of state constitutions took great pains to ensure that representation was actual. Constitutions established equal electoral districts, provided for regular elections, imposed residence requirements on voters and candidates, and empowered constituents to give specific instructions to their representatives. The traditionally underrepresented frontier regions were given either new or additional representation in the state legislatures. In this sense, the Revolution led to the redress of backcountry grievances.

Most state constitutions included bills of rights modeled after Virginia's. These documents were designed to protect the liberties of the people from grasping governmental hands, to safeguard the natural rights of the individual from would-be tyrants. The rights guaranteed were of two types: substantive, such as freedom of speech, worship, assembly, and press; and procedural, such as protection of person and property against arbitrary treatment or seizure. Guarantee of the writ of habeas corpus and prohibitions against general search warrants were typical of the latter category. The notion that government power could and should be so specifically and concretely limited was fairly radical in the eighteenth century.

The state constitutions written in 1777 and 1778 were clear departures from European practices and institutions. The flight from America of more than one hundred thousand loyalists, most of whom had been closely tied to colonial governors and British practices, paved the way for the creation of more direct democracies. But the radicalism of the American Revolution should not be overstressed. There were no mass trials and executions, no reign of terror. Some loyalists were treated roughly but acts of vengeful violence were rare. The Revolution accelerated the movement in the North for abolition of slavery, but the institution remained firmly entrenched in the South. Except for New Jersey, women remained strictly outside the political pale. In Virginia, laws providing for primogeniture and entail (limiting inheritance to a specific class or line of heirs) were abolished, but they were by the time of the Revolution observed more in the breach.

THE ARTICLES OF CONFEDERATION AND THE CRITICAL PERIOD

Creating a new central government was more difficult than framing state constitutions because there was no base on which to build. The only central government Americans had known was the British monarchy. Surprisingly little attention was paid to the project. This was so in part because Americans initially viewed the United States of America as just that, a voluntary league of independent, sovereign states. Nonetheless, there was an obvious need to legitimize the Second Continental Congress that sat almost continuously from 1775 through 1781. Though extralegal, it exercised extraordinary powers including establishing and maintaining an army, issuing currency, levying taxes, forming alliances, and defining crimes against the nation. In 1777 John Dickinson of Pennsylvania drew up a plan of union that came to be known as the Articles of Confederation. Although Dickinson's original scheme provided for a fairly strong central government, the final draft of the Articles established an edifice hemmed in with restrictions and devoid of power.

Congress stipulated that before the Articles could go into effect, all of the states would have to ratify them. That process dragged on until 1781, hamstrung primarily by disagreements over disposition of western lands. Some states through their original charters laid claim to lands extending all the way to the Mississippi River, and Virginia rather grandly insisted that it owned the entire region now known as the Midwest. States like Maryland and Massachusetts with no claims would not agree to ratify the Articles unless and until the territory beyond the Appalachians was surrendered to the national government and treated as common property. Finally, Virginia, whose patriots declared that they preferred "the good of the country to every object of smaller importance," renounced its claims, and the landless signed on.

The Articles of Confederation created what amounted to a perpetual league among independent nations. It was a confederation in the true sense of the word, the legalization of the Second Continental Congress. The national charter stated clearly that each state retained its sovereign freedom and independence and that Congress could act only in areas specifically dealt to it; all other powers were to be retained by the states. Like the Second Continental Congress, the Articles provided for a unicameral legislature with delegates elected by state legislatures and each state having one vote. On paper, Congress was given authority to control foreign affairs, declare war and make peace, coin and borrow money, raise an army, requisition funds from the several states, settle interstate disputes, govern the western territory and admit new states, maintain a postal service, and supervise Indian affairs.

In fact, the actual exercise of many of these powers was hedged with restrictions. To act in these fundamental matters, it was necessary for the national government to obtain the approval of nine states instead of a simple majority. Other powers were omitted; for example, Congress could only levy taxes and had no power to compel payment. The national legislature had no control over interstate commerce; this fundamental power was left to the states and was therefore an invitation to open competition among them. During the 1780s states erected tariff barriers and set up customs schedules against the commerce of other states. In fact, Congress had no powers of enforcement in any area; it functioned only through the will of the states. No judicial or administrative machinery existed to carry out a central will. The Articles were a logical reaction to the perceived evils of a grasping central government. Weakness and inefficiency were the prices that republicans had to pay for a system in which their liberties were safe. But an increasingly vocal minority would argue that government under the Articles was not weak and inefficient, but impotent.

REVOLUTIONARY EQUALITY AND THE ANTISLAVERY MOVEMENT

The American Revolution affected virtually every facet of life in the former colonies. It was perhaps inevitable that a movement that championed individual liberty and political democracy and that held up the equality of all human beings as a universal value should spawn an antislavery movement. Thomas Jefferson returned to Virginia and from his position as a member of the House of Delegates urged legislation providing for the gradual manumission of slaves. In 1785 the New York Society for the Manumission of Slaves was organized with the prominent jurist, John Jay, as president. By 1792 there were antislavery societies in every state from Massachusetts to Virginia. Some antislavery activists concentrated on doing away with the slave trade, others on gradual manumission, and still others on the colonization of African Americans in the interior or in some foreign land.

Although generally in a minority, the antislavery forces were active, intensely vocal, and not unsuccessful. In 1783 Maryland prohibited trafficking in human beings. In 1786 North Carolina increased the duty on imported slaves to £15 a head. In 1787 South Carolina prohibited the further importation of slaves, a measure that was, however, declared unenforceable in 1803. In 1780 Pennsylvania, a state dominated by the traditionally antislavery Quakers, provided for gradual emancipation by declaring that after a slave reached the age of twenty-eight, he or she was to become an indentured servant. During the debate over that measure Pennsylvania legislators declared that they felt called upon to demonstrate the sincerity of their professions of freedom and to exhibit their gratitude by extending a portion of their freedom to others "who though of a different color, are the work of the same Almighty hand." By 1783 the courts of Massachusetts had ruled slavery illegal, quoting the state constitution of 1780 which declared all men to have been created free and equal. By 1804 Connecticut, Rhode Island, New York, and New Jersey had passed measures providing for the gradual freeing of slaves. Abolition, however, subsequently ran afoul of the southern plantation system and the conservative backlash against democratizing forces that were sweeping the land during the 1780s.

THE DISESTABLISHMENT OF RELIGION

Revolutionary ideology not only knocked the shackles from the limbs of some African Americans, it also loosened the ties between government and religion in the United States. With its emphasis on free inquiry and liberty of conscience, Enlightenment thought militated against state-established and -supported churches. Many Revolution era Americans perceived the Church of England as an arm of the crown; indeed, one of the most inflammatory rumors that made the rounds in colonial America in the 1760s was that the church intended to set up a system of bishops in America. At the time of America's separation from England, nine of the thirteen states had an established religion: the Anglican church in New York and the South, and the Congregationalist denomination in Connecticut, Massachusetts, and New Hampshire.

Jefferson got the disestablishment movement underway when he sponsored a Bill for the Establishment of Religious Freedom in the Virginia assembly. Other state legislatures followed suit, and in Maryland, New York, the Carolinas, and Georgia where Anglicanism was identified with loyalty to the crown, disestablishment measures passed easily. Ironically, opposition to separation of the Anglican church from the state was strongest in Virginia. Conservatives there saw the established denomination as a political and social corrective to the Baptist and Methodist democrats. The disestablishment bill did not pass until 1786. In New England, Congregationalism enjoyed official state sanction into the nineteenth century. And even disestablishment states retained religious tests for voting and office holding. In New Jersey, Georgia, and the Carolinas, one had to be a Protestant to exercise the franchise. Even in historically tolerant Pennsylvania, public officials had to assent to the notion that the Old and New Testaments were the absolute word of God.

THE ADMINISTRATION OF WESTERN LANDS

The Land Ordinance of 1785

Government under the Articles scored its greatest success in management of western lands. The Land Ordinance of 1785 stipulated that the western territories be organized into no less than three nor more than seven states. The measure provided in addition that the territory be surveyed into townships of thirty-six miles square, divided into thirty-six sections of one square mile, or 640 acres. Four sections of each township were reserved for disposition by the local government and one for the support of local education. The remainder was to be auctioned off to the highest bidder, with a minimum purchase of 640 acres at a minimum price of a dollar an acre. Settlers were prohibited from occupying the land until after it had been officially surveyed so that settlement could proceed in an orderly east-west manner. Congress envisioned proceeds from sale of public land as a much needed source of revenue for the national government. In that hope it was disappointed because most frontier farmers could neither afford $640 nor cultivate 640 acres.

The Northwest Ordinance

To provide government for the Northwest Territory, Congress in 1787 passed the Northwest Ordinance. The legislation included a bill of rights to protect the basic liberties of those living beyond the boundaries of the established states—there was none associated with the Articles. The ordinance also prohibited the introduction of slavery into the Northwest. Indeed, passage of the measure marked the culmination of the brief antislavery movement that began just after the Revolution. Two years later, however, Congress passed a Southwest Ordinance without a bar to slavery. The Northwest Ordinance, then, was the first compromise between North and South over slavery. Underlying it was an understanding that the free yeomen farmers of the North would not have to compete with slave labor, but the planters of the Southwest would be given equality with planters in southern states where slavery already existed.

Most significant was the Northwest Ordinance's promise to raise the territories to eventual statehood. The original thirteen states could have held the western territories as perpetual dependencies, making itself a republican empire. There was risk in the guarantee of statehood; creating new states on an equal basis would dilute the power of the original thirteen. The western states would certainly draw labor and capital out of the East without necessarily providing an economic equivalent in the form of markets. Republican ideology and faith in the future won out, however. Under the Northwest Ordinance, statehood was to be achieved in three phases: The inhabitants of a territory were to be governed initially by a congressionally appointed governor and three judges. When the population reached five thousand, adult male landowners could elect a territorial legislature to deal with local matters, but the appointed executive would have veto power over all legislation. When sixty thousand persons resided in a territory, they could elect delegates to a constitutional convention. If Congress approved the resulting state constitution, statehood would be conferred. The decision to guarantee the western territories eventual full equality with the thirteen original states proved to be a happy one. The one glaring shortcoming of the Land Ordinance and the Northwest Ordinance was their failure to establish a mechanism for dealing with Indian claims or even recognizing those claims.

THE FRUITS OF STATE SOVEREIGNTY

The Articles of Confederation may have been an accurate reflection of the political philosophy prevailing in America at the close of the revolutionary era, but as the 1780s progressed it became more and more obvious that they had failed to establish an effective national government. During the Revolution, runaway inflation wracked the fledgling republic. Between 1776 and 1783 the value of the currency issued by the Continental Congress declined by 300 percent. Several states created agencies to regulate prices and wages, but enforcement was rare. Increasingly, housewives blamed greedy merchants for the exorbitant prices they had to pay for coffee and flour. Spearheaded by angry women, food riots featuring physical attacks on price-gouging merchants became a frequent occurrence.

Following the Revolution, the republic experienced a severe depression. Britain denied U.S. merchants access to its West Indian markets and flooded North America with cheap goods. Smuggling was an oft-resorted to option, but it made up only a fraction of the lost trade. Imports skyrocketed while exports plummeted. Between 1784 and 1786 America's debt to Britain increased by £5 million, and as a result, hard currency—gold and silver coin—flowed out of the country. So strapped for cash were the largest American banks that they called in all debts for immediate payment and refused to make new loans. With credit virtually unavailable, business activity slowed to a crawl. To make matters worse, the several states erected their own tariff barriers, thus further slowing the exchange of goods and services.

SHAYS' REBELLION

Debtors, that is, small farmers, tradespeople, mechanics, and laborers, were particularly hard hit by the depression, and during the mid-1780s they organized to defend their interests. Several states passed "legal tender" laws setting specific currency values for commodities locally produced and requiring the acceptance of such currency for payment of debts. Others passed barter laws permitting payment of taxes and debts in tobacco, cattle, or flour. In Massachusetts, however, the legislature was dominated by urban-dwelling merchants and bankers who repeatedly rejected legal tender and stay laws, measures arbitrarily extending the deadlines for payment of debts. During the 1780s nearly one-third of male heads of household were jailed for debt. During the spring and summer of 1786 several communities in western Massachusetts summoned their militias, and led by Revolutionary War veteran Daniel Shays, they closed down the local courts. At the same time, in Maryland, Pennsylvania, and other colonies, mob action intimidated judges and closed courts. In the spring of 1787 Massachusetts state militia put down the uprising in the western part of the state, killing or capturing members of Shays' army as it marched on the armory at Springfield. Fifteen leaders of the debtor insurrection were subsequently convicted and sentenced to die.

Shays' Rebellion and other similar outbreaks of violence frightened citizens of property and status. Merchants, bankers, plantation owners, and political elites began to feel that America needed a more powerful national government, one that was capable of protecting the sanctity of contracts and guarding the minority against the tyranny of the majority. In addition, businesspeople blamed Congress for its inability to force the states to lower the trade barriers among them and for its lack of success in compelling Spain and Britain to open their markets.

Meanwhile, in the West frontier farmers were literally up in arms because the national government was not strong enough to force the British to abandon the posts they operated in the Northwest Territory, something they had pledged to do in the Treaty of 1783. To make matters worse, the British were furnishing arms to Indians who were attacking American settlers on American soil. Necessary changes to the Articles, such as an amendment giving Congress limited taxing power, had proved impossible because the Articles required a unanimous vote for any revision. It became evident that the creators of the confederation had delegated too much power to the states. In addition to fostering closed economies, various states violated the terms of treaties signed between the national government and foreign nations.

One by one, prominent Americans began expressing their distress over the weakness of the national government under the Articles. "I predict the worst consequences for a half-starved limping government, always moving upon crutches and tottering at every step," George Washington declared in 1786. That same year John Jay wrote Thomas Jefferson that "the inefficacy of our government becomes daily more and more apparent," and he was then acting as the government's secretary of foreign affairs. Alexander Hamilton, a strong nationalist, decided that the country had reached "almost the last stage of national humiliation."

THE CONSTITUTIONAL CONVENTION

Out of this discontent came the Constitutional Convention, a gathering of enormous importance despite its inadvertence. In 1785 delegates from Maryland and Virginia gathered at the Mount Vernon Conference to discuss navigation of the Potomac. Nothing was resolved, and five states sent representatives to a gathering at Annapolis to discuss the deplorable state of interstate commerce. There Hamilton and James Madison convinced their fellows that problems other than commerce required attention and that the time had come for a meeting of a more fundamental sort. With the approval of the national Congress, such a gathering, which came to be known as the Constitutional Convention, met in Philadelphia at the State House in 1787. Technically, those in attendance were charged with drafting amendments to the Articles, but it was quickly decided that a completely new charter was needed. Fifty-five delegates attended, and thirty-nine signed the final draft. Rhode Island was not represented, and the representatives from New Hampshire arrived too late for significant participation.

The members of the Constitutional Convention may not have been the "demi-gods" that Thomas Jefferson called them, but they were a distinguished lot. Two future presidents, Washington and Madison, were in attendance (Jefferson and John Adams were then serving as their country's representatives to France and England respectively) plus two chief justices, and six future

Washington, Franklin, and the other "founding fathers" at the Constitutional Convention in Philadelphia in 1787.

governors. Thirty were college graduates during a period when less than 1 percent of the population had gained such distinction; most had served in the military and many were veterans of their colonial or state legislatures. Many were young—Madison was thirty-six, Hamilton only thirty-two—while Franklin was the oldest at eighty-one. Washington, a moderate fifty-five, served as the meeting's presiding officer and a symbol of the nation's sovereignty, though he contributed little to the debate.

Nearly all of the delegates represented, directly or indirectly, the great property interests of the country and notably absent were the most radical of the revolutionaries—Thomas Paine, Sam Adams, Patrick Henry, and Jefferson. Most were profoundly conservative in the sense that they regarded their task as primarily that of finding a way to preserve the American nation which they believed was on the verge of disintegration into thirteen separate entities. By European standards, however, the delegates to the Constitutional Convention were radical. They assumed that governors ought to be chosen by the governed and should be held responsible for their actions through regular election. The delegates were inclined to favor a system which would include safeguards to protect property and minority rights against the tyranny of the majority—a basic problem under the confederation. Because many of those present in Philadelphia were plantation owners, successful businessmen and financiers, or wealthy shipowners, some historians would later charge that they created a political system designed to safeguard their vested interests, but there is little evidence to support the contention. Their passion was the nation and their vision of its future.

A REPRESENTATIVE DEMOCRACY

Debate at the Constitutional Convention centered around three major issues: representation in Congress, separation of powers, and division of power between state governments and the national government. In regard to the first issue, large states insisted, not surprisingly, that representation be based on population while small states wanted each state to be equally represented. Fierce debate ensued over the competing Virginia (large state) and New Jersey (small state) plans.

The delegates compromised by creating a two-house legislature. In the Senate each state would have two delegates while representation in the House of Representatives would be in proportion to population. This, the Connecticut Compromise, was worked out largely by Benjamin Franklin. In regard to the House, slave states wanted chattel to be counted as persons while free states did not. Again, another compromise. Unconsciously underlining the absurdity of the peculiar institution, the Constitution provided that slaves would count as three-fifths of a person for purposes of both representation in the House and for the imposition of taxation by the federal government. To strike a balance between majority rule and minority rights, the Philadelphia convention decreed that state legislatures would decide how senators were to be elected (they reserved that right to themselves) while congressmen were to be selected by those persons eligible to vote for members of state assemblies.

SEPARATION OF POWERS

Under the Articles all power had been lodged in Congress. Some of the delegates to the Constitutional Convention argued that if the federal government were to be strengthened, it was unwise to have a single branch that was all powerful. As a guard against tyranny and oppression, it would be better to create three independent branches—judicial, executive, and legislative—each with its own powers but also with the ability to check the other two. The delegates created a bicameral Congress with the exclusive power to enact laws subject only to veto by the president, a veto that could, however, be overridden by a two-thirds vote of both houses. Executive authority was lodged in a president, chosen by the electoral college, itself a cumbersome compromise. The national executive would have the power to enforce laws, command the armed forces, conduct foreign affairs, and appoint subordinate executive officials and judges. The Senate, however, would have to confirm presidential appointments and ratify treaties for them to be valid. If the president were accused of "high crimes and misdemeanors," he could be impeached by the House and, if convicted by the Senate, removed from office. A supreme court whose members would be appointed, subject to congressional approval, for life would exercise the judicial function, including the power to decide all cases arising under the Constitution, federal laws, and treaties.

A NATIONAL GOVERNMENT

The final problem confronting the gathering at Philadelphia, the one that more than any other had been responsible for the existence of the Constitutional Convention, was the division of powers between the new central government and the several states. The struggle between nationalists who wanted to create as strong a central government as possible on the presumption that it would be run by the best and the brightest, and the advocates of states rights who feared that an unchecked federal government would crush the liberties of the people and even degenerate into monarchy went to the very core of the delegates' personal philosophies and political beliefs.

The document that the Philadelphia convention produced greatly increased the power of the central government without seeming to do so. The Constitution declared that the federal government should exercise no powers not expressly granted to it. It then went on to add significantly to the duties that had been assigned under the Articles, including the power to tax and to regulate interstate commerce (with the exception of duties on exports and the slave trade which was declared sacrosanct until 1808). Most important, the delegates granted to the federal government the authority to enact laws "necessary and proper" for the carrying out of its other duties. Important new restrictions were placed on the states. No longer could they regulate foreign and interstate commerce, issue paper money, or pass laws violating sanctity of contract. Finally, the new Constitution asserted that federal statutes and treaties were "the supreme law of the land" and should take precedence over all state laws and constitutions.

In addition to creating a fundamental charter that would eliminate the weaknesses of the Articles, the framers hoped to fashion a document "for the ages," to use James Madison's phrase. They succeeded. Several features have contributed to the longevity of the Constitution of the United States. The system of checks and balances, a product partly of design and partly of accident, created a government in which it would be very difficult for any person or faction to gain and exercise unchecked power. The price, a ponderous, slow-moving, and sometimes erratic political process, has seemed to most Americans a small price to pay. A liberal amending provision—additions to the Constitution may become law after passage by Congress and ratification by three-fourths of the states— appeased opponents of the Constitution both at the time and in the future. Finally, the framers of the Constitution kept the document brief and wrote it in general terms. Thus, over the years the debate in America has not been over whether to retain the Constitution but rather over what it means.

THE STRUGGLE OVER RATIFICATION

When the deliberations in Philadelphia ended in September, the Constitution was submitted to the people for their consideration. Although the Articles had required unanimous approval by the states to go into effect, the delegates, with the consent of Congress, agreed that the Constitution would become operative after nine states had ratified it. Each state held a ratification convention, and two factions quickly emerged. Those favoring ratification called themselves Federalists; those opposed, Antifederalists. The ensuing debate was frequently acrimonious and hard to reconcile. The deliberations of the Philadelphia convention had been conducted in secret, and thus the provisions of the Constitution when published in September were all the more controversial. Objections to ratification centered around two main themes: fear that the Constitution did not provide adequate protection for the liberties of the individual and a determination to protect the sovereignty of the states against a grasping, overweening central government. The Antifederalists predicted the worst consequences if the Constitution were ratified: The president would become king, a standing army would oppress and terrorize the people, and individuals would be impoverished by the combination of state and federal taxes. The Constitution was clearly an innovation, and, unable to predict the consequences, Americans trembled for their future.

Several of the states ratified quickly, especially the smaller ones which anticipated that if the federal union disintegrated, they would be swallowed up by a foreign power. In the larger states, approval came much more slowly, and the two camps were evenly divided. In Massachusetts, supporters of the Constitution changed the minds of Samuel Adams and John Hancock by promising that the first Congress would write and submit to the states for their approval a bill of rights; still, the state convention approved the Constitution by a margin of only 19 votes out of 355. When New Hampshire voted to ratify in June 1788, the Constitution technically went into effect. Virginia and New York remained outside the union, however, and it was clear that it could not survive without their participation.

In Virginia, George Washington's support helped turn the tide in favor of the Federalists, together with the knowledge that he would consent to be the nation's first president. A special courier carried the news that Virginia had voted in favor by a vote of 89 to 79 to New York where a particularly heated debate was underway. There the powerful governor, George Clinton, spearheaded the opposition, while the Federalists were led by the brilliant young Alexander Hamilton, a protégé of Washington's. To counter the Clinton family's political and economic clout, Hamilton, together with John Jay and James Madison, wrote a series of essays in support of the Constitution. Published individually in various New York newspapers, they were later collected as *The Federalist* papers, still the most compelling and thorough commentary on the Constitution in print. These essays, together with news that New Hampshire and Virginia had ratified and growing fear among New York merchants that their interests would be damaged if the state did not join the union, helped carry the day. The final vote, a month after Virginia, was 30 to 27. North Carolina which approved in November 1789 and Rhode Island which ratified in May 1790 made the vote unanimous. Seven states accompanied their acceptance with series of amendments, and in the first session of Congress, the House and Senate agreed upon twelve of those amendments, of which ten were quickly approved and became known as the Bill of Rights. Once the federal government went into operation, opposition to the Constitution began to fade. Again, controversy centered on what it meant, not on its fundamental value.

Early historians of the Constitution-making process portrayed the framers as far-sighted individuals who in creating a stable, orderly government had the long-term interests of all the people uppermost in their minds. That view has been rendered in a more sophisticated fashion by John Roche and others who argue that the creators of the nation's basic charter were conservatives but also sensitive democratic politicians who perceived what the majority wanted and wrote a document that represented those desires. A half century ago Charles Beard penned a controversial interpretation of the Constitutional Convention in which he argued that the founders of the republic were reactionary members of an American elite and that the Constitution was a document designed to safeguard the property rights and business interests of the country, both large and small. In the essay that follows, Gordon S. Wood argues that social conservatism and not economic self-interest lay at the heart of the new Constitution. Men of property and influence like Madison and Hamilton believed that the Revolution had upset the established social order, paving the way for the ascendency of licentious, opportunistic, irresponsible men. The Founding Fathers were committed to the notion of social mobility, but they also believed that if a republic were to function properly, those who rose must first acquire the attributes of social superiority—education, property, civic virtue, political and social connections. In Wood's view, then, the Constitution was designed to ensure that America would be ruled by its natural aristocracy rather than by demagogues and charlatans.

THE WORTHY AGAINST THE LICENTIOUS

Gordon S. Wood

How the Federalists expected a new central government to remedy the vices the individual states had been unable to remedy is the central question, the answer to which lies at the heart of their understanding of what was happening in the critical period. In the minds of the Federalists and of "men of reflection" generally, most of the evils of American society—the atmosphere of mistrust, the breakdown of

from Gordon S. Wood, ed., *The Confederation and the Constitution: The Critical Issues* (Lanham, MD: 1979) pp. 87–112.

authority, the increase of debt, the depravity of manners, and the decline of virtue—could be reduced to a fundamental problem of social disarrangement. Even the difficulties of the United States in foreign affairs and its weakness as a nation in the world, as Jay argued in *The Federalist,* Number 3, could be primarily explained by what the Revolution had done to America's political and social hierarchy. More than anything else the Federalists' obsession with disorder in American society and politics accounts for the revolutionary nature of the nationalist proposals offered by men like Madison in 1787 and for the resultant Federalist Constitution. Only an examination of the Federalists' social perspective, their fears and anxieties about the disarray in American society, can fully explain how they conceived of the Constitution as a political device designed to control the social forces the Revolution had released.

The most pronounced social effect of the Revolution was not harmony or stability but the sudden appearance of new men everywhere in politics and business. "When the pot boils, the scum will rise," James Otis had warned in 1776; but few Revolutionary leaders had realized just how much it would rise. By the end of the war men like Governor James Bowdoin of Massachusetts could "scarcely see any other than new faces," a change almost "as remarkable as the revolution itself." The emigration of thousands of Tories, the intensification of interest in politics, the enlargement of the legislatures and the increase in elections, the organization of new militia and political groups, the breakup of old mercantile combinations and trade circuits, the inflation and profiteering caused by the war—all offered new opportunities for hitherto unknown but ambitious persons to find new places for themselves. As John Adams noted, his own deep resentment of his supposed social superiors was being echoed throughout various levels of the society. For every brilliant provincial lawyer ready to challenge the supremacy of the imperial clique in the colonial metropolis, there were dozens of lesser men, not so brilliant but equally desirous of securing a local magistracy, a captaincy of the militia, some place, however small, of honor and distinction. With the elimination of Crown privilege and appointment men were prepared to take the republican emphasis on equality seriously. The result, as one Baltimore printer declared as early as 1777, was "Whiggism run mad." "When a man, who is only fit 'to patch a shoe,' attempts 'to patch the State,' fancies himself a *Solon* or *Lycurgus,* . . . he cannot fail to meet with contempt." But contempt was no longer enough to keep such men in their place.

Everywhere "*Specious, interested designing* men," "men, respectable neither for their property, their virtue, nor their abilities," were taking a lead in public affairs that they had never quite had before, courting "the suffrages of the people by tantalizing them with improper indulgences." Thousands of the most respectable people "who obtained their possessions by the hard industry, continued sobriety and economy of themselves or their virtuous ancestors" were now witnessing, so the writings of nearly all the states proclaimed over and over, many men "*whose fathers they would have disdained to have sat with the dogs of their flocks,* raised to immense wealth, or at least to carry the appearance of a haughty, supercilious and luxurious spendthrift." "Effrontery and arrogance, even in our virtuous and enlightened days," said John Jay, "are giving rank and Importance to men whom Wisdom would have left in obscurity." Since "every new election in the States," as Madison pointed out in *The Federalist,* Number 62, "is found to change one half of the representatives," the newly enlarged state legislatures were being filled and yearly refilled with different faces, often with "men without reading, experience, or principle." The Revolution, it was repeatedly charged (and the evidence seems to give substance to the charges), was allowing government to fall "into the Hands of those whose ability or situation in Life does not intitle them to it." Everywhere in the 1780's the press and the correspondence of those kinds of men whose letters are apt to be preserved complained that "a set of unprincipled men, who sacrifice everything to their popularity and private views, seem to have acquired too much influence in all our Assemblies." The Revolution was acquiring a degree of social turbulence that many, for all of their knowledge of revolutions, had not anticipated. Given the Revolutionary leaders' conventional eighteenth-century assumption of a necessary coincidence between social and political authority, many could actually believe that their world was being "turned upside down."

Beginning well before the Revolution but increasing to a fever pitch by the mid-eighties were fears of what this kind of intensifying social mobility signified for the traditional conception of a hierarchical society ("In due gradation ev'ry rank must be, Some high, some low, but all in their degree")—a conception which the Revolution had unsettled but by no means repudiated. In reaction to the excessive social movement accelerated by the Revolution some Americans, although good republicans, attempted to confine mobility within prescribed channels. Men could rise, but only within the social ranks in which they were born. Their aim in life must be to learn to perform their inherited position with "industry, economy, and good conduct." A man, wrote Enos Hitchcock in his didactic tale of 1793, must not be "elevated above his employment." In this respect republicanism with its emphasis on spartan adversity and simplicity became an ideology of social stratification and control. Over and over writers urged that "the crosses of life improve by retrenching our enjoyments," by moderating "our expectations," and by giving "the heart a mortal disgust to all the gaudy blandishments of sense." Luxury was such a great evil because it confounded "every Distinction between the Poor and the Rich" and allowed "people of the very meanest parentages, or office, if fortune be but a little favourable to them" to "vie to make themselves equal in apparel with the principal people of the place." "Dissipation and extravagance" encouraged even "country-girls in their market carts, and upon their panniered horses," to ride "through our streets with their heads deformed with the plumes of the ostrich and the feathers of other exotick birds." Although many, especially in the South, had expected the Revolution to lessen this kind of social chaos, republicanism actually seemed only to have aggravated it.

Most American leaders, however, were not opposed to the idea of social movement, for mobility, however one may have decried its abuses, lay at the heart of republicanism. Indeed, many like John Adams had entered the Revolution in order to make mobility a reality, to free American society from the artificial constraints Britain had imposed on it, and to allow "Persons of obscure Birth, and Station, and narrow Fortunes" to make their mark in the world. Republicanism represented equality of opportunity and careers open to talent. Even "the reins of state," David Ramsay had said at the outset, "may be held by the son of the poorest man, if possessed of abilities equal to that important station." Ramsay's qualification, however, was crucial to his endorsement of mobility. For all of its emphasis on equality, republicanism was still not considered by most to be incompatible with the conception of a hierarchical society of different gradations and a unitary authority to which deference from lower to higher should be paid. Movement must necessarily exist in a republic, if talent alone were to dominate, if the natural aristocracy were to rule. But such inevitable movement must be into and out of clearly discernible ranks. Those who rose in a republic, it was assumed, must first acquire the attributes of social superiority—wealth, education, experience, and connections—before they could be considered eligible for political leadership. Most Revolutionary leaders clung tightly to the concept of a ruling elite, presumably based on merit, but an elite nonetheless—a natural aristocracy embodied in the eighteenth-century ideal of an educated and cultivated gentleman. The rising self-made man could be accepted into this natural aristocracy only if he had assimilated through education or experience its attitudes, refinements, and style. For all of their earlier criticism of "the better sort of People" in the name of "real Merit," few of the Revolutionary leaders were prepared to repudiate the idea of a dominating elite and the requisite identity of social and political authority. . . .

In South Carolina these kinds of sentiments became particularly pronounced in the eighties; the planters found themselves confronted with widespread challenges to their authority that they had never anticipated in 1776, challenges that came from a new kind of politician, one who, as a defender proudly pointed out, "had no relations or friends, but what his money made for him." In the tense atmosphere of the mid-eighties the case of William Thompson, an unfortunate tavern-keeper who was threatened with banishment from the state by the legislature for allegedly insulting John Rutledge, became a *cause célèbre* and a focal point for the political and social animosities released and aggravated by the Revolution. Thompson's address to the public in April 1784 is a classic expression of American resentment against social superiority, a resentment voiced, as Thompson said, not on behalf of himself but on behalf of the people, or "those more especially, who go at this day, under the opprobrious appellation of, the *Lower Orders of Men.*" Thompson was not simply attacking the few aristocratic "Nabobs" who had humiliated him, but was actually assaulting the entire conception of a social hierarchy ruled by a gentlemanly elite. In fact he turned the prevailing eighteenth-century opinion upside down and argued that the natural aristocracy was peculiarly unqualified to rule. Rather than preparing men for political leadership in a free government, said Thompson, "signal opulence and influence," especially when united "by intermarriage or otherwise," were really "calculated to subvert *Republicanism.*" The "persons and conduct" of the South Carolina "Nabobs" like Rutledge "in *private* life, may be unexceptionable, and even amiable, but their pride, influence, ambition, connections, wealth and political principles, ought in *public* life, ever to exclude them from *public confidence.*" All that was needed in republican leadership was "being *good, able, useful,* and *friends to social equality,*" for in a republican government "consequence is from the *public opinion,* and not from *private fancy.*" In sardonic tones Thompson recounted how he, a tavern-keeper, "a *wretch* of no higher rank in the Commonwealth than that of Common-Citizen," had been debased by "those *self-exalted* characters, who affect to compose the *grand hierarchy* of the State, . . . for having dared to dispute with a *John Rutledge,* or any of the NABOB tribe." The experience had been degrading enough to Thompson as a man, but as a former officer in the army it had been "insupportable"—indicating how Revolutionary military service may have affected the social structure. Undoubtedly, said Thompson, Rutledge had "conceived me his inferior." But Thompson like many others in these years—tavern-keepers, farmers, petty merchants, small-time lawyers, former military officers—could no longer "comprehend the *inferiority.*" The resultant antagonism between those who conceived of such men as their inferiors, unfit to hold public positions, and those who would not accept the imputation of inferiority lay beneath the social crisis of the 1780's—a social crisis which the federal Constitution of 1787 brought to a head.

The division over the Constitution in 1787–88 is not easily analyzed. It is difficult, as historians have recently demonstrated, to equate the supporters or opponents of the Constitution with particular economic groupings. The Antifederalist politicians in the ratifying conventions often possessed wealth, including public securities, equal to that of the Federalists. While the relative youth of the Federalist leaders, compared to the ages of the prominent Antifederalists, was important, especially in accounting for the Federalists' ability to think freshly and creatively about politics, it can hardly be used to explain the division throughout the country. Moreover, the concern of the 1780's with America's moral character was not confined to the proponents of the Constitution. That rabid republican and Antifederalist, Benjamin Austin, was as convinced as any Federalist that "the luxurious living of all ranks and degrees" was "the principal cause of all the evils we now experience." Some leading Antifederalist intellectuals expressed as much fear of "the injustice, folly, and wickedness of the State Legislatures" and of "the usurpation and tyranny of the majority" against the minority as did Madison. In the Philadelphia Convention both Mason and Elbridge Gerry, later prominent Antifederalists, admitted "the danger of the levelling spirit" flowing from "the excess of democracy" in the American republics. There were many diverse reasons in each state why men supported or opposed the Constitution that cut through any sort of class division. The Constitution was a single issue in a complicated situation, and its acceptance or rejection in many states was often dictated by peculiar circumstances—the prevalence of Indians, the desire for western lands, the special interests of commerce—that defy generalization. Nevertheless, despite all of this confusion and complexity, the struggle over the Constitution, as the debate if nothing else makes clear, can best be understood as a social one. Whatever the particular constituency of the antagonists may have been, men in 1787–88 talked as if they were representing distinct and opposing social elements. Both the proponents and opponents of the Constitution focused throughout the debates on an essential point of political sociology that ultimately must be used to distinguish a Federalist from an Antifederalist. The quarrel was fundamentally one between aristocracy and democracy. . . .

The disorganization and inertia of the Antifederalists, especially in contrast with the energy and effectiveness of the Federalists, has been repeatedly emphasized. The opponents of the Constitution lacked both coordination and unified leadership; "their principles," wrote Oliver Ellsworth, "are totally opposite to each other, and their objections discordant and irreconcilable." The Federalist victory, it appears, was actually more of an Antifederalist default. "We had no principle of concert or union," lamented the South Carolina Antifederalist, Aedanus Burke, while the supporters of the Constitution "left no expedient untried to push it forward." Madison's description of the Massachusetts Antifederalists was applicable to nearly all the states: "There was not a single character capable of uniting their wills or directing their measures. . . . They had no plan whatever. They looked no farther than to put a negative on the Constitution and return home." They were not, as one Federalist put it, "good politicians."

But the Antifederalists were not simply poorer politicians than the Federalists; they were actually different kinds of politicians. Too many of them were state-centered men with local interests and loyalties only, politicians without influence and connections, and ultimately politicians without social and intellectual confidence. In South Carolina the up-country opponents of the Constitution shied from debate and when they did occasionally rise to speak apologized effusively for their inability to say what they felt had to be said, thus leaving most of the opposition to the Constitution to be voiced by Rawlins Lowndes, a low-country planter who scarcely represented their interests and soon retired from the struggle. Elsewhere, in New Hampshire, Connecticut, Massachusetts, Pennsylvania, and North Carolina, the situation was similar: the Federalists had the bulk of talent and influence on their side "together with all the Speakers in the State great and small." In convention after convention the Antifederalists, as in Connecticut, tried to speak, but "they were browbeaten by many of those Cicero'es as they think themselves and others of Superior rank." "The presses are in a great measure secured to *their* side," the Antifederalists complained with justice: out of a hundred or more newspapers printed in the late eighties only a dozen supported the Antifederalists, as editors, "afraid to offend the great men, or Merchants, who could work their ruin," closed their columns to the opposition. The Antifederalists were not so much beaten as overawed. In Massachusetts the two leading socially established Antifederalists, Elbridge Gerry and James Warren, were defeated as delegates to the Ratifying Convention, and Antifederalist leadership consequently fell into the hands of newer, self-made men, of whom Samuel Nasson was perhaps typical—a Maine shopkeeper who was accused of delivering ghostwritten speeches in the Convention. Nasson had previously sat in the General Court but had declined reelection because he had been too keenly made aware of "the want of a proper Education I feel my Self So Small on many occasions that I all most Scrink into Nothing Besides I am often obliged to Borrow from Gentlemen that had advantages which I have not." Now, however, he had become the stoutest of Antifederalists, "full charged with Gass," one of those grumblers who, as Rufus King told Madison, were more afraid of the proponents of the Constitution than the Constitution itself, frightened that "some injury is plotted against them" because of "the extraordinary Union in favor of the Constitution in this State of the Wealthy and sensible part of it."

This fear of a plot by men who "talk so finely and gloss over matters so smoothly" ran through the Antifederalist mind. Because the many "new men" of the 1780's, men like Melancthon Smith and Abraham Yates of New York or John Smilie and William Findley of Pennsylvania, had bypassed the social hierarchy in their rise to political leadership, they lacked those attributes of social distinction and dignity that went beyond mere wealth. Since these kinds of men were never assimilated to the gentlemanly cast of the Livingstons or the Morrises, they, like Americans earlier in confrontation with the British court, tended to view with suspicion and hostility the high-flying world of style and connections that they were barred by their language and tastes, if by nothing else, from sharing in. In the minds of these socially inferior politicians the movement for the strengthening of the central government could only be a "conspiracy" "planned and set to work" by a few aristocrats, who were at first, said Abraham Yates, no larger in any one state than the cabal which sought to undermine English liberty at the beginning of the eighteenth century. . . .

Nothing was more characteristic of Antifederalist thinking than this obsession with aristocracy. Although to a European, American society may have appeared remarkably egalitarian, to many Americans, especially to those who aspired to places of consequence but were made to feel their inferiority in innumerable, often subtle, ways, American society was distinguished by its inequality. "It is true," said Melancthon Smith in the New York Ratifying Convention, "it is our singular felicity that we have no legal or hereditary distinctions . . .; but still there are real differences." "Every society naturally divides itself into classes. . . . Birth, education, talents, and wealth, create distinctions among men as visible, and of as much influence, as titles, stars, and garters." Everyone knew those "whom nature hath destined to rule," declared one sardonic Antifederalist pamphlet. Their "qualifications of authority" were obvious: "such as the dictatorial air, the magisterial voice, the imperious tone, the haughty countenance, the lofty look, the majestic mien." . . .

Such influence was difficult to resist because, to the continual annoyance of the Antifederalists, the great body of the people willingly submitted to it. The "authority of names" and "the influence of the great" among ordinary people were too evident to be denied. "Will any one say that there does not exist in this country the pride of family, of wealth, of talents, and that they do not command influence and respect among the common people?" . . . Because of this habit of deference in the people, it was "in the power of the enlightened and aspiring few, if they should combine, at any time to destroy the best establishments, and even make the people the instruments of their own subjugation." Hence, the Antifederalist-minded declared, the people must be awakened to the consequences of their self-ensnarement; they must be warned over and over by popular tribunes, by "those who are competent to the task of developing the principles of government," of the dangers involved in paying obeisance to those who they thought were their superiors. The people must "not be permitted to consider themselves as a grovelling, distinct species, uninterested in the general welfare." . . .

In these repeated attacks on deference and the capacity of a conspicuous few to speak for the whole society—which was to become in time the distinguishing feature of American democratic politics—the Antifederalists struck at the roots of the traditional conception of political society. If the natural elite, whether its distinctions were ascribed or acquired, was not in any organic way connected to the "feelings, circumstances, and interests" of the people and was incapable of feeling "sympathetically the wants of the people," then it followed that only ordinary men, men not distinguished by the characteristics of aristocratic wealth and taste, men "in middling circumstances" untempted by the attractions of a cosmopolitan world and thus "more temperate, of better morals, and less ambitious, than the great," could be trusted to speak for the great body of the people, for those who were coming more and more to be referred to as "the middling and lower classes of people." The differentiating influence of the environment was such that men in various ranks and classes now seemed to be broken apart from one another, separated by their peculiar circumstances into distinct, unconnected, and often incompatible interests. With their indictment of aristocracy the Antifederalists were saying, whether they realized it or not, that the people of America even in their several states were not homogeneous entities each with a basic similarity of interest for which an empathic elite could speak. Society was not an organic hierarchy composed of ranks and degrees indissolubly linked one to another; rather it was a heterogeneous mixture of "many different classes or orders of people, Merchants, Farmers, Planter Mechanics and Gentry or wealthy Men." In such a society men from one class or group, however educated and respectable they may have been, could never be acquainted with the "*Situation* and Wants" of those of another class or group. Lawyers and planters could never be "adequate judges of tradesmens concerns." If men were truly to represent the people in government, it was not enough for them to be for the people; they had to be actually of the people. "Farmers, traders and mechanics . . . all ought to have a competent number of their best informed members in the legislature."

Thus the Antifederalists were not only directly challenging the conventional belief that only a gentlemanly few, even though now in America naturally and not artificially qualified, were best equipped through learning and experience to represent and to govern the society, but they were as well indirectly denying the assumption of organic social homogeneity on which republicanism rested. Without fully comprehending the consequences of their arguments the Antifederalists were destroying the great chain of being, thus undermining the social basis of republicanism and shattering that unity and harmony of social and political authority which the eighteenth century generally and indeed most Revolutionary leaders had considered essential to the maintenance of order.

Confronted with such a fundamental challenge the Federalists initially backed away. They had no desire to argue the merits of the Constitution in terms of its social implications and were understandably reluctant to open up the character of American society as the central issue of the debate. But in the end they could not resist defending those beliefs in elitism that lay at the heart of their conception of politics and of their constitutional program. All of the Federalists' desires to establish a strong and respectable nation in the world, all of their plans to create a flourishing commercial economy, in short, all of what the Federalists wanted out of the new central government seemed in the final analysis dependent upon the pre-requisite maintenance of aristocratic politics.

At first the Federalists tried to belittle the talk of an aristocracy; they even denied that they knew the meaning of the word. "Why bring into the debate the whims of writers—introducing the distinction of *well-born* from others?" asked Edmund Pendleton in the Virginia Ratifying Convention. In the Federalist view every man was "*well-born* who comes into the world with an intelligent mind, and with all his parts perfect." Was even natural talent to be suspect? Was learning to be en-couraged, the Federalists asked in exasperation, only "to set up those who attained its benefits as butts of invidious distinction?" No American, the Federalists said, could justifiably oppose a man "commencing in life without any other stock but in-dustry and economy," and "by the mere efforts of these" rising "to opulence and wealth." If social mobility were to be meaningful then some sorts of distinctions were necessary. If government by a natural aristocracy, said Wilson, meant "nothing more or less than a government of the best men in the community," then who could object to it? . . .

But the Antifederalist intention and implication were too conspicuous to be avoided: all distinctions, whether naturally based or not, were being challenged. Robert Livingston in the New York Convention saw as clearly as anyone what he thought the Antifederalists were really after, and he minced no words in replying to Smith's attack on the natural aristocracy. Since Smith had classified as aristocrats not only "the rich and the great" but also "the wise, the learned, and those eminent for their talents or great virtues," aristocrats to the Antifederalists had in substance become all men of merit. Such men, such aristocrats, were not to be chosen for public office, questioned Livingston in rising disbelief in the implications of the An-tifederalist argument, "because the people will not have confidence in them; that is, the people will not have confidence in those who best deserve and most possess their confidence?" The logic of Smith's reasoning, said Livingston, would lead to a government by the dregs of society, a monstrous government where all "the unjust, the selfish, the unsocial feelings," where all "the vices, the infirmities, the passions of the people" would be represented. "Can it be thought," asked Livingston in an earlier development of this argument to the Society of the Cincinnati [a hereditary society formed by Revolutionary army officers in 1783], "that an enlightened people believe the science of government level to the meanest capacity? That experience, application, and education are unnecessary to those who are to frame laws for the government of the state?" Yet strange as it may have seemed to Livingston and others in the 1780's, America was actually approaching the point where ability, edu-cation, and wealth were becoming liabilities, not assets, in the attaining of public office. "Envy and the ambition of the unworthy" were robbing respectable men of the rank they merited. "To these causes," said Livingston, "we owe the cloud that ob-scures our internal governments."

The course of the debates over the Constitution seemed to confirm what the Federalists had believed all along. Antifederalism represented the climax of a "war" that was, in the words of Theodore Sedgwick, being "levied on the virtue, property, and distinctions in the community." The opponents of the Constitution, despite some, "particularly in Virginia," who were operating "from the most honorable and patriotic motives," were essentially identical with those who were responsible for the evils the states were suffering from in the eighties—"narrowminded politicians . . . under the influence of local views." "Whilst many *ostensible* reasons are assigned" for the Antifederalists' opposition, charged Washington, "the real ones are concealed behind the Curtains, because they are not of a nature to appear in open day." "The real object of all their zeal in opposing the system," agreed Madison, was to maintain "the supremacy of the State Legislatures," with all that meant in the printing of money and the violation of contracts. The Antifederalists or those for whom the Antifederalists spoke, whether their spokesmen realized it or not, were "none but the horse-jockey, the mushroom merchant, the running and dishonest speculator," those "who owe the most and have the least to pay," those "whose dependence and expectations are upon changes in government, and distracted times," men of "desperate Circumstances," those "in Every State" who "have Debts to pay, Interests to support or Fortunes to make," those, in short, who "wish for scrambling Times." Apart from a few of their intellectual leaders the Antifederalists were thought to be an ill-bred lot: "Their education has been rather indifferent—they have been accustomed to think on the small scale." They were often blustering demagogues trying to push their way into office—"men of much self-importance and supposed skill in politics, who are not of sufficient consequence to obtain public employment." Hence they were considered to be jealous and mistrustful of "every one in the higher offices of society," unable to bear to see others possessing "that fancied blessing, to which, alas! they must themselves aspire in vain." In the Federalist mind therefore the struggle over the Constitution was not one between kinds of wealth or property, or one between commercial or noncommercial elements of the population, but rather represented a broad social division between those who believed in the right of a natural aristocracy to speak for the people and those who did not.

Against this threat from the licentious the Federalists pictured themselves as the defenders of the worthy, of those whom they called "the better sort of people," those, said John Jay, "who are orderly and industrious, who are content with their situations and not uneasy in their circumstances." Because the Federalists were fearful that republican equality was becoming "that *perfect equality* which deadens the motives of industry, and places Demerit on a Footing with Virtue," they were obsessed with the need to insure that the proper amount of inequality and natural distinctions be recognized. . . . Robert Morris, for example, was convinced there were social differences—even in Pennsylvania. "What!" he exclaimed in scornful amazement at John Smilie's argument that a republic admitted of no social superiorities. "Is it insisted that there is no distinction of character?" Respectability, said Morris with conviction, was not confined to property. "Surely persons possessed of knowledge, judgment, information, integrity, and having extensive connections, are not to be classed with persons void of reputation or character." . . .

It was not simply the number of public securities, or credit outstanding, or the number of ships, or the amount of money possessed that made a man think of himself as one of the natural elite. It was much more subtle than the mere possession of wealth: it was a deeper social feeling, a sense of being socially estab-lished, of possessing attributes—family, education, and refinement—that others lacked, above all, of being accepted by and being able to move easily among those who considered themselves to be the respectable and cultivated. It is perhaps anachronistic to describe this social sense as a class interest, for it often tran-scended immediate political or economic concerns, and . . . was designed to cut through narrow occupational categories. The Republicans of Philadelphia, for example, repeatedly denied that they represented an aristocracy with a united class interest. "We are of different occupations; of different sects of religion; and have dif-ferent views of life. No factions or private system can comprehend us all." Yet with all their assertions of diversified interests the Republicans were not without a social consciousness in their quarrel with the supporters of the Pennsylvania Constitution. If there were any of us ambitious for power, their apology continued, then there would be no need to change the Constitution, for we surely could attain power under the present Constitution. "We have already seen how easy the task is for any character to rise into power and consequence under it. And there are some of us, who think not so meanly of ourselves, as to dread any rivalship from those who are now in office."

In 1787 this kind of elitist social consciousness was brought into play as perhaps never before in eighteenth-century America, as gentlemen up and down the continent submerged their sectional and economic differences in the face of what seemed to be a threat to the very foundations of society. Despite his earlier opposition to the Order of the Cincinnati, Theodore Sedgwick, like other frightened New Englanders, now welcomed the organization as a source of strength in the battle for the Constitution. The fear of social disruption that had run through much of the writing of the eighties was brought to a head to eclipse all other fears. . . . The Federalists were astonished at the outpouring in 1787 of influential and re-spectable people who had earlier remained quiescent. Too many of "the better sort of people," it was repeatedly said, had withdrawn at the end of the war "from the theatre of public action, to scenes of retirement and ease," and thus "demagogues of desperate fortunes, mere adventurers in fraud, were left to act unopposed." After all, it was explained, "when the wicked rise, men hide themselves." Even the problems of Massachusetts in 1786, noted General Benjamin Lincoln, the repressor of the Shaysites, were not caused by the rebels, but by the laxity of "the good people of the state." But the lesson of this laxity was rapidly being learned. Everywhere, it seemed, men of virtue, good sense, and property, "almost the whole body of our en-lighten'd and leading characters in every state," were awakened in support of stronger government. "The scum which was thrown upon the surface by the fer-mentation of the war is daily sinking," Benjamin Rush told Richard Price in 1786, "while a pure spirit is occupying its place."

Still, in the face of this preponderance of wealth and respectability in support of the Constitution, what remains extraordinary about 1787–88 is not the weakness and disunity but the political strength of Antifederalism. That large numbers of Americans could actually reject a plan of government created by a body "composed of the first characters in the Continent" and backed by Washington and nearly the whole of the natural aristocracy of the country said more about the changing character of American politics and society in the eighties than did the Constitution's eventual acceptance. It was indeed a portent of what was to come. . . .

If the new national government was to promote the common good as forcefully as any state government, and if, as the Federalists believed, a major source of the vices of the eighties lay in the abuse of state power, then there was something apparently contradictory about the new federal Constitution, which after all represented not a weakening of the dangerous power of republican government but rather a strengthening of it. "The complaints against the separate governments, even by the friends of the new plan," remarked the Antifederalist James Winthrop, "are not that they have not power enough, but that they are disposed to make a bad use of what power they have." . . . What, in other words, was different about the new federal Constitution that would enable it to mitigate the effects of tyrannical majorities? What would keep the new federal government from succumbing to the same pressures that had beset the state governments? The answer the Federalists gave to these questions unmistakably reveals the social bias underlying both their fears of the unrestrained state legislatures and their expectations for their federal remedy. . . .

The Federalists were not as much opposed to the governmental power of the states as to the character of the people who were wielding it. The constitutions of most of the states were not really at fault. Massachusetts after all possessed a nearly perfect constitution. What actually bothered the Federalists was the sort of people who had been able to gain positions of authority in the state governments, particularly in the state legislatures. Much of the quarrel with the viciousness, instability, and injustice of the various state governments was at bottom social. "For," as John Dickinson emphasized, *"the government will partake of the qualities of those whose authority is prevalent."* . . . Since "it cannot be expected that things will go well, when persons of vicious principles, and loose morals are in authority," it was the large number of obscure, ignorant, and unruly men occupying the state legislatures, and not the structure of the governments, that was the real cause of the evils so much complained of.

The Federalist image of the Constitution as a sort of "philosopher's stone" was indeed appropriate: it was a device intended to transmute base materials into gold and thereby prolong the life of the republic. Patrick Henry acutely perceived what the Federalists were driving at. "The Constitution," he said in the Virginia Convention, "reflects in the most degrading and mortifying manner on the virtue, integrity, and wisdom of the state legislatures; it presupposes that the chosen few who go to Congress will have more upright hearts, and more enlightened minds, than those who are members of the individual legislatures." The new Constitution was structurally no different from the constitutions of some of the states. Yet the powers of the new central government were not as threatening as the powers of the state governments precisely because the Federalists believed different kinds of persons would hold them. They anticipated that somehow the new government would be staffed largely by "the worthy," the naturally social aristocracy of the country. "After all," said Pelatiah Webster, putting his finger on the crux of the Federalist argument, "the grand secret of forming a good government, is, to put good men into the administration: for wild, vicious, or idle men, will ever make a bad government, let its principles be ever so good."

What was needed then, the Federalists argued, was to restore a proper share of political influence to those who through their social attributes commanded the respect of the people and who through their enlightenment and education knew the true policy of government. "The people commonly intend the PUBLIC GOOD," wrote Hamilton in The Federalist, but they did not "always reason right about the means of promoting it." They sometimes erred, largely because they were continually beset "by the wiles of parasites and sycophants, by the snares of the ambitious, the avaricious, the desperate, by the artifices of men who possess their confidence more than deserve it, and of those who seek to possess rather than to deserve it." The rights of man were simple, quickly felt, and easily comprehended: in matters of liberty, "the mechanic and the philosopher, the farmer and the scholar are all upon a footing." But to the Federalists matters of government were quite different: government was "a complicated science, and requires abilities and knowledge, of a variety of other subjects, to understand it." "Our states cannot be well governed," the Federalists concluded, "till our old influential characters acquire confidence and authority." Only if the respected and worthy lent their natural intellectual abilities and their natural social influence to political authority could governmental order be maintained.

Perhaps no one probed this theme more frenziedly than did Jonathan Jackson in his Thoughts upon the Political Situation of the United States, published in 1788. For Jackson the problems of the eighties were not merely intellectual but personal. Although at the close of the Revolution he had been one of the half-dozen richest residents of Newburyport, Massachusetts, by the end of the eighties not only had his wealth been greatly diminished but his position in Newburyport society had been usurped by a newer, less well-educated, less refined group of merchants. His pamphlet, expressing his bitter reaction to this displacement, exaggerated but did not misrepresent a common Federalist anxiety.

Although differences of rank were inevitable in every society, wrote Jackson, "there never was a people upon earth . . . who were in less hazard than the people of this country, of an aristocracy's prevailing—or anything like it, dangerous to liberty." America possessed very little "inequality of fortune." There was "no rank of any consequence, nor hereditary titles." "Landed property is in general held in small portions, even in southern states, compared with the manors, parks and royal demesnes of most countries." And the decay of primogeniture and entail, together with the "diverse" habits and passions between fathers and sons, worked to retard the engrossing of large estates. The only kind of aristocracy possible in America would be an "aristocracy of experience, and of the best understandings," a "natural aristocracy" that had to dominate public authority in order to prevent America from degenerating into democratic licentiousness, into a government where the people "would be directed by no rule but their own will and caprice, or the interested wishes of a very few persons, who affect to speak the sentiments of the people." . . .

In a review of Jackson's pamphlet Noah Webster raised the crucial question. It was commendable, he wrote, that only the wise and honest men be elected to office. "But how can a constitution ensure the choice of such men? A constitution that leaves the choice entirely with the people?" It was not enough simply to state that such persons were to be chosen. Indeed, many of the state constitutions already declared "that senators and representatives *shall* be elected from the *most wise, able,* and *honest* citizens. . . . The truth is, such declarations are *empty things,* as they require *that* to be *done* which cannot be *defined,* much less *enforced.*" It seemed to Webster that no constitution in a popular state could guarantee that only the natural aristocracy would be elected to office. How could the federal Constitution accomplish what the state constitutions like Massachusetts's and Connecticut's had been unable to accomplish? How could it insure that only the respectable and worthy would hold power?

The evils of state politics, the Federalists had become convinced, flowed from the narrowness of interest and vision of the state legislators. "We find the representatives of countries and corporations in the Legislatures of the States," said Madison, "much more disposed to sacrifice the aggregate interest, and even authority, to the local views of their Constituents" than to promote the general good at the expense of their electors. Small electoral districts enabled obscure and designing men to gain power by practicing "the vicious arts by which elections are too often carried." Already observers in the eighties had noticed that a governmental official "standing, not on local, but a general election of the whole body of the people" tended to have a superior, broader vision by "being the interested and natural conservator of the universal interest." "The most effectual remedy for the local biass" of senators or of any elected official, said Madison, was to impress upon their minds "an attention to the interest of the whole Society by making them the choice of the whole Society." If elected officials were concerned with only the interest of those who elected them, then their outlook was most easily broadened by enlarging their electorate. Perhaps nowhere was this contrast between localism and cosmopolitanism more fully analyzed and developed than in a pamphlet written by William Beers of Connecticut. Although Beers wrote in 1791, not to justify the Constitution, his insight into the workings of American politics was precisely that of the Federalists of 1787.

"The people of a state," wrote Beers, "may justly be divided into two classes": those, on one hand, "who are independent in their principles, of sound judgments, actuated by no local or personal influence, and who understand, and ever act with a view to the public good"; and those, on the other hand, who were "the dependent, the weak, the biassed, local party men—the dupes of artifice and ambition." . . . [T]he best people were often overpowered in small district elections, where "the success of a candidate may depend in a great degree on the quantity of his exertions for the moment," on his becoming "popular, for a single occasion, by qualities and means, which could not possibly establish a permanent popularity or one which should pervade a large community," on his seizing "the occasion of some prevailing passion, some strong impression of separate interest, some popular clamor against the existing administration, or some other false and fatal prejudice." . . . But an entire state could not be so deluded. "No momentary glare of deceptive qualities, no intrigues, no exertions will be sufficient to make a whole people lose sight of those points of character which alone can entitle one to their universal confidence."

With a large electorate the advance toward public honors was slow and gradual. "Much time is necessary to become the object of general observation and confidence." Only established social leaders would thus be elected by a broad constituency. Narrow the electorate, "and you leave but a single step between the lowest and the most elevated station. You take ambition by the hand, you raise her from obscurity, and clothe her in purple." With respect to the size of the legislative body, the converse was true. Reduce the number of its members and thereby guarantee a larger proportion of the right kind of people to be elected, for "the more you enlarge the body, the greater chance there is, of introducing weak and unqualified men."

Constitutional reformers in the eighties had continually attempted to apply these insights to the states, by decreasing the size of the legislatures and by proposing at-large elections for governors and senators in order to "make a segregation of upright, virtuous, intelligent men, to guide the helm of public affairs." Now these ideas were to be applied to the new federal government with hopefully even more effectiveness. The great height of the new national government, it was expected, would prevent unprincipled and vicious men, the obscure and local-minded men who had gained power in the state legislatures, from scaling its walls. The federal government would act as a kind of sieve, extracting "from the mass of the society the purest and noblest characters which it contains." Election by the people in large districts would temper demagoguery and crass electioneering and would thus, said James Wilson, "be most likely to obtain men of intelligence and uprightness." "Faction," it was believed, "will decrease in proportion to the diminution of counsellors." It would be "transferred from the state legislatures to Congress, where it will be more easily controlled." The men who would sit in the federal legislature, because few in number and drawn from a broad electorate, would be "the best men in the country." "For," wrote John Jay in The Federalist, "although town or country, or other contracted influence, may place men in State assemblies, or senates, or courts of justice, or executive departments, yet more general and extensive reputation for talents and other qualifications will be necessary to recommend men to offices under the national government." Only by first bringing these sorts of men, the natural aristocracy of the country, back into dominance in politics, the Federalists were convinced, could Americans begin to solve the pressing foreign and domestic problems facing them. Only then, concluded Jay, would it "result that the administration, the political counsels, and the judicial decisions of the national government will be more wise, systematical, and judicious than those of individual States, and consequently more satisfactory with respect to other nations, as well as more safe with respect to us." The key therefore to the prospects of the new federal government, compared to the experience of the confederation of sovereign states, declared Francis Corbin of Virginia in words borrowed from Jean Louis De Lolme, the Genevan commentator on the English constitution, lay in the fact that the federal Constitution "places the remedy in the hands which feel the disorder; the other places the remedy in those hands which cause the disorder."

In short, through the artificial contrivance of the Constitution overlying an expanded society, the Federalists meant to restore and to prolong the traditional kind of elitist influence in politics that social developments, especially since the Revolution, were undermining. As the defenders if not always the perpetrators of these developments—the "disorder" of the 1780's—the Antifederalists could scarcely have missed the social implications of the Federalist program. The Constitution was intrinsically an aristocratic document designed to check the democratic tendencies of the period, and as such it dictated the character of the Antifederalist response. It was therefore inevitable that the Antifederalists should have charged that the new government was "dangerously adapted to the purposes of an immediate *aristocratic tyranny.*" In state after state the Antifederalists reduced the issue to those social terms predetermined by the Federalists themselves: the Constitution was a plan intended to "raise the fortunes and respectability of the *well-born few,* and oppress the plebians"; it was "a continental exertion of the *well-born* of America to obtain that darling domination, which they have not been able to accomplish in their respective states"; it "will lead to an aristocratical government, and establish tyranny over us." . . .

Aristocratic principles were in fact "interwoven" in the very fabric of the proposed government. If a government was "so constituted as to admit but few to exercise the powers of it," then it would "according to the natural course of things" end up in the hands of "the natural aristocracy." It went almost without saying that the awesome president and the exalted Senate, "a compound of *monarchy* and *aristocracy,*" would be dangerously far removed from the people. But even the House of Representatives, the very body that "should be a true picture of the people, possess a knowledge of their circumstances and their wants, sympathize in all their distresses, and disposed to seek their true interest," was without "a tincture of democracy." Since it could never collect "the interests, feelings, and opinions of three or four millions of people," it was better understood as "an Assistant Aristocratical Branch" to the Senate than as a real representation of the people. . . . The Antifederalists thus came to oppose the new national government for the same reason the Federalists favored it: because its very structure and detachment from the people would work to exclude any kind of actual and local interest representation and prevent those who were not rich, well-born, or prominent from exercising political power. Both sides fully appreciated the central issue the Constitution posed and grappled with it throughout the debates: whether a professedly popular government should actually be in the hands of, rather than simply derived from, common ordinary people.

Out of the division in 1787–88 over this issue, an issue which was as conspicuously social as any in American history, the Antifederalists emerged as the spokesmen for the growing American antagonism to aristocracy and as the defenders of the most intimate participation in politics of the widest variety of people possible. It was not from lack of vision that the Antifederalists feared the new government. Although their viewpoint was intensely localist, it was grounded in as perceptive an understanding of the social basis of American politics as that of the Federalists. Most of the Antifederalists were majoritarians with respect to the state legislatures but not with respect to the national legislature, because they presumed as well as the Federalists did that different sorts of people from those who sat in the state assemblies would occupy the Congress. Whatever else may be said about the Antifederalists, their populism cannot be impugned. They were true champions of the most extreme kind of democratic and egalitarian politics expressed in the Revolutionary era. Convinced that "it has been the principal care of free governments to guard against the encroachments of the great," the Antifederalists believed that popular government itself, as defined by the principles of 1776, was endangered by the new national government. If the Revolution had been a transfer of power from the few to the many, then the federal Constitution clearly represented an abnegation of the Revolution. For, as Richard Henry Lee wrote in his *Letters from the Federal Farmer,* "every man of reflection must see, that the change now proposed, is a transfer of power from the many to the few." . . .

To the Federalists the greatest dangers to republicanism were flowing not, as the old Whigs had thought, from the rulers or from any distinctive minority in the community, but from the widespread participation of the people in the government. It now seemed increasingly evident that if the public good not only of the United States as a whole but even of the separate states were to be truly perceived and promoted, the American people must abandon their Revolutionary reliance on their representative state legislatures and place their confidence in the highmindedness of the natural leaders of the society, which ideally everyone had the opportunity of becoming. Since the Federalists presumed that only such a self-conscious elite could transcend the many narrow and contradictory interests inevitable in any society, however small, the measure of a good government became its capacity for insuring the predominance of these kinds of natural leaders who knew better than the people as a whole what was good for the society.

The result was an amazing display of confidence in constitutionalism, in the efficacy of institutional devices for solving social and political problems. Through the proper arrangement of new institutional structures the Federalists aimed to turn the political and social developments that were weakening the place of "the better sort of people" in government back upon themselves and to make these developments the very source of the perpetuation of the natural aristocracy's dominance of politics. Thus the Federalists did not directly reject democratic politics as it had manifested itself in the 1780's; rather they attempted to adjust to this politics in order to control and mitigate its effects. In short they offered the country an elitist theory of democracy. They did not see themselves as repudiating either the Revolution or popular government, but saw themselves as saving both from their excesses. If the Constitution were not established, they told themselves and the country over and over, then republicanism was doomed, the grand experiment was over, and a division of the confederacy, monarchy, or worse would result. . . .

Suggested Readings

General

Willi Paul Adams, *The First American Constitutions: Republican Ideology and the Making of the State Constitutions in the Revolutionary Era* (1980).

Richard Beeman, et al., eds., *Beyond Confederation: Origins of the Constitution and American National Identity* (1987).

Linda K. Kerber, *Women of the Republic; Intellect and Ideology in Revolutionary America* (1980).

Forrest MacDonald, *Norvus Ordo Seclorum: The Intellectual Origins of the Constitution* (1985).

Jackson Turner Main, *The Antifederalists: Critics of the Constitution, 1781–1788* (1961).

John P. Roche, "The Founding Fathers: A Reform Caucus in Action," *American Political Science Review*, vol. 55 (December 1961).

Clinton Rossiter, *1787: The Grand Convention* (1973).

Thomas P. Slaughter, *The Whiskey Rebellion: Frontier Epilogue to the American Revolution* (1986).

David P. Szatmary, *Shays' Rebellion: The Making of an Agrarian Insurrection* (1980).

Gordon S. Wood, *The Creation of the American Republic* (1969) and *The Radicalism of the American Revolution* (1992).

Republicanism and Politics in the Post-Revolutionary Period

Ronald Hoffman, *A Spirit of Dissension: Economics, Politics and the Revolution in Maryland* (1987); Donald S. Lutz, *Popular Consent and Popular Control: Whig Political Theory in the Early State Constitutions* (1980); Peter Onuf, *The Origins of the Federal Republic* (1983); and Jack Rakove, *The Beginnings of National Politics: An Interpretive History of the Continental Congress* (1979).

Articles of Confederation and the Critical Period

David Brion Davis, *The Problem of Slavery in the Age of Revolution, 1770–1823* (1975); Forrest MacDonald, *E Pluribus Unum: The Formation of the American Republic, 1776–1790* (1965); Jackson Turner Main, *Political Parties Before the Constitution* (1973); and Chilton Williamson, *American Suffrage from Property to Democracy, 1760–1860* (1960).

Constitutional Convention

J. Jackson Barlow, et al., *The American Founding: Essays on the Formation of the Constitution* (1988); Christopher Collier and James Collier, *Decision in Philadelphia* (1986); Richard Morris, *Witnesses at the Creation: Hamilton, Madison, Jay and the Constitution* (1985); and Robert Rutland, *James Madison, the Founding Father* (1987).

QUESTIONS FOR DISCUSSION

1. What role did civic virtue play in American concepts of republicanism? According to proponents of that ideology, how was virtue to be maintained?

2. Identify the salient features of the Articles of Confederation. Describe the successes of the Confederation government.

3. In what ways did Shays' Rebellion highlight the weaknesses of the Articles of Confederation?
4. How did the delegates to the Constitutional Convention propose to divide power between the federal and state governments?
5. Describe the Federalist and Antifederalist positions during the ratification fight for the Constitution. Why did the Federalists succeed?
6. After reading the article by Gordon S. Wood, do you believe that the Federalist leadership advocated democracy? Explain.
7. In Wood's view, why did the Antifederalists oppose the Constitution?

C H A P T E R   S I X

THE NEW REPUBLIC, 1788–1815

GEORGE WASHINGTON

CREATING THE PRESIDENCY

As the first president of the United States, George Washington confronted circumstances which, as one historian has noted, were unprecedented in history and would never recur in the history of the American presidency. He had been elected to preside over a newborn, disorganized nation adrift in an alien and hostile world. His only guides were a constitution that left much to be worked out in practice and the discussions during the constitutional convention that he had followed closely as the presiding officer of that body. With King George III as their only point of reference in considering the chief executive of the new republic, the convention delegates looked to General Washington as the individual who, more than any other, possessed the attributes that struck the desired balance between strength and restraint.

Although Americans of all ranks idolized him as one whose career and character amply justified his reputation for integrity, dignity, candor, and republican virtue, Washington himself was awed by the burden that he had shouldered in assuming the helm of an extraordinary experiment. Though flattered to be considered the indispensable man, he succumbed to "anxious and painful sensations" as he contemplated his entry into "an unexplored field, enveloped on every side by clouds and darkness." Recognition that the extraordinary public confidence in him carried with it extravagant expectations only heightened his apprehensions. Though unable to discern where the voyage he was embarking on would lead him or what it would accomplish, he was certain of one thing: he was quitting his tranquil life at Mount Vernon for what he called an "ocean of difficulties."

George Washington entered New York to assume the office of president before an enthusiastic crowd.

But once having accepted the office that he had been elected to without a single dissent in 1788, Washington refused to allow his apprehensions to lead to a paralysis of will or a loss of direction. Rather, for him, anxiety induced extra caution and a dogged, singleminded adherence to the job of nation building. Despite his lack of expertise in public finance, political tactics, and foreign policy, Washington proved to be an honest, canny and methodical administrator and a strong, "virtuous" leader. Above all, his unique standing with the people was a priceless asset that served him and the young nation extraordinarily well.

Establishing Precedents

No sooner was Washington settled in the office of president than the agitation that erupted over titles, ceremony, and official etiquette confirmed his view that the new government would be forced to travel over untrodden ground. Every action of the president and his government, whether of small or large import, was closely scrutinized and was likely to establish precedent. When the president, plagued by hordes of visitors from breakfast to bedtime, announced a policy that limited "visits of compliment" to one hour on Tuesday and Friday afternoons and that allowed the chief executive neither to return visits nor accept invitations, critics complained bitterly that he had forsaken republicanism for the ways of a monarch. Striking a balance between free intercourse and calculated reserve was all the more difficult because of the existence of tensions between republican and monarchical strains in American political culture. For example, when Thomas Jefferson arrived in New York, the first seat of the new government, to become Washington's secretary of state, he was appalled by the aristocratic sympathies and pretensions that dominated social life in the city. The president finally devised a scheme for receiving guests that worked fairly well but did not preclude references to an American court similar to that of the British monarchy.

The Matter of Titles

All the while, Congress occupied itself with matters of etiquette and titles. Vice President John Adams, among others, proposed to surround the government with dignity and splendor and to bestow upon its officers high-sounding titles. Critics were quick to denounce all high-sounding titles as monarchism plain and simple. The model of the Roman Republic that required both simplicity and dignity as the twin standards of public conduct ultimately prevailed, and "the President of the United States" was adopted as the proper form of address for the president. Because of his public stand on the propriety of titles and matters of style and procedure, Adams never fully lived down charges that he secretly favored monarchy. One congressman gave the portly vice president a special title—"His Rotundity."

Washington's Cabinet

Since the Constitution created only the outline of the new government, the job of Congress was to fill in the details and make the government work. In the summer of 1789 Congress authorized four executive departments—state, treasury, war, and attorney general—which corresponded more or less to those in existence under the Confederation. President Washington appointed (and the Senate confirmed) Thomas Jefferson, former minister to France, as secretary of state; Alexander Hamilton, a New York lawyer and aide-de-camp to Washington during the Revolution, as secretary of the treasury; Henry Knox as secretary of war to preside over a minuscule army and a nonexistent navy; and Edmund Randolph, who, like Jefferson, had been governor of Virginia, as attorney general. In time Washington routinely convened these department heads to advise him on matters of policy, a practice that gave rise to the concept of the cabinet.

The president surrounded himself with immensely talented and independent-minded men, particularly Jefferson and Hamilton. The thirty-five-year-old Hamilton was the moving force in the administration. Born in the West Indies and the illegitimate son of a Scottish merchant, he was brilliant, quick-witted, excitable, highly knowledgeable about public finance, and sometimes indiscreet. To compensate for his lowly origins he constantly strove to achieve status, wealth, and power. Although Hamilton possessed the admiration and usually the ear of the president, Washington remained the leader of his administration.

CONSTITUTIONAL AMENDMENTS: THE BILL OF RIGHTS

High on the agenda of the new government was a series of amendments to the Constitution that became known as the Bill of Rights. Taking the lead in this effort was James Madison of Virginia who sought to fulfill earlier promises to Antifederalists and to placate their fears by pushing these amendments through Congress. He successfully thwarted efforts to alter the fundamental character of the Constitution. To the disappointment of Antifederalists, the twelve amendments approved by Congress and submitted to the states focused more on protecting the rights of individuals rather than the rights of states. Of the twelve amendments, ten were approved. These included guarantees of freedom of religion, speech, press, and assembly and protection for rights of accused persons. Only the ninth and tenth amendments represented concessions to the main fear of the Antifederalists, namely unlimited federal government power. The Tenth Amendment reserved for states or for the people those powers not specifically delegated by the Constitution to the federal government. The ten amendments that made up the Bill of Rights and became effective on December 15, 1791, helped bring North Carolina into the Union late in 1789 and Rhode Island in mid-1790. The federal Union now possessed all of the original thirteen colonies as states.

THE FEDERAL JUDICIARY

Another pressing issue that confronted the first Congress was the creation of a system of federal courts. Article III of the Constitution merely stated that the judicial power of the United States was to "be vested in one supreme court and in such inferior courts as Congress may from time to time ordain and establish." It did not even specify the number of justices to sit on the supreme bench. Because of wide differences within Federalist ranks over the scope of federal judicial power, the Judiciary Act, passed in 1789, was a compromise between the views of those such as Hamilton, who desired a powerful federal judiciary that would provide uniform civil justice, and those who feared that the state courts would be swallowed up by such a federal system. The act created a Supreme Court of six justices and a system of two circuit and thirteen district courts, all with restricted jurisdiction. Although the law fell short of the strong federal judiciary envisioned by Hamilton and others, section 25 of the law represented a victory of sorts for such a view by providing for appeals in certain instances from state courts to the federal judiciary.

THE FEDERAL TREASURY

Perhaps the most critical and certainly the most explosive issue that demanded the attention of the first Congress concerned government finance. The proposals put forward in a series of reports by Secretary of the Treasury Alexander Hamilton addressed questions of taxation, debts, a national bank, and other matters. These reports prompted deep divisions within Federalist ranks and pitted against each other those who had cooperated in drafting the Constitution and in getting it ratified. Hamilton's recommendations appeared to affect the balance of power between the federal government and the states and brought into conflict two widely different visions of the character of the republic. Hamilton's scheme envisioned a complex, commercialized society in which the business class was the most dynamic force and in which the role of states was subordinate to that of a strong, activist federal government. Such a vision of the republic diverged sharply from that embraced by Madison, Jefferson, and others who thought in terms of a simpler rural, agricultural society that emphasized the rights and powers of states. The rift within Federalist ranks over questions concerning government finance not only exposed diverging sectional interests but also sowed the seeds of the first national political parties which matured slowly, in large part because of the widespread view that parties and factions were synonymous with political corruption.

The Debt Issue

Congress received Hamilton's first set of recommendations, the *Report on the Public Credit*, in January 1790. Most members agreed that the federal government should honor its debts in order to establish public credit, but what sparked acrimonious controversy was Hamilton's recommendation about how this should be done and under what terms. To safeguard the government, the secretary made two key recommendations: the funding of the federal debt at face value and the assumption by the federal government of all state debts remaining from the Revolution. As for the $12 million debt owed foreigners, he recommended that it be paid off in full with the income from the sale of public lands in the west. The remaining debt—$45 million inherited from the Confederation and owed American citizens and the $25 million worth of states' debts—was to be funded (but not paid off) which meant that citizens who owned government securities could exchange them for new interest-bearing bonds of the same face value. Because bondholders would have a stake in the federal government, Hamilton reasoned, they would support and respect its authority. For him, public debt of manageable size was "a national blessing."

Leading the opposition to the *Report on Public Credit* was Hamilton's fellow author of *The Federalist*, James Madison, who was convinced that the funding of the debt at face value favored speculators over the more deserving original owners of government securities. A large proportion of the debt certificates issued by the Confederation went to the Revolutionary patriots who out of dire necessity had been forced to sell them to speculators at greatly devalued rates. Madison tried in vain to secure some compensation for original owners. However defensible Hamilton's refusal to discriminate between original and current owners of debt certificates may have been, it created widespread resentment, especially among those ordinary citizens who had in fact sold their certificates at great losses to speculators.

The squabble over the funding feature of Hamilton's report paled beside that calling for the assumption of state debts. In general, the attitude of members of Congress toward assumption was determined by the size of the debt of their states. Those from states, primarily in the North, with large debts supported Hamilton's proposal, while those in the South that had retired much or most of their debts opposed it. Southerners also opposed it on the grounds that it would strengthen the federal government at the expense of the states. The stalemate in Congress over the issue was finally broken when Hamilton, Jefferson, and Madison struck the so-called Compromise of 1790 by which the two Virginians agreed to help get the assumption passed in return for Hamilton's endorsement of the permanent location of the nation's capital in the South. The capital was to be moved from New York to Philadelphia and then, after a decade, to a federal district on the Potomac River. Aided by this bargain, Hamilton secured the enactment of the two major items of his report, funding and assumption, but at the cost of aggravating sectional fears and suspicions that a radically different conception of the republic was being substituted for the one embraced by those who favored an agrarian-based, states' rights republic.

Manufacturers and the Tariff

Hamilton's recommendations regarding the establishment of a mint and the levying of excise taxes on whiskey, enacted in 1791 and 1792 respectively, aroused little controversy. Congress not only authorized the establishment of a mint, but also defined the dollar as the numerical monetary unit. In his *Report on Manufacturers*, delivered to Congress in December 1791, Hamilton hoped to inspire Americans to strive for economic self-sufficiency, to survive in a world of increasing restrictions on American trade. The report recommended protective tariffs to aid "infant industries," bounties for the establishment of new industries, and awards for the invention of labor-saving machinery. As a blueprint for "a more perfect economic union," the report envisioned an agricultural south that would become indissolubly linked to an industrial-commercial north. Southerners refused to share Hamilton's optimistic prediction that such an arrangement would obliterate sectional jealousies; rather, they interpreted his report as outlining a system that consigned them and their section to the status of producers of raw materials for northern merchants, shippers, and manufacturers—a system that they equated with the one imposed by the British on the American colonies. Hamilton's *Report on Manufacturers*, designed to lay the foundation for a systematic fostering of industry by government, actually prompted little legislative response. Congress did enact a tariff, but not as highly protective as he desired. The tariff act of 1792 raised rates slightly to produce revenue rather than to protect "infant industry."

A National Bank

Of all of Hamilton's recommendations the one concerning the creation of a national bank, presented to Congress in January 1791, generated the most heated debates and created a permanent rupture within Federalist ranks. The report's call for the establishment of the Bank of the United States, patterned after the Bank of England, caused Jefferson to join Madison in openly opposing Hamilton and his vision of the republic. Hamilton proposed a national bank in which the federal government owed 25 percent of the stock and appointed five members to its twenty-five-member board of directors. Private stockholders would own the remaining stock and appoint twenty directors. The bank's directors were required to make frequent reports to the secretary of the Treasury to ensure that all regulations were observed. As the principal depository of government funds and as the fiscal agent of the Treasury in domestic and foreign operations, the bank was also to exert control on the operations of state banks. The most important function that Hamilton assigned to the bank was the issuance of bank notes which were to be the principal circulating medium of money for a society that lacked an adequate supply of specie (gold and silver coin). Since the federal government would accept these bank notes at face value in payment of taxes, it was unlikely that their value would depreciate or that citizens would redeem them in coin. In many respects, the bank was the linchpin of Hamilton's entire program, tying together the central government and the nation's commercial interests.

Under the leadership of Madison, congressional opponents of the bank likened the institution to the Bank of England and claimed that it was designed to aid the mercantile interest at the expense of the vast majority of the nation's citizens who were farmers and would derive no benefit from it. However, the main objections to the bank raised by Jefferson, Madison, and other opponents were constitutional in nature. The bank proposal, they argued, was an unwarranted and unconstitutional assertion of congressional power. Assuming a "strict construction" of the Constitution, they insisted that nowhere in the document was Congress specifically authorized to issue charters of incorporation such as that proposed in the case of the bank. Failure to follow strict construction was, in their view, the surest way for the federal government to assume unlimited power that would undermine the rights of states and threaten individual liberty. Hamilton responded by invoking the concept of "implied power" and "broad construction" of the Constitution. He insisted that Congress' authority to charter a bank was implied by Article 1, Section 2, which gave Congress the right to make all laws deemed "necessary and proper" to carry out its delegated powers.

The bank legislation ultimately passed Congress by a slim margin. Although President Washington had doubts about the measure's constitutionality, he finally accepted Hamilton's views and signed it into law in February 1791. A triumph for the secretary's "broad construction" of the Constitution, the measure chartered the Bank of the United States for a period of twenty years. As the bank demonstrated in time, "broad construction" and implied powers gave the nation the flexibility to respond to unanticipated crises and developments.

Conflict over Finance Theory

To a remarkable degree, Hamilton had succeeded in securing the enactment of a financial program that incorporated his vision of the United States—a strong central government that protected and stimulated industry and commerce and that fostered close ties between that government and men of wealth. For Jefferson and Madison, such a vision was anathema. Although both men were familiar with the workings of the marketplace and recognized that some commercial activity was essential, they distrusted large-scale commerce, cities, and especially the aristocratic pretensions of Hamilton and his followers. Jefferson prized the virtues of the independent yeomanry as providing the foundation of the republic. For him, small farmers were "the chosen people of God" in whom the Almighty had deposited "substantial and genuine virtue."

Those who shared the views of Jefferson and Madison emphasized the need for the nation's farmers to retain their independence lest their virtue be compromised. Unlike Hamilton, they did not believe that a national debt was a blessing but rather it fostered dependence and subservience and compromised personal autonomy, integrity, and virtue. Jefferson and Madison opposed Hamilton's excise tax on whiskey as an unwarranted burden on trans-Appalachian grain farmers whose staple crop could be transported more easily and less expensively when reduced to liquid form. But it was the bank that contributed most to the growing perception of the Hamiltonian financial system as a scheme to transform and even subvert the Constitution by inducing a small group of influential and wealthy individuals to support certain measures of public policy out of avarice and self-interest rather than out of any sense of selflessness and civic responsibility which was essential to the preservation of the republic as men like Jefferson and Madison envisioned it.

Within a few days after Washington signed the bank bill, Jefferson, Madison, and others initiated efforts to establish a newspaper in Philadelphia that would espouse their views and counteract Hamilton's editorial mouthpiece, the *United States Gazette*. The launching of the *National Gazette* under the editorship of Philip Freneau, a poet, provided a vehicle for the airing of a vision of the republic at odds with that of Hamilton. The battle of the gazettes not only brought to a new level of intensity the ideological struggle between what Madison called "the enemies and friends of republican government," but also marked a significant step in the evolution of the first national political parties. Within Washington's cabinet the animosity between Hamilton and Jefferson, much to the president's regret, escalated into open warfare.

DOMESTIC ISSUES

The West and Native Americans

Rising above the intensified ideological warfare and factionalism, President Washington with his enormous prestige managed to hold the young government together and to lead the nation through an era fraught with internal and ex-

FIGURE 6–1

Securing the West, 1790–1796

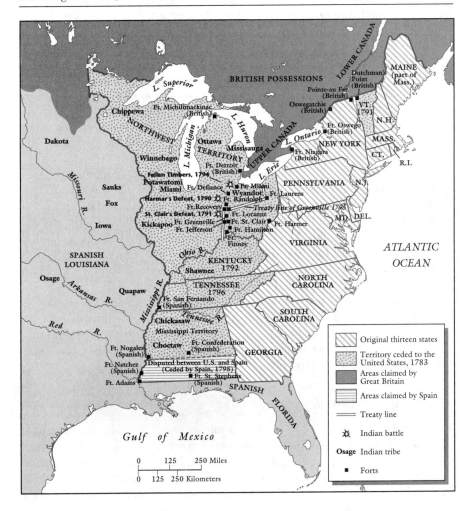

ternal crises. Unanimously reelected in 1792, he confronted a host of problems related to turmoil in the West and an increasingly menacing international environment. Isolated from the eastern states and burdened with the backbreaking task of carving farms out of the wilderness, settlers in the vast area between the Appalachians and the Mississippi also confronted multiple tribes of hostile natives—the Miamis, Shawnees, Ottawas, Chippewas, Sauks, and Fox—who resisted the white man's encroachments on their land (see Figure 6–1). When confronted by the refusal of the tribes in the old Northwest to transfer their lands, President Washington dispatched two military expeditions in 1790 to force Indian acquiescence. Both were defeated. Not until a large army under

General Anthony Wayne routed the Indians in the Battle of Fallen Timbers in 1794 were the natives forced to sign a treaty that opened much of present-day Ohio to white settlement. A degree of peace then returned to the Northwest. Not only did Wayne's assault decimate the Indians, it also challenged the presence of British troops still in the area and ultimately led to a promise that they would evacuate American soil. White Americans surged into the area to lay claim to the land. Reflecting the view of Hamilton and others who saw the sale of public lands primarily as a source of government revenue, the Land Act of 1796 required the purchase of a minimum of 640 acres at $2 per acre and the payment of the full amount within a year. Because most settlers and few speculators could afford to purchase lands under the act, the demand for more favorable terms led to additional land legislation in 1800 and 1804.

In the meantime, Washington had initiated efforts to strengthen the government's hold on the West by negotiating a treaty with Spain. Like the British, the Spaniards had persisted in efforts to provoke Indian raids and had conspired to detach the West from the young republic. Spain controlled Florida, the vast Louisiana territory, and the Mississippi River including New Orleans, a vital link with the outside world for the shipment of the produce of western settlers. In 1795 Thomas Pinckney negotiated a treaty (the Pinckney Treaty) with Spain that established the 31st parallel as the southern boundary of the United States, granted Americans free access to the Mississippi, and the right to deposit goods at New Orleans for transshipment elsewhere. The treaty also provided for the creation of a commission to settle American claims against the Spanish and a promise by each party to refrain from inciting Indian attacks on the other. Ratification of the Pinckney Treaty encountered virtually no opposition.

The Whiskey Rebellion

In the midst of attempting to resolve problems posed by Indians, the British, and the Spaniards, Washington confronted a crisis in the West involving American citizens. Throughout the backcountry farmers opposed the excise tax on whiskey which they claimed threatened their livelihood. What began as peaceful protests escalated in 1794 into large-scale resistance in western Pennsylvania known as the Whiskey Rebellion. Federal tax collectors were terrorized, federal court proceedings were disrupted, and a small force of regular troops were forced to surrender to the "Whiskey Boys."

President Washington decided to respond vigorously to the uprising, lest it spread in the backcountry from Georgia to New York where opposition to taxation was strong. When his proclamation urging the insurgents to desist failed to have the desired effect, he called for 12,900 volunteers, and received an enthusiastic response. Washington, who personally led the army, found himself at the head of a force larger than any he had commanded during the War of Independence. The rebellion quickly evaporated in the face of such an overwhelming force. Returning to Philadelphia, Washington placed Hamilton, who had accompanied him and who considered the whole affair simple lawlessness, in charge of making arrests. Rounding up about a hundred and fifty suspects, Hamilton sent twenty back to Philadelphia in chains to stand trial. Although Hamilton was certain that the government's reputation and strength had been enhanced by demonstrating its capability of compelling obedience to the law, Jefferson was inclined to take a less generous view: "An insurrection was announced and proclaimed and armed against, but never found." Madison hinted that the so-called rebellion was a mere ploy to justify the government's demand for a standing army to enforce the laws. For President Washington, however, such a show of force was essential to prove to the world that his administration was "able and willing to support our government and laws."

FOREIGN AFFAIRS: IMPACT OF THE FRENCH REVOLUTION

Shortly after Washington assumed the presidency in 1789 an event occurred in Europe that set in motion an international convulsion that profoundly affected the course of the United States for a quarter of a century. The event was the outbreak of the French Revolution which led to the establishment of a French Republic and an experiment with "liberty, equality, and fraternity." The experiment, however, degenerated into an orgy of extremism that climaxed in a bloody reign of terror, the beheading of King Louis XVI, wars with half a dozen European powers, and the rise to power of Napoleon. Following the execution of Louis XVI in 1793, a few weeks before Washington's inauguration for a second term, Britain joined Spain and Holland in a counterrevolutionary war against the revolutionary French Republic. Britain and France remained at war, except for a brief period, until the defeat of Napoleon at Waterloo twenty-two years later.

The war pitting France against Britain and Spain confronted the Washington administration with a situation that threatened the economic welfare of the nation and ultimately the existence of the republic. Convinced that the vast majority of Americans desired no part in the European conflict, Washington, on April 22, 1793, issued a proclamation of neutrality that declared the intention of the United States to remain "friendly and impartial toward the belligerent powers." But as quickly became evident, it was easier to proclaim neutrality than to maintain it. Inexorably the country was drawn into the vortex of the European storm.

The United States was a young, militarily weak country whose economic health was heavily dependent on its export trade. Both Britain and France wanted, indeed needed, American raw materials, and each was bent on preventing the other from acquiring them. As a result, each country tried to control American vessels destined for the other's ports and confiscated their cargoes. The British also impressed American sailors into service aboard their own ships because of their high demand for seamen.

Jay's Treaty

The issue of impressment, coupled with accumulated grievances against Britain, not the least of which was their continued presence in the West in forts that they should have abandoned in 1783, prompted many Americans to clamor for war to settle the score with Britain. Fully aware of the country's inadequacy to take on such a strong adversary, Washington instead sent Chief Justice John Jay to Britain in 1794 to work out a peaceful settlement of issues in dispute. The pro-British Jay brought home a treaty that made no mention of impressment and gained only two important concessions prompted in part by the American victory at the Battle of Fallen Timbers: The British promised to abandon the northwestern forts by 1796 and agreed to pay damages for the seizure of American ships and cargoes. If the British promised little, Jay conceded much, including acceptance of the British definition of neutral rights and Britain's demand for most-favored-nation treatment in American commerce. Britain continued to impress American sailors and allowed American shippers only limited access to the West Indies.

The Jay Treaty prompted outrage, especially among Jeffersonians (or Republicans as they had begun to call themselves). The treaty divided the country as few if any other issues in the history of the young republic. Despite threats that approval of the treaty might mean a break-up of the union, the Senate ratified it in 1795. Hamilton, who resigned as secretary of the Treasury in that year to attend to personal finances, rallied his followers, now known as Federalists, in support of the treaty. Despite ratification of the Jay Treaty, the public clamor refused to go away. Even the venerable Washington received verbal abuse. The division of opinion on the Jay Treaty deepened differences between the Hamiltonian Federalists and Jeffersonian Republicans and hastened the formation of two political parties. The treaty, however, may well have bought time for the United States by delaying war with Britain, and certainly it reaffirmed British recognition of American sovereignty. The pro-British position evident in the Jay Treaty not only reinforced the United States' status as an economic colony of Britain, but also drove the beleaguered French to launch a series of attacks on American shipping that resulted in the "quasi-war" with France in the late 1790s.

Responses to the French Revolution

An additional complication confronting Washington was the Franco-American alliance of 1778 which appeared to require the United States to aid France as France had aided Americans in their struggle for independence. Americans not only remembered with profound gratitude the French contribution to their independence, but they also were initially enthusiastic about the French Revolution which they viewed as the beginning of republicanism in Europe. As an admirer of French culture and a leading spokesman for republicanism, Jefferson was extravagant in his praise of the alliance between liberty and reason that was destroying despotism and tyranny in France. Jefferson's followers shared such a view. Madison even claimed that enemies of the French Revolution were "enemies of human nature."

In contrast to such views, Hamilton and his Federalist followers interpreted the developments in France as a descent into anarchy which destroyed property, law and order, and social classes, the very cement that held together civilization. For them the French revolutionaries were "mobocrats" and "levellers." Hamilton, an avowed Anglophile, renounced the 1778 alliance between France and the United States and championed Britain as the defender of order, stability, and the hierarchical society that he cherished. He described the position of Jefferson and Madison as a "womanish attachment to France and womanish opposition to Britain."

EMERGENCE OF TWO POLITICAL PARTIES

In the wake of the radicalization of the French Revolution and the controversial and indiscreet activities of Edmond Genêt, the French Republic's new minister to the United States, popular enthusiasm for the revolutionary cause cooled. Such developments, especially Genêt's utter disregard of American neutrality by commissioning privateers to attack British shipping, won converts to Hamilton's views. If domestic issues initially divided the supporters of the Constitution, events in Europe, especially the French Revolution and the Anglo-French War, contributed directly to the transformation of political factions into formal parties, the Federalist and Republican parties.

The Federalists

The Federalist party emerged out of the bloc in Congress that supported Hamilton's financial program and the commercial and business interests which benefitted by it. Ideologically, most Federalists were suspicious of the judgment and wisdom of the mass of citizens who in their opinion were prone to unchecked passion and social disorder as demonstrated by the activities of the mobs in the French Revolution. The people, in brief, could not be trusted to act in their own best interests, much less those of the nation; therefore, while the Federalists talked about the sovereignty of the people and may have been willing for the people to reign, they were unwilling for them to rule. Rejecting the egalitarian thrust of the American Revolution, they believed that people like themselves—property-owning, educated individuals who practiced self-restraint and prized order and stability—should govern so the republic would be spared democracy.

Federalists, in general, believed in a strong central government capable of acting decisively to maintain order and to restrain the popular tendency toward anarchy. To achieve such a government, they embraced Hamilton's "broad construction" of the Constitution. They detested the French Republic and agreed with Hamilton that the British system was "the best in the world." Federalism was strongest in New England and weakest in the West. Class, as much as sectional lines, distinguished it from the Republican opposition. Despite Washington's aversion to political parties and his belief that his was a nonpartisan administration, Hamilton's influence in his administration and his embrace of the Hamiltonian program enabled Federalists to make the president the symbol of their party.

The Republicans

The opposition to the Federalist program developed slowly under the leadership of Madison in Congress and Jefferson in the cabinet (until 1793). Although Madison functioned as the organizer and strategist of the Republican party, Jefferson became its symbolic head. Both articulated the widespread fear of a powerful, overbearing central government wedded to the particular interests of an economic elite that was little concerned with either the rights of states or the welfare of yeomen farmers and ordinary citizens. To preserve local and states' rights, and to protect individual liberty, they advocated the "strict construction" of the Constitution. For many Republicans, the Federalists embraced an ideology and program that smacked of monarchy, replete with "court" pageantry and talk of aristocratic titles.

Careful always to emphasize that their opposition was to the Federalist-dominated administration of Washington rather than to the Constitution, Republicans accused Federalists of shaping the American government to resemble the British monarchy which was dramatically opposed to the spirit of the Constitution. During the struggle over the Jay Treaty which he opposed, Jefferson characterized "anti republicans" (by which he meant Federalists) as made up of "old Tories, refugees, British merchants, American merchants trading on British capital, speculators and stockholders in banks and public funds, federal government officials, office hunters and 'nervous persons.'" In contrast, he wrote, landowners and laborers constituted the majority of Republicans.

Jefferson and Madison set about to awaken the country's republican sentiment, which they likened to a sleeping giant, and to provide it with the means to flex its political muscle. Among the evidence of widespread dissatisfaction with the policies of the Washington administration was the emergence of several dozen Democratic societies, essentially debating organizations, in various sections of the country, but primarily in cities. Sharply critical of the Federalist ideology and financial program, these societies represented a grassroots movement to alert citizens to keep a critical eye on the government. Spokesmen for the Democratic societies complained about the government's unresponsiveness to the needs of the people and charged that it had been corrupted by special interests.

Because these societies championed the cause of France and flourished during the tenure of the mischievous French minister, Genêt, who was elected president of the Philadelphia society, Federalists condemned them as agents of revolutionary France and its obnoxious doctrines. When President Washington suggested that the agitation of the societies was responsible for the Whiskey Rebellion, they went into decline. Although historians disagree over the exact nature of the relationship between what the president called "these self-created societies" and the Republican party, they agree that a relationship existed.

To be sure, Jefferson and Madison distanced themselves from the societies, but these organizations echoed, in more forceful language, what Jefferson, Madison, and other Republicans were saying and therefore helped publicize their views and made easier the task of organizing opposition to the administration and its Federalist policies into a viable political party. By the mid-1790s, issues large and small were being decided by partisan votes in Congress.

JOHN ADAMS

THE ELECTION OF 1796

After serving two terms, President Washington decided not to stand for re-election in 1796 and issued a farewell address which, ironically in view of future developments, condemned political parties and warned Americans against being drawn into Europe's squabbles. Though no longer viewed as a virtual demigod as he had been in 1789, he still commanded sufficient prestige and influence to prevent any candidate for the office from being foolish enough to criticize him publicly. Federalists made maximum use of Washington's veneration. Hoping that he would change his mind about retiring, Hamilton persuaded him to delay his official announcement until September 1796, two months before the electors were to meet. The purpose was to limit the time in which parties could wage formal campaigns.

The presidential election of 1796 has been described as "the first *real* contest for the presidency in American history." Yet, it was a curious contest. There were no conventions or formal caucuses, but rather an understanding among the leaders of the two parties who the candidates should be. There were no platforms, and no candidate campaigned. Even so, those in both the Federalist and Republican ranks viewed the election as a critical contest between two different political visions whose outcome would determine the future direction of the republic. The turmoil created by the violent phase of the French Revolution, the Whiskey Rebellion, and the uproar over the Jay Treaty and the Democratic societies meant that the election took place in a highly charged atmosphere in which the nonparty system urged by Washington disappeared.

Predicated on the assumption that a nonparty system would prevail, the Constitution provided a vague procedure for the selection of presidential candidates. It directed that the candidate with the greatest number of electoral votes, providing it constituted a majority, would become president and similarly the person with the second greatest number would become vice president. To rectify the problem posed by the latter in a party system, the Twelfth Amendment (1804) to the Constitution separated the balloting in the Electoral College for president and vice president.

John Adams and Thomas Jefferson

In 1796 Vice President John Adams, a Federalist with a distinguished public career—but a proud, testy individual whose independence often put him at odds with his party—considered himself Washington's heir apparent. His party concurred, and he became the Federalist presidential candidate. Thomas Jefferson, in retirement at Monticello, became the Republican candidate even though he never formally or informally accepted the nomination. His followers assumed that he would accept the presidency if elected. Various other individuals vied for the vice presidency on one party ticket or the other. Neither party reached a clear consensus on a candidate for vice president. Senator Aaron Burr of New York, despite doubts about his loyalty, enjoyed considerable support among Republicans for the office. The campaign and election abounded in power struggles and intrigues. Of all the intrigues, the most notable was that of Hamilton, who, opposed to both Adams and of course Jefferson, plotted to rig the election so that the Federalist vice presidential candidate Thomas Pinckney would get more electoral votes than Adams and therefore win the presidency. By no means the least of the Republicans' troubles was the intervention of the French minister to the United States, Pierre Adet, who intimated that only the election of Jefferson might stave off war between France and the United States. Adet's machinations greatly embarrassed Jefferson and confirmed the Federalists' suspicions that the Republicans were mere tools of France.

Victory for Adams

The presidential contest aroused great public interest, especially in the seven states (of sixteen) in which voters chose the presidential electors. Adams swept New England and won almost two-thirds of the votes in the middle states, but made a poor showing in the South; Jefferson won most of the South and West and carried Pennsylvania but showed little strength elsewhere. The Republicans' anti-British and pro-French rhetoric enabled them to attract substantial votes among immigrants, especially the Irish and French refugees from Santo Domingo. In the Electoral College Adams received seventy-one votes to Jefferson's sixty-eight which meant that because of the existing constitutional procedure the country had a Federalist president and a Republican vice president. The Federalists, however, controlled both the House and Senate. Following the election, Jefferson assumed a conciliatory position toward Adams that brought about a short-lived period of harmony and goodwill between political partisans.

THE ADAMS ADMINISTRATION

No sooner was Adams in office than he confronted a diplomatic crisis and a quasi-naval war with France that lasted throughout most of his term and destroyed any prospect of a continuation of the reconciliation between him and

Vice President Jefferson. France had suspended relations with the United States and launched attacks on American shipping on the grounds that the Jay Treaty violated the 1778 alliance between France and the United States. Compounding Adams' problems was the division within the Federalist party that owed much to the activities of Hamilton who, though out of office, attempted to function as party leader. Some members of Adams' cabinet proved to be more loyal to Hamilton than to the president. The personality differences between the two men and the president's knowledge of Hamilton's treachery during the election exacerbated the problem. Nor did Adams fully share in Hamilton's commercial-industrial vision of the republic or his stridently pro-British position. Shortly after his election, Adams reaffirmed his desire to maintain friendly relations with France—a desire difficult to implement in view of the breaking off of Franco-American relations and French depredations on American commerce.

The XYZ Affair

Confronted by an outburst of public clamor over French activities, President Adams embarked upon a two-pronged strategy. First, he secured congressional authorization for a substantial buildup in naval and military strength, including the power to call up a reserve army in the event of an invasion threat by the French. The defense legislation elated Federalists, especially Hamilton, whose martial ardor and indiscreet references to using the new army to suppress the Republican party, outraged Adams no less than Republicans. Second, the president dispatched a three-man peace mission to France to avoid war. After being treated to rebuffs and humiliation, the mission was contacted by three agents (designated as Messrs. X,Y, and Z) of French Foreign Minister Prince Talleyrand, who required a loan for France and bribes for French officials before any negotiations could begin. The American representatives resolutely refused such conditions. Their report, which arrived in the United States early in 1798, prompted Adams to denounce the French and to ask Congress to approve additional preparations for war. Without declaring war, Congress responded by cutting off trade with France, abrogating the alliance of 1778, and authorizing private and public vessels in the United States to capture French ships on the high seas. It also created a Department of the Navy and authorized the construction of new warships. In 1798 and 1799 the United States engaged in an undeclared war (quasi-war) with France centered primarily in the West Indies.

The XYZ Affair set off a wave of public hysteria and anger against France which redounded to the political advantage of the Federalists and seriously eroded public support for the Republicans. Party passions reached new heights. Street fighting broke out in various cities between supporters and opponents of France. Anti-French resolutions and petitions poured into Congress, and French nationals quickly booked passage home. President Adams, for the moment, became a popular hero as the symbol of American defiance of France.

The Republicans, all the while, viewed with alarm the provisional army which Washington had agreed to lead. His second-in-command, Hamilton, was busily organizing troops.

The Republicans feared that the army had less to do with meeting the French challenge than with destroying opposition to the Federalists and their policies. The anger against France grew so intense that it threatened the very existence of the Republican party because of its anti-British, pro-French position. With Federalists controlling all three branches of the government, Republicans could do little to influence federal policy. The militaristic drift of that policy alarmed Republicans who believed that their political opponents had exaggerated the crisis to pave the way for a war with France. Increasingly, Jefferson came to view the states as offering the only defense against the all-powerful militaristic federal government being created by Federalists who, he believed, were intent on using it to crush dissent at home.

The Alien and Sedition Acts

A series of Federalist-sponsored measures enacted by Congress in the early summer of 1798 lent credence to Jefferson's suspicions. Known as the Alien and Sedition Acts, they restricted freedom of speech and the press and the rights of immigrants. Three of these transparently partisan measures were aimed at immigrants, who tended to support the Republican party: one increased the naturalization period from five to fourteen years, another authorized the president to deport aliens considered dangerous to national security, and a third empowered the president in times of declared war to expel or imprison enemy aliens. Even more threatening to the Republicans because of its potential to stifle political dissent was the Sedition Law. The measure not only provided for punishment of any persons who conspired to oppose or impede the operation of a federal law, but also prohibited "any false, scandalous and malicious writings against the government" including either house of Congress and the president. Such a measure appeared to be a blatant attempt to muzzle the Republican press and individual critics of Federalist policy. Although President Adams never requested such laws, he contributed to the atmosphere in which they were conceived. Nor did he oppose their enactment.

Republican Response   The passage of the Alien and Sedition Acts created a storm of protest and prompted the Republicans, led by Jefferson and Madison, to take the offensive against what they considered Federalist excesses that were subverting the Constitution in ways that made the federal government an all-powerful, rather than a limited-power, government. They agreed with Republican Albert Gallatin of Pennsylvania that the Sedition Law was nothing more than an effort by Federalists to perpetuate themselves in power by eliminating all dissent and opposition. So long as the Federalists controlled the government, Republicans claimed, neither the Bill of Rights nor the system of checks and balances protected individual liberty. Jefferson and Madison, therefore, responded to the Alien and Sedition Acts by emphasizing the exercise of political power at the state, rather than the national, level and advanced a doctrine of states' rights designed to prevent the federal government from trampling on basic freedoms.

Virginia and Kentucky Resolutions   The Virginia and Kentucky legislatures directly challenged the Alien and Sedition Acts late in 1798 by endorsing manifestos on states' rights that had been written anonymously by Madison and Jefferson. Madison drafted the resolutions endorsed by the Virginia legislature and Jefferson those issued by Kentucky. These resolutions argued that the federal government had come into being through a "compact" among the states and had been endowed with certain specific powers, while each state reserved to itself "the residuary mass of rights." The states, therefore, had never surrendered their right to judge the constitutionality of federal actions and had retained the right "to interpose for arresting the progress of evil." In effect, the resolutions claimed for states the right to nullify objectionable federal laws. Jefferson and Madison raised questions about the nature of the Union that were to trouble the nation for the next six decades.

Although the Virginia and Kentucky resolutions indicated the depth of popular opposition to the Alien and Sedition Acts, they were greeted either by denunciation or silence. Even those Republicans who agreed with the ends sought by the resolutions, namely the repeal of the odious laws, feared that the forcefully worded manifestos would cause Republicans to be branded as disunionists and result in political disaster. Despite the refusal of other states to endorse the Virginia and Kentucky resolutions, popular opposition to the Alien and Sedition Acts and other Federalist-sponsored legislation persisted to such an extent that government officials in Philadelphia had the protection of armed patrols in the city. Early in 1799 the so-called Fries Rebellion erupted in the eastern counties of Pennsylvania as farmers resisted paying a direct federal tax (1798) on houses, land, and slaves. Unlike the Alien and Sedition Acts which affected relatively few people, the tax touched every property owner. President Adams responded to the "uprising" in Pennsylvania by dispatching a sizable military force to the affected area—an army that discovered no signs of rebellion. Although Republicans counseled against violence, they were quick to condemn Adams and the Federalists for overreacting with such a show of force.

THOMAS JEFFERSON

THE CAMPAIGN OF 1800

The tense atmosphere in 1799, as the two parties began preparations for a presidential election, prompted some to conclude that the republic was in peril and civil war might be imminent. But developments at home and especially abroad redirected the course of the nation's history and spared it such a fate.

The rift between President Adams and the so-called High Federalists deepened as Hamilton increasingly assumed the role of Federalist party leader, acted as if he were commander-in-chief of the nation's military forces, and conjured up grandiose plans for the acquisition of the Florida and Louisiana territories. Hamilton's presumptuousness outraged the thin-skinned Adams. For his part Hamilton considered Adams an obstructionist of "disgusting egotism" who was unfit to be president.

But even worse, in the eyes of Hamilton and the High Federalists, was Adams' rejection of a proffered alliance with Britain, dismantlement of plans for a large army in the wake of the British defeat of the French in the Battle of the Nile (1798) which removed the threat of a French invasion of the United States, and favorable response to French overtures to reopen negotiations. The departure of an American mission to Paris to settle differences with the French confirmed the suspicions of the Hamiltonian faction of the Federalist party that Adams was altogether "unreliable." By 1800 the Federalists were mired in an exchange of vituperative attacks with each other rather than with Republicans. The party entered the presidential campaign badly divided between the forces of Adams and Hamilton, a condition that encouraged intrigues and under-handed scheming.

The Republicans

Although changes in the international scene and the split in the Federalist party combined to brighten the prospects for the Republicans, neither party entered the campaign of 1800 confident of the outcome. The presidential candidates were the same as in 1796: Adams for the Federalists and Jefferson for the Republicans. The Federalist vice presidential candidate was Charles Cotesworth Pinckney of South Carolina, and Aaron Burr was again the choice of Republicans for their vice presidential nomination. Jefferson and Adams avoided direct participation in the campaign and displayed a restraint and dignity that contrasted sharply with the behavior of their supporters. Federalists depicted Jefferson as a dangerous pro-French radical and godless freethinker whose election would inaugurate a reign of terror in the United States and plunge the nation into civil war. Republicans described Adams as a tyrant engaged in a plot to subvert the Constitution and enslave the people. If the machinations of the anti-Adams Federalists played havoc with any efforts at party unity, the discovery in 1800 of a plot for a slave rebellion, known as Gabriel's Conspiracy, in Jefferson's Virginia not only struck terror in the hearts of southern slave-owners, but also posed problems for the Republicans. Federalists were quick to claim that the aborted slave insurrection had been inspired by the Republicans' embrace of French revolutionary ideas.

Jefferson's Election

After a hard-fought, bitter campaign, the Republicans decisively defeated the Federalists and gained control of both the legislative and executive branches of the federal government. The outcome of the election again revealed a strong, sectional character: the Federalists' base of support remained New England; the Republicans' support was almost solid in the area south of Maryland; and the middle states were contested ground. Despite the Republican victory, Jefferson's election was in doubt. The problem arose when Jefferson and his vice presidential running mate, Burr, received the same number of electoral votes. Republican efforts to prevent such an occurrence had gone askew. As a result, according to the Constitution, the House of Representatives was to determine whether Jefferson or Burr would become president. Though Burr had run as vice president, he let it be known that he would happily accept the presidency, and many Federalists in the House, seeing a chance to defeat Jefferson, began to rally to his support.

Convinced that Burr was "the most unfit man in the U.S. for the office of president" and alarmed by the pro-Burr activities of some of his fellow Federalists, Hamilton entered the fray to stop a movement designed to deny his old adversary, Jefferson, the nation's highest office. For Hamilton, Jefferson was by all odds the lesser of two evils, because Burr possessed a deeply flawed character and was as unscrupulous as he was ambitious. After thirty-six ballots the House chose Jefferson as president and Burr as vice president. For the first time in the nation's brief history, power was transferred from one political group to another without any disruption of domestic peace, notwithstanding the dire predictions voiced during the campaign. Jefferson later referred to the Republican triumph as "the revolution of 1800." For him, the outcome of the election repudiated the centralizing Federalist policies and ensured the preservation of the Constitution and republicanism.

THE JEFFERSON ADMINISTRATION

On March 4, 1801, Jefferson became the first president to be inaugurated in the new capital city of Washington, for which he was partly responsible. At the time, the capital was little more than a primitive village in a swampy clearing near the Potomac River, with the unfinished federal buildings scattered along stump-blocked boulevards where cattle roamed at will. Jefferson took the oath of office in the Senate chamber, the only part of the Capitol building completed. In his inaugural address, a masterpiece of political conciliation, he provided a glimpse into the course he intended to pursue. After declaring support for states "in all their rights," he promised a wise and frugal government free of burdensome debt, "honest friendship with all nations, entangling alliances with none," and reliance on a well regulated militia rather than a large standing army. In a reference that revealed his priorities and economic vision of the nation, he called for the "encouragement of agriculture and of commerce as its handmaiden." Finally, in a plea for political unity, he maintained that Americans, though referred to by different party labels, were "brethren of the same principle." "We are all republicans," he declared, "we are all federalists."

The transfer of the capital from aristocratic Philadelphia to the rustic simplicity of Washington made it easier for Jefferson to institute a new code of Republican etiquette. Even though Jefferson was an aristocrat of catholic interests
ranging from music and architecture to science and languages, he exhibited an
unpretentious lifestyle evident in his dress, informality, and impatience with the
Federalists' emphasis on pomp and circumstance. By conforming to an etiquette appropriate to republicanism rather than aristocracy, his style confounded many a European diplomat.

Domestic Programs

Federalist Control of the Judiciary   With the aid of a cabinet of Republican
activists, notably Secretary of State James Madison and Secretary of Treasury
Albert Gallatin, the new president set about to translate Republican principles
into specific policies. One issue that required immediate attention was the judiciary. Although the president's party controlled the executive and legislative
branches of the government, Federalists remained firmly ensconced in the judicial branch. The Judiciary Act, enacted in January 1801 by the lame-duck
Federalist Congress, converted the judiciary into a Federalist bastion of defense
against the victorious Republicans. The act created new judicial officers, extended the jurisdiction of the circuit courts, and reduced the number of Supreme
Court justices from six to five. In the closing days of his administration, the defeated President Adams signed commissions for the new judicial officers and designated John Marshall as chief justice of the Supreme Court.

For Republicans, a Federalist-controlled judiciary was obnoxious not only
because of the zeal it had displayed in enforcing the Alien and Sedition
Acts, but also because Federalists had long held that the Supreme Court
had the right of "judicial review," which meant that the court could either
uphold or *nullify* acts of Congress. Confronted with the dismal prospect of
having their legislative program nullified by a Federalist court, Republicans
quickly initiated a movement to repeal the Judiciary Act of 1801. By a strict
party vote, Congress in 1802 repealed the act and restored the Judiciary Act
of 1789. The Republicans also attempted, largely without success, to purge
some highly partisan Federalist judges from the federal bench, but finally
decided to abandon such a course and let time erode Federalist control of the
courts.

Marbury v. Madison   The repeal of the Judiciary Act of 1801 failed to settle
the issue of judicial review. The Supreme Court had never nullified an act of
Congress; but it had upheld the constitutionality of such legislation. It was the
possibility of the former that worried the Republicans. The Supreme Court
under the domination of Chief Justice John Marshall, a Federalist who had been
Adams' secretary of state, settled the question of the court's authority to pass on
the constitutionality of congressional legislation in a series of decisions during
his thirty-four-year tenure on the court. The first of these decisions was
rendered in the case of *Marbury v. Madison* (1803) which involved William

Marbury, one of numerous justices of the peace appointed during the closing hours of Adams' administration. Marbury, though appointed, had not received his commission before Jefferson took office. When Jefferson and Secretary Madison refused to deliver the commission, Marbury invoked a provision in the Judiciary Act of 1789 and applied to the Supreme Court to direct Madison to deliver his commission.

In a decision that revealed his skill as a political tactician, Marshall ruled that Marbury had a right to the commission but the court had no authority to force Madison to deliver it, lectured the Jefferson administration on its duty to obey the law and deliver the commission, and declared a section of the Judiciary Act of 1789 unconstitutional. "It is the province of the Judicial Department," Marshall declared, "to say what the law is." The most significant aspect of his decision was not that it denied Marbury's petition, but rather that the court for the first time struck down as unconstitutional an act of Congress. Although the court would not do so again for more than a half-century, Marshall had spoken in unmistakable terms about its right to judicial review. Jefferson, however, never agreed that Marshall had established the Supreme Court's monopoly on judicial review and contended that the other branches of the government and the people of the states had the right of such review as well. What really outraged Jefferson about Marshall's decision was his strongly worded lecture—*obiter dictum*—to Madison and hence to the president. The Supreme Court remained under Federalist domination, but Jefferson appointed three Republicans to it before he left office.

Dismantling the Federalist Program   All the while, the Jefferson administration pursued efforts to dismantle the Federalist program, at least most of it, and to replace Federalists in government positions with Republicans. Prosecutions under the Sedition Act ceased, and the law was allowed to expire in 1802. As for the Alien Acts, Jefferson refused to enforce them, and secured legislation that allowed foreigners to become citizens in five rather than fourteen years. True to promises made in his inaugural address, his administration eliminated most excise taxes including those on whiskey, trimmed the size and operations of the central government, and substantially reduced the national debt. Encouraged by the Treaty of Amiens (1802) that temporarily ended warfare between France and Britain, Jefferson slashed the military budget by reducing the army to a little more than three thousand soldiers stationed primarily in the West, and substituted a fleet of smaller and less expensive gunboats for the construction of warships initiated under the Federalists. But Jefferson, fully aware of the significance of maintaining the nation's credit, made no attempt to undo Hamilton's formula for debt funding and assumption. The tariff also remained in place which along with the sale of public lands constituted a principal source of government revenue. Despite his objections to the creation of the national bank, Jefferson as president did not complain of its existence, but rather expanded its operations and attempted to use it to woo the "mercantile interest" into Republican ranks.

Foreign Affairs

The Barbary Pirates   Even though a "wide ocean" separated the United States "from the exterminating havoc of one-quarter of the globe," as Jefferson pointed out in his inaugural address, he quickly learned as president that the avoidance of foreign entanglements was an elusive goal. No sooner had he entered office than he confronted the thorny problem of the Barbary pirates. For generations the Islamic rulers of the North African states of Morocco, Algiers, Tripoli, and Tunis had been preying on seaborne commerce in the Mediterranean. As long as America was part of the British Empire, the Royal Navy protected its shipping from these piratical depravations. With independence this was no longer true and the United States agreed to pay tribute to the so-called Barbary pirates of North Africa. The depths of degradation were reached in October 1800 when the Dey of Algiers forced a U.S. man-of-war, most inappropriately named the *George Washington*, to haul down the American flag, replace it with that of Algiers, and sail to Constantinople bearing an ambassador and gifts to the Sultan. Jefferson had no choice but to station a small fleet in the Mediterranean which provided some protection for American shipping, but did not end the payment of ransom for captured sailors.

Confronting Napoleonic France   Though he had often sung the praises of the French Revolution, if not always revolutionary France, Jefferson wished nothing so much as to play off Britain against France and keep America disentangled from European affairs. Events would not permit, however. In 1801 rumors began to filter across the Atlantic that Spain had retroceded the Louisiana territory to France. The rumors turned out to be true. The Louisiana territory was a vast and ill-defined area bounded on the east by the Mississippi, on the west by Rocky Mountains, on the north by Canada, and on the south by Spanish America. Talleyrand had managed to interest Napoleon in a scheme to reestablish French imperial power in the New World. Louisiana would act as a huge granary that would feed the French West Indies. The plan required that France recapture its colony of Santo Domingo, which had been overrun by a slave insurrection led by the indomitable Toussaint-L'Ouverture. Talleyrand's scheme became possible when in 1801 France and Britain signed a truce which was followed the next year by a formal peace, the Treaty of Amiens. Spanish Louisiana was sparsely populated and barely defended. Under the firm rule of Catholic France, the Spaniards reasoned, Louisiana would act as a barrier protecting their much more valuable possessions to the south from the avaricious Americans. Their only reservation was the possibility that the treacherous Bonaparte would turn around and cede Louisiana to a third party.

In October 1802 Spain finally signed the order transferring Louisiana to France and at that point the Spanish governor at New Orleans closed the port to American merchants and farmers who had been shipping goods down the Mississippi through the Gulf of Mexico to the east coast of the United States. Between 1785 and 1800 the population of the American trans-Appalachian

West had mushroomed. Ohio could count 45,000 inhabitants, Kentucky 220,000, and Tennessee 105,000. Most of these individuals were frontier farmers, so the Mississippi had become a commercial lifeline to them. In 1802 Americans transshipped 9 million pounds of cotton through New Orleans. News of the retrocession and closure rolled up the Mississippi provoking wild talk of an armed assault on New Orleans and secession if the national government did not intervene. Jefferson was deeply distressed, in part because he was determined to protect America's national interests and in part because these frontier farmers constituted one of the mainstays of the Republican party.

Expanding the Nation's Borders

Shortly after the Spanish commandant at New Orleans closed the port, Jefferson appointed James Monroe, a fellow Virginian and staunch Republican, as a special commissioner to join Ambassador Robert Livingston in Paris in a diplomatic effort to purchase New Orleans. Interestingly, their instructions made no mention of the Louisiana territory. They were, at a minimum, to secure the reopening of the port of New Orleans, and at a maximum the purchase of that city and the provinces of east and west Florida which Jefferson believed were part of the retrocession. To secure these territories, the American envoys were authorized to pay as much as $9,150,000.

Fortunately for the Americans, a confluence of circumstances had soured Napoleon on Talleyrand's scheme to reestablish New France. The attempt to reconquer Santo Domingo had been a disaster. Napoleon had dispatched General Charles LeClerc with an army of twenty thousand veterans to put down the slave rebellion. LeClerc took L'Ouverture in a *ruse de guerre*, but that only caused his followers to redouble their efforts. The black guerrillas together with a yellow fever epidemic destroyed LeClerc and seventeen thousand of his men. Thus the spring of 1803 saw Louisiana physically still in Spanish hands. Finally, the Peace of Amiens had proved too fragile to last. By March, Napoleon had decided that a resumption of hostilities with Great Britain was inevitable.

The Louisiana Purchase   During a negotiating session on April 11, 1803, Napoleon's representative suddenly asked Livingston: "What will you give for the whole?" Monroe arrived two days later and the terms of the Louisiana Purchase quickly emerged. Knowing full well that they were violating their instructions, the two emissaries agreed to pay approximately $15 million in cash and claims for New Orleans and a trackless wilderness that lay to the north and west. When asked if the deal included Texas and west Florida, Talleyrand declared that he did not know. He assumed, he said, that the Americans would make the best of the bargain.

The Federalists attacked the purchase agreement with vehemence and confidence. They did not want added to the Union vast new territories that were sure to be agricultural and sure to be Republican. Moreover, they understood that it would be difficult for Jefferson to justify the transaction given his strict constructionist views of the Constitution. Nowhere in that document is there a provision authorizing the president to purchase territory. Jefferson, however, swallowed his constitutional scruples and submitted the purchase agreement to the Senate as a treaty. He obviously concluded that remaining true to strict constructionism was less important than promoting his notion of an "empire of liberty" and guaranteeing the perpetuation of his vision of a virtuous agrarian republic. When the Senate gave its two-thirds approval and Congress subsequently appropriated the necessary funds, little more criticism was heard. The purchase meant that the United States acquired an additional 828,000 square miles of territory that ultimately made up a major portion of thirteen states. The results of the Jefferson administration's diplomacy were stunning, even if inadvertent. The American people had doubled their original endowment, ensuring that there would be ample room for expansion and the United States would become a great power.

Lewis and Clark Expedition   Even before the purchase, Jefferson, who had never been fifty miles west of Monticello, had planned and secured a congressional appropriation for an expedition into Spanish-owned upper Louisiana. In 1801 the president had articulated his vision of an expanding republican civilization and predicted that Americans would ultimately "cover the northern, if not the southern continent." More than his own insatiable scientific curiosity therefore prompted his desire to learn more about the immense unexplored territory beyond the Mississippi. The original purpose of the expedition was to find a useful route to the Pacific and to investigate Indian trade and diplomacy. Headed by Meriwether Lewis, Jefferson's secretary, and William Clark, the expedition embarked in May 1804. Traveling to the Pacific and back by way of the Missouri and Columbia rivers, the Lewis and Clark Expedition produced a wealth of information about the area which, in the meantime, the United States had purchased from France. Jefferson dispatched other expeditions to explore the Ouachita and Red rivers farther to the south in the Louisiana Territory. These various expeditions stimulated their interest of Americans in and ultimately the migration into the newly acquired territory (see Figure 6–2).

THE CAMPAIGN OF 1804

By 1804 President Jefferson had substantially weakened the partisan cleavages that bitterly divided the country during the previous decade. Not only had he extended the olive branch to the Federalists in his inaugural address, he had also pursued a middle-of-the-road course that enabled the Republicans to woo some moderate Federalists into their ranks, such as John Quincy Adams, son of the former president. Jefferson was certain the majority of the people supported him and his party, leaving Federalist leaders in command of an isolated and dwindling minority. Deprived of any substantive issues including the Louisiana Purchase, which increased rather than weakened Jefferson's popularity, Federalists despaired over the prospects of recouping their party's fortunes. Those

FIGURE 6–2
Explorations of the Louisiana Purchase

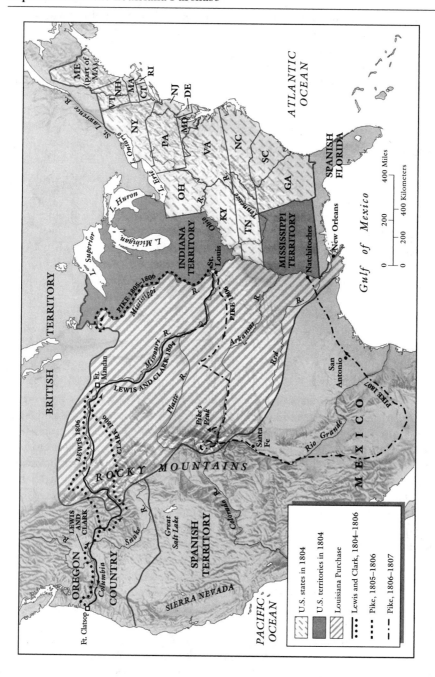

Federalists who were no more reconciled to Jefferson and his republicanism in 1804 than they had been four years earlier included extremists such as Timothy Pickering of Massachusetts, a former member of Adams' cabinet, who toyed with secession and talked of creating a northern confederacy. Pickering belonged to an ultra-Federalist group known as the Essex Junto that shared his views, but most Federalists rejected his disunion scheme and concluded that the only hope for reversing their party's decline was to await the chaos and disorder that was certain to result from the nation's excess of democracy.

Burr and the Federalist Extremists

Pickering and his fellow extremists pinned their hopes on Vice President Burr who, they believed, would be receptive to their overtures and would secure New York for their confederacy. Because of his maneuvers while the outcome of the election of 1800 was being decided by the House of Representatives, Burr was considered a traitor by the Republicans and viewed as a political outcast. In 1804 he hoped to recoup his fortunes by running for governor of New York where he counted on the support of the factious contingent of Federalists. Anti-Burr Republicans received important assistance from Alexander Hamilton, who opposed Pickering's disunionist scheme and still believed that the vice president was unfit for public office. Burr lost his bid for the New York governorship. Convinced that Hamilton was responsible for his defeat, Burr challenged him to a duel and Hamilton accepted. The two engaged in a duel on July 11, 1804, which resulted in the death of Hamilton.

Jefferson's Victory

By the opening of the presidential campaign of 1804 Jefferson had ample reason to be confident. He headed a united party and confronted a divided, demoralized Federalist opposition. His wide personal popularity owed much to the prevailing prosperity and the enthusiastic public approval of the Louisiana Purchase. Breaking with the earlier practice of a secret caucus, Republican congressmen held a public caucus to select Jefferson as the party's standard bearer and Governor George Clinton of New York to replace Burr as vice president. The Federalists, who held no caucus at all, more or less agreed through private and press discussions to support South Carolina's Charles Cotesworth Pinckney for president and New York's Senator Rufus King for vice president. The Republicans waged an effective campaign, especially in areas where the party competition was most intense. In contrast to the token efforts of the Federalists, the Republicans rallied voters by staging parades and dinners and by an effective use of the press. In the election the Federalists won the electoral vote of only Delaware and Connecticut and two electoral votes from Maryland for a total of fourteen votes to the 162 for the Republicans who had succeeded in putting together a broad-based coalition that included urban mechanics and artisans, commercial and entrepreneurial interests along the eastern seaboard, and planters and yeoman farmers in the South and West.

The duel between Alexander Hamilton and Aaron Burr in 1804 resulted in the death of Hamilton.

JEFFERSON'S SECOND TERM

Overwhelmingly reelected, Jefferson appeared to embrace a more expansive view of federal government obligations during his second term.

Domestic Issues

For example, he proposed that the surplus in the Treasury be expended on internal improvements; but convinced that the Constitution did not delegate such power to the government, he asked Congress for a constitutional amendment empowering the federal government to build a national system of roads and canals. Instead of honoring his request, Congress merely requested a report on internal improvements. Federal support for roads and canals continued to be a perennial issue, but its implementation had to await the emergence of a political faction willing to invoke the doctrine of implied powers (loose-construction) without the necessity of a constitutional amendment.

Ending African Slave Trade   Jefferson was more successful in outlawing the African slave trade. Although the president believed that blacks were "inferior to whites in the endowments of both body and mind," he admitted that under certain conditions blacks might ultimately become the equal of whites. Because slavery violated his belief that mankind was a single species and his belief in the natural rights of all people to freedom, he hoped that the system of black bondage would be abolished. But unable to rid himself of racial prejudice, he always tied the abolition of slavery to the colonization of freed blacks in Africa or the West Indies. The inhumanity of the African slave trade was the aspect of slavery, more than any other, that offended Jefferson. Not surprisingly, he recommended a federal law to prohibit the foreign slave trade beginning January 1, 1808. (The Constitution had prohibited the abolition of the slave trade before that date.) Congress followed the president's recommendation and outlawed the foreign (but not the interstate) traffic in slaves.

Randolph and the Old Republicans   Despite the overwhelming victory of the Republicans in 1804 and the shriveling of Federalist strength, party unity began to disintegrate during Jefferson's second term. The eccentric John Randolph and those known as the Old Republicans, or Quids, became increasingly alarmed at what they perceived as the expansion of federal power at the expense of the states and individual freedom. They focused their criticism on Jefferson, who, they insisted, had abandoned his own principles. Randolph openly broke with Jefferson in 1806 when the president was less than candid in making a request for a congressional appropriation that was actually to be used to pay for French influence in persuading Spain to sell Florida to the United States. Randolph exploded in indignation not at the idea of purchasing Florida, but rather at Jefferson's attempt at deception. Although Congress made the appropriation, the Republican congressional facade of solidarity was shattered. Randolph and the Quids remained a thorn in the president's side. Despite talk of a third party, they contented themselves with playing the role of obstructionists.

The Burr Conspiracy   Compounding Jefferson's problems during his second term was the so-called Burr Conspiracy which one historian has described as "an intricate melodrama with a cast of characters as large as a modern small-town telephone directory." Alienated from Jefferson and virtually read out the Republican party, Aaron Burr not only had failed to realize his ambition to be president and had been eliminated from the Republican ticket as the vice presidential candidate in 1804, but he had also been defeated in his bid for the New York governorship and was under indictment for the murder of Hamilton whom he had mortally wounded in a duel. With his political career in the East at an end, he looked westward and concocted fantastic schemes that would presumably recoup his fortunes. He devised a plan, depending on the circumstances, that involved carving out an empire in the West or conquering Mexico, or both. He enlisted the aid of General James Wilkinson, the governor of Louisiana, who was in the pay of Spain. Wilkinson's appointment as governor had been arranged by Burr. Rumors of Burr's schemes abounded, and Federalists in Kentucky twice had him indicted, but his attorney, Henry Clay, secured his acquittal. Burr sought to interest, among others, Andrew Jackson of Tennessee and Governor William Henry Harrison of Indiana in his scheme.

President Jefferson was fully aware of rumors about Burr's activities but awaited an overt act before taking action. In January 1807, as Burr approached Natchez with his rag-tail "army," he learned that Wilkinson had betrayed him and that Jefferson had ordered his arrest. Fleeing first to Pensacola, then to Alabama, he was captured and brought to Richmond, Virginia, where he stood trial for treason.

The case involved an extraordinary cast of characters including President Jefferson, who was bent on securing Burr's conviction, Chief Justice John Marshall, who was acting as judge of the Circuit Court in Richmond, and John Randolph, who was foreman of the Grand Jury. Marshall acceded to Burr's defense attorney's request to subpoena President Jefferson. Constitutional scholars agree that the two principal issues during the trial were whether the president could be compelled to honor the subpoena and whether Burr's actions actually constituted treason. Jefferson ignored the subpoena on the grounds that "the independence of the executive would be jeopardized were the president amenable to the court's writ." Jefferson's assertion of executive privilege established an important constitutional precedent as did Marshall's definition of treason. Invoking an un-Federalist "strict construction" of the Constitution's references to treason, Justice Marshall ruled that the Constitution defined treason only as the actual act of "levying war" against the republic and required two witnesses to the same "overt act." The inability of the prosecution to produce two such witnesses meant that the jury found Burr not guilty. With other charges pending, Burr jumped bail and took refuge in Europe until 1812 when he returned to New York and practiced law until his death in 1836.

Foreign Affairs

However troublesome the Burr Conspiracy and Randolph and the Quids may have been, they paled in comparison to the complex foreign affairs that dominated Jefferson's second administration. The resumption of the war in Europe in 1803, after a brief interlude, meant that Britain and France once again interfered with American commerce. British naval superiority made its attacks on American shipping especially devastating. As Jefferson well knew, the welfare of his agrarian republic depended on its ability to ship agricultural products overseas. As if the British practice of stopping and searching American ships and seizing their cargoes was not provocation enough, the Royal Navy displayed incredible arrogance by impressing American seamen into service on the pretext that they were Englishmen. Such a fate befell more than six thousand American citizens between 1803 and 1812. Jefferson sought to solve the problems with the British through means other than war, which he viewed as a threat to republican liberty by increasing the public debt, expanding government power, and destroying both lives and property. In an attempt to bring an end to depredations on American shipping by both the French and especially the British, he first pursued negotiations, then initiated a policy of "peaceable coercion."

The Embargo   Confronted by the choices of war, acquiescence in the actions of Britain and France, or a total embargo on American commerce, Jefferson opted for the latter, and Congress enacted the Embargo Act in December 1807. Supplementary legislation later attempted to plug up all loopholes in the initial act which instituted a self-imposed blockade of the nation's commerce: American vessels were prohibited from sailing to foreign ports and foreign vessels from taking on cargo in the United States until Britain and France ceased their depredations. Convinced that American products were indispensable to European nations with colonies in the West Indies and that Britain was dependent on the American market for the sale of its manufactured goods, Jefferson believed that his experiment in commercial coercion had a fair chance of success. Neither Britain nor France was significantly affected by the legislation enacted to implement the policy. For Americans, in general, but especially those in New England and the Northeast, the centers of the nation's shipping, the embargo proved to be economically disastrous. As Jefferson concluded his second term, his search for a bloodless substitute for war had proved to be in vain. His agrarian republic remained trapped in the crossfire of what had become known as the Napoleonic wars.

JAMES MADISON

THE ELECTION OF 1808

The presidential campaign and election of 1808 occurred in an atmosphere charged with outrage at the British (and French) for interfering with the commerce of a neutral power and discontent over the ineffectiveness of "peaceable coercion" measures. With Jefferson's endorsement, James Madison won the Republican presidential nomination, and George Clinton was again the party's choice for vice president. The Federalists put forward the same ticket as they had four years earlier: Charles Cotesworth Pinckney for president and Rufus King for vice president.

Madison was not without opponents within his own party. Among these were John Randolph and other Republican dissidents who promoted the candidacy of James Monroe and New York Republicans who rallied to Vice President George Clinton for the top place on the ticket. Still in disarray, the Federalists capitalized on the failure of Jefferson's foreign policy with which Madison as secretary of state had been closely identified. Younger Federalists abandoned the practice of their elders by embracing the campaign techniques of the Republicans and appealing directly to the voters. The role of partisan newspapers, nearly three hundred by 1808, was especially important in the campaign, and since most were fiercely Republican and pro-Madison, they were a major factor in Madison's election.

Despite the in-fighting within Republican ranks and the negative impact of Jefferson's policy of economic coercion, the outcome of the election was never seriously in doubt. Madison received 122 electoral votes to forty-seven for Pinckney and six for Clinton. In describing the voting pattern, one historian has concluded: "Where Republicans won, they won big; where Federalism conquered, it was close."

FOREIGN AFFAIRS

The Embargo and the Nonintercourse Act

The Federalists' defeat in the election of 1808 did nothing to dampen their hatred of the embargo which had an especially devastating impact on the northeastern part of the country. Ships rotted at their moorings, and grass began to grow on the wharves of a score of major ports. Federalist politicians pointed out that the embargo was the perfect cap to Napoleon's "continental system," the network of decrees and blockades designed to keep British ships out of European ports.

Admitting that the embargo had been three times as costly as war, Jefferson acquiesced when on March 1, 1809, Congress repealed the measure. It substituted the Nonintercourse Act, which reopened trade between the United States and the rest of the world except for those ports controlled by Britain and France.

Three days after passage of the Nonintercourse Act, Jefferson relinquished the presidency to James Madison. Barely five feet tall, "Little Jemmy" was known as a scholarly and somewhat irresolute man, but he was a skillful politician and a patriot. No sooner had he assumed office than he became involved in a neutral rights controversy with Britain. During the first weeks of the Madison administration, British Ambassador David Erskine promised, on behalf of his government, that his country's restrictions on American trade would be revoked. Thereupon Madison declared the Nonintercourse Act to be inoperable in regard to Great Britain. Several hundred ships laden with flour, tobacco, cotton, and foodstuffs departed the United States for British ports only to learn later that the foreign secretary had repudiated Erskine, recalled him, and announced that the restrictions remained in effect. Madison reimposed the Nonintercourse Act, but the damage had been done. Until the end of his tenure in office, Madison remained convinced that the British had engaged in deliberate deception.

In the meantime, Congress and the president had to devise a replacement for the Nonintercourse Act, which was scheduled to expire after one year. The measure that they came up with, Macon's Bill No. 2, proved to be one of the most unfortunate laws ever enacted by an American legislature. In a blatant effort to auction off American trade to the highest bidder, the measure reopened commerce with all the world but provided that if either France or Britain rescinded its offensive decrees, the United States, after due notification, would impose nonintercourse on the other.

Napoleon immediately informed the American ambassador in Paris that as of November 1, 1810, the Berlin and Milan Decrees were revoked. Madison took the French leader at his word and announced that all trade with Great Britain would cease in three months if that nation did not permit American ships to trade freely between nonblockaded ports. Madison persisted in such a policy despite frequent reports of French deprivations against American shipping and unfulfilled promises by Britain to remove restrictions on American trade whenever there was proof that the Berlin and Milan Decrees had actually been revoked.

Prelude to War

France proved almost as onerous to Americans on the high seas as Britain had during the Napoleonic wars, but the Britons and their Canadian colonists offended the United States in ways that France could not. For years Americans living beyond the Appalachians had complained that British authorities in Canada had been encouraging Indian tribes to attack white settlements in the old Northwest and even provided them with the arms with which to do so.

By the time Madison became president, white settlers and the principal tribes of the Northwest—the Potawatomi, Miami, Delaware, and Shawnee—had been engaged in almost constant warfare for twenty-five years. Under the terms of the Intercourse Act passed by Congress in 1790, no Native American land was to be occupied by whites that had not been ceded to the federal government through treaty. In fact, white squatters moved into Indian territory and when attacked, called on the state militia or federal military authorities for protection. The tribe involved was inevitably, if not easily defeated, forced to cede its territory, and either move farther west or become farmers on a reservation only a fraction the size of its ancestral hunting grounds.

The fortlike settlements that dotted the Ohio River Valley reflected the hostile state of Indian-American relations. American frontier farmers dared not live in isolation in the forests; it was far too dangerous. For their part the settlers refused to acknowledge that the Indians had a legitimate grievance and viewed them as heathens and savages. Efforts by American missionaries to Christianize the Indians only further divided and demoralized the trans-Appalachian tribes. Tribes became bitterly divided between Christianized assimilationists and traditionalists.

The most powerful and traditional of the tribes of the Northwest was the Shawnee. Determined to preserve their religion and to hunt and farm as had their ancestors, the Shawnee at the head of a confederation of smaller tribes and with the help of the British waged bloody warfare against frontier settlements on the Ohio. Not until the Battle of Fallen Timbers in 1794, did Americans gain the upper hand, and the Shawnees split into factions, one headed by Black Hoof who accepted Christianization and assimilation and another headed by Tecumseh who, determined to preserve the traditional Shawnee way of life, took his people farther west into the territories of Indiana, Illinois, and Michigan. Not only did American settlers flood into these territories but Governor William Henry Harrison of Indiana also concluded over a dozen treaties with the Miami, Delaware, and other tribes, despoiling them of their lands. Most of these agreements were achieved through bribery, intimidation, and trickery. Beginning in 1805 Tecumseh's brother, Tenskwatawa, known as the Prophet, began circulating among the tribes of the Indiana, Michigan, and Illinois territories urging the people to remain faithful to the ways of their fathers. At the same time, Tecumseh began molding the disaffected into a formidable military coalition with a view toward containing the spread of white civilization.

After Harrison and his fellow Indianans forced the Potawatomi and Delaware to cede three million additional acres in the Treaty of Fort Wayne in 1809, Tecumseh and his brother decided to take the offensive. By 1811 more than one thousand warriors had gathered at Tippecanoe on the Wabash in northern Indiana. Governor Harrison, who overestimated both the threat posed by Tecumseh and the Prophet and the degree to which the British were responsible for Indian unrest, organized a preemptive strike. The Indians had not intended to go to war but when attacked, they acquitted themselves well. At the Battle of Tippecanoe on November 11, 1811, Harrison's militia barely carried the day. Although Tecumseh and his followers subsequently conducted raids on settlements in Indiana and Michigan, the battle at Tippecanoe destroyed his infant alliance. Americans refused to consider the possibility that frontier greed and brutality were responsible for Indian unrest. Among the dead and wounded were found muskets with fresh English markings. "The war on the Wabash is purely British," proclaimed the *Lexington Reporter*.

Congress convened on November 14, three days following the bloodletting at Tippecanoe. The new House of Representatives was filled with first-term congressmen, most of whom were ultranationalists from the South and West who succeeded in electing to the speakership thirty-four-year-old Henry Clay of Kentucky. Clay packed key committees with superpatriots, labelled "buckskin politicians" and "coonskin Congressmen" by their detractors. Determined that the national honor be respected on both land and sea, the new congressmen from the South and West, rather than representatives from the commercial Northeast, urged confrontation with Great Britain. The former provided the margin of victory when Congress eventually voted for war.

The motives of the "War Hawks," as the press dubbed these ultranationalists from the interior, were several. Many favored hostilities because they looked forward to the conquest of Canada. Most were Republicans and many were land speculators. The addition of millions of acres of fertile territory would ensure that the republic would continue to be controlled by planters and yeoman farmers, not to mention enriching those who sold them their land.

Seizure of Canada would, in addition, put an end to British intrigue among the Indians.

If desire for Canada provoked war cries from representatives of the old Northwest, longing for Spanish Florida had much to do with the bellicosity of their brethren from the southern frontier. Because Spain was then an ally of Great Britain, war with the latter could be used to justify hostilities with the former. Land hunger and a desire to end Indian forays motivated expansionists from the South and West.

Finally, and somewhat ironically, British depredations against American shipping stirred the fighting spirit of the War Hawks. The North and East were still culturally tied to Great Britain, and if a Yankee shipowner successfully completed one voyage in three, he still made a profit. Westerners supplied much of the raw material that crowded the holds of seized ships, and the inhabitants of the trans-Appalachian West blamed Britain for a depression that gripped the region after 1808.

Most important, however, was the War Hawks' sense of honor. Impressment was a personal affront, a violation of one's honor. The proud, uninhibited debtors of the west considered it an affront to the individual, indeed an affront to the nation. America would have to go to war with Britain to avenge its honor.

THE WAR OF 1812

James Madison shared many of the prejudices against Britain of his fellow Republicans and certainly their political philosophy. He still smarted from the Erskine affair. He told congressional leaders, "Gentlemen, we must fight. We are forever disgraced if we do not." On June 1, 1812, Madison with support of his cabinet sent a war message to Congress declaring that the United States must go to war to end the barbaric practice of impressment, to force Britain to respect America's neutral rights on the high seas, and to put an end to Indian depredations on the frontier. With heavy majorities from the South and Northwest, Congress voted for hostilities.

New England never reconciled itself to the conflict, withholding its militias and selling provisions to the British. Indeed, on December 15, 1814, a group of leading malcontents gathered at Hartford, Connecticut, to draft amendments to the United States Constitution. To free New England from the alleged tyranny of the Republicans, the Hartford Convention proposed a series of amendments including one that limited presidents to a single term and another that required a two-thirds vote of Congress to declare war. Only the coming of peace quieted New England's discontent.

The United States was woefully unprepared to wage war in 1812. During the conflict the American army consisted of ten undermanned and ill-trained regiments, and volunteers did not flock to enlistment stations. In fact, the nation's effective fighting force had reached a mere thirty-five thousand by war's end in 1814. On the sea American privateers took their toll on British shipping, and American warships lost only two of fourteen major naval battles. These were mere pinpricks, however. When Britain and America finally made peace, the British Navy still consisted of eight hundred ships, while the U.S. Navy had been reduced from sixteen men-of-war to three.

American Efforts in Canada

Madison and the War Hawks believed that Canada was America's for the taking. They were wrong. Despite the fact that two out of three people living in Upper Canada (present-day Ontario) were of American origin, Canadians did not rally to their would-be liberators, but rather took up arms to repel them. In 1812 General William Hull surrendered his force of American militiamen at Detroit without a fight. General William Henry Harrison mounted another force but was defeated at Frenchtown, near the site of Hull's humiliation, in January 1813. After Oliver Hazard Perry secured control of Lake Erie in October 1813, Harrison defeated a combined Canadian-Indian force at the Thames River in October 1813. An American force mounted another invasion of Canada in the summer of 1814 but with indifferent results. When peace came at the end of the year, the Canadian-American boundary looked much as it had at the outbreak of war in 1812.

British Objectives

As long as Napoleon continued to menace Great Britain, England was unwilling to commit fully to the war in North America. In 1814, the emperor-general of France was subdued and England was free to turn its attention to America. British strategists developed a plan for a three-pronged attack. A British force would move down from Canada and subdue New England while a second army would attack and occupy the Americans' new capital, Washington. Meanwhile, a third force would capture New Orleans and move up the Mississippi.

British plans to invade and subdue the United States were only slightly more successful than American plans to conquer Canada. Captain Thomas Macdonough halted the northern expedition when he destroyed the British fleet on Lake Champlain. A British force succeeded in occupying Washington and burned several public buildings, including the president's house, then withdrew. The real objective of this mid-Atlantic onslaught was Baltimore, but after Fort McHenry guarding the harbor there successfully withstood a twenty-five-hour bombardment, the British withdrew. Some seventy-five hundred British troops subsequently descended upon New Orleans but were met there by a makeshift army of American regulars, Kentucky and Tennessee militia, free African Americans, Choctaws, and a contingent of pirates all commanded by General Andrew Jackson. After a futile and bloody assault on American breastworks, the British conceded defeat and withdrew.

The Treaty of Ghent

Normally, diplomatic negotiations between two nations cease as soon as they go to war. The War of 1812 was unusual in this respect because talks began a week after the American declaration and continued intermittently until peace came in the last days of 1814. In the fall of 1814, President Madison accepted British Foreign Minister Lord Castlereagh's invitation to send a peace commission to the Flemish town of Ghent to negotiate a peace treaty. The two sides began, typically, far apart. The British for their part demanded creation of an Indian buffer zone in the old Northwest and up-state New York. The Americans insisted upon British recognition of their definition of neutral rights and an explicit repudiation of the practice of impressment. In the end, the two nations signed on Christmas Eve, 1814 an agreement that merely restored the prewar status quo. The Treaty of Ghent made no mention of territorial cession or neutral rights. With Napoleon subdued, American neutrality no longer posed the threat to Britain that it had. Canada had proved, moreover, that it was impervious to American aggression.

In a sense, the War of 1812 ended in a stalemate, but it was a conflict with immense consequences. Psychologically, its impact was tremendous. Though Jackson's victory over the British at New Orleans came two weeks after the conclusion of the peace treaty, Americans reveled in his victory. In what one historian has called the second war for independence, Americans fought for their self-respect, for a separate identity. To their collective minds both goals had been achieved.

Impact on Native Americans

The big losers in the War of 1812 were Native Americans. Frontier expansionists and their allies in the military and federal government were able to use the conflict to further weaken Indian resistance to white encroachments on their land and culture. When in 1813 General Harrison defeated the British and Indian force at the Battle of the Thames, the great Shawnee chief, Tecumseh, died in that encounter, and with him hopes of an organized, effective resistance to white expansion also perished. Abandoned by their British allies in the Treaty of Ghent, the demoralized and divided tribes of the Northwest were no match for the land-hungry frontier people who flooded into their lands.

No less devastating was the impact of the War of 1812 on the Five Civilized Tribes—Choctaws, Cherokees, Chickasaws, Creeks, and Seminoles—in the Southwest. Here Andrew Jackson and his force of Kentucky and Tennessee militiamen mounted an assault, especially against the Creeks, who led the resistance. In the Treaty of Fort Jackson (1814) the Creeks were forced to cede 23 million acres of land, a huge tract encompassing much of Georgia and most of Alabama. As in the Northwest, the War of 1812 cleared the way for the advance of white settlement in the Southwest.

In the following essay historian Bernard Bailyn addresses a topic that has prompted considerable debate, namely the anomalies and apparent inconsistencies found in the career of Thomas Jefferson. Bailyn attempts to avoid what has been described as "the hysteria of denunciation and the hysteria of exaltation" that has characterized the discussion of these anomalies and inconsistencies from Jefferson's day to the present. He argues that Jefferson's fear of power which was the "animating spirit behind all of his thinking" was also "the ultimate source of the deepest ambiguities" that marked his career.

JEFFERSON AND THE AMBIGUITIES OF FREEDOM
Bernard Bailyn

The reputations of those who shape the fate of nations become historical forces in themselves. They are twisted and turned to fit the needs of those who follow, until, it seems, there is no actual person left, only a complex mirror in which successive interests see aspects of themselves. Of Jefferson this is doubly—trebly—true. His reputation has had what has been called a "kaleidoscopic changeability." For a century and a half it has been more fluid, more malleable than the reputation of any of the great figures of the Revolutionary generation, or indeed of anyone in American history.

The 450 crowded pages of Merrill Peterson's *The Jefferson Image in the American Mind* show the fabulous complexity of the problem that faces those who wish, as we do, to pay homage to Jefferson. Which Jefferson? The Jefferson image, Peterson writes, has been "an ill-arranged cluster of meanings, rancorous, mercurial, fertile . . . [it] was constantly evolving." Endless "errors and legends and myths" have found their way into history, and not, it seems, accidentally. The "hysteria of denunciation and the hysteria of exaltation" that have followed him through the ages were there at the start—in his own lifetime; and they were responses, in part at least, to the apparent contradictions and inconsistencies in his policies, if not his character.

Was not this fabled egalitarian, as some have claimed, a blatant "negrophobe" who placed blacks somewhere between apes and men in the evolutionary scale? He

from Bernard Bailyn, "Jefferson and the Ambiguities of Freedom," *Proceedings of the American Philosophical Society*, Vol. 137, no. 4 (Dec. 1993): 498–515.

said he sincerely loathed slavery, condemned it as "an abominable crime," a "hideous blot" on civilization which must somehow be eliminated, but he did not free his own slaves (except a few, in his will), and at the end of his life advocated the expansion of slavery into the southwestern states.

Was Jefferson not the ultimate libertarian, the passionate defender of freedom of speech, of the press, of religion, of protection against illegal searches and seizures, of the sanctity of *habeas corpus?* His passion for civil liberties radiates through his most profound state paper, the *Act for Establishing Religious Freedom.* There is nothing to compare with the elegant but emotive lyricism that lies within the formal cadences of that extraordinary document. One must read it aloud to appreciate the perfection of the rhythms and the immaculate choice of words.

> It is time enough for the rightful purposes of civil government for its officers to interfere when principles break out into overt acts against peace and good order; . . . [for] truth is great and will prevail if left to herself; . . . she is the proper and sufficient antagonist to error, and has nothing to fear from the conflict unless, by human interposition, disarmed of her natural weapons, free argument and debate— errors ceasing to be dangerous when it is permitted freely to contradict them.

But when Jefferson came to design the curriculum for the University of Virginia's law school he deliberately omitted books whose political and moral views he disapproved of, and proposed professors whose political opinions agreed with his own. In the early Revolutionary years he endorsed loyalty oaths; in suppressing the Burr conspiracy he tolerated lapses in *habeas corpus;* and in attempting to enforce his ill-fated embargo he ignored the Fourth Amendment and ruled, in certain areas and at certain times, by executive decree and the threat of armed force.

The anomalies and apparent inconsistencies seem endless. He avoided partisan debates in public, but urged others to do the opposite, and he helped support a partisan press. He was a pacifist in principle, but he argued for a retributive war against the piratical Barbary states, on the ground that if America meant to be an effective naval power "can we begin it on a more honourable occasion or with a weaker foe?" He said that a little rebellion against oppressive conditions, every now and then, would be a good thing; "the tree of liberty must be refreshed from time to time with the blood of patriots & tyrants," were his famous words. But when the Haitian people rose against their French masters, he declined, as president, to help them. He was a fervent constitutionalist, indeed a strict and narrow constructionist, especially in fighting the Alien and Sedition Acts in 1798; but five years later, in arranging for the purchase of Louisiana, he deliberately exceeded the bounds of the Constitution. "The less we say about the constitutional difficulties respecting Louisiana," he told Madison, his secretary of state, "the better"—and he added that if some political maneuvers were necessary to overcome constitutional impediments, they should be done "sub silentio."

Many of Jefferson's contemporaries idolized him, but others—many others— vilified him. Three generations of Adamses spoke of him venomously. John Adams, his lifelong friend and political opponent, in many ways venerated him, but he disagreed with him on basic principles, and declared at one point that Jefferson was as ambitious as Oliver Cromwell and so "warped by prejudice and so blinded by ig-norance as to be unfit for the office he holds. . . .As a politician he is a child and the dupe of party!" John Quincy Adams improved on his father's judgment. He conceded that Jefferson had an "ardent passion for liberty and the rights of man" but denounced him for infidelity, "pliability of principle," and double dealing. And *that* Adams's grandson, Henry, discounted Jefferson's duplicity, but wrote at length, in his monu-mental history of the Jefferson and Madison administrations, about what he took to be Jefferson's failure as a statesman, his opportunistic abandonment of principles, his willingness to "risk the fate of mankind" to justify his theories, and his fatal inca-pacity—so caught up was he, Adams said, in delusive visions of the present as a golden age—to recognize that he lived "in a world torn by wars and convulsions and drowned in blood." But it was Hamilton who was Jefferson's chief enemy in politics, and his feelings were never in doubt. Hamilton feared what he called the Virginian's fa-naticism and believed he was "crafty" and a "contemptible hypocrite." He worked feverishly for Jefferson's election to the presidency in 1800, in part because he was convinced that the alternative, Aaron Burr, would be even worse, and in part because he believed that, such was Jefferson's hypocrisy, he was unlikely ever "to do anything in pursuance of his principles which will contravene his popularity, or his interest."

So much about Jefferson seemed to contemporaries, as to many historians, anomalous and inconsistent. His appearance surprised those who came to pay their respects to the famous statesman, the sophisticated and learned savant, the friend of Lafayette, Condorcet, and La Rochefoucauld. Tall, red-headed, and freckled, dressed in ordinary, rather dowdy clothes—(yarn stockings, a British official reported with surprise, "and slippers down at the heels")—he sat casually, "in a lounging manner," perched on one hip. There was nothing, one visitor said, "of that firm collected de-portment which I expected would dignify the presence of a secretary or minister." Yet everyone recognized that his conversation was wonderfully informed and often brilliant. And why would it not be? Though he was no orator in public forums, he converse easily, and he was a fabulous polymath: politician, diplomat, architect, draftsman, connoisseur of painting, anthropologist, bibliophile, classicist, musician, lawyer, educator, oenologist, farm manager, agronomist, theologian (or rather, anti-theologian), and amateur of almost every branch of science from astronomy to zoology, with special emphasis on paleontology.

Jefferson slipped easily from role to role. His election to the vice-presidency of the United States coincided with his election to the presidency of the American Philosophical Society, a position he enjoyed far more than he did the nation's vice-presidency and which he proudly and actively held for the next eighteen years. In the midst of the ferocious struggle, in 1801, to settle the tie vote in the Electoral College—a vote, resolved only on the thirty-sixth ballot, that would elevate Jef-ferson to the presidency, transform the American government, and alter the course of American history—he calmly continued his correspondence with a professor of anatomy about the disposal of some recently discovered fossil bones that bore on disputed points of animal life in North America.

His correspondence was prodigious: the editors of the *Jefferson Papers* have located 19,000 letters written by him. They reflect extraordinary energy, a ceaseless flow of ideas on every conceivable subject, and a restless, tenacious mind, as fertile in formulating abstract ideas as in solving the most ordinary, mundane problems. Printing presses, phosphoric matches, cylinder lamps, and the shapes of plowshares fascinated him; so too did the principles of justice and the logical strengths and weaknesses of the thought of Hobbes, Hume, and Destutt de Tracy. He writes of the soil and of the heavens, and of everything in between: of economics and curtain beds; of political theory and "hydrostatic waistcoats"; of international law and carriage springs; of constitutions and macaroni machines; of poetry and pedometers. Through it all there glows his humane and generous purpose: to improve upon the inheritance; to meliorate the condition of life; to broaden the reach of liberty; and to assist in the pursuit of happiness.

Historians will never fully encompass Jefferson's protean versatility, nor will they completely resolve the paradoxes in his career and the apparent contradictions in his character. But there are a few signposts along the way to help one understand some, at least, of the basic elements in his public persona, and perhaps assess a little more accurately the complexity of his achievement.

With his enormous vitality and universal curiosity, he seemed forever young. But he was in fact thirty-three when he wrote the Declaration of Independence— almost middle-aged, by eighteenth-century standards—and though Madison was younger by only eight years and Hamilton by twelve, they seemed to belong to a different generation. By the end of 1774, when Madison, only a year from college, took his first, very minor public post, and Hamilton was still an undergraduate, Jefferson was an experienced lawyer and prosperous planter with five years of experience in the House of Burgesses behind him. They had been extremely busy years in politics. On the day he had first taken his seat in the Burgesses, he had drafted the reply to the governor's speech, and in the years that followed he wrote in quick succession several pieces of legislation, Virginia's resolution to oppose the Boston Port Act, a Declaration of Rights for Virginia's revolutionary convention, and the learned and inflammatory Instructions to Virginia's delegates to the Continental Congress. Sent to Philadelphia in 1775 as Virginia's delegate to the Continental Congress, he contributed to the drafting of the Association, which in effect set the Revolution in motion, and wrote not only the Declaration of the Causes and Necessity for Taking Up Arms but also America's reply to the British conciliatory proposals. And the next year, a month before writing the Declaration of Independence, he drew up a complete new constitution for the state of Virginia.

That he was chosen to write the Declaration is hardly surprising. It was generally known, as John Adams later recalled, that Jefferson had "a happy talent for composition." His writings, Adams said, were handed around and remarked on for their "peculiar felicity of expression." But by then Jefferson had acquired something more important than a reputation for learning and literary skill. From his voracious reading; from his extensive knowledge of law; from his acute attention to the views of his teachers and of his colleagues in politics; and from his instinctive understanding of independence as he had personally experienced it on his borderland plantations, he had developed a comprehensive view of politics, freedom, and

America's unique role in world history which would shape all of his thought and much of his actions thereafter.

It was not simply that he had helped to construct the pattern of ideas, beliefs, attitudes, and aspirations that we think of as the ideology of the American Revolution. He had personally *achieved* it—he had reached it through years of study, thought, and public controversy. To break through the barriers of the *ancien régime*, and to formulate and act on the pure principles of freedom was a triumph of enlightened thought which, he hoped, would usher in a new era in human history. In that happy time, which he felt America could now approach, legislatures would be truly representative; popular majorities would rule; the institutions of government would be strictly separated so that no person or group of people would exercise undue power; power itself would be restricted; establishments of religion would be forever banished; and the human freedoms for which mankind had yearned—freedom of speech, of the press, of worship, and the right to the security of property and to impartial judicial proceedings presided over by judges independent of political pressures—all this would be perfectly protected by the instruments of free government.

And beyond the realm of government, Jefferson glimpsed, in these early, formative years, and never lost, a vision of human felicity—a romantic vision, of sensible, hard-working, independent folk secure in their possession of land, free of the corruptions of urban poverty and cynicism, free of dependence on a self-indulgent aristocracy of birth, responsible to the common good as well as to personal betterment, educated in the essentials of free government and committed to the principles of freedom—peaceful, self-reliant, self-respecting, and unintimidated people. Occasionally the sheer romanticism of this vision would break through. "Ours," he informed Crèvecoeur in 1787, "are the only farmers who can read Homer." He was certain, after a year in France, that of the twenty million people in that country, "nineteen millions [are] more wretched, more accursed in every circumstance of human existence, than the most conspicuously wretched individual of the whole United States." In France, as elsewhere in Europe,

> conjugal love having no existence among them, domestic happiness, of which that is the basis, is utterly unknown. . . . [Their pursuits] offer only moments of extasy amidst days and months of restlessness and torment. Much, very much inferior this to the tranquil, permanent felicity with which domestic society in America blesses most of its inhabitants, leaving them to follow steadily those pursuits which health and reason approve, and rendering truly delicious the intervals of these pursuits.

These visions engrossed his mind and imagination. But he was never confident that these goals could be reached. It would, inevitably, he believed, be a constant struggle, and the outcome would always be in doubt. For along with the ideals of radical reform and the principles of freedom, he had inherited the belief, pervasive in radical thought in Britain for over a century, that freedom was in its nature a fragile plant that had been and would be, again and again, overwhelmed by the forces of power; that where freedom had survived it remained beset by those who lusted for domination. Even in Britain, its last bastion in Europe, Jefferson thought, freedom, overwhelmed by the corruption of Walpole's government early in the century, had finally been destroyed by the autocracy of George III and his junto of ministers, whose depredations Jefferson itemized so fully in the Declaration.

But the evils that had overwhelmed Britain were not unique to those once-heroic people. They arose, Jefferson believed, from human nature itself, and would take whatever form immediate situations might require. And so, though Americans had broken free from the worst evils and had set out on a new path, he knew that the realization of this vision was uncertain at best. Everything would depend on the sheer survival of the Revolutionary nation, and thereafter on its continued adherence to the principles of freedom as he had understood them in the early years of the struggle. Dangers from the inevitable counter-forces were certain to appear on all sides, and in new and unexpected forms.

But if Jefferson had been only a radical and eloquent idealist, fearful that the achievement of freedom was precarious at best, forever beset by dangers that could easily overwhelm it, he would never have played the powerful role in history that he did. Coupled—incongruously—with his soaring idealism was the realism and hard-headed pragmatism of a superb "man of business." Fantastically industrious, administratively efficient, with a true instinct for the moment to act and the moment to relent, Jefferson was a natural politician, as shrewd and calculating as the best and far more effective than most.

He tackled the most complex political and economic problems with tireless zest. He was incapable of boredom. In a six-month period in Paris he finished a detailed consular treaty with the French government, wrote a technical treatise on the American whale fishery based on data he had been methodically collecting for several years, drew up a proposal for funding the foreign debt of the United States, continued a long correspondence on outfitting American vessels in the French fleet, wrote extensively, though surreptitiously, to Lafayette on how to manage the developing revolution in Paris, drafted cunning messages to keep the United States government from being blackmailed, and sent practical advice repeatedly to an unfortunate Virginian whose family affairs were falling to pieces.

The Paris years were crowded with business efficiently handled, but his work as ambassador was preparatory to his labors as secretary of state and president. The leading student of his presidency concludes that "Jefferson brought to the presidency the most system in administration and the strongest leadership that the office had yet experienced." He had all the qualities of a successful political executive. He balanced decisiveness with accountability; he relied on discussion and persuasion rather than authority; and he was tolerant of dissenting views. "The first President to make the Cabinet system work," he established a close relationship with Congress. And beyond that, he kept in touch with the population at large, and made voters more conscious of, and involved in, the political process than they had ever been before.

All of this was the work of a natural politician and an industrious, efficient administrator—abilities not normally associated with radical idealism. But in Jefferson that unlikely association existed, and it is the key, I believe, to the complexities of his public career and to the strange oscillations of his fame. If he had been less responsive to the principles of freedom as they had emerged in the initial struggle with Britain, less committed to the vision of a golden age, and more cautious in seeking it, he might, when in positions of power, have been less likely to have had to modify or complicate or contradict his principles in attempting, in his efficient way, to effect them, and so in the end might have seemed more consistent and less likely to be thought hypocritical.

How different, in this, was he from his two younger contemporaries, who emerged on the scene after independence had been achieved and so inherited the Revolution, and took its principles for granted. Madison, Jefferson's lifelong friend, collaborator, and political ally, was quizzical and skeptical. His mind was less capacious and less elevated than Jefferson's, but more close-grained and instinctively contrary. Less learned than Jefferson, his verbal skills inferior, he was almost pedantically alert to inner complications, and so, though less adept a politician, he was more consistent. Jefferson would, if need be, jump out of a syllogism to save the major premise; Madison, less deductive, did not need such complicated gymnastics. And Hamilton, much younger in years and even younger in spirit, responded to different voices altogether—voices of a social and economic world just emerging, whose relation to Jefferson's ideals could be discordant.

So it was Jefferson—eloquent theorist and efficient politician, promulgator and custodian of the Revolution's original principles, who alone, of all the creators of independence, dominated politics into the nineteenth century—it was Jefferson who was fated, above all others, to confront the ambiguities of freedom.

From the start, and unswervingly, he argued that government must be stripped of its self-justifying power and reduced to an instrument of the people, whose voice could only be that of the majority: "the will of the majority," he said again and again, "ought to be the law." Madison too hoped that the people, not the government as such, would ultimately rule, but he believed that legislative majoritarianism could quickly lead to the destruction of the rights of minorities. For Jefferson the solution was clear: a bill of rights, which he advocated from the moment he first saw the Constitution. "A bill of rights," he wrote, "is what the people are entitled to against every government on earth . . . and what no just government should refuse or rest on inference." But Madison—who in the end would write the national Bill of Rights—pointed out to Jefferson that to enumerate human rights would be to limit their plenitude to the few items one happened to think of, and in any case, what he called "parchment barriers" had never yet prevented anyone from misusing power. Only structural balances within a government, Madison thought, pitting one force against another, could keep the misuse of power in check and so protect minority rights. Ten years later, Jefferson used the same idea in drafting the Kentucky Resolutions, which aimed to protect individual interests by pitting the states against the nation, almost to the point of nullification. But then, shortly thereafter, as president, he overrode the states rights he had earlier defended, in order to protect the nation, first from subversion, then from the dangers of foreign wars.

Why the inconsistency? There are times, he explained, when the rule of law itself must be suspended:

> A strict observance of the written law is doubtless *one* of the high duties of a good citizen, but it is not *the highest.* The laws of necessity, or self-preservation, of saving our country when in danger, are of higher obligation.

All men, he had written in his most famous pronouncement, are created equal—then why not black slaves? He agonized over the glaring, obvious inconsistency, came back again and again to the bizarre anomaly of slavery in a free state—anomaly in law, in ideology, in simple justice and humanity. His loathing of slavery was utterly sincere, and he predicted that, since "God is just [and] . . . his justice cannot sleep forever," it would one day, somehow, disappear from the face of the earth. What kept him, initially, from developing his early interest in abolition was what seemed to him to be the crippling paradox that freeing the slaves would imperil the survival of the nation's freedom. The blacks, a majority of the population in the South, lacked the qualities, Jefferson believed, that were needed to guarantee the survival of freedom: education, experience in self-government, economic independence. Whether they would ever be able to acquire these requisites of republican citizenship—whether, if their present degraded circumstances were improved and if they were "equally cultivated for a few generations," they would become the equals of any others—was a question that led him into a deeply troubling, unsure, and apologetic racism. What was clear in his mind was that the agrarian South—free of commercial, industrial, and urban corruption—was the bastion of the free republican nation. Black majority rule there would simply overwhelm the freedoms for which he struggled. "Justice is in one scale," he wrote, "and self-preservation in the other."

The problem did not diminish in time; it grew worse. Once, in the hope of at least containing slavery, Jefferson had favored limiting its geographical spread, and in fact he was largely responsible for prohibiting it in the states of the Old Northwest. But later, fearing that the growing congressional power of northern industrial and financial forces would overwhelm the country and destroy the delicate compromises of the Constitution, he changed his mind and supported the expansion of the institution, which he continued to despise and condemn, into Missouri and eventually other states in the South.

Jefferson's fear of northern economic power which propelled this strange reversal flowed from his undiminished commitment to the ideology of the Revolution in its original, pristine form. He had no need to calculate the precise political and social costs and benefits of Hamilton's financial program. He understood the threatening implications immediately; they squared perfectly with his historical memory and his political beliefs and fears. He, like radical theorists in Britain, believed it had all happened before, early in the century, in Walpole's buildup of the power of the British Treasury in collaboration with Britain's new, high-flying, ruthless banking and commercial interests. That alliance, he knew, had allowed Walpole to buy the votes he needed in the House of Commons, overthrow the famed separation of powers of the government, and usher in an age of limitless greed and political squalor.

Jefferson explained this, and its relevance to Hamilton, in his autobiographical miscellany, the *Anas*. In it he recalled his return to the United States in 1789 to become secretary of state, and his shocked discovery of Hamilton's plan for the federal government to assume the debts of the states. There was no mistaking Hamilton's purpose, Jefferson wrote. Hamilton's plan would pump money into the hands of profiteering state creditors in order to pile up "additional recruits" to the "phalanx of the Treasury." And that was not the end of the plans of the "stock-jobbing herd." Though Hamilton and his "votaries" had already become—as Walpole had been—"master of every vote in the legislature . . . the machine was not compleat. . . . Some engine of influence more permanent must be contrived," and that engine was the Bank of the United States.

Jefferson feared the bank and fought it from the start. Aside from its probable issuance of a flood of paper money that would lead to wild speculation and to the creation of a "moneyed aristocracy," and aside from its encouraging long-term national indebtedness that would in time burden the living with the extravagance of the dead, he feared the bank's political influence. He knew the historical antecedents. The bank's stockholders, like those of the Bank of England, would forever be able to manufacture a legislative majority to suit them and so corrupt the Constitution and reshape it "on the model of England." He had no choice but to fight this scheme—fight once again precisely the battle that had been fought and lost in England. The parallels are unmistakable. Hamilton, Jefferson concluded, favored monarchy "bottomed on corruption," and he made no bones about it. If you eliminated all the corruption in the British government, Hamilton said in a dinner conversation that Jefferson recalled verbatim, "It would become an *impracticable* government: as it stands at present, with all its supposed defects, it is the most perfect government which ever existed." Hamilton truly believed, Jefferson wrote, "that corruption was essential to the government of a nation," even though the whole history of eighteenth-century Britain, the whole history of Europe, revealed what consequences this kind of corruption could have.

The evils of Hamilton's program and the devastating threat it posed to the nation's freedom were clear to Jefferson from the moment he returned from France. But Hamilton's immediate goal, however erroneously and dangerously pursued, was to stimulate American economic growth, and this was something that Jefferson himself increasingly supported. His republicanism had never been naively "classical" to the exclusion of vigorous economic development or of what has been called possessive individualism, nor did his emphasis on civic virtue preclude the basic value of personal property, its preservation and enhancement. Gradually he came to value—if not the full range of entrepreneurial efforts that Hamilton had earlier promoted, or his methods—policies strangely similar to those of the Federalists. He clung to his major premise but faced realistically the rapid shifts of the economy, and made a series of adjustments.

Convinced always that "those who labour in the earth are the chosen people of God . . . the most virtuous citizens and possess the most *amor patriae*," and that the survival of freedom depends on them, he began as a radical agrarian, hoping to avoid the corruption of a debased working class and urban slums, and content for the nation to trade staples for the manufactures of others. That led him to a policy of free trade. But then he found that commercial reciprocity was not forthcoming, and so he favored, first, commercial retaliation, then protectionism, and finally the encouragement of domestic manufactures. By 1816 he concurred in a protective tariff, and wrote that "we must now place the manufacturer by the side of the agriculturist." If one did not, the results would be fatal.

> He . . . who is now against domestic manufacture must be for reducing us either to dependence on [the economies of] foreign nation[s] or to be clothed in skins, and to live like wild beasts in dens and caverns. I am not one of these; experience has taught me that manufactures are now as necessary to our independence as to our comfort.

But if that was the case, had not Hamilton's economic policies, which Jefferson had so passionately denounced, been correct from the start? He struggled to square his evolving economic views with the original principles of the Revolution that continued to dominate his thought. So he accepted manufactures; they had become necessary—but let it be *household* manufactures, he said, to keep the units small. An expanded economic role of government? Yes, but let it be chiefly the governments of the states, and the federal government only by constitutional amendment. A national bank? Perhaps: as Madison had seen when he chartered the Second United States Bank, cumulative precedent and popular usage over the years had given the bank a sanction that could not be ignored. But let it issue, not paper currency—which was "only the ghost of money," Jefferson said, "and not money itself" and which would breed speculative crazes and devastating inflation—but bills of credit and Treasury notes that would be quickly redeemed.

A highly pragmatic, tough-minded, and successful politician, Jefferson never abandoned the ideals he had so brilliantly expressed in the years before independence, and he struggled endlessly with the ambiguities they posed.

The press, he eloquently insisted, must always be free. On this he could not have been more flatly assertive, more unambiguously clear. "Our liberty depends on the freedom of the press," he wrote, "and that cannot be limited without being lost." *Again:* "Where the press is free, and every man able to read, all is safe." *And again, most famously:* "Were it left to me to decide whether we should have a government without newspapers or newspapers without a government, I should not hesitate a moment to prefer the latter." But were there *no* limits to the freedom of the press? Yes, in fact, there were. Drawing unquestioningly on the received, libertarian tradition of the early eighteenth century, which was bound into the ideology of the Revolution, he assumed that, while one could print anything one wanted to print, one was liable to legal prosecution "for *false* facts printed and published." But the question, he discovered in his years in power, was what, in matters of political opinion, is true and what is false? Who is to judge, and by what criteria? Why did not the "overt acts" doctrine of his *Act for Religious Freedom* apply in secular matters? Why would not his enemies' political falsehoods be as certainly defeated by truth as he had said false religious beliefs would be? Jefferson, reacting furiously to political attacks, adhered to his original view, which criminalized false statements, only to find himself forced to question his own basic premises. In the heat of party struggles he could only doubt, despondently, that truth could ever emerge from the contest between what he took to be an utterly ruthless, lying, scurrilous opposition press and his own right-minded publicists. At the end of his presidency he wrote that outright suppression of the press would be no more injurious to the public good than the newspapers' "abandoned prostitution to falsehood."

This was not, of course, his normal stance. He truly wished for free speech and a free press; but the complexity of these liberal goals, their inner ambiguities in application, came to him only gradually.

In the mid 1780s, recognizing the weakness and inefficiency of the federal government, he shared the view that the Articles of Confederation would have to be strengthened, but only in a few specified ways. His immediate reaction to the new Constitution when it reached him in Paris was strongly negative: its far-reaching provisions "stagger all my dispositions to subscribe" to it. "All the good of this new constitution," he wrote, "might have been couched in three or four new articles to be added to the good, old, and venerable fabrick, which should have been preserved even as a religious relique." Fearing, ever, the possible recreation of monarchy in a new guise, he was certain that a president who *could* be re-elected repeatedly, *would* be, and the result would be "a bad edition of a Polish king." Madison, who had worried through every clause and phrase of the Constitution in the most critical way possible, wrote Jefferson, on 24 October 1787, a searching analysis of the drafting and character of the Constitution. In it Madison argued that an increase in the size of a republic, far from endangering freedom by requiring an excess of power to keep order and to enforce the laws, would in fact protect freedom by dissipating animosities and multiplying factions to the point that no one interest could control the government. But Jefferson, in his reply, did not comment on this counter-intuitive idea; he reverted to the traditional fear of monarchy, elective or hereditary. Think of the Roman emperors, he wrote Madison in commenting on presidential power, think of the popes, the German emperors, the deys of the Ottoman dependencies, the Polish kings—all of them elective in some sense. "An incapacity to be elected [president] a second time would have been the only effective preventative," he said. "The king of Poland is removable every day by the Diet, yet he is never removed."

Such was Jefferson's immediate reaction to the Constitution. But soon, characteristically, as he studied the ways the Constitution would actually work, he transcended this initial response, and began to recognize the document's virtues. Within a few weeks he saw enough good in the Constitution to declare himself "nearly a neutral" on ratification. Soon thereafter he said he hoped that the requisite nine states would ratify, thus putting the Constitution into effect, but that the other four should hold out until amendments were made. Finally, after conferring with Lafayette and Paine, and convinced that the states' *recommended* amendments would quickly be enacted, he declared that outright ratification was "absolutely necessary" and that the American Constitution was "unquestionably the wisest ever yet presented to men." "We can surely boast," he concluded, "of having set the world a beautiful example of a government reformed by reason alone, without bloodshed."

So, gradually Jefferson came to accept the Constitution's basic propositions: that power could be created and constrained at the same time; that internal balances between essential rights and necessary powers could be so constructed as to be self-sustaining; that the power of a centralized, national, self-financing state could be compatible with the safety and freedom of ordinary people. The mechanics of this plan had not been the product of a grand theory. No one had designed the Constitution. It had been arrived at by an exquisitely complex process of adjustments, balances, compromises, and modifications. And therefore it is perhaps more surprising that Jefferson came so fully to accept the Constitution, and later himself to use so skillfully the executive powers that it created, than that he opposed it when it first appeared.

For the fear of power—the very heart of the original Revolutionary ideology—was an animating spirit behind all of his thinking, and ultimately the source of the deepest ambiguities. Though as president he never hesitated to use the full authority of his office, at times to use powers his opponents claimed he had no constitutional right to use, he never ceased believing that the only truly free governments were small ward-level units in which power scarcely existed and in which ordinary citizens could easily participate in government.

He struggled to eliminate aristocracies of birth and inherited wealth because, he believed, they inevitably created arbitrary power—irrational and unjustifiable power that, as he saw so vividly in Europe, could crush every impulse of ordinary people's desire for self-fulfillment. The evils of hereditary power profoundly moved him, and propelled his eloquence to extraordinary heights. In America, he wrote from France, there had never been legal distinctions among freemen "by birth or badge." Of such distinctions, "they had no more idea than they had of the mode of existence in the moon or planets." But in Europe the full horror of aristocracies of birth could be seen on every side. It was a world, Jefferson wrote,

> where the dignity of man is lost in arbitrary distinctions, where the human species is classed into several stages of degradation, where the many are crouched under the weight of the few, and where the order established can present to the contemplation of a thinking being no other picture than that of God almighty and his angels trampling under foot the hosts of the damned.

But Jefferson was an aristocrat himself. He enjoyed an inheritance of lands and slaves, and he shared the planter class's fear of mobs and of the rule of mass democracy. Salvation, for him, lay in the rule of *natural* aristocracies, elites of talent and wisdom, devoted to the public good. But he recognized that in America as in Europe the leisure and education that nurtured talent were traditionally products of inherited wealth. It followed therefore, by a logic he found compelling all his life, that a massive, systematic structure of public education that would identify and nourish native talent would be necessary if America were to retain its freedom.

His "Bill for the More General Diffusion of Knowledge" (1779) he always considered one of his most important contributions to the comprehensive revision of Virginia's laws, and he never ceased hoping that its provisions would be enacted and reproduced on a national scale. But they were not. Even in Virginia he was defeated—by parsimonious legislators; by the parochial interests of religious denominations; and by the popularity of what he called "petty *academies*" that seemed to be springing up on all sides and that inculcated in students, he said, "just taste enough of learning to be alienated from industrious pursuits, and not enough to do service in the ranks of science." Public education, "to bring into action that mass of talents which lie buried in poverty in every country, for want of the means of development," was an essential means of eliminating arbitrary power. The provision in Spain's proposed constitution of 1812 that literacy would be a prerequisite for citizenship excited his greatest admiration. "Enlighten the people generally," he said, "and tyranny and oppressions of body and mind will vanish like evil spirits at the dawn of day." But he did not live to see that dawn, nor could he conceive that a strange, unsystematic mélange of schools—public and private, parochial and secular—would one day create the universal education he so passionately desired.

Similarly, he opposed political parties, on principle, because he believed that organized political machines generated arbitrary power, power for partisan groups—selfish, power-hungry cliques, which inevitably violated the public interest. It was therefore logical for him to declare, after the bitter presidential election of 1800, that "we are all republicans; we are all federalists" since he could only think of the Federalist party not as a legitimate ruling body that differed from the Republicans on matters of policy, but as a malevolent junta (a "herd of traitors," he called them) who dream of "a single and splendid government of an aristocracy, founded on banking institutions and moneyed incorporations . . . riding and ruling over the plundered ploughman and beggared yeomanry." Once the Federalist leaders were driven from office, their followers would naturally (Jefferson believed) join the national—that is, Republican—majority. But parties survived, and for that Jefferson himself was largely responsible. To destroy the Federalist party he had had no choice but to create his own, more effective party, with devoted cadres, good organization, and an articulated program. In the process he did much, modern historians agree, "to engrain into American political life the party system, to make party government acceptable, to make party machinery a normal part of political activity, [and] to make party and patronage inseparable."

His hatred of poverty, too, was rooted in his elemental fear of arbitrary power. If he had not known from history that ignorant, idle, impoverished people were always the helpless tools of demagogues, he would have discovered it in his years in Europe. In general, his experiences there confirmed his ideological commitments, and none more than his belief that economic debasement and political tyranny go hand in hand.

He was horrified by the poverty he saw in France. A casual encounter with a beggar woman outside Fontainebleau, her tears of gratitude for the few coins he gave her, touched off "a train of reflections on [the] unequal division of property." The wealth of France, he wrote Madison, "is absolutely concentrated in a very few hands." The grandees employ "the flower of the country as servants," leaving the masses unemployed—begging and desperate—while vast lands are set aside as game preserves. He was well aware, he wrote, "that an equal division of property is impracticable," but the staggering inequality he was witnessing created such misery that, for the preservation of freedom if not for simple justice, every effort must be made legally to subdivide inherited property and to distribute it equally among descendants.

It had been for that reason in 1776 that he had written the law abolishing primogeniture and entail in Virginia, and in his draft constitution for the state he had stipulated that "every person of full age" who did not own fifty acres of land would be entitled to that amount from the public domain. The earth, he said again and again, by natural right belongs to the living and not to the dead or to their privileged descendants. Where, as in France, vast territories owned by the few are left wild while masses starve, natural right is violated, and in time those deprived of that right may well lay claim to it in ways no responsible person would favor. Poverty, Jefferson believed, was thus a political as well as a social curse; it was the foundation of an unjust concentration of political power, and led inevitably to the destruction of freedom. But he had no program for preventing the growth of poverty or for abolishing it where it existed. And he was repeatedly attacked for promoting policies that depressed the economic well-being of whole regions, chief among them his embargo of 1807–8.

That policy was devised and sustained by his idealistic passion for rational and peaceful solutions to international conflicts, but it proved to profit the rich and the unscrupulous while sacrificing the welfare of the poor. His critics were relentless. New England and the middle states, they charged, deprived of commerce and overseas markets, were devastated, but at least they could find partial relief in manufactures for a protected home market. The South, however, and Jefferson's own state in particular, had no such means of relief. "Tobacco was worthless," Henry Adams would write, relishing the irony of Jefferson's presidency in a brilliant passage of his *History,*

> but four hundred thousand negro slaves must be clothed and fed, great establishments must be kept up, [and] the social scale of living could not be reduced. . . . With astonishing rapidity Virginia succumbed to ruin, while continuing to support the system that was draining her strength. No episode in American history was more touching than the generous devotion with which Virginia clung to the embargo, and drained the poison which her own President held obstinately to her lips. . . . The old society of Virginia could never be restored. Amid the harsh warnings of John Randolph it saw its agonies approach; and its last representative, heir to all its honors and dignities, President Jefferson himself woke from his long dream of power only to find his own fortunes buried in the ruin he had made.

Fearing concentrations of power, and arbitrary power of any kind—convinced that America's experimental achievements in freedom were beset by forces that would destroy them—but endowed, himself, with an instinct for power and with exceptional political and administrative skills, and blessed with many years of active life in politics—Jefferson, more than any of the Revolution's original leaders, explored the ambiguities of freedom. If the principles that had emerged in the great struggle with Britain before 1776 had not been so clear, so luminous and compelling, in his mind; or if he had remained on the sidelines, commenting like a Greek chorus on the great events of the day, the world would have been simpler for him, the ambiguities less painful, and his reputation less complicated. As it was, he remained throughout his long career the clear voice of America's Revolutionary ideology, its purest conscience, its most brilliant expositor, its true poet, while struggling to deal with the intractable mass of the developing nation's everyday problems. In this double role—ideologist and practical politician, theorist and pragmatist—he sought to realize the Revolution's glittering promise, and as he did so he learned the inner complexities of these ideals as well as their strengths. He never ceased to fear that the great experiment might fail, that the United States might be torn apart by its internal divisions or overwhelmed by the pressures of the outside world and, like so many other nations, in the end forfeit its freedom for a specious security. But he did not despair. He hoped, with increasing confidence, that the common sense of the people and their innate idealism would overcome the obstacles and somehow resolve the ambiguities, and that America would fulfill its destiny—which was, he believed, to preserve, and to extend to other regions of the earth, "the sacred fire of freedom and self-government," and to liberate the human mind from every form of tyranny.

Suggested Readings

General

Joyce Appleby, *Capitalism and a New Social Order: The Republican Vision of the 1790's* (1984).
Roger H. Brown, *The Republic in Peril* (1964).
Stanley Elkins and Eric McKitrick, *The Age of Federalism: The Early American Republic, 1788–1800* (1993).
Donald R. Hickey, *The War of 1812: A Forgotten Conflict* (1989).
Drew McCoy, *The Elusive Republic: Political Economy in Jeffersonian America* (1982).
Forrest McDonald, *The Presidency of George Washington* (1974).
Merrill Peterson, *Thomas Jefferson and the New Nation* (1970).
James Roger Sharp, *American Politics in the Early Republic: The New Nation in Crisis* (1993).
Marshall Smelser, *The Democratic Republic, 1801–1815* (1968).
Steven Watts, *The Republic Reborn: War and the Making of Liberal America, 1790–1820* (1987).

Further Readings

EARLY REPUBLIC: Lance Banning, *The Jeffersonian Persuasion: Evolution of a Party Ideology* (1978); Noble Cunningham, *The Jeffersonian Republicans* (1963); Forrest McDonald, *Alexander Hamilton: A Biography* (1979); John C. Miller, *The Federalist Era 1789–1800* (1960).
WAR OF 1812: Robert Rutland, *Madison's Alternatives: The Jeffersonian Republicans and the Coming of the War 1805–1812* (1975).

WHIG PARTY: Thomas Brown, *Politics and Statesmanship: Essays on American Whig History* (1985); and Daniel W. Howe, *The Political Culture of the American Whigs* (1979).

OTHER WORKS: Jerald A. Combs, *The Jay Treaty* (1970); Alexander De Conde, *Entangling Alliance: Politics and Diplomacy Under George Washington* (1958); James T. Flexner, *George Washington and the New Nation, 1783–1793* (1970) and *George Washington: Anguish and Farewell, 1793–1799* (1972); John F. Hoadley, *Origins of American Political Parties 1789–1903* (1986); Richard Hofstadter, *The Idea of a Party System: The Rise of Legitimate Opposition in the United States, 1790–1840* (1969); Curtis Nettels, *The Emergence of a National Economy, 1775–1815* (1965); Robert V. Remini, *Henry Clay, Statesman for the Union* (1991); William Stinchcombe, *The XYZ Affair* (1980); James M. Smith, *Freedom's Fetters: The Alien and Sedition Laws and American Civil Liberties* (1956); and Gerald Stourzh, *Alexander Hamilton and the Idea of Republican Government* (1970).

Questions for Discussion

1. Contrast the visions of the American republic embraced by Hamilton and Jefferson.
2. Funding the national debt remains a controversial subject to this day. Explain Hamilton's funding proposal and the principal arguments against it.
3. Discuss the background and outcome of the Whiskey Rebellion and indicate its long-range significance.
4. Identify the major provisions of the Alien and Sedition Acts and discuss the principles/issues they raised and the responses to these laws.
5. If Jefferson believed that all men were created equal, how did he rationalize black slavery?
6. Identify and discuss those events and controversies that accelerated the development of political factions and ultimately political parties.
7. Explain the meaning of the title of Bernard Bailyn's essay, "Jefferson and the Ambiguities of Freedom."

The Long Shadow of Andrew Jackson: Party Politics, 1815–1844

JACKSON'S RISE TO FAME

During the thirty years between the end of the War of 1812 and the eve of the outbreak of the Mexican War, the name of Andrew Jackson (1767–1845) became inextricably linked to a formative period in the nation's history. Emerging on the national scene at the close of the War of 1812, he captured the American imagination as the hero of the Battle of New Orleans, a military victory that restored the nation's confidence and sense of destiny. Thereafter, his name became firmly fixed in the national consciousness. A contemporary characterized Jackson as the embodiment of the "the great movement of the age" and as a leader in whom Americans saw their "own image." Even those who disagreed with this assessment—and many did—were likely to admit that Jackson had left his mark upon a critical period in the nation's development and that the era which bore his name had bequeathed enduring legacies.

Born and reared on one frontier in colonial South Carolina where he fought in the American Revolution, Jackson achieved fame and fortune on another frontier located in the trans-Appalachian West, the region with which he was most closely identified throughout his adult life. Described as a "roaring, rollicking, game-cocking, horse-racing, card-playing, mischievous fellow," he read enough law to be admitted to the bar, joined the westward movement, and settled in Tennessee. There he rose to prominence as a lawyer, prosecutor, judge, land speculator, slave-owning planter, and general in the militia. Despite his rapid political ascent, Jackson by no means escaped defeats and failures, especially in his business and land ventures. For example, a land deal with a Philadelphia speculator brought him to the brink of financial ruin and almost landed him in prison. As a result of this experience, Jackson acquired a deep-seated hostility toward paper money, debts, and especially banks which he saw as accomplices in speculative ventures.

The presence of Indians on the western frontier and Jackson's encounters with them figured significantly in his early career and in the formulation of his later Indian policy. In fact, on his initial journey into the Tennessee country, Jackson and his party narrowly escaped an Indian ambush. Once established in the vicinity of Nashville, he regularly participated in military engagements against hostile Indians. Their presence all along the frontier posed a serious obstacle to westward expansion. Like most frontier residents, Jackson regarded Indians as inferior to whites and as a barbarous, untrustworthy people, but his biographer Robert Remini contends that despite such views, Jackson took a more tolerant position toward Native Americans than the majority of whites did. His most immediate concern as a resident of the trans-Appalachian West, however, was securing the frontier for whites.

Events during the War of 1812 brought Jackson widespread fame and launched his national career. As major general in the Tennessee militia, he led an army into the Southwest to subdue an uprising of Creek Indians. When his army penetrated Indian country, it launched a ferocious assault that crushed the power of the Creek Nation. Jackson's treaty with the Creeks in 1814 opened millions of acres of land to white settlers, thereby gaining for him wide recognition and respect throughout the South and West. When Jackson and his army repulsed the British in the Battle of New Orleans on January 8, 1815, "Old Hickory" emerged as an authentic American hero, a reputation that he took with him to the grave. Three years later, when the Seminole Indians in Spanish-owned Florida attacked settlers along the American frontier, Jackson pursued them across the border and seized Florida from Spain, an act that caused consternation and alarm within official circles in Washington. Following an effective defense of his military actions against charges made by Henry Clay and other critics, the affair was settled in 1819 when the United States acquired Florida from Spain. Jackson became the first governor of the new territory, a post that he vacated after a few months.

The fifty-four-year-old Jackson returned to Tennessee after his brief tenure in Florida to lay plans for realizing his presidential aspirations. With the aid of the so-called Nashville Junto, a group of politically astute and loyal friends, he plotted his strategy for winning the presidential election in 1824. Diverse groups of voters rallied to his support. His reputation as a military hero appealed to patriotic citizens generally. Westerners who saw him as one of their own were grateful for his elimination of the Creek Indian obstacle to their quest for more land. The so-called men on the make gravitated to Jackson who, as the quintessential self-made man, was an apt symbol of their own ambitions.

JAMES MONROE

Jackson laid the groundwork for his bid for the presidency during the administration (1817–1825) of James Monroe, the last of the so-called Virginia Dynasty. A dedicated Republican for whom Thomas Jefferson had served as both mentor and patron, Monroe had occupied a variety of important military, diplomatic, and political offices during the forty years prior to his election as president in 1816. Tainted by their opposition to the War of 1812 and by the secessionist sentiments voiced by some within its ranks at the Hartford Convention (1814), the Federalist party disintegrated as an effective national organization in the postwar era. In 1816 Monroe defeated the Federalist presidential candidate by winning 183 of the 217 electoral votes. He was reelected four years later with only one electoral vote cast against him. The lopsided vote, coupled with his triumphal tour of New England, prompted a Federalist editor in Boston to proclaim his administration as the beginning of an "era of good feelings." Even though Monroe's two terms witnessed an acceleration of personal and factional disputes within Republican ranks, the president himself attempted to give credence to the image of an atmosphere of harmony and public spiritedness. Firmly committed to the view of a nonpartisan chief executive first articulated by President Washington, Monroe regularly condemned the "party spirit" as destructive to republican institutions.

Monroe's most notable achievements were in the area of foreign affairs, and his name has been associated with a historic foreign policy statement, the Monroe Doctrine (see Chapter 9). In domestic policy Monroe was committed to moderate nationalism. As a former secretary of War, he strongly advocated a series of national defense measures, including the construction of more adequate coastal fortifications and the maintenance of a larger peacetime army. He also urged the adoption of a high tariff to protect "infant" industries most injured by foreign imports and recognized the need for federal aid for internal improvements such as roads and canals.

The president secured enactment of relatively little legislation to implement his recommendations, in part because they fell victim to the competing sectional interests represented in Congress. Although Congress acquiesced in his desire for improved coastal fortifications, the widespread popular opposition to large standing armies, coupled with economic considerations, ultimately led to a reduction in the size of the army to a mere six thousand men. The agricultural South led the movement that blocked efforts to enact a protective tariff, and Monroe himself contributed to the defeat of federal aid for internal improvements by insisting on a constitutional amendment before allowing the government to fund such projects. The Panic of 1819 and the economic downturn that followed also figured significantly in Monroe's failure to achieve the objectives that he outlined in his annual messages.

Because Monroe, like Madison, deferred to Congress on legislative matters and shunned the use of patronage to enhance his political clout, he seriously compromised his capacity to lead. Despite his repeated references to "the increased harmony of opinion prevailing throughout the nation," his own cabinet scarcely conformed to such an image; rather it revealed the degree to which factionalism within Republican ranks had replaced rivalry between two political parties. Because three members of Monroe's cabinet aspired to succeed him as president, they devoted their energies to mustering supporters and subordinated everything to their individual aspirations. Frustrated by the acrimonious confrontations and pursuit of individual political agendas by cabinet members, Monroe on one occasion drove his secretary of the treasury from the White House with fire tongs.

THE MISSOURI COMPROMISE

The most serious political crisis during Monroe's term erupted in 1819 when Missouri applied for statehood, an event that thrust the slavery issue into the national political arena. At the time the Union contained eleven slave states and eleven free states. Since slavery was already well established in Missouri, it was assumed that it would enter as a slave state and therefore would upset the sectional balance and open the way for the South to increase its power. While the Missouri application was under consideration, Congressman James Tallmadge, Jr., of New York proposed an amendment that would prohibit the introduction of additional slaves into Missouri and provide for the gradual emancipation of those already there. The Tallmadge Amendment set off a controversy that raged for almost two years: antislavery groups in the North rallied to its support; and southern congressmen resolutely opposed it. When Maine applied for admission to statehood as a free state, southerners promised to block Maine's application unless northerners agreed to allow Missouri to enter the Union as a slave state.

Usually sensitive to public opinion, President Monroe utterly failed to appreciate the intensity of northern antislavery opinion. The president never discussed the issue with his cabinet and left Congress to settle the matter. Speaker of the House Henry Clay and Illinois Senator Jesse B. Thomas assumed the leadership in working out a compromise that would preserve the Union intact. Their measure allowed Missouri to enter as a slave state and Maine as a free state, but to make this palatable to northerners, especially in the House, it prohibited slavery in the remainder of the Louisiana Purchase north of latitude 36°30′ which was the southern boundary of Missouri. Once the Senate approved the compromise, Speaker Clay utilized all his considerable political power and skills to get it through the House in 1820. Although a few observers, including Thomas Jefferson, viewed the Missouri Compromise as merely a temporary reprieve and believed that slavery would return to haunt the nation, most Americans hailed the compromise as a happy resolution of a crisis that threatened to destroy the Union. Few were more deeply troubled by the agitation over the Missouri-Maine question than Andrew Jackson. Kept fully informed of the congressional debates, Jackson interpreted the issue of slavery in national politics as "the entering wedge" that would destroy the Union unless the issue was consciously muted and removed from partisan politics.

POLITICAL CHANGES

Among the many changes altering American life and institutions by the 1824 election were the collapse of the first party system of Federalists and Republicans and the democratization of politics. The Federalists offered no presidential candidate after 1816 and disappeared as a national political force. The one-party hegemony that ensued meant that various factions within the Republican party competed for the presidency. Signaling the arrival of a new political culture was the overthrow of the congressional caucus which traditionally selected the party's presidential nominee. Denounced as aristocratic and undemocratic, "King Caucus" was ultimately replaced by national nominating conventions. No less significant were steps taken to open politics to more Americans. One was the reduction or elimination of property requirements for voting. Another was the introduction of written ballots to replace the custom of voting aloud. A third replaced appointive offices with elective ones. Finally, while the electoral college continued to exist and elect the president, the popular election of presidential electors replaced the practice of having them chosen by state legislatures. Such changes significantly affected the presidential campaign of 1824.

Although a rump congressional caucus chose William H. Crawford of Georgia as the Republican presidential nominee, other aspirants were nominated by state legislatures and received endorsements from mass meetings. Among them was Andrew Jackson. The other candidates, in addition to Crawford, were John Quincy Adams of Massachusetts, John C. Calhoun of South Carolina, and Henry Clay of Kentucky, all of whom were nationally known political figures and none of whom took Jackson seriously. Crawford was Monroe's secretary of the treasury; Adams, the son of President John Adams, was Monroe's secretary of state; Clay, a westerner like Jackson, was the powerful speaker of the House of Representatives and the author of the American System, a program of protective tariffs and federally funded internal improvements; and Calhoun was Monroe's secretary of War, but withdrew from the competition before the election.

JOHN QUINCY ADAMS

THE ELECTION OF 1824

In the complicated four-way contest, Jackson led with a substantial margin of popular votes, but because he received a plurality rather than the constitutionally mandated majority in the electoral college, the Twelfth Amendment required that the House of Representatives choose a president from the top three contenders (Jackson, Adams, and Crawford). Eliminated from the competition,

Clay threw his support to Adams with whom he agreed on many economic and political issues. As a result, the House chose Adams who then appointed Clay as secretary of state. Convinced that Adams and Clay had struck a "corrupt bargain" that had negated the right of the people to elect their president, Jackson resigned from the Senate, returned to Tennessee, and began preparations for the presidential race in 1828. The "corrupt bargain" united Jackson's supporters and pushed them to advocate a more democratic political process.

In organizing the opposition to Adams' administration, Jackson brought within his ranks well-placed national political figures such as Calhoun and a new breed of politicians represented by Martin Van Buren of New York who played a vital part in dispelling the popular distaste for party politics that lingered from the Revolutionary generation and was a principal strategist in reviving two-party competition. Jackson himself presided over a well-financed and effective organization in which a network of pro-Jackson newspapers articulated the campaign's central theme of the "corrupt bargain" of 1824 and the moral unfitness of Adams for the presidency. The republic, so the Jacksonians argued, had been corrupted by "special privilege" and the abandonment of virtue for which they held Adams and his secretary of State, Henry Clay, responsible.

ADAMS' ADMINISTRATION

A man of great intellect and integrity who possessed a cohesive vision of the nation's future development, Adams had been a conspicuous public figure for three decades prior to becoming president. A major objective of his foreign policy was the active pursuit of foreign trade as evident in his success in concluding nine commercial treaties. In domestic affairs he assiduously promoted a nationalistic program known as the American System, often linked to the name of Secretary of State Clay. Adams strongly advocated internal improvements such as roads and canals, a protective tariff to stimulate industry, a sound financial system based on the Bank of the United States, and the advancement of higher education and the cultivation of "elegant arts." His failure to achieve substantial portions of his program was a result of a combination of factors: The opposition of those who objected to his use of broad federal powers; the intensification of sectional rivalries; the obstructionism of the increasing number of Jacksonians in Congress who kept alive the "corrupt bargain" theme; and Adams' austere, aloof personality and disdain for partisan politics.

ANDREW JACKSON

THE ELECTION OF 1828

In 1828 Jackson confronted incumbent President Adams, the candidate of those who became known as National Republicans. The Democratic Republicans (or Democrats as they came to be called) extolled Jackson's incorruptibility, hostility to special privilege, and rise to fame and fortune from humble origins. Jackson himself remained vague on most sensitive topics and relied to a large degree on his popularity as the hero of the Battle of New Orleans. In fact, issues tended to get lost in the mudslinging that characterized the campaign. For sordidness and sheer mendacity, the campaign has few, if any, equals in the annals of politics. Jacksonians, in addition to charging Adams with having stolen the presidency in 1824, claimed that he was rich and aristocratic, wore silk underwear, and had acted as pimp for the tsar when he was minister to Russia (1809–1815). The opposition press, all the while, vilified Jackson as a bloodthirsty backwoodsman, the mulatto son of a "common prostitute," and a bigamist who had married Rachel Robards before her divorce from her first husband was final. The outcome of the election was a stunning victory for Jackson. That the voter turnout was twice what it had been in 1824 was but one indication of the democratic process taking place in American politics—a process that ultimately extended the vote to virtually all adult white males.

More than fifteen thousand citizens from all parts of the country converged on Washington to witness Jackson's inauguration as president on March 4, 1829. That Jackson was exhausted, ill, and grief-stricken by the recent death of his beloved wife Rachel in no way dampened the enthusiasm of the crowd. The chanting, cheering, boisterous throng consisted, according to one observer, of "all sorts of people, from the highest and most polished, down to the most vulgar and gross in the nation." When the sixty-one-year-old Jackson, tall, white-maned, and wrinkle-faced, finally appeared for the outdoor ceremony on the east portico of the Capitol, the shouting and applause became so thunderous that it seemed to "shake the very ground." In a ten-minute address Jackson attempted to reassure his critics and solidify his loose coalition of supporters. Repeating a campaign pledge, he promised to correct abuses that had corrupted "freedom of elections" and placed power in "unfaithful and incompetent hands."

After taking the oath of office, the new president made his way to the White House where a public reception was to be held. An immense throng surged into the Executive Mansion to catch a glimpse of the president and to partake of the refreshments. In the chaos that followed, furniture was broken, china and glassware smashed, and carpets soiled. Jackson escaped to avoid injury. Nothing like it had ever occurred before. Washington insiders, those of the elite, viewed with utter disbelief and no little disdain the behavior of the assortment of ordinary citizens—"common people"—participating in the inaugural festivities. The disorder and destruction created by the throng confirmed the worst suspicions of those who viewed Jackson's election as the elevation of brawler, drunkard, and illiterate backwoodsman to the nation's highest office. The "reign of King Mob" during his inauguration in their view was but an omen of the certain disaster that awaited the young republic under the leadership of such a vulgar *parvenu*. Even though Jackson could be cranky and obstinate and on occasion exploded into rages, he scarcely conformed to the image of a vulgarian.

Robert Cruickshank's cartoon, "All Creation Going to the White House," depicted the scene at Andrew Jackson's inauguration in 1829.

Economic and Social Changes

The economic and social transformation that accompanied the emergence of a national market economy and that produced severe tensions profoundly affected the political environment that confronted Andrew Jackson throughout his eight years as president. The conflicting demands of numerous and diverse interest groups, old as well as new, in both rural and urban America echoed loudly in the political arena. Small farmers in the West clamored for greater access to public lands, while those in the South pressed for a greater share of political power. In the Northeast and the Northwest urban labor mobilized first in local workingmen's parties and later in unions, and the evangelized middle class took up the cause of various moral and social reforms. At the same time, southern slaveholders enacted increasingly repressive slave codes in response to abolitionism and Nat Turner's slave revolt and continually pushed the cotton kingdom and its slave labor system into the trans-Mississippi West. Within such a context Jackson and his advisors, especially Martin Van Buren, secretary of state in his first administration and vice president in his second, welded together the diverse Jacksonian constituency into an effective new political party.

Rise of a New Political Party

To become a successful national party, Jacksonian Democracy had to cut across geographical sections and include a broad socioeconomic spectrum of the

electorate. Its ranks included the wealthy such as Jackson himself and the upwardly mobile as well as hardscrabble farmers and urban workers. At the heart
of the new party's ideology was the assumption of the inherent conflict between
"producing" and "nonproducing" classes, an assumption that enabled it to turn
to its advantage the fears and aspirations of those voters in the throes of adjusting to the market revolution and at the same time appeal to those largely
untouched by the revolution. Such groups included artisans, wage earners,
planters, and small farmers. Jacksonians ultimately constructed a party organization that was capable of accommodating those who had recently acquired the
vote and who demanded to participate in the political process. But the ingredient that helped make this ideology appealing to a broad segment of voters
and that enhanced the effectiveness of the Democratic organization was
Jackson himself and his immense popularity as the self-appointed spokesman
for the interests of the many against the interests of the few. It may well be
questionable whether Jackson played such a role, but what is important is that
a majority of the electorate thought he did.

If Jackson committed himself to few specific policies in the campaign of
1828, he left little doubt that he espoused "the great republican principles" of
Thomas Jefferson which assumed continual conflict between liberty and power
and between virtue and corruption. Public virtue which required a willingness
to subordinate private interests to the common good was essential to preserving
the precarious balance between liberty and power. Without virtue republicanism became "corrupted" by individuals and institutions that enjoyed power
and special privileges. Such corruption, by undermining the liberty of the ordinary citizen, would ultimately destroy republicanism itself. The "corrupt
bargain" between Adams and Clay was, in Jackson's view, a classic example of
the subversion of republican principles. The best means of combatting corruption in a society undergoing rapid and profound change, Jackson argued,
was to hold fast to majority rule, limited federal government power, and governmental protection of the interests of ordinary citizens. Whatever ambiguities
and inconsistencies may have characterized his actions as president, he remained unreconciled to what he considered economic progress predicated on
unequal privileges or the permanent domination of one group of Americans by
others who used the power of government to gain their dominance. Jackson's
aim was not to obstruct economic expansion, but rather to prevent those of
great wealth from controlling government power and using it to establish themselves as a permanent "moneyed aristocracy."

JACKSON'S FIRST TERM

Jacksonian Ideals

When Jackson entered the White House, he possessed a set of convictions
rooted in his unusual personal history and experiences in the South and West
rather than a coherent political philosophy. A product of the Revolutionary

generation, he came to office at the very moment that the nation was adjusting to the market revolution and to a new political culture that provided increasing numbers of citizens with the franchise. "Like no other figure," one historian has observed, "Jackson symbolized the American caught between the ideals of the Revolution and the realities of nineteenth century liberal capitalism." Wedded to a nostalgic vision of the early republic, Jackson often exhibited uneasiness and uncertainty in grappling with issues raised by the new socioeconomic order. The conditions under which he labored during his first administration also contributed to the ambivalence that characterized his efforts to adjust to the realities of the new order and his uncertainty in translating his set of convictions into specific policies. Surrounded by an ideologically heterogeneous cabinet prone to personal rivalry and conflict, he confronted an unruly Congress representing widely disparate sectional interests. Those in Congress identified as Jacksonians consisted of a loose coalition that included a hodge-podge of conflicting interests, ideologies, and leaders. As his set of convictions evolved into something approaching a coherent ideology, his coalition assumed the unity and discipline of a modern political party especially during his second term.

Rotation in Office   Jackson began his administration by reiterating his commitment to majority rule. "The people are sovereign, their will is absolute," he declared in his first message to Congress. To enhance the role of the people in the governing of their republic, Jackson announced his intention to implement a plan of "rotation in office" regarding appointees to government positions. Such a plan, he argued, would eliminate conditions that resulted in an elitist and corrupt "official class" whose members, unaccountable to the people, viewed their positions as a "vested right." The president claimed that the duties of civil servants should be "so plain and simple" that any reasonably intelligent citizen would be able to perform them. "It is rotation [in office]," he proclaimed, "that will perpetuate our liberty." The rotation plan created a furor among anti-Jacksonians in Congress. When a Jackson partisan in the Senate claimed that the plan was based on the idea that "to the victor belongs the spoils of the enemy," opponents denounced the "Spoils System" as nothing more than a method by which the president could reward faithful supporters. Jackson ultimately dismissed only about 10 percent of those in office when he came to power. Even his adversaries admitted that many of those whom he fired were either incompetent or corrupt. Although Jackson was by no means the first president to appoint his supporters and friends to office, he was the first to justify the practice on democratic grounds.

Conflicts in the Cabinet

The Eaton Affair   Far more troublesome and time-consuming for Jackson than the tempest over his rotation plan was the so-called Eaton Affair or "Eaton Malaria," as Secretary of State Van Buren described it. At the center of this controversy was Secretary of War John Eaton, a Tennesseean and a longtime personal friend of the president, who had married Margaret (Peggy)

O'Neale Timberlake, a young widow. In question was not merely the new Mrs. Eaton's lowly origins—the daughter of a tavern keeper—but her alleged dubious reputation and affair with Eaton prior to the death of her first husband. As gossip circulated about Peggy O'Neale, fiction mixed so generously with fact that the two became indistinguishable. Led by the wife of Vice President Calhoun, Washington's society matrons refused to treat her as a social equal and pronounced her a fallen woman unfit for inclusion in their genteel circle. The social ostracism of the Eatons deeply troubled Jackson. Peggy Eaton and the malicious gossip about her reminded him of his wife Rachel, whose life, he believed, had been shortened by just such slander. At a cabinet meeting called on September 10, 1829, to consider the Eaton Affair, Jackson finally ended the proceedings by pronouncing Peggy O'Neale "as chaste as a virgin."

The real significance of this absurd affair is that it became entangled in the struggle within the president's official family between Vice President Calhoun and Secretary Van Buren. As a result, the cabinet, already mired in political infighting, became even more sharply divided. Both Calhoun and Van Buren were intensely ambitious and sought to use their association with the popular Jackson as the means to reach the White House. Calhoun, in particular, saw Eaton and more especially his influence with Jackson as an obstacle to his own presidential aspirations. Some historians argue that Calhoun seized upon the Eaton Affair as a means to force Eaton's resignation, calculating that he could persuade Jackson to appoint a Calhounite to head the War Department. All the while, Van Buren, a widower, was extending every social courtesy to Peggy Eaton and her husband. Outraged by the treatment accorded the Eatons by Washington's social elite, Jackson came to believe that Calhoun rather than his wife was responsible for their ostracism.

John C. Calhoun   For a variety of reasons, the president had long been suspicious of Calhoun's loyalty. Not the least of these were persistent rumors that Calhoun, as Monroe's secretary of War, had supported censure of Jackson for his actions in Florida while in pursuit of the Seminoles. The vice president's failure to provide Jackson with an unequivocal denial when directly questioned appeared to confirm the rumors. To make matters worse, Calhoun published a lengthy article in a Washington newspaper in which he attempted to explain his role in the Florida incident and accused Van Buren, his arch rival for Jackson's mantle, of trying to use the Florida incident to ruin his career. As a result of this episode, Jackson was convinced more than ever that his vice president was behind efforts to exclude the Eatons from official and polite society. The growing rift between the two men obviously worked to Van Buren's advantage. At Van Buren's suggestion, Jackson revamped his cabinet; in the process he rid himself of Secretary Eaton, but more importantly, he eliminated those cabinet members who supported Calhoun.

While the political complications resulting from the Eaton Affair continued to multiply, Jackson faced a host of public issues that demanded his attention and action. Among these were internal improvements, public lands, Indian removal, and the Bank of the United States. The future of Jackson's leadership, as well as the political movement that he headed, depended upon his response to these controversial issues. Distracted by the Eaton Affair and uncertain about the proper course to pursue, Jackson made little progress during the first nine months in office in establishing his position regarding the important issues confronting the nation. Despite the conflicting sectional interests represented by Congress and the unreliability of its Jacksonian members, the president finally began to exert his leadership and define his position when the Twenty-first Congress convened in December 1829.

Land Use and Indian Issues

Public Land   Among the measures considered by Congress were those concerning public lands and internal improvements. Westerners demanded cheap land from the public domain and saw as their primary opponents northern industrialists fearful of losing their labor supply to the West. Jackson sided with the westerners and signed into law the Preemption Act (1830) that granted to squatters on certain public land preference in purchasing such land. Also of interest to westerners was the Maysville Road Bill, one of several measures sponsored by internal improvements advocates. Although the road was a link in the national road, it lay wholly within Kentucky, the home of Henry Clay.

Jackson vetoed the Maysville Road Bill on the grounds that as a "purely local" project it could not receive federal funds. Although he made clear his opposition to a federally funded system of roads and canals and vetoed other measures similar to the Maysville bill, he did not condemn internal improvements in general and, in fact, applauded the efforts of states that encouraged such projects. Sustained by Congress, the Maysville veto was the first of a dozen instances in which Jackson exercised the veto, more than all of his predecessors combined. By effectively blocking any comprehensive federal program of internal improvements, Jackson alienated many of the prime movers in the market revolution but won applause from strict constructionists and limited government advocates who interpreted his action as evidence of his commitment to traditional republican principles. But he by no means ignored the demands of the national economy: By the end of his tenure he had expended more on internal improvements than all previous presidents.

Indian Removal   While debate raged over the Maysville veto, Jackson's Indian removal legislation was making its way through Congress. The presence of Indians had long been the subject of discussion, and President Monroe had even called for their removal west of the Mississippi River, but such a plan was never implemented. Jackson was determined for removal to begin. In his view Indians simply had no rights if such rights conflicted with the security and needs of the national government. Further, Jackson argued that the removal of eastern tribes to an area west of the Mississippi was essential to preserve Indian life and culture. In his Indian removal bill, the president proposed to exchange unorganized public land west of the Mississippi for Indian lands in the East. Indians

FIGURE 7–1
Indian Removals, 1820–1840

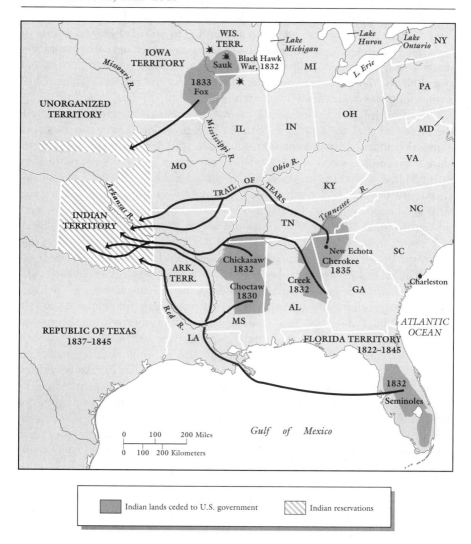

who moved would have perpetual title to their new land and would be compensated for improvements they had made on their old lands in the East. The federal government would bear the cost of their removal and assist them for the first year after removal. The bill, enacted in 1830, included an appropriation of $500,000 to cover such expenses (see Figure 7–1).

At the time Jackson occupied the White House about one hundred thousand Indians occupied approximately 100 million acres of land located in twenty-four states and territories. The so-called Five Civilized Tribes in the Southeast—the Cherokees, Creeks, Choctaws, Chickasaws, and Seminoles—had made "the most notable progress in the arts of civilized life." Whites, especially in Georgia and Alabama, deeply resented the presence of Indians, regardless of their degree of civilization, because their presence denied whites access to their land. Georgia, in particular, had been attempting to get rid of Indians within its borders. The pressure on the Indians to leave became stronger when gold was discovered on Cherokee lands in north Georgia. Seeking relief from these encroachments, the Cherokees appealed ultimately to the Supreme Court. Chief Justice John Marshall rendered two decisions.

His first decision, in the case of *Cherokee Nation v. Georgia*, rejected both the argument that the Cherokee nation was a sovereign nation and Jackson's contention that the Cherokees were subject to state law. Instead Marshall declared that Indians were "domestic dependent nations," subject not to the laws of individual states, but to those of the United States. Marshall's second decision, in *Worcester v. Georgia* (1832), enhanced the prospect of a serious constitutional crisis by ruling that all Georgia laws regarding the Cherokees were unconstitutional. Both at the time and since, President Jackson has been credited with saying: "Well, John Marshall has made his decision: *now let him enforce it!*" The statement may have sounded like Jackson, but as one biographer noted, he did not say it because "there was no reason for him to do so." Even though Jackson encouraged Georgia in its intransigence, he was nonetheless careful to avoid any action that would prompt that state to join South Carolina (which was then challenging federal authority) and thereby escalate the affair into a crisis that might jeopardize the Union itself.

In the removal measure Jackson had his first collision with the moral reformers associated with the Second Great Awakening who had long underwritten efforts to Christianize and civilize the Indians. The reformers spearheaded by Reverend Jeremiah Evarts denounced Indian removal. The president's defense of Peggy Eaton, coupled with his refusal to support the Sabbatarian (Sabbath observance) movement by closing post offices on Sunday, made their opposition to his Indian policy all the more vehement. Despite the efforts by anti-Jacksonians in Congress to exploit such opposition, the Indian Removal bill passed—but just barely.

The implementation of Indian removal dragged on throughout and even beyond the end of Jackson's tenure as president. While a minority of the Cherokees in Georgia consented to a removal agreement, the majority refused to leave their homes for the West. Jackson then sent the army to Georgia to round them up and drive them westward on what became known as "The Trail of Tears." Other tribes shared a similar fate of deprivation and suffering as they moved westward to relocate in Indian Territory (what would become Oklahoma). The Seminoles waged a war for seven years against removal. The policy of removal was no less devastating for the Indians of the old Northwest who experienced a "Trail of Death." "Whatever the intentions of those responsible for the policy," Jackson's biographer Robert Remini concludes, "the actual removal was a frightful injustice which brought sickness, starvation and death to thousands of human beings." Jackson believed, or at least convinced

Robert Lindreaux's rendition of "The Trail of Tears," the removal of the Cherokees from Georgia to present-day Oklahoma.

himself, that he had found a safe haven for thousands of Indians beyond the Mississippi where they could preserve their way of life and would constitute no threat to whites. No doubt, too, most white Americans were glad to be rid of the Indian "problem," but none were more delighted than those who profited by the surrender of more than 100 million acres of Indian land in the East.

Financial and States' Rights Issues

The Tariff Controversy   The most serious crisis that confronted President Jackson—one that raised the specter of disunion and severely tested his leadership—arose over tariffs. After the War of 1812 Congress began enacting tariff measures designed primarily to protect domestic manufacturers from foreign competition rather than to raise revenue. This trend culminated in the passage of the Tariff Act of 1828, the year before Jackson assumed the presidency. The high protective tariff, known as the "Tariff of Abominations," aroused strong opposition among those, especially in the South, who viewed it as primarily beneficial to the Northeast, the section most involved in the market revolution. Leading the opposition was South Carolina, an agricultural state in the throes of economic decline. Hard hit by the Panic of 1819, South Carolina was suffering from a drop in the price of cotton and from soil exhaustion produced by years of intensive cultivation. Convinced that the tariff act would increase the cost of both domestic and foreign manufactured goods that the state depended upon, South Carolinians tended to blame all of their economic woes on the measure. It may also be true, as some historians suggest, that a growing concern about the future of slavery figured in their opposition to the tariff. It is conceivable that some whites were alarmed by the possibility that the same federal government that imposed on them an oppressive tariff might also acquiesce in abolitionist demands and outlaw slavery. What is indisputable, however, is that before the tariff crisis had run its course it had become entangled with sectional antagonism, states' rights, and the ambitions of rival politicians.

In response to the Tariff Act of 1828, Vice President Calhoun provided his native state with a rationale for rejecting the legislation in a widely circulated pamphlet entitled *Exposition and Protest*. But because Calhoun was at the time Jackson's vice presidential running mate and hoped to succeed him, the pamphlet was published anonymously. In addition to condemning protective tariffs, Calhoun's *Exposition* developed a theory by which a state could protect itself from an oppressive central government—a device for the protection of minority rights against the tyranny of the majority. Known as the doctrine of nullification, Calhoun's theory, which received further elaboration in his Fort Hill Address (1831), represented an extreme form of states' rights. Calhoun maintained that a state could declare void federal laws that conflicted with its interests. He argued that the Union was a compact of states in which each state reserved the authority to nullify any act of Congress injurious to its sovereignty or rights. Since state conventions had created the Constitution, similar conventions could declare federal laws unconstitutional and nullify them. Only by such a procedure, Calhoun explained, could the rights of the minority be protected. Such a view stood in sharp contrast to that of Jackson who saw the Union as a creature of the people rather than the states. If the federal government refused to allow its laws to be nullified, Calhoun reluctantly conceded that a state had the right to secede from the Union. But he insisted that his doctrine of nullification had been advanced to prevent, rather than precipitate, secession. Calhoun the nationalist had become Calhoun the sectionalist.

The Nullification Crisis   With his *Exposition and Protest* and the Fort Hill Address, Calhoun had moved a dispute over a tariff act into a debate over the nature of the Union. Early in January 1830 some of the issues raised by Calhoun received an airing in the Senate during a discussion of public land sales. Senator Robert Y. Hayne of South Carolina defended slavery and states' rights and echoed the nullification theory of his friend, Calhoun. Responding to Hayne was Senator Daniel Webster of Massachusetts, who relentlessly attacked states' rights and nullification. At one point Webster shook his finger at the Senate's presiding officer, none other than Calhoun, as he declared that the Union was made up of people, not states. "Liberty and Union, now and forever, one and inseparable!" was but one of the memorable phrases in a memorable address.

Although the South Carolina legislature had approved Calhoun's *Exposition* without revealing its author, the body took no steps to nullify the tariff act. The reason for its action was the belief that Jackson was a states' rights advocate who would relieve South Carolina of its oppression as soon as he was inaugurated. Such a calculation could scarcely have been more incorrect. As one of his biographers has noted, Jackson had always subscribed to a "fuzzy kind of states' rights philosophy" which had been considerably weakened by the time he became president. In fact, the doctrine of nullification appalled Jackson who believed that although states did indeed possess rights, the destruction of the Union was not one of them. In April 1830, a banquet to commemorate Jefferson's birthday presented Jackson with an opportunity to make clear his position, especially to the nullifiers. Rising to make a toast, the president proposed: "Our Federal Union, it must be preserved." (Actually he added the word "federal" before releasing the statement to the press.) Also present at the celebration was Vice President Calhoun who responded: "The union next to our liberty most dear." The split between the two men over nullification brought an end to their relationship. Jackson chose Van Buren as his vice presidential running mate in 1832. Calhoun resigned as vice president and was elected senator from South Carolina. The final chapter in this drama occurred in the wake of the presidential election of 1832.

The Bank War   Like the tariff crisis, the so-called Bank War clarified both Jackson's political principles and conception of presidential power. A struggle that originated early in his administration, the Bank War continued until Jackson left office. The Second Bank of the United States was the successor to the original Bank of the United States whose charter had expired in 1811. The difficulties in financing the War of 1812 and the economic expansion that followed it dramatized the need for a new and larger bank. Chartered for twenty years in 1816, the Second Bank was a quasi-public institution in which the government owned one-fifth of the stock and private investors, including foreigners, owned the rest. Its board of directors consisted of five members appointed by the president of the United States and twenty elected by stockholders. The bank accepted the deposits of private individuals and served as the depository for all federal funds. It was empowered to help collect taxes, provide credit, especially to state banks, buy and sell government bonds, make commercial loans, and issue bank notes which came to constitute about 20 percent of the money in circulation in the nation. Headquartered in Philadelphia, the Second Bank ultimately had twenty-five branches located in cities scattered throughout the United States which enabled it to shift funds as necessary to different parts of the country and to exert influence on state banks. It could act as a restraint on the free-wheeling practices of state banks by insisting that they back their notes with gold and silver and by calling in the loans it made to such banks. At its best the Second Bank brought order to a chaotic banking system, provided a reliable currency, and helped finance the market revolution. At its worst it acted irresponsibly by arbitrarily restricting credit for political, rather than economic, reasons. Among those on its payroll were two well-known anti-Jacksonians, Henry Clay and Daniel Webster.

During its first two years the Second Bank acted in ways that contributed to, rather than restrained, runaway speculation. Placed under new management, the bank systematically restricted credit by calling in its loans, an act that created acute difficulties, especially in the West and in urban centers. Many Americans who held the bank responsible for the Panic of 1819 denounced it as an irresponsible "monster." With the selection of the well-educated, wealthy and highly articulate Nicholas Biddle as its president in 1823, the Second Bank generally entered upon an era marked by responsible management.

The president's dislike of banks in general and their paper money (bank notes), which he blamed for an episode that had virtually bankrupted him, rather than Biddle's arrogance, prompted him to declare war on the Second Bank. In his view the Second Bank represented the institutionalization of the "moneyed aristocracy" that thwarted the popular will and corrupted the republic. In his first annual message to Congress he included a brief reference to the bank over the objections of his advisors. He doubted both the expediency and the constitutionality of the bank (even though its constitutionality had been upheld by the Supreme Court in 1819). Specifically, Jackson accused the bank of failing to provide the nation with "a uniform and sound currency." What he did not say in his message was that he believed that bank funds were used to influence the outcome of elections, precisely the kind of corruption he associated with the "moneyed aristocracy." Congressional response to his references to the bank favored Biddle rather than the president, who was disappointed that even his partisans in Congress were divided on the issue. By 1831, however, Jacksonians in various parts of the country had begun rallying to the president's position on the bank.

Fully aware of Jackson's opposition to the renewal of the Second Bank's charter, Clay and Webster prevailed upon Biddle to apply for renewal in 1832, four years early, on the grounds that the president would not risk a veto in an election year. Clay and Webster secured congressional approval of the bank's recharter in July 1832, but they had miscalculated in believing that Jackson would not exercise the veto. "The Bank is trying to kill me, *but I will kill it*," Jackson confided to Van Buren. On July 10, 1832, Jackson vetoed the bank recharter measure with a ringing statement that denounced the bank as unconstitutional and undemocratic and called attention to the foreigners among its stockholders. The bank, he insisted, was a dangerous monopoly by which the rich and powerful bent "the acts of government to their own selfish purposes." Outraged that the message ignored the positive services rendered by the bank, Biddle denounced it as nothing more than "the fury of a chained panther biting the bars of his cage." Clay, Webster, and other National Republicans exerted their best efforts to override the veto but failed to get the necessary two-thirds majority. Whatever its shortcomings, Jackson's veto message was indisputably a masterpiece of political propaganda.

The "Downfall of Mother Bank" was a cartoon rendition (1833) of Andrew Jackson's successful war against the Bank of the United States.

THE ELECTION OF 1832

The Three-Party Campaign

Jackson's message defined at least one of the issues in the presidential campaign of 1832 which represented an important stage in the evolution of the second party system. Both parties strengthened their identity and even settled on names. The Jacksonians replaced the name Republican by calling themselves Democrats. The anti-Jacksonians became known as National Republicans for the time being. The campaign of 1832 was also significant because it introduced national nominating conventions and was the first to include a third party.

The third party originated in western New York along the Erie Canal where in 1826 a disgruntled Freemason (Mason), William Morgan, threatened to write a book exposing the secrets of the fraternal order. Arrested on a trumped-up charge, Morgan was released and shortly afterward disappeared. Allegedly he had been spirited away by a group of Masons and murdered. The public indignation over Morgan's disappearance was prompted largely by resentment of the Masonic Order as an elitist organization whose members monopolized wealth, power, and offices. The Masons' success in blocking an investigation of the affair reinforced the impression that they represented a sinister force.

Morgan's disappearance soon became the subject of mass meetings and public appeals for exposing the guilty parties. Thurlow Weed, an able editor knowledgeable in the ways of political organization, was a key figure in galvanizing the hostility toward Masonry into a political party. Entering local and state elections, the Anti-Masonic party spread rapidly, especially in the developing urban centers in upstate New York that were in the throes of the market revolution. Anti-Masons not only attacked the Masonic Order as a privileged, corrupt society but also labelled it an infidel organization that exalted reason over evangelical religion. Encouraged by their growing popularity, the Anti-Masons launched a campaign against Jackson, who was a prominent Mason. Tapping into the egalitarianism of American society, Anti-Masonry had spread into ten states, and on September 26, 1831, held the nation's first nominating convention which chose William Wirt, a former Mason who had been attorney general under Monroe, as its presidential candidate.

A little more than two months later, in December 1831, the National Republicans held their sparsely attended convention in Baltimore and selected Henry Clay as their presidential standard bearer. The party condemned Jackson's stand on internal improvements, the tariff, and the bank and attacked his "vindicative party spirit" and "inhumane" policy toward Indians. Some contemporaries believed that Clay made the bank the principal issue of his campaign. Certainly Biddle poured money into the campaign.

On May 21, 1832, the Democrats opened their convention with delegates from all states except Missouri, a showing far more representative than the other two parties. In a display of party unity and harmony the convention merely "concurred" in Jackson's renomination. The only real business was to select a vice presidential running mate. Jackson was determined that the vice presidency should go to Van Buren, both for his loyal service and as compensation for the persistent refusal of the Senate to confirm his nomination as American minister to Britain. The convention nominated Van Buren on the first ballot.

The campaign included abundant rhetoric about specific issues, ranging from the bank and the tariff to internal improvements and Indian removal. But as one historian has noted, the principal issue was concerned less with the bank per se than with "questions about power and republicanism that the effort to recharter it had raised." Clay and the National Republicans castigated Jackson for his usurpation of power, violations of the Constitution, and subversion of republicanism. In short, Jackson in their view was a dictator who threatened the very existence of liberty. The Democrats, by contrast, described the bank as a menace to popular government and equated Jackson's actions with "the cause of democracy against a corrupt and abandoned aristocracy." Democrats described themselves as allies of the working men, the poor, and ordinary citizens against the rich, powerful, and corrupt "moneyed aristocracy." Both parties staged parades, picnics, barbecues, and torchlight parades and sponsored songs and emblems. Not only were the Democrats more adept in the use of such techniques, they also proved to be more skilled in perfecting and coordinating local party organizations.

Because Jackson and Clay had been public figures so long, voters had ample opportunities to form opinions about each of them. Although the bank recharter veto may have cost Jackson votes, his personal popularity remained immense. It may be, as one scholar has noted, that voters generally trusted Jackson and distrusted Clay. In the final analysis Jackson triumphed with a stunning majority in the electoral college. Less impressive was his popular vote of 687,502 compared to the total of 530,183 received by his opponents. The results also suggest that substantial changes had occurred in the regional composition of both parties and that the Democrats, though losing two southern states, had significantly improved their standing in the North. Despite the development of new party techniques and stronger party organizations by both Democrats and National Republicans, the 1832 election did not quite mark the arrival of a full-fledged two-party system. Party politics remained fluid: the Democrats were still a coalition containing independent-minded, unreliable components; the National Republicans exhibited even less coherence.

JACKSON'S SECOND TERM

Nullification

Convinced that he had a popular mandate, Jackson in his second term moved even more decisively to implement his policies. For example, he responded forcefully to thwart South Carolina's steps toward nullification. After Jackson's reelection in 1832, South Carolina elected a convention which on November 24 passed an ordinance of nullification that declared that the tariff act of 1828, as well as a lower tariff measure enacted in 1832, would become null and void in the state as of February 1, 1833. If the federal government intervened, South Carolina would secede. President Jackson appealed to the people of his native state to act with reason, but warned them that he would not tolerate any action by the state to enforce nullification. "Disunion by armed force," he declared, "is treason." Jackson then got from Congress (but not without difficulty) the so-called Force Act that authorized him to use military force to ensure that South Carolina obeyed federal laws. Much to Calhoun's disappointment, South Carolina stood alone; other southern states adamantly refused to take up the cause of nullification. It was clear, too, that Jackson meant to use force if necessary.

In the meantime Henry Clay, Jackson's old adversary, was pushing through Congress what became the Tariff Act of 1833 which, by a gradual reduction of rates over several years, would presumably meet the demands of the nullifiers. Senator Calhoun and the president acquiesced in the measure. Clay's tariff act paved the way for the resolution of the constitutional crisis. South Carolina, following Calhoun's lead, accepted the Tariff Act of 1833, and called a convention which repealed the nullification ordinance and, in a symbolic gesture of defiance, also nullified the Force Act. Jackson weathered the nullification crisis with both his personal popularity and the Union intact. Pleased that the crisis had been resolved without the bloodshed that many predicted, he clearly realized that the sectional antagonism that the crisis exposed would probably be revived later on another issue. He predicted that the next pretext for dissolving the Union would be "the slavery question."

Financial Changes

The End of the Bank   In the wake of his reelection, Jackson also focused on finishing off the Second Bank whose original charter would not expire until 1836. He immediately began preparations to remove federal deposits from the bank, a move that encountered opposition even in his cabinet. His new policy took effect on October 1, 1833, whereby all future federal deposits would be placed in selected state banks—called "pet banks" by the opposition—and the government would draw on its funds remaining in the bank for operating expenses until they were exhausted. Biddle responded by ordering the curtailment of loans throughout the bank's branches. This sudden constriction of credit set in motion a financial panic and economic downturn. While both Jackson and Biddle engaged in bellicose rhetoric, the credit squeeze was having serious consequences throughout the country. Financial and business leaders clamored for relief. When they appealed to Jackson, he told them to take their requests to Biddle whom the president held responsible for the panic. An assortment of Democrats, all the while, advocated the creation of a new bank located in Washington, while others in New York considered creating "a ten million dollar monster" that would make their city the nation's financial center.

When the new Congress convened in December 1833, the Bank War entered a new phase. "What had begun as a straight-forward power struggle," Robert Remini has written, "sank into a morass of economic and political confusion, with some Democrats advocating a new bank and others opposing it, some favoring hard money (specie) and others violently hostile to it." In the Senate Clay, Webster, and Calhoun denounced Democrats for their blind devotion to such a tyrant as Jackson. Taking the lead, Clay pushed through the Senate a resolution censuring the president for his misuse of executive power in removing deposits from the bank. Stung by what he considered an unwarranted congressional attack on the executive, Jackson fired off a "Protest" to the Senate which described the censure as a violation of the Constitution because it charged him with an impeachable offense and only the House of Representatives could bring impeachment charges against the president. More important perhaps was Jackson's discussion of the office of president and its relation to the voters. The president, he argued, was the sole "representative of the American people," elected by them and "responsible to them." A Democratic Senate rescinded the censure in the closing days of Jackson's tenure.

The most significant outcome of the Senate censure, in particular, and the Bank War in general, was to galvanize the anti-Jacksonians, a conglomeration of National Republicans, nullifiers, anti-Masons, states' righters, pro-bank elements, high tariff advocates, and various others. Among them were the evangelical reformers in the Northeast whose initial hostility toward Jackson stemmed largely from his Indian and anti-Sabbatarian policies. Rallying to the cry of "executive usurpation," these multiple factions assumed the name Whigs, so-called after the English political party that had resisted the arbitrary power of King George III. Clay gave his blessing to the name in 1834 as various dissidents came together to oppose what the anti-Jackson press termed the tyranny of "King Andrew I." If, in the short run, the Whigs profited by defections from Jackson's coalition, the president's party in the long run benefitted from such defections which rid it of unreliable allies and made for greater homogeneity.

The Bank War, in brief, brought two-party politics to Congress where Democrats and Whigs increasingly exhibited a degree of party regularity in voting on issues that had previously been lacking. Congressional Democrats united to approve Jackson's removal of deposits. Clearly Biddle had lost the Bank War, and on the advice of Clay, Webster, and others, he reversed his credit restriction policy, and the economic crisis began to ease. In 1836 the Second Bank of the United States modified its name and became merely another state bank chartered by Pennsylvania.

Whatever Biddle's shortcomings, the death of the Second Bank left the country with a fragmented and often unstable banking system. Jackson's distribution of federal funds to selected state banks may have been in keeping with his belief in limited government and decentralized power, but it did not provide a mechanism for exercising restraint on credit operations as the Second Bank had done. For a time the president managed to achieve a degree of stability in banking through regulations issued by the Treasury Department, but a combination of events soon made it difficult to keep the system in check. True to his promise, Jackson had been able to pay off the national debt by 1835 due largely to his reduction of federal spending and the rising income from the tariff and public land sales. As the government increased its deposits in "pet banks" and as the land boom continued, the administration found it impossible to restrain such banks from fueling the speculation mania. Confronted with a surplus, runaway land speculation, and rising inflation, Jackson tried in vain to secure legislation to regulate banks and hard money. Instead Congress enacted the Deposit-Distribution Act in June 1836 which Jackson threatened to veto but ultimately signed. The measure regulated government moneys in deposit banks by imposing limits on small bank notes, by increasing the number of deposit banks by requiring at least one in every state and territory, and by providing that all money in the federal treasury in excess of 5 million dollars be distributed in installments to the states in proportion to their representation in Congress. That the number of deposit banks, under the act, increased from thirty-three to eighty-one meant an even more unwieldy and out-of-control banking system.

The Specie Circular   Deeply worried by the speculation in land and the inclination of banks to extend loans and issue bank notes far in excess of their resources, Jackson saw the omnipresent hand of the "corrupt money power" at work manipulating the earnings of honest citizens. After Congress adjourned, he issued through the secretary of the Treasury the so-called Specie Circular on July 11, 1836, which had the approval neither of Congress nor the cabinet. By decreeing that only gold and silver would be accepted in payment for public land, the circular was intended to halt the huge quantity of paper money (bank notes) flooding the country as the land speculation fever reached new proportions. Although the circular did slow land sales, the land boom continued and so did the increase in federal revenues and the expansion of the surplus. Such conditions precluded effective government control of banks and their contribution to spiraling inflation. Congress later rescinded the Specie Circular, only to have its action pocket vetoed by Jackson as one of his last official acts as president. Some historians argue that Jackson created the economic boom by destroying the bank and putting in its place the pet banks which engaged in reckless lending policies, then shut off the paper money that had fueled the speculation mania.

The Panic of 1834   At the same time that Jackson was waging war on the bank and searching for a viable fiscal policy, his administration confronted a series of disturbances related to the profound changes occurring in the nation's economy and society. The economic downturn in 1834, which marked the first decline in almost a decade of growth, created widespread unemployment. The economic boom that followed the decline brought with it a dramatic rise in inflation which posed serious difficulties for the growing population of workers in the urban Northeast and other areas under the influence of the market revolution. A combination of low wages and poor working conditions contributed to a succession of strikes, riots, and outbursts of violence. As many as two hundred strikes occurred in the Northeast and portions of the Northwest between 1833 and 1836. Ethnic and religious animosities found expression in various acts of violence ranging from anti-Irish riots to the burning of an Ursuline convent. The opposition to the abolitionists further contributed to the spreading disorder. Even the president himself received death threats and in 1835 survived an assassination attempt, one of several during his tenure in office.

Jackson and Labor

Although Jackson's references to the "humble working classes" and the corrupt "moneyed aristocracy," and his hard money policies appealed to certain elements of urban labor, the president and his party deplored the strikes and disorder. When Jackson referred to "labor," he clearly did not have in mind unskilled factory workers and day laborers for whom he had no especial sympathy. "Labor" was a broad term that he used to designate the producing classes as opposed to the nonproducing financial and commercial classes. In confrontations between labor and management Jacksonian Democrats seldom sided with the workers, and the president on occasion used troops to suppress labor riots. On a tour of the textile mills in Lowell, Massachusetts, Jackson manifested great interest in the mills' technology but paid little attention to the working conditions of the four thousand women laborers there. Although workers in some industrial cities supported Jackson and the Democratic party, those in other cities did not. Among the former were the workingmen who made up a sizable contingent of the Locofocos—so named because of their use of the new friction matches, known as Locofocos, to light a darkened hall—who were among the most radical members of the party.

Jackson and Abolitionism

If Jackson displayed little sympathy for urban workers, he was downright hostile toward the abolitionists. A slaveowner surrounded by close advisors who also owned slaves, the president did not conceal his contempt for Garrison and others who, in his opinion, were engaged in "wicked attempts" to arouse the "passions of slaves." Whatever other considerations figured in Jackson's response to abolitionism, his concern for the unity of his party was primary. He was opposed to allowing such an explosive issue as slavery to divide it. As indicated in Chapter 8, the gag rule imposed on the steady flow of abolitionist petitions in 1836 had the effect of shutting off debate on slavery.

MARTIN VAN BUREN

THE ELECTION OF 1836

The presidential campaign of that year actually got underway in 1835. Regardless of Jackson's shortcomings in other areas, he evolved into a skillful party leader and party builder. A more ideologically homogeneous cabinet (Jackson's third) that exhibited greater geographical balance helped to hold the Democrats together. Other important ingredients in transforming Jackson's followers into a unified and disciplined political party included an effective use of patronage especially in staffing customhouses, post offices, and land offices, a subsidized press, and a system of committees that provided national party coordination. When the Democratic convention met in Baltimore in May 1835, the delegates followed Jackson's wish that Van Buren receive the presidential nomination. As the vice presidential nominee, they chose Richard M. Johnson of Kentucky, a popular figure with urban workers in the East who encountered opposition among other groups because of his mulatto mistress and daughters. Jackson entered into the campaign as much as his precarious health would allow. The Democrats waged a campaign that took on the enthusiasm of a religious revival.

The Whigs were much slower to adapt to the realities of mass democratic politics. Lacking the organization of the Democrats, they remained in 1836 a disjointed, undisciplined coalition of anti-Jacksonians who had difficulty in coming to terms with political parties and electoral democracy. In general, Whigs welcomed the market revolution and an activist government to promote economic expansion, especially through underwriting Clay's American System.

They also supported so many humanitarian and moral reforms that their party became identified as a vehicle of evangelical Protestantism. That the Whigs still fell short of being a full-fledged coherent party in 1836 was evident in the strategy they chose in selecting their presidential and vice presidential candidates. Rather than a single ticket, they sponsored three sectional presidential candidates: Daniel Webster of Massachusetts; Hugh Lawson of Tennessee; and William Henry Harrison of Indiana. Their hope was to splinter the vote so that the election would be thrown into the House of Representatives.

Neither the Whigs nor the Democrats focused on pressing economic issues, as might have been expected. The bank, internal improvements, and currency were barely mentioned. The Democrats concentrated on old-fashioned republican sentiments, repeatedly referred to the rights of "the people," and attempted to justify the utility of political parties. The Whigs aired their anti-party bias by denouncing the "party spirit" and characterized Van Buren as the classic professional politician. Their effort to depict Van Buren as an opponent of slavery prompted him to become bolder in asserting his opposition to abolitionism in an effort to retain his support in the slave South. Although the Whigs attracted more voters among the wealthy, both parties garnered support among the "haves" as well as the "have-nots." The Whigs, however, fared substantially better in places that had experienced the market revolution such as the commercial areas along major transportation routes. Religion and ethnicity, some historians argue, offer the most reliable guide to party membership in the era. Evangelical Protestants, such as Presbyterians, Baptists, and Methodists, gravitated to the Whig party as did native-born Americans of British origin and an assortment of reformers influenced by the Second Great Awakening. Liturgical faiths including Lutherans, Roman Catholics, and Episcopalians tended to support the Democratic party as did recent immigrants and those opposed to government involvement in moral and religious issues. When the votes were counted, Van Buren had won by a slim margin. Because no vice presidential candidate won a majority of electoral votes, the choice fell to the Senate for the only time in the nation's history. The Democratic Senate chose Richard M. Johnson.

As Jackson departed from office in March 1837, and his handpicked successor Van Buren succeeded him, a viable two-party system was taking shape and would be fully developed by the next presidential election. Jackson remained a revered public figure whose popularity and leadership were indispensable in creating the Democratic party. Opposition to his policies and actions during his tumultuous two terms in office prompted the emergence of a coalition that evolved into the Whig party which, despite its anti-party bias, ultimately followed the Democratic model in perfecting its organization and political techniques. Appropriately, Jackson's name became inextricably linked to the Democratic party and the emergence of the nation's second political party system. As the ailing Jackson accompanied the new president down the Capitol steps following the latter's inaugural address, the appearance of the Old Hero prompted a thunderous ovation comparable to that which had greeted him eight years earlier at his own inauguration. In the words of Jackson's ally, Senator Thomas Hart Benton of Missouri, "for once, the rising was eclipsed by the setting sun."

VAN BUREN'S BACKGROUND

Martin Van Buren's accession to the presidency at the age of fifty-five was the climax to a long career in state and national politics. As much, if not more than other individuals of his generation, he deserved to be described as a professional politician. The son of a farmer and tavern keeper, he was born in 1782 in the village of Kinderhook in New York's Hudson Valley. The first president born under the American flag, he read law, established a practice in his hometown, and entered politics as a Jeffersonian Republican. He rose rapidly in the factional politics of New York at a time when the impact of the market revolution was altering the political landscape. Beginning in 1812, he occupied a succession of state and federal offices. Possessing infinite tact and superb organizational skills, he was an adaptable, practical politician rather than a dogmatic ideologue. Such traits enabled him to emerge as the dominant figure in the so-called Albany Regency, the well disciplined and powerful Republican party organization in New York. So gifted was Van Buren in the arts of compromise and political alliance making that he earned the nickname "the Little Magician."

In national politics he was closely identified for a time with William H. Crawford of Georgia whom he supported as the party's presidential candidate in 1824. Ambivalent about forces unleashed by the market revolution, he shared Jackson's views on many issues, and, no less important, was impressed by the widespread popularity of the Old Hickory. With characteristic dexterity he shifted his allegiance to Jackson and ultimately became one of the president's most trusted advisors. He rendered loyal service as Jackson's secretary of state, minister to Great Britain, and vice president. Employing political techniques that had worked successfully in New York, Van Buren was responsible, in large measure, for transforming the president's unruly coalition into a coherent and disciplined political party. Once in the White House, however, he displayed little of the political savvy that had characterized his earlier career.

ECONOMIC CRISIS

By the time Van Buren assumed the presidency, the economic boom had already crested and a bust was in the offing. A few weeks into his administration the Panic of 1837 signaled a collapse that reversed the boom and the inflation it fueled. Suddenly, Van Buren confronted an economic crisis of major proportions. A depressed economy in Britain prompted British investors who had underwritten much of the economic expansion in the United States to restrict their credit and call in their loans. This action was the immediate cause for the Panic of 1837 which, in turn, exposed the flaws in the nation's precarious economy, and heralded the onset of a depression. About a third of the labor force was unemployed by the fall of 1837 and those who retained their jobs saw their wages slashed dramatically. In New England the textile and shoe manufacturing centers virtually suspended business. Especially hard hit was the southwestern cotton frontier where planters, infected by the land speculation fever, had accumulated large debts that they could not repay. Internal improvement projects came to a halt and holders of bank notes demanded payment in silver and gold, depleting the inadequate reserves of banks to a point that specie payments had to be suspended. A degree of recovery was followed in 1839 by another panic that set in motion an economic downturn that continued into the presidential election year and beyond. The federal government itself lost about $9 million that had been deposited in pet banks.

Both Democrats and Whigs were quick to place blame for the economic crisis. The Democrats held bankers and speculators responsible for the hard times, while Whigs charged that the nation was reaping the disastrous consequences of Jackson's Bank War, which had removed the one institution capable of exercising restraint on banks and speculators.

AN INDEPENDENT TREASURY

Some Whigs and Democrats urged Van Buren to rescind Jackson's Specie Circular; others advised him to struggle on with the state bank system. Calling Congress into special session in September 1837, the president refused to heed such advice and instead proposed an Independent Treasury which would sever the unhappy relationship of the government to banks. The idea of such a divorce had been circulating for some years, and Jackson had once considered it favorably as an extension of his hard money policy. Opposed by Whigs and pro-bank Democrats, the Van Buren proposal dominated most of his administration. Not until mid-1840 did the president finally secure congressional approval of the Independent Treasury. In the meantime, Congress had repealed the Specie Circular by joint resolution in 1838.

OTHER DOMESTIC ISSUES

While Congress wrangled over his Independent Treasury bill, Van Buren performed by executive order what has been described as one of the most significant acts of his administration. He directed that no person employed on federal public works (such as navy yards) should be required to labor more than ten hours a day and that this order should take effect without a salary reduction. Whigs denounced the president for infringing on the right to work and demanded in vain that pay be reduced correspondingly.

Among issues other than the economic crisis that confronted Van Buren were those concerned with completing the Cherokee Indian removal which he inherited from Jackson and with defusing two crises that developed between the United States and Britain involving events in Canada. But everything during his administration paled beside the depression that continued to cause hardship and suffering. The president became the target of much of the rising tide of discontent spawned by hard times.

WILLIAM HENRY HARRISON

THE ELECTION OF 1840

By the presidential election of 1840 the second party system had finally emerged. The Democratic and Whig parties that entered the contest represented two fairly evenly matched national organizations. Although the politics of economic development continued to be at the center of party differences, intense cultural conflict also figured significantly in distinguishing between Democrats and Whigs. In the Northeast, Protestant workers and small producers, especially those influenced by the Second Great Awakening, responded favorably to the Whigs' combination of economic and moral appeals, while Catholic immigrants, repelled by the Whigs' embrace of temperance, Sabbatarianism, nativism, and common schools, remained faithful to the Democrats. Throughout the nation, as historian Sean Wilentz has noted, "the lines of class, ethnicity, religion, and sub-region tended to converge; cultural identities in politics—the Whigs' entrepreneurial moralism versus the Democrats' stress on personal autonomy and equal-rights—were inseparable from the ways in which the market revolution was threatening old ways of life, creating new ones, and setting large groups of Americans at odds."

The Democrats renominated Van Buren easily enough but balked at doing the same for Vice President Richard Johnson whose behavior and obsession for office had become an embarrassment. Johnson's breach of racial etiquette, coupled with Jackson's opposition, led the Democrats to leave Van Buren without a running mate and to recommend that each state vote for its favorite. The Democrats waged a campaign that reaffirmed old ideals and discussed old issues; they castigated banks, bankers, and paper money and extolled the virtues of the producing classes.

The Whigs had learned well the lessons of party organization and campaign techniques provided by the Democrats. They had considerable success in shedding their image as a potpourri of elitist malcontents and in creating a vision of democratic capitalism in which all Americans, no matter how humble their origins, could get ahead through hard work, sobriety, self-reliance, and thrift. At the same time a new generation of Whig party leaders had emerged at the state level, who were less concerned with ideological purity than with techniques for winning votes. The party's managers conducted a campaign replete with slogans, songs, broadsides, and posters that conveyed the message of democratic capitalism. In their first truly national convention the Whigs in 1840 passed over Henry Clay for William Henry Harrison as their presidential candidate because he had demonstrated vote-getting power four years earlier. John Tyler of Virginia, a former Democrat, won nomination as Harrison's vice presidential running mate.

Central to the Whig campaign was the strategy of blaming the depression on Van Buren and the Democrats. Throughout the campaign the Whigs proved to be masters of the politics of image making. They effectively portrayed Harrison, scion of the Virginia gentry and a person of considerable wealth, as a simple man of the people who preferred log cabins and hard cider. Such an image contrasted sharply with the one that they projected of Van Buren as an elegant dandy who had transformed the White House into an opulent palace while depression stalked the land. Such electioneering techniques resulted in a stunning victory for Harrison.

HARRISON AND TYLER

This decisive victory ironically was followed by four years of frustration for the Whigs. President Harrison died a month after assuming office from pneumonia which he contracted while giving his inaugural address in a freezing rain. So John Tyler became the first vice president to succeed to the presidency upon the death of the incumbent. Tyler was a Whig, but a Whig of a special sort; he was a strict constructionist devoted to states' rights and unalterably opposed to Clay's American System. Independent-minded and even stubborn, Tyler refused to be either manipulated or dominated by Clay who after the Whig victory in 1840 had assumed that the new president would defer to him. Although Tyler signed Clay's measures that repealed the Independent Treasury and raised tariff rates, he balked at Clay's bills to establish a banking institution similar to the Second Bank of the United States. Favoring a system known as the "exchequer exchange," he vetoed Clay's banking measures. When Congress refused to enact his own plan, the result was a chaotic situation for handling federal finances until the Independent Treasury was reestablished in 1846, more than a year after Tyler left office.

The political fallout from Tyler's veto of Clay's banking measures included the resignation of the entire cabinet with the exception of Secretary of State Daniel Webster. Tyler then filled the cabinet with men much like himself, namely anti-Jackson Democrats who had taken refuge in the Whig party for the lack of a better alternative. In 1844 he appointed Calhoun, who had returned to the Democratic fold, as secretary of state. The president's disregard for party in making key appointments encouraged Whigs to rally around Clay as their leader and spokesman. Whigs in Congress were so outraged by Tyler's actions, especially his veto of Clay's banking legislation, that they expelled the president from their party. Tyler may not have been as impolitic and inconsistent as contemporary critics made him out to be, but he did contribute to the chaos and confusion that characterized his administration. Alienated from the Whigs and unable to win acceptance by the Democrats, Tyler became increasingly isolated—a president without a party.

In search of an issue that would win him the Democratic presidential nomination in 1844, Tyler seized upon the annexation of Texas which had declared its independence from Mexico. Presidents Jackson and Van Buren had resisted pressure to annex Texas; both Van Buren and Clay publicly opposed Tyler's efforts. For more than four decades political leaders had managed to prevent the issues of sectional balance and the expansion of slavery from polarizing the nation and jeopardizing the Union. By the 1840s, avoiding such issues became increasingly difficult because of two developments in particular: one wing of the abolitionist movement entered the political arena and enlisted in its cause broader public support, and the northern and southern wings of the Democratic party drifted apart as a result of internal disputes and divergent constituencies. President Tyler's efforts to annex Texas failed to gain him the Democratic nomination, but they signaled the reopening of sectional antagonism and the arousal of the passions over the expansion of slavery that had been muted since the Missouri Compromise.

Few aspects of the Jacksonian Era have aroused more intense scholarly debate than the Indian removal policy identified with legislation secured by President Andrew Jackson in 1830. While much attention had been devoted to the removal of the five "civilized" tribes in the Southeast, relatively little has been focused on the fate of Indians in the old Northwest which is the subject of the following essay. The author, historian Ronald N. Satz, concentrates on the implementation of the government's removal policy rather than the motives that prompted it. After identifying four major benefits which Jackson and his successors claimed that Indians would reap as a result of removal, Satz demonstrates the vast chasm that separated their rhetoric from the actual implementation of their removal policy.

INDIAN POLICY IN THE JACKSONIAN ERA: THE OLD NORTHWEST AS A TEST CASE

Ronald N. Satz

. . . This paper is an attempt to assess the goals, execution, and results of the Indian removal policy in the 1830's and 1840's by focusing on the application of that policy in the Old Northwest. The events surrounding the removal of the Five

from Ronald N. Satz, "Indian Policy in the Jacksonian Era: The Old Northwest as a Test Case," *Michigan History* 60 (Spring 1976): 71–93.

Civilized Tribes from the South have long been, to use the words of Grant Foreman, "a chapter unsurpassed in pathos and absorbing interest in American history." This dramatic episode has, to some extent, obscured similar events taking place farther north during the same period of time. The Old Northwest provides an interesting test case for an examination of the differences between the rhetoric and the reality of the removal policy. The Indians in this region were not the beneficiaries of anything approaching the tremendous outpouring of public sympathy for the Cherokees and their neighbors in the Southeast. If the Cherokees faced a "Trail of Tears" in spite of the great volume of petitions, letters, and resolutions presented to Congress in their behalf, what happened to the Indians in the Old Northwest who lacked such enthusiastic public support?

An essential ingredient to an understanding of the Indian policy in this period is the recognition that President Jackson and his successors in the White House, the War Department, the Office of Indian Affairs, and Indian agents maintained that the removal policy would bring at least four major benefits to the Indians. These included:

1. fixed and permanent boundaries outside of the jurisdiction of American states or territories;
2. isolation from corrupt white elements such as gamblers, prostitutes, whiskey vendors, and the like;
3. self-government unfettered by state or territorial laws; and
4. opportunities for acquiring the essentials of "civilized" society—Christianity, private property, and knowledge of agriculture and the mechanical arts.

Such were the benefits that government officials claimed the removal policy would bring the Indians. As a test case of the application of this policy, let us focus our attention on events in the Old Northwest.

President Jackson asked Congress on December 8, 1829, to provide him with authority to negotiate treaties to transfer Indians living east of the Mississippi River to a western location. Jackson and his congressional supporters, in their great rush to push through such legislation, seemed unconcerned about the technical aspects of any great migration of eastern Indians to the trans-Mississippi West. Opponents of the scheme, however, raised several important questions: Would emigration be purely voluntary? Would treaty commissioners negotiate only with acknowledged tribal leaders or would land be purchased from individuals? How many Indians would go? What kind of preparations and resources would be necessary for them? What would be the specific boundaries between emigrant tribes? How would the indigenous tribes in the West react to the intrusion of new people? During the debates on the Removal Bill, Tennesseean David Crockett warned that it was a dangerous precedent to appropriate money for the executive branch without specifically knowing how the president intended to use it. Crockett warned that if Congress turned a deaf ear to the rights of the Indians then "misery must be their fate."

Unfortunately for the Indians, Congress passed the Removal Act in May 1830, and, despite the opposition of the nascent Whig party, Indian removal became a generally accepted policy in the ensuing decades. Throughout this period, congressional interest focused on patronage, partisan politics, and retrenchment to the detriment of the administration of Indian affairs. While the Whigs found it expedient to condemn aspects of the removal policy when they were struggling to capture the White House, they found it desirable to continue the policy once in office. Henry R. Schoolcraft, an Indian agent in Michigan Territory, poignantly described a serious defect of American Indian policy when he noted that "the whole Indian race is not, in the political scales, worth one white man's vote." The result of this situation, as David Crockett had warned, was misery for the Indians.

Among those who witnessed the actual dispossession of the eastern tribes in the Jacksonian era were two foreign travelers who, while not being authorities on the American Indians, nevertheless clearly recognized the deceptions involved in the treaty-making process. French traveler Alexis de Tocqueville poignantly observed that American officials, "inspired by the most chaste affection for legal formalities," obtained Indian title "in a regular and, so to say, quite legal manner." Although bribery and threats often accompanied treaty making and the formal purchases of Indian land, the United States had legal confirmation of its acquisitions. Indeed treaty negotiators were able to "cheaply acquire whole provinces which the richest sovereigns in Europe could not afford to buy" by employing such tactics as bribery or intimidation. Another European visitor, English Captain Frederick Marrayt [sic], accurately reported that "the Indians . . . are *compelled* to sell—the purchase money being a mere subterfuge, by which it may *appear* as if the lands were not being wrested from them, although, in fact, it [sic] is."

President Jackson had early indicated that his primary interest was the removal of the southeastern tribes. Although congressmen from the Old Northwest advised him following the passage of the Removal Act that the time for securing removal treaties in their region was "auspicious," Old Hickory informed them that his immediate concern was to set into motion a great tide of southern Indian emigration. Events in Illinois in the spring of 1832, however, played into the hands of the supporters of Indian removal in the Old Northwest.

In the spring of 1832, a hungry band of a thousand Sac and Fox Indians and their allies left their new home in Iowa Territory and crossed the Mississippi River en route to their old capital on the Rock River. Under the leadership of the proud warrior Black Hawk, this band, which included women and children, entered Illinois in search of food and as a means of protesting against their treatment by white frontiersmen. Mass hysteria swept the Illinois frontier with the news that the Indians had crossed the river. Governor John Reynolds called up the state militia to repel the "invasion" despite the fact that Black Hawk's band was clearly not a war party. The result was a short, bloody conflict brought on largely as a consequence of the actions of drunken state militia. The ruthless suppression of the so-called "Indian hostilities" in Illinois and neighboring Wisconsin in 1832, and the seizure of a large part of the trans-Mississippi domain of the Sac and Fox Indians as "indemnity" for the war, broke the spirit of other tribes in the Old Northwest. Under pressure from the War Department, the Winnebagos in Wisconsin soon signed a removal treaty ceding their land south of the Wisconsin River. One by one, other tribes succumbed to similar pressure.

As critics of the Removal Act of 1830 had feared, the War Department obtained many of these land cessions by bribery. Agents courted influential tribal leaders by offering them special rewards including money, merchandise, land reserves, and medals, among other things. Sometimes treaty commissioners selected chiefs to represent an entire tribe or group of bands. The Jackson administration, for example, secured the title to the land of the United Nation of Chippewa, Ottawa, and Potawatomi Indians in northeastern Illinois, southeastern Wisconsin, and southern Michigan by "playing Indian politics." Indeed, the very existence of the United Nation was the result of the government's insistence on dealing with these Indians as if they were a single unit. Yet neither the great majority of the Chippewas and Ottawas nor all of the Potawatomi bands recognized the authority of the so-called United Nation. The government's policy of dealing with the entity as the representative of all Chippewas, Ottawas and Potawatomis was a clever maneuver to oust these Indians from their lands. By working closely with mixed-blood leaders and by withholding Indian annuities, the War Department secured the desired land cessions from the United Nation in the early 1830's.

During the Jacksonian era, the War Department frequently used economic coercion as a means of securing Indian title in the Old Northwest. Since the 1790's, the department had invested funds appropriated by Congress for purchasing Indian land in state banks or stocks and had paid the Indians only the annual interest on the amount owed them under treaty stipulations. This annuity or trust fund system gave government bureaucrats virtual control over funds legally belonging to the Indians. Although Thomas Jefferson played an important role in establishing the precedent of withholding Indian annuities as a means of social control, this procedure became a standard policy after 1829.

Treaty commissioners, Indian agents, and other field officers of the War Department found that withholding annuities was a convenient means of inducing recalcitrant Indians to sign treaties and to emigrate. Commissary General of Subsistence George Gibson advised the Jackson administration, "Let the annuities be paid west of the Mississippi [River], and there is no reason to doubt that the scheme of emigration would meet with little future opposition." American officials maintained considerable influence over tribal politics by determining who would receive the annuities.

Another measure used to encourage Indians to make land cessions was the inclusion of provisions in removal treaties for the granting of land reserves to chiefs, mixed-bloods, or other influential members of the tribes. The motivation behind this practice was twofold. First, it allowed government officials to combat Indian and American opposition to the removal policy based on the fact that some Indians had demonstrated a willingness and capability of accepting the white man's "civilization." When Andrew Jackson encountered strong opposition to his efforts to remove the Cherokees and the other so-called Civilized Tribes from their Southern domain, he conceded that Indians willing to accept the concept of private property should be allowed to remain in the East on individual reserves and become citizens of the states in which they resided. Secondly and more importantly for the Old Northwest, the practice of providing reserves of land to certain Indians was an ingenious device for bribing chiefs or influential tribesmen into accepting land cession treaties and for appeasing white traders into whose hands their reserves were certain to fall.

Treaty commissioners in Indiana found it impossible to secure land cessions from the Miami and Potawatomi Indians without the approval of the Wabash Valley traders to whom they were heavily in debt. Land speculators and settlers regarded the Miami and Potawatomi reserved sections adjacent to the Wabash River and the route of the Wabash and Erie Canal as choice lands. Wabash Valley traders, Indian agents, and even United States Senator John Tipton ultimately secured most of these lands from the Indians and rented them to white settlers for high profits after the Panic of 1837. By 1840 treaties with the Miamis and Potawatomis of Indiana had provided for nearly two hundred thousand acres of individual reserves. The largest holders of these reserves were not Indians but Wabash Valley traders W. G. and G. W. Ewing and Senator Tipton. Thousands of acres of Indian land elsewhere in the Old Northwest also fell into the hands of speculators.

In spite of the fact that speculators and traders often pressured the Indians into relinquishing their reserves before the government even surveyed the ceded tribal land, little was done to protect the Indians from such swindlers. Indiana Whig Jonathan McCarty, a bitter political adversary of Senator Tipton, introduced a resolution in Congress in 1835 calling for an investigation of the handling of Indian reserves, but no action resulted. Jackson, and his successors in the White House, were anxious to tone down investigations of alleged frauds in Indian affairs in order to avoid possible political embarrassments. Even some of the staunchest opponents of the removal policy benefited directly from the sale of Indian lands. Daniel Webster, Edward Everett, Caleb Cushing and Ralph Waldo Emerson were among those who speculated in Indian lands in the Old Northwest.

In addition to granting land reserves to Indians, the War Department followed the practice of including provisions in removal treaties for the payment of Indian debts to traders as a means of promoting removal. Since the Indians relied heavily on traders for subsistence and advice in the Old Northwest, the inclusion of traders' debts was often crucial to successful treaty negotiations. Although the recognition of these debts helped to promote the signing of land cession treaties, the practice also meant that the Indians lost huge sums of money to men who frequently inflated the prices of the goods they sold or falsified their ledgers. Transactions at treaty negotiations relative to the sale of Indian land, the adjustment of traders' claims, and the like, were a complex business, yet many Indians, especially the full bloods, did not know the difference between one numerical figure and another.

The administration of Indian affairs in the mid-1830's was particularly vulnerable to criticism. The Panic of 1837 led many traders to exert political influence on treaty commissioners to have phoney Indian debts included in removal treaties. Commissioners Simon Cameron and James Murray awarded the politically influential American Fur Company over one hundred thousand dollars in alleged debt claims against the Winnebagos in Wisconsin in 1838 in return, according to rumor, for a large kickback. Only the military disbursing agent's refusal to pay the traders ultimately led to the exposure of the fraud. One eye witness to this episode subsequently claimed that it was worse than the Crédit Mobilier scandal. An English visitor to Wisconsin several years after the incident reported that the acknowledgment of traders' claims during annuity payments was still a "potwallopping affair" in which the Indians left as empty handed as when they had arrived. Both the Tyler and Polk administrations, in response to complaints from some congressmen, honest Indian agents, and concerned frontier residents, denounced the practice of acknowledging traders' debts in treaties. But the tremendous political influence of the traders, together with the War Department's emphasis on the speedy removal of Indians from areas desired by whites, led the government to follow the path of expediency. Traders continued to receive payments for their claims throughout the Jacksonian era.

If the techniques already mentioned failed to entice the Indians to emigrate, there was always brute force. The state of Indiana probably had one of the worst records in this respect. The Potawatomis ceded their last holdings in Indiana in 1836, but the treaty provisions allowed them two years to emigrate. Whites quickly began moving onto their land in order to establish preemption rights. As tension between the Indians and the whites grew, the Indiana militia rounded up the Potawatomis in 1838. When Chief Menominee, who had refused to sign the removal treaty, objected to the proceedings, the soldiers lassoed him, bound him hand and foot, and threw him into a wagon. The militia then hastily set into motion the Potawatomi exodus to the West—the "Trail of Death" along which about one hundred and fifty men, women, and children died as a result of exposure and the physical hardships of the journey. Several years later the Indiana militia also rounded up the Miami Indians in similar fashion to expedite their removal to the West.

By the end of Jackson's second term, the United States had ratified nearly seventy treaties under the provisions of the Removal Act and had acquired about one hundred million acres of Indian land for approximately sixty-eight million dollars and thirty-two million acres of land in the trans-Mississippi West. While the government had relocated forty-six thousand Indians by 1837, a little more than that number were still in the East under obligation to remove. According to the Office of Indian Affairs, only about nine thousand Indians, mostly in the Old Northwest and New York, were without treaty stipulations requiring their relocation, but there is evidence to indicate that the number of such Indians east of the Mississippi River at this time was much larger than the Indian Office reported. Indeed, there were probably more than nine thousand in Wisconsin Territory alone! The dearth of reliable population statistics for Indians during the Jacksonian era is a perplexing problem. By 1842, however, the United States had acquired the last area of any significant size still owned by the Indians in the Old Northwest. Only scattered remnants of the great tribes that had once controlled the region remained behind on reservations or individual holdings, chiefly in Michigan and Wisconsin.

The removal treaties of the Jacksonian era contained liberal provisions for emigrants and those remaining behind on reserves. They offered emigrants rations and transportation, protection en route to their new homes, medicine and physicians, reimbursement for abandoned property, funds for the erection of new buildings, mills, schools, teachers, farmers and mechanics, and maintenance for poor and or-phaned children. The treaties read as if they were enlightened agreements. Yet there were several inherent defects in the treaty-making process. One of these was the assumption that the Indian leaders dealing with the government commissioners rep-resented the entire tribe. Another was the assumption that the Indians clearly un-derstood the provisions of the agreements. Still another was the fact that the Senate often amended or deleted treaty provisions without prior consultation with tribal leaders. Although treaty stipulations were provisional until ratified by the Senate, settlers rarely waited for formal action before they inundated Indian land. While Alexis de Tocqueville noted that "the most chaste affection for legal formalities" characterized American treaty making with the Indians, he also argued that "it is im-possible to destroy men with more respect to the laws of humanity."

In spite of the favorable terms promised in removal treaties, most emigrants faced numerous hardships on their journeys to their new homes. A major reason for their misery was the system of providing them food and transportation by accepting the lowest bid from contractors. Many unscrupulous expectant capitalists furnished the Indians with scanty or cheap rations in order to make a sizeable profit from their contracts. The contractors were businessmen out to make money, and they were quite successful. Thomas Dowling, who received a contract in 1844 to remove six hundred Miami Indians from Indiana for nearly sixty thousand dollars, boasted to his brother that he would make enough profit to "rear the superstructure of an in-dependence for myself, family, and relations."

In addition to the evils of the contract system, Indian emigrants also suffered from the government's perpetual concern for retrenchment. Although removal treaties provided for the medical care of emigrants, the War Department prohibited agents from purchasing medicine or surgical instruments until "actually required" during the economic hard times after 1837. Such instructions greatly hampered the effectiveness of the physicians accompanying migrating parties. To make matters worse, emigrants from the Old Northwest, many of them weakened by their constant battle with the elements of nature en route to the trans-Mississippi West, found themselves plagued with serious afflictions. Efforts to economize in removal expenditures by speeding up the movement of emigrants also led to much suffering. The War Department ordered in 1837 that only the sick or very young could travel west on horseback or by wagon at government expense. Even before this ruling, efforts to speed up the movement of migrating parties under orders from Wash-ington officials proved detrimental to the Indians. An agent in charge of the removal of the Senecas from Ohio earlier in the 1830's, for example, wrote his superior that "I charge myself with cruelty in forcing these unfortunate people on at a time when a few days' delay might have prevented some deaths, and rendered the sickness of others more light, and have to regret this part of my duty."

Now let us examine the success of the removal policy in terms of the so-called benefits that government officials had argued it would bring to the Indians after their relocation. The first benefit was fixed and permanent boundaries outside the jurisdiction of American states and territories. Even before the Black Hawk War, the French travelers Alexis de Tocqueville and Gustave de Beaumont had voiced concern over the government's failure to establish a permanent Indian country for the northern Indians comparable to the one it was setting off west of Arkansas for the southern tribes. Sam Houston, a good Jacksonian Democrat, assured the travelers that Indian-white relations in the Old Northwest were not as critical as in the South. He pointed out that permanent boundaries were unnecessary for the northern tribes since they would eventually be "pushed back" by the tide of white settlement. Following the Black Hawk War, Houston's contention proved correct.

The history of the relocation of the Winnebago Indians from Wisconsin illustrates the government's failure to systematically plan fixed boundaries for emigrants from the Old Northwest. When the War Department pressured the Winnebagos into signing a removal treaty at the cessation of the Black Hawk War, it left them with two alternative locations. One was the so-called "neutral ground" in Iowa between the Sac and Fox Indians and their Sioux enemies to the North. This location proved too precarious for the Winnebagos who quickly made their way back to the second designated area that was within the territorial limits of Wisconsin, north of the Wisconsin River. When the Winnebagos moved into this area, they found themselves too tightly crowded together to live according to their old life styles. As a result, they frequently returned to the sites of their old villages south of the Wisconsin River.

In returning to their old homesites, the Winnebagos encountered other Indians as well as white settlers. While the War Department had induced the Winnebagos to leave southern Wisconsin in order to free them from white contact in that area, it had relocated tribes from New York there in order to free them from white contact in New York. Both the Winnebagos and the New York Indians relocated in Wisconsin soon became the victims of the great land boom that swept the territory in the 1830's as whites eagerly sought Indian land for settlement and timber.

By 1838 the Winnebagos had ceded all of their land in Wisconsin and had promised to move to the neutral ground in Iowa, but the "final" removal of the last band of these Indians in 1840 required the use of troops. For several years after their relocation, the Indian Office attempted to transfer them from Iowa to the Indian country west of Missouri. In 1841 the Tyler administration planned to have them join other northern tribes in a new Indian territory north of the present Iowa-Minnesota border and south of, roughly, the 46th parallel. This new location would appease residents of Iowa who were clamoring for the removal of the Winnebagos and settlers in Wisconsin who were anxious to expel the Winnebago stragglers and the New York Indians who had settled there. Such a northern location would also placate the citizens of Arkansas and Missouri who opposed any additional influx of Indians on their western borders. The War Department favored this plan because it would provide a safe corridor for white expansion to the Pacific through Iowa and would place the Indians of the Old Northwest far south of the Canadian border thus luring them away from British-Canadian influence.

In spite of the War Department's plans, large numbers of Winnebagos drifted back to Wisconsin during the 1840's. Efforts to relocate them in present-day Minnesota between the Sioux and their Chippewa enemies led again to Winnebago defiance. Despite the use of military force to compel them to go to their "proper homes," the Winnebagos were greatly dispersed in Wisconsin, Iowa, and Minnesota at the end of the decade to the annoyance of white settlers in those areas. The condition of these Indians clearly indicates that the War Department was lax in undertaking long-range planning for a permanent home for the tribes of the Old Northwest. The government continually reshuffled these Indians in order to make room for northeastern tribes and the growing pressures of white settlement. Whenever the white population pattern warranted it, the War Department merely redesignated new locations for the Indians. Nor did the government pay much attention to the needs of emigrants. Menominee Chief Oshkosh, in complaining about Winnebago intrusions on Menominee land in Wisconsin in 1850, cited several reasons why the Winnebagos continually left their new locations and returned to Wisconsin; these included the poor soil in their new country, the scarcity of game there, and, most importantly, their dread of their fierce Sioux neighbors.

The agony of the Winnebagos was not unique. Many other tribes faced the prospect of removing to an allegedly permanent location more than once. Continued white hostility following the Black Hawk War led the United Nation of Chippewas, Ottawas, and Potawatomis, for example, to give up their claims to northeastern Illinois, southeastern Wisconsin and several scattered reserves in southern Michigan in 1833 for a tract of land bordering the Missouri River in southwestern Iowa and northwestern Missouri. The new Potawatomi lands included the Platte Country, the region in present-day northwest Missouri watered by the Little Platte and Nodaway rivers. This area was not included in the original boundaries of Missouri in 1820. The inclusion of the Platte Country in the land designated for the Potawatomis demonstrates once again the poor planning of the War Department. In 1832 Missouri Governor John Miller had called for the annexation of this region and Missouri Senators Lewis F. Linn and Thomas Hart Benton joined him in arguing that the area was necessary for the political and economic growth of their state. Although over one hundred Potawatomis had signed the original treaty, the War Department, in its effort to appease Missourians, secured an amended treaty, signed by only seven Indians, that substituted a similar amount of land in Iowa for the Platte Country.

While the government was seeking to modify the original treaty to placate Missouri, Potawatomis who had signed that document moved to the Platte Country. The number of tribesmen there grew as small bands from Indiana continued to travel West in accordance with the provisions of the original treaty. Many Potawatomis came to view the government's new proposed location for them in Iowa as being too close to the Sioux. The Jackson administration reluctantly permitted them to settle temporarily in the Platte Country until they could find suitable sites for new villages in southeastern Iowa. There were still approximately sixteen hundred Potawatomis in the Platte Country in March 1837 when President Martin Van Buren proclaimed the area part of the state of Missouri. The War Department soon ejected them from there and resettled them in southwestern Iowa and Kansas. Government officials consolidated the Potawatomis into one reservation in north-central Kansas in 1846 and subsequently relocated them in Oklahoma during the 1860's.

The experiences of the Winnebago and Potawatomi Indians clearly indicate that the new boundaries for emigrants from the Old Northwest were far from permanent. Treaty commissioners merely reshuffled the tribes around as frontiersmen, speculators, and state officials pressured the War Department to open more Indian land to white settlement. Federal officials failed to undertake long-range planning for the establishment of permanent boundaries for the emigrant tribes from this region. The sole effort in this direction before 1848, the Tyler administration's attempt to create a northern Indian territory, failed because the War Department had neglected the needs and the desires of the Indians.

At the end of the Jacksonian era, Indian Commissioner William Medill reported that the Polk administration had begun to mark off a northern Indian "colony" on the headwaters of the Mississippi River for "the Chippewas of Lake Superior and the upper Mississippi, the Winnebagoes, the Menomonies, such of the Sioux, if any, as may choose to remain in that region, and all other northern Indians east of the Mississippi (except those in the State of New York), who have yet to be removed west of that river." Together with the removal of Indians from the "very desirable" land north of the Kansas River to a southern "colony" west of Arkansas and Missouri, Medill hoped that the concentration of the northern Indians on the headwaters of the Mississippi River would provide "a wide and safe passage" for American emigrants to the Far West. Medill's report of November 30, 1848, was a tacit admission of the government's failure to provide Indian emigrants from the Old Northwest with fixed and permanent boundaries as guaranteed by the Removal Act of 1830. Throughout this period, the exigencies of the moment determined the boundaries that American officials provided for the Indians.

The second alleged benefit of removal was isolation from corrupt white elements such as gamblers, prostitutes, whiskey peddlers, and the like. The government's lack of planning for the permanent relocation of the tribes of the Old Northwest meant that these Indians were continually in the path of the westward tide of white settlement. Although Congress passed a Trade and Intercourse Act in 1834 to protect the Indians from land hungry whites, as well as whiskey peddlers and similar groups, nothing, including Indian treaty rights, stopped the advance of white settlement. Liquor was readily available to most tribes. In 1844 Thomas McKenney, an expert on Indian affairs, reported that the Menominees in Wisconsin, who had undergone several relocations, were "utterly abandoned to the vice of intoxication." Efforts to strengthen the Trade and Intercourse Laws in 1847 failed once again to halt the liquor traffic. Frontier citizens, especially the traders and their powerful political allies, blatantly refused to cooperate in enforcing the laws.

Tribal self-government unfettered by state or territorial laws was the third benefit that removal was supposed to bring the Indians. Yet the Trade and Intercourse Acts of 1834 and 1847 placed the Indians at the mercy of the white man's conception of justice. The legislation clearly provided that American laws would take precedence over Indian laws and customs in all cases involving both groups. Since the local judicial officers in the white communities adjoining Indian settlements reflected the dominant attitudes of their respective communities and often had ties with local businessmen and traders, they were not always effective administrators of the federal laws designed to protect the Indians from whiskey peddlers or other avaricious whites. The presence of federal Indian agents and military detachments near Indian settlements, moreover, meant that the Indians were not completely sovereign. Indian agents and the commanding officers of frontier posts often played "Indian politics." They found it much easier to deal with a central tribal authority rather than a series of chiefs or headmen and encouraged the recognition of one individual as the principal tribal leader. One vehicle used to accomplish this purpose was the allocation of Indian annuities. By determining who would receive the annuities, the War Department manipulated tribal politics. The result of such efforts was the emasculation of tribal self-government.

The fourth alleged benefit of removal was "civilization." American officials involved in the formulation and execution of Indian policy argued that the Indians lacked the essentials of civilized society—Christianity, private property, and knowledge of agriculture and the mechanical arts. Indian removal, they maintained, would provide ample opportunities for the uplifting of the Indians. Yet the removal policy did not bring great benefits, in terms of the white man's "civilization," to a significant number of Indians.

The constant reshuffling of tribes to new "permanent" locations failed to promote Indian interest in the white man's "civilization." How could the Winnebagos who had suffered tremendous social and psychological strains as a result of their continuous uprooting and relocation be expected to have interest in, or make significant advances in, the adoption of Christianity or any of the other so-called prerequisites of "civilized" society? Other Indians had similar reactions.

The events surrounding the acquisition of Chippewa and Ottawa lands in Michigan demonstrate some of the reasons for the failure of government efforts to promote its "civilization" program among the Indians of the Old Northwest. In 1836 the Chippewas and Ottawas had ceded their lands with the understanding that the government would allot them permanent reservations in northern Michigan and provide blacksmiths, farmers, and teachers to help them learn white trades and farming techniques. The land cession treaty provided federal funds to accomplish the "civilization" of these Indians, but the entire project was doomed before it began.

When the Senate considered the ratification of the treaty, it amended the document so that the reserves in northern Michigan would only be temporary residences. The Indians were understandably disturbed by this unilateral alteration of the treaty, and they were reluctant to move to temporary reserves in order to clear the land and to take up farming. Commissioner of Indian Affairs Carey Allen Harris, moreover, urged that government funds for these Indians be kept to a minimum until they settled at a permanent location.

Because their "permanent" boundaries always seemed to be temporary ones, the Indians of the Old Northwest found it more convenient to live off their annuities than to labor in their fields. As Chippewa Indian George Copway lamented, "no sooner have the Indians gone on and made improvements, and our children began to like to go to the school houses which have been erected, than we hear the cry of the United States government, 'We want your lands;' and, in going from one place to another, the Indian looses [sic] all that he had previously learned." As a result of this situation, the Indians paid more attention to the fur traders than to the school teachers. The tribes in this region relied heavily on the traders for food and goods. Government officials tended to see this dependence on the traders as a sign of idleness or weakness of character. Their ethnocentricism blinded them to the fact that farming had long been women's work among these tribes. The fur trade, wild grain, and fish were traditionally much more important to the livelihood of these Indians than American agricultural products.

Other problems inherent in the "civilization program" included the personnel employed to "civilize" the Indians. Such appointments offered patronage-hungry politicians a means of rewarding their supporters. Consequently, the teachers hired to work with the Indians did not always bring altruistic motives to their jobs. Some of them were even "indolent and shif[t]less." The employment of missionaries as civilizing agents caused special problems. Interdenominational rivalries greatly impeded their work. Some Indians demonstrated open hostility to missionaries because they associated them with efforts to remove their people from their ancient homes. Presbyterian minister Peter Dougherty found that his preaching of the Gospel to the Chippewa Indians in Michigan was greatly impeded by the belief of "heathen" Chippewas that the acceptance of Christianity would lead to their removal. For several reasons, therefore, the "civilization" program actually suffered because of the removal policy.

Regardless of the intentions of federal officials, the Indian removal policy in the Jacksonian era did not bring the tribesmen the benefits that they had predicted. Scholars such as [Francis P.] Prucha, [George H.] Schultz, and [Herman J.] Viola have argued that the architects of the removal policy had thought that it was in the best interests of the Indians. If the formulators and executors of the policy actually believed this, their assumption proved erroneous for the Indians of the Old Northwest. While there was no policy of racial extermination or genocide perpetrated against the Indians of this region, there can be no doubt that the removal policy led to tribal demoralization. Whether noble intentions or nefarious ones lay behind the removal policy, the results were disastrous for the Indians. As one scholar recently asserted, "it is sometimes difficult to tell whether the Indian has suffered more at the hands of his 'friends' or at the hands of his 'enemies.'"

Frances Trollope, an English visitor to the United States, wrote in 1832 that Indian removal epitomized everything despicable in American character, especially the "contradictions in their principles and practice." "You will see them one hour lecturing their mob on the indefeasible rights' of man," she wrote, "and the next driving from their homes the children of the soil, whom they have bound themselves to protect by the most solemn treaties." American Indian policy in the Old Northwest during the Jacksonian era serves as a grim reminder of what can happen to a politically powerless minority in a democratic society. It also demonstrates that scholars must be careful not to confuse the rhetoric of government policies with the realities involved in executing these policies.

SUGGESTED READINGS

General

Lee Benson, *The Concept of Jacksonian Democracy: New York as a Test Case* (1964).
Donald B. Cole, *The Presidency of Andrew Jackson* (1993).
Richard McCormick, *The Second Party System: Party Formation in the Jacksonian Era* (1966).
Marvin Meyers, *The Jacksonian Persuasion* (1957).
Edward Pessen, *Jacksonian America: Society, Personality, and Politics* (1969).
Robert Remini, *The Life of Andrew Jackson* (1966).
Arthur M. Schlesinger, Jr., *The Age of Jackson* (1945).
John W. Ward, *Andrew Jackson: Symbol of an Age* (1955).
Harry Watson, *Liberty and Power: The Politics of Jacksonian America* (1990).
Major L. Wilson, *The Presidency of Martin Van Buren* (1984).

FURTHER READINGS

JACKSON AND HIS ERA: James S. Chase, *Emergence of the Presidential Nominating Convention 1789–1832* (1973); Ronald P. Formisano, *The Birth of Mass Politics: Michigan, 1827–1861* (1971); William W. Freehling, *Prelude to Civil War: The Nullification Controversy in South Carolina 1816–1836* (1966); Paul Goodman, *Towards a Christian Republic* (1988); Michael D. Green, *The Politics of Indian Removal* (1982); Mary W. M. Hargreaves, *The Presidency of John Quincy Adams* (1985); Lawrence F. Kohl, *The Politics of Individualism: Parties and the American Character in the Jacksonian Era* (1989); Richard Latner, *The Presidency of Andrew Jackson: White House Politics, 1829–1837* (1979); Robert J. Morgan, *A Whig Embattled* (1954); John Niven, *Martin Van Buren: The Romantic Age of American Politics* (1983); Merrill Peterson, *The Great Triumvirate: Webster, Clay, and Calhoun* (1988); Norma Peterson, *The Presidencies of William Henry Harrison and John Tyler* (1989); Robert V. Remini, *Henry Clay, Statesman of the Union* (1991) and *The Legacy of Andrew Jackson* (1988); Michael Rogin, *Fathers and Children: Andrew Jackson and the Subjugation of American Indians* (1991); Ronald N. Satz, *American Indian Policy in the Jacksonian Era* (1974); William G. Shade, *Banks or No Banks: The Money Issue in Western Politics, 1832–1865* (1972); Peter Temin, *The Jacksonian Economy* (1969); Glyndon Van Deusen, *The Jacksonian Era 1828–1848* (1959).

QUESTIONS FOR DISCUSSION

1. Describe Andrew Jackson's attitude toward Native Americans. What events in his life brought him to this position?

2. Why was the admission of Missouri to statehood so controversial? What effect did the Missouri Compromise have on the sectional dispute over slavery?

3. What did Jackson's supporters mean by the "corrupt bargain" during the election of 1824? What reforms did Jackson as president pursue in an attempt to bring about a more virtuous republic?
4. How did Vice President Calhoun and Secretary of State Van Buren attempt to use the Peggy Eaton Affair for their political purposes? Were they successful?
5. Discuss the origins and ideology of the Whig party and provide a social and economic profile of its constituency.
6. Explain Jackson's role in the tariff crisis and the Bank War and indicate what his role revealed about his conception of the presidency in particular and federal authority in general.
7. What methods did the government employ to induce Indians to cooperate with its removal schemes?

REORDERING AMERICAN SOCIETY AND CULTURE, 1825–1850

LAFAYETTE AND HIS VISIT

On August 16, 1824, the Marquis de Lafayette, the French nobleman who had played a conspicuous role in both the American and French revolutions, arrived in New York as a guest of the American people. Americans throughout the country gave him a widely enthusiastic reception. They showered him with honors, eulogies, celebrations, and an outpouring of affection. Lafayette was an authentic hero whom those of the Revolutionary generation still affectionately called "our marquis."

DEMOGRAPHIC AND ECONOMIC CHANGES

During his thirteen-month tour that took him to every state in the Union, Lafayette had ample opportunity to observe changes that had taken place since his last visit. In some respects the country in 1824–1825 was similar to the fledgling nation he had visited in 1784, but in others it was remarkably different. During the interim, the nation had adopted a constitution that established a federal union consisting of twenty-four states in 1824, vastly expanded its territory, moved the capital to Washington on the Potomac, reached a fragile truce on the slavery/sectional issue, and successfully negotiated a treacherous international minefield.

The world in which the overwhelming majority of citizens lived in 1824–1825, as it had been when Lafayette last saw America, was a world of small scale and scarcity. The majority lived outside the booming, modernizing society that was emerging in a few commercial and industrial centers. Their economic and social lives were locally oriented. Systems of barter prevailed in their subsistence or semisubsistence economy. By and large, this world of exchange was one of neighborhood relationships. Money (specie) was scarce, and for several decades after the Revolution the limited amount of gold and silver money in circulation was likely to be of foreign origin. Americans swapped goods and services and reveled in bargaining with local merchants who accepted their farm products in exchange for manufactured goods. Most farm families dealt with local storekeepers who in turn funneled farm produce to outside markets and stocked imported and manufactured goods needed by their customers.

When Lafayette arrived in the United States in 1824, industrialization was already underway. While it does not appear that he toured any of the textile manufacturing establishments, he undoubtedly was apprised of their existence. Although most of the pottery—plates, dinnerware, vases and similar souvenir pieces that commemorated Lafayette's visit—were imported from Britain, the American glass industry, which was fairly well established by 1824, provided a bountiful supply of commemorative bottles and flasks. One writer has suggested that in view of the profusion of drinking utensils produced to honor the Frenchman, it is likely that even in those taverns and inns which he did *not* visit, "he was there in spirits."

DIFFICULTIES IN TRAVEL

Lafayette could readily testify to the discomforts and risks involved in travel. Rural roads that covered the settled portion of the country were often little more than broad paths through forests. Stones and stumps made transportation at best difficult. During wet weather and in swampy areas roads became impassable. Although a few wooden bridges existed, the crossing of most rivers and streams was accomplished by fords or ferries. The difficulty in moving troops during the War of 1812, coupled with the increasing demand for an improved transportation system that accompanied the economic and demographic changes, prompted a demand for internal improvements, including roads and canals. Year after year Congress debated the issue, but a combination of constitutional objections and state and sectional jealousies thwarted the implementation of a comprehensive federal road program. As a result, people, goods, and information moved slowly.

Lafayette clearly recognized that traveling southward and westward became increasingly uncomfortable, slower, and more hazardous. For example, the trip from Cheraw to Camden, South Carolina, a distance of about sixty miles, took two days on a stagecoach that lurched and jolted on roads that were little more than rough paths. Travel on waterways was easier but not without risks. The boat which took Lafayette up the Hudson River ran aground in a fog, and the vessel that transported him up the Ohio shipwrecked near Shawneetown, Illinois. He was unharmed, but lost much of his baggage and had to spend the night ashore on a mattress that had been saved from the wreck. The experiences of the nation's honored guest who enjoyed the best travel accommodations suggest the extent of the hazards that awaited ordinary citizens who traveled either by land or water.

RELIGIOUS REVIVALISM

Lafayette's tour was so full and tightly arranged that he was forced to travel on Sundays. Such a schedule ran afoul of one by-product of the wave of religious revivalism in progress, known as the Second Great Awakening. Beginning in the 1790s among farmers and villagers in the West, the revivals gradually moved eastward and inspired a variety of reforms, including stricter Sabbath observance. Such observance came to be considered essential to public morality and social order. Sabbatarians not only launched a campaign to force private and public enterprises to cease operations on the Sabbath, but also initiated a petition campaign in an unsuccessful effort to persuade the federal government to close post offices on Sunday. Early in his tour Lafayette discovered how sensitive some Americans were about proper Sabbath observance when complaints were voiced about his Sunday travels. While such complaints were directed at those who arranged the tour rather than at the Frenchman himself, Lafayette made sure thereafter that the usual military honors and escorts were omitted during his Sunday travels.

DAILY LIFE

The texture of the physical and material life of most Americans in 1824, despite changes since the Revolution, resembled in many respects what Lafayette had encountered almost a half century earlier. Few shared even marginally in what a small minority referred to as "progress and refinement." Despite a significant rise in the per capita income, the benefits of the nation's economic growth between 1789 and 1824 were distributed unevenly with the gap between the wealthiest and poorest growing increasingly wider.

For many Americans, the social boundaries of their lives and the material comforts of their households changed only very slowly. Their dwellings were both small and poorly lighted. Far removed in size and opulence was the baronial estate of Robert Livingston located on the Hudson River in New York where Lafayette was feted at a banquet in the large greenhouse amid orange and lemon trees. By modern standards Americans were dirty and often insect-infested. Most bathed infrequently and rarely could afford store-bought soap. Body odors blended with those of the barnyards, stables, tanneries, taverns, and privies and chamber pots to fill the air with pungent and profuse smells. Food was usually coarse and heavy, and most meat was heavily salted.

Americans of both sexes possessed extremely limited wardrobes that consisted of handmade and more often than not homespun apparel. Clothing was expensive, whether calculated in terms of the labor required by spinning, weaving, and sewing that consumed much time of most mothers and wives or in terms of the cost of purchasing machine-made cloth and the charges of dress-makers or tailors patronized by more affluent citizens. Hard physical labor over long hours—sunup to sundown—was the lot of ordinary Americans of both sexes in urban as well as rural environments.

TOBACCO, ALCOHOL, AND VIOLENCE

The use of tobacco and the consumption of alcohol were so widespread that few foreign observers failed to comment on the American propensity for indulging in both. Tobacco was a relatively inexpensive, home-grown product free of heavy import duties, and in its various forms was smoked, chewed, and dipped in huge quantities. Tobacco chewing was confined almost exclusively to males who, according to one foreign visitor, engaged in "incessant, remorseless spitting." Although spittoons were omnipresent accoutrements of both public and private buildings, chewers often displayed little concern for hitting the mark. As a result, the yellow stains on floors of churches, legislative halls, and other public places bore abundant evidence of the tobacco chewers' poor marksmanship.

Alcohol was closely associated with tobacco. Observers agreed that "alternate pulls on the pipe or segar [cigar] and the glass, or intervals of drinking and chewing, were part of the daily ritual of countless men." Alcohol in the form of whiskey, beer, wine, and "hard cider" was readily available and consumed in ever larger quantities at home, in taverns, and at public occasions by both rural and urban residents. Certainly Lafayette's visit did little to reduce the consumption of alcohol in the United States which by the late 1820s had risen to an all-time high of four gallons per capita annually. The hundreds of banquets and ceremonies extended to the marquis included round after round of toasts involving alcohol in one form or another.

Often linked to overindulgence in alcohol were gambling, racing, blood sports such as cock and dog fighting, and brawling. Physical violence was a conspicuous element in American life. Men settled their differences, sometimes trifling and ridiculous, by fighting. Another way of settling quarrels and responding to insults was dueling. The death of Alexander Hamilton in a duel with Aaron Burr in 1804 resulted in driving the practice south of the Potomac. Dueling flourished thereafter primarily as a southern practice which was invoked by members of the planter class to defend their reputation, status as gentlemen, and personal honor. The practice involved elaborate ritual and precise rules. While duelists displayed decorum and self-control in the settlement of disputes, "rough and tumble elements" such as lumbermen, river boatmen, roustabouts and gamblers, frontier hunters and herders, and yeoman farmers, demonstrated no such ceremony or restraint. They admired unbridled aggression, raw physical strength, and courage in the face of pain. Brawls were often prompted by extravagant boasts, gratuitous insults, and desires for vengeance. In the southern backcountry, in particular, the emphasis was on maximum disfigurement and the severance of body parts in no-holds-barred contests in which gouging, biting, hair pulling, and scratching were altogether permissible. Gouging out an opponent's eye became the equivalent of the knockout punch in modern day boxing. A traveler into the southern back-country in 1816 recognized that he had arrived in "the region of 'gouging'" when he observed how many men lacked an eye. Although eye gouging continued long after the antebellum era, it declined as the way of life that supported the rough-and-tumble elements waned.

During his tour Lafayette observed many aspects of American life and was impressed by the changes that had occurred since the Revolution. However much he may have been impressed with such tangible evidence of the nation's material progress such as the Erie Canal, nothing attracted his admiration more than the "republican institutions" and democratic simplicity of the nation he had helped to bring into existence. As he embarked for France, Lafayette spoke in glowing terms about the happiness and prosperity of the people. Americans, he concluded, had translated republican principles into popular institutions, "founded on the plain rights of man," which served as an example to the world.

A NEW ORDER

That the United States was undergoing economic and social changes was clearly evident during Lafayette's visit. Such changes accelerated and became more widespread during the decades that followed. The transformation, especially apparent in the cities, owed much to the modernization of transportation, massive immigration from the countryside, the steady advance of industrialization, and the proliferation of production geared to mass markets. The emergence of a new order in the city involved a blending of the old, the new, and the transitional that affected everything from the distribution of wealth, residential patterns, social and class relations, and managerial practices to politics, family life, the nature of work, the character of the workplace, and the composition of the work force.

POPULATION AND WESTERN MIGRATION

Intimately linked to this new order were the nation's population growth and demographic shifts. The population of the United States quadrupled in the half century between 1790 and 1840. In the latter year it stood at over 17 million. Other than a rapid increase, population statistics revealed two other trends: a strong westward movement and migration from the countryside to towns and cities. That Andrew Jackson was the first president from the trans-Appalachian region testified to the westward shift of the population. During his presidency (1829–1837) more than a quarter of the nation's population lived west of the Appalachians. The westward movement of people from the seaboard states meant that some of these states experienced population losses. High birthrates and declining mortality rates were primarily responsible for the expanding population, but during Jackson's presidency the number of foreign immigrants entering the country began to rise, establishing a trend that would persist until the outbreak of the Civil War. Although the new immigrants, dominated by the Irish and to a lesser degree by Germans, provided a much needed source of labor for the nation's expanding economy, Irish Catholics in particular encountered prejudice and occasionally violence at the hands of Protestants.

By the 1830s changes had occurred in the condition of African Americans and Native Americans. Both the degree of slave concentration in and the geographical meaning of the South had vastly increased, as more and more slaves were employed in the cotton kingdom that pushed into the lower Mississippi Valley and beyond. Whites who had been inclined to refer to slavery as a "necessary evil" in the Revolutionary Era had begun a generation later to view it as a "positive good." Scarcely less dramatic were the changes that had occurred in the status of American Indians in the same era. In 1790 the various Indian nations effectively controlled more territory within the boundaries of the United States than the federal government did. The so-called five civilized tribes—Creeks, Cherokees, Chickasaws, Choctaws, and Seminoles—all located in the Southeast, posed special problems for the federal government in view of the demand of white settlers for their land. At the very moment that Lafayette visited Indian villages in Georgia and Alabama early in 1825, movements were underway to rid the area of Indians and to make their lands available to white farmers. Efforts to push Indians beyond the Mississippi began to succeed within a few years after they had greeted Lafayette as the "White Father" and "the Envoy of the Great Spirit."

At the same time that Americans were moving westward, they were also abandoning rural areas for towns and cities whose population increased at a rate substantially above that of the nation as a whole. New York, for example, underwent spectacular growth, surpassing Philadelphia in population by 1810 and steadily increasing its lead as the nation's largest city. Tiny villages quickly grew into towns of several thousand residents. Cities in the West such as Cincinnati, St. Louis, and Pittsburgh dramatically increased in size and economic significance. For example, Cincinnati, an Ohio river town with 2,540 inhabitants in 1810, had become the nation's third largest industrial center by 1840 with a population of 46,338. Ten years later, Cincinnati's population had risen to 115,435.

LIFE IN CITIES

Foreign visitors to the United States in the opening decades of the nineteenth century often expressed admiration for American cities, especially their open, spacious appearance and lack of congested slums. By the 1830s and 1840s the rapid growth of cities had altered the opinions of such visitors. While they commented on the hustle and bustle of the newer cities in the West, they were aware of the signs of decay in the older seaboard cities in the South and the appearance of slums in New York, Boston, and other larger urban centers in the

Northeast. Few foreign travelers failed to comment on the absence of paved streets and the omnipresent mud that characterized the rapidly growing cities in all parts of the country. Mud, according to one visitor to Detroit, was "the common topic of conversation and exceeds credibility." Everywhere garbage and waste mixed with mud, and hordes of hogs, often protected by law, roamed at will, to act as scavengers. It was not surprising, therefore, that a New Yorker in 1832 likened his city to "one huge pigsty" in which "big heaps" of mud and manure lay piled along streets for weeks at a time.

Sanitation

Throughout the antebellum era many cities attempted to cope with urban problems such as waste disposal and water supplies by invoking methods characteristic of villages and rural areas. Privies and cesspools were commonplace. In the most congested sections of cities, privies were likely to be wholly inadequate. In Cincinnati, for example, the 102 residents in one tenement in 1849 had access to only one privy. In numerous cities human waste flowed in open ditches or sewers. The inadequate disposal of waste meant that the water supply of numerous urban residents was dangerously contaminated. Only gradually did city governments assume responsibility for water and sanitation systems, many of which did not reach into densely populated slum areas until well after the Civil War.

Inadequate sanitation and the virtual absence of effective public health regulations, coupled with erroneous beliefs about the causes of disease, meant that urban dwellers regularly fell prey to an assortment of illnesses such as malaria and consumption. Most devastating of all to public health were the periodic epidemics of cholera, typhoid, and yellow fever that struck some of the nation's major cities in the antebellum era. These epidemics were sometimes interpreted in moral and class terms. Many Americans believed that the dreaded cholera epidemics, for example, were scourges of God to punish the sinful people who inhabited the slums. Echoing the sentiments of the urban elite, one New Yorker claimed that the epidemic was confined to "the scum of the city" who were "huddled together like swine in their polluted habitations." That cholera killed the rich and poor and temperate and intemperate, indiscriminately, undermined the validity of such moralistic and class explanations and prompted cities to institute public health measures designed to prevent and check the outbreak of the epidemics.

Medical Care

Despite advances in medical theory and practices, the epidemics and their causes baffled physicians. Because proof of the germ theory of disease did not occur until much later in the nineteenth century, physicians subscribed to one of several rival theories about the cause of epidemic diseases. Adhering rigidly to theories that flew in the face of evidence, they prescribed measures that were occasionally helpful but more often either useless or downright harmful.

Dan Beard's drawing of New York's "Five Points" focused on the squalor of this well-known slum.

The number of medical schools increased from six to sixty between 1810 and 1850. The absence of any sort of regulations, however, resulted in the creation of medical schools that ranged in quality from competent institutions to diploma mills. Almost any physician or group of physicians could establish a medical school and secure a state charter. Throughout the antebellum era many of those who practiced medicine possessed only such training as they acquired as apprentices to physicians who themselves were self-educated and self-certified. In the words of one historian, "bleeding, blistering, purging and puking" remained among the most widely used treatments prescribed by even the best educated physicians. Such treatments and their results help to explain why Americans so readily embraced health movements that grew up outside the medical profession and promised to decrease mortality rates by emphasizing diet, exercise, and other regimens.

Although life chances in America were considerably better than those of most European countries, sickness and death, especially among children, were frequent visitors in most households. For rural people, folk medicine often provided the sole means of treating illnesses, and both rural and urban residents consumed ever-increasing quantities of patent medicines. Dozens of such medicines which made extravagant claims as cures for an incredible array of ailments were available by the 1850s. The proliferation of these patented concoctions posed a serious threat for orthodox medical education and practitioners.

Poverty and Crime

In addition to health hazards, urban residents in the antebellum years wrestled with the problems of poverty and crime. For some Americans, poverty, like disease, was the result of individual moral failure. Poverty, in short, was punishment for vice. For example, the Baltimore Society for the Prevention of Pauperism, organized in 1820, identified four basic causes of poverty: excessive drinking, gambling, houses of prostitution, and misguided charities that encouraged the poor to believe they could get something for nothing. Some individuals who labored among the urban poor began to shift the focus from the individualistic explanation of poverty to the notion of the community's collective responsibilities to the poor whose low wages and inadequate education contributed to the perpetuation of their impoverished condition. In time the efforts of such individuals led to a more efficient organization of private charities and the enactment of laws to provide for government relief to the poor.

Many Americans linked the problem of poverty to the foreign immigrants, who began to arrive in increasing numbers in the 1830s. Immigrants arrived poor and remained poor, holding the lowest-paying jobs and living in the most wretched housing in cities. By 1852 Irish and German immigrants made up more than one half of those receiving public assistance in eastern cities. Such a condition intensified xenophobic fears and gave rise to local antiimmigrant movements that ultimately evolved into a national political party, known as the Know-Nothing party.

Closely identified in the public mind with pauperism and immigrants was the problem of urban crime. By the 1840s officials in New York and other cities became alarmed by the appearance of criminal districts and gangs similar to those in European cities. Of special concern was the proliferation of gangs of young criminals who waged war on each other and terrorized neighborhoods. That a majority of individuals arrested for crimes in general were foreign born made it all the easier to blame the rising crime rate on immigrants.

Law Enforcement

The increase in urban crime prompted actions by both private and public agencies. To address the problem of juvenile crime, Charles Loren Brace organized the Children's Aid Society in 1853 and spent most of his life attempting to move children out of undesirable circumstances in urban centers to foster homes in the West. In the public sector, cities responded to the rise in the crime rate by revamping their police systems. Since the colonial era, cities had used a combination of day policemen and night watchmen who, often hired on a part-time basis, possessed little training or discipline. Beginning in the 1840s, this system was replaced in city after city with a single centralized body of full-time, uniformed policemen. In law enforcement, as in sanitation, fire protection, and other areas, cities abandoned, often slowly and haltingly, the informal, semiprivate approach to public services that had characterized villages and small

OPENING OF THE ERIE CANAL.

A sketch depicting the opening of the Erie Canal.

towns of an earlier era for one of municipal responsibility for a broad range of such services.

THE TRANSPORTATION REVOLUTION

Urban growth and population distribution—and indeed the emergence of a national market economy—owed much to the revolution in transportation that began about 1815 and continued until the Civil War. By the end of Jackson's term in 1837 a national transportation network that linked together various sections of the nation had been established through a system of roads and canals. In addition to the National Road, begun by the federal government in 1811 and ultimately extending from Maryland to Illinois, numerous toll roads known as turnpikes, built either by states or private companies, came into existence.

Robert Fulton's introduction of the steamboat on the Hudson River in 1807 quickened interest in the possibilities of water transportation and led to a boom in canal building. More than 3,300 miles of canals, financed primarily by states, had been completed by 1840. Of all the canals constructed in America, the most famous was the Erie Canal in New York, built between 1817 and 1825. An engineering feat that proved to be a great financial success, the canal linked Lake Erie to Albany, where one might continue to New York City via the

FIGURE 8–1
Means of Transportation, 1850

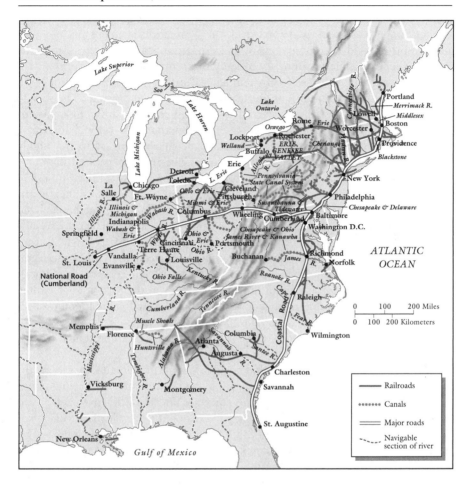

Hudson River, thereby providing New York access to the expanding markets of the West. Other systems of water transportation connected Lake Erie to the Ohio River. The network of inland waterways both increased settlement in the Northwest and stimulated trade between East and West.

By 1840 when the canal-building spree had ended, a new mode of transportation had emerged with the construction of railroads. The first company to begin operations was the Baltimore and Ohio, which opened thirteen miles of track in 1830. A little more than a decade later the United States possessed 3,300 miles of rails, almost twice as many as all of Europe. Arriving in Washington for his inauguration in 1829 in a carriage, Andrew Jackson departed the city by rail at the end of his tenure eight years later. By the outbreak of the Civil War the nation had more than 30,000 miles of rails (see Figure 8–1).

THE EMERGENCE OF THE MARKET ECONOMY

The transportation revolution, in conjunction with the expanding population, the opening of new lands and markets in the West, and the emergence of a new generation of bold entrepreneurs, contributed significantly to the rise of the market economy. The traditional economy of an overwhelmingly rural nation rested to a great extent on self-sufficient agriculture and barter. Cash crops sold either in local or distant markets gradually replaced the old system. The shift to commercial agriculture that occurred at varying rates in different areas inevitably involved money, credit, debt, and price fluctuations over which farmers exercised no control, a condition that stood in sharp contrast to the highly personal world of subsistence agriculture, barter, and the local general store.

Urban capitalists, all the while, were revolutionizing the organization and operation of the economy. They created new financial institutions such as investment and brokerage houses; commercial, savings, and land banks; and trust and insurance companies. These institutions loaned their capital to customers who invested it in projects that made the economy flourish. Corporations with numerous shareholders gradually replaced individual merchant capitalists and limited partnerships that owned entire enterprises. The liberalization of incorporation laws and the establishment of the principle of limited liability (which meant that a stockholder was liable only for the amount of his investment in case the enterprise failed) accelerated the proliferation of corporations. A principal advantage of corporations was that they could mobilize the capital necessary to underwrite ever larger enterprises.

Even so, the investment capital available was inadequate to satisfy the demands of entrepreneurs. A complicating factor was an insufficient money supply. Government alone could issue currency and the official currency was restricted to gold and silver (not paper). The amount of official currency was too small to meet the needs of business. Therefore, businessmen increasingly relied on credit provided by commercial banks. Credit from these banks usually took the form of bank notes. People borrowed bank notes from banks, and the community accepted them as money. Customers met their obligations with bank notes for which they paid the bank interest for substituting its superior credit for their own. Bank notes were backed by the general credit of the bank, some gold and silver (specie) reserve, some mortgages, and customers' promissory notes. Unfortunately, the lure of profits in the expanding economy prompted banks to issue notes far in excess of their reserves, a tendency that led to frequent bank failures and financial instability.

INDUSTRIAL BEGINNINGS

Despite the crude and often risky credit mechanisms available, conditions were ripe for the acceleration of the process of industrialization that had begun

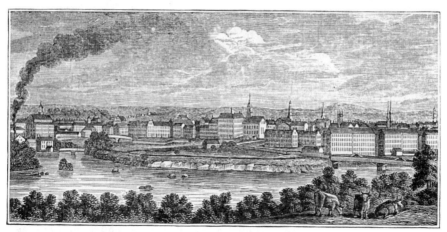

The famous textile mills of Lowell, Massachusetts, ca. 1840, as viewed from the northern side of the Merrimac River.

earlier. The embargo (1807–1809) and the War of 1812, by cutting off the supply of British manufactured goods, had encouraged investment in domestic manufacturing. The industrialization of manufacturing—the emergence of the factory system—evolved first in the Northeast. Using expertise and technology borrowed from Britain, the factory system expanded rapidly beginning in the 1820s. In time it replaced the traditional method of manufacturing that took place in the homes and shops of artisans who produced limited quantities of goods, frequently made to order for local customers. Initiated in New England's textile and shoe industries, the factory system spread throughout the Northeast and elsewhere.

The textile mills in Lowell, Massachusetts, which brought all steps in cloth production under a single roof, served as a model not merely for the textile industry but for other manufacturing operations as well. The initial paternalism of factory owners quickly gave way to more regimented and demanding work schedules, wage reductions, and fewer privileges. The introduction and widespread use of machine technology quickened the pace of production and created a demand for the manufacture of machine tools which in turn created an increasing demand for iron. As one study has suggested, "one industry forged links with another on an endless chain that ultimately expanded the production of goods and services and increased industrial output by 500 percent between 1810 and 1860." The initial phase of the nation's industrial revolution not only resulted in the efficient production of greater quantities of high quality goods and reduced economic dependence on Britain, it also raised the overall standard of living and accelerated urbanization, even though only about 14 percent of the labor force worked in manufacturing by 1850.

IMPACT OF INDUSTRIALIZATION

Such rapid and profound changes had a significant impact upon occupational and social mobility, distribution of wealth, class structure, and the internal dynamics of family life. Large numbers of workers freed from the traditional institutions of family and the craft system crowded into the urban centers. The market revolution that made possible the ascent of some into the middle class also allowed others to slip into poverty and dependency. Unable to predict which fate awaited them, many Americans harbored deep anxieties about the new order. Although some artisans successfully negotiated the shift in the locus of production from the household to the factory and entered the ranks of the new business or managerial class, many barely managed to eke out an existence. The evidence suggests that upward mobility often meant rising within the laboring class rather than moving into the middle class. For example, unskilled workers might enter the ranks of the semiskilled, and skilled artisans might improve their economic condition, but neither moved into the middle class.

The primary beneficiaries of the market revolution were merchants, manufacturers, bankers, lawyers and other professionals, and successful commercial farmers. These groups constituted a minuscule proportion of the total population. The existence of glaring disparities in wealth was most evident in urban areas. Place of residence, style of living, and even dress distinguished the haves from the have-nots in cities. Those areas most thoroughly penetrated by the market revolution provided the greatest evidence of economic disparities and well defined class lines.

IMPACT ON THE FAMILY

The separation of the household from the workplace that accompanied the rise of the factory system changed the nature, function, and size of the family. In rural areas the family remained a close-knit economic unit in which household and workplace were intimately linked and in which children were an economic asset. In urban areas the advance of industrialization undermined the traditional economic function of the family. Work was located outside the home; for lower-class families this meant that fathers, mothers, and many children under the age of fourteen left home to work long hours for low wages elsewhere. Women constituted a majority of all workers in textile mills which by the 1830s also employed twenty thousand children, mostly girls. Thousands of women took jobs as domestic servants. Work by women outside the home was considered the preserve of the lower class.

The separation of household and workplace was no less significant in altering the family life of middle-class people, that is, those standing between the very rich and the nonpropertied wage earner. The middle-class husband was expected to be the family's breadwinner. Access to readymade goods removed middle-class mothers from the production of goods, even those for household use. Among middle-class families the roles of parents were redefined and divided into public and private spheres. The public sphere of business, commerce, and politics belonged to the father; the private sphere of domestic duties and child rearing belonged to the mother.

MIDDLE-CLASS WOMEN

Within their separate sphere women, especially those in the middle class, began to develop a distinctive female culture that was encouraged by the publication of romantic novels by women, the popular magazine *Godey's Lady's Book*, and the lectures and writings of Catherine Beecher. The emergence of what is called the "cult of domesticity" assigned to women rights and responsibilities that endowed them with special virtues and relieved them of the more oppressive patriarchal arrangement that had existed earlier. Viewed as morally superior to and different from men, women were seen not so much as contributors to the family economy as the custodians of culture and morality who were primarily responsible for the management of the household and the care of children. Assigned the central role in child rearing, women became the guardians of the nation's future. The conscious choice of middle-class parents to have fewer children not only allowed families to enhance their standard of living, but also made it possible for mothers to devote more attention to each child and to increase his or her prospects for success. At the same time child-rearing practices underwent changes that emphasized affection rather than strict control, kept children at home longer, and provided them with more extensive formal education. Having to care for fewer children also allowed middle-class women greater personal freedom to move beyond the strictly domestic sphere to participate in female voluntary organizations devoted primarily to religious and charitable causes. In addition to the good works performed by such organizations, they fostered a sense of sisterhood among participants.

LABOR ORGANIZATIONS

The conditions created by industrialization caused the new urban working class to assume its own identity. By the 1830s workers had organized unions, engaged in political activities, and staged strikes in an effort to halt what they perceived as the steady deterioration of their status. Especially disturbing to workers was their perception that impersonal market forces dominated their lives. Plagued by a volatile business cycle and the specter of chronic unemployment, workers also had to cope with the problem of making ends meet in an inflationary economy in which wages failed to keep up with runaway prices. A source of great anxiety among semiskilled and especially skilled artisans was the prospect of being displaced by increasingly sophisticated machinery in factories. Focusing on specific grievances such as long hours and low wages, labor leaders in the 1820s and 1830s regularly invoked the ideology and rhetoric of the American Revolution in much the manner of President Jackson. Loudly proclaiming the virtues of freedom and equality, they denounced special privilege, monopoly, and the erosion of workers' independence which had transformed workers into "slaves of the moneyed aristocracy." The demands of urban labor scarcely matched the militancy of its rhetoric. Labor's most frequent demands included universal education, the abolition of imprisonment for debt and of "licensed monopolies," equal taxation, and election of all government officials "by the People."

In Boston, New York, Philadelphia, and other cities in which skilled artisans had formed mutual aid societies composed of members of a particular craft, these societies combined to create citywide federations to protect the endangered positions of their members. In 1834 delegates from six federations launched the National Trades' Union which later included labor groups from other cities. The initial success of a series of strikes and boycotts in the 1830s inspired other craft organizations to join in the expanding labor movement. Far less successful were attempts by organizations of unskilled and semiskilled laborers to improve their wages and hours. Even the promising prospects of the skilled artisans' organizations dimmed in the face of the concerted opposition of management, antiunion laws, court decisions, and the growth of internal union divisions prompted by racial and ethnic prejudices. Although the number of foreign-born workers in cities accelerated in the 1840s, most workers in the previous decade were native born. But even so, they were not a homogeneous group; rather, differences between skilled and unskilled workers and between those born and reared in the city and those from rural areas resulted in diverse and often conflicting assumptions, expectations, and aspirations. The large influx of European immigrants of different nationalities by the end of the 1840s intensified the diversity of the labor force.

In May 1835 the nation's first *general* strike occurred in Philadelphia when dockworkers walked off the job in protest against their long hours. Their "standout" quickly escalated into a general strike as carpenters, textile millhands, and numerous others representing a variety of trades joined the dockworkers on strike. About twenty thousand workers, both skilled and unskilled, laid aside their differences to press for the ten-hour workday. The strike quickly assumed the character of a crusade. Philadelphia's wage earners crowded the streets and parks, and indeed appeared to be everywhere except in their workplaces. Speakers denounced the "6 to 6" (sunup to sundown) work schedule as inconsistent with good citizenship, insisting that it deprived workers of opportunities for the mental improvement essential to the performance of their duties as responsible citizens. Taken aback by the scope of the strike and its effectiveness in bringing business to a standstill, a Philadelphia newspaper editor who voiced the sentiment of the city's business elite wrote: "The times are completely out of joint." According to a labor spokesman, the only people in the city who were aghast at the strike were those who made up "the blood sucking aristocracy." Within a month most of the trades involved in the strike had won the ten-hour day.

Philadelphia's general strike had significant implications both for the ten-hour movement elsewhere and for the union movement in the city. It served to galvanize efforts in other cities and towns to reduce the length of the workday into a "general demand." Inspired by the victory in Philadelphia, urban workers throughout the Northeast staged strikes. By the end of 1835 the ten-hour day had become the standard for day laborers in most cities in the region. Within Philadelphia the successful strike resulted in a sudden and dramatic increase in the membership of the General Trades' Union of the City and County of Philadelphia (GTU), a labor organization formed in 1834. The GTU was the successor to the Mechanics' Union of Trade Association organized seven years earlier and generally known as the nation's first real labor union. Although the Mechanics' Union included only skilled artisans and scarcely represented Philadelphia's working classes, it entered politics and sponsored the Working Men's party. The unrepresentative character of the organization, coupled with the poor showing of its political party in local elections, hastened its decline. The General Trades' Union filled the void left by the demise of the Mechanics' Union but the two organizations differed in several significant respects. The GTU was more highly structured, eschewed partisan politics, embraced a broader constituency that included both skilled and unskilled laborers, and sponsored a variety of education and self-improvement activities. In 1836 when the GTU mounted a campaign for higher wages, evangelical ministers and conservative editors denounced the union as a radical group bent on destroying the sacred rights of property. Labor's success in organizing and in achieving certain objectives proved to be short-lived. The Panic of 1837 and the depression that followed decimated the young labor movement, but did not eliminate workers' dissatisfaction with their lot.

CULTURAL, INTELLECTUAL, AND RELIGIOUS STRIVINGS

HIGHBROW AND LOWBROW CULTURE

The shaping of American culture owed much to those who reflected the tastes and preferences of the nation's various socioeconomic classes. Cities vied with each other in providing cultural amenities through the establishment of theaters and opera houses, museums, art galleries, and libraries. Such institutions came to be viewed as an accurate measure of a city's cultural refinement and civic pride. The driving force behind the creation of these tangible symbols of high culture was the urban elite who looked upon patronage of the arts as its special responsibility. According to one authority, the elite envisioned a cultural renaissance in which Americans would "bring European forms and concepts to new heights of achievement." In certain cities the elite groups exercised tight control over the cultural institutions that they sponsored and used them to reinforce their own lofty social status. For example, the old Knickerbocker families who established New York's Academy of Music in 1854 considered it their private preserve and for more than a generation excluded from membership the new rich whom they considered mere social upstarts, lacking in gentility and proper family credentials. The dramatic and musical performances at the Academy and similar institutions, which clearly reflected the European orientation of their sponsors, contrasted sharply with the tastes and preferences of the so-called common people.

The cultural fragmentation in the antebellum era possessed unmistakable class overtones. In theaters patronized by a cross section of the population, the seating arrangement and behavior underscored differences in class and cultural preference. The upper class occupied the expensive boxes and displayed a decorum utterly lacking among the ordinary folks who, seated in the pit and gallery, were given to shouting, stamping their feet, and engaging in occasional fistfights. Rank-and-file theatergoers were quick to demonstrate their disapproval by pelting actors, especially Europeans, with eggs and rotten vegetables. Theatrical riots were not uncommon, such as the one in New York in 1849 known as the Astor Place Riot. Such outbursts were often triggered by what the nationalistic plain people considered insults to the United States or its people uttered by "arrogant" British performers.

Minstrel Shows

Among the most popular forms of mass entertainment in antebellum America were minstrel shows. Minstrelsy had existed since the colonial era, but during the 1840s its popularity began to soar. The songs, dances, and jokes of the minstrel show swept the nation and were familiar to Americans in all sections. Minstrel performers addressed the experiences of ordinary Americans, constantly changing their routines to reflect the interests and tastes of their audiences. To an extraordinary degree, they both reflected and shaped popular thought, especially regarding the plantation, cities, African Americans, immigrants, and women's rights. Their message was invariably one that glorified American democracy and ordinary whites and that lambasted aristocrats and effete gentlemen.

Although minstrel shows have often been described almost exclusively in terms of blackfaced white entertainers who caricatured African Americans, minstrelsy initially forged positive images of ordinary whites. Such images appeared first as rustic backwoodsmen who possessed all of the admirable traits of Europeans without their corruption, decadence, and hypocrisy. Minstrel routines shifted to ethnic and racial themes in the 1840s and 1850s when concerns about the influx of immigrants and the spread of slavery into the territories intensified. As the issue of slavery moved to the center of national consciousness, blackfaced white entertainers became ascendant in minstrel shows. Through the songs and comedy routines of these performers, minstrels not only reinforced the racial prejudices of working-class whites who dominated their audiences, but also contributed enduring negative stereotypes of black Americans.

P. T. Barnum

Of all of the promoters of minstrels and other forms of mass entertainment, none surpassed Phineas Taylor (P.T.) Barnum, who became the nation's foremost show business entrepreneur. He purchased an abandoned museum in New York, renamed it the American Museum, and filled it with collections of freaks and curiosities, both real and fake. In time he offered the public a dazzling array of six hundred thousand displays and a theater, all advertised as a respectable educational institution in which patrons could view, for a single low price, everything from dramatic productions, acrobats, midgets and giants to bearded ladies, elephants, and trained fleas. Barnum consciously catered to the tastes and interests of the common people. The same techniques used in promoting the American Museum served him well in other enterprises such as his sponsoring of an American tour by Jenny Lind, "the Swedish Nightingale," in 1850 and his later circus ventures billed as "the Greatest Show on Earth."

TRANSCENDENTALISM

Coinciding with the new economic and social order were intellectual and theological trends that represented a significant break with the emphasis on Enlightenment rationalism that prevailed during the Revolutionary Era. One was Romanticism which originated in Europe and flourished in New England in the 1830s under the name of Transcendentalism. This distinctive American version of Romanticism included sufficient elements of Puritanism to endow it with a pervasive moralism. Convinced that knowledge consisted of more than what could be obtained through the senses and explained by reason and logic, Transcendentalists claimed that truth transcended the senses and could not be obtained by observation alone. They emphasized emotion and intuition, sought spiritual communion with nature, preached self-reliance, and exalted the individual. The best known Transcendentalists were Ralph Waldo Emerson, a Unitarian minister who abandoned the pulpit to become a writer and lecturer, and his circle of friends in the Boston-Concord area. One such friend was Henry David Thoreau, the author of *Walden* (1854), who roundly condemned the scramble for wealth and worldly goods that characterized the new economic and social order. In fact, he went further than Emerson in resisting what he considered the repressive forces of society. In 1846 Thoreau was jailed for refusing to pay a poll tax on the grounds that he would not contribute to the support of a government that tolerated the existence of slavery. In an essay, entitled "Resistance to Civil Government" and published three years later, he elaborated on his notion of civil disobedience by insisting upon the individual's right, indeed responsibility, to refuse to obey unjust laws. The government, he argued, had no authority to require the individual to violate his or her personal morality.

The optimism, individualism, and egalitarianism implicit in Transcendentalism were very much in evidence in Emerson's Phi Beta Kappa address at Harvard in 1837, entitled "The American Scholar," which has been termed the nation's "intellectual Declaration of Independence." "We have listened too long," he declared, "to the courtly muses of Europe." The task at hand was for Americans to free themselves from intellectual dependence on Europe by producing a distinctly American literature. Emerson was correct in detecting "auspicious signs" that such a literary revolution was in the offing. In fact, the two decades beginning in 1840 witnessed such an outpouring of significant works that they constituted a golden age of American literature, even if few of the works followed Emerson's advice in dealing with the experience of ordinary Americans and "topics of the times." Among the notable literary contributions during these years were Nathaniel Hawthorne's *The Scarlet Letter* (1850), Herman Melville's *Moby Dick* (1851), Walt Whitman's *Leaves of Grass* (1855), and the short stories of Edgar Allan Poe published in the 1840s.

THE SECOND GREAT AWAKENING

Like Transcendentalism, the wave of Protestant revivalism, known as the Second Great Awakening, exuded optimism and strove for perfectionism. More directly, perhaps, than Transcendentalism, the central message of the revival, especially as it moved into areas in the throes of the market revolution, significantly shaped the popular responses to the emergence of a new economic and social order. As the revivals moved from the West into the East, they took root especially in the boomtowns and cities along the Erie Canal during the 1820s and 1830s (see Figure 8–2).

One of the most popular revivalists active in the area was Charles Grandison Finney, a Presbyterian minister, known as "the father of modern revivalism." Beginning in 1825, Finney carried his message to the residents of Utica, Rochester, and other Erie Canal cities that were entering the market economy and coping with rapid change. In sermons that were tough, direct, and forceful, he preached a theology of millennialism and perfectionism, doctrines that emphasized human perfectibility and the duty of Christians to work toward bringing about the Kingdom of God on earth in preparation for the imminent Second Coming of Christ. Rejecting the Calvinistic concept of predestination, he declared that God had "made man a free moral agent" and that evil was the result of choices made by selfish men and women rather than innate human depravity. If Christians dedicated themselves to good rather than evil, they could convert the world and thereby eliminate sin and disorder. In brief, they could quickly bring about the millennium. Finney insisted that salvation was available to all who sincerely desired it and who demonstrated their faith by good works in this world. He demanded that some kind of relevant social action follow the sinner's conversion. By proclaiming human equality before God, his teachings joined easily with secular currents that exhibited a democratic faith in the people and a trust in feeling and intuition.

Although Finney's revivals won converts from all ranks of society, his message especially appealed to members of the new urban middle class and imbued them with a desire to impose Protestant morality on a society characterized by tensions, disorder, and violence as it attempted to adjust to a

FIGURE 8–2
The Growth of American Methodism, 1775–1850

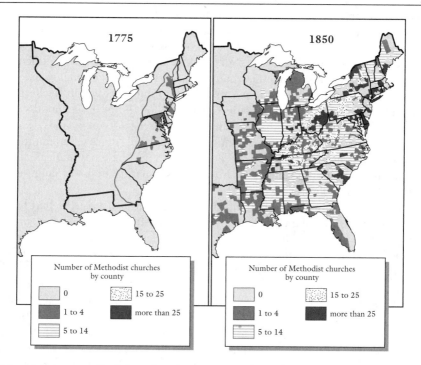

Although less evangelical than the religious movement sparked by Finney and others, Methodism nonetheless experienced a rapid growth during the Second Great Awakening. These maps also show well how rapidly the U.S. population swelled and moved into the new territories opening to the west.

new economic and social environment. According to historian Paul E. Johnson, the effort to "build a world that replaced force, barbarism and unrestrained passion constituted the moral imperative around which the northern middle class became a class." Businessmen not only abandoned old habits such as working irregular hours, consuming large quantities of alcohol, and rarely attending church for a life of temperance, steady work hours, and regular church attendance, but they also devoted themselves to persuading others, especially their employees, to follow their example.

Such a transformation bore the unmistakable stamp of evangelical Protestantism. Not surprisingly, middle-class women who were viewed as the guardians of morality played a conspicuous role in the religious revivals and the reform efforts that they promoted. The leisure and financial resources possessed by middle-class people made it possible for them to put into practice the call for good works and benevolence issued by Finney and other revivalists. Such efforts would presumably hasten the establishment of the Kingdom of God on earth, and at the same time would impose order and discipline on an unruly society. Although it is easy to exaggerate the link between revivalism and reform, one historian has observed that "when everything is said and done, it was evangelical Protestantism that provided most of the ideological and organizational foundation for antebellum reform." What is indisputable is that reform movements followed close on the heels of revivals in regions such as the Western Reserve in Ohio and the Erie Canal cities in the "burnt over district" of New York State.

One such city was Rochester, New York, which by 1830 was experiencing rapid urbanization and economic change that disrupted traditional social relationships and altered behavioral norms. Charles Finney arrived in Rochester in September of that year via the Erie Canal and for the next six months conducted a religious revival that resulted in hundreds of conversions. Among those converted were the most influential people of the city, including its prominent business leaders. By the end of the revival Finney had created a community of militant evangelicals intent on eliminating sin and inaugurating piety, order, and voluntary self-control.

While these so-called Christian soldiers waged war against the bad habits of unregenerate workingmen, such as drunkenness, Sabbath desecration, and cheap entertainments, they established churches in working-class neighborhoods and aided the deserving poor. Those workers who conformed to the expectations of their Christian employers, especially by attending church, working hard, and practicing sobriety, were far more likely to advance occupationally than those who did not. Even though hundreds of workingmen became church members and participated in the reform crusades by the mid-1830s, the majority remained outside the church and displayed little interest in the new moral code. As a result they faced insecure employment and restricted opportunities for advancement. As free moral agents, they had obviously chosen to oppose the Coming Kingdom; therefore, what was needed was more revivals to bring the unregenerate into the fold.

THE REFORM MOVEMENT

UTOPIAN SOCIETIES AND THE BENEVOLENT EMPIRE

Whatever their inspiration, numerous middle-class voluntary organizations devoted to one kind of social reform or another came into being and flourished during the Jacksonian Era. These organizations formed what has been termed the "benevolent empire," an assortment of middle-class societies and associations that shared the same or similar worldviews, tapped the same financial resources, and possessed overlapping memberships. The reform causes represented by these diverse organizations included those dedicated to promoting Sabbath observance; eliminating drunkenness, crime, and prostitution; abolishing slavery; championing the rights of women to full equality; and reforming penal and mental institutions.

Other groups chose to withdraw from society to create separate "perfect," or utopian, communities. Over one hundred utopian communities, either religious or secular in orientation, came into being in the three decades after 1820. Ideas popularized by Transcendentalism and the Second Great Awakening provided much of the impetus for the establishment of these communities. By striving for perfection in insulated groups, they sought to provide models for reform in society at large. With the exception of a few religious communities, the utopian experiments were short-lived. Disillusionment, internal discord, and financial difficulties were among the principal causes for their demise.

Conspicuous among the utopian religious communities was that founded by Joseph Smith, who claimed that the angel Moroni had led him to a set of golden tablets which revealed that Jesus had appeared in America and performed miracles in the presence of a group of ancient Hebrews residing in the New World. When this group departed from Jesus' teachings, according to Smith, God had cursed some with a dark skin. Their descendants were those whom Columbus encountered and called Indians. The inscriptions on the tablets, as translated by Smith, became *The Book of Mormon* which, published in 1830, provided the core of teachings around which Smith's community of "saints" (or religious oligarchy) was organized and over which Smith presided as "the Prophet." From time to time he received additional revelations, including one that sanctioned "plural marriage," or polygamy. To escape persecution by those who objected to such practices and condemned Mormonism for undermining the Bible, Smith and his followers moved westward and created a New Jerusalem in Illinois, where "the Prophet" was lynched by a mob. Under the leadership of Brigham Young, Smith's successor, the Mormons (The Church of Jesus Christ of Latter-day Saints) found a haven in Utah in the mid-1840s.

Another utopian religious group was the United Society of Believers in Christ's Second Appearance, better known as the Shakers. Founded by Ann Lee (Mother Ann), a former Quaker, in 1774, the society survived into the twentieth century. Eschewing worldliness, greed, and carnality in their quest for perfection, members of the society were noted for their industry and craftsmanship, especially in furniture making, and for their practices of celibacy, equality for women, and communal ownership of property. Their unconventional worship originally involved ecstatic dancing (hence the name Shakers) which ultimately evolved into ritualized patterns designed to honor God and "shake" out their sins. Their dancing at Sunday worship services contrasted sharply with their austere, work-filled existence during the remainder of the week. Their emphasis on celibacy meant that the perpetuation of the society was dependent on winning converts. The number of converts peaked during the three decades after 1830 and steadily declined thereafter.

Among the best-known secular communities were Robert Owen's New Harmony in Indiana, George Ripley's Brook Farm in Massachusetts, and John Humphrey Noyes' Oneida in New York. Perhaps the most unusual of the secular utopian communities was Nashoba established in west Tennessee in 1825 by Frances Wright, a popular writer and lecturer who directly challenged the prevailing conception of women's place in society. Like Owen's New

Harmony which Wright admired, Nashoba not only eschewed organized religion, traditional marriage, and private property, but also was biracial. In addition to whites, the community included slaves who, purchased by Wright, were to achieve their freedom by tilling the soil. Critics of Wright's experiment described it as a hotbed of paganism, free love, and race mixing. After the demise of Nashoba, Wright settled in New York where for a time she waged a vigorous campaign on behalf of the working class in its struggle against what she called the "moneyed aristocracy."

BODY REFORMERS

Existing alongside the utopian experiments and emerging from the same social and intellectual environment were reform efforts that concentrated on the private, rather than the public, sphere. These so-called physiological reformers attempted to create what historian Robert H. Abzug has described as "a sacred vision of personal life." Sharing the perfectionist motif then in vogue, they prescribed a radical change in the conception of individual holiness that promised physical and spiritual well-being and social regeneration. Among the most notable of those dedicated to "body reforms" were Sylvester Graham, creator of the Graham cracker, who advocated a scheme of living based on a vegetarian diet, physical exercise, and sexual moderation; William Andrus Alcott, whose regimen was similar to that of Graham, focused especial attention on body temperature and discoursed endlessly on ways "to keep cool"; Orson Squire Fowler and his brother Lorenzo crusaded on behalf of phrenology, a so-called science that concentrated on the study and measurement of the skull to determine an individual's mental faculties and character with a view toward enabling people to isolate and change undesirable personal traits. Wedded to the notion of the sacredness of the human body, these physiological reformers sought to alter the attitudes and physical habits of Americans in ways that would ensure their bodily health and purity. Many of those identified with temperance, abolitionism, and other reforms in the public sphere subscribed to the notions advanced by the body reformers, especially Graham.

THE TEMPERANCE MOVEMENT

Similar in some respects to the crusade for body reforms was the campaign against alcohol that was gaining momentum as Americans drank numerous toasts to Lafayette in 1824–1825. At least since the late eighteenth century various individuals and groups had voiced opposition to the widespread use of alcohol. The era between the end of the Revolution and the mid-1820s witnessed an upsurge in liquor consumption. Women as well as men drank, but women drank far less heavily. Nor was drinking confined to a particular race. Some slaveowners supplied their slaves with specified amounts of alcohol, and Indians were regularly plied with whiskey, often to cheat them out of their goods or land.

By the 1820s the evangelical piety bequeathed by the Second Great Awakening, coupled with a growing concern for the social order, especially among the urban middle classes who saw the use of alcohol by the "lower elements" as a major contributor to the instability and disorder of city life, led to the creation of the American Temperance Society in 1826, an organization that repudiated moderation in favor of total abstinence from the use of hard liquor. Some of the society's leaders lumped together drunkards, liquor dealers, Sabbath breakers, and infidels as the most serious menaces to a stable and harmonious society based on evangelical Christianity.

National in scope, the temperance crusade surpassed all other reform efforts in the size of its membership and in its longevity. Popular support for temperance, so the argument ran, would reduce the disorder and sordidness of life in burgeoning cities, raise the tone of politics, and help to preserve the moral order. Toward these ends, different temperance groups focused on different targets: Some aimed at the producers of whiskey, others concentrated on getting rid of saloons and public drunkenness, and still others made up of "exdrunkards" sought to prevail upon alcoholics to follow them in showing one's self-control. Women, in particular, were acutely aware of the curse of drunkenness and its impact on family life. Intoxicated husbands and fathers not only subjected their wives and children to physical and psychological abuse, but also reduced their families to destitute circumstances by squandering their wages in grogshops, taverns, and games of chance. It is hardly surprising, therefore, that large numbers of women of all classes rallied to the temperance banner and figured prominently in the crusade to banish alcoholic beverages and their evil consequences.

By 1834 about five thousand state and local societies were engaged in temperance activities. Two years later, the American Temperance Society reorganized to become a more effective national organization and changed its name to the American Temperance Union. Despite the objections by some involved in the cause, the temperance forces decided to use the coercive power of the state rather than rely solely upon moral suasion to achieve their aims. By 1855 all of New England, New York, and large areas of the Midwest were legally dry. Although temperance advocates by no means achieved the universal teetotalism they desired, they did succeed in substantially reducing the per capita consumption of alcohol.

EDUCATION REFORM

Public Schools

If temperance was the reform cause that attracted the largest number of adherents, the movement for free public schools resulted in the most far-reaching effort in institution building in the era. Interest in education in general and public education in particular long predated the Age of Jackson but popular support for shifting the burden of financial support for schools from parents to the state dramatically increased in the 1830s and 1840s. Among the most influential crusaders for public education was Horace Mann of Massachusetts. As secretary of the newly created state board of education and as editor of the *Common School Journal*, he promoted numerous innovations that broadened the scope of public education. Described as "spotless in character and heroic in benevolence," Mann was a staunch advocate of temperance and was identified with asylum and prison reforms. His philosophy combined his optimistic view of human nature with a desire to shape it by a rational system of education. His assumption that everyone could be taught and everyone could be improved had much in common with the millennial and perfectionist message of evangelical Protestantism. The school, Mann argued, was "the equalizer of the condition of man" and would not merely eradicate the hostility of the poor toward the rich, but remove the cause of poverty as well. He reassured those fearful that nonsectarian, public education would cause a decline in virtue and threaten the existence of the republic that public schools would free society of "the low-minded and vicious, not by their expatriation, but by their elevation." By instilling self-control, morality, sobriety, and all the Protestant and patriotic virtues in children of all classes, Mann's system also promised to produce an enlightened electorate. The *McGuffey Readers*, which first appeared in 1836 and were used widely in schools, reinforced the values articulated by Mann and other educational reformers.

The crusade for public schools won support from virtually all reform groups, including artisans, women, utopians, and phrenologists. The most crucial support, however, came from the urban middle class which saw the public school as the vehicle for unifying a fragmented society around its own values and norms and for equipping youth with the essentials for success in the new, highly competitive economic environment. For the middle class, the school seemed to offer the means for resolving social tensions without radical change. Despite the opposition of Catholics and those Protestants who feared an end to the traditional ties between religion and education, the champions of public schools inspired an educational awakening that spread throughout the Northeast. Although some southern states enacted laws creating statewide, tax-supported school systems, these often existed only on paper and went unenforced.

Lyceums and Libraries

The growing interest in education extended beyond public schools for children to include opportunities for adults to enhance and expand their knowledge. Like the public schools, the diverse efforts that promoted adult education rested on the premise, as Josiah Holbrook explained in 1826, that the diffusion of knowledge contributed to the making of good citizens and to the elevation of the "moral and intellectual taste of our countrymen." Holbrook was an early leader in the lyceum movement that provided Americans with series of public lectures by the nation's best-known writers, clergymen, scientists, and reformers. By the 1840s the lyceum movement had taken root in every section of the country and provided cities, towns, and the newer communities of the West with cultural activities that no other institution provided.

In some areas the lyceums joined literary clubs, Sunday schools, debating societies, labor organizations, and other groups in sponsoring libraries and museums, both of which figured prominently in the promotion of adult education. The formation of libraries had a long history dating to the colonial era but the increase in literacy, emergence of the new middle class, and the growth in book publishing in the 1840s and 1850s accelerated the demand for libraries. The "subscription" libraries usually limited the circulation of books to members or subscribers; others were circulating or rental libraries which made books available to all who could pay a rental fee; still others, fewer in number, were truly public libraries because they were open to all patrons without charge. Beginning with the establishment of the Boston Public Library in 1848, one large city after another created a public library to meet the insatiable demand of its citizens for books, magazines, and newspapers.

Newspapers

By no means inconsequential in the continuing education of adults were the weekly and daily newspapers that proliferated especially in the twenty years before the Civil War. The 1,266 weeklies in 1840 had increased to 2,971 by 1860; in the same era the number of dailies increased from 138 to 372. Aided by technological improvements in printing and the manufacture of paper, the cost of newspapers decreased, making them accessible to an ever wider segment of the population. The *New York Sun* became the first successful penny daily in 1833, followed two years later by the *New York Herald*. The so-called penny press initially provided extensive coverage of crime, sex, and gossip, but the *Sun* and *Herald* also pioneered in innovative news-gathering and marketing techniques. Each gradually developed a social conscience and periodically championed causes to benefit its underprivileged readers.

More appealing to the respectable folks and costing two cents were Horace Greeley's *New York Tribune*, established in 1841, and Henry Raymond's *New York Times*, founded a decade later. Both paid less attention to the sordid aspects of life and more to civic, cultural, economic and political matters, and international events. Although Raymond's *Times* prided itself on its political independence, most newspapers, dailies and weeklies, in the two decades after 1840 were highly partisan and reflected the political slant of one party or another. Indisputably the rise of the new journalism in this era contributed to the wider dissemination of information and knowledge, and therefore to the education of the American public.

THE ABOLITIONIST MOVEMENT

In 1831 William Lloyd Garrison launched *The Liberator* in Boston, an event that signaled the beginning of a new movement to rid the United States of slavery. Under the impetus of the antislavery sentiment of the Revolutionary era, northern states began to abolish slavery and some slaves had been freed elsewhere, but the status of most blacks in the South remained unchanged. Despite the waning of opposition to slavery after the Revolutionary era, antislavery societies continued to exist among both whites and free blacks in the North. Most of the white antislavery groups before 1831 endorsed some form of gradual emancipation in order to minimize economic and social dislocation. The American Colonization Society, formed in 1816, concentrated on settling freed slaves in West Africa.

Colonization and emigration schemes encountered strong opposition from free black antislavery spokespersons in the North. A host of black men and women, such as Robert Forten and Robert Purvis of Pennsylvania, Frances Watkins Harper of Baltimore and Philadelphia, and Charles and Sarah Remond of Massachusetts figured prominently in a variety of antislavery organizations at the local, state, and national levels, often serving as officers and board members. Others lectured widely to antislavery gatherings throughout the Northeast and Northwest. Black journalists in New York, Philadelphia, and elsewhere including the editors of *Freedom's Journal*, *The Rights of All*, and *The Ram's Horn* were among the most eloquent champions of freedom and equality for all black people. Some black antislavery leaders were personal friends of Garrison, and most were enthusiastic supporters of his brand of abolitionism. African Americans, in fact, made up the majority of the subscribers to his *Liberator.*

Rejecting all forms of gradualism and colonization as compromises with evil, Garrison demanded the *immediate* abolition of slavery. Determined to end what he interpreted as the North's conspiracy of silence regarding slavery, he announced in the first issue of *The Liberator* that he would not retreat "a single inch" on his demand for the immediate emancipation of all slaves. For Garrison, slavery posed a moral, not an economic issue, and its existence was the source of a pervasively corrupting influence on the republic and all its institutions. Because he considered any compromise with the "slave power" of the South as intolerable, he denounced the Constitution as an "agreement with Hell." In a similar vein he and his followers shunned the use of politics to advance abolitionism on the grounds that politics demanded unacceptable moral compromises as the price of success; they insisted upon "moral suasion" as the only acceptable means of promoting their cause. While Garrison had no blueprint for implementing "immediate" abolition and recognized that it might take time to complete, he insisted that the process should begin without delay. Always passionate and often abrasive and vituperative, Garrison infused the antislavery cause with a fervor it had previously lacked. His crusade differed in tone, social composition, and doctrine from that which had existed prior to the 1830s. The New England Anti-Slavery Society, formed in 1832, was the first organization to embrace Garrison's doctrines, followed the next year by the formation of the American Anti-Slavery Society that linked together numerous local and state abolitionist societies. Rank-and-file abolitionists were usually cash crop farmers, artisans, and entrepreneurs firmly committed to evangelical Protestantism. They belonged to the group whose status was rising in the 1830s.

Drawing its inspiration from a variety of sources, including the testimony and pleas of runaway slaves such as Frederick Douglass, abolitionism had a special appeal to young men and women whose moral imperatives were shaped by the millennial and perfectionist doctrines of evangelical Protestantism. In fact, Charles G. Finney, the revivalist, was an antislavery missionary who in 1835 joined the faculty of Oberlin College in Ohio, a center of abolitionism in the West. Among Finney's converts was Theodore Weld whose *The Bible Against Slavery* marshalled scriptural arguments to support the abolition of slavery. All the while, hundreds of middle-class women active in and influenced by the wave of revivalism included abolitionism among the reform causes that they supported. They formed their own antislavery organizations, raised money, held conventions, and distributed literature. Few women abolitionists, however, were more effective than the sisters Angelina and Sarah Grimké of South Carolina, who moved north, became Quakers, and joined the campaign against slavery. Their firsthand experience with the South's "peculiar institution" buttressed abolitionist arguments with direct and specific evidence of its inhumanity.

A manifestation of the reform impulse of the era, the abolition movement included within its ranks many of those involved in temperance and other uplift efforts aimed at bringing about the redemption of mankind and a purer phase of human history. It also relied upon the same sources of financial support. For example, the brothers, Arthur and Lewis Tappan, wealthy New York merchants who backed many of the charities associated with the "benevolent empire," provided abolitionism, through the American Anti-Slavery Society, with both money and managerial expertise. Such support was essential to the abolitionist effort to mobilize public opinion through a steady stream of propaganda broadcast through numerous newspapers, tracts, broadsides, and an expanding cadre of paid agents and lecturers. Abolitionists flooded Congress with petitions demanding an end to slavery in the District of Columbia. In 1836 southern congressmen joined with others unwilling to open debate on the divisive issue to secure adoption of a measure, known as the "gag rule," that automatically tabled all abolitionist petitions. Until 1845, the gag rule effectively shut off discussion of abolitionist demands.

The clamor of abolitionists aroused strong opposition not merely in the South, which was becoming increasingly defensive of slavery but in the North as well. Abolitionists made up only a small minority of the white population in the North and were often viewed as dangerous fanatics by the majority. A variety of motives underlay the opposition to abolitionist activities. One was economic self-interest. Some northern merchants and industrialists were reluctant to support a cause so bitterly opposed by their southern suppliers and customers. Northern workingmen believed that the freeing of southern slaves would result in an influx of blacks into the North who would jeopardize their jobs. Unquestionably, the widespread racism among northern whites inspired much of the opposition to abolitionism because it conjured up images of racial equality and even race mixing. Not even all abolitionists were able to free themselves of the pervasive racism no matter how loudly they proclaimed the "brotherhood of man." As a result tensions developed between black and white abolitionists. Frederick Douglass and other blacks involved in the antislavery movement readily recognized that the same abolitionists who were so adamant in their denunciations of a distant slave system drew the color line at home.

The opposition to abolitionism escalated mob violence. The abolitionist press reported 165 "racist mobbings" between 1835 and 1839. Garrison was dragged through the streets of Boston; Lewis Tappan's home in New York was vandalized and set afire; and Theodore Weld became known as "the most mobbed man in America." Mobs also demolished an abolitionist newspaper office in Cincinnati, razed an antislavery meeting hall in Philadelphia, murdered Elijah Lovejoy, an abolitionist editor in Illinois, and committed random acts of violence against black neighborhoods in various cities. Quick to detect a connection between the emergence of abolitionism and Nat Turner's bloody slave rebellion (see Chapter 10), white southerners not only tightened the slave codes, but also attempted to prevent the distribution of antislavery literature in their region, an effort that had the approval of President Jackson. The same violence and repression that caused some abolitionists to distance themselves from the movement radicalized others.

The overt hostility encountered by abolitionists undoubtedly contributed to the surfacing of tensions within their ranks. At the center of virtually all disputes was the irascible Garrison, who, as uncompromising as ever, employed increasingly radical rhetoric and came to advocate a much broader reform agenda, including equal rights for women, which encountered strong opposition from those fearful of weakening the focus on slavery. Even more divisive, perhaps, than the issue of women's rights was the dispute over tactics. Garrison remained wedded to moral suasion but others within the American Anti-Slavery Society maintained that politics offered a better means of eradicating slavery. Those opposed to Garrison's agenda withdrew in 1840 to form the American and Foreign Anti-Slavery Society headquartered in New York. In the same year politically minded abolitionists launched the Liberty party in time to run James G. Birney, a veteran antislavery crusader, for president. Despite the split within abolitionist ranks, their crusade continued to focus attention on slavery at a time when most national political leaders sought to ignore it.

THE WOMEN'S RIGHTS MOVEMENT

Linked to abolitionism was the emergence of an organized women's rights movement led by articulate middle-class women. The Grimké sisters, Lucy Stone, Abbey Kelly, Lucretia Mott, and other prominent leaders in the movement who played important roles in abolitionism readily perceived the striking similarity between their own conditions and those of enslaved blacks.

A women's rights rally, ca. 1850, as interpreted in a drawing by J.M. Niven.

Denied the right to vote and hold office, women occupied a position of strict dependence and inequality. The law submerged the identities of married women with those of their husbands and treated unmarried women as minors. Women were barred from higher education and most professions. Although men might treat women with politeness and gallantry, the vast majority adhered to the view that the woman's place in society was subordinate to their own. Within the abolitionist movement women regularly encountered condescending and discriminatory treatment at the hands of their male cohorts who glibly talked of human equality in referring to blacks. Garrison was a rare exception.

Beginning in the late 1820s material and cultural changes, often linked to the market revolution, altered the ways in which women viewed themselves. They increasingly assumed public roles in a variety of uplift causes. For some middle-class women, their experiences in such roles increased their discontent with the restrictions imposed on them by a male-dominated society.

On occasion specific events prompted women reformers to speak out boldly on the "woman question." For example, the Grimké sisters aroused a storm of protest in 1837 for refusing to confine their lectures to female audiences. That they dared to address audiences that included men prompted a protest from Congregationalist clergymen who insisted that "women should not speak in public and should obey men rather than lecture to them." Men and women were "created equal," Sarah Grimké declared, and women had the right to "have a voice in all laws and regulations" that governed them. She characterized the existing place of women within the family as a form of slavery. Other women active in the abolitionist movement resented their treatment at anti-slavery conventions where they were forced to sit behind screens and were denied access to offices. Such resentment prompted some women abolitionists to devote more time to ridding *themselves* of the shackles of slavery. Among them were two veteran antislavery crusaders, Lucretia Mott and Elizabeth Cady Stanton, both of whom had been subjected to overt discrimination at male-dominated abolitionist gatherings.

Led by Mott and Stanton, about a hundred women gathered at Seneca Falls, New York, in 1848 to consider their own plight. The conference issued a Declaration of Sentiments that echoed Grimké's proclamation regarding the equality of the sexes. The Seneca Falls convention drew up a lengthy list of grievances and demands including the enactment of legislation to guarantee women opportunities for education and to remove legal restrictions imposed on them such as property rights. The only resolution passed without a unanimous vote was the proposal to grant women the right to vote. Many of the delegates fully embraced separate spheres for men and women and saw no need for such a radical measure as enfranchisement. True to their promise to keep the "woman question" before the public, the Seneca Falls group continued to meet and in 1851 resolved that the right to the ballot was the "corner-stone" of the women's movement. Despite the energetic efforts of a relatively small group of women, the movement achieved few victories except in the area of property rights. Although the crusade in behalf of women persisted and grew in size, large numbers of women remained either indifferent or opposed to the drive for woman suffrage. Not until 1920 did a constitutional amendment guarantee women the right to vote.

Like the temperance, antislavery, and public education crusaders, the campaign by women to remove their legal disabilities and to secure the right to vote was a part of the wide-ranging reform ferment that characterized Jacksonian America. Despite the specific goals of the various reform groups, their efforts essentially sought to redeem and reorder a society in the throes of upheaval. The emergence of a national market economy and the wave of revivalism served as catalysts for a series of wrenching changes that affected the lives of many, if not most, Americans. The impact of such changes was greatest in the areas in the Northeast and Northwest where the market revolution was more advanced. The rise of industrialism and large-scale commercial networks disrupted the traditional economic system, altered old social hierarchies, and prompted dramatic demographic shifts. The result was widespread popular anxiety over the implications of such developments for the future of the nation. For a variety of reasons many Americans agreed with the Philadelphia editor who in 1835 observed that the times were "completely out of joint." The responses to the momentous economic and social changes produced by the market revolution were shaped, in large measure, by the version of evangelical Protestantism emphasized by revivalists such as Charles G. Finney who urged Christians to expand the boundaries of Christ's kingdom on earth. Inspired by the wave of revivalism, men and women marched forth as "holy warriors" bent on ridding the republic of every evil that impeded the coming of the millennium. Active in support of benevolent enterprises, they assumed personal responsibility for inaugurating a purer phase of human history by replacing a sinful and chaotic society with righteousness, stability, and order. Even those reformers antagonistic to political parties or excluded from the electoral process ultimately turned to politics and parties as the best means of advancing their particular cause.

In the following survey of the role of women in the pre–Civil War temperance movement, historian Ian R. Tyrrell emphasizes that their activities significantly altered women's societal position. The essay demonstrates how involvement in temperance organizations and crusades enabled women to shape their own consciousness and distinctive aspirations. The confidence and "womanly solidarity" acquired by participating in the temperance crusade found expression in a new assertiveness, especially in regard to women's rights.

WOMEN AND TEMPERANCE IN ANTEBELLUM AMERICA, 1830–1860

Ian R. Tyrrell

The links between temperance and agitation for women's rights in American history have been long recognized as profound, but historical attention has focused unduly on the late-nineteenth-century women's temperance movement and its relationship with the crusade for female suffrage. Very much less is known for the pre–Civil War years, even though women already occupied an important place in temperance agitation and despite the fact that later trends in women's temperance had their origins before the Civil War. The historical investigation of antebellum women's temperance has been hindered by the obscurity of women's agitation and its partly non-institutional character. Lacking a strong organizational focus comparable to the

from Ian R. Tyrrell, "Women and Temperance in Antebellum America, 1830–1860," *Civil War History* 28, no. 2 (June 1982):128–152.

Woman's Christian Temperance Union (WCTU), antebellum women's temperance must be approached through studies of local action, from fragmented records concerning obscure women, a good deal of whose reform activity probably took place in the privacy of their own drawing rooms and kitchens. But the elusive character of women's temperance and its institutional weakness does not negate its importance. Prior to 1860, large numbers of American women had exerted influence in the home, signed the pledge, joined male-dominated temperance societies, formed the first women's temperance organizations, and petitioned for statewide prohibition. The generation of women that reached maturity in the 1830s was the first in American history to abstain from alcoholic consumption in large numbers, and its efforts for abstinence had a large effect not only on Jacksonian men but also on their children, because it was the daughters of this first generation of abstainers who formed the Woman's Christian Temperance Union in 1874.

While recognizing the growing self-assertiveness exerted by women in temperance reform, it is equally important to understand that women's temperance emerged in the context of a larger movement that was led by and for men. To capture the character of the women's temperance movement as an independent force, it is therefore necessary to focus on the historical context of its emergence from the male-dominated movement. This struggle occurred in three overlapping but distinct phases which corresponded to changes in the social bases of temperance support and to accompanying changes in the strategies and tactics of the larger movement. These phases were (1) the evangelical-led beginnings from 1826 to 1840; (2) the popularization of reform through the Washingtonians and other self-help groups in the 1840s; and (3) the political, prohibitionist campaigns of the 1850s which forged links with the nascent women's rights movement.

The analogy with slavery—which women's rights and female temperance reformers themselves employed—may be helpful in creating an analytical framework which will illuminate the ambiguous legacy bequeathed by the larger context in which women's temperance took shape. Just as slaveholders defined the ground (and the limits) of the struggle between themselves and plantation slaves, the terrain for women's struggle for independence and autonomy within the temperance movement was defined by male power, the tactical exigencies of the larger movement, and male conceptions of female roles in reform efforts. To anticipate briefly what follows, the first temperance women took seriously the claims of evangelical clergy that women were morally superior, and they gradually turned that ideal of womanhood into a vehicle for the expression of their own aspirations. The temperance movement thus became a means for the advancement of women's consciousness and confidence and for the shattering of sexual stereotypes which limited women's participation in reform activity. Yet simultaneously, the terrain on which this struggle occurred tended to reinforce the sexual conceptions which defined and limited women's place in society. Rather than the story of an unambiguous progress toward liberal democratic freedoms or the evolution of "woman's rights," the women's temperance question saw the assertion of a distinctively female culture that emphasized conceptions of sisterhood, the moral superiority of women, and the "wrongs" done to women by male power.

If the specific contribution of temperance to women's changing societal position is to be appreciated, it is first necessary to locate women's temperance within the spectrum of women's reform activities at large. Women's work in voluntary reform was not new when temperance first began to attract their support in the 1830s. Women had participated in mission and charity work as early as the 1790s; and by the 1830s, they were deeply committed to a host of reform organizations from Bible and tract societies through the female moral reform organizations to antislavery and feminism. Like antislavery but unlike charity and mission reform, temperance included a political dimension, involving lobbying, petitioning, and public stances through pamphlets and speaking tours. Like the benevolent reforms, though, temperance was closely related to church missionary activities and was able to involve pious evangelical women without appearing to strain too far the conventional limits on female decorum. Thus, temperance represents a critical link between the religious and charitable work of women in the church and mission societies and secular reform. Though initially based on the evangelical churches, often with societies formed in church congregations, temperance became by the 1840s a reform movement which united churched and nonchurched in a program designed to improve the material condition of the whole society.

If temperance benefited from its links with evangelical churches and the benevolent crusades in gaining recruits among women, it also gained influence because temperance could encompass a number of issues of special concern to women. While the female moral reform societies drew the fire of the respectable dailies for publicizing prostitution, temperance could without any indiscretion promise social purity as a by-product of abstinence. Already in the pre–Civil War period, the grog-shop or tavern was a place of prostitution in the cities, and everywhere, in both city and country, moral reformers associated intemperance with that loss of self-control which could produce sexual indulgence.

Just as temperance had an advantage over moral reform in gaining recruits among women, so too did it have a strategic advantage over antislavery efforts, since the issues that temperance reformers advocated were of direct concern to northern women in their local communities. Judging by the content and popularity of nineteenth-century sentimental novels, fears of alcoholic husbands and of the violence and sexual abuse associated with the excessive use of alcohol were especially pressing. Although drunkenness was more common among the laboring classes in this period, heavy drinking was extremely widespread and by no means unknown in middle class and elite circles. Both the middle class reformers who patronized the temperance paper, *The Lily,* in the 1850s and the artisan and lower middle class women who joined Washingtonian societies in New York in the early 1840s believed that "the slavery of intemperance . . . at home" was a greater problem for women than Negro slavery because "a drunkard is a deliberate, voluntary savage, and he treats his wife accordingly." Slavery was undoubtedly useful in developing imagery which could capture female discontent with male domination, yet the image of the drunken husband could easily do the same, while, in addition, temperance gave women a weapon against an immediate enemy which directly affected their interests. As *The Lily* commented, "Drunkenness is not our sin alone, but it is *our particular sin—our great sin.*" In contrast, slavery seemed a more distant evil than drink for the northern evangelical women who dominated the reform constituencies of the 1830 to 1850 period.

Although inconspicuous, women were deeply involved in temperance agitation from the time of the American Temperance Society crusade (1826–36). Even the incomplete figures of the census of temperance organizations carried out by the *Journal of Humanity* in 1831 revealed twenty-four "ladies" temperance societies (all but one in the North) at a time when efforts to recruit women were only beginning. The more common pattern in this period, however, involved women participating in male-led societies. Information from temperance society membership lists and from temperance reports covering a dozen different societies, mostly in the Northeast, shows that women comprised from 35 to 60 percent of a typical temperance society in the 1830s. In no case were women excluded entirely, though the Baltimore Temperance Society restricted women to auxiliary status as members of evangelical religious congregations. Since the American Temperance Society claimed 1.5 million abstainers in the mid-1830s, even the exaggerations of partisan reformers cannot obscure the fact that probably hundreds of thousands of American women supported the temperance movement during the decade.

The evangelical reformers who first formed the American Temperance Society in Boston in 1826 quickly realized the importance of women to the success of their crusade. The Reverend Justin Edwards, the corresponding secretary of the American Temperance Society, advocated women joining temperance societies because "under the light of the gospel, which raises women in excellence of character and ability to do good, to an equality with men, every association, composed of both, will more than double its influence over the public mind." Edwards claimed credit for the fact that temperance societies granted women a participatory role, yet male temperance reformers could hardly have avoided giving women a place in their work. The temperance movement at first lacked the political base to rely on legal sanctions and initially advocated moral suasion. Any such campaign involved considerable reliance on women, because conventional thought allotted to women a special place as preservers of morality within the family. Since the temperance movement was especially interested in guarding the new generation against intemperance, it was necessary to reinforce the role of women as moral preceptors.

While Edwards and other evangelical temperance reformers were quick to welcome the influence of women, they were nevertheless careful to restrict their role within the temperance movement. Woman's "equality," according to Edwards, was located in "character" and "ability to do good"; the rightful setting for her moral influence remained "in the social circle." Edward C. Delavan, of the New York Temperance Society, asked only for "signatures" of women and the "moral influence" of mothers and daughters over the young within the family circle. There was "no sacrifice of delicacy, no stepping beyond your proper sphere," Delavan's *Temperance Recorder* told its readers. Male temperance reformers like Delavan and Edwards consistently articulated a domestic-submissive role for women in reform; they couched the women's activity in defensive terms.

The assaults of opponents of reform, if nothing else, forced male reformers into this narrow definition of women's responsibility in the temperance movement. "It has been made a subject of scornful remark that the females of our country have given their names to associations for the suppression of intemperance," complained the executive committee of the Maine Temperance Society as it strove to assure members and the public that no radical change in the position of women was contemplated. When the *Pittsfield* (Mass.) *Sun* reported that the local temperance society proposed "to swell the list of subscribers with the names of respectable females," the editor strenuously objected. "We hold this to be a satire on their sex, tending to throw the subject into ridicule."

Though male temperance reformers generally responded to such criticisms by professing the conservative aims of temperance, there is some evidence that even in the 1830s women were less willing to accept so circumscribed a role. They were not content merely to sign the pledge and to instill habits of temperance in their children and in other women. At a meeting of the Boston Temperance Society in 1834, "the ladies (who occupied the galleries), manifested unanimously their approbation" of the resolution "to abolish the liquor traffic." The uncalled-for and apparently spontaneous applause for the resolution to condemn the liquor traffic and the attempt of women to vote on the resolution from the gallery disturbed some of the male reformers, who doubted "the legality" of the proceedings. Yet within a year women had begun to outrun such restrictions on their participation. A "ladies' temperance convention" in Montpelier, Vermont, in March of 1835 indicated that women were prepared to form their own temperance groups and publicize the active role of women through the mere fact of holding such a convention. Anticipating the shift of women to a more militant attack on the intemperance of men, the convention sought "to enlist *the other sex* under the banner of *Total Abstinence*." In addition to this first known women's state temperance convention, women joined in the campaigns to refuse licenses to retailers in the northeastern states, especially Massachusetts, between 1835 and 1840.

Yet, despite the activity of women in the 1830s, their participation in temperance reform came largely through their passive presence rather than through control of their own temperance societies. In this respect they lagged behind the antislavery women, who had organized in many state and national conventions by 1837 and produced such redoubtable public lecturers as the Grimké sisters. The slow pace of public and political activity among temperance women, relative to abolitionists, bore testimony to the power within the temperance movement of Presbyterian and Congregational clergy who were conservative on the woman question. Yet it also bore testimony to the effectiveness of the evangelical image of womanhood itself in defining a (limited) role for woman in reform activity, one that emphasized her charitable and sacrificial qualities. Even those women who soon enlarged their reform role sought not to break sharply with evangelical expectations, but rather to transform the image of the pious and pure woman to new but potentially disruptive purposes.

Whereas the 1830s marked the beginning of a vocal and independent movement of women abolitionists, it was the 1840s that provided the critical point of departure for an assertive women's temperance movement. The catalyst for this transformation in women's temperance came from the economic depression of 1837–43 and the subsequent attempts of male reformers to deal with its social consequences through charitable activity and temperance proselytizing. The Washingtonian movement emerged in this context to organize new social classes and ex-alcoholics for temperance work. Alongside male Washingtonian societies devoted to redeeming ex-alcoholic men, there arose parallel Martha Washingtonian societies to extend charitable aid to alcoholics and their families. As with the earlier phase of reform, males once again shaped the strategy of reform and looked to women to aid in its implementation. The pressing need for relief of the poor called forth women to benevolent activities. Middle class male reformers still looked to women because it was "woman's place to do good." Women responded to these pleas by forming forty active societies in New York City, with six thousand members, and others in such centers as Portland, Maine; Newark and New Brunswick, New Jersey; Wilmington, Delaware; Philadelphia, Pennsylvania; New Haven and Hartford, Connecticut; and Albany, Rochester, and Utica, New York. These societies often conducted home visitations, providing clothing and food to families where the parents agreed to abstain from liquor. Naturally, the charitable work was done mostly by middle class women who had the time, the inclination, and the (modest) amounts of money required. Yet they were also able to recruit, as a more detailed examination of their membership and tactics will show, many women of artisan and working class backgrounds.

The work of the Washingtonians was supplemented in 1843 by the establishment of the mutual benefit society, the Daughters of Temperance, modeled on the male fraternal order, the Sons of Temperance. By 1848, the Daughters of Temperance embraced two hundred local chapters involving more than thirty thousand members. Nor was the Daughters the only such society: the Rechabites established a "daughters of Rechab" affiliate, and, in addition, women could choose between the Daughters of Samaria and the United Sisters of Temperance as well as a host of "ladies' temperance societies" in such centers as Harrisburg, Pennsylvania, and Seneca Falls, New York.

The forces which produced this upsurge in women's temperance were rooted in the changing character of the larger, male-dominated movement. Whereas the older temperance societies had been controlled by Presbyterian and Congregational clergy, the newer Washingtonians were dominated by lay Methodists and Baptists, as well as those of no particular religious persuasion. Secular-minded Washingtonians had no inhibitions about Biblical restrictions on the role of women, while the Methodists and Baptists gave a more important place to women's work in their missionary and benevolent societies than the Calvinists. It was the New York Methodist editor, Lorenzo Dow Johnson, for example, who replied to critics of women's temperance by writing in 1843 the first book-length defense of women's role in the movement—*Martha Washingtonianism*—and the first detailed celebration of their achievements in liquor reform.

Equally important to the rising participation of women was the changing social base of temperance support. The self-help societies had predominantly artisan and lower middle class support, and the social situation of these groups made them unable to reject practical help from women. In this context, women had the chance to assert a more independent role than hitherto. They seized the opportunity not simply to do charity work for the victims of intemperance, but to assert female over male aspirations. Thus, the larger temperance movement in its efforts at popular mobilization once again provided the arena for the development of a distinctive women's temperance movement.

The character of women's aspirations can best be understood by probing the meaning for women of changes in the social bases of temperance support. Through a study of the New York Washingtonian temperance organizations of the 1840s, the social and economic changes affecting women of lower and lower middle class backgrounds can be established. Of thirty-five women named in the Washingtonian and temperance publications as officers of Washingtonian societies or speakers at their meetings between September 1842 and March 1843, seventeen could be traced, and twelve of these were the wives of artisans or small-scale businessmen; four of the remainder were working women. That the Martha Washingtonians attracted women of the lower middle and even working classes is further suggested by the character of the mutual benefit societies that sprang from the Washingtonian revival. The Daughters of Temperance and the Rechabites, especially, were created as primitive insurance cooperatives and were patronized by wives and widows seeking to insure against bad times caused by ill health or the death of male relatives. Typical self-help societies of the Washingtonian period, we are told by the Washingtonian press, were the Ocean Union (an affiliate of the Daughters of Temperance), in which "many of the members" were "the mothers, wives, daughters, and sisters of the sailor," and the Lady Franklin Society, patronized by the relatives of printers and publishers.

This picture of the women's organizations of the 1840s contrasts quite sharply with the common view of woman reformers as members of well-to-do elites, but it does accord with the profile of male Washingtonian membership emerging from recent research. As the Washingtonians continually pointed out, they did not get support from the "upper classes" or "high society." The egalitarian thrust of temperance, particularly after the adoption of teetotalism by temperance societies in the late 1830s, drove "ladies and gentlemen" in "the higher circles" out of the movement, since it was the custom of upper class society to serve wine "at social gatherings."

The social backgrounds of Washingtonian women reveal much when considered alongside general socioeconomic change. Industrialization threatened the jobs of preindustrial artisans in the eastern cities from Baltimore to Boston. In addition, the general depression of 1837–43 threw many thousands of skilled and unskilled workers out of employment. While economic dislocation most directly affected artisan groups, many middle class people also felt the threat of insecurity which accompanied rapid economic change. The speeches of ex-drunkards before predominantly middle class audiences elicited strongly favorable responses when they dwelt upon the uncertainty of the times and emphasized how success could rapidly give way to failure if self-restraint were not exercised in the use of liquor.

Unemployment and the threat of unemployment, though a common concern of Washingtonians of both sexes, had special meaning for the wives of artisans.

Employers and charity organizations such as the New York Association for Improving the Condition of the Poor emphasized the need for self-restraint among the destitute and those threatened with unemployment. While men responded and honored the pledge, obstacles abounded. As Horace Greeley's *New York Tribune* observed, men tended to gather in taverns in times of enforced idleness, not simply to drink away their time but because the tavern served as a primitive labor exchange where jobs were advertised and employees came in search of casual labor. Thus, much of the responsibility for exercising self-restraint in artisan families fell upon the wives. Household budgets were difficult to balance at the best of times, so that in periods of economic hardship the desire of women to restrain their husbands' drinking had a rational and direct economic component. Women in effect became important though often unintended allies of employers in their efforts to impose a morality of self-discipline on male workers. The records of the New York Washington Temperance Society make clear that after the initial enthusiasm of the reformed drunkards had waned, it was the women who enlivened Washingtonian meetings and provided much of the financial assistance despite their meager resources.

While women's temperance in the 1840s thus had roots in the social and economic changes transforming the larger temperance movement, the result of women's increased participation was not merely to provide an avenue for economic self-defense but also a weapon with which women could shape their own consciousness and distinctive aspirations. These new societies constituted a resource which women could use to build their confidence and womanly solidarity. For the first time, it became common for women to speak on temperance platforms, as they did in the New York Martha Washingtonian societies, and to lead and manage these organizations themselves. Women also began to develop editorial and polemical skills through the establishment of women's temperance papers and columns for women in other temperance publications. The *New York Olive Plant* (1842) and the *New York Pearl* (1846) were the first papers designed for and edited by women in the history of the temperance agitation. In addition, such general papers as the *New York Organ,* the journal for the Sons of Temperance, established "ladies' columns" with regular female contributors.

As a result of such experiences, women gained in what the *New York Organ* called "their capacity for self-government." "Ladies' organizations" (and ladies' organizations alone) made Virginia Allen of the *New York Pearl* confident that "the world may [soon] be redeemed from its vice and misery." Sisterly solidarity was likewise promoted. Carroll Smith-Rosenberg and Nancy Cott have pointed to the development in the late eighteenth and early nineteenth century of what they call a "female world" or "woman's sphere," created and sustained through sexual segregation in the economy, religion, and women's education. Temperance societies in the Washingtonian phase and after provided an important public and institutional outlet for the phenomenon of sisterhood. Martha Washingtonians sought to create "a circle of sisters" to help resist common deprivations imposed by the male-dominated power structure of society. The cross-class character of the early Washingtonian movement among women . . . shows that the notion of a distinctive "woman's sphere" had its impact not only among the upper and middle class women . . ., but also among some women of the working classes.

Notions of sisterhood, nourished by the concept of separate sexual spheres and moral natures, could easily spill over into antimale sentiments, especially when public reform experience confirmed private beliefs in the moral obtuseness of the male sex. Women who organized for temperance could hardly fail but be impressed both by the temporizing of male reformers and by male drinking and its effects. Women had especially good reason to be incensed at male drunkenness, since heavy drinking was predominantly a male pattern of behavior in the mid-nineteenth century. The association of temperance with respectability imposed restraints on the drinking of middle class and artisan women alike, while the structure of workplace employment similarly worked against female intoxication. A good deal of the nation's heavy drinking was clearly related to patterns of work and leisure among artisans and laborers, so the increasing separation of work from the home and the restriction of employment opportunities for middle class women meant that they were not placed in the position where the opportunity to drink heavily arose.

Not only was intemperance more pronounced among men than women; the effects of (male) drinking were especially devastating for women because the law gave female dependents no adequate protection against a drunken husband or father. "Experience speakers" who addressed Martha Washingtonian audiences told of violence, abuse of children, and poverty attendant upon male drinking, not only in working class families but also on occasions among the middle classes. . . . Such narratives reminded Washingtonians of all social classes that the social problem of drinking could destroy their world at any time.

Armed with this evidence, women used their new-found opportunities in the Washingtonians, Daughters of Temperance, and other self-help temperance so-cieties of the 1840s to express their frustrations at male intemperance. Among both the well-to-do middle class reformers and the lowly artisans, women blamed what they sarcastically called "the lords of creation" for the drink problem. Drink lay at the heart of the "cruel wrongs . . . inflicted upon women" by *male* politicians, re-tailers of liquor, and drinkers. Thus, women reformers began to depict the drink problem as a glaring and critical example of the sexual subordination of women. The idea that women suffered psychological and material "wrongs" as part of this system of subordination was a commonplace in the rhetoric of articulate woman reformers in both England and America in the 1840s. Temperance, however, became an im-portant vehicle for channeling these general grievances into a specific program of reform that promised to right those wrongs by controlling male drinking.

The experience speeches of Washingtonian women and the relief activities of their societies demonstrated the thrust of this program. Its aim was to protect "the helpless mother and her children" against the abuse of male power. The Washing-tonians chose not to agitate for women's political and property rights, which seemed "so far distant" from achievement because they were dependent on the actions of (male) "legislatures and constitutional conventions." Instead, temperance women emphasized those questions which "effect our happiness more directly than the splendid privileges or immunities of a political character," especially the "right" of "every woman" to "have a sober husband." These women did not, therefore, phrase their demands in explicitly feminist terms; rather, they sought to enforce man's own announced social role as provider and protector of the family. Martha Washingtonians believed that women "suffer[ed] beyond all description from the intemperance of those that ought to protect them." Yet women reformers welcomed back the reclaimed man; they proclaimed the pledge a secure foundation for the fulfillment of a man's domestic obligations.

The Martha Washingtonians took seriously the ideology of true womanhood; they agreed that women had a special social role as preservers of the family and guardians of morality. What frustrated these women was the gap between the idealized family structure of sermons and periodical literature and the reality revealed by charity work in Washingtonian societies. In the Martha Washingtonian societies, women sought to fulfill the appointed moral role originally defined for them by men, but not through domestic submission. Rather, they sought to preserve the domestic fireside by increasingly active participation in social reform to control male drinking. In so doing, they implicitly challenged the notion, central to the true womanhood ideal, that women should remain as domestic submissives.

This campaign to control male drinking practices was not limited to organized reform activity. It also had important private and noninstitutional dimensions, though the tendency here, as in the Washingtonian societies, was for the actions of women to undermine the stereotypes and restrictions upon their conduct at the same time that women sought to preserve their special status. Beginning in the early 1840s, groups of married women began to form associations to demand that their husbands keep the pledge and threatened to withhold sexual favors if they did not. The "temperance ladies of Vermont," for example, were "said to kiss the lips of temperance men to ascertain whether they keep their pledges." We also know that young women banded together in places as far apart as Maine, North Carolina, and Iowa to agree that "we will promise marriage to no young man who is in the habit of tippling, for we are assured his wife will come to want and his children go barefoot." Others refused "to keep company" with men who were "not in favor of . . . some . . . prohibitory law."

How effective were such "sexual embargos" on the male population? In small, close-knit towns and rural communities, group action may have been partially effective. In 1852, for example, a group of young women in DeRuyter, New York, announced an embargo on young men who did not abstain and were able to get three hundred to join the local temperance society. The young man who aspired to property and respectability was forced to make professions of abstinence in order to win the hand of a suitable woman of the propertied classes. Through such informal networks and their own de facto control of the marriage market, women could influence male habits and public attitudes. In the larger cities, however, female associations could not work nearly so well. Diversity, size, and the anonymity of the city made the system impractical.

Even in the smallest towns, moreover, the embargos could only be partially effective, and the trend of liquor consumption at mid-century did not encourage continued reliance on merely moral means. The Washingtonian movement of re-formed drunkards had collapsed by 1845, and liquor consumption began to rise soon after with the introduction of lager beer brewed by German immigrants. Pre-cisely because the female associations were only partially successful in their efforts to curb male drinking, the crusade spread into overt public and political action to discourage liquor licensing and to close liquor shops.

The case of female vigilante activity in the decade after 1845 illustrates the transition in women's tactics. As early as 1834, a group of five hundred women in Elizabethtown, New Jersey, had implored the Court of Sessions not to license an ex-cessive number of liquor shops; and in the 1840s, women as far apart as Thom-sonville, Massachusetts, and Ann Arbor, Michigan, began to visit liquor sellers either to plead with them not to sell, or, more often, to threaten to have them prosecuted for violations of the liquor laws. In some cases, as in Fitzwilliam, Maine, in April 1847, women warned that they would "take the business into their own hands" if men did not prosecute. In Utica, Michigan, "having waited in vain for some legal proceedings" against a liquor seller, respectable middle class women took to the streets in July 1846 to close the shop by force. Over the next ten years, female vigilante activity against saloons spread through dozens of (mostly) small northern communities in both the East and the Midwest. . . .

The frustration that stemmed from the failure of reformers and politicians to provide legal remedies for the drink problem was paradoxically heightened by the turn to massive political, prohibitionist action after 1846. The passage of Maine Laws to suppress the sale of liquor did not necessarily entail enforcement of those laws, either by police or courts. Nor did the demand for legal remedies dissipate upon passage of such laws. The Maine Law controversy merely intensified the demand for ever more stringent laws to cope with new and more devious violations of the law. It was thus possible for women to continue to view male legislators and even some male temperance reformers as unresponsive to the demands of women for pro-tection of the home against the impact of intemperance. Whereas male prohibi-tionists had political channels in which to vent their frustration, without the vote women could not participate fully in these critical campaigns. If direct action by women against the drink trade seemed logical to some women in view of these cir-cumstances, the attack on property rights in liquor inherent in the Maine Law's pro-visions for confiscation of illegal liquor supplies provided further sanction for destructive attacks on liquor by outraged women. For all these reasons, we find that sympathy for female saloon-smashers was not limited to "fanatics" of the Carrie Nation type. Rather, many respectable women, who took no part in such pro-ceedings and themselves favored organized action to win the vote, nevertheless condoned and even encouraged the violation of property rights in liquor. "Man li-censes," Susan B. Anthony noted, but "calls on Woman" to cope with the effects of the liquor traffic. Anthony herself urged women to "strike a death blow" at the root of the evil by demanding prohibitory laws from male legislators, but Amelia Bloomer in her widely read magazine, *The Lily,* went beyond mere verbal violence to the ad-vocacy and celebration of female vigilante activity. "If the law lets loose a tiger upon her," Bloomer insisted, "she [woman] may destroy it."

Direct action gave women a more plausible way of controlling male drinking than through Washingtonian societies. The result of bar-smashing was, however, as important as its cause. Respectable women who smashed liquor shops assaulted their idealized conception as domestic submissives. Contemporary accounts of female vigilante activity make clear that its leaders and supporters were pious, middle class women, mostly the wives of evangelical ministers, doctors, lawyers, and businessmen. Like the Washingtonians, these vigilante women violated their appointed social role in order to preserve the home. . . .

Yet, despite the implications for the maintenance of existing sexual stereotypes, neither the organized activities of the Washingtonians nor the informal assaults of the vigilante women prompted denunciations from most male temperance reformers, because these attacks on male sexual and political dominance were partial and oblique. Cask-smashing was actually encouraged by male temperance reformers because it enabled them to exploit concepts of chivalry and the special status of women to destroy supplies of liquor with minimum risk of violent opposition from saloonkeepers. In many documented cases of female vigilante activity, male temperance reformers preached "war" on the liquor traffic and evoked images of violent confrontation. When women responded by taking the "war" into their own hands, sympathetic men sometimes accompanied the female vigilantes on their rampages through the saloon districts. Irish and German saloonkeepers rarely retaliated, and though the women were often arrested, they were either discharged or given only token fines which male sympathizers paid. Respectable male temperance reformers could view the saloon-smashing activities of women as examples of righteous anger against a deeply entrenched evil, as a legitimate extension of women's role as preserver of the home.

Nor did the self-help and charitable societies of the Washingtonians break completely with the traditional view of woman. These campaigns were directed toward providing charity, a traditional female role applauded by conservative churchmen. Though women spoke at temperance meetings, they utilized the traditional rhetoric of the "helper"; though women headed temperance societies, these were only local organizations devoted to gathering pledges. No national conventions were held, and the societies made no declarations of women's rights. But when in the late 1840s and early 1850s women began to demand equality within the male-dominated temperance organizations and began to agitate for political and legal rights from temperance platforms, the signs that women's temperance was becoming an autonomous and independent force would produce, particularly in the events surrounding the World's Temperance Convention in New York in 1853, considerable and hysterical opposition from the same evangelical and clerical reformers who had long implored the material and moral support of women. This vitriolic opposition did not deter women reformers from their agitation; instead, the demonstration of male prejudice, hypocrisy, and discrimination pushed some women temperance reformers into an alliance with the nascent women's rights agitation.

The newly aggressive temperance women of the fifties typically had experience in the beneficial and charitable societies spawned by the Washingtonian movement of the 1840s. It was, however, the more articulate and middle class elements that made the transition to political agitation. Cultural and practical restraints on women impaired their recruitment to political action, but so too did a split in the mid-1840s within the larger temperance movement—between Washingtonians of the artisan classes who favored moral suasion and evangelical, middle class prohibitionists. Like their male allies and relatives, middle class women in the temperance movement increasingly dissociated themselves from the Washingtonians, as did the Lady Margaret Wallace Temperance Benefit Society in 1843 in New York City. Middle class women entered the political arena in the late 1840s to campaign, first for no license and then for the adoption of the Maine Law. They did this because moral suasion had failed to eliminate the use of alcohol, especially among the lower classes, and because the Maine Law promised to eradicate the causes of drunkenness by attacking the sellers of all alcoholic beverages. Maine Law advocates argued that moral suasion had converted the respectable portion of the population and provided thereby the political support for coercive laws against the recalcitrant minority that continued to drink in defiance of respectable opinion. But just as there were male Washingtonians who refused to accept the logic of the middle class leaders of the temperance movement, there were Washingtonian women of the artisan classes who either drifted away from temperance agitation or continued their moral suasion campaigns, with diminishing strength, through such organizations as the New York chapter of the Daughters of the Rechabites.

For those women who did make the transition, the experience of the 1840s in the temperance societies proved important in two ways in shaping their new goals and tactics: in discovering the inadequacy of existing tactics and in testing the limits of male tolerance for women's independent role in reform. As women enlarged their involvement, some of them became increasingly dissatisfied with stopgap measures and began to probe the sources of their oppression. Temperance activity thus contributed to the more general questioning of "woman's place," which led to a direct challenging of the cult of domesticity among some women temperance reformers.

Susan B. Anthony began her reform career with the Daughters of Temperance, which she labeled in 1849 as "the most effectual method" of establishing sobriety in "our social intercourse." But by 1852 she proclaimed publicly that women had given much, "very much towards lessening the evil *effects* of the abomination, but they have for the most part failed to strike a *death blow* at the *root* of the evil." Thus woman's work was "to be done over, & over again." Amelia Bloomer, too, came to see the Daughters of Temperance as an ineffectual remedy; she longed for the day "when woman may have power granted her to act in such a way, that her influences may be felt, and her voice heard and heeded." The Daughters of Temperance meetings were "too often mere milk and water affairs." They had "no more effect to stop the liquor traffic than the mewings of so many kittens." Charity, benevolence, and self-help were not enough while the power structure of society excluded women and sustained the liquor interests.

The other major quarrel with the organizations of the 1840s involved questions of equality, especially the failure of the Sons of Temperance to allow women to speak from the temperance platform at annual conventions and the resistance to the demands of temperance women that they be allowed leadership roles within the organization. In fact, the Sons of Temperance refused to allow women to be members until 1854, and then only on an "associate" basis as "visitors." Not until after the Civil War did the Sons admit women on a basis of equality. When the New York Sons of Temperance refused to accept women as full participating members of their annual convention in 1852, the decision provoked a walkout from leading members of the Daughters of Temperance, who met in a separate convention to found the Woman's New York State Temperance Society (WNYSTS). Thus was born the most highly publicized of all the women's temperance societies. Presided over by Elizabeth Cady Stanton and supported by Amelia Bloomer, Susan B. Anthony, and Mary C. Vaughan, the WNYSTS gave women experience in running their own temperance organization, and they used their new platform to promote such issues as votes for women and equality before the law. With the help of *The Lily,* which under Bloomer's editorship expanded its concerns from temperance to encompass women's rights, the WNYSTS forged strong links between temperance and feminism in the early 1850s.

The creation of such societies enhanced women's confidence and consciousness but did little to upset the inequalities that had prompted their organization. Indeed, it was the heightened activity of women which produced intensified discrimination against them. Men who had earlier invited women to support the temperance cause threw up their hands in horror at the threat of women's rights agitation within the temperance movement and at the threat of women's dominance of temperance societies. At both the preliminary organizational meeting held in May 1853 and at the full session of the "World's Temperance Convention" in New York City between September 6 and 9, 1853, women faced vitriolic opposition when they sought to advance their claims for equal rights within the temperance movement. At the preliminary meeting at Brick Church in New York, attempts to have Susan B. Anthony added to the business committee led to a move, backed particularly by the evangelical clergy, to exclude women entirely from the meeting. When Antoinette Brown attempted to speak from the platform at the full convention in September, "pandemonium" reigned. So vehemently did a section of the audience object to Brown's action that the hall had to be cleared, and, subsequently, a vote of the convention affirmed the "righteousness" of the male temperance reformers who had excluded Brown. The dominant male reformers . . . feared that "woman's rights" doctrines would be publicized at their convention and thus smear with a taint of radicalism the Maine Law movement precisely at the time when it had become politically respectable. Since the leaders of the New York State Temperance Society promoted women's rights issues in their conventions and publications, the fears were understandable.

Though the purpose of male discrimination was to dissociate temperance from radical feminism, the result was to strengthen the common ground between temperance women and women's rights advocates. Women temperance reformers like Amelia Bloomer, Mary C. Vaughan, and Antoinette Brown came together with male reformers like Horace Greeley, radical abolitionists like Thomas Wentworth Higginson and William Lloyd Garrison, and women's rights advocates like Lucretia Mott and Lucy Stone to hold a "Whole World's Temperance Convention" against what they called the "Half-world's Convention" of men. Meeting in New York on September 1, 1853, the Whole World's Convention affirmed the principle of equality in temperance agitation. More than two thousand people attended the two days of meetings, and women and men were, according to the press, about equally represented. In contrast, the World's Temperance Convention a few days later saw between one and two thousand attending its daily sessions, and while the evangelical clergy were heavily represented, "a very small proportion" of participants were women. The holding of the two conventions signified a split in temperance ranks over the role of women, and the breakdown of attendance figures in the newspapers indicated the extent to which many active temperance women now supported women speaking from the temperance platform.

The alliance between women's temperance and women's rights agitation revealed in the events of the two temperance conventions was further emphasized in the aftermath of the rupture. The Ohio Woman's Temperance Convention, like the Woman's New York State Temperance Society, denounced the "tyrannical and cowardly conformation to the 'usages of society,' in thrusting woman from the platform." Nor was the significance of the World's Temperance Convention lost upon women's rights advocates. The Cleveland National Woman's Rights Convention of October 1853 gave great publicity to the temperance issue, by feting Antoinette Brown, praising the "beneficient movement" of temperance, denouncing Brown's treatment by temperance men as "a scandal," and affirming feminist support for the acceptance of woman as an equal partner in the temperance agitation.

If the experience of discrimination in antiliquor societies provided one source of temperance feminism, another lay in the changing political character of the larger temperance movement. Once again the goals of women temperance reformers were shaped in part by the larger arena in which the temperance struggle occurred. The growing popularity among male temperance reformers and their electoral supporters for a prohibitory law based on the statute enacted in Maine in 1851 made women more acutely aware than before of the precise costs of their political impotence. It was widely argued among reformers that if women voted, the liquor problem would rapidly disappear as the stringent Maine Law spread throughout the nation. Thus, organizations such as the Woman's New York State Temperance Society tended to be way stations for women on the road to a more comprehensive attack on their political and social fetters. . . .

The trend of the early 1850s, therefore, was toward the politicization of women's temperance and the advocacy of feminist issues by temperance women. Only a small minority, however, were able to complete this transition from temperance to feminism in the 1850s. While fifty thousand women in Massachusetts petitioned for the Maine Law in 1853, only two thousand demanded the suffrage at the same time. The hostility of male family members, personal inexperience, lack of confidence, physical isolation, the pressures of raising families, and general community prejudice placed obstacles in the path of an easy shift from temperance (and other reform movements) to outright feminist activity for large numbers of potential recruits.

So too did the evangelical temperance experience itself, as the careers and attitudes of many temperance women within the Woman's New York State Temperance Society indicate. Even among the members of that society who did travel the road to public feminism before the Civil War, the journey was a halting and uncertain one. The leaders of the WNYSTS became feminists during the 1850s insofar as they advocated property, legal, and voting rights for women; but rather than emphasize abstract questions of justice, they tended to offer arguments derived from their temperance experience, especially the need for women's rights in order to purify society and to raise males to the moral level of women. The majority of them also drew the line at agitating for such radical feminist issues as divorce—issues which could upset evangelical clergy and evangelical congregations that supported women's temperance in 1850s. When Elizabeth Cady Stanton attempted to commit the WNYSTS to a program of equal rights and advocated the right to divorce from the WNYSTS platform, she was deposed as president in June 1853, demonstrating that "the Temperance party in the Society was the strongest."

Leaders of the WNYSTS such as Amelia Bloomer and Mary C. Vaughan had evangelical origins. Vaughan took "Christ as our exemplar" and professed evangelical benevolence as the point of departure for reform work. Bloomer, setting out from a similar evangelical background, sought to right the "cruel wrongs . . . inflicted upon woman" by intemperance. Work in the Washingtonians, Daughters of Temperance, and similar organizations impressed upon such women an acute appreciation of the "sorrows" visited upon their "sisters" by male law and male drinkers. Both the testimony of "wronged" wives and daughters upon the temperance platform and the experience of home visitation to relieve the "suffering" of "intemperate" families helped reinforce among charity workers the bonds of sisterhood. As a corollary, their belief in their own moral superiority as a sex was confirmed by such agitation. Since women lacked power, enfranchised and legally responsible males must be held to account for women's wrongs. Though initially contemptuous of suffrage as an example of male corruption, the victories and near victories of the Maine Law period made them both mindful of the power of the franchise and resentful of their exclusion. Increasingly, these women became converts to female suffrage in order to exert more effectively what they believed was their superior moral power. The collapse of the Maine Law in the late 1850s did not lead to disillusionment with voting; temperance women were more inclined to argue that if they had had the vote, enforcement would have been more seriously attempted.

Mary C. Vaughan, who displaced Stanton as president of the WNYSTS, presents a fine example of the often reluctant but profound character of this conversion process. After disparaging the franchise while working as a Daughter of Temperance in the late 1840s, Vaughan changed her mind by September 1851 to advocate for women "the right of voting for Temperance measures"—since without the vote, "she is almost powerless in this conflict with the destroyer of so much that makes life beautiful and happy." She expressed no ambition for political office or even to exercise a general franchise, but she agreed that she could not logically deny the right of women to vote on other issues of moral concern. By 1854, this reluctant suffragist was herself deeply involved in electoral politics through her lobbying, petitioning, and campaigning for the Maine Law in New York state. She even led a group of WNYSTS workers handing out voting tickets at the polls in the general election of that year.

In their later writings and private correspondence, Stanton and Anthony denigrated the "conservative" position of the Woman's New York State Temperance Society and dismissed its efforts for prohibition and suffrage as inconsequential and unsuccessful. Nonetheless, as women's rights advocates themselves began to focus more and more on the suffrage question after the Civil War, the significance of temperance agitation for the evolving women's movement became apparent. The abolitionists had been much more important than temperance reformers in providing feminism with a small number of articulate and radical leaders, but temperance was much more instrumental in mobilizing, in the long-run and despite the many obstacles, large numbers of conservative, evangelical women who had different goals and strategies for the advancement of women. Nearly three decades of prohibitionist experience between the late 1840s and the 1870s politicized and organized behind the goal of suffrage a host of pious, middle class women, particularly from the midwestern states that increasingly dominated the temperance campaigns on the local level after the Civil War.

The organization that linked the pre- and post–Civil War women's temperance efforts was the Good Templars, founded in New York in 1851 and boasting seventy thousand members, both men and women, by 1855. Though the momentum of its activities was dissipated temporarily in the wake of the political collapse of the Maine Law agitation by 1857 and the domination of politics by the sectional and slavery controversies, the Templars returned to public prominence after the Civil War and had over 400,000 members by 1869. The Templars embodied women's aspirations by accepting them as equals in voting and office-holding within the organization and by supporting female suffrage in the political arena. Its stance on suffrage and equal rights proved increasingly attractive to members of the Daughters of Temperance, who deserted the latter organization in large numbers to join the Templars. Yet the ambiguous character of women's position within the temperance movement was especially well expressed in the Templars. Despite formal equality between the sexes, this organization still emphasized the importance of "female influence" and the "moral purity" of the "true woman" and argued that this could best be employed in "staunching the wounds of intemperance."

In the period before 1860, the process of converting temperance women to a conservative and defensive feminism, rooted in their personal experience and the ideology of feminine moral superiority, had only just begun. However, it was from the women's temperance societies of the 1850s and from the Good Templars that many midwestern suffrage leaders of the 1860s and 1870s came. After moving to Iowa, Amelia Bloomer became prominent in the suffrage agitation there, serving as president of the Iowa Woman Suffrage Society in 1871. In Indiana, the postwar suffrage leader Amanda Way had been a Good Templar in the 1850s; in Springfield, Ohio, the first president of the Springfield Woman's Suffrage Association was Eliza D. Stewart, who was also a women's temperance advocate before the Civil War and later became famous through her association with the Woman's Crusade in Ohio in

1873–74. Clarina Nichols, a prominent ally of Bloomer and Vaughan in the Woman's New York State Temperance Society in the 1850s, joined Susan B. Anthony in 1867 in the Kansas suffrage campaign; Mary Livermore, a Washingtonian in the 1840s, became in the 1860s the first president of the Illinois Woman Suffrage Association. The most famous example of a temperance woman becoming a prominent supporter of suffrage after the Civil War was, however, Frances Willard, a product of a pre–Civil War temperance family. Though she remained principally a temperance reformer, this woman probably did more than any other to popularize the suffrage cause in the 1870s and 1880s. To be sure, there were still many temperance women who did not support suffrage when the prosuffrage forces under Willard gained control of the WCTU in 1879, but the processes which would serve to make the WCTU a powerful educative force in favor of women's enfranchisement had already been foreshadowed in the pre–Civil War temperance experience. Conservative, evangelical women newly organized under the temperance banner had to experience personally the frustrations and bitterness of unrequited reform in order to be convinced that the "wrongs of women" demanded advancing women's rights.

SUGGESTED READINGS

General

Paul Boller, *American Transcendentalism, 1830–1860* (1974).

Jack Larkin, *The Reshaping of Everyday Life, 1790–1840* (1968).

Russell B. Nye, *Society and Culture in America, 1830–1860* (1974).

W.J. Rorabaugh, *The Alcoholic Republic: An American Tradition* (1979).

Mary P. Ryan, *Women in Public: Between Banners and Ballots, 1825–1880* (1990).

Charles Sellers, *The Market Revolution* (1991).

James B. Stewart, *Holy Warriors: The Abolitionists and American Slavery* (1976).

George Rogers Taylor, *The Transportation Revolution, 1815–1860* (1951).

Ronald Walters, *American Reformers, 1815–1860* (1978).

Sean Wilentz, *Chants Democratic: New York City and the Rise of the American Working Class* (1984).

FURTHER READINGS

ECONOMIC, SOCIAL, AND CULTURAL CHANGES: Arthur Bestor, *Backwoods Utopias* (1950); Carl Bode, *The American Lyceum: Town Meeting of the Mind* (1968); W. Elliot Brownlee, *Dynamics of Ascent: A History of the American Economy* (1988 ed.); Thomas C. Cochran, *Frontiers of Change: Early Industrialism in America* (1981); Whitney Cross, *The Burnt-Over District* (1950); Thomas Dublin, *Women at Work: The Transformation of Work and Community in Lowell, Massachusetts, 1826–1860* (1981); Ellen DuBois, *Feminism and Suffrage: The Emergence of an Independent Women's Movement in America, 1848–1869* (1978); Michael Fellman, *The Unbounded Frame: Freedom and Community in Nineteenth Century Utopianism* (1973); Louis Filler, *The Crusade against Slavery,*

1830–1860 (1960); Eleanor Flexner, *Century of Struggle: The Women's Rights Movement in the United States* (1975); Lori Ginzberg, *Women and the Work of Benevolence: Morality, Politics, and Class in the Nineteenth-Century United States* (1990); David Grimsted, *Melodrama Unveiled: American Theater and Culture, 1800–1850* (1968); David Jeremy, *The Transatlantic Industrial Revolution* (1981); Karen Halttunen, *Confidence Men and Painted Women: A Study of Middle Class Culture in America, 1830–1850* (1982); Paul Johnson, *A Shopkeeper's Millennium: Society and Revivals in Rochester, New York, 1815–1837* (1978); Gerda Lerner, *The Grimké Sisters of South Carolina: Rebels Against Slavery* (1967); Keith Melder, *Beginnings of Sisterhood: The American Women's Rights Movement, 1800–1850* (1977); Benjamin Quarles, *Black Abolitionists* (1969); Ian Tyrrell, *Sobering Up: From Temperance to Prohibition in Antebellum America, 1800–1860* (1979); Larzer Ziff, *Literary Democracy: The Declaration of Cultural Independence in America* (1981).

QUESTIONS FOR DISCUSSION

1. Identify and discuss the social and economic changes associated with the market revolution following LaFayette's visit in 1824.
2. What did most Americans identify as the source of poverty during the 1830s and 1840s? What steps did they take to rectify this problem?
3. Describe labor's use of strikes in the 1830s and indicate their impact on the emerging labor movement.
4. Analyze the social implications of the Second Great Awakening. Identify reform efforts inspired or shaped by these revivals.
5. Assess the role of William Lloyd Garrison in the abolitionist movement.
6. Why did many African Americans oppose the American Colonization Society?
7. Using information from the essay by Ian R. Tyrrell explain what motivated women to participate in the temperance movement and assess the significance of their role in the movement.

WESTWARD EXPANSION AND THE WAR WITH MEXICO

The Peace of Ghent that ended the War of 1812 constituted a watershed in the history of the United States. America's existence to that point had been precarious. Problems left over from the Revolutionary War, the French Revolution, and the generation of conflict that ensued, combined with America's dependence on foreign trade, meant that, like it or not, the new republic would be involved in European affairs. Given the United States' negligible army and navy, there was a continual threat during this period that the new country would be overwhelmed by one of the European monarchies. With the final defeat of Napoleon in 1815, however, the great powers would not fight another major war for a hundred years. As a result, the United States was left free to develop one of the world's most vibrant economies and to expand across the North American continent, two developments that were intimately related.

That America was innately expansionist was not surprising given the fact that it was a product of European colonization. The men and women who had made the dangerous journey across the Atlantic were deliberately trying to distance themselves from a culture that they saw as decadent and oppressive. Always before them was a vision of the ideal society, a vision that gradually expanded to include the entire North American continent. The Treaty of 1783 was an expansionist document adding a huge tract of territory between the Appalachians and the Mississippi River to the original thirteen colonies. The republican philosophy of Thomas Jefferson that came to predominate in early nineteenth-century America called for a virtually inexhaustible source of land to ensure the continuing dominance of the republic by independent, yeomen farmers. The heady nationalism spawned by the War of 1812 only served to reinforce the notion of cultural exceptionalism among Americans. In the years that followed the Treaty of Ghent, then, Americans stopped searching the eastern horizon for hostile sails and turned their gaze once again westward. There it would remain for the remainder of the nineteenth century.

THE LURE OF THE WESTERN LANDS

THE FUR TRADE

The lure that originally attracted Europeans into the interior of North America was the fur trade. From the 1670s through the 1840s French, Canadian, British, and then American trappers mined the rivers of Canada, the northwest territory, and the Oregon territory for beaver pelts, much in demand in Europe for the manufacture of hats and coats. The British-owned Hudson's Bay Company dominated this trade which depended on cooperation with various Indian tribes.

In the 1820s, American enterprises began to challenge the British and Canadians for control of the lucrative traffic in pelts. Indeed, it was an American, William Henry Ashley, who originated the rendezvous system. Each year at an appointed time, trappers would gather at a site somewhere deep in the Rocky Mountains where Ashley's Rocky Mountain Fur Company would trade guns, ammunition, tobacco, beads, cloth, and alcohol for beaver pelts. The rendezvous, modeled on Indian trade assemblages, were tumultuous, weeklong affairs during which Canadian, American, French, and Indian trappers exchanged goods, drank, gambled, and caroused. For many of these frontiersmen, the rendezvous was their sole annual contact with European or American civilization.

Mountain men such as Jedediah Smith and Jim Beckwourth, an African American, lived lives of danger and adventure. Some of these individuals were isolated, but most interacted with and depended upon local peoples. The most successful trappers learned tribal languages and married Native Americans. The melding of cultures, then, was just as typical as confrontation and warfare on the early frontier. The fur trade died in the 1840s as the beaver population failed to keep pace with the voracious hat and coat markets along the eastern seaboard of the United States and in Europe. Mountain men became artifacts of history and myth, but their exploits captured the imagination of those living to the East and generated an interest in the West that complemented the profit motives and demographic pressures impelling Americans to migrate.

EXPLORING THE INTERIOR

Government-sponsored exploration also fueled interest in the West. Following the acquisition of the Louisiana Territory in 1803, President Jefferson asked Meriwether Lewis, his private secretary and a military veteran who had served in the West, to lead an expedition across the northern reaches of this vast

Members of Native American tribes who lived in semiautonomous villages would periodically gather for rituals, ceremonies, and games. Ball Play of the Choctaw—Ball Up *by George Catlin, 1836.*

expanse. As his co-commander, Lewis chose William Clark, the son of Revolutionary War hero George Rogers Clark. Their mission was manyfold. Lewis and Clark were instructed to map the Louisiana Territory and to report on its flora and fauna. They were also to lay the groundwork for a fur-trading network that would challenge British economic power in the trans-Mississippi West.

The expedition, fifty in number, departed St. Louis in May 1804, and spent the next several months pushing their boats up the Mississippi. They wintered in present-day North Dakota with the Mandans, and in the spring of 1805 headed due west. The party barely managed to cross the Rocky Mountains ahead of the winter snows and then followed the Snake and Columbia Rivers to the Oregon coast, where they waited in vain through the winter for a rescue ship. In the spring of 1806 they reluctantly turned eastward, arriving back in St. Louis in the fall. The trip had consumed two-and-a-half years, during which the expedition criss-crossed the continent, braved the elements, and successfully negotiated with a dozen Native American tribes. They returned with a collection of maps, descriptions, sketches, and biological and botanical specimens that enriched the nation's knowledge of the Louisiana Territory and fired its imagination.

Shortly thereafter, in 1806–1807, Lt. Zebulon Pike led a party overland to the Rockies which he partially explored and mapped. In 1819–1820, an expedition under the command of Major Stephen Long toured the Great Plains, gathering information and threatening British traders and hunters. John C. Frémont, a captain in the U.S. Army, explored and mapped the overland trails to Oregon in 1843–1844. These federally initiated surveys, both economic and military in nature, were symbols of the nation's interest in the West and instruments of its settlement.

Public and private expeditions frequently included scientists, geographers, and artists who wrote, collected, drew, and painted. Karl Bodmer, who accompanied a private expedition financed by a German prince, painted a number of striking Indian portraits that were widely reproduced in the East. Although sometimes an exaggeration of reality, the landscapes of Albert Bierstadt and Thomas Moran captured the popular imagination and contributed to white America's growing romance with the West.

THE LURE OF CHEAP LAND

During the period between 1790 and 1820 the population of the United States more than doubled from 4 million to over 9 million. Augmenting the natural increase which accounted for most of the growth during this period were millions of European immigrants who flooded into the United States following the Napoleonic wars. Sometimes over the objections of eastern businessmen and industrialists, the federal government encouraged this burgeoning population to migrate to the West. In the Land Act of 1796, Congress had provided for the sale of public lands to the highest bidder with a minimum price of two dollars an acre and a minimum purchase of 640 acres. Payment had to be made within one year. The legislation established the new office of surveyor-general and directed that western lands be divided into township units of six-miles square. The federal government subsequently set up land offices at Cincinnati and Pittsburgh.

The Land Act of 1800 made it possible for settlers to buy 320 acres rather than the previous minimum of 640. It retained the two-dollar price but made credit easier. What ensued was a land boom of staggering proportions. In 1818 land sales, mostly to speculators, peaked at 3.5 million acres, an area larger than the state of Connecticut. Much of this land had been bought on credit; prices rose all out of proportion to value. In 1819 the Bank of the United States, which had directly and indirectly financed much of this speculation, decided to call a halt to the loans. The bank insisted on immediate and full repayment of loans made to state banks and refused to renew personal notes and mortgages. What resulted was the Panic of 1819. Hundreds of western banks failed, and thousands of speculators were ruined.

To reduce speculation and prevent future crises such as the Panic of 1819, Congress passed the Public Land Act of 1820. That measure ended credit and permitted a settler to buy as few as eight acres for $100, or $12.50 an acre. In the years that followed, squatters—settlers who moved onto and improved land before it was surveyed and auctioned by the federal government—pressured Washington to pass a pre-emption act. Such a law would allow squatters to purchase their land at a minimum price before it was put up for sale to the public. The Pre-emption Act of 1841 permitted those who had moved beyond the established frontier to buy 160 acres at $1.25 when their land was officially opened to settlement. The measure did not help people with less than $200, and it was subject to abuse by speculators who employed "floaters" to pre-empt land for them. Nevertheless, it was better than no pre-emption act at all and served as a further spur to western migration.

CONFLICT WITH THE EUROPEANS

THE OCCUPATION OF WEST FLORIDA

From the earliest days of the republic, American expansionists had coveted the Floridas. The end of Thomas Jefferson's presidency and the conclusion of the War of 1812 had not weakened the Republican party's determination to ensure that planters and yeomen farmers had available to them an inexhaustible supply of public land. Aside from containing millions of fertile acres, West Florida encompassed the mouths of the major rivers running through the present-day states of Alabama and Mississippi, and East Florida guarded the entrance to the Gulf of Mexico. Though Spain was weak and relatively benign, the Spanish government was, as the retrocession had shown, perfectly capable of ceding the provinces to a power willing and able to threaten American interests.

James Monroe was of the opinion that the Floridas were included in the Louisiana Purchase. Either Bonaparte and Talleyrand were unaware of the fact, he argued, or they were being disingenuous. As part of a plan to acquire both Florida and Cuba, President Jefferson declared in his inaugural address in 1805 that relations with Spain were rapidly deteriorating. He asked for a volunteer military force to deal with this menace and then secretly approached Congress for a $2 million appropriation to buy the desired territory from an intimidated Spain. Nothing, however, came of Jefferson's ploy.

James Madison was just as committed to territorial expansion as his friend and predecessor. In 1810 he began conspiring with Americans living in West Florida to separate that weakly governed and sparsely populated region from Spain. In September 1810 a band of revolutionaries overwhelmed the Spanish garrison at Baton Rouge, tore down the Bourbon flag, replaced it with a blue woolen blanket emblazoned with a silver star, and proclaimed the independence of the Republic of West Florida. Independence was not the aim of Americans living in West Florida, of course, and on October 27, Madison issued a declaration extending American jurisdiction to the Perdido River. Madrid protested but was too deeply involved in the Napoleonic wars to do anything about this assault on its sovereignty. The United States took advantage of the War of 1812 to drive the last Spanish troops out of the Mobile area.

James Monroe, another Republican, succeeded Madison in the White House in 1817 and promptly named John Quincy Adams to be his secretary of state. Adams was the son of John and Abigail, a bred-to-the-bone New Englander who was deeply influenced by his Calvinist background. He believed that the United States had been singled out by Divine Providence to civilize all of North America. Adams was devoted to the principles of republicanism; the American Revolution, he believed, was the beginning of an inevitable movement to eradicate monarchism and colonialism first from the Western Hemisphere and eventually the entire globe. The new secretary of state was a thoroughgoing nationalist, as devoted to protecting America's neutral rights and commercial interests as to expanding its territorial domain—an amphibian, one of his contemporaries called him, a creature which moved both by land and by sea.

Almost as soon as he took the oath of office, Adams initiated talks with the Spanish ambassador, Don Luis de Onis, concerning the fate of East Florida. The New Englander insisted that the Louisiana Purchase agreement coupled with the inability of Spain's provincial government to restrain hostile Indians from raiding across the border and to return runaway slaves added up to U.S. ownership of Florida. Onis vehemently disagreed, of course, and the controversy remained rhetorical until the redoubtable Andrew Jackson burst onto the scene.

As part of an effort to stop the bloody Indian forays across the border into Georgia, General Jackson was ordered with his army of three thousand into the Southeast. The War Department instructed him to put an end to the violence, even if he had to cross into Spanish territory. Jackson later insisted that he had explicit permission from the Monroe administration to use the occasion to overthrow Spanish rule in East Florida. The president would deny that contention on his deathbed, but what is clear is that the president knew of the impetuous Jackson's intent and did nothing to stop him.

In February 1818 the *"Napoléon des bois"* (Napoleon of the woods), as the French ambassador in Washington referred to Jackson, crossed into Florida from his camp on the Big Creek near Hartford, Georgia. His quarry was Chief Boleck, or "Bowlegs" as the U.S. soldiers nicknamed him, the leader of the "renegades." The Indians fled before Jackson, eluding for the most part both capture and confrontation. Two English traders who had been helping the Seminoles were not so lucky. Jackson apprehended them and after a quick court martial, hung one and shot the other. In the course of his campaign, Jackson seized first St. Marks and then Pensacola, the Spanish capital of East Florida. After claiming the province for the United States and placing one of his colonels in charge, Jackson departed for Tennessee, leaving Secretary of State Adams to deal with the irate Spanish.

THE TRANSCONTINENTAL TREATY

President Monroe quaked under Ambassador Onis' threats; he and his cabinet seriously considered repudiating Jackson's actions. Only John Quincy Adams defended him, but Adams' support was enough to stiffen the government's spine. The administration and the Republican party were committed to acquiring Florida, the secretary of state pointed out; Jackson had given them their chance. Operating on the assumption that the best defense is a good offense, Adams countered Onis' demands that East Florida be returned and compensation paid with charges that Spain's misrule in Florida fully justified Jackson's actions. If Madrid could not maintain law and order in a province so vital to America's interests, then the United States would have to. Spain, already in decline, was then having to deal with various revolutions in Central and South America. When it became clear that England would not join Spain in hostilities over Jackson's exploits, Madrid decided to part with Florida for cash rather than fight a bloody and futile war with the United States.

The Adams–Onis, or Transcontinental, Treaty actually dealt with a number of issues that had been plaguing Spanish-American relations. Some sentiment existed in the United States for the annexation of Texas, then the northernmost province of Mexico, still a Spanish colony. Onis successfully resisted Adams on the matter, however, and Texas remained part of Mexico. In the treaty, Spain gave up all claims to West Florida and ceded East Florida in return for Washington's assumption of 5 million dollars in claims by U.S. citizens against Spain. Finally, the agreement established a clear boundary between Spanish territory in North America and that claimed by the United States. The transcontinental line ran northward from the Gulf of Mexico along the Sabine River to the Red River, thence westward to the 100th meridian, north to the Arkansas River, west to the 105th meridian, and west along the forty-second parallel to the Pacific Ocean. In addition to adding considerably to the public domain, the Transcontinental Treaty eliminated Spain as a claimant to the Oregon territory, leaving only the United States and Great Britain, a development of much importance in John Quincy Adams' mind.

THE HOLY ALLIANCE AND THE THREAT OF RECOLONIZATION

The Monroe administration's war on European colonialism did not end with the Transcontinental Treaty. Between 1810 and 1818 revolution swept most of Spain's New World colonies; their bids for independence drew much attention among Americans who were convinced that their neighbors to the south wanted nothing so much as to emulate the American experience. In 1822–1823, however, Adams and his countrymen were alarmed by rumors that the Holy Alliance, a coalition of European states put together by Austrian Chancellor

Klemens von Metternich in the wake of the Napoleonic wars to combat revolution and democracy and maintain the monarchical status quo, was going to intervene in the New World to restore to Spain its lost colonies. To demonstrate its devotion to the principles of the *ancien régime*, France under Louis XVIII would lead the armada.

In 1823 Great Britain, which looked forward to trading with the newly independent Latin republics, broke with the Holy Alliance and proposed to the Monroe administration a joint warning to the continental powers not to attempt to recolonize the Western Hemisphere. The United States and Great Britain would at the same time renounce any territorial ambitions themselves. Monroe, supported by ex-presidents Madison and Jefferson, was inclined to accept the offer. Again Adams demurred. The Royal Navy was going to restrain the Holy Alliance no matter what the United States did, he argued. Why not make a unilateral statement warning against further European colonization? "It would be more candid as well as more dignified," he advised Monroe and the rest of the cabinet, "to avow our principles explicitly to Russia [which was then trying to extend Russian North America southward] and France, than to come in as a cock boat in the wake of the British man of war." In addition, Adams still coveted Cuba and Texas, and wanted to avoid any pledge that would limit future U.S. expansion.

THE MONROE DOCTRINE

The policy statement that came to be known as the Monroe Doctrine was contained in the president's regular annual message to Congress delivered in December. It comprised three principles. First, reviewing the situation with Russia in the Northwest—Tsar Alexander I had issued an edict in 1821 claiming territory southward along the Pacific coast to the 51st parallel—Monroe declared that henceforth the Western Hemisphere was off limits to any further European colonization. Thus was the noncolonization principle codified and John Quincy Adams satisfied.

Second, Greece was then struggling to escape from the Ottoman Empire, a revolution that attracted much sympathy in the United States. Indeed, some Americans insisted that it was their country's duty to come to the aid of the country from whence democracy had sprung. Adams and Monroe disagreed. Enunciating the two spheres principle, the president declared that "In the wars of the European powers in matters relating to themselves we have never taken any part, nor does it comport with our policy to do so."

Finally, while the United States promised not to interfere in the affairs of Europe, it would at the same time expect the powers to abstain from political and/or military intervention in the New World. "We should consider any attempt on [the Europeans'] part to extend their system to any portion of this hemisphere as dangerous to our peace and safety," Monroe declared.

Given that the United States was a fifth-rate power, the sweeping policy statement made by President Monroe in 1823 seemed ludicrous. Because Great

Britain wanted to continue to exploit the markets of Latin America, the Royal Navy rather than the American fleet would enforce the Monroe Doctrine. That would change, however, and the Monroe Doctrine would by the end of the century become one of the cornerstones of U.S. foreign policy.

MANIFEST DESTINY

In the years that followed, the attention of American expansionists became more specific, focusing on Texas, California, and the Oregon territory. The stated desire to restrict the spread of monarchism and colonialism on the one hand and to facilitate the extension of republicanism on the other remained the principal justifications for continental expansion. Late in 1844, as sentiment in favor of the annexation of Texas reached its peak, a New York publisher named John L. O'Sullivan coined the term *manifest destiny*. At its core was the notion advanced by John Quincy Adams that either fate or Almighty God had decreed that the United States spread free enterprise, civil liberty, and democracy from the Atlantic to the Pacific. O'Sullivan declared that any attempt by European governments to expand their influence in North America constituted a just cause for war between that nation and the United States. European colonies should continue to exist only so long as the inhabitants of those colonies were willing to be ruled from abroad. In areas of North America where there "was no absolute title against us," the United States had the right if not the duty to take the land and give it to pioneer settlers, the true repositories of republicanism and free institutions. Skeptics argued that manifest destiny was just a mask for the greed of land speculators, railroad builders, and shippers hoping to acquire ports on the west coast from which they could exploit the trade of the Pacific. Nevertheless, many Americans shared O'Sullivan's sense of mission.

THE REPUBLIC OF TEXAS

By the time O'Sullivan wrote his manifest destiny articles, the movement to annex Texas to the Union was reaching its climax. The movement had begun in 1821, when the Spanish provincial government in Mexico City issued a charter to Moses Austin to lead some three hundred families from Missouri into central Texas and settle there. Later that year Mexico declared its independence and separated from Spain. Encouraged by the moral and material aid it received from the United States and by the example of a successful republic of immigrants, Mexico continued to encourage immigration into Texas. By 1830 some eight thousand Americans were living in Coahuila-Texas, Mexico's northernmost province. From that point on, relations between American settlers and Mexico City deteriorated rapidly. A decree mandating the gradual manumission of slaves angered the numerous slaveowners in Texas. While paying lip service to Catholicism, many Texans of American origin openly practiced their Protestant faith. Following several skirmishes between settlers and Mexican troops, a provisional government of the settlers adopted a declaration of independence on March 2, 1836.

While delegates to the independence convention were meeting in San Felipe de Austin, General Antonio López de Santa Anna, dictator of Mexico, advanced into Texas at the head of four thousand troops, with the intent of crushing the insurrection. After annihilating a much smaller force of Texans at the Alamo in San Antonio, Santa Anna advanced steadily into southeast Texas. Finally, at the San Jacinto River near Galveston Bay, the Texan army under Sam Houston turned and fought. Catching the Mexicans by surprise, Houston's army killed six hundred of the enemy and captured seven hundred more, including Santa Anna. For the next ten years the Mexican government refused to acknowledge the legitimacy of the treaty Santa Anna subsequently signed at San Jacinto, a document that declared an end to the war and that recognized Texan independence, while Texas unsuccessfully sought admission to the Union. Though Andrew Jackson and his successor, Martin Van Buren, were mildly in favor of annexation, they were afraid to act for fear of arousing the rapidly growing antislavery faction in the North, an eventuality that they believed would cripple the Democratic party and perhaps even split the Union.

The Road to Annexation

Millions of dollars in debt, harassed by low-level warfare with Mexico, and vulnerable to takeover by a great power, the Texan government had no wish to remain independent and so continued to plot annexation. By the early 1840s antislavery elements were still strongly opposed to adding Texas to the Union, but a number of factors intervened to open the way to annexation. Britain, which hoped that an independent Texas would act as counterweight and barrier to an expansionist United States, openly courted the government of Sam Houston who meanwhile feigned a willingness to accept Mexican rule under certain conditions. After newly elected President William Henry Harrison died in 1841, he was succeeded by the proslavery Virginian, John Tyler. In April 1844, Secretary of State John C. Calhoun signed a treaty of annexation only to see it stalled in the Senate by Whig opposition. The Texas issue dominated the election of 1844, and after the country chose Democrat James K. Polk, an avowed expansionist, to be president, Congress in January 1845 approved the annexation by means of a joint resolution.

WINDOWS ON THE WEST

James K. Polk of Tennessee was a Jeffersonian and a Jacksonian, committed to the concept of a republic dominated by planters and independent agriculturalists. But he was also a modern man and, like John Quincy Adams, committed to expanding opportunities for American commercial interests. He looked forward not only to the annexation of Texas but to American ownership of the

Oregon territory, a region he and other expansionists anticipated would both add additional fertile acres to the public domain and furnish commercial interests with harbor sites—"windows on the west."

At stake in the Oregon dispute was a huge wilderness forty times the size of Maine, the entire area between the parallels 42 degrees and 54 degrees, 40 minutes. By the time Polk took the oath of office, the two remaining claimants to the region were the United States and Great Britain. In the summer of 1818 London and Washington had signed a treaty providing for a ten-year period of joint occupation. That agreement, which stipulated that all of Oregon should be open to settlement equally to American and British citizens, was subsequently renewed. Over the years through a natural process of settlement, the area actually in dispute narrowed to the land north and west of the Columbia River and south of the 49th parallel. During diplomatic negotiations, Britain continually maintained that it would be willing to recognize the Columbia River from its source to the point where it intersected the 49th parallel as the boundary between Canada and the United States. The United States demurred, however, because this settlement would deny it harbor sites on Puget Sound around the Straits of Juan de Fuca and the southern tip of Vancouver Island.

THE OREGON TREATY

The Democratic platform in 1844, an unabashedly expansionist document, balanced the Oregon territory, certain to produce one or more free states, against the Texas territory, sure to become one or more slave states. Polk repeated the campaign's catchiest slogan, "Fifty-four Forty or Fight," but he was clearly reconciled to giving Britain everything above the 49th parallel. The president was determined to have access to Puget Sound, however. To bluff the British into concessions, he submitted legislation to Congress in 1845 providing for the unilateral abrogation of the treaty of joint occupation. The Conservative government of Sir Robert Peel did in fact offer a settlement of 49 degrees in June of 1846, although it was acting more out of a desire for peace with the United States and the knowledge that the area south of Vancouver Island had been trapped out rather than from any sense of intimidation. Polk ignored the complaints of the 54°40′ minority in the Democratic party and submitted the Oregon Treaty to the Senate. It readily consented, and Polk signed the agreement into law on June 19, 1846.

THE ACQUISITION OF CALIFORNIA

Partly for insurance against the failure of the Oregon negotiations to bring the United States suitable port facilities and partly because he was a committed expansionist, President Polk plotted to secure California from the Spanish while he negotiated with the British over the area north of the Columbia River. The California province featured the proven harbors of San Francisco and San

FIGURE 9–1
U.S. Territories and Slave States, 1853

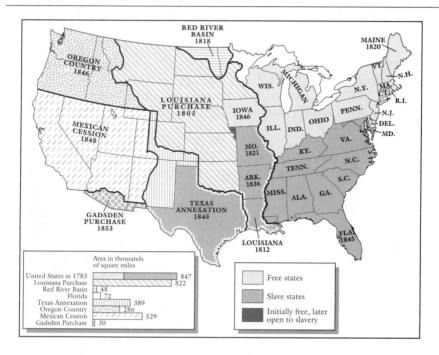

Diego. Complications arising over the annexation of Texas gave Polk the pretext to take what he wanted (see Figure 9-1).

Troubles with Mexico

Indeed, by the time Polk took the oath of office, United States–Mexican relations had reached a crisis stage. Mexico had continually threatened war with its neighbor to the north when and if it annexed Texas. And, in fact, in March 1845 the Mexican ambassador to the United States asked for and received his passports, thus severing relations between the two countries. The American ambassador in Mexico subsequently withdrew; neither side thus had official representation in the other's capital during the stormy months of late 1845 and early 1846. The rupture in relations made it virtually impossible for the two nations to settle a long-standing Texas-Mexican border dispute. During the period of Spanish-Mexican rule, the southernmost boundary of Texas had been the Nueces River. But the treaty that Santa Anna had signed under duress and an act passed by the Texas legislature claimed the Rio Grande as the border with Mexico.

Mexico City had not made much of the matter during the period of Texan independence, because it never admitted that separation had taken place. Once Texas became part of the United States, however, Polk was obligated to defend the newest state's claim, and the boundary became the focus of an international dispute. Further complicating relations were some $2 million in claims against the Mexican government filed by American citizens for damage done to property or lives during Mexico's intermittent periods of civil strife. In 1835, for example, twenty-two Americans were arrested and executed without trial for allegedly plotting against the government. Finally, Mexico City was frightened and angered by the United States' ill-concealed desire for California. Americans had been settling in the central and northern part of the province since the 1820s. In 1835 the Jackson administration offered Mexico five hundred thousand dollars for San Francisco and the area to the north, a proposal which was summarily rejected.

Mexico was right to be concerned about California. President Polk was determined to have the weakly defended and sparsely populated province, by negotiation if possible and by force if necessary. In December 1845 he dispatched a prominent Louisiana Democrat, John Slidell, to Mexico to deal with the authorities. The U.S. emissary was instructed to settle the claims issue, secure Mexican acknowledgment of the Rio Grande as the boundary with Texas, and purchase both California and New Mexico. News of Slidell's mission leaked to the press in Mexico City, however, and in the midst of a flurry of nationalist denunciations, the Herrera government refused even to speak with Slidell. "Be assured," Slidell advised Polk, "that nothing is to be done with these people until they shall have been chastized." At this point, Polk decided to force the issue. He ordered General Zachary Taylor and his considerable contingent of troops to move from Corpus Christi at the mouth of the Nueces to Brownsville at the mouth of the Rio Grande. In essence, the United States had occupied the territory in dispute with Mexico.

The Coming of War

Because California was the real object of Polk's policy and because Mexico refused to react to the Brownsville provocation, however, Polk was stymied. He met with his cabinet on May 9 and with some difficulty persuaded it to approve a war message to Congress citing unpaid claims and the rejection of Slidell. Secretary of State James Buchanan observed that he was prepared to vote for war but would feel better about the matter if the Mexicans had initiated hostilities. In a bizarre coincidence, Polk received word the next day from General Taylor that a Mexican force had crossed the Rio Grande and attacked an American foraging party, killing or wounding sixteen soldiers. The war message Polk subsequently submitted to Congress outlined twenty years of grievances culminating with the attack on Taylor's men. Two days later Congress formally declared war, empowered the president to use the army and navy, and appropriated $10 million for military purposes.

Despite an overwhelming vote for war—174 to 14 in the House and 40 to 2 in the Senate—considerable reservation existed in Congress concerning the conflict with Mexico, especially among Whigs and antislavery Democrats.

Indeed, many had voted for war only because American blood had been shed. Criticism of the president followed almost immediately. Whigs, among them first-term Congressman Abraham Lincoln, charged that Polk could have avoided war if he had so desired, and that he had deliberately provoked Mexico. As time progressed, sentiment against the war became intense, especially in the North among antislavery elements.

From all indications, Mexico in 1845 and 1846 was in an even more bellicose mood than the United States. On paper the Mexican army, heavily overstaffed with generals, was some five times the size of its American counterpart. Mexico City hoped for war between the United States and Great Britain over Oregon, and fondly recalled America's inept efforts during the War of 1812 to invade Canada. It was all delusion, of course.

The War with Mexico

Polk hoped to achieve his objectives with as little fighting as possible. Shortly after the declaration of war, he developed a military-diplomatic plan that involved seizing what he intended to purchase from Mexico and then holding it by force until the Mexican government should agree to terms. "Conquer a peace" was the term he used.

The first priority was to secure the southern boundary of Texas. General Taylor pushed across the Rio Grande and drove deep into the northern reaches of Mexico. He won a series of victories culminating with the defeat of Santa Anna's much larger force at the town of Buena Vista.

With Taylor in control of northern Mexico, General Stephen Kearny at the head of three thousand troops made his way from Fort Leavenworth, Kansas, across the New Mexico territory to Sante Fe. After capturing the Mexican garrison there, he proceeded to San Diego and then northward to Los Angeles where he joined up with Captain John C. Frémont. Even before the declaration of war, Frémont and several dozen heavily armed men, ostensibly on a scientific exploration in behalf of the U.S. government, had been conspiring with Americans living in northern California. They had already captured San Francisco and Monterey by the time Kearny arrived.

Unfortunately, Mexico refused to surrender. Much to his dismay, Polk realized that a peace treaty recognizing U.S. control of the New Mexico territory, California, and the Rio Grande would be possible only after the conquest of Mexico City. Polk named General Winfield Scott to command the expedition, and he and his soldiers captured the Gulf port of Vera Cruz in March 1847. The president had selected Scott rather than Taylor to command the expedition in part because Scott, though vain and egotistical, was a proven combat leader but also because both he and Taylor were Whigs and potential presidential candidates in 1848. Polk wanted to ensure that whatever military laurels that were to be won in the war would be divided between the two men. Shortly after Scott captured Mexico City, Polk sent Nicholas P. Trist, chief clerk of the State

Department, to Scott's camp with orders to negotiate a treaty as soon as Mexico City had been captured. Trist was a Democrat with no presidential ambitions, no political constituency, and as such was considered a safe choice.

The Treaty of Guadalupe-Hidalgo   With Trist in tow, Scott and his men made the difficult journey through the jungle and across the mountains to Mexico City. Though he had lost a leg at the battle of Buena Vista, Santa Anna had recovered sufficiently to take charge of the defense of the Mexican capital. He agreed to an armistice with Scott and Trist and accepted a ten thousand dollar payment in return for a promise to negotiate a peace treaty. Santa Anna subsequently reneged on the agreement, however, pocketed the bribe, and used the extra time to prepare the defenses of the city. The Mexican leader's efforts were all for naught. Scott's troops quickly overwhelmed the capital's defenders, and Santa Anna surrendered. No sooner had Trist begun peace negotiations with a provisional government in October than he received word of his recall. Polk had decided that the presence of a permanent envoy in Scott's camp was being interpreted as a sign of weakness by the Mexicans. Both his Mexican counterparts and Scott advised Trist to ignore the recall and to proceed with negotiations while conditions were opportune.

Following an extended dialogue, U.S. and Mexican representatives signed the Treaty of Guadalupe-Hidalgo on February 2, 1848. Mexico was forced to cede California and the New Mexico territory outright. In addition, the Mexicans recognized the Rio Grande as the southern boundary of Texas. In return, the United States agreed to pay $15 million to Mexico and assume $3.25 million worth of claims by American citizens against the Mexican government.

Polk was outraged by Trist's insubordination, but there were compelling reasons against outright repudiation of the treaty and its negotiator. First and most important, the terms of the Treaty of Guadalupe-Hidalgo conformed roughly to Polk's instructions. If he disowned it, the United States might not be able to negotiate a new one that was as favorable. Second, the Whigs, who had captured control of the House of Representatives in 1846, were in open rebellion against the war. In January 1848 that body resolved 85 to 81 that the war had been "unnecessarily and unconstitutionally begun by the President of the United States." Polk feared that if he did not act, Congress might actually cut off funding for troops in the field. Third, and somewhat contradictorily, Polk was, in early 1848, trying to spike the guns of an "All Mexico Movement." Intoxicated by U.S. military victories, extreme exponents of manifest destiny had begun a drive for the annexation of the entire country. The president recognized that the United States could not digest such a large morsel, and that any effort to do so would lead to prolonged guerrilla warfare. After Polk brought ultra-expansionists within his own party to heel, the Senate voted on March 10, 1848, to approve the Treaty of Guadalupe-Hidalgo by a vote of 38 to 14. Polk's war for empire had come to a successful military, strategic, and economic if not moral conclusion.

FIGURE 9–2
The Overland Trails, 1846

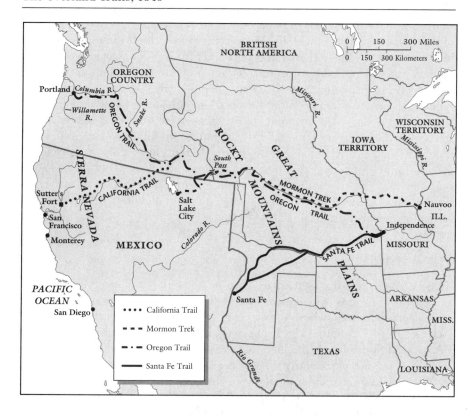

THE OVERLAND TRAILS

The achievements of American diplomats and soldiers opened the gates to a flood of immigrants from the East to Oregon and California. Before 1841 only a handful of settlers made the hard and dangerous trip across the Great Plains and Rocky Mountains to California and Oregon. In 1843 more than eight hundred migrated to the Great Northwest, and by 1845, five thousand white and black Americans lived in California and some three thousand in Oregon. With the discovery of gold in California in 1849, those numbers increased dramatically. Pioneers followed two main paths to the west coast. The overland trails crossed the northern Great Plains, followed the Platte River through Wyoming, divided into the Oregon, Mormon, and California Trails, and then crossed the Rockies. The Santa Fe Trail traversed northern New Mexico and southern Utah but because of the harsh, arid climate was not as frequently used (see Figure 9-2).

PREPARING FOR THE TRIP

Most of those who gathered in St. Joseph or Independence, Missouri, or Council Bluffs, Iowa, were members of families; indeed, many were newlyweds. Because of the hardships involved with the journey, the elderly rarely attempted the trip. Most adults ranged in age between twenty and fifty. Nor did the way west attract the very poor. The wagon, six oxen, 160 pounds of flour, 60 pounds of bacon, 40 pounds of sugar, 25 pounds of dried fruit, clothing, and other supplies that were required to sustain a family of four for the six-month journey cost a minimum of six hundred dollars. The economic burden was made somewhat lighter by the knowledge that pioneers could sell their wagon and oxen, if they survived, for as much as four hundred dollars at trail's end. Migrants almost always traveled in groups. In the early days, wagon trains might include as many as forty wagons, but after 1845 the usual number was eight to ten. Male members of the wagon train usually hired a guide or "pilot," often a retired mountain man, drew up a semimilitary constitution, and elected a leader.

THE WAY WEST

These pioneer expeditions tried to leave in April after the heavy rains which turned the trail into a quagmire, but in time to cross the mountains before winter set in. The typical train traveled fifteen miles a day as it moved through Nebraska and Wyoming. The trip across the plains past Chimney Rock and Scotts Bluff and through the last military outpost, Fort Laramie, was tedious and tiring but not particularly dangerous. Trains tried to make the South Pass in Wyoming by July in order to allow passage through the mountains before the first snows fell. The last third of the trip was the most difficult. The trail followed the Snake River through southern Idaho, a long dusty journey which featured increasingly rough terrain. Pioneers then had to traverse Oregon's Blue Mountains and, if they were successful, raft down the mighty Columbia. For river crossings, settlers had to dismantle their wagons and float them across the body of water on log rafts. Humans and animals frequently drowned.

Those going to California had to cross the virtually waterless Humbolt Sink in northern Nevada and then climb up and over the Sierra Nevada mountains. Grades were so steep that the teams of oxen had to be doubled or tripled to pull the wagons. Descents were even harder. The wagons had no brakes, so to prevent a runaway drivers frequently locked the wheels or secured their vehicles to trees and lowered them. Those who did not beat winter through the mountains often suffered a terrible fate. Members of the Donner party, for example, became snowed in and had to resort to cannibalism.

THE AMBIVALENCE OF NATIVE AMERICANS

Chances for attack from hostile Indians were also greatest during the last third of the trip, but such raids were never as frequent or extensive as popular

The traffic on the Overland Trails was immense. A present-day picture of ruts left on the Oregon Trail one hundred years ago.

literature and the movies portrayed them. Indeed, during the entire migration in which as many as five hundred thousand whites followed the Overland Trails no more than four hundred Indians and the same number of settlers died as a result of armed conflict. Most settlers never saw a hostile native; the Indians they encountered usually either ignored them or offered to help them find grass and water for their livestock. Indeed, the Sioux and other Plains Indians were far more interested in acquiring blankets, guns, and livestock through trade with the settlers than in killing them. The principal threat posed by Native Americans was theft. Young braves trained to steal ponies from rival tribes saw no reason why inhabitants of the wagon trains should be exempt.

Migrants from the East did great damage to the natives' environment, scaring off game, killing buffalo, and depleting the grasslands. Indeed, ruts from wagons driven a hundred years ago may still be seen today on the prairie and over rocky crags. In 1846 the Sioux petitioned the federal government to make compensation for damage to their hunting grounds. When that effort produced no results, they began charging settlers who passed through their territory a toll. In 1851 with traffic on the trail increasing and the number of armed clashes on the rise, federal authorities summoned representatives of various Plains tribes to a conference at Fort Laramie. There, in return for a nominal payment for damage done to their hunting grounds, the Indians agreed to confine themselves to areas north and south of the Overland Trails, thus creating safe corridors through which the settlers could pass.

LIFE ON THE TRAIL

Life on the Oregon and California Trails was characterized by an iron routine that varied only because of illness, accident, or death. Women would rise at four in the morning to prepare breakfast. The men would get up at five, eat, and begin harnessing oxen to the wagons. Males above the age of ten or so walked with the adults guiding the oxen. Women and girls rode until the latter stages of the trip when they would alight to reduce the wagon load and preserve the oxen's diminishing strength. The train stopped at noon for a hurried, cold lunch and then continued the trip until dusk. After finding a suitable spot to camp for the night, the men would circle the wagons for protection and then pasture the livestock. Meanwhile, women gathered dried buffalo chips for fuel, prepared and cooked the evening meal, mended garments, washed dishes and clothes, baked bread, and prepared bedding. After posting guards, the migrants would retire for the night, and then start the routine all over the next day.

Wagons were usually converted farm vehicles covered with canvas supported by staves. A single vehicle could carry enough provisions for a family of four, but because most pioneer couples boasted more than two children and frequently included nephews, aunts, uncles, and cousins, it was not unusual for a family to operate two wagons. Adults usually slept in the wagon for privacy with children housed in a nearby tent.

The principal cause of death, in addition to accident, was cholera, a disease characterized by diarrhea and vomiting and spread through contaminated water. Cholera dehydrated its victims, killing them within a very short period.

The stresses of travel on the Overland Trail sometimes broke up wagon trains and even families, but it generated as much solidarity as discord. Men would drive the wagons of women widowed on the trail, and families would adopt children whose parents had succumbed to illness or accident.

WOMEN AND THE WAGON TRAIN

Life on the Oregon and California Trails was particularly difficult for women because it expanded their workload in quantity and in kind, and it separated them from "civilization," which for women meant more than law, order, and culture. Civilization also meant a permanent home and the traditional domestic female mission. On the trail, there was normally a clear division of labor, with men tending the livestock, driving the wagons, guarding the camp, and doing heavy labor in general. Women washed, cooked, sewed, and bore and nurtured children. When emergencies arose, which they frequently did, women drove and repaired wagons, helped build rafts, and tended livestock. Men rarely ventured into the domestic sphere, however. Nor did the women encourage such transgression; indeed, they guarded their gender-related roles jealously. Most frequent among complaints voiced by women on the trail was the loss of Sunday as a day of rest and worship. Wagon masters generally felt that the train could not afford to lose a day to the looming winter, but women believed

The trip across the Great American Desert required months and an abundance of supplies. The Homesteader *by W.M. Carey, ca. 1850.*

that without a day off, their traditional role as guardians of society's morals and, in fact, the very integrity of the family were threatened.

With the completion of the transcontinental railroad in 1869, travel on the Oregon and California Trails effectively ended, although settlers frequently made trips north and south of the trunk line by wagon. The hundreds of thousands of pioneers who made the trip west remembered it as more dangerous and less tedious than it was. Nevertheless, the six-month trek across the continent was one of American history's great adventures. The pioneers who endured the hardships of the trail and triumphed came to embody what was best about the American spirit: sacrifice, ambition, courage, and cooperative action.

As previously noted, both contemporary critics of the Polk administration's foreign policy and historians of the Mexican War charged that manifest destiny—the notion that America had been singled out by providence to spread the blessings of republicanism across North America—was merely a cover for more mundane material and political motives. Thomas R. Hietala is a recent and comprehensive debunker of nineteenth-century American exceptionalism.

He argues that Polk and company blatantly manipulated ideology, especially America's missionary impulse, to generate popular support for policies designed to serve those occupational groups, vested interests, and bureaucracies that were crucial to the life of the Democratic party.

THE MYTHS OF MANIFEST DESTINY
Thomas R. Hietala

When John O'Sullivan coined the felicitous phrase "manifest destiny" in mid-1845, he provided Americans then and since with an invaluable legitimizing myth of empire. During the final phase of the Texas annexation crisis, he accused the European nations of "hostile interference" in American affairs, "for the avowed object of thwarting our policy and hampering our power, limiting our greatness and checking the fulfillment of our manifest destiny to overspread the continent allotted by Providence for the free development of our yearly multiplying millions." In his justification for American expansion, O'Sullivan reconciled democracy with empire while he implicitly sanctioned the dispossession of all non-Anglo peoples on the continent. During the mid-1840s, he repeatedly stressed that the United States must acquire abundant land for "the free development" of its "yearly multiplying millions"; without territorial expansion the novel experiment in free government and free enterprise might collapse.

The recurring emphasis on material factors in the Democrats' speculations about the need for expansion raises some important questions about the purported idealism of both "Jacksonian Democracy" and manifest destiny. To O'Sullivan and other Democrats, previous territorial acquisitions had been indispensable to the success of the American political and economic system. And though the Jacksonians were convinced of the superiority of popular government, they were much less certain about its viability. Their ambitions for a continental empire represented much more than simple romantic nationalism: they demanded land because they regarded it as the primary prerequisite for republican government and for an economy and society based upon individual acquisitiveness, geographical and social mobility, and a fluid class structure. These beliefs—best expressed by O'Sullivan but

from Thomas R. Hietala, *Manifest Design: Anxious Aggrandizement in Late Jacksonian America* (Ithaca: Cornell University Press, 1985), 255–272.

articulated by other Democrats as well—were crucial to most Jacksonian policies, especially those promoting territorial and commercial expansion. To consider manifest destiny in the context of such principles of political economy is a way of making more comprehensible the sustained drive for empire in the 1840s.

Misconceptions about manifest destiny still influence Americans' impressions about their nation's history. Although the civil rights struggle and the Vietnam War have led many Americans to question several of the prevailing orthodoxies of United States history, popular attitudes about the country's past—the self-concept of Americans and their definition of their nation's role in world affairs—have shown a remarkable resiliency, despite the challenges of revisionist scholars. Prevailing ideas about westward expansion are inextricably linked to the values associated with American exceptionalism and mission, fundamental components of the Jacksonian creed. The persistence of manifest destiny ideology under radically different political, economic, and military realities since the 1840s attests to the significant impact these legitimizing myths of empire have had on popular beliefs about United States history. Since continental expansion gave birth to and nurtured so many nationalistic myths, a reevaluation of the historical circumstances that spawned them is an essential exercise in the reassessment of the American past.

Complicating any separation of historical myth from historical actuality is the confusion surrounding the concept of territorial expansion as a policy implemented by national leaders and the concept of the frontier experience as a spontaneous process initiated by pioneers. Long before Frederick Jackson Turner began studying the evolution of a frontier area from "savagery" to "civilization," Americans speculated about the significance of westward expansion upon their institutions and character as well as about its effects upon the world at large. In their own minds, Americans believed that their progress provided a beacon light to a world in darkness. Moreover, though the ever-expanding frontier represented a process quintessentially American, it was also a process with ramifications for people across the Atlantic. From the very beginning of British settlement in North America, the expanding frontier and its pioneer inhabitants were as influential in historical development as were the seat of empire and its imperial officials. This preoccupation with the frontier and its impact on American character and destiny became even more pronounced after the Revolution, then reached new heights during the Jacksonian era. Images of mountain men, freedom fighters at the Alamo, wagon caravans, and prospectors rushing to California appeal more to romantic sensibilities than Calhoun's dispatches, Walker's propaganda, or Polk's devious manipulations to gain title to the Spanish borderlands. The frontiersmen deserve the pages of print that have been devoted to them, though theirs is but half the story. The epic quality of the pioneers' adventures lends sanctity to American expansion and obscures the actual dynamics of empire building. Pioneers alone did not take possession of the continent, nor did policy makers alone acquire it. Two complementary assaults by national leaders and individual pioneers achieved a continental empire during the mid-1840s.

Jacksonians exalted the pioneer as the epitome of the common man, and they celebrated American expansion as an integral part of their mission to obtain a better nation and a better world based on individual freedom, liberalized international trade, and peaceful coexistence. The Democrats equated American progress with global progress and repeatedly argued that European oligarchs were actually opposing the interests of their own people by trying to discourage the expansion of the United States. Geographically and ideologically separated from Europe, the United States, under Jacksonian direction, tried to improve its democratic institutions, utilize the land's rich resources, and demonstrate to the world the superiority of a system allowing free men to compete in a dynamic society. Consequently, the impact of the pioneering process transcended the concerns of the frontiersmen. In forming "a more perfect union" on a continually expanding frontier, Americans thought that they were actually serving the cause of all mankind.

Such a melding of exceptionalism and empire permitted the Jacksonians the luxury of righteous denunciation of their critics at home and abroad. Their domestic foes could be paired with European monarchs as spokesmen for an old order of aristocracy, privilege, and proscription; American expansionism and the Jacksonian domestic program, on the other hand, represented the antithesis of traditional systems. Since territorial acquisitions and Democratic policies fostered opportunity and democracy, they liberated men from oppressive social and economic relationships. The Jacksonians' program promised so much for so little; no wonder messianic imagery appeared so frequently in their rhetoric.

Skeptical Whigs often challenged the Democrats' sincerity, however, sensing that the Jacksonians' motives for aggrandizement were more selfish than they usually admitted. The Democrats' rhetoric proved more resilient than the Whigs' trenchant criticisms of "manifest destiny," however, and so subsequent generations of Americans have underestimated the extent and the intensity of opposition to the policies behind expansionism in the 1840s, especially the Mexican War. Enduring misconceptions about the period have not only obscured the complexities of territorial and commercial expansion during the late Jacksonian era; they have also contributed to an erroneous impression of American history during the entire century from the close of the War of 1812 to the entry of the United States into World War I. A reassessment of these misconceptions shows a greater continuity between nineteenth- and twentieth-century foreign policy than is customarily supposed. The myths of manifest destiny perpetuate an unwarranted nostalgia for times past and conceal some of the striking similarities between the past and the present. The splendid half-century of American isolation and expansion had a darker side, too. . . .

The expansionism of the 1840s acquires a new significance, however, when it is considered within the context of the cultural, social, and political factors that motivated the Jacksonians to pursue a continental empire. In promoting the acquisition of new lands and new markets, the Democrats greatly exaggerated the extent of European hostility to the United States and refused to admit the duplicity and brutality behind their own efforts to expand their nation's territory and trade. By joining their concepts of exceptionalism and empire, the expansionists found a rationale for denying to all other nations and peoples, whether strong or weak, any right to any portion of the entire North American continent. If a rival was strong, it posed a threat to American security and had to be removed; if a rival was weak, it proved its inferiority and lent sanction to whatever actions were taken by pioneers or policy makers to make the territory a part of the United States.

The confusion surrounding expansion results in part from the ambivalence of the Jacksonians themselves, who demonstrated both compassion and contempt in their policies, depending on the racial and ethnic identities of the peoples to be affected by Democratic measures. Generous and humane toward impoverished Americans and poor immigrants from Europe, the Democrats showed far less concern for nonwhites whom they dispossessed or exploited in the process of westward expansion and national development. Removal, eclipse, or extermination—not acculturation and assimilation—awaited the Indians, blacks, and mixed-blood Mexicans on the continent. Despite occasional statements to the contrary, the expansionists regarded the incorporation of nonwhite peoples into the country as both unlikely and undesirable. Without hint of hypocrisy the Jacksonians sought lenient naturalization laws and opportunities for newcomers while strenuously defending policies to separate Indians and Mexicans from their lands and programs to relocate blacks to Africa and Central America.

When expansionists did express concern for nonwhites, they did not question the basic assumptions behind racial proscription and dispossession. They trusted masters to treat their slaves humanely; they urged that the federal government compensate Indians adequately for their territorial cessions. Few expansionists, however, could see any alternative to the removal or extermination of Indians or the enslavement or proscription of blacks. Indians had no legitimate claim to land; blacks no legitimate claim to freedom. Even Free-Soilers who opposed the extension of slavery had little sympathy for the slave, arguing, in essence, that black freedom was detrimental to white status. The racism in Washington was matched by racism on the frontier: pioneers in both Oregon and California adopted restrictive measures in the late 1840s to discourage or prohibit the migration of free blacks to the far West.

The expansion to the Pacific was not primarily an expression of American confidence. Anxiety, not optimism, generally lay behind the quest for land, ports, and markets. A powerful combination of fears led the neo-Jeffersonians of the 1840s to embrace territorial and commercial expansionism as the best means of warding off both domestic and foreign threats to the United States. The Jacksonians were proponents of laissez-faire only in a limited sense, and their sustained efforts to acquire land and markets were their equivalents for what they saw as the Whigs' dangerous propensity to meddle in the domestic economy. Rather than give an "artificial" stimulus to the economy through protective duties or privileged charters, the Democrats preferred to assist American producers by means of territorial acquisitions, reciprocity treaties, improvements in the navy, and a liberal land policy. Frightened by rapid modernization in the United States, the Democrats warned that both European monarchs and the Whig opposition were threatening the Republic— the Europeans by their attempts to contain American expansion, the Whigs by their resistance to Jacksonian foreign policy and their support of legislation that would hasten industrialization, urbanization, and class polarization in the United States.

Jeffersonian ideology, especially its romantic agrarianism, its fear of industrialization, and its conviction that the United States had a natural right to free trade, contributed significantly to the ideology of manifest destiny. To the Jeffersonians and Jacksonians, American farms raised good republican citizens as well as corn, cotton, and wheat: cultivated fields produced virtuous, cultivated people. Whatever the realities of the late Jacksonian period, the expansionists insisted that agricultural societies fostered opportunity and political equality, the essential features of American uniqueness. Moreover, the neo-Jeffersonians contended that only industrial nations became international predators; agricultural countries were self-contained and did not need colonies or privileged markets. These misconceptions cloak some of the more unflattering aspects of antebellum economy and society: slavemasters, not sturdy yeomen, dominated the social and political life of the South; the country's most important export crops, cotton and tobacco, were produced by forced labor; Indians were cruelly dispossessed of their lands and often their culture to make room for American producers; "go-ahead" Americans frequently seemed more interested in land speculation schemes than in patient tilling of the soil; and the United States, like other empires, did prey upon other peoples and nations to augment its wealth, power, and security.

The fact that the United States acquired contiguous rather than noncontiguous territory makes American aggrandizement no less imperial than that of other empires of the mid–nineteenth century. The United States enjoyed several advantages that facilitated its enlargement and made it more antiseptic. Mexico's weakness, the inability of Indian tribes to unite and resist dispossession, the decline of France and Spain as colonizing powers in the New World, and geographical isolation from Europe all served the interests of the United States as it spread across the continent. In addition, the preference for an anticolonial empire embodied in the concept of a confederated Union also contributed to American success. But many Democrats wanted to venture beyond the continent, and had the party not become so divided during and after the Mexican War, the Polk administration probably would have taken steps to add Yucatán and Cuba to the United States, thereby extending the empire into the Caribbean.

The urge to expand beyond the continent was diminished by the fact that the continent itself was incredibly rich in resources. Those abundant resources provided the basis for unparalleled economic growth at home and power in relations with countries abroad. The expansionists regarded the nation's productivity as an irresistible weapon that could counterbalance the military strength of Europe. Here, again, an old Jeffersonian perception dating back to the 1790s came into play: the world desperately needed American commerce and would sacrifice a great deal to obtain it. Although the expansionists never had cause to drive the masses of Europe to starvation and revolution through an embargo on grain and cotton, their speculations on the subject showed them to be far more imperial than philanthropic in their attitudes toward their nation's wealth.

Distressed by many trends in American life, the Democrats formulated their domestic and foreign policies to safeguard themselves and their progeny from a potentially dismal future. They hoped to prevent domestic disturbances by acquiring additional territory and markets. Other measures were also devised to protect the country from various perils: the Democrats discouraged the growth of manufacturing and monopolistic banking, attempted to minimize the conflict over slavery, encouraged the sale and settlement of the national domain, and tried to discredit the efforts of dissidents to form third parties that might jeopardize the two-party system.

During the 1840s, then, national security was not "free," nor was it attained without constant effort. The expansionists utilized propaganda, personal vendetta, legislative legerdemain, confidential agents, covert military pressure, and offensive war to achieve their goals. The Jacksonians, in fact, felt as insecure in their world as their heirs felt in the 1940s, when the Soviet threat called forth a policy of ambitious containment. The insecurity of the 1840s prompted attempts to enlarge the United States; the insecurity of the Cold War prompted policies to hem in the Soviet Union. In both cases, anxiety was a major factor behind American actions.

Another myth of manifest destiny concerns the role of military power in American expansion. On May 11, 1846, President Polk informed Congress that "after reiterated menaces, Mexico has passed the boundary of the United States, has invaded our territory and shed American blood upon the American soil." War had begun, Polk observed, in spite of "all our efforts to avoid it." Much evidence, however, raises doubts about just how hard Polk tried to prevent war. Six weeks before Polk's war message, for example, Captain William S. Henry, a subordinate commander in Taylor's army en route to the city of Matamoras, noted in his journal, "Our situation is truly extraordinary: right in the enemy's country (to all appearance), actually occupying their corn and cotton fields, the people of the soil leaving their homes, and we, with a small handful of men, marching with colors flying and drums beating, right under the very guns of one of their principal cities, displaying the star-spangled banner, as if in defiance, under their very nose." This army's purpose was not limited to the defense of Texas. It is true that the United States claimed the Rio Grande as the border; it is also true that the United States, in the person of James K. Polk, claimed that the nation had a "clear and unquestionable" title to Oregon up to 54°40'. But the issue for the Polk administration was not the validity of various boundary claims, but rather the issue of whether military pressure could force Mexico to relinquish the disputed territory between the Nueces and Rio Grande, and the undisputed territories of New Mexico and California besides. The Democrats chose war to defend an unclear and questionable title in the Southwest but retreated from a supposedly clear and unquestionable title in the Northwest. The hypocrisy did not escape the Whigs.

The war promised other benefits as well. Slidell encouraged the Polk administration to prosecute the war with vigor. "The navy should have an opportunity to distinguish itself," Slidell counseled after Taylor's army had already won its laurels. "The people *must* have something to huzza about." Americans rushed by the thousands to fight in Mexico, and several congressmen begged Polk for commissions to command them. The bloodshed elevated to prominence the next two elected presidents, Taylor and Pierce, as well as the future president of the Confederacy, Jefferson Davis. In Senator Benton's words, "gunpowder popularity" often served as "the passport to the presidency" at this time. Benton himself urged Polk to name him supreme commander in Mexico: the precedent of Jackson's meteoric rise to eminence through the killing of redcoats and redskins was not lost on ambitious Democrats. Benton did not become supreme commander and he never attained the presidency. To Polk's chagrin, the war's two most celebrated generals, Taylor and Winfield Scott, turned out to be Whigs. Contrary to the Democrats' expectations, the war did not help their party at the polls.

In contrast to the turmoil of the 1850s and the ordeal of the Civil War and Reconstruction, the 1840s appear in history books as years of stunning success. Within a thousand days the United States acquired its continental empire, adding vast territories at an unprecedented rate. After World War II, several historians who studied westward expansion depicted the 1840s as a golden age in American diplomacy, a time when enlightened self-interest and adequate power and resolve to attain it guided United States foreign policy. Norman Graebner so assessed the decade, contending in 1955 that expansion to the Pacific "was a unified, purposeful, precise movement that was ever limited to specific maritime objectives. . . . It was . . . through clearly conceived policies relentlessly pursued that the United States achieved its empire on the Pacific," he concluded. Another prominent postwar scholar, Arthur M. Schlesinger, described Polk as "undeservedly one of the forgotten men of American history." Polk declared "certain definite objectives" for his term and achieved them all: a reduced tariff, an Independent Treasury, and the acquisition of Oregon and California. "By carrying the flag to the Pacific he gave America her continental breadth and ensured her future significance in the world," Schlesinger noted. Many postwar scholars who had witnessed the rise and fall of fascism only to face another menace in Cold War communism understandably assessed manifest destiny chiefly in terms of how the acquisitions had increased the wealth and power of the United States, equipping it to counter totalitarian regimes a century later. This perspective enhanced the reputations of the expansionists.

The Cold War view of manifest destiny is instructive not only for what it asserts but also for what it neglects or ignores. American policy makers in the 1840s did define the national interest in terms of acquiring land and markets, and they did find various ways to attain their ambitions. In fact, rarely have two presidents acted as audaciously as Tyler and Polk to overcome foreign and domestic opposition to their policies. The cavalier methods of the expansionists during the mid-1840s often appalled contemporaries such as the poet Emerson. "The name of Washington City in the newspapers is every day a blacker shade," he lamented in 1847, "all the news from that quarter being of a sadder type, more malignant. It seems to be settled that no act of honour or benevolence or justice is to be expected from the American government, but only this, that they will be as wicked as they dare." Cold War scholars, however, were often no more squeamish about the methods of aggrandizement than the expansionists themselves had been. Unlike Emerson and the antiwar Whigs, they seemed to accept the idea that the end justified the means.

A more detached analysis of the history of the 1840s—one less influenced by Cold War assumptions about the positive effects of nineteenth-century expansion—demonstrates how high a price was paid for the acquisitions. The expansionists' shortcomings and mistakes were as historically significant as their much touted strengths and accomplishments, for even when they attained their immediate goal, it seldom lived up to their long-term expectations. They acquired a continental empire but could not govern it. Too certain that their political institutions could resolve fundamental internal divisions and too complacent about the mounting sectional rancor over the expansion of slavery, the Democrats failed to integrate the new acquisitions into the Union and failed to keep the Union itself intact. No triumphs of technology—no quantity of railroads, steamships, telegraphs, and rotary presses—could sustain the expansive confederation. Limitations on expansion did exist, though the Democrats seemed incapable of discerning them during the 1840s. Their perceptions of the past and their fears for the future blinded them to perils in the realignment of sections and politics.

The expansionists' far-fetched notions about nonwhites precluded their thinking constructively about racial questions. By denying the likelihood of a permanent black and Indian population on the continent, antebellum Americans had difficulty preparing themselves and their descendants for racial heterogeneity in the United States. The acceptance of racial diversity as a reality of national life came largely through necessity, not choice. As most European visitors realized, racial prejudice permeated the country and transcended the sectional dispute over slavery. Americans, however, hardly seemed to question the intense racial animus across the nation; it was such a commonplace of life that it drew only isolated comment or criticism. There were many gradations of racial feeling among Americans, of course, and a small corps of radical abolitionists indicted the North for its failure to practice racial egalitarianism in the free states. But there is no denying that racial prejudice was a basic determinant of American domestic and foreign policy during the Jacksonian period.

The expansionists' ethnocentrism also sowed the seeds of future discord between the United States and the peoples of Latin America. The annexation of Texas and the Mexican War created a legacy of suspicion and anger toward the United States among peoples south of the Rio Grande. However much the United States professed to be a "good neighbor" to other countries in the hemisphere, those countries often held more ambivalent views. This tension has complicated United States relations with Latin America for well over a century and persists to the present. During much of its history the United States has reserved its diplomacy for European countries. Usually a distinct lack of diplomacy has characterized relations with Indians, Asians, and Latin Americans. . . .

Bayonet diplomacy (or "big stick" diplomacy) did not originate with Theodore Roosevelt and his interventionism in Latin America. Though not usually so described, the war against Mexico was the first instance of gunboat diplomacy. When a writer for the *Democratic Review* justified the invasion and occupation of Mexico in 1847, for example, he anticipated Roosevelt's 1904 corollary to the Monroe Doctrine. "It is an acknowledged law of nations," the *Review* writer maintained, "that when a country sinks into a state of anarchy, unable to govern itself, and dangerous to its neighbors, it becomes the *duty* of the most powerful of those neighbors to interfere and settle its affairs." Acting upon such assumptions, the United States has been doing its "duty" in Latin America for almost 140 years.

In many respects the expansionists' outlook turned out to be strikingly unrealistic. The United States was hardly overcrowded in the early 1840s: millions of acres within the existing national domain remained to be occupied and cultivated. Racial fears were also exaggerated. When southern slaves attained their freedom in 1865, no war between blacks and whites ensued. After the Civil War, scores of large cities and hundreds of factories and corporations spread across the country, yet democratic institutions and capitalism survived the transformation. Despite the undeniable hardships and radical adjustments precipitated by rapid industrialization, few Americans would argue that manufacturing weakened rather than strengthened the United States. The Democrats also overestimated the hostility of Britain. The British ministry acquiesced in the annexation of Texas; it did not incite Mexico to make war upon the United States; and it did not try to acquire California before the United States seized it in 1846. Several major premises behind the expansion of the late Jacksonian period proved erroneous.

The decade of the 1840s should be placed in a different historical context: United States policy in this crucial decade prepared the way for both late-nineteenth-century and twentieth-century imperialism. The expansion of the Tyler-Polk years, like that of the 1890s, grew largely out of a recurring domestic malaise that found expression in American aggrandizement. During both decades, ambitious and anxious policy makers welcomed war and expansion as alternatives to basic structural changes in American economics and politics. The methods of American foreign policy also suggest continuities over time. The tactics employed by Tyler and Polk to expand the empire suggest that the label "imperial presidency" should not be confined to presidents of the Cold War era: Polk, especially, acted as imperially as any of his twentieth-century successors. Democratic process and an aggressive foreign policy were as incompatible in the mid–nineteenth century as in the twentieth, as congressional critics frequently noted. In late 1846, for example, Whig Garrett Davis pointed out that the founding fathers had "entrusted to the president the national shield," but they had intentionally given the national sword and "the entire war power" to Congress. "To make war is the most fearful power exerted by human government," Davis warned, a power too momentous to be placed in any one man's hands. That admonition was out of fashion for two decades after World War II, but Vietnam gave it new meaning. In the 1840s and in the 1960s, Congress was remiss in its responsibility to scrutinize how American military power was used, for what purposes, and under what pretenses. In both cases a scheming president misled Congress into sanctioning a wider war than anticipated. Though Congress does delay while it deliberates, there are also drawbacks in granting the president the nation's sword as well as its shield: the skirmish on the Rio Grande, the attack in the Gulf of Tonkin, and, more recently, the meddling in Nicaragua, El Salvador, and Lebanon attest to that.

Orthodox historical "truths" possess considerable resiliency. By extolling the virtues and achievements of a self-conscious people, they appeal to nationalistic feeling, and through constant repetition they acquire an aura of unquestioned certainty over time. The idealism of westward expansion embodied in the concept of manifest destiny persists because it helps to reconcile American imperialism with an extremely favorable national image. The assumed benevolence and the supposedly accidental nature of American expansion are convenient evasions of the complexities of the past. In accepting the rhetoric of American mission and destiny, apologists for the expansionists of the 1840s have had to minimize or ignore much historical evidence. Perhaps more to the point, defenders of American exceptionalism and innocence have actually had to slight other crucial motives for expansion that the Democrats themselves often candidly admitted.

Though the phrase *manifest destiny* appears repeatedly in the literature of American foreign relations, it does not accurately describe the expansionism of the 1840s. It is one of many euphemisms that have allowed several generations of Americans to maintain an unwarranted complacency in regard to their nation's past, a complacency that has contributed in a fundamental way to the persistent quandary the United States has faced in trying to define a realistic role for itself in a world that seldom acts according to American precepts. Geographical isolation and a powerful exceptionalist ideology have insulated the United States from the complexities of culture and historical experience affecting other peoples, leaving Americans susceptible to myths and misconceptions at home and abroad. Often unaware of their own history, Americans frequently misunderstand foreign cultures and experiences as well. Myths and misconceptions often fill the void created by ignorance of history.

The expansionists of the 1840s should not be permitted to expropriate many of the best Americans ideals for their own purposes. Just as they manipulated the Census of 1840, the Democratic convention of 1844, and the Mexican-Texas border dispute for their own ends, so too did they exploit American exceptionalist ideology to ennoble their ambitions for riches and dominion. But rhetoric could not hide the chauvinism, aggressiveness, and design that were essential components of continental expansion. The United States used many tactics to expand its domain, and like other empires it created legitimizing myths to sanction that expansion. Some Americans, however, challenged the validity of those myths and condemned the conduct they excused. But critics of national policy seldom reach generations other than their own, for history—especially American history—often records only the dominant voices of the past. That the United States has changed dramatically since attaining its continental empire is obvious. That the American people have reassessed their basic assumptions about themselves, their national experience, and their approach to other nations is not so obvious.

Since impressions about the past affect consciousness in the present and help define possibilities for the future, the way in which historical events are interpreted significantly influences the ongoing process of defining national identity, national character, and national purpose. Because history involves both continuity and change over time, a historical work serves two crucial purposes: it provides a window to the past, and it furnishes a mirror to the present. However striking the changes in American life since the Jacksonian era, the persistence of certain principles and biases—the consistency of much of American political and diplomatic "culture" over several generations—ties the present to the past, and links both to the future. For that reason the legacy of the 1840s should be of concern to all Americans—not just historians.

SUGGESTED READINGS

General

John Mack Faragher, *Women and Men on the Overland Trail* (1979) and *Sugar Creek* (1987).

William H. Goetzmann, *When the Eagle Screamed: The Romantic Horizon in American Diplomacy, 1800–1860* (1966).

Norman A. Graebner, *Empire on the Pacific: A Study in American Continental Expansion* (1955).

Reginald Horsman, *Race and Manifest Destiny: The Origins of American Anglo-Saxonism* (1981).

Frederick Merk, *Slavery and the Annexation of Texas* (1972).

David M. Pletcher, *The Diplomacy of Annexation: Texas, Oregon, and the Mexican War* (1973).

David J. Weber, *The Mexican Frontier, 1821–1846: The American Southwest Under Mexico* (1982).

Richard White, *"It's Your Misfortune and None of My Own": A History of the American West* (1991).

FURTHER READINGS

Lure of the Western Lands

Jennifer S.H. Brown, *Strangers in Blood: Fur Trade Company Families in Indian Country* (1980); William H. Goetzmann, *Exploration and Empire: The Explorer and the Scientist in the Winning of the American West* (1966); and Frederick Merk, *History of the Westward Movement* (1978).

Monroe Doctrine

Ernest R. May, *The Making of the Monroe Doctrine* (1975); and Dexter Perkins, *The Monroe Doctrine, 1823–1826* (1927).

Manifest Destiny

Charles H. Brown, *Agents of Manifest Destiny: The Lives and Times of Filibusters* (1980); Frederick Merk, *Manifest Destiny and Mission in American History: A Reinterpretation* (1963); and Albert K. Weinberg, *Manifest Destiny: A Study of Nationalist Expansionism in American History* (1935).

Oregon

Malcolm Clark, Jr., *Eden Seekers: The Settlement of Oregon, 1812–1862* (1981); James R. Gibson, *Farming the Frontier: The Agricultural Opening of Oregon Country, 1786–1846* (1985); and Frederick W. Merk, *The Oregon Question: Essays in Anglo-American Diplomacy and Politics* (1967).

War with Mexico

Gene M. Brack, *Mexico Views Manifest Destiny* (1976); Robert W. Johannsen, *To the Halls of the Montezumas: The Mexican War in the American Imagination* (1985); and John H. Schroeder, *Mr. Polk's War: American Opposition and Dissent, 1846–1848* (1973).

Overland Trails

Sandra L. Myres, *Westering Women and the Frontier Experience, 1800–1915* (1982); James J. Rawls, *Indians of California: The Changing Image* (1984); and Kevin Starr, *Americans and the California Dream, 1850–1915* (1973).

QUESTIONS FOR DISCUSSION

1. What measures did the federal government employ to promote western migration?
2. Why did the United States seek additional lands in Spanish territory? Analyze the consequences of Andrew Jackson's exploits in Florida.
3. Identify the international events leading to the Monroe Doctrine. Why did Europe seemingly acquiesce in American demands?
4. Why were the annexations of Texas and Oregon so controversial?
5. Describe daily life on the western trail. Pay particular attention to women's attitudes toward the frontier experience.
6. According to Thomas R. Hietala, the concept of manifest destiny cloaked the nation's real motivations for territorial expansion. Identify and evaluate these motivations.
7. How have historians since World War II interpreted manifest destiny? What contemporary factors have influenced their evaluations?

CHAPTER TEN

"THE PECULIAR INSTITUTION":
Slavery and Society in the
Antebellum South

ELISHA WORTHINGTON: PLANTER

By the outbreak of the Civil War in 1861, Elisha Worthington, a native of Kentucky, had become one of the wealthiest cotton planters in the South. Like his older brothers, he migrated southwestward in search of wealth. His brothers settled in Mississippi where they became prosperous cotton planters and ultimately built mansions that stood as visible monuments to their status and wealth. Elisha joined them briefly, but in 1838 or 1839 crossed the Mississippi River into Chicot County, Arkansas, where within twenty years he carved out of the swampy, heavily wooded wilderness a sprawling domain whose acreage, slave labor force, and cotton production had few equals in the South. Whenever a portion of his land became debt-free, Worthington used it as collateral to buy more acreage and slaves. By 1860 he owned 543 slaves and four plantations that embraced 12,500 acres of incredibly fertile land along the Mississippi River. Only thirteen other planters in the South owned over five hundred slaves in that year.

The largest land- and slaveowner in a county in which slaves outnumbered whites by more than three to one in 1860, Worthington possessed an insatiable hunger for land, which meant that he was chronically in debt to individuals and banking houses in New Orleans and Louisville. His single largest loan, acquired in 1858, was in the amount of $294,000. Despite periodic flooding and fluctuations in cotton prices, the productivity of Worthington's ever-expanding acreage and slave labor force made it possible for him to meet his debt obligations. In 1860, for example, his plantations yielded 2,970 bales of cotton, as well as 31,500 bushels of corn and various other products necessary to feed his slaves and numerous cattle, horses, oxen, and mules. His profits also enabled him to build a steam cotton gin and a grist mill and to transform swamps into land suitable for cotton cultivation.

In contrast to absentee planters with extensive cotton lands in Chicot County, Worthington was a year-round resident who lived either at his Sunnyside or Redleaf plantations and usually functioned as his own manager. Unlike his brothers in Mississippi who spent protracted periods in Kentucky to escape the heat and humidity of summers in the lower South, Worthington remained in Chicot County except for short business trips to New Orleans, Louisville, or Cincinnati. On rare occasions and only for brief periods, he employed white overseers, but his was essentially a hands-on management style in which he, as owner of the land and slaves, was involved in the day-to-day operation of his plantations.

His large slave labor force was organized into "gangs" with each gang under the direct supervision of a "driver," who was a slave accountable to Worthington. Although he was protective of his slaves and provided for their basic needs, he extracted from them the maximum labor by enforcing the dawn-to-dusk work routine. Worthington obtained his large number of slaves by purchasing those living on the lands he acquired; in other words, the land and slaves constituted a single purchase. There is no evidence that Worthington ever dealt with slave traders or ever sold any of his slaves. The lack of evidence regarding his use of the whip to discipline recalcitrant slaves does not suggest the absence of physical punishment on his plantations. Regardless of the extent to which punishment was meted out, the threat was always present.

Obsessed by the desire for ever more land, slaves, and cotton, Worthington did not share the concern of some Chicot County planters for a lavish lifestyle. For example, his nearest neighbor and friend, Lycurgus Johnson, also a Kentucky native and a member of Arkansas' most powerful political family, built a residence on his Lakeport Plantation that was a local showplace. In contrast, Worthington's residences at both Sunnyside and Redleaf plantations were simple dwellings adjacent to the slave quarters. These houses were architecturally distinguishable from slave cabins primarily by being larger and slightly more comfortable.

That one of the South's largest planters and slaveowners always lived in such unpretentious residences was undoubtedly related to the fact that he remained single following a brief marriage that ended in divorce. After six months in Chicot County, his wife returned to her home in Kentucky and secured a divorce charging him with adultery. After his divorce and undoubtedly before, Worthington maintained a long-standing relationship with a female slave who gave birth to his two children, a boy and girl. He was an indulgent father who took a special interest in the education of his two children. Although his son and daughter were technically slaves, since children in the antebellum South inherited the "condition" or legal status of the mother rather than the father, Worthington enrolled both in school at Oberlin, Ohio, with instructions that his daughter be educated to "become a lady." He sent his son to a military school in France following two terms at Oberlin. Interracial sex was not uncommon in the slave South, and white planters throughout the region had so-called "shadow families" across the color line. But Worthington differed from most by recognizing his children by a slave woman as his own and accepting his paternal responsibilities.

Notwithstanding his openly biracial household and the absence of an elegant personal residence, Worthington's interest in literature, the arts, and education was probably deeper than that of many of the cotton lords who affected an aristocratic lifestyle. Largely self-educated, he read widely in diverse fields and acquired a personal library of some five thousand volumes. His love of music prompted him to acquire a piano and other musical instruments and to employ an Englishman to organize and direct a band made of his slaves. An amateur horticulturist, he took pride in the exotic plants and flowers that he grew under glass. There is little evidence to suggest that Worthington participated in the social life of the Johnsons, Hilliards, and other cotton aristocrats on nearby plantations, but he cooperated with them on matters of common concern, especially civil stability, social control, and the defense of slavery.

For a time even after the outbreak of the Civil War, Worthington continued to acquire land and to increase his cotton production. When the war came to the lower Mississippi Valley and threatened his Chicot County domain, he was determined to protect one of his largest investments, namely his slaves. In 1862 he organized a caravan of about five hundred slaves, numerous wagons, and farm animals and headed for Texas to escape the Union Army. He left behind only those slaves who were elderly or lame, and placed his mulatto son and daughter in charge of this remnant as well as of his plantations. Joining a host of other planters who took refuge in Texas, he attempted to continue to cultivate cotton as usual, except on leased land.

At the close of the Civil War, Worthington returned to Chicot County accompanied by many of his former slaves who were now freed people. In the postwar era Worthington confronted a new political, economic, and social order and an uncertain future: Slavery had been abolished and his plantations lay in ruins—overgrown by weeds and bushes and exhibiting abundant evidence of the devastation left in the wake of competing armies that traversed them. He adjusted to the new, free labor system by employing some of his former slaves in an arrangement that became known as sharecropping.

Mounting financial problems and failing health led Worthington to dispose of some of his land, notably Sunnyside, his mostly highly prized plantation and the centerpiece of his extensive cotton fiefdom. Elisha Worthington died in 1873, at age sixty-five, and was followed the next year by his son. His net worth, though radically reduced from what it had been prior to the war, was still substantial by the prevailing standards of the time and place. Because he died without a will, the distribution of his estate became the subject of a bitter

A river packet loaded with bales of cotton in the antebellum South.

and protracted legal battle between white relatives and his mulatto daughter who had cared for him and largely managed his affairs during the closing years of his life. The Supreme Court of the United States finally ruled in 1889 that his daughter should share in his estate.

The experience of Elisha Worthington as a planter in what was reputedly the second richest cotton-producing county in the nation is instructive about the society and economy of the antebellum South and the extent to which both were dependent upon and shaped by slavery, the region's "peculiar institution," as southerners termed it. Like many other white southerners and some northerners who migrated into the old Southwest in search of fortune, Worthington participated in the phenomenon known as the westward movement of the cotton kingdom, a movement accelerated by a persistent and popular quest for more and more land on which to grow more and more cotton, a crop that especially thrived in the fertile soil and long growing season of the Mississippi alluvial plain, commonly called the delta. Such quest necessitated acquiring increasing numbers of black men and women as slaves to realize the promise of wealth that cotton cultivation seemed to offer. Like many of the South's wealthy cotton lords, Worthington was a self-made man whose wealth consisted almost entirely of land and slaves. If the ownership of a minimum of twenty slaves entitled one to membership in the planter class, then Worthington's possession of more than twenty-five times that number suggests that he stood at or near the pinnacle of the slave-owning class, a status that he achieved within the two decades (1840–1860) in which southern slave society reached maturity and slaveowners no longer justified their system of human bondage as a necessary evil but rather as a positive good.

ORIGINS AND DEVELOPMENT OF SLAVERY

By the time Worthington purchased his first plantation in Arkansas in 1840, the system of slavery in the South had evolved over two hundred years (see Chapter 3). For several decades after a Dutch ship landed "20 and odd Negroes" at Jamestown in 1619, Africans appeared to have been treated as servants who would be held for a number of years, then freed in a manner similar to that of whites who entered the colonies as indentured servants. For a time their legal and social status remained fluid. Some were freed after a limited period of servitude, and a few became landowners and even slaveowners. But white indentured servants, rather than Africans, satisfied the growing demand for labor, especially in the southern colonies, until the middle of the seventeenth century. Later in the century a drastic decline in the supply of whites willing to enter indentured servitude and the restiveness of those white servants and ex-servants then in the colonies prompted colonists to substitute black labor for white. The British, having achieved naval supremacy among the European imperial powers, assumed dominance over the slave trade and were able to supply colonists with Africans to meet their need for labor. Even though the initial demand for labor may have exhibited little concern with race and color, such a condition no longer prevailed by the late seventeenth century. Beginning in 1661 with a Maryland statute, colonies enacted a succession of measures that legally sanctioned what had become the custom of enslaving blacks. Such statutes, later known as slave codes, made the slave status of Africans perpetual and inheritable, spelled out in detail the restrictions on slaves' activities, and granted white owners almost total authority over the lives of their slaves.

RELATIONSHIP OF SLAVERY AND RACIAL PREJUDICE

The relationship between race and slavery has been the subject of much debate among historians, but the issue, as Peter Kolchin has noted, was not so much whether prejudice caused slavery or slavery caused prejudice, as much as "how slavery and prejudice interacted to create the particular set of social relationships" that came into existence in the English mainland colonies. Steeped in the ways of a hierarchical society and long accustomed to viewing Africans as different—as uncivilized, heathen, and black, a color laden with negative connotations—white colonists found it all the easier to rationalize their own superiority and to justify the enslavement of Africans. Slavery, therefore, was not only a system of forced labor but also represented a set of relationships between whites and blacks increasingly defined by law, as well as custom, that provided the foundation of a caste system based on race.

SLAVERY: NORTH AND SOUTH

While slavery existed throughout the colonies, the North lacked the elements essential to large-scale agriculture, so slaves were never important to its economy. Slavery in the North, therefore, was relatively easy to abolish. In contrast, it thrived in the southern colonies where a lengthy growing season allowed an agricultural economy initially based on tobacco and rice and later on cotton to flourish. The presence of available land and an adequate supply of labor, coupled with Eli Whitney's invention of an efficient cotton gin in 1793 (which eliminated the difficulty of separating the lint from the seed) and the increasing demand of the British textile industry for cotton fiber go far toward explaining the emergence and persistence of cotton's dominance in the South. For the cultivation of cotton the region came to rely on slave labor. The table on page 388 illustrates the expansion of slavery between 1790 and 1860.

SLAVERY IN THE UNITED STATES AND THE CARIBBEAN

Of the 10 or 11 million African slaves brought to the New World from the sixteenth through the nineteenth century most were destined for Brazil and the Caribbean; only 600,000 to 650,000 arrived in what became the United States. Of this number the overwhelming majority was concentrated in the South by 1760. Unlike the slave population elsewhere in the New World, slaves on the North American mainland exhibited higher birthrates and lower mortality rates, owing in part to sufficient food, benign climate, the absence of tropical diseases, and the conditions under which they worked. Therefore, from the relatively small number of slaves introduced to the British mainland colonies, compared with Brazil and the Caribbean islands, there emerged the largest slave population in the Western Hemisphere.

By the end of the colonial era the slave society on the mainland of British America already exhibited patterns that would persist for the next three-quarters of a century and that differentiated it from that which existed in the Caribbean. In addition to being concentrated in the South, because a vast majority of slaves were American-born, they were more familiar with their environment and status. Their acculturation, in a sense, made them more tractable than newly arrived Africans whose constant resistance to a strange land and conditions prompted severe, often brutal, discipline. That slaves were scattered among numerous small slave holdings and surrounded by a large, well armed white population served as deterrents to successful slave revolts. White slaveowners were also American-born and tended to be resident, rather than absentee, masters who had often grown up with their slaves. Throughout the existence of slavery, slaveowners made up a minority of the white population. Such patterns sharply differentiated the mainland slave system from that which existed in the Caribbean.

Slave Population and Distribution, 1790 and 1860

	1790		1860	
United States	697,897	(17.8%)	3,953,760	(12.6%)
North	40,370	(2.1%)	64†	(0.0%)
regional share		5.8%		0.0%
South	657,527	(33.5%)	3,953,696	(32.1%)
regional share		94.2%		100.0%
Upper South	521,169	(32.0%)	1,530,229	(22.1%)
regional share		74.7%		38.7%
Deep South	136,358	(41.1%)	2,423,467	(44.8%)
regional share		19.5%		61.3%
UPPER SOUTH				
Delaware	8,887	(15.0%)	1,798	(1.6%)
Maryland	103,036	(32.2%)	87,189	(12.7%)
D.C.	—		3,185	(4.2%)
Virginia	293,427	(39.2%)	490,865	(30.7%)
North Carolina	100,572	(25.5%)	331,059	(33.4%)
Kentucky	11,830	(16.2%)	225,483	(19.5%)
Missouri	—		114,931	(9.7%)
Tennessee	3,417	(9.5%)	275,719	(24.8%)
DEEP SOUTH				
South Carolina	107,094	(43.0%)	402,406	(57.2%)
Georgia	29,264	(35.5%)	462,198	(43.7%)
Florida	—		61,745	(44.0%)
Arkansas	—		111,115	(25.5%)
Alabama	—		435,080	(45.1%)
Louisiana	16,544*	(51.6%)	331,726	(46.9%)
Mississippi	—		436,631	(55.2%)
Texas	—		182,566	(30.2%)

* In 1785; not included in regional or national totals.

† Includes eighteen lifetime "apprentices" in New Jersey.

From Peter Kolchin, *American Slavery, 1619–1877* (New York: Hill & Wang, 1993), 242.

"A NECESSARY EVIL"

The generation that wrote the Declaration of Independence, waged a successful revolution against Britain, and created the new republic of the United States was the first to question seriously the existence of slavery in its midst. For many Americans the presence of slaves constituted a troublesome and perplexing problem impossible to reconcile with their notions of Christian morality, egalitarian republican ideology, or capitalistic philosophy that stressed a competitive free marketplace and free labor. As a generation steeped in the culture of the

Enlightenment, it professed faith in reason, reform, and progress and spoke eloquently of natural rights, liberty, and human equality.

Even though the Revolutionary Era witnessed the beginning of the end of slavery in the North, increased the number of free blacks owing largely to the relaxation of restrictions on the manumission process, and tempered the harshness of slave life generally, the noble ideals proclaimed in the era were, by and large, applicable only to whites. In fact, the Constitution itself did not include the word *slavery*; even though it provided that three-fifths of the slaves would be counted as the basis for apportioning representatives and direct taxes among the states. The cautious, gradualist approach of the founding fathers to the issue of slavery was clearly underscored by their handling of the question of the African slave trade whose termination they believed would ultimately doom slavery. The Constitution they drafted prohibited the termination of such trade for a period of twenty years with the understanding that Congress would outlaw the importation of slaves at the end of that period.

Slaveowning southerners such as Thomas Jefferson and James Madison were profoundly troubled by the system of human bondage but believed that slavery was a necessary evil whose precipitous eradication would devastate their region. Other southerners saw no contradiction in their simultaneous defense of liberty and slavery, an intellectual feat that antislavery advocates considered sheer hypocrisy. White southerners viewed efforts to abolish slavery as infringements on their most important liberty, the right to own slaves as property. Despite the bold assertions of human freedom and equality during the Revolution and early years of the republic, the slave system in the South remained intact; it especially thrived in the lower South. In no other two decades were so many slaves imported into the country than the two ending in 1807 when Congress outlawed the international slave trade. Most of these new slaves wound up in the lower South, as did many of those of the upper South where a declining tobacco agriculture, further assaulted by the Revolution, had resulted in a surplus of slaves.

FREE PEOPLE OF COLOR

Not all blacks in the South were slaves. Although free blacks lived in the region as early as the mid-seventeenth century, their numbers did not increase dramatically until the era of the American Revolution. The 32,357 free blacks in the region in 1790 increased to 215,576 in 1820, and to 261,918 in 1860 when the South claimed more than half of the nation's total free black population. The free black caste traced its origins to various sources. Some blacks who were indentured servants became free upon completing their terms of service; others achieved freedom through military service in the colonial wars and the American Revolution. Manumissions accounted for a large proportion of the free black population. Those manumitted (or freed) by their white owners were often the natural offspring of the master by a slave mother. As a result a large percentage of free blacks were mixed bloods with substantially lighter complexions than

A view of the battery in antebellum Charleston, South Carolina.

slaves. Another source of the free black caste was self-purchase. Slaves with special skills who were allowed to hire themselves out bought their freedom and sometimes that of family members. Immigrants, especially from the West Indies, also expanded the ranks of the free black class. Once established, especially during and immediately after the American Revolution, the free black caste became the fastest growing element in the southern population by the early nineteenth century, largely as a result of natural increase.

Like slavery, the status of free people of color varied from region to region within the South. Free blacks in the upper and lower South possessed distinctive economic, social, and even complexional characteristics, which meant that their relation with both slaves and whites was different. In the lower South, for example, free blacks thought of themselves as a caste apart from slaves and whites and attached greater significance to color gradations. The concept of the three-caste society was more fully developed in New Orleans, a few other Gulf port cities, and Charleston, South Carolina, than elsewhere in antebellum America. Throughout the South free blacks acquired property and were well represented in the trades, especially in cities. Free blacks created their own churches, beneficial societies, and social and literary organizations. Although the vast majority of free blacks were poor, a few amassed considerable wealth such as Thomy LaFon and Cyprian Ricard in Louisiana, William Johnson in Mississippi, and the Ellison family in South Carolina. It was not unusual for such people to own slaves themselves. Some purchased relatives and friends, others were obviously motivated more by the desire for profit than by benevolence and treated their slaves in much the same way as white masters.

The status of free blacks in the South did not remain static throughout the antebellum era, but rather changed over time. As the slave system matured in the region the state of free blacks deteriorated until they became essentially slaves without masters. Although free blacks could make contracts and own property, they were subject to a wide variety of legal restrictions. The degree to which such restrictions were enforced varied from place to place and from time to time. But legally free blacks could not hold public office, testify against whites, or use firearms. Other laws that restricted their mobility and access to education were not uniformly enforced throughout the South.

As the white South embraced slavery ever more firmly as the cornerstone of its "superior" civilization and justified the slave system on racial grounds, free people of color became increasingly looked upon as an anomaly, as an unwanted people whose presence contradicted the whites' belief that all Africans were divinely ordained to be slaves. Beginning in the mid-1830s whites tended not only to view free blacks as indolent, improvident, and prone to criminality, but also as a menace to the system of slavery itself. Among the most serious accusations levelled at them was their role in fomenting "mischief" and even rebelliousness among otherwise docile slaves. Not surprisingly, existing laws designed to control the free black population were more rigorously enforced, more restrictions were imposed, and privileges once granted to free blacks were withdrawn. As early as 1834 and 1835, Tennessee and North Carolina, two southern states that had allowed free blacks to vote, withdrew the right to suffrage. By the 1850s, many whites in the South advocated getting rid of free blacks by returning them to slavery, arguing that slavery was their natural condition. On the eve of the Civil War several southern states enacted legislation designed to achieve such ends.

MILITANT DEFENSE OF SLAVERY

Retreating from the liberalism of the Revolutionary Era, the South increasingly became an isolated bastion of conservatism and a lonely defender of slavery as the underpinning of its way of life. The intensity of the South's feelings about slavery and its expansion into the trans-Mississippi West was abundantly evident in the controversy in 1819 and 1820 surrounding the admission of Missouri to the Union. Although the Missouri Compromise smoothed over the sectional tensions momentarily, southerners thereafter behaved as an embattled minority ever ready to defend the slave system that their "civilization" rested on and to resist all efforts to restrict its expansion westward. Fully aware that the compromise was only a reprieve and not a permanent solution, ex-president Thomas Jefferson commented on the dilemma that slavery posed for the South: "We have the wolf by the ears, and we can neither hold him nor safely let him go. Justice is in one scale, and self-preservation in the other."

In the wake of a bloody slave insurrection led by Nat Turner, the Virginia legislature defeated a plan for emancipating slaves in the winter of 1831–1832 which represented the last significant effort by white southerners to emancipate slaves. The defeat of the emancipation plan in Virginia was a clear indication of the power that the slave-owning minority exercised throughout the region.

By the 1840s southern spokesmen were displaying little of the ambivalence that characterized the thinking of Jefferson's generation; instead they enthusiastically embraced self-preservation—that is, slavery—rather than justice. Therefore, at the very moment that northern states were completing the emancipation of their slaves and the attack on human bondage was intensifying throughout the Western world, the South's course as a slavocracy appeared to be permanently fixed. The result was the spread throughout the region of a kind of siege mentality in which whites perceived themselves as victims of malevolent forces intent upon denying them the peculiar institution essential to their economy and society.

In 1831, the same year as Nat Turner's insurrection and the Virginia legislature's debate on slavery, William Lloyd Garrison launched *The Liberator* in Boston, an event that signaled the beginning of a movement to abolish slavery that grew in strength and influence over the next three decades (see Chapter 8). As the abolitionist movement gained momentum, so did the southern defense of slavery and resistance to any efforts by Congress to limit its expansion. Riding high on a wave of prosperity between 1840 and 1860, the South witnessed a substantial increase in its slave population as the new cotton lands were opened up in the lower and trans-Mississippi regions. By 1860 slaves made up about one-third of the South's total population of 12 million and represented an enormous investment of capital. Over 61 percent of the region's slaves were concentrated in the lower South by the outbreak of the Civil War.

Practical considerations, then, contributed to the development of elaborate new arguments justifying slavery and the refinement of older ones. A host of southern apologists, including some of the region's best-known writers and intellectuals, defended slavery on historical, sociological, religious, and racial grounds. Slavery, they argued, protected the liberties of whites, prevented blacks from reverting to savagery and paganism, and guaranteed social order and stability. George Fitzhugh, a major proslavery propagandist, even proclaimed that the condition of free white labor in the North was substantially worse than the lot of black slaves in the South whose masters cared for them during illness and old age and in both good and bad economic times. The defenders of slavery received important support from southern clergymen whose insistence that slavery was "ordained by God" was largely responsible for the split of Methodists and Baptists into northern and southern branches.

Such elaborate rationalizations not only constituted a response to abolitionists, but also built support for slaveowners among the white majority who owned no slaves and soothed the conscience of those slaveowners troubled by outside criticism or guilty consciences. White southerners who dared to take exception to the idea of the "positive good" concept of slavery were ostracized and in some cases left the South, as did the Grimké sisters of South Carolina and Hinton Rowan Helper of North Carolina, the author of *The Impending Crisis of the South* (1857). In the closed society that developed in the South in the decades before the Civil War, not only was the region's peculiar institution immune to criticism or even questioning, but the chances of slaves gaining freedom, by manumission or otherwise, also became increasingly difficult. Slavery had indeed become the defining characteristic of the South, a region perceived as distinctive by southerners themselves, no less than by other Americans.

THE CONTOURS OF ANTEBELLUM SOUTHERN SOCIETY

SLAVERY AND SOUTHERN DISTINCTIVENESS

The influence of slavery upon the antebellum South was both profound and pervasive and stood at the heart of the region's distinctiveness. Once a geographical expression, the South early came to be viewed as an eccentric member of the American family. Such a view had become almost universal both inside and outside the South by the late antebellum era, notwithstanding the existence of the common bonds of language, law, religion, and a commitment to republican institutions that united southerners and other Americans. The search for the source of southern distinctiveness that began in the eighteenth century and continues even today has resulted in a wide variety of conclusions that emphasize the region's climate, plantation system, ruralism, or some other attribute as primarily responsible for its sharp divergence from national norms.

But more than anything else, slavery shaped antebellum southern society and culture in ways that differentiated it from the rest of the nation and drove the wedge between North and South which led to the rupture of the Union. Slavery was more than a labor system; it was a racial caste system in which people of African descent were considered inherently inferior and unfit for freedom. The South's peculiar institution not only figured prominently in determining the region's distinctive economy, politics, ideology, and pattern of social behavior; but also profoundly influenced the contours of the region's class structure and undergirded what was called southern culture. The heavy investment in slaves seriously impeded industrialization and urbanization in particular and modernization in general. As a result, travelers regularly described the South as backward and provincial, possessing wretched roads, inadequate railroads, a high illiteracy rate, few public schools, and even fewer media for the dissemination of new ideas such as magazines and region-wide newspapers. Furthermore, the South's preoccupation, even obsession, with defending slavery did more than shut off critical discussions of that particular topic; it tended to restrict freedom of thought generally and tended to make the region unreceptive to new ideas.

For all the rhetoric about the South as if it were a single homogeneous section, there were, in fact, many Souths exhibiting wide variations in geography, topography, climate, agriculture, wealth, and slave populations. Differences existed between the upper and lower South, between hill country and lowlands, and between slaveowning and nonslaveowning whites. Despite all of the historical debate over whether this diverse South was modern or premodern—bourgeois or quasi-feudal—the truth is that it was an amalgam of all of these. The region's planters whose aggressive materialism was remarkably similar to that of northern capitalists were nonetheless different from their contemporaries to the north in their dependence on slave, rather than free labor. In the words of one historian, they juxtaposed commercial activity with a noncapitalistic labor system which accounted for the existence of many of the contradictory features of the slave South.

CLASS STRUCTURE

Historians not only have disagreed over the nature of the South's antebellum economy, but also have long debated the degree to which class antagonisms beset the region's white society. In view of the chasm that appeared to separate the interests of the plain people from those of the slave-owning class, it is scarcely surprising that so much attention has been devoted to this issue. To begin with, it is necessary to understand the minority status of slaveowners: of the 8 million whites in the South in 1860, 2 million (or one-quarter) owned slaves and only forty-six thousand qualified as planters (the owners of twenty or more slaves). Fewer than ten thousand whites owned fifty or more slaves, and to own two hundred or more slaves was exceedingly rare. In fact, 20 percent of the slaveowners possessed only a single slave. Collectively, the slave-owning class in 1860, consisting of 25 percent of the white population, dominated cotton production and owned 61 percent of the South's agricultural wealth, while the average wealth of slaveowners was almost fourteen times greater than that of nonslaveowners who grew little cotton and concentrated on food crops, and lived in small, often crude dwellings (see Figure 10–1).

CLASS TENSIONS

Nonslaveowners, who constituted a majority in the South and claimed political equality, resented the pretensions and arrogance of the slaveowning gentry and complained about the disproportionate political power exercised by the planter elite. But a combination of circumstances helps explain why the nonslaveowning class, despite its numerical superiority, posed so few challenges to the slavocracy after the early 1830s. For one thing, many nonslaveowning whites hoped one day to own slaves themselves, or they had relatives who already owned slaves. For another, those who grew cotton were dependent upon planters to gin and market it. More important was the nature of nonslaveowning whites whose diverse interests and aspirations precluded unified action. Nor was the slaveowners' role in protecting their dominant position negligible. The planter elite clearly understood that the loyalty of nonslaveowning whites, no less than that of black slaves, was essential to maintain their own authority. Their proslavery ideology, expounded in increasing numbers of publications and speeches, struck responsive chords among nonslaveowners by appealing to

FIGURE 10-1

Slavery and Staple Crops in the South, 1860

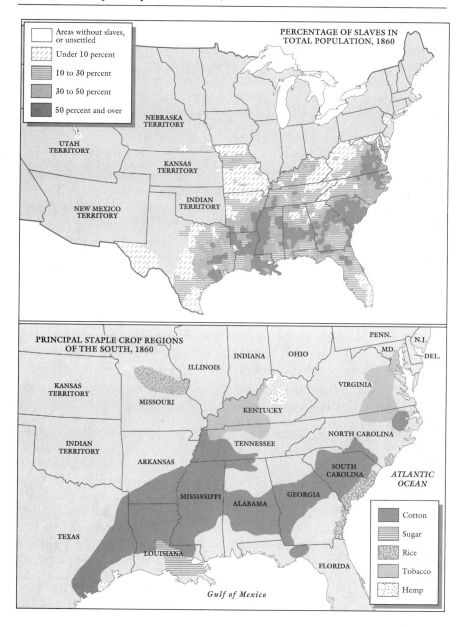

their regional patriotism and manipulating their racism. Blacks, so their argument ran, were inherently inferior beings unsuited for freedom and necessitating rigid control by whites, the master race. Such ideas confirmed the racist fears of nonslaveowning whites who had an especial horror of the prospect of living among a large population of emancipated blacks claiming social equality. Although such a strategy by the slaveowning elite did not eliminate class divisions, it sufficiently muted class tensions to ensure continued dominance by the slavocracy. By 1860 a defense of the South's peculiar institution had become tantamount to a defense of the region itself.

A HIERARCHICAL SOCIETY

The South's slave system spawned a hierarchical society based on paternalism, an ideology defined by one historian as the linking of "dominant and subordinate classes in a complex pattern of mutual responsibilities and obligations." At the head of this hierarchical society was the master of the plantation who claimed not only to adhere to an elaborate code of chivalry and honor but to preside over a peculiarly humane system of bondage. Slaveowners projected the image of benevolent Christian patriarchs who were generous toward all those dependent on them—wives, children, and slaves. They referred to their slaves as "their people," as a component of the slaveowner's household which consisted of those incapable of caring for themselves who required the guidance and control of a beneficent master. Few if any slaveowners succeeded in being both all-powerful masters of their slaves and beloved by them. In important ways, slaveowners became dependent on their slaves.

PLANTATION MISTRESS

No less idealized was the image of the plantation mistresses who were expected to be charming, gracious, and above all chaste complements to their chivalrous, but not particularly pure, husbands whose sexual liaisons with female slaves often strained marital relations. Like northern women, the southern plantation mistress occupied a separate sphere that assigned to her the rearing and educating of children, the management of a complex household and its slave staff, oversight of the health of family members and slaves and the entertainment of guests who sometimes stayed for several weeks. In addition, the plantation mistress was expected to function as the custodian of religion, morality, and culture. Often isolated on remote plantations, planters' wives lived in a private and personal world made up of family members and house slaves. Their social contacts with those outside the household were confined to people of their own class, that is, the upper class.

Chafing under the demands placed on them and the restrictions on their autonomy, more than a few planters' wives privately agreed with Susan Dabney Smedes of Alabama who claimed that a plantation mistress was "the most complete slave" on the plantation. Some plantation mistresses privately admitted that the slave system was a monstrosity; others shared the view of an Arkansas planter's wife who described slaves as "nothing but a tax and annoyance to their owners." Even so, few plantation mistresses subscribed to abolitionism; most valued the standard of living that slavery afforded them. Nor was it unusual for planters' wives to exhibit a racism and elitism equal to their husbands'.

DOMESTIC SLAVE TRAFFIC AND SLAVE-HOLDING

Following the end of the international slave trade there emerged a domestic business in buying and selling slaves that steadily expanded in scope. In towns and cities throughout the South, slave markets existed to facilitate the traffic in slaves. Although some white southerners were troubled by the existence of such institutions and more particularly the traffic in human cargo that they represented, they chose to condemn slave traders rather than the system that made possible their enterprise. Although slave traders may have been social pariahs in the eyes of some southerners, their business helped to make some individuals and companies wealthy and accelerated the movement of slaves into the new cotton regions of the lower South and West. Slave markets in Natchez and New Orleans were among the most important points of entry for slaves into these areas.

THE QUESTION OF SLAVE BREEDING

Since the smuggling of slaves into the United States from abroad after the congressional ban on the international trade accounted for only about fifty thousand of the more than 2 million slaves bought and sold in the forty years before the Civil War, the domestic slave trade essentially rested on the capacity of American slaves to reproduce themselves at a rate comparable to that of the South as a whole. The large number of slaves involved in the domestic traffic prompted abolitionists to charge slaveowners with the operation of slave-breeding farms. The subject of slave breeding has been and remains a subject of considerable debate among historians. Some recent scholars who view slavery as not merely a system of production but a system of human reproduction as well insist that slave breeding operations were widespread even though white women bore more children than black slave women in the antebellum South.

Slave breeding is at best a tricky subject, as is made clear in the testimony of William H. Heard, a Georgia-born slave who later became a bishop in the African Methodist Episcopal Church. He referred to his mother as a "breeder" because she "had children regularly" and received special treatment during pregnancy and immediately after the birth of her children. Neither regular childbearing nor such special treatment was unusual, as Heard admits. His reference to his mother as a breeder scarcely suggests that she was a part of a slave-breeding enterprise. Some slaveowners no doubt did encourage or force reproduction with the intention of profiting from the sale of the slave offspring, but the evidence is too skimpy to suggest that slave breeding for such purposes was widespread or to conclude that it constituted a major commercial enterprise.

SLAVEOWNERS' BENEVOLENCE: RHETORIC AND REALITY

The increase in the price of slaves caused by the demands for labor to cultivate the ever-expanding cotton lands in the two decades before the Civil War, coupled with the South's defensiveness in response to northern abolitionism, helped to translate at least some of the rhetoric about slaveowner benevolence into reality. Slaveowners' personal interest in the welfare of "their people" tended to increase as the cost of acquiring additional slaves and the value of those they already owned rose. Such concern was evident in the improvements in slave diet, health care, and housing and in the extension of special privileges such as those relating to hunting, fishing, gardening, and visiting neighboring plantations.

Many slaveowners also concerned themselves with the spiritual lives of their slaves once they recognized that religion could be used as a stabilizing force among the slave population. As in all matters affecting slaves, their owners attempted to exert control over their religious instruction, emphasizing biblical injunctions about being honest, moral, and faithful to masters. Such instruction was scarcely designed to alter the legal status of slaves.

The imposition of more stringent restrictions on slaves accompanied the slaveowners' increased attention to their physical well-being and religious lives. In the late antebellum period southern legislatures outlawed slave manumission and made it increasingly difficult for a slave to purchase his or her own freedom. More elaborate systems of slave patrols, designed to curb runaways and interplantation thefts and to thwart insurrectionary plots, constituted a visible sign of white authority. Often staffed by poor whites, patrols struck terror in the slave population. The simultaneous emphasis on protectiveness and restrictiveness experienced by slaves underscored the central meaning of slaveowner paternalism—the desire to make slaves more dependent and more loyal.

NO UNIFORM SLAVE EXPERIENCE

As an institution, slavery in the South was neither static nor homogeneous. To view it as an unchanging system in which there existed a single slave experience is to obscure both its evolutionary character and the diversity of conditions under which slaves lived and worked. In the 250-odd years between the arrival of the first Africans at Jamestown and the outbreak of the Civil War, slavery underwent continual legal redefinition, witnessed a dramatic growth in the numbers of bondsmen, and assumed an increasingly significant role in the politics of sectionalism. The preponderance of slaves also shifted to the lower South and trans-Mississippi Southwest.

As for the slaves themselves, they encountered a wide variety of working conditions. Large plantations, as mentioned earlier, were complex operations in which the slave workforce included house servants and skilled artisans as well as field hands. On such plantations field hands worked under highly organized labor arrangements, either the task or gang system, which often involved white overseers and/or slave drivers. In contrast, slaves residing on small farms usually worked alongside their owners. The experiences of both were vastly different from slaves in towns and cities where they labored in cotton mills, tobacco factories, iron works, and other industries. Of the approximately 140,000 urban slaves in 1860, most worked directly for their owners; others were hired out by rural owners for labor in cities. A few slaves, especially artisans, were allowed to hire out their own time, even though such a practice was illegal virtually everywhere. As a slave, Frederick Douglass considered life in Baltimore even "when most oppressive" as a "paradise" when compared with his existence on the plantation. Other variables that affected the slave experience included the personality, piety, and temperament of the master and the crop being cultivated, which determined the rigor and intensity of labor. It also made a difference whether a slave belonged to a resident or absentee owner or whether he or she belonged, as a few did, to free blacks and Indians.

Experiences might vary widely, but what did not vary was the legal status of slaves who, regarded as chattel—that is, personal property—could be disciplined at will by their owners and bought and sold like livestock. Because slaves were largely undifferentiated in social and economic status and possessed severely limited opportunities for occupational mobility, they shared much in common, including their legal status and a position of dependency. As a result, one historian has noted, the slave population "was marked by great uniformity even as it exhibited great diversity."

Methods of both motivating and disciplining slaves varied. A master who demonstrated a personal interest in the welfare of his slaves by treating them fairly, keeping families together, providing decent food and housing, and using the withdrawal of special privileges rather than the whip as a means of discipline was more likely to win his slaves' loyalty. Despite the presence of good masters, the slaves' existence was always fraught with the potential for disaster. For example, slaves were fully aware that the death of a kind master might well mean the transfer of their ownership to those prone to brutality and abuse. Even slaves who belonged to kind masters were sometimes subjected to cruel treatment by hired overseers.

The slave system in fact imposed on slaves a precarious existence in which flogging and other forms of physical punishment for infractions of plantation rules were omnipresent realities. "Fear, awe, and obedience," Frederick Douglass explained, were "interwoven into the very nature of the slave." Not all slaves felt the sting of the lash, but most had witnessed the whipping of a fellow slave and had seen the bloody lash marks—an experience that instilled fear and impressed on them the fact that they were trapped in a system which endowed their owners with tyrannical power. In explaining techniques for controlling slaves, J.H. Hammond, the South Carolina planter and politician, wrote: "We must rely more and more on the power of fear . . . to be sure we hold them [slaves] in complete check." Many slaveowners agreed that their right to use physical force to impose slave discipline was essential to the maintenance of an obedient and useful workforce. That such a view persisted after the emancipation of slaves was evident in the numerous complaints by white planters that without access to the whip it was impossible to make blacks work.

THE SLAVE COMMUNITY

Despite the use and threat of force, slaveowners never achieved total dominance over their slaves. That slaves were both persons and property created ambiguities in master-slave relationships that remained unresolved. By exploiting these ambiguities, slaves managed to secure at least a degree of autonomy. Most learned subtle ways to alter their environment. Some even learned to read, write, and figure, either surreptitiously or through the indulgence of their masters and mistresses, although slave codes prohibited the education of slaves. By employing dissimulation, playing on the master's vanity or acquiring a highly valued skill, slaves were able to survive and to create a semiautonomous community and ultimately a distinctive culture that represented an amalgam of both African and American ingredients.

SLAVES AND THE ACCULTURATION PROCESS

As we have seen, slaves imported into America were natives of different parts of Africa, primarily West Africa, and represented such a diversity of cultures, languages, and religions that they initially identified themselves not as Africans but as members of particular tribes, clans, village-states, and localities. Regardless of what else they may or may not have had in common, they shared the experience of being wrenched from their homelands, forcibly brought to an alien environment, and enslaved. As historian John Hope Franklin has noted, once these Africans of disparate backgrounds were in America, they underwent two acculturative processes simultaneously: one involved the interaction between various African cultures; the other was the Africans' interaction with Western culture. Such processes lasting over several generations resulted in the emergence of a culture that was neither African nor American, but rather a fusion of the two into an African-American culture. African influences upon this new culture were especially apparent in folktales and folk medicine, music and dance, naming practices, and religion.

CONSTRUCTING COMMUNAL BONDS

Although slaves existed in a world in which their owners prescribed minute regulations and closely scrutinized their work performance and behavior, their evenings together in their quarters, as well as their unstructured time during weekends, holidays, and inclement weather, provided escape from their omnipresent owners. At such times slaves found what historian John Blassingame refers to as their "primary environment," which provided them with "ethical rules and fostered cooperation, mutual assistance and black solidarity." In this environment, slaves learned the norms of conduct, defined roles and behavior patterns, developed a network of individual and group relationships, and acquired values and ideals that distinguished them from their masters. Beyond the view of their masters, slaves engaged in a variety of social and recreational activities including games, parties, dancing, music, cakewalks, and the sharing of folktales that strengthened social cohesion and communal bonds.

SLAVE FAMILY

Even though the slave family had no existence in law, it was one of the most significant survival mechanisms available to the slaves. For slaves, families involved a wide range of blood relations and even "fictive kin"—that is, friends who, endowed with symbolic kin function, offered solace and protection in times of trouble or family disruption. The nearly equal sex ratio among slaves in the South, in contrast to the slave population in the Caribbean, made possible the existence of monogamous families. Slaveowners encouraged such a pattern either because of their religious convictions or because of their belief that it contributed to stability and order in the slave quarters, promoted slave docility, and discouraged efforts by slaves to run away. Slaves highly valued children and perpetuated their culture by bequeathing to their offspring their own customs, mores, and ideals.

The effort to maintain stable slave families was beset by numerous, almost insurmountable, difficulties. Such families lacked legal standing and were constantly subjected to regimentation and interference by slaveowners. Especially threatening were the sexual demands of white males on female slaves, both married and single, and the disruption caused by the sale of family members. Most sexual liaisons between white men and slave women were fleeting, promiscuous relationships that sometimes produced mulatto offspring who, though often almost white in appearance, were nonetheless slaves, ignored by their white fathers and subject to sale. "Our men," Mary Boykin Chesnut, the wife of a South Carolina planter, noted in March 1861, "live all in one house with their wives and [slave] concubines, and the mulattoes one sees in every family partly resemble the white children. Any lady is ready to tell you who is the father of all the mulattoes one sees in everybody's household but her own. These, she seems to think, dropped from the clouds." If the presence of mulatto children constantly reminded plantation mistresses of their spouses' infidelity, such children provided ample evidence of the powerlessness of both slave women and their husbands.

Most devastating of all to the stability of slave families was the separation caused by sale. The domestic traffic in slaves separated numerous slave husbands and wives. A surplus of slaves in the upper South meant that many of these separations involved those who were literally sold "down the river" into the expanding cotton kingdom of the old Southwest. The wrenching experiences of husbands separated from wives and parents separated from children have received graphic descriptions in the autobiographies of ex-slaves, including Josiah Henson, who related how his mother looked on "in an agony of grief" as she witnessed her children being sold one by one. For many years after being freed, former slaves attempted to find and be reunited with family members whom they had been separated from during slavery. As late as the 1890s advertisements in search of lost relatives appeared regularly in black newspapers.

SLAVE RELIGION

If the slave family served as an important but insecure shield against the most dehumanizing aspects of slavery, slave religion also provided a means of coping with oppression and the assault on self-esteem. Like the slave family, slave religion achieved a degree of autonomy, blended African and European elements, and evolved over time. By the late antebellum period most slaveowners had concluded that religion would make slaves more docile and manageable and less likely to desire freedom. Seated in segregated sections of white churches, slaves listened to self-serving homilies by white preachers but, according to historian John Boles, they also heard "the full sermon with its message of hope and salvation" and often left worship services feeling morally superior to their owners. Boles persuasively argues that although whites were careful to emphasize that the quality of slaves' religious faith had no effect on their legal status, blacks and whites met more nearly as equals in church than anywhere else in the slave society of the South.

But slaves' exposure to conventional religion remained uneven and depended upon the piety of the slaveowner. As long as slaves worshipped with whites or under white supervision, their religious instruction was circumscribed. In their quarters and in secret places away from the watchful eyes of their masters, slaves tailored Christianity to their own needs. Slave preachers or "exhorters" pursued themes omitted from white-dominated services attended by slaves—themes that likened slaves to God's Chosen People and that promised the deliverance of the oppressed and the punishment of their oppressors. Such gatherings, as a part of what has been called the slaves' "invisible church," provided scenes of perpetual motion and intense emotion with constant singing, chanting, and shouting. The slaves' religious songs, the

An artist's rendition of a religious service in a black church in Cincinnati, Ohio, in 1857.

spirituals, did not provide evidence of contentment with their lot as some whites believed, but rather they represented, in Frederick Douglass' words, "the sorrows of his [the slave's] heart." Spirituals were also a means of expressing, occasionally overtly but more often obliquely, slaves' longing for freedom in the acceptable language of Christianity. Themes of freedom resounded in the words of spirituals such as "O Canaan, Sweet Canaan" and "Better Days Are Coming."

SLAVE RESISTANCE

Despite appearing to be reconciled to a life in bondage, the desire for freedom was universal among slaves. Slaves often talked about freedom and understood what it meant. The more slaves learned about freedom, as one writer suggested, the more desirous they were of obtaining it. No matter how much slaveowners described slaves as a childlike, docile people fully content with their lot, slaves simply refused to conform to such an image. The slaveowners' persistent anxieties about slave conspiracies and revolts suggest that they did not believe their own rhetoric and realized, as one writer noted, that "for every Sambo there might also exist a Spartacus." Rumors of slave conspiracies abounded throughout the South in the antebellum era. Few whites were unaware of the black uprising that freed Santo Domingo of French rule. Virtually all whites had heard of the abortive insurrections planned in 1800 by Gabriel Prosser, a Virginia slave; in 1822 by Denmark Vesey, a South Carolina slave who had purchased his freedom; and especially in 1831 the rebellion led by the slave preacher Nat Turner in Virginia that resulted in the death of more than fifty whites before it was suppressed. The widespread fear of slave revolts among whites, inspired by these events and encouraged by slaveowners, solidified popular support for an increasingly restrictive slave system.

Slaves recognized the great odds against the success of collective resistance, primarily because of the high ratio of whites to blacks in most of the South and the widely dispersed nature of slaveholdings. Furthermore, whites controlled the firearms and the militia. A form of slave resistance more likely to succeed involved individual rather than collective action. Usually provoked by a specific incident involving transgressions by owners or overseers, slaves resisted by direct confrontations with their oppressors or more frequently by running away. Those who chose the latter method hid in woods and swamps, disappeared into free black communities in towns and cities, or followed the North Star to a free state. Often aided by the so-called *underground railroad*, some sought refuge in Canada. The frequency with which advertisements for runaways appeared in the southern press after 1830 suggests that thousands of slaves chose this form of resistance even though it meant severing family ties and abandoning familiar surroundings.

Flight from slavery was not without great risks, especially in view of the prevalence of slave patrols. In addition, in a society that placed a premium on skin color, with white associated with free people and black with slaves, a runaway slave's color made identification easier for patrollers and search parties. Still other forms of slave resistance involved neither collective action nor individual escape; rather they took the form of more furtive tactics by those who remained on the plantation, such as feigning illness, staging work slowdowns, and committing acts of arson, sabotage, thievery, and poisoning. By adversely affecting the investments or persons of their owners, such tactics sought not so much to end the slave system as to persuade masters to make slave life more tolerable.

As the 1850s prospered, verbal exchanges between defenders of the South's slave system and northern abolitionists became sharper and more frequent, inflaming public opinion in both regions. By the end of the decade, slavery had become the focus of a highly emotional public debate. In 1858, Senator William H. Seward of New York, a leader of the Republican party, spoke of "the irrepressible conflict" between "opposing and enduring forces" represented by the North and the South. The United States, he insisted, must either become "entirely a slave-holding nation, or entirely a free-labor nation." There could be no compromise. A quarter of a century before Seward's speech a white southerner had observed that slavery had become "So interwoven . . . with our very being that no change can ever possibly be effected without a civil commotion." Such a commotion occurred in 1861 following the victory of a northern-based, antislavery Republican party.

The following selection by historian Loren Schweninger explores an aspect of slavery largely hidden from view or purposely concealed that has received scant attention from students of the antebellum South. His subject is the ownership of property by slaves. In discussing this topic he explains how the slaves' acquisition of property evolved over the years and how the internal slave economy varied from one region to another within the South. In the process, Schweninger reveals much about the diversity, complexity, and changing character of slavery.

PROPERTY OWNERSHIP AMONG SLAVES

Loren Schweninger

. . . The dynamic nature of the South's "peculiar institution," as well as its evolution from the early years of the nineteenth century until its demise during the Civil War, can perhaps be best understood by an analysis of slave property ownership. Of course, like other aspects of slavery, much of what occurred was hidden from view, or purposely concealed by masters and slaves alike, since it was illegal for bondsmen and women to own property; and compared with what has been described as a "protopeasant economy" in the British West Indies, especially Jamaica— where slaves grew much of their own food, produced many of their own necessities, and sold their surpluses more or less freely for their own profit—the South's internal slave economy remained relatively modest. Yet . . . the institutions that allowed bondspeople to accumulate property had been in place for generations; and during the nineteenth century, property ownership among slaves expanded significantly, not only in the low country of the Carolinas and Georgia, but on plantations and farms, in towns and cities, in both the Lower and Upper South. In each of these locations and regions it developed out of different circumstances and traditions and took slightly different forms. In the rural Lower South it was primarily an extension of slave gardens and livestock raising, in the Upper South primarily a result of slave hiring practices, and in urban areas it evolved from slaves being allowed to hire their own time, or in some instances, live virtually as free men and women. In both

from Loren Schweninger, *Black Property Owners in the South* (Urbana: University of Illinois Press, 1990), 30–60.

regions, as the doors to legal emancipation slowly closed during the antebellum decades, some of the most talented and ambitious slaves were able to achieve quasi-free status. Property ownership among slaves, therefore, not only tells us a good deal about cultural changes occurring in the lives of Afro-Americans but illuminates the diverse, complex, multidimensional, and evolving nature of slavery in the nineteenth century South. . . .

From the early years in colonial Virginia, blacks had been allowed to plant gardens of their own. This tradition continued during the eighteenth century, and by the early nineteenth century, the practice had spread from the tidewater of Virginia, down the eastern seaboard, and westward as slavery penetrated the areas beyond the Appalachians. Its vitality was largely due to the fact that it benefited both master and slave. From the master's perspective, blacks could use the gardens to supplement their meager diet, raising sweet potatoes, pears, pumpkins, okra, eggplant, corn, beans, collards, peas, turnips, tomatoes, and other fruits and vegetables; from the slaves' perspective this was land they could call their own and do with as they pleased. One South Carolina slave explained that while his master was cruel in many ways—seldom allowing him and the others to visit relatives on neighboring plantations, strictly forbidding the construction of a black church, and threatening to whip anyone caught reading a newspaper—he gave "every one of he plantation family so much land to plant for dey garden, and den he give em every Saturday for dey time to tend dat garden."

Some slaves used this land to plant and cultivate a few acres of a cash crop—rice, cotton, sugar, tobacco. At the end of the season, they sold their harvest to either the master or a nearby merchant. Georgia black Charles Houston planted rice on four acres allotted him by his master; in addition, he built a hog pen, a fodder bin, and a chicken coop. South Carolina's Lorenza Ezell said that on her place "All de men folks" raised a few acres of cotton "for to sell in de market." "We were never given any money," Louisiana bondswoman Octavia George recalled, "but were able to get a little money this way: our Master would let us have two or three acres of land each year to plant for ourselves, and we could have what we raised on it." Another black said that in his area slaves grew tobacco as a cash crop. In this way, he explained, several acquired sufficient means to purchase their freedom. One Alabama woman remembered how her uncles each planted a few acres of cotton. At the end of the season, they sold it to the master who paid them in cash. "My grandfather owned a cotton patch," former South Carolina bondswoman Mariah Calloway recalled, "and the master would loan him a mule so he could plow it at night." He had arrived directly from Africa, she said, and preferred working in the evenings when it was cool. Late in the autumn, he would journey to town, sell his cotton, and come back "loaded down" with cheese, sugar, tea, and dried fish.

On some plantations this internal slave economy reached surprising proportions. A group of South Carolina planters noted that in their district "negroes have every other Saturday [off], keep horses, raise hogs, cultivate for themselves every thing for home consumption & for market that their masters do." This domestic economy included planting and selling cotton. On Julien S. Devereux's Monte

Verdi estate in Rusk County, Texas, a dozen field hands used their evenings, Saturday afternoons, and Sundays to plant their own cotton. In 1850, Jesse marketed two bales weighing 1,158 pounds; Jack harvested two bales weighing about the same; Gill, Lewis, Bill, Lucius, Henry, Martin, Levin, and Stephen each raised one bale; Daniel and Scott harvested a half bale. Selling the cotton to Mt. Pleasant merchant Charles Vinzent, they purchased clothing, tobacco, hats, and other items. They also demanded partial payment in specie. "I send you $300 in gold," Vinzent wrote Devereux in 1853, "with the request to have the same distributed amongst those Negroes of yours who owned the Cotton which I bought from them." The payment to slaves for their extra crop on one plantation near Augusta, Georgia, came directly from the mistress of the estate. "Mrs. T. told me she had lately paid them [her slaves] $1,000 for their own extra crop of cotton this year—that she paid to one of the men $70," a visitor to Emily Tubman's plantation noted in 1836. "She says that there is not a more interesting set of colored people, perhaps to be found any where."

It was obvious that Devereux and Tubman, like numerous planters in the Lower South, used a combination of the task and gang systems on their plantations. Where the task system was exclusively employed, as in the cultivation of rice along the Sea Island coast of South Carolina and Georgia, slaves had even greater opportunities of accumulating property. One observer in Chatham County, Georgia, said in 1822 that blacks had "as much land as they can till for their own use." Following their work in the fields, they cultivated four or five acres of rice, corn, and cotton. A few bondsmen and women planted ten or twelve acres of a cash crop. After the harvest, they sold the crops to factors, or local merchants, or to their masters. "His slaves are sometimes his creditors to large amounts," Frederick Law Olmsted noted, after visiting Richard Arnold's plantation in Georgia; "at the present time he says he owes them about five hundred dollars."

The importance blacks attached to being able to raise their own crops, no matter how small the return, could be seen in the care they displayed toward these few acres, a devotion that far exceeded any concern for cultivating the broad fields beyond. Often they used a portion of the day on Saturday and Sunday tilling, planting, cultivating, or harvesting, and sometimes, even after twelve or fourteen hours in the field, they would spend time on their "own land." One Louisiana black recalled how she and her fellow slaves would return at dusk so exhausted they would sometimes fall into bed without supper, but when the moon was full they would spend a few more hours cultivating their tobacco patches, carefully plucking away dead leaves, gently turning over the soil, attentively digging out roots and weeds. When insects or drought destroyed their crops they often agonized at the sight of their withering fields in such emotional terms that it seemed as if a part of their own souls had withered away and died. Though they realized they could not own real or personal property without the consent of whites, or in any legal sense even with such consent—how could chattel property itself own property?—blacks believed they had certain rights of proprietorship over these fields. "A great deal [of real estate] was held by sufferance and their [the slaves'] right was most universally recognized and respected," one postwar observer acknowledged, "no advantage taken of even verbal agreement." Among the largest slaveholders, this was "a matter of honor."

Another knowledgeable white explained that many masters allowed bondspeople to own gardens and small acreages as well as various personal possessions. These practices were so universal, he asserted, that slave owners made no claim whatsoever on this property.

Some slaves on large plantations in the Lower South not only planted a few acres of a staple crop but also acquired other types of property. While this varied from plantation to plantation and region to region, blacks often owned a few personal items such as shirts, pants, shoes, watches, furniture, beehives, dogs, wagons, even firearms. "Slaves have not infrequently been known to have pistols & other dangerous weapons in their possession, and even to carry them about their persons," a Lexington District, South Carolina, grand jury explained in 1855, following the gunshot slaying of a bondsman by a fellow slave. Plantation slaves also owned hogs, cows, sometimes a horse, mule, or a few head of cattle. When Union army officers arrived in Mississippi and initiated a plan to assist former slaves in becoming independent farmers by confiscating plantation mules, horses, oxen, as well as carts, wagons, and tools, believing they belonged to the planter class, blacks protested vociferously, explaining that they had long "possessed" their own livestock and equipment. Texas slave Felix Haywood, of Bexar County, recalled how he and his father had built up a herd of seventy head of cattle by the time of the Civil War. They had begun with a few head donated to them by their owner. "My father," Haywood said proudly, "had his own brand."

If owning such a large herd was very unusual, by the end of the antebellum era a large proportion of the slaves in the low country of the Carolinas and Georgia owned farm animals and other property, and a few of them, like Haywood, were slaves of considerable means. Slave driver Paris James was described by a white planter as a "substantial man before the war [and] was more like a free man than any slave." According to the same planter, James owned a horse, eight cows, sixteen sheep, twenty-six hogs, and a wagon. Another slave livestock owner was described by a black witness as "just like a white man except [for] his color. His credit was just as good as a white man's because he had the property to back it." Other low-country slaves were considered to be "more than usually prosperous," "pretty well off," and "hardworking and moneysaving." Georgia black Alexander Steele, a slave carpenter, said his estate included four horses, a mule, and two cows, as well as large quantities of fodder, hay, and corn. He had obtained these possessions by trading for himself over a period of thirty years, and when a white planter offered him $300 for one of his prized colts, Steele refused.

Even more widespread than the ownership of livestock was the possession of money. Plantation slaves discovered several ways to earn small amounts of cash: telling fortunes, healing with roots and herbs, playing the fiddle at plantation dances and social gatherings, betting on cockfights and horse races, selling trinkets and other items to fellow slaves. Sometimes they sold poultry, meats, and liquor to free blacks, or peddled baskets and handicrafts to a nearby store owner. Masters found it virtually impossible to halt these market activities. To control their bondsmen and women in this regard the best most slave owners could do was to purchase slave produce, crops, poultry, and other items themselves. South Carolina planter Henry

W. Ravenel, who owned nearly two hundred blacks, recalled that it was a "custom" among many planters to pay cash for various slave products. On his Pooshee plantation the overseer operated a store—he called it "an institution"—which purchased "everything the negroes wished to sell, whether wanted or not," and paid them "the market price." Ravenel said the slaves received payments for Indian and Guinea corn, pumpkins, melons, ground nuts (or "pindars"), fish, eggs, chickens, and honey. "Among the more enterprising," he said, "beehives—a dozen or more, ranged under some old peachtree—would give a supply of honey or its equivalent in cash."

On a few plantations slaves could actually earn wages if they performed their tasks with extraordinary skill and dexterity. Planter James Townes was so enthusiastic about this method of creating good work habits that he urged his fellow slave owners to follow his lead. On payday, as the Negroes called it, Townes explained in an article on plantation management in the *Southern Cultivator,* his slaves were "very proud to go off with a pocket full of silver." Other slaves earned silver away from the plantation, hawking fruit to steamboat stewards, selling partridges to train conductors, peddling vegetables in a nearby town, or selling a few yards of cloth to poor whites. "Po-buckra [poor whites] come there and buy cloth from Mom," one slave in All Saints Parish, South Carolina, recalled. "Buy three and four yards. Ma sell that [and then] have to weave day and night to please obersheer." "My daddy alus had some money," a former Texas bondsman testified, "'cause he made baskets and chair bottoms and sold them." One Negro who corded wood during his spare time said that when slaves in his vicinity saw something they wanted at the store they usually did like the whites. "Us bought it."

An Alabama dental surgeon who traveled extensively in his home state confirmed this contention. He told a reporter that he frequently encountered slaves with cash in their pockets. At crossroads stores he witnessed them purchasing barrels of molasses, sugar, flour, and mackerel, as well as boxes of cheese and tobacco and sacks of coffee. Around his hometown of Fairfield slaves sometimes ordered a year's supply of groceries from Mobile, and once he espied a slave asking a merchant to change a fifty-dollar bill. "They do not like to lay up paper money," he explained, "and get their bills exchanged for silver and gold." Nor were they "fancy negroes" such as barbers, waiters, and stewards; they were just plain "plantation hands."

Although the surgeon's proslavery zeal probably caused him to overstate his case, and although slaves could acquire only small amounts of cash (he was correct, however, about their desire to "lay up" silver and gold rather than notes and paper currency), plantation slaves in the Lower South took understandable pride in being able to acquire plots of land, a few farm animals, and small amounts of money. The feeling of self-worth and independence this engendered could be seen in the proud recollection of Texas slave Scott Hooper's son who explained that his father sold his own cotton and "Dat-away, he have money and he own pony and saddle and brung chillen candy and toys and buys coffee and tea for mammy." Another black expressed the same feeling toward his stepfather who built a log house, furnished it with tables, beds, and chairs, then purchased a cloak and gown for his mother, frocks for his sisters, and coats and hats for his two brothers and himself, "all new and good, and all with money he earned in the time allowed him for sleep." It could also be seen in the enthusiasm blacks demonstrated toward earning some extra money. When a group of sugar planters near Convent, St. James Parish, Louisiana, offered cash payments to their slaves for any wood they cut during their spare time, virtually every black on the jointly owned plantation—more than one hundred—responded. In all, as shown in the "Accounts of Wood Cut in 1854" (dated July 10, 1854), they cut 2,225 cords (284,000 cubic feet), earning nearly two thousand dollars. Among the participants were "Little Joe" (a half-cord), "Old Jacob" (ten cords), and Jack Page, who cut and piled an amazing sixty-nine cords. "Poor and dependent as most of the freemen are," John Alvord, an inspector for the Freedmen's Bureau, reported in 1866, after touring states in the Deep South, "I found that a considerable number had money." A "considerable number" also owned cattle, horses, mules, and other personal items. . . .

By the end of the antebellum era, property ownership among slaves on plantations in the Lower South was fairly widespread, especially where the task system was employed. As in the eighteenth century, some owners believed that incentives, combined with force and coercion, were the best means of labor management. Away from the plantation, in towns and cities, and in manufacturing establishments of the Upper South, another labor method evolved from the colonial period which allowed slaves opportunities to accumulate property: the hiring-out system. As with the task system, hiring out provided incentives to both master and slave. With steadily rising prices for slaves and increased demands for temporary workers, masters found themselves in an enviable position. They could hire out their bondsmen and women and obtain profits ranging from 10 to 20 percent (of the slave's price) per year. While contracts concerning clothing, food, medical attention, and treatment varied, slaves hired in such a manner could often expect to earn wages for themselves if they worked beyond what was considered a normal workday. As historians Robert Starobin and Charles Dew suggest, this "Stimulant & Reward Money," as one Tennessee turnpike owner called it, was a means of labor control rather than "a step toward freedom," but blacks responded enthusiastically to even these limited opportunities. "The negroes in the swamp [cutting shingles] were more sprightly and straight-forward in their manner and conversation than any field-hand plantation-negroes that I saw at the South," one traveler said in 1856, commenting on "THE EFFECT OF PAYING WAGES TO SLAVES." There were no complaints of "'rascality' or laziness."

Hired slaves gradually came to expect some type of extra compensation. Those who were employed as dining room servants, porters, draymen, and coachmen collected tips; barbers, laundresses, and market women kept some of their earnings; skilled carpenters, masons, industrial workers, and factory hands received cash payments. While their remunerations were often small, usually a few dollars a month, observers in several Upper South cities explained that virtually all hired blacks had "prerequisites" of one kind or another. If they were called upon to do extra work, labor in the evenings or at night, or if they demonstrated unusual "fidelity," they generally expected to be compensated. Frederick Olmsted explained how this worked in the tobacco industry. "In the tobacco-factories in Richmond and Petersburg, slaves are, at this time, in great demand, and are paid one hundred and fifty to two hundred dollars, and all expenses, for a year," he said. These blacks, primarily hired hands, were expected to complete a certain amount of work, a "daily quota," and once this had been finished, they received "bonus pay." Factory managers discovered that hired blacks "could not be 'driven' to do a fair day's work so easily as they could be stimulated to it by the offer of a bonus for all they would manufacture above a certain number of pounds." As a result, slaves earned for themselves from $5 to $20 per month. Another observer said hired hands in tobacco factories earned an average of $120 annually, compared to the going rate of $1 a day for white workers. While this may have been an exaggeration, following the Civil War freed slaves in Richmond complained that their wages were less than half of what they had previously earned as hired slaves!

By the 1850s, slave hiring was a common practice in the South's major industries—hemp manufacturing, textiles, tobacco, iron production—as well as in the cities of the Upper South. In Richmond, 62 percent of the male slave-labor force was hired, in Lynchburg, 52 percent, in Norfolk, more than 50 percent, and in Louisville, 24 percent. In the South as a whole, at least 100,000 slaves (estimates range from 60,000 to 160,000) were hired each year. One industrialist who used hired blacks was William Weaver, owner of Buffalo Forge, an iron-manufacturing establishment near Lexington, Virginia. Weaver employed slave founders, colliers, miners, teamsters, woodcutters, and furnace hands—a total of nearly 100 hired blacks each year, or nearly one-half of his labor force. And, like iron makers in Tennessee, Kentucky, North Carolina, South Carolina, Georgia, Alabama, and Missouri, he offered his hired workers cash incentives. Those who were willing to cord more than the required amount of wood received forty cents per cord, the same rate at which white woodchoppers were paid. Skilled slave ironworkers could earn overwork payments for producing more than their required quota of iron, while ore-bank hands could collect for mining and washing extra ore, colliers for tending the charcoal pits at night, shoemakers for making extra pairs of shoes, and common laborers for working extra hours. What is remarkable is the manner in which Weaver's hired hands responded to these wage incentives. Most slave hands, both skilled and unskilled, used the overwork system to earn their own money. They used their wages to purchase extra clothing, tobacco, sugar, meat, coffee, liquor, and other commodities, to acquire hogs, chickens, and horses, and to pay for extra holidays with their families. In this way, historian Charles Dew notes, "a sizable number of blacks took advantage of the system to carve out something of a private and individual life for themselves."

Not all hired slaves fared as well as Weaver's ironworkers. Some were auctioned off like fieldhands and fell into the hands of harsh and oppressive masters. This was especially true of slaves turned over to the administrator of an estate following the death of a master. Others, despite extraordinary effort and diligent work habits, received only modest remunerations or did not receive the wages originally agreed upon. But even these slaves, while seeking to avoid conflict, were not completely without recourse when they felt betrayed. For three years (1799–1801),

James, a slave carpenter in Norfolk, Virginia, was hired out by his owner William Walker, earning between $2.40 and $3.50 a week for himself and his master. In 1801, however, apparently dissatisfied with the amount of his wages, James ran away, remaining at large for thirteen months. But upon his return, he was neither scolded nor disciplined; rather, his wages were increased. Others attempting to negotiate in such a manner were less fortunate. In 1846, James Armstrong, a Kentucky bondsman owned by farmer James Rudd, was similarly hired out for wages and was allowed to keep everything he earned in excess of $5.00 a week. Armstrong worked diligently, rarely missing a payment to his master. Between 1846 and 1853, Rudd kept a meticulous record of "Cash Received of James," dutifully recording each week's payment. Over the eight years, he received $1,897.65, or an average of $4.60 per week. In October 1853, however, Rudd decided to raise his own share to $7.00. Incensed by this "breach of contract," Armstrong ran away, was apprehended, and made a second break for freedom. This time he was captured, severely whipped, and cast into irons. On March 4, 1854, the once conscientious and profitable slave was sold for $1,600. . . .

Only a few months before, neither slave nor master would have predicted such an event, but the incident, agonizing to both, demonstrated what might happen if some sort of concession were not granted to a hired slave. To avoid this, some slaveholders (including Rudd) allowed their most trusted and skilled blacks to hire their own time. Self-hire had a long tradition in American slavery, stretching back to the earliest colonial period when some slaves, usually the most skilled and trustworthy, were allowed to contact a potential employer, make arrangements for wages and working conditions, and secure their own food and lodging. From generation to generation, the practice changed very little, in large measure because, as with hiring out, it benefited both master and slave. Owners did not have to pay for the slave's clothing or lodging and also saved the 5 to 8 percent fee charged by a hiring broker as well as the aggravation of taking care of the matter themselves. "I cannot now say whether the negroes will be exposed in hire or no [sic], that is at public auction," one Tennessee planter grumbled in 1813, expressing the sentiments of other slave owners. "I cannot possibly attend the hiring this year." Slaves, while required to pay their masters a monthly or yearly fee, were allowed to keep anything they earned above and beyond that amount. The famous bondsman Frederick Douglass, when he was a self-hired Baltimore ship's caulker, explained: "I was to be allowed all my time; to make all bargains for work; to find my own employment, and to collect my own wages; and, in return for this liberty, I was required, or obliged, to pay him [Douglass's master] three dollars at the end of each week, and to board and clothe myself, and buy my own calking [sic] tools." This was a hard bargain, requiring that Douglass earn twice the amount his master required, but self-hire, he asserted, had "armed my love of liberty with a lash and a driver, far more efficient than any I had before known." It was a highly valued privilege, "another step in my career toward freedom."

Unlike Frederick Douglass, most self-hired slaves were not able to extricate themselves from bondage, but they too greatly valued the privilege of managing their own time and collecting their own wages. This could be seen in their will-ingness to hire out despite the difficulties some of them faced in providing for them-selves while continuing to make payments to their masters. During periods of economic recession or depression, and in some rural areas even during more pros-perous times, slaves who lacked special skills were sometimes forced to find em-ployment wherever they could. According to one North Carolina farmer, self-hired Negroes in his neighborhood encountered difficulties earning a decent wage. "Fact is," he said, "a man couldn't earn his board, let alone his wages, for six months in the year." What did they do during the remainder of the year? "Well, they keeps agoin' round from one place to another, and gets their living somehow." Self-hired slaves who earned larger sums were sometimes forced to turn over substantial amounts to their owners. The literate North Carolina house servant and barber James Starkey, though earning a large income, was required to give most of it to his master. If allowed to work only partially for himself, he could raise his purchase price in a few years, but as long as he had wages to pay, he lamented, "it is impossible." Other blacks were allowed to hire their time only after their most productive years had long since passed. The "aged" female slave Yarico, who served Virginia farmer Thomas Wells faithfully for many years, eked out an existence "principally if not entirely" by hiring "her own labor." According to other observers, some slaves, like Yarico, would have been better off working as fieldhands on large plantations. On their own they ran the risks of harsh treatment, seizure by a slave trader, arrest by public au-thorities, and the infirmities of old age.

One of the most pernicious practices connected with self-hire was a master's holding out the promise of freedom and then drawing up a contract that was vir-tually impossible to fulfill or reneging on the original promise. Even under the best of circumstances, purchasing one's self was an enormous and risky undertaking. During the 1820s, a young male slave could buy himself for about $350 in Virginia, and about $700 in Louisiana. A generation later, with the inflation of slave prices, these costs had nearly doubled. Although the earning power of self-hired bondsmen and women appreciated considerably during the interim, during both periods it was extremely difficult for even the most frugal and dedicated black to purchase freedom papers. Even so a number of self-hired slaves exerted great effort to pay for themselves. In 1855, Mary Carrol, a young self-hired Tennessee slave who worked as a chambermaid, signed an agreement according to which she was to be advanced $600 (her appraised value) in the form of a mortgage note, and she was not to be free until she had paid the note and interest as well as premiums on a life-insurance policy and any health expenses she might incur. . . . After fifty-four months, she still owed nearly $400 on her purchase price. As if sinking deeper in quicksand, Mary Carrol's struggle to buy herself had ended only in desperate failure. Still, she was probably better off than Fanny Smith, a Virginia slave who made a verbal agreement with her master to pay for herself and her two children over a period of ten years. Shortly before the final payment she was sold.

Despite such wrenching experiences, blacks eagerly sought to hire themselves out. For whites it was simple and economical to hire slaves for certain jobs; it was often simpler and more economical to deal with the slaves themselves. But for blacks it meant the ability to earn wages, provide for their families, and gain a measure of autonomy. Several types of evidence point to the success of self-hire. One was its remarkable longevity. As early as 1712 whites in Charleston noted the presence of slaves who "go whither they will and work where they please," upon condition that so much money was paid to the master. Nearly a century and a half later Charleston residents, as well as whites in virtually every town and city and many rural areas of the Upper and Lower South, described self-hired blacks in much the same manner. In addition, by the antebellum period self-hired slaves had entered a wide range of different occupations. In urban areas of the Lower South, where free blacks often worked as skilled craftsmen, self-hired slaves became porters, draymen, market women, fishermen, boatmen, and hucksters. In New Orleans, self-hired women of color sold flowers and oranges in the streets or candy and pies in small shops. In the towns and cities of the Upper South, self-hired slaves, while working as coopers, carpenters, and millers, also loaded and unloaded steamboats, labored on the docks and along riverfronts, became servants, domestics, cooks, coachmen, and found employment as tobacco twisters, woodchoppers, and day laborers. Lastly, the increasing number of complaints, legislative petitions, and anti-self-hire laws formulated by whites in virtually every section of the South during the pre–Civil War generation reveals less about the ability of slave owners to curtail or even control the institution than about its continuing strength and vitality.

One of the primary reasons blacks remained so eager to hire themselves out was the financial benefits that could be derived from the system. Wages varied in different periods in various parts of the South, but slaves working on their own could command between $100 (for unskilled labor in the Upper South early in the century) and $500 (for skilled workers in the Lower South on the eve of the Civil War). Fluctuations could occur to the detriment (or benefit) of these slaves, during periods of economic depression (or prosperity), but generally they could expect to earn profits of between $25 and $150 per annum. One observer in Baltimore explained that slaves "let themselves out for every kind of work," paid their masters a given sum for the loss of their services, and kept only "a trifle for themselves." But in Charleston, Savannah, and New Orleans, observers said ambitious slaves were able to "save a great deal of money." Those who managed small businesses or peddled confectionery, bread, cooked fish, rice, fruit, oysters, and other commodities, or who were highly skilled as cabinetmakers, joiners, or coopers, could sometimes earn as much as white workers. The ability of some self-hired slaves to purchase luxury items such as boats, carriages, fancy clothing, or buy relatives or themselves out of bondage . . . testifies to the earning power of some members of this group. Several among them, including laborers, artisans, and businessmen, became slaves of considerable means.

The eagerness of slaves to hire their own time was perhaps best illustrated by the bondsmen and women on John Liddell's Black River plantation in Catahoula Parish, Louisiana. "I request that you would forthwith proceed to prosecute *John S. Sullivan* of Troy, Parish of Catahoula, for Hiring four of my Negro men, secretly, and without my knowledge or permission, at *midnight* on the 12th of Aug last 1849 (or between midnight and day)," Liddell instructed his lawyer, to steal away my large flatboat from my landing, and use the same in transporting lumber from Capt. Shriver's old saw Mill to his (Sullivan's) landing or store or warehouse, at troy, a distance back and forth of 6 miles, hard pulling and three miles against the current with a heavily loaded flat, thereby causing *one* of the said four negroes to become sick from . . . over exertion & exposure during the night, while striving to return home in time to prevent discovery, thereby ultimately causing death of said negro (Jake).

After Jake's death Liddell discovered to his astonishment that Sullivan had often hired his slaves, had been doing so for years, and during the past twelve months had paid them $500 in wages. "Where does this sum come from," he asked bitterly, "unless from my means, my property?"

His slaves, of course, felt differently. They viewed self-hire as an opportunity to earn spending money, even if it meant working all day, stealing away at midnight, and returning to the fields at dawn the next morning. Nor were they easily deterred; three years later Liddell was still pressing for a state law "prohibiting the employing and hiring of slaves without consent of the owners under heavy penalty." But even under the best of circumstances, self-hire sometimes strained the relations between master and slave. Although the contractual terms and amount of personal earnings slaves were allowed to keep varied considerably in individual cases, self-hire usually carried with it at least a degree of financial independence. Even slaves who reported regularly to their masters were able to manage their own money, earning their own wages and paying their owners an agreed upon sum. As a result, self-hired blacks often demonstrated an independence, self-esteem, and at times arrogance which grated on whites who believed slaves should be docile, self-deprecating, and humble. "As I have hired the boy Stephen, he is no longer authorized to trade for himself," Maury County, Tennessee, slave owner Edward H. Chappin complained in 1823, "or own any property in his own name." It seems that Stephen, without authorization, had acquired a string of horses and then established a business renting them to slaves on neighboring plantations. "I do hereby authorize the bearer of this [note]," Chappin declared, "to take in possession and deliver to me all [Stephen's] horses or other property" that might be in the hands of other blacks. On a visit to Richmond during the hiring season one foreign traveler was amused by the demands of a black domestic servant who was hiring herself out for the coming year. She demanded not only high wages, but also a number of other concessions, including the right to entertain her "friends and favourites." At length, she agreed only "to visit her proposed home and see how things looked."

Slaves who made their own financial arrangements not only felt a sense of power, however limited, but in some instances had merely occasional contact with their masters. Those who rented their time on an annual or semiannual basis sometimes moved into a twilight zone between bondage and freedom. The question of whether or not this was "undermining" the South's peculiar institution, as claimed by some contemporaries, was a specious argument considering the relatively small proportion of slaves who hired themselves out during a particular year. What is important is the willingness of slaves, whenever possible, to enter into such contracts, and the self-esteem, positive self-concepts, and attitudes of independence self-hire engendered in bondsmen and women. This was certainly true for the slave Lotty, owned by the famous Kentucky politician Henry Clay. Returning to his Ashland plantation in 1830 after serving as secretary of state, Clay sought the services of his bondswoman, an excellent house servant who had been "receiving her own hire" for about eighteen months. She was probably still with Martin Van Buren, he explained to a friend in Washington, D.C., but he could not be sure. "Will you do me the favor to look her out, and tell her I want her to return." If she displayed a "perverse or refractory disposition," he added, "be pleased to have her imprisoned until I can hear of it, and give the necessary directions." . . .

As suggested by Lotty's tenuous ties to Henry Clay, some self-hired slaves melted into the free Negro population, living and acting as free persons of color and acquiring real estate and other property. Little is known about these "virtually free slaves." This is not surprising, since even the term seems incongruous: how could slaves also be free? In some respects, of course, they could not, and even legally emancipated blacks have been termed by some historians as "Quasi-Free Negroes" and "Slaves without Masters." In addition, as their livelihoods depended upon secrecy or deception or, at the very least, a tacit illegal agreement with a prominent white slaveholder, it is extremely difficult even to identify much less uncover information about such slaves. Owners were reluctant to acknowledge that bondsmen in their charge roamed about unsupervised, undermining the controls so necessary for the slave system to function properly; the unsuspecting foreign traveler or northern visitor or southern defender of slavery believed these blacks to be either slaves or free Negroes; and free slaves themselves refused to admit, much less advertise, their situation. Consequently, the journals of the slaveholding class, descriptions by outside visitors, writings of white southerners, and to a large extent even the narratives, recollections, and autobiographical reminiscences of blacks themselves, contain only fleeting references to slaves who exercised many of the privileges of free men and women.

Yet there were slaves in the South who achieved a remarkable degree of self-sufficiency. In the Lower South, they were clustered primarily in towns and cities. In Athens, Georgia, one resident said in 1859 that there were more "free negroes manufactured and made virtually free" than there were "bona fide" free blacks in Clarke and any ten surrounding counties. A visitor to New Orleans noticed "a great many loose negroes about," slaves who seemed to be hiring their own time and earning their own living without supervision from slave owners. City officials in Charleston, Savannah, Mobile, and other urban areas told about the presence of "nominal slaves," "quasi f. n.," and "virtually free negroes" who moved about the streets seemingly oblivious to any law or regulation. While the precise number of these masterless slaves remains a matter of speculation, contemporaries in some cities believed they represented a sizable population group, at least as large as the legally free Negro population. Noting that the local courts often disregarded the spirit of an 1831 law requiring special legislative action to manumit slaves, the editor of the Natchez *Mississippi Free Trader* said that at least fifty legally enslaved bondsmen and women in the area "affect to be free." It was well known by local residents that "a large number of slaves" had been illegally manumitted; and after having "gone up the river, set foot upon the soil of Ohio or some other free or abolition State, received from them certain certificates, which are called 'free papers'; forthwith they return to Mississippi, to reside as 'free people of color.'" A longtime resident of Savannah noted in 1856, "There are, you may say, hundreds of Negroes in this city who go about from house to house—some carpenters, some house servants, etc.—who never see their masters except at payday, live out of their yards, hire themselves without written permit, etc." Others were "employed without any expression of the will of the master manifested by written permit." In his estimation, self-hired and quasi-free slaves (they were often lumped together) represented at least 10 percent of the city's total Negro population.

In the Upper South, increasing numbers of quasi-free bondsmen and women also congregated in urban areas—Baltimore, the District of Columbia, Norfolk, Richmond, Lexington, Louisville, and St. Louis. Some earned wages working in tobacco and hemp factories; a few were skilled artisans who contracted with whites as builders, carpenters, coopers, and mechanics; others worked as servants, barbers, and hack drivers. Among the nearly one thousand slaves hired yearly in Elizabeth City County, Virginia, nearly one hundred lived as quasi-free bondsmen and women including nominal slave William Roscoe Davis, who operated a small pleasure boat on Chesapeake Bay. In other cities, virtually free slaves established market stalls, traded produce, fish, and other goods with plantation slaves, and sold various commodities to whites. In the port cities of Baltimore and Wilmington and in smaller river towns, slave fishermen and boatmen, often quasi-free or hiring their time by the year, worked along the river systems, fishing and trading with plantation blacks. In Louisville and St. Louis, nearly free slaves were waiters, servants, barbers, and steamboat stewards.

In Nashville, several hundred virtually free slaves found employment as hackmen, wagoners, hostlers, confectioners, masons, builders, barbers, and laborers. Among them during the early years of the nineteenth century was a mulatto boy named John, whose activities as a self-hired slave illustrate how some Negroes managed to move into the middle ground between slavery and freedom. Taken by his owner from Charlottesville, Virginia, to Nashville, John was allowed to hire out to barge captain Richard Rapier, who transported tobacco down the Cumberland, Ohio, and Mississippi rivers to New Orleans, carrying back to Nashville sugar, tea, coffee, raisins, molasses, rum, brandy, wines, logwood, nails, tin, glass, and other commodities. Following his owner's death, John reverted to the estate of Charles Thomas, a Virginia slave owner, but the quasi-free slave remained with Rapier and accompanied his employer to Florence, Alabama, in 1819, where he continued to work as a self-hired waiter and pole boy for a full decade, before obtaining his legal freedom (with a bequest from the barge master's estate), taking the surname Rapier, and establishing a barbershop. During the antebellum period, the number of nominal slaves grew steadily in Nashville and other cities, until by the 1850s, according to some observers, they had become "a sizeable Negro population."

Although quasi-free bondsmen and women tended to congregate in towns and cities, where there were better opportunities for employment and escaping detection, some remained in rural areas as farm laborers and in a few instances as farm "owners." Usually those who became farmers did so with the acquiescence of whites since land "possession" was involved. In North Carolina, Martin County black Ned Hyman, a slave owned by John and Samuel Hyman, accumulated an estate "consisting of Lands chiefly, Live Stock, Negroes and money," worth between $5,000 and $6,000. Most of this property was listed in his free Negro wife's name. He was a "remarkably uncommon and extraordinary Negro," a group of nearly one hundred whites in his neighborhood said, and had acquired his holdings because he was "remarkably industrious, frugal & prudent." "In a word, his character stands as fair and as good—for honesty, truth, industry, humility, sobriety & fidelity[—]as any Negro they (your memorialists) have ever seen or heard of". . . . In a sparsely settled rural area of Sullivan County, Tennessee, near the Virginia border, one white farmer noted the presence of a large family of quasi-free black farmers. "Although they are Slaves yet they have been living to themselves for about 20 years," Samuel Rhea explained. "They have supported themselves on land of their masters and are tolerable farmers." William Weston, a lifelong resident of Craven County, North Carolina, recalled on the eve of the Civil War that Rebecca Sutton and her five children had taken up residence on a deserted farm near Pamlico Sound in 1818. Although a slave, "she always lived as a free woman and acted for herself," Weston testified. "She lived on my Father's Land for Several years & then lived on John Benston[']s Land. She acted for herself there also until she died."

Few nominal slaves could boast of an estate as large as Ned Hyman's, but a number entered the property-owning class. Posing as free persons of color some purchased real estate or, acting through a white protector, acquired a member of their family, even though they themselves remained legally enslaved. Other quasi-free bondsmen and women rented houses, buildings, and other property, establishing small businesses. One Nashville woman ran a laundry from her rented house in the heart of the central business district. Over the years, she saved a considerable amount of money, including $350 in Mexican gold coins, and eventually bought one of her three slave children out of bondage. Virginia slave Billy Brown, who had purchased his freedom and found a job at Hampden-Sidney College, was required by law to leave the state. Seeking to remain near his slave family, he petitioned the General Assembly: "By the course of honest industry, and careful economy," he had "acquired property, sufficient probably, with ordinary labor," to support his family for many years to come; he prayed to remain in Virginia. When his plea was rejected, Brown was forced once again to become "the property of a gentleman," although he continued to support himself "by honest industry and prudent economy." South Carolina slave Sally Patterson, the wife of a free Negro carpenter in Columbia, was listed in 1850 as a free Negro possessing $1,200 worth of real estate. In Charleston, quasi-free carpenter Joseph Elwig, who was actually owned by his father, purchased a house on Coming Street, where a number of affluent free Negroes owned homes, and was listed on the tax rolls in 1836 as a free black. Even though few of his neighbors realized that he was in reality a slave, when his father became seriously ill in 1843 Elwig was sold for $1 to his own free Negro wife so that he would not be confiscated to pay any of his father's debts. Perhaps no other act could more poignantly illustrate the anomalous condition of quasi-free bondsmen and women than a father selling his own son to ensure the son's freedom. . . .

A few partially free slaves actually established businesses. Virginia's Robert Gordon sold slack from his white father's coal yard to local blacksmiths, amassing a small fortune of $15,000 by 1846, when he purchased his freedom and moved to Cincinnati. Kentucky's Frank McWorter set up a crude saltpeter manufactory (the principal ingredient in gunpowder) in Pulaski County at the beginning of the war with Great Britain in 1812 and expanded it considerably in subsequent years as settlers poured through the region to the West. Mississippi's Benjamin Montgomery, a favorite slave of cotton planter Joseph Davis (the brother of the future president of the Confederacy), operated a retail dry goods store at Davis Bend, thirty miles south of Vicksburg, selling items to his fellow slaves in exchange for wood, vegetables, chickens, and eggs. A slave named Allen drove back and forth from the Mississippi river to the Piedmont in Virginia, vending wares from his dry goods wagon. Future Alabama congressman Benjamin Turner, while still in bondage, acquired a livery stable and considerable other property in Selma. Turner not only managed his own business but also conducted his owner's financial affairs as well. "I [ran] a livery-stable in Selma, and r[a]n omnibuses, hacks, etc.," Turner testified to the Southern Claims Commission in 1871, seeking restitution for the $8,000 worth of property he had lost at the hands of Wilson's raiders. "That was my business, and my boss [Dr. Gee] left me some business of his to look after, such as collecting money for him, and attending to his affairs as a matter of encouragement to me and to make me behave myself and not run away while the war was going on."

In Bennettsville, South Carolina, bondsman Thomas David owned a construction business, negotiating contracts, hiring day laborers (many of whom were also bondsmen), and supervising the erection of numerous houses as well as several larger buildings. "Those who were mechanics had extra privileges," a postwar investigator explained, "some of them hiring their own time, & working as master builders—hiring labourers & teaching them—making contracts for buildings &c." As early as 1802, this practice had become so prevalent in New Hanover County, North Carolina, that a group of white mechanics signed a remonstrance to the state legislature. Despite statutes forbidding such practices, slaves worked as free mechanics and undertook contracts "on their own account, at sometimes less than one half the rate that a regular bred white Mechanic could afford to do it." Sometimes these slaves hired gangs of eight to twelve other bondsmen and women who worked entirely "for their own benefit." More than a half-century later, quasi-free slave contractors in the county still controlled a large portion of the construction business. In Charleston, South Carolina, a slightly different system emerged. House servants left with the responsibility for letting out repair and building contracts when their masters journeyed to the North during the summer months hired virtually free slaves and free blacks as carpenters, builders, and masons, who in turn maintained small work gangs of nearly free bondsmen to erect outbuildings and construct houses.

Some slave entrepreneurs found it difficult to sever their ties with profit-seeking slave owners. For nearly ten years Mary Ann Wyatt of King and Queen

County, Virginia, rented herself and her five children (seven others had been sold) from her master for $45 a year while establishing a business retailing oysters to local residents. Each week during this period, she journeyed to the Rappahannock River, a distance of approximately sixteen miles, purchased two baskets of oysters, and returned to sell them in the town square. Even after she had acquired a widespread reputation as an astute businesswoman and accumulated considerable property, including a rental house, Wyatt continued to pay a monthly tribute to her master. When a local representative of the credit-rating firm of R. G. Dun and Company evaluated the barbering and confectionery business of "Edwards & Carroway" in Wythe County, Virginia, during the 1850s, he noted that the two men were "slaves who hire their time" but added that they carried on the business "in name of Jas. Saunders whom they belong to." A Tennessee slave named Jack found his master equally insistent on receiving a sizable portion of his profits. For many years "Doctor Jack," as he was known, practiced medicine in sections of south-central Tennessee "with great & unparalled success.". . . Even as his practice grew, Jack's owner, William Macon, a planter in Maury and later in Giles county, demanded the fees. Only after more than a quarter-century, perhaps after his master's death, did this gifted slave establish his own practice. An eight word advertisement in Nashville's first business directory in 1853 told of his eventual success: "Jack, Root Doctor. Office 20 N Front St."

Two popular and industrious free-slave barbers in New Bern, North Carolina, similarly forfeited most of their earnings to their owner, free mulatto John Carruthers Stanly, who had himself started out as a free-slave barber. According to Stephen F. Miller, a prominent white resident of the town, Brister and Boston were always neatly dressed and kept their shop "in good reputation." "They were purchased by your Petitioner when they were quite small and reared by him and taught the trade of a barber," Stanly said in a petition to the Craven County Superior Court. "After the increase of business compelled your Petitioner to direct his attention to other matters, he left to the care of these two slaves the management of the said establishment." During this period the shop had been under the "exclusive management of the aforesaid servants" who had faithfully collected and paid to him the "money received by them from the customers to the shop." After many years of devoted service, Stanly now hoped that the two slaves would not only be permitted to retain their earnings but would also be granted freedom papers.

Most slave business people were able to move out on their own in the early stages of their careers. In the same Nashville business directory that listed "Doctor Jack" an advertisement appeared for another enterprising slave, bathhouse owner and barber shop proprietor Frank Parrish, a bondsman originally owned by Catherine Parish, the widow of a Davidson County farmer, and later by Edwin Ewing, a lawyer and politician. As early as 1836, Parrish had advertised that customers could enjoy the luxury of "the falling spray" and the "lucid coolness" of "the flood" at his bathing establishment. He promised to receive visitors from six o'clock in the morning to ten o'clock at night. "Ladies are respectfully informed that convenient apartments have been prepared, with every accommodation for their comfort, for their exclusive use, and female servants will always be in readiness [to attend] them." At his barbershop next door, Parrish sold fancy soaps, perfumes, collars, socks, suspenders, "CURLS, PUFFS, & C., also the best CIGARS and TOBACCO." For nearly two decades prior to his formal emancipation in 1853, Parrish ran these popular and thriving businesses.

A number of black women were also to be found among the slaves who started various types of businesses. In the Lower South, female plantation slaves were involved nearly as much as the men in the retailing of various crops to their masters or to local factors. They also established stalls and small stores on the edges of towns and cities, selling various products. In the Upper South, they managed businesses as seamstresses, weavers, laundresses, and shopkeepers. One former Maryland slave recalled how his mother ran two business enterprises at the same time. "After my father was sold my master gave my mother permission to work for herself," he wrote, "provided she gave him one half [of the profits]." Within a short time, she had opened a coffee shop at the federal army garrison of Fort Washington and later operated a secondhand clothing store, selling trousers, coats, shoes, caps, and stockings to marines at the base. Despite the protests of "poor whites" in the area, she "made quite a respectable living."

Perhaps the South's most resourceful free slave was Anthony Weston, a South Carolina mechanic who built rice mills for various slave owners at the edge of the inland river systems. "In consideration of the good conduct and faithful valuable service of my mulatto man Toney by trade a millwright I have for some years past given him to himself for his time say from the middle of May to the middle of November every year," Charleston planter Plowden Weston wrote in 1826, leaving instructions that six years after his death "his whole time be given up to him" and that he should be "emancipated and set free or allowed to depart from the State." But Weston was neither emancipated, nor did he leave the state. Instead, using his earnings as a builder, he invested in real estate and slaves. Between 1833 and 1845, he purchased (in the name of his free Negro wife Maria) large amounts of real property and twenty blacks, including skilled artisans who assisted him in constructing rice mills. In 1856, one planter described a Weston-built mill as "better than any on the river." By 1860, this remarkable slave owned $40,075 worth of real estate (in his wife's name) and had become one of the most affluent blacks in South Carolina.

These quasi-free blacks who engaged in business and acquired property were highly unusual. They had a shrewd understanding of Southern society, an intuitive sense for anticipating danger, and the ability to earn a livelihood. They were also able, in some instances, to secure the aid and protection of whites. Ambitious, persevering, hard working, and astute, some of them were highly successful as business people, and even those who had achieved less success had gained a large measure of freedom and independence. They realized that only the most strenuous and persistent effort would be rewarded. For some the fear of discovery remained a constant threat; for others, what might be termed "freedom dues," payments to owners or others for the privilege of quasi-freedom, continued to be a financial burden. Yet, in virtually every city in the South and in some rural communities, legally enslaved blacks moved out on their own and established businesses. In a few instances, they led completely autonomous lives, comfortably maintained their families, moved about from place to place, and acquired real estate and other property. . . .

The acquisition of property by slaves took place in a context of master-slave relations. To understand property holding among slaves the attitudes and activities of the slaveholding class are therefore no less important than the feelings of bondsmen and women. The dilemma whites faced was as old as slavery itself: how could they inculcate the work ethic in their bondspeople without also inculcating ambition, drive, and a desire for freedom? In the struggle to solve this dilemma, they became increasingly divided. Some masters argued that allowing slaves certain freedoms would undermine the entire system; others, ignoring laws and prophecies of doom, offered their slaves incentives, including the right to own property. In the end, both sides remained steadfast in their views, but the dispute itself, as seen in the growing number of planter complaints and restrictive laws on the one hand and the increasing instances of self-hire, quasi-freedom, and property ownership on the other, revealed the complex, ambiguous, and at times intensely personal nature of master-slave relations.

It had long been assumed that slaves, as chattel property themselves, could not legally own property. During the colonial and early national periods laws had been passed making it illegal for bondsmen and women to purchase, acquire, or own various goods and commodities. Slaveholders argued that granting such privileges would not only result in robberies, thefts, and increased "trafficking in stolen goods" but also could end in the far more serious problems of slave discontent and rebellion. With the increases in property ownership among slaves during the nineteenth century, slave owners enacted new, more specific statutes to deal with the problem. In 1826, Georgia prohibited blacks from buying or selling "any quantity or amount whatever of cotton, tobacco, wheat, rye, oats, corn, rice or poultry, or any other articles, except such as are known to be usually manufactured or vended by slaves." Tennessee forbade bondsmen and women from owning a pig, cow, mule, horse, "or other such like description of property." Virginia proclaimed that anyone who bought, sold, or received "any commodity whatsoever" from a slave would be subject to thirty-nine lashes "well laid on" or a fine of four times the value of the items bought, sold, or received. Later, state lawmakers made this crime punishable by a jail sentence of up to six months. South Carolina passed an act to prevent the illicit traffic in cotton, rice, corn, and wheat, between slaves and free blacks. As late as 1864, Texas passed a law to prevent slaves from exercising "pretended ownership over property." It listed horses, sheep, cattle, goats, hogs, or any other animals "over which such negro may exercise a pretended right of ownership or on which such negro slave shall have a brand or ear mark."

Similarly, with the expansion of self-hire and quasi-freedom during the nineteenth century, slaveholders recast their eighteenth century laws to deal with these problems. These legal codes bore witness not only to the existence of these phenomena but also to the increasing importance slave owners attached to curtailing such activities among blacks. While most of the new statutes passed between 1818 and 1840 carried relatively small fines for each offense, some states, including Georgia, enacted laws with stiff penalties. "*Whereas* divers persons of color, who are slaves by the laws of this State, having never been manumitted in conformity to the same, are nevertheless in the full exercise and enjoyment of all the rights and privileges of free persons of color, without being subject to the duties and obligations incident to such persons, thereby constituting a class of people, equally dangerous to the safety of the free citizens of this State, and destructive of the comfort and happiness of the slave population," an 1818 Georgia law read, "*Be it therefore* enacted [that a fine of $500 shall be administered] for each and every offence." Several other states followed Georgia's lead. With a 1785 statute as a guide, North Carolina passed a law in 1831 to deal with the increasing number of slaves who went "at large as free men." Henceforth, masters who allowed slaves to "go at large as a freeman, exercising his or her own discre[t]ion in the employment of his or her time," would be subject to indictment and upon conviction "shall be fined in the discretion of the court." "It shall not be lawful for any person to hire to any slave the time of such slave," an 1840 Tennessee law read; or to allow bondspeople to "trade in spirituous liquors, hogs, cows, horses, or mules as a free person of color." The South Carolina Court of Appeals ruled during the 1830s that "if the owner without a formal act of emancipation permit his slave to go at large and to exercise all the rights and enjoy all the privileges of a free person of color the slave becomes liable to seizure as a derelict." At one time or another, lawmakers in virtually every southern state enacted similar codes to control slaves who enjoyed "the rights and privileges" of free blacks.

The extensive legal codes governing master-slave relations with regard to property ownership and virtually free status reflected the anxieties of whites who felt they were losing control over *their* property. The entire structure of slavery rested on the power of owners to exert complete control over their blacks. When slaves acquired property or hired their own time, they became independent and ungovernable. This problem of control, ever present in the minds of whites, was not confined to one section of the South or one type of "domestic economy" but was as deeply rooted as slavery itself. There was a direct connection between black property ownership, black initiative, and black theft, one Louisiana planter proclaimed, and on his plantation slaves would never be allowed to have anything they could call their own. When blacks possessed "stocks of horses and hogs" and exercised "all the rights of ownership in such stock," a group of Virginians noted, they were not adverse to stealing farm animals and fodder, thefts which were virtually impossible to trace. A group of Tennessee slave owners echoed these same sentiments: pass some law to prevent Negroes from "selling meats, chickens, fruits, etc., upon public days at public places," they instructed the legislature. They had experienced firsthand "the evil effects of the system now prevailing." "Every measure that may lessen the dependence of a Slave on his master ought to be opposed as tending to dangerous consequences," Edward Dudley, Timothy Barton, Jonathan Nichols, Jacob Hare, and a group of other South Carolina cotton planters explained. "The more privileges a Slave obtains, the less depending he is on his master, & the greater nuisance he is likely to be to the public." Two of the privileges they pointed to included allowing blacks to cultivate their "own cotton fields" and "trade in their own name." Forty-three years later, in 1859, a group of Hays County, Texas, slave owners offered the same opinion. "The undersigned, Grand Jurors, of the County aforesaid, Now in Session, Would Most respectfully Solicit your particular attention and ask the passage of an act of the present Legislature," J. C. Watkins, James M. Malone, John H. Cocks, and seventeen others said in a petition to the General Assembly, "to forbid Negro slaves *the right* to hold in their own name and for their own use, as property, Horses, Cattle, Land, and Stock of every description, as we see daily the baneful influence and effects on the Slave population."

But despite the web of legal restrictions, and the outcries of slave owners concerning the "baneful influence and effects" of property ownership and quasi-freedom, these practices not only continued during the antebellum period but also grew and expanded. This was due largely to the acquiescence and in numerous instances the active support of the slaveholding class. Some masters believed that encouraging initiative and individual enterprise among slaves was the best means of control, since it gave blacks something to strive for and allowed them to provide for their families. Others granted bondsmen and women certain liberties for personal, ideological, and economic reasons. Some whites who had fathered slave children felt compassion for their offspring and, though finding it difficult to manumit their progeny, did allow them to accumulate property. Though antislavery sentiments were virtually silenced following the Nat Turner rebellion, a few whites, including North Carolina Quakers and others, continued to own slaves while allowing them to "go at large as free men." One jurist called this "custom" in effect "a species of *quasi* emancipation." A substantial number of slaveholders in Maryland, Virginia, and other Upper South states, and in a few Lower South states, practiced what was referred to as "deferred manumission," allowing bondsmen and women several years to adjust to a new life and acquire property before granting them complete freedom.

Some whites who strongly defended slavery and publicly denounced quasi-freedom and self-hire found it was profitable to send blacks out on their own to earn a living. Those who owned especially talented and industrious bondsmen and women whom they trusted to be "strictly obedient to heredity" were often not adverse to sending them to towns and cities to work in various capacities. By the 1840s and 1850s many of these masters were earning good returns from their blacks who found employment in Baltimore, Norfolk, Louisville, Nashville, St. Louis, Savannah, Charleston, New Orleans, and smaller urban areas. Furthermore, it was whites who hired and paid these slaves. In 1856, a group of white builders in Smithfield, North Carolina, complained that they were constantly being outbid by free Negroes and self-hired slaves to build "houses, vessels &c." They were not only bitter about the competition from blacks but also criticized the whites who hired these construction gangs. The same was true of a group of Sumter District, South Carolina whites, who noted in 1849 that the state statute forbidding self-hire did not even apply to female slaves, yet they were often hiring themselves out and accumulating property. "The law in relation to Slaves hiring their own time is not enforced with sufficient promptness, and efficiency," a group of rural residents in the same state added a decade later, "as to accomplish the object designed by its enactment."

Not only did they flaunt the laws prohibiting property ownership and self-hire, but some masters went to great lengths to protect especially industrious slaves. "This man has served his time in my neighbourhood, and has always maintained an excellent character," Virginia planter Samuel Anderson wrote concerning one quasi-free slave. "He is a good workman and an honest and industrious man. I have no doubt that he can obtain the sanction of every man in the neighbourhood." The distinguished Virginian John Wise wrote a glowing letter in behalf of the slave Jingo of Accomac County. "His Character while a slave was a good one in every respect as far as I ever knew or heard," Wise explained. "Since he has been considered and acted as a free man it has sustained no diminution; he has lived for the last ten years within a mile of me and has supported a spotless character & one far above the generality of people of his colour for honesty, Sobriety and orderly deportment." Another black who secured similar praise was Parlour Washington, "a good industrious mechanic in the arts & trades of tanner & currier of leather and also a good shoe, boot and harness maker." Nearly one hundred Hamilton County, Tennessee, residents explained that his services were "much needed and required by the Citizens of the section of the County where he now resides." In Nashville, Ephraim Foster, a lawyer, Whig politician, and United States senator, not only allowed a few of his most trusted blacks quasi-free status but also appeared in court in behalf of his bondsmen and women. In 1818, Foster testified that the African-born Simon, who was "sober, industrious, hard working, and a firm believer in the Christian religion" should be manumitted; later, he posted bond of $1,000 for Anna, a slave who was honest, temperate, and "strictly obedient to heredity"; in 1851, he presented a petition to the court for the emancipation of his virtually free slave James Thomas, a barber, property owner, and businessman who had always maintained "an exemplary character."

In states where legal emancipations were rare, whites sometimes entered into trust agreements, promising to hold legal title to slaves while allowing them to move about freely, or purchased family members so they could remain near loved ones. South Carolina slave owner Robert Howard (not to be confused with a black slave owner of the same name) did both, when, in 1823, he purchased James Marsh's slave mother, Abby Hopton, from him for $5 (her market value was about $800) and then promised, in a deed of trust, to allow her the same rights as a free person of color. Such agreements were extralegal, or illegal, but this did not deter whites from evading or breaking the law. Even Charles C. Jones, Jr., a man of the highest probity, advised his father not to prosecute the person who had illegally hired one of his father's runaway slaves. "A prosecution would be unpleasant, tending to make the matter notorious, and would in every probability be unaccompanied by conviction," he explained. "Unless there be an obligation resting upon one for purposes affecting the general good, order, and well-being of society, the less said and done in cases of this kind the better." One southern jurist went so far as to rule (to the consternation of many slaveholders) that until illegally freed blacks were actually seized and brought to trial they must be allowed to "stand on the footing of any other free negro." Another argued that "a common reputation of freedom" was prima facie evidence of free status. "It is difficult to suppose a case," he declared, "where common reputation would concede to a man the right of freedom if his right were a groundless one." Indeed, such rulings and activities on the part of slave masters were as much a part of the fabric of antebellum race relations as the punitive and repressive laws designed to control every aspect of Negro life. . . .

It was a clear, bright morning, the second day of winter 1864, as General William T. Sherman, heading an entourage of Union soldiers, rode slowly down Bull Street in Savannah, Georgia, to the customhouse. Climbing several flights of stairs to the roof, he scanned the city—the small brick houses, the grilled gateways and half-concealed gardens, the sluggish, rust-colored Savannah river, and a smoldering, half-sunken ironclad in the navy yard—the only vestige that the city had been occupied less than twenty-four hours before by the Confederate Army. Sherman felt a sense of relief and triumph. He had led his men on one of the most successful campaigns of the war; he had reached his destination with very few casualties (only 764 men killed, missing, or wounded in an army of 65,000); he had confiscated large herds of livestock. "We started out with about five thousand head of cattle, and arrived with over ten thousand," he reported to Ulysses Grant, "of course consuming mostly turkeys, chickens, sheep, hogs and the cattle of the country." In addition, he had captured fifteen thousand first-rate mules and at least thirty thousand horses. Before his final assault northward, through the Carolinas to Richmond, he would rest his men and stock his supply wagons. In the weeks that followed Union barges, carrying thousands of hogs, sheep, horses, mules, and huge quantities of cornmeal and potatoes, moved steadily up the Ogeechee River to the narrow road at King's bridge.

Even the most loyal Savannahian had probably forgotten Sherman's month-long occupation when, some eight years later, another representative of the United States government, Special Agent Virgil Hillyer of the Southern Claims Commission, arrived in the city. Under a mandate from Congress to identify and provide restitution to Union loyalists who had lost personal property to Sherman's pillaging troops, Hillyer remained in the city nearly a year, listening to the testimony of thousands of witnesses, taking depositions from hundreds of claimants. "I know it is hard for some to realize or imagine how it was possible for slaves to own property," he wrote after several months, "[but there] are colored persons in Savannah worth their [sic] thousands; some in our market who can buy 50 or 300 head of cattle at a time, and did so before and during the war." Among them were cotton factor Monday Habersham, hostler John Butler, livery keeper Henry Wane, butcher Abram Steward, and cotton farmer Prince Kendy. These blacks had become as prosperous as many whites. Steward, for example, had leased five hundred acres from his master, owned between three and four hundred head of cattle, and had been, according to Hillyer, "the largest and most successful butcher in the Savannah market." Kendy had also rented land from his master but planted it in cotton. It was well known that Kendy's father had been the richest slave in Georgia, worth between $18,000 and $20,000, and that Kendy himself sold several bales of cotton at market each year. As if to allay any doubts about these findings, Hillyer explained that cattle and hogs multiplied rapidly, doubling in number every four or five years, and that blacks near the coast had tended livestock for many generations. Moreover, he had made every effort to verify each claim. He was convinced that most black families in southern Georgia owned a horse, mule, cattle, or other property; and that such ownership was widespread "all through the Southern States."

Coming as it did from a northern-born Unionist who was sympathetic toward freedmen and women such a report might have been viewed with suspicion, but subsequent investigators, including Virginia-born William W. Paine, a former captain in the First Georgia Volunteer Regiment, confirmed Hillyer's findings. Paine corroborated the claims of ex-slaves with the recollections of former masters. "I will [say] that if I can aid him in any degree in making the necessary proofs, I will cheerfully do so," former slave owner Charles C. Jones, Jr., wrote from New York City, concerning John Monroe's claim that he had lost cattle and horses worth $2,642. "He was one of the best Negroes I ever knew. His industry was ceaseless. He was always adding to his possessions, and surrounding himself with comforts unusual for one in his station. He had, of his own means, purchased his own and his wife's freedom prior to the emancipation proclamation." When the statements of former masters could not be procured, Paine interviewed neighbors, friends, and local residents. It took him nearly a year and a half to verify the claim of former bondswoman Linda Roberts. On January 30, 1875, she had testified that she had recently lost her husband and relied on her children and grandchildren for support, but before the war she had owned 20 head of cattle (valued at $400), 30 hogs ($150), 40 beehives ($80), 18 ducks ($9), 50 chickens ($10), 20 bushels of corn ($30), 100 bushels of rice ($200), a saddle and bridle ($20), and a horse and buggy ($260).

> I owned the property in my petition [valued at $1,159] because my husband bought it. In the first place my husband bought a mare colt which was the beginning of his raising. He planted corn & sold it to buy the mare. We raised this colt till she had a colt, she had three colts, one died. Master bought one & we kept one which we swapped for a gray mare, which the Yankees took from us. He got the cattle same as he did the horse; bought a cow and raised off her. He got the hogs in the same way, bought a sow & raised from that. He got the other things mentioned in his petition by buying, raising, & trading.

After a lengthy investigation Paine concluded, as had Hillyer, that significant numbers of slaves had owned property.

Working within the task system low-country blacks discovered many ways to accumulate property. But in various other parts of the South, on large and small plantations and in towns and cities, slaves used other means to acquire a few head of livestock, extra clothing, and small amounts of cash. Some planted staples and sold them to the master; others earned wages when they were hired out or hired themselves out; and a few gained quasi-free status. Property ownership among slaves remained small during the eighteenth century, but by the eve of the Civil War—according to the comments of slaveholders, increasing enactments to halt "pretended ownership," the recollections of former slaves, and the reports of postwar investigators—considerable numbers of slaves had become property owners.

They possessed cattle, milk cows, horses, pigs, chickens, cotton, rice, tobacco, gold and silver coin, wagons, buggies, fancy clothing, and in rare instances even real estate.

While this coincided with a declining African influence in the slave population, the motives and attitudes of slaves toward accumulating property were complex. Even those who never left the plantation saw the symbiotic relationship between ownership and autonomy, wealth and prestige, earnings and freedom. Some of them were motivated by the work ethic or a competitive impulse: they spoke of "getting ahead" and "accumulating"; they were described as "very acquisitive" or having "a passion for ownership." Yet others acquired property for show (e.g., fancy clothes), for practical reasons (a horse for visiting family members on a neighboring plantation), or as an expression of status. The drudgery and despair of perpetual enslavement aroused in some a special yearning for possessing even a few things they could call their own. In rural areas with the largest concentrations of blacks—eastern North Carolina, the Sea Islands of South Carolina and Georgia, the black belt of Alabama, the Mississippi Delta, and the sugar parishes of Louisiana—the dominant motive was probably the desire for autonomy. Indeed, by planting crops, raising farm animals, hunting and fishing, blacks could distance themselves not only from the impersonal forces of the marketplace but from their overseers and masters as well. These goals—subsistence and independence—as historian Philip Morgan suggests, were "nothing more than the central priorities of peasants throughout the world." Yet even in these regions, and more so in towns and cities and in areas with smaller concentrations of slaves (or larger numbers of free Negroes)—as in Maryland, Virginia, Tennessee, and Missouri—bondsmen and women demonstrated not only the need for autonomy but also a determination to improve themselves and provide their families with more than bare necessities. In any case, black attitudes toward property ownership had changed dramatically in only two generations.

Standing on the roof of the customhouse and looking out over a conquered city, General Sherman felt a sense of euphoria on that December day during the waning months of the Civil War. At that very moment, his troops were making their way across sluggish streams, down through cane brakes, and into cypress swamps as they marauded to accumulate provisions for a final assault against the dying Confederacy. Little did he realize, however, that some of the provisions and livestock being seized belonged to the very slaves he had marched to the sea to liberate.

Suggested Readings

General

Ira Berlin, *Slaves Without Masters: The Free Negro in the Antebellum South* (1974).

John W. Blassingame, *The Slave Community: Plantation Life in the Antebellum South* (1979).

John B. Boles, *Masters and Slaves in the House of the Lord: Race and Religion in the American South* (1988).

Bruce Collins, *White Society in the Antebellum South* (1985).
Eugene D. Genovese, *Roll Jordan Roll: The World the Slaves Made* (1974).
Nathan I. Huggins, *Black Odyssey: The Afro-American Ordeal in Slavery* (1979).
Charles Joyner, *Down by the Riverside: A South Carolina Slave Community* (1984).
Peter Kolchin, *American Slavery, 1619–1877* (1993).
James Oakes, *The Ruling Race: A History of American Slaveholders* (1982).
Kenneth M. Stampp, *The Peculiar Institution: Slavery in the Antebellum South* (1956).

FURTHER READINGS

ANTEBELLUM SOUTH: John B. Boles, *The South Through Time* (1995); Catherine Clinton, *The Plantation Mistress: Women's World in the Old South* (1982); Carl Degler, *Neither Black nor White: Slavery and Race Relations in Brazil and the United States* (1971); Clement Eaton, *The Growth of Southern Civilization, 1790–1860* (1961); Douglas Egerton, *Gabriel's Rebellion: The Virginia Slave Conspiracies of 1800 and 1802* (1993); Stanley M. Elkins, *Slavery: A Problem in American Intellectual Life* (1976); Robert W. Fogel and Stanley Engerman, *Time on the Cross: The Economics of Slavery* (2 vols., 1974); Drew Faust, *James Henry Hammond and the Old South* (1982); Elizabeth Fox-Genovese, *Within the Plantation Household: Black and White Women of the Old South* (1988); John Hope Franklin, *The Militant South* (1956); Eugene D. Genovese, *The Slaveholders' Dilemma* (1992); and *From Rebellion to Revolution: Afro-American Slave Revolts in the Making of the Modern World* (1979); Michael P. Johnson and James R. Roark, *Black Masters: A Free Family of Color in the Old South* (1984); Whittington B. Johnson, *Black Savannah, 1788–1864* (1996); Anne C. Loveland, *Southern Evangelicals and the Social Order* (1980); Donald G. Matthews, *Religion in the Old South* (1977); James Oakes, *Slavery and Freedom: An Interpretation of the Old South* (1990); Stephen B. Oates, *The Fires of Jubilee: Nat Turner's Fierce Rebellion* (1975); Leslie H. Owens, *This Species of Property: Slave Life and Culture in the Old South* (1976); Frank Owsley, *Plain Folk of the Old South* (1949); Albert J. Raboteau, *Slave Religion: The "Invisible" Institution in the Antebellum South* (1978); Mechal Sobel, *Trabelin' On: The Slave Journey to the Afro-Baptist Faith* (1979); Bertram Wyatt-Brown, *Southern Honor: Ethics and Behavior in the Old South* (1982).

QUESTIONS FOR DISCUSSION

1. Was Elisha Worthington's slave plantation typical of slave plantations throughout the South? Explain.
2. How did slavery shape the economic and social structure of the antebellum South?
3. What effect did the prohibition of the international slave trade have on the institution of slavery? Explain.
4. How did white southerners justify and rationalize the existence of slavery?
5. What methods did blacks employ to diminish some of the dehumanizing aspects of slavery?

6. Explain the origins of free people of color in the South and indicate why their status over time deteriorated rather than improved.
7. Using information from the selection by Loren Schweninger, describe how slaves accumulated property in the Deep South. What effect did ownership of property have on their lives?

CHAPTER ELEVEN

THE UNRAVELING OF THE UNION, 1848–1861

FREDERICK DOUGLASS AND THE ANTISLAVERY CRUSADE

By 1850 Frederick Douglass had become a conspicuous figure in the anti-slavery movement in both the United States and Great Britain. Born a slave in Maryland in 1818, he escaped north twenty years later, settled in Massachusetts, and quickly became a favorite on the antislavery lecture circuit under the sponsorship of William Lloyd Garrison (see Chapter 8). In 1845 he not only published the story of his life under the title *The Narrative of the Life of Frederick Douglass, an American Slave,* but also embarked on his first journey to the British Isles where for twenty months large audiences responded enthusiastically to his eloquent and passionate oratory. English friends demonstrated their admiration by raising funds to purchase his freedom.

Upon his return to the United States, abolitionists in Massachusetts became increasingly uneasy about his new self-confidence and growing independence—his determination to be his own man, free of the constraints and possessiveness of the white abolitionists. Douglass' decision to launch his own antislavery newspaper outside Massachusetts alienated him from Garrison. Moving to Rochester, New York, in 1847, Douglass launched *The North Star,* an antislavery newspaper that allowed him to establish himself as a black leader rather than as a spokesman for the Garrisonians. The momentous struggle over slavery in the territories acquired from Mexico completed Douglass' conversion to political abolitionism. Allied first with the Liberty party, he shifted his allegiance to the Free Soil party and finally embraced the Republican party.

Though Douglass worked with white abolitionists, he was keenly aware that racism was a national phenomenon and pervaded even the ranks of white

Frederick Douglass, eloquent critic of slavery and militant abolitionist.

abolitionism. Convinced that "prejudice against color is stronger north than south," he devoted a large portion of his addresses to racial discriminatory practices in the North—practices which he regularly encountered. Although northern states had abolished slavery, denounced its existence in the South, and opposed its extension into new territories, these states denied free black residents within their borders many essential rights of citizenship. Only five free states allowed blacks to vote. "It is only a slight exaggeration," historian David Potter observed, "to say that Negroes could vote where there were none to cast a ballot, but could not vote where there was actually a Negro population to be found." Before 1860 no state allowed blacks to serve on juries, and most free states required blacks to attend segregated schools or excluded them from public education. Ohio, Indiana, Illinois, and Oregon enacted laws to prevent blacks from settling within their boundaries. Everywhere, blacks were segregated in residence and employment and excluded from places frequented by white genteel society. Fully aware of this pervasive discrimination against people of his race in the North, Douglass insisted that slavery and racism were inseparable, an approach that stood in sharp contrast to the political debate prompted by the question of slavery in the territories.

AN ERA OF GROWTH AND CHANGE

Although slavery was the most controversial public issue in the United States during the decade before the Civil War, it was not the consistently all-absorbing concern of every American as it was for some abolitionists. Many were preoccupied with personal and family matters, with earning a livelihood, and with amassing wealth, or, as we have seen, focused their energies on reforms other than the antislavery cause such as temperance, women's rights, education, and improvements in prisons and mental institutions. In an age of rapid urbanization, issues such as sanitation, housing, epidemics, and crime were often the primary concerns of urban residents. In the eyes of many Americans, one of the most serious problems confronted by cities was the large influx of foreign immigrants. During the single decade of the 1850s, over 2.5 million immigrants entered the United States, more than had entered in the preceding thirty years. Two nationalities dominated: the Irish and Germans. The larger by far was the Irish contingent, mostly poor, unskilled, and overwhelmingly Roman Catholic, driven from their native land by famine. With lower horizons of expectations, the Irish worked for less and were less prone to protest long hours and low pay. Fears that the Irish and other immigrants would undercut the wages of native-born workers, coupled with growing concerns about their Catholicism and their inability to be culturally assimilated, precipitated an outburst of antiforeignism and political nativism that crested in the mid-1850s. Some of those who supported the antislavery cause also exhibited a virulent xenophobia.

Many Americans, all the while, were caught up in demographic shifts as rural inhabitants in the East sought their fortunes in the West or in cities. The lure of new, fertile lands in the West proved especially attractive to thousands of easterners. Others raced westward in search of quick riches. In fact, the decade of the 1850s opened and closed amid widespread excitement over gold rushes to California in 1849 and to Pikes Peak (in present-day Colorado) in 1859. Agriculture in the East and in the West significantly changed as the result of the introduction of labor-saving devices and machines. Such technology, coupled with the more efficient use of land and fertilizer, enabled grain farmers to increase their production so dramatically that some predicted that grain would replace cotton as the dominant factor in the economy.

Technological advances of all sorts that were either patented or perfected during the 1850s profoundly affected the lives of many Americans. Among these were Charles Goodyear's process for vulcanizing rubber; Isaac M. Singer's sewing machine capable of continuous stitching; and cast-iron stoves which replaced the open hearth for cooking and heating. The 1850s also witnessed the fanning out of telegraph lines across the continent from the Atlantic to the Pacific. Samuel F.B. Morse patented the telegraph in 1837 and constructed a line between Washington and Baltimore seven years later. By 1852 about three thousand miles of telegraph lines had been constructed and within eight years the figure had more than doubled. The role of the telegraph was especially significant in the operation of the expanding railway system.

The decade of the 1850s was a boom era in railroad construction. More than twenty-two thousand miles of track were added to the existing rail network. Much of the new construction was in the trans-Appalachian West. For example, Chicago and St. Louis became important rail centers. The explosive rail construction rerouted the flow of trade and linked the Midwest more closely with the Northeast, spawned new industries and contributed to the growth of older ones such as lumber and iron, and decreased travel time for both freight and passengers. The role of New York's Wall Street in underwriting much of the railroad expansion helped to transform the city into the nation's financial center. As the first really big business in the country, railroad companies pioneered in modern management techniques. Although the 1850s witnessed the construction of trunk lines from New York and Philadelphia to Cleveland and Chicago and the completion of a railroad linking New Orleans and Chicago at the end of the decade, the nation's rail network was by no means a fully integrated system. It involved numerous competing companies that used a wide variety of gauges, or track widths, that obstructed the efficient flow of traffic and increased the cost of trans-shipping freight.

THE ILLUSION OF A COHESIVE NATION

During the decade and a half following the end of the Mexican War in 1846, the expansion of the nation's rail system was but one of numerous factors that appeared to strengthen the cohesiveness of the republic. During this era, more than any preceding, one historian has observed, "the United States took on the qualities of a nation." But at the same time sectional rivalries and animosities intensified in ways that thwarted the strong centralizing tendencies and threatened the unity of the republic. Even though Americans may not have been as consistently preoccupied with slavery in the 1850s as we are sometimes led to believe, the issue was always present and had a way of becoming involved with all manner of other questions, including railroad expansion, that appeared to have nothing to do with slavery. Once entangled with another issue, slavery tended to swallow it up, as was the case during discussions about organizing territories acquired as a result of the Mexican War. One consequence of the war was to elevate the dispute over slavery to a level where it could no longer be contained, as political leaders had succeeded in doing since the Missouri Compromise of 1820. Efforts at containment after 1846 proved to be both temporary and illusory.

THE SLAVERY DEBATE

The Wilmot Proviso

The slavery issue reemerged publicly in August 1846 when Congressman David Wilmot added to an appropriation bill a proviso that would exclude slavery from territories acquired by the Mexican War. He introduced the provision not out of sympathy for slaves, but out of a desire to retain the new territories exclusively for free white labor unencumbered by the presence of any blacks, free or slave. He also resented the "insufferable arrogance" of the slave South in presuming to direct the destiny of the republic. Whatever his intention, the Pennsylvania congressman touched off a controversy that brought into the open sectional differences and prompted a debate which drew lines that persisted until the disruption of the Union in 1861. Much of the debate prompted by the proviso focused on Congress' authority to mandate whether a territory should be slave or free. Convinced that Congress did indeed possess such authority, northern congressmen pointed to the Northwest Ordinance of 1787 and the Missouri Compromise which outlawed slavery north of 36°30′. They especially cited Article IV, Section 3 of the Constitution which empowered Congress "to dispose of and make all needful rules and regulations respecting the territory or other property belonging to the United States."

Southern Opposition

The aging John C. Calhoun, as a spokesman for the slave South, countered with the argument that Congress did not have the right to exclude slavery from the territories, because such lands belonged to the United States as "tenants in common, or joint proprietors." Because the federal government acted as the trustee in administering territories, all citizens should be able to enter them with their property, including their slaves. What Calhoun and other southerners clearly understood was that the inability of the slave states to expand made the slave power politically vulnerable. As long as half of the states allowed slavery, the South possessed an equal vote in the Senate. But if the new territories were carved up into multiple free states, the equilibrium would be upset and the South's power destroyed. Calhoun's argument that it was unconstitutional for Congress to prevent citizens of a state from carrying their property, in other words, slaves, into any territory meant that the South Carolinian (Calhoun) considered the Missouri Compromise itself unconstitutional.

Popular Sovereignty

The question of slavery in the territories created an impasse in Congress. As long as the North and South remained deadlocked, no progress could be made toward organizing the territories. A compromise was put forward first by Democratic Senator Lewis Cass and later taken up by his Democratic colleague from Illinois, Stephen A. Douglas, which became known as "popular sovereignty." It would allow the people of a territory rather than Congress to decide the status of slavery therein. Such a procedure, Cass explained, was fair and democratic. Despite such a description, popular sovereignty was not as straightforward as it appeared. It did not, for example, specify at what point the settlers of a new territory would determine whether it would be slave or free. Many northerners argued that a territorial legislature possessed the authority to exclude slavery and could do so at the time the territory was organized, while

Calhoun and his southern followers insisted that the status of a territory as free or slave could come only upon its application for statehood. Such ambiguity in the popular sovereignty concept led to interminable wrangling and hair-splitting.

Polarization

The controversy sparked by Wilmot's proviso revealed much about the nature of the debate over slavery that raged for a decade and a half. Rather than focusing on enslaved blacks in the South, Congress ignored the larger issue of racial prejudice and dealt primarily in abstractions by concentrating on what one historian described as "the future situation of imaginary slaves in an unsettled wilderness." The fierce verbal combat over highly theoretical questions and technical constitutional issues accomplished little, other than to further polarize the North and South. On both sides of the Mason and Dixon Line references to plots, conspiracies, and intrigues became increasingly common as southerners hurled insults at the abolitionist North, and northerners reciprocated by denouncing the multiple sins of the slave power. In August 1848, members of Congress engaged in a long and bitter debate over the so-called Oregon Bill, punctuated by violent speeches and at least one challenge to a duel. As finally enacted, the bill excluded slavery from the territory. President Polk signed it but he pointed out that he did so only because it was north of the Missouri Compromise 36°30′ line.

ZACHARY TAYLOR AND MILLARD FILLMORE

THE ELECTION OF 1848

In the 1848 presidential campaign the Democrats and Whigs attempted to use the traditional strategy of evading or muting the slavery issue. Although the Democratic presidential candidate, Lewis Cass, had declared the Wilmot Proviso unconstitutional and advocated popular sovereignty, the party's platform made no explicit statement about slavery in the territories. The Whigs, who were even more evasive on the issues raised by Wilmot's Proviso, chose as their party's presidential candidate General Zachary Taylor, the hero of Buena Vista and a native southerner. Though a Louisiana slaveowner, Taylor had taken no position on public issues and had never even bothered to vote.

The most forthright position during the campaign was that of a third party, the Free Soil party, which attracted a hodgepodge of those opposed to the extension of slavery into the territories including northern "Conscience Whigs," members of the defunct Liberty party, and dissident Democrats, who combined in 1848 and nominated Martin Van Buren as the party's presidential candidate. The Free Soilers concentrated on the dangers involved in permitting the extension of slavery rather than on the evils of the existing slave system. Their poor showing in the election resulted in the disintegration of the party before 1852.

The outcome of the 1848 election, a contest that left the issue of slavery in the territories unresolved, was a victory for the Whigs and General Taylor whose triumph owed much to the support of antislavery men such as William H. Seward of New York and Abraham Lincoln of Illinois. In the interim between Taylor's election in November and his inauguration in March 1849, the crisis deepened as a result of efforts in Congress to enact a bill to abolish slavery and the slave trade in the District of Columbia.

TAYLOR AND SLAVERY IN THE TERRITORIES

When Taylor assumed office, those southerners who expected this native son and slaveholder to be supportive of their position were sorely disappointed. A political novice, the new president quickly came under the influence of Seward, an outspoken antislavery advocate and shrewd Whig politician. Although Taylor believed in slavery, he rejected Calhoun's notion that the security of the slave system in the South depended on its expansion into the western territories. He also argued that such areas were unsuited to the cultivation of staple crops such as cotton and tobacco that required slave labor. While the wrangling continued between the Calhounites, Wilmot Proviso advocates, and popular sovereignty supporters, California and New Mexico still had not been organized into territories and remained under military control. The influx of forty-niners into California in search of gold swelled the area's population to over one hundred thousand by the end of 1849.

To end the sectional deadlock, President Taylor proposed that the Mexican cession be divided into two large states, California and New Mexico (which also included most of present-day Oregon, Utah, and Colorado) and ordered military officials to speed up statehood movements in both. California quickly drafted and adopted a constitution that prohibited slavery. In December 1849 the president requested Congress to admit California as a free state as soon as possible. New Mexico would also be granted statehood upon application and, like California, would be allowed to determine for itself whether it would come into the Union as a free or slave state. In regard to the boundary dispute between Texas and New Mexico that became the focus of much debate, President Taylor recommended that the issue be left to the courts to resolve.

ESCALATION OF THE SECTIONAL CONFLICT

The South considered the president's plan untenable because it upset the existing equilibrium between the sections. A free California would tilt the balance in the North's favor, and the admission of New Mexico and Oregon as free states would consign the South to a hopeless minority status in the Senate, as it already was in the House. Interparty differences, as well as intraparty factionalism, figured in the congressional opposition to the president's proposal and prompted a variety of alternatives from both Democrats and Whigs. Many southerners viewed the situation as a supreme crisis in which slavery and the whole southern way of life was at stake. Talk of secession erupted once again. Calhoun counseled no compromise and urged the convention of southern delegates that was to meet in Nashville in June 1850 to promote secession if Congress refused to allow slaveowners the right to take their slave property into any territory. In the vein of Andrew Jackson, President Taylor let it be known that he would make no concessions to those who talked of secession and would hang anyone who threatened the Union. Calhoun was convinced that the "agitation" of the slavery question had already snapped some of the most important "cords of union."

HENRY CLAY AND THE COMPROMISE OF 1850

Into this highly volatile situation stepped the seventy-two-year-old Henry Clay, who had returned to the Senate in 1849 to propose a solution to defuse a crisis that promised to snap the remaining cords. To enhance the prospects for winning acceptance of a compromise, he enlisted the support of Massachusetts Senator Daniel Webster who, in spite of their past differences, agreed to join him in this undertaking.

In January 1850 Clay introduced his set of resolutions, known as the Omnibus Bill, that he hoped would settle all of the various points of contention over slavery. Clay's compromise included provisions designed to placate both the North and the South. Under the Omnibus Bill, California would be admitted as a free state; the rest of the Mexican cession would be organized into the two territories, New Mexico and Utah, without any restrictions on slavery which meant that Congress could not exclude slaves from these territories; the Texas–New Mexico boundary dispute was to be settled with Texas surrendering its claims in return for the payment by the United States of the Texas debt; the slave trade, but not slavery, was to be abolished in the District of Columbia; a stronger fugitive slave law would be enacted to enable the South to secure the return of slaves who sought refuge in the North; and Congress was denied the power to prohibit the interstate slave trade. The Omnibus Bill required that all components be approved as a package.

The nine-month congressional debate on Clay's compromise assumed all the attributes of high drama starring the older generation of statesmen, including the "great triumvirate" (Clay, Calhoun, and Webster), as well as the new generation of political leaders represented by Douglas and Seward. Hopes for the success of Clay's compromise were so high that the southern delegates at the Nashville Convention adjourned until the final vote on the Omnibus Bill had been taken. Many businessmen, enjoying prosperous times, earnestly desired to end the controversy over slavery and get on with making money. Despite high hopes for the success of Clay's efforts, all parts of the Omnibus Bill had the support neither of a majority in Congress nor of President Taylor. Taylor threatened a veto, but died suddenly on July 9, 1850, and was replaced by Vice President Millard Fillmore, who supported Clay's compromise as enthusiastically as Taylor had opposed it.

Douglas Rescues the Compromise

Just as it appeared as if Clay's compromise would fail because of the inability of the northern and southern sectional blocs to agree on it as a package, Senator Stephen A. Douglas, the so-called Little Giant, stepped into the breach to save the compromise with the backing of President Fillmore. As an architect of popular sovereignty, Douglas repeatedly claimed that he did not care whether the people of a new territory "voted slavery up or down." Personally, he considered slavery an outmoded, inefficient institution in disrepute in the Western world, but for him it was not a burning moral issue. Fully aware that only a minority in Congress supported all components of Clay's proposal, Douglas believed that he could get the compromise passed if the different parts were voted on separately rather than being considered altogether. Such a strategy would allow the committed minority to vote with the northern bloc for aspects of the compromise favorable to the North and with the southern bloc for those parts favorable to the South. Douglas' strategy worked, and within six weeks he secured passage of all items of Clay's original proposal. By mid-September 1850 the crisis had passed, owing in large part to the role played by a new generation of political leaders represented by Douglas.

The Compromise as a Temporary Armistice

Indisputably, the Compromise of 1850 enabled the Union to weather the storm unleashed by the Wilmot Proviso. Many Americans rightly regarded it as an extraordinary achievement. But the foundations upon which the Union remained intact for eleven more years were indeed fragile. Eighty percent of all members of Congress had opposed one or more components of the compromise. Only the swing vote of the minority committed to all parts saved the day. Although this compromise bought time, it in no way modified the North's opposition to what was viewed as the morally repulsive slave system of the South or the South's commitment to that system as a "positive good." Even though southern moderates prevailed over the "fire-eaters" at the Nashville Convention and coalitions of pro-Compromise Democrats and Whigs for a time swamped secessionist elements in southern elections, the region's basic position regarding slavery remained unchanged. The nation may well have acquiesced in the Compromise of 1850, as Stephen A. Douglas observed, but the South was more united than ever on the option offered by secession and served notice that it would exercise that option in the event of any breach in the Compromise.

Calhoun died before the Compromise of 1850 was finally enacted, but the initial debate over it deepened his despair that the South, with its agrarian society resting on a slave labor system, could continue to coexist in the Union with an industrialized, free labor North. Shortly before his death on March 31, 1850, he predicted that the rupture of the Union would "occur within twelve years or three presidential terms" and that it would probably fall apart "in a presidential election." His prophecy proved to be remarkably accurate.

UNCLE TOM'S CABIN

That northerners, no less than southerners, continued to harbor intense feelings about slavery was abundantly evident, especially among those long active in the cause of abolitionism who viewed the efforts of Clay, Douglas, and others as no more than a compromise with the forces of evil. One such individual was Harriet Beecher Stowe, a New England writer. Like other antislavery northerners, Stowe was incensed by the Fugitive Slave Law. The plot of the book, she claimed, came to her as she was participating in a communion service. Regardless of its inspiration, her *Uncle Tom's Cabin or Life among the Lowly* began serialization in a Washington antislavery newspaper in 1851 and appeared in book form the following year.

An instant best-seller, the novel could not be printed fast enough to satisfy the demand. Dramatic productions of *Uncle Tom's Cabin* appeared in theaters throughout the North. Audiences of working-class people, usually indifferent or hostile to abolitionism, were spellbound by the theatrical interpretations of Stowe's novel. Despite its flaws—contrived plot, clumsy dialect, and stereotypes of blacks—Stowe's work accurately reflected northern Protestant culture with its evangelical piety, domesticity, sentimentalism, racial prejudice, and suspicions of plantation society. Its descriptions of the tribulations endured by Uncle Tom, Eliza, and other characters who figured prominently in the plot deeply moved northern readers as a powerful indictment of both slavery and the legal system that allowed it to exist. More than any other antislavery publication, *Uncle Tom's Cabin* infuriated white southerners who viewed it as a malevolent slur on them and their society. If the northern attitude toward slavery was "never quite the same after *Uncle Tom's Cabin*," as one historian explains, neither was the southern attitude toward the North. The publication of Stowe's melodramatic, passionate novel polarized the emotions of both sections as few other events did.

FUGITIVE SLAVE ACT

Northerners who read *Uncle Tom's Cabin* or viewed dramatic productions of it could scarcely have escaped drawing a connection between its essential message and the realities that confronted them regarding the enforcement of the Fugitive Slave Act. More than any other component of the Compromise of 1850, the act directly affected the North. Despite the existence of the earlier fugitive slave law, enacted in 1793, antislavery forces in the North encountered relatively few difficulties in assisting runaway slaves. After the Supreme Court in 1843 ruled that the implementation of the act was a federal matter and states were not required to use their agencies in its enforcement, several northern states passed "personal liberty laws." These laws took advantage of the court's decision by prohibiting state officials from participating in the capture of the fugitive slaves and by denying the use of local jails for holding such slaves. The act of 1850 was both more sweeping and explicit and included

Harriet Beecher Stowe's Uncle Tom's Cabin *described in this advertisement as "The Greatest Book of the Age."*

a system of fees and penalties that encouraged federal marshals to apprehend fugitive slaves (and some free blacks) and discouraged citizens from harboring them. Antislavery spokespersons railed against the measure which Ralph Waldo Emerson pronounced a "filthy law" that he would not obey. Opponents of the act insisted that slavery was a sin and to support it was to become an accomplice in the South's great evil. Local communities in the North organized vigilance committees to assist runaway slaves in escaping to Canada; mobs rioted in protest of the act and staged dramatic rescues. Although not all northerners, probably not even a majority, were willing initially to violate or nullify a federal law, few approved of it. Clearly, the appearance of slave-catchers— "kidnappers"—in their midst served to inflame rather than calm sectional passions.

FRANKLIN PIERCE

THE ELECTION OF 1852

Despite abundant evidence that the Compromise of 1850 had not eliminated all points of contention over slavery between the sections, President Fillmore pronounced the Compromise "a final settlement" of the slavery issue. Stephen A. Douglas agreed and urged Americans to "cease agitating, stop the debate, and drop the subject." As the nation entered the presidential campaign of 1852, the finality of the Compromise of 1850 became the watchword of both Democrat and Whig leaders. Both parties attempted to convey the impression that a consensus had been achieved and slavery was no longer an issue, an impression that in reality was far from true. In 1852 the Whigs in particular were plagued by sectional divisions. Northern Whigs, who had never accepted the Compromise and opposed Fillmore as a lackey to the slave power, blocked his nomination. The convention ultimately chose General Winfield Scott, a competent military man but an inept politician, as the Whig presidential candidate. The Democrats were more successful in avoiding intraparty sectional divisions than the Whigs and selected as their standard bearer Franklin Pierce, a young, congenial former congressman and senator from New Hampshire, who enthusiastically endorsed the Compromise of 1850. Pierce benefitted not only by the fact that he had few enemies, but also by the return to the party of dissident Democrats who had formed the core of the Free Soil party four years earlier.

The triumph of Pierce and the Democrats was interpreted as evidence of nationwide approval of the Compromise of 1850 and the final settlement of the slavery question. Such an interpretation obscured more than it revealed, however. Although Pierce's electoral vote was more one-sided than any since the Era of Good Feelings, the Democrats failed to garner a majority of the popular vote in the North. The combined vote of the Whigs and the remnant of the Free Soil party was larger than that of the Democrats. Whether the election outcome constituted a bisectional endorsement of the Compromise of 1850 was open to serious question.

A fundamental alteration in the existing national party system was already underway. The Whig party had begun to unravel as a cohesive national party. The prosperity of the era made its traditional advocacy of high protective tariffs seem unnecessary or even harmful. More significant was the party's inability to reconcile differences between antislavery "Conscience Whigs" in the North and the proslavery "Cotton Whigs" in the South. As the Whigs disintegrated, a chain of events after 1852 involving the slavery question also eroded the Democratic claim as a national party and ultimately transformed it into a sectional party primarily representing the South. As a result, neither party was able to perform the unifying function in the later 1850s that had been their role in the past.

TERRITORIAL EXPANSION

Like others who insisted that the slavery question had been disposed of, President Pierce began his administration by promising to get on with other important business, especially further territorial expansion. To fulfill his promise not to be timid about expansion, Pierce inaugurated schemes to acquire various new territories, including Hawaii and Spain's island possession, Cuba. These ventures proved to be fiascos, but not before they stirred up sectional animosities over the slavery question.

Ultimately more successful were Pierce's efforts to purchase from Mexico territory that bordered the southern edge of present-day Arizona and Mexico. The area was deemed essential to the construction of a transcontinental railroad across the southern route. James Gadsden, a southern railroad promoter and friend of Secretary of War Jefferson Davis, was dispatched to Mexico to negotiate the purchase. He returned with a treaty early in 1854. Though disappointed that Gadsden had not acquired more, President Pierce nevertheless submitted the treaty to the Senate where it immediately ran into trouble. The major opposition came from free-state senators opposed to the acquisition of any more territory that might expand the area of slavery. A solid bloc of southerners in favor of the treaty finally managed to get it approved.

Railroad Politics

Not surprisingly in the boom era of railroad construction in the 1850s (see Figure 11–1), Americans became interested in building a rail line that spanned the continent. The so-called Pacific railroad had been the subject of discussion since the early 1840s, and almost everyone seemed to agree that such a project should be undertaken. The disagreement centered on the route and the eastern terminus. Visions of great wealth in construction contracts and real estate transactions prompted promoters in towns and cities up and down the Mississippi Valley to enter the competition. In general, southerners insisted upon either Memphis or New Orleans as the eastern terminus, while northerners favored Chicago. It was generally understood that such a transcontinental railroad would require federal assistance, especially land grants.

Early in the 1850s efforts by midwestern congressmen, especially those from Illinois, Iowa, and Missouri, to establish a territorial government west of

FIGURE II–I
Expansion of Railroads, 1850–1860

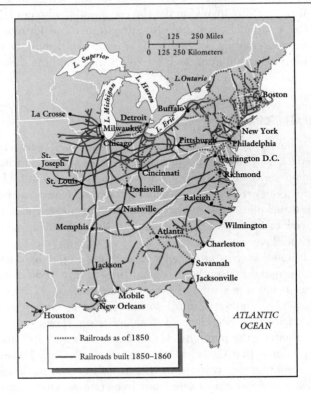

the Missouri River became entangled with the competing proposals for building a railroad to the Pacific. Senator Stephen A. Douglas, chairman of the Senate committee on territories, had long manifested an interest in organizing the remaining portion of the Louisiana Purchase, including the area north of the Missouri Compromise 36°30' line—a vast region in the heart of the continent that had remained unorganized and ungoverned for a half century. In Douglas, as one historian has explained, "railroad and territorial interests converged." He was deeply interested in the development of the territory referred to as Nebraska (running from the Missouri Compromise line to the Canadian border). Presumably the construction of the Pacific railroad across the area would promote its development. When a bill for the organization of the Nebraska territory passed by the House reached the Senate, it failed largely because of southern opposition. For southerners, too, railroad and territorial interests had become mightily mixed. Not only was the South vying for the transcontinental railroad, its spokesmen had also adopted a position regarding territories that in effect was the Wilmot Proviso in reverse—"no more antislavery territories."

The Kansas-Nebraska Act

The following year, in 1854, Douglas introduced the Kansas-Nebraska bill that incorporated features to accommodate southerners and their insistence on the right to take their slave property into any territory. As finally introduced, the bill created two territories, Kansas and Nebraska, and explicitly repealed the Missouri Compromise, leaving the voters of the two territories to determine by popular sovereignty whether slavery would be prohibited or allowed. As before, it remained unclear whether popular sovereignty meant that the status of slavery could be determined at any time or only at the time of statehood. A widespread assumption was that the measure would maintain sectional balance with Kansas, located just west of Missouri, endorsing slavery and the much larger Nebraska prohibiting it. Whatever Douglas' intentions, his bill brought sectional animosities to a new level of intensity.

After four months of bitter debate, Congress finally enacted the Kansas-Nebraska Act in May 1854, a feat that required all the eloquence that Douglas could muster, intense parliamentary maneuvering, strong southern support, and the backing of President Pierce. Rather than settling a controversy, the measure intensified it. Not only did the contest shift from Congress to Kansas where a prolonged and bloody struggle ensued between antislavery and proslavery forces, but in the North opposition to the enforcement of the Fugitive Slave Act hardened into outright resistance in the wake of the Kansas-Nebraska bill's enactment. Newspapers provided extensive coverage of rescues of fugitive slaves, while the passage of more personal liberty laws sought to slow down or prevent the return of fugitives to slavery. In the view of southerners such behavior, in addition to being overt violations of a federal law, was ample evidence not merely of the North's bad faith but of the existence of an abolitionist conspiracy as well. In brief, the Kansas-Nebraska Act set the stage for events that neither fulfilled the hopes of railroad promoters nor extended slavery as southerners desired but rather jeopardized the presidential aspirations of Douglas, undermined the existing party system, and prompted the emergence of a new political party, northern-based and antislavery, that captured the White House in six years.

Violence in Kansas

In Kansas, all the while, sporadic violence gave way to a bloody civil war. Proslavery and antislavery partisans raced into the territory, each determined to make Kansas either slave or free. Land-hungry farmers who migrated into the territory and who took little interest in the slavery issue were forced to choose sides. To complicate an already unstable situation, the federal government allowed settlers or squatters to move into Kansas before it settled claims with the ten thousand Native Americans living there or made land surveys. As a result, disputes over land claims and boundaries contributed to the chaos. Hundreds of migrants from Missouri trekked across the border into Kansas. These border ruffians, encouraged by Missouri's proslavery extremists, were determined to capture control of the territorial government.

Given their numbers, they could have done so honestly, but leaving nothing to chance, they resorted to wholesale fraud. The illegally elected proslavery legislature expelled antislavery members and enacted a stringent slave code. The antislavery settlers, provided with encouragement, financial aid, and arms by northerners, especially the New England Emigrant Aid Society, responded by organizing a rival territorial government which was also irregular. They wrote a constitution that not only outlawed slavery but excluded free blacks as well—a clear indication that an antislavery position did not mean an absence of racism.

The continuing influx of partisans including contingents from Alabama, Georgia, and South Carolina as well as from New England and elsewhere confronted a highly volatile situation in which individual acts of violence escalated into group action. The bloodshed in Kansas was widely reported in the eastern press. Although President Pierce appointed a succession of governors with the apparent expectation that they could stabilize the situation, he resolutely refused to admit that the crisis justified "the interposition of the Federal Executive." That the president singled out the "irregularities" of the emigrant aid societies in the North for public condemnation without mention of the proslavery forces seemed to indicate where his sympathy lay. By the end of 1855 "bleeding Kansas" had attracted attention throughout the nation.

John Brown and the Pottawatomie Massacre

Stories out of Kansas the following year suggested that the crisis there was worsening rather than improving. On May 21, 1856, a proslavery mob attacked the town of Lawrence, an antislavery stronghold. The destruction was so wanton that the press referred to it as the "sacking of Lawrence." No one was more outraged by the attack than John Brown, a wanderer and fanatical abolitionist who considered himself God's instrument to obliterate the sin of slavery. A recent immigrant from the North, Brown with his four sons and three other antislavery men attacked the cabins of proslavery families located on Pottawatomie Creek on the night of May 24–25. They murdered five men, left their mutilated bodies strewn about, and posted a warning that other proslavery settlers could expect the same punishment. The so-called Pottawatomie Massacre was the signal for more civil strife in Kansas as armed bands engaged in irregular guerrilla warfare.

Brown escaped legal prosecution, but not retaliation. Several hundred proslavery men later attacked and burned Osawatomie, the settlement where Brown lived. One of his sons was killed. Brown shortly thereafter returned to the East where he plotted an even more grandiose assault on the slave system. President Pierce finally appointed a highly competent governor, John W. Geary, in 1856 and promised him full military support to quell the anarchy. But the president still disavowed any intention of interfering with territorial elections. The new governor's decisiveness effected substantial, though temporary, pacification.

The Brooks-Sumner Affair

Violence related to Kansas was not confined to the geographical limits of the territory but spread to the halls of Congress as well. The day before the sacking of Lawrence, Senator Charles Sumner of Massachusetts rose in the Senate to deliver a lengthy diatribe against the slave power entitled "The Crime of Kansas" and an offensive personal attack on Andrew P. Butler, the elderly senator from South Carolina who was absent during the delivery of the philippic. Butler's young relative, Congressman Preston Brooks, also from South Carolina, felt that he was honor bound to avenge Sumner's insult to both his kinsman and his state. Arriving in the Senate chamber after its adjournment on May 22, 1856, Brooks found Sumner seated at his desk and proceeded to beat him senseless with a cane.

Although Sumner's injury appears to have been more psychological than physical, he did not return to his Senate seat until late 1859, having in the meantime been reelected as a gesture of strong support. Censured by the House despite the solid support of his southern colleagues, Brooks resigned his seat. In the words of one historian, the Brooks-Sumner episode gave the North "a dubious martyr and the South a dubious hero."

POLITICAL PARTIES IN FLUX

By the mid-1850s, the tensions produced by the slavery controversy had seriously eroded the bisectional nature of both the Democratic and Whig parties. In the wake of the Kansas-Nebraska Act the Democratic party came increasingly under the domination of its proslavery wing. Even so, the party continued to attempt to appeal to both North and South. The tensions generated by slavery proved to be fatal to the Whig organization as a national party. Lacking the cohesiveness that the Democrats had achieved under Jackson, Van Buren, and Polk, the Whigs were unable to overcome the intraparty divisiveness triggered by the Kansas-Nebraska Act. In addition, the differences between northern antislavery and southern proslavery Whigs widened at the moment that their party occupied a minority position, so they were unable to mute the slavery issue and sustain an effective national party organization. At the same time that the sectional wings of the Whig party broke apart, its northern wing disintegrated when leaders attempted to broaden the party's power base, especially among Catholics and recent immigrants, who traditionally voted Democratic. Such efforts alienated those Whigs who remained faithful to the party's commitment to evangelical Protestantism and old stock Americans.

The Know-Nothings

Among the new parties that flourished for a time in this era of political instability was one popularly known as the Know-Nothing party. The party grew out of a quasi-political secret order, the Supreme Order of the Star Spangled Banner, established in New York in 1850. Inquiries about their organization prompted members of the secret order to respond: "I know nothing," hence their popular label. In 1852 the Know-Nothings created a new political party, officially named the American party, which tapped into the longstanding prejudice against Catholics and immigrants. Not surprisingly, the Know-Nothing phenomenon coincided with a dramatic increase in the number of foreign immigrants, especially impoverished Irish Catholics. The anti-Catholicism embraced by the American Bible Society and American Tract Society fueled the popular enthusiasm for the Know-Nothings, whose platform called for the banning of Catholics and aliens from holding public office, enacting more stringent naturalization laws, and establishing literacy tests for voting.

Young native-born workers who believed that the new immigrants threatened their jobs and status rallied to the Know-Nothing standard as did other groups for wholly different reasons. Old-line Whigs in the North, traditionally committed to evangelical Protestantism and a form of nativism, deserted to the Know-Nothing ranks in droves. Southern Whigs tended to follow suit for the lack of an alternative other than the Democratic party. Antislavery and disaffected Democrats also migrated into the new party. The vacuum created by the disarray of the second-party system enabled the Know-Nothings to rise rapidly in prominence.

Apparently, few antislavery northerners who became Know-Nothings recognized the contradiction inherent in their action as did Illinois Whig Abraham Lincoln, who did not see how anyone against "the oppression of negroes [could] be in favor of degrading classes of white people." Nevertheless, in the off-year elections of 1854 the Know-Nothings won notable victories in Massachusetts, New York, Pennsylvania, and elsewhere. Massachusetts' Know-Nothing congressman, Nathaniel Banks, a former Democrat, was elected speaker of the United States House of Representatives.

Know-Nothing leaders confidently predicted late in 1855 that their party would elect the president the following year. Yet a year later their party had virtually collapsed. The reasons for its disintegration were varied: the failure to enact its nativist, anti-Catholic program; the obvious incompetence of some Know-Nothing officeholders; and objection to the party's secrecy as inconsistent with American republican principles. But slavery—and the sectional animosities it engendered—also insinuated itself into the ranks of Know-Nothingism and caused a split that signaled its failure to establish a viable national party. Northern delegates walked out of Know-Nothing conventions, first in 1855 and again in 1856, when the party refused to take a strong antislavery position. The party's remnant, primarily southern, nominated as its presidential candidate former President Millard Fillmore. Although Fillmore received over 20 percent of the popular vote in 1856, the desertions prompted by the party's stand on slavery constituted a mortal wound. Those for whom Know-Nothingism had provided a temporary home shifted their allegiance elsewhere. Many southerners joined the Democratic party, while the vast majority of northerners, especially former Whigs and assorted antislavery elements, rallied to the new Republican party.

Birth of the Republican Party

Born of political strife and shifting coalitions, the Republican party grew out of northern outrage over the Kansas-Nebraska Act. Numerous mass meetings by opponents of the measure occurred throughout the North. One group made up the Anti-Nebraska party; other groups were known by a variety of names. Ultimately, these northern antislavery groups combined and called themselves Republicans. Because of the almost spontaneous nature of the party's formation, it is difficult to speak with precision about the time or place of its birth. The name "Republican" was adopted at a convention on July 6, 1854, in Jackson, Michigan. The Republican party scarcely had an auspicious start; no important politician was involved in its founding. Abraham Lincoln, for example, protested sharply at the use of his name in connection with efforts to organize the party in Illinois. Later the party did, of course, recruit men with wide name recognition, including Lincoln and William H. Seward. In the off-year elections of 1854, Republicans and Know-Nothings acted in concert as they did later in Congress. The Republicans quickly captured control of the Know-Nothing movement in the North, welcoming its members into their ranks but at the same time rejecting Know-Nothings' nativism and anti-Catholicism. By methods that involved extraordinary skill and considerable deceit, the Republicans killed off Know-Nothingism. Although they inherited a permanent residue of nativist support, they conceded nothing that would preclude the party from seeking immigrant votes.

JAMES BUCHANAN

THE ELECTION OF 1856

The Republican convention that gathered in 1856 to nominate the party's presidential candidate included delegates who represented its diverse elements: old-line Whigs, radical antislavery men, and free-soil Democrats as well as Know-Nothings. The convention wrote a platform that opposed repeal of the Missouri Compromise and any extension of slavery, denounced the course of events in "bleeding Kansas" and demanded its admission as a free state, and called upon Congress to stamp out "the twin relics of barbarism, polygamy [a reference to Mormonism] and slavery" in all territories. The platform did not call for any interference with slavery where it already existed. Indicative of the Whig influence in the new party was the platform's support for a transcontinental railroad and other internal improvements. The convention, on the first ballot, selected John C. Frémont, a charismatic explorer and soldier ("the Pathfinder"), as the party's presidential candidate. Although Frémont may have possessed few solid qualifications for the office, he did not lack in the elements of romance and adventure so appealing to voters. Taking maximum advantage of "bleeding Kansas" and "bleeding Sumner," the party waged a vigorous campaign under the slogan "Free Speech, Free Press, Free Men, Free

Labor, Free Territory, and Frémont." Notwithstanding its lengthy, alliterative slogan, the Republican pro–Wilmot Proviso stance against the extension of slavery in the territories directly challenged the Democrats' commitment to popular sovereignty.

Convening in Cincinnati to select their presidential candidate in 1856, the Democrats passed over Pierce, whose bungling of the Kansas situation destroyed any chance of his reelection, as well as Douglas and Cass, both of whom carried too much political baggage. They chose the eminently available James Buchanan, a northerner sympathetic to the South. Despite his forty years of public service as a congressman, cabinet member, and diplomat, Buchanan had not been at the center of the public controversy over slavery. Though out of the country when the Kansas-Nebraska Act was passed, he endorsed the principle of popular sovereignty and a party platform that favored "non-interference by Congress with slavery in any state or territory or in the District of Columbia."

The older, more established Democratic party pursued a campaign that was better organized and better financed than that of the Republicans. Emphasizing that popular sovereignty offered the only fair and democratic solution to the issue of slavery in the territories, Democratic spokesmen still argued that the concept, if administered honestly and in good faith, would localize the slavery question and remove it as a disruptive issue in the national arena. That Buchanan was an experienced public servant in contrast to the untried Frémont was not lost on voters. The election resulted in a Democratic victory with Buchanan carrying five free states and all of the South except Maryland. Democrats won control of Congress in which the southern wing of the party outnumbered the northern, placing the South in a strategically dominant position. Frémont's name did not even appear on the ballot in the South, but he carried eleven free states. The outcome of the election marked the emergence of a sectionalized third-party system in which the Democrats constituted a southern party with a northern appendage, and the Republican party constituted a northern party without the slightest claim to a southern constituency.

DRED SCOTT

Votes in the presidential election of 1856 had barely been counted when the United States Supreme Court began hearing the final argument in the Dred Scott case, which brought the court directly into the center of the slavery controversy. Although many hoped that the court could settle once and for all the vexing issues related to slavery in the territories, the effect of the court's wide-ranging and controversial decision intensified rather than lessened sectional discord.

The case involved a Missouri slave, Dred Scott, whose owner had taken him first into a free state, then into a free territory; upon his return to Missouri, Scott filed suit in 1846, claiming that he was a free man because of his residence in a free state and territory. For more than a decade, while Scott remained a slave and his ownership passed to his deceased master's widow who had remarried and resided in the North, the case slowly made its way through state and federal courts. When it finally reached the Supreme Court in 1856, the justices chose to give a broad opinion dealing with the entire question of federal power over slavery in the territories.

When the court rendered its decision in March 1857, all nine justices—seven Democrats including five southerners, one Whig, and one Republican—wrote separate opinions. While there was a lack of consensus on many issues in the case, the majority agreed that Scott remained a slave. The seventy-nine-year-old Chief Justice Roger B. Taney, who wrote one of the majority opinions, ruled that Scott was not a citizen of either the United States or Missouri, and therefore had no right to sue in federal courts. He insisted no blacks, slave or free, qualified for citizenship and that in the view of the framers of the Constitution, blacks "had no rights which the white man was bound to respect." In addressing the issue of Scott's residence in free territory, he declared that slaves were property and that Congress was prohibited by the Fifth Amendment from taking property without "due process of law." Because Congress had no authority to enact legislation that deprived persons of their slave property in the territories, the Missouri Compromise had always been unconstitutional—by implication, so was popular sovereignty. Whatever the Dred Scott decision accomplished, it weakened the position of those in the center working to effect sectional adjustment.

Few Supreme Court decisions have prompted as much popular furor. Already polarized politically, the nation became polarized constitutionally. The white South was ecstatic that the court had agreed with its view that Congress had no power to prohibit slavery from any territory. In Republican and antislavery circles the decision produced dismay and outrage. The antislavery press characterized the decision as "a willful perversion" and a "deliberate iniquity." Free blacks throughout the North held meetings to protest the decision. The rally in Philadelphia, for example, passed resolutions that placed the responsibility for the decision on the slave power and "its doughfaced allies at the North" and reminded the nation of the past "patriotic services of colored men in the defense of the country" as one evidence that blacks were indeed entitled to citizenship and its rights.

Republican party leaders attacked the court's decision but without directly urging defiance. Instead, they insisted that because the court had neither the need nor the right to decide on congressional authority over slavery in the territories, that portion of the decision was mere *obiter dictum* and not binding as the law of the land. Another strategy, pursued by Senator William H. Seward and others, maintained that the decision itself was part of a slave power conspiracy between the prosouthern executive and prosouthern judiciary to negate the wishes of the majority of the people. Although President-elect Buchanan had committed a breach of propriety in urging the justices to render a broad, rather than a narrow, decision, direct evidence to support the widely circulated charges of a proslavery plot involving the president and court is at best skimpy. Nevertheless, Republicans capitalized on the conspiracy theory and warned that it only remained for the proslavery court to rule that no free *state* could exclude slaves, since such exclusion would also deprive citizens of their property rights. To ensure that such a calamity would not occur, some Republicans promised that their party would win control of the national government, pack the court with antislavery justices, and reverse the Dred Scott decision.

CONFUSION IN KANSAS

Convinced that popular sovereignty, if impartially applied, offered the best chance of resolving the slavery-in-the-territories controversy, Buchanan turned his attention first to the situation in Kansas where bloodshed had ended but strife had not. The president believed that it was essential for him to solve the Kansas imbroglio in a way that would prove the viability of popular sovereignty and at the same time deprive the Republicans of one of the most potent propaganda weapons in their antislavery arsenal. To implement his plan to tranquilize Kansas and admit it as a state as quickly as possible, he dispatched his old friend, Robert J. Walker, to the territory as governor.

Walker had scarcely assumed his new post when the already complex political situation in the territory became even more confusing as the proslavery and antislavery factions intensified their struggle for control of Kansas' future as a state. Elections called by one faction were boycotted by the other, and voting fraud was rampant. When the territory elected delegates to a constitutional convention in June 1857, the antislavery forces refused to participate on the grounds that the proslave element had rigged the whole process. The proslavery document that emerged from the convention held at Lecompton, hence known as the Lecompton constitution, guaranteed the rights of owners of slaves already in Kansas to hold their property in perpetuity. Instead of submitting the entire constitution for popular approval as President Buchanan had indicated, the convention decreed that voters could only choose between two versions of it. One version contained a clause allowing the entry of additional slaves into Kansas; the other prohibited the entry of more slaves. Either way, voters had to accept the constitution itself which included objectionable features other than the recognition of slavery already existing in the territory. Because antislavery voters refused to participate in the vote on December 21, 1857, the provision for the admission of more slaves passed by a vote of 6,143 to 569, out of an electorate of twenty-four thousand. Following this alleged proslavery triumph, the Kansas territorial legislature, under the control of the antislavery faction, scheduled another referendum on the entire constitution for early January 1858. It was defeated by a large majority. There seems little doubt that the vast majority of Kansas voters were opposed to slavery.

Response to the Lecompton Constitution

The Lecompton constitution aroused strong opposition within the president's own party. Stephen A. Douglas denounced it as a dishonest, fraudulent implementation of the doctrine of popular sovereignty. He served notice on Buchanan that he would oppose any administration effort to have Kansas admitted as a state under the Lecompton constitution. Governor Walker, too, declared that the document was a swindle designed to cheat the antislavery majority in Kansas. Despite such advice, Buchanan accepted the Lecompton constitution and the vote on it in December as legitimate. The speedy admission of Kansas under the proslavery constitution, the president maintained, would "restore peace and quiet to the whole country," while its rejection would be "keenly felt" in the fourteen slave states. Aside from the role of southerners in his cabinet and in his social life, the president had other reasons to be sensitive to the feelings of the South. He was, after all, the titular head of the party in which southerners constituted the dominant wing.

On February 2, 1858, the president submitted the Lecompton constitution to Congress with a message that urged its approval and that denounced the antislavery forces in Kansas for maintaining an illegal government. Senator Douglas, who was up for reelection and could ill afford to support the Lecompton constitution, broke with the administration and joined its opponents in waging a battle against it. The president and the southern Democrats virtually read Douglas out of the party, and the president used every power and device at his command to win congressional approval of the constitution. The administration forces in the Senate held firm, but enough Democrats in the House joined Republicans to prevent approval without an amendment that required another popular vote on the Lecompton constitution in Kansas. The Senate finally concurred in the amendment.

Buchanan and his allies, especially southerners, reasoned that Kansas voters would approve the proslave constitution rather than delay statehood until the territory's population reached the required ninety thousand. Such a calculation proved to be wholly erroneous. Kansas voters overwhelmingly defeated the Lecompton constitution on August 2, 1858. By 1860, only two slaves remained in Kansas which entered the Union as a free state the following year. The extent of the damage done to the Democratic party by Buchanan's Kansas policy became abundantly evident in the elections of 1857 and 1858.

THE PANIC OF 1857

Compounding the problems of the Democrats was the Panic of 1857 that struck suddenly in the fall of that year accompanied by the usual bank failures and suspension of specie payments. The economic slump ended more than a decade of prosperity. Economic concerns suddenly assumed greater importance. Aware that past economic downturns had helped their party by fomenting hostility toward bankers and paper money, Democrats sought, for a time, to divert attention away from sectional issues by invoking traditional Jacksonian rhetoric against monopolies and aristocratic bankers. President Buchanan blamed the panic on the excesses of banks and called on state governments to curb them.

Like almost everything else in the 1850s, the economic recession was drawn into the sectional conflict. When the slump proved to have a more severe impact on northern agriculture and industry than on the economy of the South, southerners were encouraged to boast even louder that their slave-based economy was superior to that of the free-labor North. Zealous secessionists concluded that an independent southern nation was economically viable. Senator James H. Hammond of South Carolina claimed that no one would dare "to make war on cotton" because without the South's great staple the entire "civilized world" would collapse. "Cotton is king," he exclaimed. In the North, in contrast, manufacturers and farmers blamed hard times on the southern-dominated Democratic party and specifically held southerners responsible for lowering the tariff earlier in 1857. Such northerners, as well as many in the West and Midwest, looked with favor on Republicans' efforts to broaden their party's power base by advocating higher (protective) tariffs, federally funded internal improvements, and free grants of 160-acre homesteads to actual settlers. That such homesteads were to be available to immigrants who had not yet become citizens helped Republicans to eliminate the taint of nativism that lingered from their earlier association with Know-Nothingism. When imports fell during the recession, causing tariff receipts to decline so drastically that the Buchanan administration had to resort to deficit spending, the Republicans were quick to lay the blame on the lowered tariff rates and the financial mismanagement of the Democrats. In brief, the Democrats failed both to turn the economic crisis to their political advantage and to use it to divert attention from the sectional controversy. Instead, the Republicans capitalized on the panic and its consequences.

THE SPLINTERING OF THE DEMOCRATIC PARTY

Far more significant for the Democratic party was the damage caused by Buchanan's dogged support of the Lecompton constitution. So disruptive were the consequences that the party's claim to being the last remaining political organization with substantial support in both the North and South was called into question. Beginning with the elections in the fall of 1857 and continuing more dramatically in those held the following year, Democratic fortunes at the polls declined precipitately. In the North, Democrats who had been unalterably opposed to the Lecompton constitution as an outright swindle and deeply offended by Buchanan's efforts on its behalf, ran separate candidates or aided Republicans against proadministration Democrats. Throughout the North and Midwest, Buchanan Democrats suffered one defeat after another.

The differences between the president and Senator Douglas remained as deep as ever, so much so that Buchanan and his allies in the party tried in vain to defeat Douglas' bid for reelection in Illinois in 1858. Disappointed by the failure of their efforts to admit Kansas to the Union as a slave state, southern Democrats soured on popular sovereignty and especially on Douglas, whom they viewed as a traitor because of his opposition to the Lecompton constitution. In the campaign for reelection, the Little Giant faced both the opposition of those within his own party and a formidable Republican challenger, Abraham Lincoln.

THE LINCOLN-DOUGLAS DEBATES

A former Whig who had joined the Republican party in the wake of the passage of the Kansas-Nebraska Act, Lincoln was born in humble circumstances in Kentucky and grew up on frontier farms in Indiana and Illinois. Largely self-educated, he pursued a variety of occupations, served in the Black Hawk War, and ultimately became a lawyer. He entered politics at an early age and served eight years in the Illinois legislature and a single term in Congress. Shortly after joining the Republican party he received substantial support for the party's vice presidential nomination in 1856. Depicting himself as the underdog, Lincoln entered the senatorial race two years later against an opponent who was a highly visible and influential political leader. Their physical appearances presented a study in contrasts: Lincoln was a lanky six-footer with a brooding expression and unruly hair, whose apparel bordered on the shabby; Douglas, short, portly, and fashionably attired, always exuded an air of self-confidence and cockiness.

Douglas accepted Lincoln's challenge to a series of public debates on the issues of slavery and the sectional controversy. They met in seven sites around the state of Illinois to engage in the celebrated Lincoln-Douglas debates that received close attention in the nation's press. Lincoln's performance combined conservatism with moral indignation, reforming zeal, and passionate sincerity in ways that broadened his appeal to Republicans both inside and outside Illinois. He explained that he did not consider blacks his "equal in many respects—certainly not in color, perhaps not in moral or intellectual endowment," but a black person was the equal of "every living man" in "the right to eat the bread, without leave of anybody else, which his own hand earns." A basic difference between him and his opponent, Lincoln argued, lay in their disagreement over the moral dimension of slavery. He considered slavery a moral wrong, while Douglas did not.

In the debate at Freeport, Illinois, Lincoln asked Douglas a question designed to expose the inconsistency between the Dred Scott decision and the doctrine of popular sovereignty. Could the people of a territory, he asked, legally exclude slavery prior to the formation of a state constitution? Douglas responded by asserting that slavery could exist only with the protection of the police power of the government; therefore if the people of a territory refused to pass a slave code, slavery would never be established there. Even though Douglas had made almost identical assertions earlier, his response to Lincoln's question became known as the Freeport Doctrine or Freeport Heresy in the South.

In a close contest Douglas won reelection, but he was more than ever unacceptable to southern Democrats, a fact that did not bode well for his presidential aspirations. Although the Democrats retained control of the Senate, their party was badly fractured as it faced the next presidential election. The Republicans, by contrast, fared well, winning a plurality in the House and finding a new leader in Abraham Lincoln. Despite his loss to Douglas, Lincoln achieved great national prominence as a result of his role in the widely publicized Illinois Senate race and he was soon being touted for the Republican presidential nomination in 1860.

Early in 1859, with the Kansas imbroglio pushed off center stage and the return of economic prosperity, an uneasy calm returned to the political arena. But the persistence of deep differences between the North and the South was evident everywhere, especially in the northern resistance to the enforcement of the Fugitive Slave Act, the continuing debates over the Dred Scott decision, the disparate responses to *Uncle Tom's Cabin*, and the steady stream of bellicose rhetoric that flowed from both proslavery and antislavery extremists. The forces of moderation at the nation's political center that managed to give the country the appearance of being calm for the first three-quarters of 1859 were at best weak.

JOHN BROWN AND THE HARPERS FERRY RAID

Just how fragile such forces were became apparent in the wake of an assault on the federal arsenal in Harpers Ferry, Virginia, on the night of October 16, 1859, by John Brown and his army of eighteen men, including five blacks. The zealot responsible for the Pottawatomie Massacre three years earlier had returned to the East where he enlisted the aid of prominent antislavery spokesmen in his increasingly obsessive drive to destroy slavery. After months of fund-raising and planning, Brown and his army staged a surprise attack on the arsenal in the sleepy Virginia village. The purpose of their bold act was to incite a general slave rebellion throughout the South. But the operation was so poorly planned and so unrealistic in its objective that it was doomed to failure. No uprising of slaves materialized, and a contingent of marines under Colonel Robert E. Lee easily routed Brown's army and captured Brown himself, who was tried, convicted, and sentenced to death. To the end, Brown remained firmly convinced of the rightness of his deed. Brown was hanged on December 2, 1859.

Impact of the Raid

The impact of the Harpers Ferry raid can best be measured, as one scholar has noted, in terms of social psychology. All of the simmering sectional animosities came to the surface. Passions ran high for months. The emotional polarization of the nation was complete. Many northerners considered Brown a martyr who died in an effort to free the nation's slaves. Even abolitionists wedded to nonresistance and moral suasion expressed admiration for him. But those quickest to disassociate themselves from Brown's raid were the moderate and conservative leaders of the Republican party, including Lincoln. To separate themselves

An artist's rendition of the federal arsenal at Harpers Ferry, Virginia, the scene of John Brown's raid in 1859.

from "rank abolitionism," Republicans organized anti-Brown protest meetings in various northern cities. Such multiple Republican responses to the Harpers Ferry raid made it all the easier for southerners to blur distinctions between moderate Republicans like Lincoln and the party's more extreme elements.

Not surprisingly, the white South was outraged by Brown's act and shocked by the tolling of church bells in northern cities on the day of his execution. The Harpers Ferry raid revived and strengthened the South's long-standing fear of slave insurrections. Brown's plan "to purge this land with blood" conjured up memories of the bloody insurrection in Santo Domingo and especially Nat Turner's rebellion in Virginia. Rumors of slave plots abounded, and vigilante groups quickly organized to do battle against them. Further contributing to the rising tide of hysteria in the South was the chorus of shrill rhetoric emanating from extremists, or fire-eaters, who interpreted the Harpers Ferry raid as a plot hatched by "the nigger abolitionism of the black Republicans." Assurances by Lincoln and other moderate Republicans that it was the work of a madman acting alone fell on deaf ears in the South, especially in view of the captured correspondence that revealed Brown's extensive ties to prominent northern abolitionists the so-called Secret Six. As far as white southerners were concerned, the fire-eaters had it about right—abolitionism and Republicanism were but two different labels for those determined to crush slavery, even if it meant consigning all whites in the South to a fate of murderous butchery. For white southerners the time for compromise had passed. The preservation of the Union required nothing less than an ironclad guarantee of the rights of slaveowners.

ABRAHAM LINCOLN

THE ELECTION OF 1860

The Breakup of the Democratic Party

The opening of the Democratic convention to nominate the party's presidential candidate in April 1860 occurred in an atmosphere of such tension and excitement that passion often triumphed over reason. That the convention met in Charleston, South Carolina, a hotbed of secessionism, only served to exacerbate the tense atmosphere. Spokesmen for the two wings of the party aired the complete repertoire of sectional differences, often in fiery oratory that scarcely contributed to party harmony. For example, William L. Yancey of Alabama, long a leading fire-eater, delivered a lengthy defense of the most extreme southern position and laid down nonnegotiable demands. When it became clear that the Douglas Democrats would never agree to such demands, Yancey led the state delegations of the entire lower South in walking out of the convention. Although the Douglas Democrats had sufficient strength to defeat the South's effort to secure a guarantee for slavery in the territories, they could not muster the two-thirds vote required to nominate Douglas as the party's presidential candidate. When, after ten tumultuous days, it was apparent that the deadlock could not be broken, the convention adjourned with the understanding that it would reconvene in Baltimore, a border city, in June 1860. In the meantime, those delegates who had walked out in Charleston scheduled a convention in Richmond. In the end, the Baltimore convention nominated Douglas and the Richmond convention nominated Buchanan's vice president, John C. Breckinridge. Sectional dissension had finally shattered the sole remaining political party with claims to a national constituency.

The Constitutional Union Party

A week before the Charleston convention adjourned, a new party, called the Constitutional Union party, was born. As early as 1858 a gathering in Washington, made up of old Whigs and American party members, had laid plans for a national race two years later. Senator John J. Crittenden of Kentucky, Henry Clay's successor, spearheaded the movement to create a third party. His hope was to pull together old Whigs, who still possessed substantial strength in the border states, and conservative Democrats and Republicans to form a moderate center party that would provide an alternative to the southern sectionalism of the Democratic party and the northern sectionalism of the Republican party.

For Crittenden the Union-saving mission once identified with Clay and the Whigs still had a role to play in American politics.

In a harmonious convention in Baltimore that included delegates from twelve of the fifteen slave states and eleven of the eighteen free states, the Constitutional Union party nominated as its presidential candidate John Bell of Tennessee. A lifelong Whig from a border state, Bell had served as a congressman and speaker of the House, United States senator, and secretary of war. Although he was a slaveholder, he was not a vocal exponent of the political rights of slavery and had voted against the Lecompton constitution. The Constitutional Union party, intent on diverting attention away from the vexing issues involved in the sectional controversy, sought to focus on its Union-saving mission.

Lincoln's Nomination

On May 16, 1860, the Republican convention opened in Chicago. During the four years since their debut on the national political scene, Republicans had perfected their organization, assumed a more conservative or moderate position on slavery, and broadened their constituency by appealing to both immigrants and various economic interests. By 1860 the Republicans had moved beyond being the single-issue, free-soil party that they had been four years earlier. Although the platform adopted by the party convention in 1860 denounced disunionism, the reopening of the African slave trade as proposed by a few southern fire-eaters, and the extension of slavery in the territories, it also condemned John Brown's raid, promised no interference with slavery in those states in which it already existed, and advocated a wide range of internal improvements, a protective tariff, and a homestead act.

At the opening of the Republican convention William H. Seward of New York was clearly the front-runner in the competition for the Republican presidential nomination. That he ultimately failed to capture the prize owed much to the liabilities he had accumulated over twenty years as a highly visible figure in both the Whig and Republican parties. However much he had moderated his antislavery stand, his lingering image as an uncompromising foe of slavery—one who referred to the "irrepressible conflict" between slavery and freedom—did not conform to the party's moderate position in 1860. More important was the recognition by party managers that Seward was weakest in "doubtful states" such as Pennsylvania, Indiana, and Illinois, precisely the states needed for a Republican victory. The convention ultimately nominated Abraham Lincoln, whose star had risen dramatically during and after the senatorial race with Douglas. Lincoln's other assets included his strength in the "doubtful states," a moderate position on the slavery issue, and a shrewdly managed campaign for the nomination.

The Campaign

The campaign of 1860 was extraordinary in many respects. First, voters confronted four major candidates for president who provided them with clear-cut choices: Breckinridge stood for congressional protection of slavery in the territories; Lincoln, depicted as "Honest Abe," the champion of the common man, conceded the constitutional right of the southern states to preserve slavery within their borders, but insisted that Congress prohibit slavery in the territories; Douglas, still committed to popular sovereignty, offered the Freeport Doctrine as a means of circumventing the Dred Scott decision and thereby ensuring that slavery remained a local issue; Bell appealed to the Union and the Constitution which, for many voters, offered no real solution to the controversies over slavery. Second, the four-way contest actually evolved, as one historian has observed, "into two two-way contests, one between Lincoln and Douglas in the free states and the other between Bell and Breckinridge in the slave states." Campaigns in the past had generated distorted images and misunderstandings, but those in 1860 regarding the South's perception of Lincoln and the North's failure to appreciate the mood of the South had fateful consequences. In campaigns waged by all candidates the real possibility of a breakup of the Union was often either obscured or ignored. Republicans, in particular, refused to take seriously the steady flow of secession talk from southern spokesmen. For many Republicans the South was bluffing. When the votes were counted, Lincoln had won the election with only 39 percent of the popular vote but with a clear majority of the electoral votes. He had become president of the United States, including the ten slave states in which his name had not appeared on the ballot.

The distorted image of Lincoln that prevailed in those states was that of a flaming incendiary abolitionist and inveterate enemy of the South bent on destroying the slave system. In the highly charged atmosphere of late 1860 no amount of persuasion could convince the South that Lincoln was in reality a cautious, conservative Republican without any intention of making a direct assault on the region's peculiar institution. The outcome of the election exposed, as never before, the predicament of the South, namely its inability to prevent the North from controlling the federal government. The choice of Lincoln as president meant that the South's moment of decision had finally arrived—either secede or reach some sort of accommodation that would preserve the Union.

PRELUDE TO CIVIL WAR

Secession

In view of its past experience in nullification and secession, it is not surprising that South Carolina was the first southern state to reach a decision. On December 20, 1860, a convention passed a secession ordinance. Six Deep South states—Alabama, Mississippi, Florida, Georgia, Louisiana, and Texas—quickly followed with secession ordinances. The secession of seven states suddenly transformed the controversy over slavery into a debate over the Union and the survival of the republic. If most northerners considered slavery as wrong, they viewed secession as treason and something not to be tolerated. Through the act of secession, the South united the North as it had never been united on the slavery issue. Frederick Douglass, among others, expressed the fear that the Lincoln administration's preoccupation with the preservation of the Union would cause the abolition of slavery to fall by the wayside.

Formation of the Confederacy

On February 4, 1861, delegates from the seven seceded states gathered in Montgomery, Alabama, and launched the Confederate States of America. Less than two weeks later, Jefferson Davis was inaugurated president of the provisional government. Though deeply interested in the happenings in Montgomery, the upper South and border states of Virginia, North Carolina, Tennessee, and Arkansas hesitated to cast their lots with the new Confederacy. A variety of considerations made them reluctant to rush into joining a united South. Among these were economic ties with the North, the presence of proportionately fewer slaves than the lower South, and the widespread existence of unionist sentiment especially among their large nonslave-holding white population. The upper South and border states assumed a wait-and-see posture in the hope that a settlement could be reached that would keep the Union intact.

Final Efforts to Save the Union

Efforts to achieve such a settlement had begun as soon as South Carolina officially seceded. Having convened on December 3, 1860, Congress joined others in trying to save the Union. Panaceas and compromise solutions advanced by congressmen of all political persuasions piled up in such huge quantities that each house chose a committee to sift through them and report those that seemed most promising. For a moment, the compromise offered by the venerable Senator John J. Crittenden appeared to be feasible. Crittenden called for a revival of the Missouri Compromise by guaranteeing federal protection of slavery south of the line 36°30' and the prohibition of slavery north of the line; compensation to owners of runaway slaves; enforcement of the Fugitive Slave Act and the repeal of the North's personal liberty laws; and a constitutional amendment that would forever guarantee slavery in the District of Columbia and in any state where it already existed. Southerners refused to support the Crittenden Compromise unless Republicans accepted it in advance. When President-elect Lincoln rejected the idea of allowing slavery to spread into any additional territories, Crittenden's final effort at union saving collapsed. No more successful was the so-called Peace Convention called by the Virginia legislature that gathered in Washington on February 4, 1861, the same date that the Confederacy was born in Montgomery.

In his message to Congress on January 8, President Buchanan not only urged Congress to prescribe "a distinct and practical proposition for conciliation," but also revealed that his position regarding the seceded states had stiffened. In fact, he had refused South Carolina's demands that federal

FIGURE 11–2
Southern Secession

The Progress of Secession
(Circled numbers indicate order of secession)

	Border slave states that did not secede
	States that seceded after the fall of Fort Sumter
	States that seceded before the fall of Fort Sumter
	Union states

fortifications in Charleston harbor be evacuated. To reinforce the garrison at Fort Sumter where various federal forces in the harbor had been concentrated, he first considered sending a warship but was persuaded to dispatch instead a less menacing unarmed merchant vessel. The *Star of the West*, loaded with arms, ammunition, and two hundred men, left New York on January 5, 1861, bound for Charleston. Upon its arrival in Charleston harbor, South Carolina batteries opened fire on the vessel. Federal troops at Fort Sumter were on the point of returning the fire when the *Star of the West* turned back and sailed out of the harbor. President Buchanan chose to ignore this act of war. During the closing weeks of his administration, as the last of the compromise efforts collapsed, federal arsenals and forts in much of the South were seized, but the federal government remained in possession of Fort Pickens at Pensacola and Fort Sumter at Charleston.

On March 4, 1861, the day of Lincoln's inauguration, thousands of soldiers were stationed in and around Washington because of the fear of violence. Amid this military display and the atmosphere of apprehension, Lincoln delivered an inaugural address that exhibited a spirit of conciliation and friendliness toward the South. Again he assured the South that he had no intention of interfering with slavery in the states where it existed, but secession was not an option because the Union was perpetual. No government, he declared, "ever had a provision in its organic law for its own extermination." Although there would

Fort Sumter, South Carolina, was the scene of action in 1861 that began the Civil War.

"be no invasion" and "no use of force," Lincoln emphasized that he fully intended to "hold, occupy and possess property and places belonging to the
[federal] government." Each section in the dissolving Union had its own interpretation of Lincoln's inaugural address: Many southerners regarded it as an
act of war; northerners tended to believe that it was a peace offering. For a time
after the inauguration nothing much seemed to happen and the Lincoln administration, for many Americans, began to resemble that of his predecessor.
But appearances, in this instance, were deceptive.

The day after his inauguration Lincoln received word that the federal
garrison at Fort Sumter was running short of supplies and was being surrounded
by Confederates. Though reluctant to force the issue at Fort Sumter by sending
provisions, Lincoln recognized that the preponderance of northern opinion had
crystallized against further concessions to the South. He was also aware of a congressional resolution reminding him of his duty "to hold and protect the public
property of the United States." He abandoned the idea of evacuating Fort
Sumter and informed the governor of South Carolina that supplies were being
sent to reprovision the garrison. The response of the Confederacy was to demand
the surrender of Fort Sumter. When the fort's commander refused, Confederate
forces opened fire just before dawn on April 12, 1861, which meant that the
South fired the first shot in what became the nation's bloodiest war. Within a little
more than twenty-four hours, federal forces surrendered and the Confederate
flag was hoisted over the ruins of Fort Sumter.

Any lingering hopes for a last-minute adjustment that would preserve the
Union and avert a full-scale war evaporated with the rapid sequence of events
that followed the firing on Fort Sumter. Lincoln immediately proclaimed the

lower South in a state of insurrection and called for seventy-five thousand volunteers from the free states to suppress the rebellion. Interpreted as a declaration of war, the president's call for troops ended the watchful waiting of the upper South states. Virginia, Arkansas, North Carolina, and Tennessee decided to leave the Union and join the Confederacy (see Figure 11–2), but only after deliberations that exhibited considerable regret and no little misgiving. Unionist sentiment persisted, especially in the mountainous areas of each state. The western, nonslave-holding counties of Virginia that refused to abide by the decision to join the Confederacy ultimately became the state of West Virginia. In three other states—Maryland, Kentucky and Missouri—the issue of secession triggered protracted and bitter struggles. Even though all three remained in the Union, the struggles over secession created divisions that were slow to disappear.

The role of John Brown in the events leading to the Civil War has been the subject of a large body of historical literature. In the following selection, historian David M. Potter traces Brown's career and explores the ties between him and northern abolitionists who supported his assault on the federal arsenal at Harpers Ferry, Virginia, in 1859, and shared his belief that slaves in the South would be prompted to rise up in revolt by such an assault. Potter views the Harpers Ferry raid; Brown's capture, trial, and execution; and the North's response as virtually severing whatever remained of the "psychological ties of union."

HARPERS FERRY: A REVOLUTION THAT FAILED

David M. Potter

If Lincoln and Douglas in 1858 caused a considerable part of the American public to think about the philosophical aspects of slavery, John Brown in 1859 focused attention dramatically upon its emotional aspects. The emotional aspects proved to be much the more powerful of the two.

from David M. Potter, "Harpers Ferry: A Revolution That Failed," in *The Impending Crisis, 1848–1861* (New York: Harper & Row, 1976), 356–384.

Hardly anything can be said with certainty about John Brown, but it appears that he was taught to hate slavery by his father and gradually became increasingly committed to the fight against it, although until his Kansas adventures at the age of fifty-six, he spent most of his life in pursuits such as farming, running a tannery, raising sheep, speculating in land, driving cattle, and acting as agent for a wool company. It also appears that he was a man of very high abstract standards—rigorously moral, condemning wrong, despising weakness. But he did not live up to his rigid standards, and his life was checkered with episodes that must have been very hard on the self-respect of a man of such exacting righteousness. He gave a bill of exchange on the Bank of Wooster for money which he did not have. He secretly mortgaged a piece of land which he had already pledged as security to a man who had sustained a loss of $6,000 by signing a note for him. He was subsequently sent to jail for refusing to relinquish the land to the legal owner. He induced a woolen company to make him its agent and to advance him $2,800 with which to buy wool, then used the money for his own purposes. He escaped criminal prosecution for this act by promising to make restitution, which was never made. He was sued no less than twenty-one times, usually for defaulting on financial obligations.

Throughout the years when these episodes occurred, he constantly expressed the most pious ideals and high-minded convictions. In some men such a discrepancy between words and acts would indicate deliberate deception and knavery, and indeed this has been attributed to Brown. From the full record of his life, however, it appears that he did have very high standards but was unable to live up to them. Until his fifty-sixth year, "Old Brown" had failed at every enterprise to which he set his hand and had repeatedly violated his own principles. It further seems likely that in order to avoid facing this reality, he began to create an image of himself as a man who was immune to ordinary human frailties—a man of iron in physical endurance; a deeply purposeful man, with dedication unrelieved by any element of levity, or self-indulgence, or even casualness; a man of deeds and not of words. Perhaps most people have attributed such superhuman qualities to themselves in occasional compensatory fantasy, but the remarkable fact about John Brown is that he began to act as if he really had these characteristics, so that after a while, the fantasy became, in a sense, the reality, except that the outward qualities of strength—of heroic endurance, inspiring leadership, and relentless purpose—concealed inner qualities of weakness—of flawed judgment, homicidal impulse, and simple incompetence. John Brown never did develop the basic human capacity of making his means serve his ends, and his ultimate triumphant failure was built upon the accident of his survival to face trial after Harpers Ferry.

The more Brown yearned to dedicate himself, the more he turned to antislavery as the overriding purpose for his life. To say this is not to suggest a doubt that the antislavery cause could take possession of a man by its own inherent moral strength. But in any case, John Brown really began to make a career of antislavery after the Pottawatomie massacre. For three years, from 1856 to 1859, he gave up all other pursuits and devoted himself exclusively to developing his plans for military operations against slavery, either in Kansas or elsewhere.

Brown had no money of his own, and since a military company cannot function without equipment and supplies, he soon discovered the irony that his dedication to a life of military action had in fact committed him to an occupation which was one part fighting and several parts fund raising. For some thirty months, between January 1857 and July 1859, he spent approximately half his time traveling about soliciting money. He made seven trips to Boston, five trips to Peterboro, New York, to see Gerrit Smith, and numerous visits to other places, so that he became a kind of circuit rider, frequently forced, as he himself felt, to beg in a humiliating way for the support that would enable him to operate. With this aid, he was able to keep together a little band of about a dozen devoted young men, to hire at inadequate wages an English adventurer named Hugh Forbes as an instructor in military drill, and to order one thousand pikes for a purpose which seemed obscure when he bought them. Between himself and his financial backers there was fairly constant tension, for he kept waiting for them to give enough to enable him to act, and they kept waiting for him to do something with what they had already given before they gave more.

When Brown embarked upon this career early in 1857, he was fresh from nearly four months of "military service" of the bushwhacking variety in Kansas, and his purpose was not at all unusual. Kansas was full of free-lance fighting men, operating with bands which they had raised themselves. Brown was one of them, and what he wanted initially was to equip and lead a crack military company of about fifty men to continue fighting the battles which were then being waged in the territory. His own experiences in the Kansas strife and the killing of his son Frederick by a proslavery man may have fortified his purpose, or he may by this time have developed an *idée fixe* unrelated to ordinary emotions. In any case, antislavery men in the East had given him very limited financial help when he first migrated to Kansas in 1855, and he now conceived the idea of appealing to these same sources for support in his project. He procured two letters from Charles Robinson, the free-state "governor" of Kansas, expressing thanks for "your prompt, efficient and timely action against the invaders of our rights" and urging all "settlers of Kansas" to "please render Captain John Brown all the assistance he may require in defending Kansas from invaders and outlaws." Armed with these, he set out for the East in October 1856. At Chicago, he met with members of the National Kansas Committee; in Ohio, Salmon P. Chase provided him with a letter of general commendation; and in Springfield, Massachusetts, he obtained a letter of introduction to Franklin B. Sanborn, a well-connected young schoolteacher and antislavery worker in Boston. He arrived in Boston on January 4, 1857.

Brown's reception was an immense personal success and a great financial disappointment. The elite of Boston had a deep ideological commitment to the cause of freedom in Kansas, and they probably felt some guilt that most of their support had been merely rhetorical. They were prepared, therefore, to lionize a genuine Kansas fighting man, and John Brown filled the role to perfection with his grim silences, his expressions of contempt for words rather than deeds, and his picturesque frontier dress, including a bowie knife in his boot which he had taken from a notorious proslavery bushwhacker. Here was a man hunted by his enemies, who always went armed and who barricaded himself in his room at night, even in Boston. Sanborn, the young schoolteacher, was completely captivated, and became a disciple; he took Brown to see Dr. Samuel Gridley Howe, famous throughout the country for his work with the blind and for other philanthropies, and Theodore Parker, probably the foremost clergyman in the United States. Very soon, Brown had met many of the eminent figures of Boston: Amos A. Lawrence, the textile magnate; George L. Stearns, another man of property; Thomas Wentworth Higginson, a young Unitarian parson of Brahmin family; Dr. Samuel Cabot, Wendell Phillips, William Lloyd Garrison (whose doctrine of nonresistance prevented a close relation with Brown), and a little later Henry David Thoreau and Ralph Waldo Emerson (in both of whose homes Brown stayed as a guest), as well as Bronson Alcott.

John Brown's stiff angularity of posture, of manners, and of speech reminded the highly literate Bostonians of certain familiar literary, historical, and biblical images. Brown was a Highland chief, a Cromwellian Covenanter, an Old Testament prophet. They saw him as, by nature and instinct, a man of action, utterly devoid of artistry and rhetoric, and they never sensed at all that he was, in some ways, more of an artist and a man of words than any of them. He had romanticized himself quite as much as others romanticized him, and though not widely educated, he was aware of the relevance of Highland chiefs and prophets as models for his own image, and as alternative personae for the John Brown whose earlier persona had been a shabby and unsatisfactory one. John Brown's nature, holding the mirror up to art, captivated the literati by his consummate "naturalness." Thus, Thoreau saw him as a man of "rare common sense and directness of speech," and Bronson Alcott wrote, transcendentally, "I am accustomed to divine men's tempers by their voices—his was vaulting and metallic, suggesting repressed force and indomitable will." Emerson made him virtually a noble savage: "A shepherd and herdsman, he learned the manners of the animals and knew the secret signals by which animals communicate."

Personally, Brown in Boston was a *succès fou*. The Boston intellectuals suspended their ordinary critical faculties where he was concerned, and ultimately this suspension was to have grave consequences. But though they idealized him and welcomed him in their homes, they did not raise very much money for him. Once the effort fell through to get $100,000 for him by act of the Massachusetts legislature, he was reduced to small gifts—a little better than handouts—and to a contingent promise from George Stearns of $7,000 to subsist one hundred volunteer-regulars *if* it became necessary to call that number into service in Kansas. As limited gifts came in, he found himself under increasing pressure to go back to the territory and engage in some of the direct action which was supposed to be his forte. Therefore, by June he was on his way west to Iowa, and in November he crossed over into Kansas again.

Kansas in November 1857 was a very different place from the territory he had left in October 1856. Robert J. Walker had replaced John W. Geary as governor; fighting had died down; and free-staters had won a majority in the new legislature, thanks to Walker's decisive action in throwing out fraudulent returns. The antislavery party had nothing whatever to gain at this point from a resumption of the border wars. They remembered unpleasantly what Brown had done at

Pottawatomie (something the Bostonians did not know); they regarded him as a troublemaker; and they conspicuously failed to welcome his return. Brown saw that Kansas was no place for him, that his career as a Kansas guerrilla was played out, and he left the territory after less than two weeks, going back again to his base at Tabor, Iowa.

At this point, Brown faced a difficult and crucial decision. He had either to abandon his role as an antislavery warrior, admitting another failure, or to redefine his mission. He gave his answer at Tabor in late November or early December to the nine men who had accompanied him there. His ultimate destination, he told them, was the state of Virginia. This must have come as a shock to them, and several of the men were disposed to argue, but Brown's hypnotic eloquence won them over.

At first glance, it would appear that Brown had seized upon the Virginia scheme as a desperate alternative when the adventure in Kansas drew toward an unavoidable close. But upon closer scrutiny, one perceives that the Allegheny Mountains had long held great fascination for this strange, disguised romanticist. Kansas was only a detour on the path of his destiny. Apparently, the possibility of basing himself in the mountains and operating from there to emancipate the slaves in Virginia had been the main topic of discussion when he first visited with Frederick Douglass, the foremost Negro in America, in 1848. Also, Brown's daughter, half a century later, asserted that the plan of an invasion from the mountains had been freely discussed in their home as early as 1854. Brown was gathering information on slave insurrections as early as 1855. But there is no evidence of any explicit plans or commitments until August 1857, just before his return to Kansas. At this time he told his associate, the English soldier of fortune Hugh Forbes, of a plan to invade Virginia and free the slaves, and Forbes challenged the practicability of the plan. But Brown continued with his project nevertheless, and after November it emerged as a grandiose and revolutionary scheme, wholly unlike his participation in the homemade wars of Kansas. Again he would need money, and this time it was a project which could not be advocated before a legislature. Many of the people he had appealed to previously were too mild to be approached on this matter, and Brown despised the timidity of most of the abolitionists, in any case. But there were some men in Boston whom he felt that he could trust. He started east again in January 1858.

Early in February, he revealed his scheme to Frederick Douglass, who had been both a slave and a fugitive and who had a realistic understanding of what was involved. Douglass warned him against the plan, but Brown did with this as he did with all advice—he ignored it. Later in the same month, at Gerrit Smith's home in Peterboro, New York, he unfolded to Smith and to Franklin Sanborn a plan for a campaign in slave territory somewhere east of the Alleghenies to set up a government that would overthrow slavery. Sanborn accurately described it as "an amazing proposition, desperate in its character, wholly inadequate in its provision of means," and he might have added, profoundly illegal in its purposes. Smith and Sanborn tried to induce him to give it up, but when he proved unyielding, they rallied to his support, and as he soon wrote to his family, "Mr. Smith & family go *all* lengths with me."

From Peterboro, Brown went on to Boston, where he met five of his staunchest supporters, George L. Stearns, Franklin B. Sanborn, Thomas Wentworth Higginson, Theodore Parker, and Samuel Gridley Howe. To them also he unfolded his plan, and all of them agreed to raise money for his support. These five, together with Gerrit Smith, became known as the "Secret Six," and it was their rather limited aid which finally enabled Brown to strike his blow at Harpers Ferry.

The five are remembered chiefly as genteel intellectuals and philanthropists: Howe, a pioneer in care for the blind and the mentally retarded; Parker, a Unitarian clergyman of astonishing erudition and scholarly eminence; Higginson, another Unitarian, living at the very hub of the Brahmin society to which he had been born, and later the "dear preceptor" of Emily Dickinson; Stearns, the richest man in Medford, the husband of Lydia Maria Child's niece, close friend of Sumner, and the patron of all good causes; Sanborn, a younger man, a hard worker who became secretary of every group he joined, and who ultimately made a career of exploiting his relation with great men whom he had hero-worshiped—Brown, Howe, Emerson, Thoreau, and Bronson Alcott. But at the time, all were notable as unusually militant antislavery men. Howe, Higginson, and Sanborn had all been to Kansas. Stearns had been one of the foremost raisers of funds for the purchase of Sharps rifles. Parker had been head of the Boston Vigilance Committee which was committed to resisting the Fugitive Slave Law by violence if nonviolent methods failed. The other four were also members. Stearns and Parker had concealed fugitives in their homes. Higginson, the most extreme, personally led an attack to rescue Anthony Burns from the Boston Court House in 1854, and three years later, he sponsored a "Disunion Convention" at Worcester.

In the end, news of the Harpers Ferry raid threw four of the Secret Six into panic at the thought of being implicated. Parker was dying in Europe, and only Higginson stood firm, neither disclaiming his association with Brown nor taking flight, nor destroying his correspondence. Yet even Higginson in later years tended to minimize the revolutionary character of Brown's plans, and indeed it was never certain whether he had any carefully formulated plans, or, if he did, to what extent he actually adhered to them after he went to Maryland. Further, he was so secretive—and so distrustful of some of his supporters—that one cannot assume that he revealed his plans—especially to men who frankly stated that they did not want to know too much in detail. Thus, controversy turns on three questions: (1) whether Brown had fixed plans, (2) whether he revealed them, and (3) whether the revelations were understood by those to whom they were disclosed. These questions will always leave some aura of uncertainty, but the fact is that there was never as much uncertainty about *what* Brown proposed to do as about *how to interpret it.* He proposed to take an armed force into Virginia, rally the slaves, place weapons in their hands, and resist by force any effort to prevent their being freed. Such action could hardly have failed to result in a bloody slave insurrection, and indeed Howe, Smith, and Parker all talked about it in those terms. It would, on the other hand, be possible to argue that the slaves would not resort to violence unless the whites made efforts to subjugate them, in which case the slave masters and not the slaves would be responsible for any violence that ensued. Also, one could cling to the idea that Brown intended to recruit a large number of slaves and hurry them north to freedom, rather than to precipitate a large-scale insurrection in the slave states. Brown's own statements illustrate the ambiguity in the project, for soon after his capture he asserted that freeing the slaves was "absolutely our only object," but he admitted in the next breath that he had taken a prisoner's money and watch, and that "we intended freely to appropriate the property of slaveholders to carry out our object." Again, in the famous speech on the occasion of being sentenced to death, he admitted a "design on my part to free the slaves," suggesting that this might be accomplished simply by spiriting the slaves away. "I never did intend murder or treason," he said, "or the destruction of property or to excite or incite slaves to rebellion, or to make insurrection." Later still, he amended this second statement by saying, "I intended to convey this idea, that it was my object to place the slaves in a condition to defend their liberties, if they would, without any bloodshed, but not that I intended to run them out of the slave states." No doubt Brown meant to make the point that his primary purpose was to free slaves and not to kill slaveholders. Still, it was a tenuous distinction to say that slaves would be encouraged to defend their freedom but not incited to insurrection; or that a governmental arsenal would be seized, its defenders overpowered, and its arms taken but that no treason was intended; or that bloodshed would be avoided but that the property of slaveowners would be seized. Brown's disclaimers amounted to the assurance that no persons would be killed unless they interfered with what Brown was engaged in doing. In this sense, any one of the Six could have asserted that he had not meant to support an insurrection. But all of them knew that Brown intended to strike with armed men, to take slaves from their masters by force if necessary, to take hostages, and to prevent the masters from regaining control over the slaves. They should have known, and probably did know, that this amounted to starting a servile insurrection, whatever it might be called. Parker and Higginson—and, for a while, Howe and Smith—seem to have been willing to recognize this reality frankly. They regarded slavery itself as a kind of war which gave philosophical justification to resistance by the slave.

It is pertinent that the word "treason" was first applied to them not by their accusers but by themselves. Not only was Higginson, in his own words, "always ready to invest in treason," but Sanborn, at almost the same time, said, "The Union is evidently on its last legs and Buchanan is laboring to tear it in pieces. Treason will not be treason much longer, but patriotism." The fact that the Six did not reveal the plan to other antislavery men suggests their awareness that it was strong medicine; their skittish insistence that Brown should refrain from informing them about details of his plan testified to their recognition of the illegality of his intended measures.

Perhaps the clearest indication of how much they knew, however, is an indirect one. Early in 1858, two bombshells, in the form of letters from Hugh Forbes, hit Howe and Sanborn. Brown had never told them about Forbes, but clearly he had told Forbes about *them,* for Forbes related that Brown had employed him to drill troops and had spoken of his financial support in Boston, but had not paid him what was promised. Forbes held Brown's backers responsible for this default. He also disparaged Brown's judgment, demanded to be paid or put in charge of the whole operation, and threatened to sell his secrets to the New York *Herald* if he were not recompensed. The Six did not yield to this blackmail, but the important point was that they learned, almost inadvertently, not what Forbes knew about Brown, but what he knew about them—which only Brown could have told him. Sanborn, explaining the whole matter to Higginson, wrote that Forbes knew "what very few do [know]—that the Dr. [Howe], Mr. Stearns and myself are informed of it—How he got this knowledge is a mystery." In short, Sanborn and Howe knew enough about Brown's plans to be deeply concerned that anyone else should be aware of their knowledge.

In spite of many subsequent efforts to make it appear that Brown was engaged simply in a "raid," in which he intended only to snatch a few slaves and quickly slip away to some hideout in the Virginia mountains, it is clear that his enterprise was meant to be of vast magnitude and to produce a revolutionary slave uprising throughout the South. The first proof of this lies in a "Provisional Constitution" which Brown imprudently presented to a group of some thirty-five Negroes and a few white men at Chatham, Ontario, in April 1858. This document was so strange that a question must arise as to the sanity of its framer. But with its provisions for confiscating all the personal and real property of slaveowners, and for imposing martial law, and for maintaining an elaborate government over a large area, it clearly contemplated a sustained military occupation of an extensive region in which slavery would be overthrown. Since Brown never expected to have more than fifty or a hundred men in his striking force, and since he later gave military commissions to thirteen out of seventeen of his white followers (though to none of the five Negroes), it is evident that the large army necessary to this operation would have to be composed of slaves who had thrown off their bondage. The second proof lies in his decision to seize the armory at Harpers Ferry, Virginia. Harpers Ferry was in a difficult location, and it was clearly more risky to attack federal property than private property. The only thing to be gained by seizing the armory was weapons, and since Brown's own little band already had far more guns than they needed, one can only conclude that he intended to place arms in the hands of large numbers of slaves.

If all had gone according to plan, Brown would have struck in the summer of 1858, but at the last moment Hugh Forbes threatened to sink the project by revealing all of the secret plans. Forbes had joined the enterprise in the belief that Brown could make it highly lucrative by tapping large wealth in New England (Brown may once have believed this himself). Later, when Brown could give him only a few hundred dollars for many months' service, and when he became disillusioned by the mistakes in Brown's planning, he defected and went to Senators Henry Wilson (in person) and William H. Seward (by letter) with information about the plot. Wilson reacted by sending Howe a very sharp letter, with pointed inquiries about why the Kansas Committee was mixed up in an affair like this, and with warnings that it would seriously injure the antislavery cause. The Six promptly held hurried meetings at which they transferred property from the Kansas Committee to Stearns so they could deny that the Committee was involved, and then, over the protests of Howe and Higginson, they instructed Brown that he must suspend his plan and go west.

Higginson thought the enterprise would never be revived, and with anyone but Brown as leader, it probably would not have been. Certainly the postponement was dangerous, not only because of the difficulty of keeping the little band together during an indefinite delay, but also because it seemed unlikely that the precarious secrecy of the plot could be preserved much longer. A number of Brown's young followers had talked and written indiscreetly; many Ontario Negroes must have known about the "convention" at Chatham; Forbes had already let his tongue wag; and the security precautions of the Secret Six might have seemed amateurish even to a small boy. Moreover, one of Brown's followers, John H. Cook, was already at Harpers Ferry, where he soon found a job and a wife. Brown was acutely fearful that Cook would talk too much.

Perhaps only a mad project could have survived, but, in any case, this one did. Brown went back to Kansas for the third and last time in June 1858, and in December he led a raid into Missouri in which his followers killed one slaveholder, took a certain amount of livestock and property, and liberated eleven slaves whom they then carried east in midwinter, across the northern prairies, all the way to Ontario. This was perhaps the most successful operation Brown ever engaged in. After another three and a half months of fund raising and delay, he then went to Maryland and rented a farm five miles from Harpers Ferry. There he settled down and waited three and a half months longer for additional men and money, which, for the most part, never arrived. By mid-October he had twenty-two followers and probably recognized that his little force never would be any stronger. On the evening of October 16, he set out with all but three of these men, marched down toward the Potomac with a wagonload of arms, cut the telegraph wires, crossed the bridge, captured the watchman guarding the bridge, and moved into Harpers Ferry. With no difficulty whatever, he seized the armory and rifle works. He then sent out a detail to capture two slaveholders of the neighborhood along with their slaves. One of these was Colonel Lewis Washington, a great-grandnephew of George Washington, and Brown told his men to be sure to bring in one of the family heirlooms, the sword which Frederick the Great had presented to George Washington. This mission was accomplished, and the detail, with its prisoners, was back at the armory by daybreak. Meanwhile, at about 1:00 A.M., Brown's men had stopped a Baltimore and Ohio train and inadvertently killed the Negro baggage master, but had later allowed the train to go on its way.

At morning, as the employees at the armory straggled in for their day's work, Brown took a number of them prisoner, and he tried to send a detail back to his farm to move some of the military equipment from there to a schoolhouse nearer the Ferry. But otherwise he sat down and waited. In his own mind, he was waiting for the slaves to rise, but in reality, he was waiting for the slow-moving forces of organized society to get into motion and to overwhelm him. By midmorning, the local militia of nearby towns in Maryland and Virginia were on their way to the Ferry, and the president of the Baltimore and Ohio Railroad had decided to risk being made a laughingstock by reporting to Washington the incredible information that an insurrection was in progress at Harpers Ferry. Also the local inhabitants began to seize the initiative. At first they had lain very low, assuming quite logically that no one would dare seize a government arsenal without a large force at his back. But now they began a desultory firing in the direction of the armory.

By midafternoon of October 17, the militia companies had arrived and gained control of both bridges. Outpost details that Brown had placed were killed or driven in or had escaped, and Brown himself was forced to hole up in the engine works. By ten o'clock that night, Lieutenant Colonel Robert E. Lee, United States Cavalry, with his aide Lieutenant J. E. B. Stuart, had come to command all federal forces in the area.

The engine house could have been captured that night, within twenty-four hours of the beginning of the raid, but Lee, very much the professional soldier, was in no hurry. He preferred to observe protocol, giving the Virginia troops a chance to lead the assault if they wanted to (which they did not), giving the insurrectionists a chance to surrender, and taking precautions to avoid shooting any of Brown's prisoners. The next morning, he sent Stuart to parley with the leader of the insurrectionists, and as they talked through a crack in the engine house door, Stuart, who had served in Kansas, was astonished to recognize John Brown of Osawatomie. Up to this time, no one on the outside had known who was attacking. A few moments later, when Brown refused to surrender, Stuart stepped aside and waved in a detachment of twelve marines who charged with fixed bayonets, without firing a shot. In a few moments it was all over. One marine and two of Brown's men were killed in the assault. Brown himself would have been killed if his assailant, Lieutenant Israel Green, in command of the detachment, had not been armed only with a decorative dress sword which inflicted some painful but not very serious wounds. Altogether, Brown's men had killed four people and wounded nine. Of his own small force, ten were dead or dying; five had escaped the previous day, and seven were captured.

Technically, Brown's operations had been almost incredibly bad. Leading an army of twenty-two men against a federal arsenal and the entire state of Virginia, he had cut himself off from any chance of escape by moving into a position where two rivers walled him in, as if in a trap. Leading what purported to be an utterly secret operation, he had left behind him on the Maryland farm a large accumulation of letters which revealed all his plans and exposed all his confederates; as Hugh Forbes wrote, "the most terrible engine of destruction which he [Brown] would carry with him in his campaign would be a carpet-bag loaded with 400 letters, to be turned against his friends, of whom the journals assert that more than forty-seven are already compromised." After three and a half months of preparation, he marched at last without taking with him food for his soldiers' next meal, so that, the following morning, the commander in chief of the Provisional Army of the North, in default of commissary, was obliged to order forty-five breakfasts sent over from the Wagner House. For the remaining twenty-four hours, the suffering of Brown's besieged men was accentuated by acute and needless hunger. His liaison with allies in the North was so faulty that they did not know when he would strike, and John Brown, Jr., assigned to forward additional recruits, later stated that the raid took him completely by surprise. If, as is sometimes suggested, this indicated the disordered condition of Brown, Jr.'s mind rather than lack of information from his father, it still leaves the question of why such a crucial role should have been entrusted to one whose mental instability had been conspicuous ever since Pottawatomie. Finally, the most bizarre feature of all is that Brown tried to lead a slave insurrection without letting the slaves know about it. It is as clear as it is incredible that his idea of a slave insurrection was to kidnap a few slaves, thrust pikes into their hands while holding them under duress, and inform them that they were free. He then expected them to place their necks in a noose without asking for further particulars. As Abraham Lincoln later said, with his disconcerting accuracy, "It was not a slave insurrection. It was an attempt by white men to get up a revolt among slaves, in which the slaves refused to participate. In fact, it was so absurd that the slaves, with all their ignorance, saw plainly enough it could not succeed."

Lincoln also said, "John Brown's effort was peculiar." With all that has been written about whether John Brown was "insane," this is perhaps as exact as it is possible to be. But let it be said briefly, first, that insanity is a clear-cut legal concept concerning a mental condition which is seldom clear-cut; and second, that the insanity explanation has been invoked too much by people with ulterior purposes— first by those who hoped to save Brown's life, then by Republicans who wanted to disclaim his act without condemning him morally, and finally by adverse critics who hoped to discredit his deeds by calling them the acts of a madman. The evidence shows that Brown was very intense and aloof, that he became exclusively preoccupied with his one grand design, that he sometimes behaved in a very confused way, that he alternated between brief periods of decisive action and long intervals when it is hard to tell what he was doing, that mental instability occurred with significant frequency in his family, and that some believed he had a vindictive or even a homicidal streak with fantasies of superhuman greatness. Also, Pottawatomie should be borne in mind. From all this, one may clearly infer that Brown was not, as we now say, a well-adjusted man. But the strongest element in the case for his madness is the seeming irrationality of the whole Harpers Ferry operation. In lay terms, a man who tried to conquer the state of Virginia with twenty-two men might be regarded as crazy. Was Brown crazy in these terms?

This question presents a difficulty, for if a belief in the possibility of a vast, self-starting slave insurrection was a delusion, it was one Brown shared with Theodore Parker, Samuel Gridley Howe, Thomas Wentworth Higginson, and a great many others whose sanity has never been questioned at all. It was an article of faith among the abolitionists that the slaves of the South were seething with discontent and awaiting only a signal to throw off their chains. Gerrit Smith believed it, and two months before Brown's attempted coup he wrote, "The feeling among the blacks that they must deliver themselves gains strength with fearful rapidity." Samuel Gridley Howe believed it, and even after Brown's failure and when war came, he wrote that twenty to forty thousand volunteers could "plough through the South & be followed by a blaze of servile war that would utterly and forever root out slaveholding and slavery." Theodore Parker believed it, and wrote after Harpers Ferry, "The Fire of Vengeance may be waked up even in an African's heart, especially when it is fanned by the wickedness of a white man; then it runs from man to man, from town to town. What shall put it out? The white man's blood." Thomas Wentworth Higginson believed it and suggested that white men were foolish to be shaved by Negro barbers. "Behind all these years of shrinking and these long years of cheerful submission," he added, "there may lie a dagger and a power to use it when the time comes." As J. C. Furnas has expressed it, there was a widespread "spartacus complex" among the abolitionists, a fascinated belief that the South stood on the brink of a vast slave uprising and a wholesale slaughter of the whites. "It is not easy, though necessary," says Furnas, "to grasp that Abolitionism could, in the same breath warn the South of arson, rape, and murder and sentimentally admire the implied Negro mob leaders brandishing axes, torches, and human heads." If Brown believed that the South was a waiting pyre, and that twenty-two men without rations were enough to put a match to it, the belief was one of the least original notions in his whole stock of ideas. Thus the Boston *Post* spoke much to the point when it said, "John Brown may be a lunatic [but if so] then one-fourth of the people of Massachusetts are madmen."

The *Post* certainly did not intend to shift the question from one concerning Brown's personal sanity to one concerning the mass pathology of the abolitionists. A historian may, however, regard the latter as a legitimate focus of inquiry, especially now that it is recognized that rationality is by no means a constant in human society. But any question about whether the abolitionists were in touch with reality must carry with it a recognition that the Spartacus complex was by no means confined to the abolitionists. Southerners shared it in the sense that they were ever fearful of slave insurrection and were immensely relieved to learn that the slaves had not flocked to Brown's support. Clearly they had felt that it might be otherwise.

A year and a half later, when the Civil War came, experience proved that the slaves were not as resentful or as bloodthirsty as the abolitionists thought, and though they decamped in droves from their plantation homes, the path which they chose to freedom was not the path of insurrection, rapine, and butchery. In the light of the Civil War experience, it seems justifiable to say that Brown had been wrong in supposing that the slaves were ripe for revolt. Yet even this conclusion has to be qualified by the fact that Brown did not submit his own hypothesis to a fair test. He did not give the slaves a chance to show how they would react to an insurrection. In spite of all Brown's pretense of having made a deep study of Spartacus, Toussaint, and other practitioners of the art of slave revolt, he managed his plans in a way which Toussaint or Gabriel Prosser, not to mention Denmark Vesey, would have scorned. More than a year before he struck, Hugh Forbes warned him that even slaves ripe for revolt would not come in on a plan like his. "No preparatory notice having been given to the slaves," he said, "the invitation to rise might, unless they were already in a state of agitation, meet with no response, or a feeble one." But Brown brushed this aside: he was sure of a response, and calculated that on the first night of the revolt, between two hundred and five hundred slaves would rally to him. This expectation explains a great deal—why Brown dared to start a war with an army of twenty-two men, why he wanted the weapons at Harpers Ferry, why seventeen of his men held officers' commissions, why he carried no rations with him, why he had taken the trouble to frame a provisional constitution and get it adopted, and most of all, why he did nothing but wait at the arsenal on October 16 while his enemies gathered to beset him.

To Brown and the abolitionists, the plan seemed perfectly reasonable, and the literati of Boston admired him extravagantly as a man of action for attempting it. But to Frederick Douglass and the Negroes of Chatham, Ontario, nearly every one of whom had learned something from personal experience about how to gain freedom, Brown was a man of words trying to be a man of deeds, and they would not follow him. They understood him, as Thoreau and Emerson and Parker never did.

Two of Brown's sons were killed at Harpers Ferry. If he had been killed also, as he certainly would have been but for the inadequacy of Israel Green's dress sword, the impact of his coup would probably have been very much diminished, for the general public did not sympathize with promoters of slave insurrections, and it might quickly have dismissed Brown as a mere desperado. But he was not killed, and he surpassed himself as few men have ever done, in the six weeks that followed. The most striking testimony to his superb behavior was the fact that he extorted the complete admiration of the Virginians. They had regarded all abolitionists as poltroons, but Brown showed a courage which captivated southern devotees of the cult of courage in spite of themselves. Governor Henry A. Wise, a Virginian far gone in chivalry, was perhaps worse smitten than any of them. "He is a bundle of the best nerves I ever saw, cut and thrust and bleeding and in bonds," said Wise. "He is a man of clear head, of courage, fortitude, and simple ingeniousness. He is cool, collected, and indomitable, and it is but just to him to say that he was humane to his prisoners." Later, refusing to have Brown examined for insanity, he said, "I know that he was sane, and remarkably sane, if quick and clear perception, if assumed rational premises and consecutive reasoning from them, if cautious tact in avoiding disclosures and in covering conclusions and inferences, if memory and conception and practical common sense, and if composure and self-possession are evidence of a sound state of mind."

The admiration of the Virginians for Brown's gameness, of course, would not prevent them from trying him and hanging him for his offense, and he recognized this fact calmly without waiting for sentence to be pronounced. As he did so, he had composure and unselfishness enough to recognize that the manner of his death might be a great service to antislavery, and he prepared to die in a way which would glorify his cause. Harpers Ferry had been another failure after a lifetime of failures, but he still faced one more test—the wait for the gallows—and, while this might seem a harsher one than all the others, he knew that this was a test he would not fail. "I have been whiped as the saying is," he wrote to his wife, "but am sure I can recover all the lost capital occasioned by that disaster, by only hanging a few moments by the neck; & I feel quite determined to make the utmost possible out of a defeat."

Description can hardly do justice to his conduct. He was arraigned with excessive promptness, while still suffering from his wounds, and was indicted and brought to trial on the day of the arraignment, one week after his capture. The trial lasted one week, after which he was sentenced to be hanged one month from the date of sentence. This haste was shocking by any standards and appalling by modern standards of infinite prolongation, but it was generally agreed by Brown and others that the trial was conducted fairly and with a rough justice. During the trial, where Brown lay wounded on a pallet, and later, while awaiting execution, he handled himself with an unfailing dignity and composure. Apparently he never flinched from the hour of his capture until the moment of his death. His conduct deeply affected his jailer, won the hearts of his guards, and made a profound impression on millions of people who stood the death watch vicariously with him as his execution approached. On the occasion of his sentence, he responded with one of the classic statements in American prose:

> . . . it is unjust that I should suffer such a penalty. Had I interfered in the manner in which I admit, and which I admit has been fairly proved—for I admire the truthfulness and candor of the greater portion of the witnesses who have testified in this case—had I so interfered in behalf of the rich, the powerful, the intelligent, the so-called great, or in behalf of any of their friends, either father, mother, brother, sister, wife or children, or any of that class, and suffered and sacrificed what I have in this interference, it would have been all right. Every man in this Court would have deemed it an act worthy of reward rather than punishment.
>
> This Court acknowledges, too, as I suppose, the validity of the law of God. I see a book kissed, which I suppose to be the Bible, or at least the New Testament, which teaches me that all things whatsoever I would that men should do to me, I should do even so to them. It teaches me, further, to remember them that are in bonds as bound with them. I endeavored to act up to that instruction. I say I am yet too young to understand that God is any respecter of persons. I believe that to have interfered as I have done, as I have always freely admitted I have done, in behalf of His despised poor, is no wrong, but right. Now, if it is deemed necessary that I should forfeit my life for the furtherance of the ends of justice, and mingle my blood further with the blood of my children and with the blood of millions in this slave country whose rights are disregarded by wicked, cruel, and unjust enactments, I say, let it be done.
>
> Let me say one word further. I feel entirely satisfied with the treatment I have received on my trial. Considering all the circumstances, it has been more generous than I expected. But I feel no consciousness of guilt. I have stated from the first what was my intention, and what was not. I never had any design against the liberty of any person, nor any disposition to commit treason or incite slaves to rebel or make any general insurrection. I never encouraged any man to do so, but always discouraged any idea of that kind.

In its broad historical effects, John Brown's death was significant primarily because it aroused immense emotional sympathy for him in the North, and this sympathy, in turn, caused a deep sense of alienation on the part of the South, which felt that the North was canonizing a fiend who sought to plunge the South into a blood bath.

When John Brown was hanged at Charlestown, Virginia, on December 2, 1859, the organized expressions of sympathy in the North reached startling proportions. Church bells tolled, black bunting was hung out, minute guns were fired, prayer meetings assembled, and memorial resolutions were adopted. In the weeks following, the emotional outpouring continued: lithographs of Brown circulated in vast numbers, subscriptions were organized for the support of his family, immense memorial meetings took place in New York, Boston, and Philadelphia, a memorial volume was rushed through the press, and a stream of pilgrims began to visit his grave at North Elba, New York. The death of a national hero could not have called forth a greater outpouring of grief.

If this outburst of national mourning—for it was nothing less—had been confined merely to expressions of admiration for Brown's courage and sorrow for his death, perhaps the ultimate significance might have been less. Society allows everyone a considerable measure of eulogy in lamenting a death, and probably no one would have objected very seriously when young Louisa May Alcott wrote:

> No breath of shame can touch his shield
> Nor ages dim its shine.
> Living, he made life beautiful,
> Dying, made death divine.

But it quickly appeared that the celebration of the memory of John Brown was not so much a matter of mourning for the deceased as it was of justifying his purposes and damning the slaveholders. Two days after he was sentenced, the *Liberator* exhorted its readers to "let the day of his execution . . . be the occasion of such a public moral demonstration against the bloody and merciless slave system as the land has never witnessed," and this is, in fact, what it became. Wendell Phillips struck the note of castigation, which was sounded almost endlessly, when he declaimed, before Brown's death, "Virginia is a pirate ship, and John Brown sails the sea, a Lord High Admiral of the Almighty, with his commission to sink every pirate he meets on God's ocean of the nineteenth century. . . . John Brown has twice as much right to hang Governor Wise as Governor Wise has to hang him."

The moral effect of condemning the slave system was achieved partly in an indirect way by extravagant veneration of Brown. In phrases which are well remembered, Emerson declared that Brown would "make the gallows as glorious as the cross." Thoreau compared him to Christ and called him "an angel of light." Garrison said that the huge assembly by Tremont Temple in Boston was gathered to witness John Brown's resurrection. But in many cases, abolitionist speakers and writers went beyond the mere glorification of Brown to an explicit approval of the idea of slave insurrection. Garrison announced, "I am prepared to say 'success to every slave insurrection at the South and in every slave country.' And I do not see how I compromise or stain my peace profession in making that declaration." Wendell Phillips, speaking on "The Lesson of the House [*sic*]," said, "The lesson of the hour is insurrection." The Reverend George B. Cheever thought it "were infinitely better that three hundred thousand slaveholders were abolished, struck out of existence," than that slavery should continue to exist; the Reverend Edwin M. Wheelock believed that Brown's mission was to "inaugurate slave insurrection as the divine weapon of the antislavery cause" and that people should not "shrink from the bloodshed that would follow." To him, Brown's activities had been a "sacred and radiant treason," and to the Reverend Fales H. Newhall the word treason had been "made holy in the American language."

The Albany *Argus* tried to assure the public in general and the South in particular that these pronouncements were not at all representative. "It is the fashion," it said, "to impute to the Clergy as a body, sympathy with the sectional intolerance of the day. Nothing can be more false or more unjust. . . . The divines who preach 'killing no murder' are few indeed. In the city of New York, Cheever (who is a pensioner upon the British Anti-Slavery Societies); in Brooklyn, Beecher; in Boston, one or two of the same kidney, and in the interior some scattered imitators, are all of the clergy engaged in this crusade." To support the *Argus,* a great deal of evidence could be adduced to show that responsible opinion in the North did not support the devotees of insurrection. Two leading Republicans, Abraham Lincoln and William H. Seward, both repudiated Brown's act—Lincoln saying that although Brown "agreed with us in thinking slavery wrong, that cannot excuse violence, bloodshed and treason," and Seward that Brown's execution was "necessary and just," although pitiable. Within a year, the Republican platform of 1860 would characterize Brown's coup as "among the gravest of crimes." Also, many men not Republicans organized Union meetings, at which such eminent figures as John A. Dix and Edward Everett tried to offset the impression that all northerners sympathized with Brown.

But to the South, these reassurances were not convincing. The Republican disclaimers smacked of tactical maneuvers to avoid losing the votes of moderates; it was hard to see in Republican ranks any real regret about Brown except regret that he had failed. As for the Union meetings, they helped very little. They were too obviously inspired by northern merchants, partly motivated by fear of losing southern trade; and they took too much of a proslavery tone. By defending slavery, they made it appear that the North was divided between advocates of slavery and advocates of slave insurrection, with no middle group which opposed slavery but also opposed insurrection and throat-cutting as remedies for slavery.

Despite all efforts to explain Brown away, the South knew that what had happened at Harpers Ferry represented far more than the fanatical scheme of one man and a handful of followers. It knew that vast throngs of people had turned out to honor Brown's memory; knew that the Massachusetts legislature had very nearly adjourned on the day of his execution; and knew that Joshua Giddings could count on thousands of votes in Ohio whenever he ran for office, in spite of the fact—or perhaps because of the fact—that he had said he looked forward to the hour "when the torch of the incendiary shall light up the towns and cities of the South, and blot out the last vestiges of slavery." The discovery of much of Brown's correspondence at the farmhouse in Maryland quickly brought to light the fact that he had enjoyed support in high quarters in the North. Indeed, with the names of Howe, Parker, Emerson, and Thoreau among his supporters, it was clear that he had had the backing of the cultural aristocracy of New England. It was also clear from the behavior of the Secret Six that a significant part of this elite was committed to attitudes which went far beyond mere opposition to slavery and made the union of the states seem a questionable relationship indeed. These attitudes included hostility to the Union and hatred of the white South. The southerners of 1859, of course, did not know all that was later revealed. They were not aware that Franklin Sanborn had praised Brown by calling him "the best Disunion champion you can find," or that if Thomas Wentworth Higginson had had his way, Brown would have followed through on his original plan to seize Harpers Ferry a year earlier. But it *was* publicly known that Higginson had collaborated with Garrison in his disunion convention in 1857, that Gerrit Smith had advised antislavery men in Kansas to fight the federal troops, and that Wendell Phillips was denouncing the American eagle as an American vulture. They knew Theodore Parker as one of Brown's supporters, but they did not know that Parker, after Harpers Ferry, had written: "It is a good antislavery picture on the Virginia Shield: a man standing on a tyrant and chopping his head off with a sword; only I would paint the sword-holder black and the tyrant white, to show the immediate application of the principle." They did not know how far the Six had shared Brown's guilt, but they did know that Gerrit Smith had had a mental breakdown because of his fears that someone would find out, and that Franklin Sanborn and Samuel Gridley Howe had fled to Canada to escape interrogation, while Higginson refused to go before a congressional committee. They did not know that Higginson had seriously discussed an expedition to rescue Brown, although they did know that rescue rumors had been rife in the North.

Plainly, some of the leading intellectuals in the North had subsidized Brown to lead a slave insurrection, and when he paid the penalty for this act, he had been mourned more than any American since Washington. The South, realizing this fact, questioned whether the American Union was a reality or merely the shell of what had once been real. As for Brown's courage, said the Baltimore *American,* this proved nothing. "Pirates have died as resolutely as martyrs." As for Brown's high principles, said Jefferson Davis, his actual mission was "to incite slaves to murder helpless women and children."

If we may believe John W. Burgess, there was a revolution of opinion in the South within six weeks after Harpers Ferry. Unionist sentiment, which had remained robust up to that time, suddenly began sinking as the South saw itself isolated and beset in a union with fellow citizens who would turn loose upon it the horror which it dreaded too much to name. For many southerners, this hazard meant only one thing: those who are not for us are against us. "We regard every man in our midst an enemy to the institutions of the South," said the Atlanta *Confederacy,* "who does not boldly declare that he believes African slavery to be a social, moral, and political blessing."

By this definition, nearly every man in the North was an enemy. James M. Mason of Virginia said in the Senate that "John Brown's invasion was condemned [in the North] only because it failed." Jefferson Davis declared that the Republican party was "organized on the basis of making war" against the South. A Mississippi legislator warned his constituents, "Mr. Seward and his followers . . . have declared war on us." The governor of South Carolina informed the legislature that the entire North was "arrayed against the slaveholding states." These were well-worn phrases, but John Brown gave them a new meaning. It was hard for a southern Unionist to answer the statement of the Richmond *Enquirer* that "the Northern people have aided and abetted this treasonable invasion of a Southern state," hard to refute C. C. Memminger of South Carolina when he said, "Every village bell which tolled its solemn note at the execution of Brown proclaims to the South the approbation of that village of insurrection and servile war."

But if the South was friendless externally, at least it had solidarity internally. "Never before, since the Declaration of Independence," proclaimed the Sumter,

South Carolina, *Watchman,* "has the South been more united in sentiment." This unity must now be used to protect the South: Governor William H. Gist felt that if the South did not "now unite for her defense," southern leaders would "deserve the execration of posterity." Robert Toombs was more specific: "Never permit this Federal government to pass into the traitorous hands of the black Republican party." The Mississippi legislature passed resolutions declaring that the election of a president by a party unprepared to protect slave property would be a cause for the southern states to meet in conference and that Mississippi stood ready to help Virginia or other states to repel such assailants as Brown. With a presidential election only nine months away, this injunction was neither vague nor abstract. But the Baltimore *Sun* did not even need to wait for an election. It announced that the South could not afford to "live under a government, the majority of whose subjects or citizens regard John Brown as a martyr and a Christian hero, rather than a murderer and robber." The governor of Florida also thought that he had seen enough: he favored an "eternal separation from those whose wickedness and fanaticism forbid us longer to live with them in peace and safety."

Two Richmond newspapers effectively summarized what had happened in Virginia and the South. On October 25 the *Enquirer* observed, "The Harpers Ferry invasion has advanced the cause of disunion more than any other event that has happened since the formation of its [sic] government." A month later, the *Whig* declared, "Recent events have wrought almost a complete revolution in the sentiments, the thoughts, the hopes, of the oldest and steadiest conservatives in all the Southern states. In Virginia, particularly, this revolution has been really wonderful. There are thousands upon . . . thousands of men in our midst who, a month ago, scoffed at the idea of a dissolution of the Union as a madman's dream, but who now hold the opinion that its days are numbered, its glory perished."

Certainly the psychological ties of union were much attenuated at the end of 1859. Harpers Ferry had revealed a division between North and South so much deeper than generally suspected that a newspaper in Mobile questioned whether the American republic continued to be a single nation or whether it had become two nations appearing to be one.

SUGGESTED READINGS

General

Don E. Fehrenbacher, *The Dred Scott Case: Its Significance in American Law and Politics* (1978).

William Freehling, *The Road to Disunion: The Secessionists at Bay* (1990).

William E. Gienapp, *The Origins of the Republican Party, 1852–1856* (1987).

Holman Hamilton, *Prologue to Conflict: The Crisis and the Compromise of 1850* (1964).

Michael F. Holt, *The Political Crisis of the 1850s* (1978).

Stephen B. Oates, *To Purge This Land with Blood: A Biography of John Brown*, 2nd ed. (1984).

David M. Potter, *The Impending Crisis, 1848–1861* (1976).

James Rawley, *Race and Politics: "Bleeding Kansas" and the Coming of the Civil War* (1969).

Joel H. Silbey, *The Partisan Imperative* (1985).

Kenneth M. Stampp, *And the War Came: The North and the Secession Crisis, 1860–1861* (1970).

FURTHER READINGS

ISSUES AND EVENTS DURING THE ERA, 1848–1861: William L. Barney, *The Road to Secession* (1972); Stanley W. Campbell, *The Slave Catchers* (1970); Steven Channing, *Crisis of Fear: Secession in South Carolina* (1970); William J. Cooper, *The South and the Politics of Slavery, 1829–1856* (1978) and *Liberty and Slavery: Southern Politics to 1860* (1983); Richard N. Current, *Lincoln and the First Shot* (1963); David Donald, *Charles Sumner and the Coming of the Civil War* (1960); Robert F. Durden, *The Self-Inflicted Wound: Southern Politics in the Nineteenth Century* (1985); Don E. Fehrenbacher, *Prelude to Greatness: Lincoln in the 1850s* (1962); Eric Foner, *Free Soil, Free Labor, Free Men: Ideology of the Republican Party Before the Civil War* (1970) and *Politics and Ideology in the Age of the Civil War* (1980); Thomas F. Gossett, *Uncle Tom's Cabin and American Culture* (1985); Harry V. Jaffa, *Crisis of the House Divided: An Interpretation of the Lincoln-Douglas Debates* (1959); Robert W. Johannsen, *Stephen A. Douglas* (1973); Paul Kleppner, *The Third Electoral System, 1853–1892* (1979); John Mc-Cardell, *The Idea of a Southern Nation: Southern Nationalists and Southern Nationalism 1830–1860* (1979); William S. McFeely, *Frederick Douglass* (1991); Thomas D. Morris, *Free Men All: The Personal Liberty Laws of the North, 1780–1861* (1974); Chaplain W. Morrison, *Democratic Politics and Sectionalism: The Wilmot Proviso Controversy* (1967); Roy F. Nichols, *The Disruption of American Democracy* (1948); Joel H. Silbey, *The Shrine of Party: Congressional Voting Behavior, 1841–1852* (1967); Kenneth Stampp, *America in 1857* (1990); Benjamin Thomas, *Abraham Lincoln: A Biography* (1952); Gerald W. Wolff, *The Kansas-Nebraska Bill* (1977).

QUESTIONS FOR DISCUSSION

1. Explain the Wilmot Proviso and its significance.
2. Identify the principal provisions of the Compromise of 1850 and the Kansas-Nebraska Act and explain their significance in the sectional dispute over slavery.
3. Discuss the origins of the Know-Nothing party, its appeal, and rapid decline.
4. Discuss the origins of the Republican party and explain its success in the presidential election of 1860.

5. Discuss the main thrust of the Dred Scott decision and the reception of the decision in the North and the South.
6. How did Abraham Lincoln's election spark the Civil War? Was the war inevitable? Why or why not?
7. Was the Harpers Ferry raid well planned? What was John Brown attempting to accomplish? Was there method to his "madness"?

THE CIVIL WAR

In February 1861 President-elect Abraham Lincoln made the long journey from Springfield, Illinois, to Washington, D.C. He attempted to enter the city inconspicuously, some said because he was an unassuming man, others because he feared assassination. The crowds that greeted him no doubt included hostile and even murderous southern sympathizers, but the vast majority cheered him. One question was on all minds: Would there be war? Lincoln was asked that crucial query again and again. His answer, invariably put in parable form, was that one should not cross a river until one came to it. History brought the new president and the nation to the point of decision within weeks. In April 1861 North and South joined in four long, bloody years of war.

To Lincoln the task ahead was nothing more or less than preservation of the Union; all other issues including slavery were subordinate to it. Most northerners agreed with him. Not until the fall of 1862 would the president issue an emancipation proclamation. Lincoln wanted to do nothing during the early stages of the war to undermine loyalists in the border states. Moreover, he realized that, aside from abolitionists, most northerners and Republicans were racists who cared little about the plight of the slaves. Indeed, working-class fears of economic competition from manumitted bondsmen remained intense. And yet, by 1862 the war was freeing tens of thousands of slaves, some of whom sought refuge with Union armies and some of whom fled to the North. Gradually human rights replaced reunification as the primary justification for the war. Lincoln's rhetoric reflected the change. In 1862 he proclaimed that "If I could save the Union without freeing any slave, I would do it, and if I could do it by freeing some and leaving others alone, I would do that. What I do about slavery and the colored race, I do because I believe it helps to save the Union." In the Gettysburg Address delivered in 1863, he declared that the conflict then reaching its climax was a trial to determine if a nation "conceived in Liberty,

Lincoln's nomination for the presidency by the Republican party pointed to its commitment to preservation of the Union and exclusion of slavery from the territories. The soon-to-be-president on the eve of the election.

The war took a terrible toll on the president. Lincoln in 1865.

and dedicated to the proposition that all men are created equal" could endure. His message resonated throughout the North, and the Civil War become a great crusade for human rights.

APRIL 1861: WAR BEGINS

LINCOLN AND THE SECTIONAL CRISIS

Judging by his inaugural address the new president believed that he could preserve the Union without war. Ignoring the seceded states, he declared, "I therefore consider that in view of the Constitution and the laws, the Union is unbroken. . . . The power confided to me will be used to hold, occupy, and possess the property and places belonging to the Government, and to collect the duties and imposts; but beyond what may be necessary for these objects, there will be no invasions, no using force against or among the people anywere." Lincoln further asserted that his administration would not attempt to interfere with the institution of slavery in the southern states, and the federal government would continue to insist on observance of the Fugitive Slave Act. If hostilities came, Lincoln announced, they would have to be initiated by the rebellious factions in the southern states.

The firing on Fort Sumter left Abraham Lincoln no choice. He duly called for seventy-five thousand militia to put down the rebellion. The overriding goal for Lincoln, as for the vast majority of northerners, shifted from preservation to restoration of the Union. During his presidency he would subordinate all—civil liberties, political popularity, human life—to the the great, overriding goal of restoring the Union. The task the backwoods lawyer from Illinois had set for himself would be horrendously difficult.

SECESSION

Following the assault on Fort Sumter and Lincoln's call for volunteers, Virginia, Tennessee, North Carolina, and Arkansas seceded and joined the Confederacy. Civil war erupted in Missouri and Kentucky over the issue; both states provided the South with thousands of soldiers but in the end stayed loyal to the Union. So did Maryland and Delaware, and their choice proved to be crucial. Kentucky bracketed the all-important Ohio River. Missouri not only bounded the Mississippi but controlled major overland routes to the West. Delaware was nothing less than the gateway to Philadelphia, while Maryland surrounded the nation's capital on three sides. Finally, the sixty-three northern and western counties of Virginia, made up largely of slaveless upcountry farmers, seceded from that state and subsequently became the free state of West Virginia.

Northern Advantages

The North anticipated a short war—ninety days to judge by Lincoln's first call up of soldiers—and a comparison of North and South on the basis of population, agriculture, manufacturing, transportation infrastructure, and other vital indices would seem to validate that optimism. The population of the North in 1860 was 19 million and that of the South 9 million of whom 3.5 million were slaves. As far as agriculture was concerned, the South surpassed its adversary in total acreage, but the North claimed more improved land. In 1860, northern farmers produced three times the amount of flour meal as their southern counterparts.

In the all-important category of railroad track mileage, the North exceeded the South 19,700 to 10,500, but the disparity was greater than even these figures indicate. Three trunk lines including the Baltimore and Ohio and New York Central linked the Atlantic seaboard with the Great Lakes and the Ohio and Tennessee river valleys. Of these, the Confederacy controlled none. In addition, the North could claim over one hundred thousand manufacturing enterprises against the South's eighteen thousand.

In no area was federal supremacy greater than seaborne commerce. By the middle of the nineteenth century Yankee clipper ships were challenging Britain for control of trade with the Pacific rim, while traditional carriers plied their wares in Europe, the Caribbean, and Latin America. American shipping in 1860 totalled more than 5 million tons, the vast majority of it carried in the hulls of northern ships. As the war progressed, it seemed as if the North could arm, feed, clothe, and transport its troops as it pleased while logistics became an increasingly debilitating problem for the Confederacy. In the end, the North was able to claim 2 million soldiers to the South's eight hundred thousand.

Southern Advantages

In the short term, however, the South could claim a number of advantages. First, the manpower disparity did not immediately translate into an edge on the battlefield. The regular army of the United States numbered a mere sixteen thousand, and most of those were stationed in the West or along the Mexican border. The thousands of militia and volunteers who flocked to the stars and stripes would require months of training. Southern volunteers, by contrast, were accustomed to the outdoors, to riding, to firearms, and to fighting, the last a conspicuous characteristic of southern culture.

Second, at the outset, the Confederate Army enjoyed superior leadership. Over one-quarter of the regular army's officer corps resigned and joined the Confederacy. Conspicuous among them was Robert E. Lee, an experienced, imaginative soldier who would serve as commander of the Army of Northern Virginia from 1862 through 1865. Though not particularly keen on secession, the Virginian could not imagine abandoning his kith and kin in their hour of need. General Winfield Scott actually offered command of federal forces to Lee, who had graduated second in his class at West Point, but Lee opted for the Confederacy instead.

Third, the nature of the war seemed to favor the South. Confederate soldiers were fighting for their homes and families; they could claim to be defending their homeland against foreign invasion. Indeed, all the South had to do was maintain the status quo while the federals would have to invade and subdue their enemy. The Confederacy would enjoy internal lines of communication and supply, and would be fighting on familiar terrain. At the outset, Confederate volunteers were generally able to feed and arm themselves, and even supply their own mounts. With great satisfaction did the Confederacy draw parallels between the coming civil conflict and the Revolutionary War.

Fourth, the economic discrepancy, which was eventually to decide the outcome of the war, seemed not so important at the beginning. As mentioned above, the southern soldier initially brought to camp what he needed to subsist and fight, each man his own quartermaster. In addition, slaves constituted a huge labor force that would keep farm and plantation running and in the process free white male heads of household to fight. And the cornerstone of the economy was King Cotton. Southerners reasoned that the dependence of French and British textile mills on southern cotton would provide leverage sufficient to compel those two European powers to recognize the Confederacy and break the northern blockade of the South.

A MODERN WAR

Although James K. Polk during the Mexican War served as something of precedent, Abraham Lincoln was the first modern wartime president. Congress was not in session when the new chief executive took the oath of office, and he was grateful for it. Indeed, he postponed its convening until July in order to give himself a freer hand. In the spring of 1861 Lincoln issued decrees expanding the military budget, imposing a naval blockade on the South, and calling up state militias. Above all he wanted to hold the border states in the Union, and he was determined to do whatever was necessary to achieve that goal. When in August 1861 the federal commander in Missouri, General John C. Frémont, issued an order freeing the slaves, Lincoln countermanded it. At the same time, the president authorized the suspension of habeas corpus in Maryland so that Confederate sympathizers could be detained indefinitely.

Lincoln understood that his role as commander-in-chief during a civil conflict was far different than it would have been during a foreign war. If ever Clausewitz's aphorism that war is an extension of politics was true it was during the Civil War. Lincoln had to defeat the military rebellion by force while he simultaneously struggled to persuade the Confederate states to rejoin the Union.

Technology and Strategy

Technology and strategy combined to make the Civil War the bloodiest in American history with a total of 630,000 deaths due to wounds and disease by the time the last shot was fired. New weaponry was partially responsible. Rifled barrels replaced smooth bore muskets. The number of misfires dropped from 411 per thousand to 5. Soldiers could kill at a quarter of a mile; the effective range of the musket had been one hundred yards. With rifle and cannon able to decimate enemy ranks at long range, bayonet charges were few and far between. As one soldier who took part in the bloody assault on Port Hudson in 1864 observed, "Many men in the regiment never laid eyes on a Rebel during the whole action."

In addition, strategic thinking was still fixated on the Napoleonic era when the tactic of direct attack by massed infantry became entrenched in the military mind. Thus did carnage reign. Defensive positions bristled with rifles and artillery loaded with grapeshot—a combination of minié balls, chain, and nails—which acted as huge sawed off shotguns. General D.H. Hill described the effect at Malvern Hill: "As each brigade emerged from the woods, from 50 to 100 guns opened upon it, tearing great gaps in its ranks. Most of them had an open field half a mile wide to cross, under the fire of field artillery and heavy ordinance. It was not war—it was murder."

FINANCE AND SUPPLY

Once it became apparent that the war would not be over in ninety days the principal preoccupation in Washington became organization and finance. The

War Department faced the unprecedented task of arming, feeding, clothing, and transporting seven hundred thousand troops. Initially overwhelmed, the federal government had to rely on the states, many of which raised volunteer units and then contracted directly with shoe and clothing factories to outfit them. Private patriotic and aid societies solicited enlistments, raised money, and collected food and clothing. Though the War Department under Edwin M. Stanton eventually mastered the arts of mass procurement and supply, these volunteer efforts remained crucial. The battlefield and home front were thus intimately intertwined from the beginning.

The intermingling of the public and private also characterized finance but with less felicitous results. Lincoln regarded money as the province of Congress and not the executive, and he relied upon the House and Senate to raise the funds necessary to conduct the war. Understandably, given the fact that no national banking system existed, Congress turned to private financiers for help. Philadelphia banker Jay Cooke issued patriotic calls for the purchase of war bonds and eventually sold $400 million worth, keeping a "fair commission" for himself. As of 1865, the federal government had borrowed over $2.5 billion.

In addition, in August 1861 Congress imposed the nation's first income tax, a flat 3 percent on incomes $800 and above. But even this did not suffice to meet the government's needs.

A National Monetary System

Reluctantly, Secretary of the Treasury Salmon P. Chase agreed to issue paper money. In February 1862 Congress passed the Legal Tender Act creating a national currency. Because of its color the new money was called "greenbacks." The Legal Tender Act facilitated financing of the war but led to inflation. The 80 percent decline in the value of federal currency during the Civil War caused immense suffering among the working class and among those on fixed incomes, but in the end proved bearable.

Chase's decision to issue paper currency served a secondary purpose: creation of a national currency. Prior to the Legal Tender Act money had consisted of coins and state bank notes. In 1863 Congress enacted the National Bank Act which forbade state banks from issuing their own currency and forcing them to apply for charters from the federal government. Thus did the war centralize the financial system and give the federal government immense power over it, a development that would never have occurred had southern states' rights advocates still been in Congress.

JEFFERSON DAVIS AND THE CONFEDERATE GOVERNMENT

Meanwhile, in the South, provisional president Jefferson Davis was attempting not to preserve but to create a union. Given the fact that an extreme states' rights philosophy underlay secession and rebellion, his task was doomed to failure from the beginning. Though he had served in a national cabinet, was a veteran of the Mexican War, and had considerable administrative experience, Davis did not compare favorably with Lincoln. He possessed none of his northern counterpart's political shrewdness nor his persuasive powers.

A native of Kentucky, Davis had moved with his family to Mississippi where he became a wealthy cotton planter. Many of the aristocrats in and around Richmond viewed him as uncouth nouveau riche. Lincoln, the country lawyer, suffered similar snubs and expressions of contempt in Washington, but managed to exert his will on the government and war effort in spite of them.

To avoid controversy, Davis excluded some of the ablest men of the South from his cabinet. Ironically obsessed with democracy, the Confederate president appointed a member from each of the six original states, excluding Mississippi which he represented. When wealthy plantation owners refused to finance the war, Davis would not coerce them nor would he chastise those state governments that refused to supply or adequately equip their militias.

A Rich Man's War

The Confederacy was conspicuous for its failure in the areas of finance and manpower mobilization. The Davis government refused to impose a uniform tax until 1863 and by then it was too late. Richmond chose to finance the war by borrowing and issuing paper money. By war's end inflation had reached 9,000 percent, wrecking the economy and demoralizing the population of the South.

Like the North, enlistments in the Confederate army fell off sharply after the first months of the war. In 1862 the Congress in Richmond, whose C.S.A. constitution paralleled exactly the U.S. Constitution except for the explicit condonement of "negro slavery," enacted the nation's first draft law. It obligated every able-bodied man between the ages of eighteen and thirty-five for three years of military duty. The upper limit was later extended to age fifty. Purchase of substitutes not of draft age was allowed, as it was in the North. But unlike the North where the price for a substitute stabilized at around $300, in the South it soared to as much as $10,000. Most divisive was the provision in the draft law exempting one white male on every plantation that worked twenty or more slaves. It seemed increasingly to working-class southerners that they were mere pawns in a rich man's war.

FIRST BULL RUN (MANASSAS)

In Washington and Richmond pressure mounted throughout March 1861 for a quick, decisive victory. Davis agreed to allow General P.T.G. Beauregard to gather his troops in Virginia and southern Maryland at Manassas junction about twenty-five miles west of Washington. To counter this move, Lincoln ordered General Irvin McDowell and his thirty thousand largely untrained troops to move south and confront Beauregard. Anticipating a quick victory, and a subsequent march on Richmond, a number of congressmen and their ladies drove out to witness the battle.

On July 21, 1861, on the banks of a meandering tributary of the Potomac River called Bull Run the naivete and optimism that had so far characterized attitudes on both sides were shattered. McDowell and Beauregard, who had been West Point classmates, attempted to turn each other's left flank. The federals nearly succeeded in overwhelming the Confederate fortifications, but when southern reinforcements under General Joseph E. Johnston rolled in by train from the west, the Union advance was checked. It was during this action that Colonel Thomas Jackson, a former professor at the Virginia Military Institute, earned the nickname "Stonewall" by holding his ground under heavy onslaught. The Union retreat disintegrated into a rout. Roads to Washington clogged with exhausted and wounded soldiers and panicked spectators.

Almost as demoralized by the bloody battle of First Bull Run as the federal troops, Beauregard and Johnston's forces were unable to follow up their victory. The following day a summer downpour rendered the roads impassable. Army Chief of Staff Winfield Scott had predicted to Lincoln that victory in the war would require 300,000 men and three years. Bull Run gave him instant credibility.

PLANNING FOR THE LONG HAUL

Confronted with the prospect of an extended conflict, Lincoln and his generals developed a three-phase strategy. The Army of the Potomac, reformed after Bull Run, would remain in eastern Virginia to protect the capital and menace Richmond. The federal navy would tighten its blockade of the South, cutting it off from foreign munitions and other vital manufactured goods. Finally, in what was dubbed an "anaconda" strategy, federal armies would seize the Mississippi, Tennessee, and Cumberland river valleys, thereby dividing and strangling the Confederacy (see Figure 12–1). The Confederate approach was simpler. If Lee and his lieutenants could hold the U.S. military at bay for a sufficient period, Britain and France, starved of cotton, would surely intervene and break the Union blockade. Meanwhile, a war-weary northern public would force Lincoln to sue for peace.

The Union Blockade

During the first year of the war major military encounters occurred on the high seas and in the West. To break the Union blockade, the Confederacy sheathed a captured Union steamship (the *Merrimac*) in iron and unleashed it on the fleet blockading Chesapeake Bay. The federal vessels proved defenseless against the newly dubbed C.S.S. *Virginia's* battering ram and guns. "Who is to prevent her from dropping her anchor in the Potomac . . . and . . . battering down the halls of the Capitol?" asked one alarmed Navy Department official. The very next day, however, the Union ironclad *Monitor,* described by one observer as a giant floating shingle, arrived on the scene and engaged the *Virginia.* The two vessels fought to a draw, and the *Virginia* retreated to its lair at Norfolk. When

FIGURE 12–1

Principal Military Campaigns of the Civil War

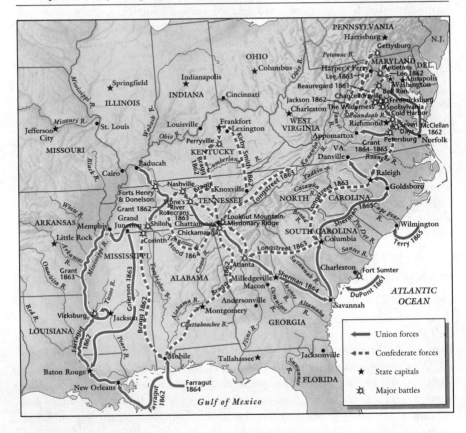

the Confederates were forced subsequently to abandon the port, the "scourge of the Union" was destroyed.

Actually, the Union blockade did not pose a significant threat to southern shipping until 1863. At the outset of the war the U.S. Navy had but thirty-three ships with which to patrol thirty-five hundred miles of coastline. During the first year of the war only one-eighth of the Confederate vessels attempting to run the gauntlet were captured. By 1865 this percentage had increased to one-half. From 1863 through the end of the war, the blockade succeeded in denying the South much needed armaments and other manufactured goods.

The War in the West

The man in charge of the North's anaconda was Ulysses S. Grant, a slight, dishevelled, unassuming man who had once resigned his commission because of a drinking problem. Confronting Grant, whose twin headquarters were at Cairo,

To counter the threat posed by the C.S.S. Merrimac *to the Union blockade of the Confederacy, the North built its own ironclad, the U.S.S.* Monitor. *The officers of the* Monitor *shown on the deck of the vessel.*

The First Naval Conflict between Iron Clad Vessels, *a lithograph produced by Endicott & Co., 1862.*

Illinois, and Paducah, Kentucky, was General Albert Sidney Johnston, a huge Texan known for his discipline and bravery. To block any and every move by the enemy, Johnston stretched his forty thousand men across 150 miles of western Kentucky. During the opening weeks of 1862 Grant moved to take advantage of the paper-thin Confederate lines. His troops marched southward along the Tennessee and Cumberland rivers supported by gunboat flotillas. In February, Union forces captured Fort Henry on the Tennessee and Fort Donelson on the Cumberland, the latter battle resulting in the surrender of twelve thousand Confederate troops. Grant's victories made him an instant hero in the East; the press nicknamed him "Unconditional Surrender" Grant, his initials conveniently corresponding to the ultimatum he had given the Confederates at Donelson. Fame, he was soon to learn, was fleeting.

APRIL 1862: THE SOUTH GAINS MOMENTUM

SHILOH

Grant's next objective was Corinth, Mississippi. Victory and momentum had made him careless, however. While approaching Corinth, he stationed his men between two creeks, tributaries of the Tennessee, on a vulnerable plateau. Exhorting his men to show themselves "worthy of the women of the South," Johnston attacked early on the morning of April 6. Catching the federals asleep or at breakfast, rebel troops killed hundreds and pinned the rest against the river bank. Nevertheless, with the help of artillery situated across the river and fire from the Union gunboats, Grant managed to hold his ground. That night, reinforcements arrived in a torrential downpour. Grant and his steel-nerved subordinate, William Tecumseh Sherman of Ohio, rallied the troops and drove the Confederate force into Corinth. The northern force was too battered to pursue, however.

Johnston's forces succeeded in halting Grant's advance, but they had suffered heavy losses, including Johnston who fell in battle. Nevertheless, the eastern press regarded Shiloh as something of a Confederate victory and turned on Grant claiming that his drunkenness had been responsible for the setback. Lincoln prevented his dismissal—"I can't spare this man; he fights"—but Grant was temporarily relieved of command, and the Union offensive in the West stalled. Shiloh was the bloodiest battle in American history. The twenty-five thousand combined casualties exceeded the total for the Revolutionary and Mexican Wars combined. But, in fact, this was to be the first of dozens of such savage encounters.

MCCLELLAN AND LEE

In the aftermath of Bull Run, Lincoln replaced McDowell with General George B. McClellan, a West Point classmate of Stonewall Jackson. McClellan was handsome, egotistical, and charismatic. For nine months following the Union debacle at Bull Run, McClellan collected and trained troops. When urged to action by an increasingly impatient Lincoln, the general repeatedly cited superior Confederate forces. "If General McClellan does not want to use the army I would like to borrow it," an exasperated Lincoln remarked. Finally, the president ordered his commander to move on Richmond by February 22, Washington's birthday.

Suddenly emboldened, McClellan declared that he would occupy the Confederate capital within ten days. Taking advantage of the fact that Fort Monroe on the Atlantic tip of the peninsula separating the York and James rivers was in Union hands, McClellan decided to attack from the east. Instead of days, however, his maneuvering consumed months. Nevertheless, by the end of May 1862, the Army of the Potomac could hear Richmond's church bells.

Confederate commander Joseph E. Johnston had merely been biding his time, however. On May 31 he attacked the Union army on the south bank of the Chickahominy River. In the ensuing Battle of Fair Oaks, only the arrival of reinforcements prevented the decimation of McClellan's positions. Fierce fighting in which Johnston was severely wounded left both armies battered and exhausted.

At this point fifty-five-year-old Robert E. Lee assumed command of the Army of Northern Virginia. Impeccably dressed, reserved in demeanor, always gentlemanly, Lee was a tiger on the battlefield. His first name, one of his lieutenants remarked, should have been Audacity. Duty, he once remarked, was the "sublimest word in our language."

As soon as he took command, he struck hard at McClellan, who had retreated north of the Chickahominy. The Army of the Potomac retreated back down the peninsula with Lee and Stonewall Jackson in hot pursuit. The Confederates attempted a knockout blow at the Battle of Malvern Hill on July 1, but were prevented from overtaking the retreating McClellan by artillery entrenched on the hilltop and fire from Union gunboats in the Potomac. Disgustedly, Lincoln ordered McClellan back to Washington. He was to merge his forces with those of General John Pope, called in from the West to take charge of defending the capital.

SECOND BULL RUN (MANASSAS)

With McClellan on his way back to the capital, Lee decided to leave a token force to defend Richmond and to strike Pope before the two Union forces could be united. In the Second Battle of Bull Run, fought on almost the exact same spot as the first, Jackson led Pope into a trap. Thinking that he was dealing only with a moderate size force, Pope attacked. Thirty thousand Confederates under James Longstreet then smashed the Union flank. Pope's shattered formations abandoned the field and in the days that followed regrouped in positions around Washington. Lincoln dispatched Pope to Minnesota to fight Indians and once again named McClellan commander of the Army of the Potomac.

ANTIETAM

In the aftermath of Second Bull Run Lee persuaded President Davis to allow him to carry the war into the North, a move that the Confederacy believed would further undermine northern morale and perhaps elicit recognition from the European powers. In September 1862 he led his troops into western Maryland and headed for Pennsylvania. As luck would have it, a Confederate officer left a copy of Lee's orders wrapped around a bundle of cigars in camp, and a detachment of Union soldiers discovered them.

McClellan, who had moved northward to shadow and counter Lee, discovered that he vastly outnumbered his adversary, Lee having dispatched Stonewall Jackson to capture Harpers Ferry. For sixteen crucial hours the ever-cautious McClellan delayed, allowing Lee to consolidate his position near Antietam Creek on the Virginia-Maryland border. Finally, on September 17, 1862, McClellan's forces attacked. Just as it appeared that the Confederate ranks would break, General A. P. Hill arrived with a division of reinforcements. Although his men had force-marched from Harpers Ferry, a trip of sixteen hours, they leaped into the fray attacking McClellan's flank. The carnage was terrible: the day's fighting left five thousand dead and eighteen thousand wounded. "Where the line stood," wrote a Georgia veteran, "the ground was covered with blue. I could have walked on them without putting my feet on the ground." Late in the afternoon the fighting ended. Antietam was regarded as a victory for the Union only because Lee's army was halted on its march north.

Lee's forces regrouped south of the Potomac. For six weeks, Lincoln waited in vain for McClellan to attack. Exasperated, the president relieved his principal commander and assigned him to recruiting duty in New Jersey.

GREAT BRITAIN AND THE CIVIL WAR

Antietam was hardly a smashing battlefield victory for the Union but it proved to be of immense diplomatic value. Lincoln and Seward believed that they had to keep Great Britain neutral at all costs. Opinion in the former parent country was divided. The British upper classes identified with the southern aristocracy, while the middle and working classes, concerned with democracy and human rights, initially favored the North. A number of British manufacturers believed that they would benefit from an independent Confederacy; consequently members of this powerful group supported the South.

On April 19, 1861, Lincoln had proclaimed a maritime blockade of the seven seceded states, and the British admiralty ordered its officers in American waters to observe a strict neutrality. Shortly afterward, the Confederacy dispatched envoys to London and Paris to apply for loans, solicit diplomatic recognition, and promote the idea of armed intervention. Davis and his colleagues were certain that King Cotton would provide the leverage necessary to achieve recognition at least. Although in 1860 the British textile industry depended on the South for 80 percent of its raw fiber, King Cotton proved to be a mere commoner, however. The outbreak of war saw a 50 percent oversupply of the commodity in Britain. The surplus extended to the manufactured product; thus did the industry actually welcome the South's self-imposed boycott. During the war smugglers, like the fictional Rhett Butler of *Gone with the Wind*, ran some 1.5 million bales past the Union blockade. Further, the British developed new sources in India and Egypt.

Far more important in raising the specter of British intervention was humanitarian sentiment. Many Englishmen felt revulsion at the unprecedented carnage associated with Civil War battles. It seemed to many in England that the only humane thing to do was intervene and broker a peace. Accordingly, on September 14, 1862, Lord Palmerston, then prime minister, noting that the northerners "had got a very complete smashing" at Second Bull Run, wrote Foreign Secretary Earl Russell proposing that Britain and France force Washington to accept an arrangement "on the basis of a separation." Then on September 23, Palmerston received word of Lee's drive northward into Maryland. If the North sustained a defeat, Great Britain should act "while the iron is hot," he told Russell; if not, it should reconsider the whole matter.

The bloody stalemate at Antietam, and Lee's withdrawal to the south chilled British interventionists. McClellan had failed to destroy the Army of Northern Virginia, but the North was much stronger than many Britons realized. In effect, Antietam crushed southern hopes of European intervention.

FREDERICKSBURG

Ever determined to carry the fight to the enemy, Lincoln appointed the modest, personable Ambrose E. Burnside as commander of the Army of the Potomac. Burnside, best known for his sidewhiskers, had twice turned down the command on the grounds that he was not up to the job. But he could not resist when duty called the third time. And if President Lincoln wanted him to fight, he would fight. Moving southward, Burnside crossed the Rappahannock River on December 13, 1862. On that blustery cold day, the massive Union army approached Lee's forces dug in behind stone fences on Marye's Heights just west of Fredericksburg, Virginia. Six times Burnside sent his infantry across the mile of bottomland in front of the Confederate lines. Six times the blue ranks were chewed to pieces by artillery and musket fire. When the smoke had cleared, a weeping Burnside was left to contemplate twelve thousand Union casualties and Lee's army still in place. The Army of the Potomac limped back across the river.

As 1862 drew to a close, the war had stalemated in both East and West. Morale in the North reached a low ebb. The press vied with northern Democrats who called for a negotiated settlement and radical Republicans who wanted a more vigorous prosecution of the war, in denouncing Lincoln. It was at this low point that Abraham Lincoln chose to issue the Emancipation Proclamation, arguably the most significant social policy decree in the history of the republic.

THE EMANCIPATION PROCLAMATION

In 1858 Lincoln, then a candidate for the U.S. Senate, had asserted that "a house divided" could not long endure and that the United States would eventually have to become either all slave or all free. Upon his inauguration as president, however, he had promised not to interfere with slavery where it existed. Though it roused the bitter ire of abolitionists at home and abroad, Lincoln hewed to that line during the first two years of the war.

His reasons were several. Initially, he wanted to give loyalists in the southern states every opportunity to defeat the secessionists. Radical Republicans increased their clamor on behalf of emancipation, but Lincoln realized that they were a minority. Indeed, most Republicans were more concerned about keeping slavery out of the territories than with abolishing it in the South. They did not believe African Americans to be the social or intellectual equals of whites. Moreover, northern working-class fears of job competition from free blacks was intense.

Policy aside, however, Lincoln and the North were faced with the reality that the war was emancipating the slaves. By the fall of 1862, tens of thousands of runaways, known as contrabands, had flooded into Union lines. As a result, Lincoln edged closer to a formal emancipation proclamation. To return the fugitives to slavery was unthinkable. Moreover, Lincoln reckoned that emancipation would give the North a "higher cause" for which to fight and thus improve morale. Finally, a decree freeing the slaves would remove the backbone from the South's domestic workforce. Following the Battle of Antietam, Lincoln in September 1862 issued a preliminary emancipation proclamation. If the southern states did not desist in their rebellion as of January 1863, he would declare all of their bondsmen "forever free." That, of course, did not happen, and on New Year's Day Lincoln issued the Emancipation Proclamation.

In truth the famous decree was hardly a clear-cut affair. It applied only to the states in rebellion. Slaveholders in the border states were legally entitled to hold on to their chattel. Abolitionists were appalled. Secretary of State Seward sardonically summed up the situation: "We show our sympathy with slavery by emancipating slaves where we cannot reach them and holding them in bondage where we can set them free." Despite the ambiguity of Lincoln's statement, black leaders praised the Emancipation Proclamation. "We shout for joy that we live to record this righteous decree," declared Frederick Douglass, former slave and the voice of black America. Douglass and other spokesmen and women for the black community anticipated that the proclamation would either encourage southern slaves to flee to Union lines or to refuse to work for their masters. They were correct in both cases.

Plight of the Contrabands

During the Civil War approximately one-half million slaves, one-seventh of the total, fled to Union lines. Following the Emancipation Proclamation, a large number of the men enlisted in the military service. For those who did not enlist and for black women and children, life was extremely difficult. The ex-slaves, called freedmen, were housed in filthy refugee camps and suffered from disease, exposure, and general neglect. "The children are all emaciated to the last degree," observed one northern missionary, "and have such violent coughs and dysenteries that few survive."

Most Union troops were prejudiced against blacks; they viewed the ragged, hungry contrabands as a nuisance at best. In the Sea Islands, General Butler employed the runaways building fortifications and doing other menial chores, but in the Mississippi Valley where most of the contrabands were concentrated, freedmen were employed on plantations leased by loyal planters. To relieve themselves of the burden of caring for the contrabands, commanders of federal troops often forced freedmen to sign contracts that they did not understand and that compelled them to live and work in conditions that did not differ much from slavery.

African-American Soldiers

Early in the war free blacks had attempted to enlist in the Union Army but to their bitter disappointment had been rebuffed. During the course of the war, pressure built on the Lincoln administration to allow African Americans to participate in the struggle to restore the Union. With emancipation, the president decided that opening the service to blacks was both inevitable and wise. The proclamation included a provision permitting enlistment in both the army and navy. In the end, some two hundred thousand African Americans served under the stars and stripes, constituting approximately one-tenth of the Union Army and Navy.

Although fears that white racists in northern cities would riot at the sight of blacks in uniform proved unfounded, black soldiers did suffer from discrimination and segregation while bearing arms for their country. Initially, they received ten dollars a month while their white counterparts were paid thirteen. Not until June 1864 did the War Department intervene and equalize pay. African Americans served in all-black units commanded by white officers.

Conventional wisdom among northern officers was that black Americans possessed neither the courage nor intelligence to serve in combat. Thus, initially "buffalo soldiers," as the Indians later called them, dug trenches, drove wagons, and performed other menial chores. Inevitably, however, black troops were pressed into combat. In 1863 almost half of the Fifty-fourth Massachusetts Volunteers, commanded by abolitionist Robert Gould Shaw, perished in an attack on Fort Wagner, South Carolina. Although poorly trained and equipped, African-American troops fought ferociously and courageously in the struggle for Vicksburg. As a result most white officers changed their opinion, and tens of thousands of black soldiers saw action. Some thirty-seven thousand died fighting for their country.

African-American soldiers were, of course, anathema to white southerners. The sight of former slaves clad in blue uniforms, armed with muskets,

African-American soldiers played an increasingly significant role in the Union war effort. A photograph of Company E, Fourth Colored Infantry at Fort Lincoln, 1865.

and engaged in the effort to liberate their own people, was as repulsive to Confederates as it was thrilling to black southerners. During the first months after the Emancipation Proclamation, various Confederate voices promised execution if blacks fighting for the Union were captured. At Fort Pillow in Tennessee Confederate troops executed 262 black prisoners of war, but atrocities declined precipitously when President Lincoln threatened retaliation.

Since the early days of the republic, African Americans had pressed their government for the right to bear arms in the knowledge that it would be difficult to deny full citizenship to those who had served in the armed services. Frederick Douglass exaggerated when he observed that "no power on earth can deny that he [the black veteran] has earned the right to citizenship"; participation in the military coupled with the Emancipation Proclamation and the Thirteenth Amendment, a constitutional provision outlawing slavery that was passed by Congress in 1865, marked the beginning of a new, more hopeful chapter in the African American's struggle for equal rights.

MEDICAL CARE, HYGIENE, AND THE ROLE OF WOMEN

In the areas of finance, logistics, and particularly medical care both the Union and Confederacy were initially quite dependent on volunteer agencies. Medical practices were still primitive at the time of the Civil War. Many soldiers who

Revelations concerning mistreatment of Union prisoners of war reinforced northern animosity toward the Confederacy. The issuing of rations at Andersonville, Georgia, August 17, 1864.

might otherwise have recovered if doctors had known about antiseptic procedures, died of infection, especially gangrene. Because army camps were frequently overcrowded and filthy and because adequate sanitary measures were not taken, as many soldiers died of typhoid, pneumonia, diphtheria, and malaria as from enemy fire.

The medical corps on both sides of the Mason-Dixon line lagged far behind other branches of the service in both size and technological know-how. At the Battle of Pea Ridge in northwest Arkansas in 1862, the wounded lay so long in the field that a number were eaten by wild boars. At Shiloh it rained heavily the day after the battle causing scores of wounded to either drown or die of exposure. Prisoners of war suffered from mistreatment and neglect in both the North and South. In 1864 at the Confederate prison camp of Andersonville in southwestern Georgia, for example, thirty-three thousand men were crowded into a facility designed for ten thousand. Forced to live in an open stockade, nearly one hundred died every day during the scorching summer.

From the outset women in both the North and South formed volunteer associations to raise money, sew clothes and quilts, and make bandages for the men serving in the field. As of 1863, the Women's Central Association for Relief could claim seven thousand chapters throughout the North. They provided an estimated $15 million worth of food, medical supplies, and clothing to the

Union Army as well as food, shelter, and transportation to soldiers on leave. In 1861 President Lincoln authorized the formation of the United States Sanitary Commission. This organization, comprised almost entirely of men, sent five hundred agents into the field to advise soldiers on proper latrine construction, water treatment procedures, and healthy food preparation.

In conjunction with women experienced in the nineteenth-century reform movement, most notably Dorothea Lynde Dix, the Sanitary Commission forced the armed services to accept women as paid army nurses. Initially, there was as much resistance outside of military hospitals as inside. Nursing had always been standard duty for American women, but not outside the family. Caring for the bodily needs of strange men would corrupt the morals of American women, critics proclaimed. The reformers persisted, however, and before war's end more than three thousand northern women had served as paid army nurses. Among the most notable were Clara Barton, founder of the American Red Cross, and Mary Ann "Mother" Bickerdyke, who took on the military establishment in the West, dismissing incompetent employees and ordering the construction of bathing facilities and sanitary hospitals.

Women assumed the roles of volunteer quartermasters and nurses in the South as well as the North. There was even more resistance to women nurses in the Confederacy than in the northern states because females had played much less conspicuous roles in public life than their northern counterparts. Necessity prevailed, however. During the Seven Days' Battles of 1862 the fighting threatened to engulf Richmond. The streets were glutted with thousands of wounded Confederates because there was no room in the hospitals. The women of Richmond set up roadside hospitals to provide at least food and shelter. From that start, middle-class women insisted on playing their part in the Confederate medical corps.

APRIL 1863: THE PENDULUM STARTS TO SWING

NORTHERN DISCONTENT

Politics

The Civil War overshadowed but did not eradicate politics in the North. The Republicans who won the 1860 election were determined not only to prevent the spread of slavery into the territories, but also to enact their Whiggish platform. The elimination of southern congressmen and senators, who were nearly all Democrats and opponents of big government, cleared the way for the Republicans to succeed. The Morrill Tariff passed in 1861 had nearly doubled the prewar tariff rate by 1865. During the war Congress chartered the Union Pacific and Central Pacific Railroads. The former was to build westward from Nebraska and the latter eastward from California. With their joining, the nation would have its first transcontinental railroad. The West enjoyed special attention from the Republican majorities. Under the Homestead Act passed in

1862, settlers could claim 160 acres of land, and if they worked their acreage for five years and built a house on it, the tract was theirs for a small fee. Passed that same year, the Morrill Land Grant Act awarded states vast tracts of public land to be used to finance the construction of agricultural and mechanical colleges.

Northern Democrats protested this growth in national power—in effect the fulfillment of Henry Clay's American Plan—but they were unable to stop the legislative juggernaut. Though Stephen A. Douglas and the Democrats had claimed 44 percent of the popular vote in 1860, the party was deeply divided between war Democrats, who like Stephen Douglas insisted there was no middle road between patriotism and treason, and peace Democrats who denounced the draft, martial law, and the alleged abuse of power by President Lincoln. The leader of the Copperheads, as the Republicans referred to the peace Democrats, was Clement Vallandigham, a former Ohio congressman, who advocated a negotiated peace and threatened a western secession if the Lincoln administration did not comply. Vallandigham and his fellows played on the racist sentiments of the urban working class, insisting that the Emancipation Proclamation would flood northern cities with cheap black labor. In 1862 Lincoln had declared that any and all citizens interfering with or discouraging enlistment were subject to arrest and indefinite detention. Eventually more than twenty thousand individuals were arrested, most of whom were never charged with a specific crime or brought to trial. Vallandigham was seized and deported to the South.

At the same time Lincoln battled the Copperheads, he was forced to deal with deep divisions within his own party and growing social unrest throughout the North. The radical Republicans continued to gain strength and to voice criticism of Lincoln for being too timid. They focused first on the Emancipation Proclamation and then on harsh treatment of the South at war's end. The division was reflected not only in Congress but in the cabinet in the personages of Salmon P. Chase and William H. Seward. In 1862 the Radicals created a joint Committee on the Conduct of the War, which attempted to interfere with the actions of the executive in its handling both of the war and dissent.

Economics

Politics aside, by 1863 the North was seething with discontent. The Civil War caused something of an economic boom, but the wealth created was very unevenly distributed. The iron-making, boot, textile, and farm implement industries, just to name a few, boomed. The Borden company made a fortune selling canned milk to the government, while the McCormick brothers' reaper revolutionized farming and made some farmers rich. For most, however, the Civil War spelled hard times. The 15 percent annual inflation rate dramatically reduced living standards, particularly for the working class. Wages rose only half as fast as prices and as a result coal miners, railroad engineers, and more than a dozen other groups formed unions during the war. Management fought back by blacklisting union organizers and employing women, immigrants, and African Americans as strikebreakers.

The Draft

Equally as inflammatory was conscription, first introduced in July 1863. The draft law was originally intended to stimulate reenlistment and provide additional volunteers. Soon, however, it became apparent that the federal government needed to enlist the eligible forcibly with the aid of armed marshals. Nearly all northern Democrats had voted against the draft law, and they made much political profit out of the provisions for substitution. Those draftees who chose not to enlist could pay other men to fight for them. Three hundred dollars, the going price for a substitute, was equal to a year's wages for a blue-collar worker, Democrats pointed out. In fact, only 7 percent of those called actually served. Twenty-five percent hired substitutes and another 45 percent were excused, usually for health reasons. Nevertheless, many more poor men served than rich men, and the draft process was frequently marred by favoritism and prejudice.

During the spring of 1863 occasional outbursts of violence marred the recruiting process, but then in mid-July elements of the New York working class, many of them Irish immigrants, rose up en masse. For a week they burned, looted, and lynched. Order was restored only after regular units of the U.S. Army were rushed in from Gettysburg. When the smoke cleared, a black orphanage lay in ruins, and 105 people had perished, many of them black.

The draft had touched off the rioting but more profound causes lay at the heart of the unrest. The Civil War merely aggravated the frustration of the poor; working-class New Yorkers took out their frustration against African Americans because they believed them to be the cause of low wages and job competition, and more simply because they were an available and vulnerable target. Ironically, the single most important factor relieving pressure on draft-age whites was the enlistment of two hundred thousand African Americans.

SOUTHERN DISTRESS

If northern society was showing signs of stress by 1863, Confederate society was threatening to disintegrate. In violation of his cherished democratic principles, Jefferson Davis was forced to enlarge the power of the central government and rule through decree in such crucial matters as manpower, allocation of raw materials, and transportation. Yet he refused to follow Lincoln's example by vigorously suppressing dissent. As a result, it flourished. In 1864 Davis' own vice president, Alexander Stephens, took the lead in suggesting a negotiated settlement to the war. At the same time, states' rights governors ignored requisitions for troops, money, and materiel.

The war changed the way southerners lived even more than it did northerners. The region's largest cities swelled with soldiers, refugees, and bureaucrats. The population of Richmond tripled as the Confederate bureaucracy swelled to seventy thousand.

Changing Gender Roles

Many of the bureaucrats were women, so-called government girls, who were forced to serve in the workforce because of the manpower shortage. Gender roles on farm and plantation also changed dramatically because of the war. As white masters and overseers departed to fight, white women were left behind on the plantation to cope with shortages, raise crops, and manage slaves. The wives of yeomen farmers did not enjoy the benefit of slave labor or of mechanization, which was largely a northern phenomenon. Planting and harvesting were backbreaking, frustrating chores for those who remained behind.

Politics, Economics, and Basic Survival

Conscription and inflation were issues that ate away at the heart of southern nationalism. Commoners everywhere railed at the high cost of substitutes; yeomen farmers were particularly galled by the provision in the draft law exempting those who owned twenty or more slaves. Inflation was so great that it virtually destroyed the Confederate currency by war's end. In 1864 in Richmond eggs sold for six dollars a dozen and butter for twenty-five dollars a pound. All but the very rich were reduced to begging. Inflation coupled with the increasingly effective northern blockade led to starvation in some areas. In 1863 some three hundred women and children armed with clubs, knives, and pistols staged a bread riot in Richmond. They smashed windows and broke into bakeries and grocery stores, carrying away bread and other foodstuffs. The Davis administration had to threaten to use force before the crowd would disperse. During the last year and a half of the war working-class southerners and yeomen farm families became preoccupied with survival. Tens of thousands refused either to pay taxes or to respond to the draft. By 1865 the desertion rate in the Confederate Army was running at 40 percent.

Peace sentiment grew apace in the South in 1864. More than a hundred meetings were held in North Carolina alone calling for negotiations. But Jefferson Davis would have none of it. The absence of a two-party system in the Confederacy made the framing of alternatives difficult. Davis was in firm control of Congress and he equated negotiation with treason. Thus the war moved inexorably toward its conclusion.

CHANCELLORSVILLE

The Union defeat at Fredericksburg damaged but did not destroy the Army of the Potomac. As successor to the disgraced Burnside, Lincoln picked one of his more voluble assistants, Joseph E. Hooker. Known as a hard drinker and tough talker, "Fighting Joe" declared following his appointment that God had best have mercy on Robert E. Lee because he could not. Hooker's plan was a good one, but it failed in execution.

The new Union commander led his 130,000 troops northwest and then south across the Rappahannock and Rapidan rivers, his goal being to turn Lee's left flank. The Confederates deduced what was happening and moved to block. Lee positioned his main force to confront Hooker while sending J.E.B. Stuart's cavalry to harass his lines of communication. When subsequently Hooker lost contact with Lee's army he panicked and ordered his troops to retreat to Chancellorsville, a crossroads just south of the Rapidan.

Typically, Lee decided to seize the initiative. He dispatched Stonewall Jackson to assault Hooker's exposed right flank and then moved his remaining forces to attack directly. Lee struck with all he had on the late afternoon of May 2. Hooker's troops were encamped on the edge of a dense wooded area called the Wilderness. The Union lines broke but the densely thicketed forest coupled with nightfall kept the Confederates from following up. The next day the battle resumed, and after a day of furious fighting Hooker and his army retreated northward across the Rappahannock. Chancellorsville was a clear-cut Confederate victory, but Lee had suffered twelve thousand casualties and lost Jackson who in the confusion of battle had been shot by Confederate pickets.

VICKSBURG

While Lee and Hooker bloodied each other at Chancellorsville, Grant, who had been reinstated as Union commander in the western theater, had begun his advance down the Mississippi. Two major fortresses still remained in Confederate hands: Vicksburg, Mississippi, and Port Hudson, Louisiana. Situated on bluffs two hundred feet above the river, Vicksburg with its garrison of thirty thousand troops was a formidable obstacle. The city was protected on the west by the river and on the north by a forest and swamp. The only avenue of attack was across a dry neck of land to the east and south.

Positioned at Memphis well to the north of Vicksburg, Grant had to find a way to circle around and approach from the southeast. He moved down the river and then departing at Milliken's Bend led his army overland south and east to Grand Gulf well south of Vicksburg. Meanwhile, Union gunboats successfully braved the batteries at Vicksburg and rendezvoused with Grant, helping him and his men across the river. The federals moved east and captured Jackson before laying siege to Vicksburg. For six weeks the city suffered in Grant's iron grip. With starving soldiers and townspeople reduced to eating insects and rats, Confederate General John C. Pemberton surrendered his thirty thousand troops on July 4. Shortly thereafter Port Hudson fell to Grant, and the entire Mississippi from Cairo, Illinois, to Louisiana was in Union hands. The Confederacy was irreversibly split.

News of Grant's siege of Vicksburg prompted Lee to undertake a diversionary thrust into the North. The Confederate cabinet was divided on the

The fall of Vicksburg to Grant's forces in July 1863 gave the Union control of the entire Mississippi River. In the honeycomb of trenches depicted here, Confederate defenders sought refuge from continuous Union bombardment.

wisdom of the move, but Lee insisted that his offensive would not only relieve pressure on Vicksburg but also elicit recognition from the European powers. At any rate, he argued, war-ravaged Virginia would no longer support his army. Hooker wanted to take advantage of Lee's departure to descend on Richmond, but Lincoln rebuked him. "Lee's army, and not Richmond, is your true objective," he told him and then promptly replaced Hooker with General George G. Meade, a Philadelphia aristocrat. Meade's army moved northward, paralleling the advance of the Army of Northern Virginia. The federals were careful to keep themselves between Lee and Washington, D.C.

GETTYSBURG

Gettysburg, Pennsylvania, was not deliberately selected as the decisive battle of the Civil War. Confederate troops foraging for shoes ran into Union cavalry in the village. Both sides called for reinforcements and within twenty-four hours the two armies were in place. Union forces outnumbered Confederates, 90,000 to 75,000. Lee's troops drove the Union advance guard out of the town proper, but the loss was a federal blessing in disguise.

Meade's army occupied defensive positions on high ground east of Gettysburg. The Union line resembled a fishhook, the shank running south-north

Charges by massed troops across open fields produced massive casualties at the Battle of Gettysburg in July 1863. Here members of the Twenty-fourth Michigan Infantry lie where they fell.

along Cemetery Ridge with the hook to the north curling eastward around Culp's Hill. Lee rejected advice to take up defensive positions southwest of the Union army, thus blocking its escape route to Washington. On July 2 Lee pounded the Union flanks with some success. Because Stuart's cavalry was un-accountably absent, Lee suffered from lack of information concerning the extent of damage to enemy positions. The Confederates fought fiercely in the assaults which culminated in hand-to-hand fighting, but the federals, who out-numbered their adversary, were equally as tenacious.

On July 3 Lee decided on a frontal attack. At three in the afternoon General George E. Pickett's three divisions emerged from the woods and converged on Cemetery Ridge across more than a mile of open ground. At seven hundred yards Union artillery opened up. Those of Pickett's men who were not felled by grape and cannister died in a withering hail of rifle fire. Of the thirteen thousand–man force, more than half had been killed, wounded, or captured. "All this has been my fault," Lee observed remorsefully.

When Lee withdrew into Virginia on July 4 he had lost seventeen generals and one-third of his men. Total casualties at Gettysburg ran to fifty-one thousand. Meade was too battered and stunned to follow up his victory, or the Civil War might have ended in July 1863.

CHICKAMAUGA AND CHATTANOOGA

With Lee and Meade momentarily immobilized, the focus of battle shifted to Chattanooga, the railhead for all of eastern Tennessee and the gateway to northern Georgia. The first week in September Union General William Rosecrans took the city and then pursued General Braxton Bragg's army into northern Georgia. The Confederates, for once outnumbering the enemy 70,000 to 56,000, made their stand near Chickamauga, an Indian word meaning "river of death." The Battle of Chickamauga would have turned into a rout had it not been for the determination of General George H. Thomas, a Virginia unionist, to hold the right flank at all costs. Battered, Rosecrans retreated to Chattanooga, and Bragg laid siege to the city. Lincoln urged Rosecrans to hold fast and dispatched Joe Hooker to the scene to relieve the siege. At the same time Grant and Sherman arrived from the West with reinforcements. Grant drove through the Confederate siege lines opening up a supply route to the beleaguered Rosecrans. After Grant replaced Rosecrans with Thomas in late November, Union forces broke out of Chattanooga. Following Confederate defeats at Lookout Mountain and Missionary Ridge, Bragg abandoned the field.

GRANT'S STRATEGY

In March 1864 Lincoln called Grant to Washington and made him overall commander of Union forces. Grant decided to accompany the Army of the Potomac under Meade and named his long-time lieutenant, Major General William Tecumseh Sherman, to be commander of the West. Grant and Lincoln decided that the twin goals of the Union in 1864 would be destruction of Lee's army in the East and annihilation of the remaining Confederate forces under General Joseph Johnston in Georgia.

As the combatants soon learned, Grant was a different type of general. His predecessors had been in constant search of a decisive battle, a knockout blow. After four years of bloody but indecisive encounters, Grant recognized that the Civil War was a war of attrition. He would attack continually, harassing the enemy, eating up his troops and supplies, and destroying his morale. Victory, he declared, would belong to the side "which never counted its dead." And given northern superiority in manpower and materiel, victory was inevitable. In addition, at Grant's behest war became total. He ordered his generals to destroy any and all civilian property of military use.

APRIL 1864: THE NORTH GAINS MOMENTUM

THE WILDERNESS AND COLD HARBOR

In May 1864, the Army of the Potomac, numbering 115,000, engaged Lee's forces, numbering 65,000, in the Battle of the Wilderness near Chancellorsville. Grant attacked and after two days of bloody battle in the tangled underbrush withdrew slightly to the east and then moved south. At Spotsylvania Court-house the two armies engaged in five days of carnage. Again Grant swung to his left and moved south. "I propose to fight it out along this line if it takes all summer," he wrote Washington. The Union army absorbed more casualties, but Lee was running out of replacements.

The first week in June the Army of Northern Virginia and the Army of the Potomac clashed again at Cold Harbor. In less than half an hour, the en-trenched Confederates killed seven thousand attacking federals. Though battered, Grant's army slid to the left and advanced on Petersburg, a railhead connecting Richmond with the rest of the South. Lee dug in to defend the South, but instead of attacking Grant laid siege. While his troops were ade-quately supplied by Union vessels moving up the James River, Lee's shivering troops starved in their muddy trenches.

ATLANTA

The Confederate commander in the West, Joe Johnston, was a master of evasion and escape. He gradually retreated toward Atlanta hoping to stretch Sherman's supply lines and then draw him into a disastrous battle. President Davis wanted attack rather than retreat, however, and he replaced Johnston with General John Bell Hood, the impetuous Texan who had lost the use of an arm at Get-tysburg and part of a leg at Chickamauga. Hood, Lee once observed, was "all lion, none of the fox." Though he had to be strapped to his horse, Hood led three attacks from his base in Atlanta on Sherman's advancing troops. All met with bloody repulse, however, and Hood was forced to evacuate Atlanta, which Sherman took on September 2, 1864.

THE CAMPAIGN AND ELECTION OF 1864

Sherman's victory in Georgia could not have come at a better time for Abraham Lincoln. Only with great difficulty had the backwoods lawyer from Illinois won the Republican nomination in 1860. As the 1864 nominating con-vention approached, the radicals flayed him for being too tardy with the Emancipation Proclamation and for planning to reincorporate the occupied parts of Arkansas, Tennessee, and Louisiana into the Union. They were de-termined that the states of the South be treated as conquered provinces. Treasury Secretary Salmon P. Chase announced his candidacy, but he and the Radicals overplayed their hands. By the time the Republican convention met, Lincoln's managers were firmly in control, and he was nominated on the first ballot. The Democrats selected the popular George B. McClellan to be their standard bearer, but the party was deeply divided between peace De-mocrats (Copperheads) and individuals like McClellan who wanted to fight on until the Confederacy was completely vanquished. Still, as late as August, Lincoln was predicting his own defeat. The fall of Atlanta undermined the antiwar movement in the North, and Lincoln swept to easy victory, capturing 212 out of 233 electoral votes.

SHERMAN'S MARCH TO THE SEA

Meanwhile, General Sherman had decided to "make Georgia howl." The ultimate practitioner of total war, Sherman was determined to march to the sea and in the process destroy every weapon, every granary, every animal, and every building that might be of any use to the enemy. Before leaving, his troops burned much of Atlanta to the ground. "War is cruelty, and you cannot refine it," he told the mayor of that unfortunate city. Starting on November 16, Sherman led his sixty-two thousand men on the 285-mile journey to Savannah. Flanked by cavalry, four columns of infantry advanced across a front twenty to sixty miles wide, destroying everything in their path. In their wake deserters from both sides looted at will.

Hood had fled northwestward into Tennessee, hoping to draw Sherman away from the undefended Deep South, but the Union commander refused to take the bait. He did dispatch George Thomas with thirty thousand men to keep track of Hood. Thomas did more than that. On November 30 at the Battle of Franklin, Union forces shattered wave after wave of Confederate infantry. A week later Hood suffered another defeat at Nashville which effectively ended southern resistance in the West.

On December 22, Sherman had delivered Savannah to Lincoln as a Christmas gift. Early in 1865 he crossed into South Carolina, the first state to secede, and one, Sherman observed, that "deserves all that seems in store for her." His troops subsequently burned twelve towns to the ground, including Columbia, the capital, as they marched northward.

APRIL 1865: THE WAR ENDS

PETERSBURG

News of Sherman's devastating march through Georgia deepened the despair of Lee's troops then under siege at Petersburg. His ranks thinned by desertion, disease, and battle, Lee decided to try to break out and join Joe Johnston's army in North Carolina. Lee pulled out of Petersburg but soon found his path blocked by General Philip Sheridan's cavalry. Lee wheeled to face Grant, but despite his troops' willingness to fight, decided to end what had become senseless slaughter.

LEE SURRENDERS

On April 9, 1865, Palm Sunday, Lee donned his dress uniform and met with Grant, splattered with mud and smoking a cigar, to work out the terms of

The Wilmer McClean family and home, 1861.

surrender. Four days later outside Appomattox Courthouse, just east of Lynchburg, Virginia, the Confederates, flanked by ranks of Union soldiers, laid down their arms. A Union officer recounted the scene: "On our part not a sound of trumpet . . . nor roll of drum; not a cheer . . . but an awed stillness rather." Grant pardoned Lee's twenty-six thousand men and sent them home with their horses and mules "to work their little farms." Lee was not so lucky. Early in the war, the federals had seized his wife's plantation, overlooking Washington, D.C., and converted it into a cemetery for Union soldiers (Arlington National Cemetery). On April 18 Joe Johnston surrendered to Sherman near Durham, North Carolina. The nation's longest, bloodiest conflict was over.

Debate over why the South lost the Civil War, or conversely, why the North won, has preoccupied more historians for a longer period of time than perhaps any other issue in American history. Some analysts focus on diplomacy, some on generalship, some on disparity in material wealth, and some on politics north and south of the Mason-Dixon line. While Reid Mitchell argues that all of these factors were contributory, it was the perseverance of the rank-and-file

Union soldier and the reasons for that perseverance that provide the key to understanding the outcome of the conflict.

THE PERSEVERANCE OF THE SOLDIERS
Reid Mitchell

Why did the Union win its war against the Confederate Rebellion? I find myself giving the same answer that Richard Current gave in his essay for *Why the North Won*—that, "As usual, God was on the side of the heaviest battalions." What I would like to suggest, however, is that having the heaviest battalions does not proceed automatically from having the greater population, wealth, or resources. I'd also like to suggest that the battalion—or the company and the regiment—might be the right unit of analysis to answer the question of Union victory. The ideology and the morale of the Union soldier made a key contribution to Union victory; one reason the Union could triumph was the perseverance of its soldiers.*

I do not want to go so far as to say that Union superiority made Union victory inevitable, but I will say it made it probable. James McPherson is right to point us toward a consideration of the element of contingency—things could have gone differently, on the battlefield and elsewhere, and those differences could have produced a Confederate victory. But it is no assertion of inevitability to argue that the odds were more than a little in favor of the Union.

The Union's heavier battalions are usually figured in material terms. The loyal states had a population advantage of five to two over the Confederacy—and that is counting slaves as part of the Confederate population, which is questionable

from Reid Mitchell, "The Perseverance of the Soldiers," in Gabor S. Boritt, ed., *Why the Confederacy Lost* (New York: Oxford University Press, 1992), 109–132.

---

* Throughout this essay I have consciously avoided the habitual use of "the South" and "southern" as synonyms for "the Confederacy" and "Confederate." Not all Southerners were Confederate; indeed, with roughly 10 percent of southern whites Unionist and virtually the entire black population in favor of Union victory, it seems reasonable to conclude that almost half the South welcomed Confederate defeat.

mathematics. The value of real and personal property in the states remaining in the Union was three times that in the Confederate states. More important, the value of Union manufactures—as the two sides prepared to fight one of the first industrial wars—was more than ten times greater than those of the Confederacy. And the list can go on—comparative banking facilities, the railroad network, value of food crops, and so on.

These material bases are by themselves insufficient explanations for Union victory. We have learned all too well in the second half of the twentieth century that being a powerful and wealthy industrial nation does not ensure victory against a weaker agrarian nation. The Confederacy had many advantages—a vast terrain, the capacity to put a higher percent of its white population in arms, the opportunity to remain on the defensive. One advantage it rejected as too dangerous, however, was the opportunity of fighting a guerrilla war—the one kind of warfare most likely to defeat the Union army. Once the Confederacy decided on conventional warfare, the heaviest battalions would win—as long as the Union was willing to prosecute the war.

This is the point where we are all too likely to rush ahead into good old-fashioned military history—battles and leaders—or into a study of the Union as an industrial giant and claims that the Civil War was the first modern war, or into an analysis of the social history of the South between 1861 and 1865. Let me slow us down to consider the sometimes neglected step of mobilization, because the formation and cohesion of armies—getting those heaviest battalions into the field and keeping them there—were crucial to Union victory. We must avoid treating the northern will to fight, in 1861 or in 1864, as foreordained.

A question asked during the Vietnam era may be helpful here: What if they gave a war and nobody came? What would have happened if the people of the Union had not supported the war? Specifically: What would have happened if the men of the North had not volunteered in droves in 1861? The answer is that despite the material superiority that the Union possessed there would have been no war at all—Confederate independence would have been a fact. In 1861, the Union government, frantic to establish its supremacy over the states of the South, lacked much ability to coerce the states of the North.

The reasons we have trouble imagining this have to do with our status as twentieth-century Americans. One is nostalgia. We want to look back to the Civil War as something romantic. We associate draft resisters and popular discontent with the Vietnam era, not the Civil War. We do not even consider that the people of 1861 could have decided not to support the war. Another reason we assume that the citizens of the Union would contribute the manpower required of them is because we fail to comprehend just how severe these demands were. Forever after the Civil War when the Federal government has made war, it has been more cautious about asking for so many men in proportion to the population—one reason for the so-called hundred division gamble in World War II. (The U.S. Army wanted more men but the government judged that political realities would permit no more than 100 divisions to be called to service.) A third reason is our familiarity with a powerful national state. The Federal government routinely requires us to do lots of things and most of us grumble and acquiesce. It is hard for us to imagine that the people of 1861 might have refused to serve in the mass armies of the Civil War. Yet the Union government of April 1861 was hardly the United States government of December 1941. The states, not the Federal government, created those mass armies; and for the first half of the war, men entered the armies voluntarily.

The way in which localities and states raised the troops is sometimes treated as an unfortunate concession to localism. In the absence of both a Federal apparatus for raising large numbers of men and any national tradition for such a procedure, the Federal government probably could not have mobilized the armies directly. Statewide mobilization was hardly a concession to localism; it was a necessity. The Federal government was dependent on the states. Many Americans had dealt with no other United States official than the local postmaster.

When Lincoln issued his first call for troops in April 1861 he acted not from the constitutional right to raise armies—a right limited to Congress in any case—but from a statute that permitted him to order out the various state militias. While the Federal government seemed to dither in indecision, the state governors enlisted more soldiers than the War Department knew what to do with. Arguably, what saved Washington, D.C., itself, in its isolation in the first weeks of the war, was not any energy or decision on the part of the Federal government, but the speed and vigor with which Massachusetts governor John Andrew raised and organized troops, the characteristic decisiveness and uncharacteristic military competence of Massachusetts militia general Benjamin F. Butler, and the initiative and hustle of the northern volunteer soldier.

Why did these men of 1861 rush into the armies? Why were they so eager that the War Department could not keep up with the enlistments and that various northern states complained that other states were being allowed to contribute more soldiers than they were? There are many reasons that men enlisted—youthful high spirits, community pressure, the overpowering enthusiasm. But the volunteers of 1861, who continued to compose the bulk of the Union army throughout the war, were motivated by ideology as well.

Their principal incentive was their love for the Union. To them, the Union meant both the ideals of liberty and democracy that they believed unique to the United States, and the government that would uphold those ideals. They agreed with Abraham Lincoln that secession, by threatening to tear down the only existing government based on these ideals, threatened to destroy the ideals themselves. They also felt that the Union was a precious legacy, handed down to them by the Revolutionary fathers. Defending it was in many ways a familial duty, something a son owed the generations before him. In February 1862, Private Wilbur Fisk testified to the emotional strength of the ideology of Union. On night-time picket duty in northern Virginia, the soldiers marveled at their position. "When we reflect that we are standing on the outer verge of all that is left of the American Union, and nothing but darkness and Rebellion is beyond, and that we are actually guarding our own homes and firesides from treason's usurpations, we feel a thrill of pride that we are permitted to bear a part in maintaining our beloved Government." The Union was a man's family writ large.

Furthermore, some soldiers of 1861 were not only pro-Union but anti-slavery as well. Perhaps only 10 percent of the Union army, they nonetheless contributed additional fervor to the Union cause. As the war continued, anti-slavery grew among the soldiers. When Lincoln issued the Emancipation Proclamation at the start of 1863, it did dishearten some soldiers, who began complaining that the war for the Union had become a war for blacks. But in general, the army was heartened by the Emancipation Proclamation, seeing it as a sign that the government—recognizing that secession was based on slavery—was willing to take the necessary means to win the war and destroy both secession and slavery. The Emancipation Proclamation invigorated the war effort.

Beyond its impact on white volunteers, emancipation was an ideological source of strength in other ways. The Emancipation Proclamation destroyed the possibility of European intervention in the Civil War. It established that what had looked to some liberals like a war for self-determination against a central government was actually a war of slavery against freedom. The Confederacy's ideology of slavery did it no good in the international arena. Just as important, emancipation opened the door for black enlistment within the Union army. The significance of black soldiers is sometimes underestimated, partly because their presence in the army is only just entering the realm of national myth and partly because they made up less than 10 percent of the army all told. In fact, however, in the concluding months of the war, black troops were more than 10 percent of the army still in the field. The union won its victory with the aid of black soldiers. Emancipation was a crucial first step in both the decision to recruit blacks and in the black decision to support a war for a Union that historically had not done much for them.

But that was a little later in the war. In 1861 and 1862 the men of the Union army were white and they were volunteers. In a war where men enlisted for a confusing multiplicity of terms—three-month enlistments, nine-month enlistments, one-, two-, and three-year enlistments—getting men into the army did not guarantee keeping them in the army for the duration. That was a problem that would particularly concern the Lincoln administration during the winter of 1863–64. Another question was more immediate in 1861–62: "How would the Union use its power to defeat the Confederacy?" That question proved difficult for the Union to answer and out-and-out impossible for many of the leading commanders, most notably George McClellan. The innovations in military technology that marked the Civil War were not matched by comparable innovations in tactical thinking. Applying the superior force that the Union possessed seemed impossible for Union generals.

George McClellan at least had strategic brilliance on his side. His Peninsula campaign certainly should have worked; the demonstrable fact that George McClellan was gutless served to discredit his plan. As a result of Seven Pines and the Seven Days, the Confederate army defending Richmond lost more than 26,000 men—nearly 30 percent of its available forces. The Army of the Potomac lost slightly more than 20,000, only about 20 percent of its forces. The strategy of taking up a position where the Confederates had to launch frontal assaults was justified—or would have been if McClellan had not panicked and retreated.

After McClellan, Union generals in the East favored "the direct approach"—march overland to Richmond seeking a decisive battle that would destroy Lee's army. But if McClellan showed that brains were not enough, Hooker and Burnside showed that guts were not either—or at least not the kind of moral courage that could commit troops to one battle in the hopes that one battle was all it took to win the war. These generals were unable to see what to do after a defeat—which makes one wonder if they would have known what to do after a victory. Thus Pope is defeated at Second Bull Run, McClellan is immobilized by victory at Antietam, Burnside and Hooker are immobilized by their defeats at Fredericksburg and Chancellorsville, and Meade has little idea what to do with his victory at Gettysburg. In fact, the Union fundamentally decided to have its principal army, the Army of the Potomac, act as a shield against Lee's army, while its armies in the West won campaigns and conquered territory.

Until Grant came east. Grant recognized the material basis of Union superiority, and planned to bring "the heaviest battalions" into play methodically. His was a strategy not of battles or campaigns, but of war. Russell Weigley said of Grant: "He developed a highly uncommon ability to rise above the fortunes of a single battle and to master the flow of a long series of events, almost to the point of making any outcome of a single battle, victory, draw, or even defeat, serve his eventual purpose equally well."

Grant believed in hitting the principal Confederate armies with concentrated forces. Because of the Union's material base, he could do this. He also believed that the way to apply this superior force was to fight every day in every theater of the war. Under his direction in 1864, all Union armies began an advance, eliminating the Confederacy's earlier advantage of using interior lines to shift troops around to where the threat was greatest. As Lincoln told him and he told his commanders, "Those not skinning can hold a leg." This was a war of annihilation based on the recognition that to beat the Confederacy, its armies must be destroyed. Grant's army then was the point of the spear, and leaning behind it was the weight of superior northern population, industrial base, agricultural production, wealth.

It worked, but the human cost was immense. In fact, the human cost was so great that it threatened to undermine the military strategy, because it threatened to sicken the Union to the point it would have been unwilling to continue the war. Yankee Private Wilbur Fisk had his tongue carefully placed in his cheek when he said, "The more we get used to being killed, the better we like it." Let's consider the casualties that earned Grant his reputation as butcher. During the first month of the 1864 campaign, as the Army of the Potomac ground its way from the Rapidan through the Wilderness to the nightmare of Cold Harbor, it suffered approximately 55,000 casualties—about the total strength of the Army of Northern Virginia at the start of the campaign. In the process, it inflicted 32,000 casualties—a ratio of roughly 5 to 3, which is higher than the 5 to 2 superiority that the Union possessed over the Confederacy, and is not an unreasonable proportion considering the advantages that the defense had in Civil War battles.

Still, it is a little glib, even cold-blooded, to say that these are reasonable casualties. They are certainly higher in proportion to the population than the United

States would accept today. So we must remember the material and ideological bases of Union superiority. First, as high as this proportion was, it was lower than what the Confederacy suffered. Second, the northern people believed that saving the Union was worth it, certainly more than the American people thought victory in Vietnam was worth its casualties, and more than Confederates thought that independent nationhood was worth the casualties Grant's armies were inflicting. Nonetheless, it was a near thing. If Sherman had not captured Atlanta on the eve of the 1864 presidential election, it is possible that Lincoln and the pro-war party would have been defeated.

The soldiers' ideology continued to motivate them through the hellish second half of the war. Furthermore, by the middle of the war, many soldiers had developed even stronger loyalties to keep them in the army. These were loyalties to their fellow soldiers, specifically to the men they served with in their messes, companies, and regiments. The jargon that military thinkers use for this kind of loyalty is small-unit cohesion. All armies at all times count on it. Added to the ideology of 1861, the small-unit cohesion of 1864 created the tenacity that kept soldiers in the army so that the Union could keep an army in the field.

Perhaps the best way to understand small-unit cohesion is think of the company as a substitute family. That, at least, is how the soldiers themselves came to feel about it. The months of service that turned volunteers into veterans also created in them dependence on their fellow veterans, indeed even a love—any other word would be inadequate—for their fellow soldiers. Leaving the army meant leaving behind men with whom one had served, suffered, and risked one's life. The affections of this substitute family competed with the claims of the family a soldier had left at home.

The loyalty the soldiers displayed extended beyond that owed to the living. As befitted "a nation founded in blood," soldiers felt bound to the dead as well—to, in Lincoln's phrase in the First Inaugural, "every patriot grave." Specifically, they felt obliged to those men who had served by their sides and were now gone, having died in the hospital or battlefield or having been sent home wounded, some of them maimed for life. Like their own families, or the perpetual Union they fought to preserve, their military families included the living and the dead. Abandoning the war meant making a mockery of their sacrifices.

In the winter of 1863–64, the Union government made every appeal—and used every bribe—it could think of to persuade soldiers already in the army to re-enlist. These were the best soldiers the Union had, impossible to replace and just as impossible to keep against their wills. Without them there would be no spring campaign in 1864. There was none of the naïve enthusiasm of 1861 to call on; these men had lost any illusions about war. Over half of them re-enlisted.

That in itself suggested the commitment of the rank and file to the cause of the Union, but as a sign of this commitment it was surpassed by the soldiers' vote in the fall elections. This re-enlistment was crucial for army cohesion, but it took place before the bloody spring campaigns, with the heavy loss in life, the failed and sometimes senseless frontal assaults that eventually led to soldiers displaying a Cold Harbor syndrome and officers complaining that the men would not press attacks home. Still, even after the dreadful summer campaigns in Virginia, where the armies invented modern trench warfare around Petersburg, the soldiers of the Union voted overwhelmingly for Abraham Lincoln and the Republican party in the 1864 election—voted, indeed, for the continuance of the war.

How did the Union succeed in employing its heaviest battalions? The Union succeeded because the men who made up those battalions volunteered to be employed, not just in 1861 when they did not know better, but in 1864 as well.

Yet here we come to a question that should give us pause. Did not all the factors that created cohesion within the Union army operate as thoroughly in the Confederate army as well? The Confederate armies were built on volunteers. The experience of fighting together should have created the same small-unit loyalties in the Confederate army, and in fact it did create the same loyalties. Nonetheless, by the end of the war the Confederate armies were dissolving. By the spring of 1865, lack of men wrecked the Confederate war effort.

In April 1865, Robert E. Lee attributed the defeat of the Army of Northern Virginia—which immediately led to the surrender of all Confederate armies—to its "moral condition." "The operations which occurred while the troops were in the entrenchments in front of Richmond and Petersburg were not marked by the boldness and decision which formerly characterized them." What caused this moral condition was "the state of feeling in the country," and particularly, "the communications received by the men from their homes, urging their return and the abandonment of the field." "From what I have seen and learned, I believe an army cannot be organized or supported in Virginia, and as far as I know the condition of affairs, the country east of the Mississippi is morally and physically unable to maintain the contest." And a less well-known soldier, Charles Fenton James, wrote his sister in February 1865 about how soldiers, listening to "the voice of despondency," started to desert. "The only fear that I ever felt was that the spirit of the people and the army might flag."

It would be comforting to believe that it comes down entirely to a question of ideology—that the Confederate soldier, motivated by an ideology of freedom that was really an ideology of slavery, lacked the inner resources needed to fight the war to a successful conclusion. Or, as is sometimes asserted, that Confederate soldiers forced in the army or duped into the army, had no significant ideological motivation at all. The superior cohesion of the Union army could then be attributed to the superior morality of Union ideology.

A moment's reflection will show us, however, that this line of thought will lead to justifying the old adage that historians are camp followers of successful armies. The ability of an ideology to sustain sacrifice is hardly dependent on its moral correctness. People have endured much for bad causes. The Confederacy itself is a case in point.

Nonetheless, the Confederacy did suffer from ideological and structural weaknesses, and they were key to Confederate defeat. By ideological weakness, I am not referring to states' rights. While I do not share Emory Thomas's vision of the Confederacy as the first centralized, socialistic state—if the Confederacy was a socialist state, it was the first example of the failure of socialism—I do believe that the

Confederacy's story reveals a considerable willingness to innovate within government and to create an unprecedented Federal authority. What I call the ideological weakness and principal structural weakness was the fact that the Confederacy was created as a means to defend racial slavery.

Let me give an example in terms of the very way the Confederacy chose—had to choose—to fight its war for independence. Confederate leaders insisted on organizing a conventional army and fighting a conventional war, rather than exploiting the Confederacy's potential for unconventional—guerrilla—war. Yet there was a nasty war within a war in Missouri, guerrilla operations under John Singleton Mosby and others in northern Virginia, and bushwhacking throughout the South behind Union lines. Many southern whites proved willing to adopt guerrilla warfare—what Michael Fellman perceptively calls "self-organized warfare." The Confederacy did not. With painful exceptions, the Union did not have to fight the Civil War as a war of what we now call "counter-insurgency." It is idle to speculate, but I doubt that the Union could have won the war if the Confederacy had decided to wage it as a guerrilla war. The Union certainly did not succeed in putting down what might be called the postwar guerrilla activity that took place during Reconstruction. But in 1861 the Confederacy did not choose to fight a guerrilla war—because, in large part, it did not seem possible to fight a guerrilla war and keep slavery intact.

Just as important, slavery meant that the Confederacy went to war with its population divided. Far more so than in any other American war, the soldier in the field could not count on the unified support of the civilians back home. What I would like to consider here is the way that the Confederacy's weakness on the home front—including the problem of racial slavery but considering other factors as well—undermined the loyalties of its soldiers in the field. Why did the soldiers go home in 1865?

Let's start with common sense. One reason that Confederate soldiers became demoralized was death—death in the camp and hospital, death on the battlefield, death in defeat, and even death in glorious victory. The surest way to demoralize a man is to kill him. And a lot of men went home in the spring of 1865 because they foresaw the inevitability of defeat and did not see any reason to wait around and be killed. You may call it demoralization or lack of southern will, but I would call it common sense. If it was demoralization, it would have infected anyone who could count.

But Yankees, we know, can count even better. If, on the one hand, Union forces inflicted higher casualties proportionately on their Confederate counterparts, Confederate forces, on the other, were inflicting numerically higher casualties on the Yankees. There was nothing particularly cheery about the death toll in the Civil War no matter which side a soldier might be on. Yet, as we have seen, the Union kept its armies together more far more successfully than did the Confederacy.

Confederate soldiers deserted for many reasons. Low rations made men fear for their health and doubt the ability of the Confederate government to survive. One North Carolina soldier considered deserting because the prospects for victory were so slim; he wrote his wife to "tell the children that I cant come to see them unless I runaway." Another soldier wrote, "I am tired of so much fiting for they is some part of the permotac army most allers afiting." He was war-weary—"I am tired of hering guns let alone fiting"—and he worried for his family, "my little boy was sick and Eliza was give out wek with the rumitiz." One of the most important reasons for Confederate desertion was the tug of home.

"I want you to come home as soon as you can after you get this letter." This plaintive cry of a Confederate woman moves us well over a hundred years after she wrote it; imagine its impact on her husband. Indeed, some diehard Confederates began blaming southern women for men's desertion. "Where is the virtuous woman of the eighteenth century?" lamented Buck Long. "Oh! that she was still in our land to scorn and drive from door to door the cowardly deserter." Charles Fenton James told his sister, "Desertion takes place because desertion is encouraged, because the name 'deserter' has ceased, in a great measure, to be a reproach and disgrace." It was the women who should make it a disgrace: "The women of the Confederacy have the power, if they have the will and determination to save the country." The Reverend John Paris, who preached a sermon—and then published it—at the mass execution of twenty-two deserters, said that most of the men executed had been persuaded to desert by an "appeal from home."

Did Confederate husbands love their wives more than Yankees did? Even a hot-blooded southerner like myself will not argue that. Sergeant Caleb Blanchard assured his wife, that "no man loves his wife better than I," and the letters to and from home testify to the depth of love of most Union soldiers for the families they left behind. But Confederate soldiers left their Confederate wives—and Confederate mothers, sweethearts, daughters, fathers, sons, family and friends—at higher risk than did Union soldiers. And as the war went on, the dangers that the people back home faced grew more widespread. Confederate soldiers found themselves torn between two duties: one to the Confederacy, one to their families. After 1864 some Confederates saw the war as likely to end in defeat; others saw it as unlikely to end at all. Not surprisingly, more of them chose their duty to their families over their duty to the Confederacy, even over their duty to their fellow soldiers.

To a large degree, the dangers that called the soldiers home came from the fact of war itself. Food was in all too short supply throughout the Confederacy. Inflation made Confederate money almost worthless—and the soldiers were paid so little to begin with. Clothes, when available, were expensive; medicine was unaffordable. Most of the grown men—the grown white men—were in the army and left the burden of farming and other work to women, the young, and the elderly. The people of the South faced a very real danger of malnutrition, even starvation. The toll the war took on the health of the non-combatant has never been successfully measured, but it must have been immense.

Other fears came directly from the Union army. As the Federal troops headed south, particularly as Sherman marched through Georgia, Confederates recognized the prospect that those they left at home would soon find Yankee soldiers on their streets, in their farmyards, and even inside their houses. The Union army was an army of invasion, seemingly irresistible everywhere except the territory just north of Richmond. How could a man protect his family when he was hundreds of miles away?

Sergeant Edwin H. Fay told his wife that "if you desire it my dearest one I will come home at any cost[,] for I hold that my first duty is to my family, my country is secondary." Indeed, his correspondence sometimes seemed intended to raise in her the fears that would lead her to call him back home. When Union forces began operating in the vicinity of Minden, Louisiana, his hometown, he advised her to wear a pistol at all times; if a Yankee insulted her to "blow his brains out." He wrote her the story of Yankees trapping two ladies in their parlor and then raping two slave women to death before their eyes. Sergeant Fay's wife never did instruct him to desert—perhaps to his disappointment.

William L. Nugent was initially optimistic about the impact of Union occupation, assuring his wife "I judge you will not be in any danger at home." The Yankees would compel her to give up her slaves, but they would also "compel them to obey & respect you." But soon he advised her to leave her home, if the Union forces set up a contraband camp in the vicinity—"anything but being kept in close proximity to a camp of demoralized negroes."

The women and children left behind faced more than hard times and the threat of Union armies. They faced the increasingly sure destruction of slavery; they lived among a people newly free. Southern institutions of racial oppression had been rationalized as a necessary means to control a savage people. Now the men who had been the force behind the laws of slave control were in the army, far from their homes.

Slavery, said Alexander H. Stephens in his most quoted line, was the cornerstone of the Confederacy. It was the institution that the Confederacy had been created to protect; in turn, some Southerners argued that it was the institution that would protect the Confederacy. The Confederacy could field such a high proportion of its white men precisely because loyal black men and women could be expected to perform the other labor necessary for the South to function, only because the slaves were contented and would not rebel.

And yet . . . and yet. The Old South had been fiercely afraid of slave rebellion, rebellion that might fall most heavily on women and children. And wartime slave management was not simply a concern but a matter of policy: the so-called "twenty nigger" law that exempted those men who owned or oversaw twenty or more slaves from the draft was designed to ensure effective plantation management. While slavery supposedly freed up white men to fight Yankees, slavery also required enough white men be left behind to see that the slaves did not free themselves.

The fact was, however, that the number of strong, active white men left behind to manage the plantation economy, govern the slaves, and protect white women was inadequate. Slave management was a burden that fell increasingly on women. The assurances of slave faithfulness and of black docility were never more needed. And they had never been harder to believe. Masters learned that slaves had never loved slavery. One soldier, for example, received a letter from his wife "stating that his Negroes were killing up his hogs, dogs, chickens, & c. and cutting up generally." Soldiers learned of incidents of violence, black against white; they feared for their families in a countryside filled with Yankees and newly freed blacks; even the calmest whites acknowledged a rising level of independence and assertiveness among blacks—they called it insubordination, ingratitude, and sauciness.

These were the factors that undermined the cohesion of the Confederate army—not simply death and defeat but the fears men had that their families would be crushed as traditional southern society came crashing down around them. The men who answered their wives' calls and went home were hardly cowards, nor were the realists who saw the handwriting on the wall. I can only rejoice that their good sense took away from Jefferson Davis and Robert E. Lee the means of prosecuting an immoral war. The point must be made—had the Confederate soldiery remained in the field, the war would have continued, and almost certainly would have grown in brutality. And had that soldiery not gone home but headed to the hills to pursue guerrilla warfare, the war could have dragged on indefinitely—and the Confederate soldier would have come home to no home at all. If the Union army's cohesion made Union victory possible, lack of cohesion accounted for the timing of Confederate defeat. In December 1864, Lincoln spoke of the Confederate president Jefferson Davis, saying, "Between him and us the issue is distinct, simple, and inflexible. It is an issue which can only be tried by war, and decided by victory." Lincoln cast the prospect of victory and defeat as a matter of Union and Confederate will. "If we yield we are beaten; if the Southern people fail him, he is beaten."

Lincoln's December 1864 message to Congress came after the Union army had taken Atlanta and after Union voters, including the rank and file of the army, had elected him to another four years in office. He used the message to boast of the vitality of the Union, seemingly stronger after four years of war. He pointed out "that we have *more* men *now* than we had when the war *began;* that we are not exhausted, nor in process of exhaustion." The Union could "maintain the contest indefinitely." In manpower and in the other materials of war, the Union still had the heaviest battalions. More important, "the public purpose to re-establish and maintain the national authority is unchanged, and, as we believe, unchangeable." Without that resolution, the heaviest battalions could not have been brought into play. That resolution was the cause of Union victory and Confederate defeat in 1865.

So let's honor the resolution of the common soldiers and allow one of them to offer us our conclusion. Union private Wilbur Fisk, whose words we opened with, often spoke with the accents of Abraham Lincoln. In April 1864, as the Army of the Potomac prepared to begin the bloody Wilderness campaign, Fisk wrote home that in this Rebellion, "the people have not Rebelled against the few, but the few have Rebelled against the people." The "proud slaveholder" wished to destroy the government of the people and create a new nation built on slavery. Could the slaveholders' Rebellion succeed? Fisk asserted that "If the North will do her duty, we answer, Never! And the North *will* do her duty." The North would destroy the Confederate armies, the Confederate government, and the Confederate institution of slavery. Wilbur Fisk was sure of ultimate Union victory because he was sure of the perseverance of the Union soldier. "Never in a war before did the rank and file feel a more resolute earnestness for a just cause, and more invincible determination to succeed, than in this war; and what the rank and file are determined to do everybody knows will be done."

Suggested Readings

General

Dudley Cornish, *The Sable Arm: Negro Troops in the Union Army* (1956).

Paul D. Escott, *After Secession: Jefferson Davis and the Failure of Confederate Nationalism* (1978).

Shelby Foote, *The Civil War: A Narrative*, 3 vols. (1958–1974).

George M. Fredrickson, *The Inner Civil War: Northern Intellectuals and the Crisis of the Union* (1965).

Alvin M. Josephy, Jr., *The Civil War in the American West* (1992).

James M. McPherson, *Battle Cry of Freedom: The Civil War Era* (1988).

Philip Shaw Paludan, *"A People's Contest": The Union and Cival War, 1861–1865* (1988).

James L. Roark, *Masters Without Slaves: Southern Planters in the Civil War and Reconstruction* (1978).

Daniel E. Sutherland, *The Expansion of Everyday Life, 1860–1876* (1989).

Geoffrey C. Ward, Ken Burns, and Ric Burns, *The Civil War: An Illustrated History* (1990).

Secession Crisis

Steven A. Channing, *Crisis of Fear: Secession in South Carolina* (1970); Michael P. Johnson, *Toward a Patriarchal Republic: The Secession of Georgia* (1977); D.M. Potter, *Lincoln and His Party in the Secession Crisis* (1942).

Military Engagements

Albert Castel, *The Guerilla War* (1974); William C. Davis, *The Duel Between the First Ironclads* (1975); Joseph T. Glatthaar, *The March to the Sea and Beyond: Sherman's Troops in the Savannah and Carolinas Campaign* (1985); James M. McPherson, *Ordeal by Fire* (1982); James M. Merrill, *William Tecumseh Sherman* (1971); Stephen W. Sears, *Landscape Turned Red: The Battle of Antietam* (1983); Wiley Sword, *Shiloh: Bloody April* (1974).

Impact of War on American Society

John R. Brumgardt, ed., *Civil War Nurse: The Diary and Letters of Hannah Ropes* (1980); William J. Kimball, *Starve or Fall: Richmond and Its People 1861–1865* (1976); Eugene C. Murdock, *One Million Men: The Civil War Draft in the North* (1971); Daniel E. Sutherland, *Seasons of War* (1995); C. Vann Woodward, ed., *Mary Chesnut's Civil War* (1981).

Government and Politics During Wartime

Curtis A. Amlund, *Federalism in the Southern Confederacy* (1966); Charles R. Lee, *The Confederate Constitutions* (1963); James M. McPherson, *Abraham Lincoln and the Second American Revolution* (1990); Hubert H. Wubben, *Civil War Iowa and the Copperhead Movement* (1980).

African Americans and the Civil War

Herman Belz, *A New Birth of Freedom: The Republican Party and Freedmen's Rights, 1861–1866* (1976); Ira Berlin, et al., *Slaves No More: Three Essays on Emancipation and the Civil War* (1992); John Hope Franklin, *The Emancipation Proclamation* (1963); Louis S. Gerteis, *From Contraband to Freedom: Federal Policy Toward Southern Blacks, 1861–1865* (1973).

QUESTIONS FOR DISCUSSION

1. Compare and contrast the capabilities of the South and the North to wage war in 1861.
2. Compare and contrast the steps taken by the Union and Confederate governments to mobilize their manpower and economic resources. What effect did these measures have on the home fronts?
3. Why was the South so successful in the early stages of the war? Analyze Robert E. Lee's contribution to the Confederacy.
4. What motivated Abraham Lincoln to issue the Emancipation Proclamation? What did it accomplish?
5. Describe the roles played by African Americans and women in the war effort.
6. How did Ulysses S. Grant change Union strategy and what were the consequences of those changes?
7. Using information from the article by Reid Mitchell explain why the North won the Civil War. What other factors were important in your opinion?

THE POLITICS OF RECONCILIATION, 1865–1877

The decade that followed the Civil War was a crucial period in the nation's history. The War Between the States had decided through force that the Union would endure and that slavery would not, but it left a number of other questions unanswered. What would be the political, economic, and social status of the millions of African Americans whom President Lincoln had emancipated in 1863? What effect would the end of slavery have on the free labor force, on social stratification among white southerners, and on the whole fabric of American life? The course of Reconstruction would decide the fate of the two major political parties and determine to a degree whether or not the United States would continue down the path toward economic integration. The Civil War both destroyed and preserved. Those who triumphed believed that they had an opportunity to create a new social and political order, but they would be surprised by the resiliency of those who had been defeated and their determination to return to the past.

THE REALITY OF FREEDOM

Slavery had begun to crumble in many areas of the South before the Emancipation Proclamation or the final surrender of Lee's forces in 1865. Thousands of slaves fled to Union lines and became contraband. In other areas, remote from the battlefield, slaves only learned months, sometimes years, after the Emancipation Proclamation that they were free. The newly liberated reacted to their freedom in a number of ways. Some confronted their owners: One Virginia slave sought out her mistress on the veranda of the plantation house, declaring "I'se free. Yes, I'se free. A'int got to work fo' you no mo'." Others tested and expressed their freedom by leaving their former plantation and moving about the countryside. Observers reported enormous numbers of freedmen crowding roads in the South in the summer and fall of 1865. "If I stay here I'll never know I am free," a South Carolina black told his former mistress. Whites quickly discovered that the deference and humility they had come to expect from African Americans had evaporated. No longer did blacks tip their hats or move off the sidewalks. Some freedmen returned to the environs of their old plantations to be with friends and family while others moved away permanently.

The immediate aftermath of the war saw a shift of the black population in the South to areas already heavily populated by blacks. Attracted by African-American churches, schools, and fraternal societies as well as the protective presence of federal troops, freedmen flocked to southern cities. Indeed, during the first five years after the Civil War, the black population of the South's ten largest cities doubled.

Emancipation provided former slaves with the opportunity to renew or strengthen family ties. Thousands set out in search of wives, husbands, children, and parents who had been sold away. They walked hundreds of miles, placed ads in newspapers, and queried federal and local officials. For every joyous reunion, however, there was a story of frustration and tragedy. Many relatives had disappeared forever, died, or started new families. Husbands and wives took advantage of emancipation to legitimize their relationships. Union chaplains performed thousands of marriages in the months after Lee's surrender.

Not surprisingly, black families absorbed the gender roles of the dominant white culture. Black males had been able to fight in the Union Army during the Civil War; Reconstruction found them voting, serving on juries, and holding office. For black women as for white, these roles were closed. Union officials designated African-American men as heads of household, and black women took their places as keepers of hearth and home. For years following the end of the war, white landowners complained about their inability to persuade black women and children to work in the fields. Former bondswomen preferred to stay home and spend more time with their children and to support their families by cooking, sewing, and gardening, activities that had been severely restricted by fieldwork during slavery. At the same time, because black families everywhere lived below the poverty line, women had to work outside the home as domestics, seamstresses, laundresses, and even as field hands. They did so of their own free choice, however. Freedom did not bring release from dawn-to-dusk labor or from economic insecurity, but it gave to black families the autonomy they had never had during slavery.

A number of former slaves wanted nothing more to do with plantation life and sought work in mines, on ranches, in mills, and on the railroads. The vast majority, however, hoped to continue in the line of work they knew best—farming. In the aftermath of the war, freedmen took the position that the land they had worked for years as slaves rightfully belonged to them; participation in the treasonous rebellion had forfeited any claim the plantation owners had, claimed the freedmen. The typical African-American family in the South hoped above all else for a house, barn, cow, mule, and enough land to support itself. And, in fact, the Freedmen's Bureau Act of 1865 provided that abandoned land be divided into forty-acre plots and leased for three years with an option to buy. By 1866, however, the federal government had halted efforts to confiscate and divide southern plantations; indeed, Washington ordered the eviction of tens of thousands of slaves who had set up shop on their former masters' lands. A few African-American heads of household were able to purchase farms, but most had to hire out as agricultural laborers.

The twin pillars of the black communities that emerged in the South following emancipation were churches and schools. Prior to the war black Christians, slave and free, were compelled to attend white churches where they were segregated in separate pews or in balconies and denied any role in governance. Most all-black congregations had white ministers. Complaining that the principal message white Christians had for blacks was "Slaves obey thy masters," bondsmen and -women in rural areas raised up their own black preachers who presided over clandestine services. After the war, blacks deserted white churches in droves. In 1865 in South Carolina forty thousand blacks attended white churches; a year later that number had dwindled to a few hundred. In cities and on former plantations, freedmen pooled their resources to build houses of worship. By 1866 Charleston's African-American population had formed ten autonomous churches: two Episcopalian, two Presbyterian, one Baptist, and five Methodist. The most popular denominations were the African Methodist Episcopal and the Baptist. Blacks were attracted particularly by the latter's emphasis on congregational independence, democracy, and emotional spiritualism. Over time churches became more than religious centers, serving as the organizational basis for burial and insurance societies, festivals, and political organizations.

Slave codes had prohibited the education of bondsmen, a prohibition that African Americans felt to be particularly onerous. Observers remarked on how avidly freedmen sought to educate themselves following the war. A number of free blacks and a handful of slaves had managed to learn to read, write, and compute; in the months after the war they organized hundreds of makeshift schools. Education was clearly a priority for the Freedmen's Bureau; by 1869 it was operating three thousand schools and teaching over 150,000 students. Half the teachers employed in these institutions were white—volunteers from northern religious societies like the American Missionary Association—but half were black. The federal government and private charitable organizations helped found colleges such as Hampton, Fisk, and Tougaloo to train black teachers. African Americans responded by raising $1 million for school construction.

Emancipation, then, was a turbulent, exhilarating experience for African Americans; it was also anxiety-producing. Consciously or unconsciously, freedmen understood that the vast majority of southern whites were still committed to white supremacy, and if the federal government and Union Army did not intervene, their former masters would try to restore societal and economic patterns that had prevailed before the war. That meant nothing less than return to bondage.

LINCOLN'S PLAN OF AMNESTY AND RECONSTRUCTION

Abraham Lincoln had never recognized the right or fact of secession. From the outset of the Civil War he argued that merely a state of rebellion existed in certain southern states. He furthermore insisted that the president rather than Congress or the Supreme Court should establish conditions under which the federal government would resume normal relations with those states that had seceded. On December 8, 1863, he issued his Proclamation of Amnesty and Reconstruction. In it he offered to pardon any former Confederates who would take an oath to support the Constitution of the United States. Certain classes of high-ranking officers in the Confederate military and government were excepted from this general amnesty. The president's decree further stipulated that when the number of citizens equal to one-tenth of the votes cast in the national election of 1860 had taken the oath and established a government, the state's congressmen and senators would be seated. Lincoln's plan excluded all African Americans from participation in oath taking, voting, or holding office. In his second inaugural address in 1864 the Great Emancipator had committed the nation to a peace based on "malice toward none." Unfortunately for his plan, a substantial majority of northerners and Republican legislators still harbored deep malice toward those who had fomented the Confederate rebellion.

JOHNSON'S PLAN OF RECONCILIATION

With Lincoln's assassination in April 1865, the mantle of national leadership fell upon the shoulders of Vice President Andrew Johnson. Because he was a staunch Unionist and a bitter enemy of the planter aristocracy which dominated the politics of his native Tennessee, many anticipated that the new president would reverse Lincoln's lenient policies toward the South. They were mistaken. Though a loyal citizen of the United States, Johnson was not antisouthern, however, and he subscribed to the honored southern dogma of states' rights. A former slaveowner himself, he was certainly not a believer in the equality of all men. Ex-Confederate leaders played on Johnson's deep-seated inferiority complex and with flattery and promises of political support persuaded him to grant amnesty to former Confederates who would take an oath of loyalty to the Constitution and federal laws. Moreover, under his plan of reconciliation, all that the seceded states had to do to reinstate themselves as full-fledged members of the Union was to repudiate the Confederate debt, ratify various antisecession acts, and approve the Thirteenth Amendment outlawing slavery.

President Johnson further endeared himself to the sons and daughters of Dixie by hamstringing the efforts of the Freedmen's Bureau to provide ex-slaves with a degree of economic independence. Created by Congress in 1865, the Bureau of Refugees, Freedmen, and Abandoned Lands was to aid refugees and freedmen by furnishing tents, food, and medical supplies, establishing schools, supervising contracts between the former slaves and their employers, and managing confiscated or abandoned lands. After the passage of the Southern Homestead Act in 1866, the bureau hoped to assist African Americans in obtaining farms under its terms—"forty acres and a mule." No sooner had he come to power than President Johnson ordered that lands seized by the advancing Union armies and distributed to ex-slaves by the bureau be returned to their Confederate owners.

THE SOUTH'S REACTION

A wave of optimism swept the South in the wake of presidential reconstruction. The states of the former Confederacy showed no hesitation in repealing various acts of secession, but no thought was given to granting African Americans the right to vote. Legislatures in the reconstructed states enacted various "Black Codes." Similar to the laws that governed free African Americans before the war, these statutes entitled freedmen to own property, bear witness, sue and be sued in court, and contract legal marriages. Interracial unions, however, were outlawed, and African Americans were forbidden to carry firearms and possess alcoholic beverages. Black vagrants and those who broke labor contracts were everywhere subject to fine and imprisonment. In some states, black people who could show no means of support could be hired out by the courts to do labor in the fields. Complementing these legal efforts to maintain white supremacy were a rash of whippings, mutilations, and murders of former slaves.

CONGRESSIONAL REACTION

Congressmen and senators returning to Washington in December 1865 were well aware of the alarming events transpiring in the South. Because their constituents were not ready to forgive and forget, and because presidential reconstruction seemed sure to restore Democratic dominance throughout Dixie, the Republican majority had come to have grave doubts about Johnson's program. The Radicals, a minority within the Republican party, were for the most part former abolitionists genuinely committed to full citizenship for the freedmen of the South. Led by Thaddeus Stevens of Pennsylvania and Charles Sumner of Massachusetts, they insisted that the former Confederate states be treated as conquered territories and that they be readmitted to the Union only on the condition that the great plantations be broken up and distributed among the freedmen or that African Americans be guaranteed the right to vote—or both.

Congress blocked Johnson and the ex-Confederates by refusing to seat the senators and congressmen elected under presidential reconstruction. After receiving testimony concerning the mistreatment in the South of freedmen, northerners, and southern loyalists, Congress passed a bill to extend the life and enlarge the functions of the Freedmen's Bureau. When President Johnson vetoed it, the Republican majority voted to override in July 1866. Perhaps most important, Congress passed and submitted to the states the Fourteenth Amendment to the Constitution. Its crucial sections defined citizenship and enjoined the several states from depriving its citizens of life, liberty, and property without due process of law; it guaranteed to every citizen equal protection under the law; and it proposed to deny representation in the House of Representatives to states refusing male inhabitants the vote in proportion to the number of males in those states who were denied the franchise.

Racial Violence

In the summer of 1866 race violence swept the South. After several jostling incidents in Memphis, white mobs joined police in an indiscriminate attack on the black population. Only after three days of total mayhem was the federal military commander able to restore order. Forty-six black men, women, and children lay dead while eighty were grievously wounded. One white was injured. As sporadic beatings, shootings, and lynchings continued, northern blood boiled, and Congress prepared to bring the South and its patron in the White House to heel.

Radical Reconstruction

In March 1867, Congress passed measures which, taken together, came to be known as Radical (or congressional) Reconstruction. The former Confederate states were divided into five military districts. Each district was to be commanded by a military officer with enough force at his disposal to maintain peace and enforce the law. As soon as was practicable, the military governor was to call elections to state conventions in which all adult males who were not disfranchised for participation in the rebellion were to be eligible to vote. This massive grant of voting power to a people who but two years before had been slaves was an unusual and remarkable historical event. When the qualified electors had ratified a constitution providing for adult male suffrage, when Congress had approved it, and when the state in question had ratified the Fourteenth Amendment, it could be readmitted to the Union (see Figure 13–1).

Tenure of Office Act

On the same day that it established the conditions for reunion, Congress passed the Tenure of Office Act. The measure was designed to discipline President Johnson and to prevent him from dismissing from the government officials who

FIGURE 13–1
Reconstruction in the South

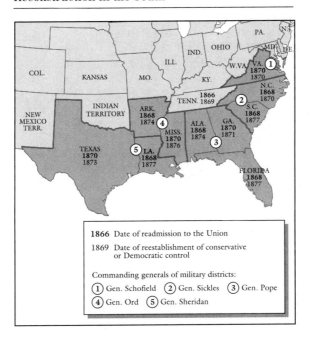

1866 Date of readmission to the Union

1869 Date of reestablishment of conservative
      or Democratic control

Commanding generals of military districts:

(1) Gen. Schofield   (2) Gen. Sickles   (3) Gen. Pope

(4) Gen. Ord   (5) Gen. Sheridan

were favorably inclined toward Radical Reconstruction, especially Secretary of War Edwin Stanton. Under the Tenure of Office Act, the president could not dismiss cabinet members or other officers without the express approval of Congress.

Presidential and Congressional Parrying

Enraged, President Johnson vetoed both the Radical plan for Reconstruction and the Tenure of Office Act only to have his vetoes immediately overridden. As Congress challenged him for control of Reconstruction policy during late 1866 and early 1867 Johnson had become more intemperate in word and deed. Just prior to the midterm elections he had stumped the Midwest, campaigning against Republican candidates who opposed his southern policy. He denounced Radical Reconstruction as an attempt "to Africanize half of our country." Talk of impeachment was rampant in Washington throughout early 1867. The Radicals held hearings that produced ample evidence that the president had refused to enforce laws designed to protect freedmen and Unionists in the South, but they could not agree on legal grounds for action. Johnson gave it to them when in January of 1868 he dismissed Secretary of War Stanton. The next month Thaddeus Stevens brought charges of impeachment in the House against the president for violating the Tenure of Office Act.

The Radical managers of impeachment pressed their case vigorously. Benjamin Butler declared that the president was trying to overthrow Congress and establish a dictatorship. To indicate how desperate the situation was in the South, he waved a nightshirt allegedly stained with the blood of an Ohio carpetbagger who had been flogged by Mississippi ruffians. Thereafter, whenever Republicans urged legislation to establish greater federal control over the South, opponents would accuse them of waving the bloody shirt. The charges of wrongdoing brought by the House centered on the accusation that Johnson had been "unmindful of the high duties of his office" and that he had attempted to bring Congress into "contempt and reproach." In effect, the Radicals defined "high crimes and misdemeanors" as a refusal to accept Congress' definition of the division of powers within the federal government. Predictably, when Johnson was tried before the Senate in May, he was acquitted. The nation breathed a sigh of relief at having avoided the trauma of removing a chief executive from office. Radicals could console themselves with the knowledge that Johnson had but a few months left in his term.

ULYSSES S. GRANT

THE ELECTION OF 1868

In the 1868 presidential election the Republicans chose as their nominee Ulysses S. Grant, the commander of the Union Army. A celebrated war hero, Grant was not closely identified with the Radical wing of the party and, as a political novice, had not yet accumulated powerful enemies. The Democrats selected as their standard bearer the wartime governor of New York, Horatio Seymour. In the end the Democrats were no match for the financial resources of investment bankers Henry and Jay Cooke, the cartoons of Thomas Nast in *Harper's Weekly*, and the Republicans' claim that they had saved the Union. Grant swamped Seymour. Close upon the Republican triumph came passage of the Fifteenth Amendment by Congress. Within a year the necessary states had ratified it. The right to vote, proclaimed the new amendment, "shall not be denied . . . on account of race, color, or previous condition of servitude."

EXPANSION AND DEPRESSION IN THE AGE OF *LAISSEZ-FAIRE*

The Civil War served as a major stimulus to the economy of the North, as the federal government pumped millions of dollars into the private sector. Government purchases during the period from 1861 to 1865 laid the foundation for the modern meat packing, milk processing, and railroad industries. The expansion that began during the war continued into the Reconstruction period, laying the basis for the industrial revolution. Between 1860 and 1880 three million immigrants arrived in the United States providing cheap labor to burgeoning industries and consumers of goods produced by those industries. By

1873 American manufacturers were producing 75 percent more than they had in 1860. The true engine of economic expansion during the immediate postwar period was the railroad. Between 1865 and 1873 America witnessed the construction of 35,000 miles of new track, much of it in the Midwest and West. The completion of the first transcontinental line in 1869—the Central Pacific and Union Pacific were joined by silver and golden spikes at Promontory Point, Utah, in 1869—made possible much of this growth as smaller, subsidiary lines branched off from the trunk. During the presidencies of Ulysses S. Grant railroading became the United States' leading business, serving as the country's principal means of capital formation and facilitating the peopling of the West.

This unparalleled economic expansion coupled with a laissez-faire attitude on the part of the government led to widespread corruption. Again, railroads led the way. In an effort to promote construction, Congress and state legislatures gave the railroad companies direct cash subsidies and millions of acres of public land. In order to continue and increase these subsidies, lobbyists distributed free passes, discounted stock, and even paid cash bribes to public officials in positions to help them. In 1872 Vice President Schuyler Colfax was forced to resign when implicated in the Credit Mobilier scandal. The Credit Mobilier was a dummy construction company set up by the principal stockholders of the Union Pacific to attract additional federal subsidies. In return for favorable votes, prominent Republicans, including Colfax, received stock in the bogus firm. Increasingly, state Republican parties took the spoils of federal patronage as their organizing principle, abandoning ideology and the issues of union and citizenship. Disgusted with the majority's dalliance with the spoils system and its corruption, a powerful and increasingly influential minority organized a faction they dubbed the Liberal Republicans. Led by intellectuals such as E.L. Godkin, editor of the *NATION*, and eastern patricians such as Charles Francis Adams, the Liberal Republicans called for laissez-faire to be carried to its logical conclusion. Corruption stemmed from government efforts to aid economic growth. As Godkin put it: "The government must get out of the 'protective' business and the 'subsidy' business and the 'improvement' and the 'development' business . . ." The Liberal Republicans were elitists who wanted to limit the franchise to the educated and who favored immigration restriction. Champions of Jeffersonian individualism, they insisted that the government leave not only businessmen to their own devices, but the freedmen as well. Government intervention was evil no matter what the justification.

Following a period of rapid and sustained expansion, the economy went into a tailspin in 1873. In September of that year the banking house of Jay Cooke and Company declared bankruptcy when it was unable to sell stock in the Northern Pacific Railroad. More than a hundred other concerns followed suit, and by 1876 half the nation's railroads had defaulted on their bonds. The eighteen thousand business failures that transpired between 1873 and 1876 threw millions of people out of work. Thousands of desperate Americans took to the road in search of employment; conservative men of affairs viewed these "tramps" as threats to social stability. In the countryside, thousands of farmers were driven into peonage by falling prices and decreased demand. The social unrest generated by the Panic of 1873 was intensified by the insensitivity of the federal government. In 1874 President Grant, a staunch friend of bankers and corporate executives, vetoed a congressional measure that would have authorized a modest issue of new greenbacks, the paper money printed by the federal government during the Civil War to help pay for government purchases. Debtors were convinced that currency inflation would help them by increasing wages and commodity prices while keeping their debts constant. Creditors believed the same thing. The depression that followed the Panic of 1873 continued for sixty-five months, the longest downturn in American history.

THE NEW SOUTHERN ELECTORATE

By 1870 all of the ex-Confederate states had been readmitted to the Union. Initially, the Republican governments elected under Radical Reconstruction were made up of freedmen and Unionists, both northern and southern. They had their faults, but they were hardly the unmitigated villains that the former Confederates portrayed them as. Aided by the Freedmen's Bureau agents and the Union League, a patriotic organization established during the war, the commanders of the military districts set about registering the hundreds of thousands of eligible ex-slaves and providing them with a minimum of political education.

The African Americans

Most of the seven hundred thousand males who were old enough to vote were in an understandably poor position to participate in a democracy. Because it had been a crime before the war to teach slaves to read and write, most were illiterate. But in the postbellum South a core of educated and experienced African Americans was available to help bridge the chasm between slavery and freedom. South Carolina had Francis L. Cardozo, educated in Glasgow and London, and state supreme court justice J.J. Wright, a former member of the Pennsylvania bar. Florida's secretary of state, Jonathan Gibbs, had earned a degree from Dartmouth. Many more were self-educated or had occupied positions of leadership within the slave community. From this educated and responsible element came the African Americans who contributed to the writing of the new constitutions and who participated in the Reconstruction governments. Tens of thousands of southern blacks voted in the presidential election of 1868 and were responsible for giving Grant his majority in the popular vote.

What was surprising about the African Americans who held power was their lack of vindictiveness. They favored removing disabilities from ex-Confederates who were willing to obey the law, and they attempted no revolution in the social sphere.

*During and after Reconstruction, Confederate loyalists
portrayed a South oppressed by Union soldiers and
exploited by northern politicians and businessmen.
This view is supported by an 1872 cartoon which
appeared in the British publication,* Puck.

The Carpetbaggers

Joining African Americans in the new southern electorate were thousands of
white and black northerners who came South following the war. Many were
former Union soldiers, lured by the cheap land and potential for economic
growth they had encountered during their campaigning in Virginia, Georgia,
Tennessee, Louisiana, and other southern states. This group also included
federal agents, philanthropic teachers who manned the dozens of schools established for freedmen following the war, and opportunistic businessmen. Ex-
Confederates referred to them as "carpetbaggers," a name meant to imply that
as transients, they had no stake in southern society. In reality, these teachers,
preachers, merchants, farmers, and mechanics brought with them millions of
dollars to invest, and most of them came determined to settle permanently.
They were interested in economic development and law and order. Although
some were no more enlightened in their racial views than native white southerners, they supported the African Americans' right to vote as a means for
maintaining Republican supremacy.

Southern Loyalists

The third group eligible to vote and participate in the governments established under Radical Reconstruction were southerners not disfranchised for participation in the rebellion. The ex-Confederates reserved a special hatred for this group which they referred to as "scalawags"—runty, neglected cattle—suggesting at once both meanness of spirit and material poverty. These were the people who had smarted for years under a system which gave every advantage to the planter class; they had opposed secession as a suicidal effort to save a labor system that impoverished and denigrated white workers.

These three groups which played such a prominent role in Radical Reconstruction were never the monolithic threat they were accused of being. Although the warriors of the Lost Cause complained bitterly of "nigger rule," black southerners did not hold office in proportion to their numbers. African Americans never controlled a single state convention or government. Carpetbaggers were in a minority in every state except Mississippi. More often than not, these two groups and the native white Unionists worked at cross purposes. Some were conservative in race relations and some liberal; some were conservative economically and some liberal.

RADICAL RECONSTRUCTION UNDER SIEGE

In many respects the new constitutions written by the reconstructed southern states were superior to those they replaced. The states assumed responsibility for many social services that had formerly been left to local officials and private initiative. Most established universal suffrage and free public education, and financed the construction of hospitals and other institutions for the care of the indigent, homeless, and physically handicapped. All contained liberal provisions for the establishment of private corporations, especially railroads, and the expansion of the state's industrial and natural resources. Womens' rights were expanded. For the first time, South Carolina had a divorce law on its books.

Counter-Reconstruction

Despite these accomplishments, the state governments set up under Radical Reconstruction were engaged from the outset in a constant, losing struggle for survival. The key to the Republicans' ability to retain power in the South was the freedman's vote, but the Republican majority in Congress failed to provide the former slaves with the two prerequisites for long-term participation in the democratic process: substantial education and economic independence. The agents of the Freedmen's Bureau and Union League who came south after the war taught African Americans the mechanics of voting and frequently told them whom to vote for, but they were not able to furnish the training and knowledge necessary to enable freedmen to grapple with the complex issues of the day. For African Americans educational opportunity consisted of a handful of black colleges established by northern philanthropists, Hampton and Fisk, for example, and public school systems that very quickly began to discriminate against black children. Moreover, conspicuously absent from the Reconstruction statutes were provisions breaking up the great landed estates of the South and dividing them among the black farmers who had tilled them as slaves. In most instances freedmen had to go back to work for their old masters as wage laborers or tenant farmers. The contracts that they signed coupled with their illiteracy and penury rendered them vulnerable to all sorts of pressure from the ex-Confederates to vote the way they were told or not to vote at all.

Another great weakness of the Republican coalition in the South was that it had come to power in part at the behest of the federal government in Washington. Its hope, never realized, was that it would come to represent a new, politically conscious alliance of indigenous working people. Their prejudices and pocketbooks threatened, members of the once powerful class of planters, as well as many new landowners, chose to regard the Republican governments as fraudulent and alien. The South, they declared, was an occupied country.

THE CONSERVATIVE RESURGENCE

Conservatives in the former Confederate states began gathering strength in the late 1860s as new amnesties, individual pardons, and defections from the ranks of loyal white southerners began to swell their ranks. A prime tool used by the planter class was the Ku Klux Klan. The KKK began as a small fraternal anti-black association in Tennessee in 1865. It described itself as an institution of "chivalry, humanity, mercy, and patriotism." In the spring of 1867, delegates from several states met in Nashville, elected former Confederate general Nathan B. Forrest as Grand Wizard, and sent its members back to their states determined to use any method to destroy Radical Reconstruction. Dressed in white sheets and peaked white hoods, they rode through the countryside in the middle of the night rousting politically active freedmen from their beds. If burning crosses and threats did not suffice, the Klansmen resorted to torture and execution. Violence was visited on carpetbaggers and scalawags as well, but the Klan and its aristocratic, cavalier sponsors were particularly effective in pressuring white Republicans through social ostracism and economic boycott.

REPUBLICAN CORRUPTION

Unfortunately for their credibility, the Republican governments in the South were increasingly guilty of fiscal irresponsibility and corruption. Public debts doubled and tripled in the South as taxes were increased to pay for new schools, roads, and hospitals. As one state treasurer after another absconded with public funds, legislators accepted bribes from railroad entrepreneurs in return for lucrative state subsidies. But this was the era of Ulysses S. Grant and New York's Boss Tweed who, as head of a political machine that lived off graft and bribery, typified abuse of the public interest by elected officials. Corruption, embezzlement, and speculation constituted a national way of life. The tragedy of public immorality in the southern states was that the Republican governments there could least afford it—politically as well as financially.

THE FIFTEENTH AMENDMENT

The Republican effort to institutionalize equal rights for blacks peaked in 1869 and 1870 with passage by Congress and ratification by the states of the Fifteenth Amendment to the Constitution. That addition to the basic law of the land barred any state from denying citizens the right to vote on the basis of race, color, or previous condition of servitude. A more extreme version would have guaranteed the vote to all adult males, but it was defeated on the grounds that it involved the federal government too deeply in the affairs of the states. Thus the states were free to enact or keep on the books literacy tests, poll taxes, and property qualifications. These restrictions extended theoretically to all citizens but would in the future be employed specifically to disfranchise African Americans.

American suffragists were bitterly disappointed that the Fifteenth Amendment did not extend the vote to women as well as ex-slaves. A militant wing of the feminist movement headed by Susan B. Anthony and Elizabeth Cady Stanton were so offended that the amendment made gender an explicit qualification for voting that they lobbied against it. Led by Lucy Stone, the other branch of the movement supported the constitutional bar on racial discrimination, arguing that "the Negro's hour" had come, and women could afford to rejoice for African Americans and wait their turn. The dispute was so bitter that it divided the suffragist movement for years to come.

THE LESSENING OF FEDERAL CONTROLS

By the middle of the 1870s the vengeful mood that underlay Radical Reconstruction in the North had been replaced by one "more understanding" of the South. Whitelaw Reid, the journalist who had found the South arrogant and defiant in 1865, was much more charitable five years later. Immediately after the Civil War the vast majority of citizens had wanted Dixie to do penance for splitting the Union and causing four long years of war. They demanded that the South reject its cavalier social system. African-American suffrage and equal rights were the clubs with which the North tried to beat the South to its knees. By the seventies that animosity, the only thing that would have made any real difference in saving Radical Reconstruction, was rapidly diminishing.

Following impeachment proceedings, Congress was relatively inactive on the Reconstruction front. The growing Democratic minority in both houses found support among a new generation of Republican leaders typified by James G. Blaine, the junior senator from Maine, and in 1874 and 1875 they defeated bills designed to increase the federal supervision of elections. Blaine and his cohorts urged the Republican party to put Civil War and Reconstruction issues behind it, and concentrate on economics. They wanted to build a political following in the South by appealing to the economic views of former Whigs driven into the Democratic party by the slavery controversy. Leave blacks and whites alone to work out their own destiny, and appeal to the high-tariff, prointernal improvement views of southern businessmen, the new leadership argued.

President Grant displayed little enthusiasm for Radical Reconstruction. Between 1869 and 1874 he used his pardoning power freely. In 1874 he refused to send troops into Mississippi to help the Republican administration of Governor Adelbert Ames maintain law and order. The South would resent federal interference so intensely, he claimed, that it would be counterproductive.

In its chief concerns the Supreme Court seemed also to reflect the mood of the times. During the crucial months following the launching of Radical Reconstruction, the justices avoided the great issues of the day, those of the status of the former Confederates, the southern states, and the freedmen. Instead, they concentrated on questions of property, the impact of industrialization, and the role of the government in the expanding economy. In 1873, the court ruled that the Fourteenth Amendment protected privileges and immunities of persons as citizens of the United States but not as citizens of the several states. If, as the court argued, most civil rights were derived from state, rather than federal, citizenship, the Fourteenth Amendment would provide little protection to individuals who might suffer from state laws that restricted their privileges and immunities or deprived them of their rights completely.

RUTHERFORD B. HAYES

THE ELECTION OF 1876 AND THE COMPROMISE OF 1877

By 1876 the conservatives or "Redeemers," as they referred to themselves, were in power in all but three of the ex-Confederate states. The national election of 1876 was universally perceived to be crucial to the future of the republic. The Democrats, out of power for twenty years, were determined to cast off the stigma of treason. The Republicans claimed to be weary of crusading and were seeking another basis on which to make their appeal to the voters. Among other things, the outcome of the election would determine the future of the political parties, the ultimate fate of the Reconstruction program, the status of the freedmen, and perhaps even the fate of the Union itself.

The Republicans nominated Rutherford B. Hayes, a Civil War general and three-time governor of Ohio. With an unblemished reputation and a long association with the cause of civil service reform, he was the perfect nominee for a party beset by scandal. The Democrats staked their hopes on the widely respected reform governor of New York, Samuel J. Tilden. He had gained a national reputation as a crime fighter by helping to smash the notorious Tweed Ring which had corruptly governed New York City for a generation. During the Civil War Tilden had been a staunch Unionist. As the presidential campaign unfolded, Republican orators cast caution to the wind and concentrated on the old issues of war and Reconstruction. Cried one Republican canvasser, "Every man that shot Union soldiers was a Democrat. The man that assassinated Abraham Lincoln was a Democrat. . . . Soldiers, every scar you have got on your heroic bodies was given you by a Democrat."

The early election returns seemed to indicate a victory for the Democrats. Tilden had 184 electoral votes, only one short of the number needed for election. But there was still hope for Hayes. The vote in the three southern states still unredeemed—Louisiana, South Carolina, and Florida—was disputed. If the Republicans could count on all the electoral votes of these states plus one contested vote in Oregon, their candidate would win. In each of the states in question both sides claimed a victory. In each case, however, the state canvassing boards were in the hands of Republicans, who after rejecting the Democratic claims, approved the Republican electors. Not surprisingly, the Democrats cried foul, and their electors met to cast their votes for Tilden.

To break the gridlock that threatened America's electoral process, Congress appointed a bipartisan electoral commission to settle the issue. That body, composed of five members from the Republican Senate, five members from the Democratic House, and five members of the Supreme Court, refused to overturn the decisions of the canvassing boards and awarded all the disputed electors to Hayes. Infuriated, Tilden's supporters promised to obstruct the counting of the votes. Because Hayes' election had to be certified by both houses of Congress and because the House was controlled by the Democrats, a stalemate loomed.

Convinced that Tilden's election would result in what they referred to as "home rule," the vast majority of white southerners had voted Democratic. But when it appeared that Hayes might win, southern leaders decided to salvage what they could. Southern businessmen and bankers, many of them former Whigs, approached supporters of Hayes, himself a former Whig, with offers of help in the electoral crisis in return for a live-and-let-live policy toward the South. In the short run that meant withdrawal of federal troops that were propping up the Republican governments of South Carolina and Louisiana. In the long run it meant abandonment of the freedmen and northern compliance in the nullification of the Fourteenth and Fifteenth Amendments. But there was an economic aspect to the "Compromise of 1877" as well.

In the sharecrop/crop-lien system, southern planters found an economic substitute for slavery. Black sharecroppers pose before the landowner's barn, ca. 1870–1880.

Already ravaged by the war, the economies of the former Confederacy had been especially hard hit by the Panic of 1873 and the depression that followed. The region was in desperate need of capital to rebuild roads, harbors, and factories, and to finance a southern transcontinental railroad. The national Democratic party, traditionally the party of agriculture, low tariffs, and laissez-faire, had steadfastly opposed government subsidies. Republicans suggested to southern conservatives that if they would accept Hayes' inauguration, they could then count on Republican votes for the economic reconstruction of the South. As a sign of good faith Hayes' party helped southern congressmen and senators pass the Texas and Pacific Railroad bill in January 1877. Subsequently, when northern Democrats began to lay plans to obstruct the inauguration of Hayes after the electoral commission's decision, they found themselves deserted by their southern colleagues.

THE HERITAGE OF RECONSTRUCTION

So 1877 saw the former Confederate states back in the Union under conditions very favorable to those who had led the secession movement and fought the Civil War. Within the states themselves, the "Redeemers," self-styled saviors of the South, continued to resort to ruse, conspiracy, and intimidation to control the electoral process. Politically, the South retreated further from democracy and proceeded to institutionalize the policies by which they had overthrown Reconstruction. The tactics the southern aristocracy employed to maintain themselves in power such as last minute changes in polling places, long, complicated ballots, and literacy tests served to reduce both the black and white electorate.

Economically, the Redeemers found a suitable substitute for slavery in the sharecrop, crop-lien system. Most freedmen and many poor white farmers were forced to enter into contracts with the planters under which the landowners would furnish the land and the croppers the labor. At harvesttime the two parties would divide the crop. Inevitably, the farmer would have to use his share to pay off the country store, owned almost always by the planter, for the seed, machinery, and other necessaries he or she bought on credit during the year. Inevitably, the illiterate croppers found themselves deeper and deeper in debt to the country store. In many ways the sharecrop system was superior to slavery, as far as the planters were concerned, because it involved less obligation on the planters' part. For many former slaves, freedom meant the right to starve to death, but none would have traded it for a life in shackles. The first step toward equality and opportunity had been taken.

The following essay, a chapter from Leon Litwack's Been in the Storm So Long, *describes the conditions and forces at work in the South that combined to keep African Americans in an exploited, servile status, even though they had been emancipated. He focuses especially on the paternalism that characterized so much northern philanthropic activity among freed blacks and shows how the Freedmen's Bureau became a servant of the planting aristocracy rather than a protector and educator of the ex-slaves.*

BACK TO WORK: THE OLD COMPULSIONS
Leon F. Litwack

Although the former slaveholders constituted a small minority of the white population of the South, nearly everyone still looked to them for leadership and supported the urgent need to impose controls on the newly freed blacks. To play on
white fears of the Negro, moreover, as most planters recognized, served an important function in maintaining their own supremacy and in muting class antagonisms. Despite the abolition of slavery, the attitudes, fears, and assumptions which
had helped to shape and reinforce that institution for over two centuries remained
virtually unaffected. When the Freedmen's Bureau commissioner in Mississippi and
Louisiana commented on the state of white opinion in the post-emancipation South,
he invited attack as a northern partisan but the evidence was altogether too compelling to discount his conclusions:

> Wherever I go—the street, the shop, the house, the hotel, or the steamboat—I
> hear the people talk in such a way as to indicate that they are yet unable to
> conceive of the negro as possessing any rights at all. Men who are honorable in
> their dealings with their white neighbors will cheat a negro without feeling a single
> twinge of their honor. To kill a negro they do not deem murder; to debauch a negro
> woman they do not think fornication; to take the property away from a negro they
> do not consider robbery. The people boast that when they get freedmen affairs in
> their own hands, to use their own classic expression, "the niggers will catch hell."
>
> The reason of all this is simple and manifest. The whites esteem the blacks their
> property by natural right, and however much they may admit that the individual re-
> lations of masters and slaves have been destroyed by the war and by the President's
> emancipation proclamation, they still have an ingrained feeling that the blacks at
> large belong to the whites at large, and whenever opportunity serves they treat the
> colored people just as their profit, caprice or passion may dictate.

No doubt some southern whites might have thought this a crude characterization
of their thinking, but nearly every white man and woman readily agreed to the
wisdom of restraining and controlling black men and women in ways that were not
thought to be necessary for themselves. . . .

Despite a white rhetoric that doomed the freedmen to self-extinction, most
planters needed and demanded their labor. And despite all the talk about a childlike

from Leon F. Litwack, "Back to Work: The Old Compulsions," in *Been in the Storm So Long: The Aftermath of
Slavery* (New York: Knopf, 1979), 364–386.

race, most whites expected blacks to work and behave like mature adults. Although the war and emancipation had, in the view of whites, filled the heads of their former slaves with unrealistic expectations and rendered their labor erratic, they refused to give up on them altogether, at least not until time-honored remedies proved ineffectual. Whether he had ever owned slaves or not, almost every white man remained convinced that only rigid controls and compulsion would curtail the natural propensity of blacks toward idleness and vagrancy, induce them to labor for others, and correct their mistaken notions about freedom and working for themselves. Claiming an intimate and exclusive knowledge of the Negro's character ("We are the only ones that understand the nigger"), the former slaveholder demanded the necessary force to back up the traditional rights of authority over "his people," including the punishment of deviant behavior. Without compulsion of some kind, the experiment in free labor could not succeed. It was as simple as that.

The self-evident truth which the planter class now imparted to the freed slaves was that they must either work for white folks or starve. That advice differed in no significant way from what Federal officials had been telling blacks since the moment of liberation. "When that lesson has been thoroughly learned and inwardly digested," a Macon newspaper declared, "the negro may perhaps be of some value." Whatever sympathies Northerners pretended for the Negro, southern whites assumed they could not object to a principle so universally accepted. "All we want," a South Carolina planter told a northern visitor, "is that our Yankee rulers should give us the same privileges with regard to the control of labor which they themselves have." When pressed for his understanding of northern labor controls, he indicated that laborers were bound by law to make an annual contract and could be punished for any violations. Told that no such laws existed in the North, the planter seemed incredulous. "How do you manage without such laws? How can you get work out of a man unless you compel him in some way?" The visitor replied that "Natural laws" sufficed, with the best laborers commanding the best wages. "You can't do that way with niggers," the planter immediately retorted. . . .

The urgency of the situation seemed obvious enough. To plant a crop without knowing how many laborers might be around to harvest it made postwar agricultural operations a highly risky venture. Henry W. Ravenel, for example, thought no planter would want to engage in such operations "without some guarantee that his labour is to be controlled & continued under penalties & forfeitures." To make the free labor system work, some planters suggested that the ex-slaves be apprenticed to their former masters or to an employer of their choice. The apprenticeship laws enacted by a number of states imposed such controls on blacks under eighteen years of age who were orphans or whose parents could not or refused to support them. Such laws provided some planters with a cheap supply of involuntary labor (if he were deemed a "suitable" person, the former owner of the minor was given preference); at the same time, the arbitrary power these laws usually gave to the courts to bind out such children without the consent of their parents revived the specter of families forcibly separated.

The idea of apprenticing nearly four million ex-slaves to their former masters never received serious consideration. Nor did the proposals to distribute the freed blacks equally around the country or to colonize them elsewhere make any sense to planters who desperately needed laborers. Anxious to regain control over their blacks, but not entirely indifferent to northern reactions, the planter class preferred to establish a docile black labor force in the guise of fulfilling their Christian duties and obligations to those who had once served them so well. Claiming sympathy for their former slaves, they demanded the controls necessary to make them once again "happy and prosperous." To control and regulate the freedmen was to advance and protect the best interests of this unfortunate race, to help them restrain their "worst passions," to redeem them from certain relapse into semi-barbarism, to save them from "inevitable failure," to disabuse their minds of false illusions, and to assist them in finding their proper place in postwar southern society. "If they cannot (as they never can) occupy the places of legislators, judges, teachers, &c.," a North Carolina planter explained, "they may be useful as tillers of the soil, as handi-craftsmen, as servants in various situations, and be happy in their domestic and family relations. . . . It is our Christian duty to encourage them to these ends." That was putting the best possible face on the legislation adopted by most of the ex-Confederate states to regulate the freedmen—laws that came to be known collec-tively as the Black Codes.

To the white South, the principle seemed altogether clear and fair-minded: "Teach the negro that if he goes to work, keeps his place, and behaves himself, he will be protected by *our* white laws." Although borrowing heavily from antebellum re-strictions on free Negroes, as well as from northern apprenticeship laws and Freedmen's Bureau and War Department regulations, the Black Codes were still very much a product of postwar southern thinking, both a legal expression of the lingering paternalism (to protect the ex-slave from himself) and a legislative re-sponse to immediate and pressing economic problems. While the Codes defined the freedman's civil and legal rights, permitting him to marry, hold and sell property, and sue and be sued, the key provisions were those which defined him as an agricultural laborer, barred or circumscribed any alternative occupations, and compelled him to work. "Upon this point turns the entire question," a South Carolina newspaper said of the principle of compulsion, "and as that is decided, so is the safety or ruin of this country." If the Codes did not reestablish slavery, as some northern critics charged, neither did they recognize the former slaves as free men and women, entitled to equal protection under the law. As if to underscore how little had changed, a South Carolina law defined the two parties to a labor contract as "servants" and "masters."

Although the laws differed from state to state, the underlying principles and the major provisions remained the same. If found without "lawful employment," a freedman could be arrested as a common vagrant, jailed and fined; if unable to pay the fine, he would be hired out to an employer who in turn assumed the financial li-ability and deducted it from the laborer's wages. The Mississippi law also defined as vagrants any blacks unable or unwilling to pay a new tax to support Negro indigents, while the Alabama code included as vagrants "any runaway, stubborn servant or child" and any laborer "who loiters away his time" or fails to comply with the terms of his employment. Several of the codes also set down the hours of labor (from sunrise to sunset), the duties, and the behavior expected of black agricultural workers. . . .

Rather than expedite the slave's transition to freedom or help him to realize his aspirations, the Black Codes embodied in law the widely held assumption that he existed largely for the purpose of raising crops for a white employer. Although the ex-slave ceased to be the property of a master, he could not aspire to become his own master. No law stated the proposition quite that bluntly but the provisions breathed that spirit in ways that could hardly be misunderstood. If a freedman decided that agricultural labor was not his special calling, the law often left him with no practical alternative. To discourage those who aspired to be artisans, mechanics, or shopkeepers, or who already held such positions, the South Carolina code, for example, prohibited a black person from entering any employment except agricultural labor or domestic service unless he obtained a special license and a certification from a local judge of his "skill and fitness" and "good moral character." This provision, of course, threatened to undermine the position of the old free Negro class which had once nearly dominated the skilled trades in places like Charleston. With unconcealed intent, the Mississippi law simply required special licenses of any black wishing to engage in "irregular or job work." To discourage freedmen who aspired to raise their own crops, Mississippi barred them from renting or leasing any land outside towns or cities, leaving to local authorities any restrictions they might wish to place on black ownership of real estate.

By adopting harsh vagrancy laws and restricting non-agricultural employment, the white South clearly intended to stem the much-feared drift of freedmen toward the cities and to underscore their status as landless agricultural laborers. Even as Mississippi forbade them to lease lands outside towns or cities, local ordinances there and in neighboring Louisiana made black residency within the towns or cities virtually intolerable if not impossible. The ordinance adopted in Opelousas, Louisiana, deservedly served as a model and inspiration for other communities. To enter the town, a black person needed his employer's permission, stipulating the object of the visit and the time necessary to accomplish it; any freedman found on the streets after ten o'clock at night without a written pass or permit from his employer would be subject to arrest and imprisonment. No freedman could rent or keep a house within the town limits "under any circumstances," or reside within the town unless employed by a white person who assumed responsibility for his conduct. To hold any public meetings or to assemble in large numbers for any reason, blacks needed the mayor's permission, as they also did to "preach, exhort or otherwise declaim" to black congregations. Nor could they possess weapons or sell, barter, or exchange any kind of merchandise without special permits. A freedman found violating these ordinances could be punished by imprisonment, fines, and forced labor on the city streets. . . .

With the adoption of the Black Codes, the place of the ex-slave in postwar southern society had been fixed in law, his mobility checked, his bargaining power sharply reduced, and his rights of appeal hedged with difficulties. Any freedman who refused to work at the prevailing wage in a particular area could be defined as a vagrant, and there was little to protect him from combinations of employers setting wages and conditions. To many in the North, the Codes smacked of the old bondage, and even some southern whites thought them ill-advised, impractical, or at least badly timed. *"We showed our hand too soon,"* a Mississippi planter conceded. "We ought to have waited till the troops were withdrawn, and our representatives admitted to Congress; then we could have had everything our own way." Unmoved by the criticism they anticipated, the authors of the Florida code thought it "needless to attempt to satisfy the exactions of the fanatical theorists—we have a duty to perform—the protection of our wives and children from threatened danger, and the prevention of scenes which may cost the extinction of an entire race." The special committee preparing the Mississippi code conceded that some of the proposed legislation "may seem rigid and stringent" but only "to the sickly modern humanitarians."

To the former slaves, whose opinions carried little weight, the Codes clouded the entire issue of freedom and left them highly dubious of what rights if any they could exercise without fear of arrest or legal harassment. In petitioning the governor, the freedmen of Claiborne County, Mississippi, thought it necessary to ask for a clarification: "Mississippi has abolished slavery. Does she mean it or is it a policy for the present?" By barring them from leasing or renting land, the petitioners charged that the legislature had left them with no choice but to purchase land, knowing full well that "not one of us out of a thousand" could afford the price of even a quarter of an acre. If any of them deserted an employer because of cruel treatment, they could be arrested and forcibly returned to him. How could this be reconciled with their newly won freedom? "Now we are free," they insisted, "we do not want to be hunted by negro runners and their hounds unless we are guilty of a criminal crime." . . . The petitioners assured the governor of their willingness to work for anyone who treated them well and paid them adequately; they reminded him, too, of how the slaves had stood by their white families in troublesome times. Although they recognized the presence of some "good and honest" employers among the whites, such men were "not the majority" and the "good" employer could be easily intimidated and "put down as a negro spoiler." Finally, the petitioners thought Jefferson Davis, a fellow Mississippian, should be set free, if only because "we [know] worse Masters than he was. Although he tried hard to keep us all slaves we forgive him." . . .

The Black Codes proved to be short-lived, largely because the South had moved precipitately, impetuously, and carelessly. Although Federal officials, both in the Freedmen's Bureau and the Union Army, had implemented labor policies which were strikingly similar, the Codes were deemed too blatantly discriminatory and overly repressive. Not long after the Codes were adopted, Federal officials ordered many of them suspended, nearly always on the grounds that freedmen should be subject to the same regulations, penalties, punishments, and courts as whites. Several of the state legislatures, too, had second thoughts about their actions, particularly after the initial insurrection panic subsided and the labor situation improved; the legislators themselves repealed or revised some of the more obnoxious clauses, and the Codes passed by a number of states in 1866 proved less harsh. . . .

If the Codes were dead, the sentiment which had created them was still very much alive. Whether enforced, set aside, or amended, the Black Codes had revealed how the ruling class expected to perpetuate that rule. The setback, then, could be viewed as but temporary, a concession to expediency. If statutes proved unavailing in returning the ex-slaves to the fields and kitchens where they belonged, economic necessity and the enforcement of contracts could achieve the same goals within an ideological framework familiar and acceptable to the North. Neither during slavery days nor in the immediate postwar years, moreover, did the planter rely entirely on legislative enactments to maintain the order and discipline he deemed essential. When it came to managing blacks, experience taught him that the place to establish his authority was in the field and the kitchen, not simply in the courthouse.

Faced with troublesome laborers after the war, a Louisiana sugar planter mused over the changed situation and how he would have dealt with such problems in better days. "Eaton [an overseer] must find it very hard to lay aside the old strap— As for myself, I would give a good deal to amuse myself with it, a little while. I have come to the conclusion that the great secret of our success was the great motive power contained in that little instrument." Few of the former slaveholders would have disputed that observation. To maintain a disciplined and docile labor force, they had long acknowledged their reliance on "the power of fear." Nor had the emancipation of the slaves lessened the need to exercise their traditional prerogatives. "They can't be governed except with the whip," one planter explained. "Now on my plantation there wasn't much whipping, say once a fortnight; but the negroes knew they would be whipped if they didn't behave themselves, and the fear of the lash kept them in good order."

When Federal officials suspended the newly enacted Black Codes, southern whites greeted the decision with predictable expressions of dismay but few were altogether surprised and some felt the states had acted foolishly. But when Federals in some regions reprimanded employers for using the whip on black laborers or forbade any kind of corporal punishment, that was truly hard to accept—even to comprehend. "I know the nigger," a Mississippi planter pleaded with a Freedmen's Bureau official. "The employer must have some sort of punishment. I don't care what it is. If you'll let me tie him up by the thumbs, or keep him on bread and water, that will do. . . . All I want is just to have it so that when I get the niggers on to my place, and the work is begun, they can't sit down and look me square in the face and do nothing."

To manage black laborers, numerous planters agreed, was not unlike handling mules; both could be stubborn, even insolent, and experience suggested that they were most serviceable and contented when they had "plenty of feed, plenty of work, and a little licking." What these planters now demanded was simply the necessary authority to exact the fear and the deference always considered essential to racial control. Like the Black Codes, corporal punishment would benefit the blacks by restraining their worst passions and forcing them to acknowledge authority. "A nigger has got to know you're his master," a Georgia planter still insisted, "and then when he understands that he's content." Still another former slaveholder attributed his postwar success in managing thirty-five freedmen to their *fear* of punishment: "You see I never let myself down to 'em."

If the old discipline in any way contradicted the new freedom, few of the former slaveholders cared to admit it. To them, emancipation had only made more urgent the need to exercise traditional authority. Although employers made less use of the whip than before the war, they managed to find equally effective and less controversial alternatives. After serving a fifteen-day jail sentence for lashing a former slave ("was there ever such a damned outrage!"), a South Carolina planter claimed to have "larnt a trick" that exacted the proper respect of his blacks. "I jest strings 'em up by the thumbs for 'bout half an hour, an' then they are damned glad to go to work." Since the Union Army used that method to discipline its own men as well as recalcitrant blacks, the South Carolinian obviously expected no interference. Fearful of whipping their freed slaves, lest they lodge a complaint with Federal officials, some planters took out their frustrations in verbal abuse. "Can't lick free niggers, but I don't know if there's any law ag'in cussin' 'em, and I believe it does 'em a heap o' good," a Georgian suggested to a group of fellow planters. "It's next best to lickin'. Jest cuss one o' 'em right smart for 'bout five minutes, and he'll play off peart." Unfortunately for this planter, emancipation had left him without a black to curse and he could only fantasize about how to bring the freedmen under control. "I should like to lick a hundred free negroes jest once all 'round. If I didn't bring 'em to know their places, I'd pay ten dollars apiece for all I failed on."

The degree to which emancipation altered the day-to-day behavior and temperament of the former slaveholder became a matter of immediate concern to black men and women. On numerous farms and plantations, they soon discovered that the potential of the white family for volatile behavior had in no way been abated and it seemed like the old times again. Katie Darling, a former Texas slave, remembered staying with her "white folks" for six years after the war "and missy whip me jist like she did 'fore." If Anna Miller perceived any change in her master after emancipation, it was only his rapid mental deterioration. "De marster gets worser in de disposition and goes 'roun' sort of talkin' to hisse'f and den he gits to cussin' ev'rybody." Within a year after vowing that he would not live in a country "whar de niggers am free," her master killed himself. . . .

Although Federal officials were inclined to overlook how an employer chose to discipline his laborers, the blacks themselves refused to be passive spectators. If a planter relied on the old discipline, confident that fear and punishment could still maintain a captive labor force, he might discover that his intended victims, often his former slaves, no longer felt compelled to submit. After what they had endured as slaves, they saw no reason to tolerate such treatment as freedmen. "Damn him," a South Carolina black remarked after an altercation with his old master, "he never done nufin all his damned life but beat me and kick me and knock me down; an' I hopes I git eben with him some day." In Mississippi, an overseer who responded to a disobedient field hand by threatening him with an ax suddenly found himself facing the laborer's daughter and several other blacks, all of them holding axes. "I had to run for my life," the overseer testified. On the Brokenburn plantation in Louisiana, John B. Stone, the highly temperamental son of the mistress, shot a black youth after an argument in the fields. That so infuriated the other hands that they turned upon Stone and might have killed him had not some others intervened. Still, Kate Stone would never forget the sight of her brother being escorted to the house by "a howling, cursing mob with the women shrieking, 'Kill him!' and all brandishing pistols and guns." The family thought it best to send John away to school, at least until a semblance of calm had been restored. Upon his return, he seemed a much-changed and subdued young man. "He never speaks now of killing people as he formerly had a habit of doing," his sister wrote of him.

If open resistance invited severe reprisals, the freedmen could exercise the power to withhold their labor or leave the premises and never return. The ties that kept former slaves on the plantation were often so tenuous that an employer's threat or attempt to inflict punishment might end the relationship altogether. Faced with the imminent loss of their laborers, many a former master and mistress suddenly became "very con'scending" after the war, learned to address their blacks in terms of respect, and banished both the whip and the overseer. "I told my overseer the old style wouldn't do,—the niggers wouldn't stand it,—and he promised better fashions," an Alabama planter remarked; "but it wasn't two days before he fell from grace, and went to whipping again. That just raised the Old Scratch with them; and I don't blame 'em." In explaining the changed attitudes of their old masters, some former slaves suggested that fear itself could have been a motivating factor. "He never was mean to us after freedom," a former Tennessee slave recalled, along with the many beatings she had once endured. "He was 'fraid the niggers might kill him." Rather than trust their former master to exercise proper judgment, many blacks extracted from him, as a condition of employment, assurances that he would refrain from corporal punishment and discharge the overseer.

By these and other demands, the freedmen suggested the need not only to abolish the relics of bondage but to give substance to their position as free workers, with the same rights and prerogatives they had observed white laborers exercising. Nowhere would they manifest this determination more vividly than in the new economic arrangements they worked out with their employers. Unfortunately, the former slaveholding class seemed in many respects less equipped to make the transition to freedom than their former slaves. No matter how hard some tried, few of them were capable of learning new ways and shaking off the old attitudes. Even if they could, they found themselves increasingly trapped into an untenable position. Desperately needing to exact enough labor from their former slaves to meet a brutally depressed market, employers now encountered free workers who looked first to their own subsistence and refused to work up to an exploitative level they deemed incompatible with their new status. When these conflicting needs created an impasse, as they often did, the employer class was forced to look elsewhere for the kind of compulsion and guidance that might once again produce a stable and tractable labor force. How ironic that none other than the much-hated Yankee conquerors should have ultimately shown them the way.

Not long after Federal authorities set aside the Black Code of South Carolina, Armisted Burt, who had helped to frame the new laws, noted with obvious satisfaction that the Union commander had ordered freedmen to contract with an employer or be sentenced to hard labor on public projects. "I have no doubt the Yankees will manage them," he concluded. The confidence he expressed was not misplaced. No matter how much whites chafed under military rule and occupation, the planter class—native whites and northern lessees alike—often acknowledged its indebtedness to the Union Army for controlling the otherwise restless and rebellious dispositions of the freed slaves. After conversing with the local commander on steps that had been taken to suppress a feared black uprising, the manager of a plantation in low-country South Carolina breathed much easier: "Our people object to the troops being sent here. I thank God they are here." No sooner were cases of "insubordination" reported to Federal authorities, a Georgia clergyman and planter informed his sister, than forceful steps were taken to suppress the troublemakers. "The effect has been a remarkable quietude and order in all this region. The Negroes are astounded at the idea of being whipped by Yankees. (But keep all this a secret, lest we should be deprived of their services. I have not called on them yet, but may have to do so.)"

If the Black Codes had not been the edicts of legislatures dominated by ex-Confederate leaders, they might not have suffered the fate of nullification. The problem lay not so much in specific provisions as in what the total product came to symbolize to the victorious North—white southern intransigence and unrepentance in the face of military defeat. But the suspension of the Codes in no way diminished the need to reactivate and control black labor. Almost every Federal official recognized that necessity, and Union commanders moved quickly to expel former plantation hands from the towns and cities, to comply with the requests of planters to force their blacks to work, and to punish freedmen for disobedience, theft, vagrancy, and erratic labor. "Their idea of freedom," the provost marshal of Bolivar County, Mississippi, said of the recently freed slaves, "is that they are under no control; can work when they please, and go where they wish. . . . It is my desire to apply the Punishments used in the Army of the United States, for offenses of the Negroes, and to make them do their duty." Empowered to settle disputes between employers and laborers, the provost marshals invariably sustained the authority of the planters. In Louisiana, for example, plantation laborers testified to the hopelessness of appealing any grievances they might have to the nearest Federal official:

Q: Have you any white friend, in your parish, who will support your claims or take your defense?

A: We have no white friends there.

Q: Have you any colored friend who could do so?

A: No colored man has any thing to say; none has any influence.

Q: Is not the Provost Marshal a protector for your people?

A: Whenever a new Provost Marshal comes he gives us justice for a fortnight or so; then he becomes acquainted with planters, takes dinners with them, receives presents; and then we no longer have any rights, or very little.

If Union officers eschewed the whip as an instrument of slavery, they did not hesitate to employ familiar military punishments to deal with "disorderly" blacks. "What's good enough for soldiers is good enough for Niggers," a sergeant told a

Florida woman who had expressed shock over seeing her "negligent" servant hung up by the thumbs. Upon witnessing a similar punishment meted out to two laborers he had reported for loitering on the job, a South Carolina planter heard them plead to be flogged instead. But if Yankee "justice" dismayed or surprised some native whites, a Mississippi hotelkeeper marveled at the way the local provost marshal had dealt with a "sassy" black who refused to work. "We've got a Provo' in our town," he boasted, "that settles their hash mighty quick. He's a downright high-toned man, that Provo', if he is a Yankee. . . . He tucked him [the black] up, guv him twenty lashes, and rubbed him down right smart with salt, for having no visible means of support." That evening, the black victim returned quite willingly to his job.

Since the early days of occupation, Federal authorities had shared with planters a concern over how to keep the ex-slaves in the fields and impress upon them the necessity of labor. "The Yankees preach nothing but cotton, cotton," a Sea Islands slave exclaimed, voicing the dismay of many blacks over how quickly their liberators returned them to the familiar routines. Soon after the troops occupied a region, Union officers confronted the problem of what to do with the "contrabands" pouring into their camps. Although many of them were conscripted for military service and labor, the vast majority found themselves working on abandoned and confiscated plantations. The Federal government supervised some of these plantations, while leasing most of them to private individuals, including a number of northern whites intent on maximizing profits as quickly as possible. Thomas W. Knox, a white Northerner who tried his hand at plantation management, characterized most of his colleagues in the business as "unprincipled men" who had little regard for the former slave. "The difference between working for nothing as a slave, and working for the same wages under the Yankees," he observed, "was not always perceptible to the unsophisticated negro." Small numbers of black farmers also managed to obtain leases, all of them eager to demonstrate the feasibility of free and independent labor. The most successful of such experiments took place at Davis Bend, Mississippi, where blacks secured leases on six extensive plantations, including two belonging to Joe and Jefferson Davis; the blacks repaid the government for the initial costs, managed their own affairs, raised and sold their own crops, and realized impressive profits.

Whatever the promise of Davis Bend, neither the Union Army nor the Freedmen's Bureau thought to question the basic assumption underlying the discredited Black Codes—that the ex-slaves were fit only to till the land of others as agricultural laborers and that only compulsion would exact the necessary work and discipline. The proven success of black lessees at Davis Bend and elsewhere, no matter how widely applauded, failed to stem the steady drift toward restoration. Even before the termination of the war, loyal planters and those who took the oath of allegiance to the United States government were permitted to retain their plantations and to work the blacks on a wages or shares basis; Federal officials intervened only to provide planters with the necessary laborers, to suppress any disorders, and to provide guidelines for the management of the ex-slaves. In the view of some Union officers, only if the former master and his former slaves agreed to a separation should the blacks be permitted to leave the plantations on which they had worked. That was how Emma Holmes interpreted Federal policy in her region, and her mother accordingly reported to the local Union officer a black man who had taken a job elsewhere: "By yesterday morning he had found out the Yankees were his masters, and he walked back here to his work."

Based on early experiences with the freedmen, the labor system established during the war by successive Union commanders in Louisiana proved far more typical of the Federal approach than the short-lived Davis Bend experiment. To meet the problem of growing numbers of black refugees and of plantations disrupted by black defections and erratic labor, General Nathaniel P. Banks promised to return the ex-slaves to the fields and to enforce "conditions of continuous and faithful service, respectful deportment, correct discipline, and perfect subordination on the part of the negroes." The regulations he issued manifested precisely that spirit: a contract system binding the ex-slaves to the land, compensating their labor with wages or shares, and assuring them of just treatment, adequate rations and clothing, medical attention, and education for their children. Although the freedman could select an employer, he was bound to him for the remainder of the year, during which time he was expected to perform "respectful, honest, faithful labor." To encourage compliance, one half of his wages would be withheld until the end of the season; any black refusing to enter into a contract, violating its terms, or found guilty of "indolence, insolence, and disobedience" would forfeit his pay and be subject to military arrest and employment without wages on public works. Conceding little else to emancipation, the new rules forbade employers from flogging their laborers or separating families; in numerous instances, however, freedmen were returned to their old masters with little concern for their subsequent treatment.

Even if conceived in "a benevolent spirit," the labor system envisioned by these regulations struck some black critics as "freedom by toleration" and a "mitigated bondage" analogous to Russian serfdom. That was how the *New Orleans Tribune*, the articulate organ of the free colored community, chose to characterize the new rules. "Strange freedom indeed! Our freedmen, on the plantations, at the present time, could more properly be called, mock freedmen." If a laborer were truly free, the editor observed, he should be able to choose his place of residence and his trade or occupation, negotiate his own terms with an employer (including wages, conditions, and term of service), and bring court action against anyone who tried to defraud him; moreover, he should be paid the full value of his labor, not a wage stipulated by planters' meetings or Federal rules. Under the current regulations, the editor contended, blacks would have to work for wages which barely sustained them. But that deplorable fact seemed even less important than the ways in which the new system perpetuated and enforced the dependency of the freedmen on their former masters:

> He does not wear his own clothes; but, as the slave, he wears his master's clothes. He does not eat his own bread, the bread he won by the sweat of his brow; he eats his master's bread. He is provided for like the mules and cattle on the plantations. And it is said that this is the way some people intend to follow to make men!

Finally, black critics thought it highly ironic but not altogether surprising that such a labor system should have been instituted and defended by white men who never ceased to display their abolitionist credentials as evidence of their good faith. "I

despise a man who pretends to be an abolitionist, and who is only a deepskin abolitionist," a black clergyman told a meeting in New Orleans called to protest the
labor regulations. "We have good friends, who will work with us till this country be
a free country; but we have unfaithful friends also. A wolf came, one day, among
sheep, in sheep's clothing; but he had a strange foot, and the sheep wondered at that.
We, too, are ready to watch this foot."

In defending the labor system of Louisiana, a Union officer not only alluded to
his "life-time Anti-Slavery" but curtly dismissed the black critics in New Orleans as
"a class of colored people who, with all their admirable qualities, have not yet forgotten that they were, themselves, slaveholders." But if the urban black elitists could
be dismissed, Federal authorities would still have to contend with the black laborers
themselves, most of whom had never read a newspaper and needed no one to
remind them of the oppressive nature of the system under which they were now
told to work. The kind of resistance they undertook varied from mass defections to
open revolt; most of them, however, took out their grievances in the erratic work
habits about which their employers continued to complain. Rather than submit to
the new regulations, the blacks on a plantation south of New Orleans threw down
their tools, vowed they would never work under such terms, and "left in a body." In
Plaquemines Parish, field hands lodged the familiar complaint that they had not yet
received their share of the previous season's crops; when they then refused to
work, a civilian police officer attempted to arrest the ringleaders, only to find
himself "beset upon by at least twenty—with hoes, shovels and hatchets" and forced
to leave. Whether directed at specific labor regulations or reflecting general conditions, such outbreaks in Louisiana and elsewhere in the South would require the
continued intervention of Federal authorities.

Neither the charges of black critics nor the resistance of black laborers effected any significant changes in a labor system calculated to subordinate black labor
to white planters and lessees. The advocates of that system persisted in the assumption that only coercion and rigid controls could assure the triumph and vindication of free labor in the South. When in mid-1863, at General Banks's request, two
abolitionists evaluated the labor system of Louisiana, they reported with praise that
on those plantations where the regulations had been faithfully implemented, the
black laborers appeared to be "docile, industrious, & quiet." By 1865, the initial
experiment in labor relations undertaken in Louisiana had evolved into a system
of contracts between laborers and employers not unlike that being instituted
elsewhere in the occupied South under the auspices of Federal authorities. Although
the format and the specific terms might differ, the nature of the relationship remained essentially the same, as did the role of the Federal government and the
sources of black discontent. . . .

With the end of the war, the Bureau of Refugees, Freedmen and Abandoned Lands
(commonly known as the Freedmen's Bureau) undertook to complete the transition to "free labor" initially begun under the direction of the Union Army. "The
freedmen in a few instances are doing well," Thomas Smith reported in November
1865, not long after he had assumed his post as a Bureau subcommissioner in

charge of northern Mississippi. He found many of the freedmen to be "indolent," some of them "disrespectful and totally unreliable," and almost all of them "greatly in need of instruction." But like most Bureau agents, he thought his primary concern was not to make literates of the freed slaves but to teach them to be reliable agricultural laborers. "They have very mistaken notions in regard to freedom. . . . They ask, 'What is the value of freedom if one has nothing to go on?' That is to say if property in some shape or other is not to be given us, we might as well be slaves." He needed to disabuse their minds of such notions while at the same time restoring their faith in the former masters. "The colored people lack confidence in the white man's *integrity*; they fear that, were they to hire to him, and work for him, that he would not pay them for their labor. . . . The more quickly, and the more perfectly, *that* confidence is restored, the better will it be for all classes." He could conceive of no more important task he faced in his new position.

If "instruction" could cure the propensity of the ex-slaves toward "indolence" and "unreliable" labor, the agents of the Freedmen's Bureau eagerly assumed the role of teachers and disciplinarians. The lessons they imparted seldom varied and rarely departed from what Union officers and planters had been telling the slaves since the first days of liberation. "He would promise them nothing, but their freedom, and freedom means work," General Oliver O. Howard, the Bureau commissioner, explained to the freedmen of Austin, Texas, and he offered them, too, the classic maxim of nineteenth-century employers: "The man who sits about the streets and smokes, will make nothing." That very morning, Howard said, he had attended church services in different parts of the city and had heard a black clergyman and a white clergyman preach the gospel of love. "Oh, if you will only practice what you preach," the commissioner told the freedmen, "it will all be well." But if they refused to work, a Bureau officer warned the blacks of Mississippi, they should expect neither sympathy, love, nor subsistence. "Your houses and lands belong to the white people, and you cannot expect that they will allow you to live on them in idleness." Nor should the ex-slave expect the state or Federal government "to let any man lie about idle, without property, doing mischief. A vagrant law is right in principle. I cannot ask the civil officers to leave you idle, to beg or steal. If they find any of you without business and means of living, they will do right if they treat you as bad persons and take away your misused liberty." . . .

No doubt many Bureau agents took comfort in the impact of their message. "The Negro is often suspicious of his former master and will not believe him," the subcommissioner in Jackson, Mississippi, observed, "but when assured by the Federal authorities that he must go to work and behave himself, he does so contentedly." That made it all the more imperative, he thought, "for the good of the Negro and the peace of the Country," to have Bureau representatives visit every part of their districts. The manager of a plantation in Bolivar County, Mississippi, heartily agreed. "If you would send an agent here to look into matters, and give some advice, I would be pleased to have him make his quarters with me for a week or two." With unconcealed enthusiasm, a planter near Columbia, South Carolina, welcomed the advice a Bureau official gave to his laborers. "You're their best friend, they all know," he told him, "and I'm very glad you've come down this way." The planter had good reason to be grateful. Until the official's visit, the freedmen had thought they owned the plantation.

Acting in what they deemed to be the best interests of the ex-slaves, the strongest and proven advocates of the freedmen's cause admonished them to prove their fitness for freedom by laboring as faithfully as they had as slaves—and even more productively. "Plough and plant, dig and hoe, cut and gather in the harvest," General Rufus Saxton urged them. "Let it be seen that where in slavery there was raised a blade of corn or a pound of cotton, in freedom there will be two." Along with Saxton, few whites were more committed to the freedmen than Clinton B. Fisk, a Bureau official who subsequently helped to found one of the first black colleges. And he doubtless thought himself to be speaking in their best interests when he advised the freedmen to remain in their old places and work for their former masters.

> You have been associated with them for many years; you are bound to the old home by many ties, and most of you I trust will be able to get on as well with your late masters as with anyone else. . . . He is not able to do without you, and you will, in most cases, find him as kind, honest, and liberal as other men. Indeed he has for you a kind of family affection. . . . Do not think that, in order to be free, you must fall out with your old master, gather up your bundles and trudge off to a strange city. This is a great mistake. As a general rule, you can be as free and as happy in your old home, for the present, as any where else in the world.

Consistent with such advice, Freedmen's Bureau officials made every effort to rid the urban centers of black refugees and to force them back onto the plantations. (Ironically, the very presence of the Bureau in the towns and villages had induced many ex-slaves to settle there, thinking they might be more secure with Federal protection nearby.) A successful Bureau officer in Culpeper, Virginia, was able to report that "this village was overrun with freedmen when I took charge here, but I have succeeded in getting the most of them out into the country on farms. The freedmen are, almost without an exception, going to work, most of them by the year."

Having been established to facilitate the transition from slavery to freedom, the Bureau faced an admittedly immense task. With limited personnel and funds, it was forced to operate on a number of levels, providing the newly freed slaves with food rations and medical care, assisting them in their education, helping to reunite families, relocating thousands of ex-slaves on abandoned lands, and transporting still more to areas where the scarcity of labor commanded higher wages. In its most critical role as a labor mediator, the Bureau set out to correct abuses in contracts, establish "fair" wage rates, force employers to pay what they had promised, and break up planter conspiracies to depress wages. "What we wish to do is plain enough," a Bureau officer in North Carolina announced. "We desire to instruct the colored people of the South, to lift them up from subserviency and helplessness into a dignified independence and citizenship." . . .

Whatever directives flowed out of the national office, the crucial power of the Freedmen's Bureau rested with the state and local officials, many of whom were former soldiers and officers who looked upon their positions as sinecures rather than opportunities to protect the ex-slaves in their newly acquired rights. The competence of individual agents varied enormously, as did the quality of the commitment they brought to their jobs. Under difficult, even hazardous circumstances, some Bureau agents braved the opposition of native whites as well as Federal authorities to protect the freedmen from fraud, harassment, and violence; among these agents were whites imbued with the old abolitionist commitment and a small group of blacks, including Martin R. Delany, B.F. Randolph, and J.J. Wright, all of them holding posts in South Carolina. But many of the field agents of the Freedmen's Bureau coveted acceptance by the communities in which they served and became malleable instruments in the hands of the planter class, eager to service their labor needs and sharing similar views about the racial character and capacity of black people and the urgent need to control them. The *New Orleans Tribune* tried to be as sympathetic toward the Freedmen's Bureau as its observations would permit: in the midst of a hostile population, the agents had little choice but to act cautiously; their acquaintances were almost always whites and each day they were subjected to "false impressions and misrepresentations." Under such conditions, the editor charged, the legitimate grievances of black laborers were understandably "treated with contempt"—that is, if they were considered at all. In a recent visit to Amite City, in St. Helena Parish, he found that most of the blacks were unaware of the presence of the Bureau. "The representatives of the federal power are lost in the crowd," the editor observed; "and feeling themselves powerless, they are wasting time the best they can, and do not hurt the feelings of any body." To "make Abolition a truth," he suggested that black troops be stationed there. "Up to this time, Emancipation has only been a lie—in most of our parishes."

No matter how a Bureau agent interpreted his mission, the tasks he faced were formidable. At the very outset, the extent of territory for which he was responsible reduced his effectiveness. "My satrapy," a South Carolina agent recalled, "contained two state districts or counties, and eventually three, with a population of about eighty thousand souls and an area at least two thirds as large as the state of Connecticut. Consider the absurdity of expecting one man to patrol three thousand miles and make personal visitations to thirty thousand Negroes." The questions an agent needed to answer and act upon were equally demanding. If a slaveholder had removed his blacks during the war to a "safe" area, who bore the responsibility for returning them to their original homes? If blacks had planted crops in the master's absence, who should reap the profits? Could a former master confiscate the personal possessions a black had accumulated as his slave? If a black woman had borne the children of a master, who assumed responsibility for them in freedom? Could the ex-slaveholders expel from their plantations the sick and elderly blacks no longer able to support themselves? Compared to the numerous disputes involving the interpretation of contracts, the division of crops, and acts of violence, these were almost trivial questions, but even the best-intentioned agents had few guidelines to help them reach a decision. The Bureau officer, a South Carolina agent recalled, needed to be "a man of quick common sense, with a special faculty for deciding what not to do. His duties and powers were to a great extent vague, and in general he might be said to do best when he did least."

No sooner had he taken office than the typical Bureau agent found himself besieged by planters wanting to know what terms and punishments they could impose on their blacks. That would constitute the bulk of his work, along with the many complaints of freedmen who had suffered fraud, abuse, and violence at the hands of their employers. Unfortunately, few Bureau agents possessed the ability, the patience, or the sympathy to deal with the grievances of the freedmen, even to recognize their legitimacy, and the ex-slave had no way of knowing what to expect if he should file a complaint. To do so, he might have to travel anywhere from ten to fifty miles to the nearest Bureau office, where he was apt to find an agent "who rides, dines, and drinks champagne with his employer" and viewed any complainant as some kind of troublemaker. Even the more sympathetic agents were not always able to consider the freedman's grievances with the seriousness they deserved.

> The majority of the complaints brought before me came from Negroes. As would naturally happen to an ignorant race, they were liable to many impositions, and they saw their grievances with big eyes. . . . With pomp of manner and of words, with a rotundity of voice and superfluity of detail which would have delighted Cicero, a Negro would so glorify his little trouble as to give one the impression that humanity had never before suffered the like.

. . . Even where a Bureau official tried to act on behalf of a freedman, he might find himself frustrated by military authorities, whose support he needed to enforce his decisions but whose sympathies often lay with the native whites. In some regions, military officers not connected with the Bureau collected fees for approving labor contracts and paid little attention to the provisions. Captain Randolph T. Stoops, the provost marshal in Columbia, Virginia, readily conceded his lack of concern in such matters but thought it perfectly justified. "As to the price of labour I have nothing to do with it. The citizens held a meeting some time since and made a price to suit themselves. . . . When Farmers bring the negro before me to have written agreements between them whatever price is agreed upon between them I enter on the article and consider them bound to fulfill the agreement whatever it may be." Often over the protests of sympathetic Bureau agents, military authorities permitted employers to mete out punishments to recalcitrant blacks or imposed their own form of discipline. That was how Captain Stoops dealt with the problem of blacks "swarming the streets" of the town in which he was stationed. "There being no jail or place of confinement I resorted to the wooden horse and making them work on the streets. Such punishment I found beneficial for in a short time I found almost every negro for some distance, had gone to work and was doing well. . . . Fright has more to do with it than anything else."

To keep the freed slaves on the old plantations and to force them into contracts with an employer doubtless helped a local Bureau official to win a degree of toleration in an otherwise hostile community. But at the same time, he easily persuaded himself that he was acting in the best interests of the freedmen. After all, the Bureau officer in Vicksburg observed, wherever the freedmen were "submissive and perform the labor they contract to do in good faith," the native whites treated them "with kindness." If the blacks themselves remained unconvinced of the Bureau's good intentions, an official could reason that they had only recently been released from bondage and were in no position to know what was best for them. The more the freedmen resisted their advice, the more Bureau officials insisted on it, justifying their positions by the number of ex-slaves they had induced to return to work. Upon assuming his post in Jackson, Mississippi, Captain J.H. Weber found the city "full to overflowing with stragglers from the plantations." He immediately ordered the troops under his command to round up the "stragglers" and put them to work on the city streets.

> The result was surprising; it stopped in short order the influx of stragglers, and saved the soldiers the labor of cleaning up the City. The stragglers began to learn, and those coming in learned from them that they could not remain here in idleness—they went back to their homes contented to go to work again. I have gathered up in this way, more than three hundred, and as planters and others have called for laborers, I have turned those thus gathered up over to them . . .

With equal satisfaction, a Bureau officer in southern Mississippi boasted that his "presence and authority," backed by troops when needed, had "kept the negroes at work, and in a good state of discipline." If it had not been for the Bureau, he added, "I feel confident there would have been an uprising upon the part of the negroes."

Established to ease the ex-slaves' transition to freedom, the Freedmen's Bureau ultimately facilitated the restoration of black labor to the control of those who had previously owned them. "They are, in fact, the planter's guards, and nothing else," the *New Orleans Tribune* concluded, almost two years after expressing its initial doubts about the Bureau. "Every person acquainted with the regime of our country parishes knows what has become of the Bureau's agencies and the Agents." The potential for a different course of action had been present from the outset. Although the President's liberal pardon policy necessarily frustrated any radical redistribution of land, the Freedmen's Bureau had been in a position to effect significant changes in labor relations, particularly during the chaotic aftermath of emancipation. "In my opinion," a Bureau official wrote from Meridian, Mississippi, in June 1866, "you could inflict no more severe punishment on a planter than to take from him the negroes that work the place. They will do anything, rather than this, that is possible or reasonable. They feel their utter helplessness without them to do the work." But even the best-intentioned of the commissioners and local agents manifested their sympathy for the freedmen in curious and contradictory ways, embracing a paternalism and a contract labor system that could only perpetuate the economic dependency of the great mass of former slaves.

"Philanthropists," a black newspaper observed in 1865, "are sometimes a strange class of people; they love their fellow man, but these to be worthy of their assistance, must be of an inferior kind. We were and still are oppressed; we are not demoralized criminals." Nor did black people need to be reminded to avoid idleness and vagrancy; the repeated warnings, preached by native whites and Federal authorities alike, were all too reminiscent of the white preacher's sermons during slavery. After all, the newspaper concluded, "the necessity of working is perfectly understood by men who have worked all their lives."

Suggested Readings

General

Michael Les Benedict, *A Compromise of Principle: Congressional Republicans and Reconstruction* (1974).

Dan T. Carter, *When the War Was Over* (1985).

Richard N. Current, *Those Terrible Carpetbaggers: A Reinterpretation* (1989).

Eric Foner, *Reconstruction: America's Unfinished Revolution, 1862–1877* (1988).

William S. McFeely, *Grant: A Biography* (1981).

Eric L. McKitrick, *Andrew Johnson and Reconstruction* (1988).

George C. Rable, *But There Was No Peace: The Role of Violence in the Politics of Reconstruction* (1984).

James L. Roark, *Masters Without Slaves* (1977).

Kenneth Stampp, *The Era of Reconstruction, 1865–1877* (1965).

C. Vann Woodward, *Reunion and Reaction*, rev. ed. (1956).

Overview of Reconstruction

John Hope Franklin, *Reconstruction After the Civil War* (1961).

Congressional and Presidential Reconstruction and the Constitutional Issues

Richard H. Abbott, *The Republican Party and the South, 1855–1877* (1986); Michael Kent Curtis, *No State Shall Abridge: The Fourteenth Amendment and the Bill of Rights* (1990); Eric Foner, *Politics and Ideology in the Age of the Civil War* (1980); Peyton McCrary, *Abraham Lincoln and Reconstruction* (1978); Earl M. Maltz, *Civil Rights, the Constitution, and Congress, 1863–1869* (1990); Hans L. Trefousse, *Andrew Johnson* (1989).

African Americans in the Aftermath of Slavery

James D. Anderson, *The Education of Blacks in the South* (1989); Barbara J. Fields, *Slavery and Freedom on the Middle Ground* (1985); Eric Foner, *Nothing but Freedom* (1983); Herbert G. Gutman, *The Black Family in Slavery and Freedom* (1976); William S. McFeely, *Frederick Douglass* (1989); Lynda J. Morgan, *Emancipation in Virginia's Tobacco Belt* (1992); Joel Williamson, *After Slavery* (1965).

Life in the Postwar South

Jacqueline Jones, *Soldiers of Light and Love: Northern Teachers and Georgia Blacks, 1865–1873* (1980); Michael S. Perman, *The Road to Redemption* (1984); Michael Wayne, *The Reshaping of Plantation Society* (1983); Jonathan M. Wiener, *Social Origins of the New South* (1977).

Compromise of 1877 and the End of Reconstruction

William Gillette, *Retreat from Reconstruction, 1869–1879* (1979); C. Vann Woodward, *Reunion and Reaction; The Compromise of 1877 and the End of Reconstruction* (1956).

QUESTIONS FOR DISCUSSION

1. Assess Andrew Johnson's role in Reconstruction. Was he an aid or a deterrent to national reconciliation?
2. How was Congress able to seize control of the reconstruction process? What were the consequences of this change?
3. Describe the political relationship of African Americans, poor whites, and carpetbaggers in the newly reconstructed governments. Was this Republican coalition successful? Why or why not?
4. How did southern Democrats "redeem" the South?
5. Discuss and analyze the events leading up to the Compromise of 1877.
6. According to the selection by Leon Litwack, how did the Freedmen's Bureau become the tool of southern planters?
7. Was Reconstruction a success? Why or why not?

CHAPTER FOURTEEN

THE INDUSTRIAL REVOLUTION

In 1876 Americans celebrated the first century of the nation's independence with an infinite variety of activities. None, however, compared in scope to the celebration in Philadelphia, the site of the Centennial Exhibition which lasted for five months and attracted nearly 10 million visitors. Located in Fairmount Park, the exhibition consisted of a conglomeration of huge buildings, spectacular fountains, and numerous statues and monuments. Although its original purpose was to focus attention on the nation's achievements as revealed by its "arts, manufacture and products of the soil and mine," the most popular exhibits were those displaying an array of scientific and technological marvels. By all odds the favorite with visitors was the huge Corliss Steam Engine that weighed more than a million and a half pounds and that powered other exhibits. On display also was an assortment of machines and inventions for combing wool, spinning cotton, and printing newspapers as well as sewing machines, Pullman Palace Sleeping Cars, and an operating model of Alexander Graham Bell's telephone.

A visit to the exhibition convinced the novelist William Dean Howells that the American genius spoke most freely in machinery and technology, which for the time being took precedence over art and literature. For the aging poet John Greenleaf Whittier, who reluctantly agreed to write a centennial hymn but refused to visit the exhibition, the whirling machines at Philadelphia resembled nothing so much as the snake in the Garden of Eden. Whether the mechanical sights at the exhibition inspired optimistic forecasts of unparalleled progress or gloomy prophecies of the end of the republican dream, few failed to recognize that they represented forces which would transform American society.

POSTWAR INDUSTRIALIZATION

The process of industrialization that began early in the nation's history quickened in tempo and broadened in scope so dramatically after the Civil War that the postwar generation is commonly called the Age of the Industrial Revolution. By 1890, just as farm production reached unprecedented levels, the annual value of manufactured goods surpassed that of agricultural products, and nearly 60 percent of the labor force worked in nonagricultural jobs. By the end of the century the nation's railroads spanned the continent and linked together all sections in a transportation network whose rail mileage exceeded that of all European countries. Coinciding with this industrial expansion was the spectacular growth in the nation's population which increased from 31.5 million in 1860 to almost 76 million in 1900. Much of this population growth centered in cities. In the 1880s alone, eighty-eight cities doubled in size. Unevenly distributed geographically, urban growth was most evident in areas undergoing rapid industrial development, such as the Northeast and the Great Lakes region.

THE CAUSES OF RAPID INDUSTRIAL EXPANSION

A combination of circumstances and conditions existed in the post–Civil War decades which help explain the speed with which the industrial revolution occurred in the United States. Endowed with an abundance of natural resources essential to industrialization, such as iron and coal, the nation also possessed an adequate labor supply and available capital, from both domestic and foreign sources, for the financing of costly enterprises such as railroads and factories. Government policies and court decisions encouraged unrestricted economic development. Also important in promoting American industrialization was the existence of ample markets for manufactured goods, both at home and abroad. Nor was the nation lacking the technological expertise from Western European nations, which had industrialized earlier, but Americans themselves had traditionally been preoccupied with machines and gadgets, largely because of the country's historic shortage of labor. In the late nineteenth and early twentieth centuries the inventions of Alexander Graham Bell, Thomas A. Edison, George Westinghouse, George Pullman, and a host of others revolutionized industry, transportation, and communication. Many inventions patented before the Civil War came into use on a large scale in the postwar era. Finally, Americans embraced the work ethic and the notion of an open society in which every individual had an opportunity to achieve success. The public perception was that the careers of Andrew Carnegie, John D. Rockefeller, and other "captains of industry" confirmed the validity of their idea of the "self-made man," a concept popularized in the fiction of Horatio Alger. Inspired by desires to reap profits and impose order on a chaotic, unstable economy, many captains of industry were exemplars of the work ethic who displayed great ingenuity and skill in organizing complex industrial enterprises. If their methods in the marketplace often diverged sharply from traditional ethical practices, their private lives with few exceptions conformed to the tenets of Victorian morality.

The Railroads

The driving force behind the rapid industrialization of the United States was a rail system that tied together the country's vast geographic domain. By the end of the Civil War the nation had approximately thirty-five thousand miles of rails, virtually all located east of the Mississippi River. Despite two severe economic depressions, in the 1870s and 1890s, the rail network, including five transcontinentals, underwent such dramatic expansion that by 1900 the United States had 193,000 miles of railroads (see Figure 14–1). A succession of technological improvements enhanced the railroads' efficiency, safety, and profitability. Among these were the shift from iron rails to those made of more durable steel and the use of the coupler and airbrake.

The construction of railroads required huge amounts of investment capital. Although private capital, including a substantial amount from European sources, accounted for the bulk of funds consumed by railroads, government at all levels in the United States also provided assistance. The Pacific Railway Act of 1862, with its revisions in 1864, extended credit and made donations of public land to companies engaged in building transcontinentals. The joining of the Union Pacific and Central Pacific at Promontory, Utah, in 1869 marked the completion of the first transcontinental railroad. No less generous to railroads were state and local governments which provided loans, tax exemptions, and other forms of aid. Plagued by mismanagement, wasteful practices, overexpansion, and national economic fluctuations, railroads were chronically in need of bailout loans. Investment bankers, most notably J. Pierpont Morgan, who provided such loans, reorganized the nation's railroads, beginning in the 1890s, into seven systems that came to control almost two-thirds of the rail mileage in the United States.

Although much of the rhetoric about railroads depicted them as powerful agents of progress and civilization, their operation and management prompted much public criticism. Rising in tempo and severity, this criticism focused on fraudulent construction contracts, stock manipulation, rate policies, and various other issues. Indisputably, railroad companies were guilty of many of the charges made by their critics, but the government got reduced rates in transporting troops, freight, and mail on rail lines that received federal aid, and railroads also ultimately repaid government loans. More important, especially in the case of the transcontinentals, much of the land granted to rail companies acquired value as a result of the railroad's arrival. As a principal colonizer of the West, the railroad was both a cause and consequence of the westward movement. Regardless of the benefits derived from the construction of the rail system, increasing public pressure for government regulation of railroads prompted Congress in 1887 to enact the Interstate Commerce Act. Though important as a precedent in federal

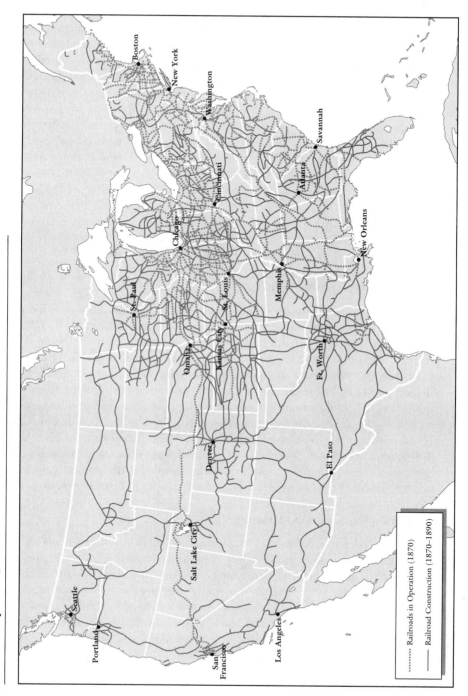

FIGURE 14–1
Railroad Expansion, 1870–1890

regulation, the law failed to eliminate practices that critics considered undesirable, in large part because of its vague language.

Whatever the abuses and misconduct of railroads, their construction and operation contributed in diverse ways to the emergence of a new industrial order. Not the least of these was their role in revolutionizing the nation's distribution system and in tying together all sections of the United States into a single economic unit. In addition, railroads reduced transportation costs, stimulated industrial developments through their enormous consumption of steel and other manufactured products, provided employment directly and indirectly to thousands of workers, inspired and used a wide range of new technologies, and accelerated the mobility of both people and goods. As the nation's first big business, railroads served as models for the large-scale enterprises that emerged in the late nineteenth century. If the railroad was decisive in shaping the modern American business organization, it was also the one aspect of the late-nineteenth-century industrial revolution which most thoroughly captured the American imagination. In the words of the poet Walt Whitman, the rail locomotive was "the modern emblem of motion and power—the pulse of the continent."

The Communication Revolution

During the period of rapid railroad expansion, the nation also experienced a revolution in communication. By 1861 telegraph lines extended across the continent. Often constructed alongside rail lines and operated by numerous competing companies until consolidated into the Western Union shortly after the Civil War, the telegraph made possible instantaneous communication between distant points and especially facilitated the operation of railroads. Even more important to speedy communication was the telephone, use of which spread rapidly in the quarter of a century after Alexander Graham Bell demonstrated his invention at the Centennial Exhibition in 1876. By the turn of the century, 1.3 million telephones were in service, and long-distance calls were commonplace. The communications network, coupled with the transportation system, provided the essential prerequisites for rapid industrial growth.

Corporate Expansion and Monopolies

With railroad companies as their organizational models, entrepreneurs created industrial enterprises of immense size, scope, and complexity. Ownership became separated from management. Companies owned and managed by individuals or a few partners gave way to large, rationally organized corporations owned by hundreds, even thousands, of stockholders and managed by salaried employees, who made up a new managerial class. Operating in a boom-and-bust environment characterized by disorder, unpredictability, and periodic depressions, corporate leaders in the late nineteenth century not only pursued a variety of strategies to achieve cost-effectiveness, greater production, and maximum profits; they also sought to impose order and stability on an unruly economy. In the pursuit of such objectives, some industries—especially the stronger, more ad-

The busy Union Pacific Railroad station in Omaha, Nebraska, in the late nineteenth century.

vanced ones, such as steel and oil refining—succeeded in eliminating their competitors. Some captains of industry engaged in stock manipulation, price-fixing and rigging, political bribery, and a variety of other unsavory practices.

The takeover of small companies, whether by means fair or foul, had the effect of concentrating enormous power in the hands of a few mammoth corporations. Once in monopolistic control of an entire industry, a corporation obviously found it easier to put into practice the principle of charging more than what the traffic would otherwise bear. The size and power of such corporations created alarm and outrage among a public accustomed to a simpler world of smaller economic units. Although Congress enacted the Sherman Antitrust Act in 1890 in response to popular demands to curb the abuses of corporations and to ensure the continuation of competition, corporate mergers in industry continued, even accelerated, in the 1890s under the direction of investment bankers who performed similar functions for railroads. By 1900 a few large companies dominated virtually all major facilities of production and distribution. Ten years later, fewer than 1 percent of the nation's companies produced 44 percent of its manufactured goods.

THE EFFECTS OF INDUSTRIALIZATION

By the turn of the century the captains of industry and their cohorts, the investment bankers, had succeeded in transforming the United States into the most productive industrial nation in the world (see Figure 14–2). Through the use of new technologies, machines, and sources of energy, organizational and

FIGURE 14–2
Industries and Resources, 1900–1920

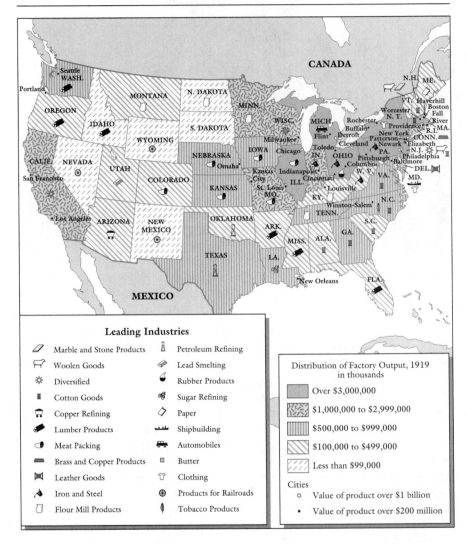

Leading Industries

▱	Marble and Stone Products	⚒	Petroleum Refining
🐑	Woolen Goods	◈	Lead Smelting
✳	Diversified	◔	Rubber Products
▮	Cotton Goods	◒	Sugar Refining
🗜	Copper Refining	◇	Paper
✒	Lumber Products	⚓	Shipbuilding
◑	Meat Packing	🚐	Automobiles
▬	Brass and Copper Products	◻	Butter
▣	Leather Goods	⛕	Clothing
⚒	Iron and Steel	⊕	Products for Railroads
◻	Flour Mill Products	◍	Tobacco Products

Distribution of Factory Output, 1919
in thousands

- Over $3,000,000
- $1,000,000 to $2,999,000
- $500,000 to $999,000
- $100,000 to $499,000
- Less than $99,000

Cities
- o Value of product over $1 billion
- • Value of product over $200 million

marketing innovations, and assembly line and other manufacturing techniques they created remarkably efficient systems of mass production and mass distribution—systems whose effects were pervasive.

The social consequences of the industrial revolution were especially evident in the changes in the family, the condition of women, and the class structure. Traditional family life was father-centered and home-centered, but the separation of work from the home and a family setting meant that fathers spent long hours in distant industrial workplaces. To supplement the family income and to make ends meet, lower-class women in increasing numbers also left home to work in factories and mills. Although the labor of children was exploited shamelessly by some industries, children in an industrial setting were generally less of an economic asset than they were on the farm; hence a decrease in the size of the family accompanied industrialization. In middle-income families the combination of fewer children and more labor-saving technology in the home freed women to engage in a variety of civic organizations and/or to enter white-collar jobs and professions.

Notwithstanding the popularity of Horatio Alger's tales of rags-to-riches, growing up in poverty in the late nineteenth century was not in the least conducive to the accumulation of great wealth. This is not to imply an absence of upward mobility but rather to suggest that there was also much downward mobility as well as a sizable population of permanent transients, that is poor people constantly moving from place to place and rarely factored into mobility statistics. Much of the upward mobility occurred among those who moved from the lower into the middle class, in large part because industrialization created a disproportionately large number of new positions in the middle-income ranges, especially managerial and clerical jobs and new skilled trades such as machinists.

Although scholars continue to disagree over whether industrialization made class lines more or less rigid, it is indisputable that the struggles for precedence at the top of the social scale between the old elites and the new rich sometimes assumed titanic proportions. In New York, for example, the struggle was especially fierce, pitting the old families such as the Livingstons and Beekmans, who placed as much emphasis on continuity and ancestry as on money, against the newly minted millionaires represented by the likes of the Vanderbilts and Goulds whose credentials consisted almost wholly of their wealth and penchant for conspicuous consumption. When the old elite refused to share control of the city's Academy of Music, the Vanderbilts and their circle sponsored the Metropolitan Opera which opened in 1883. The first *Social Register* which appeared five years later attempted to impose order on the chaos in high society by identifying those of both the new and old elites presumed to be entitled to social recognition and preference.

Though unevenly distributed, the material benefits of industrialization were sufficient to preclude mass support for socialism or other efforts to redirect the American socioeconomic order. The small radical organizations such as the Socialist Labor party of Daniel Deleon attracted little support among industrial workers. More successful was Eugene Debs' socialist movement launched late in the 1890s that won converts in certain industrial cities, but even so the vast majority of the labor force remained wedded to capitalism and traditional values.

Americans were often ambivalent and confused about the implications of large-scale industrialism and only slowly became reconciled to the changes that it brought about. Critics regularly pointed out that corporate enterprises rarely allowed social and human considerations to interfere with the pursuit of profits. To be sure, industrialization involved great costs in both human and natural resources. But in time the spread of the idea of philanthropy did ameliorate some of the social injustices and inequities. As articulated in 1899 by Andrew Carnegie in an essay entitled "The Gospel of Wealth," the new philanthropy was to avoid outright charity in favor of gifts that would enable people to help themselves. As a result, the captains of industry and business funneled their gifts to educational and medical institutions, libraries, recreational facilities, and even the arts.

THE LABOR FORCE

The triumph of industrialism in late nineteenth-century America owed much to the presence of an adequate labor force. Several developments in the era reversed the nation's historic shortage of labor. One was the use of machines to replace human labor both in the factory and on the farm. Much of the surplus farm population created by the mechanization of agriculture found employment in industry. At the same time, most of the foreign immigrants flooding into the country, as well as increasing numbers of women and children, entered the industrial labor market.

In April 1886 Andrew Carnegie, the steel mogul, rhapsodized about the relationship between labor and capital in the United States in an essay in *Forum* magazine. He praised labor unions as beneficial to both labor and capital, pronounced as sacred the right of workers to organize, and proclaimed the arrival

Andrew Carnegie, the steel mogul, at his desk, ca. 1890.

The construction of streetcar tracks in Washington, D.C., in 1891.

of the American worker to a position of equality with the "purchaser of his labor." Although such rhetoric reflected Carnegie's lifelong effort to reconcile the egalitarianism of his Scottish boyhood with his role as a multimillionaire industrial employer of tens of thousands of workers, it bore little resemblance to reality. The more than thirty-six thousand strikes that occurred in the quarter of a century after 1881 appeared to contradict Carnegie's picture of sweetness and light between labor and capital.

Published a few weeks before the violent eruption of labor unrest at Haymarket Square in Chicago early in May 1886, Carnegie's essay ironically appeared not on the eve of an era of labor-management harmony but rather at the very moment that widespread disorder erupted on the labor front. His musings, especially his reference to strikes and lockouts as ultimate absurdities, would return to haunt him in a very personal way six years later. The reorganization of the separate entities of Carnegie's empire into the Carnegie Steel Company, the largest in the world, on July 1, 1892, coincided with the company's involvement in a bloody and brutal conflict with the workers at its steel plant at Homestead, Pennsylvania. A lockout of workers by management as part of a strategy to crush the steel workers' union, coupled with a strike, paralyzed the huge Homestead plant until the Carnegie Company, backed by the state militia, imported enough immigrants and blacks as strikebreakers to reopen it. The failure of the Homestead Strike figured significantly in thwarting efforts to unionize the steel industry for many years.

The sources of labor's discontent in an era of rapid industrialization were both numerous and complex. Even though average wages did rise, such statistics obscure the fact that large segments of the labor force were regularly unemployed without access to relief from either private or governmental sources. Even in an ordinary year it was not unusual for a third of all industrial workers to be unemployed for as much as three or four months, a phenomenon created in large part by the volatile nature of the economy. In a similar vein, statistics regarding the average decline in the hours of labor can also be misleading. More rigid workplace rules and fewer breaks in the work schedule accompanied shorter hours. Because of the heavy investment in expensive machinery, a loss of time meant a loss of money for an industry. To maximize profits, industrialists established production quotas and instituted a piecework system, whereby a worker's wage was determined by productivity rather than by hours of labor. Pressure was applied to meet quotas which, if met, were then increased. Driven to the state of exhaustion by such an arrangement, workers became even more prone to accidents. The combination of unfamiliar machines and the absence of safety devices made some industries notoriously dangerous places to work. Each year thousands of workers were killed and seriously injured with little or no recourse for compensation.

The loss of the workers' autonomy on the factory floor, the reorganization of the work process, and the existence of dangerous conditions were by no means the only sources of labor's discontent. The expansion of industrial operations, along with changes in the design and control of work, resulted in larger, more impersonal workplaces in which labor came to be treated as a commodity rather than as a collection of human beings. The divorce of ownership from management in large-scale enterprises radically altered the environment in which labor operated. The manager of an industrial plant was no longer its owner but a salaried employee whose primary concern was meeting production schedules. Lost in this change was the paternalistic concern of an owner for his workers and the ability of workers to bargain individually. No component of the labor force was more profoundly affected by the Industrial Revolution than artisans and craftsmen, whose skills were often made obsolete by sophisticated machinery, leaving them with the options of either sliding downward to the status of an unskilled worker or learning a new skill. The displacement and degradation of the elite of the workplace was a potent factor in creating a profound sense of grievance within the ranks of labor.

LABOR'S EFFORTS TO ORGANIZE

If, as has often been noted, industrial capitalism gave rise to powerful labor unions in the United States, it is no less true that labor's quest for effective national organizations proved to be protracted and difficult. One obstacle was ideology. Unlike their European counterparts, American workers lacked a class consciousness that translated into the idea of labor solidarity: instead they accepted the idea of a profit-oriented society, thought of themselves as would-be capitalists awaiting the big chance, and believed that the surest way to advance was through individual initiative rather than collective action. Nor were they unaffected by the widespread tendency to equate unions with violence, foreigners, and radicalism. Encouraged by industrialists, such notions appeared to be validated by the terrorist activities of a secret society of coal miners in Pennsylvania, known as the Molly McGuires, in the 1870s, Chicago's Haymarket Riot of 1886, and the violent Homestead Strike in 1892. Small wonder, then, that the American labor movement was basically conservative and persistently encountered problems in staying organized.

Considerations other than ideology, of course, accounted for the slow development of broad-based, effective labor unions. One was the opposition of management, which engaged in a variety of antiunion activities, including the use of blacklists and yellow dog contracts. Local, state, and federal governments were also antiunion and often intervened in labor disturbances on the side of industrialists as they did in the Great Railway Strike (1877), the Haymarket Riot, the Homestead Affair, and the Pullman Strike (1894). Labor's limited experience with unions, much less with the type of organizations required to be effective in the era of the new industrialism, also posed obstacles to unionization. Such labor organizations as existed at the end of the Civil War were narrowly based craft unions whose membership represented less than 10 percent of the industrial wage earners. As industry expanded, so did the size of the unskilled workforce, which had no place in the elitist organizations of skilled workers.

No one knew better than Andrew Carnegie the disunity that characterized American industrial labor. "There are more grades and ranks in labour," he observed, "than in educated society." Carnegie also understood the extent to which the heterogeneous nature of the labor force deterred unionization. Into his steel plants poured a hodgepodge of native-born whites and blacks from both urban and rural backgrounds and an ever-increasing number of foreign-born workers, representing a variety of cultural traditions, religious preferences, languages, and prejudices. Racial, ethnic, and religious animosities divided rather than unified workers as did the barriers to communication created by their diversity of languages. Further complicating the task of organizing strong and stable unions were patterns of social mobility which produced an industrial workforce characterized by widely disparate levels of expectations. Not surprisingly, the fragmentation of industrial labor produced a succession of competing ideas about organizational strategies and goals.

The three best-known unions organized after the Civil War reflected the differences in labor philosophies. The first, the National Labor Union (NLU), founded in 1866, embraced political action as the means to advance the workers' cause. Wedded to the Jacksonian ideal of an economy made up of small, independent producers, the NLU invoked the rhetoric of abolitionism in denouncing the wage slavery of modern industrialization and advocated a scheme of worker-controlled cooperatives to rescue the toiling masses. Allied with various other reform groups, the union sponsored a third party in 1872 which barely made a ripple in the election. The NLU disappeared during the depression of the 1870s.

Filling the void was the Noble and Holy Order of the Knights of Labor, organized in 1869, whose bent toward reform resembled that of its predecessor, even though it displayed less interest in political action. Initially, a secret ritualistic society opposed to the use of strikes, the Knights rejected the trade union model as too narrowly based and attempted to organize into a single union everyone who toiled, regardless of sex, race, or skill. The only exceptions were those such as lawyers, bankers, and a few others considered immoral despoilers of the working class. Its aim was to replace the exploitative, competitive system of industrialism with a "cooperative commonwealth." The organization had a membership of nearly three-quarters of a million workers by the mid-1880s; it abandoned its secrecy and ritual, and ironically began to function more like a trade union. Just as the Knights' popularity crested, the union suffered a rapid decline. Flaws in its organizational structure and decision-making process, and its inability to maintain the solidarity of its polyglot membership during the antiunion hysteria created by the Haymarket Riot combined to reduce its effectiveness as a broad-based union. By 1900 the Knights of Labor had virtually disappeared and with it the idea of one big union of all workers and the vision of an inclusive workingmen's democracy to replace the exploitative, competitive system of industrial capitalism.

The successor to the Knights was the American Federation of Labor (AFL), founded in 1886 and headed by Samuel Gompers, its architect and guiding spirit, from the beginning (except for a year) until his death in 1924. Except for its advocacy of the eight-hour day and immigration restriction, the AFL bore little resemblance to its two predecessors. Intensely practical in its approach, the union accepted the wage system and rejected any notion of a grand association of all workers. As a coalition of existing trade unions, it consisted almost entirely of skilled craftsmen who excluded blacks, recent immigrants, and women from their ranks. Placing a low priority on reform and political activities, the AFL focused on the bread-and-butter issues of wages, hours, and working conditions and considered the strike as the most valuable weapon in securing for labor an equitable share of the fruits of industrial capitalism. For Gompers, the central goal was to obtain sufficient power for the AFL in the workplace to compel employers to accept the principle of collective bargaining. In the pursuit of this goal the union centralized authority in the hands of national officials and used increased union dues not only to build up a treasury to aid workers in times of unemployment and strikes, but also to ensure a well disciplined membership less likely to cave in under pressure and to prevent constituent trade unions from acting at cross purposes.

The staying power of the narrowly based AFL stood in sharp contrast to that of its predecessors. Although it possessed a membership in excess of 1.5 million in the early years of the twentieth century, it remained an organization of the aristocracy of labor, closed to unskilled workers and slow to adapt to the changing organization and requirements of the workplace. Despite occasional successes in winning concessions from the management, labor unions remained weak throughout the late nineteenth century. By 1900 only a tiny fraction of the American workforce held membership in any labor organization.

FIGURE 14–3
Sources of Immigration

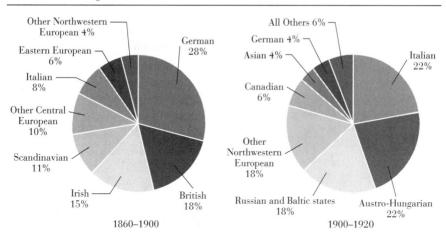

Other Northwestern European 4%
Eastern European 6%
Italian 8%
Other Central European 10%
Scandinavian 11%
Irish 15%
British 18%
German 28%

1860–1900

All Others 6%
German 4%
Asian 4%
Canadian 6%
Italian 22%
Other Northwestern European 18%
Russian and Baltic states 18%
Austro-Hungarian 22%

1900–1920

SOURCE: Data from *Historical Statistics of the United States, Colonial Times to 1970* (White Plains, NY: Kraus International, 1989), pp. 105-109

IMMIGRANTS IN THE LABOR FORCE

Throughout the era of the industrial revolution an increasing proportion of the nation's labor supply consisted of foreign-born peoples. The United States was, of course, a nation of nations and had welcomed immigrants from the beginning, but in the late nineteenth century those coming into the country changed both in terms of numbers and places of origin. In its first century, the United States attracted immigrants primarily from northern and western Europe, especially Great Britain, Ireland, Germany, and Scandinavia. Although the old immigrants continued to come to America, the new immigrants from southern and eastern Europe—Italy, Russia, Poland, and the Balkans—began to arrive in ever larger numbers in the 1880s. By 1910 almost 8.5 million new immigrants had settled in the United States (see Figure 14–3). Except for the East European Jews, these people came from rural areas and were generally poor. A majority were young males in their prime productive years who, upon entering the industrial labor force, readily accepted the least attractive, lowest-paying jobs and often served as strikebreakers. Even though their living and working conditions were often appalling, the new immigrants, with their lower expectations, found life in the United States far superior to that in southern and eastern Europe.

The arrival of so many new immigrants who diverged sharply from the prevailing white Protestant norm aroused concern among native-born Americans. Predominantly Roman Catholic and Jewish in religion, these immigrants tended to be swarthy in complexion, spoke a variety of unfamiliar languages, often embraced anticapitalistic ideologies, and generally appeared far more alien to the dominant culture than the old immigrants. That the new immigrants flocked to industrial cities and established themselves in a mosaic of ethnic enclaves made them all the more conspicuous and different. The alien qualities of the flood of immigrants pouring into the country, especially those from southern and eastern Europe, convinced many natives that they could never be assimilated into American society and indeed posed a threat to democracy. Fed by a complex of political, economic, and religious fears, hostility toward immigrants took many forms, some subtle and others overt. Among the more tangible expressions of this prejudice were the American Society for the Suppression of Jews, the anti-Catholic American Protective Association, the Immigration Restriction League, and the restrictionist crusades of labor unions. After almost two decades of agitation, the antiimmigrant forces triumphed in the era of World War I. The postwar decade witnessed the enactment of legislation that ended the nation's tradition of unlimited immigration.

THE EMERGENCE OF THE MODERN CITY

The concentration of immigrants, as well as native-born migrants, in large urban centers was but one indication that the modern city was a product of industrialization. Centered there were factories, mills, and sweatshops, large pools of labor and consumers of manufactured products, headquarters of corporate giants, financial institutions, and systems of transportation, communication, and marketing. As industry expanded in scope and scale, cities increased in size, complexity, and impersonality. Characterized by incredible motion and mobility, both physical and social, the new industrial city also witnessed the emergence of a complex of tensions and rivalries between, and even within, the diverse ethnic, racial, and economic groups concentrated there.

The emergence of urban America prompted by the industrial revolution brought in its wake multiple problems related to housing, transportation, health, and public services. That Americans embraced a philosophy of laissez-faire and lacked experience in governing and managing large, complex metropolises ensured that such problems would not be solved systematically or quickly. The spectacular, chaotic growth of older cities and the mushrooming of new ones, in fact, occurred without planning or direction. The result was the multiplication of squalid slums, noise, smoke, and opportunities for political corruption. Foreign observers regularly remarked on both the misgovernment and ugliness of American cities. Not until the early twentieth century did the United States witness nationwide campaigns to improve the quality of life in cities through systematic planning, structural reforms, and beautification efforts.

The modern metropolis contrasted sharply with the preindustrial city. Lacking either inexpensive public transit or well-defined business, industrial, and residential districts, the preindustrial city was a compact walking city in which rich and poor, native and foreign-born peoples lived in close proximity to each other and to their workplaces. The mature industrial city presented an entirely different picture. It was a new type of urban community that developed distinct districts—business and banking, industrial and residential—and separated people according to ethnicity, nationality, and social status. The industrial city expanded in two directions simultaneously: vertically and horizontally. Improvements in structural steel, glass and other building materials and the invention of the electric elevator combined with the creativity of architects to make possible the nation's first skyscrapers—a development encouraged by the soaring cost of urban real estate. No less dramatic was the city's horizontal expansion, due in large part to cheap public transportation provided by cable cars, electric trolleys, or streetcars to suburbs. The emergence of these satellite cities, linked to but separated from the city itself and often fiercely protective of their independence, significantly altered the social geography of urban America. A sorting process occurred as the more affluent took refuge in the cleaner, quieter, greener suburbs, leaving behind the poor, immigrant, and blue-collar peoples to cope with the overcrowded tenements, smoke, noise, and traffic congestion of the city. By the turn of the century, large American cities contained multiple residential districts, clearly identified by class, ethnicity, and race. With few exceptions, the farther the residence was from the inner city, the more prestigious its address, a pattern that would persist into the late twentieth century.

The new industrial cities, despite the confusion that accompanied their emergence, permanently altered the face of the nation and created a new American both sociologically and psychologically distinct from his or her rural counterpart. By 1910 nearly half of the nation's population was classified as urban. Notwithstanding the popular nostalgia for the agrarian republic of the past and frequent expressions of anticity prejudices, the United States by the turn of the century was indeed an industrial nation of cities, an authentic expression of American pluralism.

THE RURAL REGIONS OF AMERICA

The more than half of the nation's population which lived in rural America in 1900 exhibited both antipathy toward the alien culture of the industrial city and an irresistible attraction to its bright lights. Despite such ambivalence, rural Americans both contributed to and were profoundly affected by the processes of industrialization and urbanization taking place in the country. The predominantly rural, agricultural West and South provided raw materials for the industries concentrated in the Northeast and Great Lakes region which in turn marketed an infinite variety of manufactured products, including farm implements and machinery, in the West and South. Such products dramatically altered the quality of life in these rural regions.

In the late nineteenth century, neither the West nor South possessed the combination of ingredients necessary to undertake large-scale industrial development. The sparsely populated West contained vast areas of uninhabited territory. A combination of developments in the late nineteenth century prompted a westward shift of the nation's population. The discovery of gold and silver in the

FIGURE 14-4
Indian Reservations, 1875 and 1900

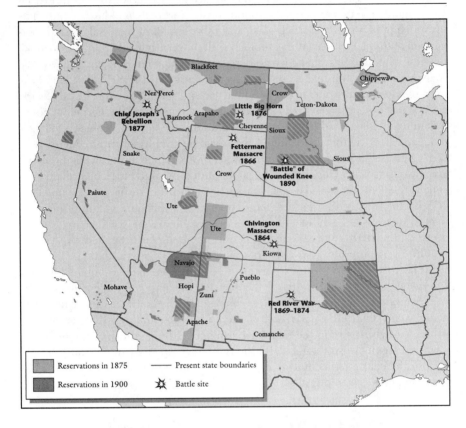

West attracted easterners in search of quick riches; others rushed westward to take advantage of the cheap land made available by the Homestead Act (1862). Trapped between a mining frontier moving eastward from the coast of California and an agricultural frontier advancing westward from the Mississippi, Indians on the Great Plains mounted disunified efforts to retain their lands in the area—efforts defeated by the United States Army (see Figure 14–4). Federal legislation not only consigned the remaining Indians to reservations and sought to transform them into farmers, but also aided railroad construction in the West. Agriculture, especially wheat growing, flourished in an area once known as the "Great American Desert"; six new western states entered the Union in 1889–1890; towns multiplied and those along railroads grew into small cities. The census of 1890 revealed that the traditional concept of a western frontier had come to an end.

All the while, the post–Civil War South, devastated by the conflict and burdened with the consequences of defeat, persisted in its antebellum preoccupation with cotton cultivation.

Beginning in the 1880s, the South embraced the so-called New South doctrine, a formula for economic development that envisioned industrialization as the key to solving the region's poverty. Because the South lacked the capital to finance industrialization, New South boosters turned to northern capitalists. But northern investment in southern industry came with a hefty price tag, namely the imposition of restrictions to ensure that southern industrialization was subservient to, rather than competitive with, the industrial Northeast. To be sure, the South witnessed an increase in cotton mills, timber-related enterprises, and other low-wage, labor-intensive industries that buttressed its status as an economic colony of the North. Not even the extravagant claims of New South enthusiasts could obscure the fact that the South entered the twentieth century as an overwhelmingly rural, agricultural region mired in poverty, illiteracy, and the politics of race. Both the South and West underscored the uneven distribution of industrialization in late-nineteenth-century America.

In the following essay, Maury Klein, the biographer of Jay Gould and the author of numerous other works relating to the Industrial Revolution in late-nineteenth-century America, assesses the various images of the robber barons that emerged over time. For better or worse, he argues, these business leaders were not only products of their culture but reflections of it as well.

THE ROBBER BARONS
Maury Klein

It is now well over a hundred years since the Industrial Revolution began to transform every facet of American life, and we still do not comprehend the full meaning of that process. No other revolution in man's long history caused such sweeping and fundamental changes as those wrought by the interaction of industrialism, science, and technology. The results of this startling transition from an individualistic agrarian society to a highly organized industrial one have been at best a mixed blessing. Small wonder, then, that several generations of Americans, hard pressed to be kept abreast of their fast-changing world, have viewed the pioneers of industrialism with mingled emotions.

from Maury Klein, "The Robber Barons," *American History Illustrated* (October 1971), 13–22.

The early stages of industrial development in the United States took place in an environment unusually free from social and legal restraints. It tended to be fluid in form, chaotic, ruthless, and highlighted by the spectacular exploits of individual participants. Out of this titanic struggle, this clash of iron wills and grand visions, there emerged a complex landscape strewn with astonishing productivity, broken dreams, and a new sense of organization to order and systematize the gains that had been made.

The whole of this experience was simply too much for most observers to fathom. It was clear that a new society with new institutions and relationships was emerging, but it was so vast and intricate as to defy description. The ideals, values, and attitudes of an earlier America did not easily fit this new context, yet they could not easily be abandoned. Unable to interpret this strange society comfortably in old terms or find acceptable new ones, most Americans resorted to a traditional tactic. They tried to understand the new order and its institutions in terms of the men who seemed to be responsible for creating them.

It is hardly surprising, therefore, that their interpretation of business leaders depended upon their reaction to the industrial experience itself. To most Americans, two conspicuous developments characterized the new industrial order. One was the fantastic increase in production and productivity, which seemed to promise a future blessed with material abundance and freedom from want. Many Americans regarded this horn of plenty as the very essence of progress, the natural reward for a free and enterprising people.

Unfortunately, the second obvious fruit of industrialism, the concentration of this new wealth into a few hands, threatened to contradict this rosy vision. It was to be expected that some men would profit more than others from their contribution to the new order, but the scale of their rewards and the extent of their personal power were unprecedented. Before long, critics arose to challenge both the wisdom and the justice of allowing a select few to reap so unequal a share of the new wealth regardless of who they were or what they had done.

Defenders of the industrial and financial moguls conceded their enormous profits but denied they were excessive. They pointed to the benefits such men had bestowed upon society as a whole: more goods of better quality at lower prices, cheaper and more efficient transportation, new markets, a dazzling variety of products, more jobs, and higher wages.

One noted businessman, Edward Atkinson, sounded this theme in a speech delivered in 1886. Discussing the railroad system developed by Cornelius Vanderbilt, he admitted that the commodore earned about fourteen cents profit on every barrel of flour shipped over his lines. But at the same time he saved shippers and consumers alike even greater sums and thereby lowered the price of flour. "Did Vanderbilt keep any of you down," Atkinson challenged, "by saving you two dollars and seventy-five cents on a barrel of flour while he was making fourteen cents?"

From the beginning, then, Americans tended to interpret the industrial experience in terms of its apparent authors. Enterprising and energetic men had devised new organizations and methods of production, new products, and modes of distribution.

They came to be regarded as "industrial statesmen" by those who applauded their contribution. Critics of the new order deplored its unequal distribution of wealth, the questionable methods used to gain supremacy, and the tawdry consequences that resulted from the scramble for riches. They viewed the "industrial statesmen" not as pioneering innovators but as predators, industrial pirates, or later, robber barons.

The origin of the term "robber barons" is not entirely clear, but after 1900 it became so widely used as to become synonymous with American business leaders of the late 19th century. For decades these polar extremes of industrial statesmen versus robber barons shaped the boundaries of the debate over American industrial development. That is not surprising, for after all the entrepreneurs personified the glories, agonies, and complexities of the new orders.

No specific business leader neatly fitted either extreme label. Even their severest critics admitted that the robber barons made positive and often valuable contributions to national economic development. On the other hand, admirers of the industrial statesmen recognized that the most creative entrepreneurs some-times resorted to shady practices or made serious mistakes of judgment. The disagreement centered rather upon their role and impact upon American life. Since the record of any individual was a mixed one, the problem became one of drawing a proper balance.

At first the robber baron advocates had the better of the argument. The growth of huge monopolistic enterprises produced deep public apprehension over the power wielded by big corporations in the economy. Most people associated these organizations with specific individuals, who promptly became the targets of intense criticism. The activities of these businessmen were often colorful and spectacular. Indeed, the very scale upon which they operated made them mysterious and awesome figures, capable of influencing the destinies of thousands of people by their manipulations.

Like all American heroes they loomed larger than life in the public imagination. They were men of large ambitions who pursued their grand visions with relentless vigor. They seemed to possess all the attributes of many earlier public idols: courage, cunning, shrewdness, and above all, boldness. Most men harbored great dreams but lacked the means and the will to achieve them. Not the robber barons. They seemed to transcend the limitations of mere mortals. True, they could be ruthless and unscrupulous. They manipulated men and laws alike to suit their purpose. But they had the daring to get what they wanted, and that earned them the grudging admiration even of their critics.

These critics distinguished between two broad types of robber barons. The first kind might be called industrial pirates, for they were considered predators in the truest sense. They were essentially manipulators interested only in advancing their own fortunes at the expense of whatever individuals and institutions they touched. They cared little for creating anything of lasting value. Their function was parasitic and their contribution to economic development minimal or nonexistent. They were engaging rogues, colorful, dynamic, and exciting, but primarily plunderers and destroyers.

Of all the robber barons Jay Gould best personified this type in the view of most critics. Frail of stature and racked with consumption, he earned from Matthew

Josephson the sobriquet "the Mephistopheles of Wall Street." Endowed with a brilliantly analytical mind, he mastered the intricacies of financial manipulation with a thoroughness and verve unmatched by any of his peers. Coldly calculating in his approach, he worked as a loner, allying himself with others whenever necessary to achieve a given end but refusing to be bound by considerations of loyalty or friendship.

Like most loners, Gould's ultimate purposes and innermost thoughts remained unfathomed. He pursued his immediate objectives with remorseless logic. He seemed uninterested in possessing power or glory or acclaim. Neither social interests nor the desire to erect enduring monuments structured his quests. He was a dark, mysterious genius with a penetrating eye for unearthing the realities of a financial opportunity. He was, perhaps, the ultimate technician, dedicating his talent and intensity only to the game itself.

The examples of his genius were numerous and legendary. He possessed a gift for turning every situation to his own advantage regardless of the consequences to the enterprise or his associates. His venture into New York City's rapid transit system in 1881 illustrates his style. Sensing the future value of that property, Gould determined to seize control of the two companies then existing, the Manhattan Elevated and New York Elevated Railways. His chief weapons were to be the courts, the New York *World*, a newspaper he had purchased in 1873, and Western Union Telegraph Company, which he had just acquired in a recent coup. His tactic was to harass the management and convince the stockholders to sell out cheaply.

In May 1881, New York's Attorney General Hamilton Ward, a Gould henchman, opened proceedings for bringing suit to annul the charter to Manhattan Elevated on behalf of the state. The *World* promptly launched a campaign against the company's owners in which charges of insolvency and conspiracy flowed freely. At the same time the telegraph wires buzzed with rumors and carefully garbled messages. The curiosity of Wall Street and the general public, at first casual, mounted steadily.

While the *World*'s editorial and financial writers hacked away mercilessly at the company, Gould's lawyers launched a barrage of writs and injunctions. A friendly judge prepared to petition for bankruptcy; the Manhattan Elevated's stock dropped from 57 to 29 in short order. At that point Gould and his allies, including the eminent Cyrus Field, began to buy the stock until they held controlling interest. Abruptly the journalists and lawyers ceased their onslaught and declared the company solvent in its new hands. The stock advanced steadily with the help of covert boosts from the controlling syndicate.

Once in command Gould installed Field as titular head of Manhattan Elevated and increased the company's capitalization. Most of the new funds went into the syndicate's pockets and fares were raised to ten cents to carry this heavier capital burden. When these events aroused public indignation, Field wavered before the outcry. Despite Gould's objection he determined to lower fares to a nickel and persuaded some stockholders to support him. To bolster his position, Field also began to buy large amounts of Manhattan Elevated stock.

Annoyed by Field's defection, Gould joined with a favorite partner in the syndicate, Russell Sage, to lay a typically cunning snare. They cheerfully sold shares to Field until he had by their calculations overextended himself, whereupon they led a devastating raid upon the market. The price of Manhattan Elevated broke almost in half and destroyed Field's credit, leaving him ruined and helpless. Gould and Sage then stepped forward with an offer to relieve Field of his Manhattan Elevated securities at bargain basement prices. Although the transaction cost him millions, Field had no choice but to accept and retire from the company.

The Manhattan Elevated venture revealed Gould at his predatory best. He manipulated men, media, and the courts to achieve control of a company. Once in command he deranged its finances to suit his own needs. His mismanagement of an enterprise was a deliberate, calculated course of action. Having wrung maximum personal profit from the company, he would gracefully retire leaving in his wake a gutted and bankrupt enterprise. Occasionally he might return to the same victim again, as he did with the Union Pacific Railroad. With only one venture, the Missouri Pacific system, did he remain long enough to develop some real interest in its long-term success or failure.

It was easy for critics to denounce the Jay Goulds and their associates as robber barons or industrial pirates. They defied the law, ignored social and business custom, and cared nothing for the enterprises they exploited and frequently wrecked. Unhampered by ethical restraints, they ruined their adversaries by resorting to deceit and stealth. They seemed to take everything and give nothing.

The same objections could not be leveled against the second type of robber baron. He was the businessman referred to as an "industrial statesman" by those who rejected the robber baron argument. An observer who viewed the businessmen of the era in a more favorable light would likely make a careful distinction between a Jay Gould on one hand and an Andrew Carnegie or John D. Rockefeller on the other.

The main difference between the two types was that Carnegie and Rockefeller and their breed were builders rather than wreckers. They accumulated vast personal fortunes but they also founded huge enterprises and remained closely identified with them. They dealt with basic products, improved their quality, lowered their price, and increased their output. They pioneered a host of technological innovations that revolutionized American industrial production. They devised new organizations and techniques to administer enterprises on an unprecedented scale.

In short, these entrepreneurs forged the basis for our modern complex industrial society. Neither their critics nor their defenders denied them this role, but they interpreted its results and by-products differently. What separated critics and defenders, then, were not differences of fact so much as differences of values. In their arguments each side emphasized different aspects of the same careers. Naturally the critics concentrated on negative qualities while the defenders stressed the more positive achievements.

The varying treatment of John D. Rockefeller is a good case in point. As the nation's most conspicuous symbol of big business, Standard Oil probably received more publicity than any other corporation in America. Alternately praised and damned, it drew fire from virtually every quarter. Almost invariably, however, critics and defenders alike regarded the company as the creature of its founding genius. Any evaluation of Standard Oil soon evolved into an analysis of Rockefeller himself.

The defenders saw in Rockefeller's career an unparalleled success story, a definitive episode in the American Dream, and an invaluable contribution to American economic development. He personified the saga dearest to the American's heart: "the poor boy who rose to riches through hard work and determination." To his strong dedication and self-discipline he added a deep religious piety. Lean of body and ascetic in tastes, he considered work a duty and had few pleasures beyond it.

As a businessman Rockefeller was unrivalled. Once having decided to enter the petroleum industry, he stayed with it for the rest of his business career. He first conceived the notion that the best way to stabilize the erratic petroleum industry was to "organize a commonly owned unit on a national scale." In patient, methodical fashion he worked toward that goal. Always amenable to new ideas, he succeeded in persuading other talented men, many of them former rivals, to join his combination and work together.

Rockefeller concluded that refining offered the best chance for stability and growth in the chaotic oil industry. He started a refinery in Cleveland in 1865 and five years later formed the Standard Oil Company of Ohio. From the beginning the company pursued an expansionist policy. It acquired other refineries such as Long Island Oil Company, and vital auxiliary enterprises making such products as lumber, paint, barrels, siding, lighters, tankage, tank cars, and warehouses. As Rockefeller acquired rival refineries, he often convinced able men in these firms to join Standard's management.

The parent company rapidly became a community of interests turning all its energy toward the quest for stability. Utilizing every resource at hand, including market connections, leases, railroad rebates, patent and trademark controls, and pooling mechanisms, Standard relentlessly made its operations more efficient. It made a superior product, sold it for less, and drove its competitors into bankruptcy or induced them to join the combination. By 1881 Standard possessed more than forty subsidiary firms and threatened to become administratively unwieldy unless some new organization was devised.

Rockefeller and his peers met this challenge by forming the great Standard Oil Trust. The new organization contained numerous weaknesses but at least permitted the development of fully centralized managerial control over a multi-state operation at a time when no Federal incorporation law yet existed. Two new organizations were created in 1882 for this purpose: Standard Oil of New Jersey and Standard Oil of New York. New managerial techniques, based on the committee system, were evolved to run the trust's far-flung operations efficiently.

The new organization prospered mightily. Directed by its brilliant, tightly disciplined officers, the trust developed a solidarity and efficiency of management unmatched by companies that were much smaller and less complicated. In this task Rockefeller acted not as dictator but as chairman. He did not issue orders but rather acted as team captain, presiding over meetings where policy was debated and decided by consensus. His genius lay in his ability to keep his officers working together in an atmosphere of discipline, frankness, and mutual respect. To ensure this team effort, all the trust's top managers were installed in one building at 26 Broadway in New York.

By the 1880's Standard Oil had become the largest and most powerful corporation in the nation. Strict attention to detail steadily reduced costs even while the trust expanded its activities. New processes were introduced and integrated, new products were developed, and quality steadily improved. Slowly the company branched into marketing; later it would integrate backward into oil production. Rockefeller constantly spurred his colleagues toward a policy of large volume and narrow profit margins. To achieve this end he did not hesitate to use price-cutting at both national and local levels.

In 1884 Standard owned 77 percent of America's refining capacity and marketed nearly 85 percent of its total petroleum products. There would be no complete monopoly, however, for the growth of large rival firms steadily reduced Standard's proportional share of the facilities and the market even though Standard continued to grow as well. By 1892 the company had achieved full vertical integration—controlling its products from the wells to the consumer.

To Rockefeller's defenders, the Standard Oil colossus was to be admired as both an unparalleled success story and a monument to the free enterprise system. It provided the public with a variety of quality products formerly unavailable to people at prices they could afford. Rockefeller and his cohorts had imposed stability upon a once chaotic cutthroat industry. They had rationalized and organized a vital sector of American economic development and given it an important position in foreign and domestic markets. They had created thousands of jobs, stimulated the development of many new industries, and pioneered in significant administrative and technological innovations. They were, in short, agents of progress, and their contribution to society was beneficial.

The critics thought otherwise. Conceding Standard's positive achievements, which elevated Rockefeller above a predator like Gould, they still portrayed its officers as robber barons and in many ways more dangerous types. First of all, they condemned his tactics and lack of business ethics. That he was pious and devoutly Christian did not in the least excuse his ruthlessness. He marched to his goals with the conviction of a crusader. Lacking any doubt in the righteousness of his cause, he was reputed to have said, "I had our plan clearly in mind. It was right. I knew it as a matter of conscience. It was right between me and my God. If I had to do it tomorrow I would do it again in the same way—do it a hundred times."

What he did was simply to crush anyone or anything in his way. He undersold competitors into bankruptcy and compelled them to join the combination or be destroyed. He broke every attempt by the oil producers to organize themselves while he spurred the refiners into unity and consolidation. He coerced the railroads into giving Standard rebates on not only its own oil but on that of its competitors as well. Through such devices as the notorious South Improvement Company he conspired to monopolize the oil industry, ruin those who opposed him, and extract maximum profits from a helpless public. He was accused of spying on his rivals, sabotaging their businesses, and maintaining a small army of agents for whatever dirty work needed to be done.

The results of Rockefeller's tactics outraged the critics no less than the tactics themselves. However successful and efficient his operation, it prospered on the ruins of smaller, less competent enterprise systems; he had destroyed the system itself by eliminating its cornerstone, free competition. Once Standard had established its dominance, smaller firms could never again compete in the industry except as hirelings of Standard or as a component of some gigantic rival corporation.

In either case Rockefeller had driven the industry to organize into huge companies whose survival depended upon sheer size and strength. No place was left for the little man or the independent operator except at the pleasure of the giants.

Once in command, these giant corporations could conspire to control prices and production. The public was virtually helpless to affect their policies even through anti-trust legislation. The economic power accumulated by Standard and by Rockefeller personally rendered them impervious to social or political pressure. They were truly robber barons holding sway over a captive public. Whatever their contribution to "progress," they were the new ruling class.

Virtually the same characterization was applied to Carnegie, Philip Armour, Gustavus Swift, Henry Havemeyer, Cornelius Vanderbilt, E. H. Harriman, and the other "constructive" robber barons. The fact that many of them had been poor boys who made good, that some were pious Christians with simple tastes, or that several gave most of their fortunes away to worthy causes made no difference in their essential impact upon American life. They were charged with perverting the free enterprise system, destroying economic opportunity, fostering a grossly unequal distribution of wealth, and callously exploiting smaller businessmen, workers, and consumers alike.

Most of these indictments against the robber barons were actually indictments against the industrial process itself. In praising or condemning these business leaders, critics and defenders were reacting to the vast changes wrought in American life by the economic revolution. Thus they held the robber barons personally responsible for what had occurred, and identified them as the primary agent of change.

More often than not this response was heavily charged with emotion. Men felt deeply the bewildering complexities of an emerging industrial society. Few could divine any coherent order in the process, much less comprehend the meaning of it all. Politicians, writers, businessmen, and philosophers alike, as they strove to glimpse the future, wavered erratically between visions of Utopia and apocalypse. How could it be otherwise at a time when man's destiny was hurtling him down a new and unknown course? The broad underlying causes could not always be grasped, but someone had to be held accountable whether as saints or devils.

For much of the 20th century this emotional, individualistic interpretation prevailed among businessmen, politicians, scholars, and anyone else who thought about the matter. Within the past twenty years, however, the whole industrial experience has been re-examined in a different light. The new approach, seeking to be more analytical and objective, tried to neutralize the virulent controversy over the role of the robber barons by focusing attention upon such underlying themes as organizational and institutional development.

The effect of this new approach upon the image of the robber barons was profound. It did not alter that image so much as soften and blend it. Most businessmen were acknowledged to have been both pirates and pioneers. They differed only in degree, not in kind. The important point, however, was that they were now seen more as creatures of their environment than creators of it. They remained the leading actors in the drama of American industrial development, but their roles were reduced in scope and fitted into a much broader landscape.

The new approach played down the significance of individual exploits and es-capades, however spectacular they may have been. It stressed instead the growth of organizations on an unprecedented scale as the most important fact of the industrial era. The robber barons had achieved power, fame, and fortune by creating and dominating great corporations, but the instruments eventually succeeded in di-minishing the influence of individual men in any sector of society.

How did this happen? In simple terms, the early industrial era, with its lack of social and legal restraints, had pitted businessmen against each other in savage com-petition. To gain advantages they joined together, pooled their resources, and devised new organizations to increase their leverage. The scale of combat grew steadily as did the size of the markets over which they fought. Technological break-throughs revolutionized production techniques and fostered operations of gigantic proportions.

These operations required large labor forces and massive amounts of capital. They also required new organizations and administrative techniques if they were to be run efficiently. Slowly but steadily business became bureaucratized along the lines marked out by Standard Oil. The power of these organizations gave them immense advantages in their dealings with individuals or weaker institutions. Partly for this reason other sectors of society began to organize on a large scale. Once the federal government's vital role in social and economic issues was acknowledged, its bu-reaucracy swelled steadily. Workers joined unions, professional men formed their own groups, and before long nearly every kind of interest group found it necessary to form some kind of organization.

The corporation was only the most dominant and conspicuous of the organi-zations that structured American life. Their total impact upon existing relationships and institutions was enormous and far-reaching. Above all, they dwarfed the impact of individual action and minimized the ability of men to bring about change. For or-ganizations, unlike men, could endure forever and tended to perpetuate themselves once they were created. They were not easily destroyed and resisted modification if only because of their bulk and complexity. To effect any meaningful action or change men could no longer work alone. They had to join together either to capture ex-isting organizations for their own use or else create new ones to suit their purposes.

In this context the robber barons assume still another image. They can be seen as the last generation of giants in American history. This status alone would make them cultural heroes of a sort regardless of the extent to which their actions were condemned or despised. It is not that men have grown smaller since the Gilded Age. It is rather that they have grown more numerous, that they no longer operate in so unrestrained an environment, and that the institutions of society dwarf them as never before in human history.

It is true that men still accumulate vast fortunes and wield enormous power. It is also true that the United States produces cultural heroes of an incredible number and variety. But none of them could ever have the tremendous influence upon the nation's development that the robber barons exerted. The size and scope of existing institutions limit both their power and freedom of action.

That is why the most important fact about the robber barons may be that they were the last generation of American leaders to function in a relatively free and fluid environment. In a sense they were the last of those rugged individualists so cherished in American folklore. The brilliance with which they played the game changed its rules forever. Born into an open environment that stressed personal profits as the prime reward of achievement, they performed so well as to destroy the very system that had provided them opportunity. They were taught to compete vigorously and they understood that competition produces some winners but many more losers.

The successful entrepreneurs also saw that to win the game they had to destroy not only their competitors but competition itself. They accomplished this end with ruthless brilliance and in the process erected huge organizations to protect their supremacy and insure stability. Having done this, the entrepreneurs doomed their own breed to extinction. They had closed the system. Business leadership of the future would be dominated by managers, administrators, and bureaucrats.

Scarcely had the legendary robber barons passed from the scene when, in the public's eye, their places were filled by faceless, anonymous executives. The new business leaders were often able, competent men, but hardly the stuff of which cultural heroes are made. Only an occasional maverick like Henry Ford seemed a worthy successor to the Carnegies and Rockefellers, but for that very reason Ford seemed ill-suited to the times in which he lived.

To a large extent, then, the robber barons in all their images have remained prisoners of folklore. They were often judged not for what they were but for what they represented in an age of agonizing transition. For all its material benefits, industrialism produced a host of difficult and unpleasant problems which defy solution to this day. The robber barons were denounced for their part in creating these problems and their indifference to them. Critics bitterly castigated their lack of social conscience and responsibility, an approach which reinforced the image of the businessman as predator or parasite.

Certainly this lack of concern for the broader consequences of their actions was unfortunate, but it was after all part of the value system upon which they were reared. They had been taught to pursue their own interests, and nothing in the American credo specifically charged successful businessmen with being responsible for national problems. Like most men, the robber barons accepted the existing rules of the game and modified them whenever possible to suit their own purposes. In other words, they did exactly what the prevailing system encouraged them to do, and in that sense they were not only products of their culture but reflections of it as well.

Because their role was so conspicuous and crucial, the robber barons bore the brunt of odium in an age confused by change. As a group they might be considered the first scapegoats of our confrontation with the greatest revolution in human history. They were sharply called to account for their part in a movement that created both material progress and social dislocation. They were natural targets for a people unable and somewhat unwilling to come to terms with the vast implications of this new age.

Thurman Arnold understood the contradiction inherent in this response. What he wrote in 1937 about the trusts might be applied equally to their creators as well:

> . . . the anti-trust laws were the answer of a society which unconsciously felt the need of great organizations, and at the same time had to deny them a place in the moral and logical ideology of the social structure. They were part of the struggle of a creed of rugged individualism to adapt itself to what was becoming a highly organized society.

Upon the course of that struggle can be charted the changing image of the robber barons. And it is by no means ended.

Suggested Readings

Paul Arvich, *The Haymarket Tragedy* (1984).
Robert Bremner, *American Philanthropy* (1988).
Melvyn Dubofsky, *Industrialism and the American Worker* (1975).
John Higham, *Strangers in the Land: Patterns of American Nativism* (1955).
Samuel P. Hays, *The Response to Industrialism* (1975).
Richard Hofstadter, *Social Darwinism in American Thought* (Rev. Ed., 1955).
Matthew Josephson, *The Robber Barons* (1934).
Richard C. Kirkland, *Industry Comes of Age* (1961).
Glenn Porter, *The Rise of Big Business* (1992).
Robert H. Wiebe, *The Search for Order, 1877–1920* (1966).

Further Readings

LATE NINETEENTH-CENTURY ECONOMIC DEVELOPMENT: Alfred D. Chandler, *The Visible Hand: The Managerial Revolution in American Business* (1977); Carl N. Degler, *The Age of the Economic Revolution, 1876–1900* (1977); John A. Garraty, *The New Commonwealth, 1877–1890* (1968); Edward C. Kirkland, *Dream and Thought in the Business Community, 1860–1900* (1964); Harold Livesay, *Andrew Carnegie and the Rise of Big Business* (1975); George R. Taylor and Irene Neu, *The American Railroad Network, 1861–1890* (1964); Olivier Zunz, *Making America Corporate, 1870–1920* (1990). LABOR: Leon Fink, *Workingmen's Democracy: The Knights of Labor and American Politics* (1983); Gerald Grob, *Workers and Utopias* (1961); Herbert G. Gutman, *Work, Culture, and Society in Industrializing America* (1976); Paul Krause, *The Battle for Homestead 1880–1892* (1992); David Montgomery, *The Fall of the House of Labor: The Workplace, the State, and American Labor Activism, 1865–1925* (1987); David T. Rodgers, *The Work Ethic in Industrial America* (1978). IMMIGRATION: Roger Daniels, *Coming to America: A History of Immigration and Ethnicity in American Life* (1990); Alan Kraut, *The Huddled Masses: The Immigrant in American Society, 1880–1921* (1982). URBANIZATION: Blake McKelvey, *The Urbanization of*

America, 1860–1915 (1963); Raymond Mohl, *The New City: Urban America in the Industrial Age 1860–1920* (1985); Eric Monkkonen, *America Becomes Urban* (1988). WEST and SOUTH: Walter P. Webb, *The Great Plains* (1931); Gilbert Fite, *The Farmer's Frontier, 1865–1900* (1966); C. Vann Woodward, *Origins of the New South, 1877–1913* (1951); Paul M. Gaston, *The New South Creed: A Study in Southern Mythmaking* (1970); James C. Cobb, *Industrialization and Southern Society* (1984).

QUESTIONS FOR DISCUSSION

1. Identify and discuss the circumstances and conditions that promoted rapid industrialization in the late nineteenth century.
2. Do you agree or disagree that railroads were the driving force behind the industrial revolution? Explain.
3. Did the federal government get anything in return for aiding the construction of railroads? If so, what?
4. Discuss the impact of the industrial revolution on the family, the condition of women, and the class structure.
5. Identify and discuss the sources of labor's discontent in the late nineteenth century. Explain this discontent in an era in which average wages rose.
6. Compare and contrast the Knights of Labor and the American Federation of Labor (AFL). What features and characteristics of the AFL explain its staying power?
7. How did the new immigration differ from the old? Explain.
8. Identify the most striking differences between the industrial city and the preindustrial city.
9. Do you consider "robber barons" an appropriate label for the late-nineteenth-century leaders of industry and business? Explain.

CHAPTER FIFTEEN

GILDED AGE POLITICS, 1877–1897

JAMES A. GARFIELD

On the evening of July 1, 1881, President James A. Garfield was in high spirits as he strolled across Lafayette Square to visit Secretary of State James G. Blaine before leaving on his summer vacation the following morning. The solution of both personal and political problems that had plagued him for the past several months undoubtedly accounted for his lighthearted mood. His wife had survived a serious illness and was recuperating at the seashore. A tumultuous session of a cantankerous Congress had finally adjourned, and the president had reason to be pleased that he had fared so well in the political skirmishing. While little legislation of any significance had been enacted, the president had succeeded in refunding the national debt which saved taxpayers about 10 million dollars.

Chosen as a compromise candidate in the Republican convention of 1880, Garfield differed little philosophically from his Democratic opponent, General Winfield S. Hancock. Both waged campaigns that focused on personalities and manipulated symbols related to the past, especially the Civil War, rather than on problems arising from the new economic order. Those dissatisfied with the mirror images reflected by the two major parties had the option of voting for the Greenback-Labor party, as 3.4 percent of them did. In an election in which over 79 percent of the eligible voters cast their ballots, Garfield emerged victorious with fewer than ninety-five hundred more votes than Hancock.

No comparable period in Garfield's previous career as an educator, Union officer in the Civil War, politician in his native Ohio, and veteran member of the U.S. House of Representatives had caused more frustration than the few months following his inauguration as the twentieth president on March 4, 1881. His problem stemmed not from any national or international crisis but rather from the political conundrum posed by Congress. His own party barely controlled the House, and the Democrats and Republicans were precisely matched in strength in the Senate with each party having thirty-seven members. Perhaps more exasperating to Garfield was the continual struggle between two factions in his own party, the Stalwarts headed by Senator Roscoe Conkling of New York, and the Halfbreeds led by Senator James G. Blaine of Maine. The factional warfare involved few differences in principles and policies; rather it focused on efforts by each faction to gain control of the party and to distribute patronage. The appointment of Blaine as secretary of state set the president on a collision course with the colorful and vindicative Conkling. The machinations of Secretary Blaine hastened a showdown between the president and Senator Conkling which occurred in a contest for control of patronage in the New York Customhouse with its staff of fifteen hundred employees. Accustomed to viewing this patronage plum as his private preserve, Conkling refused to assume the role of supplicant before the president while Garfield was determined to demonstrate that he was chief executive of the nation rather than "the registering clerk of the senate." Garfield carried the day and Conkling resigned from the Senate. The conviction that he had protected executive prerogatives concerning appointments undoubtedly contributed to the president's good humor as he entered Secretary Blaine's house on that warm July evening.

Unnoticed by Garfield was a solitary, shabbily dressed figure sitting on a park bench in Lafayette Square, Charles Julius Guiteau. A self-styled "lawyer, theologian, and politician" and "a Stalwart of the Stalwarts," Guiteau suffered from severe psychological problems. Rising from his park bench, he primed his .44-caliber ivory-handled revolver, and began following the president with the intention of shooting him before he disappeared into Secretary Blaine's doorway. For whatever reason, no shot was fired.

For weeks Guiteau had badgered the president and the secretary of state to appoint him to a diplomatic post as a reward for his contribution to Garfield's election, a contribution that consisted solely of a three-page speech that was never delivered. Nevertheless, Guiteau became such a nuisance at the White House and State Department that he was barred from both. Inclined toward increasingly bizarre behavior and violently opposed to Blaine, he concluded that his divinely inspired mission was to remove the president by assassination to ensure the triumph of the Stalwarts through the elevation to the White House of Vice President Chester A. Arthur, a political associate of Senator Conkling. Guiteau's failure to fire his pistol in Lafayette Square appears to have strengthened his resolve to dispose of the president.

On the morning of July 2, 1881, Garfield went to the Baltimore and Potomac Railway station to await the special car that would take him north on his vacation. Suddenly Guiteau appeared, pulled out his revolver, and shot the president twice in the back. Boasting loudly that he was a Stalwart, the assassin was led off to jail while Garfield was rushed back to the White House. Despite occasional evidence of improvement, the president never recovered from the gunshot wounds and died on September 19, 1881, a little more than six months after his inauguration. Garfield's death at the hands of a disappointed office seeker not only elevated Arthur to the presidency but also gave a sense of urgency to the existing movement for civil service reform. The result was the passage in 1883 of the Pendleton Act, legislation designed to address the evils of the spoils system.

THE STRUGGLE FOR POWER BETWEEN THE PRESIDENT AND CONGRESS

The experiences of James A. Garfield during the single year between his nomination as the Republican presidential candidate in 1880 and his death six and a half months after assuming the nation's highest office cast into bold relief many of the distinctive attributes of the American political system in the late nineteenth century. Among the characteristics of national politics and government most frequently cited are those relating to the weakness of presidents and the dominance of Congress. Both presidents and Congress reflected the popular belief in individualism, laissez-faire, and social Darwinism which in practice meant a negative government—that is, the best government being the one which governed least.

PATRONAGE

Patronage (appointments of the party faithful to office) took precedence over the formulation of public policy and the enactment of significant legislation. Patronage consumed the time and energy of both presidents and members of Congress and occasioned some of the most acrimonious struggles between the legislative and executive branches of government. With varying degrees of success, post-Reconstruction presidents strove mightily, as Garfield did, to protect what they considered executive prerogatives over appointments. Even Garfield, who subscribed to the theory that the spoils of office belonged to the victorious party, came to resent the extent to which office seekers monopolized his time. No one, of course, was more preoccupied with the spoils of office than Senator Conkling who, throughout his two decades as a powerful figure in Congress, never drafted a single bill nor had his name attached to a significant piece of legislation. Conkling may well have been an extreme example, but numerous others prominent in the affairs of the House and Senate for lengthy periods almost equalled his record.

CONGRESSIONAL SUPREMACY

Congress emerged as the dominant branch of government during the tumultuous era immediately after the Civil War and retained such a status for almost a quarter of a century. Symbolic of congressional supremacy was the

Tenure of Office Act, a measure that required the concurrence of Congress in the removal of federal officials appointed by the president with the approval of the Senate. Though modified two years later, the law nonetheless remained in effect until Democratic president Grover Cleveland finally secured its repeal in 1887. But with or without the Tenure of Office Act, real political leadership rested not in the White House but in a congressional clique made up primarily of senators who headed powerful state machines. Because the control and distribution of political appointments was the glue that held together these machines, the so-called senatorial oligarchy was preoccupied with patronage. Skilled in the use and manipulation of rules and procedures, the ruling clique dominated most important House and Senate committees. Convinced that the president should confine himself to obeying and executing laws, congressional leaders managed to restrict the executive to a subordinate role in the governing process by allocating to themselves all matters of policy and legislation. The frequency with which the Senate rejected presidential appointments and ignored executive recommendations, even when both were of the same party, was eloquent testimony of congressional supremacy. The minuscule White House staff throughout the late nineteenth century suggested that not much was expected of the president other than dispensing patronage.

Ironically, congressional government did not result in the enactment of important laws, much less the pursuit of a coherent legislative program, that addressed issues raised by the emerging industrial-urban society. Despite its dominance in the federal government, Congress was ill-equipped to pursue a vigorous legislative agenda. Widespread adherence to the doctrine of laissez-faire and the belief in a negative government, coupled with the existence of incredibly complicated rules and procedures (especially in the House) figured significantly in preventing the systematic pursuit of such an agenda. Generally, the Democrats controlled the House and the Republicans the Senate, and not until the 1890s did any president enjoy the luxury of having his own party in control of both houses of Congress throughout his tenure. The result was a protracted period of gridlock.

PARTY POLITICS

In an era of extraordinarily high voter turnout and intense party loyalty, the two major parties were evenly matched in political strength nationally. Each party consisted of coalitions of regional interests and ideological groups or factions with different and often conflicting objectives. Small wonder that critics found American political parties lacking in "distinctive tenets." Fear of disturbing intraparty equilibrium prompted Democrats and Republicans to engage in the politics of evasion. Both wrote ambiguous platforms, selected presidential candidates who posed no serious threats to the status quo, and usually manipulated symbols of the past or focused on personalities and scandals rather than addressing more substantive issues that might risk unleashing intraparty divisions.

NATIONAL POLITICS

Few, if any, presidential campaigns equalled the one in 1884 in focusing so exclusively on personality and scandal. Preempting discussion of policy issues were allegations regarding the personal conduct and morality of the two candidates, Republican James G. Blaine, who was accused of accepting bribes from railroads while a member of Congress, and Democrat Grover Cleveland, who, depicted as a drunkard and libertine, was charged with being the father of an illegitimate son. Such politics of evasion gave rise to numerous issue-oriented third parties such as those that embraced prohibition, various currency proposals, and other questions of popular concern.

The intensely partisan campaigns waged by both major parties in the late nineteenth century constituted a form of mass entertainment. Even though only males could vote, entire families attended rallies, torchlight parades, picnics, barbecues, and florid speeches that were standard features of political campaigns. The principal purpose of the campaign ballyhoo was to galvanize the party faithful rather than to win new converts from the ranks of the opposition, and the faithful turned out in record numbers on election day, as evidenced by the almost 80 percent of qualified voters who participated in the presidential election of 1880. Off-year elections attracted a smaller number of voters, but still upwards of 60 percent.

The outcome of national elections, however, often hinged on the votes of a half dozen "doubtful" states, especially New York and Ohio. For obvious reasons, both parties lavished a disproportionate amount of their effort and resources on winning these states. Most presidential and vice presidential candidates in the late nineteenth century came from the "doubtful states" in the Northeast and Midwest.

Although James Bryce, an astute British observer, complained that American political parties lacked the ideological distinctiveness of their counterparts in Europe, he admitted that both Democrats and Republicans had "traditions" and "tendencies." Such traditions and tendencies, so evident in appeals to memories of a heroic past and to party figures who inhabited that past, served as cement to hold together the disparate elements that made up each of the two major parties. As the self-proclaimed heirs of Thomas Jefferson and Andrew Jackson, Democrats tended to favor states' rights and limited government. Linked historically to the antislavery movement, Republicans identified theirs as the party that waged the Civil War, saved the Union, and freed the slaves. Republicans more than Democrats tended to favor using government to advance economic, especially industrial, development.

On most important policy issues such as civil service reform, monetary measures, and railroad and trust regulation, differences appeared most dramatically not in the official stance of the two parties but rather in the positions assumed by factions within them. The one issue which rather consistently separated parties was the tariff. In general, Republicans supported a high tariff to protect America's "infant industries" (hence called the protective tariff), while Democrats for the most part favored a low tariff. Each party claimed that its tariff formula was essential to national prosperity. Unlike the two preceding presidential campaigns, the one in 1888 was an issue-oriented contest known as "the great tariff debate." The campaign pitted Democrat Grover Cleveland, a low tariff advocate, who was making a bid for reelection, against Republican Benjamin Harrison, an exponent of protectionism. Reflecting upon his narrow defeat, Cleveland remained convinced that his emphasis on a lower tariff "was right" from the standpoint of principle, but admitted that it may not have been the best strategy from the standpoint of party politics.

STATE AND LOCAL POLITICS

Even more than official party positions on national issues, such as the tariff or even the political traditions of the two major parties, state and local politics provided important clues to differences between Democrats and Republicans. The emotional intensity of party loyalties was often more evident at the state and local levels, because here party affiliation involved not merely economic interests but regional identity such as existed in the South, and issues of class, race, nationality, and a complex of cultural ingredients, notably religion, as well. Generally speaking, Republicans considered themselves as the party of middle-class respectability which attracted the support of old stock northern Protestants. Inclined to use the coercive powers of the state to impose middle-class standards of conduct and morality on society, Republicans supported legislation to enforce prohibition, observance of the Sabbath, and restrictions on immigration and to strengthen public schools at the expense of parochial schools. African Americans voted the Republican ticket out of gratitude for emancipation. For the lack of a viable alternative, they continued to vote Republican long after the party had abandoned them.

In contrast, the Democratic party (outside the South) tended to attract the support of Catholics, newer immigrants, and urban political bosses and their machines. Generally opposed to government regulation of individual behavior, Democrats waged fierce battles with Republicans over such matters as prohibition and observance of the Sabbath. But nowhere were the political struggles over cultural issues more intense than in the area of education where contests regularly occurred over the teaching of foreign languages, the use of Protestant or Catholic Bibles in schools, and compulsory attendance at public schools. The intense popular feelings about such issues heightened party loyalties and accounted in part for the remarkably large turnout of voters for elections.

POLITICAL UPHEAVAL

The twenty-year stalemate between two evenly matched national political parties came to an end in the 1890s largely as the result of the convergence of two events: the entry into politics of a vigorous farm protest movement known as Populism and the onset of a devastating depression. The upheaval of the 1890s did not occur suddenly or without warning. Beginning at least as early as the 1870s and increasing in number during the 1880s, commentators from fields as diverse as journalism, literature, the new social sciences, and religion pointed out flaws in the emerging industrial-urban society.

Dissatisfaction with the response of the major parties to problems raised by the new socioeconomic order prompted a succession of independent political movements by groups whose agendas represented widely disparate and often antagonistic ideologies. At one extreme were so-called "best men" or Mugwumps. Consisting primarily of educated, upper-class residents of the urban East, the best men embraced the philosophy of laissez-faire and limited government and held firmly to the idea that men of talent, like themselves, should manage the affairs of state.

Convinced that public service had fallen into the hands of the most incompetent elements of both major parties and disdainful of urban political machines, they rejected the notion that all men were equal or equally worthy of power, least of all the hordes of immigrants pouring into the nation's cities. Failing in their efforts to restrict the suffrage, the best men focused their energies on voter education and especially civil service reform, which presumably would guarantee efficiency and expertise in government by elevating individuals like themselves in public service. Shunning third parties, these elite reformers chose to remain within the two-party system as independents with the right to switch parties or support the candidates of their choice when necessary, as many Republican best men did in 1884 because of their belief that the party's presidential candidate, James G. Blaine, was a symbol of corrupt machine politics.

At the other extreme of the ideological spectrum from the urban elitist reformers were numerous, if less socially prominent, groups whose dissatisfaction with the political status quo led them to launch third parties. Especially significant were efforts by agrarian and urban laborers to win access to political power. For example, in the wake of the Haymarket Riot of 1886, the Knights of Labor entered the political area under a variety of party labels and achieved considerable success at the local level. But such success was short-lived. Like the Prohibition, Greenback, and other third parties in the late nineteenth century, the workingmen's parties soon disappeared in an environment so thoroughly dominated by the major parties.

THE FARMERS' MOVEMENT

By 1890 few segments of the population had accumulated more grievances, real and imagined, than American farmers. Convinced that their traditional status was being preempted by those associated with the new industrial order, they suspected that the government was indifferent, if not downright hostile, to agrarian interests. Not only did farmers find themselves competing in an

A farm family on the western frontier, ca. 1880.

international market, but the opening up of new farmlands, especially in the West, as well as advances in scientific agriculture and the use of expensive labor-saving farm machinery, conspired to produce a surplus of agricultural products, drive prices down, and thus increase farm indebtedness. Farmers may well have exaggerated their plight, but they did have legitimate grievances such as a steady decline in profits, a burdensome and discriminatory taxation system, and high transportation costs.

The crisis was especially acute among cotton farmers in the South because of the steady decline in the cotton prices throughout the late nineteenth century. Under the crop-lien system (the practice of mortgaging unharvested crops) in the South, debts mounted; mortgage foreclosures proliferated in many agricultural regions, and the number of landless tenants and sharecroppers dramatically increased.

Farmers searched frantically for the causes and cures of their plight. No more inclined to assume responsibility for their predicament than other groups, they blamed railroads, banks, corporations, and an indifferent government. Frustrated by their lack of bargaining power and political leverage, they viewed themselves as Americans in the process of being dispossessed. They responded by overcoming the obstacles posed by their physical isolation and penchant for individualism to organize for collective action in what historian Lawrence Goodwyn has described as "the largest democratic mass movement in

American history." The search for a solution to the farm crisis prompted them to embrace a wide range of strategies, from currency inflation, farmer-owned cooperatives, and railroad and corporate regulation to a variety of political and tax reforms.

The Grange and the Greenback Party

An early farm organization was the Grange (Patrons of Husbandry). Founded in 1867, the Grange began as a social and educational organization but rapidly broadened its scope to include farm cooperatives and political action. In politics the so-called Grangers achieved considerable success in gaining control of state legislatures and in enacting laws to regulate railroads and warehouses. The failure of Grange cooperatives and the return of greater prosperity, however, caused the organization to decline dramatically in membership and influence by the late 1870s. Numerous farm organizations came into existence in the following decade. Some Grangers gravitated to the Greenback party which elected fourteen members to Congress in 1878. Two years later the Greenback candidate for president, James B. Weaver of Iowa, a former Granger, garnered almost 306,000 votes. Focusing on various currency reforms, including the circulation of more greenback and silver money and the adoption of the income tax, the Greenback party disintegrated a few years after its defeat in the 1880 election.

The Farmers Alliance

A broader-based farm protest movement had emerged by the late 1880s as the agricultural crisis continued to worsen. Known as the Farmers Alliance, the movement benefited by the experience of the Grangers, Greenbackers, and similar groups and even borrowed items from their agendas, including monetary inflation (silver and greenbacks) and cooperatives for buying and selling, but provided a more comprehensive program to cure the ills of farmers. Founded in Texas in the mid-1870s, the Alliance, as well as other farm organizations, spread throughout the South where thousands of farmers sank deeper into debt as cotton prices plummeted. When the cooperative movement fell prey to the same forces that had crippled the Grange's cooperatives (inept management and discrimination by wholesalers, railroads, and bankers), southern farmers rallied to the Alliance's subtreasury plan as the remedy for their plight. This plan called for a system of federal government warehouses in which farmers could store nonperishable crops and borrow up to 80 percent of their value until prices warranted sale on the open market.

In 1888 the Alliance and similar organizations combined to form the Southern Alliance. In the meantime, another regional protest organization, the Northwestern Alliance, had come into existence in the Midwest where farmers had witnessed a steady decline in grain prices. By 1890 the Alliance movement had spread far and wide over agricultural regions of the country, owing largely to its strong leadership and success in recruiting discontented farmers into its ranks.

The failure of Congress to enact the subtreasury plan in that year, coupled with the continued deterioration of the farm economy, was the signal for the Alliance to launch a third party. Led by Kansas where the name People's party (Populist) was first used, other midwestern states saw the rise of various independent farmers' parties in 1890. In the heavily Democratic South, many whites were unwilling to risk participating in a third party for fear of opening the way for "Negro rule" and the restoration of "black and tan" Republican rule of the Reconstruction era. Those white southerners who did embrace the third party idea, such as Tom Watson of Georgia, tended to be among its most uncompromising spokesmen.

THE POPULIST PARTY

Despite the complications of race and politics, as well as economic differences which separated the southern and midwestern farmers, a national People's party, universally called the Populist party, was formally launched in Omaha in July 1892. Although the Populist convention attracted an assortment of reformers including labor union representatives, women suffrage advocates, and followers of Henry George's single tax scheme and Edward Bellamy's socialistic "Nationalism," the gathering was first and foremost an assemblage of disaffected farmers. An atmosphere of religious fervor pervaded the Omaha convention as one speaker after another described Populism as dedicated to reclaiming "the Government in the name of the People" and to abolishing an economic system in which "the fruits of the toil of millions are boldly stolen to build up colossal fortunes for a few." "If liberty fails here," one Populist orator claimed, "it fails forever."

The Omaha platform restated many earlier Alliance demands, and reflected farmers' view that an increased money supply would raise agricultural prices and thereby enable them to escape their indebtedness. Therefore, the platform called for the free and unlimited coinage of silver, which would presumably aid debt-ridden farmers. It also advocated government ownership of railroads, telegraph, and telephones; revocation of the land grants to railroads; and enactment of an income tax and the subtreasury scheme.

The platform praised devices of direct democracy such as the initiative, referendum, and popular election of U.S. senators. In a frontal attack on the policy of laissez-faire, it also called for extending governmental powers as much as needed to end poverty and injustice. To attract labor support, the Populists endorsed the eight-hour day, immigration restriction, and abolition of Pinkerton industrial detectives. The convention nominated James B. Weaver of Iowa, a Union veteran and former Greenback congressman, as the Populist presidential candidate, and James G. Field of Virginia, a Confederate veteran, as his vice presidential running mate.

Joined by a band of colorful and dramatic orators such as Mary E. Lease of Kansas and Tom Watson of Georgia, the Populist presidential candidate launched an energetic campaign. Despite promises to erase Mason and Dixon's line, Weaver discovered on the campaign trail in the South that white voters could be less than cordial to a former Union officer. No less than sectionalism, issues of race, class, and traditional party affiliation posed problems for the new party in its initial national campaign. Weaver's emphasis on the themes implicit in the Omaha platform, especially free silver, antimonopolism, and egalitarianism, was not without popular appeal, though. He polled more than a million votes in the 1892 presidential election, and for the first time since the Civil War a third party broke into the electoral college.

GROVER CLEVELAND

THE 1892 ELECTIONS

Populists elected ten representatives, five senators, three governors, and numerous candidates for state legislatures and local offices. Such a showing spurred the party's leaders to look forward to an even better performance in the off-year elections in 1894 and to capturing the White House two years later. Their initial success and exaggerated expectations tended to obscure two ominous developments, however: the declining membership in the Farmers Alliance, the central base of the party's support, and the switching of parties by many voters in 1892, shifting not to Populism but to the Democratic party.

Although easterners in both of the two major parties expressed alarm at the agrarian uprising and attempted to portray Populists as hayseed socialists or lunatics or both, the presidential campaign in 1892 between incumbent Republican president Benjamin Harrison and Democrat Grover Cleveland ignored the issues raised by Populism and again focused on the tariff. Harrison and the Republicans were in political trouble, in part because of the popular discontent over the high protective tariff, the McKinley Tariff of 1890, which was perceived as the cause of a rise in the cost of living. The image of the Republican Congress, the so-called "Billion dollar Congress," as a spendthrift body that wiped out the treasury surplus by its generous appropriation measures, added to the party's woes. Another reason for the decline in Republican popularity was a wave of strikes and labor disturbances, the most serious of which was the affair at Andrew Carnegie's steel plant in Homestead, Pennsylvania. Cleveland and the Democrats exploited these developments and insisted that the nation's prosperity required a lower tariff. The outcome of the election was a decisive Democratic victory which once more placed Cleveland in the White House.

Economic Crisis

Cleveland had scarcely assumed office in 1893 when a financial panic devastated financial markets and thus touched off the most severe depression of the nineteenth century. The nation's gold reserve dipped below 100 million dollars which was considered essential to maintain the gold standard and public confidence in the nation's currency system. A dedicated "gold bug,"

Cleveland was profoundly disturbed by the continued hemorrhaging of the gold reserve and blamed the panic and depression on the Sherman Silver Purchase Act of 1890 which required the government to purchase 4.5 million ounces of silver a month (about the total output of American silver mines) to be paid for in notes redeemable in gold or silver, but in practice only in gold. With single-minded persistence Cleveland set about repealing the Sherman Act as the only action needed to cure the depression. He succeeded in getting the measure repealed, but at heavy costs. Indeed, the president expended great political capital to no good end because repeal had no impact on the economy. Cleveland's campaign against the Sherman Act alienated two powerful groups, the silver mine owners and the agrarian interests who demanded more, rather than less, silver money in circulation. In brief, Cleveland's dogged insistence on repeal sharply divided his own party.

Thereafter, a succession of unfortunate developments plagued the Cleveland administration, including the passage of a tariff measure (the Wilson-Gorman Act) he disliked but allowed to become law without his signature, and the treasury's purchase of gold to bolster the reserve from the very bankers whom many referred to as the "money monsters of Wall Street." While the economic crisis worsened, Cleveland remained inflexible in his belief that his responsibility was to keep the government solvent and the gold standard secure. It was not, he believed, his responsibility to provide federal relief to ameliorate suffering. Further undermining his popularity and deepening his alienation from all but the most conservative faction of his own party were two actions taken in 1894: the use of federal troops to break the Pullman strike and the administration's response to "Coxey's army," a group of unemployed people who marched on Washington to petition the government to provide work through a federal road-building project. Its leader, Jacob S. Coxey, and his associates were arrested, and members of his army were beaten.

Saddled with an unpopular president and a divided party, the Democrats suffered such serious losses in the elections of 1894 that they slipped into a minority position from which they would not recover for a generation. The elections of that year witnessed a substantial increase in the Populist vote, but ironically a decrease in the number of offices held by Populists. Despite Populist rhetoric about capturing the White House in 1896, the movement had already crested. Essentially an agrarian movement, Populism had little appeal for industrial workers and urban residents, despite efforts to attract their support. The real winners in the election of 1894 were the Republicans who depicted their party as the party of prosperity and identified the Democrats with economic distress and depression and the Populists with dangerous radicalism.

Gold Versus Silver: The Battle of the Standards

The devastating depression of the early 1890s, coupled with the wide-ranging Populist critique of and challenge to corporate capitalism, prompted Americans to think seriously about the nature of their society and government and to question whether democracy and economic equality were possible in the new industrial-urban order. As is often the case, public debate came to focus on specific issues that served as symbols of widely divergent views. As the presidential election of 1896 approached, the debate came to concentrate on the currency issue—gold versus silver—which represented far more than disagreement over the money question. Advocates of the gold standard equated gold with fiscal responsibility, stability, property rights, sanctity of contracts, morality, and even patriotism. Any tampering with the gold standard, therefore, placed civilization in peril. On the contrary, advocates of silver linked silver money, "the people's money," to democracy and to liberation, especially of the debtor classes enslaved by gold, which allegedly imposed unreasonable restrictions on the currency in circulation and the availability of credit to ordinary citizens. The publication of two pro-silver propaganda tracts, William H. Harvey's *Coin's Financial School* (1894) and Ignatius Donnelly's *The American People's Money* (1895), and the pro-gold responses to them set the terms of the debate of "the battle of the standards" in the presidential campaign of 1896.

WILLIAM McKINLEY

THE 1896 PRESIDENTIAL CAMPAIGN

There was little question about whom the Republicans would choose as their presidential candidate when they held their convention that year. Governor William McKinley of Ohio, a former congressman and author of the Tariff of 1890, had carefully and expertly prepared the way for his nomination with the help of Mark Hanna, a wealthy, retired businessman. The Republicans came out unequivocally for the gold standard and any thoughts McKinley may have had about soft-pedaling the issue among pro-silver western Republicans, were quickly abandoned. Republican publicists described McKinley as the "advance agent of prosperity" who would rescue the country from the depression caused by Cleveland and the Democrats. Republicans linked patriotism and the flag to the gold standard which, along with a protective tariff, was considered essential to the return of prosperity.

In contrast to the calm that marked the proceedings that selected McKinley, the Democratic convention turned out to be a free-for-all between rival forces within the party. One faction represented eastern conservative elements, the Bourbons (Cleveland or Gold Democrats), who had long dominated the party; the other consisted primarily of agrarians from the South and West who espoused free silver and significant portions of the Populist agenda. That the latter group carried the day and wrote a pro-silver platform meant that the Democratic party underwent nothing short of an internal revolution in 1896.

The extent of this change was evident in the selection of William Jennings Bryan, a young Nebraska congressman, as the party's presidential nominee. First recognized as a pro-silver spokesman during the debates over the repeal of the Sherman Act, Bryan mesmerized the convention with his "Cross of Gold" speech denouncing the gold standard; thereafter, in Mark Hanna's words, he talked "silver all the time." In contrast to McKinley who waged a "front porch campaign" from his home in Ohio while others spoke and wrote in his behalf, Bryan embarked on a speaking tour in which he traveled eighteen thousand miles and delivered six hundred speeches to audiences totalling 5 million people.

Convinced that the two major parties would adopt conservative platforms and either embrace the gold standard or equivocate on the currency issue, Populist leaders decided to hold their convention last. Many Populists disapproved of the emphasis placed on the silver issue on the grounds that at best it distorted the meaning of their agenda. By the time the Populists convened in St. Louis to nominate a national ticket, their dreams of capturing the White House and inaugurating a new, more democratic order as an alternative to the emerging corporate state had been dashed. Always more a movement than a disciplined political party, Populism not only had passed its peak and failed in efforts to attract the support of urban labor, but Bryan and the Democrats had also appropriated many of its ideas, including the silver issue. The crisis that confronted Populists as they gathered in convention brought to the surface tensions and fissures that had always characterized their ranks. Ultimately, the convention endorsed Bryan, then nominated Tom Watson of Georgia as its own vice presidential candidate, because delegates were led (or misled) to believe that the Democrats would support him rather than the eastern banker who had been placed on the ticket with Bryan. "Fusion" with the Democrats proved to be an act of suicide by the party which had mounted the most formidable agrarian protest in American history. By the time the presidential campaign got underway, Populism no longer posed a serious threat to the two major parties.

The triumph of William McKinley and the Republicans in the election of 1896 signaled the completion of the process of party realignment that had been in progress since the opening years of the decade, a process prompted largely by the rise of Populism and the onset of a major depression. Unable to combat charges that linked their party with the economic crisis effectively, Bryan and the Democrats failed to forge a farm-labor coalition and failed to carry a single urbanized state in the election. No less significant was the fact that thousands of Democrats in 1896 switched their party allegiance to the Republican party which emerged as the majority party, a status it would continue to occupy for a generation. That the White House and both houses of Congress were controlled by Republicans in 1897 marked the end of the Gilded Age politics of stalemate and the beginning of the new order of Republican ascendancy at the national level. Prosperity gradually returned, but ironically, for reasons that had little to do with the gold standard, which the Republicans finally wrote into law in 1900.

THE RISE OF A NEW POLITICAL ORDER

The political system in which McKinley handily won reelection in 1900 differed significantly from that in which Garfield had barely gained possession of the White House twenty years earlier. By the turn of the century the era of close national elections was over, and the Republican party was the choice of a majority of the electorate. The new political order also exhibited greater institutional balance between the legislative and executive branches of government and a closer relationship between the business community and the Republican party. The pageantry and extravaganza that were integral parts of party campaign strategies in the 1880s gradually gave way to an emphasis on "educational politics" which concentrated on the mass distribution of literature, party organization, and the use of polls and personal appeals. Shifts in party allegiance among voters during the 1890s signaled a decline in the emotional intensity of partisan loyalties.

Another significant change in voter behavior was the steady decline in turnout on election days, a trend that continued through the 1920s. There is no easy or simple explanation for this phenomenon. In the late nineteenth and early twentieth centuries legal and extra-legal devices disfranchised African Americans in the South (and in the process many poor whites) but the decline in voting was a national rather than a regional phenomenon. So thoroughly did the Democrats prevail in the South and the Republicans in the Northeast and Midwest that voters in these regions may well have perceived little reason to exert the effort to vote. Another possible explanation for the decline in voting may be related to proliferation of issue-oriented and special-interest organizations through which voters chose to influence public policy rather than political parties. Whatever the reason, party voting, according to one historian, never "again enjoyed the privileged position in public life it had during the nineteenth century."

....

In the following essay Robert S. Salisbury forthrightly challenges what he terms the traditional view that no substantive differences on issues separated the Democrats and Republicans in the Gilded Age. His challenge relies heavily on an analysis of congressional roll call votes and on material drawn from political handbooks and manuals by Edward McPherson, a Republican congressman from Pennsylvania, long-time clerk of the House of Representatives, and a prominent figure in the national Republican party. While admitting that the motivation for the differences in the behavior of the two parties is not easily explained, the author nonetheless concludes that the Republican party's emphasis on an activist, positive government committed to the national interest contrasted sharply with the Democratic party's "sterile negativism" and concern for the parochial interests of states and localities. He suggests that the Republican party's sympathy for underprivileged groups such as African Americans, women, Indians, and Chinese immigrants contradicts the traditional view that the party abandoned its Civil War idealism for reaction and corruption in the postwar era.

THE REPUBLICAN PARTY AND POSITIVE GOVERNMENT: 1860–1890

Robert S. Salisbury

. . .This article will offer evidence refuting the traditional view of the Gilded Age, that there were no substantive differences on issues separating the two major parties. Rather, a majority of both Democrats and Republicans maintained a consistent stance throughout this period on such questions as the desirability of governmental intervention in the nation's economic and political system; the regulation of private behavior by governmental coercion; the advisability of governmental spending; and attitudes toward such discriminated-against groups as blacks, Indians, women, and Chinese immigrants. The tenacity with which both Democrats and Republicans upheld their respective positions on these and other substantive issues, belies the view that neither party hewed to any consistent principles.

Throughout the period 1860 to 1890, both the Republican and Democratic parties remained consistent in their respective approaches to public affairs. Born in the throes of sectional crisis, the Republican party espoused a policy of governmental intervention in both the public and private spheres. By the public sphere is meant the nation's economic and political institutions, while the private sphere refers to those questions of lifestyle such as alcoholic consumption, sexual mores, and religious practices. Positive action on behalf of economic development, a propensity to expend public monies, assistance to various underprivileged groups, regulation of private behavior, and the supremacy of national authority over that of the several states, constituted the Republican credo of an active government. In sharp contrast, the Democratic party stood for the following doctrines: cultural, political and economic laissez faire; "personal liberty"; opposition to all "sumptuary" laws; individualism; localism; states rights; and retrenchment/"economy." In 1876, New York Democrat Clarkson Potter perhaps best captured the distinction between the two parties:

> One for having the government power do much; the other for having them do little; one for having the exercise of government centralized, the other for having it localized. One, the party which would hold up the weak, aid the feeble, and protect the needy; the other, a party insisting that, beyond preserving order and adminis-

from Robert S. Salisbury, "The Republican Party and Positive Government: 1860–1890," *Mid-America: An Historical Review, 68* (January 1986), 15–34.

tering justice, government should interfere with the action of its citizens as little as possible; and that while the general government should prescribe those regulations which affect the whole people, local affairs should be left to the people of the localities.

During the Civil War and Reconstruction era (1860–1870), the two parties divided on those issues stemming from the internecine conflict and its aftermath. With the attack on Fort Sumter, the Republican party became the unswerving defender of the Union's inviolability and stout champion of the expansion of national authority vis-à-vis that of the states. Although initially opposed only to the extension of the "peculiar institution," the Republican party evolved, under the exigencies of wartime, into an organization committed to the conferral of nothing less than full citizenship upon the newly freed slaves and Northern blacks. This policy of support for black aspirations looking toward racial equality and justice was exemplified by the Republican voting record in Congress during this period. Over the bitter objections of the Democratic party, both in Congress and out, the Republican Congressional majority enacted into law such measures as the Thirteenth, Fourteenth, and Fifteenth Amendments to the Constitution; the 1866 Civil Rights Act; the Freedmen's Bureau; and the various Reconstruction Acts in an attempt to translate into reality the dream of a color-blind society. Almost without exception, support for these Administration proposals came exclusively from Republican Representatives and Senators in the nation's capital. In fact, opposition to black aspirations for equal rights constituted the one substantive issue on which Congressional Democrats retained the greatest roll call unity during these years.

In addition to manifesting an often virulent strain of racism, Democrats throughout the Civil War and Reconstruction years displayed their essential negativism on other issues. Such Republican war measures as conscription, suspension of *habeas corpus*, the imposition of loyalty oaths, enlistment of black soldiers into the Union Army, arrest of dissenters, and military censorship of newspapers received almost no support from Congressional Democrats on the relevant roll call votes. For its advocacy of these war-induced measures, the Lincoln Administration was sharply condemned by Democrats, who accused the federal government of violating the Constitution and individual rights. Republican activism in the economic sphere also came in for Democratic censure. Issuance of almost half a billion dollars of paper money or "greenbacks" unbacked by gold; provision of federal assistance for construction of internal improvements such as canals and railroads; establishment of a national banking system, and the concommitant taxation out of existence of the paper currency of state banks; passage of a protective tariff; enactment of a dizzying array of wartime taxes, including the nation's first income tax—these Republican-sponsored measures were opposed by a majority of House and Senate Democrats hewing to their party's traditional position of economic laissez faire and hostility toward Republican interventionism.

This same distinction between Republican activism and Democratic negativism manifested itself on House and Senate roll calls during the ensuing years 1870 to 1890. One contentious issue concerned the responsibility of the federal government to assist the nation's economic development. Seeing nothing wrong in extending governmental assistance to the private economic sector, the great majority of Congressional Republicans supported, while Democrats tended to oppose, such programs as federal land grants to railroads and subsidies to the merchant marine.

Yet another indication of the Democrats' predilection for limited government was the party's consistent attitude toward the tariff. By 1890, their advocacy of tariff reduction had become the Democrats' principal economic policy. This emphasis aptly summarized the party's free market and laissez faire orientation. In sharp contrast, the Republicans became increasingly identified with the doctrine of protection, claiming it was essential for two reasons. On the one hand, Republicans argued the high tariff wall allowed America's "infant industries" to prosper without having to face the potentially ruinous competition posed by the massive importation of cheap foreign products. The G.O.P. claimed repeatedly that the Democratic policy of "free trade" would eventuate in just such destructive competition for American industry, leading to the bankruptcy of numerous domestic firms. Secondly, Republicans stressed that through governmental imposition of high tariff rates, the American worker's job was protected from competition with goods produced by the "pauper labor" of Europe. Party orators admonished workers that if they wanted to retain their present high standard of living, the Republican policy of protectionism had to remain inviolate. Indeed, Republicans attributed much of the nation's current prosperity to the beneficient results of the protective system instituted by the G.O.P. in 1861. The equation was simple: free trade and/or low(er) tariffs meant economic hardship and unemployment; protectionism resulted in good times and plenty of work. Republican support for the protective tariff thus accorded with that party's activist bent, and inclination to stimulate the nation's economy by means of governmental intervention in the market place.

Throughout this entire twenty year period, the Democrats in both chambers displayed a decided penchant for budget cutting and "economy" when confronting the annual appropriation bills. The majority of Congressional Republicans, however, manifested a much broader conception of the national welfare by supporting these appropriation measures, whether substantive or miscellaneous/incidental against the sustained attacks of Democratic "economizers". Although exceptions did exist, Republicans tended to support, and Democrats tended to oppose, governmental expenditures when they came up for a roll call vote on the House and Senate floors.

The Democrats' persistent hostility to funding the nation's armed forces during this period is illustrative of the party's overall reluctance to spend public monies. A substantial majority of Democrats voted both to reduce the size of the Army and to slash expenditures for the Navy when the occasion presented itself in Congress. Republicans, on the other hand, remained consistent in their support of the nation's military establishment by voting overwhelmingly to increase the Army's manpower ceiling and to fund the construction of additional vessels for the Navy.

Another issue over which the two parties sharply divided concerned the desirability of granting federal pensions to veterans of past wars and their dependents. A solid majority of Democrats consistently opposed the various pension proposals, while Republicans were well-nigh unanimous in their support of the veterans and their families receiving their just due from the government. Given the pervasive laissez faire ethos of late nineteenth-century America, such pension payments were the nearest equivalent to our present-day welfare checks.

The Republican party was also more inclined to support the concept of federal assistance to public education. An especially revealing vote occurred in 1880 when Republicans defeated a motion by the Democrats (reflecting that party's inveterate aversion to federal regulation and/or oversight) to eliminate the United States Commissioner of Education's discretionary authority over distribution of the school funds to the respective states and territories. This particular piece of legislation would have provided for federal aid to education from the proceeds of public land sales and the surplus revenues of the Patent Office. In order to receive these funds, the states and territories were required to file detailed reports with the Commissioner of Education concerning their common school systems. The Commissioner of Education would then have the discretionary authority to certify which units were eligible to receive the federal funds. Again in 1884, Democrats attempted unsuccessfully to eliminate federal oversight regarding distribution of the school funds—in this bill, no monies could be disbursed until the Secretary of the Interior had received the mandatory reports from the states and territories regarding their systems of public education. With their strong belief in localism and limited government, Democrats found this stipulation for federal regulation of education highly objectionable. On three occasions during the 1880s—in 1884, 1886, and 1888—a bill providing for federal financial assistance to public schools passed the Republican-controlled Senate only to be bottled up in committee by the Democratic House leadership.

The propriety of federal intervention to maintain law and order in the various states was yet another issue which sharply differentiated the two parties. Resistance to federal intervention constituted a unifying doctrine around which the disparate elements of the Democratic party coalesced. Republicans were especially concerned that the purity of the ballot box be preserved against Democratic fraud and violence, in the North as well as the South. G.O.P. spokesmen emphasized that through their "shotgun" and "tissue-ballot" tactics of carrying elections, Southern Democrats were attempting to secure what they had failed to win in four bloody years of fratricidal conflict: the nullification of federal authority, and its replacement by the pernicious doctrine of states rights. Consequently, such measures as legislation to suppress the Ku Klux Klan and other terroristic organizations; President Grant's suspension of *habeas corpus* in certain Southern counties for the purpose of quashing mob violence; enactment of federal laws safeguarding voting and other civil rights in the states all elicited a virtually straight-party division in Congress—Republicans supporting and Democrats opposing, the supremacy of national authority over that of the several states.

In addition to taking a jaundiced view of the Republican propensity to intervene in the public sphere, Congressional Democrats also opposed their counterparts' proclivity to regulate private behavior. For example, the liquor issue was a constant source of controversy between the two parties. Republicans supported and Democrats opposed, those resolutions mandating an investigatory commission of the alcoholic liquor traffic. Democrats took the view that liquor consumption was a purely personal affair with which the government (at least on the federal level) had absolutely nothing to do. Republicans felt otherwise, believing that Congress had the obligation to determine the social, economic, and political costs of the liquor trade.

A controversy touching on both religion and lifestyle concerned the Mormon sect and its practice of polygamy in Utah Territory. Relevant Congressional roll call votes demonstrate conclusively that what support existed for the Saints and their "relic of barbarism" (in the words of the 1856 Republican platform) came almost entirely from Democrats eager to defend the principles of cultural autonomy, personal liberty, and no sumptuary laws. Consequently, a majority or substantial minority of Democrats opposed those Congressional measures which sought to punish polygamists (such as denying them the right to serve on juries, vote, and hold office), and to place the Mormon sect and Utah Territory under tighter federal control. Republicans, on the other hand, were deeply disturbed by what they viewed as the Mormons' monopoly of political power in Utah, the alleged discrimination which gentiles faced in Mormon-dominated courts, and the sect's apparent attempt to establish a theocracy in the territory. Mormonism represented an affront both to the Republicans' conception of sexual morality, and to their belief in the supremacy of federal authority. Thus, Congressional Republicans were well-nigh unanimous in their resolve to tighten federal authority over both the Mormon sect and the government of Utah Territory.

The strict partisan division on the 1876 Constitutional amendment proscribing public aid to sectarian institutions (Republicans in favor, Democrats opposed), further illustrates the Republican party's conviction that government possessed an inherent right to intervene in what most Democrats regarded as the inviolate and intensely personal sphere of religion. Although not mentioned specifically in the amendment's language, this measure was directed principally against Catholic schools.

A final issue touching on the regulation of private behavior by government concerned the attempt to ban the advertising of lottery tickets. A majority of Republicans supported this effort to legislate morality, while a majority of Democrats opposed the measure as an unwarranted interference by government in a matter best left to the individual. Again, the respective party stances on all these issues—Mormonism/polygamy, aid to sectarian institutions, the liquor question, and the banning of lottery advertisements—typifies Republican activism and Democratic negativism concerning the right of government to regulate private behavior.

One of the more interesting findings to emerge from a study of party divisions during this twenty-year period concerns the Republican and Democratic responses to the following discriminated-against groups in American society: blacks, women, Chinese immigrants, and Indians. Of the four groups, those issues dealing with black aspirations occasioned the greatest partisan cleavage on the relevant Congressional roll calls. These votes reveal that Republicans overwhelmingly favored black demands for equality and justice, whether this meant support for integrated schools in the Sumner Civil Rights Bill; retention of the clause outlawing racial discrimination for jury selection in the same bill; election law enforcement in the South; integration of the nation's armed forces; establishment of a minimum annual quota of black cadets at West Point; a ban on racial discrimination aboard interstate commerce carriers; elimination of all racial discrimination in the nation's agricultural colleges; funding predominantly black schools in the District of Columbia; and endorsement of the mulatto P.B.S. Pinchback for the disputed U.S. Senate seat from Louisiana. On the other hand, the states rights, negative government, racist orientation of the Democrats militated against their supporting any federal intervention on behalf of blacks. In fact, Democrats were even more cohesive on those issues than Republicans, presenting an almost unanimous opposition to black aspirations for justice and equality.

Congressional reaction of the two parties to the 1879–1880 "Exodus" movement, involving the migration of thousands of Southern blacks to the North and West, is most instructive for illuminating their fundamentally different responses to black aspirations. Fleeing from the intolerable conditions of political, economic, and social oppression prevalent in the former Confederacy, these black migrants settled primarily in Kansas, with the remainder locating in such states as Nebraska, Iowa, and Indiana. Democrats blamed this migration on the presence of "outside agitators," making the fatuous claim that black discontent in the South was due neither to economic hardship nor political oppression. Rather, Democrats singled out Republican politicians and Northern relief societies as the culprits in luring away thousands of contented blacks from their homes in the sunny South to the frozen plains of Kansas. Republicans, however, recognized the movement for what it was: a desperate attempt on the part of a terror-stricken people to flee the daily violence and humiliations inflicted on them by Southern Bourbons.

Women were another underprivileged group to experience the Democracy's opposition to their demands for equality and justice. Roll call votes granting women the right to vote in Pembina (Dakota) Territory; according women the right to practice law before the federal courts; establishing a permanent Congressional Committee on the Rights of Women Citizens; proposing a Constitutional amendment enacting nationwide woman suffrage; and granting statehood to Wyoming in 1890 with that territory's constitution providing for woman suffrage (since 1869), invariably found Republicans and Democrats on opposite sides. The majority of Republicans supported these measures, while a majority of Democrats voted against equal rights for women.

Chinese immigrants fared substantially better at the hands of Congressional Republicans than they did with the Democrats. In 1879, Congress bowed to nativist sentiment and passed a bill stipulating that no more than fifteen Chinese passengers per ship would be allowed to enter the United States. This exclusionist measure abrogated unilaterally the 1868 Burlingame Treaty, which had allowed unrestricted immigration between the United States and China. On final passage of the bill, an overwhelming majority of Democrats supported, while a narrow majority of Republicans opposed, the measure. By a margin approaching four to one, House Republicans then voted to sustain President Hayes' veto of the Fifteen Passenger Bill. Democrats voted to override the President's veto by a margin of nearly six to one. Three years later, Congressional nativists were successful in passing the 1882

Chinese Exclusion Act. This iniquitous measure contained the following discriminatory provisions: a suspension of Chinese laborer immigration for a ten year period; a complicated system of certification and registration for those Chinese non-laborers wishing to enter the United States; a definition of "Chinese laborers" which included both skilled and unskilled workers, and those Chinese employed in mining; and a denial of American citizenship to all Chinese residing in the United States. Again, the two parties divided quite predictably: a majority of Democrats voting in favor of both versions of the measure and its discriminatory amendments, a majority of Republicans voting against the bill and its racist provisions. Especially striking was the Senate vote on the motion to deny American citizenship to resident Chinese: Democrats supported this amendment unanimously, while Republicans opposed it by a margin of five to one.

Key Senate roll call votes on Indian policy during this period also assume a distinctive partisan coloration. A majority of Republican Senators opposed transfer of the Indian Bureau from the Interior to the War Department, thus endorsing the concept of continued civilian control over Indian affairs; voted against abolition of the reformist Board of Indian Commissioners, a group of nine unpaid philanthropists established in 1869 to consult with, and offer advice to, the Indian Bureau; supported the granting of United States citizenship to Indians; and in general, voted to retain or increase the amounts stipulated for such annuities as Indian education and subsistence. By way of contrast, a majority of Democrats voted for transfer of the Indian Bureau from civilian to military control; voted to abolish the Board of Indian Commissioners; opposed the conferral of U.S. citizenship upon native Americans; and, in general, voted against, or to reduce, the annual Indian service budgets.

Democratic negativism was personified by the actions of the party's only President during this period. In office from 1885 to 1889 and having no constructive legislative program to enact, Grover Cleveland put into practice the negative government, laissez faire precepts of his party. Federal benevolence to Union veterans struck Cleveland as mere "charity" and "paternalism," whose only result would be to sap their recipients of that sturdy individualism and self-reliance so essential to the maintenance of a free government. Accordingly, Cleveland vetoed hundreds of private pension bills during his first Presidential term on the grounds the recipients had not demonstrated the required need for such payments (i.e., proving that their disabilities were service-related). The first President to ever veto a private pension bill, Cleveland's repeated blows for "economy" in government received the plaudits of the nation's Democratic and Independent press. In 1887, the President vetoed a $10,000 appropriation providing free seeds to drought-stricken Texas. Defending his action, Cleveland maintained:

> I can find no warrant for such an appropriation in the Constitution, and I do not believe that the power and duty of the General Government ought to be extended to the relief of individual suffering which is in no manner properly related to the public service or benefit. A prevalent tendency to disregard the limited mission of this power and duty should, I think, be steadfastly resisted, to the end that *though the people support the Government, the Government should not support the people.* . . .

Federal aid in such cases encourages the expectation of paternal care on the part of the government, and weakens the sturdiness of our national character, while it prevents the indulgence among our people of that kindly sentiment and conduct which strengthens the bonds of a common brotherhood.

Finally, as if to dramatize the traditional Democratic demand that the federal government should withdraw its interference with the national economy—the separation of business and government—Cleveland devoted his entire 1887 Annual Message to a call for tariff reduction.

Republican activism reached its zenith during the Benjamin Harrison Administration. The two years (March 1889 to March 1891) of the Fifty-First Congress marked only the second time since 1875 (the other period being 1881 to 1883) when Republicans simultaneously controlled the House, Senate, and the Presidency. Given this opportunity to enact their program, Republicans went to work with a zeal which contrasted sharply to the Democratic torpor and inaction of previous sessions. Four laws of major importance were passed. The 1890 Sherman Silver Purchase Act redeemed party pledges to "do something" for the interests of silver. Under provisions of the law, the Treasury was required to purchase 4,500,000 ounces of silver bullion per month. In payment, Treasury certificates of full legal tender would be issued. These certificates in turn, were redeemable in gold or silver coin at the option of the Treasury Secretary. The 1890 McKinley Tariff Act increased the general level of customs duties to their highest rates ever, many of the duties assuming prohibitory levels. In this instance, Republicans made good their promise to safeguard both American industry and workers from the deleterious impact of cheaper foreign goods invading the domestic market. The 1890 Dependent Pensions Bill granted bounties to virtually all individuals associated with the Union war effort. A record of 90 days service, an honorable discharge, and proof of a veteran's physical disability, whatever its origin, were the only requirements for pension eligibility. Expenditures rose and the pension list grew by leaps and bounds, but the Republicans had fulfilled their campaign pledge of assisting "the boys in blue". In a revealing letter, Harrison's Commissioner of Pensions, James Tanner, noted that to the Democrats, "the surplus is sacred and ought not to be depreciated, even to keep the old soldiers from starving". Tanner then went on to express the Republican position that the Treasury surplus be allowed to "disappear" into needy hands, where it would do the most good:

What I was able to do in the case of the old lady you were interested in, I will, please God, if my life be spared, do in many other cases. . . . I am beginning to think that I have some of the powers of the alchemist; for circumstances favor me so that I am able to transmute some of the coin of the republic into God's sunshine, and send it streaming into the homes of the deserving and the suffering.

The 1890 Sherman Anti-Trust Act declared illegal every "contract, combination in the form of trust or otherwise, or conspiracy, in restraint of trade or commerce among the several States, or with foreign nations." Dissolution of guilty trusts, fines and imprisonment, and the award of triple damages to successful plaintiffs constituted the stiff penalties imposed for violation of the law. During the 1890s, adverse court decisions, the Spanish-American War, economic dislocation resulting from the 1893 Depression, no body of legal precedent, and an inadequate staff in the Justice Department all served to cripple the law's enforcement. After the turn of the century, however, the Sherman Act took on a new vigor and has guided all subsequent antitrust policy in this country. This particular legislation made America almost the only industrial power to regulate business combinations.

In addition to enacting these four major pieces of legislation, the Republican Congress established a territorial government for Oklahoma, increased appropriations for the Army and Navy, admitted two new states (Idaho and Wyoming) to the Union, increased spending on public works projects and subsidies to business, and passed a law requiring the inspection of meat products intended for export. When Congress adjourned on October 1, 1890, that body had passed a record number of 1,085 bills during the first session of the Fifty-First Congress just completed.

In an era which did not reward electorally that party advocating racial justice, Republicans came close to passing two measures primarily intended to benefit blacks. The first of these was the Blair Bill providing for federal aid to public education. Since the distribution of funds would be based on the number of illiterates in each state or territory, Southern blacks stood to benefit most by the legislation. On three previous occasions—in 1884, 1886, and 1888—the bill had passed the Republican-controlled Senate only to be pigeonholed by the Democratic House. In March of 1890, the bill's sponsor, New Hampshire Senator Henry Blair, made a final, unsuccessful attempt to enact his pet project. This time, it was the Senate which reversed its three earlier votes, defeating the measure by a margin of 32 (24 Republicans and 8 Democrats) to 36 (20 Democrats and 16 Republicans). The second piece of legislation to fail of passage was the Federal Elections Bill providing for federal supervision of Congressional elections. Although applicable to the entire nation, the legislation was primarily aimed at ending the wholesale disfranchisement of blacks in Southern elections. By a vote of 155 to 149, the bill passed the House. With the exception of one Union Laborite, all the affirmative votes were cast by Republicans; only two Republicans opposed the measure. In the Senate, however, the bill was defeated by the defection of six conservative Republicans who joined with the Democratic minority. Similar to the House vote, no Democrats supported the Federal Elections Bill on the decisive Senate roll call. Although the education and fair election measures went down to defeat at the hands of a Democratic-conservative Republican coalition, a large majority of Congressional Republicans did support both bills.

The Republican reward for presiding over one of the most constructive Congressional sessions in American history was to suffer a disaster at the polls in November, 1890. Democrats charged the Republicans with legislating too much, and decried the free-spending ways of the "Billion-Dollar Congress". Criticizing the increase in Congressional expenditures, Democrats calculated that Republicans had spend that much money in pensions, subsidies, and appropriations. Without notable success, Republican orators defended their spending record, claiming America was "a Billion Dollar Country". Democrats claimed that the higher rates of the McKinley

Tariff meant higher consumer prices. The Federal Elections Bill also came in for its share of abuse, with Democrats conjuring up the specter of federal bayonets at each polling place. Attempts by Republican pietists in the Midwest to implement prohibition, Sunday-closing laws, mandatory school attendance, and the compulsory teaching of certain subjects in English alienated those voters opposed to governmental "meddling" in private behavior. Republicans saw an aroused electorate decisively repudiate their party's three-decade-long espousal of governmental activism in both the public and private spheres. Instead, voters had opted for the traditional Democratic doctrine of negativism.

That there were these different approaches to the issues displayed by the Republican and Democratic parties seem conclusively established by an analysis of the relevant roll call votes throughout this period; the question of motivation remains much more difficult to disentangle, however. Consequently, it is possible to assume a more critical or cynical interpretation of the Republican voting record than has been taken above. This is especially the case when considering the Republican stance toward various minority groups such as blacks, Indians, women, and Chinese immigrants. While Republicans were more sympathetic to these discriminated-against groups, Democrats were more so to others—especially the large numbers of Catholic immigrants who came to America during these years. Resentful of Republican attempts to impose morality by statute on such issues as prohibition, Sunday-closing laws, and compulsory school attendance, many Catholics avidly embraced the party of personal liberty and cultural autonomy. Certainly, many contemporary readers would find it difficult to square the alleged Republican concern for "justice" with the party's efforts in the late 1880s and early 1890s to restrict parochial schooling in Wisconsin and Illinois. Then, too, it is conceivable that Republicans were more sympathetic toward Chinese immigrants because the latter represented a cheap source of alternative labor to Catholic immigrants such as the Irish and Italians, who were already predominantly Democratic in their politics. Similarly, Republican efforts on behalf of blacks, rather than representing any idealistic commitment to equal rights, could be viewed as motivated by crass political expediency—an attempt to defend a large and sympathetic voting bloc in a hostile area of the nation.

It would be most accurate to say, however, that Republican motives were a mixture of both idealism and political calculation regarding the various groups discussed above. In this regard, the example of blacks is most instructive. By supporting a free ballot and an honest count, denouncing Democratic voting abuses in the South, and endorsing the concept of federal aid to public education (which because of their proportionately higher rates of illiteracy, would aid Southern blacks most of all), the great majority of Congressional Republicans did not entirely abandon the blacks. The G.O.P. most assuredly did combine both a genuine interest for the welfare of black Americans, along with a keen appreciation of the latters' potential as a voting bloc which could revive flagging Republican electoral fortunes. What needs to be stressed is that even this ambivalent stance put Republicans light years ahead of the Democratic position of racism and oppression. Blacks preferred the Republican position on race, however flawed, to the Democratic alternative which, at best, meant a hands-off attitude of indifference to racial matters, or, at worst, a degeneration into the savage Bourbon violence which spurred black migration from the South to the North starting in 1879. When the Democrats, during Cleveland's second term in office, found themselves in control of the Presidency and Congress for the first time since 1861, they repealed in 1894 all but seven of the forty-nine sections of the 1870–1871 Enforcement Acts providing for federal protection of black voting rights.

This same point can be made for the other discriminated-against groups—Indians, women, and Chinese immigrants. Whatever can be said regarding Republican motives, it remains an uncontestable fact that a majority of G.O.P. Congressmen and Senators consistently supported the aspirations of these groups with their votes on issue after issue. On the other hand, a solid majority of Democrats in Congress just as consistently opposed, by their votes, the hopes of these groups for greater equality and justice in Gilded Age America. However equivocal the Republican stance might on occasion be, it was infinitely preferable to the standard Democratic response—that of a sterile negativism to the groups in question. Then, too, although many contemporary readers would condemn as bigoted the Republican effort to mandate that the curricula of both public and private schools be taught in English, the G.O.P. had a ready response to Democratic charges that such laws violated the right of parents to educate their children in accordance with each family's beliefs and values. Republicans countered by asserting that "since the success of universal suffrage and of popular government requires universal intelligence," it was essential that school authorities have the power to regulate the curriculum of private/parochial in addition to public schools. Although debatable in and of itself, such an argument in favor of universal educational standards was at least consistent with the Republican philosophy of government stressing the primacy of the national interest over that of the various states and localities.

A study of this period thus reveals the post–Civil War era to be more complicated than that view which postulates an unbridled descent of the Republican party from wartime idealism to Gilded Age reaction and corruption. With its persistent belief in positive government, and its more sympathetic (compared to the Democrats) stance towards the plight of such underprivileged groups as blacks, Indians, women, and Chinese immigrants, the Republican party emerges in a more favorable historiographical light.

Suggested Readings

John M. Dobson, *Politics in the Gilded Age: A New Perspective on Reform* (1972).
Lawrence Goodwyn, *Democratic Promise: The Populist Moment in America* (1976).
Stanley P. Hirshon, *Farewell to the Bloody Shirt: Northern Republicans and the Southern Negro, 1877–1893* (1962).
Morton Keller, *Affairs of State: Public Life in Nineteenth Century America* (1977).
Paul Kleppner, *The Cross of Culture: A Social Analysis of Midwestern Politics, 1850–1900* (1970).

Robert D. Marcus, *Grand Old Party: Political Structure in the Gilded Age, 1880–1896* (1971).

H. Wayne Morgan, *From Hayes to McKinley: National Party Politics, 1877–1896* (1969).

David J. Rothman, *Politics and Power: The United States Senate, 1869–1901* (1966).

John S. Sproat, *"The Best Men": Liberal Reformers in the Gilded Age* (1968).

Tom E. Terrill, *The Tariff, Politics and American Foreign Policy, 1874–1901* (1973).

FURTHER READINGS

POLITICS IN THE GILDED AGE: Geoffrey Blodgett, *The Gentle Reformers: Massachusetts Democrats in the Cleveland Era* (1966); Charles Calhoun, *The Gilded Age: Essays on the Origins of Modern America* (1996); Justus D. Doenecke, *The Presidencies of James A. Garfield and Chester A. Arthur* (1981); Paul Glad, *McKinley, Bryan, and the People* (1964); Lewis Gould, *The Presidency of William McKinley* (1980); Ari Hoogenboom, *Outlawing the Spoils: A History of the Civil Service Reform Movement* (1968); Richard J. Jensen, *The Winning of the Midwest: Social and Political Conflicts, 1888–1896* (1971); Paul Kleppner, *The Third Electoral System, 1853–1892* (1979); J. Morgan Kousser, *The Shaping of Southern Politics: Suffrage Restriction and the Establishment of the One-Party South, 1880–1910* (1974); Michael McGerr, *The Decline of Popular Politics: The American North, 1865–1928* (1986); Samuel McSeveney, *The Politics of Depression* (1972); H. Wayne Morgan, *William McKinley and His America* (1963); Joanne Reitano, *The Tariff Question in the Gilded Age: The Great Tariff Debate of 1888* (1994); Homer Socolofsky and Allan Spetter, *The Presidency of Benjamin Harrison* (1987); Richard E. Welch, *George Frisbie Hoar and the Half Breed Republicans* (1971) and *The Presidencies of Grover Cleveland* (1988); R. Hal Williams, *American Politics in the 1890s* (1978). POPULISM: O. Gene Clanton, *Populism: The Humane Preference in America, 1890–1900* (1991); Robert C. McMath, *American Populism: A Social History* (1993); Jeffrey Ostler, *Prairie Populism: The Fate of Agrarian Radicalism in Kansas, Nebraska and Iowa, 1880–1892* (1993); Norman Pollock, *The Populist Mind* (1967).

QUESTIONS FOR DISCUSSION

1. Identify and briefly explain the principal attributes of national politics in the Gilded Age.
2. What differences in principle and policy distinguished Republicans from Democrats in the Gilded Age? Discuss.
3. What did the presidential election of 1884 reveal about Gilded Age politics?
4. Discuss the grievances of American farmers in the late nineteenth century.
5. Discuss the rise of the Populist party and the principal features of its platform. Explain its decline.
6. Explain how President Grover Cleveland responded to the depression of the 1890s.

7. Discuss the issue or issues that separated Republicans from Democrats in the presidential election of 1896 and analyze the consequences of the election's outcome for both parties.

8. In his essay what evidence does Robert S. Salisbury present to support his view that the Republicans in the late nineteenth century, more than the Democrats, demonstrated a belief in positive government and exhibited sympathy for underprivileged groups?

CHAPTER SIXTEEN

THE NEW EMPIRE

As the year 1890 dawned, foreign affairs seemed a very minor concern to most Americans. The nation was immersed in the triumphs and tragedies of the business age. The industrial revolution was in full swing. The hero-villains of the age were immensely successful entrepreneurs like John D. Rockefeller and Andrew Carnegie. Farmers struggled with declining prices and mortgage foreclosures. Blue-collar workers confronted a radically altered factory system and new scientific management theories that seemed designed to exploit and depersonalize them. Urbanization with its teeming slums, mass transit problems, and machine politics transfixed intellectuals and would-be reformers. In the West, white Americans occupied themselves with felling trees and Indians, as one insensitive wag put it. The nation thrilled with excitement as the last spike was driven into the first transcontinental railroad. And it worried over the periodic crashes, depressions, and strikes that seemed to belie corporate America's contention that the millennium was just around the corner. Indeed, foreign diplomats complained to their home chanceries that Americans paid no more attention to what was happening in Russia or China or France than they did to another planet in the solar system.

In 1891 the State Department was housed in the new State-War building in Washington, a massive contemporary castle that shocked architectural traditionalists, but it occupied only one part of one wing. The foreign policy establishment consisted of one secretary of state, three assistant secretaries, one very versatile translator, and seventy-six other employees. This meager contingent stood as a seeming monument to the insignificance of foreign policy in the national scheme of things. Yet, beneath the surface powerful forces were at work that would propel the United States onto the world stage by the end of the decade. In 1898 America would go to war with Spain, its first conflict with a

621

European power since the War of 1812, and as a result of that encounter, it would acquire island possessions in the Caribbean and the Pacific.

OVERSEAS EXPANSION

The decision to join Britain, Germany, Japan, and the other imperial powers in acquiring overseas possessions was not as great a break with tradition as at first it seemed. Continental expansion was a prominent feature of nineteenth-century American history (see Figure 16–1).

The expansionist impulse, fueled by the notion that America had been singled out by God or destiny to rid the hemisphere of colonialism and bring the blessings of liberty and democracy to the less fortunate peoples of the world, culminated with the Mexican War. With the acquisition of New Mexico territory and California, the United States rounded out its continental boundaries, but popular interest in expansion did not end with the Treaty of Guadalupe–Hidalgo.

The notion that America had a mission to spread its institutions to other peoples—manifest destiny—remained a powerful part of the American psyche. The Buchanan administration came very close to annexing Cuba, and William Seward, President Lincoln's secretary of state, was an ardent expansionist. He failed in his effort to acquire Santo Domingo but persuaded Tsarist Russia to sell Alaska. There was, then, a continuing expansionist impulse that slowed in the late nineteenth century not only because the nation was preoccupied with domestic affairs, but also because new ground rules had to be developed as the United States made the transition from continental to overseas expansion.

ECONOMIC DIMENSIONS

The changing nature of the American economy also contributed to the burst of diplomatic and military activity that marked the end of the century. The early stages of the industrial revolution did indeed take much air out of the expansionist impulse. Even the poorest American dreamed that he or she could live the rags-to-riches Horatio Alger myth. Businessmen had enough to occupy them exploiting the continent's natural resources and abundant labor pools. But by the mid-1890s some of the consequences of the national economy's unparalleled growth had become apparent. Throughout its history the United States had been a net exporter of raw materials and a net importer of manufactured goods. The more economically advanced nations of Western Europe sought out American markets and raw materials, and determined the terms of trade.

By the 1890s, however, America's ability to produce industrial exports had increased dramatically. In 1897 the value of manufactured articles exported by the United States exceeded that of those imported. That same year the value of exports over imports stood at $286 million, the largest in history. These and other figures convinced industrialists that, under truly competitive conditions,

Figure 16–1

Colonial Possessions, 1900

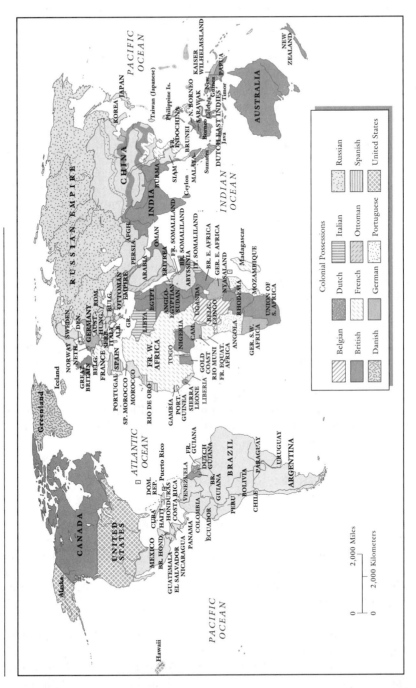

they could outsell their foreign rivals anywhere in the world. As the century came to a close, industrialists and financiers began pressuring various administrations and their State Departments to help them secure markets abroad that would absorb surplus capital and products. Especially attractive were the underdeveloped areas of Asia and Latin America. In response to this perceived need, businessmen-diplomats began prowling the highways and byways of international commerce, and Washington began taking an intense interest in securing markets, bases, and sources of raw materials.

PSYCHOLOGICAL DIMENSIONS

There was, finally, a psychological dimension to the expansionism of the 1890s. Americans were extremely conscious of the fact that they had reached the status of a great power in terms of population, agricultural output, and industrial production. In the late nineteenth century the universally recognized badge of great power status was overseas possessions.

As Americans developed the attributes of a great power, they craved colonies, the trappings of a great power. The growing desire to enter the race for overseas territory was also a reaction to the dullness and drabness of industrial life. With the disappearance of the Western frontier, Americans were very much in need of a romantic outlet. The decade of the 1890s was in many ways a desperately unhappy time. The Panic of 1893, the Homestead and Pullman strikes, and the bitterly divisive election of 1896 caused many Americans to question the soundness of their institutions. By contrast, empire building was an exciting, exhilarating diversion. It could, many believed, bring the nation together. Empire would be a reaffirmation of the soundness of the American creed of republicanism, free enterprise, and individual liberty. Even the most downtrodden citizen could gain vicarious satisfaction by identifying with a virile young nation exercising an expansionist foreign policy.

PROPAGANDISTS FOR EMPIRE

During the 1890s a collection of intellectuals, military officers, and politicians developed a multifaceted rationale as well as a detailed plan for implementing an imperial foreign policy. Foremost among these were the social Darwinists. Academics, Protestant clergymen, and journalists primarily, they insisted that the evolutionary principles of survival of the fittest and natural selection were applicable to the international as well as the natural environment. Nations, like organisms, must either compete for the necessities of life and grow, or be pushed aside by the strong to wither and die. The United States, they proclaimed, had survived and prospered because it possessed superior characteristics.

Combining the Social Gospel with Darwinian theory, clergymen argued that American expansion was both inevitable and good. Indeed, the nation had a moral responsibility to uplift and civilize the less fortunate people of the world, enabling them to enjoy the blessings of liberty and democracy. In 1885 the American Home Missionary Society forged an important link between religious duty and manifest destiny by publishing *Our Country: Its Possible Future and Its Present Crisis* by Josiah Strong, a Congregational minister. He saw the Anglo-Saxon as the ultimate victor in the struggle for existence which the pressure of population upon the means of subsistence caused. That triumph was pleasing in the sight of God, Strong claimed, because Americans were "living examples of the merits of civil liberty and spiritual Christianity." There were in this justification for expansion strong strains of racism and cultural exceptionalism.

Adding their voices to the social Darwinists were a group of naval expansionists who explained to the nation how to make the switch from continental to overseas expansion. In 1890 Captain Alfred T. Mahan published *The Influence of Sea Power on History* and in 1897 *The Interest of America in Sea Power.* The first told the story of Britain's use of naval power to build the greatest colonial empire the world had ever seen, and the second was a blueprint for the construction of an American overseas empire. Mahan realized that the United States could not rival England at once. The planting of colonies was the last step, not the first.

Initially, Mahan declared, the government should focus on building enough warships to control the waters around the North American continent. Next, it must deny to potential enemies certain strategic sites within its defensive perimeter. Finally, it must occupy key positions along the main water routes of the world. In a series of widely read magazine articles he called attention to the strategic features of the Caribbean, the need to build a U.S.–controlled isthmian canal there, and the changes in commerce and warfare that the interoceanic canal would bring about. He linked together Cuba, the Isthmus of Panama, and Hawaii in a single system of bases and waterways that was allegedly vital to American security.

The social Darwinists and naval expansionists found a receptive audience in a group of young, ambitious Republican politicians who decided to use overseas expansion as a vehicle to carry them to national prominence. Theodore Roosevelt, soon to accede to the presidency, and Senators Henry Cabot Lodge (R–Massachusetts) and Albert Beveridge (R–Indiana) worked energetically and successfully to sell the Republican party and the American people on the idea of using naval power to build an empire. By the middle of the decade, both parties had committed to a naval building program and the Republicans went on record favoring the annexation of Hawaii and the construction of a Central American canal. Whereas Strong and Mahan were primarily intellectuals who developed the justification for expansion, Roosevelt and Lodge were men of political action who sold the ideas of others to their party and eventually their nation. By the end of the decade, isolationism and anticolonialism were still very prominent themes in the thinking of many Americans, but the imperialists had made great strides and planted seeds which blossomed into empire in Latin America and East Asia.

A TRIFLE EMBARRASSED.

Uncle Sam.—Gosh! I wish they wouldn't come quite so many in a bunch; but, if I've got to take them, I guess I can do as well by them as I've done by the others!

Racism was an important part of the anti-imperialist argument. That element is portrayed in this political cartoon entitled, "A Trifle Embarrassed."

THE SPANISH-AMERICAN WAR: EXPANSIONISM OR HUMANITARIANISM?

In 1898 the United States went to war with Spain and as a result acquired island possessions in the Caribbean and the Pacific. The catalyst for that conflict was American concern for the people of Cuba who were then struggling to free themselves from the yoke of Spanish colonial rule. Americans had long been interested in Cuba because of its strategic location athwart the entrance to the Gulf of Mexico and because of the economic value of its broad, fertile acres. Several times during the nineteenth century the United States seemed to be on the verge of annexing Cuba, but the resistance of the Spanish coupled with fears in the North that the island would be divided into one or more slave states prevented such a move. Spanish rule in Cuba was harsh; the parent country oppressed and exploited the Cubans mercilessly. In 1868 an insurrection erupted which elicited much sympathy in the United States, but preoccupation with the problems associated with Reconstruction precluded intervention. Spanish authorities managed to drive rebel leaders into exile in 1878, but anticolonial feelings continued to run high, and in 1895 civil war erupted on the island once again.

The insurgents in Cuba resorted to tactics typical of guerrilla warfare: They refused to wear uniforms, resorted to assassinations and bombings, and extorted money from property owners. To quash the rebellion, Spanish military authorities rounded up, or reconcentrated, noncombatants in areas in which the guerrillas were particularly active and herded them into fortified stockades. Spanish soldiers then killed anyone caught outside the stockades and destroyed all plant and animal life that could be of possible use to the insurgents. Poor hygienic conditions in the camps led to the deaths of hundreds of women, children, and elderly people. Atrocities associated with the Cuban insurrection were widely reported in the United States by members of the "yellow press," the name given to the new mass media that appealed to the semieducated working- and lower-middle-class public. Joseph Pulitzer, publisher of the *New York World*, and William Randolph Hearst, who owned and operated the *New York Journal*, ordered their reporters to describe every gory detail of the Cuban conflict, and their papers subsequently boomed. In 1898 America was a nation looking for a cause, and many citizens believed that ending the bloodshed in Cuba was that cause.

Two events pushed the United States and Spain to the brink of war. In January 1898, the Spanish ambassador wrote a private letter to a friend in Havana that was very critical of President William McKinley who had just delivered a bellicose address to Congress blaming Spain for the bloodshed in Cuba. In effect, the letter called McKinley a spineless politician. Hearst procured a copy of Erique Dupuy de Lome's correspondence and on February 9 published it verbatim on the front page of the *Journal*. A wave of outrage swept the nation. Five days later an American battleship, the U.S.S. *Maine*, blew up in Havana harbor killing 250 men. Though the Spanish had least to gain from destroying the vessel, the yellow press, Congress, and the American people generally blamed them for the disaster.

With Congress threatening to declare war even in the absence of a presidential invitation, McKinley issued an ultimatum. He demanded first that Spain give up the policy of reconcentration, second that it declare an armistice to last until October 1898, and third that if by that date no settlement with the Cubans had been reached, both sides would accept American arbitration. Spain, which was approaching the end of a three hundred–year decline in power, agreed to the first demand but procrastinated on the second and third. Exasperated, McKinley went to Congress in April and asked for the authority to intervene militarily in Cuba to put an end to the conflict. With little opposition, the House and Senate voted for war. At the same time, however, Congress passed the Teller Resolution which stated that the United States was taking up arms in behalf of Cuban independence and would not seek to annex the island when Spain had been defeated. It was a self-denying pledge that some would come to regret.

The war in Cuba was quickly over. The Spanish military waged war on both land and sea, but proved weaker even than the ill-prepared Americans. The twenty thousand–man U.S. force, clad inappropriately in woolen winter uniforms, suffered almost as many casualties from its own spoiled rations as from Spanish bullets. In August the two sides signed an armistice which imposed a cease-fire and transferred the island of Puerto Rico from Spain to the United States. Significantly, America suddenly had an island possession in the Caribbean.

After the war, sentiment built in the United States for annexation of Cuba as well. The Teller Resolution prevented that, but the McKinley administration devised a scheme which converted Cuba into an American protectorate. Under the terms of the Platt Amendment to the Army Appropriations Bill of 1902 Cuba could not enter into an agreement with a third party without Washington's permission, the United States was entitled to intervene in Cuba at any time to maintain law and order, and Cuba agreed to cede land to its northern neighbor for the construction of a naval base. American occupation forces compelled the Cuban government against its will to include the terms of the Platt Amendment in the Cuban constitution of 1902. During the next thirty years the United States would land troops repeatedly on the island to protect a government in power, usually one that was friendly to American business interests.

EMPIRE IN THE PACIFIC

The Spanish-American War led to empire in the Pacific as well as in the Caribbean. In the summer of 1898 President McKinley persuaded Congress to annex the Hawaiian Islands, then ruled by a native monarchy, to keep the islands out of Spain's hands. As soon as war was declared, Washington ordered Commodore George Dewey, commander of the U.S. Asiatic fleet, to seize the Philippine Islands, then a colonial possession of Spain. Dewey's ironclads destroyed the Spanish fleet, wooden-hulled and sail-powered, in Manila harbor on May 1. When the fighting ended in August, however, the United States possessed only the capital city; the rest of the archipelago was either in Spanish or insurgent hands.

Nevertheless, the McKinley administration acted as if the Philippines were America's to dispose of. During the fall and winter of 1898 pressure built on the president to retain the island group. Businessmen insisted that the Philippines would serve as an ideal base of operations for penetration of the potentially enormous China market. Naval expansionists insisted that the United States needed the Philippines so the American navy and merchant marine could have their own refueling and resupply station in the Pacific. Finally, American Protestant leaders, ignoring the fact that the islands had been Catholic for three hundred years, declared that it was America's duty to civilize and Christianize the Filipinos.

McKinley, not a man to struggle against the prevailing political currents, instructed American peace commissioners, then negotiating in Paris with the Spanish to demand cession of both the Philippines and Guam. The Spanish protested, but so complete had been their military defeat that they were helpless. The Treaty of Paris, concluded in 1899, transferred both the

Philippines and Guam to the United States. Anti-imperialists in the Senate, arguing that the Philippines were remote and hard to defend and that imperialism and democracy were incompatible, attempted to block ratification. They fell one vote short.

The decision to retain the Philippines led to both short- and long-term difficulties. The Filipinos, who had chafed under Spanish rule no less than the Cubans, believed that the war would result in their independence. When they discovered that they would just be exchanging their Spanish overlords for American ones, they turned on the U.S. occupying force. For two years guerrilla warfare raged, and not until the United States adopted the tactic of reconcentration did the insurrection collapse in 1902. More important, annexation and subsequent American efforts to protect its sphere of interest led to a half-century of rivalry with Japan that would produce the bloodiest war in human history.

THE OPEN DOOR

American businessmen looked forward to utilizing the nation's Asian possessions to exploit the China market, but it seemed that that market might disappear before they could act. As the Spanish-American War was coming to a close, Britain, Russia, Germany, France, and Japan were busily carving up China and Southeast Asia into spheres of influence. These spheres, which generally included a port and the contiguous area to the interior, were exclusive trading zones from which businesspeople of third nations were excluded.

In 1899 some two hundred U.S. businesses with an interest in trading with China formed the American Asiatic Association and pressured the McKinley administration to ensure that they would have the opportunity to trade with East Asia. In the fall of 1899 Secretary of State John Hay and his Asian advisors drafted a series of private notes to the great powers asking them publicly to commit to the principle of equality of trade opportunity. American businesses assumed that given a level playing field they could always outsell their competitors from other nations.

Though Britain, Germany, Japan, and the other powers had no intention of opening their spheres, Hay went ahead and announced in March of 1900 that equality of commercial opportunity was a fait accompli in Asia. It was not, but once committed to the principle, the United States would work throughout the rest of the twentieth century to advance it.

No sooner had Hay issued his declaration, known as the first open door note, than another threat to the open door materialized. In the spring of 1900 a group of young, patriotic Chinese (the Society of the Heavenly Fist, dubbed Boxers by the Western press) rose up against the massive foreign interests in China. They burned foreign property and killed missionaries and businesspeople. For fifty-five days, non-Chinese survivors holed up in Beijing (then Peking). The powers assembled an international force, relieved the siege, and in August crushed the rebellion. Hay, fearful that Germany, Japan, Britain, and the other participants would use the occasion of their intervention to completely dismember China, issued a second open door note. In July 1900 the secretary of state declared that thenceforward the United States would work to preserve the territorial integrity and political independence of China. Thus did America proclaim its willingness and ability to protect the world's most populous nation, a community of some 600 million souls situated halfway around the world.

BALANCE OF POWER AND THE "BIG STICK"

Theodore Roosevelt, who acceded to the presidency upon McKinley's assassination in 1901, was an avowed expansionist, but he viewed different regions of the world differently. He took a balance of power approach to European affairs—that is, he regarded the emergence of any one power capable of dominating the continent as dangerous to American interests. Because that was Great Britain's policy as well, and because of that nation's naval power and proximity to Europe, the Roosevelt administration generally contented itself with supporting London's diplomatic initiatives. Roosevelt took a balance of power approach to Asian affairs as well, but because of American interests there, he believed that the United States would have to serve as arbiter, playing one great power off against another as Britain did in Europe. In this way, the United States might succeed in protecting the Philippines and keeping the economic and political door at least partially open in China. The Caribbean basin and Latin America in general were, to Roosevelt's mind, a U.S. sphere of interest. He was determined to maintain order there, to protect American economic and strategic interests, and to prevent an extra-hemispheric power from establishing a base of operations (see Figure 16–2).

In 1904 the Russo-Japanese War erupted as those two powers struggled for control of Manchuria, an economically underdeveloped but potentially rich province of China. Japan, a densely populated, industrializing power, was determined to secure control of the region to exploit its raw materials and markets. Russia no less than Japan viewed domination of Manchuria as its manifest destiny and steadily expanded its interests in northern Manchuria until they clashed with Japan's in the south. As Japan won victory after victory, Roosevelt became concerned about the balance of power in Asia and about China's survival. In the summer of 1905 he sponsored a peace conference at Portsmouth that ended the conflict, and in 1908 in the Root-Takahira Agreement tacitly recognized the Japanese sphere of influence in Manchuria in return for Japanese recognition of American dominance over the Philippines.

THE PANAMA CANAL

Roosevelt was an acquaintance and something of a disciple of Alfred Thayer Mahan. Like Mahan, the president believed it imperative that the United States build and operate an isthmian canal. Indeed, he envisioned a canal treaty with

FIGURE 16–2

The United States in Central America, 1895–1934

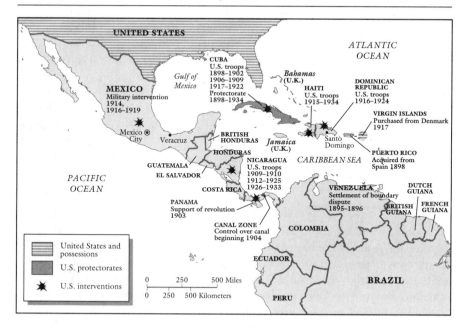

one or another of the Central American republics as the crowning achievement of his first administration. Most interested observers in the United States favored Nicaragua over the other prospective site, Panama (then the northernmost province of Colombia). Nicaragua was closer to the United States, and to the untrained eye the engineering problems seemed less daunting. An international consortium dominated by powerful American interests—the New Panama Canal Company (NPC)—owned rights to a canal site in Panama, however, and had actually begun construction. The NPC desperately wanted Congress to select Panama, and in response to lobbying efforts by the company's representatives, it did. In 1902 Congress appropriated $80 million to pay for a canal and authorized the president to begin negotiations with the government of Colombia. If he encountered difficulties, however, he was to switch to Nicaragua.

Colombia viewed the canal site as one of its principal natural resources. When the United States offered $10 million and $250,000 a year for a six-mile-wide strip, it balked. Under the proposed agreement, the NPC would receive $40 million. Bogotá proposed that the total—$50 million—be split between the NPC and Colombia. Roosevelt exploded. He refused to admit that as a sovereign nation, Colombia had the right to negotiate the best terms possible. Instead of counteroffering or using negotiations with Nicaragua to pressure Bogotá, the Roosevelt administration began conspiring with a group of

Panamanians who wanted to detach the province from Colombia and conclude a Panamanian-American canal deal. In November 1903 that faction, aided by U.S. money and military might, ousted Colombian authorities, proclaimed independence, and signed the Hay–Buneau Varilla Treaty (Philippe Buneau Varilla was a major shareholder in the NPC who persuaded the Panamanians to name him ambassador to the United States) with the United States. Under the terms of this, the first Panama Canal Treaty, the United States paid $10 million down and $250,000 a year for a ten-mile-wide strip to be held "in perpetuity." Roosevelt, who made no secret of his contempt for most Latin states, had taken what he wanted in the Panama Canal affair without any regard for Colombian sovereignty. The United States had intervened in Colombia's internal affairs and in the process generated deep apprehension throughout Latin America concerning its big stick diplomacy and Yankee imperialism in general.

The Roosevelt Corollary

As soon as work began on the Panama Canal—it was completed in 1914—it became the heart of the new American empire. Roosevelt and succeeding presidents were determined to protect this economic and strategic lifeline from potential adversaries who could hold it hostage in peacetime or attack it in wartime. Progressive Era presidents were particularly concerned about the financial instability of the various republics whose shores were washed by the Caribbean. Most were ruled by military dictators who oppressed their respective populations and ran up huge debts with British, French, German, and Italian bankers. The United States feared that defaults by these irresponsible tyrants would provide the opportunity for one or more of the great powers to intervene and establish protectorates and military bases from which the canal could be threatened.

In December 1904, President Roosevelt announced a sweeping policy designed to deal with such an eventuality. Roosevelt realized, he said, that the "insurrectionary habit" of these "wretched republics" imposed certain obligations on the United States. In what became known as the Roosevelt Corollary to the Monroe Doctrine, the president declared that "chronic wrongdoing . . . may in America, as elsewhere, ultimately require intervention by some civilized nation, and in the Western Hemisphere the adherence of the United States to the Monroe Doctrine may force the U.S. . . . . in flagrant cases of such wrongdoing or impotence, to the exercise of an international police power."

Dollar Diplomacy

William Howard Taft, who succeeded Roosevelt in the presidency in 1909, realized that his predecessor's interpretation of the Monroe Doctrine could lead to repeated and prolonged military intervention into Latin American affairs. To avoid such eventualities, he and his secretary of state, Philander Knox, hit upon the idea, as Taft put it, of "substituting dollars for bullets." In Latin America the administration hoped to persuade U.S. investors to buy up the debts owed by various republics to European creditors. When the military strongman governing Nicaragua, José Zelaya, was overthrown in 1911, the United States compelled the new government to accept such a financial agreement. The fruits of dollar diplomacy, as the Taft administration's foreign policy was dubbed, were bitter, however. When in 1912 an insurrection broke out against the government of Adolfo Díaz, American bankers who had invested in Nicaragua pressured the Taft administration to come to its aid. Civil disorder threatened their investments and property, and they insisted that they were entitled to protection. Late that year a contingent of U.S. Marines landed in Nicaragua to restore order; they remained there until 1925.

THE NEUTRALIZATION SCHEME

Similarly, the Taft administration hoped to use investment capital to keep the open door partially open in China. An American railroad entrepreneur, E.H. Harriman, as part of a scheme to construct a worldwide transportation system, attempted to purchase first the Japanese-owned South Manchurian railway and then the Russian-owned Chinese Eastern railroad. He was rebuffed in both cases and turned to the State Department for help. The Taft administration thereupon devised a plan which it believed could accommodate Harriman and further the long-range goals of America's East Asian policy. In the Neutralization Scheme, the United States attempted to buy control of both the South Manchurian and Chinese Eastern and then sell them to the Chinese government, thus restoring Chinese sovereignty in Manchuria and reopening the area to American businessmen. Japan and Russia refused to sell, however. In fact, the Taft administration's diplomacy drove the two powers together. They reached an agreement clearly delineating their respective spheres and tightly closing them to citizens of third powers.

MORAL IMPERIALISM

During his successful bid for the presidency in 1912 Woodrow Wilson denounced both the big stick and dollar diplomacy. While safeguarding America's legitimate strategic and economic interests, the Democratic nominee promised to raise diplomacy to a higher plane. It would be the policy of the United States under his administration, Wilson declared, to spread the principles of democracy and equality of opportunity around the globe. Wilson was initially most concerned about Latin America. He regarded the Latin habit of governing through military coup as deplorable. "We hold . . . that just government rests always on the consent of the governed," he declared, "and that there can be no freedom without order based upon law and upon the public conscience and approval." Because of its idealism and aggressiveness, Wilson's approach to foreign affairs was dubbed "missionary diplomacy." Mexico provided an early laboratory for the new president's idealism.

THE MEXICAN REVOLUTION

Between 1876 and 1911 Mexico was ruled by the dictatorial Porfirio Díaz who, supported by large landowners, the Catholic church, and the military, oppressed and exploited the nation's millions of peasants. In 1911 a revolutionary movement headed by Francisco Madero and committed to democracy, land reform, and an end to foreign exploitation overthrew Díaz. But then, in 1913, just as Woodrow Wilson was coming into power, Victoriano Huerta, one of Madero's generals, ousted the president, had him killed, and established a full-fledged military dictatorship.

Wilson was appalled at this lawless derailment of the Mexican revolution, and he decided not to sit idly by. He announced that the United States would withhold diplomatic recognition from the new regime and privately informed Huerta that formal ties would be reestablished only if and when Mexico held free presidential elections and Huerta was not a candidate. The Mexican leader, of course, rejected that proposal. Still Wilson was not dissuaded. Remnants of Madero's Constitutionalist movement headed by Venustiano Carranza were then in open revolt against Huerta. To help the rebels, Wilson ordered the U.S. Navy to blockade the Mexican coast so Huerta could not import arms and other materials from abroad.

In April 1914 upon hearing that a German transport laden with arms was headed for Vera Cruz, Wilson ordered armed intervention. American Marines stormed the port killing two hundred Mexicans in the process. In his effort to "teach the South American republics to elect good men" Wilson had intervened militarily in a neighboring state with which the United States was at peace and with which it had very significant economic ties.

In the summer of 1914 Argentina, Brazil, and Chile sponsored a conference on the Mexican crisis at Niagara Falls on the Canadian-American border. The Wilson administration used that meeting as cover to withdraw American troops from Vera Cruz. Later that year Carranza ousted Huerta, and the first truly democratic revolution in Mexico's history got underway. Wilson withheld recognition until he was sure that Carranza proved himself a fit instrument of democracy. Formal diplomatic ties were restored in 1915, but Wilson's diplomacy left a bitter heritage. Mexicans, even those committed to the principles of the revolution, were deeply offended by U.S. policy. Intervention for whatever reason was imperialism, Latinos insisted, and Mexicans resented the assumption implicit in missionary diplomacy that they could not rule themselves.

Thus did the United States build overseas empire, both formal and informal, during the period from 1890 through 1914. Inspired by its expansionist history and notions of American exceptionalism and reacting to perceived economic and strategic interests, America acquired island possessions in the Caribbean and Pacific, proclaimed itself guardian of the open door in China, and intervened repeatedly in various Western Hemisphere republics to maintain stability and protect the investments of U.S. citizens. During the

Progressive Era, the United States realized its dream of becoming a world power with all of the burdens and benefits that that status involved.

The causes and consequences of the Spanish-American War continue to be hotly debated. A number of historians have argued that American intervention into the Cuban-Spanish conflict was pointless and needless. No vital American interests were involved; rather the war and the imperial consequences that followed were the product of a jingoistic press and public and a weak president. In the following selection, John L. Offner argues that the war was both necessary and inevitable. The clash between Spanish colonialism and Cuban nationalism was irreconcilable. If the United States had not intervened, the insurrection would have dragged on for many more years. As far as the United States was concerned, electoral politics—the desire of the Republicans to keep Bryan and the Democrats out of the White House in 1900—was the primary factor in the nation's decision to go to war. Though committed to peace, McKinley, whom Offner portrays as a sincere, effective public servant, was overwhelmed by Spanish and Cuban inflexibility and the desires of his own party.

AN UNWANTED WAR: THE DIPLOMACY OF THE UNITED STATES AND SPAIN OVER CUBA, 1895–1898

John L. Offner

The war for Cuban independence that began in February 1895 involved three participants—Cuba, Spain, and the United States. Each witnessed the events in Cuba from its own historical and national perspective, viewpoints that differed widely and that still color the histories of each nation. To understand the diplomacy of the Spanish-American War, one must appreciate these differing perspectives.

from John L. Offner, "The Cuban Revolution," in *An Unwanted War: The Diplomacy of the United States and Spain Over Cuba* (Chapel Hill: University of North Carolina Press, 1992), 1–16.

For the leaders of the Cuban revolution, the . . . [struggle] that began . . . in 1895 represented the renewal of a war for independence that had started in 1868. All the leaders had taken part in the earlier Ten Years War, and although they had ended armed struggle in 1878, many had never ceased to dream of Cuban independence. Nevertheless, from 1878 to 1895, changes had taken place in Cuba that affected the renewal of the war. During these years, rationalization of the Cuban sugar industry and the end of its forced labor system altered the fundamental economic and social conditions on the island. Abolition of Cuban slavery during the 1880s coincided with a severe depression in the cane sugar industry. European nations were expanding beet sugar production, which decreased the international market for cane sugar and caused a fall in the price. Toward the end of the 1880s, however, the Cuban sugar industry had begun a revival based largely on American markets and capital. Mechanization of mills and transport resulted in larger cane plantations and more efficient sugar-refining mills.

As sugar exports shifted from Europe to North America, much of the innovation was paid for by American dollars. Part of the increase in U.S. investment in the Cuban sugar industry resulted from many Cuban, Spanish, French, and British plantation owners acting to protect their property by becoming naturalized American citizens. But native Americans made some of the largest investments in land, mills, and transportation. Edwin F. Atkins of Boston, for instance, acquired the twelve-thousand-acre Soledad Plantation, which he valued at about $1 million. In 1892 Atkins joined Henry O. Havemeyer of the American Sugar Refining Company in purchasing the Trinidad interests for $600,000, the largest single investment of that year. Atkins, one of Cuba's largest sugar producers, became an active lobbyist in Washington. After the Cuban revolution resumed in 1895, Atkins lobbied against the insurgents and for continued Spanish sovereignty.

Prosperity came to the island's sugar plantations in the early 1890s. As Cuban sugar production and exports soared, large amounts of new American capital were attracted to the island, further accelerating the rationalization of the industry. The boom was cut short in 1895 by changes in U.S. and Spanish tariff legislation, the general economic decline of the 1890s, and the onset of the Cuban revolution. Cuban sugar production peaked in 1894/95 at just over a million tons, and the U.S. market absorbed more than 91 percent of it. By contrast Spain imported slightly more than 2 percent of Cuba's crop. In 1895 American imports fell to 769,000 tons, and the following year they skidded to 235,000 tons, by this time reflecting the devastating effects of the Cuban revolution. Alarmed by the accelerating economic collapse, some Cuban planters looked to Madrid for relief through tariff negotiations with Washington; many others defined their future in terms of autonomy in economic affairs or annexation to the United States.

There were many causes of the Cuban revolution. Working-class Cubans existed in extreme poverty on the fringe of the sugar and tobacco industries. Recently freed slaves faced continued economic and social repression. Social and economic injustice fed the long-smoldering political sources of rebellion. The 1890s depression caused additional economic hardship. Many Cuban leaders who had started the 1860s rebellion and who now lived in exile in Spanish America or the

United States still longed for independence. Spain's failure to provide autonomy as promised in 1878 weakened Cuba's political moderates. During the late 1880s, expatriate revolutionaries began a new campaign for independence. José Martí organized and directed the movement, and General Máximo Gómez became its military head; closely associated was Antonio Maceo, a charismatic Afro-Cuban general. Martí inspired Cuban-American emigré communities in the United States and kept in close contact with Gómez and Maceo, the former having returned to his native Santo Domingo and the latter in exile in Costa Rica. In 1892 Martí capped his organizational efforts with the formation of the Cuban Revolutionary Party, and in the following months Cubans contributed funds for the renewal of the revolution and encouraged rebellion on the island. Because of Spanish vigilance and several false starts, the timing of the outbreak of the Cuban war was delayed until February 1895. When the struggle finally began, the Cuban sugar industry was just starting to feel the effects of a slowdown. Several weeks later, when Gómez, Martí, and Maceo landed on a beach in eastern Cuba, the Cuban sugar plantations had completed the 1894/95 harvest and were laying off laborers, many of whom joined the independence fight. *Cuba Libre* was the cry that rallied the rebels. No longer seeking autonomy under the Spanish flag, they demanded independence and social justice.

United against Spain, the revolutionary leaders were divided in how they saw their future relations with the United States. Insurgent opinion ranged from fear of U.S. annexation to willingness to consider a close association with the American neighbor. Martí was apprehensive over the signs of growing U.S. interest in Hawaii and the Caribbean. One of his goals was to secure Cuban independence before the United States projected an annexationist policy toward the island. Gómez and Maceo were also wary of U.S. interest and believed Cubans could win independence without American intervention.

But Tomás Estrada Palma, who briefly had been president of the Cuban Republic during the Ten Years War, believed that a special relationship with the United States was inevitable and desirable. When Martí died in 1895 in a military clash in Cuba, the civilian leadership of the Cuban Revolutionary Party fell largely to Estrada Palma. He reasoned that since the United States provided the only large market for Cuban sugar, the island's prosperity required commercial access to the United States. Moreover, the immense destruction of the Cuban war necessitated new capital investment, which after independence could come only from the United States.

Another divisive issue for the Cuban insurgents was the design and direction of the revolutionary leadership and future government. The possibility existed that at the end of a successful war, governmental power would be in the hands of victorious military caudillos. Before the rebellion began, Martí argued for civilian control, but Gómez and Maceo were wary of outside interference, recalling the failures of the Ten Years War. Gómez, a stubborn and dictatorial general who liked to issue political proclamations, was suspected of political ambitions, despite his promises that after the war he would accept civilian authority. Maceo, a politically attractive leader, was more openly contemptuous of civilian government, although he pledged to follow Gómez's lead. Covering these conflicting views was a loose agreement worked out by Martí, Gómez, and Maceo over how the revolutionary movement was to be directed and what its outcome should be. When Martí died, the new Cuban civilian leader, Estrada Palma, exercised little influence over Cuba's military leaders. In addition, Estrada Palma questioned the ability of the Cuban masses to govern themselves in an orderly way and to protect property. Although an ardent champion of independence from Spain, he believed that at the end of the war some form of association with the United States would be essential to ensure Cuban political liberty. Thus, Gómez, a tough field commander, and Estrada Palma, a civilian diplomat in New York City, did not have an understanding on how Cuba should be ruled.

Cuba's racial makeup was another factor affecting the diplomacy of the war. The island had a large population of Afro-Cubans. The census of 1887 recorded 1,631,687 people; nearly one-third were of African descent. Most had been freed from slavery during the 1880s, and many lived in squalor on the fringe of plantation society. The ranks of the Cuban revolutionary army contained large numbers of Afro-Cuban soldiers. Upper-class Spaniards and Cubans—planters, merchants, and professionals—often described the war against Spain as a racial and social struggle for control of the island, a struggle that pitted black against white, poor against rich, and rural against urban. There were predictions that if Spain left Cuba, the island would descend into anarchy, racial warfare, and ultimately division into two parts, much like Santo Domingo. As a result some propertied Cubans and Spanish, who feared a triumphant Afro-Cuban army, wanted annexation to the United States.

As the Cuban rebellion engulfed the island, Gómez employed a strategy of destroying the Cuban economy in order to persuade the Spanish to leave, thereby increasing upper-class fears of property destruction, banditry, and anarchy. After losing the Ten Years War, Gómez had brooded over the failure, concluding that the next rebellion must be more savage if it was to succeed. So he set out to turn the island into an economic desert that would become such a burden on the Spanish that they would withdraw. During the Ten Years War the rebellion had been confined to the eastern and mountainous portion of the island and therefore had never crippled the island's economy. This time widespread popular participation contributed to Gómez's military successes which carried revolutionary troops from the eastern to the western tip of Cuba and allowed them to torch the island's wealth.

Initial insurgent successes in Cuba were matched by the broad support the Cuban Revolutionary Party obtained in the United States and other nations. Martí had successfully organized thousands of Cubans residing abroad, many naturalized Americans. Involved in clubs and committees, workers, businessmen, and professionals contributed time and money to the patriotic cause. Political support was strongest in Florida and New York City, where most emigrant Cubans lived. Another important unit, under the leadership of Dr. Ramón Betances, a Puerto Rican physician, was located in Paris, France. Betances hoped the war would unify Cuba and Puerto Rico into a single republic. Exiles in France provided significant financial support for the revolution, and Betances sometimes held covert talks with Spanish agents.

Cuba's major civilian leaders lived in New York City. Estrada Palma was the delegate of the Cuban Revolutionary Party and the chief diplomatic agent of the Republic of Cuba. Benjamín Guerra was the party treasurer; Gonzalo de Quesada

Arôstequia, the party secretary, held the post of Washington lobbyist; and Horatio Rubens, a North American, functioned as legal counsel. All were American citizens. Of these Cuban leaders, Estrada Palma was much older. Since release from a Spanish prison, he had taken up residence in a small New York State community [Central Valley] and taught school. He lived frugally and was respected for his personal honesty and integrity. Rubens, young, ebullient, and full of his self-importance, was passionately caught up in the drama of the revolutionary events. He was eager to provide spirited leadership to the Cuban cause. Quesada was also young and carried into prominence by the independence movement. He frequently represented the Cubans, meeting in Washington with American congressmen sympathetic to the island's independence. All together, the Cuban organization was popularly known as the Junta. It promoted the revolution through public appeals, meetings, financial campaigns, press releases, political lobbying, and outfitting filibustering expeditions for Cuba. During the fall of 1895 the Cubans adopted a constitution and formed a government, which never had as much authority as the military field commanders or the party officers living abroad.

The success of the military efforts in Cuba and the political and financial support overseas were impressive but inadequate to win Cuban independence. Gómez and Maceo initially carried the war across the island, crippled the Cuban economy, and held the support of the Cuban people, achieving far more in one year than during the entire Ten Years War. Nevertheless, the Spanish killed Martí in 1895 and Maceo the next year, which were grievous losses to the revolution. More important, Gómez was unable to drive the Spanish from the island. With a small army, never totaling more than forty thousand men and divided into small, poorly armed units scattered across the island, Gómez could not confront the Spanish in a decisive battle or force them from their entrenched fortifications associated with towns and cities. The Cuban army had no artillery and relied on machete charges, which were ineffective against trenches and barbed-wire emplacements. Thus the war settled down to one of attrition and destruction, with the insurgents roaming over much of the countryside and harassing Spanish troops and outposts where possible. Avoiding large battles, Gómez decimated the Cuban economy; his military success lay in Spain's inability to defeat his army or strategy. Gómez believed that, in time, economic strangulation would free Cuba, but time became the issue; how long and at what human and economic cost would it take to free Cuba?

Estrada Palma also had difficulty in bolstering the revolution. Although the Junta enjoyed American popular approval, it was impossible to transform the many meetings, marches, and press accounts into enough soldiers, guns, and medicines so that Gómez could win the war. Congress passed belligerency resolutions, but the executive branch failed to act; and financial campaigns never raised sufficient funds to satisfy the needs of Gómez. Of seventy-one filibustering expeditions outfitted in the United States, only twenty-seven reached Cuba. Supplies arrived in Cuba from other Caribbean ports, but Estrada Palma and the emigrés were unable to deliver the guns, ammunition, and quinine needed to end the war. Gómez was largely dependent on the men and materiel he obtained within Cuba to keep his army in the field.

Just as the Cubans were unable to bring the war to a quick conclusion, the Spanish also failed to do so. Spain had changed greatly since the independence struggle had begun in the 1860s. The first Cuban rebellion had coincided with many years of peninsular political upheaval that had shaped Spanish political and economic society during the last third of the nineteenth century. A coup in 1868 unseated Queen Isabel II, who had reigned since 1833, and unleashed years of political turbulence on the peninsula. Spanish political factions could agree neither on the choice of the next monarch nor on the definition of what powers the monarchy should have. Thus political cleavages divided monarchists, republicans, clericals, militarists, provincial nationalists, and urban and rural elements. The years of political upheaval ended in 1875 with the restoration of the Bourbon monarchy. Alfonso XII, the son of Isabel, gained the throne through the efforts of the army, led by General Arsenio Martínez de Campos, and the support of professional politicians, headed by Antonio Cánovas del Castillo. The new king agreed to accept constitutional restrictions, thus meeting one of the major demands of political liberals. Cánovas then worked to decrease the influence of the army in politics and thereby end the recurring military coups carried out by *pronunciamientos,* political proclamations of leading generals. He believed that Spain should have a two-party system, which would allow for peaceful changes of ministries and thereby end the revolutionary plots and coups. He encouraged all politicians to accept the restored monarch and the 1876 constitution and to participate in Spanish political life. Those who refused were largely excluded from office—Carlists (supporters of Don Carlos as monarch), republicans, and some provincial autonomists, particularly Catalonians and Basques of the north.

Cánovas's solution to Spain's political disorders lasted into the twentieth century; it defined the governmental system and established the generation of politicians that the United States faced in 1895. The leadership of the Spanish government came from an oligarchy of wealthy, landed, and often titled politicians who controlled local and national offices both through appointments and elections. The monarch had the important powers of selecting the head of the cabinet, dissolving the Cortes [representative assembly], and decreeing new elections. When Alfonso died of tuberculosis in 1885, this authority fell to María Cristina, his Austrian wife, a Hapsburg, who held it until her only son, Alfonso XIII, became sixteen in 1902. Although a foreigner, untrained in Spanish politics, and little loved by her Spanish subjects, the young queen regent took her position seriously. She was intelligent and diligent. Her primary goal was to conserve the Spanish throne for her son. By 1895 the queen regent was an important political presence in Spain's governing councils.

The new Spanish political system contained managed national elections. When Spain's principal political figures—the monarch, cabinet ministers, generals, and loyal opposition leaders—decided that a particular cabinet had reached an impasse solvable only by dismissal, the monarch would select a new prime minister and give him the necessary decree to hold new elections. The incoming prime minister and his interior minister would appoint urban and rural officials throughout Spain who could be counted on to provide an election majority. These officeholders and election managers were called *caciques.* When candidates for office were determined, a few spaces were reserved for the opposition. Often only one person ran for each office, and the results of the election came as no surprise; sometimes they were published before the election occurred. Obviously the Spanish electoral system was not democratic; it was not designed to be so. Rather it allowed for peaceful changes of ministry, an opposition voice in the Cortes, and freedom from military coups, thereby bringing order and centralized control to Madrid after years of political upheaval.

During the Restoration, two governing political parties emerged, the Conservatives and the Liberals. Cánovas led the Conservatives until his assassination in 1897. He tended to be closer to the military officers and ultra-clericals. The Liberals were headed by Práxedes Mateo Sagasta, who retained direction of the party until his death in 1903. Before 1868, Liberal politicians had been excluded from office, and they had generated much of the revolutionary instability of the 1870s. When the Liberal Party entered office, it pressed for a large number of reforms. Opposing ultra-clericals, Liberals sought greater freedom of religious conscience and expanded secular education. One progressive goal, the elimination of slavery, was provided by Cánovas just before he left office in 1881. Liberals also promoted a free press, union legality, and an expanded suffrage. Universal male suffrage, adopted in 1890, was corrupted by the electoral system, yet during the 1890s more people voted, and municipal elections in particular became more responsive to the ballot box. Sagasta also attempted to reform bloated military budgets, but his efforts chiefly alienated the officers. Despite political differences, Liberals and Conservatives shared a common determination to make the Restoration succeed, thereby ending military coups and securing centralized authority throughout Spain. Conservatives accepted limited liberal reform, and Liberals supported the restored monarchy. Thus Cánovas and Sagasta alternated in the office of prime minister from 1875 to 1899, the *turno pacifico*, which brought internal peace and over two decades of stability to Spain.

Though Cánovas and Sagasta shared much, they had contrasting personalities and did not work easily or closely together. Born of lower-middle-class parents in southern Spain, Cánovas came to represent the large landholders of Andalusía. He was a brilliant intellectual, a prominent historian by age twenty-five, who moved easily in the highest social circles and was the center of attention at Madrid salons. A forceful public speaker, he commanded attention by his sparkling intellect. Hardworking, ambitious, and shrewd, he was Spain's most important nineteenth-century politician.

Sagasta had no intellectual pretensions, and to Cánovas, he was barely literate. Born in 1825 in Torrecilla of middle-class parents, he was educated as an engineer. The young Sagasta entered politics as a progressive, championing ideas that were out of favor in Isabel's Spain. Faced by repression, Sagasta turned revolutionary, attempting coups, manning barricades, and leading civil guards. After being imprisoned and exiled, he turned to foreign plotting and edited a revolutionary journal. On his return to Spain, he took an important part in the agitated political events of the post-Isabel years. Sagasta held several cabinet posts, including foreign minister, and was prime minister in 1875 when Martínez de Campos and Cánovas overthrew the government and placed Alfonso XII on the throne. In the years that followed, Sagasta decided to accept the constitutional Bourbon monarchy; other progressive politicians approved his decision and rallied to the new order. From these supporters Sagasta formed the Liberal Party, which he held together until his death. More retiring than Cánovas, Sagasta shunned the social circles and avoided the Madrid salons. Instead he worked ceaselessly to unify the party factions.

By the 1890s the Restoration was showing signs of old age. Cánovas and Sagasta had brought many beneficial changes to Spain but now seemed more involved in retaining office than adopting new programs. Each man was having greater difficulty holding together a group of politicians with which to form a ministry. Cánovas's major political supporter and election manipulator, Francisco Romero Robledo, left his political following. A blatantly corrupt municipal election in Madrid had caused such an outcry against Romero Robledo that the two men separated. Moreover, Francisco Silvela, who supported greater local rule and honesty in government, had left Cánovas's entourage. After Cánovas's death, Silvela bested Romero Robledo and others to become the leading Conservative. Sagasta also had difficulty harmonizing his coalition of politicians. Antonio Maura broke with him over the issue of autonomy for Cuba, and Germán Gamazo, Maura's father-in-law, coveted Sagasta's leadership role. Moreover, with the resumption in the 1890s of colonial wars in Cuba and the Philippine Islands, military leaders had become more important and assertive in Madrid politics. The aged Martínez de Campos and other generals who led the colonial campaigns, such as Camilio García de Polavieja and Valeriano Weyler y Nicolau, assumed greater prominence.

By 1895 there were many peninsular political and economic issues affecting the Cuban war and Spain's diplomacy with the United States. Spanish politicians, mindful of earlier revolutionary turbulence, were united in trying to maintain political authority at the center against all divisive threats. The fundamental point of the Restoration was the continuation of the Bourbon constitutional monarchy. Restoration politicians feared a return to *pronunciamientos* and saw a threat in generals who might turn to coups; but junior officers and common soldiers tended to listen to Republican politicians. On the fringe of Spanish politics were the Carlists, who longed to change the monarchy in their favor by wrapping themselves in the flag of ultra-nationalism and ultra-clericalism. Don Carlos lived in Venice, but he had many Spanish supporters in northern rural Catalonian and Basque villages. Carlists often made common cause with disaffected provincial autonomists and ultra-clericals. When the Cuban war began, Carlists divided: some supported military suppression by Weyler and believed Madrid was fighting to defend the faith in Cuba; others saw in Spanish military failures the opportunity to overthrow a discredited regime. The Spanish government carefully monitored Carlist activities and successfully held them in check. Another group of excluded politicians were the Republicans, who were strongest in urban areas. Inherently opposed to monarchy, they were largely excluded from office, yet they had leaders of national stature. In a crisis, urban workers, soldiers, and junior officers might form behind them to end the Restoration. Republicans, however, were even more divided by the Cuban war than the Carlists. Some took a fraternal interest in the aspiring insular republic, but others, needing the support of the army, took a strong stand against the Cuban Republic. Thus many Carlists and Republicans supported military repression of the insurrection.

Part of the political scene in Spain was the unfettered press. Journalists enjoyed press freedom, and a few newspapers, such as *El Imparcial,* provided broad news coverage and political independence. The bulk of them, however, were allied to a particular politician or party and provided limited news slanted to what their owners wanted. As the war developed in Cuba and the threat of U.S. intervention grew, newspapers often glorified Spanish heroism, patriotism, and noble behavior and characterized Americans as greedy Yankees lacking military virtues. As a result, many Spaniards had unrealistic expectations, believing their navy had a superior fighting spirit and would be victorious.

The Restoration also affected the colonial administration of Cuba and helped to define Madrid's response to the *Grito de Baire.* To obtain a settlement in 1878, the Spanish government promised autonomy to the insurgents but subsequently failed to provide it. Restoration politicians, suppressing the local aspirations of Catalonians and Basques, were unwilling to extend autonomy to Cubans. If Madrid granted home rule to Cuba, some peninsular provincial leaders might demand the same status, and local control would inevitably weaken the power of managed national elections. Instead, Spanish politicians chose to regard Cuba as an inherent part of Spain, much as Asturias or Andalusia. As late as 1893, Antonio Maura presented to the Cortes a Cuban autonomy plan, which Cánovas and Sagasta sharply rejected. The Restoration system allowed Cuba to send members to the Cortes, but insular elections were just as cynically controlled as peninsular ones. On the island a political organization of Spanish officials and community leaders, the Constitutional Union, dominated the administrative process through appointed offices and corrupt elections. Moreover, the bloated military regime found the colonies an opportunity for offices, promotions, and personal financial gain. This regime was unresponsive to Cuba's basic social and economic problems.

In addition, Madrid regulated Cuban trade to benefit Spanish industrial and agricultural interests. During the last third of the nineteenth century, Spain experienced some industrial development. Barcelona's expanding and high-priced textile production, sheltered by high tariff walls, profited from the Cuban market, and Spanish wheat farmers enjoyed flour sales to Cuba. At the same time, Spain encouraged domestic beet production, with the result that Cuba's cane sugar exporters faced declining peninsular sales. Although Spain had an unfavorable balance of trade with the outside world, soaring Cuban sugar sales to the United States helped offset the nation's unfavorable import account. Madrid never solved the problem of rising Spanish exports to the island and decreasing imports from it; indeed during the 1890s, tariff changes worsened the imbalance.

When the Cuban rebellion began, Cánovas, who became prime minister a few weeks after the outbreak, sent Martínez de Campos to Cuba. Arriving in April, the captain general, who had negotiated the end of the previous Cuban uprising, quickly realized that the scope of the new insurrection was much greater than the last and that a political solution modeled after that of 1878 was out of the question.

Pressured by *peninsulares* (Spaniards residing in Cuba) for a military solution, he advised Cánovas in July that he was unwilling to wage all-out war, which would involve a massive loss of life; instead he suggested that General Valeriano Weyler, a vigorous and ruthless officer, assume the command.

Weyler arrived in Cuba in February 1896, bringing with him authority to fight war with war. During the campaign, about two hundred thousand Spanish troops went to Cuba; in addition, Weyler could count on an additional fifty thousand spirited Spanish and Cuban *voluntarios*. Weyler initiated a plan of warfare designed to eliminate insurgency from the economically developed western and central portions of the island and to restrict it to the eastern mountainous region, where it could be gradually reduced. He divided the island into several war zones, separated by north-south military barriers of trenches, barbed wire, and watchtowers. His plan was to concentrate his forces in the west to defeat the insurgents there and to use the military barriers to prevent insurgent reinforcements from the east. After reestablishing control of the west, he intended to move his troops to the central portion of the island, where they would end that insurgency, thereby containing the remaining Cuban forces in the eastern portion of the island, sealed off by a military barrier. During 1896 Weyler realized some successes. He reduced insurgency in the western zone but did not completely eliminate it. The central region became more secure, but insurgent bands still roamed widely throughout much of the area and often crossed the military barriers. Weyler's troops killed Maceo in December 1896, which raised Spanish hopes. Despite his determined efforts and some successes, however, Weyler did not end the insurrection in the western two-thirds of Cuba, and he never reduced the eastern stronghold. Gómez remained in the field and continued to harass Spanish military units and destroy economic assets.

Associated with Weyler's failed military campaign was his civilian reconcentration program designed to separate insurgents from civilians. To cut off manpower, food, supplies, and information from the insurgents, Weyler ordered the peasants to leave their homes and villages and to relocate in towns and cities where the Spanish military could control them. The order was first directed at only a portion of the island, but in a few months it was expanded to include most of the island's rural population. He also called for a cessation of sugar production and tobacco exports in an effort to prevent Cuban planters from bribing insurgents to allow their businesses to operate. Weyler's directives, added to those of Gómez, rapidly reduced the island's productive capacity. More important than the collapse of the economy was the plight of unemployed *reconcentrados* in the fortified towns. Within months about four hundred thousand rural refugees entered concentration sites that were unprepared to receive them. The *reconcentrados* lacked housing, food, sanitation, and medical care. The results were predictable; indeed, Martínez de Campos had foreseen the inevitable effects even as he placed the plan before Cánovas in 1895. Starvation and disease soon gripped the island, and by 1897 the concentration centers had become death camps, with tens of thousands dying and thousands more living under the threat. The fate of the *reconcentrados* grew more grim with each passing month. In 1896 the numbers affected were relatively small, but by 1897 the condition of the *reconcentrados* had reached disaster proportions.

As Spain increased its military pressure on Cuba, Cánovas tried to negotiate a settlement with the insurgents. During 1896 he initiated secret talks with Betances in Paris and continued the meetings sporadically until April 1897. The Cubans rejected an offer of autonomy, one of suzerainty, and a request to pay $200 million for their independence.

By the spring of 1897, Spain's military and diplomatic campaigns had produced limited results at an extremely high cost. The Cuban insurgents were entrenched in eastern Cuba and able to disrupt economic life throughout most of the island. About 250,000 Spanish soldiers and Cuban volunteers had failed to defeat Gómez; some had died in combat, and tens of thousands had succumbed to tropical diseases; makeshift hospitals were filled with sick and dying troops. Those able to fight were insufficient to mount large-scale operations to search out and destroy insurgents. To this military failure were added the thousands of Cuban civilians who had perished in reconcentration camps and the thousands more condemned to starvation, disease, and death. On the peninsula, Cánovas and Weyler were encountering political opposition as Liberals decried military methods and called for a political settlement based on home rule. Abroad, the U.S. government was increasing its demands for an early settlement.

The United States also had changed since the Ten Years War, but some things remained constant. The geographic situation of Cuba was the same; the island, located about ninety miles from the Florida coast, commanded vital sea lanes to the Gulf of Mexico and had many fine natural harbors. It had a subtropical setting for its rich and well-watered soil, which offered a basis for a commercial exchange of sugar and other subtropical products for North American foodstuffs and manufactures. Another constant was the American belief that Spain was decadent and declining and that its remaining colonies would inevitably strike off their chains. Deeply imbued with nineteenth-century liberalism and a belief in progress, Americans identified with Cuba's struggle for political and economic freedom. But American views of Cuban independence were tempered by racism and bigotry, since many opposed annexing Cuba because of its African heritage, Creole population, and Catholic faith.

A significant development since the Ten Years War was the enormous change in relative strength between Spain and the United States, a difference that was evident in nearly every phase of economic life. Spain lagged farther and farther behind in population growth, technological development, manufacturing and mining output, transportation improvements, agricultural production, and financial strength. These economic resources affected military power as well; by 1898 the new American navy outclassed the Spanish fleet.

American economic development during the latter half of the nineteenth century encouraged businessmen and government officials to reappraise commercial and investment opportunities abroad. Periodic economic depressions had sharpened American awareness of the importance of foreign markets to secure national prosperity. Sugar dominated American interest in Cuba, but there were also substantial investments in mining, cattle ranches, and tobacco. The exact amount of investment is unknown, but Americans considered it important. Secretary of State Richard Olney, for instance, estimated U.S. investment at $50 million, and although this was exaggerated, his figure was accepted as a measure of the significance of American economic interest. Moreover, investment was rising rapidly in the 1890s; the largest single annual increase, $1.2 million, came in 1892. More accurate figures were available for commerce; customs data showed a rapid growth in American-Cuban trade, which peaked at just over $103 million in 1893. These figures, $50 million in investment and $100 million in trade, were often cited to illustrate America's economic involvement in Cuba.

Cuba became part of the American political scene of the 1890s as both U.S. political parties faced instability and unprecedented challenges. During the late 1870s and 1880s, the parties had been closely matched. The balance of the 1880s, however, gave way to political turbulence during the next decade as voters shifted traditional party allegiances. New political movements and parties challenged both Republicans and Democrats, who suffered humiliating defeats at the polls. The first to feel the new currents were the Republicans in the 1890 election. Democrats had a field day as 238 gained seats in the House of Representatives, compared with a mere 88 Republicans. William McKinley was among those swept out of Washington. Traditional politicians found little comfort in the formation of the Populist Party in 1891, which, through fusion with discontented Democrats and Republicans, won stunning victories in the West and South. The 1894 election, which took place during the depression and amid bitter partisan divisions, resulted in a rout for the Democrats.

These seesaw election returns set the stage for the presidential election of 1896, the most hotly contested one in twenty years. A coalition of Democrats and Populists formed behind the candidacy of William Jennings Bryan on a platform of silver coinage, which terrified eastern business interests. The contest divided both political parties as silver Republicans supported Bryan and as gold Democrats backed McKinley. Unprecedented campaign innovations, Bryan's extensive electioneering throughout the nation, and Mark Hanna's massive financing, changed the character of presidential campaigning. Although McKinley won, Republican politicians feared another election debacle and expected future desperate contests.

Into this unstable and passionate political scene came the Cuban issue. Politicians of all stripes tried to use the Cuban insurrection to promote their cause. Republicans, Democrats, and Populists weighed in on the side of Cuba's insurgency, demonstrating their enthusiasm in public meetings and congressional debates. It was left to the presidents, Cleveland and McKinley, to try to find a way to accommodate popular politics at home to diplomatic responsibilities abroad. . . .

Suggested Readings

David L. Anderson, *Imperialism and Idealism: American Diplomats in China, 1861–1898* (1986).

Robert L. Beisner, *From the Old Diplomacy to the New, 1865–1900*, 2nd ed. (1986).

Charles S. Campbell, Jr., *Transformation of American Foreign Relations, 1865–1900* (1976).

Walter Lafeber, "The American Search for Opportunity, 1865–1913," in *The Cambridge History of U.S. Foreign Relations*, ed. Warren Cohen (1993).

Gerald F. Linderman, *The Mirror of War: American Society and the Spanish-American War* (1974).

Stuart Creighton Miller, *"Benevolent Assimilation": The American Conquest of the Philippines, 1899–1903* (1982).

Thomas J. Osborne, *"Empire Can Wait": American Opposition to Hawaiian Annexation, 1893–1898* (1981).

Louis A. Perez, Jr., *Cuba Between Empires, 1878–1902* (1983).

Tom E. Terrill, *The Tariff, Politics and American Foreign Policy* (1973).

David F. Trask, *The War with Spain in 1898* (1981).

The Spanish-American War

Jules R. Benjamin, *The United States and the Origins of the Cuban Revolution* (1990); H.W. Brands, *Bound to Empire: The United States and the Philippines* (1992); Willard B. Gatewood, Jr., *"Smoked Yankees" and the Struggle for Empire: Letters from Negro Soldiers, 1898–1902* (1971); Ernest R. May, *Imperial Democracy: The Emergence of America as a Great Power* (1961).

Expansion of the American Empire into the Pacific

Warren I. Cohen, *America's Response to China*, 2nd ed. (1980); Jane Hunter, *The Gospel of Gentility: American Women Missionaries in Turn-of-the-Century China* (1984); Akira Iriye, *Across the Pacific: An Inner History of American–East Asian Relations* (1967); Thomas J. McCormick, *China Market: America's Quest for Informal Empire, 1893–1901* (1967); Charles E. Neu, *The Troubled Encounter* (1975).

Theodore Roosevelt and Latin America

Howard K. Beale, *Theodore Roosevelt and the Rise of America to World Power* (1956); Richard H. Collin, *Theodore Roosevelt's Caribbean* (1990); Walter LaFeber, *The Panama Canal* (1979); Lester E. Langley, *The Banana Wars* (1983); David Mc-Cullough, *The Path Between the Seas: The Creation of the Panama Canal, 1870–1914* (1977).

Woodrow Wilson, Missionary Diplomacy, and the Mexican Revolution

Peter Calvert, *The Mexican Revolution, 1910–1914* (1968); Lloyd Gardner, *Safe for Democracy: The Anglo-American Response to Revolution, 1913–1923* (1984); P. Edward Haley, *Revolution and Intervention: The Diplomacy of Taft and Wilson with Mexico, 1910–1917* (1970); Arthur S. Link, *Woodrow Wilson: Revolution, War, and Peace* (1979); Robert E. Quirk, *An Affair of Honor: Woodrow Wilson and the Occupation of Veracruz* (1962).

QUESTIONS FOR DISCUSSION

1. Discuss the events leading to war with Spain in 1898 and evaluate America's military performance during the war.

2. Describe the events leading up to the open door notes. Could these policy statements be considered multinational agreements? Why or why not?

3. Analyze Roosevelt's diplomacy in the Panama Canal affair and discuss the consequences of the Roosevelt Corollary.

4. How was dollar diplomacy applied to Latin America and China? Assess its effectiveness.

5. Discuss the Mexican-American crisis of 1913–1916. How did Wilson's policy exemplify missionary diplomacy?

6. According to the selection by John L. Offner, what tactics did Cuban rebels employ in their fight for independence from the Spanish?

7. Offner claims that certain domestic events in America led to a declaration of war against Spain. What were they?

CHAPTER SEVENTEEN

PROGRESSIVISM:
The Many Faces of Reform

THEODORE ROOSEVELT

No one greeted the declaration of war with Spain in 1898 more enthusiastically than Theodore Roosevelt, an aristocratic young New Yorker, who was assistant secretary of the Navy in the administration of President William McKinley. Previously he had served as a member of the Civil Service Commission and as a police commissioner in New York City. An ardent expansionist, unwilling to remain an armchair warrior in Washington, he resigned his position to join a volunteer cavalry regiment composed of cowboys, Indian fighters, and Ivy League polo players and steeplechase riders.

STATE VISION

Relishing what he termed the "great adventure" in Cuba, Roosevelt emerged from the military campaign as the hero of San Juan Hill. His newly acquired fame propelled him into Republican politics in New York where the party desperately needed a candidate who was both virtuous and attractive. Roosevelt won the Republican nomination for governor, and despite the apprehension of party bosses about the choice of one already widely known as a reformer, New Yorkers elected him governor in the fall of 1898. During the next two years Roosevelt mastered the mechanics of political power and perfected a distinctive political technique and style. The governorship completed his preparation for national leadership.

NATIONAL VISION

Chosen as McKinley's vice presidential running mate in 1900, Roosevelt proved to be a colorful and effective campaigner. An enthusiastic defender of the Republican party's policy of overseas expansion, he contributed significantly to the party's triumph over William Jennings Bryan and the Democrats in a campaign in which imperialism was proclaimed "the paramount issue." Less than six months after his inauguration as vice president, Roosevelt succeeded to the presidency as a result of McKinley's death at the hand of an assassin.

A SYMBOL OF PROGRESSIVISM

Despite the tragedy that brought Roosevelt to the presidency, few Americans failed to detect that his accession to the office signaled "the dawn of a new day." The youngest of the U.S. presidents, he and his six rambunctious children enlivened a theretofore dull White House. Not since Thomas Jefferson had a president exhibited greater intellectual curiosity and possessed literacy in so many fields as Roosevelt. The scope of his interests enabled him to shift with ease from plotting political strategy to an informed discourse on Icelandic literature or a discussion of an obscure zoological question.

If Roosevelt resembled Jefferson in the range of his intellectual interests, his political ideas owed far more to Alexander Hamilton. An advocate of a strong, active central government, he possessed a broad view of the presidential office and achieved some of his goals through a dramatic use of executive authority.

Though a gradualist and moralist with a deep reverence for social order and historical continuity, he was never simply a defender of the status quo. Whether Roosevelt should be classified as a conservative or reformer—or perhaps a "conservative progressive"—is complicated by the Rooseveltian personality that combined contradictory impulses. A background of wealth, lofty social status, and education instilled in him a strong sense of stewardship which he translated to mean an obligation to serve, inspire, and lead those who, unlike himself, did not belong to the "governing class." He both revered the past and looked confidently to the future. Significant reform, he believed, came through steady, continuous growth rather than through radical alterations likely to have disruptive effects. His was the pursuit of a middle way to protect "orderly liberty" from tyranny on the one hand and anarchy on the other. During his seven and a half years as president, Roosevelt, more than any other individual, came to symbolize the national reform ferment known as progressivism. His youth, moral fervor, and skill in public relations combined to make him a highly visible and often controversial spokesman for reform.

INFLUENCES OF A NEW WORLD

When Roosevelt moved into the White House in 1901, the United States was a vastly different nation than it had been at the time of his birth forty-two years earlier. Victory in the Spanish-American War had resulted in the acquisition of a far-flung empire and the establishment of the country as a world power, while dramatic economic and demographic changes had gone far toward transforming the United States into an industrial nation by 1900. Changes of such magnitude left in their wake a host of problems, as well as a sense of uneasiness, especially among middle- and upper-class Americans who believed that the nation confronted a serious social crisis. A succession of developments and events during the decade immediately prior to Roosevelt's accession to the presidency intensified their anxieties. Among these were a devastating depression; the emergence of both Populism and Eugene Debs' Socialist party; numerous strikes and the rise of small, but violent, unions; the arrogance of large corporations; and the assassination of President McKinley by an anarchist.

THE GOALS OF PROGRESSIVISM

The search for a way both to ensure the material bounty of industrialism and preserve the principles and values of a democratic society was the concern of the progressive movement, a variegated and diffuse reform effort that evolved and expanded throughout the first two decades of the twentieth century. Never a cohesive movement with a single reform agenda, progressivism embraced a wide variety of reforms that were sometimes overlapping and contradictory. Unlike rural-based Populism in the 1890s, progressivism emerged and evolved in an era of relative prosperity. Despite its debt to Populism, however, progressivism possessed an urban cast and reached its fullest maturity in American cities. Although members of the middle and upper-middle classes, including intellectuals, politicians, clergymen, social workers and business people, assumed leadership roles, progressive reforms in time attracted the support of a sufficiently broad spectrum of the population to give them appeal across class, cultural, and even ethnic lines.

As heirs to a reform tradition that reached into the distant American past, progressives borrowed from widely disparate sources both at home and abroad. Inspired by modern science and its potential for improving the human condition, they utilized the methods and tools of social science in the pursuit of their objectives; in fact, a reliance on experts, statistics, and data collection, as well as an emphasis on efficiency and rational planning, were important components of their strategies. They embraced the twin gospels of morality and efficiency, and, like Theodore Roosevelt, implored Americans to be "upright . . ., practical and efficient."

Progressive rhetoric was intensely moralistic and robustly optimistic. But this rhetoric was sometimes misleading. Progressives, for example, regularly made claims in the name of "the people," when in fact they meant people like themselves. References to the "common good" had different meanings to different progressives. If there was an intellectual commitment more or less universal within progressive ranks, it was faith in human progress and belief in the basic goodness of individuals. The existence of evil, most agreed, was the result of defective institutions and/or oppressive environments rather than the work of inherently evil human beings. The progressive mission, then, was to reform society and institutions in ways that would allow people to live richer, fuller, and more harmonious lives, an objective summarized in the term "social efficiency." To achieve such ends, progressives implemented policies based on what they called "universal models," that is, ideal examples applicable everywhere. Such models were the results of statistics, surveys, and other data often collected and prepared by individuals trained in the new social sciences. Confident of their own instincts and degree of enlightenment, progressives had no doubt that the responsibility for determining the proper alterations in society was theirs. Nor did they doubt that an informed, rational citizenry would agree.

MOTIVES BEHIND THE REFORMS

No single motive was universally operative among progressives, but rather a wide range of different impulses and considerations, from altruism to self-interest and a desire for social control, inspired individuals and groups to participate in reform efforts. Humanitarian concerns inspired some reformers, especially those steeped in the values and ethics of Christianity as articulated by advocates of the Social Gospel. For them, reform provided a means of translating their religious faith into action. Such progressives have been termed "ministers of reform" and their activities as "reforms of the heart." Their quest for social justice appeared in many guises, from a multifaceted crusade in behalf of children to campaigns focusing on housing, health, education, and problems of the urban poor. The quintessential advocate of social justice was Jane Addams, the founder of Hull House in Chicago, a settlement house that ministered to the least fortunate of the city's population and inspired similar enterprises throughout the United States. The settlement house was only one example of voluntary associations that were often on the cutting edge of the reform efforts. Such organizations, especially, were responsible for important progressive accomplishments.

Other progressives acted out of fear or self-interest. The display of corporate arrogance, coupled with eruptions of anger and violence in the 1890s, conjured up images of class warfare, socialism, and other heretical doctrines; hence, alterations in American society and institutions were necessary to save the nation from consequences certain to result from the widening gulf between the few "haves" and the many "have-nots." Scarcely less disturbing for some progressives was the perceived threat posed by the immigrant masses (18 million between 1890 and 1920) who inhabited the sprawling slums of American cities. Such people were viewed both as the primary cause of the "urban problem" and as a menace to democracy. Reform as applied to them often meant social control and immigration restriction.

A MORE COMPLEX SOCIETY

But whether it was the old middle class in the throes of a status revolution or a self-conscious new middle class struggling to gain ascendancy that energized the reform movement, its rank and file consisted of Americans who were aware, however vaguely, that the turn of the century had ushered in a new and different society that was more complex, interdependent, and impersonal than the one in which their immediate forebears had lived. Despite high employment rates, increasing personal income, and other evidences of a flourishing economy that fed optimism and confidence, there also existed a gnawing "sense of vulnerability"—a mood of uneasiness spawned by the perception that individuals no longer exercised control over their own destinies, but rather had become pawns of impersonal forces.

Of all the impersonal forces perceived as threats to the individual, the powerful corporation, in popular opinion, was the most ominous. The common people saw themselves as hostages or victims of what were variously referred to as "vested interests" or "malefactors of great wealth." Such a perception created a public mood that was receptive to reforms which promised to cut through the impersonality of modern industrial life to protect or extend the rights of individuals. Progressive reforms, either directly or indirectly, held out such a promise. Therefore, if the means employed by progressives sometimes appeared radical, the ends they sought were, more often than not, conservative.

MUCKRAKERS

Among those who articulated, interpreted, and gave focus to the anxieties that troubled Americans at the beginning of the twentieth century was a group of talented journalists, who wrote principally for inexpensive, popular magazines, and were called "muckrakers" by Roosevelt. Among the most notable muckrakers were Ida Tarbell, Lincoln Steffens, Samuel Hopkins Adams, and David Graham Phillips. Their exposés, appearing in *McClure's*, *Collier's*, *Ladies Home Journal*, and comparable publications, explored a wide range of topics from corruption in city government, health-threatening foods and medicines, and corporate skullduggery to the exploitation of labor, the horrors of immigrant ghettos, and the venality of United States senators.

Convinced, as were progressives in general, that social change could be achieved through education, muckrakers made publicity a primary instrument of reform. They sought to educate the public by laying bare "the shameful facts," fully confident that a rational citizenry, properly informed, would take action to correct problems such as economic and social inequities, inefficient and unresponsive government, and reckless exploitation of human and natural resources. Although muckrakers did not cause or create the progressive movement, they raised public awareness, articulated popular indignation, and indicated the directions that reform efforts should take.

Widespread discontent with the status quo, which crystallized during the turbulent and economically depressed 1890s, meant that the public was all the more receptive to the muckrakers' exposés. In particular their disclosures reawakened and refashioned the old fear that privileged business corrupted politics and government.

GOVERNMENTAL ACTIVISM

Convinced that the nation confronted a social crisis that threatened the historic promise of American life, progressives of widely different backgrounds concluded that laissez-faire had to be replaced by government activism. Government alone, they believed, had the power to preserve economic and political freedom by ridding the new industrial order of its flaws. Progressive reformers had no intention of destroying industrial capitalism; rather their aim was to make adjustments to ensure that it operated more equitably and efficiently and conformed to what they considered basic American principles. Confident of their ability to achieve such goals through the application of a combination of the "scientific" method and Christian ethics, they first devoted themselves to capturing control of the organs of government, and once in control, they not only attempted to utilize political devices and instruments that would guarantee what they usually termed "the people's rule," but also invoked government power to mitigate and humanize some of the worst aspects of industrial life.

WOMEN'S ACTIVISM

The shaping of the progressive agenda and the achievement of its objectives owed much to the activities of women and their organizations. In 1890 white women's clubs had united in the General Federation of Women's Clubs, followed six years later by the formation of the National Association of Colored Women. Both consisted primarily of educated, middle-class women who had originally organized societies and clubs for the purpose of self-improvement. By the turn of the century, women's organizations had begun to shift their focus to social and cultural change. In addition to championing women's suffrage, they mounted campaigns that established libraries, hospitals, parks and playgrounds, and juvenile courts, as well as improved schools, sanitation, and public health facilities. As municipal housekeepers, women came to recognize the limits of local charity in addressing national problems of industrial society. Moving beyond moral suasion to become sophisticated participants in the political process, they urged greater social responsibility on the part of the state and ultimately succeeded in having much of the social policy of their voluntary organizations embraced by government. Their efforts were critical in the passage of legislation dealing with everything from child labor, public education, and prohibition, to factory and tenement inspection, pure foods and drugs, and conservation.

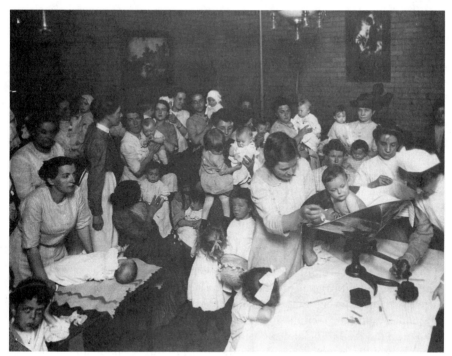

A baby clinic operated by the Infant Welfare Society in Chicago, ca. 1911.

TYPES OF REFORM

Broadly speaking, progressive reforms fell into four categories: changes designed to make the government more efficient, honest, and responsive to the popular will; more stringent regulation of business to protect the interests of consumers, workers, and small business people; efforts to improve the quality of life in the burgeoning cities; and the use of the coercive power of government to impose middle-class standards on personal behavior and morality. The final category included measures designed to eliminate gambling, dance halls, prostitution, liquor, and opium (drugs) as well as laws in a few states requiring the sterilization of certain criminals, sex offenders, and mentally deficient persons.

Of the efforts to achieve social control few, if any, attracted as much attention as the prohibition movement. The campaign against alcoholic beverages began in the nineteenth century as a moral crusade, but progressives brought it to fruition by marshaling scientific evidence to demonstrate the evils of alcohol. Therefore, the "liquor traffic" came to be linked to gambling, poverty, corrupt politics, rowdyism, violence, disregard for the Sabbath, inefficiency, disease, and a host of "kindred evils."

THE POLITICS OF REFORM: LOCAL TO NATIONAL GROWTH

The initial stimulus for reform legislation came largely from special interest organizations such as those dedicated to good government, social uplift, and consumer concerns rather than from political parties which in time embraced, in varying degrees, the progressive agenda. Constantly shifting alliances and coalitions in pursuit of one reform or another characterized progressive politics. Politically, progressivism flowed upward from the local level through the states to the federal government. Reform flourished first and most dramatically in American cities. The organization of the National Civic Federation in 1900 signaled a new era of urban reform. The bossism, corruption, and inefficiency that were characteristic of so many municipal governments and so graphically exposed by muckrakers, ultimately set in motion organized political efforts to reform and restructure city government. Such efforts led to demands for honest, efficient officials, impartial representation, expanded social services, equitable taxation, regulation of public utilities, and other changes.

Often rallying around a charismatic political figure, municipal reformers either wrested political control of major cities or seriously challenged those long entrenched in power. Some introduced structural reforms such as the city manager and the commission form of government as devices to promote efficiency and to focus official responsibility. Because changes in city charters and taxation usually required approval of state legislatures, municipal reformers took their campaigns to state capitals under the slogan "home rule for cities."

In some respects the reform movement at the state level was the most critical politically, because state legislatures not only determined the scope of reform that could be achieved at the local level, but because they elected U.S. senators, they were also critical in determining the extent of reform legislation at the federal level. Parading under a variety of labels such as the "Wisconsin Idea" or the "Oregon System," statewide progressive crusades gradually captured control of the organs of state government. As the progressive movement evolved, it attracted an expanding constituency. A few reformers began to appear in the House of Representatives by the middle of the first decade of the twentieth century. Their appearance in the Senate where the terms were six, rather than two, years in length was more gradual.

The progressive presence at the national level received an important boost in 1901 with the elevation of Theodore Roosevelt to the presidency. The mere fact that Roosevelt continually talked about reforms that needed to be instituted meant that his presence in the White House provided progressivism with the wherewithal to have a national impact. But confronted by a conservative Congress, jealous of its prerogatives and hostile to vigorous White House leadership, Roosevelt moved cautiously but steadily during his first term. Prior to 1905 when he was "president by accident," Roosevelt's most significant political achievement was his success in capturing control of the Republican party. Although he wrung a few concessions from Congress, his most dramatic activities, such as trust-busting and settlement of the coal strike, were those that did not require congressional approval.

ROOSEVELT'S REFORMS

ANTITRUST ACTION

By the time Roosevelt reached the White House, he was convinced that monopolistic corporations posed an ominous threat to the nation. His main task, he noted a little later, was to discover "methods of controlling the big corporations without paralyzing the energies of the business community." In addressing the problem of big business, Roosevelt invoked the existing Sherman Antitrust Act (1890) as the basis for a suit against the Northern Securities Company, a railroad combine which had come into existence after a no-holds-barred struggle that had elicited much unfavorable publicity. The court ruled in the government's favor and for the first time ordered the dissolution of a corporation for violating the Sherman Act.

During his presidency a total of more than forty antitrust suits were instituted against mammoth corporations. Though labelled the "trust buster," Roosevelt ultimately concluded that the solution to the trust problem lay in federal regulation rather than in efforts to break up large corporations. Ever the moralist, he distinguished between good and bad trusts, not on the basis of their size because he believed that big corporations were essential to modern industrial capitalism, but rather on the basis of their conduct. To assist him in making such distinctions, he got Congress in 1903 to approve the establishment of the Bureau of Corporations with the power to investigate interstate corporations.

LABOR DISPUTES

Three months after instituting an antitrust suit against the Northern Securities Company, Roosevelt made dramatic use of executive authority by mediating a serious labor crisis prompted by a strike of miners in the anthracite coalfields of Pennsylvania. In May 1902, over fifty thousand miners belonging to the United Mine Workers went on strike demanding wage increases, the eight-hour day, and recognition of the union. The principal owners of the mines were several railroad companies whose spokesmen adopted an intransigent position toward the labor agitators responsible for what they termed an "insurrection."

The federal government had intervened in strikes previously, but always, either directly or indirectly, on the side of management. Federal intervention under Roosevelt represented a significant departure from such an approach. The first indication of his different strategy was his summons of representatives of both union and mine owners to a White House conference in a futile attempt at presidential arbitration of the dispute. Outraged by mine owners' arrogance and adherence to a divine right property doctrine, Roosevelt threatened to seize and operate the mines, even though his advisors warned that he lacked the constitutional authority to do so. Deeply concerned about the dwindling supply and rising price of coal and especially about the impact on Republicans in the fall elections of 1902, the president ultimately secured a settlement of the strike that granted the miners a wage increase and reduction in hours but not recognition of their union. Although claims that Roosevelt's action in the coal strike was proof that he was a champion of labor and consumers and a foe of business were exaggerated, his strategy established an important precedent by injecting the federal government as a third party to major labor disputes.

Elected president in his own right in 1904, Roosevelt pushed for reform legislation becoming bolder and more effective thereafter, as was evident in legislation to regulate railroads and to protect and promote public health. Although the Hepburn Act of 1906 involved considerable compromise on Roosevelt's part, it was nonetheless an extraordinarily significant piece of legislation which revitalized and substantially expanded the powers of the Interstate Commerce Commission. No less indicative of Roosevelt's contribution to the enlarged regulatory role and activism of the federal government was his success in securing the enactment of the Pure Food and Drug Act and Meat Inspection Act of 1906 which banned the manufacture and sale of mislabelled, adulterated, or unsanitary foods and drugs. All the while, he overhauled the machinery of the executive department, making it more efficient and honest, served notice on what he called "the wealthy criminal class" that their crimes would no longer go unpunished, and inspired a national crusade to conserve natural resources.

ENVIRONMENTAL CONSERVATION

Among the most impressive and enduring achievements of Roosevelt's administration were his efforts in behalf of conserving the nation's forests, land, water, wildlife, and other natural resources. As an outdoorsman and naturalist, Roosevelt had taken a keen interest in conservation long before becoming president. Beginning in 1901, he rarely missed an opportunity thereafter to promote the cause of conservation. Through executive action under the provisions of existing laws or the implied authority of the presidency, he added 150 million acres to government reserves. All the while he functioned as an evangelist who marshaled the support of a wide variety of influential organizations on behalf of his crusade. The nation, for the first time, acquired a comprehensive conservation policy as a result of efforts by the president and a small group of government officials committed to rational planning, scientific management and use of resources, and the gospel of efficiency rather than mere preservation. Prominent among this group was Gifford Pinchot, the head of the U.S. Forest Service.

THE EXPANDED PRESIDENTIAL ROLE

Although the list of reform legislation secured by Roosevelt was admittedly short, it was substantial, considering the political context within which it was achieved and the issues it addressed. Roosevelt's significance lay not in the quantity of legislation he secured, but rather, as a contemporary explained, it

Theodore Roosevelt, an enthusiastic advocate of conservation, was photographed during a visit to Yosemite National Park.

lay in his success in making reform respectable. Using the White House as "a bully pulpit," he functioned superbly as an educator and publicist for progressivism. In the process, he was not only a major contributor to the reform agenda, but also responsible for establishing the central role of the federal government in the implementation of that agenda. When Roosevelt left the White House in 1909, not the least of his legacies was a redefinition of the office of president.

WILLIAM HOWARD TAFT

REFORM AND A GROWING CONSERVATISM

During the tenure of Roosevelt's hand-picked successor, William Howard Taft, who easily triumphed over Democrat William Jennings Bryan in 1908, the progressive movement continued to expand and evolve in spite of the fact that Taft's primary concern lay not so much in securing additional reforms as in what he termed placing "the circle of law" around those instituted by his predecessor. Lacking the flair for drama, political skill, and popular appeal of Roosevelt, Taft also had the misfortune to be president when his party split into warring factions. The result was that he got caught in the crossfire between the progressive (Insurgent) and conservative (Old Guard) wings of his party.

The struggle over the Payne-Aldrich tariff bill dramatized the division within Republican ranks. Unlike Roosevelt who steered clear of the tariff, Taft boldly confronted the issue, demanded a lowering of tariff rates, and called Congress into special session in March 1909 to enact a new tariff law. Insurgent Republicans mounted a well orchestrated campaign to thwart what they perceived as the effort of the Old Guard to maintain a tariff favorable to special interests. The outcome of the struggle was a measure which scarcely constituted a substantial downward revision as called for by the president. That Taft acquiesced in and signed into law a measure so radically altered by Old Guard senators alienated the Insurgents from the White House. For many Insurgents, Taft's later reference to the measure as "the best tariff ever passed by the Republican Party" was proof that the president had joined the ranks of the party's conservatives. Reinforcing such a perception was Taft's passive role during the Insurgents' successful struggle to curb the power of Speaker Joseph G. Cannon, an Old Guard stalwart, and to "democratize" the rules of the House of Representatives. For his part, Taft came to view the Insurgents as untrustworthy, even dangerous, men whom he treated as the party's unwanted stepchildren.

Although feuding between the White House and congressional insurgents deepened the divisions among Republicans and complicated the enactment of legislation, the reform record of Taft's administration was by no means as barren as some contemporary critics charged. Among the reform measures that Taft secured from Congress were those establishing a system of postal savings banks, the Appalachian Forest Reserve, and the Children's Bureau which possessed broad authority over all matters affecting minors. Of especial significance was the Mann-Elkins Act (1910) that further expanded the powers of the Interstate Commerce Commission and created a commerce court to expedite appeals from the Commission's rulings. The Mann Act of 1910, by outlawing the transporting of women across state lines for "immoral purposes"—the "white-slave traffic"—represented a major victory for antivice reformers. In four years Taft initiated more antitrust suits and withdrew more public land than Roosevelt did in seven and a half years. Ironically, it was a highly publicized dispute over conservation between Taft's secretary of the Interior Richard Ballinger and Roosevelt's appointee Gifford Pinchot that led to the open break between Roosevelt and Taft. With Pinchot's encouragement Roosevelt became convinced that his hand-picked successor was undermining what Roosevelt had called "my policies."

REPUBLICAN RUPTURE AND DEMOCRATIC VICTORY

The internecine conflict within Republican ranks, coupled with the rupture in the Roosevelt-Taft friendship and the newly discovered vitality of the

Democrats, spelled disaster for Republican candidates in the congressional elections of 1910. Bored with private life and opposed to Taft's renomination, Roosevelt acquiesced in pleas from progressive Republicans and agreed to seek the party's presidential nomination in 1912. Failing to defeat Taft at the Republican convention, Roosevelt became the standard bearer of a third party, known as the Progressive party, created by Insurgent Republicans and others. A divided Republican party opened the way for the Democrats to capture control of the White House under the leadership of Woodrow Wilson, the party's presidential nominee.

TWO VERSIONS OF POLITICAL PROGRESSIVISM

Overshadowing the lackluster Taft during the campaign, Roosevelt and Wilson occupied center stage with a spirited debate over their respective versions of progressivism, known as the New Nationalism and the New Freedom.

ROOSEVELT'S NEW NATIONALISM

Roosevelt's New Nationalism, based on the assumption that economic concentration was an inevitable attribute of modern industrialism, called for a federal government sufficiently powerful to exercise vigorous regulation of big business and endorsed a wide range of social justice measures such as the abolition of child labor, suffrage and minimum wage for women, health and safety standards for labor, and a system of "social insurance."

WILSON'S NEW FREEDOM

Reflecting a commitment to limited government, small businesses, and free competition, Wilson's New Freedom tended to equate bigness in business with badness and to favor breaking up monopolistic corporations rather than creating big government to regulate them. Wilson's references to social justice were sympathetic but not specific. In a crowded field of presidential aspirants that included Roosevelt, Taft, Eugene Debs of the Socialist party, and an assortment of others, Wilson won the election of 1912 by polling 42 percent of the popular vote.

WOODROW WILSON

MATURITY OF PROGRESSIVISM

Progressivism on the national level came to maturity during the presidency of Wilson. A highly respected scholar and educator who had served as president of Princeton University, Wilson was a native of the South and scion of one of the region's notable Presbyterian families. A Democrat initially wedded to states' rights and limited government, he was a favorite of the party's conservatives. But by 1910 when he was overwhelmingly elected governor of New Jersey, Wilson had shed much of his conservatism. A strong political leader, he secured the enactment of a wide-ranging reform program during his term as governor. The growth of reform sentiment and the expansion of the progressive agenda during the first dozen years of the twentieth century, coupled with the foundation laid by Taft and especially Roosevelt, enabled Wilson to achieve an impressive array of reform legislation during his first term as president.

ECONOMIC REFORMS

Changes in the tariff, banking system, and corporate regulation were top priorities of Wilson's initial legislative program.

A Lowered Tariff and a Graduated Income Tax

In securing legislation that embodied the desired changes the president indisputably proved his effectiveness as a politician. He won congressional approval of the Underwood-Simmons Act (1913) which substantially lowered tariff rates and imposed a graduated income tax as authorized by the newly ratified Sixteenth Amendment.

The Federal Reserve Act

Although there was popular clamor for banking reform to modernize the banking system and destroy the concentration of the "money power" on Wall Street, there was no unanimity about how such reform was to be implemented. Wilson's mastery of political maneuvering was nowhere more evident than his engineering the passage of the Federal Reserve Act (1913) that contained features of the disparate proposals put forward by various interest groups. It was, without question, one of the most significant and enduring achievements of Wilson's administration. The decentralization feature of the act provided a system of regional federal reserve banks, while the centralization feature imposed federal supervision by creating a Federal Reserve Board. One of the most important provisions of the measure was authorization of a new, flexible currency, known as federal reserve notes, that would expand or contract in volume in response to the needs of the economy. Whatever its deficiencies, the Federal Reserve Act brought order and coordination to a chaotic banking system and for the first time provided an efficient clearinghouse for checks.

Antitrust Legislation and the Federal Trade Commission

No less complex than the problems posed by the banking reform were those involved in the passage of legislation regarding monopolistic corporations. Wilson's formula for harnessing corporate power, as spelled out during the presidential campaign of 1912, found expression in the Clayton Antitrust Act (1914) which replaced the Sherman Act (1890) as the nation's basic antitrust law. Because the Clayton Act exempted labor unions from prosecution under antitrust legislation, Samuel Gompers of the American Federation of Labor described it as "Labor's Magna Carta."

A month prior to the passage of the Clayton Act, Congress enacted the Trade Commission Act. Enthusiastically supported by the president, this measure created a new regulatory agency, the Federal Trade Commission (FTC) that more nearly reflected the philosophy of Roosevelt's New Nationalism than it did Wilson's New Freedom. Designed as a federal watchdog, the new agency was empowered to investigate violations of antitrust statutes, to require periodic reports from interstate corporations, and to issue cease and desist orders when it discovered the existence of unfair trade practices. Wilson's enthusiasm for the FTC indicated that he had substantially shifted his position on the trust issue, a shift that focused on the regulatory, rather than the trust-busting, approach.

A Rejection of Additional Reforms

Despite the significance of the legislation enacted during Wilson's first eighteen months in the White House, many groups of Americans considered his legislative agenda woefully incomplete. Wilson refused to support measures prohibiting child labor and providing rural credits (long-term, low-interest-rate government loans to farmers). Proponents of women's rights, including suffrage, also expressed disappointment with the president's inaction regarding their concerns. African Americans whom Wilson had courted in the campaign of 1912 held him responsible for allowing the spread of segregation within the federal government. As one African-American spokesman noted, the president had instituted a New Freedom "for whites" and "a new slavery" for blacks. The clamor of these groups and social justice advocates in general was of little avail, for Wilson rejected all pleas for additional reforms, at least until the fall elections of 1914 allowed him to assess the direction of the political wind. Taking place in the midst of an economic slump and after the outbreak of the Great War in Europe in August 1914, the elections resulted in a resurgence of Republican strength generally and a reduction in Democratic majorities in Congress.

POSITIONING FOR REELECTION

Military Preparedness

Although war orders from Europe stimulated the American economy and allowed Democrats to claim credit for the return of prosperity, Wilson was well aware that a reunited Republican party—still the majority party—posed serious difficulties for his reelection in 1916. Further complicating the political scene for both parties was the emergence of foreign policy issues, involving

America's rights as a neutral power, German submarine warfare, and the question of military preparedness (see Chapter 6). The result was a demand for a military buildup which Wilson initially opposed as unnecessary and needlessly provocative. But in view of events in 1915, particularly the sinking of the *Lusitania* that cost the lives of 128 Americans, Wilson cautiously altered his stand on "preparedness" and endorsed a substantial increase in the nation's armed forces.

Continued Domestic Reforms

Despite efforts to justify his shift in terms of "preparedness for peace," most progressives in both parties viewed Wilson's support of national defense measures with disfavor. At the same time they, along with various other groups, notably farmers, pressured the administration to include their domestic demands in his legislative agenda. No one was more keenly aware than Wilson that the support of such constituencies was essential to his reelection.

During the first ten months of 1916, while Congress was busy enacting his national defense legislation, Wilson pursued a course that enhanced his reputation as a progressive and broadened his appeal to include labor, farmers, and other socioeconomic elements of the population. His strategy enabled him to create a coalition that ultimately assisted in winning reelection.

In January 1916, Wilson appointed to the Supreme Court Louis D. Brandeis, a Jew and a widely recognized advocate of various social justice causes. After a bitter six-month struggle, which included abundant evidence of Anti-Semitism, the Senate confirmed Brandeis' appointment. The elevation of Brandeis to the nation's highest tribunal was only the beginning of what appeared to many as a vastly expanded version of the original New Freedom.

Nowhere was Wilson's metamorphosis more evident than in the matter of government credit for farmers which two years earlier he had pronounced unacceptable as special class legislation. In 1916 his support secured the passage of the Federal Farm Loan Act which created a system of Land Banks to make available to farmers long-term, low-interest-rate loans. The Warehouse Act (1916) also addressed rural credits by embodying an idea reminiscent of the Populists' subtreasury scheme: It authorized government-licensed warehouses to issue negotiable receipts for farm products deposited with them. Like others increasingly dependent on motor vehicles, farmers welcomed the passage of the Federal Highways Act (1916) which allocated funds on a dollar-matching basis to states for the construction of highways that met certain federal standards.

Although Wilson earlier had allowed a federal child labor bill to die for the lack of his support, he won congressional approval in 1916 of a law prohibiting the shipment in interstate commerce of goods produced by underage workers. Social workers, social justice organizations, and labor unions greeted the new law with great enthusiasm. Organized labor in particular had reason to be pleased with Wilson's expanded version of the New Freedom. The president was largely responsible for the enactment of the Federal Compensation Act, a model

Children at work in a factory, ca. 1915. The presence of large numbers of children in industrial establishments prompted a national crusade against child labor.

workers' compensation measure for federal employees, and more significantly the Adamson Act which averted a nationwide strike by railroad workers by guaranteeing them the eight-hour day.

The Revenue Act

One of the most significant measures enacted by Congress in 1916 and signed by the president on September 8 was the Revenue Act. Designed in part to pay the cost of military preparedness and denounced by critics as a "soak the rich" scheme, the act dramatically increased taxes on large incomes, raised inheritance taxes, and imposed a special levy on the munitions industry. It also created a bipartisan tariff commission which increased the role of the president in tariff-making. While Wilson's part in the passage of the Revenue Act, except for the tariff commission provision, was limited, the fact that he signed it endeared him to workers, farmers, and various others, especially those who argued that since the rich profited by military preparedness, they should bear the burden of the costs.

THE 1916 PRESIDENTIAL CAMPAIGN

In 1916 the Democrats by acclamation nominated Wilson for a second term. They also adopted his platform that Wilson's biographer describes as embracing "internationalism abroad and bold nationalistic progressivism at home." Both Wilson and the party quickly learned, especially by the enthusiastic response to remarks by the convention's keynote speaker, that peace sentiment in the nation was both broad and deep. Summarized in the slogan "He Kept Us Out of War," the peace theme became the Democrats' most popular campaign issue, all the more so when linked with Wilson's progressive record.

Unable to latch onto a theme with mass appeal, the Republicans wrestled with a perplexing situation. Divisions within the party caused by neutrality and preparedness tended to offset whatever unity resulted from the disbanding of the Progressive party. Theodore Roosevelt's return to Republican ranks and more particularly his noisy bid to become the party's standard bearer posed difficulties for Republican leaders who were convinced that his nomination would be suicidal. Their task, according to one historian, was to find a candidate "who was progressive enough to placate reformers, conservative enough to reassure the right wing, firm enough on neutral rights to keep the East happy, and pacific enough to retain the midwestern and western peace advocates, German-Americans, and progressives."

Such a formidable task fell to Charles Evans Hughes, a Supreme Court justice and former governor of New York who was selected as the Republican presidential candidate. Whatever Hughes' shortcomings, he came much closer to filling the party's needs in 1916 than did Roosevelt. The Republican platform on which Hughes campaigned made concessions to a few reforms, but straddled more divisive issues such as preparedness and neutrality. In addition to lambasting the Democrats' revenue and labor laws, Hughes criticized Wilson for what he termed his failure to take a stronger stand against violations of America's neutral rights. Such efforts proved inadequate to defeat Wilson, who not only wrapped himself in the flag but also donned the multiple mantles of peace, progressivism, preparedness, and prosperity.

As the presidential campaign neared conclusion—a campaign that had employed all the latest advertising and publicity techniques including billboards, films, and photo opportunities—the outcome still remained uncertain. Indeed, the first election returns indicated a Republican victory, but Democratic gains in the West, especially California, were sufficient to return Wilson to the White House for another four years.

If in 1916, Wilson "advanced toward progressivism without becoming an advanced progressive," as historian Lewis L. Gould has remarked, his administration had brought the reform movement at the national level to fruition. Under his leadership the Democratic party underwent a metamorphosis, from a commitment to the idea of limited government and localism to an acceptance of a broader use of federal power and a broader national outlook. Although the Democratic coalition of 1916 proved to be fragile and of short duration, Wilson contributed significantly to the evolution of the modern Democratic party. By the time of his inauguration for a second term in March 1917, foreign affairs dominated the national agenda. The following month the United States entered World War I on the side of the Allies.

WAR AND PROGRESSIVISM

The American experience in the war significantly affected progressivism. Despite references by some reformers to the "social possibilities of war," the conflict undermined some of the principal assumptions of progressivism. The slaughter of millions of people scarcely seemed to confirm the progressives' belief in the goodness and rationality of people. The persecution of citizens at home in the anti-German crusade and the subsequent Red Scare which occurred with governmental encouragement eroded progressive assumptions about the benevolent state. Within the ranks of progressivism itself the conformist, coercive tendencies, apparent especially in prohibition and antivice crusades, tended to eclipse the generous, humane impulses under the stress of war. As the national mood evidenced symptoms of moral fatigue, and dissent in all forms became identified as radical and revolutionary, the climate that had nourished vigorous reform efforts evaporated. While the eclipse of the reform impulse in the postwar era was never as complete as sometimes assumed, its visibility was diminished and its victories less noteworthy.

PROGRESSIVE ACCOMPLISHMENTS AND LEGACIES

Much of the progressive agenda had been achieved by 1917. Not only did progressives secure an enormous amount of legislation at the local, state, and federal levels that affected virtually every aspect of American life, they also added four amendments to the U.S. Constitution: the Sixteenth (income tax); the Seventeenth (direct election of United States senators); the Eighteenth (prohibition); and the Nineteenth (woman suffrage—see Figure 17–1). The political struggles during the Progressive Era produced enduring legacies, including those that altered how policy was made, public business was conducted, and campaigns were waged.

DIRECT DEMOCRACY

Nevertheless, progressive success in reinvigorating political democracy, disciplining big business, and solving social ills was not only more limited than their rhetoric suggested, but sometimes also had unanticipated results. Their direct democracy devices such as the initiative, referendum, and recall, for example, became instruments that enabled well financed special interest groups to negate reform goals. Whether progressives intended it or not, their actions increased bureaucratic decision-making remote from ordinary citizens.

If progressivism witnessed an increased faith in the ability of government to correct society's ills, it also displayed an aversion to party politics and especially to corrupt bosses and machines. Despite its emphasis on democracy, voter

FIGURE 17-1
Woman Suffrage Before 1920

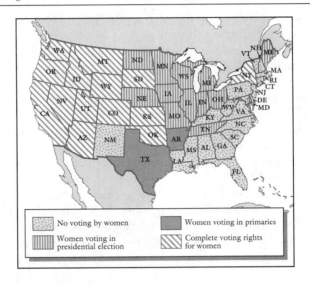

participation in the election process, for whatever reasons, declined in the first two decades of the twentieth century.

NATIVE AMERICANS

The disinherited and unorganized were not so much actors in the progressive drama as the objects of reform actions. Native Americans, for example, were subjected to official actions designed to de-Indianize them. The federal policy toward Native Americans, as advocated by the Indian Rights Association and other humanitarian organizations, collectively known as "Friends of the Indian," had been established in the last quarter of the nineteenth century and essentially remained in effect until the New Deal of the 1930s. Predicated on misguided idealism, this policy had two basic goals: the assimilation of Indians into American society, a process that required the abandonment of their traditional culture; and the termination of the Indians' status as special wards of the government which involved, among others, the abolition of the Bureau of Indian Affairs in the Interior Department.

A major step toward implementing these goals was the passage of the Dawes Act in 1887. Much amended in the following decade, the law initiated the breakup of reservations and the dissolution of communally held tribal lands. Reservations were to be divided into parcels of land allotted to individual Indians who, upon assuming ownership, became American citizens. The Dawes Act, coupled with educational and religious indoctrination programs, constituted a frontal assault on tribal unity and culture by attempting to transform the nation's oldest inhabitants into self-supporting farmers and ranchers who

A science classroom at the Carlisle Indian School, ca. 1915, an institution funded by the federal government and located in Carlisle, Pennsylvania.

adhered to the individualistic ethic and "the habits of civilized life." In brief, the Friends of the Indian and the government had put in place policies and programs designed to create an Indian that conformed to the popular image of the ideal citizen.

Despite ample evidence by the opening years of the twentieth century that the de-Indianization efforts were largely ineffective, the approach continued to possess widespread support among influential whites. President Roosevelt's commissioner of Indian Affairs, Francis E. Leupp, shared the Friends' basic objectives regarding Indians and parted company with them primarily on how best to achieve those objectives. Leupp played an important role in the passage of the Burke Act of 1907 which modified the Dawes Act, especially in separating land allotments to Indians from the bestowal of citizenship. He also insisted that Indian schools be located on reservations rather than elsewhere as the Friends desired. Although Leupp and his successor in the Progressive Era may have taken the first steps toward the eventual elimination of the misguided Indian reform theories held by the Friends, such steps scarcely constituted a fundamental change in the government's Indian policy. Reduced in numbers, their tribal cohesion severely weakened, and unable to stem the advance of white civilization, Native Americans remained an isolated and impoverished people increasingly plagued by high incidences of alcoholism, unemployment, and petty crimes.

AFRICAN AMERICANS

All the while, both legal and extra-legal discrimination against African Americans, the nation's largest racial minority, continued and multiplied without interruption. The so-called Atlanta Compromise, articulated in a speech in 1895 by Booker T. Washington, the head of Tuskegee Institute in Alabama, outlined a formula of race relations that prevailed for decades. Washington counseled blacks to abandon politics and civil rights agitation and to concentrate on economic self-help. Publicly acquiescing in segregation, Washington assured blacks that the accumulation of property and wealth would ensure the acquisition of all civil and political rights. Therefore, the primary educational need of African Americans was vocational training such as that offered at Tuskegee rather than higher learning (liberal arts). Because powerful whites shared this view, Washington became the beneficiary of white philanthropy which greatly enhanced his power and influence, especially among blacks. Despite his efforts to suppress all dissent from his accommodationist philosophy, his formula of race relations never won universal endorsement in the black community.

Ultimately Washington's critics rallied around W.E.B. DuBois, a Harvard-educated scholar/activist and founder of the anti-Washington Niagara Movement. Like many white reformers of the Progressive Era, DuBois was an elitist who placed great faith in the methods and findings of the social sciences in his assault on racial inequality. Convinced that African Americans, no less than other groups, would "be saved by their exceptional men" whom he labeled "the Talented Tenth," DuBois maintained that blacks were entitled to every right "political, civil, and social" belonging to other freeborn Americans and that until such rights were received by blacks he "would never cease to protest and assail the ears of America."

The struggle between Washington and DuBois took place within an environment characterized by the wholesale disfranchisement of blacks, the existence of separate and grossly unequal educational opportunities for African Americans, and the regular occurrence of diverse forms of racial violence throughout the South and by the spread of extra-legal Jim Crowism elsewhere in the country. Booker T. Washington's accommodationist philosophy enjoyed great popularity among whites during the Progressive Era.

Although the plight of African Americans did not occupy a place of priority on the progressive agenda, white reformers did not altogether ignore it. A series of articles by the muckraker Ray Stannard Baker exposed the pervasiveness of racial discrimination. These articles, collected and published in book form under the title *Following the Colorline*, appeared in 1908, the year in which a bloody race riot occurred in Springfield, Illinois.

Shocked by the outbreak of a race riot in the North, a group of prominent whites representing the elite of progressive reform organized the National Association for the Advancement of Colored People (NAACP) in 1909–1910 to address the nation's race problem. In its early years whites shaped the agenda and strategy of the organization. The only black official in the initial NAACP was DuBois, the director of publicity, who disbanded his Niagara Movement and ultimately succeeded in forcing the new organization to assume a position of forthright opposition to accommodationism and all forms of racial discrimination. The death of Washington in 1915, accompanied by the expansion of black membership in the NAACP and its success in whittling away at the legal structure of Jim Crowism, marked the beginning of a new epoch in African-American history and American race relations.

Whatever the shortcomings of progressivism, its impact on American society was profound and long lasting. Progressive reformers identified significant issues and raised many of the right questions. But in part because of their effort to reconcile the new corporate order with their idealized (and hence nonexistent) version of a nineteenth-century system of morality and ethics, some of their solutions proved too simplistic, impermanent, purely symbolic, or difficult to enforce, and others had unintended consequences. Even so, their emphasis on an active, positive role for government, especially in the social arena, proved to be an enduring legacy.

In the following selection John C. Burnham describes and analyzes the social hygiene movement during the Progressive Era. Essentially an effort to alter American attitudes toward sex, the movement was inspired by both moral fervor and science. Its attempt "to impose social change from above" was, according to Burnham, typical of progressive reforms.

THE PROGRESSIVE ERA REVOLUTION IN AMERICAN ATTITUDES TOWARD SEX

John C. Burnham

In the optimistic and melioristic progressive atmosphere of the early twentieth century, many reform movements flourished. The supporters of each one attempted

from John C. Burnham, "The Progressive Revolution in American Attitudes Toward Sex," *Journal of American History*, 59 (March 1973), 885–903.

in some specific way to alter institutions and beliefs characteristic of their culture in that period. Of all progressive reform movements, the most extraordinary was the social hygiene movement, a campaign to change American attitudes toward sex. As a typical reform movement it illustrates how people of the progressive generation attempted by manipulating the social environment, especially through the use of education, to change attitudes and behavior. The unusual quality of the movement derives from both the ambitious nature of the goal and the extent to which the reformers succeeded. The so-called revolution in morals became one of the lasting legacies of progressivism to American life.

Reformers directed their campaign against two fundamentals of Victorian morality, the conspiracy of silence, and the double standard. In 1914 William T. Foster, president of Reed College, described what he and others had been combating:

> Throughout the nineteenth century the taboo prevailed. Certain subjects were rarely mentioned in public, and then only in euphemistic terms. The home, the church, the school, and the press joined in the conspiracy. Supposedly, they were keeping the young in a blessed state of innocence. . . . [But] An abundance of distressing evidence showed that nearly all children gained information concerning sex and reproduction from foul sources,—from misinformed playmates, degenerates, obscene pictures, booklets, and advertisements of quack doctors. At the same time the social evil and its train of tragic consequences showed no abatement. The policy of silence, after many generations of trial, proved a failure.

Foster's appraisal was accurate, at least for the middle classes. There were important exceptions to the rule of euphemism and silence, the most notable of which were seduction themes in literature and scandal stories and advertisements of quack doctors that appeared in the newspapers. But, on the whole, social prohibitions against any open discussion of sex-related matters were surprisingly well observed. As late as 1899, when Denslow Lewis, a distinguished Chicago physician, attempted to discuss "the hygiene of the sexual act" at the meetings of the American Medical Association, the famous Baltimore gynecologist, Howard Kelly, objected. . . . The association refused to publish Lewis' paper.

Like the conspiracy of silence, the double standard of conduct—for women, strictest purity, and for men, considerable freedom to indulge their "inherent bestiality" before and outside of marriage—was subject to reservations and exceptions as a general social standard. Many members of evangelical churches or otherwise well-bred young men did not use prostitutes, but hewed to a higher standard. Perhaps the best known example was Theodore Roosevelt, who confided to his diary at the time of his engagement, "Thank heaven I am absolutely pure." Such behavior was exceptional, however, for it was a common, if ancient, belief, held and taught even by physicians, that sustained continence is injurious to a man's health. Advocates of the double standard could cite the most venerable opinion, including that of Augustine: "Suppress prostitution, and capricious lusts will overthrow society."

By 1900 pressure was mounting against the social stability embodied in the conspiracy of silence and the double standard. One set of forces, acting through a purity movement, undermined the double standard. Another set of forces, working through sophisticates and rebellious intellectuals, tended to break the conspiracy of silence. In the Progressive era the opponents of the double standard and the conspiracy of silence were fused and absorbed into the social hygiene reform movement as it acted to initiate the revolution in sexual standards.

Many factors contributed to the movement to purify American life. The most central was the small town religious idealism that shaped the aspirations and even behavior of many Americans. Women often took seriously their claim to moral superiority, and many of them, along with male uplift leaders, joined the international campaign to keep governments from legally sanctioning prostitution. Anti-prostitution efforts created the white slavery scare that expressed itself in a sensational literature as well as the Mann Act of 1910. But another and more significant result of the battle against "commercialized vice" was a general social movement dedicated to purifying American life, particularly by means of rearing children of both sexes to lead pure lives. By 1895 these "purity groups" had created a well-defined and identifiable movement. They endorsed not only personal purity and public stands against immorality but also rescue work to save "fallen women" and their patrons. Moreover, the advocates of purity backed feminism; a limited kind of moral sex education to protect children from vice and disease; and vigorous local and specific campaigns against prostitution, pornography, and suggestive literature. The purity reformers were remarkably successful, particularly in the suppression of "impure" publications and discussions. They sustained and guarded the conspiracy of silence.

By the early twentieth century, the anti-prostitution campaigns were more sophisticated and inclusive. Yet the progressive reformers retained the same concern for home training as a meliorative measure. The idea of a totally purified society, too, was common to both the religiously inspired reformers before 1900 and their secular counterparts after 1900. The progressives, however, recognized that the problem was not with the individual prostitute or pimp, but with the large-scale business that exploited public women. The reformers of the new century also connected the elimination of the red light district with social efficiency and municipal reform. The bordello was only one among many noxious social institutions fought by the progressives—temperance, housing, wages, and many other reforms were inseparable parts of the promise of American life.

. . . The first evidence of a new standard of morality for the twentieth century appeared in discussions of divorce, one of the troublesome questions that fulfillment raised. Divorce, and remarriage, especially, required modifications in the Victorian image of the sexless woman protected by a double standard. The well-publicized "revolution in morals" of the 1910s and 1920s involved primarily changes in the nature of acceptable and expectable female behavior. Throughout the previous century American writers had recognized that in addition to embodying purity and idealism, the American girl had impulses that could "electrify" both herself and her male counterpart. By 1900 authors of fiction and drama with increasing frequency were suggesting that a woman has a sexual existence in addition to her spiritualizing and uplifting role.

A number of intellectual rebels in the United States went further than conventional literati who dealt with family, romantic love, divorce, and fulfillment. To confirm the right of women to sexual as well as economic, political, and social equality, they appealed to European propagandists and exemplars of frankness. To late Victorians, Henrik Ibsen, George Bernard Shaw, Émile Zola, and other literary innovators appeared bold and iconoclastic. . . . For the educated, therefore, an impressive array of both radical and more respectable writers had suggested thinking about "the sexually unthinkable." . . .

By the opening years of the twentieth century, social changes embodied largely in advances by both purity and anti-purity forces foreshadowed innovations in American attitudes toward sex, particularly the conspiracy of silence and the double standard. But the revolution in the ways that middle-class Americans coped with sex grew out of an independent reform movement that a group of conservative medical specialists created.

The physicians who founded the social hygiene movement were impelled to their crusade not so much by the general sentiments that usually energize reform movements but rather by new scientific discoveries about venereal diseases. Syphilis had long been known as a dangerous disease. Generally those afflicted knew that they had it and took treatment until the obvious symptoms disappeared. The other major venereal disease, gonorrhea, was regarded as little dangerous as a bad cold. Both maladies were considered by early Victorians to be the result of immorality, and there was widespread opinion that God utilized these diseases to punish sin. As a result, sympathy for those affected was rare.

During the course of the nineteenth century, medical technology brought to light horrifying facts about these illnesses. Syphilis had complications that no one had suspected; it lay behind major diseases of every organ of the body, even, for example, types of arthritis, degenerative nervous disorders, and paresis, a peculiarly grisly form of mental illness that caused "almost mortal terror" among physicians, in the words of a Providence psychiatrist of the day. Gonorrhea also turned out to be a dangerous and deadly infection, the cause of diseases, especially women's diseases, the nature of which medical authorities had theretofore not guessed. Moreover, the known prevalence of venereal illnesses increased, and a huge fraction of the population appeared to be infected. Most terrifying of all was the fact that the obvious symptoms proved no safe guide as to the presence or absence of the versatile microorganisms responsible for the illnesses. In some cases the victims reaped an appalling harvest of wild oats twenty or twenty-five years after infection.

Physicians dealing with syphilis and gonorrhea became particularly disturbed when they discovered that many victims of these sad afflictions were not men who took advantage of the double standard but women and children whose purity was beyond question. The doctors spoke therefore of "syphilis of the innocent." The innocent were wives whose husbands had infected them. There were children, too, who had so to speak "inherited" the disease from their parents at birth, if, indeed, they were not stillborn. The innocent included people of all ages whose infections were not associated with sex at all but with a chaste kiss, a wet nurse, a common towel. The diseases appeared to threaten not only the family but also the individual, sexless person. In many areas squeamish citizens cooperated with medical personnel who campaigned to secure legislation to outlaw the ubiquitous common drinking cup.

By the turn of the twentieth century, what had only a few decades earlier seemed just one of many public health problems, emerged as an intolerable menace to society. Physicians, especially specialists, expressed their concern through articles in professional journals and papers presented at professional meetings. . . . By 1903 the American Medical Association had a committee on the prevention of venereal maladies. By and large the various medical commentators advocated, as steps toward prevention, the education of the public and/or compulsory medical inspection of prostitutes in the continental fashion. Both ideas were controversial, indeed, unpopular, and the physicians kept the discussion almost entirely within the profession. Because of popular prejudice some hospitals refused to admit venereal disease patients. The doctors therefore made treatment of the ill a third aspect of the program, but again they found that they were dealing with general social attitudes, not just medical practice.

The physicians were stymied primarily by the advocates of purity. On only one occasion had inspection of public women been tried in the United States. St. Louis passed an inspection ordinance in 1870, but in 1874 the forces of righteousness succeeded in nullifying it. Furthermore, as anti-prostitution writers pointed out, it was not clear that inspection was effective.

The extreme concern of medical leaders, however, made a number of them so desperate that they were willing to fight the purity groups and their own doubts, and they advocated inspection measures that they hoped would pass for public health legislation. The major reason that the doctors could not produce change was the conspiracy of silence; they were afraid to disclose publicly what they knew. The whole profession was placed in the tragic situation of being unable to warn potential victims of the dangers they faced. The man who discovered that physicians need not stand helpless in this predicament was a dignified and most eminent specialist, Prince A. Morrow of New York. . . .

Morrow had given few indications of his potential as a social reformer. . . . The only clear symptom was his work in 1880, at the age of thirty-four, in translating a book, *Syphilis and Marriage,* by the world renowned French syphilographer, Jean-Alfred Fournier. Fournier described in frightening detail the tragic consequences that follow when a person infected with syphilis marries. Fournier believed that physicians should persuade such persons to postpone marriage until after the most rigorous treatment. Morrow in the introduction to the translation remarked on the importance of Fournier's book to "family and society." But otherwise there is very little evidence of Morrow's opinions in those years. In 1885 his remarks in a manual on venereal diseases showed him to be pessimistic about preventing those afflictions. In the light of the St. Louis experience, he dismissed inspection of prostitutes as "practically a failure" in this country. For prophylaxis he offered only the commonsense observation that chances of infection were diminished if a prostitute were visited early in the evening before she had much business. In the same book, however, his description of a newborn syphilitic baby, although objective, left no doubt that he harbored strong feelings about what he saw in his practice.

In 1893 Morrow edited a collective work on syphilis written by a number of specialists. He was especially impressed by an article in that book by another New York doctor, Samuel Treat Armstrong, who wrote about the public health aspects of syphilis. Armstrong had set about gathering statistics and information about infection rates, intending to show that legislation requiring the medical inspection of public women would control the spread of syphilis. He was surprised to discover that the body of medical opinion, including his own, was mistaken; nowhere had inspection controlled the disease over a period of time. The only suggestion that Armstrong was able to make then—the one picked up by Morrow—was that society expedite the treatment of every infected person, particularly by opening hospitals to venereal cases.

A few years after this work appeared, Morrow in 1899 attended, at his own expense, the first of two international conferences held in Brussels to consider the public health aspects of venereal diseases. Many of the physicians and public health officials attending the Brussels meeting concluded that venereal diseases were more prevalent than was generally believed and that inspection of prostitutes was not effective. The resolutions of the conference aimed at improving inspection systems and educating the public concerning the dangers of venereal infection.

In the wake of this meeting Morrow began his career as a social reformer by presenting a powerful address to the New York County Medical Society. He declared that the principal sufferers from syphilis and gonorrhea were either innocent women and children or unwitting youngsters who had no idea of the dangers to which they exposed themselves. Morrow despaired of wiping out prostitution, but urged improving social conditions and the wages of women and prosecuting the merchants of flesh who made money off the social evil. Again he suggested prophylaxis by the direct means of treating all of those afflicted. He also thought that young men ought to be warned about the dangers of the diseases. After hearing Morrow the society appointed a committee to investigate the subject further, and Morrow was named chairman. The committee gathered some statistics about the high incidence of venereal diseases, and, presumably under Morrow's guidance, stressed in their report education and treatment—and not inspection of prostitutes—as the best means of preventing venereal diseases.

Morrow and his committee asserted that they were not utopians and that they accepted the inevitability of commercial immorality. "Prostitution," they wrote, "is inherent in the human race; it cannot be annihilated, it is a necessary evil in our social system." But Morrow was now unmistakably committed to agitation for social reform. . . .

Morrow was active in organizing the second Brussels conference, which met in 1902. The delegates there heard reports by members of a French group, the French Society of Sanitary and Moral Prophylaxis, founded in 1900 by Fournier, who had successfully undertaken an educational campaign to warn youth against venereal diseases and to urge infected persons to seek treatment. After the meetings Morrow was asked to found such an organization in the United States. At the time he was busy writing *Social Diseases and Marriage,* which emphasized "moral and educational influences," as the most efficient means of preventing disease, and it was not until May 1904 that he made a public plea for an American organization.

Morrow proposed that the organization include not only medical men but also prominent laymen, leaders of opinion especially, for the problem was moral as well as medical. . . . Morrow attacked directly the tendency of society to conceal and ignore this "Social Peril," as he styled it, and he proposed an organization to educate the public.

Morrow later spoke of the indifference and prejudice that he fought in those early days. He talked to innumerable people and wrote letters endlessly. It was almost another year, February 8, 1905, before he called an organizational meeting. Only twenty-five people responded to his call to meet at the New York Academy of Medicine. . . . In his address to the group, Morrow advocated a program of action that involved new ideas. He proposed that the society be the source of a forceful propaganda campaign to expose and publicize the dangers of venereal diseases and to eradicate prostitution.

Morrow's proposal to end prostitution was especially startling, since only a few years before, he had helped to draft a committee report that had characterized the abolition of prostitution as utopian. Now, however, Morrow denounced even inspection of public women and asked the new organization to eliminate commercial venery by means of changing moral standards, specifically by destroying the double standard of conduct. Morrow was not yet allied with the purity movement, but he thought that the propaganda of his new organization should appeal to the public concern about preserving the family, a concern that, he pointed out, had been aroused by publicity about the divorce problem. Although his listeners may have been "half-hearted," they nevertheless constituted themselves the American Society of Sanitary and Moral Prophylaxis. . . .

In spite of Morrow's hope to include lay leaders, five sixths of the organizers and a similar proportion of the 120 charter members were physicians; and the movement remained primarily medical in membership and support for some years. Quickly a number of affiliated organizations appeared all over the country—most of them organized under the auspices of local medical societies. In general the response of individual physicians in every region was beyond any reasonable expectation. . . . A large number of eminent physicians were sympathetic to what became Morrow's program, but they did not take the action that he did. Once he spoke up, however, they were willing to follow him into the treacherous areas of education and morals.

The ambitions of these reformers stand as a monument to the power of the progressive reform impulse. Morrow and other leaders of the early social hygiene movement—almost all of them leading physicians—could hardly be characterized as other than conservative in their attitudes. None, certainly, was an extremist. Yet these doctors were aware that they were undertaking to bring about fundamental changes in prevailing opinion and attempting to alter, . . ."deep-rooted customs and habits of thought." They sought to break the conspiracy of silence, to eradicate incorrect folk beliefs concerning venereal diseases, and to convince the entire manhood of the nation that continence was entirely compatible with health. Most radical of all, they were bent on improving morals—something that centuries of religious training had failed to achieve.

What drew the doctors to support Morrow was his emphasis on education as a preventive measure in fighting venereal diseases. He and his colleagues and supporters therefore set about propagandizing both other physicians and the general public. So successful was Morrow's publicity campaign that the social hygienists soon began to influence the purity movement.

As early as 1904, 0. Edward Janney, president of the American Purity Alliance, and himself a physician, said that while he hoped that eventually moral influences and reforms such as improving economic conditions would bring about purity, these forces acted only slowly. "The one method of relief, at once correct in theory and prompt in bringing about an improvement," he asserted, "is Education." . . .

By 1906 the editor of the *Philanthropist* not only took note of the early social hygiene societies but also urged that they be supported. Within a year this journal, although still stressing immorality and white slavery, was now increasingly emphasizing education and citing the work of Morrow and his allies. Early in 1908 the American Purity Alliance announced a new objective. To the usual ". . . devoted to the Promotion of Social Purity, the Better Protection of the Young by Prevention of Vice and the Prevention of its Regulation by the State" were added the significant words: "Its Work is Educational and Preventive." By 1911, the successor magazine, *Vigilance,* was predominantly devoted to education. The other leading purity journal, *Light,* showed a slower but parallel commitment to sex education.

In the years before World War I institutional amalgamations paralleled convergence of programs. In 1911 two of the major purity organizations, the American Purity Alliance and the American Vigilance Committee, elected the same officers, and the next year the two consolidated to form the American Vigilance Association, which was dedicated to fighting prostitution and educating the young about dangers of immorality. Many of the medically oriented groups that had followed Morrow's lead met in 1910 and elected him president of a new national organization, the American Federation for Sex Hygiene. After Morrow's death in 1913, the two forces, medical and purity, merged formally and symbolically, in 1913–1914, to form the American Social Hygiene Association. . . .

The coalition of moral and sanitary reformers marked the purity leaders' surrender of the conspiracy of silence. It is important to spell out exactly what was surrendered. Purity leaders had long advocated providing children with moral training and a modicum of sexual instruction so as to prepare them for life's dangers and temptations. As early as the 1890s many of them were stressing that "innocence is not ignorance." In that decade a large number of sex education books appeared.

Purity people, however, and Morrow's social hygienists interpreted differently the meaning of sexual enlightenment. The former believed primarily in using the home as the agency of education; they did not wish to disturb the prohibition on public discussion of sexual matters. Morrow and other physicians wanted to use all possible social institutions, including schools and the press, for education and propaganda aimed at both adults and children. Medical men were particularly eager to get the ill to take treatment; purity groups were never comfortable with using blunt propaganda such as that which the social hygienists soon had posted in many public rest rooms.

The tone of the writings of the two groups also tended to differ. Purity materials were usually pious and positive; their authors believed that "the physiological facts of reproduction may be clothed in delicate language and surrounded by an atmosphere of sacredness and self-reverence that will render the knowledge thus obtained a guarantee of right conduct." Examples were often from nature—bees and flowers—and the rhetoric had a religious flavor, emphasizing the beauty of God's creation and the vague dreadfulness and guilts of uncleanliness of mind and weakness of will. Because purity writers maintained that bad thoughts lead to bad deeds, they warned against the former more vigorously than the latter.

Many tracts from the American Society of Sanitary and Moral Prophylaxis groups took over rhetoric and reading lists intact from the well-established purity literature for children, but Morrow's medical groups also showed a tendency to accept clean, respectful, and monogamous sexual intercourse in fairly straightforward terms and to emphasize the hazards of actions rather than thoughts. This set of attitudes turned out to be compatible with advocating sexual fulfillment, as later liberated writers who adopted social hygiene ideas showed. Purity people were apt to put a great deal of emotional content into discussions of the dangers of masturbation. Morrow and his group, in part because they were more open in their discussions, painted frankly what fate awaited those who actually had sexual intercourse. . . .

Both the venereologists and the purity people were, like other progressives, attempting to impose middle-class standards on the total population by means of education. The purity people were aiming chiefly at a clientele susceptible to religious-moral appeals, those who were largely middle class in attitude. Morrow and his compatriots, by contrast, were greatly concerned about the working as well as the middle classes, and a significant part of their propaganda, including a number of graphic "exhibits," was aimed at frightening people with bad thoughts and wicked tendencies into refraining from sexual activity—to surrender something now in the hope of greater rewards in kind later. Purity people accepted this kind of "education" only slowly and reluctantly.

When the American Federation for Sex Hygiene resolved to join in with the purity groups, the majority in the governing council represented only a minority of Morrow's forces. The Federation, however, as an anonymous observer wrote at the time, had "lost its real leader and spirit." The official statement of one constituent society reflected the new emphasis: "the actual dealing with disease has gradually sunk more and more into the background of our Society's activities. . . ." Instead the social hygiene groups were emphasizing moral rather than sanitary prophylaxis. The purity people were always suspicious of the medical interest in preventing and treating diseases among the immoral. When World War I mobilization raised urgent and immediate public health questions, the doctors once again tended to overshadow the purity forces. A deep split occurred, for example, over the question whether or not army medical authorities should furnish soldiers with prophylactic devices that would make immoral conduct safe.

. . . The fact remains that the first revolution in American attitudes toward sex came only after Morrow stepped forth to lead the new campaign against both the conspiracy of silence and the double standard. Physicians and purity workers found themselves drawn together under his leadership. The medical groups which originally joined him in societies for "sanitary and moral prophylaxis" crystallized much opinion, and it was only after the doctors began their campaign that others joined. A number of educators, for example, who had been giving sex education talks covertly now spoke openly. Of those anxious for reform Morrow alone had the courage to speak out, and his actions had momentous effects.

Morrow's challenge to the double standard is still affecting American life. In his own day the forces that he mobilized compelled the ancient institution of prostitution to retreat in the realm of morals and the domain of law enforcement. Reformer Jane Addams of Chicago proclaimed that Americans had developed a new conscience sensitive to the ancient evil, and the success of the anti-prostitution and social hygiene physicians in convincing their colleagues and the public that continence was compatible with health signified a remarkable change in middle-class attitudes. The whole effort, of course, hinged on the promise that with proper sex education marriage would bring sexual fulfillment. Undoubtedly the most striking tangible alteration in American social life in the Progressive era was the decline of the traditional red light or segregated district in American cities.

In city after city so-called "vice commissions" of citizens investigated and recommended that the universal system of toleration give way to repression. The spontaneity with which the segregated districts disappeared in the years around 1910 is truly remarkable. Beyond the roles of municipal reform, feminist agitation, the purity crusade, and the white slavery scare, social hygiene propaganda was the vital factor in the demise of the old order. Not only were the publications of the various social hygiene societies and leaders available but also local medical reform groups often assisted vice commission personnel. Morrow's name appeared conspicuously in almost all of the commission reports, and typically they advocated the program of the social hygiene movement: suppression of vice, treatment of the ill, and, above all, education and propaganda. Because action followed the reports, Morrow and his followers were well aware that they were playing an important part in progressive reformism. . . .

The most dramatic breach in the conspiracy of silence was the exposure of children to sex education outside the home. Many of the purity people never surrendered their beliefs that parents should enlighten their own children. The bulk of the purity groups, however, finally joined the social hygienists in advocating that public agencies, particularly schools, carry on a general program of sex education. In 1912, and only after having avoided the subject before, the National Education Association resolved:

> We believe that the time has arrived when normal schools and teachers' colleges should give adequate courses of instruction in sex hygiene, with the view ultimately, of the introduction of similar instruction into the courses of study in public schools.

Implementing sex education stirred up more controversy than advocating it. The physicians who had initiated the movement insisted that the subject of venereal diseases be included, and others wanted the psychology of sex in addition. That biology, physiology, and reproduction should be a part of the curriculum seemed generally acceptable among those who favored the idea at all, although many advocates wanted various types of material taught earlier or later. There was no agreement on how much frankness should be included, and reactions to sex education therefore varied largely according to the understanding of how much would be taught and by whom and when.

In the rush to equip teachers, clergymen, physicians, and parents with information suitable for the children, large numbers of books, pamphlets, and articles appeared, along with bibliographies of suggested readings. The quantity of such material was striking, but even more striking was the variety. . . .

School instruction in sexual matters did engender much opposition. The *Nation,* for example, represented a certain type of liberal opinion appalled by the thought of a school teacher's imparting sexual knowledge. Conservatives, such as John A. Sheppard, a clergyman of Jersey City, declared that "Just at present our ears are dinned with the fad of sex hygiene. Its introduction into the schools is discussed throughout the country. If ever there was a system diabolically devised to injure our youth, and to make them voluptuaries, this is by far the most effective." Still others saw sex education as only one aspect of the general breaking of the conspiracy of silence and denounced it along with other public recognitions of the existence of sexuality.

Such conservatives were not altogether unrealistic in their appraisal of what was happening. As soon as the physicians had convinced a number of prominent Americans that for the sake of health and morals sexual subjects ought to have public exposure, social rebels took advantage of the social hygiene crusade to sanction as educational whatever might be written. In the *Masses,* for example, writers repeatedly discussed sex for the sake of defiantly discussing sex. . . .

Those who wished to bring matters sexual into the public arena and did so in the wake of the social hygiene movement paid a price for their new freedom of discussion: moral idealism had to accompany the discussion. The progressive generation was more than friendly to combining idealization with sex, particularly in advocating romantic love. Walter Lippmann, who often voiced the aspirations of many younger progressives, wrote in 1914:

> . . . Our interest in sex is no longer to annihilate it, but to educate it. . . . And there is an increasing number of people who judge sexual conduct by its results in the quality of human life. They don't think that marriage justifies licentiousness, nor will they say that every unconventional union is necessarily evil.

Lippmann and others were clearly opposed to the double standard as well as the conspiracy of silence.

The extent of the impact of the social reformer physicians upon many aspects of American civilization is illustrated best by their venture into drama. Eugène Brieux, the famous French playwright, had written a play, *Les Avariés,* to show the tragic consequences that follow when a man ill with venereal disease marries. . . . After it was translated into English and published under the title, *Damaged Goods,* Thomas N. Hepburn, a Hartford physician and one of Morrow's lieutenants, in 1912 obtained permission to order 10,000 copies of the play to be used for propaganda purposes in the United States. Not content with that, Hepburn worked with the famous actor and manager, Richard Bennett, to produce the play on Broadway in 1913, with Bennett in the leading role. At first performed before a private matinee audience, *Damaged Goods* then was shifted to a night bill and became a notable commercial success. Late in September the play moved to the Blackstone Theater in Chicago, where it was sponsored by the local social hygiene society in conjunction with the local anti-prostitution organization. It also played in Washington. Even with such respectable backing the play met criticism as well as much praise for its frankness. . . . The financial success of *Damaged Goods,* according to drama critic W. H. Denny, led to "a rush on the part of managers and authorities to provide the public with plays on kindred subjects, called vice plays. . . ." That such plays—often European in origin—were available was a symptom of the presence of forces besides the social hygiene movement at work inimicable to the taboos.

The intense reaction to *Damaged Goods* and the other dramas that followed in its wake showed that all the purity forces were far from reconciled to the program of "education" envisaged by the medically oriented social hygienists. A writer in the New York *Herald* traced the opposition to those who were uncomfortable that the new "white slavery" plays "are showing up the connection of the politicians and office-holders and so-called respectable men with these disorderly houses." More fundamentally the conservatives objected that all of the plays, in the words of Roman Catholic poet and journalist Joyce Kilmer, "take the responsibility of sin from the individual and place it upon society." Many purity people simply doubted that the plays and the moving pictures that followed them were educational. The audiences came for sensational purposes, according to New York journalist Hans von Kaltenborn. . . .

The social hygiene reformers were not always pleased by the Pandora's box of sexual discussion that they had opened. The doctor who was president of the original New York organization in 1914, E. L. Keyes, Jr., declared that "As the primitive centre for discussion of sex in this country, we must assume at least some of the blame for, and be the first to protest against, the flood of 'Sexology' amidst which we struggle for breath today." He made it clear, however, that he and his group had no regrets if they had coincidentally encouraged rebellious intellectuals and other free souls who advocated that everyone read Ellis. First of all, he said, the social hygiene movement at its most medical stood for high morality, not free love, and certainly not prostitution. Second, he continued, bringing sex into the open was a relatively superficial change, despite the emotion that the subject engendered.

Like other progressives, the social hygiene reformers were fundamentally conservative. Compared to preserving the nation's health and guarding the home and the sacred institution of the family, upholding the conspiracy of silence and the double standard seemed of secondary importance. As Morrow observed after reviewing what he himself had seen in medical practice to be a result of venereal diseases, no system of morals that fostered such evils could possibly be right.

The physicians' campaign to break the conspiracy of silence and eliminate the double standard of morality stands as a classic example of a progressive reform movement. Like other progressive reformers, Morrow and his group were inspired by moral fervor and sought to impose social change from above. They were if not patrician reformers upper middle-class reformers. The impact of science in inspiring them was particularly striking. New knowledge about the cause of a large amount of human misery suggested that it might be obliterated if only social conditions permitted. The doctors never gave up the idea that a large part of prevention consisted simply of treating the ill. The progressive mood contributed the idea that it was no longer necessary to endure and ignore evil, not prostitution and certainly not disease.

SUGGESTED READINGS

John Milton Cooper, Jr., *The Warrior and the Priest: Woodrow Wilson and Theodore Roosevelt* (1983).

Robert Crunden, *Ministers of Reform: The Progressives' Achievement in American Civilization* (1982).

Allen F. Davis, *Spearheads for Reform: The Social Settlements and the Progressive Movement, 1890–1914* (1967).

Dewey W. Grantham, *Southern Progressivism* (1983).

Samuel P. Hays, *Conservation and the Gospel of Efficiency* (1959).

Richard Hofstader, *The Age of Reform from Bryan to FDR* (1958).

Arthur S. Link, *Woodrow Wilson and the Progressive Era, 1910–1917* (1954).

George Mowry, *The Era of Theodore Roosevelt and the Birth of Modern America* (1958).

Robert H. Wiebe, *The Search for Order, 1877–1920* (1967).

FURTHER READINGS

THE PROGRESSIVE ERA: John W. Chambers, *The Tyranny of Change: America in the Progressive Era, 1900–1917* (1980); John M. Cooper, *Pivotal Decades: The United States, 1900–1920* (1990); Alan Dawley, *Struggles for Justice: Social Responsibility and the Liberal State* (1992); Gabriel Kolko, *The Triumph of Conservatism* (1963); Arthur S. Link and Richard L. McCormick, *Progressivism* (1983); David Noble, *The Progressive Mind, 1890–1917* (1981). SPECIFIC REFORMS and INDIVIDUAL REFORMERS: John Blum, *The Republican Roosevelt* (2nd ed., 1977); Mina Carson, *Settlement Folk; Social Thought and the American Settlement Movement* (1990); David Chalmers, *The Social and Political Ideas of Muckrakers* (1964); Noralee Frankel and Nancy Dye, *Gender, Class, Race and Reform in the Progressive Era* (1991); Lewis L. Gould, *Reform and Regulation: American Politics, 1900–1916* (1986); Louis R. Harlan, *Booker T. Washington: Wizard of Tuskegee 1901–1915* (1967); Charles F. Kellogg, *NAACP: The History of the National Association for the Advancement of Colored People, 1909–1920* (1967); David L. Lewis, *W.E.B. Du Bois: Biography of a Race, 1868–1919* (1993); Roy Lubove, *The Progressives and the Slums* (1962); Nathan Miller, *Theodore Roosevelt: A Life* (1991); Bradley Rice, *Progressive Cities* (1977); Ruth Rosen, *The Lost Sisterhood: Prostitution in America 1900–1918* (1982); David J. Rothman, *Conscience and*

Convenience: The Asylum and Alternatives in Progressive America (1980); James H. Timberlake, *Prohibition and the Progressive Movement, 1900–1920* (1963); Walter I. Trattner, *Crusade for Children* (1970).

QUESTIONS FOR DISCUSSION

1. How did progressivism resemble and differ from Populism?
2. Who were the muckrakers, and what was their role in the reform movement known as progressivism?
3. Identify and analyze the goals and limitations of progressivism.
4. Describe and assess the role of women in the progressive movement.
5. Assess the place of Presidents Theodore Roosevelt and Woodrow Wilson in the national progressive movement. What contributions did each make to it?
6. "The presidential election of 1912 confronted voters with two versions of progressivism." Explain the meaning of this statement.
7. The Progressive Era added four amendments to the U.S. Constitution. What were they, and how did they reflect the progressive agenda?
8. Did the plight of African Americans receive attention from progressives? Explain.

CHAPTER EIGHTEEN

THE END OF INNOCENCE:
The United States and World War I

America's decision to participate in the Great War, as World War I was called at the time, marked the end of an era. Isolationism had been the dominant impulse in U.S. foreign policy since the founding of the republic. The United States would attempt to retreat within the Western Hemisphere once again during the 1920s and 1930s, but would find that it could not. America's economic might, its far-flung interests, and the destruction of the European balance of power meant that the United States would be a major player in Europe and Asia for the remainder of the twentieth century.

EVENTS LEADING UP TO THE GREAT WAR

THE POLARIZATION OF EUROPE

By 1910, Europe had divided into two rival alliances: the Central Powers consisting of Austria-Hungary and Germany; and the Triple Entente made up of Great Britain, France, and Imperial Russia. The polarization of European politics was the result of a series of bi-national (i.e., two-power) rivalries. Germany had burst upon the world scene as a modern, unified state following the Franco-Prussian War in 1870–1871. Recognizing that unification of the German principalities would forever relegate France to second place on the continent, Napoleon III had fought a disastrous war with Prussia, which spearheaded the movement for German unification. Following its victory, Prussia occupied Paris, forced France to pay an indemnity, and seized the border province of Alsace-Lorraine. For the next forty years an entire generation of French politicians maintained themselves in office by promising a war of revenge against Germany. Franco-German relations were subsequently punctuated by one war scare after another.

Determined to take its place in the sun, the new German Empire entered the race for overseas colonies with a vengeance. Military and diplomatic agents of William II struggled to carve out concessions and annex territory in West Africa, the Middle East, and Asia. Germany's colonial ambitions and its avowed determination to build a navy second to none inevitably brought it into conflict with the world's greatest imperial power, Great Britain. British diplomats labored to contain German expansion in the underdeveloped regions of the world, while the Admiralty embarked on a vigorous naval building program to ensure that the Royal Navy remain the largest in the world. As the twentieth century dawned, many Europeans were predicting war between the two naval superpowers.

The third bi-national rivalry, between Austria-Hungary and Russia, actually supplied the spark that set off the Great War. Since the time of Peter the Great, Russia had maneuvered to extend its influence in the Balkans to gain port facilities in the eastern Mediterranean. As the various ethnic-national groups in that troubled region rebelled against their Turkish overlords in the late nineteenth century, Russia had come to their aid with money, diplomatic influence, and, in the case of Bulgaria, troops. To extend their influence and establish client states in the region, the Russian tsars had posed as champions of national self-determination. By definition, Russian machinations posed a threat to the Austro-Hungarian Empire, a polyglot entity made up of some twenty-five ethnic groups. Not only did the principle of national self-determination threaten the integrity of the empire, but the state of Serbia, whose chief sponsor was Russia, acted as a magnet attracting Serbs living in the Austrian principality of Bosnia-Herzegovina.

On June 28, 1914, Archduke Francis Ferdinand, the heir to the Austrian throne, was assassinated in Sarajevo, the capital of Bosnia, by Serbian nationalists. Immediately, the Austro-Hungarian government issued an ultimatum to the Serbian government demanding, among other things, the right to cross freely into Serbia in search of terrorists and separatists. Austria's demands and Serbia's rejection of them brought the two alliance systems into play. By the beginning of August, Austria-Hungary and Germany were at war with Russia and France. Germany's subsequent invasion of neutral Belgium, the first stage of its thrust toward France, caused Great Britain to join the Allies—the new name for the Triple Entente—and declare war on the Central Powers, which were soon joined by Turkey and Bulgaria. The war spread around the world as Japan, allied with Britain, seized Germany's Far Eastern possessions. The British Commonwealth countries of Canada, Australia, New Zealand, and South Africa likewise intervened, dispatching troops to Europe and the Middle East and conquering German colonies in Africa and the South Pacific. In 1915, Italy entered the war on the Allied side, and in 1916 Romania followed suit (see Figure 18–1).

AMERICA'S PREJUDICED NEUTRALITY

In the United States, the prevalent reactions to the outbreak of hostilities in Europe were shock, surprise, and thankfulness that Americans were not in-

FIGURE 18–1

Europe Goes to War

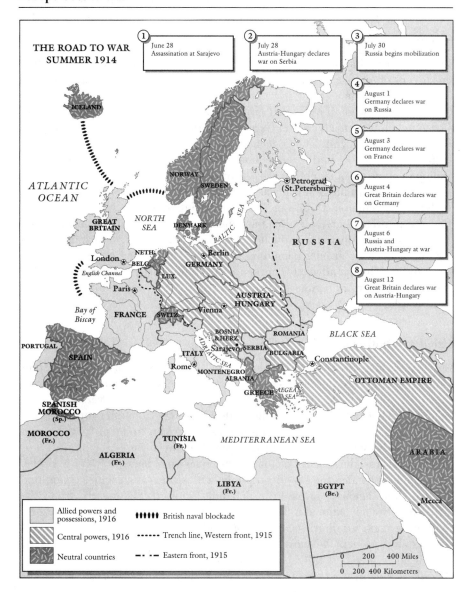

THE ROAD TO WAR
SUMMER 1914

① June 28
Assassination at Sarajevo

② July 28
Austria-Hungary declares
war on Serbia

③ July 30
Russia begins mobilization

④ August 1
Germany declares war
on Russia

⑤ August 3
Germany declares war
on France

⑥ August 4
Great Britain declares war
on Germany

⑦ August 6
Russia and
Austria-Hungary at war

⑧ August 12
Great Britain declares war
on Austria-Hungary

Allied powers and
possessions, 1916

♦♦♦♦♦ British naval blockade

Central powers, 1916

----- Trench line, Western front, 1915

Neutral countries

– · – · Eastern front, 1915

0   200   400 Miles

0   200 400 Kilometers

volved. The Great War spawned new, terrible machines of mass destruction—the airplane, the submarine, mustard gas, the tank, the modern machine gun, and trench warfare. Americans watched in horror as the combatants slaughtered each other by the thousands in northern France. President Woodrow Wilson and his secretary of state, William Jennings Bryan, shared their countrymen's determination to remain aloof from the fighting. In August of 1914 Wilson issued a public statement urging Americans to "be neutral in fact as well as in name . . . impartial in thought as well as in action."

Supporters of the Central Powers

But America was a nation of immigrants, many of whom traced their origins back to one or another of the combatants. Though they might remain neutral in word and deed, they could not control their sympathies. Adherents of the Central Powers were in a decided minority but still significant. There were in the United States some 8 million German Americans, most of whom lived in the Midwest and Southwest. They rejected the Allied contention that a militaristic, aggressive Germany had been primarily responsible for starting the war. Joining them were some 5 million Irish Americans who resided primarily in the nation's cities. Irish nationalism was reaching its peak, and Britain's crushing of the Easter Rebellion in Dublin in 1916 fired the hatred of Irish Americans who took the position that Great Britain's enemy was automatically their friend. Wealthy German Americans launched a propaganda campaign, hiring speakers and commissioning articles defending the fatherland and promoting the cause of neutrality. Though advocates of the Central Powers had some success in criticizing the autocratic regime of Tsar Nicholas II, they were fighting a losing, uphill battle.

Allied Sympathizers

Most Americans saw the war through Allied eyes. News from the battlefront came by way of transatlantic cables, all of which were controlled by Great Britain after the Royal Navy severed those belonging to the Central Powers. The great majority of citizens entertained either mild or strong sympathies for the Allies. History, language, and tradition caused most Americans to identify with Great Britain. The way Germany fought the war also played into Allied hands. For many Americans, the decisive factor was the invasion of neutral Belgium. British propagandists regaled the American public with stories of atrocities committed by "the Hun" against "brave little Belgium." Ignoring the eastern front, the British and French claimed to be fighting for democracy, decency, and Western civilization against militarism, aggression, and barbarism.

Despite President Wilson's sincere desire to keep the United States out of the war, most members of his administration were clearly pro-Allies. Probably the only real neutral was Secretary of State William Jennings Bryan. His evangelical Christian faith caused him to approach international relations as an idealist and a virtual pacificist. His most frequently delivered lecture in the years prior to the outbreak of war was "The Prince of Peace," which argued that all but a few wars in history—the American Revolution and the Civil War were exceptions—were wrong and that world leaders must create machinery for the peaceful settlement of disputes. Robert Lansing, who would replace Bryan as secretary of state in 1915, was publicly pro-British while Colonel Edward

House, Wilson's unofficial advisor, was decidedly anti-German. America's ambassador to Great Britain, Walter Hines Page, was a thoroughgoing Anglophile who served as much as an apologist for the Allied cause as an impartial representative of American interests. Even Wilson possessed an innate pro-British bias. His doctoral dissertation, *Congressional Government*, was a comparative study of the American congressional and British parliamentary systems in which he argued that the former ought to acquire attributes of the latter.

Economic Ties to the Allies

Reinforcing America's cultural and intellectual ties to the Allies was a developing pattern of international trade that ultimately gave the United States an economic stake in an Allied victory. As 1914 opened, the nation teetered on the edge of a major depression. The war in Europe at first disrupted trade and threatened to plunge America into a depression. Very quickly, however, the Allies, who controlled the transatlantic sea lanes, began to make massive purchases of armaments and raw materials in the United States. By 1915 the economy was booming under the stimulus of these expenditures. As Allied purchases increased geometrically, London and Paris' supply of gold and dollars dwindled to nothing.

In the spring, the French government approached J.P. Morgan, head of America's largest investment banking firm, about floating a $100 million loan. Chastened by previous assaults on his trusts by the Roosevelt and Wilson administrations, Morgan inquired at the State Department as to the propriety of the transaction. Not surprisingly, Bryan, who had spent much of his career railing at "bloated financiers," denounced money as the worst type of contraband (commodities which under international law it was illegal for a neutral to sell to a belligerent). The problem with the State Department's ban on loans was that it quickly imperiled the health of the economy. After Bryan resigned over another issue, Wilson rescinded the State Department prohibition on loans to the warring powers. In August, with the administration's approval, Morgan extended a $500 million line of credit to the French. By the time the United States entered the war, American financiers had loaned the Allies some $2 billion, compared to $27 million loaned to Germany. U.S. bankers were sure to lose their investment if Britain and France were defeated. Cultural and economic factors ensured that the United States would not enter the war on the side of the Central Powers.

NAVAL WARFARE AND AMERICAN NEUTRAL RIGHTS

The decision between war and peace, between remaining neutral and joining the Allies, was determined by events on the high seas. Both Britain and Germany, the two principal naval powers involved in the Great War, violated American neutral rights, but they did so in vastly different ways. That difference would prove to be crucial.

As it had since its emergence as a great power in the seventeenth century, Great Britain attempted to use its control of the seas to starve its enemies into submission. Soon after the war erupted, Britain imposed a naval blockade on the Central Powers. Its massive battle fleet patrolled the Atlantic, the North Sea, and the Mediterranean stopping neutral ships and seizing their cargoes if they were destined for a port controlled by Germany or its allies. The Royal Navy offended neutral sensibilities by stationing its ships in mid-ocean, rather than outside enemy ports declared blockaded, as international law required, and expanded the list of contraband, traditionally limited to items used on the battlefield, to include raw materials such as petroleum, cotton, and food. The United States which, as a third-rate naval power with a first-rate merchant marine, had traditionally insisted on maximum leeway for neutrals to trade with belligerents, strongly protested British seizure of its ships. Because British policy did not threaten American lives and because the government bought most of the cargoes that it seized, U.S. reaction was limited and restrained. There was never any chance that British violation of American neutral rights would be a *casus belli* (cause of war). This was clearly not the case with Germany.

Submarine Warfare

Except to fight the indecisive Battle of Jutland in 1916, the German fleet did not venture in force from its home ports. The only real service the surface fleet rendered was to keep elements of the Royal Navy on continuous duty in the North Sea. Thus, the only weapon available to Germany to break the Allied blockade was the submarine. The sub, as a new weapon, was not covered by existing rules of warfare. Under international law when surface cruisers encountered enemy merchant vessels, they were to fire a warning shot, remove the crew, and only then sink the vessel. Early in the war, German U-boat commanders tried to follow the rules of naval warfare; the results were disastrous. On the surface the thin-skinned submarines were very vulnerable. Most British merchant vessels were armed with deck guns and could match the submarines' firepower. Very quickly, the German high command realized that if the sub was going to be an effective weapon, it would have to torpedo while submerged and leave the merchant crew to fend for itself.

In February 1915, Germany announced to belligerents and neutrals that in response to Britain's blockade and its widespread violation of neutral rights, the Imperial Navy was going to treat the waters around the British Isles as a war zone. All Allied vessels venturing into that area were liable to be sunk by German submarines. The announcement made it clear that neutral vessels were exempt, but warned, ominously, that in time of war, mistakes were easily made. President Wilson responded by declaring that Germany would be held "strictly accountable" for any damage to American property or loss of life resulting from submarine activity in the war zone.

Sinking of the *Lusitania*

Because German U-boat commanders were under explicit orders not to attack neutral vessels, the crisis in German-American relations began to fade. Then,

Nothing did more to alienate Americans from the Central Powers than the sinking of the Lusitania. *Here an artist's rendering with the caption "The Greatest Sea Crime on Record" depicted the sinking.*

on the morning of May 7, 1915, a German submarine torpedoed and sank the British passenger liner *Lusitania* within sight of the Irish coast. The 1,198 people killed included 128 Americans. On the day that the *Lusitania*, the Cunard line's largest, newest, and most luxurious ship, sailed from New York, notices put up by the German Consulate had appeared at dockside warning passengers that they were traveling aboard a belligerent ship and would be entering a war zone. None paid heed, sure that Germany would never be rash enough to sink an unarmed passenger liner.

The attack on the *Lusitania* was an accident of war. In his postwar account of the affair, the commander of the U-20 wrote that he was low on fuel and heading back to his home base when he spotted a four-stacked vessel flying the British flag lying low on the horizon. Taking a gamble, he dispatched at extremely long distance his single remaining torpedo. It was only when the U-boat commander approached and saw the name *Lusitania* emblazoned on the doomed vessel's stern that he realized what he had done.

A storm of outrage swept America. "It is a deed for which a Hun would blush, a Turk be ashamed, and a Barbary pirate apologize," declared New York's *The Nation*. Angry though they were, the American people and their president hoped that the incident would not lead to war. A *Literary Digest* poll taken shortly after the sinking showed that only six out of one thousand respondents favored a declaration of war. Three days after the destruction of the *Lusitania* Wilson addressed a large crowd in Philadelphia and told them that sometimes nations like men could be "too proud to fight." The bellicose former president, Theodore Roosevelt, along with the Allied governments, was deeply disappointed.

Wilson's Dilemma

In the wake of the sinking of the *Lusitania* Wilson faced a choice of policy. He had, after all, told Germany that it would be held accountable for any loss of American life or damage to American property. Actually, the submarines posed very little threat to U.S. commerce. At the beginning of 1915, the Germans possessed only twenty-one U-boats, and they were slow, clumsy vessels with limited weaponry. The real danger was the vulnerability of American citizens who traveled as passengers and crew on Allied merchant vessels. Two poles of opinion formed within the administration as to how best to respond. Bryan advocated a passive neutrality. To spare Americans the terrible carnage then reigning in Belgium and France, Bryan argued, the president should prohibit American vessels from entering the war zone or American citizens from traveling on belligerent vessels. Robert Lansing, counselor of the State Department and its second in command, urged a more aggressive stance. It would be a betrayal of American interests and tradition not to demand that Germany respect the right of Americans to travel where they wanted and trade with whom they wanted whether in war or in peace. Colonel House, a wealthy Texan and Democratic party power broker who had become one of Wilson's most trusted confidants, agreed. Wilson did not want war, but he could not bring himself to abandon America's traditional defense of neutral rights. He sent a toughly worded note to Germany demanding an apology and a promise not to attack unarmed passenger liners in the future. After some delay, Berlin gave the required assurances, and the crisis once again began to fade. Reluctantly, Bryan resigned in protest on June 8, 1915.

Out of the controversy over America's proper posture toward the Great War and its future role in the international community came the three basic philosophies which would determine U.S. policy for the rest of the twentieth century: (1) Bryan and his followers were basically isolationists. Overseas investments, military bases, and alliances would involve the United States in the great power politics and imperial clashes that had plagued the nation-state system since its founding. Physically isolated and economically self-sufficient, the isolationists argued, the United States should focus on perfecting its domestic political institutions and social system. (2) Theodore Roosevelt represented the nationalist point of view. The United States clearly had legitimate strategic and economic interests abroad, but they were specific and limited. America ought to play an active role in world affairs, but it should operate on a case-by-case basis and maintain its freedom of action. (3) Taft and the international lawyers who gathered around him were proto-internationalists. Without some mechanism for the peaceful solution of conflict and an international military force to back it up, the world would continue to suffer from periodic cataclysms like the Great War. Before the fighting in Europe ended, Woodrow Wilson would take the notion of collective security, broaden and deepen it, and articulate it into a compelling vision of an economically and strategically interdependent world.

In the short run, the submarine controversy with Germany remained Wilson's overriding concern. In late March 1916, a German U-boat attacked the English Channel steamer *Sussex*, injuring several Americans. Frightened and angry, Wilson threatened to sever diplomatic relations with Germany unless its government promised not to attack all unarmed merchantmen without giving prior warning. The American ultimatum touched off a heated debate in Berlin. To accede would be to relinquish the submarine as a weapon and to give up hope of breaking the Allied blockade. But to refuse was to risk bringing the United States into the war. Because the German high command anticipated victory on the battlefield by late 1916 and did not want anything to detract from that goal, it agreed to a surrender. Germany subsequently promised not to attack without warning, but reserved the right to resume submarine warfare in the future if circumstances dictated.

Somewhat belatedly, Wilson realized that his public demands in the wake of the *Lusitania* and *Sussex* affairs had transferred the initiative for war from Washington to Berlin. Given his tough statements, if Germany decided to resume all-out submarine warfare, the president would have little choice but to go to Congress and ask for a declaration of war. Consequently, he maneuvered frantically in late 1915 and early 1916 to bring the war to a close before the United States could be drawn in. In December 1915, he dispatched Colonel House to Europe to broach a plan for a mediated settlement of the war, but none of the belligerents felt comfortable enough with their relative battlefield positions to enter into negotiations.

While he maneuvered desperately to end the war in Europe before the United States could be drawn in, President Wilson continued with his preparedness program. In 1916, Congress passed massive funding bills to beef up the army and navy, and resoundingly defeated proposals by congressional allies of Bryan designed to keep American citizens off Allied ships. These debates revealed a marked shift by the two major parties in their foreign policy positions. Democrats had generally followed Bryan's lead in opposing a more assertive, interventionist role in world affairs. In the preparedness and neutrality votes, however, they sided with Wilson and embraced the notion of an activist foreign policy. Those same votes witnessed a decline of Rooseveltian nationalism within the Republican party—the same party which had ardently supported the Spanish-American War and the acquisition of the Philippines. Led by Robert LaFollette, William Borah, and other progressive isolationists, the Republicans would gradually abandon imperialism and come to advocate strategic and economic self-sufficiency.

THE ELECTION OF 1916

Politicians and people of affairs were forced to divert their attention from the war in Europe momentarily and focus on the presidential election of 1916.

Wilson and the Democrats did not face the contest with a great deal of confidence. The Republican party had healed the Taft-Roosevelt split that had cost it the election in 1912. Wilson could not forget that he had won with but 42 percent of the vote. Quietly ignoring Theodore Roosevelt, the Republicans nominated the popular, attractive former governor of New York, Charles Evans Hughes, thus further discouraging the Democrats. But then in the keynote address at the Democratic convention in St. Louis, ex-Governor Martin Glynn of New York electrified the delegates with an offhand reference to the president's success at avoiding war. After the delegates repeatedly stood and cheered, Democratic propagandists translated Glynn's remark into "He kept us out of war!" Somewhat against his will, then, Woodrow Wilson campaigned in 1916 as the peace candidate.

The election was extremely close. Wilson won with 49 percent of the popular vote to Hughes' 46 percent, but the tally in the electoral college was 277 to 254. A number of historians have speculated that the peace issue turned the tide for the Democrats.

WILSON'S SEARCH FOR PEACE

Wilson was glad of his victory but troubled that he had been forced to campaign as the peace candidate. "I can't keep this country out of war," he remarked. "Some damned little German lieutenant can plunge this nation into war through a calculated outrage." In the fall of 1916, he pressed ahead with a peace offensive in another effort to end the war before the United States could be drawn in. On December 18, 1916, Wilson dispatched a peace note to the combatants asking them for a candid statement of their war aims. The note, made public two days later, asserted that there was no essential difference between those aims—peace and self-determination—and hence no reason to continue hostilities. Wilson's initiative touched off a frantic debate in the belligerent capitals. Both sides had secretly worked out a peace program that called for their defeated enemies to give up territory and pay indemnities. In January 1917, the British sent a diplomatic, noncommittal reply; the Germans brusquely told the Americans not to meddle in the internal affairs of other nations.

Deflected but not discouraged, President Wilson made a surprise appearance before the Senate on January 22, 1917, to outline a peace program rooted in his vision of a new international order. He called for peace without victory, the guarantee of fundamental rights and safeguards for all nations—equal sovereignty, freedom from aggression, freedom of the seas, and eventual disarmament—and the establishment of a league of nations to enforce the peace. He held out hope that the principles of collective security and free trade would usher in an era of peace and ever-increasing prosperity.

Wilson's call for peace without victory fell on deaf ears. Even before he addressed the Senate, Germany had decided on a resumption of all-out submarine warfare. Berlin realized that this step would inevitably bring the United States into the war, but it reasoned that the Central Powers could defeat the Allies before America could make its presence felt on the battlefield. By 1917 the German submarine fleet had grown to such a size that the high command believed it capable of actually blockading Britain and France, cutting them off from the munitions and raw materials needed to fight the war. The strategists in Berlin had miscalculated.

AMERICA ENTERS THE WAR

On January 31, 1917, the German ambassador informed the State Department that submarine war would commence against all shipping the next day. The news sent shock waves through the United States. On February 3 Wilson severed diplomatic relations with Germany, but shrank from asking Congress for a declaration of war. Perhaps, he hoped, Berlin was bluffing. It would be best to await events. Then, on February 28, American opinion was further inflamed against the Central Powers when several newspapers published verbatim the text of a telegram that German Foreign Minister Alfred Zimmerman had sent to the German Embassy in Mexico City. He warned of the approaching resumption of submarine warfare, and he instructed his diplomats to approach their host government about an alliance in case Germany found itself at war with the United States. The cable offered Mexico the territory it had lost to the United States as a result of the Mexican War of 1848—territory which included the states of Texas, New Mexico, and Arizona. The telegram had a stunning effect on American opinion; it brought the war close to home and seemed to confirm the warnings of those who had been arguing that Germany would stop at nothing short of world domination. The Zimmerman telegram, together with the collapse of the Tsarist regime in Russia and its replacement by a pro-war parliamentary democracy, helped unify the nation behind a declaration of war when it finally came.

When, in fact, German submarines began attacking U.S. merchantmen in the war zone around the British Isles, Wilson called a special session of Congress for April 2, and he authorized limited naval action against German submarines. In a dramatic address on the evening of the second, Wilson asked Congress to recognize that a state of war already existed because of the hostile action of the German Navy. The United States, he said, was going to war to protect American lives and property and to defend its definition of neutral rights. But there were loftier goals. This was to be a great crusade "to make the world safe for democracy." It was a war to end wars, because out of it would come a league of nations dedicated to collective security and economic and social justice around the world. For Woodrow Wilson, armed neutrality without formal belligerency would bring all the costs of war without any of the benefits. Most importantly, active participation in the conflict would enable the United States to shape the peace and make concrete his vision of a new world order.

MOBILIZING FOR WAR

Though America did not enter the Great War until 1917, its commitment was swift and complete. On the home front the most immediate task, aside from re-cruiting and training troops, was to organize the economy. Though Woodrow Wilson was devoted to private enterprise and the virtues of a regulated economy, he like his advisors recognized that the demands of waging modern war would require massive government intervention into and control over the private sector. It would simply not do to leave decisions regarding manpower, material, and production priorities up to individual corporations. In 1917 Wilson created the War Industries Board (WIB) to deal with these matters, but that agency was only marginally effective until the successful stock broker and Wall Street speculator Bernard Baruch assumed control in 1918. Relying alter-nately on flattery and threats, Baruch persuaded private industry to accept WIB guidelines. The financier's power became such that he was able to determine prices, output levels for steel and other industries, allocation of raw materials, and a thousand other details of industrial life. The WIB operated with sur-prisingly little friction; hundreds of "dollar-a-year" businessmen flocked to Washington to aid in the war effort. In partnership with the WIB, American in-dustry increased its overall output by 20 percent during the war.

U.S. participation in the Great War stimulated experiments in state making in other areas as well. A federal Fuel Administration under Harry A. Garfield invented daylight savings time to cut down the use of electricity and oil for lighting, forbade the operation of motor vehicles on certain days, and shut down nonessential factories one day a week to conserve desperately needed coal. So powerful was Garfield that he was able to close all factories located east of the Mississippi for four days in January 1918 in order to divert coal to mu-nitions ships stranded in New York harbor. Without actually taking them over from their owners, the federal government assumed supervisory power over the nation's railroads and integrated them into a single system.

Food was at a premium during World War I. The dramatic new re-quirements of the U.S. expeditionary force as well as the ongoing needs of America's allies and liberated areas placed huge strains on U.S. agriculture and agribusiness. To head the newly created Food Administration, Wilson chose the respected mining engineer and the hero of the Belgium relief effort, Herbert Hoover. As part of the effort to encourage American farmers to produce more, Hoover raised and fixed prices. He proclaimed "wheatless" and "meatless" days and sent five hundred thousand volunteers door-to-door to persuade American housewives to plant victory gardens. Responding to the Food Admin-istration's goading and incentives, wheat farmers increased production from existing lands and planted tens of thousands of additional acres.

The Wilson administration was no less determined to make labor a member of the war team than he was business. Samuel Gompers, president of the American Federation of Labor, was an enthusiastic member of the Council of National Defense, and he formed a committee within the labor movement to generate support for the war. Gompers was something of a chauvinist, declaring the Great War at one point to be a "wonderful crusade," but he also saw in the conflict an opportunity to obtain higher wages and better working conditions for his members. The administration proved surprisingly cooperative. The president personally endorsed the notion of an eight-hour day, and in early 1918 he asked Harvard law professor Felix Frankfurter to head up a War Labor Board (WLB). In fact as well as in word the WLB supported the concept of collective bargaining. On two occasions, Frankfurter's agency secured a government takeover of companies that refused to bargain with unions in good faith. Real wages rose during World War I, and union membership increased from 2.7 million in 1916 to 4 million in 1919.

U.S. government and Allied purchases stimulated the American economy, and that coupled with the loss to the labor force of tens of thousands of white males created unprecedented employment opportunities for women and ethnic minorities. Some change occurred in the kinds of jobs that women held—in electrical equipment manufacturing, the aircraft industry, and agricultural implement factories women constituted a fifth of the workforce—but generally they simply became office workers and retail clerks in greater numbers. The number of women in the workforce held steady at around 8 million throughout the war. Most female workers were young and single; there was no mass migration from the hearth and home by homemakers into the workforce. Moreover, after the war, many of the new jobs that had been created were taken over by returning veterans. Still, on the whole, the war created a rising level of expectations among American women and a willingness to challenge long-established norms concerning dress, sex, and vocation.

AFRICAN AMERICANS AND WORLD WAR I

The Great War combined with a number of other factors to affect profoundly the lives of African Americans. Between 1914 and 1920 nearly five hundred thousand blacks moved from farms and towns in the South to large urban areas in the Midwest and Northeast. Cleveland's African-American population grew by 300 percent, Detroit's by 600 percent, and Gary, Indiana's, by a whopping 1,284 percent. A number of factors contributed to the Great Migration as this, one of the most significant demographic episodes in the nation's history, was called. There was first the ongoing hostility of southern whites to blacks. Political disfranchisement, economic exploitation, and inequality under the law were permanent features of southern life during the first quarter of the twentieth century. Those African Americans who dared protest or who were even suspected of committing crimes were beaten or killed. Indeed, spurred on by the sight of black soldiers in uniform, mobs lynched forty-eight African Americans in 1917, sixty-three in 1918, and seventy-eight in 1919. Not all of these illegal executions occurred in the South, but a disproportionate number did. Positive incentives for the mass exodus existed as well. The outbreak of war in Europe all but ended immigration, and the booming war industries in the Midwest and North needed semiskilled workers. Beginning in 1916, labor agents working for these concerns spread out across the South advertising jobs and promising high wages and good working conditions. Entire families of African Americans gathered up their belongings and headed north. Deprived of its traditional cheap source of labor, the white South retaliated against those who remained which, of course, accelerated rather than staunched the flow.

Black migrants found conditions in New York, Philadelphia, Chicago, and other cities better than in the South in some ways and worse in others. A female domestic in the North could earn $1.50 to $2.00 a day plus meals and transportation, a wage that it would take a week to earn in the South. Cotton picking paid around $.50 a day while many factory jobs paid $3 a day. Some families came north, but the majority of those who came were young and unmarried. The men went to work in steel mills, coal mines, meat-packing houses, or railroad yards. Women became maids, laundresses, or seamstresses. Life was in some ways more secure for the new "urban Negro," but it was also impersonal and lonely. It became, moreover, increasingly violent. Fearful for their jobs, covetous of scarce housing, and vulnerable to the racist appeals of opportunistic politicians, white northerners turned on their new neighbors. In 1917 a race riot in East St. Louis left thirty-nine blacks and nine whites dead, and six thousand African Americans homeless. In July 1919, the month the final peace treaty was signed, outbreaks of racial violence in Washington, D.C., and Chicago killed forty-four people.

THE WAR AND MEXICAN AMERICANS

Under pressure from farmers and ranchers in the Southwest who were responding to government incentives to grow more crops and raise more livestock, the immigration authorities relaxed restrictions along the U.S.–Mexican border. As a result between 1917 and 1920 more than one hundred thousand Mexicans flooded into the Southwest. They worked as migrant farm laborers or migrated to the the cities of the West. Often persecuted and ostracized, Mexican Americans formed barrios or ghettos in these urban areas.

THE BACKLASH OF INTOLERANCE

Wars generally breed demands for conformity, superpatriotism, and abuse of civil liberties, but World War I was exceptional for its excesses in these areas. Immediately after Congress voted for war, President Wilson created the Committee on Public Information (CPI) and asked George Creel, a seasoned journalist and former muckraker, to head it. Creel applied himself with a vengeance to the task of selling the war. Altogether the CPI employed fifteen thousand speakers, artists, and writers, including Ida Tarbell and Ray Stannard Baker, to incite the populace to sacrifice for the great crusade then underway in Europe. Selling the war, Creel declared, would be "the world's greatest adventure in advertising."

The heart and soul of the CPI's effort on the home front were the seventy-five thousand "four minute men" who were prepared to speak to social clubs, churches, or theater goers on the virtues of patriotism and the righteousness of the struggle in Europe. Initially, the CPI instructed its personnel to stick to the facts, but by 1918 Creel and his associates were stressing the depravity of "the Hun," portraying Germany and Germans as innately autocratic, brutal, and predatory. The burgeoning movie industry produced, with CPI support, movies like *The Beast of Berlin* and *The Prussian Cur.* This wave of propaganda and the intolerance that naturally accompanies war generated intense hatred towards German Americans and all things German. Sauerkraut was renamed "liberty cabbage" and dachshunds became "liberty pups." A number of schools dropped German from the curriculum; the state board of education in California called it a language of "autocracy, brutality, and hatred." Symphony orchestras responded to Wilson and Creel's appeals to patriotism by banning the works of Brahms, Bach, and Beethoven. More seriously, numerous German Americans were persecuted and even killed merely because they had been born in Germany.

Those Americans who dared openly to oppose the war suffered grotesque violations of their civil liberties. "Woe to the man or group of men that seeks to stand in our way in this day of high resolution," warned President Wilson. But some could not be intimidated. Many German Americans believed that the fatherland was no more guilty of starting the war than any of the other participants, and they were reluctant to send their sons off to kill their kinsmen. After British authorities brutally crushed an Irish nationalist uprising in 1916, Irish Americans could muster little sympathy for the war. The American Socialist party called a special national convention to condemn the conflict in Europe and the Wilson administration's decision to participate in it. The Great War had been started by the bankers and munitions makers of the nations concerned and was being fought solely for their benefit, the Socialists declared. The great majority refused to recognize the right of these individuals and groups to dissent.

The Espionage and Sedition Acts

In 1917 Congress passed the Espionage Act and the following year the Sedition Act. The former imposed maximum sentences of twenty years for persons found guilty of aiding the enemy, hindering recruitment, or encouraging disloyalty. The latter measure, much more dangerous, promised fine and imprisonment for any person convicted of using "disloyal, profane, scurrilous, or abusive language" about the government, the flag, or the uniform. A provision in the Espionage Act gave to the postmaster general the power to censor the mails. By war's end, he had banned more than four hundred periodicals, including editions of the *New York Times* and the *Saturday Evening Post.* In 1918 a federal court convicted Eugene V. Debs, head of the Socialist party, of espionage for publicly denouncing capitalism and the war. He ran for the presidency in 1920 from his prison cell in Atlanta and garnered more than a million votes. Eventually, life became dangerous for any person or group suspected of holding "radical" political views. The International Workers of the World (IWW), a left-leaning labor union active in the West, had not come out openly against the war, but its members were subjected to persecution anyway. In Arizona an angry mob aided by law enforcement officials rounded up more than a thousand IWW members (nicknamed "Wobblies"), loaded them on boxcars, and dumped them in the desert.

Groups and individuals protested the widespread violations of civil liberties brought on by participation in the Great War. The Civil Liberties Bureau, forerunner of the American Civil Liberties Union, was formed in response to various outrages. Most Americans either participated or condoned the orgy of nativism and intolerance. In 1919 the Supreme Court by a vote of 7 to 2 upheld the Sedition Act, declaring that the right to free speech was not absolute. The persecutions, beatings, and prosecutions of those who were or who were thought to be different, including African-American veterans, continued for more than a year after the war was over. In their patriotic zealotry, Woodrow Wilson and his fellow Americans overlooked the fact that the republic was founded upon the principle of liberty as well as democracy.

THE AMERICAN EXPEDITIONARY FORCE

In deciding in January 1917 to wage all-out submarine warfare, the German government gambled that their blockade could starve the British Isles and the British and French armies into submission before the United States could become a factor in the fighting. It was a gamble that did not pay off. It was true that the United States Army was in deplorable condition at the outset of the war. The two hundred thousand officers and men were equipped with three hundred thousand outdated rifles, 1,500 machine guns, and two field radios. The Army General Staff did not even have a war strategy for Europe; Wilson had forbidden his top military personnel from providing for such a contingency lest the plans be revealed and American neutrality compromised. Thousands volunteered for the army, but Wilson's advisors told him that victory would require at least a million men. At the behest of the White House, therefore, Congress passed in May 1917 the Selective Service Act. The "draft," as it was called, required all men between the ages of 21 and 30 (later increased to 18 and 45) to register for military service. Twenty-four million American males registered with the Selective Service System. Of these, 2.8 million were called, about 12 percent of the total. Some in Congress criticized conscription as a system of involuntary servitude, but Wilson defended it as the most democratic of systems. The entire nation had volunteered, he declared; the draft merely decided who would go.

When the United States entered the war, the Allies were being pushed back on every front. Two French offensives in the spring of 1917 failed, and the Germans inflicted a decisive defeat on the British in Flanders during the summer. That fall the Russian provisional government under Alexander Kerensky collapsed to be replaced by the Bolsheviks, a radical faction of the Russian socialist movement dedicated to the destruction of private property and the creation of a worker-peasant state through armed insurrection. The new communist regime took Russia out of the war freeing tens of thousands of German and Austrian troops for action in the west.

In the spring of 1918 sixty-four German divisions attacked the British-French salient at Picardy. Within days the Central Powers had reached a point on the Marne River only fifty miles from Paris. French authorities considered evacuating the capital, but Allied forces counterattacked. Twenty-seven thousand Americans blocked the Germans at the town of Chateau-Thierry. A month later, troops of the American Expeditionary Force (AEF) under General John J. Pershing cleared the Germans out of Belleau Wood, a vital strongpoint. Having unified themselves under a Supreme Command, the Allies pressed their advantage. In July with a million U.S. troops in the field a major counterattack got underway. On September 12, 1918, five hundred thousand Americans together with a French force expelled the Germans from the St. Mihiel salient, twelve miles south of Verdun. Two weeks later the nine hundred thousand–man AEF struck the German line between the Argonne Forest and the Meuse River. The Central Powers held briefly and then broke. When the Americans captured the enemy's main rail supply route in the west, the Germans began falling back all along the line.

TRENCH WARFARE

Americans, blessed with fifty years' respite from the horrors of total war, approached the conflict in Europe with a certain romantic naivete. Illusions were soon shattered by the realities of trench warfare. Pinned down by rapid-fire machine guns, gas, and long-range artillery, soldiers spent months in cold, wet, lice-ridden trenches only hundreds of yards apart. Their existence was reduced to long periods of miserable boredom punctuated by bursts of absolute terror. Periodically, the troops in the trenches were called upon to go over the top to assault the enemy. The results were inevitably disastrous. The German offensive at Verdun in 1916 took the lives of six hundred thousand men; twenty thousand British soldiers died in the first day of the Battle of the Somme. When they were not being slaughtered on the battlefield, soldiers were being afflicted with influenza, trenchfoot, and other diseases and blasted into a state of shell shock by the earthshaking artillery bombardments.

WILSON'S FOURTEEN POINTS

Even before the United States entered the war, Wilson outlined his peace program in a speech delivered to Congress in January 1917. Running throughout the Fourteen Points, the name given to the president's vision of the postwar world, were three themes. First was peace without victory. If the world was not to be plunged into another cataclysm like the one then raging in Europe, the victors would have to refrain from imposing a harsh peace on the vanquished. Dismemberment of the defeated nations or imposition of reparations payments that distorted their economies would create a thirst for vengeance and sow the seeds of another war. Second, Wilson insisted that the principle of self-determination govern any peace settlement. If the various ethnic and linguistic groupings throughout the world did not ultimately enjoy the right to determine their own form of government and to control their own destiny, there would be revolution and violence. Indeed, the suppression of this impulse had led directly to the outbreak of the Great War. Third, the president called for the establishment of an international collective security organization in which the peace-loving nations of the world would band together not only to combat aggression but also to eliminate the roots of war such as socioeconomic insecurity and political repression.

After the United States entered the war, a government agency, the Committee on Public Information, spread Wilson's ideas not only in America but throughout the world. The principles underlying the Fourteen Points were favorably received at home and abroad, but leaders of the Allied nations had signed a series of secret agreements in 1914 and 1915 in which they committed themselves to partitioning Austria-Hungary, stripping Germany of its colonies and some of its European territory, and saddling the defeated nations with a huge reparations burden. They were certain that their respective populations, having borne the brunt of the war, would insist on an extremely harsh peace.

GERMANY SUES FOR PEACE

In the late summer of 1918 the Imperial German Command informed civilian leaders in Berlin that if they did not sue for peace, the army would disintegrate and Germany would be helpless to fend off an Allied invasion. Using intermediaries, representatives of the German government contacted the Wilson administration and asked for peace negotiations based on the Fourteen Points. After securing a commitment from the Central Powers to lay down their arms and evacuate all occupied territory, the Wilson administration with some difficulty persuaded British, French, and Italian leaders to agree to a cease-fire and a peace settlement based on his program. On November 11, 1918, representatives of the principal combatants signed an armistice in Marshall Ferdinand Foch's railcar in the forest at Compiègne. The Great War was over.

World War I set a new precedent for carnage. Weapons such as the machine gun, long-range artillery piece, the hand grenade, and poison gas took a deadly toll. Nearly 9 million combatants died, and 20 million suffered disabilities. France lost half of its male population between the ages of twenty and thirty-two. American losses, by comparison, were light, 48,909 dead and 230,000 wounded. Of the 2 million Americans who served, nearly four hundred thousand were African Americans. Of these, half served overseas. Though segregated into separate units, frequently assigned to menial tasks at the outset of the war, and most often commanded by white officers, black soldiers saw combat and distinguished themselves. Indeed, the French government awarded the Croix de guerre, the nation's most important military decoration, to entire units for their bravery.

The Germans believed that they would be able to participate in the peace negotiations that followed their surrender. They were mistaken. The Allied armies occupied Germany to the Rhine River and the British Navy blockaded that nation's ports. The general peace conference was scheduled to open in January 1919, and neither Germany, Austria-Hungary nor any other of the Central Powers was invited to attend.

THE PARIS PEACE CONFERENCE

The end of World War I left Woodrow Wilson relieved and exhilarated. He sensed that his moment in history had arrived. The enemy had been defeated and the world stood ready to embrace his vision of a peace based on justice, fair play, and collective security. He determined to let nothing stand in his way. The cease-fire in Europe coincided with mid-term congressional elections in the United States. Ignoring the fact that the party in control of the White House usually loses ground in the House and Senate, Wilson campaigned vigorously for various Democrats implying that his party was the only fit instrument for peacemaking. The Democrats lost control of the Senate by one seat, thus giving the Republicans a majority on the Senate Foreign Relations Committee, the body that would have to pass on any peace treaty that the president brought home from Paris. Thus did Wilson take a long step toward making the peace settlement a partisan issue.

PREPARATIONS FOR THE CONFERENCE

Throughout November and December 1918, the president and his advisors worked feverishly to prepare for the forthcoming conference. To head the American delegation, Wilson chose himself. He was widely criticized at the time for his decision. Sitting presidents simply did not venture outside the United States. But the Fourteen Points were his creation, and the other Allied powers were sending their heads of state. In light of these and other factors, his decision to go himself was justifiable. This was not true of Wilson's choice of fellow delegates. The five-man official delegation included Secretary of State Robert Lansing, General Tasker Bliss who had been America's representative on the supreme Allied war council, Colonel House, and Henry White, a career foreign service officer and the only Republican on the delegation. Under the Constitution the Senate of the United States must approve by a two-thirds vote any treaty negotiated by the executive. That body was then in the hands of the

Republican party, and the president would have been well served by naming one of its Republican members to the delegation. But he did not.

FIRST PHASE: THE LEAGUE OF NATIONS

President Wilson and his entourage of delegates and experts sailed aboard the *George Washington*. Before the peace conference opened at Versailles, the Paris suburb that was home to eighteenth- and nineteenth-century Bourbon monarchs, the president toured the Allied capitals where he was given a hero's welcome. The English, French, and Italians were merely grateful for U.S. intervention, but Wilson mistook their adulation for support for the Fourteen Points.

The Paris Peace Conference opened amidst mass confusion. Twenty-seven countries were in attendance; there were over one hundred official delegates with thousands of support staff. Quickly the principal powers agreed to break the conference down into a Council of Ten with two delegates each from the United States, Great Britain, France, Italy, and Japan. Japan and Italy subsequently played a major role in settling only those issues that affected them directly. The great decisions at Versailles were made by Wilson, French Premier Georges Clemenceau, a devout nationalist determined to render Germany forever incapable of waging war again, and British Prime Minister David Lloyd George, a wily and pragmatic politician with an eye always to improving his country's strategic and economic situation.

At Wilson's insistence the first phase of the conference focused on drafting and ratifying the covenant, or charter, of the League of Nations, the president's collective security organization. Aware that support for a league was thin or nonexistent among the other delegates, Wilson was determined to secure their approval before he expended his political capital on other issues. Moreover, to his mind the League would compensate for compromises and possible injustices that might appear in the treaty proper. Indeed, over time the world body would be able to correct those injustices.

In late February President Wilson returned to the United States to attend to some domestic chores while the conferees in Paris enjoyed a recess. He was in a triumphant mood. The delegates to the Paris Peace Conference had approved his plan for a collective security organization, and the world seemed poised on the brink of a new era of peace and prosperity. His advisors warned him that the Senate was in a rebellious mood and counseled him to do some fence-mending. He duly had the members of the Senate Foreign Relations Committee to the White House, but rather than consulting them, he lectured the assembled solons on the virtues of his peace program. Shortly before Wilson's departure for Europe and the second phase of the conference, Senator Henry Cabot Lodge, chairman of the Foreign Relations Committee and Wilson's bitter enemy, circulated the Republican Round-Robin Note, a statement by thirty-nine senators and senators-elect that they would not vote to approve the covenant of the League as it stood. Wilson not only ignored the note, but in a dockside speech virtually dared the Republican-controlled Senate to defy him.

Despite promises of a democratic, openly run conference, most major decisions at Versailles were made in secret by the "Big Four." Here Wilson, Lloyd George, Clemenceau, and Orlando discuss the proceedings outside the Hall of Mirrors.

SECOND PHASE: THE TREATY OF VERSAILLES

The second phase of the Versailles Conference dealt with the substance of the peace treaty, that is the territorial, monetary, and political conditions that would prevail in postwar Europe and Asia. It was a complex and difficult process involving long negotiations and inevitable compromises. Indeed, President Wilson had to retreat on two of his most cherished principles: peace without victory and national self-determination. Wilson's experts told him that Germany could afford to bear a reparations burden of from $10 to 12 billion. Clemenceau and to a lesser extent Lloyd George were in a vengeful mood. They wanted literally to make Germany pay the cost of the war and in the process forever cripple its economy. Following a long struggle, the principals agreed to refer the matter to a reparations commission that would meet after the conference proper had ended. That body ended up imposing a $33 billion debt on Germany, a debt that ultimately contributed to the runaway inflation and political instability that toppled the Weimar Republic.

The French premier wanted not only to subvert Germany's economy but to dismember the country. He proposed that France take back Alsace-Lorraine and also annex everything up to the Rhine River. Wilson balked at this gross violation of the principle of national self-determination. After threatening

FIGURE 18–2

Postwar Europe and the Near East

to leave Paris and withdraw support for any peace treaty that was signed, Wilson managed to persuade Clemenceau to trade annexation of the Rhineland for temporary occupation and transformation of the region into a demilitarized buffer zone. In the east, however, East Prussia was separated from the rest of Germany and large tracts of German territory were given to Poland and the newly created state of Czechoslovakia. In the final peace treaty, Germany lost nearly a tenth of its population and an eighth of its territory (see Figure 18–2).

Woodrow Wilson returned to the United States in July 1919 aware that he had been forced to make important concessions to those who did not share his vision of the postwar world. He was in no mood to compromise any further. Public opinion polls in the United States taken in the summer of 1919 indicated that anywhere from two-thirds to three-fourths of those questioned favored

U.S. membership in a League of Nations. The president was confident that if Senate Republicans tried to block his peace program, he could rally the American people and sweep their opposition away.

DOMESTIC OPPOSITION TO THE TREATY

Despite public opinion polls and the president's confidence, important groups inside and outside the Senate opposed ratification or favored modification of the Treaty of Versailles. A group of Republican senators led by Henry Cabot Lodge were determined to modify the covenant of the League. Lodge hated Wilson and would have opposed the treaty on purely personal grounds if for no other. But the Lodge Republicans were reacting to other considerations. Wilson had made no effort to involve the Republican party in the peace process, to build a bipartisan consensus. Politically, the GOP (Grand Old Party; i.e., Republican) was almost bound to offer an alternative. Finally, these individuals were nationalists. They saw no reason why the United States should surrender its freedom of action and be committed by a majority of the League members to a course of action that was perhaps not in its interests.

Also in the Senate were a group of isolationists, dubbed "irreconcilables" by the press, who were opposed to membership in an international organization under any conditions. Led by William Borah of Idaho, the fourteen Republicans and one Democrat insisted that the United States ought to focus on domestic problems of poverty, ignorance, corporate wrongdoing, and political corruption. What went on in the rest of the world really had no bearing on American interests strategically and economically defined.

Criticisms by Immigrant Groups

There were certainly groups outside the Senate opposed to the Treaty of Versailles. German Americans regarded the peace agreement as unjust and were angry at Wilson for leading the nation into war against the "fatherland." Irish Americans were upset because the treaty did not provide the immediate and unconditional independence of Ireland. Italian Americans complained that the nation of their origin did not receive its just share of the spoils. They were upset especially that Fiume and Trieste at the head of the Adriatic went to the newly created state of Yugoslavia. Finally, many liberals such as journalist Walter Lippmann were angry that the treaty violated the principles of national self-determination and peace without victory.

Debate in the Senate

The debate in the Senate dealt with the territorial and economic provisions of the treaty proper but principally with the terms of the covenant of the League of Nations. Like the present-day United Nations, the League consisted of three main branches: a general assembly consisting of all members, a secretariat or administrative branch, and a council of the League with permanent and rotating members. Article X of the covenant provided that when the council found that a state of aggression existed, it could call upon member states first for economic sanctions against the aggressor, and if they were not effective, contributions to an international military force that would do battle to defend the victims of aggression. It was here that the Lodge Republicans insisted that the U.S. Constitution, which gives to Congress the right to declare war, had been violated. Lodge proposed a series of reservations or amendments to the covenant, the most important of which stated that the United States would not go to war to defend another member of the League without the express consent of Congress. Thus was the stage set for one of the great political confrontations in American history.

Upon his return in July, Wilson submitted the treaty to the Senate as the law required, and it was duly referred to the Foreign Relations Committee. Lodge perceived that popular support for the League was broad but thin and that with the passage of time the American people would lose interest in the issue. Delay, he decided, was the best tactic. To that end he read the entire 264-page treaty to a mostly empty committee room which consumed two weeks and then held open public hearings which took another six.

Wilson's Appeal for Support

As autumn approached, Wilson became increasingly concerned. Indeed, he sensed that Lodge's tactics were working and that the public was losing interest. Against the advice of his family and physician, aware that the war had exhausted the president and that his health was fragile, Wilson decided to embark on a strenuous cross-country speaking tour to rally the American people behind his peace program. The presidential train departed Washington on September 3. The tour got off to a slow start in the predominantly isolationist Midwest, but picked up steam in the West. Wilson delivered probably his best speech at Pueblo, Colorado, on the fifteenth, but collapsed that evening. His wife, Edith Boling Wilson, ordered the train back to Washington. Two weeks later the president suffered a debilitating stroke and for seven months he lay secluded in his bedroom, cut off from the outside world except for his wife and a few select associates. Wilson participated in the last stages of the treaty fight and his mind was generally clear, but he had taken himself out of the public and senatorial eye at a crucial juncture.

While Wilson was on his speaking tour, Lodge reported the treaty out of committee. The reservations were attached to the covenant by a straight party vote and the Senate took its first ballot in November. After due deliberation, Wilson ordered his supporters in the Senate to vote against the treaty with the Lodge reservations. The United States either surrendered part of its freedom of action, its sovereignty, for the common good or it did not, he reasoned. Collective security would not work if national legislatures had the right of veto over military action by the League. With the irreconcilables and Democrats voting nay, the treaty with reservations went down by a vote of 55 to 39. The way was then clear for a vote on the treaty without reservations. The Democrats and Republicans simply switched sides, and the treaty was defeated by a vote of 53 to 38. A huge public outcry arose. Eighty percent of the Senate favored membership in the League in one form or another, but that hallowed body seemed unable to find common ground. In March a third vote on the treaty with the Lodge reservations attached was taken. Wilson remained firm in his commitment to a League with the covenant as he had originally negotiated it, and once again ordered Senate Democrats to vote nay. A number deserted the president but not enough. Forty-nine senators voted yes but thirty-five no, seven votes short of the two-thirds required. So it was that when the experiment in world government that Woodrow Wilson conceived held its inaugural session in Geneva, the United States was absent.

Many historians subsequently blamed World War II on America's absence from the League. Had it lent its economic and military might to the organization, it could then have stood up to Germany, Italy, and Japan, and nipped aggression in the bud. Much of the blame for the stalemate that kept the United States out of the League has been laid on Woodrow Wilson and his stubborn refusal to compromise. In the ensuing essay Lloyd Ambrosius examines the issue of Wilson's health and its impact on his decision making during that crucial period in 1919.

WOODROW WILSON'S HEALTH AND THE TREATY FIGHT, 1919–1920

Lloyd E. Ambrosius

Confusion and controversy have surrounded both the state of Woodrow Wilson's health and the reasons for U.S. rejection of the Versailles treaty. Scholars have reached no consensus on either of these questions, and certainly not on the nexus

from Lloyd E. Ambrosius, "Woodrow Wilson's Health and the Treaty Fight, 1919–1920," *The International History Review*, Vol. IX, No. 1 (February 1987), 73–84.

between them. Specialists in medicine and psychology, as well as historians and political scientists, have entered into this scholarly controversy, offering conflicting interpretations of the president's physical and psychological condition, and especially its impact on his political leadership in 1919 and 1920. Anyone seeking to understand the politics of peacemaking in the United States after the First World War must, therefore, take into account the condition of Wilson's mind and body: his political personality—however it was shaped—was a significant factor in the fight over the League of Nations.

Internal contradictions marked Thomas A. Bailey's interpretation of the treaty fight. In *Woodrow Wilson and the Great Betrayal* (1945), he placed primary responsibility on Wilson and the Democrats, rather than Senator Henry Cabot Lodge and the Republicans, for defeating the League. Bailey concluded that "the treaty was slain in the house of its friends rather than in the house of its enemies. In the final analysis it was not the two-thirds rule, or the 'irreconcilables,' or Lodge, or the 'strong' and 'mild reservationists,' but Wilson and his docile following who delivered the fatal stab . . . This was the supreme act of infanticide. With his own sickly hands Wilson slew his own brain child." In another passage Bailey summarized more explicitly the effect of the president's illness on this act of infanticide, asserting that "Wilson's physical and mental condition had a profoundly important bearing on the final defeat of the treaty." Bailey seemed to agree with the retrospective judgement of Senator Gilbert M. Hitchcock, the Democratic minority leader during the treaty fight, who had concluded that "I shall always believe ratification would have been possible if Wilson's health had not given way; when that tragedy occurred, not even his best friends could exercise any considerable influence on him." Hitchcock thus attributed the treaty's failure to the president's intransigence, the tragic consequences of his stroke in 1919. Bailey elsewhere in his book, however, repudiated the logic of Hitchcock's argument and, in so doing, contradicted himself. He stated: "Some apologists for Wilson claim that if he had not collapsed he would have compromised with Lodge. Perhaps so, but there is nothing to support such a view in his public utterances, in his private papers, or in his character."

Bailey thus offered the contradictory conclusions that Wilson's health vitally affected the outcome of the treaty fight, and that it did not. The only way he might have reconciled these two conclusions would have been to argue that a healthy Wilson could have forced Lodge and the Republicans to accept the League without their reservations. If they had acquiesced in his demand for unqualified ratification, then he could have achieved his goal without compromising with Lodge. But Bailey did not present this case, and there is no evidence to warrant it.

Sigmund Freud and William C. Bullitt enlivened the controversy with their psychological study of *Thomas Woodrow Wilson* (1966). Collaboration during the early 1930s between the Viennese founder of psychoanalysis and the U.S. diplomat produced this critical study, a crude application of psychoanalysis to history: Freud contributed his theory, and Bullitt offered his experience and knowledge of Wilson. They argued that during the treaty fight he was suffering from "an extraordinary mental disintegration," the consequence of unresolved conflicts in his personal life. One conflict originated in his childhood, emerging from his ambivalent relationship with his domineering father, Joseph Ruggles Wilson, a Presbyterian clergyman. Freud and Bullitt claimed that Wilson was afflicted throughout his life by "the conflict between his passivity to his father and his aggressive activity against his father, and that his mental equilibrium depended on his ability to beat Lodge into submission and to repress his knowledge of the truth about the Peace Conference." During the treaty fight the Republican senator was "a father representative." The president's need to repress his knowledge about the negotiations in Paris, in the Freud-Bullitt view, arose from his tremendous guilt over the concessions he had made to the Allies. Wilson was, in other words, desperately seeking "to escape the scourgings of his Super-Ego." This was the other internal conflict that afflicted him; suffering from a "father fixation" and a guilty conscience, he sought release in 1919 by offering himself as a sacrifice, identifying himself unconsciously with Jesus Christ as "the Saviour of the World." He preferred death to compromise with Lodge. According to Freud and Bullitt, Wilson's neurosis—which was now "very close to psychosis"—accounted for his political failure during the treaty fight.

This interpretation presupposed the accuracy of Bullitt's view of the peace conference. He claimed, in his letter of resignation from the U.S. delegation on 17 May 1919, that Wilson could have achieved his vision of "a new world order" if he had openly appealed to world public opinion rather than secretly surrendering the Fourteen Points. "That you personally opposed most of the unjust settlements, and that you accepted them only under great pressure, is well known," Bullitt wrote to the president. "Nevertheless, it is my conviction that if you had made your fight in the open, instead of behind closed doors, you would have carried with you the public opinion of the world, which was yours; you would have been able to resist the pressure and might have established the 'new international order based upon broad and universal principles of right and justice' of which you used to speak." This view of Wilson's failure in Paris undergirded the analysis of Freud and Bullitt, who saw the president's acute psychological problems in 1919 as the consequence of his "moral collapse" during the peace conference, especially since he denied this reality even to himself. "His mental life from April to September 1919, when he collapsed completely and permanently, was a wild flight from fact," they claimed. Underlying this dubious interpretation was the assumption that the Versailles treaty substantially violated the Fourteen Points and that Wilson could have forced the Allies to accept his own position. But the reality of the peace conference was otherwise, as he recognized more clearly than either of them. The psychological interpretation of Freud and Bullitt therefore rested upon an inaccurate historical foundation.

Before publication of the Freud-Bullitt study, Alexander L. George and Juliette L. George had offered a similar, but more sophisticated, analysis of Wilson's political personality. They employed Freudian psychology, following the lead of the political scientist, Harold D. Lasswell. They, too traced the president's psychological problems to his childhood, emphasizing his father's negative contribution to his low self-esteem. "At the root of Wilson's numerous blunders, both in negotiating the Treaty and later in attempting to secure its ratification," argued the Georges in *Woodrow Wilson and Colonel House* (1956), "was his complicated personal involvement in the objective of an idealistic peace and a new world order." His inner needs drove him to attempt immortal work and to seek domination. He could not compromise with Lodge, another father figure, during the treaty fight, and because power provided compensation for his low self-esteem, the president sought political domination over the senate. "So now," the Georges concluded, "he did not *want* to reach a compromise agreement with the Senate. He wanted to defeat the Senate, and especially Lodge. If he could not overcome his enemies, it would be less painful to him to sacrifice the Treaty than to make concessions. He could relieve his sense of guilt for having provoked his own defeat by picturing himself martyred in a great cause and by seeking vindication from 'the people'—a vindication for which he strove to his dying day." Thus, according to the Georges, Wilson's psychological problems explained his refusal to compromise with Lodge, and the consequent failure of the United States to ratify the treaty and join the League.

Another political scientist, James David Barber, embraced the Georges' interpretation, giving it a new label. In his book on *The Presidential Character* (1972), he grouped Wilson with Herbert Hoover and Lyndon Johnson as active-negative presidents: they were all energetic and active leaders who did not enjoy political life. With grim determination, they pursued power to the point of their own destruction. Like the Georges, Barber traced the origins of presidential compulsion to early experiences of childhood, adolescence, and young adulthood, agreeing with them that "Wilson attempted to compensate for low self-esteem by dominating his social environment with moralistic rhetoric." This search for power and perfection, Barber concluded, created within Wilson "the psychological context for his stubborn, self-defeating behavior in the League fight."

Neurologist Edwin A. Weinstein offered an alternative to these Freudian interpretations of Wilson's personality, but on one point agreed with the Georges and Barber as well as with Freud and Bullitt: they all concurred that, for Wilson, the pursuit of victory was more important than success. His power motive was greater than his desire for any particular achievement. But Weinstein rejected the Freudian conclusion that Wilson's yearning for power arose from his troubled relationship with his father; instead, he argued that the president's Calvinist ethic furnished the source of his hard work and self-confidence. "This orientation," Weinstein nevertheless conceded, "sometimes led to overconfidence and rigidity, and to greater concern for success and victory than for the nature of the achievement itself." But he did not regard this as a pathological condition in the Freudian sense. In Weinstein's diagnosis, Wilson's neurological illness caused the negative changes in his personality after 1906, and especially in 1919 and 1920. He had suffered a series of little strokes before his massive stroke on 2 October 1919, and denial of his disability further contributed to Wilson's abnormal behavior. "Following his stroke," Weinstein observed, "the outstanding feature of the President's behavior was his denial of his incapacity." In other words, the psychological consequences of brain damage accounted for his inability to function normally during the treaty fight.

Historian Arthur S. Link immediately noted the implication of the neurologist's diagnosis for reinterpreting the treaty fight. Answering the question of whether he thought Wilson's stroke might explain his uncompromising stubbornness, Link wrote:

I do. A few years ago one could have argued both ways. But Dr. Edwin A. Weinstein's broad-gauged medical history of Wilson argues persuasively that his 1919 stroke was a massive one, caused by the occlusion of the main artery on the left side of his face. According to Weinstein, Wilson's behavior during the Treaty fights [sic] was typical of the behavior of a person who had undergone such an experience. He became irritable, proud, defensive, rigid, dogmatic, unyielding. Wilson was different after the stroke; his refusal to compromise, his stubborn insistence upon having the whole or nothing even though he might have got two-thirds is altogether typical of a stroke victim.

Thus Link joined the controversy over the president's health on Weinstein's side.

Weinstein and Link, with the clinical psychologist James William Anderson, launched a direct attack on Freudian interpretations of Wilson in the *Political Science Quarterly*. Criticizing particularly the Georges' book, they presented a positive image of Wilson's relationship with his father and added the dimension of his relationship with his mother. They offered the diagnosis of developmental dyslexia as an alternative explanation for his slowness in learning to read, that is, a physical rather than emotional explanation for his childhood problem. Reiterating that Wilson suffered from a series of strokes in 1896, 1900, 1904, and 1907, they claimed that these contributed to his rigidity as president of Princeton during the controversies over the quad plan and the graduate college. Wilson's behavior after his later massive stroke followed the same pattern. Weinstein, Anderson, and Link thus concluded: "In October 1919 he had a massive stroke that completely paralyzed the left side of his body and produced mental attitudes and personality changes which were important factors in his failure to obtain ratification of the Treaty of Versailles."

In his medical and psychological biography of *Woodrow Wilson* (1981), Weinstein elaborated his findings. "It is the author's opinion," he wrote, "that the cerebral dysfunction which resulted from Wilson's devastating strokes prevented the ratification of the Treaty. It is almost certain that had Wilson not been so afflicted, his political skills and his facility with language would have bridged the gap between the Hitchcock and Lodge resolutions, much as he had reconciled opposing views of the Federal Reserve bill in 1913, for example, or had accepted the modifications of the Treaty suggested in February, 1919." Not only Link, but other historians, including Charles E. Neu and John Milton Cooper, Jr., found in Weinstein's argument a persuasive explanation for the president's behavior during the treaty fight.

But Weinstein and his collaborators failed to persuade the Georges. In reply, they questioned his diagnosis of developmental dyslexia and of little strokes, noting quite correctly the dearth of credible evidence. Dr. Michael F. Marmor, an ophthalmologist from whom they had obtained an opinion, challenged Weinstein's thesis that Wilson had suffered a series of little strokes over the years: in his judgement, there was insufficient medical evidence to prove this hypothesis. In *The New England Journal of Medicine,* he accused Weinstein of violating the adage that physicians should not think of zebras when they hear hoofbeats, that is, that they should use common sense rather than imagine the most far-fetched diagnosis of a patient's illness. Marmor buttressed the Georges' conclusion that Wilson's political personality was not caused by long-term neurological illness. Adhering to their original interpretation, the Georges rejected Weinstein's explanation of Wilson's intransigence during the treaty fight. They acknowledged that his October 1919 stroke undoubtedly affected Wilson's behavior, but discounted its political significance:

> Whatever the nature of the brain damage he sustained in the fall of 1919, it altered neither his grasp of his problem with the Senate nor his strategy to deal with it. He had struck his unyielding position long before October 1919—a position that anguished practically everyone who cared personally about him or supported U.S. entry into the League of Nations. Wilson's conduct in this respect after the stroke was entirely consistent with his behavior before it. Both before and after, ample warnings were conveyed to him of the all but inevitable consequences of his refusal at every turn to compromise. Both before and after the stroke, he rejected these warnings, using the same arguments against compromise and cogently communicating them from his sickbed. The stroke seemed not to modify his behavior one whit in this respect.

On this crucial point, the Georges reached the correct conclusion: Wilson maintained his inflexible position from the beginning of the treaty fight to the bitter end. Long before he suffered his stroke in October 1919, he had decided to take an all-or-nothing stance in dealing with the senate. When he returned to the United States in February during the middle of the peace conference, he called upon the Democrats to turn the League into a partisan issue. He was in no mood to make any substantial concessions, and showed no inclination to compromise with the Republicans even after they signed the round robin. Although he called for some modifications in the covenant after returning to Paris, the president did not accept all of the changes that Republicans had suggested in February 1919, or at any other time. By the end of the peace conference, he had also firmly resisted the most substantial demands for revision that the Germans and the British presented: he was strongly committed to the treaty, including the covenant, without further revision. In his official presentation of the treaty to the senate, he claimed that it represented God's will. Making that assertion hardly indicated flexibility on Wilson's part. In his meetings with individual senators and with the senate foreign relations committee during July and August 1919, he rejected all requests for significant compromise. He maintained this uncompromising stance during his speaking tour of western states before his collapse. This clearly-established pattern of Wilson's behavior before the October 1919 stroke provided no basis for expecting that he would have compromised on any significant point with the Republicans.

As an opinion, Weinstein's view cannot be refuted, nor does it need to be: no historian can disprove a counterfactual statement of opinion. No evidence is available to prove that Wilson, if he had not suffered a massive stroke in 1919, would not have compromised with the Republicans; however, the whole pattern of the president's leadership revealed his inflexibility. At no time, either before or after his stroke, did he show any willingness to accept either amendments or reservations to the Versailles treaty in the resolution of ratification. He was willing only to consider a separate interpretative resolution. As long as Wilson persisted in rejecting reservations in the legally-binding resolution of ratification, there was no prospect of bridging the gulf between his position and that of Republican senators. The issues were far more fundamental than the particular words in the different reservations: no facility with language could resolve them. At stake was the balance between the executive and legislative branches of the U.S. government in determining its foreign policy, as well as the policy itself. These were real issues on which even a healthy Wilson could not in all probability have convinced the senate to surrender in 1919 and 1920.

None of the psychological and medical explanations of the president's political behavior is fully satisfactory. Wilson and Lodge recognized that real differences divided them, and neither was willing to compromise his basic position. These differences had emerged long before the peace conference or the president's massive stroke. Freud and Bullitt as well as Weinstein and Link neglected to account for this element of continuity throughout the post-war years. Because the president had adopted his all-or-nothing stance before April 1919, his so-called "moral collapse" could hardly explain his rigidity during the remainder of the treaty fight. Freud and Bullitt overlooked this fundamental problem. Nor could Wilson's massive stroke sufficiently account for the failure of his political leadership after October 1919: Weinstein and Link ignored that his subsequent public behavior followed the same pattern as before. A Freudian interpretation of Wilson's childhood might help explain his presidential character, but the historical evidence is inconclusive, and Link and Weinstein correctly noted this deficiency in the Freud-Bullitt study as well as the Georges' book. Fortunately, for an understanding of Wilson's role during the treaty fight, it is largely irrelevant whether childhood experiences with his father or mother, or other formative influences, shaped his political personality. It is, however, essential to comprehend the interaction between the president and other leaders, such as Lodge, and to place this personal dimension within the larger historical context. As Bernard Brodie observed in a review of the Georges' book: "It is one thing to observe compulsive behavior and identify it for what it is; it is quite another to find the original causes."

While Link and Weinstein, on one side, and the Georges and Marmor, on the other, continued their dispute, the psychiatrist Jerrold M. Post offered the most persuasive synthesis. He agreed with the Georges and Marmor that the evidence is insufficient to support Weinstein's unequivocal diagnosis of developmental dyslexia and of a series of little strokes. But he also criticized the Georges for overemphasizing Wilson's father and neglecting his mother, for both parents had contributed significantly to his character. From Wilson's relationship with both parents, he had acquired not only high aspirations but also his self-defeating behavior. His massive stroke in 1919 magnified this negative propensity, but did not create it. Post thus correctly emphasized the element of continuity in the president's political behavior throughout the treaty fight.

An accurate analysis of Wilson's personality requires an understanding of the historical context in which he operated. While the treaty cannot be comprehended without regard for his psychological and physical condition, neither can his presidential character be explained without regard for the external environment of American progressivism. One of the most important features of this context for Wilson was the emergence of the Social Gospel in the United States, as he interpreted U.S. participation in the world war within the framework of his Christian faith. A Social Gospel theologian, George D. Herron, published a book entitled *Woodrow Wilson and the World's Peace* (1917), proclaiming the kingdom of God on earth as the ultimate goal of the president's foreign policy. After reading the book, Wilson applauded "Herron's singular insight into all the elements of a complicated situation and into my own motives and purposes." As a good Presbyterian, the president called the League's constitution a covenant and located its headquarters in Calvinist Geneva. From this perspective, while officially submitting the Versailles treaty to the senate, he proclaimed that it fulfilled God's progressive destiny for the United States. Given his understanding of the U.S. mission, Wilson naturally suffered from despair as he realized that neither the Old World nor the U.S. senate would conform to his vision of internationalism. In this context, he entrusted the League's fate to God. In a speech during his western tour in September 1919, the president reaffirmed his belief in Divine Providence and confessed that, if it were not for his faith, he would go crazy. Link and Weinstein, the Georges, and Freud and Bullitt, all quoted these presidential statements as evidence for their various interpretations, yet it is not necessary to accept their medical or psychological analyses to understand Wilson's hope and despair: these were the normal consequences of his religious convictions, not the pathological results of "moral collapse" or neurological illness. His theology misled the president into a false understanding of international relations, as Reinhold Niebuhr would later argue, but this was not a uniquely personal failure.

Another important feature of the historical context during this era of American progressivism was the pervasive search for control. Science and technology had enabled Americans to conquer nature by the beginning of the twentieth century, and they now hoped to achieve the same success in human relations. Industrialization and urbanization had created a new society, which required the government to play a more active role both at home and abroad; within a changing nation and a revolutionary world, progressive Americans hoped to avoid uncontrollable chaos or anarchy. They wanted control of the trusts, or social control, at home as well as collective security abroad. Seeking orderly progress, they preferred reform to revolution, and it was in this spirit that Wilson created the League of Nations. He epitomized the American search for control, but he was not unique: other Americans shared this progressive perspective. Perhaps his personal experiences as a child, resulting in low self-esteem and a strong power motive, contributed to the president's desire to dominate the senate during the treaty fight, but this Freudian explanation is, at best, insufficient and, at worst, inaccurate. It failed to account for the pervasive striving for control that characterized progressive Americans, not all of whom, surely, had domineering fathers. In Wilson's case, moreover, recognition of the failure of American progressivism to transform the world undoubtedly contributed to his inflexibility during the treaty fight. These were social, not merely personal, responses to the external environment of the modern world.

For a comprehensive understanding of the treaty fight, historians of U.S. foreign relations must take into account Wilson's health. The condition of his mind and body undoubtedly influenced his political leadership, but other factors in the historical context after the First World War contributed even more to the president's failure to achieve U.S. ratification of the Versailles treaty. The leading protagonists in the scholarly controversy over his health, focusing too narrowly on psychological or medical problems, neglected the external environment of American progressivism and the realities of international affairs. As a consequence, their explanations for the treaty's defeat in the senate are inaccurate, and even their interpretations of Wilson's personality are inadequate. It is time for scholars to view the president as a whole person within the historical context of the modern world.

SUGGESTED READINGS

Lloyd E. Ambrosius, *Woodrow Wilson and the American Diplomatic Tradition* (1987).
Kendrick Clements, *William Jennings Bryan: Missionary Isolationist* (1982).
John M. Cooper, Jr., *The Warrior and the Priest* (1983).
Ross Gregory, *The Origins of American Intervention in the First World War* (1971).
David M. Kennedy, *Over Here: The First World War and American Society* (1980).
Thomas J. Knock, *To End All Wars* (1992).
N. Gordon Levin, Jr., *Woodrow Wilson and World Politics: America's Response to War and Revolution* (1968).
Arthur S. Link, *Woodrow Wilson: Revolution, War, and Peace* (1979).
Arno J. Mayer, *Politics and Diplomacy in Peacemaking: Containment and Counterrevolution at Versailles, 1918–1919* (1967).
William C. Widenor, *Henry Cabot Lodge and the Search for an American Foreign Policy* (1980).

FURTHER READINGS

The Great War

John Coogan, *The End of Neutrality* (1981); John M. Cooper, Jr., *The Vanity of Power: American Isolationism and the First World War* (1969); Patrick Devlin, *Too Proud to Fight: Woodrow Wilson's Neutrality* (1974); Frederick C. Luebke, *Bonds of Loyalty: German Americans and World War I* (1974); Ernest May, *The World War and American Isolation, 1914–1917* (1966).

United States at War

Arthur E. Barbeau and Henri Florette, *The Unknown Soldiers: Black American Troops in World War I* (1974); Robert Ferrell, *Woodrow Wilson and World War I* (1985); Daniel M. Smith, *The Great Departure: The United States in World War I, 1914–1920* (1965); Russell Weigley, *The American Way of War* (1973).

The Domestic Front

John Chambers, *To Raise an Army: The Draft Comes to Modern America* (1987); Maurine Greenwald, *Women, War, and Work* (1980); James R. Grossman, *Land of*

Hope: Chicago, Black Southerners, and the Great Migration (1989); William Preston, *Aliens and Dissenters: Federal Suppression of Radicals, 1903–1933* (1963).

The Versailles Peace Conference

Charles Mee, *The End of Order, Versailles, 1919* (1980); Klaus Schwabe, *Woodrow Wilson, Revolutionary Germany, and Peacemaking* (1985); John M. Thompson, *Russia, Bolshevism, and the Versailles Peace* (1967); Arthur Walworth, *America's Moment: American Diplomacy at the End of World War I* (1977).

Wilson, the Senate, and the Struggle over Ratification

Frederick Calhoun, *Power and Principle* (1986); L.W. Martin, *Peace Without Victory* (1958); Emily Rosenberg, *Spreading the American Dream* (1982); Ralph Stone, *The Irreconcilables: The Fight Against the League of Nations* (1970).

QUESTIONS FOR DISCUSSION

1. Identify the cultural and ideological loyalties of the American public at the outbreak of World War I in Europe.
2. Was the Wilson administration impartial in thought as well as in action? Explain.
3. Compare and contrast British and German policies toward neutral shipping during World War I.
4. Describe and assess the three basic foreign policy philosophies that developed during World War I.
5. Wilson claimed that America entered the war "to make the world safe for democracy." What government actions on the home front caused his critics to doubt this claim?
6. What did Wilson mean by "peace without victory"? Why was he unable to achieve his goal?
7. What explanation does Lloyd E. Ambrosius offer for Wilson's stubborn refusal to compromise during the struggle for ratification of the Treaty of Versailles?

THE "NEW ERA": 1919–1932

The decade between the end of the Great War and the beginning of the Great Depression occupies a special place in the American imagination. Mention of it is likely to conjure up the image of a pleasure-seeking, iconoclastic society inhabited by an assortment of characters from F. Scott Fitzgerald novels, who "had grown up to find all Gods dead, all wars fought, all faiths in man shaken." The image includes flappers dancing the black bottom or Charleston, affluent young men racing around in sleek roadsters, and jazz musicians performing in clubs or speakeasies in which booze flowed freely despite prohibition. Rejecting what they perceived as the blue-nose Victorianism of their elders, those included among the "flaming youth" are often remembered primarily for their devil-may-care spirit and shocking sexual behavior. Although relatively few Americans of any age conformed to such an image, those who did succeeded in winning for the postwar era labels such as Roaring Twenties, Jazz Age, and Era of Wonderful Nonsense.

THE ECONOMY IN THE 1920s

While other labels such as the Prosperity or Dollar Decade suggest that the 1920s witnessed profound economic changes, they too can be misleading by implying that all of American society shared equitably in a sustained prosperity. The fact is that the decade began with economic instability and ended in a catastrophic depression.

Immediately after World War I Americans went on a buying spree. During wartime, wages had been high, but wage earners were unable to buy the consumer products, such as automobiles and household appliances, that they wanted and could afford. The release of this pent-up purchasing power after the war not only stimulated the economy but also fed a runaway inflation. The end of the buying spree in 1920, coupled with the termination of war contracts and the economic recovery of European nations that had been prime markets for American goods, resulted in a sharp recession. Accompanying a precipitous drop in industrial production was an increase in unemployment and widespread strikes. With notable exceptions, most areas of the economy began to recover in 1922, and an uneven prosperity continued for seven years.

Industrial production in the 1920s increased so dramatically that it is known as the era of the second industrial revolution. Not only did industrial wages, salaries, profits, and dividends rise substantially, but consumer credit and the consumption level of the average American family also soared to unprecedented heights. Mass production and mass consumption of everything from automobiles to toiletries, accompanied and made possible by phenomenal advances in technology and a new emphasis on advertising and salesmanship, created such a booming economy that for some, like Herbert Hoover, the abolition of poverty was not only possible, it was also probable.

But despite widespread prosperity and popular veneration of industrial and business leaders credited with bringing it about, a large segment of the American population remained throughout the 1920s in an economically depressed condition. Among these were farmers who, geared to high prices and high production levels during World War I, were not only mired in debt at war's end but also confronted changing markets, international competition, and the recurrent problem of overproduction. Although postwar prosperity was far more characteristic of cities than of rural America, it eluded even those urban residents employed in declining industries such as coal mining, textiles, and railroads.

If Prosperity Decade must be used with caution as a label for the 1920s, so must "normalcy," a term used by President Warren Harding in calling for a return to "a regular, steady order of things" in the wake of World War I. Events following the war brought little comfort to those who desired a quick and orderly transition from war to peace. A haphazard, chaotic demobilization process, a wave of strikes, wild fluctuations in the economy, bitter wrangling over the League of Nations, and the removal of effective presidential leadership, caused by Woodrow Wilson's debilitating illness, combined to produce turbulence rather than stability.

Hardly anyone in America was "in a normal state of mind," Senator James Reed of Missouri observed in August 1919. Rather, the nation was suffering from "shell shock." Such a psychological condition was the result of almost two decades of frenetic reform activity followed by the rigorous discipline imposed by war and the stress prompted by the postwar disorder. Furthermore, American involvement in the war had been too brief to exhaust the fighting spirit and reservoir of hate for all things German that had been so successfully nurtured by government agencies and private patriotic organizations.

THE RED SCARE

Once the foreign enemy had been defeated, the unspent wartime emotion found an outlet in the Red Scare which reached its most convulsive stage in 1919–1920. Fueled by an antiforeignism that originated early in the nation's history and by post–World War I anxieties, the Red Scare came to involve more than merely a campaign to rid the nation of alleged threats posed by the existence of small, disorganized Communist parties in particular or by ideological radicals in general. Leading the anti-Red crusade was President Wilson's attorney general, A. Mitchell Palmer, who exhibited little concern for civil rights in staging the so-called Palmer Raids against individuals and organizations suspected of harboring what he considered un-American ideas. Self-appointed patriots, both inside and outside the government, cast a wide net under the slogan "One hundred percent Americanism," which exploited racial, ethnic, and class prejudices. Theirs was a movement to revitalize the nation by purging it of alien influences blamed for the postwar labor unrest, race riots, a so-called crime wave, violations of prohibition, radical utterances, and virtually anything else that did not conform to one hundred percent Americanism. The resumption of large-scale immigration after the war, coupled with a downturn in the economy, served only to enhance the shrillness of those determined to cleanse the nation of un-American impurities.

Among those considered dangerous to the nation because of ideological impurities were two obscure Italian immigrants and self-proclaimed anarchists, Nicola Sacco and Bartolomeo Vanzetti. Accused of a murder and payroll robbery that occurred in South Braintree, Massachusetts, on May 5, 1920, the two men were tried and convicted even though the evidence linking them to the crimes was at best circumstantial. Much of the courtroom drama, in fact, centered on their radical beliefs and foreign birth. After exhausting all appeals the two men were executed in 1927. The Sacco-Vanzetti case attracted international attention and prompted the aging French novelist Anatole France to write an emotional *Appeal to the People of the United States.* Often considered the most enduring symbol of the Red Scare the case nonetheless has remained the subject of intense debate. When the governor of Massachusetts issued a public apology on the fiftieth anniversary (1977) of the execution of Sacco and Vanzetti, he was roundly condemned by a host of politicians and private citizens.

Although the hysteria engendered by the Red Scare subsided early in the 1920s, its influence was felt throughout the decade and even afterward. By linking radicalism with organized labor and foreigners, the Scare figured significantly in the decline of unions and provided momentum to the movement for immigration restriction that had been in progress since the late nineteenth century. The restriction movement scored a major victory in 1924 with the passage of the National Origins Act that not only slowed the influx of immigrants in general but also discriminated against those from southern and southeastern Europe—precisely the people whom one-hundred percenters considered most alien, unassimilable, and radical. As the decade progressed, it was obvious that the Red Scare had created an atmosphere which stifled social reform, encouraged a narrow nationalism, and promoted the growth of organized efforts to thwart cultural trends of the postwar decade considered undesirable, alien, or both.

A TIME OF MANY CHANGES

Of all the many labels applied to the 1920s undoubtedly the most accurate and descriptive is "the New Era." Certainly, few Americans during the decade failed to realize that they were living through an era of rapid change. The culmination of a half century of social, economic, and intellectual changes, coupled with those set in motion by World War I, had gone far toward producing a new America.

The war itself served as a major catalyst for change, bringing unprecedented government control of the economy, the triumph of large-scale industrial organization and extraordinary growth in the power and size of the federal government. With the war also came a vast increase in the productive capacity and physical plant of manufacturing, a redefinition of the relationship between government and business, and a new emphasis on scientific management.

THE CHANGING LABOR FORCE

Defense industries attracted thousands of Americans away from the farm to the city. Large numbers of women who assumed jobs previously held by men achieved a degree of independence that quickened their desire for further liberation. Black men rallied to the call for troops and participated in the war to make the world safe for democracy in an effort to win first-class citizenship for the blacks at home. All the while, blacks of both sexes moved northward in search of jobs and greater opportunities. But the outbreak of race riots in 1917–1919 pointed up the degree to which anti-black prejudice was a national rather than merely a southern phenomenon. Organized labor, with government support, achieved many of its long-standing objectives—gains that were not to be quietly surrendered after the war. From the wartime experience, then, emerged many of the ingredients that went into the making of a postwar New Era.

REACTION TO THE CHANGES

Some embraced the New Era with enthusiasm as signaling the arrival of another stage in American progress. Others exhibited a good deal of ambivalence. For example, Henry Ford, whose inexpensive automobile did more to transform the old culture into a new one than almost anything else, remained throughout his career torn between the past and the future. Still other

Americans displayed no such uncertainty and denounced the changes of the New Era as nothing short of abominations. In this category belonged Baxter F. McClendon, a traveling evangelist, who, deeply troubled by what he termed "this age of new things," observed: "We have new thought, new voices, new books, new theology, new psychology, new philosophy, new religion and everything hell can suggest and the devil can concoct." Whether one approved or disapproved of trends in the postwar era, everyone recognized that theirs was an "age of new things." In fact, the adjective *new* was liberally applied during the 1920s.

The New Woman

As was frequently the case in the use of the word, references to the "new woman" of the 1920s did not apply to American women in general, but rather to a relatively small segment of the female population. To be sure, women had acquired the right to vote by the Nineteenth Amendment, but contrary to the predictions of anti-suffrage leaders, its impact on politics was slight. Women not only proved to be no more inclined to vote than men, but when they did, they usually voted like their spouses or male relatives. While the Nineteenth Amendment had little effect on politics, it appears to have deprived the women's movement of a unifying force. The division among women on issues that directly affected their lives was especially pronounced in regard to the Equal Rights Amendment (ERA) which declared that "men and women shall have equal rights throughout the United States."

Promoted by Alice Paul and the National Woman's party, the amendment was first introduced in Congress in 1923 but was never able to secure a favorable committee report and therefore failed. Many women such as Jane Addams and Florence Kelley, who earlier had secured legislation for the protection of women, opposed ERA as the work of extremists whose efforts would harm, rather than help, women. Women tended to be more successful in promoting measures related to good government and the welfare of mothers, children, and consumers. For example, women were primarily responsible for the passage of the Sheppard-Towner Act of 1921 which provided federal assistance for the establishment of state programs for maternal and infant health care. But among the most vocal critics of the legislation was Margaret Sanger, the veteran advocate of birth control, who condemned it for failing to provide for "family limitation." The Sheppard-Towner programs ceased in 1929 when Congress cut off funding.

For many Americans the term "new women" referred to a small minority who focused on securing changes in the private, rather than the public, sphere—that is, women who rebelled against Victorian constraints and the traditional double standard applied to the behavior of the two sexes. By their actions, speech, and dress they directly challenged conventional notions of feminine decorum. Especially shocking for some of their elders was their flaunting of what was termed their sexual freedom. Such behavior attracted much attention, but was confined to a relatively small group of younger middle-class women in urban areas. Most women scarcely conformed to such an image, preferring instead to concentrate on marriage, a family, and a home. Those who entered the workforce, as increasing numbers did in the 1920s, still experienced systematic discrimination in wages and opportunities.

The New Negro

The term "New Negro" was also an urban phenomenon that although used widely was applicable to a relatively small percentage of the nation's African-American population. But like the New Woman, the New Negro was not only of symbolic significance but also bequeathed influential legacies. Most of the individuals and organizations associated with the New Negro were concentrated in one section of New York City, known as Harlem, the capital of black America in the 1920s. During the decade and for a time afterward an assortment of race-conscious black writers, artists, and musicians rediscovered and embraced African and African-American culture. Among the most notable participants in the Harlem Renaissance were Langston Hughes, Jean Toomer, and James Weldon Johnson, who were a part of the nation's well-educated mulatto elite. Heirs to a long tradition of leadership in the black community, leaders of the Harlem Renaissance, according to Joel Williamson, shifted from a mission of "carrying white culture to the Negro mass to one of picking up black culture within the Negro world and marrying it smoothly to the white culture they knew so well." By accepting black culture and blending it with white culture in the Negro world, the Renaissance literati and artists contributed significantly to a separate culture that was neither wholly black nor wholly white, but a combination of the two—a distinctive African-American culture.

In addition to being the center of a black cultural awakening, Harlem was also the home of those who were in the vanguard of the new activism and militancy emerging in black America. One such individual was W.E.B. DuBois, a founder of the National Association for the Advancement of Colored People (NAACP) and the editor of its magazine, *The Crisis*. Reflecting the cultural dualism associated with the Harlem Renaissance, with which he was closely identified, DuBois demanded both first-class citizenship for blacks and a racially integrated society in which they retained their group identity, thereby accommodating what he described as the "two-ness" of black people in the United States. An elitist and a militant racial reformer, DuBois represented an organization supported primarily by middle- and upper-class blacks and whites.

DuBois' approach to race and race relations differed dramatically from that of Marcus Garvey, a native of Jamaica and the head of the Universal Negro Improvement Association which, headquartered in Harlem, appealed to poor, lower-class blacks in urban America. A charismatic figure with a gift for pageantry and display, Garvey preached the doctrines of racial separatism and black nationalism, and urged black Americans to return to their glorious homeland in Africa. He described DuBois and others in the NAACP as snobs and as black people trying to be white. DuBois, in turn, considered Garvey a buffoon and a dangerous demagogue skilled in playing on the ignorance of the black masses. Although Garvey's back-to-Africa movement disintegrated in the wake of his arrest and conviction for fraud in 1925, his emphasis on black separatism, shorn of any of the ambiguity of DuBois' "two-ness," created a legacy that was to resurface in the black nationalist movements of the 1960s. All the while, the NAACP persisted in its struggle, primarily through courtroom battles, to dismantle the segregationist legal structure and to secure for blacks the rights of first-class citizenship.

CHANGING VALUES AND PERSPECTIVES

The New Era, according to Walter Lippmann, witnessed "a vast dissolution of old habits." But neither their dissolution nor replacement occurred without a noisy struggle between the prophets of the New Era whose values and perspectives had been shaped by an urban, industrial environment and the champions of traditional rural, small-town culture and ideals. Their head-on collisions over issues such as prohibition, religion, moral standards, public schools, science, ethnicity and race, and immigration filled the air with the sounds of combat.

Prohibition

The fact that the Eighteenth Amendment which outlawed the production and sale, but not consumption, of alcoholic beverages, went into effect in 1920 did not mean that the struggle over prohibition had come to an end. Opposed by a substantial portion of the population, especially urban working-class and ethnic groups, the "noble experiment" proved to be easier to initiate than to enforce. The flourishing of bootleggers and the widespread patronage they attracted lent credence to the idea that prohibition encouraged a public willingness to tolerate lawbreaking in general. That mobsters such as Al Capone included bootlegging in their diversified, illicit operations and readily resorted to violence to protect their turf seemed to support the notion that prohibition was responsible for a crime wave in the 1920s.

The issue assumed a prominent place in the political arena during the presidential campaign of 1928 when Alfred E. Smith, the Democratic candidate and quintessential representative of urban America, forthrightly opposed the Eighteenth Amendment as an exercise in hypocrisy. As a "wet," Roman Catholic of Irish immigrant parents, who grew up on New York's East Side, Smith symbolized, as few other national political figures, the values and attitudes that were anathema to prohibitionists. The repeal of the "noble experiment" in 1933 suggested that prohibitionists, like others intent upon imposing rural small-town standards on the nation in the postwar decade, were fighting a losing battle.

The Ku Klux Klan

Among those groups which rallied to the support of prohibition was the Ku Klux Klan, a patriotic, fraternal order established in Georgia in 1915 and modeled after the post–Civil War society of the same name. Flourishing in the atmosphere generated by the Red Scare, the organization wrapped itself in the flag, paraded around burning crosses, and combined prayer and patriotism with acts of bloody brutality in its crusade on behalf of Protestant fundamentalism, white supremacy, and "moral purity." A self-proclaimed order of "the plain people . . . not highly cultured . . . but entirely unspoiled and not de-Americanized," the Klan aimed its heaviest artillery at blacks, Catholics, Jews, foreigners, radicals and moral transgressors of whatever race or religion. Spreading far beyond the South into the Midwest, Far West, and even eastern cities, the organization claimed a membership of several million and exerted considerable influence in local and state political contests and even in the Democratic national convention of 1924. Plagued by scandals, financial corruption, and the imprisonment of the nationally prominent Indiana Klan leader, who was convicted of manslaughter and rape, the organization declined in both membership and influence in the last half of the 1920s.

Religion: Modernists Versus Fundamentalists

Because many Americans troubled by the New Era were convinced that the battle to preserve traditional values would be decided on the religious front, it was not surprising that few of the cultural clashes of the 1920s generated more noise than the so-called war in the churches between fundamentalists and modernists. Fundamentalists subscribed to doctrinal statements known as "fundamentals," the most important of which was the belief in a divinely inspired, errorless Bible, including the Genesis account of the creation of man. Fundamentalists transformed their battle for the Bible into a battle for civilization—a civilization shorn of the uncertainties and ambiguities of the New Era. Modernists, lacking any precepts comparable to the "fundamentals," attempted to retain the substance of the historic faith without a literal reading of the scriptures. Theirs was an effort to make Christianity spacious enough to embrace modern knowledge, including scientific knowledge. Modernists tended to interpret scripture symbolically rather than literally and thereby to accommodate Darwin's theory of evolution as "God's way of doing things."

    In time, the theory of evolution became the focus of the modernist-fundamentalist controversy in which fundamentalists transformed evolution into a catchall, code word for the totality of error in modern America. Evolution, so the fundamentalist argument ran, shattered the premise and authority of an errorless Bible, transformed man from a creature in God's image into a mere animal, and encouraged him to exalt the attributes of his brutish (ape) ancestors. By such tactics fundamentalists linked the modernists' accommodation of the evolution theory to "godless education," "creeping secularism," sexual immorality, rising divorce rates, Bolshevism, and virtually everything else they found reprehensible in the postwar decade. Their organized efforts to gain control of the major Protestant denominations and to outlaw the teaching of evolution in public schools prompted a succession of noisy, highly emotional struggles both in church councils and state legislatures.

The most dramatic event in the struggle was the so-called "Monkey Trial" in Dayton, Tennessee, in July 1925, in which a high school football coach and sometime science teacher, John T. Scopes, was convicted of violating the state's antievolution statute enacted earlier that year. The Tennessee Supreme Court upheld the constitutionality of the "monkey law" but reversed the judgment against Scopes on technical grounds.

For eight days the little Tennessee town was the scene of "the biggest and best newspaper story" since World War I in which the drama focused on a confrontation between two disparate sets of values or worldviews. The two most conspicuous figures at the trial were Clarence Darrow, an agnostic and big-city criminal lawyer, who represented Scopes, and William Jennings Bryan, the folk hero of rural America, who assisted the prosecution. The presiding judge was a lay preacher of the fundamentalist persuasion. On hand for the drama were famous scientists and theologians who rubbed shoulders with journalists from all parts of the world, including H.L. Mencken, of the *American Mercury* and the high priest of irreverence in the 1920s, who delighted in poking fun at the religion of the "yokels" and "gaping primates" of the Tennessee countryside. Through a pioneer effort in remote-control broadcasting, Chicago's radio station WGN kept Americans informed of "the strange happenings" in Dayton, which, according to one journalist, was a country village located "forty miles from the nearest city and a million miles away from anything urban, sophisticated and exciting."

The modernist-fundamentalist controversy subsided in the wake of the Scopes Trial. The death of Bryan shortly afterward deprived the fundamentalist, antievolutionist crusade of its most effective leader. Thereafter, the movement became diffused among rival organizations and individuals whose sensationalism alienated even its supporters. Failing to capture control of a single major Protestant denomination or to hold back the tide of New Era values, fundamentalism had largely disappeared from the headlines by 1930. Though quiescent, fundamentalists thereafter devoted their efforts to the creation of their own churches, seminaries, Bible colleges, and religious organizations. Ill-equipped to arrest what they perceived to be the steady advance of secularism in the New Era, they staged a strategic retreat, reorganized, and mounted another crusade later following World War II under the banner of "creation science."

Influence of the Cities

Religious fundamentalists and other Americans who crusaded for a restoration of traditional standards and ideas correctly linked the cultural and social trends of the New Era that they found so disturbing to the city. Concentrated in the city were those forces and institutions, such as technology, consumerism, corporations, bureaucracies, and progressive education, responsible for the transformation of American life and culture. Urban America was seen by some as the source of the modernism that had infected Protestantism. That the city was also the home of Roman Catholics, an ever-expanding number of African Americans, and a large foreign-born population, not to mention political radicalism, labor unions, dance halls, liquor, and sexual permissiveness, made it all the more objectionable to those wedded to what was called "the old time religion" and super-patriotism. For such Americans, cities represented new versions of Sodom and Gomorrah.

CHANGING DEMOGRAPHICS

The decade of the 1920s witnessed a milestone in a demographic trend long in existence: The census of 1920 revealed that for the first time in the nation's history more people lived in towns and cities than in the country (see Figure 19–1). As the decade progressed, so did the tempo of urbanization. While the share of national wealth represented by agriculture steadily declined, that represented by cities vastly increased. In the physical sense cities expanded both vertically and horizontally: Skyscrapers, such as the Tribune Tower in Chicago and the Empire State Building in New York, made possible largely by technological breakthroughs, came to dominate the central districts of large cities, while suburbs proliferated around the fringes of major urban areas. The movement of the affluent white middle class to suburbia meant that the least mobile, poorer segment of the urban population—ethnic and racial groups—was left in the inner city.

Residents of urban and suburban America were at the center of the mass culture and consumer market that characterized the 1920s. Evidence that the locus of the national experience had shifted from rural to urban America appeared in the pejorative references to the "yokels," "rubes," and "hicks" who inhabited the countryside and to the stultifying atmosphere of villages and small towns. The millions who left the rural areas for urban America did not, of course, suddenly or automatically shed the attitudes and values shaped by their earlier experience. Urban residents in general displayed throughout the decade a nostalgia for the rural, small-town past that was fast disappearing and constructed suburban homes by the thousands whose architecture reflected that nostalgia.

NEW TECHNOLOGIES

No less than urbanization, a combination of technological advances, accessible electric power, new marketing and distribution mechanisms, and the application of concepts of scientific management and industrial efficiency marked

FIGURE 19–1
Urbanization, 1920

the 1920s as a new era. Mass production, especially in new industries, such as automobiles, radios and movies, meant that the benefits of modern technology reached more Americans than ever before. The public's insatiable appetite for mass-produced items revolutionized the home, workplace, communication, travel, leisure, and virtually every aspect of life. Within three years after the establishment of the first commercial radio station, KDKA in Pittsburgh, in 1920, there were over five hundred such stations. By the end of the decade Americans owned more than 10 million radios and spent almost a billion dollars annually on radio equipment. In the same period the average weekly attendance at movies exceeded 100 million and, like radio, spawned a billion-dollar industry. Movies became a principal arbiter of American taste, style, fashion, and even morals. They reinforced the pursuit of pleasure and contributed significantly to what has been termed the sexual revolution of the 1920s. Movie stars such as Charlie Chaplin, Mary Pickford, and Douglas Fairbanks were better known by the American public (and certainly better paid) than the president of the United States.

An urban street scene, ca. 1925, displaying the nation's diverse population, various means of transportation, and bustling industrial economy.

But none of the technological marvels of the decade had more pervasive implications than the automobile. Small wonder, then, that one of the most popular heroes in the 1920s was Henry Ford, whose assembly-line production techniques made the Model T affordable even to working-class families. Charles A. Lindbergh was a lanky, shy stunt pilot whose solo transatlantic flight in 1927 not only was interpreted as a symbol of the spirit of our people but also signaled the arrival of the new aviation industry. Ford and Lindbergh were the heroes of a society whose existence had become inextricably linked to machines and technology.

BUSINESS

The theory and assumptions that underlay the New Era economy represented an amalgam of ingredients drawn from the Gilded Age and the Progressive Era. Replacing the corporate arrogance, cutthroat competition, and hypocritical insistence on laissez-faire of the late nineteenth century were concerns for the consumer, a favorable public image of the business community, and industrial cooperation, especially through trade associations that promised something called the "New Competition."

THE NEW GOVERNMENT–BUSINESS RELATIONSHIP

The experiences of business and industrial leaders who staffed federal agencies during World War I figured significantly in revising the relationship between government and business. Impressed by the positive role that government could play in promoting economic development without interfering with it, the postwar business and industrial spokesmen sought, with considerable success, to use government as a facilitator, coordinator, and catalyzer for, rather than a regulator of, the economy. In the Progressive Era, government had become the senior partner in the government-business relationship, but in the 1920s it relinquished that position to business. Thereafter, rather than busting trusts, the federal government either tacitly approved or actively encouraged corporate mergers. The result was that one hundred corporations accounted for one-half of the nation's industrial production by 1929.

PUBLIC RELATIONS AND THE VALUE OF THE EMPLOYEE

As corporations grew larger and larger, the expanding body of public relations and advertising experts in their employ strove mightily to convince the public that business was enlightened, socially responsible, and dedicated to the economic welfare of all citizens. Not only did these publicists tout their clients' philanthropies and involvement in community activities, they also made much of their efforts to achieve a contented workforce by instituting higher wages, shorter hours, and more favorable working conditions.

Widely cited as evidence of the enlightened character of New Era business were the so-called "welfare capitalism" programs instituted by companies to provide a wide range of benefits including paid vacations and insurance, retirement funds, and stock participation plans. Such benefits, along with "company unions" in the form of workers' councils and employee-representation plans, were designed, in large measure, to eliminate labor unions. Although the ballyhoo over enlightened capitalism in the 1920s may well have been more image than reality, it encouraged popular veneration of business and industrial leaders. Elevated to the position of authorities on a wide range of matters beyond economics, these leaders presumably could and certainly did provide definitive answers to questions on politics, morality, and almost any other subject.

POLITICS

In national politics the Republican party dominated the New Era. The collapse of Wilson's coalition, coupled with a split between its urban and rural wings which was exacerbated by issues such as the prohibition and the Ku Klux Klan, left the Democratic party in disarray. Although the Republicans controlled the White House and Congress throughout the 1920s, the Democrats became the primary beneficiaries of a political realignment that occurred as the decade progressed. In an era of rapid urbanization the Democrats managed to capture a preponderance of the urban vote. Immigrants, new voters, and first-time voters rallied to the Democratic banner. By the end of the decade the party which a few years earlier seemed near extinction had revived sufficiently to pose a serious challenge to continued Republican dominance.

WARREN G. HARDING

Public weariness with a decade and a half of reform activities, followed by wars and postwar economic dislocation, figured significantly in the overwhelming victory of the Republican ticket headed by Warren G. Harding, the affable senator from Ohio who was the presidential candidate, and Governor Calvin Coolidge of Massachusetts, the vice presidential candidate. Coolidge's nomination owed much to a public statement he issued during the Boston police strike of 1919 which gained for him widespread popularity. "There is no right," Coolidge declared, "to strike against the public safety by anybody, anywhere, any time."

Convinced that the president should function primarily as a facilitator and adjudicator rather than a forceful leader who bent Congress to his will, Harding, nonetheless, insisted on a cabinet made up of what he called the "best minds." Such minds were represented in his cabinet by Secretary of Commerce Herbert Hoover, Secretary of State Charles Evans Hughes, and Secretary of Agriculture Henry Wallace, whose views differed dramatically from those of their Old Guard colleagues such as Secretary of the Treasury Andrew Mellon. Tensions within the cabinet often taxed Harding's talents as an adjudicator. In addition, the president faced a cantankerous Congress in which Old Guard Republicans resolutely opposed anything that they interpreted as an infringement on their prerogatives or as a perpetuation of Wilson's New Freedom. Other than the Democratic minority, the most troublesome element in Congress was the so-called Farm Bloc, a contingent of rural midwestern Republicans (joined occasionally by southern Democrats) known as the "Sons of Wild Jackasses" because of their continual braying about rural distress. Nevertheless, the president managed to establish the broad outlines of the foreign and domestic policies that his two Republican successors would pursue throughout the remainder of the 1920s.

In foreign affairs, Harding interpreted his election to mean that Americans had not only repudiated Wilson's League of Nations, but had also rejected the prospect of any future international crusades that would commit the nation to military action. In lieu of Wilson's formula of peace through international organization, the Republican approach focused on peace through disarmament, as evidenced by agreements that grew out of the Washington Conference (1921–1922), and by an effort in 1928 to outlaw war by treaty.

In domestic policy, Harding's administration was openly pro-business. Its aim, according to the president, who invoked a Wilsonian phrase, was "a new freedom from too much government in business and not enough business in government." In pursuit of such a goal, Harding promoted government economy, especially in vetoing a veterans' bonus bill and in securing passage of the Budget and Accounting Act (1921); sponsored high tariff legislation; and allowed Secretary of the Treasury Mellon to embark upon a tax program that called for the lowering of taxes on corporations and large personal incomes on the theory that such a policy would provide incentives to expand the economy through job-producing and profit-making investments. Because Mellon remained in office throughout the 1920s, he ultimately succeeded in putting in place many of his tax formulas.

Only after Harding's sudden death in August 1923 did Americans become aware of the scandals that riddled his administration. Although there was no evidence of Harding's complicity in any of the scandals, a Senate investigating committee uncovered widespread theft and bribe-taking among government officials appointed by him. Two cabinet officials were charged with an assortment of illegal activities: Attorney General Harry Daugherty escaped conviction by a hung jury, but Secretary of the Interior Albert B. Fall was not so fortunate and became the first cabinet officer in American history to go to prison for malfeasance in office. Fall's conviction resulted from what became known as the Teapot Dome scandal in which he accepted bribes in return for allowing two large oil companies access to the nation's oil reserves at Teapot Dome in Wyoming and Elk Hills in California. Despite the exposure of such scandals, the public mourning of Harding's death indicated that he was an extraordinarily popular president who came close to achieving his desire to be the "best loved," if not the "best," president.

CALVIN COOLIDGE

In contrast to the outgoing, personable Harding, his successor in the White House, Vice President Calvin Coolidge, was a dour, taciturn New Englander whose so-called genius for inactivity made him almost as popular. Whatever their differences in personality, their policies were virtually identical. Decisively elected in his own right in 1924 in a campaign in which he confronted a divided Democratic party and a third party—the Progressive party—headed by Robert LaFollette, the veteran progressive from Wisconsin, Coolidge presided over the high tide of industrial prosperity in the 1920s. He largely ignored the persistent farm crisis and vetoed the cumbersome McNary-Haugen Farm Bill as unworkable. Opposed to anything that smacked of government competition with private enterprise, he fought the effort by Republican Senator George Norris of Nebraska to have the government sell electricity generated by the federally sponsored Wilson Dam on the Tennessee River at Muscle Shoals, Alabama. Although Coolidge failed to have the dam sold to a private company, he succeeded in stalling Norris' plan for the Muscle Shoals project to generate and sell electric power. Of his accomplishments as president, Coolidge took the greatest pride in his reduction of the national debt, a feat made possible not only by what was termed "Coolidge prosperity," but also by the reduction or elimination of federal government programs.

Few, if any, public figures surpassed Coolidge in giving voice to the materialistic orientation of American culture in the 1920s. Most famous for his observation that "the business of America is business," he also declared that "brains are wealth and wealth is the chief end of man." In typically terse fashion Coolidge announced that he did "not choose to run for president in 1928." Few politicians equalled his sense of timing, political skill, or just plain good luck: Cast into national prominence by the Boston police strike of 1919, he won the Republican vice presidential nomination the following year; the unexpected death of Harding elevated him to the presidency, an office that he vacated six months before the crash of 1929.

HERBERT HOOVER

The Republican presidential candidate in 1928 was Herbert Hoover, a wealthy mining engineer with a distinguished record of public service, who soundly defeated his Democratic opponent, Alfred E. Smith. Smith's Catholic religion and opposition to prohibition caused the Democrats to suffer losses especially in the South, but in view of the prevailing prosperity it is probable that no Democrat could have won the presidential election in 1928. As secretary of commerce for the previous seven years, Hoover was one of the architects of Republican prosperity. More than either of his immediate predecessors, he possessed a firm grasp of the intricacies of New Era economic philosophy and of the relationship between a robust national economy and a stable international order. Convinced that the nation was passing through an economic restructuring phase, he dedicated himself to the elimination of poverty and waste through a process that combined private initiative with government assistance.

His philosophy rested on two principles: individual self-help and voluntary cooperation. These principles underlay his emphasis on the self-regulation of business assisted, but not directed or imposed by, the government. Enlightened self-interest would presumably motivate businessmen to pursue such regulation in order to achieve economic stability and order. Described by his public relations team in 1928 as the great engineer, efficiency expert, able administrator, humanitarian, and even "miracle man," Hoover appeared to be precisely the individual needed to perpetuate Coolidge prosperity. He proclaimed the arrival of a new day in his inaugural address.

Events proved that his concerns about being oversold as a worker of economic miracles were not unfounded. Less than six months after his inauguration, the prosperity bubble burst in the fall of 1929 with a resounding stock market crash which heralded the onset of the Great Depression. Stock prices plummeted wiping out stock fortunes except for a few like Joseph P. Kennedy and Bernard Baruch, two well-known investors who early detected the weaknesses in the market and got out before the crash. A brief rally misled many into believing the worst had passed, but it soon became apparent that the economy had grave problems. The collapse of the international economy only worsened the domestic crisis.

Economic Conditions That Set the Stage for the Stock Market Crash

Despite references to the permanence of prosperity, the New Era economy abounded in flaws. Not the least of these was the inability to maintain the purchasing power necessary to sustain an ever-rising level of mass production. The failure of consumption to keep up with production resulted largely from the uneven distribution of wealth, encouraged by federal tax policies and by the imbalance between industrial wages and profits, with the latter rising far in excess of the former. Needless to say, the plight of farmers and workers in declining industries prompted a precipitous decline in the purchasing power of both. The saturated markets caused by overproduction in certain industries, such as automobiles and construction, the overextension of credit even for speculation in overvalued stocks, and the slowdown in international trade prompted in part by high tariff policies contributed to the economic collapse.

The Great Depression

Confronted by a crisis of monumental proportions, President Hoover initially invoked the strategies that had worked so well for him during the 1920s, but such strategies proved to be wholly inadequate. Voluntary and cooperative efforts, no matter how enthusiastically encouraged by the government, simply could not cope with the deepening crisis. Privately sponsored soup kitchens and breadlines were quickly taxed beyond their capacities to provide food for the needy. By mid-1932 thousands of families were destitute. About two hundred thousand residents of Chicago converged on the Loop in a hunger march, chanting "We want bread." Neither city governments nor private charities possessed the resources to respond to the rising numbers of needy people that accompanied industrial layoffs and shutdowns. In the countryside farmers suffered from the twin tragedies of drought and depression. Huge dust storms rolled across the plains darkening the sky and depositing silt over a vast area of the United States. In the Midwest Milo Reno's National Farm Holiday Association resorted to direct action in attempting to stop the flow of milk and food to cities in an effort to call attention to the farmer's plight. Although Hoover initiated a federal public works program and secured from Congress the legislation necessary to create the Reconstruction Finance Corporation (1932) to extend federal credit to banks, insurance companies, and various industries, ordinary Americans were inclined to describe his efforts as "too little, too late."

As the depression worsened, the president became increasingly rigid and isolated, a lonely individual whose political influence and reputation as an economic miracle man had evaporated. His use of military force in 1932 to disperse the Bonus Marchers, veterans of World War I who converged on

Washington to demand passage of a veteran's bonus bill, destroyed whatever remained of his reputation as a humanitarian.

Rarely has a president's popularity plummeted so dramatically in so short a time. Unable to shed the image of a do-nothing chief executive in the face of a worsening crisis, he became the butt of cruel jokes, and his name became synonymous with the most devastating and prolonged economic disaster that the nation had ever experienced. The depression not only destroyed the reputation of the president, it also seriously tarnished that of businessmen and industrialists who in the New Era had enjoyed enormous prestige.

In the following selection James J. Flink describes and analyzes the influence of the automobile, and what he terms "automobility," on American society and economy in the decade of the 1920s. Flink makes effective use of the important sociological study, Middletown (1929), by Robert and Helen Lynd.

THE CAR CULTURE
James J. Flink

With his characteristic flair for understating the spectacular, President Warren G. Harding said in his April 12, 1921, message to Congress that "the motorcar has become an indispensable instrument in our political, social, and industrial life." An anonymous resident of Muncie, Indiana, was more accurate when he exclaimed to the Lynds, "Why on earth do you need to study what's changing this country? I can tell you what's happening in just four letters: A-U-T-O!". . .

During the 1920s automobility became the backbone of a new consumer-goods-oriented society and economy that has persisted into the present. By mid-1920s automobile manufacturing ranked first in value of product and third in value of exports among American industries. In 1926 United States motor vehicle factory sales had a wholesale value of over $3 billion and American motorists spent over $10 billion that year in operating expenses to travel some 141 billion miles. The automobile industry was the lifeblood of the petroleum industry, one of the chief

from James J. Flink, *The Car Culture* (Cambridge, MA: MIT Press, 1975), 140–145, 148–151, 156–159, 161–162, 164–165, 167–168, 176–181.

customers of the steel industry, and the biggest consumer of many other industrial products, including plate glass, rubber, and lacquers. The technologies of these ancillary industries, particularly steel and petroleum, were revolutionized by the new demands of motorcar manufacturing. The construction of streets and highways was the second largest item of governmental expenditure during the 1920s. The motorcar was responsible for a suburban real estate boom and for the rise of many new small businesses, such as service stations and tourist accommodations. In 1929, the last year of the automobility induced boom, the 26.7 million motor vehicles registered in the United States (one for every 4.5 persons) traveled an estimated 198 billion miles, and in that year alone government spent $2.237 billion on roads and collected $849 million in special motor vehicle taxes. . . .

The automobile culture became truly national in the 1920s as significant early regional differences in automobility lessened. California led the nation in 1929 as it had in 1910 in ratio of population to motor vehicle registrations. It remained true as well that the leading regions in motor vehicles per capita were still the Pacific and West North Central states and that the South continued to lag behind the rest of the country in adopting the automobile. But the gap among the various regions of the United States had closed appreciably by 1920. . . .

Another indication that the automobile culture had become national by 1920 was that automobile ownership was beginning to approximate the distribution of population along a rural-urban dimension. . . . A survey of car ownership among over 4.1 million American families conducted in 1927 . . . showed only slight differences in the percentage of families owning automobiles in cities of various sizes. . . .

The only thing that prevented the American automobile culture of the 1920s from being universally shared was the inequitable income distribution of Coolidge prosperity. It seems significant . . . that almost half of American families still did not own a car in 1927, the year the market for new cars became saturated and the replacement demand for cars for the first time exceeded the demand from initial purchasers and multiple-car owners combined. . . .

The market for automobiles among the lower-income brackets by 1924 was thus conceived by the industry's main trade association primarily as a dumping ground to solve what was known as "the used car problem." From the beginnings of the industry, most automobile manufacturers and dealers had encouraged owners to trade up to higher-priced models or to keep up with technological improvements and changing fashions by replacing their cars long before they were ready for the junk heap. Owners in turn expected a generous trade-in allowance. The problem was that the depreciation was great because used car prices were fixed at the maximal amounts that new, less affluent classes of purchasers could afford to pay. . . . By the mid-1920s, when the market for cars was becoming saturated, most dealers were selling more used cars than new models. . . .

Although even used cars that brought a mere $10 to $25 profit to the automobile dealer were beyond the reach of almost half of all American families in 1927, still other households operating on marginal incomes skirted insolvency and sacrificed essentials for personal automobility. . . . The Lynds found in 1929 that many working-class families in Middletown were mortgaging homes to buy cars, that "a working man earning $35.00 a week frequently plans to use one week's pay each month as payment for his car," and that "the automobile has apparently un-settled the habit of careful saving for some families." "We'd rather do without clothes than give up the car," a working-class mother of nine told the Lynds. "I'll go without food before I'll see us give up the car," said another working-class wife em-phatically. . . .

Advertising undoubtedly played an important role in booming automobile sales beyond the bounds of sanity in the 1920s. The automobile industry during the decade became "one of the heaviest users of magazine space as well as of newspaper space and of other types of mediums . . . the expansion in the adver-tising of passenger cars and accessories, parts and supplies in 1923 being particularly noteworthy." Expenditures for automobile advertising in magazines alone climbed from $3.5 million in 1921 to $6.2 million in 1923 and to $9.269 million in 1927.

Automobile advertisements incredibly managed to make irresistible to an in-creasing number of American families in the 1920s a combination of time payments on the family car, a mortgaged home on the outskirts of town, and the inevitable traffic jam that accompanied the Sunday afternoon drive. As the utilitarian virtues of the product came to be taken for granted by the consumer, automobile adver-tisements gave more emphasis to making the consumer style conscious and to psy-chological inducements to buy cars. . . .

Although some expensive items, such as pianos and sewing machines, had been sold on time before 1920, it was time sales of automobiles that set the precedent during the twenties for a great extension of consumer installment credit. By 1926 time sales accounted for about three-fourths of all automobile sales. And as the market for automobiles approached saturation after 1925, the finance companies, fearing they had overextended credit for automobile purchases and wishing to di-versify their risks, played an active role in encouraging installment purchases of many other types of merchandise. . . . Motorists early came to support higher and annual registration fees as one means of securing better roads. For the same reason, there has consistently been almost no public opposition to the gasoline tax. The gasoline tax was innovated in Oregon, New Mexico, and Colorado in 1919 as a means of raising money to meet matching funds for road construction that the federal government made available to the states after World War I. By 1925 gasoline taxes had been imposed by forty-four states and the District of Columbia. By 1929 all states collected gasoline taxes, which amounted to some $431 million in revenue that year, and rates of three and four cents a gallon were common. . . .

"Among the many factors which contributed toward the expansion of local taxes [between 1913 and 1920], probably no single one, price inflation aside, ex-ercised a more potent influence than did the automobile," reported the President's Research Committee on Social Trends in 1933. "This taking to wheels of an entire population had a profound effect on the aggregate burden of taxation." Staggering highway expenditures, the bulk of which came directly out of the motorists' pockets in use taxes, accounted for only part of this increased tax burden. The committee found that "it was not merely in its influence on highway costs that the automobile affected the size of the tax bill. Its use in cities created serious problems of traffic congestion and increased crime. Motorized police and traffic control became important items of increased expenditure. Moreover, . . . the motorcar was responsible for a spreading out of the population of cities toward the peripheral or suburban areas. This movement helped to swell the volume of local taxation, since schools and other public facilities had to be provided anew in these outer areas, despite the under-utilization of such facilities in older areas where population declined. In the rural sections of the country, good roads and the motor bus stimulated the growth of the consolidated school, thus putting within the reach of farm children an educational offering which approached the urban standard. In terms of educational returns per dollar spent, it was much more economical than the little one-room school. Nevertheless, it involved a larger absolute amount of expenditure and rural tax rates rose accordingly." The committee concluded that, "since the changes which came with the motor era are inextricably bound up with other types of change, it is impossible to state in dollars and cents just how much the automobile has cost the taxpayers of the country."

This was indeed an ironic outcome from the adoption of an innovation whose proponents had claimed, less than a generation before, would lower the cost of living. . . . But by the late 1920s our historical experience was proving that these and most other early predictions about the benefits of mass personal automobility were erroneous.

The President's Research Committee on Social Trends noted that "car ownership has created an 'automobile psychology'; the automobile has become a dominent influence in the life of the individual and he, in a very real sense, has become dependent on it." . . .

Automobility was undoubtedly the major force unifying Americans in the period between the two world wars. Despite comments in the automobile trade journals in the early 1920s recognizing that "illiterate, immigrant, negro and other families" were "obviously outside" the market for motorcars, there was agreement that "every clear-thinking American, be he rich or poor, realizes that in a measure, the automobile and its manufacturers are helping to solve the labor and social problems of the future," as well as "the tendency of the automobile to bring into intimate and helpful contact sections of our population which normally would never meet." The automobile outing and the automobile vacation became national institutions in the 1920s. By 1926 some 5,362 "motor camps" dotted the American countryside, and an avalanche of tourists who never before had traveled more than a few miles from home began to descend on distant national parks, forests, and points of historic interest. The new mobility of the labor force and long-distance trucking decentralized the location of industrial plants, opened up the Pacific Coast and the Southwest to commercial development, knit regional economies more tightly together, and promised eventually to abolish class and ethnic, as well as sectional, differences. . . .

There was ample evidence by the 1920s that the national individualized automobile culture was destructive of the beneficial as well as the repressive aspects of "community." "The mobility afforded by the new modes of transportation combined with . . . periodic waves of employment, unemployment, and reemployment to diminish the tendency for the workers in a given factory to live together immediately about the plant," observed the Lynds. "The trend towards decentralization of workers' dwellings means that instead of a family's activities in getting a living, making a home, play, church-going, and so on largely overlapping and bolstering each other, one's neighbors may work at shops at the other end of the city, while those with whom one works may have their homes and other interests anywhere from one to two-score miles distant." The breakdown of the neighborhood was also evident in that "the housewife with leisure does not sit so much on the front porch in the afternoon after she 'gets dressed up,' sewing and 'visiting' and comparing her yard with her neighbors,' nor do the family and neighbors spend long summer evenings and Sunday afternoons on the porch or in the side yard since the advent of the automobile and the movies." . . .

. . .[B]y 1929 it was evident to the Lynds and many others that any tendency of automobility to bring the family together was "a passing phase"—although an increasing number of people did tend to find the Sunday drive preferable to attending church. . . .Although no one has ever proved that the back seat of a Model T was more convenient or comfortable than a haystack, of thirty girls brought before the Middletown juvenile court for so-called "sex crimes," nineteen named an automobile as the place where the offense occurred, and a Middletown judge explained a dwindling red-light district by pointing out that "the automobile has become a house of prostitution on wheels." . . .

Although in theory the family car could bring husbands, wives, and children together in their leisure-time activities, the divorce rate continued to climb in the 1920s, and intergenerational conflicts between parents and children reached a new height during the decade. There is no evidence that the motorcar contributed to the divorce rate, but then neither did it, as early proponents of automobility expected, stop the divorce mill from grinding. That the motorcar undercut parental authority, on the other hand, is unequivocal. . . .

The main things that automobility symbolized were material prosperity through a higher standard of living, individual mobility, and an improvement in the quality of life through a fusing of rural and urban advantages. If one excludes the obviously great payoff for such economic interest groups as the automobile and oil industries, real estate developers, and contractors, the realities of the automobile revolution fell far short of its proponents' promises for most Americans. As we have already seen, what the individual gained from automobile ownership was at the expense of undermining community and family, and it invited anonymity and anomie. Improvements in the quality of life through a fusing of rural and urban advantages also proved illusory.

. . ."[G]rass-roots Americans" undoubtedly benefitted more than the urban masses from personal automobility. The motorcar and improved roads increased rural land values, lessened the drudgery of farm labor, ended rural isolation, and brought the farm family the amenities of city life, the most important being far better medical care and schools. In a day when "busing" has come to be associated in the minds of many Americans with an alleged lowering of educational standards, it seems particularly pertinent to point out that in the 1920s and 1930s the daily busing of farm children long distances to consolidated schools was hailed as a significant forward step in achieving educational parity between rural and urban schools.

These benefits of the school bus and the Model T notwithstanding, the cityward migration of farm youth was not stemmed, as auto enthusiasts promised it would be. Even more important, the family farm was already being killed off in the 1920s by a combination of the farm tractor, corporate agriculture, and the propensity of bankers to foreclose mortgages that had been incurred to finance the farmers' automobility. . . .

Some 135,000 suburban homes in sixty cities were already chiefly dependent on motor vehicle transportation by 1922, and the exodus of the middle class and businesses accelerated as the automobile culture matured in the 1920s. Massive conversion of the central city to accommodate the motorcar was thus paradoxically undertaken as its cost and problems were avoided by the escape to suburbia that automobility encouraged. *Motor* enthused that, in making possible the proliferation of suburban country clubs, the motorcar had "added a new phase of growing social importance to the social life of this country." But a more significant development in American social life was that the central city increasingly came to be an isolated ghetto of the deprived of American society as the middle class retreated to a modified version of the Jeffersonian vision of a nation of yeoman farmers. The implications of this progressive bifurcation of American society into urban ghettos and middle-class residential suburbs would not become apparent to the middle class, unfortunately, until the deterioration of living conditions in the central city manifested itself in widespread riots during the mid-1960s.

Automotive safety, on the other hand, was already recognized as a major problem by the mid-1920s. Although improved roads and better control of motor vehicle traffic progressively reduced the number of fatalities per miles of automobile travel in the 1920s, more automobiles traveling at higher speeds meant a mounting toll of fatalities, injuries, and property damage in absolute figures. In 1924, automobile accidents accounted for 23,600 deaths (including the deaths of 10,000 children), over 700,000 injuries, and over a billion dollars in property damage—"regarded as one of the big economic problems of the day" by *Motor Age*.

The automobile industry consistently turned out cars with more horsepower that were capable of higher speeds than could be driven legally, much less safely, on the highways of the day. The industry also put styling ahead of safety in automotive design. Newspaper accounts of accidents frequently mentioned the failure of steering mechanisms, brakes, tires, and other components. Yet the NACC Traffic and Safety Committee analysis of 280 automobile accident fatalities in 1924 traced only 7 to a defect in the vehicle. . . .

Automobility was the driving force behind Coolidge prosperity, and the boom of the 1920s was shattered with the saturation of the market for new cars after 1925. It would be simplistic, of course, to say that market saturation in the automobile industry "caused" the Great Depression in the sense that it was a sufficient condition for what occurred. There are too many variables involved that are too complexly interrelated. What I am arguing here is that automobility played a key role in creating the most important necessary conditions underlying the Great Depression and that this role has not been recognized adequately by historians. Undoubtedly, the great affection that Americans have had for automobility has mitigated against perceiving that the automobile revolution contributed much to bringing about the worst socioeconomic crisis in American history.

It would be nice to know precisely when automobile manufacturers and dealers began to get uneasy about conditions. Walter P. Chrysler said that "early in 1929 it had seemed to me that I could feel the winds of disaster blowing." . . . Yet Charles W. Nash, in an address delivered to the annual meeting of the National Automobile Dealers Association (NADA), had said as early as 1925: "I read something the other day in an ad where a fellow was boohooing the idea of the saturation point. I am going to say to you men tonight, regardless of the fact that I will be contradicted . . . that the saturation point was reached two years ago; not now but two years ago." Nash thought the industry had reached "the point of the survival of the fittest" and added that "production must be limited to fit the demand."

Although better roads and the Model T got rural America out of the mud in the 1920s, automobility was also in large part responsible for the depressed condition of agriculture, which involved a ruinous combination of overproduction of staple crops and higher fixed prices for equipment and chemical fertilizers. Along with the farmer's automobile came the widespread displacement of farm horses by the tractor, which necessitated a switch to artificial fertilizers, encouraged the use of other expensive machinery to increase productivity, displaced farm workers, and usually involved a mortgage on the family farm. Ultimately, automobility made the small family farm obsolete. The Hoover Committee on Recent Economic Changes, for example, pointed out that "the most dramatic and probably the most significant single factor which has entered into the productive situation of agriculture within the last few years has come with the increased mechanization of the farm, primarily as a result of the internal combustion engine." The number of tractors in use on American farms increased from 147,600 in 1919 to over 825,900 by 1929. . . . The committee concluded that the tractor "permits enormous economies in the production of staple agricultural products, but its effective utilization demands larger operating units and a more specialized type of economic organization; it permits also of a considerable release of manpower."

For many businesses, too, the automobile boom of the 1920s was either illusory or deleterious. Especially on short-haul passenger traffic, the motor vehicle cut heavily into the business of the railroads. "The steady decline in railway passenger traffic since 1920 is evidence that the competition of motor vehicles is severe," reported the Hoover Committee in 1929. "The automobile is being used more and more on relatively short trips, both for business and pleasure, that formerly were made by rail. The public has recently shown a decided preference for the motor coach over the steam railway coach and the trolley car." . . .

The unsettling impact of the motor vehicle on retailing and wholesaling was significant. By opening up much larger trading areas, automobility killed off the village general store and lessened deposits in small local banks. The big mail-order houses—Sears, Roebuck and Montgomery Ward—were forced to assume the new business risks involved in opening chains of retail stores. Before the advent of the automobile, the mail-order houses had catered to the isolated rural population. Retailing "had been concentrated into the center of cities and towns into which all avenues of transportation funnelled." But, as Robert E. Wood, the former general merchandise manager at Montgomery Ward who became vice-president of Sears, Roebuck, explained, "When the automobile reached the masses, it changed this condition and made shopping mobile. In the great cities Sears located its stores well outside the main shopping districts, on cheap land, usually on arterial highways, with ample parking space." Downtown merchants in medium-sized cities saw business move to the periphery of town or the metropolis and were forced to specialize in a single line of goods. . . . These developments in retailing completely unsettled wholesale trade. Competition became much sharper among wholesalers, and many firms found they could no longer operate economically in the expanded trading areas brought about by automobility. . . .

Nor did the automobile boom of the 1920s mean prosperity even for most of the automobile industry. By the mid-1920s, . . . most automobile dealers were breaking even or losing money. In the 1920s the franchised dealership system became universal, wiping out the wholesalers who had served as middlemen between the automobile manufacturers and the dealers in the early days of the industry. With the closure of entry into automobile manufacturing in the 1920s and the solidification of the industry into an oligopoly of giant corporations, most small automobile producers, and with them most parts and accessories manufacturers, faced ruin. . . .

There was indeed some justice in the outcome that the main benefits of the automobile boom accrued to a relatively small number of capitalists, for the boom was mainly due to vast capital expenditures to reshape the American economy and society to fit the motor vehicle—something largely accomplished by the late 1920s. During the decade the production of capital goods and nonresidential construction rose much more rapidly than the production of commodities designed for direct consumption, including residential construction. This huge, rapid expansion in capital investment undoubtedly encouraged an unrealistic emphasis upon the priority of savings for investment. And it encouraged this at the expense of demands for better income distribution and great increases in personal disposable income.

The paradox confronting Americans by the late 1920s was that, while the automobile boom was the product of capital investment, automobility had caused a concomitant shift to a new consumer-goods-oriented economy and society. The diffusion of mass-production techniques (innovated in the automobile industry) tremendously increased the output of all commodities. Even more important, "the great expansion in the automobile and electrical industries had far reaching effects in diverting the consumers' purchasing power from old to new products and placing in the hands of consumers stocks of durable products which have a slow rate of obsolescence and which, consequently, need to be replaced only after a lapse of considerable intervals of time." During the twenties the production of such durable consumer-goods items increased 72 percent, compared with an increase of less than 15 percent in the production of more staple, perishable commodities.

Personal disposable income did not increase sufficiently and income distribution was inadequate during the 1920s to support the phenomenal increase in the
production of durable consumer goods with low replacement demand. The decade
was a time of relatively full employment, and the real wages of workers employed in
manufacturing rose about 17 percent between 1919 and 1929. However, per capita
disposable income rose only about 9 percent during that period, and the rise was
fairly well concentrated in the upper-middle- and upper-income brackets. Despite an
almost 50 percent gain in manufacturing output, contrary to the optimistic predictions of Henry Ford and other apostles of industrial efficiency, the number of
workers employed in manufacturing remained constant—the big gain in new employment being in relatively poorly paying service trades. The collapse of the trade
union movement after the 1920–1921 recession was one important reason why
workers did not share adequately in the gains of the automobile boom. Wages and
prices remained relatively stable from 1922 to 1929, freezing the level of demand for
an ever-increasing amount of consumer goods. On the other hand, net corporate
profits soared from $3.9 billion in 1922 to $7.2 billion in 1929, and bank deposits,
almost wholly from the upper-middle and upper classes, increased from $41.1 billion
to $57.9 billion. These excessive savings lacked productive outlets for investment, so
they became the main source of the runaway bull market of the late 1920s. . . .

SUGGESTED READINGS

Frederick Lewis Allen, *Only Yesterday* (1931).

Susan D. Becker, *The Origins of the Equal Rights Amendment: American Feminism
Between the Wars* (1981).

David Burner, *The Politics of Provincialism: The Democratic Party in Transition,
1918–1932* (1968).

Paul A. Carter, *Another Part of the Twenties* (1977).

Nathan Huggins, *Harlem Renaissance* (1971).

William E. Leuchtenberg, *Perils of Prosperity, 1914–1932* (1958).

Robert K. Murray, *The Harding Era: Warren G. Harding and His Administration*
(1969).

Robert Sobel, *The Great Bull Market: Wall Street in the 1920's* (1968).

George E. Webb, *The Evolution Controversy in America* (1994).

Joan Hoff Wilson, *Herbert Hoover: The Forgotten Progressive* (1975).

FURTHER READINGS

OVERVIEWS of the NEW ERA: Ellis W. Hawley, *The Great War and the Search for
Modern Order: A History of the American People and Their Institutions,
1917–1933* (1979); John D. Hicks, *Republican Ascendancy, 1921–1933* (1958);
Glen Jeansonne, *Transformation and Reaction: America, 1921–1945* (1994);
Michael Parrish, *Anxious Decades: America in Prosperity and Depression,
1920–1941* (1992). SOCIAL, CULTURAL, and PSYCHOLOGICAL ASPECTS of

the ERA: Loren Baritz, *The Culture of the Twenties* (1970); Erik Barnouw, *A Tower in Babel* (1966); Dorothy Brown, *Setting a Course: American Women in the 1920s* (1987); David Chalmers, *Hooded Americanism: The History of the Ku Klux Klan* (1965); Stanley Coben, *Rebellion Against Victorianism: The Impetus for Cultural Change in 1920s America* (1991); Lynn Dumenil, *The Modern Temper: American Culture and Society in the 1920s* (1995); Paula Fass, *The Damned and the Beautiful: American Youth in the 1920s* (1977); Willard B. Gatewood, *Controversy in the Twenties: Modernism, Fundamentalism, and Evolution* (1969); John Higham, *Strangers in the Land: Patterns of Nativism, 1860–1925* (1955); Nathan Huggins, *Harlem Renaissance* (1971); Robert K. Murray, *Red Scare* (1955); Andrew Sinclair, *Prohibition: The Era of Excess* (1962); Robert Sklar, *Movie-Made America* (1975). ECONOMICS and POLITICS: Guy Alchon, *The Invisible Hand of Planning: Capitalism, Social Science, and the State in the 1920s* (1985); Irving Bernstein, *The Lean Years: A History of the American Worker, 1920–1933* (1960); Peter Fearon, *War, Prosperity, and Depression: The U.S. Economy, 1917–1945* (1987); Donald McCoy, *Calvin Coolidge: The Silent President* (1967); Robert K. Murray, *The Politics of Normalcy* (1973); Burl Noggle, *Teapot Dome: Oil and Politics in the 1920s* (1963); James W.W. Prothro, *Dollar Decade* (1954); Albert U. Romasco, *The Poverty of Abundance: Hoover, the Nation, the Depression* (1965).

QUESTIONS FOR DISCUSSION

1. The 1920s have been referred to as "the Prosperity Decade" and the age of "normalcy." Explain whether these labels are accurate or appropriate.
2. Explain the origins of the Red Scare and its impact.
3. Describe the mood of the 1920s that contributed to the flourishing of the Ku Klux Klan.
4. Identify and analyze the principal issues in the presidential election of 1928. Why did the Republicans win?
5. Identify the ingredients of the prevailing economic philosophy called the "New Competition" and what it signified about a change in the relationships between government and business.
6. Describe and analyze the status of organized labor in the 1920s.
7. What factors and circumstances contributed to the collapse of Republican prosperity during and after the crash of 1929?
8. James J. Flink argues that the automobile was "the backbone of a new consumer-goods-oriented society and economy." What evidence does the selection from his book *The Car Culture* present in support of this argument?

CHAPTER TWENTY

ROOSEVELT'S NEW DEAL

FRANKLIN DELANO ROOSEVELT

Almost one hundred thousand persons gathered in the vicinity of the east front of the Capitol on Saturday, March 4, 1933, to witness the inauguration of Franklin D. Roosevelt as president. The dreary weather seemed to reflect the popular mood as Americans attempted to survive what has become known as the "winter of despair." Shortly before noon President Herbert Hoover and President-elect Roosevelt traveled in an open limousine from the White House to the Capitol, despite the cold, damp weather. Because Hoover proved unresponsive to Roosevelt's attempts at conversation, a strained silence characterized their short trip down Pennsylvania Avenue.

In his inaugural address that provided a glimpse into his extraordinary ability to establish rapport with the American people, Roosevelt referred to "a stricken nation in the midst of a stricken world," but expressed supreme confidence in the ability of Americans to weather the depression and restore prosperity. "Let me assert my firm belief," Roosevelt declared, "that the only thing we have to fear is fear itself, nameless, unreasoning, unjustified terror which paralyzes needed efforts to convert retreat into advance." Rejecting the rules of the "previous generation of self-seekers" who provided false leadership and worshipped at the feet of material wealth, he promised an administration that would "apply social values more noble than monetary profit." Convinced that his election was a mandate for "direct, vigorous action," he also promised to "act and act quickly" in presenting to Congress "detailed measures" for implementing programs that would "put people to work," aid farmers, provide relief, halt mortgage foreclosures, and impose strict supervision over banks and investment houses. The president's address prompted frequent and enthusiastic applause, but at no point was it as thunderous and prolonged as when

Roosevelt explained that, if necessary, he would seek extraordinary presidential power to meet the economic crisis, power equal to that bestowed on presidents in wartime.

To be sure, Roosevelt spoke in generalities, and his inaugural address was lacking in details about the specific measures he intended to take to combat the worst depression in the nation's history. But his generalities, coupled with an air of confidence and the promise of a responsive federal government, were sufficient to reassure Americans that they had made the right choice in November 1932 in rejecting Hoover and electing Roosevelt. It was, according to the writer of one of the half-million letters received at the White House within a few days after the inauguration, Roosevelt's "human feeling for all of us" that gave people hope where little had existed before. Unlike his predecessor, the new president possessed a "first-class temperament" and a combination of other qualities that made people trust him and rally enthusiastically to his support, fully confident that he had their interests at heart.

HIS EARLY YEARS

Born in 1882 at Hyde Park, New York, Franklin Roosevelt was the scion of a patrician family of Dutch ancestry. Educated at Harvard College and Columbia Law School, Roosevelt exhibited the optimism, noblesse oblige, belief in progress, and other values characteristic of the genteel society of late-nineteenth-century America. On March 17, 1905, he married Eleanor Roosevelt, a distant cousin and the favorite niece of Republican president Theodore Roosevelt.

AN EMERGING POLITICAL LIFE

Roosevelt had little taste for the practice of law and determined to pursue a career in politics. After two terms in the New York legislature where his commitment to progressive reform broadened, he was appointed assistant secretary of the Navy by President Woodrow Wilson. His post in the Navy Department not only provided valuable experience in dealing with the federal bureaucracy, patronage, and competing interest groups but also widened his circle of acquaintances and enhanced his national reputation. Chosen as the Democratic vice presidential candidate in 1920, he proved to be a valuable asset to the ticket headed by Governor James Cox of Ohio whom he sometimes overshadowed during the campaign. Following the defeat of the Democrats, Roosevelt returned to New York to practice law and serve as a vice president of the Fidelity and Deposit Company.

POLIO SHAPES HIS CHARACTER

Without warning in August 1921, Roosevelt was stricken with polio, an illness that permanently crippled both legs and forced him to wear heavy steel braces for the remainder of his life. Refusing to succumb to the psychology of invalidism, he learned to conceal the frustration caused by his crippled legs, vastly increased the strength of his upper body, and became more expansive and radiant than ever. Gone were much of the arrogance and impatience so evident earlier in his career. As his wife astutely observed, Roosevelt's suffering had caused him "to have a greater sympathy and understanding of the problems of mankind." His experiences at Warm Springs, Georgia, where he spent much time in the 1920s in an attempt to "swim himself back to health" in the water of the natural springs, reinforced his newfound identity with others who were disadvantaged. Here he encountered other paralytics and came to know the economically disadvantaged residents of the north Georgia hill country. His experiences at Warm Springs helped to shape federal programs during his tenure as president.

Fears that polio had ended Roosevelt's political career proved to be unfounded. He achieved a limited degree of mobility. Gradually resuming his business and political activities, he was a conspicuous figure at the Democratic national convention in 1924, where he delivered a memorable nomination speech for Governor Alfred E. Smith of New York. Although Smith failed to get the nomination and the Democrats suffered another defeat in their bid for the White House, Roosevelt's political stock rose dramatically. His speech, display of courage, and irresistible radiance made a lasting impression on convention delegates.

The convention of 1924 marked the beginning of Roosevelt's political comeback. Four years later, he was again chosen to nominate Smith as the Democratic candidate for president and drafted by New York Democrats to run for governor. While Smith lost the election to Republican Herbert Hoover, Roosevelt won the New York governorship in what was indisputably a Republican year. Reelected by a landslide in 1930, Roosevelt as governor identified in a general way with early-twentieth-century progressivism, surrounded himself with liberal reformers such as Frances Perkins and Harry Hopkins, and mastered the art of public relations, especially through his effective use of radio. When the devastating effects of the Great Depression settled upon the country, few if any governors responded more forcefully than Governor Roosevelt to the deepening economic crisis.

THE 1932 PRESIDENTIAL CAMPAIGN

That he had emerged by 1932 as a dominant contender for the Democratic presidential nomination owed much to his activities, as well as those of aides and allies, preceding the convention in Chicago. By promising the vice presidency to John Nance Garner of Texas, speaker of the House and a presidential hopeful, Roosevelt survived a serious "Stop Roosevelt" movement and won the nomination. Shattering precedent, he flew to Chicago to accept the nomination in person. In his acceptance speech he promised the American people "a new deal." The ensuing campaign between Roosevelt and Hoover could scarcely be described as exciting. Although Roosevelt traveled extensively, constantly displaying his radiant smile and air of self-confidence, he took few risks and spoke primarily in general, even vague, terms about how he intended to combat the economic crisis. He did, however, lay the blame for the depression at the feet of Hoover and the Republican party. Because Americans tended to share this view, they rejected Hoover and elected Roosevelt by a landslide. Although the Socialist and Communist parties were convinced that the severity of the economic crisis would expose the bankruptcy of capitalism and prompt a massive shift in popular support to their causes, American voters proved to be "less radical than the left hoped and the right feared." They rejected the revolutionary alternatives offered by Socialist and Communist candidates and opted for a capitalist system shorn of its defects.

ROOSEVELT'S FIRST TERM

At the time of Roosevelt's inauguration in March 1933, the economy was near collapse, and a mood of despair gripped much of the country. A quarter of the workforce was unemployed, and home mortgage foreclosures were occurring at an alarming rate. Depositors, frightened by the increasing number of bank failures, were staging runs on banks to withdraw funds which further weakened a banking system near collapse. In fact, the banking system was in such disarray that the banks had been closed in thirty-eight states. Agriculture after a decade of decline had reached bottom; charitable and philanthropic agencies had exhausted resources to feed the long lines of hungry people that increased daily. Hunger marches in major cities were but one sign of suffering visible everywhere.

IDEOLOGICAL SOURCES

Roosevelt did not enter office with any master plan for solving all the problems that faced the nation, but his lack of ideological inhibitions meant that he had few qualms about using federal power to alleviate human suffering and to correct what he perceived as grievous flaws in the economic system. Nor was he averse to experimentation to achieve the desired results.

The ideological sources of the New Deal were as numerous as they were diverse. The host of economists, former social workers, businessmen, young lawyers, and others who converged on Washington to participate in the establishment of a new social and economic order represented a bewildering array of economic philosophies and policy perspectives. Among them were fiscal conservatives wedded to government economy and balanced budgets, advocates of deficit government financing to expand mass purchasing power, and devotees of expensive federal social programs. Some who had been identified with the early-twentieth-century reform movement embraced ideas related either to Theodore Roosevelt's New Nationalism or Woodrow Wilson's New Freedom;

others involved in the mobilization effort during World War I brought with them strong views on government-business cooperation and fully appreciated the analogy that Roosevelt drew between combatting the depression and fighting a war; still others represented a younger generation that had come of age in the postwar years.

The diversity of the New Deal, however, was nowhere more apparent than in the Roosevelt cabinet which consisted of a mixture of "deserving Democrats," urban liberals, rural conservatives, and innovative social reformers. Among the most fertile sources of ideas for New Deal policies and programs was a small, inner circle of presidential advisors known as "the brains trust" whose personnel changed as the emphasis of the Roosevelt administration shifted.

Notwithstanding the intellectual contributions of numerous individuals and groups, Franklin Roosevelt remained the central figure in the New Deal. As its spokesman and symbol, he was the one who gave it what coherence it possessed and who got proposals enacted into law. Presiding over and reveling in the clash of ideas that swirled about him, he functioned as a synthesizer who on occasion awed subordinates by blending together sharply conflicting positions. By diffusing responsibility among subordinates, he remained the final arbiter and ultimate decision maker. Some have argued that Roosevelt was incapable of sustained thought and possessed more style than substance, but no one has questioned his mastery of the art of politics, his skills in communication and public relations, and his fine-tuned sensitivity to the shifting moods of the public and Congress.

THE STRATEGY

The intellectual crosscurrents within the Roosevelt administration not merely contributed to the appearance of chaos, but also resulted in contradictory legislative initiatives. Nevertheless, there early emerged the outlines of a multi-pronged strategy for combatting the depression, a strategy that the president considered consistent with his aim of rescuing and strengthening the capitalistic system.

To alleviate the suffering of millions of unemployed Americans, the administration initiated relief programs that took various forms, ranging from direct dole to the creation of jobs for the jobless. Such programs were viewed as temporary expedients which would become unnecessary as the economy improved. Therefore, central to the early New Deal strategy for lifting the nation out of its crisis was legislation intended to bring about industrial and agricultural recovery.

TWO NEW DEALS

In his pioneer history of the Roosevelt administration published in 1944, Basil Rauch introduced the concept of two New Deals. According to Rauch, the first New Deal lasting from 1933 through 1934 was basically conservative, and its primary aim was economic recovery. Based on the philosophy of economic scarcity, its immediate objective was higher prices for industry and agriculture. The first New Deal primarily benefitted big agriculture and big business. Rauch contended that the second New Deal in the years after 1934 was devoted largely to permanent reform. Based on the philosophy of economic abundance, it had as its primary objective the increased purchasing power and social security of the whole population. Its principal beneficiaries were labor unions and small farmers. According to Rauch, pressures from the left prompted Roosevelt to shift from the basically conservative approach of the first New Deal to the liberal program of social and economic reforms of the second. The two–New Deals interpretation, in various forms and shadings, prevailed for most of the generation after its first appearance and continues to be invoked by those seeking to make sense out of the ideological twists and turns exhibited by the Roosevelt administration, even though most scholars agree that New Deal initiatives do not lend themselves to such a neat, orderly arrangement.

Whatever the inconsistencies and jumble of policy perspectives exhibited by the New Deal, Roosevelt indisputably moved with dispatch on multiple fronts during the first one hundred days of his administration. Never before in the nation's history had so much significant legislation been proposed by a president or passed by Congress in so short a period of time.

BANK REFORMS

On his second day in office, Roosevelt declared a banking holiday which closed all banks to forestall the total collapse of the banking system and halt the erosion of public confidence in the nation's financial structure. He summoned Congress into special session for March 9, 1933, to enact the Emergency Banking Act which, in addition to legalizing the bank holiday, authorized the reopening of solvent banks. Three days later, Roosevelt delivered the first of his many "fireside chats," radio broadcasts to the American people, to explain in simple language the nature of the banking problem and the steps taken to solve it. The public heeded the president's request that money be deposited in reopened banks. Within a matter of weeks the banking crisis had passed.

On June 16, 1933, the last day of special session of Congress, Roosevelt signed the Glass-Steagall Banking Act which separated commercial and investment banking, expanded federal regulation of the banking system, and created the Federal Deposit Insurance Corporation (FDIC) to insure accounts of up to $2,500. Although originally opposed to the concept of federally insured bank deposits, Roosevelt acquiesced in the FDIC in the face of demand by a public all too familiar with bank failures. When the FDIC emerged as one of the most popular New Deal measures, the president claimed credit for its enactment. In coping with the banking problem, Roosevelt opted for a middle course by resuscitating the existing system rather than either nationalizing banks or letting the crisis run its course. Critics who claimed that he could have nationalized banks soon learned that the president's bold actions were often means to achieve conservative ends.

Evicted sharecroppers with their scant belongings on the side of a highway in 1939.

IMMEDIATE MEASURES TO INCREASE REVENUES

Two other measures that received Roosevelt's attention in the first days of his administration related directly to promises he had made during the campaign. One was the Beer-Wine Revenue Act which accelerated the end of prohibition by legalizing the sale of beer and light wines. A few weeks earlier Congress had submitted to the states the Twenty-first Amendment which, ratified in December 1933, ended the "noble experiment." A second measure that addressed a campaign pledge by Roosevelt was the Economy Act which authorized the president to reduce both veterans' benefits and federal workers' salaries. Such expenditures constituted a significant part of the federal budget but affected a minuscule percentage of the population. In response to the Economy Act, a second Bonus Expeditionary Force (BEF) converged on Washington to protest. To defuse a potentially explosive situation Roosevelt furnished tents and mess halls for the Bonus Army, and his wife Eleanor, a social activist who served as conscience of the New Deal, visited their encampment. One veteran succinctly summed up the differences in the approaches of Roosevelt and his predecessors in his remark: "Hoover sent the army; Roosevelt sent his wife." The second BEF dispersed shortly after Mrs. Roosevelt's visit, which was an early example of the public role that Eleanor Roosevelt would play throughout her husband's administration. Beyond the usual ceremonial activities, she spoke out on a wide variety of social issues, identified with the plight of African Americans, the poor, and other disadvantaged groups, and on occasion became the center of controversy.

RELIEF PROGRAMS

No issues confronting the Roosevelt administration in 1933 were more pressing than those concerning relief for millions of needy Americans. The response was a variety of programs hastily organized to address the needs of various groups of people.

The CCC

One such program which demonstrated Roosevelt's willingness to experiment was the Civilian Conservation Corps (CCC) designed to address the problem of jobless youths by putting them to work on reforestation, soil erosion, and other conservation projects. Created through the cooperative efforts of the Army and various federal agencies, the CCC was open to unemployed, single males between the ages of eighteen and twenty-five who were paid thirty dollars a month, of which twenty-five went home to families to spend and thereby stimulate the economy. Initially denounced by some critics as a "form of sovietism," the CCC ultimately became one of the New Deal's most popular programs. By the time it was ended in 1940 it had enrolled more than 2.5 million youths whose monuments were hundreds of projects that contributed to "the preservation and purification of the land, the water, the forests, and the young men of America."

The NYA

A second New Deal program to aid youth of both sexes, created by executive order in 1935 as a part of the new Works Progress Administration (WPA), was the National Youth Administration (NYA) which complemented the CCC by assisting young people to remain in school through providing grants to colleges and schools for part-time employment of students, an early version of work-study. The NYA not only enabled students to complete their education but also kept them off an already glutted labor market. For young people who were not attending school but unemployed, the agency established vocational training programs to provide them with marketable skills.

The HOLC and the EFMA

Among other Americans who received relief from the New Deal during its first hundred days were those threatened with the loss of homes and farms by mortgage foreclosure. The ineffectiveness of Hoover's Federal Home Loan Bank Act (1932) prompted Roosevelt to seek and obtain new legislation which authorized the Home Owner's Loan Corporation (HOLC) to provide government refinancing of mortgages for distressed owners. Although the HOLC rescued the real estate market and the construction industry, it also ultimately helped refinance one out of every five mortgaged urban private residences in the United States.

The Emergency Farm Mortgage Act (EFMA) complemented the HOLC by providing government refinancing of farm mortgages which allowed thousands of rural Americans to save their farms. Few actions by the Roosevelt administration did more to garner the gratitude of the middle class and strengthen its stake in the New Deal than federal assistance in preventing the loss of the homes and farms.

The FERA and the CWA

The most comprehensive relief measure during the first hundred days was the Federal Emergency Relief Act (FERA), enacted in May 1933 and patterned on the relief effort that Roosevelt had inaugurated as governor of New York. Harry Hopkins, the social worker who had headed that effort, was placed in charge of the FERA which initially channeled a half-billion dollars in federal relief grants to state and local agencies.

Deeply concerned about the effects of government dole on the pride and morale of people, Hopkins worked feverishly to devise work projects for the unemployed to avoid the degradation of having to accept handouts. All the while, he tried desperately to cut through the bureaucratic snarls, patronage politics, and the incompetence of state and local agencies to get relief to those citizens in the most dire circumstances.

No matter how much Hopkins exhorted, cajoled, and threatened, however, it soon became apparent as winter approached that the FERA was inadequate to meet the demands for relief. At his urging Roosevelt created the Civil Works Administration (CWA) by executive order. Viewed as a stopgap agency, the CWA was a strictly federal operation designed to put people to work as quickly as possible. As head of the CWA, as well as the FERA, Hopkins attempted to generate projects on which to employ those in need of relief.

Although the haste with which the CWA was organized and put in operation took its toll in terms of expenses, political interference, and outright graft, the agency at its peak employed 4.2 million people on thousands of projects. Such projects included building or improving roads, schools, playgrounds, and airports in addition to developing parks, clearing waterways, laying sewer lines, and employing teachers in rural schools and urban adult education classes. Pumping a billion dollars of purchasing power into the economy by the time it was dismantled in the spring of 1934, the CWA had gotten the country through the severe winter of 1933–1934. Despite its popularity, Roosevelt, as always, was concerned about costs and welcomed the end of the CWA and resumption of the relief burden by the FERA.

AGRICULTURAL REFORMS

The New Deal's efforts to stimulate economic recovery centered in two of the most important measures of the first hundred days. The first of these tackled the crisis in agriculture. Few if any other economic groups had been so devastated by the depression as American farmers whose net income in 1933 was only one-third what it had been in 1929.

Working closely with Secretary of Agriculture Henry A. Wallace, Roosevelt gave priority to farm legislation. Although the New Deal's first hundred days witnessed the enactment of the Emergency Farm Mortgage Act and the Farm Credit Act which reorganized the agricultural credit system and expanded the amount of credit available to farmers and farm cooperatives, the centerpiece of Roosevelt's efforts to stimulate agricultural recovery was the Agricultural Adjustment Act. A complex measure of far-reaching significance, it combined ingredients from a potpourri of agricultural policies dating back at least to Populism. It also included a host of new devices that gave the secretary of agriculture a wide choice of options for combatting the farm crisis. Such options included marketing agreements and quotas, government-subsidized agricultural exports, and federal loans on storable crops as well as a plan for crop reduction. The enactment of the law owed much to Roosevelt's successful juggling of a medley of conflicting proposals and his skillful bargaining with farm organizations to craft an omnibus measure that had their endorsement.

The basic objective of the Agricultural Adjustment Act was to restore to farmers the purchasing power they had possessed during 1909–1914, the golden age of agriculture. The primary means of achieving this objective was the elimination of the mounting crop surplus and its depressing effect on farm prices by limiting production under a domestic allotment scheme for basic commodities such as cotton, wheat, corn, and tobacco. The incentive for farmers to reduce acreage under cultivation was government subsidies, known as "benefit payments." In brief, the government would pay farmers to curtail production in order to raise prices and thereby enhance their purchasing power. The cost of the program was to be borne by a tax on processors of agricultural products. The implementation and operation of this complex law was the responsibility of the Agricultural Adjustment Administration (AAA), an agency endowed with vast powers. In Roosevelt's words, the New Deal's approach to the farm crisis represented a "new and untrod path."

The initial action of the AAA was to order the one-time destruction of 10 million acres of cotton and 6 million newly born pigs. Even though the purpose was to prevent additional surpluses in already glutted markets, these actions stunned a public which interpreted it as unnatural, even immoral, in view of the millions in need of clothes and food. A more persistent problem for the AAA was the internal squabbling within the agency among personnel who disagreed on which one of the main alternatives for combatting the farm depression provided by the Agricultural Adjustment Act should be emphasized. Throughout 1933 and 1934 the AAA invoked various alternatives and continually refined and modified the farm program.

Despite such problems, agricultural prices did rise sharply. That the farmers' purchasing power in 1935 was almost 90 percent of what it had been in 1909–1914 meant that the New Deal could boast that it was well on its way to achieving its primary objective. Such claims, however, obscure how unevenly the benefits of "agricultural adjustment" were distributed; large farm operators received the lion's share of the subsidies, which in the rural South in particular were used to increase farm mechanization. The combination of mechanization and crop reduction resulted in the displacement of thousands of tenant farmers and sharecroppers who, in many instances, sought work in cities where the labor market promised little relief.

Much to the delight of the processors of farm products, the United States Supreme Court in January 1936 declared the Agricultural Adjustment Act's processing tax unconstitutional on the grounds that it was an improper exercise of federal power because it forced farmers to regulate agricultural production. By depriving the government of funds with which it expected to finance the agricultural program, the court's decision destroyed Roosevelt's hope of balancing the budget. Immediately, the president sought to replace the Agricultural Adjustment Act with a law that would in effect achieve the same ends. Deeply concerned about soil conservation as a result of the destruction caused by the dust storms in a large drought-stricken area known as the "Dust Bowl" and fully aware that the federal courts tended to look with favor on conservation laws, the Roosevelt administration persuaded Congress to enact the Soil Conservation and Domestic Allotment Act which paid farmers for not planting soil-depleting crops and for sowing instead soil-building grasses and legumes.

INDUSTRIAL REFORMS

At the same time that the New Deal wrestled with problems posed by the farm depression, it was attempting to stimulate industrial recovery through a complex measure known as the National Industrial Recovery Act (NIRA), a proposal that fused ideas of economic recovery with those of social reconstruction. It embodied ideas of a planned economy, industrial self-government, and government-business cooperation as well as a promise to protect labor. To end cutthroat competition and facilitate industrial cooperation it suspended the antitrust laws. Drawing upon the experience of the War Industries Board in World War I, the first sections (Title I) of the act proposed both to raise prices to a profitable level by limiting production to actual needs and to guarantee labor a reasonable workweek and living wage. Title II of the act authorized a Public Works Administration with a fund of 3.3 billion dollars for construction projects.

Confident that the NIRA measure would fulfill its promise of restoring industrial prosperity, Roosevelt characterized it "as the most important and far-reaching legislation ever enacted by Congress." He appointed Hugh Johnson, a loud, hard-drinking, and majestically profane West Point graduate who had been a member of the War Industries Board, to head the National Recovery Administration (NRA), the agency charged with implementing Title I of the measure. The primary means of achieving its objectives were codes to fit every trade and industry. These codes would regulate production, prices, wages and trade practices. Committees representing management, labor, and the public drafted such codes which, upon being approved by the NRA and the president, had the force of law. A massive publicity campaign that equated support of the NRA with patriotism kicked off the code-making process.

The NRA "blue eagle" symbol was displayed prominently in the window of this restaurant.

The irascible Johnson was a whirlwind of activity, often shooting from the hip, as he drafted codes, secured the approval of the president, and implemented regulations. Partially as a result of such haste, codes exhibited abundant evidence of sloppiness and a startling lack of uniformity. The NRA's attempt to obtain codes even for industries of small economic value, such as the dog food and burlesque theatrical industries, only further contributed to the bureaucratic morass into which code making sank. More importantly, big business and industry gained concessions from Johnson that allowed them to dominate the code-making process with the result that they fixed prices, allowed minimum wages to become maximum wages, disregarded the provisions for the forty-hour workweek, and replaced veteran employees with lower-wage new ones.

Not surprisingly, Roosevelt's plan for industrial recovery prompted protest from a wide variety of sources, including labor unions, small businesses, consumers, women, and African Americans who claimed to be discriminated against or in some way harmed by NRA activities. To head off a congressional investigation, Roosevelt appointed a review board to evaluate the operation of NRA codes. The board presented a scathing report in 1934 that substantiated many of the complaints against the industry-dominated codes. In the wake of this report Johnson resigned. The president's attempt to reorganize and revitalize the administrative structure of his industrial recovery program proved to be unsuccessful. The death of the NRA came in May 1935 when the Supreme Court declared Title I of the National Industrial Recovery Act unconstitutional on the grounds that it delegated legislative power to the president and regulated intrastate transactions which had only an indirect effect on interstate commerce.

FINANCIAL REFORMS

As important as the relief measures and agricultural and industrial recovery measures were, they by no means constituted the sum of New Deal action during the first hundred days. In an effort to raise prices and ease the debt burden, Roosevelt manipulated the currency, devalued the dollar, and took the country off the gold standard. Taking advantage of the fallout from the stock market crash, he secured the enactment of the Securities Act which provided limited federal supervision of new investment securities by requiring advanced disclosure of information about new stock issues. He completed the process of securities reform the following year with the Securities Exchange Act which broadened federal supervision over all securities being traded, old as well as new, and created the Securities and Exchange Commission (SEC), a federal agency to police the stock and securities market.

THE TVA

Finally, Roosevelt took up the cause of the Muscle Shoals project on the Tennessee River, a cause championed by Senator George Norris and other Republican progressives in the 1920s, and persuaded Congress to establish the Tennessee Valley Authority (TVA), a measure that went far beyond what Norris had proposed. The TVA represented an experiment in social planning and regional rehabilitation for the Tennessee River Valley. Its central feature involved the construction of multipurpose dams that not only assisted in flood control, but also generated inexpensive electric power and provided a "yardstick" by which to ascertain reasonable electric rates to be charged by private power companies (see Figure 20–1). TVA also oversaw the manufacture of fertilizer, soil conservation and reforestation projects, the transformation of the Tennessee into a navigable river, and, as it turned out, a limited amount of social experimentation.

POLITICAL RESPONSE TO THE NEW DEAL

By the time of the fall elections of 1934 there were signs of economic recovery even though the country remained mired in depression and 12 million Americans were still unemployed. The New Deal initiatives on so many fronts in 1933–1934, coupled with the president's personality and expressions of

FIGURE 20–1

The Tennessee Valley Authority

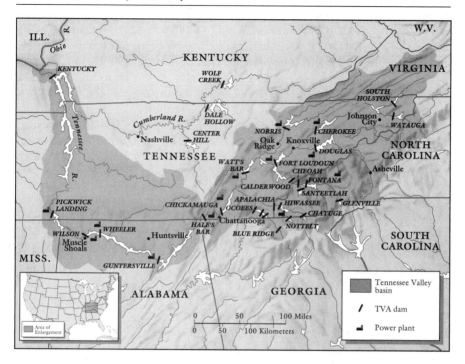

optimism, had lifted the nation's spirits. As the economy improved, though, political disunity increased. Although the *New York Times* reported that the 1934 elections destroyed the "right wing of the Republican Party," conservative Republicans joined anti–New Deal Democrats to organize the American Liberty League. An organization dominated by wealthy businessmen, the League dedicated itself to the defeat of Roosevelt and his New Deal. While the activities of the League were a nuisance, the rumblings on the left were of more concern to Roosevelt. The outcome of the 1934 elections revealed both the immense popularity of the president and the rising tide of radicalism which threatened to push him farther to the left than he ever intended to go.

Evidence of such radicalism appeared in the campaigns of former Socialist Upton Sinclair in California and the Progressive and Farmer-Labor parties in Wisconsin and Minnesota. No less ominous was the clamor generated by Senator Huey Long of Louisiana, the Roman Catholic "radio priest" Father Charles E. Coughlin, and a retired physician, Francis E. Townsend, who rose to prominence with his plan for a federally funded retirement program that garnered wide support among the elderly. Both Long and Coughlin who had originally been enthusiastic Roosevelt supporters turned violently against the president. Convinced that the depression had been caused by an international conspiracy of bankers, Coughlin denounced Roosevelt for his refusal to destroy the existing American banking community and his failure to accept the priest's various panaceas for economic recovery. Coughlin's anti–New Deal rhetoric was not without appeal to his nationwide radio audience; at the very least it encouraged the belief that Roosevelt's approach to recovery was too timid.

Unlike Townsend and Coughlin, the flamboyant Senator Long had presidential aspirations and won considerable popular support with his "Share Our Wealth" plan. Long's plan called for sharply graduated taxes, the limitation of income to a million dollars a year, and the redistribution of wealth to provide all families with a guaranteed annual income. The appeal of such schemes, accompanied by a wave of strikes in 1934, appeared to confirm the existence of widespread popular unrest, stemming from impatience with the New Deal's failure to take bolder, more radical steps to bring about recovery.

THE SECOND NEW DEAL: SOCIAL PROGRAMS

Always sensitive to changes in the popular mood, Roosevelt responded by abandoning efforts to cooperate with the business community and, beginning in 1935, undertook another round of recovery and reform initiatives with an emphasis on social reform and social justice. Political pressures as well as the influence of new personnel in the "brains trust," especially Thomas G. Cochran and Benjamin C. Cohen, nudged Roosevelt to undertake what has been called the "Second New Deal." Not only did the president expedite the enactment of pending legislation, but he also advocated measures that were so crafted as to steal the thunder of his critics on the left without being considered radical departures from the American tradition. The legislation of the Second New Deal may have been deemed revolutionary by the American Liberty League, but compared to the proposals put forward by Coughlin, Long, Townsend, and others, such measures appeared to a majority of voters as the essence of moderation.

THE WPA

In January 1935 Roosevelt signaled the arrival of the Second New Deal in his State of the Union Address. Because the rate of unemployment remained extraordinarily high, he proposed as the first order of business the expansion and reorganization of relief efforts through a huge program of emergency public employment for the jobless, a program that provided jobs rather than handouts for the unemployed. In April 1935, Congress appropriated $4.8 billion for the president to spend largely as he desired in reducing unemployment. Roosevelt divided the funds among many agencies, but a little more than one third ($1.4 billion) went to the newly created Works Progress Administration (WPA) headed by Harry Hopkins. Unlike the FERA, which made work relief grants to states, the new agency placed relief workers directly on the federal payroll.

Devoted largely to construction projects, the WPA also included programs for unemployed actors, writers, artists, and musicians that combined relief with the promotion of cultural nationalism.

Although the WPA spent over $10 billion and employed 8.5 million people before being phased out in 1943, it fell far short of Roosevelt's goal of providing jobs for all of the nation's jobless, created make-work projects of little value, and ultimately became entangled in politics. Ridiculed by critics as "boon-doggling" run riot, the WPA became the butt of numerous anti–New Deal jokes about paying "lazy bums" to lean on shovels or engage in leaf-raking activities. Despite its defects, the agency did represent a bold departure whose achievement was impressive. Its construction activities alone resulted in building over 650,000 miles of roads, 125,000 public buildings, 8,200 parks, 853 airports, and numerous bridges. Communities, large and small, benefitted by WPA construction as well as its artistic and cultural projects.

THE WAGNER ACT

The Roosevelt administration may well have been "riding at anchor" in the spring of 1935, as one writer has suggested, but when the Supreme Court struck down the NIRA in May, the president suddenly resumed the role of the bold leader. Before the end of the summer Congress had approved what he termed "must" legislation regarding labor, social security, banking, and taxation. The labor bill had been introduced by Senator Robert Wagner of New York in 1934, but had initially been blocked by Roosevelt who considered it special interest leg-islation that ran counter to his pursuit of national unity. The president switched his position on the bill in 1935 after the court's invalidation of the NIRA elim-inated guarantees to labor. The National Labor Relations Act (Wagner Act) not only replaced the NIRA's Section 7-A by guaranteeing workers' right to organize and bargain collectively through unions of their choice, but also prohibited man-agement practices that interfered with union activities and created the National Labor Relations Board to enforce the provisions of the measure. In addition to winning labor's support for Roosevelt, the Wagner Act accelerated the movement to unionize mass production industries. Later in 1935, John L. Lewis of the United Mine Workers and other industrial union spokesmen within the American Federation of Labor (AFL) organized the Committee on Industrial Organization to challenge the AFL's commitment to craft unionism. Out of this committee within the AFL ultimately emerged a separate union, the Congress of Industrial Organizations (CIO), which embraced the concept of unionizing all workers in a single industry rather than along craft lines.

THE SOCIAL SECURITY ACT

The same Congress that passed the Wagner Act in the summer of 1935 also re-sponded to Roosevelt's request for social security legislation by enacting the Social Security Act, a measure of enduring significance that became the centerpiece of the New Deal's welfare state. Systems of national social insurance had existed in the industrialized countries of Western Europe since the late nineteenth and early twentieth centuries and had been advocated by various groups and individuals in the United States for decades. By the 1930s about half of the states had some form of pension or unemployment insurance system, but most programs were grossly inadequate. The growing popularity and appeal of the ideas of Huey Long and Francis Townsend suggested that Americans were ready to abandon their historic assumptions about the government's social responsibility. The administration's social security bill incorporated many of the proposals recommended by a committee established in 1934 and chaired by Secretary of Labor Perkins. Although critics on the right condemned it as rank socialism, the measure was, in fact, conservative and considerably less than comprehensive. It failed, for example, to include farm laborers, domestics, occasional workers, and some others who were in greatest need of assistance.

The law signed by the president on August 14, 1935, created a system of unemployment insurance, old age pensions, and assistance for the blind, deaf, and disabled, as well as dependent children. Adhering to the American system of federalism, the measure provided that all these programs except old age pensions were to be administered by the states which would determine the benefits to be paid so long as they reached a certain minimum. Both the unemployment insurance and old age pensions were to be self-funded programs financed by payroll taxes levied on both employers and employees. According to Roosevelt, this method of financing involved more politics than economics. "With those taxes in there," he declared, "no damn politician can ever scrap my social security program." The immense popularity of the Social Security Act suggested the extent to which it deflected criticisms leveled at the New Deal by Long, Townsend, and others who complained about the administration's insensitivity to the needs of the aged, unemployed, and disabled. Compared to their panaceas, the social security measure made Roosevelt appear as the essence of moderation.

ADDITIONAL REFORMS

Within two weeks after the passage of the Social Security Act, Congress enacted three other pieces of legislation which Roosevelt had included on his "must" list. One concerned tighter regulation of the public utilities industry, especially its holding companies. Forced to compromise in the face of strong opposition, Roosevelt ultimately succeeded in getting congressional approval of the Public Utilities Holding Company Act. In addition to being "a bold stroke against bigness" which unraveled the pyramids of holding companies characteristic of electric utilities, the law sought through tighter federal control to discourage fraud and inefficiency.

Another New Deal proposal enacted in August 1935 was the Banking Act which, despite strong opposition, constituted the most important revision of the Federal Reserve System since its establishment under Woodrow Wilson. It curtailed the autonomy of the regional reserve banks, concentrated power in the Federal Reserve Board, and substantially increased federal control over the banking system.

Finally, Congress responded to Roosevelt's demand for a new revenue act which would encourage "a wider distribution of wealth" by enacting the so-called "Soak-the-Rich Tax." Although the law scarcely deserved such a label, it sharply increased inheritance taxes and placed a surtax on net incomes over $50,000 a year. While the new law by no means precluded the amassing of great wealth, it did serve to take much of the wind out of sails of taxation schemes such as those included in Huey Long's "Share-Our-Wealth" program.

In addition to social security and labor laws, Roosevelt further endeared himself to those whom he called "the forgotten man" by issuing executive orders creating the Rural Electrification Administration (REA) and the Resettlement Administration (RA). Through low-cost government loans to nonprofit cooperatives established by farmers, the REA provided electric power to rural America. Few, if any other, New Deal measures altered the way of life for so many citizens. Created by consolidating components of other New Deal agencies, the RA represented an attempt to address the problem of rural poverty. The agency resettled farmers attempting to eke out an existence on depleted lands on to federally sponsored cooperative farm communities and established model suburban towns, known as Greenbelt towns. The underfunded RA was later reorganized as the Farm Security Administration.

ROOSEVELT'S SECOND TERM

THE 1936 PRESIDENTIAL ELECTION

Although evidences of the depression were omnipresent as the nation entered the presidential campaign of 1936, virtually all economic indices suggested how much better off Americans were than they had been four years earlier. Roosevelt had reason to be optimistic about his reelection, but he did not anticipate the magnitude of his victory. The New Deal's reform efforts, especially those in 1935, largely eliminated the threat posed by dissidents on the left. Roosevelt welcomed the challenge of the Liberty League and other conservative critics whom he described as greedy "economic royalists."

Clearly, Roosevelt was in control of the Democratic party which not only readily accepted his platform, but also acquiesced in his desire to repeal the century-old rule whereby presidential nominations required a two-thirds vote of the convention delegates—a rule cherished by the South as a device for the region to exercise a minority veto over the party ticket. In accepting his nomination, Roosevelt reaffirmed his commitment to reform and proclaimed that "this generation of Americans has a rendezvous with destiny."

Entering the campaign in disarray, the Republicans nominated as their presidential candidate Governor Alfred Landon of Kansas, a moderate progressive and the only Republican governor reelected in 1934. Despite the best efforts of Republican publicists to promote their candidate as a "liberal Coolidge," a humane, but thrifty, wonder worker, Landon faced an uphill battle. Few political leaders had captured the popular imagination as Roosevelt had by 1936. A mill hand in North Carolina spoke for many Americans when he declared: "Mr. Roosevelt is the only man we ever had in the White House who would understand that my boss is a sonofabitch."

Although Roosevelt shied away from disturbing the racial status quo, African Americans as beneficiaries of the New Deal relief programs abandoned the Republican party to rally to the president's support. Along with the urban masses, labor unions, and southern and western farmers, African Americans constituted an important component of the "Roosevelt coalition" that emerged in 1936 and persisted for a generation.

Roosevelt had put together a winning coalition—one that resulted in a landslide victory in which he carried every state except Maine and Vermont. For the first time in forty years the Democrats became the nation's majority party. Overwhelmingly endorsing the activist government represented by the New Deal, voters not only gave Roosevelt a popular mandate to continue his reform efforts, but they also provided him with top-heavy Democratic majorities in both houses of Congress.

The adoption of the Twentieth Amendment to the Constitution in 1933 meant that Roosevelt's inauguration for a second term occurred on January 20, 1937, rather than in March. Although the weather—a driving rain—was little more hospitable than that four years earlier, the condition of the nation's economy, not to mention the mood of the people, exhibited vast improvement over that confronting Roosevelt at his first inauguration. In his second inaugural address the president noted that in spite of substantial recovery, one-third of the nation's population remained "ill-housed, ill-clad, ill-nourished." Because indications were that Roosevelt intended to press on with a reform agenda, especially in addressing the needs of the unfortunate one-third of the population, his first act was altogether unexpected.

JUDICIAL REFORM

On February 5, 1937, little more than two weeks after his inauguration, the president forwarded to Congress without warning a judiciary reorganization bill. The measure provided that whenever any federal judge reached the age of seventy who had served ten years or more and failed to retire, the president might appoint an additional judge. No more than fifty judges could be appointed under the act, and the maximum size of the Supreme Court was fixed at fifteen. The latter provision was the crux of Roosevelt's plan; it would have allowed him to expand the existing nine-member Supreme Court by six justices. Roosevelt justified his bill on the grounds of crowded dockets, and the physical inability of the aged justices on the Supreme Court to perform their duties. In a fireside chat with the American people on March 9, 1937, he stoutly defended his court reform plan as a method "to save our national constitution from hardening of the judicial arteries" and from a supreme court that acted "not as a judicial body but a policy making body." Although the president's address had a positive impact on his radio audience, his court-packing scheme touched off a storm of controversy in Congress and left in its wake a political atmosphere that threatened the expansion of his New Deal agenda.

Frustrated and angered by the Supreme Court's invalidation of so much New Deal legislation, including the AAA and NIRA, the president feared that none of his important social and economic reforms would pass the scrutiny of the justices. He was especially concerned about the fate of the Social Security Act and the National Labor Relations Act. Even though the sudden appearance of his so-called court-packing plan created the impression that it was a scheme hastily contrived after his reelection, he had, in fact, been considering judicial reform for over two years. Fully cognizant of the public veneration of the court, he opted for enlarging the court's membership, a method sanctioned by precedent and presumably Constitutional. Whether Roosevelt should make the court a campaign issue in 1936 prompted a sharp division of opinion among his strategists. Except for a vague reference in the platform to the possibility of "a clarifying amendment" to the Constitution to enable Congress to safeguard economic security, court reform did not figure in the campaign.

The crescendo of protest that greeted Roosevelt's proposal suggested that it had struck a nerve. For some it appeared to lend credence to the charge of "caesarism" hurled at Roosevelt by critics on the right. The anti–New Deal press joined the fray, charging the president with deception and duplicity. Republicans waged a quiet, largely invisible, campaign against the court-packing plan but left the public fracas in Congress to members of the president's own party. Large numbers of Democrats, including some usually reliable New Deal supporters, deserted Roosevelt for the first time. Suddenly the president discovered that the top-heavy Democratic majority in Congress had become altogether unreliable.

Despite the best efforts of Senate majority leader Joseph T. Robinson of Arkansas, who allegedly had been promised a seat on the Supreme Court, the president's court-packing measure aroused strong, outspoken opposition from liberal as well as conservative Democrats in the upper house. In the meantime, the court itself removed much of Roosevelt's reason for the measure by reversing itself on certain legal issues and doctrines and by upholding the constitutionality of both the Social Security Act and the National Labor Relations Act. The resignation of Justice Willis Van Devanter in May 1937 provided Roosevelt with the opportunity to appoint a pro–New Deal replacement who would convert the liberal minority on the court to a majority. The sudden death of Senator Robinson on July 14, 1937, eliminated any hope that the president's Judicial Reorganization Bill could be pushed through Congress. The emasculated measure that was finally enacted and halfheartedly signed by Roosevelt concerned only lower court procedure and retirement benefits.

The president later remarked that in the struggle over his court bill he lost the battle but won the war. To be sure, a succession of deaths and resignations by justices enabled him to turn the court into a liberal tribunal that upheld New Deal legislation. But winning the war proved to be costly for the Roosevelt administration. Despite its Democratic majority, a sullen Congress was no longer inclined to do the bidding of the White House. Southern Democrats, resentful of the place occupied by labor and northern urban groups in Roosevelt's Democratic party, increasingly cast their lot with Republicans against their own party leader.

ECONOMIC DOWNTURN

The furor over the court-packing plan had not subsided when the Roosevelt administration confronted a crisis from another quarter—a sharp downturn in the economy replete with falling stock prices, declining industrial production, and rising unemployment. Critics were quick to label the recession "the Roosevelt Recession" and to cite it as evidence that the New Deal, for all its spendthrift policies, had failed to cure the depression.

Even though Roosevelt blamed the recession on business monopolists and profiteers, his own decision in June 1937 to sharply reduce funding for federal programs was largely responsible for the downturn in the economy. Only when the economy continued to deteriorate in the spring of 1938 and many Americans found themselves in a situation similar to that of 1932–1933, did Roosevelt concede that the recession was more than a "corrective dip."

A $33 billion appropriation from Congress enabled him to resume large-scale federal spending, especially for public works projects, which reversed the economic decline. Accompanying the resumption of federal spending was a trust-busting crusade orchestrated by members of the Roosevelt administration who believed that the activities of industrial monopolies posed serious obstacles to the New Deal recovery program. The president acquiesced in the crusade, but refused to heed the advice provided early in 1938 by British economist John Maynard Keynes who encouraged him to undertake massive deficit spending to achieve an economic recovery equal to pre-1929 levels, an achievement that had to await World War II.

INCREASED UNIONIZATION

In addition to the repercussions of the bitter court fight and the recession, the growing militancy of labor contributed to the New Deal's "sea of troubles." The rapid unionization of industrial labor, especially under the leadership of the CIO, enabled workers to win victories against some of the nation's largest corporations, including United States Steel and General Motors.

The occasional outbreaks of violence that accompanied union activities, the passionate rhetoric of union spokesmen, and especially the tactic of the sit-down strikes used successfully by the United Auto Workers outraged many middle-class Americans. For them the strikers' lack of respect for private property smacked of labor radicalism of the European variety. In effect, the aggressiveness of unions tended to lend credence to charges by right-wing conservatives that the labor movement was a creature of the New Deal and an instrument of its radicalism. That Roosevelt assumed a position of neutrality in regard to the sit-down strikes only served to confirm such perceptions. The momentous redistribution of power represented by the growing strength of organized labor also aroused the outspoken opposition of conservative, especially southern, Democrats in Congress who were no longer reluctant to oppose the president.

The combined impact of the court-packing battle, recession, and sit-down strikes did much to thwart Roosevelt's plans to aid the third of the nation that remained "ill-housed, ill-clad, [and] ill-nourished." In fact, Congress meted out rough treatment to the president and his programs in 1937 and 1938, especially those New Deal agencies with politically weak constituencies. Roosevelt's "must" legislation no longer received the special deference it once had, and some of his recommendations, including "seven little TVA's" and a bill to reorganize the executive branch, failed to be enacted. Especially significant in blocking the extension of New Deal reforms was a group of conservative Democratic senators (dominated by southerners) who had forged a bipartisan coalition with Republicans in mid-1937. Ironically, Roosevelt himself remained immensely popular with rank-and-file Americans who consistently displayed their deep affection for him as he traveled about the country. Such popular affection prompted even those Democratic congressmen and senators opposed to an expanded New Deal agenda to scramble for places on the presidential train and to seize every opportunity to be photographed with Roosevelt.

THE WANING OF THE NEW DEAL

Although the conservative renaissance and unreliability of the Democratic majority in Congress during the late 1930s posed serious difficulties for Roosevelt, his second-term achievements were still substantial. To be sure, some of the measures enacted in 1937 and 1938 had been slowly making their way through the legislative mill for some time. In 1937 Congress enacted the National Housing Act and the Farm Tenant Act which did benefit those Americans who fell within the category of the ill-housed and ill-fed. The Housing Act created the United States Housing Authority with $800 million to lend to local governments for slum clearance, public housing, and rent subsidies.

While the housing law addressed an urban problem, the Farm Tenant Act focused on rural poverty by providing assistance to poor farmers, tenants and sharecroppers, and migratory farm workers. The act created the Farm Security Administration (FSA) which abandoned the program of moving farmers to better land initiated by the Resettlement Administration and emphasized instead the creation and protection of the small family farm. The FSA provided loans to tenants for the purchase of land and grants to small farmers for improvements and debt payment. At best, both the Housing Act and the Farm Tenant Act were modest beginnings in addressing problems of the urban and rural poor.

The major legislative achievements of the New Deal in 1938 were the so-called second Agricultural Adjustment Act and the Fair Labor Standards Act. The farm measure was a response to bumper crops with renewed surpluses and declining farm prices during the recession. It not only used the principle of soil conservation payments as the means to restrict acreage in staple crops but also included provisions for restrictions on the amount farmers could sell (marketing quotas) and federal crop insurance. The act granted extensive authority to the secretary of agriculture in the matter of acreage allotments and subsidies and established the ever-normal granary plan whereby farm surpluses were stored until prices rose to acceptable levels.

The labor measure, known as the wages and hours bill and introduced by Alabama Senator Hugo Black in May 1937, encountered strong opposition from southern industrial spokesmen, the AFL, and conservative ideologues. Extensively revised, the measure as finally enacted exempted numerous workers including those in agriculture and in retail and service occupations. As signed by the president on June 25, 1938, the Fair Labor Standards Act provided for a minimum wage of twenty-five cents an hour, a maximum work-week of forty hours, and overtime rates for hours beyond the maximum. The act prohibited the labor of children under sixteen. While it did not radically alter existing practices except in the South, the law provided protection for the lowest paid and unorganized workers.

POLITICAL MANEUVERING

Angered by the obstructionist tactics of conservative Democrats, Roosevelt embarked upon a mission to mold the Democratic party into the New Deal image. Urged on by a group of advisors known as the elimination committee, the president belatedly decided to purge the party of anti–New Deal dissidents in the fall elections of 1938. His purpose was to rid the party of those who rode to office on his coattails but once in office voted against his program. Roosevelt barnstormed the country aiding liberal New Deal Democrats against conservative anti–New Deal incumbents, but his late entry into the campaign meant that he found party leaders already committed to the support of individuals whom he opposed. Despite the president's success in defeating John J. O'Connor of New York, an ardent anti–New Dealer who chaired the House Rules Committee, the purge was a failure. Not only was there widespread resentment over the president's interference in state elections, but the reelection of those whom Roosevelt had opposed only served to harden their resistance to his New Deal. The aborted purge, like the court fight, prompted cries of caesarism from critics who compared Roosevelt's activities to the antics of Adolf Hitler and Joseph Stalin.

The elections in the fall of 1938 offered little comfort to Roosevelt and the New Dealers. For the first time during Roosevelt's presidency, the Republicans gained ground and substantially reduced the Democratic majorities in Congress from 229 to 93 in the House and from 56 to 42 in the Senate. The fall elections essentially marked the end of the New Deal's domestic reforms. In his State of the Union Address in 1939 Roosevelt proposed no additional reform measures. By that date the threat of international crisis slowed the pursuit of new social and economic programs.

In the following selection, Harvard Sitkoff assesses the impact of the New Deal on African Americans. Despite its failures and unfulfilled promises, the New Deal elicited widespread praise and endorsement among the nation's largest racial minority. Sitkoff argues that President Franklin D. Roosevelt "acted in ways that had the unintended consequence of laying the groundwork for the Second Reconstruction."

THE NEW DEAL AND RACE RELATIONS
Harvard Sitkoff

Perhaps no aspect of the New Deal appears more anomalous or paradoxical than the relationship of Afro-Americans and the administration of President Franklin Roosevelt. On the one hand are the facts of pervasive racial discrimination and inequity in the recovery and relief programs, coupled with the evasiveness of New Dealers on civil rights issues. On the other hand, there is the adoration of FDR by blacks and the huge voting switch of Afro-Americans from the party of Lincoln to the Roosevelt coalition between 1932 and 1940. Faced with this enigma, some historians have concluded that Roosevelt gulled blacks in the 1930s, seduced them with rhetoric and gestures that left untouched the actual harm perpetuated by New Deal neglect and political cowardice. Others conjecture that the blacks' positive opinion of Roosevelt in the thirties had little to do with any effort the New Deal made to improve race relations and everything to do with the desperate need of

from Harvard Sitkoff, ed., *Fifty Years Later: The New Deal Evaluated* (Philadelphia: Temple University Press, 1985), 93–111.

Afro-Americans for the New Deal programs designed to aid the unemployed and the poor, regardless of color. . . . Both interpretations have greatly enriched our historical understanding of blacks and the New Deal. . . . But, both interpretations omit the impact of the New Deal on civil rights in the context of the prevailing racial conservatism of the period. However limited and tentative they may seem in retrospect, the New Deal's steps toward racial justice and equality were unprecedented and were judged most favorably by blacks at the time. Their significance is the theme of this essay.

Certainly no racial issue or matter had greater priority for blacks in the 1930s than the opportunity to earn a living or to receive adequate relief. The Great Depression devastated Afro-Americans, who were disproportionately mired in farm tenancy or who were the "last hired and first fired" in industry. At the bottommost rungs of the economic ladder, no group was in greater need of governmental assistance simply to survive. Accordingly, every civil rights organization and Afro-American leader scrutinized the various New Deal programs for their material effect on blacks. They found much to condemn. Blacks were never aided to the full extent of their need. New Deal legislation and local administration often resulted in discrimination against blacks or their exclusion from benefits. And, at times, the New Deal augmented the educational, occupational, and residential segregation of Afro-Americans.

However much blacks hoped for a new deal of the cards from Roosevelt, they found the deck stacked against them. The heritage of black poverty and powerlessness brought them into the Depression decade without the wherewithal to overcome at the local level those insisting that they remain the lowest social class or to prevail over their opponents at the national level in a political system granting benefits mostly on the power of the groups demanding them. Largely due to the measures taken by Southern state legislatures at the turn of the century to disenfranchise blacks, they could do little to lessen the President's dependence for New Deal legislation and appropriations on the white southerners who held over half the committee chairmanships and a majority of the leadership positions in every congressional session during the thirties. The very ubiquity of the worst depression in American history, moreover, limited the possibility of a major New Deal effort to remedy the plight of blacks. Hard times defined Roosevelt's mandate and kept the pressure on the New Deal to promote the economic recovery of middle-class America rather than to undertake either the long-range reform of the structural bases of poverty or to engage in a protracted effort to vanquish Jim Crow. In addition, the traditions of decentralization and states' rights further undermined the effort of blacks to gain equitable treatment from the New Deal. Despite the laudable intent of many Roosevelt appointees in Washington, those who administered the New Deal at the state and local levels, especially in the South, saw to it that blacks never shared fully or fairly in the relief and recovery projects.

Thus the National Recovery Administration (NRA) quickly earned such epithets as "Negroes Ruined Again," "Negro Run Around," and "Negro Rights Abused." The NRA wage codes excluded those who toiled in agriculture and domestic service—three out of every four employed blacks—and the administrators in Washington connived to accept spurious occupational classifications for black workers, or their displacement by white employees. Denied the benefits of the NRA's effort to raise labor standards, blacks nevertheless felt the impact of the NRA as consumers by having to pay higher prices for most goods. Similarly, the Agricultural Adjustment Administration (AAA) . . . eschewed safeguards to protect the exploited landless black peasantry and acquiesced in the widespread cheating of croppers out of their share of the subsidy to planters, or the wholesale eviction of tenants whose labor was no longer needed. Those who had traditionally oppressed blacks in the South also controlled the local administration of the Tennessee Valley Authority (TVA), and the consequences were the same. . . .

The early relief and welfare operations of the New Deal proved to be only marginally more beneficial to blacks. The Civilian Conservation Corps (CCC) allowed local officials to choose the enrollees, and, not surprisingly, young black men were woefully underrepresented. They were also, in the main, confined to segregated CCC units and kept out of the training programs that would lead to their advancement. Moreover, despite the laudable intentions of Harry Hopkins, the Federal Emergency Relief Administration and the Civil Works Administration succumbed to the pressure brought by angry whites who thought that blacks were being spoiled by direct relief or were earning more on work-relief than white laborers in private enterprise. . . . Especially in 1933 and 1934, discrimination was rife and blacks depended on the mercy of the lily-white personnel in local relief offices. Similarly, the New Deal's capitulation to racial prejudice became manifest in the refusal to admit blacks in the subsistence homestead program; the failure to prohibit racial discrimination in unions protected by the National Labor Relations Act; the passage of a Social Security Act with enough loopholes to exclude two-thirds of all Afro-American workers in 1935; and the encouragement of residential segregation by the Federal Housing Administration.

Gradually, however, counterforces pushed the New Deal toward a more equitable treatment of blacks. A clear demonstration by blacks of their determination to achieve full, first-class citizenship seemed foremost among the interrelated reasons for that transformation. On a scale, and with an intensity, unknown in any previous decade, a host of black advancement and protest organizations campaigned for racial justice and equality. More blacks than ever before marched, picketed, rallied, and lobbied against racial discrimination. They boycotted businesses with unjust racial practices. The National Association for the Advancement of Colored People (NAACP) and the National Urban League adapted to the mood of militance. . . . New militant organizations such as the National Negro Congress and Southern Negro Youth Congress prodded the more moderate black groups to greater aggressiveness and amplified the volume of the growing movement for black rights. Simultaneously, the Negro vote in the 1930s developed into a relatively sizable and volatile bloc that politicians of both major parties in the North could no longer ignore. A marked upsurge in the number of blacks who registered and voted resulted from the continuing migration of Afro-Americans from the South to the cities above the Mason-Dixon line, and from the new immediacy of government to the life of the common people during the New Deal. Concentrated in the states richest in electoral votes, the black vote began to be ballyhooed as a balance of power in national elections. . . . Northern big-city Democrats became especially attentive and displayed unprecedented solicitude for black needs. At the same time, the power of the South within the Democratic party declined; Dixie Democrats prominently joined in the conservative criticism of the New Deal; and racism became identified with fascism. One result was that northern Democrats ceased to support their southern brethren in opposing black rights.

Augmenting these developments, members of the radical left and the labor movement in the thirties preached the egalitarian gospel to millions of white Americans. Communists and the Congress of Industrial Organizations, in particular, advocated an end to racial discrimination and insisted on the necessity for inter-racial harmony. Their desire for strong labor unions or class unity, unhampered by racial divisions, propelled them into the forefront of mainly white organizations pressing for civil rights. White southern race liberals, although few in number, joined the fray, stressing the connections between economic democracy in the South and the cause of black rights. . . . These trends, in turn, gained from the changes in the 1930s in the academic and intellectual communities. Biologists refuted the doctrines of inherent and irremediable racial differences. Social scientists started to un-dermine white racism by emphasizing environment rather than innate character-istics. . . . A new ideological consensus began to emerge, an American creed of treating all people alike, of judging each person as an individual.

Roosevelt could neither ignore what these occurrences portended, nor dis-regard the strength of the forces arrayed against racial reform. He understood that however much black powerlessness had decreased and white hostility to blacks had begun to diminish, the majority of white Americans still opposed desegregation and equal opportunities for blacks. He knew that to combat the worst depression in the nation's history he needed the backing of the southern Democrats who wanted no modification of traditional racial practices. Roosevelt, the consummate politician and humanitarian, therefore, husbanded his political capital on racial matters, doing what he thought was right, if it would not cost him dearly. Above all, he avoided an all-out confrontation with those whose support he deemed necessary. Always the fox and never the lion on civil rights issues, Roosevelt nevertheless acted in ways that had the unintended consequence of laying the groundwork for the Second Recon-struction.

After 1934, although Jim Crow remained largely intact, blacks gained a much fairer, but still far from fully adequate, share of New Deal benefits and services. In the CCC the percentage of black enrollees rose from 3 percent in 1933 to 6 percent in 1936 to nearly 10 percent in 1937, and to over 11 percent in 1938. . . . By the start of 1939, some 200,000 blacks had served in the Civilian Conservation Corps, and when the CCC ended in 1942 the number stood at 350,000. In addition, over 40,000 blacks who had entered the Corps as illiterates had learned to read and write.

The National Youth Administration (NYA) directly aided another 300,000 black youths. Like other New Deal agencies, the NYA accepted segregated projects in the South, employed a disproportionate number of blacks in servile work, and lacked the resources to assist Afro-Americans to the extent their privation required. Yet the fervor of Aubrey Williams, head of the NYA until it ended in 1943, led that agency to hire black administrative assistants to supervise black work in every southern state, to forbid either racial or geographic differentials in wages, and to an insistence that black secondary and college students in every state receive aid at least in proportion to their numbers in the population. The NYA also employed more blacks in administrative posts than any other New Deal program, and Afro-Americans annually received between 10 and 20 percent of NYA's appropriations.

With a zeal similar to that of Williams, Dr. Will Alexander, the chief of the Farm Security Administration (FSA) managed to insure benefits for black farmers that were roughly proportionate to their percentage of farm operators. Overall, blacks received about 23 percent of the New Deal's farm security assistance. This was achieved only because FSA officials in Washington kept constant pressure on local authorities to prevent racial discrimination. But the FSA could never convince Congress to appropriate the funds needed to make more than the slightest dent in the problem of needy and displaced tenant farmers. By 1940, . . . the FSA had placed a mere 1,393 black families on its resettlement communities and had provided tenant purchase loans to only 3,400 blacks. Even this minimal effort, however, earned the FSA a reputation as a "disturber of the peace," and the top place on the southern conservative's "death list" of New Deal programs.

Equally vigilant on matters of race, Secretary of Interior Harold Ickes, who ran the Public Works Administration (PWA), employed a quota system on government construction projects to root out discrimination against black laborers. . . . The quota was effective in diminishing discrimination. It led to the admission of hundreds of skilled blacks into previously lily-white southern construction trade unions. . . . Similar quota systems would later be adopted by the U.S. Housing Authority, the Federal Works Agency, and the President's Committee on Fair Employment Practices.

Ickes' concern for racial fairness also led to the PWA expenditure of over $45 million for the construction and renovation of Afro-American schools, hospitals, and recreational facilities. The nearly $5 million granted for new buildings at black colleges increased their total plant value by more than 25 percent. In addition, the PWA loaned municipalities and states more than $20 million to build and repair scores of schools, dormitories, auditoriums, and gymnasiums for blacks. Of the 48 PWA housing projects completed by 1938, 14 were solely for Afro-Americans and 15 for joint black-white occupancy. Blacks occupied one-third of all PWA housing units and 41,000 of the 122,000 dwelling units built by the U.S. Housing Authority (USHA). The determination of the PWA and USHA to be racially fair and to meet the black demand for public housing also led them to charge blacks a lower monthly average rent than they did whites, and to set a higher maximum family income for blacks than whites as the cut-off for admission to the housing projects.

Likewise, the concern for black welfare of Harry Hopkins was manifest in the constant efforts of officials in the Works Progress Administration (WPA) to forbid racial discrimination by local relief authorities in assigning jobs to the unemployed and in establishing wage rates. Hopkins did not succeed in ending such practices in the South, but as the Urban League proclaimed: "It is to the eternal credit of the administrative offices of the WPA that discrimination on various projects because of race has been kept to a minimum and that in almost every community Negroes have been given a chance to participate in the work program." . . .

Blacks, long accustomed to receiving little more than crumbs, largely accepted the New Deal's half a loaf. The continuance of discrimination and segregation appeared secondary to the vital importance of work-relief, public housing, government-sponsored health clinics and infant care programs, NYA employment to keep a child in school, a FSA loan to purchase a farm, or new educational facilities in the neighborhood. Primarily because of the PWA and WPA, the gap between both black unemployment rates and black median family income relative to whites diminished during the 1930s, and the percentage of black workers in skilled and semi-skilled occupations rose from 23 to 29 percent.

In no small part because of the myriad of New Deal programs that improved the nutrition, housing, and health care available to Afro-Americans, black infant and maternal mortality significantly decreased, and black life expectancy climbed from 48 to 53 years in the 1930s. Over 1 million blacks learned to read and write in New Deal–sponsored literacy classes. . . .

Summing up the prevailing Afro-American response to the New Deal efforts to relieve black distress, the *Pittsburgh Courier* editorialized that "armies of unemployed Negro workers have been kept from the near-starvation level on which they lived under President Hoover" by the work provided by the WPA, CCC, PWA, and other federal projects. It acknowledged the unfortunate continuation of racial discrimination and the New Deal's failure to end such practices. "But what administration within the memory of man," the *Courier* concluded, "has done a better job in that direction considering the very imperfect human material with which it had to work? The answer, of course, is none."

Blacks expressed their thankfulness for the uncommon concern the Roosevelt Administration showed for their well-being, and for the direct material assistance that enabled them to endure the Depression. The very novelty of simply being included—of being considered and planned for—elicited praise in hundreds of letters written to the White House and to New Deal agencies. As a group of black social workers visiting Hyde Park proclaimed: "For the first time Negro men and women have reason to believe that their government does care." That sentiment was bolstered time and again by the battles that Alexander, Ickes, Williams, and other New Dealers waged in pursuit of a more equitable deal for blacks, by their overt disdain for racist attitudes and practices, and by their public championing, in articles and speeches, of the cause of racial justice and equality. Blacks viewed their actions with hope as symbolic of a new high-level governmental disposition to oppose racial discrimination.

Blacks in the 1930s also applauded the success of these New Dealers in en-larging the roster of Afro-Americans working for the government. The number of blacks on the federal payroll more than tripled during the Depression decade. The proportion of black government employees in 1940 was twice what it had been in 1930. In addition, the Roosevelt Administration unprecedently hired thousands of blacks as architects, engineers, lawyers, librarians, office managers, and statisticians. This was viewed at the time as "the first significant step toward the participation of Negroes in federal government activity," and as "representing something new in the administration of our national affairs." To insure further steps, the Administration also abolished the Civil Service regulations that had required job seekers to des-ignate their race and to attach a photograph to their application forms. Some New Deal officials desegregated the cafeterias, restrooms, and secretarial pools in their agencies and departments; others highlighted their abhorrence of Jim Crow by having blacks and whites work at adjoining desks.

Roosevelt also reversed two decades of diminishing black patronage. He ap-pointed over one hundred blacks to administrative posts in the New Deal. Previous administrations had, at best, reserved a handful of honorific and innocuous positions for loyal Negro party leaders. Roosevelt selected a large number of nonpartisan black professionals and veterans of the civil rights movement and placed them in formal positions of public importance so that both government officers and the Afro-American community regarded their presence as significant. Popularly referred to as the Black Cabinet or Black Brain Trust, these black officials had considerably more symbolic value than actual power. They rarely succeeded in pushing the New Deal further along the road to racial equality than it wished to go. Most of their efforts to win greater equity for blacks were defeated by interest groups that were better able to bring pressure to bear on Roosevelt. But their very being and prominence, Roy Wilkins of the NAACP noted, "had never existed before." This fact alone elicited howls from white southerners that "Negroes were taking over the White House," which was hardly the case. Still, the presence of the Black Cabinet, like Roosevelt's selection of William Hastie as the first Afro-American federal judge in American history, hinted at a New Deal determination to break, however timo-rously, with prevailing customs of racial prejudice. As Mary McLeod Bethune, di-rector of the NYA's Division of the Negro Affairs, emphasized during the thirties, such appointments were not "tokenism" but the essential first steps in making the government aware of black needs and in planning policies that would help the race.

The Black Cabinet certainly did raise the level of national awareness of racial issues. The race advisers appointed by Roosevelt articulated the problems of blacks, the ultimate goal of integration, and the specific responsibility of the federal gov-ernment in the area of civil rights, both within the corridors of the various agencies in which they worked and in the public conferences and reports they generated. "At no time since the curtain had dropped on the Reconstruction drama," wrote Henry Lee Moon of the NAACP, "had government focused as much attention upon the Negro's basic needs as did the New Deal." . . . Even Ralph Bunche, who was perhaps the New Deal's severest black critic, admitted at the end of the 1930s that the New Deal was without precedent in the manner in which it granted "broad recognition to the existence of the Negro as a national problem and undertook to give specific consideration to this fact in many ways."

Roosevelt appointees also stirred the hopes of Afro-Americans by establishing precedents that challenged local white control over blacks. The National Advisory Committee on Education, which was appointed by Roosevelt, called in 1938 for specific guarantees that federal grants to states for education would be spent equitably for black as well as white schooling. No government body had said that before. . . .

The New Deal, indeed, substantially expanded the scope of the federal government's authority and constricted traditional states' rights. . . . This alteration in the system of federalism augured well for black hopes of future federal civil rights actions, as did the emergence of a new conception of positive government . . . which guaranteed every American a minimally decent economic existence as a matter of right, not charity, and which assumed the role of the protector of weak interests that could not contend successfully on their own.

Roosevelt's appointments to the Supreme Court immediately sanctioned the expansion of federal power over matters of race and strengthened the rights of blacks. After FDR's abortive attempt at "court packing" in 1937, the personnel on the Supreme Court changed swiftly and power passed into the hands of New Dealers, who articulated a new judicial philosophy which championed the rights of racial and religious minorities and formulated new constitutional guarantees to protect civil rights. As a result, both the number of cases involving black rights brought before the federal courts and the percentage of decisions favorable to black plaintiffs leaped dramatically. What would culminate in the Warren Court clearly began in the Roosevelt Court. With the exception of James Byrnes, Roosevelt's eight appointees to the Court were truly partisans of the cause of civil rights. . . . Their decisions . . . signaled the demise of the separate-but-equal doctrine established by Plessy v. Ferguson (1896). . . .

Although not a presidential appointee, Eleanor Roosevelt certainly made the most of her position as First Lady to link the civil rights cause with the New Deal. Working quietly within the administration, at first, Mrs. Roosevelt influenced her husband and numerous agency heads to be more concerned with the special needs of blacks. Gradually her commitment became more open and visible. Functioning as an unofficial ombudsman for blacks, she goaded bureaucrats and congressmen into lessening racial discrimination in federal programs, and acted as the main conduit between the civil rights leadership and the higher circles of the New Deal and the Democratic party. Repeatedly breaking with tradition, Eleanor Roosevelt openly entertained Afro-American leaders at the White House, posed for photographs with blacks, and publicly associated herself with most of the major civil rights organizations and issues. . . .

"Nigger Lover Eleanor," as some whites derided her, squarely placed her authority and prestige behind the drive for civil rights legislation in President

Roosevelt's second term. Delivering the keynote address at the first meeting of the Southern Electoral Reform League, she emphasized the necessity for a federal act to end all poll tax requirements for voting. Mrs. Roosevelt also publicly endorsed the quest for antilynching legislation, and sat prominently in the Senate gallery during the efforts of northern liberals to invoke cloture and shut off the southern filibuster of the 1938 Wagner-Van Nuys-Gavagan antilynching bill. In the same year Eleanor Roosevelt also helped to organize the Southern Conference for Human Welfare. At its opening session in Birmingham, Alabama, she defied the local segregation ordinance, conspicuously taking a seat on the "Colored" side of the auditorium. White supremacists immediately condemned the First Lady's act as "an insult to every white man and woman in the South." But in the Negro press, Eleanor Roosevelt's disdain for Jim Crow was a "rare and precious moment in the social history of America." Further stirring the wrath of white supremacists and gaining the admiration of blacks, Mrs. Roosevelt began to denounce racial discrimination in the defense program. In 1939, she publicly decried the bigotry of the Daughters of the American Revolution when that organization refused to rent its Constitution Hall for a concert by the famous black contralto, Marian Anderson. Mrs. Roosevelt then used her "My Day" newspaper column to explain why she could no longer remain a member of a group practicing such discrimination and, working with her husband and the NAACP, she arranged for Marian Anderson to sing her concert in front of the Lincoln Memorial. . . .

Such highly publicized actions of Mrs. Roosevelt, as well as the President's increasingly more egalitarian gestures and rhetoric, had a vital impact on blacks in the 1930s. Although Franklin Roosevelt shied away from any direct challenges to white supremacy, the very fact that he frequently invited blacks to the White House, held conferences with civil rights leaders, and appeared before Afro-American organizations indicated to blacks that they mattered. It was a start. Mindful of political realities, blacks sought progress, not perfection. They understood that no president would act boldly and unyielding on black rights until a majority constituency for dramatic change had emerged. Until then, symbolic actions would count, for they played an important role in educating and persuading, in inspiring hope and commitment.

Accordingly, the civil rights leadership and their allies in the 1930s utilized the President's association with the campaigns for antilynching and antipoll tax legislation to mobilize future support. Their public complaints to the contrary, these black rights spokesmen recognized the insurmountable barriers to cloture being voted in the Senate and the necessity for Roosevelt to maintain the backing of the southern leadership in Congress. They knew he would not jeopardize his relief and defense programs for a futile attempt at civil rights legislation. Accordingly, blacks extracted the greatest possible advantages from what the President said and did, however lukewarm and timorous.

On the poll tax, Roosevelt publicly supported the legislative efforts for its abolition. . . . In a public letter Roosevelt vigorously endorsed the antipoll tax movement in Arkansas. At a press conference in 1938 he opposed the use of poll taxes: "They are inevitably contrary to the fundamental democracy and its representative form of government in which we believe." No legislator or informed citizen doubted where the President stood on this matter. In part, this helps to explain why the House of Representatives in 1941 voted to pass an antipoll tax bill by a better than three-to-one margin.

Similarly, the President aided the civil rights movement on antilynching, both with public statements to influence mass opinion and private pressures on the Senate to get it to consider legislation, but Roosevelt would neither place the anti-lynching bills on his list of "must" legislation, nor intervene with the Senate leadership to end the filibusters that doomed the proposals from even coming to a vote. Over a coast-to-coast radio hook-up, early in his administration, Roosevelt denounced lynching as "a vile form of collective murder." . . . No president had ever spoken like that before. . . . Only Roosevelt, [W.E.B.] DuBois concluded, "has declared frankly that lynching is murder. We all knew it, but it is unusual to have a President of the United States admit it. These things give us hope."

More ambiguously, Roosevelt in 1934 authorized Senators Edward Costigan and Robert Wagner to inform the Majority Leader "that the President will be glad to see the anti-lynching bill pass and wishes it passed." And, in 1935, he requested that the Majority Leader permit the Senate to consider the bill. The half-heartedness of Roosevelt's support did nothing to avert the inevitable southern filibuster that killed the measure in 1935. Meanwhile, Roosevelt's private encouragement of others to keep up the fight led to a protracted and bitter wrangle over antilynching legislation in 1938. A far cry from the charade of 1935 in which both sides went through the motions, the two-month-long talkathon of 1938 smacked of fratricide. The southern senators overwhelmingly blamed the New Deal for provoking the civil rights issues that alienated the South from the Democratic party. . . .

The result in Congress notwithstanding, black leaders gained significantly from the struggle against lynching and from the President's involvement in the cause. Lynchings declined from a high for the decade of twenty-eight in 1933 to eighteen in 1935, six in 1938, and two in 1939. To ward off federal legislation, most southern states made greater efforts to prevent lynching and enacted their own bills to stop the crime. At the end of the decade, Roosevelt established a special Civil Rights Section of the Justice Department and empowered it to investigate all lynchings that might involve some denial of a federal right. And, in no small part because the public identified the crusade against lynching with the First Family, the campaign for federal legislation attracted new supporters and allies to the black cause who would stay to fight against discrimination in the defense program, segregation in education, and the disfranchisement of Afro-Americans. . . .

Roosevelt's overtures . . . also showed in the series of precedent-shattering "firsts" that he orchestrated in the 1936 campaign. Never before had the Democrats accredited an Afro-American as a convention delegate; in 1936 they accorded thirty blacks that distinction. For the first time, additionally, the national party in 1936 invited black reporters into the regular press box; chose a black minister to offer the convention invocation; selected blacks to deliver the welcome address and one of the speeches seconding Roosevelt's renomination; and placed a black on the delegation to notify the Vice President of his renomination. Yet another significant event at the convention occurred when liberals and New Dealers wiped out the century-old rule, utilized by the South as a political veto, which required the Democratic nominee to win two-thirds of the delegates' votes in order to obtain the nomination. The white South recognized the threat and resented the intrusion. And its fears of a future attempt by the New Deal to alter race relations were heightened when Roosevelt pointedly campaigned before black audiences and promised that in his administration there would be "no forgotten races" as well as no forgotten men. Then in the 1940 presidential race, Roosevelt affirmed his desire to include blacks evenhandedly in defense training and employment, promoted the first black to the rank of Army Brigadier General, and insisted that, for the first time, the Democrats include a specific Negro plank in the party platform, pledging "to strive for complete legislative safeguards against discrimination in government services and benefits."

However circumspect this New Deal record seems today, for blacks in the thirties it meant change for the better. The mixture of symbolic and substantive assistance, of rhetoric and recognition, led blacks to cast their ballots overwhelmingly for Roosevelt once the New Deal began. After voting more than 70 percent for Herbert Hoover in 1932, a majority of black voters deserted the Republican party for the first time in history in 1934, about two-thirds of the Afro-Americans registered in 1936 entered the Roosevelt coalition, and nearly 68 percent of all black voters in 1940 went for FDR. This [was a] startling shift in the black vote. . . .

Virtually every civil rights spokesman stressed both the value of new government precedents favorable to blacks and the manner in which the New Deal made explicit the federal government's responsibility in the field of civil rights. Editorials in the black press and journals frequently reiterated that the New Deal had ended the "invisibility" of the race problem and had made civil rights a part of the liberal agenda. Perhaps most importantly, blacks in the thirties lauded the manifold ways in which the New Deal reform spirit ushered in a new political climate in which Afro-Americans and their allies could begin to struggle with some expectation of success. . . .

These developments did little to change the concrete aspects of life for most blacks in the 1930s. The New Deal failed to end the rampant discrimination against blacks in the North, who were living in ghettos that had turned to slums and who were twice as likely to be unemployed as whites. The Roosevelt Administration also failed to enfranchise black southerners, to eradicate segregation, or to elevate the great mass of blacks who remained a submerged caste of menials, sharecroppers, unskilled laborers, and domestics. These facts cannot be gainsaid. The New Deal record on race is replete with failures and timidity, unfulfilled promises, and insufficient effort. The New Deal did not fundamentally transform the economic, legal, or social status of Afro-Americans.

But for the millions of blacks who hung FDR's picture on their walls, who kept voting for Roosevelt, and naming their children after him, something vital did begin in the New Deal, breaking the crust of quiescence that had long stifled even the dream of equal opportunity and full participation in American life. The New Deal gave blacks hope. . . . The barely visible flicker of black hope at the start of the New Deal would shine brightly as the United States mobilized for World War II.

Suggested Readings

Anthony Badger, *The New Deal: The Depression Years, 1933–1940* (1989).
Roger Biles, *A New Deal for the American People* (1991).
Alan Brinkley, *Voices of Protest: Huey Long, Father Coughlin, and the Great Depression* (1982).
James M. Burns, *Roosevelt: The Lion and the Fox* (1956).
Paul Conkin, *The New Deal*, 2nd ed., (1975).
William E. Leuchtenburg, *Franklin D. Roosevelt and the New Deal, 1932–1940* (1963).
Robert S. McElvaine, *The Great Depression: America, 1929–1941* (1984).
Lois Scharf, *Eleanor Roosevelt: First Lady of American Liberalism* (1987).
Arthur M. Schlesinger, Jr., *The Age of Roosevelt*, 3 vols. (1957–1960).
Nancy J. Weiss, *Farewell to the Party of Lincoln* (1983).

Further Readings

THE GREAT DEPRESSION and the NEW DEAL: Caroline Bird, *The Invisible Scar* (1966); Alan Brinkley, *The End of Reform: New Deal Liberalism in Recession and War* (1995); Frank Freidel, *Franklin D. Roosevelt*, 4 vols. (1952–1973); Edward R. Ellis, *A Nation in Torment: The Great American Depression, 1929–1939* (1992); Michael Parrish, *Anxious Decades: America in Prosperity and Depression, 1920–1941* (1992); Dixon Wector, *The Age of the Great Depression, 1929–1941* (1948). SPECIAL ASPECTS of the ERA: Sidney Baldwin, *Poverty and Politics: The Rise and Decline of the Farm Security Administration* (1969); Bernard Bellish, *The Failure of the NRA* (1978); William R. Brock, *Welfare, Democracy, and the New Deal* (1988); Sidney Fine, *Sit Down: the General Motors Strike of 1936–1937* (1969); Kenneth Finegold and Theda Skocpol, *State and Party in America's New Deal* (1995); Frank Freidel, *FDR and the South* (1965); Ellis W. Hawley, *The New Deal and the Problem of Monopoly* (1966); Jonathan Harris, *Federal Art and National Culture: The Politics of Identity in New Deal America* (1995); Mark Leff, *The Limits of Symbolic Reform: The New Deal and Taxation, 1933–1939* (1984); Michael Parrish, *Securities Regulation and the New Deal* (1970); James T. Patterson, *The New Deal and the States* (1969); Richard Pells, *Radical Visions and American Dreams: Social and Cultural Thought in the Depression Years* (1973); John Salmond, *The Civilian Conservation Corps* (1967); Harvard Sitkoff, *A New Deal for Blacks* (1978); George B. Tindall, *The Emergence of the New South 1913–1945* (1967); Stanley Vittoz, *New Deal Labor Policy and the American Industrial Economy* (1987); Susan Ware, *Partner and I: Molly Dewson, Feminism, and New Deal Politics* (1987).

QUESTIONS FOR DISCUSSION

1. Explain the concept of the two New Deals and how historians have distinguished between the "first" and "second" New Deals. Is the concept valid? Explain.
2. Identify the principal sources of New Deal ideas and the historical precedents for New Deal actions.
3. How did the Roosevelt administration respond to the banking and unemployment crises between 1933 and 1935?
4. Explain the New Deal's approach to the agricultural crisis in 1933 and the basic objectives of its early farm legislation. How did the New Deal later attempt to address the plight of tenant farmers and sharecroppers?
5. Identify the most vocal critics of the New Deal, on both the right and left, by 1935, and explain the nature of their criticism.
6. What was the court-packing plan? Analyze its impact.
7. Identify the various components of the Roosevelt coalition that enabled the president to win reelection in 1936 by an overwhelming majority. How did this coalition alter the status and configuration of the Democratic party?
8. First define what the term "welfare state" means to you, then explain whether in your opinion the New Deal created a "welfare state."
9. What evidence does Harvard Sitkoff's essay provide in support of its view that while the New Deal failed fundamentally to alter the economic, legal, and social status of African Americans, it gave them hope and prompted them to idolize President Roosevelt?

CHAPTER TWENTY-ONE

FROM ISOLATIONISM TO GLOBALISM:
The United States and World War II

The peace structure established by the Treaty of Versailles was one of the shortest-lived in modern history. It took but twenty-one brief years for the world to move from one cataclysm to another, even greater one. The factors responsible for the coming of World War II are multitudinous, complex, and arguable. The Treaty of Versailles had humiliated Germany but left it with the sinews of power. The Great Depression swept the world, creating economic and social insecurity and distracting the victors of World War I, the very nations who had assumed responsibility for enforcing the peace. The global economic crisis stimulated the growth of fascism throughout the world, but particularly in Germany, Italy, and Japan.

Though it was the world's most formidable economic power and one with vast military potential as well, the United States retreated from its responsibilities as a great power. Following a brief effort at the outset of his administration to involve the United States at least indirectly in various collective security enterprises, President Franklin Roosevelt abdicated in the field of foreign affairs, leaving the stage to isolationists inside and outside Congress. Not until Europe actually went to war did Roosevelt act to warn his countrymen of the dangers of fascism and national socialism. Over a two-year period, the administration presided over a massive mobilization movement and implemented a program of aid to the Allies. Still, the United States did not actually go to war with the Axis powers, led by Germany, Japan, and Italy, until Japan bombed Pearl Harbor.

EMERGENCE OF THE AXIS POWERS

Three expansionist nation-states emerged during the interwar period to threaten the status quo: Nazi Germany, Fascist Italy, and Imperial Japan. Germany craved revenge for the harsh peace imposed upon it by its conquerors in 1919, while Italy felt that it had not received the spoils it deserved for its role in defeating the Central powers. Meanwhile, following a brief flirtation with democracy, Japan fell under the sway of extremists in the military who argued that the nation's survival as a great power depended upon its ability to build a far-flung empire. Although they were deeply divided ideologically, all three powers shared the common objective of upsetting the existing balance of power.

GERMANY

By far the greatest threat to the status quo was Nazi Germany. Wracked by inflation and humiliated by its loss in the Great War, the Weimar Republic proved susceptible to the lure of political extremists of every stripe. The most ruthless and dangerous of these was Adolf Hitler, an Austrian ne'er-do-well who founded and led the National Socialist party. Racism, imperialism, and totalitarianism were the three fundamental aspects of Nazism. In 1933, promising to save Germany from communism and restore the nation to its rightful position as an international power, Hitler became chancellor of the Weimar Republic.

Those few who had read *Mein Kampf*, Hitler's autobiography and statement of political beliefs, understood that he blamed the Jews for Germany's problems and envisioned a world dominated by the "pure" Aryan race whose homeland was Germany. Unfortunately, most Germans and virtually no foreigners had bothered to explore the new leader's past and his credo. Once Hitler occupied the chancellorship, he and his storm troopers terrorized and persecuted opposition parties into extinction. In 1935, Hitler renounced the disarmament provisions of the Versailles Treaty, and the following year he ordered German troops to occupy the Rhineland, a region in western Germany that, under the terms of the 1919 peace, was supposed to remain forever demilitarized. Though he had ordered his generals to retreat at the first sign of resistance by the Western democracies, Britain and France refused to enforce the provisions of the Versailles Treaty.

ITALY

Plagued by political fragmentation, poverty throughout its southern regions, and diplomatic impotency, Italy embraced Benito Mussolini and the Fascist party in 1922. Once in power, Mussolini outlawed all other political parties and established the corporate state whereby all facets of the economy were planned and controlled by the state acting in coercive concert with business and labor. In foreign affairs, Mussolini promised nothing less than the restoration of the Roman Empire. Referring to the Mediterranean as *"mare nostrum"*—our sea—he promised to absorb eventually all those lands washed by its waters. As a first, preparatory step, Mussolini in 1935 invaded the strategically important but militarily insignificant kingdom of Ethiopia. That nation occupied the western shoulder of East Africa and guarded Europe's trade routes with Asia. With the League of Nations standing idly by, the fully mechanized Italian Army defeated Emperor Haile Selassie and his horse-mounted spearmen—although with some difficulty. After that, Mussolini cast his imperial gaze on Yugoslavia and southern France.

JAPAN

Japan constituted the third great threat to world peace in the 1930s. A densely populated island nation lacking in the natural resources necessary to support its modern industrial economy, it had to look beyond its shores for petroleum, iron ore, zinc, lead, rubber, as well as for markets to absorb its surplus production. Liberals in Japan argued that the nation's goals could be achieved through peaceful, economic expansion, but they gradually lost out to militant nationalists, centered in the army, who insisted that Japan must physically annex neighboring territories in order to be secure. In 1931 Japan seized Manchuria from China, and then in 1937 went to war with Jiang Jieshi's Nationalist regime. Meanwhile, Japanese expansionists spoke ominously of a Greater East Asian Co-prosperity Sphere.

ALLIED APPEASEMENT

Opposing the European have-not nations were the victors of World War I—Britain, France, and the host of smaller countries created by the peace treaty such as Czechoslovakia and Poland. In the Far East, the European colonial powers plus the United States, committed to the open door policy since America's acquisition of the Philippines, stood in Japan's way. In reacting to this threat, the democracies, both imperial and nonimperial, had two ways open to them. They could seek to nip aggression in the bud by confronting the have-not powers at the outset with full military force, or they could act on the assumption that the leaders of the fascist nations were reasonable individuals with legitimate grievances, and appease them. Britain, France, and their allies chose the latter course in no small part because it was the path of least resistance. They would argue subsequently, however, that if only the United States had thrown its weight behind collective security, either within the context of the League of Nations or without, that confrontation rather than appeasement would have been the policy of choice.

AMERICAN ISOLATIONISM

Whatever the European democracies might or might not have done, the United States was in fact deeply isolationist during the 1930s and tacitly supported a policy of appeasement. Franklin Roosevelt did not personally share the perspectives of Senators William Borah and Robert LaFollette, or economist-historian Charles Beard, all of whom believed that European powers and Japan were enmeshed in an endless cycle of conflict that had no bearing on American interests. As a member of the eastern aristocracy, he had traveled widely in Europe, was pro-British, admired his nationalist cousin Theodore Roosevelt, and as assistant secretary of the Navy under Wilson, displayed a streak of imperialism. Nonetheless, Roosevelt was elected to pull the country out of the Great Depression. He had no intention of turning congressional isolationists against his New Deal programs by pursuing aggressively interventionist policies in Europe and the Far East. After a brief and unsuccessful campaign to get an arms embargo measure through Congress in 1933, a bill that would have empowered the president to cut off arms sales to aggressors while allowing them to their victims, Roosevelt abandoned the field to the isolationists.

REACTIONS AGAINST THE GREAT WAR

The gathering war clouds in Europe and the Far East stimulated America's desire for peace and noninvolvement. Basically the mood of the public was one of deep disillusionment with the results of the Great War. Americans read Erich Maria Remarque's *All Quiet on the Western Front* and watched the movie based on it. They absorbed the dual message that war is horrible and that no one nation was responsible for the carnage of 1914–1918. When Wilson's dreams of peace without victory and a new world order failed to materialize, many concluded that Americans had fought and died for nothing. A group of historians emerged to portray the Great War as a mistake, criticizing Wilson for sacrificing American neutrality and portraying the United States as a dupe of the British. Walter Millis' *America's Road to War, 1914–1917* which advanced this thesis became a nonfiction best-seller.

REACTIONS AGAINST CORPORATE PROFITEERING

Reinforcing this view was the work of Senator Gerald Nye of North Dakota. For two years his Senate committee investigated the role played by American munitions makers in the war. The Nye committee proved that giant corporations such as DuPont reaped enormous profits from the war. Though there was no proof, Nye went further, charging that war profiteers had been responsible for intervention. Americans were then blaming businessmen and financiers for the Great Depression. It was easy for them to believe that the "merchants of death" were responsible for World War I as well.

COLLEGIATE PACIFISM

Reinforcing and reflecting the isolationist impulse was a mood of pacifism on the nation's college campuses. A poll conducted by a leading Ivy League institution indicated that 72 percent of those queried opposed compulsory military service during wartime. Princeton University students formed the Veterans of Future Wars, a parody of veterans organizations, and a cross-section of collegians signed pledges that they would never fight under any circumstances. Beginning in 1934 students and faculty staged one-day antiwar walkouts on campuses all across the country. This pacifist protest became an annual spring rite until war erupted in 1939.

LEGISLATING AGAINST WAR

Isolationist sentiment crystallized in a series of neutrality acts passed by Congress from 1935 through 1937. In 1935 Senator Nye and a colleague introduced legislation banning arms sales and loans to nations at war. They argued that if Congress could outlaw activities that had led to involvement in the Great War, America could avoid entanglement in future conflicts. The State Department protested that such legislation would hamstring American foreign policy, but President Roosevelt refused to intervene. In August 1935 Congress passed the ban on munitions sales and prohibited travel aboard belligerent vessels. In 1936 it outlawed loans, and in 1937 Congress made all three measures permanent.

Franklin Roosevelt's views during this period continue to be a source of debate. A number of his advisors argued that passage of the neutrality legislation would send a dangerous signal to would-be aggressors: They could do as they wished and the United States would acquiesce. The measures denied Washington even the option of bluff. Privately, Roosevelt expressed some of the same reservations. Following the outbreak of the Spanish Civil War in 1936 and the Sino-Japanese War in 1937, he publicly denounced "the epidemic of world lawlessness" and called for an international effort to "quarantine" the aggressors. At the same time, he signed the neutrality legislation without protest and declared during the 1936 presidential campaign his undying hatred for war. Whatever his private hopes for international cooperation against aggression, Franklin Roosevelt had no intention of challenging the powerful isolationist movement.

THE OUTBREAK OF WAR IN EUROPE: 1938–1939

It was not coincidental that Adolf Hitler launched his expansionist program in the spring of 1938. The Führer's stated goal was reincorporation of all German-speaking peoples into the Third Reich. After absorbing Austria, the Nazis turned their attention to the Sudetenland of Czechoslovakia, a strip of territory along that nation's western boundary added by the architects of Versailles to give the new state a defensible frontier. The 3.5 million Germans who inhabited the Sudetenland ached for reunion with the fatherland.

Throughout the summer and early fall, Hitler accused the Czech government of persecuting his countrymen, and he massed troops along Germany's eastern border. The besieged Czechs appealed to Britain and France, both of whom had a treaty commitment to defend the infant republic from aggression, to intervene. After intensive personal diplomacy, British Prime Minister Neville Chamberlain arranged a European summit conference at Munich in late September. Significantly, no representative of the Czech government was in attendance. There the Western democracies turned over the Sudetenland to Hitler in return for a promise not to seek an additional foot of European territory. Chamberlain returned home to be hailed by the British people as the prince of peace. Roosevelt cabled tersely, "Good man!"

Very quickly were the British and French disabused of their illusions concerning Hitler. In the spring of 1939 he broke his Munich pledge; German troops overran the remainder of Czechoslovakia, and the Führer annexed a state that had no historical or cultural relationship to Germany. That summer, Hitler signaled his next target by denouncing the Polish government for persecuting Germans incorporated into that state by the Treaty of Versailles.

Recognizing belatedly that Hitler was bent on nothing less than the domination of all of Europe, British diplomats tentatively approached the Soviet Union about an anti-German alliance. Convinced that the communists and Nazis, bitter enemies throughout the 1930s, could never make common cause, the United Kingdom proceeded at a leisurely pace. Unbeknownst to them, German and Soviet diplomats had been holding top secret, high-level talks. In August, the two nations shocked the world by publishing the Nazi–Soviet Nonaggression Pact. Its public provisions stated simply that the two nations promised never to make war on each other. Its cynical secret protocols stipulated that if Germany found itself at war with Poland, the Red Army would come to its aid. In the wake of victory, Germany would annex the eastern two-thirds of Poland and the Baltic state of Lithuania while the Soviet Union would be entitled to absorb the western one-third of Poland as well as Estonia and Latvia. To no one's surprise, Germany invaded Poland in September. When Hitler refused to respond to a twenty-four-hour ultimatum to withdraw, Britain and France declared war.

With the outbreak of hostilities, Roosevelt officially proclaimed neutrality as the law required, and the Neutrality Acts went into effect. No less than British and French leaders, the president recognized the threat posed by Germany as the events of 1939 unfolded. During that fateful summer he sounded out Congress about modifying the arms embargo measure to allow the United States to help bolster those who stood in Hitler's path. He could not even get past the Senate leadership. In November, following the outbreak of war, however, the president called Congress into special session and persuaded it to substitute cash-and-carry for the compulsory ban on arms sales. Under the proposed regulations, belligerents could purchase arms in the United States if they paid cash and carried the goods in their own ships. Evenhanded in outward appearance, the proposal would aid the Allies, as Britain, France, and the host of smaller countries that sided with it were called, because the Royal

Navy controlled the surface of the Atlantic. Public opinion strongly supported the president, and Congress passed the legislation by wide margins.

AMERICAN RESPONSE
TO THE EUROPEAN WAR: 1939–1941

Though President Roosevelt and most Americans sympathized with those fighting the Axis—the name given to the coalition of Germany, Italy, and Japan after those three powers signed an anti-comintern pact in 1937—it would be two years before the United States entered the war. During that period, however, America moved from a state of neutrality to nonbelligerency (a non-fighting ally of the anti-Axis powers) to a state of undeclared war with Germany in the winter of 1941. Roosevelt was determined to move carefully. He understood that Germany in particular posed a mortal threat to America's vital interests, but he was determined not to lead a divided nation into what was sure to be a cataclysmic war.

ISOLATIONISM VS. INTERVENTIONISM

From 1939 through 1941, a debate raged within the United States between those who were convinced that the war in Europe had no bearing on the national interest and those who believed that America's very survival depended upon its indirect and, if necessary, direct participation in the war. In the fall of 1940 isolationists formed the America First Committee. Included in the America First movement were German and Irish Americans, conservative nationalists such as Republican Senator Robert A. Taft of Ohio, aviator Charles Lindbergh, and former president Herbert Hoover. Though isolationism was Midwest-centered and made up largely of business-oriented opponents of the New Deal, it included former progressives and elements of the extreme left.

Political insurgents such as Borah and William Langer of Minnesota joined with neo-Marxists such as Charles Beard to espouse the merchants of death thesis. Until Hitler invaded the Soviet Union in 1941, even the Communist party of the United States mouthed the isolationist line. America Firsters, as the isolationists were called, argued that the United States was safe and secure within the Western Hemisphere. They likened the Atlantic and Pacific unto two great moats and argued that the wars in Europe and the Far East were indigenous and perpetual.

Confronting the isolationists were the interventionists who organized their own mouthpiece, the Committee to Defend America by Aiding the Allies. Included in this group were Anglo- and Franco-Americans and those who could trace their origins to one or another of the nations victimized by the Axis powers. Ideologically, interventionists tended to be liberal New Dealers, and politically, they were generally Democratic, although members of the eastern, liberal wing of the Republican party supported all-out aid to the Allies. Because of lingering disillusionment with Wilsonian internationalism, the interventionists tended to downplay ideology and collective security. Instead, they emphasized that once the Axis overwhelmed contiguous areas, the fascist coalition would turn to the Western Hemisphere. In view of the airplane and modern warship, the Atlantic and Pacific were not moats but highways. It was better for the United States to act while it still had allies, argued William Allen White, the Kansas newspaper publisher who had founded the Committee to Defend America, than to wait and face the aggressors alone.

THE FALL OF FRANCE

Although the arguments put forward by the interventionists were compelling, events on the battlefield had a much greater effect on American opinion. Germany and the Soviet Union quickly gobbled up Poland, but for the next six months there was very little action. During this, the period of the "phony war," the combatants sat behind their respective fortifications and waited. Then in April 1940, the German Army seized Denmark and Norway. The following month Hitler unleashed his "blitzkrieg" (lightning war) against the French and British expeditionary force in France. Employing tanks, mobile infantry, and dive bombers in close coordination, the German Army pushed deep into northern France and drove a wedge between French and British forces. Three weeks after the British expeditionary force escaped across the English Channel from Dunkirk, France surrendered.

The fall of France had a dramatic impact on American opinion. As the Luftwaffe battered London and other British cities night after night, everyone anticipated a German invasion of the United Kingdom, an operation that most feared would succeed. Frightened by the crisis in Europe, Congress increased the defense budget from $2 billion to $10 billion. The president asked for and in September obtained Senate and House approval for a peacetime draft, the nation's first. Citing the international emergency, Roosevelt ran for an unprecedented third term in 1940. After he won, the president responded to Prime Minister Winston Churchill's plea for help in the Battle of the Atlantic. German submarines were sinking a large percentage of Allied freighters carrying goods purchased in the United States. In December 1940, by executive order Roosevelt transferred some fifty surplus destroyers to Great Britain in return for permission to build bases on eight British possessions in the Western Hemisphere. The destroyers-for-bases deal, he told isolationists, was just part of the effort to perfect the defenses to Fortress America.

THE LEND-LEASE BILL AND AMERICAN NONBELLIGERENCY

By the spring of 1941, the Roosevelt administration was no longer able to avoid a confrontation with the isolationists in Congress. Churchill, with whom Roosevelt had struck up an almost daily correspondence, wrote thanking the president and his countrymen for the opportunity to purchase the planes, bullets, and guns that were enabling Britain to hold its own against the Axis. Unfortunately, he reported, by the late summer his country would run out of gold and dollars with which to keep the life-giving flow of supplies going. The president and his advisors responded by asking Congress to pass the Lend-Lease Bill. Under this deceptively titled measure, the United States would "lend" or lease munitions, raw materials, machinery, and other items to those nations fighting aggression. Senator Taft remarked that lending bullets or food to someone was like lending chewing gum; you really did not want it back. His colleague, Senator Burton K. Wheeler, declared Lend-Lease to be the "administration's triple-A [Agricultural Adjustment Act] in foreign policy." It was designed to "plow under every fourth American boy." Nonetheless, following a vigorous debate, both houses of Congress passed Lend-Lease by wide margins. At that point, the United States became a nonfighting ally of those struggling against the Axis. Over the course of the war, the United States provided the British Empire with over $25 billion in Lend-Lease aid and billions more to other nations fighting against the Axis.

In the euphoria that followed enactment of the Lend-Lease program, many interventionists urged the president to cast caution to the winds and authorize U.S. naval vessels to escort Allied transports in the Atlantic and even to permit American merchant vessels to carry goods to and from Europe. Still fearful of outstripping public opinion, however, Roosevelt would only agree to authorize "neutrality patrols" in the western half of the Atlantic. Although Hitler had given his sub commanders strict orders not to attack American vessels, incidents were bound to occur. In September, a German U-boat fired on an American destroyer carrying supplies to GIs stationed in Iceland. President Roosevelt went on a national radio hookup, angrily denounced this "unprovoked" attack, and issued his "shoot-on-sight order." Not until after the war did the American people learn that the U.S. destroyer had been following the German submarine, broadcasting its position to nearby British warships.

UNDECLARED WAR

On October 17, 1941, a German submarine damaged the U.S. destroyer *Kearny*; ten days later, another U-boat torpedoed and sank the *Reuben James*, killing more than one hundred American seamen. When in November Congress acceded to the administration's request to remove the "carry" from cash-and-carry, and American destroyers began convoying U.S. and British warships, the United States and Germany found themselves involved in an undeclared naval war.

Step by careful step Franklin Roosevelt had moved the United States from a status of neutrality to nonbelligerency to undeclared war. Interventionists accused him of being too timorous, isolationists of deceitfully leading the nation to the brink of a war that had no bearing upon its interests. Though a formal declaration of war with Germany seemed unavoidable by December 1941,

Roosevelt, remembering that a poll taken in September indicated that 80 percent of the American people wanted to stay out of the war, was loath to take that final step. Events in the Pacific took the matter out of his hands.

JAPANESE EXPANSION AND THE COLLAPSE OF THE OPEN DOOR

The outbreak of war in Europe had proved to be a great boon to Japanese expansionists. Suddenly, Britain, France, the Netherlands, and Belgium were removed from the balance of power. Following the outbreak of the Sino-Japanese War in 1937, Japan had managed to capture much of coastal China, but Jiang Jieshi (Chiang Kai Shek) and his armies retreated to the vast interior and managed to hold their enemies at bay. Meanwhile, the militarists in Tokyo turned their attention to the European colonies in the East Indies and Southeast Asia, territories that were rich in rubber, tin, and petroleum and that had been rendered defenseless by the war in Europe.

In the summer of 1940, the Roosevelt administration attempted to use economic leverage to contain Japanese expansion. That nation's economy was heavily dependent upon the United States for petroleum, scrap iron, and steel. The State Department announced a licensing and quota system and prohibited the export of high-octane aviation fuel altogether.

Unintimidated by these partial sanctions or perhaps provoked by them, the Japanese pressured the government of occupied France, located in the city of Vichy, to permit occupation of northern Indochina. Tokyo claimed the move was necessary to cut off supplies from India and Burma to Jiang Jieshi, but Britons and Americans feared that this was the first step toward converting the area into a Japanese colony. Under the thumb of Hitler, who was hoping for Japanese cooperation in a planned attack on the Soviet Union, the Vichy government gave its permission. Then on September 27, 1940, Germany, Japan, and Italy signed the Tripartite Pact pledging that if a nation not then at war with one of the signatories entered the fray, the other two would declare war on it. The pact served to link Japan with Nazism and fascism for the first time in the minds of many Americans, making it part of a worldwide totalitarian threat.

The failure of diplomacy in the spring of 1941 set the stage for the surprise attack on Pearl Harbor. In an effort to end U.S. economic sanctions and to obtain American approval for a Japanese sphere of interest in the Pacific, Tokyo ordered its ambassador, Admiral Kichisaburo Nomura, to enter into negotiations with Secretary of State Cordell Hull. The positions taken by the two men proved irreconcilable. While Nomura insisted that the United States accord his nation a free hand in the Far East, Hull ended each session with a moral lecture on the evils of aggression. In June, the talks were broken off.

JAPAN MOVES SOUTHWARD

On June 22, 1941, Germany disavowed the Nazi-Soviet Nonaggression Treaty and invaded the Soviet Union. Hitler's latest move again benefitted Japan, which had been constrained in its expansionist plans by the presence of an uncommitted Soviet Union to its north. Though Berlin wanted Japan to join in the attack on the seat of world communism, Tokyo decided to move south. In July, Japanese troops invaded southern Indochina. The Roosevelt administration learned of Japan's move even before it had been made. Using a decoding device known as MAGIC, U.S. intelligence had broken the Japanese diplomatic-military code in the spring. Washington responded to the occupation of southern Indochina by slapping a total embargo on trade with Japan on July 25 and seizing Japanese assets in the United States. At this point Japan had approximately a twelve-month supply of petroleum. If it did not secure new sources before the end of that period, its economy and war machine would grind to a halt.

In October General Hideki Tojo, an army militant, became premier of Japan, and plans for further expansion into the East Indies and war with the United States got underway. To mask war preparations Japan sent yet another envoy to Washington to negotiate. The two governments traded proposals that essentially restated the positions that Hull and Nomura had taken in the spring. MAGIC enabled American diplomats to evaluate Japan's proposals and declare them unacceptable even before they were presented by Japanese diplomats in Washington. Roosevelt's military advisors pled with him to avoid steps that would lead to war. They needed time to shore up woefully inadequate defenses in the Philippines. Secretary of State Hull refused to compromise, however, and on November 26 he sent a stiff ten-point reply that called for, among other things, an immediate Japanese withdrawal from China.

ATTACK ON PEARL HARBOR

Unbeknownst to U.S. intelligence—in spite of MAGIC—a huge Japanese task force had left its base in the Kuril Islands on November 25 headed for Pearl Harbor. As the Japanese battle group, shrouded in secrecy, steamed toward its objective shrouded in secrecy, Japanese diplomats delivered their country's reply to Hull's ultimatum on December 6. Naval intelligence actually decoded the fourteen-point reply faster than the clerks in the Japanese Embassy. When he read Japan's rejection of Hull's terms, Roosevelt declared, "This means war!" On the seventh, war warning messages were sent to American outposts in the Pacific, but it was too late. On the morning of December 7, 1941, Japanese dive-bombers and mini-subs caught the U.S. Pacific fleet bottled up within Pearl Harbor. The surprise attack sank or crippled eight battleships. In one brilliant tactical stroke, the Japanese had momentarily destroyed American naval power in the Pacific.

The Japanese attack on Pearl Harbor, an operation which took the lives of twenty-four hundred American personnel, unified the nation in behalf of war as

The Japanese achieved complete surprise at Pearl Harbor, but the attack united the American people and helped ensure the eventual defeat of the Axis. Here U.S. battleships and cruisers take direct hits.

nothing else could have done. Certain that if the Japanese attacked U.S. territory, it would be the Philippines, the Roosevelt administration and its commanders in the Pacific had been taken unaware. Nevertheless, the American people rallied behind their government. Addressing a joint session of Congress the following day, the president declared December 7 "a date which will live in infamy" and asked for a declaration of war. With only one dissenting vote, both houses acceded. On December 11 Germany and Italy declared war on the United States. The debate between isolationists and interventionists was at long last moot.

THE U.S. ENTERS THE WAR

AXIS DOMINATION

When the United States entered the war, the Allied cause was desperate. Hitler and Mussolini controlled the entire continent of Europe (see Figure 21-1).

FIGURE 21–1

The Height of German Expansion, 1938–1942

German warplanes continued their nightly assault on British cities to the west, while on the eastern front the Wehrmacht penetrated deep into the Ukraine and Caucasus in the spring of 1942. In North Africa, General Erwin Rommel's Afrika Korps had pushed the British eastward into Egypt to the point where he was in a position to threaten the Suez Canal.

The situation was equally as grim in the Far East. Pearl Harbor was just a cover for Japanese amphibious landings in Southeast Asia and the East Indies. American forces in the Philippines under General Douglas MacArthur attempted to block the Japanese advance but were quickly overwhelmed. After occupying Malaya and the Dutch East Indies, Japanese forces invaded New Guinea and Burma, pushing undermanned and ill-equipped British units back all along the front. From these vantage points, they were in a position to threaten India and Australia. The military void created by the destruction of the U.S. Pacific fleet allowed Japan to perfect its system of island defenses in the central Pacific.

RESURGENCE OF THE ALLIES

In late 1942 and early 1943, however, the Allies began to turn the tide by winning a series of major battles. Because of the attack on Pearl Harbor most Americans favored a Pacific-first strategy. The tens of thousands of volunteers who flocked to enlistment booths believed that they would be sent west to avenge the "day of infamy." The U.S. Navy did, in fact, favor a Pacific-first strategy, but to Britain's great relief, President Roosevelt and his chief of staff, General George Marshall, decided to continue with the Europe-first approach that had prevailed since the passage of Lend-Lease. In the spring of 1942 Soviet Foreign Minister Vyacheslav Molotov traveled to Washington to appeal to President Roosevelt to open a second front in Europe at once. The Russians were then being driven out of the Ukraine and Caucasus by 3.3 million German troops. To the subsequent dismay of his military chiefs, Roosevelt promised that Allied troops would engage the Germans and Italians in the west before the year was out. In November 1942, American soldiers splashed ashore in Tunisia and Algiers. After a brief flurry of fighting the Vichyite soldiers occupying these North African territories laid down their arms. In the months that followed, British Field Marshall Sir Bernard Montgomery halted Field Marshall Erwin Rommel's advance on the Suez Canal. Following his defeat at El Alamein, the "Desert Fox," as Rommel was called, moved westward toward Tunisia. American forces under General George S. Patton survived a sharp defeat at Kasserine Pass in Tunisia and subsequently linked up with Montgomery. Caught between the Americans and British, the last German soldiers in North Africa surrendered in May 1943.

THE BATTLE OF STALINGRAD

While the Allies were clearing North Africa of Germans one of the most important battles of the war was raging on the eastern front. With the Germans preparing to advance into Central Asia, the Red Army decided to make its stand at Stalingrad. From August through November 1942, the German Sixth Army laid siege to the city. Tens of thousands of noncombatants perished, but the Soviets refused to give way. As the bitter Russian winter descended on the battle, the Red Army took the offensive. On February 2, 1943, the Germans, having lost 140,000 men, surrendered. Though much remained to be done, the tide of battle had turned in the east.

THE SECOND FRONT ISSUE

Following the Battle of Stalingrad, the Russians looked expectantly to the west, hoping for an Anglo-American assault on occupied Europe. Although plans for a direct attack across the English Channel had gotten underway in 1942, British and American leaders continued to disagree over the wisdom of the plan. Winston Churchill and most of his military advisors preferred a prolonged bombing campaign, economic strangulation, and attacks along the southern periphery of Axis-controlled Europe, what the prime minister referred to as the enemy's "soft underbelly." Though committed to a cross-channel invasion, Roosevelt and his advisors compromised. In July 1943, American and British troops invaded Sicily, the large island lying off the tip of the Italian boot. As Patton and Montgomery's troops swept across Sicily, anti-Axis Italians overthrew Mussolini, and a new government under General Pietro Badoglio sued for peace. On September 8 Italy surrendered unconditionally, but German troops occupied the north, freed Mussolini from prison, and installed him as head of a puppet regime. Hours after Italy's surrender, Allied troops landed at Salerno and began their slow, costly advance toward Rome. Not until May 1944 did American forces under General Mark Clark break through German defenses. The climactic battle of that campaign, the struggle for the mountaintop abbey-fortress of Monte Cassino, was one of the bloodiest of the war. With the capture of Rome on June 4, 1944, the stage was at last set for Operation Overlord, the Allied cross-channel invasion.

THE STRUGGLE FOR THE PACIFIC

As Eisenhower's forces closed in on the Germans, American sailors and marines were struggling to turn the tide in the Pacific. Relying on MAGIC, U.S. intelligence learned that a Japanese naval task force intended to seize Port Moresby on the southern tip of the island of New Guinea. If that campaign were successful, the outer defenses of Australia would have been breached. The U.S. aircraft carriers *Lexington* and *Yorktown* intercepted the Japanese fleet assigned to attack Port Moresby. In a furious air-to-ship battle the Americans lost the *Lexington*, but the Japanese also lost a carrier and more important, called off their raid on Port Moresby. In that sense, the Battle of the Coral Sea, as it was known, was an Allied victory.

The struggle for control of the Pacific would be determined by the aircraft carrier, floating air bases from which the combatants could project their power hundreds of miles. Coral Sea stopped the Japanese advance to the south, but it was the Battle of Midway in June 1942 that turned the tide of war. At the same time that Admiral Yamamoto dispatched a flotilla to capture Port Moresby, he sent another, larger fleet to attack and seize Midway Island, a vantage point from which the Japanese could once again threaten Hawaii. Again prewarned by MAGIC, the American carriers, or "flattops," lay in wait northeast of Midway. After hours of furious engagement, an attack squadron of thirty-seven

American dive-bombers broke through the clouds and caught four Japanese carriers with their planes on deck where they were being refueled and rearmed. Without air cover and their decks littered with fuel and bombs, the Japanese vessels were perfect targets. U.S. bombs and bullets ignited huge explosions killing thousands and sinking three Japanese aircraft carriers immediately. A fourth went under shortly thereafter. The Battle of Midway crippled the Japanese carrier fleet and threatened its air superiority in the Pacific. Between 1942 and 1944 Japan could build and launch only four new carriers; American shipyards produced fourteen.

MOBILIZING THE WAR EFFORT

As Admiral Yamamoto had predicted, the war was won on the home front. Altogether American industry turned out more than twice as many goods during the war than the German and Japanese economies combined. The totals for 1942 alone were 8 million tons of shipping, forty-five thousand tanks, and sixty thousand planes. Plants that had lain idle during the depression suddenly were running at full capacity. To meet wartime demands, industrialist Henry Ford built the huge Willow Run plant in Michigan which at the height of its output employed forty-two thousand workers and turned out a B-24 bomber every hour. Henry Kaiser's California shipyard was able to lower the time required for the construction of a merchant vessel from 105 to fourteen days. Though the situation on the battlefield remained bleak, it was clear by the end of the first year of the war that American industry could produce planes, tanks, and guns at a much faster clip than the Axis could destroy them.

Nor was manpower a problem. By the time of the Japanese attack on Pearl Harbor, the draft had been in effect for almost a year. At that point Congress extended the term of military service to cover the duration of the war. Eventually 15 million American men and women would serve in the armed forces; that still left some 60 million adults to operate the nation's factories and farms. Indeed, the war had the unintended effect of ending the depression, producing full employment, and bringing into the workforce groups previously marginalized, namely women, African Americans, and Hispanic Americans.

INFLUENCE ON WOMEN AND MINORITY GROUPS

Rosie the Riveter

World War II forced Americans to change their attitudes toward gender roles in the workplace. In the first place, women constituted a significant portion of the armed forces. Approximately two hundred thousand women enlisted into the Women's Army Corps (WAC) and its naval equivalent, Women Accepted for Volunteer Emergency Service (WAVES). The Marines, Coast Guard, and other branches enlisted women as well, though in lesser numbers. In the second

Women played a major role on the home front, contributing to an Allied victory and raising their level of expectations. Here female riveters labor in a defense plant.

place, female Americans took up the slack in the civilian workforce created by the enlistment and drafting of millions of men and the expansion of industry. Using Rosie the Riveter, an attractive model dressed in overalls, as a come-on, the federal government encouraged women to abandon hearth and children and become sheet metal workers, millers, welders, lumberjacks, machinists, and stevedores. The number of women employed in the workforce increased from 14 million in 1940 to 19 million in 1945. By 1944 a third of all American females were employed outside the home. Although women continued to be paid less than men for the same work, the average paycheck for female workers increased during World War II by 50 percent. The chance to "get out of the kitchen" and earn money gave American women a sense of independence that they would be loath to give up after the war.

African Americans and World War II

At the outset of hostilities African-American leaders demanded that their people be given a prominent role in the war effort and that there be no discrimination in either the military or the defense effort. Eventually, more than a million black Americans served in the armed forces but nearly all were enlisted men who served under white officers. Secretary of the Navy Frank Knox typified the attitude of the white power structure when he defended his decision to bar blacks from the ranks of petty officers by declaring that there was no way that "men of the colored race" could maintain discipline among "men of the white race." African-American soldiers were much less likely to see combat than their white counterparts. The army and even more so the navy relegated them to menial jobs. There were some gains. In 1940 officer candidate schools were desegregated except for the Air Force. At Tuskegee Institute in Alabama a separate flight school turned out nearly six hundred black flyers, many of whom went on to establish distinguished combat records.

In February 1941 A. Philip Randolph, the aggressive head of the Brotherhood of Sleeping Car Porters, threatened a massive march on Washington unless President Roosevelt issued a comprehensive executive order banning discrimination in the defense industry and in the armed forces. Fearing internal discord at a time when the country was threatened with war, the administration persuaded Randolph to call off his march in return for an executive order requiring nondiscrimination clauses in all defense contracts and creating a Fair Employment Practices Committee to police the private sector. These measures did have some impact. The number of African Americans working for the federal government jumped from sixty thousand to two hundred thousand by war's end. Eventually some 2 million blacks were employed in war-related industries.

The lure of industrial employment drew African Americans out of the South by the hundreds of thousands. Specifically, between 1940 and 1950 three hundred thousand migrated to the West, and five hundred thousand each to the Midwest and Northeast. This dramatic population shift created severe racial tensions in a number of urban areas and helped convert civil rights into a national rather than a purely regional issue. As white and black war workers competed for scarce housing and scarcer goods, resentments mounted. On a hot Sunday evening in the summer of 1943, black and white bathers traded insults at the Belle Island recreation park in Detroit. The next day a full-scale race riot erupted. For twenty-four hours absolute mayhem reigned. When the National Guard finally intervened, twenty-three blacks and nine whites lay dead. Later in the year only the personal intervention of Mayor Fiorello LaGuardia prevented a similar outburst in Harlem.

Whites sensed correctly that African Americans intended to use the war, a crusade for freedom and democracy according to government propaganda, to permanently knock down racial barriers in the workplace, the voting booth, and public facilities. Participation in the military and expanded economic opportunity generated a new sense of confidence and militancy in African Americans. NAACP membership leaped from fifty thousand to four hundred and fifty thousand. In 1944 in *Smith v. Allwright* the Supreme Court ruled Texas' white primary unconstitutional. The high court found that the

Democratic party primaries were part of the electoral process opened up to blacks by the Fifteenth Amendment. Thus did the United States take the first great step toward enfranchising its colored minorities.

Hispanic Americans and World War II

Hispanic Americans experienced some of the same upward social and economic mobility during the war that African Americans did. Tens of thousands of Americans of Mexican descent left rural areas in California, Texas, and New Mexico for jobs in the cities in the aircraft and petroleum industries. Wages were lower than those paid to whites, and unions sometimes resisted penetration of the workforce by this new group, but Hispanic Americans benefitted nonetheless. Though there was not strict segregation in the armed forces, many Chicanos served in the Eighty-eighth Division, the highly decorated "Blue Devils" who won such acclaim in the Italian campaign. Aside from the "Zoot-Suit" riots of 1943 in which white sailors attacked Mexican-American youths in Los Angeles dressed in their distinctive long jackets and baggy pants, white racism directed toward Hispanics was generally economic and social rather than physical.

Persecution of the Nisei

The ethnic group that fared the worst during World War II—largely as a result of World War II—was Japanese Americans. The war with Japan brought smoldering antioriental sentiment on the West Coast out into the open. The consensus there and elsewhere was that Issei (naturalized Americans born in Japan) and Nisei (persons of Japanese ancestry born in the United States) were loyal to the emperor and that all were potential spies and saboteurs. In response to these exaggerated fears, President Roosevelt issued orders creating War Relocation Camps. Altogether 120,000 Japanese Americans were forcibly rounded up and sent to ten hastily built camps in seven western states. They were forced to abandon their homes and sell their businesses at cut-rate prices. In the camps the Issei and Nisei lived in tar paper shacks surrounded by barbed wire and armed guards.

Victims of the War Relocation Camps filed suit in federal court claiming that the government was violating their civil liberties. In 1944 a divided Supreme Court ruled that incarceration of Japanese Americans was justified in wartime on grounds of national security. Beginning in 1943 individuals could escape the camps by swearing an oath of allegiance to the United States and taking a job away from the West Coast. During the two years that followed thirty-five thousand internees left the camps, but at war's end some five thousand Japanese Americans returned to Japan. The detention centers, monuments to the hypocrisy of a nation claiming to be fighting for democracy and the rule of law, remained open until March 1946, and not until 1983 did the government admit its mistake.

THE DEMOGRAPHICS OF WAR

Ethnic Americans of color were not the only group compelled by the war to pull up stakes and move. Tens of thousands of young men left home for training camps and then service overseas. Some 9 million Americans moved to cities not only in the Northeast and Midwest but the West Coast and Gulf Coast as well to work in the defense industry. Cities in California, Texas, Alabama, and Florida became boomtowns as shipyards, aircraft factories, and munitions plants fed their economies. The population of California alone grew by 2 million during the war. This mass migration resulted in fattened paychecks but considerable discomfort as well. The country experienced a severe housing shortage. Entire families were forced to live in a single boardinghouse room. Prefabricated and trailer houses served as uncomfortable abodes for tens of thousands of defense workers and their families.

WORLD WAR II AND THE AMERICAN ECONOMY

The necessities of war led to massive intervention by the federal government into the domestic economy. The state of emergency proclaimed in 1941 gave the president emergency powers to allocate manpower and resources. To convert American industry to produce for war, Roosevelt created in 1942 the War Production Board (WPB) with Donald Nelson as its head. The affable Nelson, a former Sears, Roebuck executive, quickly found himself bypassed by the military who preferred to deal directly with defense contractors. To the ire of the public, the WPB began approving lucrative cost-plus contracts to produce scarce items and huge tax breaks through rapid depreciation for businesses building new plants. Equally unpopular was the Office of Price Administration whose task it was to control inflation. Military demands created shortages in the domestic economy from sugar and coffee to rubber and gasoline. New automobiles were unobtainable. The government began rationing gasoline in 1943. Not all was confusion and waste, though. During the war the federal government created fifty-one plants to manufacture synthetic rubber. The Office of Scientific Research and Development employed thousands of scientists who were responsible for developing such crucial weapons as the proximity fuse, the bazooka, the high-altitude bomb sight, radar, and sonar.

Massive wartime expenditures by the federal government rolled through the economy creating consolidation and expansion in the private sector and prosperity up and down the socioeconomic scale. The gross national product doubled from 1940 to 1945. The biggest businesses were most efficient and hence able to acquire the most government contracts, thus growing bigger. In 1942 alone three hundred thousand concerns went under in the United States. Nevertheless, despite tax incentives and huge profits earned during the war, the rich did not grow disproportionately richer. Excess profit taxes and a 94 percent rate on the very wealthy limited income growth for the rich to 20 percent. For the first time in the twentieth century, the lowest quarter of wage earners gained ground at a faster rate than the upper quarter.

"DR. WIN-THE-WAR": THE 1944 ELECTIONS

World War II produced a decisive shift to the right in domestic politics. Widespread prosperity did away with the economic unrest and class hostility that underlay much of the New Deal. The electorate became increasingly aggravated over government intrusion into their lives. Price controls, rationing, and a hundred other irritations combined to create a "throw the rascals out" mentality. Republicans also benefitted from low voter turnout due to absent servicemen and the inability of newly displaced workers to vote. As a result, in 1942 the Republicans won forty-four seats in the Senate, nine in the House, and captured the governorships of California and New York. GOP legislators joined with conservative southern Democrats to turn the country to the right. In 1943 alone Congress abolished the Works Projects Administration, the Civilian Conservation Corps, and the National Youth Administration.

The conservative turn in American politics spelled troubled for organized labor. Unions made significant gains during the war, but strikes in 1943 and 1944 by the United Mine Workers with the irascible John L. Lewis at their head prompted Congress to pass the Smith-Connally War Labor Disputes Act. That measure authorized the president to seize plants essential to the war effort, required unionwide votes before strikes, and prohibited unions from making political contributions. In 1944 Florida and Arkansas passed so-called "right-to-work" laws which were emulated by a number of other states in the years to follow.

Ever sensitive to the shifting tides of public opinion, Franklin Roosevelt announced that "Dr. New Deal" had given way to "Dr. Win-the-War." To better prepare himself and the Democratic party for the 1944 presidential contest in which he would be competing for an unprecedented fourth term, Roosevelt dumped his liberal vice president, Henry Wallace, in favor of the more conventional, conservative senator from Missouri, Harry S Truman.

To challenge Roosevelt, the Republicans picked New York Governor Thomas E. Dewey, who had made his name in politics as a crime-fighting prosecuting attorney. Dewey represented the more liberal, internationalist wing of the party, and he made it clear that if he were elected, there would be no reversion to isolationism. In domestic policy the GOP candidate also adopted a me-too approach. American voters were not impressed. Roosevelt swamped Dewey in the electoral college by a vote of 432 to 99. The electoral vote was closer; the president's margin of 3.6 million was the smallest of his four elections.

CLOSING THE CIRCLE IN THE PACIFIC

Meanwhile, in the Pacific American forces had begun the long, arduous process of rooting the Japanese out of their strongholds. The first task was to pry loose the imperial army from its positions on the north coast of New Guinea. U.S. Army and Marine units under General MacArthur, fighting in the stifling, mosquito-infested jungles that comprised most of the South Pacific, had secured a foothold on the eastern coast of New Guinea by January 1943. At that point, the Combined Chiefs had to decide on a grand strategy for the Pacific. MacArthur wanted to advance from his positions on New Guinea and retake the Philippines from which he had been forced so ignominiously a year earlier. Admiral Chester Nimitz, however, wanted to use naval and air power to advance directly across the Pacific taking key Japanese-held islands and finally besieging Japan itself. The military chiefs decided to combine the approaches, authorizing MacArthur to proceed with his assault on the Philippines while Nimitz was to advance across the central Pacific thus protecting MacArthur's northern flank.

After an American task force destroyed eight Japanese troop ships and ten of the war vessels guarding them, Tokyo decided that it was too risky to try to reinforce its island outposts. This in turn made it possible for Nimitz to adopt the tactic of "leapfrogging" whereby American forces attacked and overwhelmed certain island fortresses but bypassed others leaving them isolated and useless. Nimitz' island-hopping campaign began in the fall of 1943 with Tarawa in the Gilbert Islands. In one of the fiercest battles of the war nearly one thousand marines lost their lives rooting out four thousand Japanese, almost all of whom fought to the death. From bases on the Gilberts, planes from the Seventh Air Force were able to attack Japanese positions in the Marshall Islands to the north. In June 1944, American forces were able to secure control of the Marianas, the last great island chain guarding the approaches to Japan. In the Battle of the Philippine Sea, fought on June 19 and 20, 1944, U.S. ships and planes destroyed three more Japanese carriers and nearly three hundred enemy aircraft. From the Marianas, B-17 bombers were at last able to launch attacks on the home islands themselves.

As American Marines struggled to take the Marianas, another U.S. task force assaulted the Philippines. On October 20, 1944, General Douglas MacArthur splashed ashore on the island of Leyte in the Philippines, announcing dramatically to assembled journalists: "People of the Philippines: I have returned." Meanwhile, the Japanese high command, desperate to avoid being cut off from vital supplies in Southeast Asia, ordered three separate battle fleets to converge on Leyte. What ensued beginning on October 25 was the largest naval battle in history. The United States won a decisive victory, destroying most of what remained of Japanese sea power. From that point on, Japan was forced to rely on "Kamikaze," or suicide air force units, for strategic defense. Kamikaze pilots inflicted serious damage but were not able to stop the Allied juggernaut. By the end of the year General MacArthur had reconquered the Philippines, and early in 1945 U.S. Marines paid a huge price in casualties but managed to capture the southern islands of Okinawa and Iwo Jima. The stage was set at last for the final battle.

OPERATION OVERLORD: THE WAR IN EUROPE

While U.S. Marines island-hopped their way across the Pacific, American, British, and Canadian planners were preparing for an assault on Fortress Europe, as the German-occupied west was referred to in the press. Because the United States was supplying the major portion of the men and materiel for the Allied war effort in the Western European and Pacific theaters by 1943, it called the strategic shots. Churchill's pleas for continued attacks on the periphery of Europe were thrust aside. Chief of Staff George C. Marshall and the supreme Allied commander in Europe, Dwight Eisenhower, were free to proceed with their plans for a cross-channel invasion. For two years in Great Britain, the Americans, British, and Canadians amassed and trained 3 million troops, stockpiled millions of tons of equipment, and assembled an armada of landing craft in Great Britain in preparation for Operation Overlord. On June 6, 1944, the Allies struck, landing on the Normandy coast, chosen because it possessed no natural harbor sites and was therefore relatively lightly defended. The Allied armada that Eisenhower had assembled was the largest the world had ever seen. Overlord's 6,483 ships spewed forth 176,000 men and fifteen hundred tanks. The ferocity of the fighting varied as American forces splashed ashore on Utah and Omaha beaches and the British and Canadians landed at Gold, Juno, and Sword. At Omaha the American First Division suffered heavy casualties. The twelve thousand Allied planes assigned to Overlord quickly overwhelmed the 169 German fighters available to defend Normandy. During the night, three divisions parachuted down behind German lines. As British, American, and Canadian troops advanced inland from the beaches, the two forces linked up. A week later more than three hundred thousand troops were pushing the Germans back all along an expanding front. On August 25, Paris surrendered, and by September, Allied troops had reached the Rhine River. At this point General Eisenhower ordered a halt so that coalition troops could rest and resupply. Gasoline was in especially short supply. In December, Hitler decided to take advantage of the pause, and he threw most of his remaining tank divisions into a daring counter-attack. Taking advantage of bad weather which denied the Allies air cover, German armor and infantry blasted through a weak point in Eisenhower's lines in the Ardennes forest. Hitler hoped to thrust all the way to the coast, thereby cutting off and isolating up to a third of the Allied army. The German offensive created a huge bulge in the Allied line, hence the name Battle of the Bulge. The 101st Airborne Division dug in, however, and held out at the crucial crossroads town of Bastogne in Belgium. Clearing skies finally permitted the air cover necessary for Eisenhower to take the offensive. The Battle of the Bulge had halted the Allied advance but it had greatly damaged the German military's ability to defend German soil.

VICTORY IN EUROPE

The end of the war in Europe came quickly if not easily. The Russians launched a massive offensive in mid-January and swept across the Oder River toward

FIGURE 21–2

Allied Advances and the Collapse of German Power

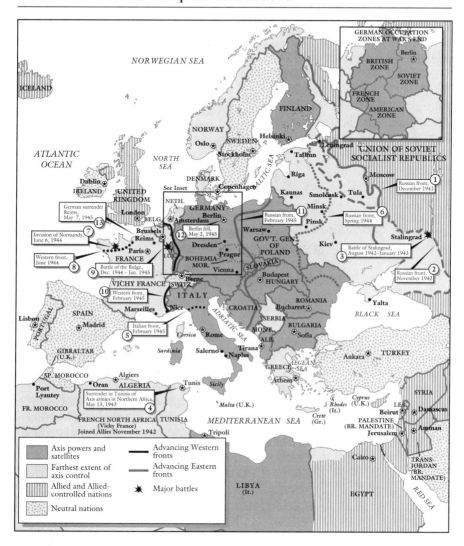

Berlin. American troops under the command of General Omar Bradley crossed the Remagen Bridge on the Rhine on March 7, 1945. In his capacity as supreme commander, General Eisenhower overruled the British, who wanted to occupy Berlin before the Russians. Instead, the Western Allies advanced across a broad front, capturing the Ruhr Valley, the industrial heart of Germany, and meeting the Russians at the Elbe. With the Red Army advancing on the outskirts of Berlin, Adolf Hitler committed suicide on April 7. A week later, General Eisenhower accepted the unconditional surrender of all German forces (see Figure 21-2).

THE HOLOCAUST

As American, British, and Canadian soldiers moved across Germany, the Allies' worst fears about the fate of Europe's Jews were confirmed. Anti-Semitism was one of the guiding principles of National Socialism, and in 1941 Nazi leaders set in motion the "final solution" to what they perceived to be the Jewish problem. During the next four years German intelligence agents, secret police, and SS troops rounded up millions of Jews, and forced them into concentration camps in which inmates—men, women, and children—were systematically starved, beaten, and gassed. Eventually 6 million Jews perished in Auschwitz, Buchenwald, and dozens of other camps. The Holocaust consumed, in addition, four million others, including gypsies, homosexuals, and the mentally ill. "We are told that the American soldier does not know what he is fighting for," declared General Dwight David Eisenhower, supreme commander of Allied forces. "Now at least he will know what he is fighting against."

THE YALTA CONFERENCE

As the war progressed, it became evident that the Big Three—the United States, Great Britain, and the Soviet Union—had very different expectations concerning the world that would emerge after the Axis had been defeated. Winston Churchill and his advisors were practitioners of the art of balance-of-power politics. They insisted that the fate of Europe would continue to determine the fate of the world. Churchill looked forward to the quick rehabilitation of France, Germany, and Italy to prevent an ambitious imperial power, namely the Soviet Union, from being able to dominate the continent.

Indeed, the British leader favored an Allied thrust up through the Balkans to block the advance of the Red Army into Central Europe. For his part, Stalin believed that because his country had borne the brunt of the war in Europe, it ought to be free to carve out a sphere of interest in Eastern Europe and the Near East. Specifically, the Soviet Union was determined to establish communist regimes throughout Eastern and Central Europe. These would serve as buffers protecting Russia from ever being attacked again by would-be Napoleons or Hitlers. They could also be used as springboards for spreading Marxism-Leninism.

Franklin Roosevelt originally favored the "Four Policemen" concept in which the United States, Britain, the Soviet Union, and China would rule their respective regions, promoting democracy and defeating aggression. In 1944, he embraced Wilsonian internationalism, although his version of the League of Nations would be dominated by the victorious powers just as surely as would have been the world of the Four Policemen. Roosevelt, moreover, favored postponing discussions concerning boundaries, reparations, and spheres of influence for as long as possible lest the Grand Alliance be rent asunder. By the end of 1944, this was no longer possible.

When it became clear in early 1945 that Nazi Germany's defeat was only months away, Roosevelt finally agreed to a full-dress diplomatic conference to discuss the shape of the postwar world. Accordingly, the Big Three gathered at the Crimean resort of Yalta in late February. At this point, the Red Army was within fifty miles of Berlin. With much of Eastern Europe within his grasp, Stalin was in a strong bargaining position. In the Declaration of Liberated Europe, each of the Big Three promised to hold free elections in their zones of occupation as soon as possible, but they provided no means of enforcement. Germany was divided into zones of occupation, with the Russians in control of the eastern third, the British the northwestern third, and the Americans the southwestern third. France was given control of a small area in the west. Stalin promised to enter the war against Japan as soon as Germany surrendered. In return, Roosevelt assured the Soviet leader that his country would receive the Kuril Islands, Outer Mongolia, and portions of Manchuria in any peace settlement. The president was being told at the time that Russian participation was crucial. There were 2 million Japanese soldiers in the home islands and another 1.5 million in Manchuria. The final offensive would be a long, bloody affair (see Figure 21-3).

VICTORY IN THE PACIFIC

Indeed, the United States approached the final stages of the Pacific war with apprehensive determination. Following the Battle of Midway, American strategists had fashioned a plan for victory whereby Douglas MacArthur, based in New Guinea, would advance on the Philippines while Admiral Chester Nimitz striking out from Hawaii, would move on the key Japanese islands in the Central Pacific. In 1944 Nimitz swept through the Gilbert, Caroline, and Marshall islands, establishing bases for further advance and building airstrips from which B-29s could begin their devastating bombardment of the Japanese home islands. Meanwhile, MacArthur landed on the island of Leyte in the Philippines on October 20, and by the end of the year Japanese-occupied Manila had fallen. In early 1945, U.S. marines captured the key southern Japanese islands of Okinawa and Iwo Jima. The stage was set for the final assault.

The fateful decisions surrounding the war in the Pacific were made not by Franklin Roosevelt, but by his vice president, Harry S Truman. The strain of fighting the Great Depression and World War II proved too much for Roosevelt's polio-ravaged body. He died suddenly on April 12 at his retreat at Warm Springs, Georgia. Harry Truman actually had three options available to him for ending the war in the Pacific. The first involved a conventional invasion with an American force led by MacArthur moving up from the south and a combined Anglo-American army descending toward Japan from the Aleutians. D-Day was set for November. Estimates were that the final campaign would last a year and cost a minimum of one hundred thousand casualties. The second, urged upon Truman by a group of diplomats, was to offer Japan a negotiated settlement. That nation was suffering terribly from Allied bombing and would surely surrender, they argued, if assured that it could retain the institution of emperor. At the Potsdam Conference, Truman and Clement Attlee, who had replaced Churchill as prime minister, urged Japan to surrender, but promised no concessions in return.

FIGURE 21–3

The Pacific Theater

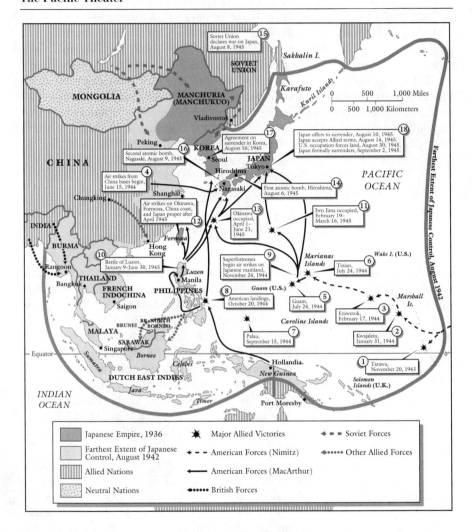

THE DECISION TO USE THE BOMB

The third alternative for ending the war in the Pacific was to shock Japan into surrendering through use of an atomic bomb. Early in the war Roosevelt had authorized creation of the top secret Manhattan Project, a $2 billion crash program to split the atom and produce a nuclear explosive device before Hitler's scientists could.

Following dramatic breakthroughs at nuclear research laboratories in Oak Ridge, Tennessee, Hanford, Washington, and Los Alamos, New Mexico, U.S. atomic scientists set off an atomic reaction in the New Mexico desert on July 16, 1945. That first device produced a blinding fireball and a mushroom cloud that rose forty thousand feet in the sky. Informed of this success while at Potsdam,

Perhaps the most controversial decision of the war was to force Japan's
surrender with the atomic bomb. The awe-inspiring mushroom cloud rises
over Hiroshima.

President Truman ordered the Air Force to select suitable targets and use the bomb to bring the war against Japan to a close as quickly as possible.

On August 6 the *Enola Gay* dropped a single bomb on the military-industrial target of Hiroshima. At least sixty thousand died in the initial blast, but still Japan did not surrender. On August 8 the Soviet Union entered the war. The United States dropped a second bomb on the city of Nagasaki on August 9 with equally devastating effect. On August 14, Japan surrendered unconditionally.

Some historians would later charge that the United States had bombed Japan primarily to intimidate the Soviet Union with whom relations were rapidly deteriorating. But President Truman maintained that in view of Pearl Harbor, the American people would never have permitted a negotiated settlement, and that any weapon that saved the lives of U.S. servicemen deserved to be used.

During the twenty-five years following the end of World War II, historians struggled to identify and evaluate Franklin D. Roosevelt's role during the crucial months of 1941 when America was still nominally neutral and the Axis powers were expanding rapidly through Europe and Asia. Some portray the president as a farsighted leader who carefully led an isolationist nation into a realization of the mortal threat it faced and of America's commonality of interest with Great Britain. Others portray him as a foreign affairs novice who was swept along by events and who, by acting earlier and more decisively, could have stopped Japanese aggression and perhaps even have saved France and prevented the Battle of Britain. They fault him particularly for failing to educate the public about the dangers of fascism and Axis aggression. Still others depict Roosevelt as a pawn of the British. Roosevelt had every intention of involving America in the war in Europe, they claim, and deceived the American public about his intentions while he secretly manipulated events to make U.S. entry seem inevitable.

Waldo Heinrichs' 1988 study, Threshold of War, *depicts Roosevelt as a farsighted, informed, and generally courageous leader who sought to contain Japan in the Pacific while forming a common front with Britain and the Soviet Union against Germany and Italy. That the common front led to American belligerency was not the product of a sinister plot, but a realistic reaction to a very real threat.*

THRESHOLD OF WAR: FRANKLIN D. ROOSEVELT AND AMERICAN ENTRY INTO WORLD WAR II

Waldo Heinrichs

At New London on Monday, August 4, President Roosevelt boarded the yacht *Potomac* ostensibly for a cruise along the New England coast, but after a day of well-publicized boating and fishing in Buzzards Bay he slipped into nearby Vineyard Sound to rendezvous with Admiral King's flagship *Augusta*. Early the next morning he boarded the heavy cruiser, which, with another heavy cruiser and five destroyers, immediately departed for Newfoundland. Steaming at high speed in spite of fog, the

from Waldo Heinrichs, "August–September: Crossing the Threshold," in *Threshold of War: Franklin D. Roosevelt and American Entry into World War II* (New York: Oxford University Press, 1988), 146–179.

task force arrived at Argentia on August 7, one day before Churchill's earliest possible arrival in the *Prince of Wales* and two days before the scarred British battleship entered the bay. Though the American Lend-Lease base was on British territory, Roosevelt was determined to welcome the prime minister to North America.

During the trip and the wait, the president received radio messages corroborating news accounts of the German slow-down in Russia. [Undersecretary of State Sumner] Welles arrived by air on August 8 with the latest intelligence. Dispatches indicated that the cool and skeptical attitude maintained by the embassy at Moscow was changing. On August 2 it had reported that the German drive had halted or slowed and that the Russians were manifesting "definite optimism." Three days later it judged that "determined and courageous Soviet resistance" as well as the need for resupply had brought a respite, which the Soviets were likely to put to good use and further delay the German advance. Such a delay, the embassy concluded, would have a vital bearing on the "ability of the Soviet armies effectively to engage the bulk of the German armies until the advent of winter" and if necessary to withdraw eastward while continuing to fight. . . .

On arrival at Argentia the president called a conference of his military advisers, including Marshall, Stark, and Arnold, and gave them a glimpse of his intentions. Prominent in the review was his decision to increase the number of B-17s in the Philippines from a squadron of nine planes to a group of thirty-six. "That was a distinct change of policy," Arnold later reminisced. "It was the start of a thought to give General MacArthur weapons for offensive operations." A squadron of B-17s could do little more than assist in the defense of the islands, but a group could attack or threaten Japanese territory. To use General Marshall's words to his British opposite, General Sir John Dill, at the coming conference, the reinforcement of the Philippines would act as a "serious deterrent" to Japan, especially in the winter months which were more suitable for high-altitude bombing. Roosevelt furthermore stated his intention to send twenty-eight P-40s a month to Russia for September, October, and November. That the Philippines project was linked in the president's mind with the Russian situation is indicated by the fact that Arnold in his outline notes of the meeting placed the dispatch of the B-17s alongside the dispatch of the P-40s to Russia under the overall heading of "Russia." The object was not simply to deter a southward advance but a northward advance as well.

Boarding the *Augusta* immediately upon arrival in the *Prince of Wales* was "Hurry Upkins" [presidential aide Harry Hopkins] with full reports of his talks in Moscow. Wasted by illness but fiercely determined, Hopkins had flown back to Scotland in time to join Churchill for the voyage to Argentia. In conversations on July 30 and 31 he had found Stalin cooperative, forthcoming, and vitally concerned to secure help from the democracies. Hopkins undoubtedly found it curious to hear the leader of the Soviet state, which Churchill had described that spring as "an amoral crocodile lurking in the depths," condemn Hitler Germany for lack of moral standards, but now, at least, views of Germany coincided.

At their second conference, with Maxim Litvinov as translator the only other person present, Stalin gave the first detailed exposition of the progress of the war so far provided the West. "Merely because German forces pierce the Russian line does not mean the Russians are lost," he pointed out. Soviet mechanized forces were fighting far forward of their lines and with partisans were seeping in between the Panzers and the follow-up infantry. This infiltration forced the Germans to disperse their tanks and infantry to protect their lines of communication. With this difficulty and the lack of good roads, the Germans were finding that "moving mechanized forces through Russia was very different than moving them over the boulevards of Belgium and France."

Pressure on his army in the last ten days had considerably lessened, Stalin went on; the Germans were tired. It would be difficult for them to continue the offensive after September 1 when the heavy rains began, and after October 1 they would have to go on the defensive for the winter. "He expressed great confidence that the line during the winter months would be in front of Moscow, Kiev and Leningrad— probably not more than 100 kilometres away from where it is now." To capture the bulk of Soviet munitions plants, German forces would have to move 150 miles east of these centers. For the May 1942 campaign Stalin expected to mobilize 350 divisions. In rough comparison (the U.S. division was bigger), Roosevelt expected to have twenty divisions ready by the end of 1941. Stalin's assessment contained much that was true about the battle at the moment. Needless to say, it was as positive as he could make it and far more positive in claims for the future than the staggering losses and bad generalship of the Red Army and the strength of the replenishing Wehrmacht justified.

The most urgent Soviet needs, according to Stalin, were light antiaircraft guns, aluminum for planes, machine guns and rifles, and for the longer term tanks, planes, steel, oil, and other matériel already requested. Stalin urged American entry into the war and the most intimate cooperation, even to the extent of welcoming an American army on the Russian front and sharing Soviet tank designs. But by the next spring, he said, the problem of supply would be acute.

Hopkins carried out the president's instruction to deal with Soviet requests for aid in two categories: what could be delivered immediately—largely token quantities; and what could be shipped for a war that lasted into 1942. Long-term needs, Hopkins advised the Soviet leader, could be addressed at a conference in Moscow, at which American, British, and Soviet representatives would allocate munitions according to the strategic value of each front as well as national interests. Taking his cue from Stalin's statement that the Soviet front should be stabilized by October 1, and mindful that it would be "very unwise" to hold a conference until it was established "whether or not there was to be a front," Hopkins tentatively suggested a meeting about that date. The Russians were to be given maximum encouragement to fight on with token American assistance now and hopes for 1942 until the immediate outcome was clear. What could then be offered would be far more substantial and encouraging than the pittance that could be provided now.

Hopkins also conferred with Foreign Minister V. M. Molotov about Japan, the latter betraying considerable unease about the possibility of a Japanese attack on Siberia. He gave Hopkins the impression that "the Japanese would not hesitate to strike if a propitious time occurred." The one thing which would prevent it, said the

Soviet, was some kind of American warning—meaning, Hopkins supposed, a statement that the United States would come to Russia's assistance if Russia were attacked by Japan. Hopkins replied that his government shared these concerns but had no desire to be provocative. Nevertheless, he would convey this message to the president.

The dominant cast of Argentia was gray, from the bleak, misty hills and cove to the warships riding at anchor. Enlivening the scene were pinpoints of color in flags, uniforms, and gleaming brasswork and the hum of small boats scuttling between the British battleship and the American cruisers. In spite of the convenience of the remote spot as a secret rendezvous, the symbolic value of an Atlantic meeting, and the delight both principals took in a naval encounter, the disadvantages were considerable. The difficulty of shuffling officials between ships, the constant burden of protocol for dignitaries aboard warships, and the wariness each side had of the other—strangers with differing purposes, one at peace, the other at war—led to a feeling of disorganization and desultory, fragmented decision-making. This sense of aimlessness, however, and the lack of immediate dramatic results should not belie the significance of the conference.

Argentia was a critical juncture in the evolution of Roosevelt's world policies. Churchill was right in saying that something big was happening, "something really big," and it was not just the cementing of personal ties from the principals on down and the tears welling up during the singing of "Onward Christian Soldiers" at a common divine service on the afterdeck of the *Prince of Wales,* with American and British sailors intermingled under the big guns. The importance of Argentia lay not in radical departures and vivid consequences but in the congealing of tentative policies devised in response to the recent great changes in world politics and the balance of forces.

Roosevelt's chief purpose at Argentia was to establish the political basis for waging and winning the war. Not that he was seeking war. Rather, he was about to embark on courses of action in the containment of Japan and protection of the Atlantic which carried distinct risks of war, but which he nevertheless regarded as crucial for the nation's security. He desired a public declaration of fundamental American convictions about the conditions of peaceful world order, the sort of peace his countrymen would feel justified entry into the war. At the same time he wanted it framed as a joint statement with Great Britain, not issued unilaterally like Woodrow Wilson's Fourteen Points. He sought an international standard, a banner for the anti-Axis coalition to rally around, and a promise for subjugated peoples.

But first he wanted an answer to his question of July 14 as to whether Britain had made any secret commitments to the Soviet Union or any of the governments-in-exile regarding postwar territorial changes. London's silence on this score was disturbing. However, Sir Alexander Cadogan, permanent under secretary of the Foreign Office, came with assurances. In a long talk with Welles on the first day of the conference, only a short time after the president and prime minister had first met, he said Britain had promised Yugoslavia in March to allow reconsideration of the status of Italian-owned Istria after the war, hardly a "firm commitment," he pointed out, but he solemnly pledged that this was the only territorial undertaking his government had made. Welles and Roosevelt were satisfied.

Negotiation of a joint declaration of purpose was not completed until the day of departure, but there was never any likelihood of failure; that, said Hopkins, was "inconceivable." The Atlantic Charter, as it came to be known, was mostly a re-statement of familiar Wilsonian principles: non-aggrandizement, self-determination (with the "wish" for restoration of sovereignty and self-government to peoples "forcibly deprived of them"), freedom of trade, freedom of the seas, abandonment of force, disarmament, and ultimately, in some form, a world security organization. Point Six offered a gentle vision of world peace after the destruction of "Nazi tyranny," one providing "all nations the means of dwelling in safety within their own boundaries, and . . . assurance that all the men in all the lands may live out their lives in freedom from fear and want." The only serious disagreement arose over free trade, with Churchill insisting that he must make an exception for existing agreements for trade preference within the Commonwealth, and Welles repre-senting the deep-set convictions of Hull and his advisers in favor of an unconditional open door. Roosevelt settled the matter by siding with Churchill.

The Atlantic Charter was unremarkable because most people in the United States and Britain took for granted most of what it said. No other vision of world order had any standing. The strength of the Charter lay in the sharp contrast it drew between the multilateral world vision of the democracies and the self-serving aims of the Axis.

Churchill's chief purpose at Argentia, of course, was to range the United States as closely as possible with Britain, and it was his particular concern to do this in respect to Japan. The British government's preferred course of action was to secure a guarantee of assistance from the United States, give one to the Netherlands for the East Indies, and use these as the basis of an explicit warning to Japan of war against further encroachment. . . . Of particular concern at this time were Japanese designs on Thailand, the next domino after southern Indochina. The British reported they had a secret message from the Thai prime minister that the Japanese were demanding under threat of force military as well as economic concessions. Japanese bases on the Kra isthmus would uncover the defenses of Malaya. The War Cabinet in London un-derstood that Congress, not the president, had the power to declare war, but still be-lieved (and so informed Churchill aboard the *Prince of Wales*) that Roosevelt might be induced to present an oblique war warning which they could join in.

Churchill agreed. The Americans were told that Britain had just given a pledge of assistance, limited to the forces at Britain's disposal in the region, to the Netherlands in case of Japanese attack on the East Indies. Now how far could the Americans go respecting an attack on the Dutch and a movement into Thailand? Churchill proposed simultaneous British, American, and Dutch warnings to Tokyo that any further encroachment by Japan in the southwest Pacific would result in countermeasures by those countries even though these might lead to war. Further, according to the Churchill draft, the United States would warn Japan that if the British went to the assistance of the Netherlands, the president would request au-thority from Congress to give them aid.

Roosevelt preferred a less precipitate approach. He had not changed his mind about the need for firmness in dealing with Japan. The period of "extreme patience" had come to an end, Welles told [British diplomat Sir Alexander] Cadogan. Roosevelt was expanding the air reinforcement of the Philippines. He promised Churchill to maintain trade restrictions in full force, though he did not explain what that meant, whether limiting Japan to peacetime use of oil or continuing to withhold funds for any oil exports. The trick, as it must have seemed to him, was to curtail oil exports as much as possible without provoking Japan by a formal ban. Furthermore, while at every step now Roosevelt was stiffening policy, he was one to preserve as much flexibility as the situation permitted. The British did not learn then or for some time thereafter that trade had been suspended just before he left Washington.

In Welles' view the time for warnings had passed. Only a few days earlier he had pointed out to the minister-counselor of the Japanese embassy, who was returning to Japan to report personally to Prince [Prime Minister Fumimaro] Konoe, that if Japan persisted in its drive for overlordship in East Asia and the south Pacific, hostilities were bound to ensue between their two countries. Given its recent sharply increased opposition to Japan, Welles told Cadogan, the American public was not likely to tolerate a Japanese attack on the East Indies. Of course the American was describing an historical process whereas the British, seeking deterrence, wanted sterner stuff. Nevertheless, a warning on the British model would in fact have been superfluous, for the principal Japanese decision-makers had already concluded that an attack on Malaya or the Dutch East Indies was bound to lead to war with the United States.

Roosevelt understood that a Japanese attack on the Dutch East Indies would result in war. He said as much on the eve of the conference: if Japan attacked there, "we are vitally interested and will do our utmost to get them out." But he was also undoubtedly influenced by his belief that the American people had not reached the point of supporting a declaration of war against Japan or Germany and that it would be unwise to commit them farther down this road than they had reached by themselves. It seems unlikely, however, that he regarded this as a hindrance, for it fitted his own fundamental belief that sound policy derived from American interest. British and American interests, while congruent, were not identical. He spoke of a vital interest in the Dutch East Indies but not in Singapore. He preferred to take responsibility for escort operations in the western Atlantic rather than to send an American destroyer force to the British Isles and to set his own course in adopting sanctions against Japan. Yet he was not a nationalist rather than an internationalist; he was both. He sought the most intimate cooperation, in fact coordination, with Churchill. But he resisted formal combination and commitment. Always he insisted on preserving control of the allocation of American resources and the timing and nature of American responses to Axis aggression.

Roosevelt's main difference with Churchill was his reluctance to bring matters to a head. He wanted a drying up of Japanese oil supplies rather than a formal severance of trade, a sobering realization not a sudden shock. A war warning, too, might precipitate matters when delay was vital. He wanted at least thirty days for Anglo-American reinforcement, in which the first echelon of Flying Fortresses might reach the Philippines and, as Churchill reported, "we may improve our position in the Singapore area."

An opportunity to play for time had just appeared. On August 6, Nomura had delivered to Hull, now back at his desk, a Japanese reply to the president's suggestion of the neutralization of Indochina, which had been lost in the swirl of events at the end of July. The Japanese picked up Roosevelt's proposal and offered a deal: Japan would promise not to extend its military presence beyond French Indochina and would remove its troops from Indochina upon settlement of the China war provided the United States would halt its military buildup in the region, restore normal trade relations, and use its good offices to bring about negotiations with Chiang Kai-shek. This would have been the worst kind of Munich. In return for America's relaxing all pressures, Japan would promise no further expansion. But the southern Indochina move would have to be accepted—and thus somewhat validated—until the United States facilitated an end to the China war. Roosevelt and Churchill agreed the terms were impossible, but Roosevelt was interested in the fact that the Japanese couched their proposal as a response to his own and that they offered negotiations. He proposed to take up the offer and enter into discussions on condition that the Japanese make no move while the talks were in progress. He would make no concessions and relax no pressures but, as a Foreign Office official described it, "keep the Japanese in play" for the next one to three months.

Although he had no intention of appeasing Japan, Roosevelt finally concluded he had to appease Churchill. After divine services on the *Prince of Wales* the prime minister cornered Welles and pleaded with him "in the most emphatic manner" for a "clear-cut" warning. This was the only hope of preventing a war, he warned, in which Japanese cruisers would play havoc with British imperial communications in the Indian Ocean. Such a blow "might be almost decisive" to his government.

The next day, Roosevelt outlined his delaying tactics and then agreed to a war warning substantially in accord with Churchill's draft. He would tell Nomura that, if Japan refused these conditions for talks or made further advances, "in his belief" the United States would take certain steps in spite of his realization that these "might result in war." The warning was not quite as unconditional as the British desired, but it used the word *war*. Furthermore, the president included Thailand in his neutralization proposal, in spite of the fact that before the conference he affirmed that an advance into Thailand should not be occasion for war. Presumably he was being educated on the strategic importance of southern Thailand. And he was prepared to extend the warning to include a Japanese attack on the Soviet Union and to so inform Moscow. Welles, however, more interested in the negotiations than the warning, advised a weaker statement of unlimited applicability. The two principals approved. . . .

Roosevelt went to Argentia fully expecting to confirm the taking over of convoy escort operations in the western Atlantic. This was to be a fruit of the conference, a result of agreement about war aims, and so it was. Churchill took the initiative in his enthralling review of the war situation aboard the *Augusta* the first evening of the conference. The Royal Navy, he said, needed to withdraw its fifty-two destroyers and corvettes from escort operations in the western Atlantic to bolster convoy protection along the Gibraltar and West African routes where submarines were now concentrating. The Americans readily agreed. Roosevelt had told his advisers before Churchill arrived that the United States must protect cargoes as far as Iceland, in fact east of Iceland. Upon sending Hopkins to London in July he had given him a map torn from the *National Geographic* upon which he had drawn a line encircling Iceland some 200 miles to the east, about halfway to the Faroe Islands, and then running west and south as before along the 26th meridian. This was to be the zone of operations. Each convoy must contain at least one American or Icelandic flag ship. American war vessels would be restricted to convoy protection, a responsibility broadly though vaguely defined: it would be too late for escorts to start shooting after an attack began, the president told his advisers. The two navies aimed at starting American escort on September 1.

Iceland had manifold strategic advantages: as a base for North Atlantic escort operations, as a link in the bomber ferry route, and now as the staging point for Arctic convoys to Russia. This last was a perilous route funneling a thousand miles between the Arctic ice and German air and naval forces in northern Norway, but in Stalin's judgment it was the best. . . .

Iceland was also the northern bastion of the Atlantic line described in Roosevelt's speech of May 27. The new front in Russia eased but by no means dissolved the president's concern for protection of the Atlantic. A stabilization of the front in the Soviet Union during the winter, the desired outcome, would have the disadvantage of permitting Hitler to withdraw the few divisions needed for a campaign through the Iberian Peninsula to northwest Africa. The situation in Spain, Churchill warned, was going from bad to worse. Hopkins returned from Argentia "much churned up over the likelihood of the Germans or Spain making a drive to the south, including the Atlantic islands—the Azores, Canaries, Cape Verdes."

. . . The Atlantic barrier was no less a matter of vital interest to Roosevelt in August than it had been in May. From Argentia he ordered implementation of plans to augment the Iceland garrison in early September. Numbers were less a problem, however, since the British, with invasion fears eased, were willing not only to retain their own contingent but also slightly reinforce it. Now only 5,000 instead of 10,000 American troops were needed to reinforce the Marine brigade already present. . . .

The *Prince of Wales* left Argentia on August 12 escorted by American as well as British destroyers. Memory of this heartening naval clasp was soon lost in the North Atlantic mists as the British party and, later, official circles in London, weary of two years of war and one year of lonely struggle, canvassed the meager concrete benefits of the meeting. The Soviet bid for vast quantities of American war matériel along with their own needs and those of the American armed services added up to far more than the Americans could produce. The two leaders followed Hopkins' advice in suggesting to Stalin a meeting at Moscow about October 1 to decide how, when, and where among the three nations war supplies should be allocated. Russia was indeed a "welcome guest," as Churchill said, but it was a "hungry table," and in view of the president's passionate concern to sustain the Soviet war effort, British leaders were deeply worried about having their own requirements met, especially for their forthcoming Mideast offensive.

The Atlantic Charter and the promised war warning were fine, but where was the substance? The United States Navy was taking over convoy protection in the western Atlantic—where U-boats were scarce. The Stars and Stripes would not be flying at Londonderry and Gare Loch after all, though work on the bases would continue. The destroyers as well as long-range submarines of the ABC-1 war plan would remain closer to home. No more Catalina patrol planes, the type that had spotted the *Bismarck,* were available. Furthermore, the new American battleships would not be available for assignment to Gibraltar or anywhere else until the end of the year. In builder's trials the new lightweight machinery and hull form of the *Washington* and *North Carolina* had produced severe vibration in the propeller shafts at high speed which affected the fire control systems. "The problem must have been terrifying," says one authority, because all battleships being built and some cruisers were following the same design. Experts advised substituting new propellers with fewer blades. These experiments would take months. So with no more American battleships coming from the yards or the Pacific, the Royal Navy would gain no substitutes for any battleships it might send to Singapore. It was not difficult to imagine that Roosevelt intended to supply the war to a limited extent indeed and otherwise stand on the sidelines.

The East Asian picture was no more encouraging. The Americans were asking the British to reduce their allocations of certain items to permit strengthening of the Philippines, which they argued would assist Singapore. The Admiralty doubted the practical value of the B-17 reinforcement of the Philippines. Americans had, they thought, "rather exaggerated hopes of the effect of operations, particularly air, from the Philippines against a Japanese expedition to the South China Sea." Given the American refusal to accept plans for the defense of the "Malay Barrier" and British ignorance of how far Roosevelt was prepared to go in restricting oil shipments to Japan, the party aboard the *Prince of Wales* may well have voyaged eastward with a sinking feeling.

Yet it would have been the wrong feeling. The importance of Argentia was less what the two leaders agreed to than what Roosevelt himself concluded. A burgeoning but still tentative interest in supplying the Soviet Union became a firm determination. In fact, maintaining a Russian front against Hitler became the centerpiece of his world strategy, with large consequences in all theaters. He was ready to enter the Battle of the Atlantic at the risk of war, tipping from most benevolent neutrality to active belligerency, in order to forward supplies to the Soviet Union no less than Britain. He was taking advantage of Hitler's drive to the east and refusal to accept the American challenge on the Atlantic to intervene with less risk of war. Avoiding a confrontation with Germany reduced the chances of war with Japan. He thereby kept in abeyance the vast claims on American production a declaration of war would entail. But it is hard to believe that he did not understand that sooner or later, one way or the other, this course of action would lead to war.

So far as Japan was concerned, he had three possible courses of action: the passive, the soft, and the hard. The passive route was simply to do nothing to provoke Japan, either by an oil embargo or by Asian reinforcements, in order to bring the full weight of American power to bear against Germany. But he undoubtedly perceived this to be the riskiest course, for it not only left the resources of Southeast Asia and Britain's connections to Australia and New Zealand at Japan's mercy but also offered no discouragement to a Japanese attack against the Soviet rear. The soft choice meant coming to an agreement with Japan which at least offered the possibility of preventing a further southward advance by some concession ending the China war, but at great cost to the American reputation as guarantor of nations resisting aggression, and probably with heightened risk of a Japanese attack northward once its southern flank was secure. He was moving along the third course, the hard policy, estimating it no doubt the least risky: severe containment of Japan risked war, but in that event more likely a southward than the more critical northward attack. Meanwhile, the draining of Japan's oil supplies would progressively reduce its capacity for war. The risk would decline as American military power increased and in time far surpassed that of Japan.

The decisions of the Atlantic Conference period were bold departures, and President Roosevelt surely did not take them without trepidation. So far American public opinion had been mobilizing behind his policies. However, administration confidence in public support received a rude shock on August 12, the last day of the conference, when word came that the House of Representatives had extended the Selective Service Act by a margin of one vote. The slimness of victory did not really signify a relapse into isolationism, but it indicated the limits of interventionism. Extension of the draft was an issue of great political sensitivity because many felt honor-bound to the conscripts to limit their service to the original term of one year. The vote drew these as well as hard-core isolationists, most Republicans and all Roosevelt-haters. It also drew the complacent. News readers of later July and early August could gain the impression that the Germans had met their match in Russia and that maintaining a large army for defense of the Western Hemisphere, which after all was the rationale for the draft, was no longer urgent. So the temptation to turn a deaf ear to Roosevelt's and Marshall's warnings and entreaties was powerful.

Still, a margin of one was enough. American mobilization stayed on course. According to a *Fortune* poll, 72 percent of Americans believed Hitler would try to conquer the world and 58 percent that armed intervention was necessary to defeat him. A poll in Montana indicated that the most outspoken isolationist, Senator Burton K. Wheeler, would be defeated in an election now by at least 100,000 votes. The index of production rose steadily. The steel industry reached full capacity and mills worked through the July 4 weekend. Shortages began to appear. In two instances, at North American and Federal Shipbuilding, the military services took over plants to prevent longer work stoppages.

Public opinion and domestic political considerations generally could not be ignored. Neither could international political and strategic requirements and military capabilities. So far Roosevelt had managed to keep his various autonomous imperatives in rough harmony. As he moved to a global framework of policy, this became increasingly difficult to do.

The president returned to Washington on Sunday morning, August 17, refreshed and buoyant from his ocean voyage and settled course of action. Preceding him was Welles with the war warning and preceding Welles was a message asking [Secretary of State] Hull to set up a meeting with Nomura. The secretary of state, who was naturally averse to showdowns, and his advisers strongly disapproved of the warning for the same reason the president had been dubious about it: threatening language risked provoking Japan in a situation in which delay seemed imperative. . . .

The Japanese government had now asked for a conference between Premier Konoe and President Roosevelt in Hawaii. The idea was not new. . . . Ambassador Nomura, who doubted that the Americans would be moved by anything but concrete proposals, had reintroduced it in a conversation with the secretary of state on August 8, but so gingerly that Hull virtually ignored it. MAGIC, however, showed that Nomura was acting under instructions and that his government attached great importance to the proposal. According to intercepts, the Konoe cabinet believed that the only way to relieve the "critically tense" situation was for the leaders to meet, "lay their cards on the table, express their true feelings, and attempt to determine a way out. . . ." On August 16, Nomura urged on Hull a return to the more comprehensive framework of the conversations conducted in the spring and interrupted in July as a preliminary to a leaders' meeting, and indicated that his government "would make concessions in order to avoid war."

It was very hard to say no. Conceivably the Japanese were having a change of heart, though Roosevelt doubted it. They were more influenced by the sway of battle in Russia than by regard for the United States, he told Lord Halifax. Even so, finding out seemed wise, and resuming the talks offered the further opportunity of weakening Japan's ties with the Axis at the delicate moment when the United States was intervening in the Battle of the Atlantic. Above all, a return to the Hull-Nomura format of the spring, in all its complexity with the added inducement of a culminating leaders' meeting, was likely to win more time for containment than discussions pivoting on the neutralization of Indochina. The previous talks had, after all, consumed three months. But a blunt war warning was not likely to create a mood conducive to extended discussions, so Roosevelt accepted the weaker version.

The president saw Nomura on Sunday afternoon, August 17, only a few hours after his return. The meeting really consisted of two conversations divided by a pause: one admonitory, the other conciliatory. First Roosevelt read the State Department's version of the warning, which no longer insisted upon an unconditional Japanese commitment to remove its forces from Indochina, nor referred to the Indochina neutralization proposal and British support for it, nor warned against advance in specific places or directions. Most important, the warning itself did not use the word "war" or "conflict." It simply said that, if Japan made any further advances, the United States would have to take whatever steps were necessary to safeguard the rights and interests of its citizens and its safety and security. . . .

Moving to the second part of the conversation, Roosevelt showed how the Japanese move into southern Indochina had led to a breakdown in diplomacy, then painted a fair picture of the possibilities for peace on American principles and an open door for trade and resources in the Pacific region. If Japan was prepared to abandon its expansion and embark on such a program, Roosevelt went on, his government would, as requested, consider resumption of the Hull-Nomura conversations and seek to arrange a time and place for a meeting of high officials. The president said he preferred San Francisco or Seattle because a journey to Hawaii would take too long and he was not permitted to fly. Juneau or Sitka in the Alaska panhandle might be an alternative, he said. But while dangling the hope of a leaders' meeting before Nomura, Roosevelt let it be known that distance was a problem, and he could not promise attendance. Furthermore, a critical condition, first the United States required a "clearer statement" of the Japanese government's "attitude and plans."

To the British, Roosevelt tried to minimize his weakening of the warning. Informing Lord Halifax of the proposal for a meeting with Konoe, he claimed that the warning he delivered was similar to the Argentia draft. But Halifax checked the wording with Welles, and Churchill soon knew better.

Publicly the prime minister gloried in the common aspirations and promised co-operation of Argentia: as he had journeyed home, he said, "overhead the far-ranging Catalina airboats soared, vigilant, protecting eagles in the sky." "We shall not be denied the strength to do our duty to the end," he assured his war-weary countrymen. Turning to Asia he scathingly denounced Japanese military "factions" which were "seeking to emulate the style of Hitler and Mussolini as if it were a new wave of European revelation." Japanese armies had been "wandering" about China for years bringing "carnage, ruin, corruption." Now they threatened the southwest Pacific and he was "certain that this has got to stop." Cleverly placing America out front as Japan's principal antagonist, he praised the "infinite patience" with which it was trying to work out a settlement, but if trouble came, he warned, Britain would "of course" range itself "unhesitatingly at the side of the United States." The Japanese press reacted to the speech with "almost unprecedented violence in tone," [Ambassador Joseph] Grew reported.

Churchill was depicting in rhetoric the common front he had failed to secure in secret diplomacy, and with some success. The New York Times, under the four-column headline CHURCHILL WARNS JAPANESE TO "STOP" OR FACE BRITISH-AMERICAN COALITION, commented that the British leader had confirmed what many suspected: that the two governments had decided at Argentia to take the "strongest sort of line" with Japan.

Behind these rhetorical flourishes, the British government grew increasingly critical as it examined the American backslidings and the paltry tangible results of Argentia. Particularly disillusioning were Roosevelt's frequent public assurances that he had not made any commitments at the conference and that the nation stood no closer to war. On August 28, Churchill, aiming at Roosevelt, wrote Hopkins a most despondent letter. He spoke of a "wave of depression" in the cabinet and informed circles over apparent American disinclination to become involved. "If 1942 opens with Russia knocked out and Britain left again alone all kinds of dangers may arise," he warned. That night, he said, thirty U-boats lay in a line from eastern Iceland to northern Ireland but east of the 26th meridian, beyond current American responsibility. In the past two days submarines had sunk 25,000 tons of shipping. The implication was clear that the Battle of the Atlantic could still be lost while Americans guarded its western reaches. He ended by saying that he would be grateful for "any sort of hope." If the British ever reached the conclusion that the United States would not somehow, sometime join the fray, Hopkins warned Roosevelt, "there would be a very critical moment in the war and the British appeasers might have some influence on Churchill."

Churchill was keeping one step ahead of the American navy, which was moving as fast as possible to enter the Battle of the Atlantic within the limitations agreed to at Argentia. The president, having taken his decision, left implementation to the navy; admirals were not summoned to the White House in August as they had been in July. Nevertheless, over a month passed before escort began. The navy planned to start September 1, but administrative and logistical problems forced post-ponement. . . .

Great difficulty occurred in getting ships to the right place at the right time. Ice-landic and American-flag merchantmen, one of which Roosevelt still insisted had to provide a figleaf of neutrality for each convoy, were a particular problem. Adequate numbers of American vessels only began departing from New York on August 27. Some Icelandic vessels were so slow they endangered their escorts; others ignored escorts and steamed off alone.

A division of responsibility was arranged with the Americans taking fast (HX) convoys and the Royal Canadian Navy the slow (SC) from a point south of New-foundland to a rendezvous with British escorts south of Iceland and then back again with convoys of empty ships. But the Canadians, with too few vessels and too few with adequate range, had to retain some of the British escorts to carry out their side of the bargain.

The measured activity of the Atlantic Fleet before the Argentia conference gave way to a rush for position afterward. Within a week Admiral [Ernest J.] King [com-mander of the U.S. Pacific Fleet] ordered the fleet train from Newport to Casco Bay, Maine, the nearest American anchorage to the convoy routes. The Support Force commander established himself at Argentia. Destroyer tenders, repair ships, oilers, and other auxiliaries followed or moved on to Iceland. At Casco Bay, King set up a destroyer pool, dissolving the neat division and squadron organization, so that escort units could be filled out on the basis of readiness and a mixture of old and new destroyers. From there units moved up to Argentia near the convoy meeting point or were pre-positioned in Iceland for the westbound convoys.

By mid-September thirty-three destroyers, every one the Atlantic Fleet com-mander could get his hands on, and the Coast Guard cutter *Campbell* were ready for merchant vessel escort at the northern bases. Another sixteen were due by the end of October and six more by the end of the year, leaving a bare minimum to escort warships, one division (four ships) to patrol the Caribbean, and a sonar training di-vision at Key West which Admiral King coveted. He had barely enough vessels to begin the task: six escort groups of five destroyers each. Canadian units had even fewer. King planned to increase the number to seven groups of at least six each, and allow a layover in Boston, but storm damage and machinery breakdowns were con-stantly whittling down the number available to meet the inexorable convoy schedules.

So urgent was the need for destroyers that peacetime criteria for efficiency were dispensed with. Gunnery proficiency was below that of the Pacific Fleet and, for recently completed destroyers, unsatisfactory. In machine gun practice in August even veteran Support Force squadrons were scoring virtually no hits because of lack of practice ammunition. U.S.S. *Ericsson, Nicholson,* and *Mayo* reported for escort duty with no gunnery practice at all. Injuries among crews unfamiliar with weapons and equipment were "far too many in number." Few destroyers were equipped with radar and fewer still experienced in its use. U.S.S. *Babbitt,* hurrying to duty, received its underwater sound detection gear not in a dockyard but at Casco Bay from a tender.

As the fleet readied, the war moved back toward it. The number of operational U-boats increased from sixty-five in July to eighty in October and the number on station rose past thirty, permitting the U-boat command to form a wolfpack of fourteen boats, Group Markgraf, for Greenland-Iceland waters. These began entering the western Atlantic on August 18 and by early September were neatly positioned in rank and file to sight any plume of smoke in the hundreds of miles of convoy routes lying southeast of Greenland and southwest of Iceland. At the same time the German naval command began super-encyphering U-boat locations within encyphered messages, delaying ULTRA [British decoding device] by as much as four days and temporarily masking U-boat deployment. Atlantic Fleet destroyers were entering far more dangerous waters than could have been imagined a month earlier.

The nearly inevitable encounter occurred September 4 some 125 miles southwest of Iceland between U.S.S. *Greer,* a World War I destroyer, and U-652, cruising on the northern flank of Group Markgraf. *Greer* was sailing alone carrying mail and officer passengers to Reykjavik from Boston and Argentia. Informed by a British patrol bomber of a submarine in its path it proceeded to hunt and find the boat and pursue it tenaciously for the next several hours, in full compliance with orders to trail and report U-boats in the American defense zone. U-boats were forbidden to initiate attacks on American warships, but the submerged U-652, unable to identify the nationality of its pursuer and believing depth charges dropped by the plane had come from the destroyer, finally fired two torpedoes in self-defense, which *Greer* dodged. The American destroyer responded with depth-charge attacks and further pursuit until called off at twilight. The quarry, shaken but not damaged, continued westward to join in a pack attack on September 9–11 on SC-42, which was desperately trying an end-run to the north, close to Greenland. U-652 claimed as probably sunk two of the sixteen vessels lost from that devastated convoy.

The *Greer* incident greatly facilitated arrangements for escort of convoy. The incident allowed removal of the restrictions under which it would be conducted. President Roosevelt on learning of the encounter immediately ordered the navy to "eliminate" the submarine, and destroyers were ordered down from Iceland before the search was called off.

The following day, September 5, the president met with Admiral King and Admiral Stark among others and authorized the beginning of outward-bound escort September 16 and escort back from Iceland of the first convoy available whether fast or slow. Destroyers were ordered out again from Iceland on September 12 to assist battered convoy SC-42. Then Roosevelt permitted destroyers to escort convoys without American or Icelandic-flag ships and the Royal Canadian and Royal navies to escort American ships as far as Iceland. A few days later he authorized attack on German and Italian warships anywhere in the western Atlantic, including Iceland and a broad belt of ocean to its east. Mere presence of a submarine or raider was now grounds for attack. By September 16, when the first American escort group, Task Unit 4.1.1, met the first American-escorted convoy, HX 150 out of Halifax, the United States Navy was in a state of full belligerency in the western Atlantic.

As he had done in his radio address of May 27 before the Iceland venture, so now before taking this next big step Roosevelt made a powerful presentation of his views and intentions to the American people and sought their support. His plans for a broadcast were interrupted by the failing health and then death of his mother the weekend of September 6–7. He was with her when she died at Hyde Park on Sunday, and he remained for her funeral. Meanwhile the speech went through draft after draft at the State Department and White House. Hopkins brought the latest draft to the presidential train in New York as it was returning to Washington, and that evening and the next morning Roosevelt refined it and tested it on congressional leaders. On Thursday evening, September 11, he broadcast a major state paper setting out the basis for intervention in the Battle of the Atlantic and, if that followed, war with Germany. The speech went out in his familiar, reassuring voice and vivid, colloquial idiom to a nation of family homes gathered around their radios. He aimed his message abroad as well, to the nations and peoples fighting Hitler and particularly to the British, described by Churchill as so very discouraged with the lack of tangible results from the Atlantic meeting.

Claiming correctly that the submarine fired first on the *Greer* and with deliberate intent to sink it, the president was silent about what the U-boat captain must have regarded as hostile pursuit. Roosevelt did not rest his case on the ambiguities of the chase, however, but placed the incident in the larger context of German U-boat warfare and American devotion to the freedom of the seas. The *Greer*, he insisted, was on a "legitimate mission" to Iceland, an American outpost protecting waters through which passed ships of many flags carrying food and war matériel provided by the American people as an essential part of their own defense. If the U-boat had been unable to identify the destroyer, as the Nazis claimed, and still fired, this reflected a policy of indiscriminate violence, as proven by such other attacks as the sinking of the *Robin Moor* and stalking of the U.S.S. *Texas* in June, and the recent sinkings of the Panamanian freighter *Sessa* and the American freighter *Steel Seafarer*.

These acts of "piracy" were all part of a Nazi plan for domination of the seas wherein no American ship could travel without the "condescending grace of this . . . tyrannical power." A counterpart was Nazi subversion of governments in Latin America aiming at ultimate control of the Western Hemisphere and a "permanent world system based on force, terror, and murder." The Monroe Doctrine was too self-limiting for Roosevelt, however; the immediate issue, he insisted, was freedom of shipping on the high seas, the settled policy of the United States since Presidents John Adams and Thomas Jefferson cleared the Caribbean of privateers and the Mediterranean of corsairs. The line of supply to the enemies of Hitler would be maintained at all costs and by active defense: "When you see a rattlesnake poised to strike, you do not wait . . . you crush him." The American navy would protect "not only American ships but ships of any flag" in American defensive waters. "Let this warning be clear," he concluded: "From now on, if German and Italian vessels enter the waters, the protection of which is necessary for American defense, they do so at their own peril." ROOSEVELT ORDERS NAVY TO SHOOT FIRST, the banner headline of the New York Times reported the next day.

The president was evasive about the precise manner in which the navy would provide protection. In fact [Secretary of War] Stimson himself did not learn of the escort system until September 25. Nonetheless the determination to use force and the justification for it had been forthrightly declared to the American people, and their reaction was powerfully supportive. Approving "in general" the "shoot on sight" directive were 62 percent of those interviewed by Gallup, disapproving 28 percent.

Once restrictions on escort eased, the British, Canadian, and American navies were soon getting much "mixed up together," to use Churchill's apt phrase. Even before the Greer incident, the battleship H.M.S. Rodney teamed up with the American carriers Wasp, Yorktown, and Long Island in search of a German raider, possibly the cruiser Prinz Eugen, which British intelligence feared had broken out again and which had been supposedly sighted east of Bermuda. The search was in vain. The president's orders to shoot on sight in the western Atlantic included German surface raiders as well as aircraft overflying Iceland. . . .

Shortly after Argentia, the German offensive resumed and soon sweeps and plunges by Panzer and motorized forces were taking huge bites out of the Red Army. The Soviets now were paying the price for the rest and replenishment of German forces in late July and early August. Army Group North cut Leningrad's communications, besieged the city and prepared to storm it. In the center the decision was to defer the attack on Moscow. Guderian's Panzer army swung south and with easier supply on a lateral front drove in behind the massive, inert concentration of Soviet forces—two-thirds of a million men—at Kiev. Opposite him, from Army Group South, Kleist's Panzer group crossed the Dnieper and gathered mass to strike north, meet Guderian, and seal off Kiev. Further south, Runstedt's columns fanned out across the Ukraine to encircle Odessa, cut off the Crimea, and capture the great bend of the Dnieper where it pokes eastwardly toward the industries of the Don basin. Beyond the Don lay the Caucasus and the Volga. Every major city of European Russia was imperiled except, for the moment, Moscow.

Western observers were slow to grasp the grim reality as the optimism of early August persisted. The American embassy in Moscow, now determinedly hopeful where it had been persistently skeptical, considered the reverses in the Ukraine as no worse than one battle lost. It warned that the capture of Rostov, where the Germans could turn the corner into the Caucasus, would be most serious, but pointed out on August 23 that winter would begin in sixty days. Soviet destruction of the great dam at Zaporozhe on the Dnieper, their emblem of proletarian progress, showed that Stalin's scorched earth policy was in "deadly earnest." The American legation in Switzerland, estimating German casualties of 1,400,000 (British estimates were 2,000,000), saw no sign of the breaking of Russian morale, fronts, or command. General Mason-Macfarlane, the British observer at Moscow, reported after a visit to the front that Russian morale and equipment were excellent, though he acknowledged that the situation in the south was "precarious." The *New York Times* reported the Russians holding or gaining on August 24, 25, 28, 31, September 1, 3, and 4. Only the American military attaché in London, with access to British intelligence, which in turn was based partly on ULTRA, pointed out the grave danger of the envelopment of Kiev.

So after weeks of sanguine reports, news of this "lurch into disaster in the Ukraine," as one authority has described it, came as a shock to Roosevelt, especially delivered as it was in a letter from Stalin to Churchill which was passed on to Washington on September 5. The situation, the Soviet chief said, had "considerably deteriorated" in the past three weeks because the Germans had transferred thirty to thirty-four divisions and great numbers of tanks and aircraft from the west. They did so "with impunity," he continued acidly, because they recognized that the danger in the west was a bluff. Their strategy was to smash their enemies singly, first the Soviet Union, then Britain. Now more than half the Ukraine was gone, and the enemy was at the gates of Leningrad. He ticked off the losses: the Krivoi Rog iron-ore district and metallurgical works in the Ukraine. Out of production for months because of evacuation were an aluminum factory on the Dnieper, another at Tikhvin in the north, an automotive factory and two aircraft factories in the Ukraine, and two automotive factories and an aircraft factory in Leningrad.

The only answer to this "mortal menace" was a British second front in the Balkans or France, a guarantee of 30,000 tons of aluminum by October, and monthly shipments of 400 aircraft and 500 tanks. Without this help, the Soviet dictator concluded in brutal candor, Russia would be defeated or so weakened it would be unable to help its allies by active operations. In conveying the message, Churchill informed Roosevelt that Soviet Ambassador Ivan Maisky in London had used language "which could not exclude the impression that they might be thinking of separate terms." With that language the American government was already familiar. In a dispatch Washington received August 27, Anthony Biddle, ambassador to several governments-in-exile in London, had reported Maisky as saying that the Soviet Union would make peace unless the United States entered the war and the British opened a second front.

Churchill responded to Stalin with equal candor that a second front that year was impossible and the next year indeterminable. The best he could offer was a buildup of forces in the Middle East, which, after the defeat of Axis forces in Libya, would "come into line on your southern flank," some undefined operation "in the extreme North when there is more darkness," and further battering of Germany from the air. Lacking a fighting front to offer, the British government stretched itself on war supplies. Churchill said he would try to expedite the Moscow conference on supply and promised on the spot, from British production, one-half of Stalin's request for tanks and planes with the hope that the Americans would supply the other half. He apologized to Roosevelt for presuming on American aid, explaining that the "moment may be decisive."

These were the exigencies when Roosevelt met with the admirals on September 5 to decide arrangements for escort of convoy. On the immediate issue of reinforcing the Middle East the president decided to meet the prime minister halfway: he would provide transports for one division and ten to twelve cargo ships. The troop ships would be the navy's largest and fastest: the former luxury liners *United States, America,* and *Manhattan.*

Roosevelt was no less determined to provide the Soviet Union with all possible war matériel than he had been before the Argentia conference. Upon his return from Argentia in the wake of the House vote barely extending the draft, he warned reporters against a natural tendency to slacken in delivery of goods when the Russians were succeeding. This, he said, was "terribly, terribly dangerous." He established the priority of Russian supply in the most authoritative and deliberate way in a letter to Stimson on August 30: "I deem it to be of paramount importance for the safety and security of America that all reasonable munitions help be provided for Russia, not only immediately but as long as she continues to fight the Axis powers effectively." . . .

The competitors for American supply were in fact "dividing a deficiency." War production in 1941 was still less than 10 percent of total production and less than two-thirds of British-Canadian, which it would not surpass until the last quarter of 1942. Because of design changes, B-17 production halted and the United States produced exactly one heavy bomber in July 1941. Better than half the military planes produced were trainers, and there were scarcely any spare parts. The United States had on hand eighty medium tanks and expected to complete 450 in the July-September quarter as against 10,790 by the end of 1942. It expected to produce 230,000 tons of shipping in the same quarter; the army calculated that defeat of Germany would require the 10.8 million already planned through 1943 and an additional 13.1 million tons.

From September 8 to the end of the month, intense and at times bitter struggles over priorities and allocations occurred between the White House and the army, the army and navy, the Americans and British at London, and the Anglo-Americans and Russians in Moscow. Roosevelt carefully monitored the action and imposed his will at crucial moments to ensure that the outcome would be acceptable to the Soviet government.

Bitterest of all was the battle over tanks. Stalin asked for five hundred a month, or 4,500 through June 1942, and the British promised half. Under pressure to match the British offer of 2,250, the U.S. Army agreed to stretch out the equipping of the 3rd, 4th, and 5th Armored Divisions and fifteen independent tank battalions and postpone activation of the 6th Armored Division. This sacrifice and severe cutbacks in British allocations yielded 1,524 medium and light tanks, or precisely two-thirds of the matching offer. The British protested, whereupon the president ordered a doubling of tank production and an increase of 25 percent in deliveries, to the anguish of the U.S. Navy, which feared that a higher priority for tanks would reduce the armor plate available for warship construction. With a greater supply promised, at least on paper, the British agreed to make up the difference in immediate deliveries in return for a larger quota of American tanks later. On this basis Stalin's demand for 500 tanks a month could be met. In the meantime the Soviet demand had risen to 1,100 a month, but in the end Stalin settled for five hundred.

With this sort of juggling and some highly speculative promissory notes on future production and delivery, the British Commonwealth and United States came forward with responsive offerings at Moscow on September 28. They would meet Stalin's original requests for aircraft and tanks in full. Canada would provide one-half the aluminum sought, and the Americans would study the possibility of providing the rest. Counterbalancing modest amounts of other weapons, the British and Americans offered 90,000 jeeps and trucks, as well as a wide array of finished metals and raw materials, and large amounts of wheat and sugar. Britain and the United States assured production but not delivery, leaving the enormous problem of transportation to joint responsibility and the future. Payment was a problem since Roosevelt was not quite ready to extend Lend-Lease to the Soviet Union on account of anti-Soviet public opinion, but by patching together credits and old purchases the Treasury Department tided over the interim. Stalin sent word he was "much gratified."

. . . Stimson and General [George C.] Marshall understood Roosevelt's concern for aid to the Soviet Union and his disposition, as Churchill explained to Stalin on August 28, "to take [a] strong line against further Japanese aggression whether in the South or in the Northwest Pacific." Marshall aimed his argument for holding on to American bombers and developing American strategic air power directly at these presidential concerns. In his brief for a conference with the president on September 22, next in priority after preparing task forces for defense of the Atlantic islands was the air reinforcement of the Philippines. The brief read: "Rush buildup of air power to Philippines . . . to restrain Japan from advance into Malaysia or Eastern Siberia.

What American planes might deter heavily depended on how far they could reach. The B-17C, the version sent in September, had a combat radius with a half-load of bombs of 900 miles. Formosa, Shanghai, even Okinawa, were within striking distance, but not the home islands of Japan. The B-17E, however, the new version to be sent thereafter, had a somewhat longer reach which might place Kyushu, the southern island of Japan, within striking distance. The army's War Plans Division began a special study of these and other strategic possibilities of air power in the Philippines on September 16.

Enthusiasm for the project did not wait. The B-17s authorized at Argentia, which would bring the total in the Philippines to thirty-five, prepared to move in October. The day the first nine B-17s arrived in the Philippines, Marshall ordered a second group of thirty-five across in December—as soon as it had new planes—for a total of seventy. The Air Corps was pressing for more, asking MacArthur how many could be accommodated on existing fields in three months and how many in six. . . .

The oil embargo and air reinforcement of the Philippines were both meant to halt Japanese expansion but there the similarity ends. The reinforcement project aimed at making a Japanese attack northward or southward too costly and risky. This deterrent effect itself was speculative and would not in any case be fully realized for several months when runways were extended and planes, ground personnel, munitions, and gasoline arrived. Therefore it might prompt Japanese action before the military capability was in place. Nevertheless, the aim of the rein-forcement was to encourage Japanese inaction. The oil embargo, however, if fully im-plemented and joined in by the British and Dutch, would have an immediate and growing impact and carry beyond deterrence to coercion. The clock would be ticking toward the moment when Japan would lack the fuel to send armies and fleets into battle and it would have to attack, change its aims, or subside in influence. It would suffer severe penalties from inaction.

The decision on an oil embargo was closely held and deviously managed. Action proceeded not in the formal realm of peacetime quotas and proclamations re-stricting export, for on paper Japan was supposed to receive some quantities of some kinds of oil, but in the shadowy world of inaction, circumvention, and red tape.

Upon the freezing of Japanese assets in July, the United States required both export licenses and licenses to withdraw funds to pay for the exports. Before leaving for Argentia, Welles had directed [Assistant Secretary of State Dean] Acheson to withhold action on exchange licenses for the time being, in effect while the president and he were absent. Most export licenses were denied, but a few were approved, and these came before the Foreign Funds Control Committee, which before long would have to give reasons for delay. Then, as Acheson later explained to Sir Ronald Campbell of the British embassy, the committee "discovered by accident the technique of imposing total embargo by way of its freezing order without having to take decisions about quotas for particular commodities." In anticipation of the freezing order, Japanese banks had sequestered dollars in the United States and Latin America. Aware of this plunge into cash and foreign accounts, the committee insisted that these funds be used before releasing frozen assets. The Japanese demurred.

This was the state of affairs Acheson reported to Welles the day before the president returned from Argentia. Undoubtedly either by phone or in person on August 21 or 29, when he saw the president alone, Welles reported the situation to Roosevelt, and no countervailing directive was issued. Japanese trade, Acheson noted on August 20, was "a matter of confidential discussion between the President and Secretary Hull." On September 5, a day Hull had lunch with the president, the secretary of state gave departmental sanction to these stalling maneuvers. The United States had imposed an embargo without saying so. It was in a position, said Acheson, to point out to the Japanese that they had "imposed [an] embargo upon themselves by their lack of loyalty to [the] American freezing order." . . .

Trade did not stop immediately. One ship was allowed as ballast a cargo of low-grade lubricating oil, asphalt, cotton, and cocoa beans. Some iron ore moved to Japan from the Philippines, some cotton to Japanese-occupied China. Dollars and yen were unfrozen to pay diplomatic staffs.

The stall only gradually surfaced. For weeks the British and Dutch were left in ignorance of the American intent. They learned September 13 that the embargo was "practically absolute" but that Hull wanted no publicity "which might demonstrate the completeness of the present embargo or suggest greater severity." On Sep-tember 26, Acheson apologized for the problems caused by the "somewhat oppor-tunist measures" he had been obliged to follow, and he finally explained to the

British and Dutch how the embargo worked and urged them to achieve the same result. They were already well on the way. Certain Indian trade with Japan posed a problem, and Britain was anxious to secure as much magnesium as possible from Japan for the making of incendiary bombs, but Japan's trade outside its orbit in East Asia had been practically closed down by October.

With the single exception of a stringent war warning, Roosevelt by October had fulfilled the commitments he made at Argentia. He had reaffirmed and indeed reinforced and extended the new policy directions he had chosen in the wake of the German attack on Russia. He had entered the Battle of the Atlantic, though on his own terms, extended the best aid possible to the Soviet Union, begun the buildup of a deterrent force in the Philippines, applied maximum economic pressure against Japan, and entangled the Japanese in complex and prolonged diplomatic talks. He had established, if not a formal alliance, an intimate political relationship with Great Britain. He had chosen courses risking war in the belief that alternative courses seemed riskier to American vital interests. The central dynamic of his policies was the conviction that the survival of the Soviet Union was essential for the defeat of Germany and that the defeat of Germany was essential for American security. This more than any other concern, to his mind, required the immobilization of Japan.

No single decision or day marked the point when Roosevelt crossed over from benevolent neutrality to belligerency and risk of war. The process was complex and extended from late July to mid-September. One particular day, however, seems to epitomize the transition: Friday, September 5, 1941. This was the day following the *Greer* incident when he ordered the start of convoy escort, the day he received Stalin's ominous message and promised his three best transports for reinforcement adjacent to the Russians in the Middle East. It was also the day Secretary Hull formalized within government the undercover embargo and when the first B-17s departed for Manila and the 19th Bombardment Group was ordered to follow in October.

SUGGESTED READINGS

John Morton Blum, *V Was for Victory: Politics and American Culture during World War II* (1976).

John Dower, *War Without Mercy: Race and Power in the Pacific War* (1986).

Susan M. Hartmann, *The Home Front and Beyond* (1982).

Gregg Herken, *The Winning Weapon* (1980).

Warren F. Kimball, *The Juggler* (1991).

Eric Larrabee, *Commander in Chief: Franklin Delano Roosevelt, His Lieutenants, and Their War* (1987).

Martin J. Sherwin, *A World Destroyed: The Atomic Bomb and the Grand Alliance* (1975).

Gaddis Smith, *American Diplomacy During the Second World War, 1941–1945*, 2nd ed. (1985).

Ronald H. Spector, *Eagle against the Sun* (1984).

Randall B. Woods, *A Changing of the Guard: Anglo-America, 1941–1946* (1991).

Further Readings

The Origins of World War II in Europe

P.M.H. Bell, *The Origins of the Second World War in Europe* (1986); Keith Eubank, ed., *World War II: Roots and Causes*, 2nd ed. (1992); David E. Kaiser, *Economic Diplomacy and the Origins of the Second World War* (1980); Gerhard L. Weinberg, *The Foreign Policy of Hitler's Germany: Starting World War II, 1937–1939* (1980).

Isolationism and America's Response to War

Wayne S. Cole, *Roosevelt and the Isolationists, 1932–1945* (1983); Robert A. Divine, *The Reluctant Belligerent* (1979); Frederick Marks, *Wind Over Sand: The Diplomacy of Franklin Roosevelt* (1988); Bruce Russett, *No Clear and Present Danger* (1972); James C. Schneider, *Should America Go to War* (1989).

Japanese Expansion

Michael A. Barnhart, *Japan Prepares for Total War: The Search for Economic Security, 1919–1941* (1987); Herbert Feis, *The Road to Pearl Harbor* (1964); Akira Iriye, *The Origins of the Second World War in Asia and the Pacific* (1987); James William Morley, ed., *The Fateful Choice: Japan's Advance into Southeast Asia, 1939–1941* (1980); H.P. Willmott, *Empires in the Balance: Japanese and Allied Pacific Strategies to April 1942* (1982).

Strategy and Diplomacy in the European Theater

George Herring, *Aid to Russia, 1941–1946* (1973); Ronald Schaffer, *Wings of Judgment: American Bombing in World War II* (1985); Mark Stoler, *The Politics of the Second Front, 1941–1943* (1977); Russell P. Weigley, *Eisenhower's Lieutenants: The Campaign for France and Germany, 1944–1945* (1981).

The War in the Pacific

Clay Blair, Jr., *Silent Victory: The U.S. Submarine War Against Japan* (1975); Gordon W. Prange, *At Dawn We Slept: The Untold Story of Pearl Harbor* (1981); John Toland, *The Rising Sun: The Decline and Fall of the Japanese Empire* (1970); William T. Youngblood, *Red Sun Setting: The Battle of the Philippine Sea* (1981).

The Home Front and Cultural Diplomacy

Alison R. Bernstein, *American Indians and World War II* (1991); Roger Daniels, *Prisoners Without Trial: Japanese Americans in World War II* (1993); Holly Cowan Shulman, *The Voice of America: Propaganda and Democracy, 1941–1945* (1990); William M. Tuttle, Jr., *Daddy's Gone to War: The Second World War in the Lives of America's Children* (1993); Harold Vatter, *The U.S. Economy in World War II* (1985); Allan M. Winkler, *Homefront, U.S.A.* (1986)

The End of the War and the Decision to Use the Atomic Bomb

Gar Alperovitz, *Atomic Diplomacy: Hiroshima and Potsdam* (1985); Diane Shaver Clemens, *Yalta* (1970); Leon Sigal, *Fighting to a Finish* (1988); Michael B. Stoff and Jonathan F. Fanton, eds., *The Manhattan Project* (1991).

The Holocaust

Deborah Lipstadt, *Beyond Belief: The American Press and the Coming of the Holocaust, 1933–1945* (1993); David S. Wyman, *The Abandonment of the Jews: America and the Holocaust, 1941–1945* (1984).

QUESTIONS FOR DISCUSSION

1. Describe the isolationist impulse as it existed in the United States during the 1930s. How was this spirit manifested in Congress?
2. Discuss the significance of the Nazi-Soviet Pact.
3. Compare and contrast the isolationist and interventionist positions as they developed in 1941. On which side of the debate did Roosevelt most nearly belong? Explain.
4. Despite laws to the contrary, Roosevelt aided the Allied powers against the Axis forces. What methods did the president employ?
5. Did the Japanese accomplish their goal in attacking Pearl Harbor? Why or why not?
6. Discuss the impact of World War II on women and Americans of African, Hispanic, and Japanese descent.
7. Evaluate President Harry S Truman's decision to use an atomic bomb to end the war with Japan. Were there any other feasible options?
8. Compare and contrast American and British goals during the drafting of the Atlantic Charter (Argentia Conference). According to historian Waldo Heinrichs, how significant was the final document? Explain.

CHAPTER TWENTY-TWO

THE ORIGINS OF THE COLD WAR

In the spring of 1945 the United States joined with the other victorious powers to establish the United Nations. American participation in this new collective security organization seemed to mark the end of isolationism and the triumph of Wilsonian internationalism. Yet, the U.N. was formed in a way that ensured that the five permanent members of the security council—Britain, France, the United States, the Soviet Union, and China—would dominate its proceedings. In addition, the unconditional veto accorded members of the Security Council coupled with provisions exempting "internal matters" from U.N. action and sanctioning regional security organizations meant that it would be very difficult for the new organization to act unless the major powers were unified. Indeed, the charter did more to preserve the principle of national sovereignty than to establish world government.

Roosevelt and Truman perceived correctly that whatever the provisions of the U.N. charter, the key to peace in the postwar world was keeping the Grand Alliance intact after the fighting had stopped. But for ideological, geopolitical, and historical reasons, that proved impossible. Joseph Stalin was determined to extend Soviet power as far into Europe as he could by establishing indigenous communist regimes that were loyal to Moscow. The Soviet leader viewed the Anglo-American call for immediate free elections in all occupation zones as a hostile act, since governments chosen in this way were bound to be noncommunist. Britain and belatedly the United States came to perceive the Soviet Union as a totalitarian, imperial threat bent on dominating first Europe and then the entire world. Stalin and communism, in the view of the Western democracies, were no different from Hitler and Nazism. The result of this confrontation was the division of Europe and the onset of the Cold War.

SEEDS OF DISCORD

Soviet mistrust of the Western democracies was heightened at the outset by their attempts to use economic and atomic diplomacy to pressure the Kremlin. At war's end, the Russian economy, built so laboriously and brutally during the 1930s, lay in ruins. Between 15 and 20 million Russians had died during the period from 1941 through 1945. The fighting destroyed thirty thousand factories, and agricultural output fell by 50 percent. The situation was so difficult that Stalin was loath to withdraw the Red Army from Eastern Europe lest it rebel over the lack of housing and jobs in the USSR. The Soviet Union desperately needed outside aid to rebuild and maintain a degree of political stability.

The United States, which emerged from World War II as by far the richest nation in the world, recognized Russia's plight and attempted to take advantage of it. In January 1945, as the war entered its final stages, the Kremlin requested a $6 billion reconstruction loan. The Roosevelt administration agreed in principle, but as relations between Washington and Moscow cooled, the Americans gradually pared their offer down to $1 billion. In the end, Stalin rejected the United States' veiled demands for concessions in the Soviet zones of occupation, and negotiations collapsed. In addition, in May 1945 even before the end of the war in Europe, the Truman administration ordered an immediate and complete cutoff of Lend-Lease aid to its Russian ally. When Stalin protested this "brutal" action, the president turned on the Lend-Lease spigot once again. Upon Japan's surrender in August, the program came to a final and unconditional end.

During World War II Roosevelt and Churchill chose not to inform Stalin of the Manhattan Project, the Anglo-American effort to build an atomic weapon ahead of the Germans. Unbeknownst to them, however, Soviet double agents in Canada and Britain penetrated the nuclear research programs and kept the Kremlin informed. Alarmed by Anglo-American secrecy, the Soviets started their own atomic program in 1943. By the time Truman informed Stalin of the weapon's existence at Potsdam, the Soviets were well on their way to developing their own weapon. Following the war, proponents of international cooperation within the Truman administration developed a disarmament plan which called for atomic powers to turn over in order fissionable material, processing plants, and finally stockpiles of international weapons to an international agency. Before it was officially presented to the U.N., that plan was modified by Bernard Baruch, the conservative financier whom Truman selected as his first representative on atomic energy. Baruch was responding to Army Chief of Staff Dwight Eisenhower who argued that in light of the rapid demobilization of U.S. armed forces, the country could not then limit its ability to produce atomic bombs. Under the Baruch Plan, the United States would keep its weapons unless and until the other atomic powers agreed to relinquish their fissionable materials and agreed to thorough inspection. Soviet representatives to the U.N. recognized the Baruch Plan for what it was—a scheme to perpetuate the American monopoly on atomic weapons—and they summarily rejected it.

THE DIVISION OF EUROPE

Meanwhile, in Germany, temporary zones of occupation quickly hardened into permanent boundaries. Determined to make Germany pay for the damage done to the Soviet economy, the Kremlin began taking reparations in the form of industrial plants, agricultural output, and forced labor. At the same time, the British, French, and Americans had made the decision to block the Russians from taking products from their zones. The United States and Great Britain merged the areas under their control and called for a unified Germany. Fearing a resurgence of German power, the Soviets laid the foundations for a communist republic in the east. In turn, France, the United Kingdom, and the United States made plans to transfer their authority to an independent West Germany.

One by one, communist regimes replaced coalition governments in Romania, Bulgaria, Hungary, and Poland. Soviet occupation authorities followed a similar pattern in each country. In the weeks following ouster of the Nazis, the Red Army established coalition governments composed of various prewar parties. Included in each were representatives of the local communist organization which, though small in number, had played a conspicuous role in the resistance. In each case, the communists were given control of the ministry of the interior which in turn supervised the state police. Invariably, the police discovered plots against the government by the other parties, jailed their leaders, and outlawed them. This process continued until there was just one. The communist regimes thus established in Eastern Europe were totally subservient to Moscow.

AMERICA'S AMBIVALENCE TOWARD SOVIET EXPANSION

The Truman administration was for a variety of reasons initially reluctant to confront the Soviets in Central Europe and the Near East. During the first year after the war, America's 11 million-person armed force dwindled to 2 million. Americans were tired of war; they wanted to get back to their families, to working and prospering, to dying in bed instead of on some distant battlefield. There was a tendency to place too much faith in the United Nations. Four years of propaganda had portrayed the Russians as America's gallant allies and Stalin as friendly old "Uncle Joe." Most Americans found it difficult to make the transition to thinking of the Russian leader as another Hitler bent on world domination. In addition, not only was Truman inexperienced and uninformed concerning world affairs, he picked as his first secretary of state James F. Byrnes, a man who was better known for his ability to deal with Congress than with wily foreign diplomats.

THE IRON CURTAIN SPEECH

Gradually during 1946, American attitudes began to harden. The first week in March Truman arranged for Winston Churchill to deliver a major speech on foreign affairs at Westminster College in Missouri. With Truman on the speaker's stand, Churchill declared that an "iron curtain" had descended across Europe from the Baltic to the Adriatic. Behind that frontier, the forces of communist totalitarianism ruled. The Soviet Union was an inherently expansionist power and the forces of international communism would sweep over Europe if the United States did not intervene. Indeed, he said, the only thing that could avert the destruction of Western civilization was American military and economic might. He called for the creation of an Anglo-American military establishment to protect Western Europe from further communist expansion. Some labeled Churchill a warmonger, but others remembered that he was the same man who had warned Europe against the dangers posed by Nazism and fascism in the 1930s.

THE IRANIAN CRISIS

The same week that Churchill spoke, Truman quietly forced the Soviets to abandon a scheme to gain economic and political control of Iran. In 1943 the Soviets had occupied the northern part of that strategically and economically important country. When World War II ended, the Russians refused to leave and began laying plans to merge the Azerbaijani region of Iran with the Soviet Republic of Azerbajain. When the Soviets attempted to gain control of Iran's oil industry as well, the government in Teheran appealed to the United Nations and to the United States. In March 1946 President Truman warned the Soviet Union against either military or political aggression against Iran and moved the U.S. Mediterranean fleet to the Persian Gulf. At that point, Stalin backed down.

ORIGINS OF THE CONTAINMENT POLICY

In January 1947, Truman replaced the South Carolinian as secretary of state with General George C. Marshall, the architect of Allied victory over the Axis. The naming of a military man to fill America's top diplomatic post was quite unusual, but Marshall had absolute respect for the hallowed democratic principle of civilian control of the military. He was, moreover, an excellent administrator. Determined to convert the State Department into a body capable of making long-range policy as well as dealing with immediate crises, he named a trio of qualified assistants. Marshall tabbed Dean Acheson to be undersecretary. A tough-minded Anglophile, Acheson believed that the United States ought to assume Britain's nineteenth-century role of arbiter of world affairs. With the example of Western appeasement of Hitler at Munich in 1938 always in mind, Acheson opposed appeasement and insisted that America negotiate only from strength. As assistant secretary for economic affairs, Marshall selected the Houston cotton broker and ardent economic internationalist, Will Clayton. Trade and aid were crucial, Clayton argued, to preserving the economy of the noncommunist world. To head the newly formed policy planning staff, the secretary chose George Kennan, a career diplomat and seasoned student of Russian culture and politics. He was intensely distrustful of the men who ran the

Kremlin and believed that if the Western democracies did not take adequate military and political measures, the Soviets would overrun all of Europe.

In February 1947 Kennan published an article in the prestigious journal *Foreign Affairs* entitled "The Sources of Soviet Conduct." It was nothing less than a call to arms. Russia's wartime and postwar advance on Europe was simply another chapter in the never-ending story of the effort by the barbaric peoples of the Asiatic heartland to overrun Western civilization, he wrote. Because the United States was part of this civilization and because the Western democracies had been gravely weakened by the war, America would have to intervene. The best approach would be containment, a policy of less than war itself but of opposing force with force, of drawing a line, establishing a defensive perimeter and telling the Russians, "Thus far you shall go and no farther." Actually, Kennan believed that because American resources were limited and that certain areas were of greater economic and strategic importance than others, the United States should stress some areas over others—Europe and the eastern Mediterranean, for example. An opportunity to implement the new approach was not long in coming.

DECLARATION OF COLD WAR

THE TRUMAN DOCTRINE

In late February 1947, Great Britain informed the United States that for financial reasons it was going to have to begin dismantling its outposts in the eastern Mediterranean and cutting off aid to its allies in that area. Since the construction of the Suez Canal, the region had been vital to Great Britain, whose lines of communication with its far-flung Asian and Far Eastern empire bisected the region. Its announcement that it was withdrawing signaled Britain's demise as a great power, a development which presaged both long-term and short-run problems for the Western democracies. Starting in 1944, the pro-Western Greek monarchy had been fighting a bitter civil war against an insurgent force that included a significant contingent of communists and that received aid from communist Yugoslavia. In addition, Turkey was then being pressured by the Soviet Union to grant it permission to build bases on the Bosporus and elsewhere in the country. To better make his point, Stalin massed several divisions of the Red Army along the Soviet-Turkish border. Marshall, Acheson, and Kennan quickly decided that the United States would have to assume Britain's role in the eastern Mediterranean.

On March 12, 1947, the president addressed a joint session of Congress. He asked for $400 million in emergency aid for Greece and Turkey. More important, he requested approval for the containment strategy George Kennan had just outlined. "It must be the policy of the United States," Truman declared, "to support free peoples who are resisting attempted subjugation by armed minorities or by outside pressure." In the debate that followed, some administration critics pointed out that the Greek government was undemocratic, corrupt, and reactionary and that Turkey was not a democracy and had remained neutral during the war. Why not allow these totalitarian regimes to be absorbed by another autocratic power? State Department spokesmen could only reply that under noncommunist regimes, democracy and progress were at least possible; under communism they were not. Within days, Congress had overwhelmingly approved the Truman Doctrine. The civil war in Greece ended in less than two years, and Turkey succeeded in resisting pressure from the Kremlin. America's announcement that it would resist external communist aggression and internal communist subversion, however, set the stage for a global confrontation with the Soviet Union.

THE MARSHALL PLAN

In the summer of 1947 the focus of the Cold War shifted to Western Europe, an area of far greater strategic importance to the United States than Eastern Europe or the Near East. Two years after the end of the fighting, France, Britain, Italy, and the low countries had still not recovered from the war's devastation. In an article in the *New York Times*, Hanson Baldwin reviewed the "plague and pestilence, suffering and disaster, famine and hardship" that gripped the region. Bombing and ground warfare had destroyed most of Western Europe's industry and much of its agricultural base. Drought had killed most of the 1946 wheat crop, and the severe winter of 1946–1947 had cut the prospects for the crop of 1947. Unemployment in France ran into the millions, and in England the coal shortage was so great that power had to be shut off for hours each day. Political extremism had historically flourished in such environments, and by 1947, there was a very real danger that the French and Italian Communist parties would be able to assume control of their respective countries through the electoral process. It seemed that if the United States did not act, all of Europe would drift into the communist orbit. At stake was the industrial balance of the world.

At a commencement address at Harvard, Secretary Marshall outlined a plan for the U.S.-financed rehabilitation of Western Europe. In his speech, Marshall urged the European nations to draft a coordinated plan and then present it to American officials. He made it clear the offer extended to all of Europe including Eastern Europe and the Soviet Union to the Urals. Apparently, the secretary of state was gambling that the Soviets and their satellites would not accept because it was clear that Congress would never fund a project that financed communist regimes. And, in fact, when representatives of the European states assembled in Paris in July, the Soviet representative walked out. The Kremlin subsequently forbade its client states to participate. Over the next four years the United States poured $17 billion into Europe. The Marshall Plan coupled with military aid rendered after the outbreak of the Korean War helped turn Western Europe's economy around. By 1952 industrial production had increased 30 percent over prewar levels and agricultural output 11 percent.

American policymakers decided that economic deprivation would spawn social instability and political extremism. German workers paid by Marshall Plan funds reconstruct a bombed-out building in Berlin, ca. 1948–1952.

With the return of prosperity, the appeal of the French and Italian Communist parties began to decline. The Marshall Plan also served U.S. economic interests. With the revival of its economy, Western Europe became America's largest trading partner.

THE NORTH ATLANTIC TREATY ORGANIZATION

The Truman Doctrine and Marshall Plan were America's declaration of Cold War, its promise to provide economic and military aid to those nations threatened by international communism. In 1949 the United States went one step further and committed American troops to the defense of Western Europe. Fearful that the Soviet Union would use its superiority in conventional forces in a military assault on the Western democracies, Great Britain, and France, together with Belgium, the Netherlands, and Luxemburg, signed the Brussels Treaty in 1948 providing for collective self-defense.

FIGURE 22–I

A Divided Germany and NATO

Then in 1949 in response to a request from Europeans that the United States demonstrate its willingness to shed blood for the common good, President Truman called for the creation of an Atlantic defense community. On April 4, 1949, in Washington, the United States joined with Canada, Iceland, Denmark, Norway, Portugal, Greece, Turkey, and the Brussels powers to create the North Atlantic Treaty Organization (NATO, see Figure 22–1). Its key clause stated that "an armed attack against one or more . . . shall be considered an attack against them all." In 1950, Truman named Dwight D. Eisenhower to be supreme NATO commander, and he sent four American divisions to Europe to form the corps of a NATO army.

It was clear that these troops were to serve as a tripwire if Soviet troops attacked. In effect, Western Europe had been placed behind an American atomic shield. There was no evidence of a Russian plan to invade the west, but the Soviets continued to maintain hundreds of divisions in Eastern Europe and East Germany. Caught up in the Munich analogy, American officials felt that they could not gamble that units of the Red Army were there for purely defensive purposes. The creation of NATO led directly to the formation by the Soviet Union and Eastern Europe of the Warsaw Pact and heightened tensions throughout the world.

THE COLD WAR IN ASIA

By 1949 the notion prevailed among most Americans that they and their allies faced an international communist threat directed from the Kremlin and bent on world domination. They made little or no distinction between Marxist-Leninist ideology and Soviet imperialism. When China, the most populous nation in the world, fell to the communists in 1949, both government officials and the general public in the United States assumed that the Kremlin was responsible. The triumph of the Chinese Communists under Mao Ze-dong greatly intensified public and official anxiety in the United States and led directly to the Korean War.

THE FALL OF CHINA

When the War in the Pacific ended in August 1945, there were two governments in China—one under Jiang Jieshi headquartered in Nanking and the communist regime under Mao Ze-dong who controlled much of the north. For a year an uneasy truce prevailed between the two governments, and then full-scale civil war erupted. Despite superiority in manpower and materiel, the Chinese Nationalists were driven off the mainland within two years and forced to take refuge on the island of Formosa (Taiwan).

Jiang's defeat sent shock waves through the United States. Republicans blamed the Truman administration. Following the war, the United States had funneled $2 billion to Jiang's army and still it had collapsed like a house of cards. In reality, American policy had had little impact on the Chinese situation. Primarily responsible for the Nationalists' defeat was the fact that Jiang had lost touch with the people. His regime had become corrupt and exploitive. Promotion in the military depended upon loyalty to General Jiang Jieshi and not competence. In contrast, Mao and Zhou Enlai, his chief lieutenant, governed areas under their control fairly, if autocratically, instituting land reform and an equitable tax structure. Most important, the Chinese

Communists convinced the masses that they were the true promoters of Chinese nationalism, that they were capable of unifying and stabilizing the country and gaining it the international respect it deserved. The Soviets did furnish the Chinese Communists with some $2 billion worth of munitions and equipment taken from the Japanese, but Stalin, who preferred a weak and divided China, advised Mao and Zhou to abjure armed conflict. Least important was American policy. The Truman administration provided aid without forcing Jiang to institute reforms, but there was little the United States could have done to have halted the civil war or prevented a Nationalist defeat.

NSC 68 AND THE GLOBALIZATION OF THE COLD WAR

Nonetheless, the United States reacted as if it were responsible for the Chinese Communist takeover of the mainland and that it had the power to prevent the spread of communism anywhere and everywhere else. After the Soviet Union exploded an atomic device in 1949, Truman ordered the military to go ahead with development of a hydrogen bomb. At the same time, Acheson ordered the policy planning staff, now headed by Paul Nitze, to come up with a new defense policy.

The premise underlying NSC 68, as the new edition of containment became known, was that Marxism-Leninism was inherently totalitarian and imperialistic and that the Soviet Union was determined to impose its will on the entire world. Nitze advocated a massive expansion of American military power so the United States could meet the threat posed by Soviet communism whenever and wherever it appeared. NSC 68 insisted that the U.S. economy could support a military budget that absorbed up to 50 percent of the GNP, and it recommended that the defense budget be increased from $13 billion to $45 billion.

KOREA DIVIDED

Before the globalist policies inherent in NSC 68 could be carried out, however, the Cold War spread to the Korean peninsula and heated up. From 1905 to 1945 Korea was a Japanese colony. The Allies made a verbal commitment to Korean independence during World War II, and in June 1945, to clear the area of Japanese, Soviet troops occupied the area north of the thirty-eighth parallel and U.S. forces the territory south of that line. As the Cold War intensified, however, the thirty-eighth parallel became an impermeable barrier. The communists installed a people's republic in the north, and American authorities presided over the election of the staunchly anticommunist Syngman Rhee in the south.

Paradoxically, at the same time Nitze and his staff were preparing NSC 68, Dean Acheson was attempting to reduce American commitments in East Asia. In response to pressure from conservatives such as Senator Robert Taft and former president Herbert Hoover who were arguing for a more limited role for the United States in world affairs, the undersecretary announced in January

1950 that South Korea was henceforward outside America's strategic perimeter. Its defense was a matter for the U.N. Other statements by Acheson and General Douglas MacArthur, commander of U.S. forces in the Far East, indicated that Taiwan was also not among those nations that the United States would defend from attack. MacArthur declared repeatedly that it would be madness for the United States to fight a land war on the mainland of Asia.

THE KOREAN WAR

North Korea Invades

On June 25, 1950, the army of the communist republic of North Korea crossed the thirty-eighth parallel in an effort to reunify the country. Syngman Rhee's forces fled in confusion. Two days later, Truman met with his top advisors: Korea and Taiwan were to be brought back within the American defense perimeter, he declared. The president ordered MacArthur to use troops under his command to ensure that the South Korean army was not driven entirely off the peninsula.

Subsequently, with U.S. help, Rhee's forces were able to establish and protect an enclave around Pusan. The following week, the United States and its allies on the U.N. Security Council presented a resolution condemning North Korean aggression and calling upon members to contribute to a military force to defend South Korea. The Soviet representative to the U.N. was then boycotting council meetings because, at the insistence of the West, the world organization was refusing to seat Red China. As a result, the resolution authorizing U.N. military intervention into the Korean conflict passed. On July 8 MacArthur was named to head the multinational force that was to help the South Koreans defeat aggression.

MacArthur Counterattacks

Allied forces, made up primarily of South Korean and U.S. troops, were initially forced to cling to an enclave around Pusan on the southeastern tip of the peninsula. In the fall, however, MacArthur staged a daring amphibious landing at the port of Inchon on the west coast halfway between the thirty-eighth parallel and the southern tip of Korea. The assault was a success, and MacArthur's troops established a beachhead. In the weeks that followed, U.S. Marines and army personnel in cooperation with Republic of Korea troops pushed out from Pusan and Inchon. Confronted with this two-pronged offensive and Allied firepower, the North Korean Army began to retreat, a retreat that quickly turned into a rout.

China Enters the War

As MacArthur's troops neared the prewar boundary between North and South Korea, the Truman administration faced a dilemma. Should the U.N. command stop at the thirty-eighth parallel or should it continue northward to the Yalu

The beginning of a successful beachhead at Inchon, Korea, 1950.

River and reunify the country? MacArthur strenuously recommended the latter course, and Truman's advisors in Washington soon concurred, arguing to the president that it would be impossible to maintain an independent and secure South Korea as long as the communists were in control of the North. And, of course, the temptation to roll back the frontiers of communism in East Asia was irresistible.

By the second week in November, MacArthur was within sight of the Yalu River, the boundary separating North Korea from China. The Supreme Commander predicted that American troops would be home by Christmas. In choosing to forcibly reunify Korea, the United States had opted to ignore warnings sent out by Communist China that it would not tolerate such a move. With the bitter Korean winter setting in, three hundred thousand Chinese troops crossed the border and smashed the two U.N. columns that had penetrated deep into North Korean territory. In his haste and overconfidence, MacArthur had had these two spearheads advance so quickly that they outran their logistical and reserve support. There was, moreover, little connection between the two. The communists killed or captured a large number of American soldiers; a remnant of MacArthur's force fought its way to the coast and escaped while the rumps of the columns retreated before the advancing Chinese (see Figure 22–2).

FIGURE 22–2
The Korean War

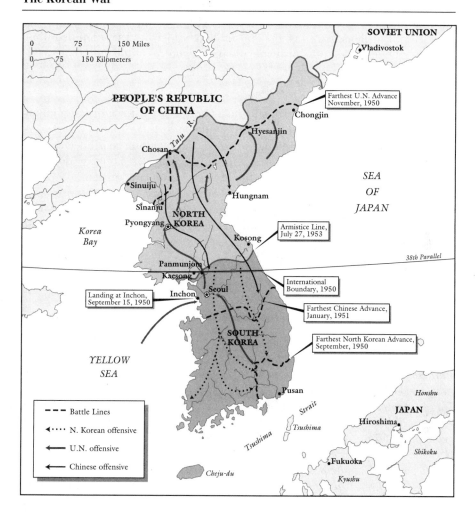

Truman's Dilemma

Massing its reserves and utilizing its superior firepower, the U.N. command halted the communist offensive, but only after the Red Chinese and North Koreans had advanced well below the thirty-eighth parallel. Slowly, painfully, the Allies advanced up the peninsula once again until they reached a line corresponding roughly to the prewar boundary. This time President Truman chose to stop and seek a peace based on the restoration of prewar boundaries. General MacArthur protested this decision so vehemently that Truman felt it necessary to relieve him of his command. The general returned to the United States to a hero's welcome. Republicans in Congress succeeded in launching an official investigation of the circumstances surrounding MacArthur's dismissal, but the administration succeeded in defending its decision to stop at the thirty-eighth parallel and in demonstrating that in publicly criticizing the administration, the general had violated the principle of civilian control of the military.

An Uneasy Peace

Meanwhile, in October 1951 armistice talks began in the town of Panmunjom located between the U.N. and communist battle lines. Talks quickly deadlocked over the question of how to exchange prisoners, and fighting continued sporadically through the next year and a half and became an issue in the 1952 election. Dwight Eisenhower, the Republican candidate, promised that if elected, he would act at once to end the war. The Republicans did indeed win, and in the spring of 1953 Secretary of State John Foster Dulles made veiled threats to expand the war dramatically if the Chinese and North Koreans did not agree to an armistice. Whether in response to these threats or out of war weariness, Pyongyang and Beijing agreed to exchange prisoners, and the guns fell silent in Korea on July 27, 1953.

The causes of the Cold War have attracted more attention since the 1960s than any other single issue in American history. Orthodox historians take the view that the Soviet Union and Communist China were totalitarian, expansionist powers bent on dominating the world. As it had during World War II, the United States interposed its power between the Soviet Union, Communist China, and the noncommunist world in order to protect its strategic and economic interests and to preserve freedom and democracy throughout as much of the world as possible.

Revisionists challenge this view, insisting that the Soviet Union was a devastated, defenseless nation in 1945 and that its aggressiveness stemmed from justifiable suspicion of the capitalist, Western nations led by the United States. Similarly, they portray Jiang Jieshi as a corrupt warlord with fascist tendencies, while Mao Ze-dong and his colleagues come across as autocratic but genuinely committed to a strong, egalitarian China. Like the Soviet Union, China after 1949 was weak and its policies defensive.

Postrevisionists see the Soviet Union and Communist China as expansionist, autocratic threats to Western civilization, but imply that mistakes and contradictions in American policy simultaneously antagonized the Soviet Union and opened Eastern Europe to communist domination.

Bruce Cumings is the leading revisionist authority on the origins of the Korean War. In the interpretation that follows, he argues that the South Korean government of Syngman Rhee was more a creation of the American government designed to contain communism in East Asia than a true expression of the

Korean populace's will. Moreover, he insists that rolling back the Bamboo Curtain (the Asian version of the Iron Curtain) was a viable policy option being considered by the Truman administration well before the war broke out. MacArthur's initial success in a sense presented Washington with an opportunity to do what it already wanted to do.

THE COURSE OF KOREAN-AMERICAN RELATIONS, 1943–1953

Bruce Cumings

Internationalism, Containment, Rollback: A Sketch

In conventional accounts of the cold war, the Roosevelt administration is identified with a naïve internationalism, the Truman administration with a realistic containment, and the Eisenhower/Dulles administration with unsettling rollback policies. FDR's globalism, exemplified by the United Nations organization and the "four policemen" (the United States, USSR, Great Britain, China) who would regulate the peace, gave way to Truman's narrower conception of containing the Soviet Union, first in Greece and Turkey (1947) and then in East Asia (1950). When the Republicans assumed power in 1953, John Foster Dulles proclaimed a new policy of "liberation," or rollback, accompanied by loud rhetoric about "positive action" against communism to replace the alleged defeatism and negativism of containment; Dulles met his deserved rebuke in 1956, when the Soviets invaded Hungary and the United States could do nothing to implement its support of rollback, thus showing the policy to have been empty.

This account of policies and people is fallacious and misleading. Only the Truman administration pursued actual rollback policies, and only in Korea. From 1945 to 1950 American policy moved through the entire gamut, beginning with the inherited Rooseveltian globalism, narrowing to containment by early 1946, and moving into a phase of potential rollback in the summer of 1949. After the Korean

from Bruce Cumings, "The Course of Korean-American Relations, 1943–1953" in Bruce Cumings, ed., *Child of Conflict: The Korean-American Relationship, 1943–1953* (Seattle: University of Washington Press, 1983), 3–57.

War began, the opportunities of the fighting opened the way to the only implementation of rollback, and the only occupation of Communist-held real estate in the postwar era. The Korean peninsula, far from being a distant backwater, was instead the center of all this action. Close attention to the Korean case therefore goes beyond Korean-American relations: it tells a tale, if not the tale, of the cold war. . . .

Rollback

Rollback was the preferred strategy of those elements wholly dissatisfied with internationalism, and partially dissatisfied with containment; it got its strongest voicing in the early 1950s but its only actual implementation in 1950. Since it barely existed in both theory and practice, unlike the other two visions, it is the hardest to sketch satisfactorily. A world free of communism was its ideal, leading to compromises on other fronts. . . .

In the wake of the atomic attacks on Japan, several American officers attached to the State-War-Navy Coordinating Committee (SWNCC), including Dean Rusk, found a line at the thirty-eighth parallel that could divide U.S. and Soviet occupation responsibilities in Korea. This occurred on the night of August 10–11, 1945. Stalin's response was to say nothing—the first of several anomalies in Soviet policy toward Korea, leading up to the fall of 1950. Why anomalous? Because the Soviets had entered Korea on August 8 and could have enveloped the peninsula long before the Americans could arrive.

SWNCC planners were desirous of stopping the southward flow of Soviet power in Korea; thus they wanted a line as far north as practicable, one that included the capital at Seoul. (Given American capabilities, no line was practicable if the Soviets resisted.) Thus the decision was political. The U.S. military was more reluctant, noting that no forces for occupation were anywhere near Korea. Although the decision came in harried times, it was a logical follow-on to planning that had linked the control of Korea to Pacific security as early as November 1943.

The reluctance of the American military to occupy Korea presaged another consistent pattern: the State Department wished to define Korea as important to U.S. security, but military planners sensed the limits of American military power and wondered if this peninsula were all that important in the context of global U.S. security concerns. Such worries came up again in 1947 and 1950, as we will see. Later in August 1945 yet a third pattern in American policy toward Korea was etched in: with the actual occupation, policy would increasingly be subject to decisions made on the scene rather than in Washington. State Department planners were too far off and too preoccupied with other matters to grab the reins of policy. Those on the scene quickly came to think that they knew better, and so sought to exclude the State Department. Thus "high policy," to speak in such terms, dallied behind Korean realities—usually by at least six months—and all too often the tail wagged the dog.

A month after the Korean problem was disregarded at Potsdam, the United States had sponsored a rush into Korea and had acquired, so it seemed, some sort of commitment to defend at least a part of Korea against Soviet encroachments or a Soviet-sponsored regime. This scramble into Korea, and this seeming commitment, had the support of virtually all government agencies concerned with the matter, from the president on down. Gen. John R. Hodge, occupation commander, not only understood this mandate but learned, also in late August, that his problems would include not simply the Soviets, but Korean revolutionaries released by the thousands from Japanese prisons after August 15. Such political prisoners joined others in setting up labor unions, political parties, "people's committees," and a host of peace-keeping forces that nearly supplanted the Japanese by the time the Americans arrived. Hodge knew this because of "a flood" of messages exchanged with Japanese commanders in Seoul who spoke darkly of Communists running rampant and desired an early American entry to prevent "the transfer of authority from the Japanese hand."

Hodge thus, from the day he arrived, set about eliminating this domestic, indigenous revolutionary force, something that so greatly disordered the U.S. occupation, that the indigenous Left and its fortunes became the touchstone against which virtually all occupation policy was judged from 1945 to 1949 (the occupation did not actually terminate until June 1949, almost a year after the Republic of Korea was proclaimed). This meant that the cold war arrived in Korea in September 1945, with a de facto containment policy toward the Soviets in the north and a counterinsurgent policy in the south. Within the first three months of the occupation such policies led to, among other things, the surreptitious return of Syngman Rhee to Seoul (through an end run around State Department opposition), the revival of the very substantial Korean element of the Japanese national police, the utilization of Korean colonial bureaucrats in all departments, the extraordinary and insubordinate act of establishing National Defense Forces for the south alone (in October 1945), and finally moves toward the creation of a separate southern administration that would merge selected exile nationalists (Syngman Rhee and Kim Ku, mainly) with the colonial bureaucracy. . . .

Although by early 1946 Hodge backed off from formally creating a separate southern regime, in effect a separate southern entity existed from December 1945 on; by August 1946 its Korean leaders were already questioning American "interference" in their activities. This same entity became the political basis for the ROK regime in 1948; very little changed during 1946 and 1947. What were the consequences of this early, precipitate action?

First, the southern regime was almost entirely an American creation, much more so than with the Nationalists in China or the successive regimes in South Vietnam. Second, the occupation intervened time and again in the countryside, either with U.S. tactical troops or with American-directed Korean police, to suppress the opponents of this regime. Thousands died as a result of such actions, and indeed in the autumn of 1946 four of the eight southern provinces erupted in bloody conflict. . . . Third, the bolstering of this regime as a bulwark against communism in the north created a containment policy. . . . The thirty-eighth parallel became a line drawn in the dirt behind which were constructed dikes and edifices in the form of military, police, and civil bureaucracies, all with the main goal of stopping the southward flow of revolution, or the northward flow of counterrevolution. . . .

By September 1946, Korea had become rather important, at least in the mind of one of Truman's high advisers. Clark Clifford's important, top secret report of that month argued that "the U.S. should support and assist all democratic countries which are in any way menaced or endangered by the U.S.S.R."; in discussing certain "trouble spots" he turned first to East Asia: "This country should continue to strive for a unified and economically stable China, a reconstructed and democratic Japan, and a unified and independent Korea." Such countries "will require diligent and considered effort on the part of the U.S. if Soviet penetration and eventual domination is to be prevented." The paper also argued for global policies, not ones linked only to the preservation of a non-Communist Western Europe.

Such thinking led directly to the Truman Doctrine in early 1947, marking among other things a formal commitment to containment in Europe, and in Greece and Turkey. For a time it appeared that it would also be extended to Korea. On March 5, 1947, Secretary of War Robert Patterson addressed a letter to the Secretary of State, saying that Greece and Turkey were "only part of a much larger problem"; he thought it "important and urgent" to survey situations elsewhere in the world "which may require analogous financial, technical, and military aid on our part." This prompted a study of Korea, then getting about $100 million per annum in all expenses connected with the occupation. An interdepartmental committee came up with a report, submitted to the secretaries of state and war, which argued that containment should be extended to Korea and that the large sum (for that time) of $600 million be appropriated for "a positive political, cultural, and economic program." . . .

On April 4, Secretary Patterson responded to such thinking by dropping a bombshell: the United States should "get out of Korea at an early date"; all measures should have early withdrawal as their goal. He noted that the occupation was a great drain on War Department funds, that Congress was not likely to provide $600 million for Korea, and if it did this would be a drain on other needed funds. He suggested either that the United States set up and recognize a separate southern government, or take the problem to the United Nations, both as methods of getting out. . . .

With this argument Patterson set the terms of a debate that would last down to 1950, in which the State Department argued for what might be called the *political-strategic* interest of the United States in Korea, while military departments at times recognized the political value, but tended not to say much about it and instead to argue that the *military*-strategic value of Korea was nil: it would be bypassed in a general war, and so the troops should come out. The situation was one in which the State Department defined the political value of Korea as high, with the fairly unsubtle suggestion that the occupation was botching the political aspect by supporting the Korean right-wing; whereas the military, tired of paying for a thankless struggle, and worried about world-wide limits to U.S. power, retreated to a narrow general-war-based definition of Korea's value to the United States. . . .

Dean Acheson, by then an under secretary of state, had somewhat different ideas. He told a secret congressional hearing in 1947 that "we have drawn the line in Korea." His point was that containment should be applied where it could work, but not where it would simply drain American blood and treasure. In a cabinet meeting in March 1947, for example, when queried as to why, if containment were the policy, the United States would want to pull out of China, Acheson responded, "Fundamentals of problems the same [in China]. The incidences are different." The "incidences" in Korea were such that containment might work; in any case, as we have seen, the occupation had been trying to make it work.

These disputes over whether containment should apply to Korea, or whether the United States ought to cut its losses, were put off with the acceptance of SWNCC 176/30, "United States Policy in Korea," implemented in mid-August 1947. This document argued that "The U.S. cannot at this time withdraw from Korea under circumstances which would inevitably lead to Communist domination of the entire country. The resulting political repercussions would seriously damage U.S. prestige in the Far East and throughout the world. . . ." The suggested course of action was to take the Korean problem to the United Nations General Assembly in the fall of 1947, assuming (as virtually all Americans in Seoul and Washington had since early 1947) that the second round of U.S.–Soviet Joint Commission talks would fail. . . .

The move to the UN was a grand success in lining up multilateral backing for American policy in Korea, although the Americans (in Washington and Seoul) had constantly to cajole and threaten the delegates on the UN Temporary Commission on Korea (UNTCOK) to get them (1) to agree to serve, over Soviet objections; (2) to hold an election in the south only, when their mandate was to hold it throughout Korea; (3) to validate that the May 10, 1948, National Assembly elections were conducted in a "free and fair" atmosphere (given that all delegates knew the election would bring Syngman Rhee and the rightist Korean Democratic party to power); (4) finally to recognize the Republic of Korea as "the only such government" in Korea organized under UN sponsorship—something that the Rhee regime immediately used as tantamount to official UN recognition. But the policy was also a failure, in that it not only accomplished but gave blessing to the final division of Korea and the separate southern regime that had been created, in its essentials, in the fall of 1945. In other words, the UN sanctioned a division and a regime that internationalists (John Vincent being the best single example) had fought against since early 1945. The reasons this could happen are two, and simple: (1) the United States utterly dominated the UN during this period; (2) both containment thinkers and internationalists were united by an irreduceable minimum goal: Korea or a part of it should be kept out of the Soviet orbit, for otherwise the security of the Pacific would be threatened. . . .

The Baiting Game

With U.S. policy poised between withdrawal (option A) and the ironclad guarantee of commitment (option C), two obstreperous Asian dictators sought to bait a far-off and seemingly reluctant guarantor. Chiang K'ai-shek and Syngman Rhee urged full U.S. backing for the southern side in their respective civil wars. Chiang could not get American policy to bite, and he ended up on Taiwan (still dangling bait). Syngman Rhee dangled bait all during 1949. A third dictator, Kim Il-sung, also sought support for his side of the civil war, in a bargaining relationship with the Russians *and the Chinese*—a matter we will get to shortly.

1948 was a year that changed the East Asian context of American policy profoundly. Most important, the Nationalists lost the civil war in China. The victory of Mao's forces had a tremendous impact on all actors in the East Asian milieu. For Americans, including George Kennan, it suggested a stiffened policy in areas contiguous to China. For Syngman Rhee and his allies, it struck terror in their hearts. For Kim Il-sung and his allies, it was the headiest thing that had happened since the capitulation of the Japanese Empire. Next in importance, the reverse course for Japan set in, giving the United States a strong commitment there and raising fears among Japan's old enemies. The spring crises in Czechoslovakia and Berlin suggested to Americans a Soviet policy willing to probe with force at the periphery of its empire. Within South Korea the old battles between the State Department and the occupation also ended; General Hodge was replaced in late August 1948, and a new ambassador, John Muccio, became the head of the American mission in Seoul. . . . Muccio was a cold warrior who got along well with the military, and rarely if ever questioned the harsh repression that was daily fare under the Rhee regime. All of these changed circumstances combined to suggest once again the virtues of containment in Korea.

On December 17, 1948, the chief of the Division of Northeast Asian Affairs in the State Department, Max Bishop, penned a top secret memorandum that fit Korea into previous considerations. He wanted a careful review of NSC 68 in view of the changed situation. On Japan, he remarked, "Should communist domination of the entire Korean peninsula become an accomplished fact, the islands of Japan would be surrounded on three sides by an unbroken arc of communist territories . . . we would be confronted with increasing difficulties in attempting to hold Japan within the United States sphere. . . ."

Should Korea be lost, the United States "would have lost its last friend on the continent" with China's fall; "failure to face up to these problems in Korea could eventually destroy U.S. security in the Pacific." Bishop suggested a "positive effort" aimed, in Truman Doctrine terms, "to develop in non-Soviet northeast Asia a group of independent people . . . who, on an economically viable basis, are capable of successfully resisting communist expansion." Bishop was close to the Japan lobby and this statement reflected its views on Korea. Like Kennan, Bishop also noted that there was in Northeast Asia "one of the four or five significant power centers in the world." Then he asked the containment question: "Whether communist expansion in northeast Asia had already reached the point at which the security interests of the U.S. require positive efforts to prevent further expansion." But he also introduced a new question: "Whether the communist power system, already brutally frank and outspoken in its hostility to the U.S., must be *caused to draw back* from its present extensive holdings" (my emphasis). Elsewhere, in the National Security Council (NSC), the Economic Cooperation Agency (ECA), and the CIA, Japan's economic revival raised a similar question: how Japan could be viable without its previous Asian territories, how it could function except as a drain on American resources without its old "natural" economy. Japan needed an economic hinterland, and from 1948 to 1950 American planners sought it in Manchuria, Korea, Taiwan, and Southeast Asia. Such thinking also suggested the virtues of rollback, at least in some of these regions. Thus, a rollback option had been suggested, and now the choices were four: cut bait, containment, ironclad guarantee, and rollback.

. . . The firmest advocate of rollback was Syngman Rhee. As early as June 1946 he had publicly argued for a "northern expedition" to kick the "Communist bandits" out of the north; he used the same Chinese characters that Chiang did for the northern expedition in the 1920s *(pukbŏl* or *beifa)*. At about the same time he found a small coterie of unofficial American backers to support his plans for a separate southern government and a march north. Americans familiar with South Korea since 1945 knew that not only Rhee, but his nationalist rival Kim Ku, and such other right-wing Koreans with experience in the Chinese Nationalist military as Yi Pŏm-sŏk and Yi Ch'ŏng-ch'ŏn, had grandiose plans not only to attack north but to keep on going into Manchuria, to open a new front in alliance with Chiang in the Chinese civil war. . . .

American policy, clearly, would not commit to Rhee's provocative rollback strategy. But during this same period—summer 1949—U.S. policy began to congeal around containing an overt North Korean attack, and by December 1949 this policy had arrived with new options, one of which was rollback. This assertion directly reverses the conventional historiography, but new documentation requires such a reversal, in my view. On June 27, 1949, the Department of the Army drew up a top secret schedule of options in the event of "a possible full scale invasion from North Korea subsequent to withdrawal of U.S. troops from South Korea." The possible courses of action included (a) emergency evacuation of American nationals in Korea; (b) presentation of the problem to the United Nations Security Council for emergency consideration; and (c) "to initiate *police action* with U.N. sanction by the introduction of a military task force into Korea composed of U.S. units and units of other member nations of the U.N. with the objective of restoring law and order and restoration of the 38th parallel boundary inviolability" (emphasis added). The paper recommended adopting options (a) and (b) as policy, but option (c) was deemed "unsound militarily" and should be considered only if "all other methods have failed." The JCS subsequently stated its agreement with these judgments. Thus the military stuck to its long-standing judgment that Korea was the wrong place to make a stand—but now with the single caveat, unless all else fails. . . .

From the fall of 1949 to the spring of 1950 was, as Acheson aptly put it, "the NSC 68 period." It was, in other words, the time when the State Department and NSC pursued a major—perhaps the major—reorientation of postwar global policy, resulting in the famous NSC 68 document. Simultaneously the same agencies developed NSC 48, "The Position of the U.S. with Respect to Asia," approved by Truman in its second revised form as 1949 drew to a close. This document was, in effect, an NSC 68 for Asia policy. Although this documentation has been available since the mid-1970s, most analysts have missed the interesting dialectic between containment and rollback policies that runs through both documents.

In its final form NSC 48/2 included for the first time an expressed commitment to extend containment to Asia: "For the foreseeable future . . . our policy must be to contain . . . the power and influence of the USSR in Asia." But there was another phrase as well, in the second ellipsis: "to contain and *where feasible to reduce* the power and influence of the USSR in Asia" (emphasis mine). Although Korea was not mentioned in this context, the logic of the new policy meant that the policy of containment pursued in Korea since August 1945 had won final sanction. But what about the suggestion of *reducing* Soviet power and influence? Was this an insignificant addendum? The deliberations leading up to the adoption of NSC 48/2 show that it was not. In conjuring the realm of the feasible, policy makers had rollback in their minds. . . .

NSC 68, adopted in effect if not formally in April 1950, contained similar references both to containment all along a global communist periphery, and to rollback. Soviet mischief might mean global war, or it might mean "limited objectives"; in any case the United States must "apply force" to counteract such activity. But containment was not conceived passively: "As for the policy of 'containment,' it is one which seeks by all means short of war to (1) *block* further expansion of Soviet power, (2) expose the falsities of Soviet pretensions, (3) *induce a retraction* of the Kremlin's control and influence and (4) in general, so foster the seeds of destruction within the Soviet system that the Kremlin is brought at least to the point of modifying its behavior. . . ." (emphasis added). Later on the document referred to "the checking and rolling back" of the Kremlin's drive, "to check and to roll back" its attempt at world domination, the taking of "dynamic steps to reduce the power and influence of the Kremlin," and so on. In short, the dialectic between containment (passive bulwarks) and rollback (dynamic action) was nearly identical to that in NSC 48. . . .

. . . The drafters thought the revived Japanese economy would require an Asian hinterland in order to function. This was an idea that ran like a thread through much of the reverse course planning. We have already seen that Kennan immediately grasped the *strategic* logic of reviving Japan: it should be reintroduced in Northeast Asia as a counter to the Soviet Union in classic balance-of-power fashion. But the NSC 48 drafters, and other agencies such as the ECA and the CIA, saw an *economic* logic as well. In this they were joined by elements of the private sector in the Japan lobby, representing banking and high-technology industries that did not fear Japanese competition. . . .

Southeast Asia was the main candidate for Japan's hinterland in the period from 1948 to 1950, but there were some suggestions that the old hinterland might be more appropriate, if Korea, Manchuria, and Taiwan could be kept out of or wrested back from Communist hands. Thus an ECA memorandum in Acheson's papers, dated November 3, 1948, argued that "North China and Manchuria constitute the one area of vital importance to the U.S." in Asia; "the Japanese proved it to be the key to control of China," and without the resources of the area, "there would literally be no hope of achieving a viable economy in Japan." The author noted "the strategic and economic relationship of North China and Manchuria with Korea and Japan." Thus, "our first concern must be the liberation of Manchuria and North Korea from communist domination." . . .

Stretching from the Pacific ports of North Korea through Manchuria into North China was the only well-developed industrial structure in Asia outside of Japan, with heavy industries such as steel, iron, petrochemicals, automobiles, and hydroelectric generation, newly installed by Japan in the 1930s and early 1940s. The parsimonious industrial-structure logic of Kennan's containment policy (we had four, they had one) would seem to make this Northeast Asian complex more important for Japan than Southeast Asia: here was Japan's true "natural" economy, the result of its imperial policies over four decades. I have found only scattered evidence that the "liberation" of this region had anything to do with NSC 48, or with the march north after the Korean War began. The most one can say is that the rollback logic mingled security and economic considerations inextricably, and that both the security and the economic advantages of rollback were more obvious in Northeast than in Southeast Asia.

The more important points about rollback in 1949 are two: first, such contingency planning cleared the way for the adoption of containment in Asia, by making containment seem to be a compromise rather than a wholly new policy. . . .

Rollback talk also had great value in domestic politics. It would steal an issue from the Republican Right, while bringing Republican moderates such as Dulles into a much more stable coalition behind American cold war policy. Indeed, it was during the "NSC 68" period that Dulles joined the Truman administration, and it is then—not in 1953—that he began talking about "positive action," the rollback metaphor. . . .

[Two] more facts need to be established. First, as mentioned earlier, throughout most of 1948 and 1949 a guerrilla struggle existed in the south, and after May 1949 it was punctuated by numerous engagements along the thirty-eighth parallel. By April 1950, however, . . . this guerrilla effort was virtually extinguished and border incidents also tailed off to nothing after March 1950. Second, major transfers to North Korea of Korean soldiers who had been fighting in the Manchurian campaigns with the People's Liberation Army (PLA) occurred in 1949 and early 1950. . . . Within North Korea the regime recruited soldiers using entirely nationalist appeals, with no reference to China or the Soviet Union, and not much to socialism.

Although the origin of the Korean People's Army cannot be discussed further here for reasons of space, the point to remember is that battle-hardened Koreans directed this army, using highly nationalistic appeals; Chinese influence was greater than Soviet influence from 1946 on (the year the army began forming), and yet this was a Korean rather than a puppet army. In 1950 the Soviets shipped tanks and other materiel to North Korea, *primarily to compete with the Chinese for influence,* just as they do today. The DPRK gets it high-technology military items from the USSR, the depth of its experience is with China, but its heart is thoroughly Korean. I believe, although I cannot at this point prove, that the conventional battles of the Korean War began because the North wished to unify the peninsula and provide thereby the basis for an authentically revolutionary-nationalist regime that could resist domination by outside forces, including the Soviets and the Chinese. Furthermore it is my view that the ostensible "Korean War" subsequent to June 25 was in fact a denouement, not a beginning; it was a civil and revolutionary struggle fought over issues that were joined immediately after liberation in 1945, moving through a political phase in 1945–46 in which revolutionaries sought to establish people's committees in North and South, into a phase of mass rebellion in the fall of 1946, then into a period of unconventional warfare from early 1948 to the beginning of 1950, and finally to a phase of conventional warfare that began in the summer of 1949 on a small scale, then moved into a quiet period of waiting as both North and South sought backing from their guarantors for a conventional assault, and then into hot war as the People's Army, in MacArthur's phrase, "struck like a cobra" and nearly enveloped the peninsula within weeks. I also think that this last phase was initiated by Kim Il-sung and his allies over *at best* Stalin's acquiescence and *at worst* over his objections. Subsequent Soviet behavior in the fall of 1950 supports such an interpretation, as we will see. Had the United States not become involved, the June war would have been a denouement to the previous period. All of this, of course, is subject enough for another article. . . . When war came in the form of frontal invasion, with only the barest attempts to claim provocation, American involvement was a foregone conclusion. All high officials at Blair House were unanimous for intervention, minus a few military demurrals about committing ground troops. A formerly top secret JCS study of the decision to intervene put the argument simply, and correctly: the rapidity of the decision is itself evidence that the Truman administration was "already pledged" to defend South Korea. State Department intelligence officials also got together in record time (mid-afternoon, June 25 Washington time) in a thorough discussion of the situation that was heavily loaded toward intervention.

The NSC 48 decision, and the June 25 decision, were decisions for containment. Containment was a classic option B between those who favored rolling back communism and those who favored the internationalist measures we have discussed; containment was a convenient fall-back point that did not necessarily compromise the ultimate goals of rollback or internationalist accommodation. For all practical purposes, this compromise was forced in Korea in 1945. By late 1949, Washington's policy makers gave final approval, in effect, to the actions Hodge and others had taken since 1945 to forge an anti-Communist bulwark in the South. Strangely, however, the containment compromise did not last long. North Korea's lunge forward opened up the realm of the feasible: the first postwar opportunity to reduce Communist-held territory. . . .

But what if the offense had its headquarters in P'yŏngyang and not Moscow? Stupid is not an adjective that I have ever considered applying to Joseph Stalin. Kim Il-sung was not stupid, either, but he and his allies were—and remain today—extraordinarily incapable of attributing subtlety to American policy; for them the United States was just another imperialist among the many that have bedeviled Korea. Furthermore Kim was and is fixated on Korea and the desire to reunify his divided country. If we make the assumption that Acheson was not simply constructing a defense, but a particular defense that would encourage action in one place and not another, Kim may have played into his hands. Stalin, on the other hand, gave apparent lukewarm support to the endeavor and then pulled back, both in June 1950, when he pulled advisers back, and in the subsequent course of the fighting, when according to Khrushchev he failed to provide North Korea with the wherewithal for victory. Stalin had a policy similar to Acheson's in regard to Socialist allies along the containment periphery. Support them, if Russian interests are not hurt, abandon them (e.g., the Greek guerrillas) if they are, but in any case leave a realm of ambiguity that does not commit Soviet might. Above all, make a mess here, make a mess there (Korea, Indochina) in the hope that the Americans would be drained in a hemorrhage of blood and treasure. . . .

. . . In fact the rollback policy drew together a far more broadly based coalition behind Korea policy than had ever existed before. It healed splits between internationalists, containment advocates, baitcutters, and rollbackers, leaving only some isolated internationalists in its wake. Had the successes of the march north not been so fleeting, the coalition would have included Japan- and Europe-firsters seeking an Asian hinterland with China- and Asia-firsters hoping to recapture China for Chiang; they were all in support of rollback after the September 15 Inch' ŏn landing. This rollback coalition would later have been strained over the question of whether to go beyond the Yalu, with the Asia-firsters in support and the Europe-firsters opposed, fearing that this would bring World War III. Or, a unified Korea under American auspices might have temporarily stabilized domestic conflict over foreign policy, until rollback met a failure elsewhere. With the Chinese intervention, however, the United States did not get a unified Korea but thought it was about to get World War III, judging from the panic and alarm in the Truman cabinet. Eventually the fighting stabilized around the thirty-eighth parallel again, the crisis passed, and with it went rollback as a viable American policy. From that time until the 1960s and the Bay of Pigs, containment was the preferred policy of the Truman and Eisenhower administrations, rollback nothing more than rhetoric.

Until the Inch' ŏn landing, there was no unanimity among high policy makers. John Foster Dulles was among the first to call for rollback, on July 14. The PPS [Policy Planning Staff] argued a week later, however, that the Kremlin would intervene to protect North Korea, which in turn led to an "emphatic dissent" by John Allison, director of the Office of Northeast Asian Affairs. At the end of July, the Department of Defense submitted a paper arguing for rollback and showing a touching regard for Korean aspirations for unification—something rarely seen in American policy before or since, and explicable solely by the opportunities of the fighting in Korea. This paper, however, also argued that the fighting provided "the first opportunity to displace part of the Soviet orbit," and thus linked rollback thinking with the realm of feasibility pointed to in NSC 48/1. Then in Allison's top secret paper of August 12, the NSC 48/1 phraseology was patent: "Since *a basic policy* of the United States is *to check and reduce* the preponderant power of the USSR in Asia and elsewhere, then UN operations in Korea can set the stage for the non-communist penetration into an area under Soviet control" (emphasis added). This phrase reappeared several more times in top secret planning prior to the move north. Still, however, there was no unanimity; Kennan and the CIA, among others, continued to oppose a march north. Up to the Inch' ŏn landing, U.S. policy had determined only to wait until the moment arrived, when the realm of the feasible might present itself, or might not; the decision would be taken accordingly.

MacArthur's brilliant success carried everything before it in Korea, and everything behind it in Washington. It stimulated a consensus on rollback so broad that it stretched all the way from MacArthur to internationalist John Vincent, the main antagonist in the State Department of the Korean Policy of the occupation and the military. On October 7 Vincent weighed in from exile in Bern, saying "Personally, I believe we should cross the 38th parallel when set to do so irrespective of whether Chou En-lai is bluffing or not." Another archetypal liberal who suffered the wrath of the McCarthyites, O. Edmund Clubb, remarked that he hoped the Chinese would get a good bloodying if they dared to intervene. . . .

. . . [W]hat of the Soviets during this period? We have seen that Stalin originally acquiesced in the thirty-eighth-parallel decision in August 1945. A second seeming anomaly occurred in December 1948, when he withdrew Russian troops from the North, something quite contrary to Soviet satellite policy in these years, and therefore contrary to the usual assumption that North Korea was a docile Soviet tool. Third, Stalin watched as tens of thousands of Korean soldiers who fought with the Chinese Communists entered North Korea in 1949 and 1950. To a consummate realist who had once inquired how many divisions the Pope had, this would only indicate a likely skewing of North Korea toward China. Fourth—and still unexplained—was the Soviet absence from the UN Security Council in June and July 1950. Last, and most important, why did the Soviets apparently do little or nothing when MacArthur moved into North Korea? The various drafts of NSC 81 in September 1950 argued that the United States should not go north if the Soviets even *threatened* intervention, let alone if they actually intervened. NSC thinking was the mirror image of its assumption that Stalin had ordered the attack. During the fall of 1950, according to the available documentation, the Soviet Union was virtually mute (save some propaganda blasts that cost them nothing) while China and India made most of the representations to the Americans about the march north. Nor did the Soviets order the Chinese into Korea, according to the best scholarship and documentation on the subject. So what was the Soviet "commitment" to North Korea? One can hazard a guess that it was not comparable to the U.S. commitment to South Korea, and of a distinctly different order from Soviet commitments to key states on its East European periphery; also that Stalin was willing to allow an adventurous Kim Il-sung to stew in the juice of his own provocations; last, that Soviet behavior in the fall of 1950 must inevitably reflect back on its role in June 1950. Stalin did *not* order the only attempt since 1945 to pierce through by force of arms the containment periphery. Therefore one hazards a final guess: that Kim Il-sung and his Korean allies moved in June 1950 not at Stalin's order, but to unify their country, revolutionize the South, and thereby provide the basis for a self-contained national communism that could resist great power pressure from any source, including China and the Soviet Union. After the war this peculiar blend of Korean nationalism and Marxism-Leninism developed in the North alone, and therefore on a much slimmer base.

As for American policy, and the three sketches at the beginning of this article, we may note the following. First, the post-Inch'ŏn successes of the fighting in Korea healed splits among these three currents, making for a broad coalition behind rollback. Had it worked—had the Chinese not intervened—the coalition would have held until another rollback debacle occurred. Second, given that it did not work in Korea, a revisionist history had to emerge: MacArthur, the lone wolf, would be blamed for the failures, while Dulles would again merge comfortably with the broad middle, while using rollback rhetoric to sate the outraged appetites of the Republican right wing. But, third and most important, the failure of Korean rollback meant that decisive limits had been placed on "positive action" for at least a decade, making containment the vastly preferable policy for the liberal elites then in control of U.S. foreign policy.

Containment in fact, albeit with rollback rhetoric, became the policy of the quiet years of the Eisenhower administration. Liberal rollback had failed, but it was blamed on Asia-first rollbackers like MacArthur. And so MacArthur slowly faded from the scene, but not without some uproarious pulling and hauling in domestic American politics, as the rollback constituency fought back against the reversal of verdicts on who was to blame for the debacle in the frigid North Korean hinterland.

Suggested Readings

Bruce Cumings, *The Origins of the Korean War, 1945–1947* (1981) and *The Roaring of the Cataract, 1947–1952* (1990).

John Lewis Gaddis, *The United States and the Origins of the Cold War, 1941–1947* (1972).

Michael Hogan, *The Marshall Plan: America, Britain, and the Reconstruction of Western Europe, 1947–1952* (1987).

Akira Iriye, *The Cold War in Asia* (1974).

Melvyn P. Leffler, *A Preponderance of Power: National Security, the Truman Administration and the Cold War* (1992).

Ernest R. May, ed., *American Cold War Strategy: Interpreting NSC 68* (1993).

Wilson D. Miscamble, *George F. Kennan and the Making of American Foreign Policy, 1947–1950* (1992).

Michael Schaller, *The American Occupation of Japan* (1985).

Randall B. Woods and Howard Jones, *Dawning of the Cold War: The United States Quest for Order* (1991).

Daniel Yergin, *Shattered Peace: The Origins of the Cold War and the National Security State* (1977).

Further Readings

Overviews, Biographies, and Bi-national Studies

Terry H. Anderson, *The United States, Great Britain and the Cold War, 1944–1947* (1981); Kai Bird, *The Chairman: John J. McCloy* (1992); Michael M. Boll, *Cold War in the Balkans* (1984); Warren Cohen, *America in the Age of Soviet Power, 1945–1991* (1993); John Lewis Gaddis, *Strategies of Containment* (1982); James L. Gormly, *The Collapse of the Grand Alliance, 1945–1948* (1987) and *From Potsdam to the Cold War: Big Three Diplomacy, 1945–1947* (1990); Deborah Welch Larson, *Origins of Containment: A Psychological Explanation* (1985); Ralph Levering, *American Opinion and the Russian Alliance* (1976); Thomas Alan Schwartz, *America's Germany* (1991).

The Truman Doctrine, Marshall Plan, and NATO

Timothy P. Ireland, *Creating the Entangling Alliance: The Origins of NATO* (1981); Howard Jones, *A New Kind of War: America's Global Strategy and the Truman Doctrine in Greece* (1989); Lawrence Kaplan, *NATO and the United States* (1988);

Alan S. Milward, *The Reconstruction of Western Europe, 1945–1951* (1984); Imanuel Wexler, *The Marshall Plan Revisited* (1983); Lawrence S. Wittner, *American Intervention in Greece, 1943–1949* (1982).

The Cold War in Asia

Dorothy Borg and Waldo Heinrichs, *Uncertain Years: Chinese-American Relations, 1947–1950* (1980); Gordon H. Chang, *Friends and Enemies* (1990); Rosemary Foot, *The Wrong War* (1985); Marc S. Gallicchio, *The Cold War Begins in Asia* (1988); Gary Hess, *The United States Emergence as a Southeast Asian Power, 1940–1950* (1987); Michael Schaller, *The American Occupation of Japan* (1985) and *Douglas MacArthur: The Far Eastern General* (1989); Nancy Bernkopf Tucker, *Patterns in the Dust* (1983).

QUESTIONS FOR DISCUSSION

1. Account for Soviet mistrust of the Western democracies at the conclusion of World War II.
2. What steps did the Soviet Union take to bolster its economy and protect its political integrity? How did the American government respond to Russian territorial demands?
3. What relationship did the Truman Doctrine and the Marshall Plan bear to the American policy of containment?
4. Why did China fall to the communists in 1949?
5. How did NSC 68 differ from George Kennan's version of containment? What were the domestic implications of NSC 68?
6. Evaluate General Douglas MacArthur's prosecution of the Korean War.
7. According to Bruce Cumings in *Child of Conflict*, why did the United States follow a policy of rollback during the Korean War? Explain what that term meant and evaluate its effectiveness.

THE FAIR DEAL
AND THE SECOND RED SCARE

POSTWAR AMERICA

The United States emerged from World War II in a sober but optimistic mood. The disillusionment that had pervaded the nation following the Great War was not in evidence. Further revelations concerning the Holocaust convinced Americans that the Axis powers had constituted not only a threat to Western civilization but were the very embodiment of evil. Congress and the Truman administration rejected isolationism and declared their support for a new world order based on collective security and the creation of an interdependent world economy that would bring prosperity to all. In 1950 the Truman administration adopted NSC 68 and thereby committed the United States to combat communism throughout the globe. When later that year, North Korea invaded the South, the United States intervened, acting on the assumption that the attack was authorized by and represented an expansion of Sino-Soviet communism.

At the same time, Americans were tired of war, of violence, of rationing, of intrusive government. They wanted to return to normal family life and the pursuit of material gratification. As a result, the U.S. military was quickly demobilized, and a conservative coalition in Congress abruptly ended wartime controls on the economy and blocked efforts to expand the New Deal. Women and ethnic minorities, especially African Americans, anticipated that wartime opportunities would extend into the postwar period, but they were mistaken. The white, male-dominated power structure demanded that blacks, Hispanics, and women resume their normal, restricted roles in national life. In part, the movement to return to and sustain the status quo was fueled by a wartime prosperity that continued unabated into the 1950s. Rising incomes and relatively

861

full employment propelled many working-class Americans up into the middle class and eliminated the economic and class tensions that had driven the New Deal.

The rush to internationalism, the willingness to assume a leading role on the world stage stemmed from the fact that many Americans believed that the defeat of the Axis signaled the beginning of a long period of peace and tranquility in international affairs. The emergence of first the Soviet Union and then Communist China as totalitarian threats to areas deemed vital to U.S. interests shattered that illusion. Within two years of the end of World War II the United States had assumed leadership of a noncommunist coalition dedicated to the containment of Soviet and subsequently Chinese imperialism as well as Marxism-Leninism. The proximity of this new crusade to World War II, coupled with the Soviet explosion of a nuclear device in 1949 and the "fall" of China to the communists, led to a second red scare in the early 1950s. Anticommunism became a major if not dominant feature of American life, one that would distort politics, foreign policy, and popular culture for years to come.

DEMOBILIZATION AND RECONVERSION

Most economists and government officials anticipated that the end of hostilities and reconversion to a peacetime economy would produce a new economic downturn. Indeed, many operated on the assumption that the huge expenditures that accompanied World War II rather than initiatives and programs of the New Deal had pulled the country out of the Great Depression. They were, to their delight, wrong. A number of programs and forces cushioned the shock of demobilization and reconversion. Unemployment pay and other Social Security benefits eased veterans back into the workforce. The Servicemen's Readjustment Act of 1944, known as the GI Bill of Rights, provided $13 billion in college, vocational training, housing, and business incentives for returning veterans. By 1947 more than 1 million former servicemen were attending college under the GI Bill. Finally, the pent-up consumer demand for scarce goods coupled with the release of billions of dollars of forced wartime savings stimulated the private sector creating hundreds of thousands of jobs.

The primary economic problem facing the nation in the late 1940s was not depression, but inflation. Business desire for higher profits coupled with organized labor's demands for higher wages combined to frustrate the Truman administration's efforts to keep the economy on an even keel. The president believed that labor was entitled to modest increases and that management ought to be able to absorb those increases without raising prices. Business and industry rejected their workers' demands for raises, running as high as 30 percent in some sectors, and the country was swept by a wave of bitter strikes. Choosing to blame the unions, Truman used sweeping powers granted to the executive during the war, seized the nation's principal coal mines, shut down by John L. Lewis' United Mine Workers, and threatened to draft striking rail workers into the army. Meanwhile, Congress refused the president's requests to extend the life of the Office of Price Administration (OPA), the wartime agency that was empowered to set prices for all products. Runaway inflation gripped the nation. Congress belatedly resurrected the OPA, but only for a short period. Following the mid-term elections of 1946, the administration agreed to end all controls except on rents, sugar, and rice.

THE BABY BOOM AND HOUSING PROBLEM

Although the American economy boomed in the months and years following the end of World War II, the sudden return of several million servicemen created painful dislocations. Families long delayed swelled the birthrate which exploded from 19.4 per thousand in 1940 to 24 in 1946 and did not fall off again until the 1960s. Four-child rather than two-child families became the norm in America. Future analysts would give the name "baby-boom generation" to this bulge in the demographic curve.

The tens of thousands of new families produced by demobilization had a most difficult time finding proper housing. Because of the depression there had not been a good year for new housing starts since 1929. The industry was simply not prepared for the demand. Pollster Elmo Roper estimated that 19 percent of families were doubled up, while another 19 percent were looking for housing. To deal with the problem, President Truman named Wilson Wyatt to be federal housing expediter. Wyatt set a goal of 1.2 million new dwellings for 1947, but the housing industry, shackled by outdated technology and lack of capital, proved unable to respond. Many young families had to make do with dreadful prefabricated shelters. By 1950, however, the housing industry had responded to the challenge. The ingenuity and profit motive of builders and real estate entrepreneurs coupled with thirty-year mortgages at 4.5 percent interest rates made available through the Federal Housing Administration and the Veterans Administration produced a housing boom that acted as one of the principal engines of the economy.

HALTING ADVANCES FOR AMERICAN WOMEN

The months following V-J Day were a time of upheaval and mixed emotions for American women. Ecstatic over the end of hostilities and the return of loved ones, they were at the same time disturbed by forces that seemed determined to rob them of the social and economic gains they had made during the war. Veterans wanted their jobs back, and they got them. By 1946, 2.25 million women had left their jobs, and another million were laid off.

Unemployment proved only temporary, however. Pent-up consumer demand coupled with massive savings fueled a postwar boom in consumer products. There were more women working in 1950 than in 1940, 28 percent of the workforce versus 24 percent. But women who reentered the workforce lost the seniority and benefits they had earned during the war, and they were usually unable to reacquire positions in manufacturing and management.

For the most part they moved into lower positions that paid less. They were nurses rather than doctors, teachers rather than superintendents, secretaries rather than executives. The post–World War II workplace was heavily segregated by gender. Seventy-five percent of working women labored at female-only jobs, a higher figure than in 1900. Cultural pressures for American women to return to homemaking, to defer to males in the private as well as the public sphere, were tremendous.

CHANGING OPPORTUNITIES FOR MINORITIES

War's end eroded the economic gains made by African Americans and Hispanics as well. At the height of the war the shipbuilding industry had employed more than two hundred thousand ethnic minorities; by the end of 1946 that number had shrunk to less than ten thousand. Following the end of hostilities the federal government temporarily ended the bracero program, a U.S.–Mexican agreement under which Mexican laborers were given short-time visas to work in war industries in North America; nevertheless, the South and Southwest experienced a labor surplus in the immediate postwar period. Just as they had following World War I, black veterans found that many Americans resented rather than appreciated their service and expected them to accept quietly a return to second-class citizenship.

HARRY S TRUMAN

Harry Truman's great dream as president was to broaden and deepen the New Deal programs of FDR, a somewhat ironic goal given the fact that Roosevelt and much of New Deal Washington had shunned Truman during the 1930s. A typical son of the Midwest, Truman had grown up on a farm near Kansas City. Following his graduation from high school he served as an artillery officer in France during the Great War. Failing in a series of business ventures, Truman decided to enter politics in 1924. He was subsequently elected county judge and U.S. senator with the help of the infamous Pendergast machine which dominated the political life of Kansas City, Missouri. Though Truman was an ardent New Dealer, the Democratic administration would have nothing to do with him until he was reelected on his own in 1940. Roosevelt chose him as his running mate in 1944 because Truman was acceptable to various factions within the Democratic party.

By his own admission, Truman was not the best equipped person in the country to be president. He was somewhat undereducated, had no experience in foreign affairs, and had been shut out of the decision-making process by Roosevelt. He tended to analogize between Kansas City politics and international affairs, seeming always to want to simplify the complex. He was given to clichés such as "The buck stops here," and he carefully cultivated the image of a no-nonsense, practical, decisive public leader. In truth he was intensely unsure of himself, especially during the first two years of his administration. Truman's emphasis on personal loyalty led to charges, partially true, of cronyism. Finally, he was given to intemperance in public statement, occasionally lapsing into profanity when provoked.

On the positive side, Harry Truman was a man of integrity and courage, devoted to the interests of his country. He was an experienced administrator and a fairly effective politician. He understood budgetary matters and the political process. In foreign affairs he proved, after his first two years in office, a tough-minded defender of the nation's economic and strategic interests as he perceived them. In the domestic sphere Truman was an authentic New Dealer believing that the government has a responsibility to care for those unable to care for themselves and to ensure fair play in the marketplace. He was, moreover, a lifelong crusader against discrimination based on race or religion. Though initially tentative, Truman was always tough in a crisis; he had no intention of giving in to antireformists at home or would-be aggressors abroad.

THE CONSERVATIVE COALITION

Within six months of Roosevelt's death, Truman and Republicans in Congress joined by conservative, mostly southern Democrats, were locked in a bitter struggle over aspects of economic and social policy. In September 1945, the president called on the House and Senate to revive the reform program that had been sidetracked by World War II, including extension of Social Security to cover farm and other workers, increase in the minimum wage, creation of a national health insurance system, and reorganization of the executive branch. Instead, Congress rejected the president's attempt to extend the New Deal and enacted the most far-reaching anti-union bill ever passed by a national legislature.

The leader of the conservative coalition in Congress was Senator Robert A. Taft. "Mr. Republican," a dour legal and parliamentary genius, was America's most outspoken champion of business interests, a trenchant foe of the welfare state, and a constitutional strict constructionist. Taft and the conservative coalition wanted above all to redress the alleged imbalance between labor and management created by the National Labor Relations Act. Angered by the wartime strikes carried out by John L. Lewis and the United Mine Workers, the public was in an anti-union mood.

Over the protests of the Truman administration and liberal Democrats, Congress in June 1947 passed the Taft-Hartley Act. It outlawed the "closed shop"—the practice in unionized plants of requiring membership of all employees—and certain "unfair" practices such as jurisdictional strikes and secondary boycotts. It permitted employers to sue for breach of contract and authorized the president to impose "cooling off" periods during strikes that imperiled the nation's health or safety. Finally, the measure compelled unions to submit annual financial statements to the secretary of labor, forbade union contributions to political parties, and required union officials to submit affidavits swearing that they were not members of the Communist party. Declaring

Taft-Hartley to be nothing less than a measure of class warfare, Truman vetoed it only to see his veto immediately overridden by both houses of Congress.

THE ELECTION OF 1948

Thomas Dewey and the Republican Party

Harry Truman's modest physical appearance, his lack of formal education, his failure to get his program through Congress, and his occasional public profanity combined to reinforce the popular notion that he was not fit to govern. Out of the White House since 1932, the Republicans looked forward to the election of 1948 with a great deal of anticipation. The conservative wing of the party preferred Taft, but the feeling among the moderate majority was that he was too austere and would prove to be a poor campaigner. Party leaders approached the hero of Normandy, Dwight D. Eisenhower, but he had not decided whether he was a Republican or a Democrat. Thus it was that the Republicans turned to the man who had led them to defeat in 1944, Governor Thomas E. Dewey of New York. Dewey had compiled a progressive record as governor and firmly supported the policy of containment. GOP leaders consoled themselves with the thought that Truman was no Roosevelt. The party's 1948 platform endorsed most of the New Deal reforms as an accomplished fact and approved the administration's bipartisan foreign policy. Essentially, what Dewey promised was a cleaner, more efficient administration.

Henry Wallace and the Progressive Party

Meanwhile, the Democratic party was being torn apart by internal disputes. Leading the charge against Truman and the Democratic establishment was former secretary of agriculture and vice president, Henry A. Wallace. Champion of the blue-collar worker and small farmer, both black and white, Wallace charged that the Democratic party had been taken over by big business and southern segregationists. The country's foremost proponent of Soviet-American friendship, Wallace vehemently attacked the Truman administration's decision to get tough with the Soviet Union. In 1947, he organized the Progressive Citizens of America and notified the world that he would run on a third party ticket.

The platform of the Progressive party called for gradual nationalization of basic industries and full civil rights for black Americans. The Progressives were grievously damaged when it was revealed that the party included communists and communist sympathizers. When challenged by reporters, Wallace declared that he would accept help from whatever quarter it was offered.

Democratic Discord

Democratic liberals, newly organized into the Americans for Democratic Action, maneuvered desperately to avoid choosing between Wallace and

Truman. They quietly approached General Eisenhower, but he rebuffed them. He identified the Democratic party with big government and deficit spending, and he was opposed to both.

To make matters worse, southern Democrats were up in arms over the president's civil rights program. Truman had been a staunch opponent of the Ku Klux Klan in Missouri, and in 1947 at his behest, a prestigious commission had produced a study of race relations in America entitled *To Secure These Rights*. It was a searing indictment of segregation and discrimination and a resounding call for federal action to ensure that African Americans were accorded their constitutional rights. Truman enthusiastically endorsed its findings and recommendations.

When the Democratic convention assembled in Philadelphia in July, the long-anticipated fight between liberals headed by Mayor Hubert Humphrey of Minneapolis and the conservative, southern wing of the party erupted. After a bitter floor fight the convention adopted a civil rights plank demanding a Fair Employment Practices Commission and federal antilynching and anti–poll tax legislation. Delegates from Dixie made good on their promise to bolt if the party made a commitment to civil rights and immediately walked out of the convention. A few days later, the exhausted remainder nominated Truman, largely because, a number of journalists observed, they had no other choice.

Meanwhile, disgruntled southern Democrats gathered in Birmingham, Alabama, waved Confederate flags, paid homage to Jefferson Davis, and founded the States Rights Democratic party. The Dixiecrats, as the southern dissidents were subsequently labeled, nominated South Carolina Governor J. Strom Thurmond for president. The segregationists hoped that they could capture enough electoral votes to throw the election into the House of Representatives where they might strike a sectional bargain which would preserve their beloved racial system.

TRUMAN'S CAMPAIGN

Harry Truman was one of the few people in the country who thought he could win reelection. Following his nomination, he flew to Philadelphia to address the Democratic delegates in the wee hours of the morning. In a spirited acceptance speech, he condemned the "do-nothing" Eightieth Congress, which was Republican dominated, and promised to call it into special session to enact the progressive planks in the Republican platform. Since the GOP majority was dominated by Senator Taft and the conservative wing of the party, the president knew that it would continue to do nothing, revealing, hopefully, that Dewey's campaign promises were nothing more than that—promises.

While Congress fretted and fumed and Dewey conducted a mild, essentially "me-too" campaign, Truman embarked on a strenuous whistle-stop campaign. Unbeknownst to his challengers, Truman had developed a winning strategy for 1948. His advisors knew that to succeed, he needed the midwestern and

Most political pundits predicted a Republican victory in 1948. Here a sign outside the Bellevue-Stratford Hotel prematurely predicts a Dewey victory.

western farm belts. Fortunately for Truman, the New Deal agricultural programs continued to make the administration popular with farmers. His strategists assumed correctly that the key to carrying American cities was securing the support of labor unions and African Americans. Truman's veto of Taft-Hartley and his advocacy of the suggestions contained in *To Secure These Rights* gave him a leg up with both these groups. Casting aside his prepared texts, the president lambasted the Republicans and did his best to keep alive memories of the Great Depression. "Give 'em hell, Harry," shouted the increasingly responsive crowds.

Virtually every observer picked Dewey to win; the archconservative *Chicago Tribune* even went so far as to print an extra with banner headlines announcing Dewey the winner. In one of the most stunning political upsets in American history, Truman captured 24 million popular votes and tallied 303 votes in the electoral college. Dewey garnered 21 million popular and 189 electoral votes. The Republicans were stunned. Angry and frustrated, party leaders promised themselves that never again would they run a "me-too" campaign.

THE FAIR DEAL

In his annual message to Congress in January 1949, President Truman launched what he called his Fair Deal. Over the next year, the now Democratic-controlled House and Senate handed him a number of victories. They increased the minimum wage from 40 to 75 cents an hour and extended the Social Security Act bringing 10 million new workers under its provisions. Truman's greatest victory for the disadvantaged was the Housing Act of 1949 which appropriated large sums to clear slums and build 810,000 units of low cost housing over the next six years.

There were defeats. In the wake of a gigantic lobbying effort by the American Medical Association, Congress rejected the president's plan for national health insurance. Led by the conservative coalition, the House and Senate also turned back the so-called Brannan Plan which would have established a guaranteed income for farm families. Most disappointing for Truman was Congress' obstructionism in the area of civil rights. Year after year, former Dixiecrats managed to defeat his antilynching, anti–poll tax and Fair Employment Practices legislation. The president was able to frustrate segregationists to an extent by issuing executive orders. In 1948 he signed decrees that outlawed discrimination in the civil service and promoted integration of the armed services.

THE ROOTS OF ANTICOMMUNISM

Much of Truman's second administration was dominated by the Korean War and the hunt for communist subversives who had allegedly penetrated not only the federal government, but also the nation's colleges and its communication and entertainment industries as well. During the New Deal and World War II, communists and communist sympathizers entered public service freely. During the 1930s and World War II communism did not, after all, inspire the hysterical fear that it did after the onset of the Cold War. Responding to charges by the House Un-American Activities Committee that subversives had penetrated to the very core of the federal bureaucracy, President Truman ordered the FBI to conduct a comprehensive investigation. By the close of 1947 more than two thousand communists and fellow travelers had resigned from the federal government; 221 were indicted for espionage.

THE HISS CASE

Public anxiety continued to mount, however, and when the president and some of his closest policy advisors were placed in a compromising position by a sensational spy case—the trial of Alger Hiss—the stage was set for one of the most terrifying witch-hunts in American history. Hiss was a member of the Ware group, a Washington-based cell of Soviet espionage agents. A scion of the eastern aristocracy, Hiss had seemed above reproach, rising through the ranks of the Roosevelt and Truman administrations to hold a high position in the State Department. In 1948, he was president of the Carnegie Endowment for Peace. That year, Whitaker Chambers, a former Soviet agent, told the House Un-American Activities Committee that Hiss had passed him secret documents ten years earlier. Hiss denied the charges and sued Chambers for libel. In the ensuing trial, Chambers produced microfilm of State Department documents that Hiss had allegedly passed him. Indicted by a New York grand jury, Hiss again denied that he was a Soviet spy. When correspondence with Chambers was proven to have been written on Hiss' typewriter, he was indicted and subsequently convicted of perjury.

The Hiss case might not have had the impact that it did had not President Truman come to his defense. Assured by many of his advisors about Hiss' integrity, he dismissed the charges against the former State Department official as "a red herring." When pressed to denounce his friend and former colleague, Dean Acheson refused, declaring "I do not intend to turn my back on Alger Hiss."

The Hiss case was just the most sensational of a series of spy revelations. On February 15, 1946, Canada announced the arrest of twenty-two persons who had illegally passed on information to Soviet intelligence operatives. Hiss was convicted of perjury in 1948. The next year Klaus Fuchs, a British scientist who had worked in Los Alamos on the atomic bomb project, confessed that he had spied for the Kremlin. In 1950 nine Americans were arrested for passing on atomic secrets to the enemy. Julius Rosenberg, the alleged spymaster, and his wife, Ethel, were executed for treason in 1953.

JOSEPH R. MCCARTHY

It was perhaps inevitable that unscrupulous politicians would seek to take advantage of the mounting red scare. In the fall of 1950 Richard Nixon used the Hiss case to smear his Democratic opponent and win election to the Senate. But the chief exploiter of anticommunist hysteria was the junior senator from Wisconsin, Joseph R. McCarthy. McCarthy first won election to the Senate in 1946 largely on the basis of a trumped-up war record. With no legislative accomplishments to his credit, he began searching desperately for an issue that would keep him in the Senate. With the instinct of a born demagogue, he seized on the communist infiltration issue with a vengeance. On February 9, 1950, he told a Republican women's club in Wheeling, West Virginia, that the State Department was infested with communists and that he had a list of their names. Because of his mumbling no one could be sure whether or not he had said 205, or fifty-seven, or "a lot." At a subsequent address, he claimed that eighty-one Reds occupied positions of trust in the State Department.

Back in the Senate, several of his colleagues asked for proof. Instead of producing any, McCarthy, a burly, heavy-browed man, asserted that Owen

Lattimore, a professor at Johns Hopkins University who had advised the State Department on Far Eastern affairs, was a top espionage agent. When the FBI concluded that there was no proof, the Wisconsin demagogue turned on Philip Jessup, U.S. representative to the United Nations.

In the summer of 1950, the Senate appointed a special committee under Millard Tydings to investigate McCarthy's charges. The Tydings Committee quickly concluded its investigation and reported that the senator's claims "represent perhaps the most nefarious campaign of half-truth and untruth in the history of the Republic." But McCarthy was not subdued. Using a composite photograph purporting to show Tydings and the American Communist party head, Earl Browder, in rapt conversation, McCarthy helped defeat Tydings for reelection from Maryland in 1950. Tydings' defeat, in turn, sent a ripple of fear through the Senate and House.

McCarthyism Triumphant

When the Republicans gained control of Congress in 1952, McCarthy became head of the Committee on Government Operations. He used its permanent subcommittee on investigations to launch a nationwide reign of terror. He continued to hammer away at government officials, labeling Dean Acheson and George Marshall "executioners" of Jiang Jieshi and the Chinese Nationalists. But he cast his net more widely to include academics, actors, and journalists. After he accused the Voice of America of spreading communist propaganda, he dispatched two self-important young red-baiters on his staff, Roy M. Cohn and G. David Schine, to Europe to cleanse the Voice of America and U.S. libraries operated by the United States Information Agency. By 1953, McCarthy had helped create an atmosphere in which neighbor was informing on neighbor, colleague on colleague. People accused of communist connections or sympathy were assumed guilty until proved innocent.

McCarthyism hit those areas of American life that were most public—entertainment, the media, government, and academia. The second red scare (the first occurring in 1919 following the end of the Great War), beginning with HUAC's highly publicized investigation of the movie industry in the late 1940s, led to the creation of a blacklist, an unofficial list of actors, writers, and directors suspected of communist sympathies. Suddenly, such individuals found it impossible to find work. The same was true of radio and the infant but burgeoning television industry. Only a few hundred of the 250,000 people who taught at junior- and senior-level colleges in 1952 were dismissed for suspected communist leanings or for refusing to take the prescribed loyalty oath, but the fears that McCarthyism inspired had a blighting effect on intellectual inquiry. Students and teachers became afraid to even discuss Marxism as a historical, economic, or social phenomenon. The civil service and foreign service were most directly affected. According to one estimate there were 2,700 dismissals and 12,000 resignations between 1947 and 1956 that were directly attributable to the anticommunist hysteria.

McCarthyism thrived on innuendo and false charges. Senator McCarthy demonstrates to a Senate committee and a TV audience the pervasive influence of the Communist party in the United States.

The Demise of McCarthyism

The end of the post–World War II red scare came rather quickly in 1954 when McCarthy challenged the U.S. Army. Angry that it had not granted Schine an exemption from military service, McCarthy "uncovered" a spy ring in the Signal Corps which was headquartered at Ft. Monmouth, New Jersey. When Secretary of the Army Robert Stephens refused to testify and to turn over records that McCarthy wanted, the nation's number one red hunter branded all concerned cowards and traitors. The army counterattacked by filing twenty-nine charges against McCarthy, Cohn, the permanent subcommittee's counsel, and others. Chief among the accusations was that McCarthy had sought a commission and special treatment for Schine.

Hearings were held by the Committee on Government Operations with Senator Karl Mundt in the chair. Because the proceedings were televised, Americans could witness McCarthy's browbeating, big lie tactics for the first time. "Have you no shame?" Army counsel Joseph Welch asked McCarthy incredulously when he implied that one of Welch's young aides was a communist. Although nothing substantive came out of the Army–McCarthy hearings, they provided political momentum to a movement in Congress that led to official censure of McCarthy in December 1954. McCarthyism subsided, but the anxieties of the Cold War coupled with the nation's innate conservatism meant that rabid anticommunism with its periodic tendency to focus on traitors within would remain an important part of American culture.

Much has been written about McCarthy and McCarthyism. Some historians have focused on the anxieties generated by the Cold War; others have honed in on the Wisconsin senator's unique skills as a demagogue. Robert Griffith in his widely read book, The Politics of Fear, *credits both of these factors but argues that without the willingness of moderate as well as conservative Republicans to put their ethical qualms aside and make use of McCarthy for partisan political purposes, neither the man nor the movement would have had the monumental effect on America that they did.*

THE RISE OF JOE MCCARTHY*
Robert Griffith

The rise of Joe McCarthy took only a few short months. In February he was an undistinguished and indistinguishable midwestern senator. By July he had become a symbol of Republican extremism and a political force of major proportions. What follows is an attempt to describe and to understand that meteoric rise.

It should be clear by now that the "Communist issue" was a staple of postwar Republican campaign oratory, and that McCarthy had said little more than his party colleagues across the nation. It is easy to see that the anti-Communist crusade demanded a leader of McCarthy's temerity. It has been somewhat less evident that even more important was the quiet, cautious, and yet continuous support the senator received from his own party. "Communism-in-government" was a Republican issue, and one the G.O.P. could ill afford to lose in its battle against the Democrats. McCarthy's support among Republicans grew proportionately with his increasing identification with this issue, and this in turn contributed to his rising power and influence.

McCarthy's true significance lay in the fact that he brought to this thoroughly conventional political issue his own thoroughly unconventional personal qualities—a

from Robert Griffith, *The Politics of Fear: Joseph R. McCarthy and the Senate* (Lexington: The University Press of Kentucky, 1970), 52–114.

*Note that footnotes have been omitted.

flair for self-dramatization, a superb sense of press-agentry, and a stubborn unwill-ingness to back down. He would later recall that Republicans had been yelling "treason" for some time, but that their notices had been buried in the want ads. The way to get action, he declared, was to change the "treason" to "traitors." From Wheeling, McCarthy had headed West for a speaking engagement in Salt Lake City. By the time he reached Denver, reporters had in hand a State Department denial of his first charges. McCarthy scoffed at the statement and told reporters he had "a complete list of 207 [sic] 'bad risks' still working in the State Department." When he arrived in Salt Lake City a few hours later, he told the newsmen that he would be glad to furnish the names to the State Department if only the department would open the loyalty files of the "fifty-seven" who were "card-carrying Communists."

By February 11, when McCarthy reached Reno, Nevada, the pressure was building. He was met by a telegram from Deputy Undersecretary of State John E. Peurifoy demanding any information McCarthy might have. Another senator might have drawn back, allowed the issue to cloud, and then sought out a strategic retreat. But not McCarthy. From Reno he telegraphed the president that in spite of the "blackout" on loyalty files he had been able to compile "the names of 57 Com-munists" in the State Department. He demanded that Truman revoke the directive closing the files to Congress and charged that "failure on your part will label the Democratic Party of being the bedfellow of international communism."

While Deputy Undersecretary of State Peurifoy denied the McCarthy accu-sations one by one, the senator, not visibly perturbed, left Reno for a dinner speech in Huron, North Dakota, and there the issue hung for the next week.

THE ANATOMY OF A SPEECH

I have given Senators the fullest, most complete, fairest resume of the files that I possibly could.

JOE MCCARTHY

Early on the evening of February 20 McCarthy appeared on the floor of the Senate clutching a bulging and battered tan briefcase. In it were photostatic copies of some 100-odd individual dossiers prepared in 1947 from the State Department loyalty files by a team of investigators from the House Appropriations Committee. The list included past and present employees of the department as well as a large number of applicants. Of the original 108 singled out by the House investigators, only about forty remained with the department, and all of these had received full field investi-gations by the FBI. The "derogatory information" in most, but not all, of these cases pertained to alleged Communist or left-wing activity. Several involved alleged in-stances of homosexuality; one was the case of a Bible student from Ohio Wesleyan University whom the investigators believed had been *too thoroughly investigated;* and another concerned an elderly Russian emigré who had been refused em-ployment. . . .

The list then was hardly new, nor was it entirely accurate. The individual case summaries contained a goodly number of unconfirmed and unsubstantiated allegations. They reflected both the professional bias of the State Department's security force and the political bias of the House investigators digging out material for the Republican Eightieth Congress. Whatever the faults of the "Lee list," it was a godsend for McCarthy, and he turned upon it with his exceptional talent for compounding distortion upon distortion. At no point did he admit that he was reading to the Senate from a badly outdated committee file. Instead, he told his colleagues that he had pierced the "iron curtain" of State Department secrecy and with the aid of "some good, loyal Americans in the State Department" had compiled an alarming picture of espionage and treason. He read to the Senate "81" of these cases. Well, not quite 81. He skipped 15, 27, and 59; 7 and 99 were the same; and in cases 21 through 26 he merely repeated himself. . . .

But these misrepresentations were minor compared to the manner in which he twisted and distorted each individual case to wring from it the most sinister and sensational implications. Sometimes he would only omit a line or two. Thus in "case no. one" he neglected to mention that a full field investigation had developed "nothing derogatory." In "case no. six" he omitted the sentence: "On January 7, 1947, a memorandum summarizing the investigation stated that nothing had been developed tending to affect adversely the subject's loyalty." In "case no. 46" he cited a State Department report of March 22, 1947, raising questions as to the individual's loyalty, but left out a subsequent memorandum of June 18, 1947, in which the security officer concluded: "It is not believed by this office that the information at hand raises a reasonable doubt as to (subject's) loyalty to the United States and, accordingly, security clearance is recommended.". . .

At other points, the enormity of his lie was staggering. Compare, for example, the following (Lee case no. 40):

> This employee is with the Office of Information and Educational Exchange in New York City.
>
> His application is very sketchy. There has been no investigation. (C-8) is a reference. Though he is 43 years of age, his file reflects no history prior to June 1941.

McCarthy case no. 36:

> The individual is 43 years of age. He is with the Office of Information and Education. According to the file, he is a known Communist. I might say that when I refer to someone as being a known Communist, I am not evaluating the information myself. I am merely giving what is in the file. This individual also found his way into the Voice of America broadcast. Apparently the easiest way to get in is to be a Communist.

McCarthy could not even keep his "facts" straight in the case of a man whom he cited as an example of "a good, loyal American" who had been refused employment with the Voice of America. This proved, he declared, that "unless one has a communist background one cannot qualify for a position with the Voice of America."

Neither the senator nor the House investigators found it significant that the gentleman in question was nearly seventy years old, and perhaps a little elderly to be starting out in the civil service.

In short, the speech was a lie; it demanded, especially of those Republican partisans who, like Senator Homer Ferguson, must have realized the enormity of McCarthy's fraud, a willing suspension of disbelief.

SENATE RESOLUTION 231

The atmosphere of the Senate all day was one of awareness on both sides that a partisan issue might be developing.

WILLIAM S. WHITE

The McCarthy speech was fantasy, but the political byplay which surrounded it was very real. Behind the facade of Senate decorum stormed a potentially explosive party debate. Majority Leader Scott Lucas and the Democrats did their best to harry McCarthy. Lucas tried to pin him down: Was it "205" Communists as he had declared in Wheeling? Or only "57" as he now told the Senate? And if there were "57 card-carrying Communists" in the State Department, who were they? But McCarthy eluded his pursuers, first offering, then refusing to turn over any names to his Democratic interrogators. Lucas then told the Senate that there would be no vote on the cotton bill, the pending question when McCarthy rose to speak, and as he had anticipated, the Chamber quickly emptied.

Minority Leader Kenneth Wherry and the Republicans labored hard on McCarthy's behalf. They vigorously protested the absence of many senators, and McCarthy himself finally called for a quorum. When the necessary number failed to answer the bells, Lucas then moved for a recess, but was defeated 16-18 on a straight party-line vote. Lucas had no alternative but to send out the sergeant at-arms to compel attendance, the first time in five years that this expedient had been necessary.

During the "friendly questioning" the Republican professionals of the "Communist issue" took McCarthy in hand. Homer Ferguson helped him stumble over difficult matters of internal security procedures, and Ferguson, Owen Brewster, and others drew out the controversial files issue and the argument over Congress's right to papers originating in the Executive Department. Karl Mundt contributed the thought that the State Department policy of allowing "Communists" to resign enabled them to infiltrate other government agencies.

Most of the burden of backstopping McCarthy fell to Minority Leader Wherry, who threw Republican support behind a suggestion that "an appropriate committee of the Senate make a thorough investigation" of McCarthy's charges. The Nebraska senator even suggested that the inquiry be assigned to the Appropriations Committee, whose chairman, the ultraconservative Democrat Kenneth B. McKellar of Tennessee, would have given substantial aid to the Republicans.

McCarthy's performance and the Republican support it received were enough to trigger the investigation. The Democratic leadership met in caucus the following morning, and when the Senate convened, Majority Leader Lucas introduced Senate Resolution 231, authorizing an investigation of McCarthy's charges. Sensing that the demands for an investigation would be irresistible, the Democrats stole a march on their opposition. The Lucas resolution, moreover, gave jurisdiction of the investigation to the moderate Foreign Relations Committee rather than to the conservative-led Appropriations Committee.

The Republicans were prepared with a counterstrategy. They first sought to broaden the inquiry. Homer Ferguson, who had investigated the Commerce Department during the Eightieth Congress, demanded that the investigation include "any other agency of the Government concerned with the intercourse of the United States with other nations." Although Lucas rejected this proposal, he compromised by expanding the investigation to include persons who "are, or have been, employed by the State Department," and by agreeing to delete specific references to McCarthy's charges. . . .

Wayne Morse of Oregon insisted that the hearings be conducted in public so that any person accused of disloyalty might have the right to confront his accusers. Even Morse, however, conceded that the committee might take preliminary evidence and testimony in executive session, and he finally agreed to a rather vague amendment proffered by Massachusetts Republican Leverett Saltonstall, which was duly incorporated by Lucas into the resolution.

The final Senate resolution authorized "a full and complete study and investigation as to whether persons who are disloyal to the United States are, or have been employed by the Department of State."

THE MCCARTHY LOBBY

Congress cannot function today without lobbyists.

SENATOR ESTES KEFAUVER

McCarthy had joined the communist issue, but it remained for him to exploit the materials which nearly five years of Republican attacks had produced. In the interim between the passage of Senate Resolution 231 and the beginning of the hearings on March 8, he had to develop a major indictment of the State Department and the Democratic administration. The "cases" which he had read to the Senate on February 20 were a poor start. Some had never been employed by the department and others were long gone. His preposterous exaggerations would show up rather badly under close examination, and it would be especially embarrassing if he could not produce the names which he had "held in his hand."

He reserved a room at the Library of Congress and set his staff members to digging into old congressional investigations. He badgered fellow congressmen for documents and materials on the Communist issue, and some, including

Congressman Richard M. Nixon, allowed him to use their files. He even added to his staff a former FBI man, Donald Surine, who had been cashiered from the service. Mc-Carthy also sought the aid of a heterogeneous collection of individuals and groups which might be described as Washington's "anti-Communist lobby."

Most senators are faced with a staggering load of legislative and political re-sponsibilities, and their professional staffs are notoriously overworked. Any senator who would play a large role in the affairs of state must almost of necessity depend upon lobbies of one sort or another for the technical aid which they offer. From a friendly lobby a senator might receive a variety of assistance ranging all the way from research and speechwriting to press relations. A lobby will very often line up wit-nesses for a congressional hearing and sometimes even coach them on what they will say. While the American public has traditionally frowned upon the existence of lobbies, they are probably indispensable, given the present structure of congres-sional government. . . .

For Senator McCarthy this vacuum was filled by a loose coalition of right-wing journalists and zealots. They were not a "lobby" at all in the strictest sense of that word. They did not register as such with the secretary of the Senate, nor did they have the organizational coherence which usually characterizes a modern lobby. Nor were they really "McCarthy's." They existed well before the senator made his sudden appearance as a national figure, and they continued to exist well after his equally sudden demise. Nevertheless, they provided for McCarthy all the essential services which lobbies have at their disposal and, as in the case of traditional lobbies, the relationship proved mutually beneficial.

In the forefront of the "McCarthy lobby" was a large group of right-wing news-papermen. It would later be said that "during the McCarthy exposures a whole new group of reporters arose who worked closely with him and his staff." In fact these newsmen were active long before the senator from Wisconsin discovered com-munism as an issue. They were the closest thing that Washington had to "experts" on the Communist issue, and they provided McCarthy with quick leads and ele-mentary research. . . .

McCarthy already had connections with Colonel Robert R. McCormick, and in the weeks and months which followed his speech at Wheeling this relationship became ever closer. In addition to Edwards and Walters, McCarthy was aided by Walter Trohan, an important columnist for the McCormick papers, by most of the staff of the *Washington Times–Herald,* and by a host of commentators and analysts on the McCormick-owned Mutual radio network.

Even more important was the support of William Randolph Hearst, Jr., and his large publishing empire. Like the McCarthy-McCormick alliance, the relationship between the newspaper heir and the senator was one of mutual expedience. Mc-Carthy desperately needed the semblance of proof to support his charges, and the Hearst people wanted a forum for their own rare view of current events. Columnists such as George Sokolsky, Westbrook Pegler, and especially Fulton Lewis, Jr. (who also broadcast for the Mutual network), all worked intimately with the Wis-consin senator, turning up leads, "hot tips," and that peculiar brand of pseudoev-idence on which the Communist controversy thrived. Other Hearst employees, including Ken Hunter, Howard Rushmore, Lawrence Kerley, and Ray Richards, also did footwork for the senator.

The most valuable appendage of the Hearst organization was J.B. Matthews, whom the publisher had snatched up after his sojourn as staff director for the Dies Committee and now employed as a "researcher." It was from Matthews's private files (especially his personal copy of "Appendix Nine" of the Dies Committee) that McCarthy collected the material he first took before the Senate subcommittee.

A third major figure in the "McCarthy lobby" was the mysterious yet ubiquitous Alfred Kohlberg. For thirty years an importer of Chinese textiles, Kohlberg became a prodigiously energetic anti-Communist zealot during the mid-forties and the most persistent exponent of the thesis that China had been betrayed to the Communists by a sinister cabal of State Department officials. . . . Although his main concern was American policy in China, his interests spanned a broad range of extremist causes. He was the financial "angel" behind *Plain Talk,* a periodical whose contributors fancied themselves as the "intellectual right." He also financed the magazine's successor, *The Freeman,* and was indirectly involved in the organization of *Counter-attack,* a newsletter edited by three former FBI agents. The research and editorial staffs of all these Kohlberg-subsidized publications were apparently placed at McCarthy's disposal.

Kohlberg supplied McCarthy with voluminous "documents" to support his (and McCarthy's) thesis of conspiracy in high places. Much of this material was from Kohlberg's profuse writings on the China controversy, but the lace merchant also had access to the files of the Chinese Nationalist secret police, and—through the good offices of a government clerk—to the files and minutes of the Civil Service Commission's Loyalty Review Board. . . .

The Tydings Committee was indeed one to inspire confidence among Democrats and supporters of the administration. If they had hoped for a smooth and decorous investigation, however, their expectations were quickly shattered. The hearings opened on March 8 amid a scene of bewildering confusion and tumult. Tydings immediately demanded that McCarthy produce the name of "case 14" and identify the "high State Department official" whom McCarthy charged had shielded the man. The question was designed to embarrass McCarthy and put an end to his efforts at dissimulation. . . .

For the first few weeks McCarthy was scraping rock bottom; only his unique and overblown sense of drama, together with the sensational coverage given his charges in the press, saved his act from complete collapse. The first "case" he pulled out was that of Dorothy Kenyon, a distinguished and liberal lawyer from New York City. Miss Kenyon had not been among those mentioned by McCarthy in his Wheeling speech, nor was she on his list of "81" cases presented to the Senate. She was not even in the State Department, though she had served from 1947 to 1949 as a United States delegate to the United Nations Commission on the Status of Women. She had belonged to a large number of liberal left-wing, and in some instances "front" organizations, and the famous "Appendix Nine" of the Dies Committee had listed twenty-eight such groups behind her name. McCarthy began his presentation: "This lady has been affiliated with 28 Communist front organizations."

McCarthy named eighteen of these organizations in two days of testimony. Senator Hickenlooper added six more a few days later.

It is difficult to recapture the enormity of McCarthy's performance. One begins with his sources. Appendix Nine listed some twenty-eight organizations with which Miss Kenyon had been "affiliated," and McCarthy produced from the files of J. B. Matthews a number of photostats "documenting" these connections. Of the twenty-eight, only a half-dozen had ever been "cited" by the attorney general as "Communist fronts," and in no instance did Miss Kenyon's "affiliation" postdate this listing. . . .

All this McCarthy ignored, and as was so very characteristic of him, the weaker his case, the more inflated his rhetoric. Thus while most observers would conclude that the dates of Miss Kenyon's alleged affiliations were a little dusty with age, Mc-Carthy found in this evidence that her "Communist activities" were not only deep-rooted "but extend back through the years." A 1938 letterhead, he triumphantly proclaimed, showed an affiliation "going back 12 years." . . .

The attack on Dorothy Kenyon was symptomatic of McCarthy's desperation and audacity. No one then nor since has been able to suggest that Miss Kenyon was anything but a generous and liberal citizen. She called McCarthy "an unmitigated liar," and the senator never proved the contrary.

McCarthy also took an offhand swing at United States Ambassador at Large Philip C. Jessup, accusing the diplomat of "an unusual affinity" for Communist causes. Jessup had been under fire for some time from right-wing Republicans because he had testified as a character witness for Alger Hiss and because he was identified with the administration's Far Eastern policy. Richard Nixon had recently dubbed him "the architect of our far-eastern policy," a title McCarthy would later bestow upon others. Unlike Miss Kenyon, Jessup was a very real and high-ranking American diplomat. But McCarthy's "case" against the ambassador, as developed by Senator Hickenlooper during a committee session on March 20 and elaborated by McCarthy in a Senate speech on March 30, was pathetic. They accused Jessup of membership in six "Communist fronts." Of the six, Jessup had not been affiliated with two, and two more were not fronts at all. As for the remaining pair, he had been briefly connected with each, well before they were "cited" as Communist fronts, and in the company of many other distinguished citizens. Only one of these, the American Russian Institute, had been listed by the attorney general and Jessup had not even been a member; he had been among the sponsors of a dinner the group held in 1944.

In his Senate speech of March 30, McCarthy also repeated a number of charges originally made against Jessup by Alfred Kohlberg. In 1949 Kohlberg had charged Jessup with being "the initiator of the smear campaign against Nationalist China and Chiang Kai-shek [Jiang Jieshi], and the originator of the myth of the 'democratic' Chinese Communists." . . .

McCarthy also gave the committee the name of Owen Lattimore, a Far Eastern scholar who was then director of the Walter Hines Page School of International Relations at Johns Hopkins University. Although Lattimore had served only briefly in the State Department, he had been one of the main targets in Alfred Kohlberg's battle over the Institute of Pacific Relations and had been frequently attacked by

Kohlberg in the years which followed. Lattimore would later become the center of controversy, but in this first presentation, McCarthy said little that was not already public knowledge. . . .

McCarthy also attacked Harlow Shapley, the director of the Harvard Observatory, and Frederick L. Schuman, a professor at Williams College. Both men were ardent left-wing activists, but they were scarcely subversive in any recognized meaning of that term. Moreover, they had only the most tenuous of relations with the State Department. Shapley had served from 1947 to 1950 as a representative of the United States National Commission for UNESCO. Schuman's only contact had been a 1946 lecture to Foreign Service officers during an orientation program. Both men had been the target for HUAC, CUAC, and other congressional critics, and McCarthy now followed suit by listing the various "front" affiliations of each.

Finally, McCarthy turned to John Stewart Service, who like Owen Lattimore would later figure as a protagonist in the hearings. The charges against Service were a rehash of all the old accusations: Patrick Hurley's declaration before a Senate Foreign Relations Committee in 1945 that Service had worked to undermine American policy in Asia, the *Amerasia* case, and so forth. McCarthy drew at great length from an article by Emmanuel Larsen in *Plain Talk*, and he noted that the Civil Service Commission had only recently ordered another loyalty hearing for Service.

The sum of McCarthy's "nine public cases" was not impressive. Of the nine, only four were in the State Department, and all four had been carefully checked by the department's security force. Each of them, moreover, offered strong and persuasive rebuttal to McCarthy's charges.

This first phase of the Tydings investigation ended amid increasingly sharp Democratic attacks on McCarthy and a growing uneasiness among "liberal" Republicans over the senator's failure to prove his charges. Henry L. Stimson, who had served as secretary of state under Herbert Hoover and later as secretary of war under Franklin Roosevelt, wrote a long and eloquent letter to the *New York Times* expressing the concern of many over the extreme partisanship exhibited by McCarthy and other Republicans in their attacks on the Department of State. "The man who seeks to gain political advantage from personal attacks on a Secretary of State," declared Stimson, "is a man who seeks political advantage from damage to his country." With the exceptions which one might anticipate, the nation's press was generally cool to the McCarthy performance, and even such veteran redbaiters as Eugene Lyons discounted the senator's claims.

Still, the Wisconsin senator had not fared altogether badly. The Republican leadership had naturally been cautious. They had been taken by surprise by his original accusations, and they still feared that the charges might somehow boomerang and destroy a good political issue. The Republican caucus had explicitly declined to make the charges a party issue, but McCarthy received growing support from his colleagues as the hearings proceeded. Within the subcommittee both Hickenlooper and Lodge worked to give him the advantage. . . .

Even more important was the growing publicity which McCarthy was attracting. There is a maxim to the effect that a politician should never worry about what the papers are saying, but only when they are not saying anything. If this is true, then McCarthy had good cause for rejoicing. The bitter wrangling of the committee hearings, their thinly veiled adversary character, the drama of McCarthy's accusations and in turn the attacks which were leveled at him, all created an irresistible news source. Even such staid and conservative journals as the *New York Herald Tribune* and the *New York Times* gave the hearings extensive front page coverage. . . .

AGENTS AND ARCHITECTS

I believe you can ask almost any school child who the architect of our eastern policy is, and he will say, 'Owen Lattimore.'

JOE McCARTHY

The second phase of the Tydings investigation was precipitated by McCarthy's sensational charges against Owen Lattimore and took place amidst an increasingly bitter debate over American policy in China. The Communist victory in China had shocked many Americans, and some who still nurtured the illusion of American omnipotence abroad sought to blame this "catastrophe" upon those who made and executed United States foreign policy. For Republicans such as Senator William F. Knowland of California and Congressman Walter H. Judd of Minnesota, the "China issue" became the lever for breaking up the bipartisan consensus which had shaped national policy since the end of World War II. And as the restraining influence of Arthur Vandenberg declined, the tempo of partisan debate steadily increased.

President Truman was enraged by McCarthy's charges and by the continuing Republican attacks on the Department of State. When Senator Styles Bridges confided to reporters that he and other Republicans planned to "go after" Acheson, the president wrote a long letter to the New Hampshire Republican, appealing as an "old-time personal friend and Senate colleague" for the senator to weigh carefully "this unwarranted attack on bipartisan foreign policy." By the time Bridges received the letter he had already launched a major attack on the secretary of state. Two days later, at a press conference, reporters coaxed the angry president into charging that the partisan attempt "to sabotage bipartisan foreign policy" by Bridges, Wherry, and McCarthy was the Kremlin's "greatest asset."

Whatever else the president may have intended, the immediate result of his remarks was further to inflame his congressional critics and to force McCarthy more firmly than ever upon the Republican leadership. Taft denounced the attack as "bitter and prejudiced" and praised McCarthy as "a fighting marine" who had been "slandered" by the president.

On the same day that Truman lashed out at the Republicans from his vacation White House in Palm Beach, McCarthy made his second major speech on "communism-in-government," concentrating exclusively this time on the Far East and charging that China had been "betrayed" by a State Department "more loyal to the ideals and designs of communism than to those of the free, God-fearing half of the world." The speech reflected the strong influence of Alfred Kohlberg and Walter Judd, both of whom were supplying McCarthy with material on the "China issue." In it Mc-Carthy repeated his earlier charges against John Stewart Service, Philip C. Jessup, and Haldore Hanson. His main target this time, however, was Owen Lattimore.

Lattimore had never been a regular member of the State Department in the strictest sense, though he had held several government posts and was a respected authority on Far Eastern affairs. . . . As a specialist in Far Eastern studies he had been active in the Institute of Pacific Relations and at one time edited its magazine, *Pacific Affairs*. He had been on the editorial board of *Amerasia* from 1937 to 1941, though he was never active in its management.

Although Lattimore had originally been a warm supporter of Chiang Kai-shek, he became increasingly critical of the Nationalist leader during the mid-1940s and increasingly sympathetic toward the Generalissimo's Communist opposition. This earned for him the wrath of Chiang's highly vocal supporters in this country, and in particular that of Alfred Kohlberg and the "China lobby." Kohlberg charged, by implication and innuendo, that Lattimore was a Communist and a traitor; and these charges were repeated intermittently throughout the late 1940s by right-wing journalists and politicians. . . .

Then on March 21 the senator told eager reporters that he was prepared to name the "top Russian espionage agent" in the United States. Tydings immediately called an emergency session of the subcommittee, which met behind closed doors to hear the senator's charge. It was a farce, except for the seriousness which the committee was forced to accord McCarthy. He had absolutely nothing new. . . .

By the time McCarthy made his Senate speech of March 30, he was already backing away from his sensational spy charges of a few days before. ("I fear in the case of Lattimore, I have perhaps placed too much stress on the question of whether or not he has been an espionage agent.") Drawing on material supplied by Alfred Kohlberg, he now returned to his earlier charge that Lattimore was "the principal architect of our far-eastern policy" and as such had subverted both American and Chinese interests. He presented to the Senate the affidavit of a former Communist (later identified as Louis Budenz) whom he declared would testify that Lattimore had belonged to the party. He read a statement by another unidentified ex-Communist (Freda Utley) which asserted that Lattimore was "very obviously receiving instructions from the Soviet Union" when he visited Moscow in 1936. He read portions of a letter Lattimore had written in 1943, purportedly showing Lattimore's "pro-Communist" inclinations, but when other senators pressed him to place the entire letter in the *Record,* he refused, replying that it was still "classified." It was an angry session. Democratic Senators Herbert H. Lehman, Dennis Chavez, Hubert H. Humphrey, Clinton P. Anderson, and Brien McMahon were all on their feet at one point or another, and the easily aroused New Hampshire Republican Charles Tobey nearly exploded when McCarthy refused to place the Lattimore letter in the *Record.* The galleries were crowded and noisy, and at one point McCarthy was applauded in defiance of Senate rules.

By the time Lattimore first testified before the subcommittee, the drama of his appearance had already been intensified by the increasingly vehement Republican attacks upon the administration's foreign policy in China. If Alger Hiss could be made the symbol of the New Deal generation, perhaps Lattimore might serve as a scapegoat in the China debate. The day before Lattimore testified, Senator William F. Knowland attacked him in a major Senate speech comparing the professor's many books and articles to the Communist party "line."

The subcommittee convened on April 6 in the large, marble-pillared Senate caucus room. Newsmen reported the largest crowd since Wendell Willkie had packed the same room when testifying in favor of lend-lease shortly before World War II. Lattimore, a bespectacled, slightly balding man with a sharp professorial air, denounced McCarthy's charges as "base and contemptible lies." He accused the Wisconsin senator of serving as the willing tool of the "China lobby." He defended himself against each of McCarthy's specific accusations and introduced into the record letters from Chiang Kai-shek and Madame Chiang warmly praising his services. At the end of the hearing, Tydings announced that four of the committee members had examined Lattimore's loyalty file and found no evidence indicating that he was or ever had been a Communist. Lattimore was loudly applauded at the end of the hearing. Obviously, he had won this round, but the fight was far from over.

The fact that Louis F. Budenz would testify in the Lattimore case had been an open secret in Washington for some time. In his speech of March 30, McCarthy had promised he would produce a witness who would testify that Lattimore was a Communist, and as early as April 1, Lattimore had telegraphed Budenz, asking him to disavow the statements which were being attributed to him. Following Lattimore's emphatic testimony, the press continued to buzz with rumors that Budenz would come forth to "identify" Lattimore, and on April 11 McCarthy confirmed that subpoenas had been served on the onetime editor of the *Daily Worker*. The growing intensity of the party debate, together with the careful press agentry which preceded Budenz's appearance, created a mood of tense expectancy and apprehension. The demand for seats was almost unprecedented, and veteran political observers declared that the testimony would play an important role in the future of Senator McCarthy and the Communist issue with which he was increasingly identified. . . .

Budenz appeared before the Tydings Committee on April 20, 1950. The hearing resembled a scene by Nathanael West. The caucus room was choked with spectators, nearly 700 in a space designed to hold less than half that number. There were senators and congressmen, high administration officials, and other less distinguished onlookers. The giant klieg lights blazed away, making the room insufferably hot. The television and newsreel cameras whirred constantly, and there were flurries of popping explosions as the photographers rushed about. Occasionally a microphone would shriek out of control, adding to the noise and confusion.

Budenz began in a quiet, ordinary voice. His remarks were long, discursive, and at some points incoherent, but there emerged from his testimony at least four specific accusations. He declared that Lattimore was a member of a Communist cell within the Institute of Pacific Relations; that in 1943 he had been told by party headquarters that the "line" on Chiang Kai-shek had been changed to opposition and hostility; that at the time of Henry Wallace's trip to China in 1944, Budenz was told "to consider Owen Lattimore as a Communist"; and finally that he, Budenz, had been informed that Lattimore had "been of service" in the *Amerasia* case.

Senate Republicans eagerly grasped the Budenz testimony, declaring that it went far toward proving their charges and that the Lattimore case "looks like another Alger Hiss case." Even such a moderate as Ralph Flanders got up in the Senate to note that the investigation had "taken a more serious turn.". . .

Budenz had been in frequent contact with Alfred Kohlberg for some years, and only recently had conferred with him about the Lattimore case. It is more than probable that all of Budenz's charges concerning the China question (including the 1949 article for *Colliers*) sprang not at all from the ex-Communist's facile memory, but rather from the fertile imagination of the China merchant. Budenz merely served to legitimize these accusations and give them an aura of authority. And though Budenz was very vague and evasive, it also turned out that he had conferred with Robert Morris, a right-winger hired at the instigation of the Republicans on the subcommittee as assistant counsel, and with Charles J. Kersten, a former Wisconsin congressman who was working for McCarthy. Budenz's background, moreover, was such as to raise very serious questions as to his reliability as a witness, even though he told the subcommittee that because of the Catholic sacrament he was able to gain redemption for the sins of his past and was therefore "a different man than 5 years ago.". . .

Next came Freda Utley, a shrill and excitable ex-Communist who testified that although Lattimore was not a spy, he had been a "Judas Cow" who had led other innocents to the slaughter. Miss Utley had been a member of the British Communist party during the late 1920s, later moving to the Soviet Union, where she married a Russian. She left during the mid-1930s, when her husband was caught up in the Stalinist purges, and came to this country. She soon drifted into the extreme right-wing politics of the America First committee. She was a member of Alfred Kohlberg's China Policy Association and a contributor to the Kohlberg-subsidized journal, *Plain Talk*. She told the committee that "the Communist cancer must be cut out if we are to survive as a free nation. Perhaps in this operation some healthy tissues on the fringe will be destroyed." She never specified whether Lattimore was "on the fringe" or not, but like Budenz she offered no corroboration of any sort. At one point the exasperated Tydings declared: "We don't want opinion evidence here. We want facts, f-a-c-t-s. We are getting few of them."

Lattimore appeared for a second time before the committee. As before, the caucus room was crowded, though on this occasion the crowd was not nearly so partial toward Lattimore. The professor denied each of the specific accusations made by Budenz and Utley, and he attacked the credibility of both.

Senator McCarthy had produced no evidence to support his contention that Lattimore was the "top Russian espionage agent" in America. Even Budenz and Utley had denied this. Nor had he been able to prove his second thesis, that Lattimore was the "architect of our far eastern policy." Excepting the very dubious and unsubstantiated testimony of Budenz and Utley, there was nothing to show that Lattimore was a Communist at all. At the very worst, the sharp-tongued little professor was a "fellow traveler," although McCarthy had not even proved this.

Nevertheless, McCarthy emerged from the Lattimore hearings stronger than before. Whatever the probative value of the Budenz testimony, it was greedily seized upon by Republican partisans as proof of G.O.P. charges of long standing, and by the end of April close observers discerned a steady growth of support for McCarthy from within his party. His charges had become inextricably caught up in the acrimonious debate over America's "failure" in China, and hardly a day passed without an attack on the Department of State. The "Communist issue," moreover, appeared to be gaining momentum all across the country. In Florida, Congressman George A. Smathers defeated the veteran Democratic Senator Claude Pepper in a scurrilous primary campaign based on charges that Pepper was too friendly with Communists and Negroes. Willis Smith followed suit in his successful attempt to unseat North Carolina Senator Frank P. Graham, and both Democrat Manchester Boddy and Republican Richard M. Nixon used the Communist issue in their campaign against Helen Gahagan Douglas in California.

In the middle of April the administration rallied its forces for a counteroffensive against the Republican right in general and McCarthy in particular. Vice President Alben Barkley denounced all those who would "abridge our freedom" and "sow rumors and suspicions among us." Senate Majority Leader Scott Lucas pleaded for an end to the "angry wrangling" over foreign policy. Even the aging Tom Connally was drawn out by the attacks on United States foreign policy and shouted across the Senate that the Republican charges against the Department of State were "base slander." Secretary of State Acheson compared McCarthy to the Mad Slayer of Camden, New Jersey, and called for an end to the "filthy business" which was destroying public confidence in the State Department. The president himself denounced the Wisconsin senator before a dinner gathering of the Federal Bar Association, and other administration supporters echoed his charges. . . .

It was clear that the confidence with which Tydings had begun the investigation had evaporated in the face of McCarthy's growing support. In early March he had sarcastically told McCarthy that as the "man who occasioned this hearing" he, McCarthy, would get one of the most thorough investigations in the history of the Republic. He had patronizingly referred to the senator as "this boy" in executive session. Now he was worried and apprehensive. At a meeting in the office of the Senate secretary, Leslie Biffle, on May 8, 1950, he appealed to fellow senators to "go after McCarthy." Senator William Benton, a freshman Democrat from Connecticut, took the floor on the following day to denounce McCarthy as a "hit-and-run propagandist of the Kremlin model." A few days later, the veteran New Mexico lawmaker, Dennis Chavez, made a vehement attack on Louis Budenz. Speaking as a Roman Catholic, Chavez accused Budenz of "using the Cross as a club" and hiding behind it to conduct a campaign of smear and vilification.

McCarthy thrived upon such attacks and the publicity which they brought him, and he turned upon his adversaries his own unparalleled skills at vituperation. He denounced all the "egg-sucking phony liberals" whose "pitiful squealing . . . would hold sacrosanct those Communists and queers" who had sold China into "atheistic slavery," and he pledged himself to the task of driving out the "prancing mimics of the Moscow party line in the State Department." He charged that Lucas and Chavez were "dupes" of the Kremlin and were spewing "its malignant smear." He accused Tydings and McMahon of conducting "Operation Whitewash." He railed at Acheson and Jessup as "dilettante diplomats" who "whined" and "whimpered" and "cringed" in the face of communism. He declared that former Secretary of State George C. Marshall was "a pathetic thing" who was "completely unfit" for high office. . . .

THE RISE OF JOE MCCARTHY: WHY?

It all comes down to this: are we going to try to win an election or aren't we.

TOM COLEMAN

How to explain the rise of Joe McCarthy? The answer is necessarily complicated. There has always been a fear of radicalism in this country and what I have called the "anti-Communist persuasion." Following World War II America found itself in a world increasingly polarized between East and West, and hung upon a precarious "balance of terror." Joe McCarthy made his appearance at a singularly propitious moment in this postwar devolution, when events both at home and abroad (the conviction of Alger Hiss, the fall of Nationalist China) provided interested partisans with ready issues. Nor was it possible to gainsay the senator's own unique contributions—his overblown sense of drama, his talent for political invective, his willingness to "raise on the poor hands." And he seemed to have touched a popular nerve with his appeal to rid the government of "Communists and queers."

More important was the Communist issue itself, with its readymade style and slogans, even with its own "lobby." McCarthy's real triumph in these first months was in identifying himself with this issue. The phrase "McCarthyism"—first coined by the senator's opponents—assisted in this process. For most liberals, "McCarthyism" meant reckless attacks on individuals from the privileged sanctuary of the Senate. For extremists such as Fulton Lewis, Jr., "McCarthyism" was "Americanism," a phrase faintly reminiscent of something Earl Browder once said. In fact, "McCarthyism" was shorthand for the issue of "communism-in-government," a preeminently Republican issue which served as the cutting edge of the party's drive for power. And as the public, press, and politicians all came to identify McCarthy with this issue, the senator won steadily increasing support from his party.

From the very outset McCarthy had the backing of a small but strategically located group of conservative Republicans to whom the Communist issue had long been important. This group included Kenneth S. Wherry, the Republican floor leader, Bourke B. Hickenlooper, who aided McCarthy from within the Tydings Committee, Karl E. Mundt, Homer Ferguson, Owen Brewster, William E. Jenner, and others. As McCarthy began to concentrate his attacks on American policy in China, he also won over the support of hard-line "Asia Firsters" such as William F. Knowland and Styles Bridges, as well as isolationists such as George W. Malone.

From the beginning the McCarthy charges had represented a potentially powerful Republican campaign issue, and although the Senate Republicans never made these charges party policy, Republican leader Robert Taft urged McCarthy to press on with the attack. Truman's blast at the Republican right on March 30 seemed to confirm this movement and reporters saw in Taft's reply ("The only way to get rid of Communists in the State Department is to change the head of government.") the emerging G.O.P. battlelines for 1952. . . .

All Republicans, of course, did not share this idea of party strategy. From time to time senators such as Ralph E. Flanders of Vermont, H. Alexander Smith of New Jersey, and Leverett Saltonstall of Massachusetts would exhibit some uneasiness over the senator's "bare-knuckle" tactics. Republican governors James H. Duff of Pennsylvania, Alfred E. Driscoll of New Jersey, and Earl Warren of California strongly criticized the senator, and the president of Columbia University, Dwight D. Eisenhower, warned that calling names was a "behind-the-iron-curtain trick" and that Americans should not be suckered into calling anyone a Communist "who may be just a little bit brighter than ourselves." The most spirited Republican dissent was the celebrated "Declaration of Conscience" made by Senator Margaret Chase Smith and six other Republican senators. Senator Smith charged that the Senate had been "debased to the level of a forum of hate and character assassination sheltered by the shield of Congressional immunity" and she declared that she did not want to see the Republican party ride to victory on "the Four Horsemen of Calumny—Fear, Ignorance, Bigotry and Smear."

But the tide of party politics was running heavily against the moderates. Senators Taft, Wherry, Brewster, and Bridges spoke for the Republican majority when they praised McCarthy and urged him to continue his attacks; even such moderate Republicans as H. Alexander Smith and Alexander Wiley were unwilling to follow the lead of Margaret Chase Smith and the small group which signed the "Declaration of Conscience." The New Jersey senator later recalled that the Declaration "raised the issue pretty severely," and that while he felt it was a "beautiful job" he still intended to "try and convert McCarthy rather than get him reprimanded publicly." Alexander Wiley confided to his son that McCarthy's techniques were "rather vicious," but publicly he issued a press release calling on the Truman administration to stop trying to "smear McCarthy.". . .

The response of the Democrats to McCarthy was more complicated, but they too contributed to his growing power and influence. It was not that McCarthy lacked vocal enemies—he did not, at least during the spring and summer of 1950. But most of these opponents were members of the Truman administration. In the Senate, only twelve Democrats spoke out against McCarthy.

Senators Tydings, Green, and McMahon were drawn into the McCarthy opposition primarily because they were members of the Tydings Committee, Scott Lucas because he was majority leader, and a few stalwarts such as Dennis Chavez of New Mexico because of the call by Tydings and others to rally behind the party banner. The remainder were members of the rather small and as yet ineffectual liberal bloc—Herbert H. Lehman of New York, William Benton of Connecticut, Harley M. Kilgore and Matthew M. Neely of West Virginia, Clinton P. Anderson of New Mexico, Hubert H. Humphrey of Minnesota, and Paul H. Douglas of Illinois.

The rest of the Senate was silent. In the aftermath of the Hiss case and the China debacle, both Dean Acheson and the State Department were exposed to all manner of partisan attack; and many Democrats, especially the Southern conservatives, were unwilling to defend them. Some of this reluctance was ideological, some of it was political, some of it was even personal—they didn't *like* Dean Acheson. In

July the Senate Democrats did rally for a party line vote on the Tydings Committee Report, but this was the last display of Democratic unity on the McCarthy issue until December 1954. Confronted by the issues and emotions symbolized by Joe McCarthy, most Democrats preferred to acquiesce. . . .

Suggested Readings

William C. Berman, *The Politics of Civil Rights in the Truman Administration* (1970).
Barton J. Bernstein, ed., *Politics and Policies of the Truman Administration* (1970).
Robert J. Donovan, *Conflict and Crisis: The Presidency of Harry S. Truman, 1945–1948* (1977).
———— , *Tumultuous Years: The Presidency of Harry S. Truman, 1949–1953* (1982).
Robert H. Ferrell, *Harry S. Truman and the Modern American Presidency* (1983).
Robert Griffith, *The Politics of Fear* (1970).
Alonzo Hamby, *Beyond the New Deal: Harry S. Truman and American Liberalism* (1973).
Maeva Marcus, *Truman and the Steel Seizure* (1977).
Norman D. Markowitz, *The Rise and Fall of the People's Century: Henry A. Wallace and American Liberalism, 1941–1948* (1973).
Thomas C. Reeves, *The Life and Times of Joe McCarthy* (1982).

Further Readings

Postwar American Culture and Society in the Immediate Postwar Period

Michael Barson, *"Better Dead than Red!" A Nostalgic Look at the Golden Years of Russiaphobia, Red-Baiting, and other Commie Madness* (1992); Paul Boyer, *By the Bomb's Early Light: American Thought and Culture at the Dawn of the Atomic Age* (1985); Ruth Schwartz Cowan, *More Work for Mother* (1983); Landon Y. Jones, *Great Expectations: America and the Baby Boom Generation* (1980); Glenna Matthews, *"Just a Housewife"* (1987); Keith W. Olson, *The GI Bill, the Veterans, and the Colleges* (1974); Stephen J. Whitfield, *The Culture of the Cold War* (1991).

Domestic Politics and Reform

Jack S. Ballard, *Shock of Peace* (1983); Andrew J. Dunar, *The Truman Scandals and the Politics of Morality* (1984); Robert James Maddox, *From War to Cold War: The Education of Harry S. Truman* (1988); Irwin Ross, *The Loneliest Campaign* (1968); Allen Yarnell, *Democrats and Progressives* (1973).

McCarthyism

Michal R. Belknap, *Cold War Political Justice: The Smith Act, the Communist Party, and American Civil Liberties* (1977); Richard M. Freeland, *The Truman Doctrine and the Origins of McCarthyism* (1972, 1985); Richard Fried, *Nightmare in Red* (1990); Stanley I. Kutler, *The American Inquisition* (1982); Peter L. Steinberg, *The Great "Red Menace": United States Prosecution of American Communists, 1947–1952* (1984).

QUESTIONS FOR DISCUSSION

1. Describe economic and demographic conditions in the United States at the close of World War II.
2. In what ways did the status of women and minorities deteriorate after the war?
3. Assess Harry S Truman's qualifications for the presidency in 1945. How did he win the 1948 presidential election?
4. Was Truman's Fair Deal effective? Explain.
5. Discuss the Alger Hiss case and its impact on American politics and society.
6. What role did the army play in the downfall of Joseph McCarthy?
7. Using information from Robert Griffith's essay on the rise of McCarthy, describe the senator from Wisconsin's tactics as he searched for communist sympathizers in government. Identify McCarthy's principal sources of support.

THE EISENHOWER ERA

The decade of the 1950s was a period in American history characterized by outward calm and deep inner anxiety. The American people responded to the anxieties of the Cold War by electing a moderately conservative president who symbolized stability and strong leadership in international affairs and maintenance of the prosperous status quo in domestic affairs. The Eisenhower administration contained communism at home and abroad and consolidated the social and economic gains made during the 1930s and 1940s. While white Americans spent their money on a variety of spectacular new consumer goods and embraced an optimistic, feel-good variety of Christianity, African Americans launched the modern civil rights movement, a movement that would shake the republic to its foundations as it confronted the contradiction of a democracy relegating a substantial portion of its citizenry to permanent second-class citizenship.

DWIGHT D. EISENHOWER

THE ELECTION OF 1952

As the election of 1952 approached and America's frustration with the Korean War drove Harry Truman's popularity downward, leading Republicans once again struggled to position themselves for their party's presidential nomination. Because he was a two-time loser, Governor Dewey could not run himself, but he and his moderate allies were determined to keep the nomination from Senator Taft, a figure they regarded as both reactionary in domestic affairs and neo-isolationist in foreign policy. In desperation they approached General Dwight D. ("Ike") Eisenhower, president of Columbia University on leave and supreme commander of NATO.

The intensely ambitious Eisenhower was a novice at conventional politics. His military background and orthodox midwestern views convinced him, however, that he was a Republican. After some delay he accepted the offer of GOP moderates to back him for the presidency. His decision to challenge Taft, he confided to friends, grew primarily out of a desire to save the country from the perils of isolationism. Although the Taft people dominated the Republican National Committee, they were outmaneuvered at the national nominating convention. Eisenhower's nomination on the first ballot embittered the Taftites who threatened to sit out the election. The Republican nominee subsequently healed the breach and took a long step toward winning the election by meeting with Taft in New York and agreeing to his "articles of co-operation."

Meanwhile, Senator Estes Kefauver broke with the Truman adminis-tration and announced his candidacy for the Democratic nomination. The president kept the party in suspense about his own intentions until March 30 when he announced that he would not seek what would amount to a third term. Thereupon, Truman and his advisors launched a concerted campaign to draft Adlai Stevenson, the enigmatic governor of Illinois, a man who was rhetorically liberal, philosophically moderate, and coy to the point of perverseness. Stevenson refused to commit until after the Democratic convention assembled. He finally agreed to run, however, and with the president's backing, received the nomination. The Democratic platform endorsed the achievements of the Truman administration and called for the extension of existing Fair Deal programs and the enactment of new ones.

The American people were sick of the Korean War which continued to drag on despite the fact that armistice negotiations had been underway since 1951. Though they supported containment, Americans naturally tended to identify the anxieties of the Cold War with the previous administration. An increasingly conservative country was tired of Democratic appeals to middle-class guilt and to economic grievances that for most whites had ceased to exist. They were, in short, ready for a change.

The Eisenhower campaign quickly picked up steam and appeared headed for a runaway victory when in mid-September the Democratic National Com-mittee published reports that Eisenhower's running mate, Richard Nixon, had used an $18,000 political slush fund for his personal use. Fighting off efforts by the general's advisors to dump him, Nixon made a maudlin appeal to the American people over the new medium of television. He had done nothing wrong, he told the nation. The only gift his family had received was their little dog, Checkers, and they were going to keep him. The "Checkers speech" was a brilliant stroke. Eisenhower quickly welcomed the Californian back on board. When the final ballots were counted, Eisenhower had outpolled Stevenson 33 to 27 million. The country was war weary, and the Democrats failed to hold two important elements of the old New Deal voting coalition—farmers and south-erners.

ALL ABOUT IKE

Dwight Eisenhower assumed the presidency with some serious handicaps. Only Zachary Taylor entered the White House with less exposure to civilian life, and his example was not encouraging. Born in Denison, Texas, and raised in Abilene, Kansas, Eisenhower had managed to obtain an appointment to West Point despite the fact that his father was a mere creamery worker. From West Point student, to tank instructor during the Great War, to serving as aide to Douglas MacArthur, to supervising the Normandy invasion, Eisenhower's only experience outside the army had been as president of Columbia University, and that had not been a happy one. His long military career had stunted his intellectual growth and created a tendency to rely too heavily on the initiative and good judgment of his subordinates. On the plus side, as supreme commander of allied forces in Europe, Ike had directed one of the largest, most complex military operations in history. More significant, he had demonstrated considerable political skills in holding the British, French, and Canadians in a smoothly working alliance. He seemed born for responsibility.

Eisenhower's mind was like his personality, "just plain American," one of his contemporaries wrote. Indeed, the new president was "standard American" almost to the point of caricature. He liked westerns, bourbon, bridge and poker, golf, fishing, gardening, and hunting. His admiration of the successful businessman was so unabashed that it reminded history buffs uneasily of Ulysses S. Grant. Ike's political philosophy seemed orthodox Republican to the core: devotion to free enterprise and a balanced budget, a respect for states' rights, and a distrust of the welfare state. Yet, he agreed with the moderate wing of the party that the New Deal should stand. Defining his position as "modern Republicanism," the president claimed that he was "conservative when it comes to money and liberal when it comes to human beings."

DOMESTIC PROGRAMS

CONSERVATISM WITH A CONSCIENCE

In domestic affairs, Eisenhower tended to delegate authority to his cabinet which, during the early years of the administration, was dominated by conservative businessmen; "eight millionaires and a plumber," one wag dubbed it after Eisenhower named Martin Durbin of the Plumbers and Steamfitters Union to be secretary of labor. The leading figures in this citadel of orthodoxy were Ohio industrialist George Humphrey who immediately ejected economists from the Treasury Department and announced that the new administration would spare no program in its effort to balance the budget. Heading the Defense Department was former General Motors president Charles E. Wilson.

In the midst of his campaign to hold down Pentagon spending, he announced that "what was good for our country was good for General Motors, and vice-versa." Ezra Taft Benson, conservative farm market specialist and bulwark of the Mormon church, headed Agriculture.

The conservatives in the Eisenhower administration were as good as their word. Tax reductions went into effect for individuals and corporations on January 1, 1954, and the administration succeeded in cutting government spending during fiscal 1954 by $6.5 billion. Acting upon the conservative Benson's advice, the administration reduced farm price supports dramatically. All too quickly did these fiscal conservatives learn that a too rigorous application of deflationary policies was counterproductive. Indeed, when recessions developed in 1954 and 1957, Eisenhower abandoned his goal of a balanced budget and authorized increased federal spending and easier credit as part of an effort to restore prosperity. These steps along with modest increases in New Deal welfare programs led to a steady growth in the federal budget from $29.5 billion in 1950 to $76.5 billion in 1960. Ike managed to balance the budget only three out of his eight years in office, but compared to his successors, he was the epitome of fiscal responsibility.

THE INTERSTATE HIGHWAY ACT

Perhaps the Eisenhower administration's most significant and revealing achievement was the creation of the interstate highway system. By the 1950s it had become clear that America's system of overland transportation was in dire need of attention. Chronically strapped for funds, the nation's privately owned railroad system had steadily cut passenger service and failed not only to build new tracks but to maintain old. The existing network of highways, built and maintained by state or local authorities, was clearly inadequate to serve a growing population spread across a vast continent.

Unwilling to consider outright nationalization of the railroads or even the substantial subsidies that modernization would have required, the administration instead threw its weight behind the Federal Highway Aid Act of 1956. The measure authorized construction of four- and eight-lane, controlled-access highways linking the nation's major cities. This, the interstate highway system, was to be completed by 1970 at a cost of $27.5 billion. In effect, the representatives of auto manufacturers, trucking firms, and construction companies out-lobbied rail interests. Among other things the battle over transportation pointed up the fact that the traditional dichotomy which had identified big government with liberalism and limited government with conservatism was fast becoming obsolete. Despite Republican rhetoric, the real issue was not whether government was big or small, but rather whose interests it served.

FOREIGN AFFAIRS

FROM ROLLBACK TO CONTAINMENT

Despite his campaign rhetoric, Eisenhower was not fundamentally unhappy with the policy of communist containment overseas. He believed in the existence of a monolithic communist conspiracy directed from the Kremlin which had as its ultimate objective world domination. Cunning and ruthless, the Soviet communists were willing to resort to intimidation, subversion, and, if the United States did not maintain its defenses, military aggression. The president did not share the Republican right wing's obsession with the threat of domestic communist subversion; the principal threat was abroad and was best met through formation of military alliances and programs of economic and military aid. John Foster Dulles, the corporate lawyer and Dewey advisor whom Eisenhower selected as his secretary of state, fully shared these views. Articulate, bright, and tremendously energetic, Dulles was the author of a number of books and pamphlets on international affairs. Yet Dulles, who was a prominent Presbyterian layman, insisted on taking a self-righteously moralistic stand against communism in public. Playing to the conservative gallery, he wielded such epithets as immoral, enslavement, and banditry when talking about the Soviet Union.

During the campaign of 1952 Republican campaigners had promised that if their candidate were elected, the United States would roll back the Iron Curtain in Europe and unleash Jiang Jieshi to liberate the Chinese mainland from the communists. Events quickly revealed those pledges to be nothing more than political rhetoric. When in the summer of 1953 workers in East Germany rioted to protest working conditions and lack of bargaining power, and the Soviets crushed the rebellion with tanks and machine guns, Washington could only deplore the course of events behind the Iron Curtain. When in 1956 Hungarian freedom fighters took to the streets of Budapest to try to rid their country of its Soviet occupiers, the American response was the same. Though the CIA had encouraged the rebellion, Washington refused to respond to the Hungarians' pleas for military intervention and even delivery of arms and other supplies. Similarly, during the various Taiwanese crises of the 1950s the administration acted to restrain rather than unleash Jiang Jieshi.

AMERICA AND THE FIRST INDOCHINESE WAR

The administration's conservative approach to combating the spread of communism was perhaps best revealed in its response to the crisis in Indochina. From 1882 until 1941 Laos, Cambodia, and Vietnam composed French Indochina, France's richest and most important colony. Forced to relinquish control to the Japanese following its surrender to Germany in 1941, the French returned to Southeast Asia in 1946 determined to regain their lost provinces.

The war in the Pacific gave a strong fillip to anticolonial movements throughout the area, and Indochina was no exception. Shortly after Japan's surrender, Ho Chi Minh, leader of the Vietminh, a broadbased but communist-led resistance movement, proclaimed from Hanoi the existence of a new nation, the Democratic Republic of Vietnam. His ultimate goal was unification and independence for all of Vietnam. The French, however, were determined to reclaim their colonial empire and with the help of British and Chinese Nationalist occupation forces, reinfiltrated the country. In 1946 war erupted between the French and the Vietminh. By 1954, the French had been largely driven out of the Vietnamese countryside. With war weariness mounting in France, Paris agreed to a general peace conference on Southeast Asia to be held in Geneva.

On the eve of the meeting, a decisive battle raged for control of the French garrison at Dien Bien Phu situated on the Laotian border in North Vietnam. In March, the French government requested an American air strike to relieve its beleaguered and outgunned garrison. Although Dulles and the chairman of the Joint Chiefs of Staff favored such a move, others in Eisenhower's entourage urged the president not to intervene unilaterally. When Britain refused to participate, Eisenhower told the French that continued economic and arms aid was the most they could hope for. It would, he said, be a "tragic error to go in alone as a partner of France." Dien Bien Phu fell to the communists in the spring of 1954, and shortly thereafter the Geneva Conference divided the country at the seventeenth parallel. A pro-Western regime emerged in Saigon to rule the south, while Ho and the communists, operating out of Hanoi, prevailed in the north.

THE NEW LOOK AND MASSIVE RETALIATION

The principal foreign and defense problem confronting Eisenhower, Dulles, Humphrey, and Wilson was how to reconcile a reduced defense budget with a militantly anticommunist posture around the globe. Humphrey and Wilson were afraid that the globalist responsibilities inherent in NSC 68 would cause the United States to spend itself into bankruptcy. The answer that they came up with was the policy of strategic deterrence, or what Dulles referred to as massive retaliation. According to this scenario, the administration would concentrate its funds on the Air Force, specifically the Strategic Air Command and its fleet of nuclear armed bombers. Pursuing a diplomatic strategy of brinksmanship, the United States would have to convince the communists that it was willing to use nuclear weapons in virtually any situation, even anticolonial "wars of liberation" that the communists attempted to coopt.

Two problems were inherent in massive retaliation and brinksmanship. To be successful, the American threat had to be credible. The Soviet Union exploded its own atomic device in 1949, and by 1954 both superpowers had detonated hydrogen bombs. With the launching of Sputnik in 1957, the Soviets closed the so-called bomber gap and achieved parity in delivery systems. From that point on, the United States was faced with the very real threat of nuclear annihilation if it launched its attack. The Eisenhower defense policy also seemed to deny the United States flexibility of response. American interests and the threats they faced around the globe were not uniform. The defense of some areas was more important and necessitated greater risks than others. Reliance on atomic weapons did not permit subtle distinctions.

THE SUEZ CRISIS

In addition to the threat of massive retaliation, Dulles proposed to contain communism through a series of alliances; indeed, it appeared that the secretary of state was intent on building a military fence around the Sino-Soviet sphere of influence. In 1955 Dulles traveled to Manila to preside over the creation of the Southeast Asia Treaty Organization (SEATO). Britain, France, Australia, New Zealand, the Philippines, Thailand, and Pakistan promised to view an attack on any one of them as a threat to their own peace and safety. That same year the United States presided over creation of, but did not join, the Middle East Treaty Organization (METO subsequently renamed CENTO) which included Turkey, Iraq, Britain, Pakistan, and Iran. Alliance building proved to be an ineffective strategy. The Soviets sought to project their power not through military aggression but rather through forging ideological links with anti-colonial revolutionary movements in developing areas and providing non-Western governments with economic and military aid. Nowhere were the flaws in administration policy more apparent than in the Suez crisis of 1956.

A number of factors contributed to instability in the Middle East and thus to converting it into a Cold War battleground. The first was the region's colonial history. For centuries the region stretching from Egypt to Iraq had been ruled by the Turks. World War I broke that bond, but Britain and France in effect replaced the Ottoman Empire when the League of Nations named them protectors of Egypt and the newly created states of Palestine, Iraq, Transjordan, and Lebanon. By the close of World War II the Middle East seethed with anti-Western hatred. That sentiment was reinforced by the fact that the Arabs viewed the United States and its European allies as champions of Zionism, the international movement to establish a Jewish homeland in Palestine.

In May 1948, the British officially withdrew from Palestine, which it had been administering as a U.N. mandate, whereupon Zionists in Palestine proclaimed the existence of a Jewish state, Israel. The Truman administration immediately extended diplomatic recognition, but the Palestinians aided by the Arab states of the region declared war. The Israeli army quickly routed their foes driving a million Palestinians from their homes.

From 1948 onward the humiliated Arab states refused to recognize Israel, tried to strangle the new state economically, and continually threatened to annihilate Israel in a second war. Finally, the maldistribution of the region's oil reserves contributed to unrest in the Middle East. By the 1950s Arab rulers with petroleum deposits had worked out arrangements with Dutch, British, and American companies under which they received 50 percent of all profits earned from extraction and refining. Unfortunately, those nations with the largest and poorest populations—Egypt, Syria, and Jordan—had no oil and had to stand by and watch a relative handful of royal family members in Saudi Arabia, Kuwait, and Qatar grow obscenely rich.

Nowhere was Arab nationalism stronger than in Egypt where in 1952 the corrupt King Farouk had been replaced by Col. Gamal Abdel Nasser. Nasser wanted to raise the living standard of his impoverished people and to make Egypt the center of a Pan-Arab movement that would destroy Israel and end Western influence in the Middle East.

In 1955 he obtained a pledge from the Eisenhower administration of $56 million in aid to help build the High Aswan Dam, a project that would increase Egypt's arable land by one-third. When, however, Nasser mortgaged his country's 1956 cotton crop in a huge arms deal with Communist Czechoslovakia and formally recognized Beijing as the government of China, Secretary Dulles withdrew the offer in July 1956. In retaliation Nasser nationalized the Suez Canal which was then owned and operated jointly by the British and French. Humiliated and threatened by the action, London and Paris plotted intervention. On October 29, 1956, the Israeli army invaded the Sinai peninsula to destroy Palestinian guerrilla bases operating on Egyptian territory. Britain and France immediately announced that they would not permit the fighting to overwhelm the canal and appealed to both sides to keep their troops ten miles on either side of the waterway. When Nasser refused, the two Western powers dropped paratroops into Egypt and seized the canal.

The aggressive action of their European allies left the United States in a quandary. The Eisenhower administration could hardly condone blatant military aggression without further alienating the Arab world, but Britain and France were its two principal allies in the contest with the forces of international communism. On October 30 the United States placed a resolution before the Security Council calling on Israel and Egypt to stop fighting and on Israel to withdraw its troops. Britain and France vetoed this and a similar Russian resolution. Making the most of the situation, Moscow threatened to send volunteers into the area and rain missiles on London and Paris. Eisenhower responded by announcing that the United States would use force to prevent Soviet intervention. The U.N. subsequently negotiated a cease-fire, British and French troops withdrew, and the Egyptians began administering the canal fairly and efficiently.

A CHANGING AMERICAN CULTURE

NEW CONSUMERISM

While the Cold War made the 1950s a decade of anxiety in foreign affairs, Americans were able to console themselves with mass consumption and social conformity at home. As America moved into the postindustrial era, consumption became a virtual obsession. The proportion of homeowners in the population increased by 50 percent during the period from 1945 to 1960, and almost everyone owned an automobile.

A wide variety of new gadgets were available for purchase; in 1947 the Polaroid Land camera, developed by Edwin H. Land, went on sale. The first camera with its own darkroom, the Polaroid could turn out a picture in seconds and was an instant success. Spending on advertising increased 400 percent and almost tripled the amount the nation spent on education. Producers of consumer products spent millions of dollars glorifying consumption and then reaped huge profits satisfying the need that they had created. Unconsciously harking back to the early colonial period when Puritan burghers insisted that material success was a badge of divine favor, advertisers preached that possession of the latest model car and the newest type of refrigerator was not only fun but positively moral.

In the new consumer culture, shopping became a major recreational activity. The shopping center replaced the town square as the focal point of community life. In 1945 the nation could boast but eight of these modern marketplaces, but by 1960, four thousand. Leading the charge to the malls were adolescents. The baby-boom generation enjoyed more disposable income than any of its predecessors and generated a special market which included transistor radios, teen fashions, and 45-rpm vinyl records.

THE ENTERTAINMENT INDUSTRY

A new medium made it possible for Old Gold cigarettes, Chevrolet automobiles, and General Electric washing machines to render themselves irresistible to the American public—television. In fact, acquiring a television set in itself became a badge of consumerism fulfilled. In 1946 there were only eight thousand primitive black-and-white machines; by 1960 45.8 million high quality sets adorned 90 percent of the nation's households. *TV Guide* became the fastest growing periodical of the 1950s, and the "electronic hearth" transformed the way Americans lived. Instead of reading, exercising, conversing, or congregating, the nuclear family gathered faithfully before "the tube" to watch their weekly mystery or variety shows.

As the TV audience increased, hour-long theatrical productions multiplied to include "Playhouse 90," "Robert Montgomery Presents," and the "Hallmark Hall of Fame." Situation comedies were popular from the start: "Mr. Peepers" with Wally Cox was set in a high school, while "The Life of Riley" starring William Bendix featured a family with a working-class background. Nothing, however, could match the popularity of "The Honeymooners" with Jackie Gleason and "I Love Lucy" starring Lucille Ball. Comedy extravaganzas such as Sid Caesar's "Your Show of Shows" and straight variety productions such as "The Ed Sullivan Show" attracted legions of devoted followers. By the mid-1950s high quality dramas were increasingly replaced by westerns, police thrillers, and the ubiquitous quiz show, most notably "The $64,000 Question" and "Twenty-One."

A "typical" American family gathered around its electronic hearth, ca. 1955.

The TV changed the way Americans thought, dressed, and acted. The new medium made its adherents at once more cosmopolitan and more provincial, more active and more passive. Americans were more aware of what Marshall McLuhan would call "the global village," but they also substituted vicarious for real experience. Sitcoms, westerns, and variety shows became placebos that insulated the common man from the hurts and anxieties of human existence.

Threatened with extinction by television, the motion picture industry at first fought the new medium and then accommodated. Cinemascope provided Technicolor, three-speaker moving pictures whose impact on the senses television could never match. Another way to compete was to screen things that TV dared not show. In 1956 Elia Kazan's *Baby Doll* and *The Man with the Golden Arm*, starring Frank Sinatra as a drug addict, failed to receive the motion picture censor's seal of approval but made money anyway. The following year the French film *And God Created Woman* featured a nude Brigitte Bardot and opened the floodgates. In general during the 1950s, though the quantity of films fell, quality did not. *From Here to Eternity, On the Waterfront, Bridge on the River Kwai,* and *A Streetcar Named Desire* would become classics.

A MOBILE SOCIETY

Proliferation of automobiles had almost as great a cultural impact as the spread of television. In 1947 Congress authorized the construction of thirty-seven thousand miles of additional highways, and by the end of the 1950s work on Eisenhower's interstate highway system was well underway. As a result, Americans began traveling in unprecedented numbers. Car production sky-rocketed from 2 million in 1946 to 8 million in 1955. As they struck out for a national park, the seashore, or the mountains, mobile Americans transformed the tourist industry into a phenomenon of the masses. Thousands of service stations sprang up across the nation to provide fuel and basic creature comforts. Walt Disney started the first major theme park—Disneyland—in California. Motel and hotel receipts increased 2,300 percent during the fifteen years following World War II. Well-to-do Americans traveled abroad, more than 8 million in the 1950s.

THE RISE OF SUBURBIA

The dramatic increase in car ownership was in part responsible for another major development in postwar America—suburbia. In 1947 William Levitt, an aggressive New York developer, purchased twelve hundred acres of cheap Long Island farmland and built 10,600 houses. The inexpensive three-bedroom homes were sold almost at once. Within a year the development boasted a population of forty thousand. Other Levittowns followed in Pennsylvania and New Jersey, and construction entrepreneurs all over the country began their own subdivisions. Suburban housing was dreadfully uniform and monotonous. But suburban developments filled a need. By insuring loans for up to 95 percent of the value of a house, the Federal Housing Administration made it easy for a contractor to borrow money to construct low-cost homes and for young couples to buy them.

The housing boom—13 million new homes were constructed in America between 1950 and 1960, 11 million of them in suburbia—prompted one of the largest mass migrations in American history. At the height of the great European exodus of the late nineteenth century, 1.2 million people came to the United States each year. During the 1950s the same number moved to suburbia annually. By 1960 18 million Americans had carved out a niche on the "crabgrass frontier." Many of these suburban enclaves grew up outside the nation's major urban areas—New York, Philadelphia, Chicago—but many were built adjacent to Miami, Memphis, Dallas, and Albuquerque—the capital centers of the burgeoning "Sun Belt."

CHANGING PERSONAL ROLES

The Drive to Conformity

Suburbia both symbolized and reinforced one of the dominant characteristics of postwar American society—the demand for conformity. America's shift from

The housing shortage was solved but the cost was architectural sterility and monotony. An advertisement for Levittown shows tract houses.

an industrial to a postindustrial state was marked by the emergence of a powerful new managerial class. These specialists in management, marketing, and finance were linked to the vast corporations and conglomerates for which they worked by rising salaries and benefits but also by a culture that emphasized loyalty and conformity. IBM and other companies expected their employees to dress conservatively, live conservatively, and vote conservatively. The traditional "inner-directed" self-made American was replaced by salaried managers who were "other-directed," to use sociologist David Reisman's terms. To move from group to group in an increasingly differentiated bureaucracy, the organization man suppressed his individuality, spurned conflict, and sought guidance and approval from the environment around him or her.

The Cult of Domesticity

A skyrocketing birthrate reinforced a veritable cult of feminine domesticity that emerged during the 1950s. Women who had entered the workforce in droves during World War II and functioned as factory workers, traffic cops, and managers were told to return home and prepare to be the perfect helpmate to their returning veteran-husbands. An article entitled "Home Should Be More Wonderful Than He Remembers It" lectured women on their postwar roles. Magazines, motion pictures, popular literature, and advertisements depicted the ideal woman of the 1950s. According to *Life* and *Reader's Digest*, she was "pretty and popular," a mother of four who had married in her late teens, well dressed, well groomed, an emotional and sexual helpmate to her husband, den mother, PTA activist, efficient homemaker, and pal to her fellow-housewives. If women lacked a sense of fulfillment, they could turn to sewing, canning, or flower arranging. The career woman was distinctly out of fashion.

At the heart of what Betty Friedan later called "the feminine mystique" was the notion of the indispensable female. The flywheel of modern society, so the argument ran, was the housewife and mother. Her unconditional, nurturing love was a haven from the competitive, dog-eat-dog world of factory and office. The ideal suburban wife—efficient, beautiful, loving—existed to help the organization man reach new levels of success and fulfillment. Educators, politicians, ministers, and, indirectly, popular television shows broadcast the message that the modern woman should limit her horizons to hearth and husband. In short, the high priests of American culture proclaimed simultaneously that women were superior to men and that they existed solely to enhance and enrich the existence of men. Even *Life* magazine, which in 1956 had touted the "ideal" middle-class woman, observed in 1959 that once her children were raised, the suburban housewife was left only with a mind-numbing round of club meetings and card parties.

A Sexual Revolution

The decade of the 1950s was an unlikely setting for a sexual revolution, but it served as the stage for one of modern history's greatest sexual revolutionaries, Alfred C. Kinsey. An established biologist at Indiana University, Kinsey turned in the late 1930s to the study of human sexuality. In 1938 he organized a course on marriage and family life and began compiling sexual histories of his students. The Kinsey reports published from 1948 through 1955 demolished many myths about sexuality, the primary one being that women were incapable of enjoying sex and submitted to it only for purposes of procreation. He also asserted that heterosexuality and homosexuality were not alternatives but poles at each end of a continuum along which all human beings fell.

A Religious Revival

The forces of conformity that were so strong during the early postwar period coupled with the anxieties of the Cold War led to a religious revival that was simultaneously intense, pervasive, and amorphous. Overall, church membership increased from 64.5 million (49 percent of the total population) in 1940 to 125 million (64 percent) in 1965. All religions and denominations gained, but leading the way were Roman Catholics, Baptists, and southern Pentecostals.

Observers noted during the 1950s a blending of the secular culture and institutionalized religion. Led by Norman Vincent Peale, whose *Power of Positive Thinking* sold millions of copies, many contemporary religious figures concentrated on quieting the American middle class' anxieties in the nuclear age. Peale offered a simple how-to course in personal happiness. Shun negative thoughts, trust in God, be joyful and enthusiastic, he preached. The fruits of such an approach would be not only spiritual but also secular. Indeed, his relentlessly optimistic version of Christianity promised to make the practitioner "a more popular, esteemed, and well-liked individual." In an earlier era Protestantism had demanded constant, agonized soul-searching, but by the 1950s it had become for many, according to Russell Kirk, a religion amounting to "little more than a vague spirit of friendliness, a willingness to support churches—providing these churches demand no real sacrifices and preach no exacting doctrines."

There were, of course, serious alternatives to this syrupy, sin-free approach to religion. The 1950s witnessed a new interest in revivalism and fundamentalism. One of the most striking preachers of the period was a young, well dressed Baptist evangelist named Billy Graham. In sincere sermons that stressed the sovereignty of God and the absolute wisdom of the Bible, the charismatic Graham drew hundreds of thousands of Americans to huge amphitheaters such as New York's Yankee Stadium and Madison Square Garden. Meanwhile, the intelligentsia was drawn by the preachments of Reinhold Niebuhr and Paul Tillich, Protestant theologians who attacked the feel-good religion propounded by the dominant culture. Niebuhr, who taught and preached at the Union Theological Seminary in New York, was the towering theological and philosophical figure in the movement known as Christian neo-orthodoxy. He attacked the materialism, complacency, and conformity that seemed to permeate postwar America. Humans were called upon not to ensconce themselves in a cocoon but to love the world and assume some responsibility for its problems.

THE CULTURE OF POVERTY

Despite the affluence of the postwar period, substantial segments of the population were cut off from the American dream. Various studies showed that 20 percent of all Americans lived below what was considered the poverty line, $3,000 for a family of four in 1960 and $4,000 for a family of six. The economic boom that followed World War II saw no significant redistribution of income. Indeed, the percentage of the nation's wealth owned by the richest 5 percent of the population actually increased during this period from 20.2 percent in 1950 to 21.4 percent in 1956. Poverty in America was deepest and widest among four groups: African Americans, increasingly isolated in inner-city ghettos, mill and factory workers in New England and the Carolinas, those who lived in the Appalachian coal region that stretched from western Pennsylvania to northern Georgia, and residents of the rural South, both black and white.

In 1962 Michael Harrington published an influential book entitled *The Other America* in which he revealed in cold statistics and passionate prose that there existed in the nation a "culture of poverty." Only education, employment opportunity, and minimum levels of social and economic security would allow the poor to improve their lot, but there was no way for them to access these essentials. Those living in slums and depressed areas like Appalachia were cut off from educational opportunity, medical facilities, and meaningful employment. Poor, ignorant, helpless, and ignored, they were locked in a vicious circle in which poverty denied opportunity, and lack of opportunity perpetuated poverty. To make matters worse, television and advertising constantly reminded the disadvantaged of the world that lay forever beyond their reach.

CULTURAL REBELLION

Postwar Literature and the Beat Generation

Much of the best in postwar literature reinforced sociologist David Reisman's image of middle America as a mindless, conforming mass without a central core. In Arthur Miller's play, *Death of a Salesman*, the central character, Willy Loman, is an aging, confused traveling salesman who had centered his life on acquiring material possessions by means of personal magnetism, positive thinking, and hustle, and had raised his two sons, Biff and Happy, to do likewise. This superficial salesman awakes near the end of his life's journey to discover that his boss deems him a failure and that his life is bereft of meaning and valid relationships. *Death of a Salesman* and other plays by Edward Albee and Tennessee Williams as well as novels such as *From Here to Eternity* by James Jones, *The Invisible Man* by Ralph Ellison, and John Updike's *Rabbit, Run* portray what George Tindall has termed America's "brooding sense of resigned alienation."

A small group of these alienated intellectuals, led by Jack Kerouac, attempted an existential as well as artistic rebellion against the conforming culture. Kerouac's novel *On the Road* and Allen Ginsberg's *Howl & Other Poems* invited those turned off by "I Love Lucy" and Levittown to drop out and experiment. Kerouac was a handsome, working-class youth who went to Columbia on a football scholarship but soon immersed himself in alcohol, sex, and rebellious behavior. Beat was both a literary and social movement. Beat writers denounced mainstream literature and rationalistic criticism. The roots of authentic literature, they argued, were spontaneity, emotional release, eastern religion, and intuition. The beats (or beatniks as they came to be known to the larger culture) sought personal rather than social or political solutions to theirs and society's problems. They despised technology and derided both professionalism and specialization. Through esoteric art forms, drug experimentation, relentless sex, eastern religion, and vagabondage, the beats sought to escape what they perceived to be the horror of American middle-class existence.

Rock 'n' Roll

A much more pervasive form of cultural rebellion was rock 'n' roll. In 1952 a Cleveland radio disc jockey featured rhythm and blues on a new program entitled "Moondog's Rock 'n' Roll Party." Moondog, whose real name was

Alan Freed, employed the term to refer to the type of dancing associated with the music, and in 1954 moved his operation to New York. That same year Bill Haley came out with the revolutionary "Rock Around the Clock," the theme song for the popular movie, *Blackboard Jungle*, and the rock 'n' roll movement was underway. The music stirred white middle-class youth, and as a result, barriers separating white and black music began to fall on all sides.

What record producers and studios really wanted and needed was a white performer who could present black music forms to white teenagers. The answer to their dreams appeared in the personage of Elvis Presley, a poor white truck driver from Tupelo, Mississippi. He taught himself the guitar, learned the R&B style, and by 1954 was performing on regional radio shows around the South. His personal appearances featured a bump and grind routine that American parents equated with the sexual act but that he attributed to the revivalist preachers of his youth. In 1956 Presley's "Don't Be Cruel," "Love Me Tender," "Heartbreak Hotel," and "I'm All Shook Up" sold more than 15 million records.

THE SECOND RECONSTRUCTION: THE CIVIL RIGHTS MOVEMENT

Not all Americans conformed; not all could conform. One of the driving forces behind the creation of the suburbs was the desire of white middle-class Americans to avoid having to live with the hundreds of thousands of African Americans who flooded into eastern and midwestern cities during the depression and World War II. Indeed, despite heroic service in the workplace and on the battlefield, black Americans were as segregated and discriminated against in the years immediately following World War II as they had ever been. Yet currents of change were stirring. The war itself gave African Americans new experiences and skills and instilled in them a rising level of expectations. The spread of the Cold War to developing, nonwhite areas of the world made institutionalized racism a huge handicap for the United States as it competed for the allegiance of the peoples of Asia and Africa. Even though President Truman had been unable to secure any significant legislation, he had succeeded in adding civil rights to the liberal agenda. From the 1948 Democratic convention onward it would be an integral part of the party's reform program.

BROWN V. BOARD OF EDUCATION

The cutting edge of the civil rights movement that burgeoned during the 1950s was, not surprisingly, the Constitution of the United States. From its inception in 1909, the nation's leading civil rights organization, the National Association for the Advancement of Colored People (NAACP), devoted its attention to filing suit against organizations, institutions, and governmental entities that denied African Americans equal treatment under the law and due process as guaranteed by the Fifth and Fourteenth Amendments.

Following World War II, NAACP lawyers, led by Thurgood Marshall, tackled the crucial issue of segregation in the nation's public schools. Challenging *Plessy v. Ferguson*, the 1896 Supreme Court case which upheld the doctrine of separate but equal, Marshall cited black sociologist Kenneth Clark and others to show that separate schools could never be equal because they imparted a sense of differentness and inferiority to African-American children. In 1952, he filed suit in behalf of the parents of Linda Brown, a black Topeka, Kansas, girl who had been denied entrance to an all-white school even though she lived only blocks away. On May 17, 1954, newly appointed Chief Justice Earl Warren announced the court's unanimous decision. The court agreed with the NAACP and Brown's parents. "Separate educational facilities are inherently unequal," Warren declared; such artificial distinctions implied second-class status and were likely to damage the "hearts and minds" of black children irreparably. Aware of the difficulty of overturning racial barriers in the segregated South and anxious to avoid social upheaval, Warren and the court ordered that desegregation proceed "with all deliberate speed" and left implementation to lower courts.

WHITE BACKLASH

Integration of public education made an auspicious start when several border states moved to comply but then bogged down in the Deep South. Local white citizens' councils formed to fight the Brown decision; Virginia's Senator Harry F. Byrd coined the term "massive resistance" as a rallying cry for the white supremacists; and in 1956, 101 congressmen and senators signed the Southern Manifesto, which denounced the court's decision as "a clear abuse of judicial power." Eisenhower's ambivalence toward court-ordered integration further encouraged local school boards to disobey or subvert the law. Although not a racist, Eisenhower did not believe that racial harmony could be created through federal coercion. He hated confrontation and insisted that progress could be achieved through reason, prayer, and the efforts of well-intentioned individuals. The point he missed was that African Americans were ready to sacrifice harmony to achieve their rights under the law. Though he worked quietly to desegregate federal facilities, he could never bring himself publicly or privately to endorse the Brown decision.

THE LITTLE ROCK CRISIS

The rising tide of white resistance and the president's timidity paved the way for the first great crisis of the post-Brown era: the closing of the public schools

Army National Guardsmen escort black students into Central High School, Little Rock, Arkansas, 1957.

at Little Rock, Arkansas. Arkansas was hardly the most racist of the southern states. In fact, its governor, Orval Faubus, had established a reputation as a liberal on socioeconomic questions, including race. When the crunch came, however, Faubus proved to be an opportunist who believed that his political future could best be secured by siding with the white supremacists.

Under a plan devised by the Little Rock School board, nine black children were scheduled to enter Central High School when it opened the first week in September. Citing the threat of violence by mobs opposed to integration, Faubus on September 3, 1957, sent 270 Arkansas National Guardsmen to deny entry to the "Little Rock Nine," as the press subsequently dubbed them. Mayor Woodrow Mann denounced Faubus' "interference." The governor, he said, "had called out troops to put down trouble where none existed." A federal judge ordered the guardsmen removed, and the African-American students attended class. When an angry mob surrounded the building shouting racist slurs, Faubus' prediction of trouble seemed a self-fulfilling prophesy.

The governor refused to use force at his command to protect the beleaguered children, prompting Eisenhower to declare, reluctantly, that he would use "whatever force was necessary" to see that the law of the land was respected. One thousand U.S. Army paratroops descended on Little Rock and defended the Little Rock Nine from racist mobs that ran as large as fifteen hundred. The students finished out the year, but Little Rock authorities closed the school for the 1958–1959 term.

THE CIVIL RIGHTS ACT OF 1957

Although Eisenhower was not an enthusiastic supporter of the Brown decision, his administration was responsible for the passage of the first significant piece of civil rights legislation since Reconstruction. Working through Senate Majority Leader Lyndon Johnson, the Justice Department secured passage of the Civil Rights Act of 1957. The measure created a permanent Commission on Civil Rights and affirmed the federal government's duty to ensure African Americans' right to vote. The bill did not provide for specific enforcement procedures, however.

THE MONTGOMERY BOYCOTT

Perhaps the toughest task facing black civil rights leaders in the twentieth century was convincing their brethren that they controlled their own fate, that if they were ever to defeat oppression by the white majority, they would have to take matters into their own hands. In the mid-1950s, that message began to register, and as a result civil rights became an authentic mass movement. On December 1, 1955, in Montgomery, Alabama, "the cradle of the Confederacy," a black garment maker, Rosa Parks, refused to give up her seat to a white and move to the back of the bus. She was duly arrested. The next night, black community leaders led by the young, charismatic Martin Luther King, Jr., gathered at his Dexter Avenue Baptist Church to form the Montgomery Improvement Association (MIA) and launch a massive bus boycott.

The original goal of the boycott was simply to force the bus authority to make seating available on a first come, first served basis, but after Mrs. Parks decided to appeal her conviction, its objective became the judicial invalidation of Alabama's segregated seating law. An effective carpooling system enabled the protesters to bring the municipal transport system to the verge of bankruptcy. King was arrested for orchestrating the boycott and black leaders were subjected to threats and isolated instances of violence. After a year of harassment by Montgomery police and intense economic and psychological pressure from the white majority, the boycott remained in place. In 1956 the Supreme Court ruled the state's segregated coach law unconstitutional.

MARTIN LUTHER KING, JR., AND
NONVIOLENT CIVIL DISOBEDIENCE

The civil rights movement that began in Little Rock and Montgomery was significant for its inclusion of working-class blacks. The twin institutional anchors of the movement were the NAACP and the black churches. Its philosophical basis initially was nonviolent civil disobedience as articulated by Rev. King. Educated at Morehouse College and Boston University, where he earned his Ph.D. in religion, the young Baptist preacher drew upon the Gospels, the civil disobedience writings of Henry David Thoreau, and particularly the experience of

The sit-in was adopted by youthful civil rights activists from the CIO and other non-violent protest movements. African-American students stage a lunch counter sit-in, ca. 1964.

Mahatma Gandhi in combating British imperial authority in India. "Passive resistance and the weapon of love," he told the MIA at the height of the boycott, were the keys to victory. If black Americans were to win respect for their rights as citizens and human beings, they must confront their white oppressors peacefully, returning hate with love. By refusing to acquiesce in the Jim Crow system of discrimination and segregation, King explained, African Americans would force white America either to destroy them or accept them as equals. The ultimate goal for King was to reunite a broken community through the power of Christian love. "We will soon wear you down by our capacity to suffer," he told his antagonists, "and in winning our freedom we will so appeal to your heart and conscience that we will win you in the process." A year after the successful Montgomery boycott, King founded the Southern Christian Leadership Conference (SCLC) to lead the fight against institutionalized racism.

In early 1960, another spontaneous event added momentum and an important new constituency to the civil rights movement. Four students from North Carolina Agricultural and Technical College in Greensboro sat down at a Woolworth's lunch counter and refused to move after being denied service. The sit-in movement spread to other cities—Raleigh, Charlotte, Little Rock, Nashville, and Birmingham—and to other types of facilities—wade-ins at public swimming pools and kneel-ins at churches. In April 1960, the mostly student participants, black and white, in the sit-in movement formed the Student

Nonviolent Coordinating Committee (SNCC). From this point on, the SCLC and SNCC would constitute the cutting edge of the civil rights movement. Nonviolent demonstrations subjected participants to water hoses, beatings, repeated arrest, police dogs, and in some cases murder by white vigilante groups. But their activities dominated the national media and stirred the conscience of a nation.

Most early accounts of the civil rights movement of the 1950s centered on the charismatic personality of Martin Luther King, Jr., and the complex, pervasive web of official and unofficial racism that confronted him and his associates. In his analysis of the Southern Christian Leadership Conference and its role in the early years of the Second Reconstruction, Adam Fairclough reveals that circumstance, politics, and shifting perceptions among various social classes, occupations, and regions made the civil rights movement as variegated and subtle a phenomenon as the racist system it was combating.

THE PREACHERS AND THE PEOPLE: THE ORIGINS AND EARLY YEARS OF THE SOUTHERN CHRISTIAN LEADERSHIP CONFERENCE, 1955–1959

Adam Fairclough

"The preachers took over from the teachers," recalled Malcolm B. Johnson, longtime editor of the Tallahassee *Democrat,* some two decades after the event that had shattered the tranquillity of Florida's capital and, like its more famous counterpart in Montgomery, Alabama, transformed the relationship between black and white.

Before the bus boycott of 1956–1957 contact between the races in Tallahassee had been characterized by the tacit acceptance of segregation by both groups. The

from Adam Fairclough, "The Preachers and the People: The Origins and Early Years of the Southern Christian Leadership Conference, 1955–1959," *The Journal of Southern History,* Vol. LII, No. 3 (August 1986), 403–427.

most influential blacks had been educators—high school principals and college presidents—who deferred to white sensibilities and pandered to white paternalism with all the tact and finesse of seasoned diplomats. When blacks began to boycott the segregated buses, therefore, whites of influence instinctively turned to the black leaders whom they knew best, the teachers, to end the protest quickly and quietly. Thus in an honest attempt to mediate, editor Johnson asked a noted and respected high school principal to select five or six "responsible" Negroes with whom the city and the bus company could do business—with the understanding, of course, that the principle of segregation was not negotiable. To his shock and discomfiture, however, Johnson found himself confronted by a roomful of angry blacks who resisted the usual evasive courtesies and insisted upon pressing their demands. The figures with whom white officialdom preferred to deal could not stop the boycott—blacks were not only rejecting the status quo, they were also following new leaders. And the latter refused to observe the old rules: they were not interested in white paternalism; they regarded deference as demeaning; above all, they were uncompromising in their opposition to segregation.

Most of these new leaders were clergymen. The Inter-Civic Council, set up to coordinate the boycott, had six ministers among its nine officers and was led by the Reverend C[harles]. K[enzie]. Steele. The same pattern had appeared in Montgomery, where the boycott organization, the Montgomery Improvement Association (MIA), was top-heavy with men of the cloth. In Birmingham, too, clergymen dominated the organized opposition to segregation. The preachers were indeed taking over from the teachers.

White leaders, dumbfounded by the sudden emergence of hitherto obscure figures, refused to acknowledge their legitimacy. These new men, they reasoned, must be radicals, communists, outsiders—self-seeking parvenus whose hold over their followers rested on a clever combination of duress, demagogy, and deceit. But however much whites ignored, denigrated, or persecuted them, the new leaders won respect and support from ordinary blacks and became forces to be reckoned with. And out of the protest movements in Montgomery, Tallahassee, and Birmingham came a new civil rights organization, the Southern Christian Leadership Conference (SCLC), founded in 1957. Described by one member as "'a bunch of Baptist preachers'," by another as "'a movement, not an organization'," SCLC was an unusual, unorthodox, and in some ways even bizarre outfit. Even so, it left an indelible mark on the South. After a slow and faltering start SCLC became a dynamic force within the civil rights movement and one of the most effective pressure groups in American history.

The formation and subsequent importance of SCLC reflected a basic fact about leadership in the southern black movement: ministers wielded influence out of all proportion to their numbers. Such prominence owed much to the economic facts of life. Most blacks, educated or not, depended on a white landlord or employer; they could ill afford to be identified as "troublemakers." To oppose segregation was to invite eviction, loss of livelihood, and loss of credit. Teachers were notoriously vulnerable to economic retribution: in some southern states they could be fired merely for advocating integration or belonging to the National Association for the

Advancement of Colored People (NAACP). College teachers were more difficult to get rid of, but they too might be squeezed out of their posts for challenging the status quo. But churches were owned and controlled by blacks themselves, and ministers could be fired by their congregations alone. With a high degree of economic independence, preachers enjoyed a freedom of speech and action denied to the majority of blacks. The vital connection between economic safety and black leadership is also suggested by the occupations of prominent laymen in the civil rights movement. Many, if not most, were self-employed businessmen and professionals whose clientele was wholly or mainly black: doctors, dentists, lawyers, undertakers, and storeowners. Like ministers, these laymen experienced economic security that gave them the latitude to defy white opinion. It was ironic that segregation, by helping to create a self-sufficient black middle class, inadvertently nurtured its leading adversaries; the most effective opponents of segregation were often its principal black beneficiaries.

The appearance of church leadership in movements against segregation reflected a shift in black attitudes rather than a bold initiative by preachers. The relationship between clergy and community was one of symbiosis rather than one of leaders and followers. . . .

Thus the impulse that led to the civil rights movement came from outside the church and was nurtured by politics. In Montgomery, for example, in the period before the bus boycott, among the most prominent black activists numbered a sleeping-car porter and union official, E[dgar]. D. Nixon; a businessman, Rufus A. Lewis; and a college teacher, Jo Ann Robinson. All three headed political clubs that in the early 1950s became increasingly vociferous in articulating black demands and grievances. One issue that they repeatedly raised was segregation on city buses: between 1953 and 1955 they met city and bus company officials on at least four occasions to complain about abusive drivers and about company policies that made blacks stand over empty seats or surrender their seats to whites. Mrs. Robinson's group, the Women's Political Council, took the lead in these meetings, and the conviction that black votes had helped to elect at least one of the city commissioners encouraged it to adopt an increasingly forthright stand. Clearly, the bus boycott was no bolt from the blue.

The inception of the boycott underlines the fact that the original dynamic came from without the church, not from ministers but from laypeople. The contribution of Rosa Parks should not be overlooked. Her decision to choose arrest rather than humiliation when driver James F. Blake ordered her to surrender her seat on December 1, 1955, was not the impulsive gesture of a seamstress with sore feet. Although she was shy and unassuming, Rosa Parks held strong and well-developed views about the iniquities of segregation. Long active in the NAACP, she had served as the secretary of the local branch at the time E. D. Nixon was president. In the summer of 1955, moreover, she had spent two weeks at the Highlander Folk School in Monteagle, Tennessee, an institution that assiduously encouraged interracial amity. Founded and run by Myles Horton, a white radical, Highlander flouted the local segregation laws and gave black and white southerners a virtually unique opportunity to meet and mingle on equal terms. "For the first time in my adult life," Parks recalled, "I found out . . . that this could be a unified society. . . ." Her protest on the Cleveland Avenue bus was the purposeful act of a politically aware person. It was also part of a groundswell of discontent among Montgomery's black population.

Plans for a mass protest were well advanced by the time the church entered the picture, with the Women's Political Council again taking the initiative. Upon learning of Parks's arrest, Jo Ann Robinson immediately suggested a boycott and spread word of the plan through the women's club; she also took the decisive step of running off 40,000 handbills from a mimeograph machine at Alabama State College. The black ministers who met on the evening of December 2 to discuss the boycott were thus confronted, as J. Mills Thornton III has pointed out, with a fait accompli. And it was not until December 5 that Martin Luther King, Jr., became president of the boycott organization; by the time he made his first speech as leader, blacks had been off the buses for a day.

The ministers took over the leadership of the boycott with obvious reluctance. As King later confided to a friend, the protest would never have gotten off the ground but for Nixon, lawyer Fred D. Gray, and the Women's Political Council. The fact that they selected King, a virtual newcomer, to be their spokesman is perhaps the most revealing comment on the timidity of the local clergy. As Mrs. A. Wayman West, Jr., put it, "the ministers who didn't want the presidency of the MIA . . . were just chicken, passing the buck to Dr. King." Nevertheless, the formation of the Montgomery Improvement Association brought preachers into the vanguard of the protest, and they remained there for the duration.

Why did the leadership pass so swiftly from laypeople to clergymen? The latter's economic independence explains much; as Professor L[awrence]. D. Reddick of Alabama State College put it, the more vulnerable teachers were obliged to remain "discreetly in the background." Equally important, ministers were pushed to the forefront because the principal activists, Nixon, Lewis, and Robinson, knew that blacks could be far more effectively mobilized en masse through the pulpit than they could through politics. The existing political clubs were tiny: there were only 2,000 registered voters out of a total black population of 50,000. They were also, quite often, at loggerheads. As Rufus A. Lewis put it, "It was a small group working over here for this reason and another small group working over there for that reason. . . . They were not thinking of bringing in the mass of the folks." The church, by contrast, extended throughout the community, bridging political factions and spanning social classes. As an organizational tool it was second to none. In a city with neither a black radio station nor a widely read black newspaper, it provided the information network. It also furnished the meeting places, the fundraising machinery, and the means of organizing an alternative transportation system.

The prestige of the church reinforced its utility. It was the oldest and most respected institution in the black South. Central to their culture, the symbol of their historical experience, the expression of their hopes and aspirations, the church gave blacks a sense of solidarity, self-identity, and self-respect. When it came to arousing and manipulating an audience, the black preacher had few rivals. "I had never truly understood the meaning of the term 'collective experience'," wrote the sociologist John Dollard in 1937, "until participating in a well-planned Negro revival service. . . . In the Negro churches it is a case of every man with the preacher and the boundaries of the self are weakened." Through the church the boycott harnessed the emotionalism and theatricality of black religion. The morale-boosting mass meetings, with their hymns, sermons, and "pep talks," provided entertainment and a sense of involvement. "With the help of those preachers who could preach and those other folks who could pray," remembered the Reverend S. S. Seay, "we kept the churches filled." Its links with the church gave the boycott coherence, respectability, and religious fervor.

It might still be wondered why the black ministers of Montgomery, with their record of political passivity, accepted the leadership that was thrust upon them. They did so in part because they simply did not realize what a Herculean task lay before them. Most, King included, had been skeptical about the boycott's chances of success; had the first day been a flop, they doubtless would have quietly but quickly disengaged themselves. But with the buses practically empty and support for the protest solid, they were forced to continue. Nobody, in any case, expected the boycott to last long; after all, the MIA did not seek the abolition of segregation, merely equality of treatment within the existing system. The MIA knew that other cities in the Deep South, notably Mobile and Atlanta, had already conceded the principle of "first come, first served" segregated seating—white passengers taking seats from the front towards the rear, and blacks sitting from the back towards the front. This arrangement eliminated the need for blacks having to surrender their places to whites or being made to stand while reserved "white" seats remained empty. Blacks in Montgomery would only need to stay off the buses for a week or two, at most, to achieve this eminently reasonable goal. In Baton Rouge, where blacks had staged a bus boycott in June 1953, it had taken precisely seven days. . . .

If white officials in Montgomery had shown the same degree of flexibility as those in Baton Rouge had, they could have ended the boycott within days *and* preserved segregated seating. Their intransigence, however, not only prolonged the boycott but also persuaded the MIA that there could be no fair solution within the framework of segregation. When negotiations broke down, both the city and the bus company having spurned any compromise acceptable to the blacks, the MIA confronted the stark alternatives of pressing on with the boycott or backing down. If popular support had ebbed or crumbled, the latter might have been the only realistic alternative. As it was the degree of black solidarity made such an admission of defeat unthinkable. "They are determined never to return to jim crow buses," King marveled. "The mass meetings are still jammed and packed and above all the buses are still empty."

Thus the obstinacy of the white authorities and the enthusiasm of the black population trapped the ministers in their leadership role; if they dropped out, they would be branded as cowards and traitors. As the protest went from strength to strength, moreover, they began to enjoy that role. By early 1956 the boycott was attracting national and international publicity. In February it reached the front page of the New York *Times,* and in March King's trial drew reporters from England, France, and India. Although many of the news stories focused on King—a fact that caused not a little jealousy and resentment—the other leaders shared some of the limelight; initially cagey about revealing their identities, they now enjoyed the prestige conferred by extensive media coverage. As the boycott lengthened the MIA's leaders won the respect and affection of the black population; when the city prosecuted them under Alabama's rusty antiboycott law, they became popular heroes. Each repressive act by white officialdom tightened the bonds of pride and trust between the preachers and the people. . . .

Most accounts of the civil rights movement depict the Montgomery bus boycott as the decisive initiating event. They also suggest that the protest in Montgomery sparked a wave of similar boycotts—not only in Tallahassee, but also in Atlanta, New Orleans, Birmingham, Mobile, and other cities. The reality, however, was much more complicated. It is undeniably true that the events in Montgomery, to quote August Meier and Elliott Rudwick, "made an extraordinary impression on Afro-Americans across the country." But they did not immediately spur blacks to take direct action against segregation. Most of the "boycotts" supposedly modeled on Montgomery were not boycotts at all in the sense of sustained mass protests. Only in Tallahassee did events roughly parallel those in Montgomery. It is true of course that blacks in Tallahassee knew about the Montgomery bus boycott and that Steele, who had been a pastor in Montgomery before moving to Florida, was well in tune with events there. But to describe the Tallahassee boycott as a mere imitation, or copy, of the more famous Montgomery boycott would be an oversimplification. As one of Steele's colleagues, the Reverend K. S. Dupont, put it, "Montgomery was not a spark-plug for Tallahassee. Tallahassee was its own spark-plug." Too much emphasis on the Montgomery protest also obscures the significance of the earlier Baton Rouge boycott. It is inaccurate to claim, as Coretta King did, that Montgomery was the birthplace of nonviolent direct action. As Meier and Rudwick have argued, the fact that such a claim could be made, and that the Montgomery boycott was organized in ignorance of the events in Baton Rouge, suggests that necessity, rather than precedent, explains the rise of nonviolent direct action.

The origins of the civil rights movement, and of the Southern Christian Leadership Conference, must be sought in all three protests: Baton Rouge, Montgomery, and Tallahassee. In each case the target, the method, the type of organization, and the style of leadership were virtually identical. Only the goals differed—in Baton Rouge the protesters settled for equality within segregation (or something close to it), while in the other two cities they came to insist upon complete desegregation. The obvious explanation for this distinction is *Brown* v. *Board of Education* (1954), the momentous decision whereby the U. S. Supreme Court turned its back on the "separate but equal" principle and declared that segregated public schools were unconstitutional. Without doubt, *Brown* had a tremendous influence upon black aspirations. Yet the impact of the decision in the short-term—and, in light of the later agitation for "Black Power," in the long-term as well—was not so clear-cut. After all, the original demand of the MIA had not been for desegregation but rather "the right, under segregation, to seat ourselves from the rear forward on a first come, first served basis." As late as April 1956, nearly three months after it filed its desegregation suit, the MIA indicated that it was still willing to settle on these terms. Even in Tallahassee, when two years had elapsed since *Brown*, blacks hesitated before openly declaring for integration.

What accounted for this hesitation? Thornton has suggested that black southerners did not yet possess that robust confidence in the federal judiciary that they later acquired; in Montgomery, the boycotters had been uncertain that the courts would sustain them if they attacked segregation itself. Other explanations come to mind. Blacks generally assumed that the dismantling of segregation would be a long, protracted business; few could foresee that it would be swept away, in its legal forms at least, within a decade. In 1955–1956 it still struck many as quixotic to demand an immediate end to segregation. Then again many blacks harbored reservations, ranging from mild uneasiness to outright opposition, about the use of direct action to change the law. To dismiss these dissenters as "Uncle Toms" is neither accurate nor enlightening. In Tallahassee, for example, many of the doubts about the efficacy of the boycott came from within the ICC. As the Reverend David H. Brooks put it, "'I don't believe a negative boycott without legal basis [*i.e.,* court action] is going to get us very far. We're just wasting time charging the City Commission with not granting us integration'." Brooks, it should be added, remained a staunch supporter of the ICC in spite of his reservations. This debate over the relative merits of legalism and direct action became a central theme within the civil rights movement.

If, as Thornton has suggested, it was the intransigence of the white authorities that converted the initially mild demands of the boycotters into an uncompromising insistence on desegregation, then *Brown* could be judged as important for its effect upon whites as for its impact on blacks. For that decision inadvertently unleashed a wave of racism that drowned out the voices of moderation and compromise. Throughout 1955, wrote Numan V. Bartley, "the Deep South sank deeper into hysterical reaction. . . ." Adamant opposition to black demands and strident denunciations of the NAACP dominated political debate as office seekers fell over themselves to defend "white civilization." . . .

The very modesty of their original demands helps to explain why the boycotters did not wish to be identified with the NAACP. True, there was an element of necessity in this, for the NAACP was not the best instrument for conducting a mass protest such as a bus boycott. But political considerations were equally important: many blacks opposed the idea of fighting under the NAACP's banner. Contrary to a commonly held view, black southerners created organizations like the MIA and the ICC not because they considered the NAACP too conservative, but because many thought it too radical. They knew, moreover, that whites regarded the NAACP as the source of all evil and, except insofar as they harassed it, refused to have any dealings with the organization. Thus the boycotters created purely local bodies not only to appease conservative blacks but also out of deference to white hostility to the New York–based NAACP. Whites might negotiate with "local" Negroes; at least, they would not reject negotiation out of hand. They would not on the other hand sit down at the table with the NAACP under any circumstances.

It was doubly ironic then that the bus boycotts in Montgomery and Tallahassee were laid at the NAACP's door, exposing the organization to yet greater persecution. Most white southerners simply refused to believe that local protests against segregation were exactly that. Given the racist premise that blacks were happy and contented, the only rational explanation for the boycotts lay in the machinations of some external force or forces. Whites in Montgomery, wrote Alistair Cooke, re-garded King as "'the cat's-paw of the NAACP'. . . ." So pervasive was this habit of thinking that even Governor Collins—no demagogue—in one of his public statements blamed the Tallahassee bus boycott on the NAACP. Many other whites took this line of thinking several stages further, attributing the South's racial problems to a diabolical conspiracy masterminded by the communists. In the words of one Florida legislator who urged Collins to investigate the NAACP's subversive links, "the Communists have very adroitly brought this situation into being and the blame for its entirety should be placed squarely where it belongs." If the level of of-ficial harassment is anything to go by, white southerners saw the NAACP as the most potent threat to their racial supremacy. In blaming it for the bus boycotts, however, they were shooting at the wrong target. And the fact that their persecution of the NAACP inadvertently strengthened local protest organizations compounded the irony. The Birmingham-based Alabama Christian Movement for Human Rights (ACMHR), led by the Reverend Fred L. Shuttlesworth, came into being as a direct response to the suppression of the NAACP by the state authorities.

These three groups, the MIA, the ICC, and the ACMHR, formed the nucleus of the Southern Christian Leadership Conference. But if the raw materials for SCLC lay in the South, the organizational concept came from the North. SCLC was the brainchild of three New Yorkers, two blacks and a white, who had offered their services to King during the Montgomery bus boycott and had become convinced, after seeing the movement at close quarters, that that pattern of mass organization represented the wave of the future.

Of the three, Bayard Rustin was the most important. Born in Chester, Penn-sylvania, nearly twenty years before King, Rustin was an illegitimate child brought up by a Quaker grandmother. He had an unusual political background in which pacifism and socialism formed the central, intertwined strands. In the 1930s he joined the Young Communist League (YCL) in New York, but left the party like so many others after the 1939 Hitler-Stalin pact. He afterwards joined the Socialist party and con-tinued his career by working for the Fellowship of Reconciliation (FOR), a pacifist organization. In 1942 he helped set up the Congress of Racial Equality (CORE), an offshoot of the FOR that tried to use Gandhian tactics of passive resistance—CORE coined the term "nonviolent direct action"—against racial discrimination. Rustin also assisted A. Philip Randolph, the black trade-union leader, in his "March on Washington Movement" for fair employment practices, a collaboration that marked the beginning of a long and close friendship between the two men. The draft put a temporary stop to Rustin's activities, and he spent the last two years of the war in jail as a conscientious objector. The year 1949 saw him on a North Carolina chain gang, after participating in a bus trip organized by CORE and the FOR (the "Journey of Reconciliation"), to highlight the fact that segregation in interstate travel was still being practiced by the South in defiance of the U.S. Supreme Court. In 1948 he had worked with Randolph campaigning against segregation in the armed forces.

By the time of the Montgomery bus boycott Rustin had become an official of the War Resisters' League and one of the leading lights of American pacifism. He was also reckoned something of an expert on Gandhian tactics, and it was in this capacity that he volunteered his services to King in February 1956. Rustin discovered that King was "very simpatico to discussing the whole question of nonviolence." Arriving during the critical week that saw the indictment of the entire MIA leadership, Rustin suggested the emphasis on "passive resistance" that was evident in King's speech to the packed mass meeting of February 23. His presence in Montgomery, however, soon became a matter of notoriety in the eyes of local whites once they discovered Rustin's past involvement with the YCL and the details of his 1953 arrest on a morals charge. After receiving some worried phone calls from local black leaders, A. Philip Randolph, who had initially encouraged Rustin to contact King, discussed the situation with a group of socialist, pacifist, and civil rights leaders. All agreed that Rustin should leave Montgomery forthwith.

Although forced to work behind the scenes in New York, Rustin stayed in touch with King and helped to mobilize northern support for the boycott. Among other things, he was a founder of "In Friendship," an organization created in early 1956 for the purpose of helping "victims of racial terror"—blacks in the South who found themselves without jobs or homes as a consequence of their civil rights activity. One of its aims was to make giving to the civil rights movement "respectable"; to appeal to the kind of organization—trade unions, church bodies—that regularly contributed to causes like the Red Cross, Radio Free Europe, and the United Jewish Appeal. In May "In Friendship" staged a rally in New York's Madison Square Garden that marked one of the first occasions in which prominent entertainers such as Tallulah Bankhead and Sammy Davis, Jr., lent their talents to the civil rights cause. The event raised several thousand dollars for the MIA. However, "In Friendship" proved less significant for its fundraising activities, which were short-lived, than for the role of its three founders, Rustin, Ella J. Baker, and Stanley D. Levison, in the inception and subsequent history of the Southern Christian Leadership Conference.

Like Rustin, Ella J. Baker had come of age politically during the Great Depression. She was five years older than Rustin and had grown up in North Carolina. After graduating from Shaw University in Raleigh she moved to New York, settling in Harlem. There she worked under the WPA, but she found employment at the national office of the NAACP shortly before the war, first as a field secretary and later as director of branches. While a field secretary she had worked to build up the NAACP branch in Montgomery and thus became well acquainted with E. D. Nixon and other local activists. During these years she also became friendly, to use her own words, "with people who were in the Communist Party and all the rest of the Left forces."

Stanley D. Levison came from a completely different background in terms of class and race, although he shared the same political milieu. Born in 1912 of Jewish parents, Levison trained as a lawyer and qualified for the New York Bar. Over the years, however, various business interests occupied most of his time, and he built up a substantial income. A staunch Roosevelt Democrat, he involved himself in a variety of liberal groups, notably the American Jewish Congress and the NAACP. His activities in the latter introduced him to Ella Baker, and the two soon discovered that they shared a similar political outlook. Levison too moved in circles that brought him into contact with communists, and in the early 1950s he belonged to that relatively small band of liberals who attempted unsuccessfully to thwart official efforts to suppress the Communist party. Later, when questioned about his past, he shrugged off these associations: "in the 1930s and 1940s you could scarcely have been an intellectual in New York without knowing some [Communists]." According to a recent study by David J. Garrow, however, Levison was not only a conscious "fellow traveler" but had also been "closely involved in CP financial activities between 1952 and 1955. . . ." If true, it seems unlikely that Levison ever disclosed this fact to King. The latter knew perfectly well, on the other hand, that Levison, like Rustin and Baker, was firmly on the "left." King in fact harbored no aversion to radicalism, having been exposed to Marxism as a student and having noted that both capitalism and Marxism "each represents a partial truth."

As the Montgomery bus boycott unfolded Rustin, Baker, and Levison discussed the possibility of using it as the launchpad for a new civil rights organization. That a new organization was needed they all agreed; none of the existing groups could effectively promote mass action in the South. The NAACP had the members and the machinery, but its national leadership frowned upon mass action, especially if it involved civil disobedience or direct action. Its bureaucratic framework, moreover, made it slow-moving and difficult to mobilize in a crisis. The Congress of Racial Equality, on the other hand, while passionately committed to nonviolent direct action, had failed to attract a mass following. Indeed, by 1955 CORE seemed moribund. Both these organizations, Rustin argued, shared two fundamental weaknesses: they were northern-based and had interracial leadership. Nonviolent protest in the South would be best promoted by an indigenous, black-led organization that, although fully committed to integration, did not make a fetish of interracialism. "In Friendship" had originally been closely aligned to the NAACP, but by the latter half of 1956, Baker recalled, "We began to talk about the need for developing in the South a mass force that would . . . become a counterbalance, let's call it, to the NAACP." SCLC was conceived as a means of capitalizing on what had developed in Montgomery in terms of mass action. As Levison put it, the object was "to reproduce that pattern of mass action, underscore mass, in other cities and communities."

Rustin put the organizational ball in motion by asking C. K. Steele to call publicly for a conference of southern Negro leaders, thus forcing King's hand. Steele declined, but he did undertake to back such a call if it came from King himself. Finally, on New Year's Day, 1957, Steele, King, and Shuttlesworth made the announcement, sending about one hundred invitations to a conference on transportation and nonviolent integration to be held at King's father's church in Atlanta, Ebenezer Baptist, on January 10 and 11. About sixty people responded. Furnished with working papers by Rustin (who impressed Steele as "a very brilliant person"), the participants, representing practically every southern city, agreed to establish a "Southern Leadership Conference on Transportation and Non-Violent Integration." Rustin scheduled another meeting for February 14 in New Orleans. There, in the Baptist church of A. L. Davis, about one hundred people voted to make the organization permanent, and in August at its first annual convention it adopted the name by which it is still known: the Southern Christian Leadership Conference. The theme of this convention, "To Redeem the Soul of America," became SCLC's official motto. . . .

What kind of people sat on SCLC's board? The directors were all black. Two-thirds of them were ministers, although this proportion declined over the next decade. The lay minority included a dentist, a pharmacist, a professor of history, several businessmen, and an official of the International Longshoremen's Association. Only one woman sat on the board—a fairly accurate indication of the role of women in SCLC generally. All but a handful of the ministers were Baptists, a fact only partially explained by the numerical preponderance of black Baptists in the South. True, Baptists made up perhaps two-thirds of the church-going population; "the Baptists had the masses of the people and what we needed at that time was the masses," admitted S. S. Seay, one of the few Methodists on the board. Even so, Methodists accounted for only one in five of the ministers and were clearly underrepresented. The journalist Louis E. Lomax claimed that denominational bigotry explained the disproportionate influence of Baptists and that there was "a good deal of mumbling among Methodists about this. . . ." Clannishness, however, would be a more accurate explanation: Baptists all but monopolized the leadership because they knew each other and tended to stick together. One can easily detect, for example, an "old boy network" made up of graduates of Morehouse College in Atlanta and Alabama State College in Montgomery: these two institutions accounted for eight of SCLC's nine original officers, if one includes Samuel W. Williams, a professor at Morehouse, and L. D. Reddick, who taught at Alabama State.

Three other characteristics of SCLC's founders should be noted. First, they all came from the urban South: none resided in a town smaller than Valdosta, Georgia, or Clarksdale, Mississippi, and most lived in the dozen largest cities. With a few exceptions the civil rights movement originated in the cities and only later, in the early 1960s, penetrated the rural Black Belt. Second, the ministers in SCLC were representative in some ways but unrepresentative in others. Social activists tend to be a self-selecting minority and in that sense atypical. The black clergymen who took part in the civil rights movement were certainly atypical of the black clergy as a whole, the vast majority of whom, in the words of one authority, were "primarily interested in their pastoral role. . . . [and] have little apparent interest in . . . the general citizenship status of their own parishioners, to say nothing about that of the Negro masses." During the Birmingham protests of 1963—one of the most highly organized and successful of all the civil rights campaigns—only about twenty of the city's 250 black ministers participated.

In a larger sense, however, the socially conscious minority could be considered far more representative than the uninvolved majority. As the bus boycott movements had dramatically illustrated, blacks would respond en masse, and with enthusiasm and determination, to vigorous antisegregationist leadership. Activists like King and Steele reflected the opinions of black southerners far more accurately than did the much larger group which abstained from the struggle. Finally, as defined in terms of education, occupation, wealth, and social standing, most of SCLC's founders came from the relatively small upper-middle class. Few had failed to graduate from college; many had higher degrees and seminary training. The ministers pastored large, well-established churches and belonged to the social elite of the black community. In short, SCLC's founders were among "the best and the brightest" of the black clergy and professional class. . . .

By any objective appraisal King made a massive contribution to the success of the boycott. But if his role in Montgomery explained his elevation to SCLC's presidency, something else is needed to account for the fact that SCLC, the organization, never managed to establish a separate identity from King the individual. SCLC was not only dominated by King, its very structure appeared to be built around him. On paper the board of directors functioned as SCLC's governing body; in practice, as far as policy was concerned, it acted as a rubber stamp. Consisting for the most part of King's own nominees, it rarely questioned and even more rarely opposed the policies and statements that King placed before it. "Like the black church," Bayard Rustin has written, "the structure of the SCLC was autocratic. . . . major decisions rested with Dr. King." Equally striking was the extent to which SCLC framed its public image and public appeal around the King persona: King was unique and indispensable, a black leader—*the* black leader—of heroic proportions. Men like Steele and Shuttlesworth received little public exposure; there was no attempt to "build them up" or portray them as figures comparable in stature to King. Indeed, King treated the other officers of SCLC with unconscious disdain. In 1965, for example, when he nominated Ralph Abernathy to succeed to the presidency should anything befall him, he did not bother to consult Steele, SCLC's vice-president. The absence of democracy in SCLC eventually became a major source of internal discord.

But these problems lay in the future. When SCLC was set up in 1957, Rustin and Levison structured it so as to capitalize on the prestige that had accrued to King as a result of the Montgomery bus boycott. The press had singled out, magnified, and thereby distorted his role in that protest. Nevertheless, as L. D. Reddick noted, "the influence of the press in focusing upon King . . . was decisive in shaping the image that took form in the public mind." The Montgomery bus boycott became synonymous with King's name, and SCLC was designed to build upon that name. Its King-centered structure was no accident: Rustin and Levison deliberately decided to project King, through SCLC, as a national leader.

The philosophy of nonviolence was a crucial facet of the role that Rustin conceived for King. At the start of the boycott King had emphasized New Testament morality without ever linking it to Gandhian or pacifist doctrines. But with the encouragement of Rustin and others, particularly Glenn E. Smiley of the FOR, he decided to avow nonviolence as a fundamental principle and began, in the words of biographer David L. Lewis, "to lace his discourses with Gandhian terminology." In April 1956 in his first published article, he insisted that "the only way to press on is by adopting the philosophy and practice of non-violent resistance." He elaborated on this argument in his first book, *Stride Toward Freedom* (1958), in which he seriously asserted that blacks would be able to convert their white oppressors into friends if they accompanied their protests with redemptive love: "We will soon wear you down by our capacity to suffer. And in winning our freedom we will so appeal to your heart and conscience that we will win you in the process." Thus the lion, he argued, might be persuaded to lie down with the lamb.

Blacks in Montgomery were confused by the Gandhian philosophy. To some extent, it is true, the idea of loving the enemy accorded with their Christian beliefs. They might also appreciate the practical wisdom of refraining from violence. But the majority of blacks were not pacifists and considered the notion of converting the segregationists through love and self-sacrifice faintly ridiculous. Meier and Rudwick are probably right, therefore, in arguing that the growing appeal of nonviolent direct action for blacks had little to do with the Gandhian doctrines that King and others read into it. Those doctrines did, on the other hand, appeal to many whites. Nonviolence not only enamored King to Rustin's own circle, the pacifist fringe, but also endeared him to more mainstream figures like Eleanor Roosevelt and Chester Bowles, former American ambassador to India. Equally important, it enhanced the general impression of King as a man of peace and moderation. As Rustin well knew, the concept of nonviolence was ideologically neutral; it gave a patina of respectability to the politically suspect tactic of mass direct action—a crucial consideration in the McCarthy era. Thus the right-of-center organ of Republican publisher Henry R. Luce, *Time* magazine, could put King on its front cover with an approving inside feature. *Time*'s story quoted King's views on clothes ("'I don't want to look like an undertaker, but I do believe in conservative dress'.") and concluded that its subject "avoids the excesses of radicalism. . . ."

Throughout 1957, 1958, and 1959 Rustin and Levison worked quietly in the background to polish King's image as the evangelist of nonviolent resistance. They helped King with his speeches; they scrutinized his articles and arranged for their publication; they gave editorial assistance on *Stride Toward Freedom*. Even when thus burnished, King's prose tended to be dull, flat, and platitudinous. Nevertheless, King was sufficiently erudite and the concept of nonviolent direct action sufficiently novel to establish the hero of Montgomery as a kind of philosopher-statesman. Widespread public exposure enhanced this reputation; Rustin and Levison not only proffered literary assistance but also arranged speaking engagements and helped to introduce King to people and organizations across the liberal spectrum. Harris Wofford recalled of this period that "Rustin seemed ever-present with advice, and sometimes acted as if King were a precious puppet whose symbolic actions were to be planned by a Gandhian high command."

The projection of King as an American Gandhi soon brought wider recognition. In 1957 Kwame Nkrumah invited King to Ghana's independence celebrations, and the resulting trip yielded the additional dividend of an introduction to Vice-President Richard M. Nixon and a subsequent visit to the White House. King's reputation received another fillip in May of that year when the executive secretary of the NAACP, Roy Wilkins, agreed to share the platform with King and A. Philip Randolph at an outdoor rally in Washington (the Prayer Pilgrimage) organized by Rustin, Levison, and Baker. Confirmation of King's status as a "national" Negro leader came in June 1958 when he met President Dwight D. Eisenhower as part of a black delegation that included Randolph, Wilkins, and Lester Granger, the head of the National Urban League. In 1959, after recovering from an assassination attempt that had resulted in a serious stab wound near the heart, King visited India where he met Prime

Minister Jawaharlal Nehru and immersed himself in Gandhian folklore. By now King had achieved a unique kind of status. It was far from clear exactly who or what he represented—he had no political or organizational base—yet he was honored by universities, courted by politicians, indulged by foreign heads of state, and consulted by the president.

Thus far, however, King's personal prestige had not been translated into concrete support for SCLC, which suffered from chronic money problems. With no dues-paying members and no systematic fundraising program, most of SCLC's financial support had to come from the affiliates, and contributions were quite small—forty-six dollars from Charles Gomillion, head of the Tuskegee Civic Association; fifty dollars from the Interdenominational Ministerial Alliance of Durham, North Carolina. Some money arrived from sympathetic whites: former Senator Frank P. Graham of North Carolina, for example, sent twenty-five dollars. And a trickle of money came from abroad; Canon John Collins, dean of St. Paul's Cathedral, was an early contributor. The donation of $11,000 from the United Packinghouse Workers of America was an exceptional windfall; for its first few years SCLC operated on a shoestring. As late as 1960 its budget barely exceeded $60,000, and its staff consisted of Ella Baker, the executive director, plus two secretaries. . . .

Other people also criticized King's tendency to exalt his own role and shared Baker's concern about SCLC's organizational weakness. Stanley D. Levison, perusing the manuscript of *Stride Toward Freedom,* cautioned King against implying that "'everything depended on you . . .'"; as it stood, his account of the bus boycott conveyed an impression of egocentricity. L. D. Reddick, the historian from Alabama State who sat on SCLC's board, proffered similar advice in his 1959 biography of King, *Crusader Without Violence.* There was a growing feeling, he wrote, that King was "taking too many bows and enjoying them . . . forgetting that victory at Montgomery had been the result of collective thought and collective action." This, plus his obvious liking for fine clothes, expensive restaurants, and first-class hotels, placed a question mark over his sincerity; even some of his colleagues "felt that he was bent on making a fortune." King was also "too much in motion," Reddick thought, "flying about the country, speaking almost everywhere." The clear implication was that he should spend less time junketing and making speeches and more time on SCLC.

Dissatisfaction with SCLC's progress came to a head in October 1959 when the board of directors, prodded by Baker, took a long, hard look at the organization's direction. SCLC had received virtually no publicity, the board lamented. It had barely scratched the surface in the field of voter registration. It had failed to concert action among the local affiliates. It had held too many speech-filled conferences, too close together, leaving no time for analysis and long-term planning. It had not yet developed a "positive, dynamic, and dramatic program." Finally, it was the board's view that King had yet to give "the maximum of his time and energies to the work of the SCLC."

This reappraisal led to a number of measures. Bayard Rustin agreed to serve as part-time public relations director with the understanding that he would "quietly resign" in the event of any embarrassing publicity about his past. The number of board meetings was cut from three to two a year, the number of conventions from two to one. Recognizing that SCLC's thirteen-member administrative committee was too large and too difficult to assemble to function effectively, the board appointed a subcommittee of five to assist Baker in working out a program for 1960. This small inner group consisted of four clergymen—Sam Williams, Ralph Abernathy, Fred Shuttlesworth, and Joseph E. Lowery (one of the few Methodists on the board)—and one layman, L. D. Reddick. Finally, King agreed to resign his pastorate in Montgomery so that he could move to Atlanta and devote more time to SCLC. Henceforth he would share the pastorate of Ebenezer Baptist Church with his father, an arrangement that freed him from the obligation to preach every Sunday. It also had the added advantage of enabling SCLC to utilize Ebenezer's spacious education building, just a hundred yards or so up Auburn Avenue.

What accounted for SCLC's poor showing during its first years? King's administrative inexperience clearly played a part, but this factor should not be exaggerated. Notwithstanding the strictures of Ella Baker, it made good sense to build up King's personal prestige even at the cost of diverting his energies from organizational matters. After all, at this stage King was SCLC's only real asset. Some of SCLC's problems were the usual kind of "teething troubles" that invariably afflict new organizations. For example, it inevitably took time to establish a stable group of officers, for some of the board members soon lost interest or for various other reasons ceased to participate. T. J. Jemison of Baton Rouge decided that his activities with the National Baptist Convention, which he would eventually head, left him no time for his duties as SCLC's secretary. Fred Shuttlesworth of Birmingham took over this post. A. L. Davis of New Orleans, SCLC's second vice-president, also dropped out, to be replaced by Joseph E. Lowery of Mobile. These changes underscored the fact that Alabama was SCLC's principal base.

The limitations imposed by SCLC's structure proved to be long-term defects. The local affiliates were independent bodies subject to no organizational discipline. Moreover, like churches of the same denomination everywhere, each Negro Baptist congregation was a sovereign body, impervious to outside interference. Requesting the affiliates' cooperation was one thing, getting it quite another. In practice it proved impossible to mobilize them behind a common program. When it came to taking initiatives, moreover, King had to be careful not to tread on the toes of local leaders. Men like Shuttlesworth and Steele were proud, sensitive, egotistical individuals who, to quote Louis E. Lomax, "saw themselves as potential Martin Luther Kings, and . . . did not want his organization moving into their parishes to capture the power and the glory. . . ." They might seek SCLC's help, and they might invite King to speak, but they would not brook interference in their own bailiwicks. As Steele emphatically stated in 1978, there had never been any question of King telling him what to do during the Tallahassee bus boycott. "We didn't have that because . . . I considered Tallahassee beyond Montgomery. I still think that."

SCLC's lack of impact owed most perhaps to the fact that nonviolent direct action did not immediately catch on. There was a three-year gap between the end of the Montgomery bus boycott and the beginning of the student sit-in movement. SCLC had no idea that when direct action finally became a South-wide phenomenon, it would single out for attack "white only" department store lunch counters. As indicated by its original title—the Southern Leadership Conference on Transportation and Non-Violent Integration—SCLC's first goal had been to spread the example of Montgomery by stimulating bus boycotts in other cities. But with the important exceptions of Tallahassee and Rock Hill, South Carolina (where a boycott put the transit company out of business), no other sustained bus boycotts took place. In cities like New Orleans, Atlanta, and Mobile, good-faith compliance with court-ordered desegregation made long boycotts unnecessary. "What happened," Levison recalled, "was that in some of the cities victory came very fast. The city power structure . . . decided they didn't want to go through a Montgomery. So they quietly desegregated buses. And, therefore, a great wave of boycotts didn't develop." This in part explained SCLC's shift to voter registration at the end of 1957.

Even when cities ignored *Browder* v. *Gayle,* as Baton Rouge did, blacks did not immediately organize boycotts. In cities like Miami they were too few proportionately to prosecute a boycott successfully and did not attempt to do so. Elsewhere the repressive climate, combined with timid or erratic leadership, defused the boycott as an effective weapon. In Birmingham, for example, police intimidation, disunity among black leaders, and the difficulty of devising alternative transportation in such a large city militated against a successful bus boycott. When Shuttlesworth tried to launch one in October 1958, it fizzled out after a few weeks.

Many black leaders also resisted the suggestion that mass direct action should become a standard tactic. Some regarded the concept of direct action as dangerously radical, others simply thought legal and political action far more effective. Indeed, in some ways the Montgomery protest strengthened the argument for legal action; desegregation had come about in response to an MIA suit, not the boycott itself. In addition, the precedent established by *Browder* v. *Gayle* meant that other suits challenging bus segregation would be upheld by the federal courts; boycotts would be superfluous. Thus many of the "boycotts" often bracketed with Montgomery and Tallahassee were no more than one-day protests designed to provoke the necessary arrests on which to base a legal challenge. Such for example was the Atlanta boycott—a rather decorous affair in which a group of black ministers led by the Reverend William Holmes Borders got themselves arrested and then filed suit in federal court. Their action even had the tacit support of Mayor William B. Hartsfield and the Atlanta Transit Company. The latter, the three parties agreed, would mount a token legal fight and then bow to court-ordered integration. Borders made no attempt to boycott the segregated buses during the two years that it took the case to wind its way through the courts. Similar tactics prevailed in New Orleans, Memphis, Baton Rouge, and Savannah.

Proposals to use mass direct action against segregated theaters, motels, restaurants, lunch counters, and so on aroused even stronger misgivings. Few blacks doubted that they had a clear right to withdraw their patronage from a business or public service; they could spend their money as they pleased. But it was one thing to boycott segregated buses and quite another to "sit in" or otherwise physically to intrude upon the premises of a private business. That involved deliberately breaking the law, courting arrest, and risking fines and incarceration. True, all state and local segregation laws were of dubious constitutional standing in light of *Brown* and *Browder v. Gayle*. There seemed to be a clear distinction, however, between public services on the one hand and private businesses on the other. The latter might not have the right to appeal to the public authorities to enforce segregation, but might not tradesmen, acting as individuals, have a right to refuse service to whomever they pleased—even when those they turned away always happened to be blacks? The right of private individuals to practice racial discrimination was a legal gray area which involved the sensitive and—especially in the South—emotional issue of property rights. And it was ground upon which many blacks preferred not to tread.

It would be wrong to suppose that opposition to the "sit-in" type of tactic existed wholly or even mainly within the NAACP. On the contrary, even after the Montgomery and Tallahassee bus boycotts most black adults disapproved of deliberate civil disobedience. In the early 1960s this opposition drastically declined, but only *after* the success of the student sit-in movement had been established. In 1960 the initial reaction of most parents had been to oppose the sit-ins.

The postboycott histories of the MIA and the ICC underlined this reluctance to embrace the tactics of physical confrontation. In Montgomery the MIA evinced little enthusiasm for directly challenging other aspects of segregation; further progress in desegregation had to wait until the Civil Rights Act of 1964. King's influence waned, and according to one study "reversion to accommodation as the leadership form . . . was an accomplished fact within eighteen months after the boycott." It was a similar story in Tallahassee, where Steele proved unable to persuade the board of the ICC to endorse civil disobedience or the "jail without bail" tactic. Ministers like Steele, it should be added, often came under pressure from their congregations to limit or tone down their civil rights activities. "It's been all I could do to stay here," Steele lamented in 1978.

The difficulties involved in mobilizing blacks behind more radical tactics cannot be attributed to conservative attitudes alone. No matter how they felt about such tactics, the economic facts of life constrained most blacks. Economic reprisals had been relatively uncommon during the bus boycotts. The nature of the protest itself afforded some measure of anonymity and protection; it was difficult to visit retribution upon an entire community. Arrest on a sit-in, a picket line, or a demonstration, on the other hand, invited economic disaster. Apart from the cost of bail (usually exorbitant), legal fees (often considerable), and fines (frequently heavy), there was the real possibility of a spell in jail. Either way, fine or jail, arrestees faced the likelihood, often amounting to a near certainty, of losing their jobs. Again and again during the course of the civil rights movement, SCLC was confounded by the fact that relatively few blacks would take part in its protests if the protests entailed a high risk of arrest.

Only in 1960, when black students entered the fray in large numbers, did a broad assault on segregation become possible. In the late 1950s the campuses were quiet. A sociologist who taught in a black college in Augusta, Georgia, noted that "apathy and indifference" prevailed among the students, an observation that could be applied to the great majority of such institutions. It was only a matter of time, however, before the combination of rising expectations and relative immunity from white sanctions galvanized black students in rebellion against the color line. The role of the students at Florida A&M in the Tallahassee bus boycott was, in retrospect, a clear portent.

The student sit-ins solved none of SCLC's organizational problems. But they did infuse it with new blood, new dynamism, and new tactical concepts. The difficulty of mobilizing black adults remained, but the demonstration in 1960 that parents would eventually rally in support of their children pointed toward an answer. During the heyday of the civil rights movement young people—children and teenagers—furnished the most eager and numerous volunteers for jail. "They are your militants," Steele observed. "They are your soldiers." The tactics of nonviolent protest still had to be refined, but SCLC soon learned that the surest way to mobilize the adults was first to involve their children. Young people made up the initial phalanx, the entering wedge. In 1960, however, the great campaigns lay in the future. SCLC had the bare bones of an organization, little more. "For a time," wrote Claude Sitton of the New York *Times*, "it seemed doubtful that the conference would amount to much."

Suggested Readings

Charles C. Alexander, *Holding the Line: The Eisenhower Era, 1951–1962* (1975).
Stephen E. Ambrose, *Eisenhower: Vol. II, The President* (1984).
David L. Anderson, *Trapped by Success* (1991).
David J. Garrow, *Bearing the Cross: Martin Luther King, Jr., and the Southern Christian Leadership Conference* (1986).
Fred I. Greenstein, *The Hidden-Hand Presidency: Eisenhower as Leader* (1982).
Peter L. Hahn, *The U.S., Great Britain and Egypt, 1945–1956* (1991).
George H. Nash, *The Conservative Intellectual Movement in America: Since 1945* (1976).
Chester J. Pach, Jr., and Elmo Richardson, rev. ed., *The Presidency of Dwight D. Eisenhower* (1991).
Stephen G. Rabe, *Eisenhower and Latin America* (1988).
Mark H. Rose, *Interstate: Express Highway Politics, 1941–1956* (1979).

Further Readings

Domestic Politics During the Eisenhower Era

Piers Brandon, *Ike* (1986); Robert F. Burk, *Dwight D. Eisenhower* (1986); Herbert Parmet, *Eisenhower and the American Crusades* (1972); Gary W. Reichard, *The Reaffirmation of Republicanism: Eisenhower and the 83rd Congress* (1975); Harold G. Vatter, *The U.S. Economy in the 1950s* (1962).

The New Look and Brinksmanship

Robert Divine, *Eisenhower and the Cold War* (1981); Richard Immerman, ed., *John Foster Dulles and the Diplomacy of the Cold War* (1990) and *The CIA in Guatemala* (1982); Diane Kunz, *The Economic Diplomacy of the Suez Crisis* (1991); Roger Louis and Roger Owen, eds., *Suez 1956* (1989).

Popular Culture During the 1950s

James L. Baughman, *The Republic of Mass Culture* (1992); William Boddy, *Fifties Television* (1990); John K. Galbraith, *The Affluent Society* (1963); Albert Goldman, *Elvis* (1981); Robert Wuthnow, *The Restructuring of American Religion* (1988).

The Civil Rights Movement During This Period

David Chappell, *Inside Agitators* (1994); Charles Eagles, ed., *The Civil Rights Movement* (1986); Stephen B. Oates, *Let the Trumpet Sound* (1982); J. Harvie Wilkinson, *From Brown to Bakke: The Supreme Court and School Integration, 1954–1978* (1980); Juan Williams, ed., *Eyes on the Prize: America's Civil Rights Years, 1954–1965* (1987).

QUESTIONS FOR DISCUSSION

1. What factors led to Dwight D. Eisenhower's election as president? Assess his qualifications for the office.
2. Trace the course of the First Indochinese War. How did the Eisenhower administration respond?
3. How effective was John Foster Dulles' policy of brinksmanship? Identify its weaknesses.
4. Discuss the Suez Crisis and evaluate American policy during that episode.
5. What factors contributed to the affluence and poverty that characterized American society during the 1950s?
6. Assess the tactics employed by civil rights activists. How effective were they in achieving their goals?
7. How does Adam Fairclough evaluate the leadership of the Southern Christian Leadership Conference?

CHAPTER TWENTY-FIVE

THE POLITICS OF VISION:
The Presidency of John F. Kennedy

As the decade of the 1950s came to a close, America seemed directionless, dispirited, and increasingly anxious. Liberals—those committed to peaceful change, to social justice at home and abroad—had struggled to reconcile their idealism with the realities of Cold War America. The evil that underlay Hitler's death camps, the doomsday implications of Hiroshima, and the grinding competition of the Cold War left liberals shaken and confused. Menaced at home by the unreason of Joseph McCarthy's anticommunist witch-hunt and abroad by Soviet imperialism, the reform impulse had given way to television sitcoms, gray flannel suit conformity, and guilt-free religion. Nevertheless while America was and continued to be politically conservative, it was still a dynamic society typified by growth, change, and energy. Sometime toward the close of the 1950s Americans seemed to have decided that eight years of holding the line, clinging to the status quo was enough. There emerged in the land a renewed longing for direction and purpose. Suddenly energized, liberals cast aside their pessimism and set forth once again on their perennial search for a brave new world.

JOHN F. KENNEDY

Born on May 29, 1917, John Fitzgerald Kennedy was the second son of Joseph P. and Rose Fitzgerald Kennedy's nine children. Joe Kennedy was a self-made Boston Irishman who had attended Harvard College and then made a fortune in the stock market, producing movies, and importing liquor. His courtly, attractive wife was the daughter of John F. ("Honey Fitz") Fitzgerald, mayor of

Boston. Their second son, John, attended Choate Academy and Harvard. Soon after World War II erupted, Jack, as he was known to his friends, enlisted in the navy. He subsequently won a commission and became a PT boat commander in the South Pacific. In an incident that Joe, Sr., took care to publicize, Jack's boat was sliced in two by a Japanese destroyer on August 2, 1943. Demonstrating the courage and coolness under fire that was to mark his presidency, Kennedy guided his surviving crew to a nearby island and then after spending days in the water, secured their release.

Though somewhat reluctant, Jack Kennedy agreed in 1946 to run for the House of Representatives from Massachusetts' Eleventh District. His shy good looks, quiet charm, and war record coupled with his family's money and organizational talents carried the day. Kennedy's three terms in the lower house were distinguished primarily by the conservatism of his views. He opposed big government, favored a balanced budget, and supported containment of communism. Like his father, Jack frequently expressed sympathy for Joe McCarthy and his anticommunist crusade. Then in 1952 Kennedy took Henry Cabot Lodge, Jr.'s, Senate seat away from him. That he lost the vice presidential nomination to Senator Estes Kefauver in 1956 did him no harm, given the Democratic ticket's disastrous defeat at the hands of Eisenhower and Nixon; indeed, his run at the vice presidential nomination brought him the visibility he needed to capture the presidential nomination in 1960. By the time he made his successful bid for the presidency, Kennedy had moved to the political left, managing to convince Democratic liberals during the campaign that he was truly committed to social and economic justice for all and to vigorous but peaceful competition with the forces of international communism.

The new administration reflected Kennedy's aura of youth and energy. The major cabinet posts were filled by liberal activists—Connecticut governor Abraham Ribicoff as secretary of health, education, and welfare; labor lawyer Arthur Goldberg as secretary of labor; and Arizona congressman Stuart Udall as secretary of the interior—while the White House staff featured such tough-minded liberals as Theodore Sorenson and Kenneth O'Donnell. Unlike Eisenhower, Kennedy relied heavily on academics and intellectuals for advice. But the president's personality was perhaps his best asset. Cool, urbane, and self-effacing he charmed reporters with news conferences that were witty and fact-filled, while he infused the American people with a new sense of purpose.

DOMESTIC AGENDA

THE NEW FRONTIER

In his acceptance speech at the final convention session at Los Angeles, John F. Kennedy, the forty-three-year-old nominee from Massachusetts, placed himself and his New Frontier program squarely in the middle of the American reform tradition. "Woodrow Wilson's New Freedom promised our nation a new political and economic framework," he told the delegates. "Franklin Roosevelt's New Deal promised security and succor to those in need. But the New Frontier . . . is not a set of promises—it is a set of challenges." He issued a call to arms to Americans, especially young people and intellectuals, many of whom had been alienated from public life during the Eisenhower years, to join with him in attacking ignorance, poverty, prejudice, and inequality.

To the surprise of many, however, President Kennedy's domestic program did not fare well. There were many reasons. Kennedy had won by a razor-thin margin over his Republican opponent in 1960, Richard Nixon. The election results enabled conservatives to claim throughout his term in office that he lacked the popular mandate necessary for sweeping social and economic reform. Mike Mansfield succeeded Lyndon Johnson as Senate majority leader, and following his death, House Speaker Sam Rayburn was succeeded by John McCormack of Massachusetts. Mansfield was timid and ineffectual, while McCormack was out of sympathy with much of the administration's agenda. In addition, not only was Kennedy not a good congressional politician, he made very poor use of Vice President Lyndon Johnson, who was. The president's brother Robert, who became attorney general, and other New Frontiersmen held the Texan in fierce contempt. Of the twenty-three bills the president sent to Congress in 1961, sixteen were defeated outright.

Nevertheless, there were significant legislative successes. As the country wallowed in a recession, the White House persuaded Congress to expand Social Security benefits, raise the minimum wage to $1.15 an hour, extend unemployment benefits for another thirteen weeks, and pass a $4.88 billion omnibus housing bill. The administration's major legislative achievement in 1962 was passage of the Trade Expansion Act which gave the president wide powers to negotiate the lowering of trade barriers and led to a 35 percent reduction in tariffs between the United States and Western Europe. With some difficulty, the president and his aides persuaded the House and Senate to establish a privately owned and financed corporation to administer a communications satellite system capable of relaying television and telephone signals around the world. Critics charged that the bill was just a huge giveaway to International Telephone and Telegraph and other communications conglomerates, but it passed nonetheless, and Telstar became a reality.

THE SPACE PROGRAM

The Communications Satellite Act of 1962 was a product of ITT's political clout but also the administration's determination to press ahead with a space program. During the 1960 election campaign the Kennedy camp had scored points with the voters by charging that the launching of the Sputnik satellite by the Soviets in 1957 indicated that the Republicans had neglected to develop a missile program and thus placed the United States at a disadvantage in the Cold War. Early in 1961 Soviet astronaut Yuri Gagarin circled the earth in a space capsule, presenting worried Americans with further evidence of the alleged missile gap. But then on May 6, 1961, Commander Alan B. Shepard was launched into suborbital space from Cape Canaveral. His three hundred–mile trip was the first in a series of successful, manned space flights. The same month Shepard made his historic flight, Kennedy urged Congress to make a commitment to putting a man on the moon by the end of the decade. Legislators responded by doubling the National Space and Aeronautics Administration's budget in 1962 and then again in 1963.

THE ECONOMIC PROGRAM

Though corporate profits during the early 1960s rose 67 percent, compared to a 13 percent rise in personal income, the business community was generally hostile to the Kennedy administration. In part, that animosity stemmed from the president and Labor Secretary Goldberg's efforts to control inflation. In 1962, the administration helped avert a strike in the crucial steel industry by supervising the signing of a contract between the major producers and the steel workers in which labor made only modest demands and industry agreed not to raise prices. Ten days later, Roger Blough of United States Steel announced a $6 per ton increase. Five other large firms announced identical increases the following day. Kennedy was furious. "My father always told me that all businessmen were sons-of-bitches, but I never believed it till now," he confided to his aides. Denouncing the steel companies for flaunting the public interest, Kennedy ordered the Defense Department to award new contracts only to those companies who held the line on prices. Within seventy-two hours Blough and his fellow executives rescinded their orders.

The economy improved during the early years of Kennedy's tenure in the White House, but not to the extent that the administration hoped for or desired. Gross income increased, but unemployment hovered at a disappointingly high 5.5 percent. Pockets of intense poverty, particularly in the rural South and urban Northeast, persisted. The GNP, though healthy, lagged behind that of Europe. Much of America's prosperity was being fueled by the $6 billion increase in the arms budget in 1961—a product of the burgeoning arms race with the Soviet Union—and spending on the space program. By 1962, over half the federal budget was devoted to space and defense. These trends eventually persuaded the president to follow the recommendations of Walter W. Heller, chairman of the Council of Economic Advisers, and other liberal economists who were urging a substantial reduction of taxes even in the midst of prosperity. Early in 1963 he proposed to Congress that the federal government cut taxes by $10 billion over the next three years. Passed in 1964 after a year of often bitter debate, the "new economics" did in fact provide a significant boost to the economy.

EXTENDING THE FAIR DEAL

Heading the Kennedy administration's social agenda were education and health care. During the 1960 campaign the Democrats, again using Sputnik and the alleged missile gap, blasted the Eisenhower administration for neglecting America's schools and those who taught and learned in them. In 1961, Kennedy submitted legislation that would provide $2.3 billion to public schools for construction and teachers' salaries and another $3.3 billion for higher education. Catholic leaders, angered that the bill did not cover parochial schools, joined with southerners, fearful that federal aid to education would be used to coerce them into accepting integration, to prevent passage. Early in 1962 the president threw his support behind the King-Anderson bill to provide federally funded health care for the elderly. Financed chiefly by payroll deductions and administered by the Social Security system, Medicare would provide medical insurance for workers over sixty-five. Private health insurers and the American Medical Association denounced the proposal as "socialized medicine" and launched a massive lobbying campaign to defeat it. Kennedy went all out to win approval, at one point addressing a mass rally of senior citizens at Madison Square Garden, but Congress caved in to the special interests and tabled Medicare indefinitely.

THE KENNEDYS AND CIVIL RIGHTS

THE FREEDOM RIDES

The Kennedy brothers, especially Robert, were committed to the crusade for nondiscrimination and equality under the law for African Americans. But the president and his advisors also wanted to retain as much political support among southern whites as possible. In the spring of 1961 the Congress of Racial Equality headed by civil rights veteran James Farmer planned a series of freedom rides to test southern compliance with recent court orders banning segregation on buses and in terminals engaged in interstate travel. The SCLC and several branches of the NAACP decided to lend financial aid.

Farmer and the other organizers anticipated confrontation; indeed, that was the purpose of the operation. "Our intention," he later declared, "was to provoke the southern authorities into arresting us and thereby prod the Justice Department into enforcing the law of the land." The organizers of the freedom rides notified the FBI and the Justice Department of their plans but never received any reply.

The first week in May thirteen riders, both black and white, split into two groups and departed Washington, DC, for Alabama and Mississippi. They encountered only sporadic harassment until they reached Anniston, Alabama. There a white mob smashed windows and slashed tires. Outside of town, en route to Birmingham, the bus was firebombed. The mob reassembled, surrounded the bus, and beat the freedom riders with clubs and pipes as they fled the burning vehicle. SCLC workers from Birmingham barely managed to rescue the bruised and bleeding riders.

On May 20, 1961, a fresh group of twenty-one riders, having assembled and trained in Nashville, boarded a bus in Birmingham destined for Montgomery. All was quiet when the vehicle pulled into the capital city's terminal, but as the passengers disembarked, they were surprised and attacked by a white mob; this assault left one white rider paralyzed from the neck down. Montgomery police stood by as the brutality unfolded.

Television footage and news photos of the carnage at Montgomery shocked the nation and the world. The freedom rides were at last front-page news. Gradually the Kennedy administration succumbed to pressure to intervene. When a collection of enraged whites surrounded Montgomery's First Baptist Church in an attempt to break up a rally in behalf of the freedom riders, Attorney General Kennedy sent in four hundred federal marshals to prevent bloodshed. The Justice Department eventually petitioned the Interstate Commerce Commission to issue clear rules prohibiting segregation on interstate carriers. CORE proclaimed victory in its battle against Jim Crow on the highways, but Farmer and other civil rights leaders continued to be dismayed by the reluctance with which the Kennedy administration supported the constitutional rights of African Americans. Events at the University of Mississippi in the fall of 1962 did not serve to allay those misgivings.

RACIAL VIOLENCE IN MISSISSIPPI

In September the university with the backing of Governor Ross Barnett rejected the application of James H. Meredith, an African American, for admission. Meredith had obtained a federal court order requiring Ole Miss to register him; consequently the Justice Department was forced to intervene. On the twenty-eighth a U.S. court of appeals found Barnett guilty of civil contempt. Two days later Meredith was escorted onto the University of Mississippi campus by U.S. marshals. Over the radio, Barnett encouraged resistance to the "oppressive power of the United States," and an angry mob of several thousand whites, many of them armed, laid siege to the campus on September 30. In the ensuing violence two men were killed; the marshals, several of them severely wounded, were able to hold off the rioters only with the help of three hundred federalized National Guardsmen. On October 1 Meredith began attending class, but the Oxford campus continued to be the scene of segregationist protests and disruptions.

Indeed, Mississippi seemed trapped in a vicious cycle of racial protest and violence. The summer following Meredith's forced entry into Ole Miss a sniper gunned down civil rights leader Medgar Evers outside his home in Jackson, Mississippi, and in 1963 a church bombing in Birmingham left four young black girls dead. Dissatisfied with the federal government's timidity, Martin Luther King, Jr., led a freedom march on Washington where he delivered his incomparable "I have a dream" speech to two hundred thousand onlookers. Administration officials participated in the march, but in the end the only real legislative achievement in the civil rights arena during the Kennedy years was passage in 1962 of the Twenty-fourth Amendment to the Constitution barring the poll tax as a requirement for voting in federal elections.

KENNEDY AND THE COLD WAR

The Kennedy administration's indifferent record in the social and economic sphere was due to the president's relative inexperience with congressional politics, the narrowness of his margin of victory, and the strength of entrenched interests, as well as the fact that from the outset he gave top priority to foreign affairs. The constant threat of nuclear war, the spread of the Cold War to developing areas as Nikita Khrushchev threw his support behind wars of national liberation, and specific crises in Berlin and Cuba may have dictated such a course, but the president was predisposed to foreign affairs anyway. His senior paper at Harvard, later turned into a book, was a study of European appeasement entitled *While England Slept*. During his tenure in the Senate he secured a seat on the Foreign Relations Committee and became one of the country's most outspoken cold warriors. In his inaugural address, which featured foreign affairs, he issued a ringing call to arms: "Let every nation know . . . that we shall pay any price, bear any burden, meet any hardship, support any friend, oppose any foe to assure the survival and success of liberty."

The president's appointments reflected his determination to win the Cold War. His choice of Dean Rusk, an unassertive protégé of George Marshall, signaled Kennedy's determination to be his own secretary of state. To be secretary of defense he chose former Ford Motor Company head Robert McNamara, who believed the Soviets could be defeated through technology and scientific management. The new NSC advisor, McGeorge Bundy, and his deputy, Walt Rostow, were academics who prided themselves on their pragmatism and toughness.

There was from the outset a basic contradiction in the foreign policies of John Fitzgerald Kennedy. He and his advisors insisted that they were out to make the world safe for diversity, that under their leadership the United States would abandon the status quo policies of the past and support change, especially in the developing world. The Kennedy people did not object to Eisenhower's intervention into the internal affairs of other nations, but to the fact that it usually intervened ineptly and always to prop up the status quo. According to Arthur Schlesinger, Jr., Kennedy fully understood that in Latin America "the militantly anti-revolutionary line" of the past was the policy most likely to strengthen the communists and lose the hemisphere. He and his advisors planned openings to the left to facilitate "democratic development."

At the same time, the administration saw any significant change in the world balance of power as a threat to American security. Kennedy, Bundy, Rusk, and McNamara took very seriously Khrushchev's January 1961 speech offering support for "wars of national liberation"; it was, they believed, evidence of a new communist campaign to seize control of anticolonial and other revolutionary movements in economically underdeveloped regions.

The person who generally supplied key assumptions behind the perception of threat for the new administration was Walt Rostow. As a prominent member of the so-called Charles River school of development economists centered at

Harvard and M.I.T. in the 1950s, Rostow had become convinced that the future struggle between communism and capitalism would take the form of contests to demonstrate the relevance of each ideology to the development process in the Third World. Rostow liked to describe communists as "scavengers of the modernization process." If the Third World was not to succumb to the siren's song of Marxism-Leninism, with all the implications that that would pose for the international balance of power, then the United States and other "developed" countries would have to demonstrate that economic progress could take place within a democratic framework.

COUNTERINSURGENCY AND NUCLEAR DETERRENCE

Intent on putting the Soviets on the defensive, the new administration persuaded Congress to launch the largest peacetime arms buildup in the nation's history. When completed, America's awesome new nuclear arsenal would include one thousand Minuteman solid-fuel ICBMs (up from sixteen at the close of the Eisenhower administration) and thirty-two Polaris submarines carrying 656 missiles.

Determined to create an alternative to the policy of massive resistance, McNamara set out to strengthen conventional forces as well. The Pentagon quickly developed plans to add five combat-ready Army divisions, three tactical air wings, and a ten-division reserve. To fight Khrushchev's wars of national liberation, Kennedy and his advisors embraced the new tactic of counterinsurgency. To train newly created Special Forces units to beat communist guerrillas at their own game, facilities at Fort Bragg, North Carolina, were greatly expanded. The object of this multi-billion-dollar buildup ($6 billion in 1961 alone) was the new strategy of "flexible response." The president could choose from a variety of military options in dealing with an international crisis rather than having to rely on the threat of nuclear annihilation in every instance (see Figure 25–1).

THE BERLIN CRISIS

John F. Kennedy's decision to focus on foreign affairs was prophetic; his term in office was punctuated by one confrontation after another with the forces of international communism. In June 1961, the leaders of the Soviet Union and the United States held a summit conference in Vienna. The ongoing problem of Berlin dominated their discussions. In an effort to stop the rearmament of West Germany and to halt the flow of skilled workers from communist East Berlin to the western sectors of the city, Khrushchev announced that his country was going to sign a separate peace treaty with the German Democratic Republic (GDR), the communist government of East Germany. Realizing that the German Democratic Republic was certain to cut off overland access from West Germany to West Berlin, Kennedy warned his adversary against such a step. The United States had gone to war twice to defend Western Europe, he said, and would do so again.

Figure 25–1
The Cold War

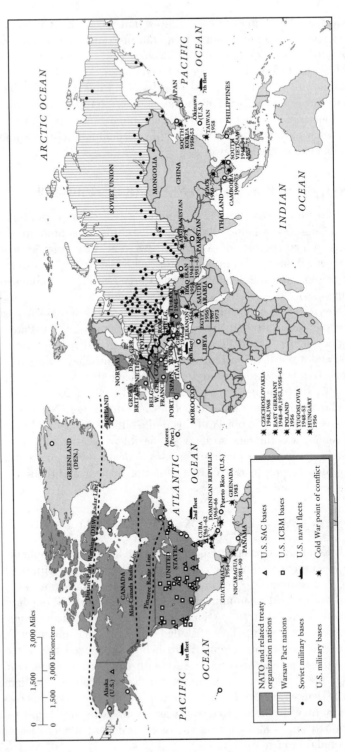

To stop the massive outflow of humanity from the east, communist authorities constructed a wall dividing Berlin.

With reports circulating in the press that Khrushchev had bullied him in Vienna, Kennedy decided to do some intimidating himself. On July 25, he delivered an impassioned television address to the American people. Declaring Berlin to be vital to the defense of the free world, he announced that he was asking for $3 billion more in defense spending to include construction of a nationwide system of defense shelters, and calling up a hundred and fifty thousand National Guardsmen and reservists to active duty. Aware of American nuclear superiority, Khrushchev beat a strategic retreat.

In August, Soviet occupation troops and East German soldiers began building the Berlin Wall to staunch the flow of emigrés to the west. The Soviet Union did in fact sign a separate treaty with East Germany, but the GDR made no move to cut off overland access to West Berlin. Neither side had won a victory, but Kennedy believed that he had demonstrated to friends and foes alike America's determination to honor its commitments. Credibility would become an increasingly important concept in the Cold War.

CUBA

The Bay of Pigs

In 1959, Cuban revolutionaries led by the charismatic Fidel Castro overthrew the corrupt and dictatorial regime headed by Fulgencio Batista. As Batista, his foreign bank accounts filled with wealth extorted from the Cuban people, fled to exile, Castro and his band of revolutionaries rode into Havana to take possession of the country. Certain that the Cuban military remained pro-U.S., Washington rushed to extend recognition and American businesses in the Ever Faithful Isle paid their taxes a year in advance. By 1960, however, the Cuban revolution had taken a sharp turn to the left. The new regime outlawed rival parties and jailed dissidents. Castro confiscated millions of dollars of private property, American and Cuban. Victims of government persecution and nationalization fled to Florida and other areas on the Gulf Coast.

With the encouragement of the Eisenhower administration and the help of the CIA, fourteen hundred Cuban exiles formed themselves into a military unit and began training in secret bases in Honduras. If they could stage a successful amphibious landing, they believed, the Cuban people would rally to their cause and overthrow Castro.

Soon after he was inaugurated, Kennedy was briefed on the plan. The CIA and Joint Chiefs of Staff urged him to reaffirm Eisenhower's commitment of U.S. naval and CIA support for the mission. The exiles were armed and ready to go. Castro had made no secret of his conversion to Marxism-Leninism and was then receiving massive aid from the Soviet Union. Kennedy's political advisors reminded him that he had castigated Eisenhower for permitting a Soviet satellite to be established "on our very doorstep." In addition, if the exiles were thwarted, they would return to the United States and claim that the Democrats lacked the courage to follow through on a Republican initiative.

Armed and transported by U.S. personnel, the Cuban exile brigade landed at the Bay of Pigs on April 17, 1961. They fought bravely and well, but soon faced some twenty-five thousand Cuban soldiers. The Honduran training bases had been a poorly kept secret, and Castro was fully prepared. With their ammunition running out and with Castro's air force in control of the skies over the beaches, the insurgents appealed for U.S. intervention. Kennedy refused, and as a result the nine hundred surviving exiles were forced to surrender at the end of the second day. The president was stunned by the collapse of the Bay of Pigs operation and by the torrent of criticism that engulfed him. On a national television hookup, he accepted personal responsibility for the raid but remained unrepentant. Clearly, he was sorry not for having violated the sovereignty of a neighboring country but for having failed to achieve Castro's ouster. Kennedy harassed his Cuban adversary for the remainder of his administration, imposing a trade embargo and tacitly authorizing several CIA assassination attempts.

The Cuban Missile Crisis

In response to U.S. aggression against their ally, the Soviets began a massive arms buildup in Cuba during the summer of 1962. Ostensibly, the move was made to protect Castro from another U.S.–sponsored invasion, but the twenty-four medium range (one thousand miles) and eighteen intermediate range (two thousand miles) missiles gave the Soviet Union and its Cuban ally more than a defensive capability in the Western Hemisphere. More than likely, Khrushchev's gamble was the result of pressure from his generals who were alarmed at the massive expansion of America's nuclear arsenal.

The communists tried to keep construction of the missile sites secret, repeatedly lying to the president and his brother, Robert. Tipped off either by the CIA or Cuban exiles as to the existence of the missile sites, GOP congressional leaders demanded an investigation. U-2 spy plane photos taken on October 14 revealed the alarming truth. American intelligence indicated that if the sites were completed and armed, the Soviets and/or Cubans would be able to rain nuclear destruction down on as many as eighty U.S. cities.

Huddling with his advisors on an almost continuous basis throughout the next two weeks, Kennedy considered a variety of options that ranged from an immediate air strike and invasion to acquiescence in the buildup. Gradually, the White House settled on a naval blockade, or quarantine, of Cuba to prevent the arrival of missiles and warheads. U.S. diplomats would then demand the removal of existing equipment; if the communists refused, the military would invade and dismantle the sites forcibly. On the evening of October 22, the president revealed the existence of the bases to the American people, denouncing their construction as "a clandestine, reckless, and provocative threat to world peace." He announced the blockade, demanded the removal of the missile bases, and made it clear that if warheads were launched from Cuba, the United States would retaliate against the Soviet Union.

For the next six days, the world teetered on the brink of Armageddon. Castro mobilized his armed forces, the United States began assembling an invasion force of a quarter of a million men, and Soviet missile transports headed toward the blockade of ships set up by the U.S. Navy around Cuba. On Wednesday, October 24, the Soviet ships went dead in the water. Over the next seventy-two hours, the White House and Kremlin exchanged a flurry of communications. Kennedy rejected a proposal whereby the Russians would agree to dismantle their bases in Cuba in return for a pullout of American Jupiter missiles from Turkey. Blustering and bluffing all the way, Khrushchev finally agreed on Sunday, October 28, to remove the missile sites from Cuba in return

A U-2 reconnaissance photograph showing the placement of Soviet rocket installations in Cuba.

for a U.S. promise not to invade Castro's communist republic. Infuriated, the Cuban leader subsequently refused to permit U.S. personnel to verify that launchers and missiles were being sent back to the Soviet Union. When, however, Russian naval commanders pulled back tarps on their ships to permit aerial inspection of the dismantled equipment, President Kennedy ordered an end to the naval blockade on November 20. The Cuban Missile Crisis was over.

America's 1962 confrontation with Cuba left a mixed legacy. Alarmed by just how close their nations had come to engaging in nuclear war, Kennedy and Khrushchev agreed to the installation of a hot line so that they and their successors could communicate directly and immediately if a similar situation developed in the future. The crisis gave a mild impetus to advocates of peaceful coexistence in both countries. In the late summer of 1963 the United States and the Soviet Union signed a nuclear test-ban treaty. At the same time the crisis and America's perceived victory strengthened the conviction of war hawks in the United States that the only way to deal with the communists was through the threat of force. Humiliated by the Cuban Missile Crisis, the Russian defense establishment swore "never again" and embarked on a crash naval and missile construction program. Within five years the Soviet Union possessed the nucleus of a modern navy and actually exceeded the United States in the number of ICBMs it possessed.

VIETNAM

Lost in the drama of the Berlin and Cuban crises was the growing American commitment to support and defend a noncommunist government in the far-off land of South Vietnam. After both Moscow and Beijing recognized Ho Chi Minh's government as the legitimate ruler of all of Vietnam in 1950, the United States concluded that the Democratic Republic of Vietnam (DRV) was a Sino-Soviet satellite and that Ho was a puppet of Stalin and Mao Ze-dong. Throughout the 1950s the Eisenhower administration poured economic and military aid into Vietnam. South Vietnam president Ngo Dinh Diem, a principled, patriotic man, briefly attempted land and constitutional reform, but he proved unsuited to the task of building a social democracy. A devout Catholic and traditional mandarin by temperament and philosophy, he distrusted the masses and had contempt for the give-and-take of democratic politics. Increasingly, he relied on his family and loyal Catholics in the military and civil service to rule a country in which 90 percent of the population was Buddhist. His brother Nhu used the Can Lao party, the press, and the state police to persecute and suppress opponents to the regime. As corruption increased and democracy all but disappeared, a rebellion broke out in the South against the Diem regime. In 1960 the DRV decided to give formal aid to the newly formed National Liberation Front, the name assumed by the anti-Diemist revolutionaries.

Kennedy and Diem

A variety of factors combined to ensure that President Kennedy would attempt to hold the line in South Vietnam. He viewed the conflict in South Vietnam as one of Khrushchev's wars of national liberation, a test of his administration's resolve just as much as Berlin or Cuba. Kennedy and his advisors fully accepted the domino theory whereby the fall of one government in a particular region threatened by communism was assumed to lead to the fall, in turn, of each of the other noncommunist governments in the area. His agreement in 1961 to the neutralization of Laos, a landlocked nation wracked by communist insurgency, further strengthened his resolve to hold the line in South Vietnam. In the fall of 1961, as the guerrilla war intensified, Rostow and the president's military aide, General Maxwell Taylor, returned from a fact-finding trip to South Vietnam to recommend the dispatch of eight thousand combat troops. The president decided against direct military intervention, but he ordered an increase in aid to Diem and the introduction of additional military advisors. The number of American uniformed personnel grew from several hundred when Kennedy assumed office to sixteen thousand by 1963.

Despite American aid, the Diem regime became increasingly isolated from the masses. Bribes and intimidation by civil servants and military officials alienated peasant and urban dweller alike. Law 10/59 which the government pushed through the rubber stamp national assembly gave Nhu's police and special forces the power to arrest and execute South Vietnamese citizens for a wide variety of crimes including black marketeering and spreading seditious rumors about the government. By 1963 the nation teetered on the brink of chaos with the Viet Cong (the military branch of the NLF) in control of the countryside, students and intellectuals demonstrating in Saigon and Hue, Buddhist monks burning themselves in protest, and high-ranking military officers hatching a variety of coup plots.

Shortly before his own assassination in November 1963, Kennedy tacitly approved a military coup in Saigon which led to the deaths of both Diem and Nhu. The president sensed that the United States was on the verge of plunging into a morass from which it could not extricate itself. Only the South Vietnamese themselves could establish a broad-based, noncommunist government and make the sacrifices necessary to sustain it. Without that commitment, all the American aid in the world would be for naught. And yet, he was unwilling for both political and strategic reasons to stand by and see Vietnam fall to the communists. Not only would America's credibility with its allies be damaged, there would be a Republican-led anticommunist backlash at home that could possibly produce a new wave of McCarthyism.

Because of the profound dangers involved, historians have repeatedly dissected the Cuban Missile Crisis in an effort to discover the forces and factors that brought the world to the edge of nuclear war. Traditional accounts of the event assert that Khrushchev ordered missiles into Cuba to discredit Kennedy, to shift dramatically the world balance of power in favor of the Soviet Union, or to signal to the United States that the Kremlin would not tolerate covert or overt efforts to overthrow Fidel Castro. These historians have faulted Kennedy for overreacting to the missile buildup or for mishandling the crisis after it had begun, but they have given little credence to the notion that Kennedy was committed to the Cuban leader's ouster by whatever means.

In the interpretive piece that follows, Thomas G. Paterson describes the ongoing efforts of the Kennedy administration to overthrow the Castro government. John and Robert's obsession with the revolutionary regime in Havana was unreasonable, Paterson argues. It was, to use J. William Fulbright's phrase, "a thorn in the side, not a dagger in the heart." And, finally, the stationing of Soviet missiles in Cuba grew out of Castro's recognition that if the Kennedy administration could not assassinate him through subversion, it would once again resort to direct military action. In short, Paterson writes, "The origins of the October 1962 crisis derived largely from the concerted U.S. campaign to quash the Cuban revolution."

SPINNING OUT OF CONTROL: JOHN F. KENNEDY, THE WAR AGAINST CUBA, AND THE MISSILE CRISIS

Thomas G. Paterson

"My God," muttered Richard Helms of the Central Intelligence Agency, "these Kennedys keep the pressure on about [Fidel] Castro." Another CIA officer heard it straight from John F. and Robert F. Kennedy: "Get off your ass about Cuba." Defense Secretary Robert McNamara remembered that "we were hysterical about Castro at the time of the Bay of Pigs and thereafter." As someone said, *Cuba* became one of the four-letter words of the 1960s.

A knowledgeable and engaged President Kennedy spent as much time on Cuba as on any other foreign-policy problem—or more. Cuba stood at the center of his administration's admitted greatest failure, the Bay of Pigs, and its alleged greatest success, the missile crisis. Why did President Kennedy and his chief advisers indulge such a fixation with Cuba and direct so many U.S. resources to an unrelenting campaign to monitor, harass, isolate, and ultimately destroy Havana's radical regime? One answer springs from a candid remark by Robert F. Kennedy, who later wondered "if we did not pay a very great price for being more energetic than wise about a lot of things, especially Cuba." The Kennedys' famed eagerness for action became exaggerated in the case of Cuba. They always wanted to get moving on Cuba, and Castro dared them to try. The popular, intelligent, but erratic Cuban leader, who in January 1959 overthrew the U.S. ally Fulgencio Batista, hurled harsh words at Washington and defiantly challenged the Kennedy model of evolutionary, capitalist development so evident in the Alliance for Progress. As charismatic figures charting new frontiers, Kennedy and Castro often personalized the Cuban-American contest. To Kennedy's great annoyance, Castro could not be wheedled or beaten.

Kennedy's ardent war against *fidelismo* may also have stemmed from his feeling that Castro had double-crossed him. As a senator, Kennedy had initially joined many other Americans in welcoming the Cuban Revolution as an advancement over the "oppressive" Batista dictatorship. Kennedy had urged a "patient attitude" toward the new government, which he did not see as communist. Castro had in fact denied repeatedly that he was a communist, instead proclaiming his allegiance to

from Thomas G. Paterson, ed., *Major Problems in American Foreign Relations, Vol. II: Since 1914* (Lexington, MA: D.C. Heath, 1995), 495–507.

democracy and private property. But in the process of legitimizing his revolution and resisting U.S. pressure, Castro turned more and more radical. Americans grew impatient with the regime's highly charged anti-Yankeeism, postponement of elections, jailing of critics, and nationalization of property. The president rejected the idea that intense U.S. hostility toward the Cuban Revolution may have contributed to Castro's tightening political grip and flirtation with the Soviet Union. Nor did Kennedy and other Americans wish to acknowledge the measurable benefits of the revolution—improvements in education, medical care, and housing and the elimination of the island's infamous corruption that once had been the American Mafia's domain. Instead, Kennedy officials concluded that Cuba's was a "betrayed revolution."

Richard N. Goodwin, at the time a young White House and State Department official, provided another explanation for the Kennedy fixation with Cuba. He remarked that "the entire history of the Cold War, its positions and assumptions, converged upon the 'problem of Cuba.'" Indeed, the Cold War dominated international politics, and in the zero-sum accounting of the time, a loss for "us" meant a gain for "them." As Cuban-American relations steadily deteriorated, Cuban-Soviet relations gradually improved. Not only did Americans come to believe that a once loyal ally had jilted them for the tawdry embrace of the Soviets; they also grew alarmed that Castro sneered at the Monroe Doctrine by inviting the Soviet military to the island. When Castro, in late 1961, declared himself a Marxist-Leninist, Americans who had long denounced him as a communist felt vindicated. American leaders began to speak of Cuban membership in the "Sino-Soviet bloc," thus providing communists with a "spearhead" to penetrate the Western Hemisphere. From the moment of victory, Castro had called for Cuban-style revolutions throughout Latin America, and Havana had sent agents and arms to other nations to kindle radical fires. Castro's revolutionary mission happened to coincide with Nikita Khrushchev's alarming statement that the Soviet Union supported wars of national liberation worldwide. Cuba came to represent the Cold War in the Western Hemisphere.

In addition to the Kennedy style and the Cold War, domestic politics influenced the administration's Cuba policy. In the 1960 presidential campaign, Kennedy had seized the Cuban issue to counter Richard Nixon's charge that the inexperienced Democratic candidate would abandon the Chinese islands of Jinmen (Quemoy) and Mazu (Matsu) to communism and prove no match for the hardnosed Khrushchev. "In 1952 the Republicans ran on a program of rolling back the Iron Curtain in Eastern Europe," Kennedy jabbed. "Today the Iron Curtain is ninety miles off the coast of the United States." . . .

Overarching all explanations for Kennedy's obsession with Cuba is a major phenomenon of twentieth-century world history: the steady erosion of the authority of imperial powers, which had built systems of dependent, client, and colonial governments. The strong currents of decolonization, anti-imperialism, revolutionary nationalism, and social revolution, sometimes in combination, undermined the instruments that the imperial nations had used to maintain control and order. The Cuban Revolution exemplified this process of breaking up and breaking away. American leaders reacted especially hostilely to this revolution not simply because

Castro and his 26th of July Movement taunted them or because domestic politics and the Cold War swayed them but because Cuba, as symbol and reality, challenged U.S. hegemony in Latin America. The specter of "another Cuba" haunted President Kennedy, not just because it would hurt him politically but because "the game would be up through a good deal of Latin America," as Under Secretary of State George Ball put it. The Monroe Doctrine and the U.S. claim to political, economic, and military leadership in the hemisphere seemed at stake. As Castro once remarked, "The United States *had* to fight his revolution." . . .

Eisenhower failed to topple Castro, but American pressure accelerated the radicalization of the revolution and helped to open the door to the Soviets. Moscow bought sugar, supplied technicians, armed the militia, and offered generous trade terms. Although the revolution's radicalization, given Cuban conditions, was probably inevitable, it was not preordained that Cuba would end up in the Soviet camp. Hostile U.S. policies helped to ensure that outcome. Revolutionary Cuba needed outside assistance to survive. "Russia came to Castro's rescue," Ambassador Philip Bonsal has concluded, "only after the United States had taken steps designed to overthrow him."

To be sure, Kennedy inherited the Cuban problem from Eisenhower. But he did not simply continue his predecessor's anti-Castro policies. Kennedy greatly exaggerated the Cuban threat, attributing to Castro a capability to export revolution that the Cuban leader never had and lavishing on him an attention he did not deserve. . . .

The questions of whether and under what conditions to approve an exile expedition dominated the president's discussion of Cuba in his first few months in office. Although Kennedy always reserved the authority to cancel the operation right up to the moment of departure, his choices pointed in one direction: Go. National security affairs adviser McGeorge Bundy later said that the president "really was looking for ways to make it work . . . and allowed himself to be persuaded it would work and the risks were acceptable." . . .

The Bay of Pigs plan began to unravel from the start. As the brigade's old, slow freighters plowed their way to Cuba, B-26 airplanes took to the skies from Nicaragua. On April 15, D-Day-minus-2, the brigade pilots destroyed several parked planes of Castro's meager air force. That same day, as part of a preinvasion ploy, a lone, artificially damaged B-26 flew directly to Miami, where its pilot claimed that he had defected from the Cuban military and had just bombed his country's airfields. But the cover story soon cracked. Snooping journalists noticed that the nose cone of the B-26 was metal; Cuban planes had plastic noses. They observed, too, that the aircraft's guns had not been fired. The American hand was being exposed. The president, still insistent on hiding U.S. complicity, decided to cancel a second D-Day air strike against the remnants of the Cuban air force.

Shortly after midnight on April 17, more than fourteen hundred commandoes motored in small boats to the beaches at Bahía de Cochinos, where they immediately tangled with Castro's militia. But some commandoes never made it, because their boats broke apart on razor-sharp coral reefs. Castro's marauding airplanes shot down two brigade B-26s and sank ships carrying essential communications equipment and ammunition. Fighting ferociously, the brigade nonetheless failed to establish a beachhead. Would Washington try to salvage the mission? Kennedy turned down CIA appeals to dispatch planes from the nearby USS *Essex,* but he did permit some jets to provide air cover for a new B-26 attack from Nicaragua. Piloted this time by American CIA crews, the B-26s arrived an hour after the jets had come and gone. Cuban aircraft downed the B-26s, killing four Americans. With Castro's boasting that the *mercenarios* had been foiled, the final toll: 114 of the exile brigade dead and 1,189 captured; 150 Cuban defenders dead.

"How could I have been so stupid, to let them go ahead?" Kennedy asked an assistant. Stupid or not, Kennedy knew the answers to his own question. First, he dearly sought to oust Castro and to score a victory in the Cold War. Second, his personality and style encouraged action. Always driven to win, Kennedy believed (as one aide put it) "that his disapproval of the plan would be a show of weakness inconsistent with his general stance." . . . Third, fear of nasty political repercussions influenced the president. Told to disband, brigade members might have refused to give up their arms or might even have mutinied. In any case, Republicans would have scorned a weak-kneed administration. . . .

Failures in intelligence, operations, decisionmaking, and judgment doomed the Bay of Pigs undertaking. Arrogant CIA architects knew too little about the landing site and assumed too much about Cuba. The CIA also failed to assassinate Fidel Castro. As one CIA official admitted, the agency intended "that Castro would be dead before the landing." . . .

Kennedy and his advisers believed that the invasion would ignite a popular revolt against an unpopular government. Yet no rebellion erupted. Kennedy also assumed that, should the brigade prove incapable of taking territory, it could melt into the mountains and become a guerrilla army. But the mountains lay eighty miles away, with impassable swamps between. The guerrilla option proved impossible. As well, Kennedy officials nurtured the fiction that American participation could be hidden and plausibly denied. "Trying to mount an operation of this magnitude from the United States," a CIA official later wrote, "is about as covert as walking nude across Times Square without attracting attention." Until his decision to cancel the second strike, Kennedy nonetheless clung to the fiction of deniability. . . .

Defeat did not chasten the administration. On April 20 the beleaguered president spoke out. "Let the record show," he boomed, "that our restraint is not inexhaustible." Indeed, the United States intended to defend the Monroe Doctrine and carry on a "relentless" struggle with communism in "every corner of the globe." In familiar words, Kennedy declared that "the complacent, the self-indulgent, the soft societies are about to be swept away with the debris of history. Only the strong . . . can possibly survive." Attorney General Robert Kennedy remarked that the Bay of Pigs "insult needed to be redressed rather quickly."

Critical to understanding the missile crisis of fall 1962 is the relationship between post–Bay of Pigs U.S. activities and the Soviet-Cuban decisions to place on the island missiles that could strike the United States. In May 1962 Soviet and Cuban officials first discussed the idea of deploying nuclear-tipped missiles on the island; in July Raúl Castro, in Moscow, initialed an agreement: in late August and early

September, during a trip by Che Guevara to Moscow, the two nations put the accord into final form.

After the Bay of Pigs, the Kennedy administration launched a multitrack program of covert, economic, diplomatic, and propagandistic elements calculated to overthrow the Castro government. This multidimensional project prompted the Cuban-Soviet decisions of mid-1962. Secretary of Defense Robert McNamara said later: "If I had been in Moscow or Havana at that time [1961–1962], I would have believed the Americans were preparing for an invasion." Indeed, Havana had to fear a successful Bay of Pigs operation conducted by U.S. forces.

Encouraged by the White House, the CIA created a huge station in Miami called JM/WAVE to recruit and organize Cuban exiles. In Washington, Robert Kennedy became a ramrod for action. At a November 4, 1961, White House meeting, the attorney general made his pitch: "Stir things up on the island with espionage, sabotage, general disorder." The president himself asked Colonel Edward Lansdale to direct Operation Mongoose—"to use our available assets . . . to help Cuba overthrow the Communist regime." Operation Mongoose and JM/WAVE, although failing to unseat Castro, punished Cubans. CIA-handled saboteurs burned cane fields and blew up factories and oil-storage tanks. In a December 1961 raid, for example, a seven-man team blasted a railroad bridge, derailed an approaching train, and torched a sugar warehouse. One group, Agrupacíon Montecristi, attacked a Cuban patrol boat off the northern coast of the island in May 1962. Directorio Revolutionario Estudiantil, another exile organization, used two boats to attack Cuba in August. Alpha 66 attacked Cuba on numerous occasions. CIA agents contaminated goods leaving European ports for Cuba, and they bribed European manufacturers to produce faulty equipment for Cuba—as when a German industrialist shipped off-center ball bearings. British-made Leyland buses were sabotaged, too. These spoiling operations compelled the Castro government to divert scarce resources from economic and social programs to coastal defense and internal surveillance. They also pushed Cuba toward greater dependence on the Soviet Union.

By 1962 more than two hundred anti-Castro, Cuban exile organizations operated in the United States. Many of them banded together under the leadership of José Miró Cardona, the former prime minister. Miró Cardona met with President Kennedy in Washington on April 10, 1962, and the Cuban exile left the meeting persuaded that Kennedy intended to use U.S. armed forces against Cuba. Indeed, after Miró Cardona returned to Miami, he and the Revolutionary Council—the government in exile—began to identify possible recruits for a Cuban unit in the U.S. military.

The CIA, meanwhile, devised new plots to kill Castro with poisonous cigars, pills, and needles—to no avail. Did the Kennedys know about these death schemes? Robert Kennedy learned about them in mid-1962, and his biographer Arthur M. Schlesinger, Jr., claims that the attorney general ordered an end to assassination projects. But they did not end. The president apparently never directly ordered the assassination of Castro—at least, no trail of documents leads to the Kennedy White House. But of course, nobody uttered the word *assassination* in the presence of the president or committed the word to paper, thereby honoring the principle of plausible deniability. Advisers instead simply mentioned the need to remove Castro. "And if killing him was one of the things that was to be done in this connection," assassination was attempted because "we felt we were acting within the guidelines." So bespoke the CIA's Richard Helms. President Kennedy may or may not have known about the assassination plots, but he did set the general guidelines.

Intensified economic coercion joined forces with these covert activities. The Kennedy administration banned most imports of Cuban products in February 1962. Washington also pressed its North Atlantic Treaty Organization allies to support the "economic isolation" of Cuba. The embargo hurt. Cuba had to pay higher freight costs, enlarge its foreign debt, and suffer innumerable factory shutdowns because industries could no longer obtain spare parts once bought in the United States. . . .

The Kennedy administration engineered Cuba's ouster from the Organization of American States in early 1962. The expulsion registered loudly in Havana, which interpreted it as "political preparation for an invasion." By spring 1962, moreover, fifteen Latin American states had answered Washington's call to break relations with Cuba.

At about the same time, American military planning and activities—some public, some secret—demonstrated a determination to cripple the Castro government. Operation Mongoose director Lansdale noted in a top-secret memorandum to the president that he designed his schemes to "help the people of Cuba overthrow the Communist regime from within Cuba and institute a new government." But he asked: "If conditions and assets permitting a revolt [timed for October 1962] are achieved in Cuba, and if U.S. help is required to sustain this condition, will the U.S. respond promptly with military force to aid the Cuban revolt?" Lansdale gave the answer he preferred: "The basic plan requires complete and efficient support of the military." Another contemporary document, this one from the chairman of the Joint Chiefs of Staff, General Maxwell Taylor, noted in the spring of 1962 that the Operation Mongoose plan to overthrow the Cuban government would be undertaken largely by "indigenous resources" but recognized "that final success will require decisive U.S. military intervention." Because the plan also required close cooperation with Cuban exiles, it is likely that Castro's spies picked up from the leaky Cuban community in Miami at least vague suggestions that the U.S. military contemplated military action against Cuba. As CIA agents liked to joke, there were three ways to transmit information rapidly: telegraph, telephone, and tell-a-Cuban.

American military maneuvers heightened Cuban fears. One well-publicized U.S. exercise, staged during April, included 40,000 troops and an amphibious landing on a small island near Puerto Rico. Throughout 1962 some noisy American politicians called for the real thing: an invasion of Cuba. In summer 1962, moreover, the U.S. Army began a program to create Spanish-speaking units; the Cuban exiles who signed up had as their "primary" goal a "return to Cuba to battle against the Fidel Castro regime."

By the late spring and early summer of 1962, then, when Havana and Moscow discussed defensive measures that included medium-range missiles, Cuba felt besieged from several quarters. The Soviet Union had become its trading partner, and the Soviets, after the Bay of Pigs, had begun military shipments that included small arms, howitzers, machine guns, armored personnel carriers, patrol boats, tanks, MiG jet fighters, and surface-to-air missiles (SAMs). Yet all this weaponry, it seemed, had not deterred the United States. Given the failure, moreover, of Kennedy's multitrack program to unseat Castro, "were we right or wrong to fear direct invasion [next]?" asked Fidel Castro. As he said in July 1962, shortly after striking the missile-deployment agreement with the Soviets: "We must prepare ourselves for that direct invasion."

Had there been no exile expedition at the Bay of Pigs, no destructive covert activities, no assassination plots, no military maneuvers and plans, and no economic and diplomatic steps to harass, isolate, and destroy the Castro government in Havana, the Cuban missile crisis would not have occurred. The origins of the October 1962 crisis derived largely from the concerted U.S. campaign to quash the Cuban Revolution. To stress only the global dimension (Soviet-American competition), as is commonly done, is to slight the local or regional sources of the conflict and thus to miss the central point that Premier Nikita Khrushchev would never have had the opportunity to install dangerous missiles in the Caribbean if the United States had not been attempting to overthrow the Cuban government. This interpretation does not dismiss but incorporates the view, predominant in the scholarly literature, that the emplacement of nuclear missiles in Cuba served the Soviet strategic goal of catching up in the nuclear-arms race. Rather, the interpretation in this essay emphasizes that both Cuba and the Soviet Union calculated that their interests would be served by putting medium- and intermediate-range rockets on the island. Havana hoped to gain deterrent power to thwart an expected American invasion, and Moscow hoped to enhance its deterrent power in the Cold War and save a new ally. From Castro's perspective, the United States would not start a local, conventional war out of fear that it would then have to risk a nuclear war.

"We'd carried out the Bay of Pigs operation, never intending to use American military force—but the Kremlin didn't know that," Defense Secretary Robert Mc-Namara recalled. "We were running covert operations against Castro" and "people in the Pentagon were even talking about a first strike [nuclear policy]. . . . So the Soviets may well have believed we were seeking Castro's overthrow *plus* a first strike capability. This may have led them to do what they did in Cuba." . . .

Why did the Cubans and Soviets decide on medium (MRBM) and intermediate (IRBM) missiles, with ranges of 1,020 and 2,200 nautical miles, respectively, instead of on a military pact, nonnuclear, conventional forces, or weapons that might meet the U.S. definition of "defensive"? The answer is that the Cubans sought effective deterrence. One is reminded of similar American thinking, near the end of the Second World War, that the Japanese were so fanatical that only the threat of annihilation from the atomic bomb would persuade them to surrender. The Cubans, in fact, looking for an immediate deterrent effect, had wanted to make the 1962 missile agreement public, but the Soviets, guessing that the deployment could be camouflaged until the missiles became operational, preferred secrecy.

On October 14 an American U-2 plane photographed the missile sites in Cuba, thus providing the first hard evidence, as distinct from the reports of exiles, that the island was becoming a nuclear base. "He can't do that to me!" snapped Kennedy when he saw the pictures two days later. He had warned the Soviets that the United States would not suffer "offensive" weapons in Cuba, although the warnings had come after the Cuban-Soviet decision of early summer. The president convened his top advisers shortly before noon on October 16. His first questions focused on the firing readiness of the missiles and the probability that they carried nuclear warheads. The advisers gave negative, although tentative, answers. All agreed that the missiles could become operational in a brief time. . . .

For the next several days, Kennedy's advisers, named the Executive Committee (ExCom), met frequently in tight secrecy and discussed four policy options: "talk them out," "squeeze them out," "shoot them out," or "buy them out." In exhausting sessions marked by frank disagreement and changing minds, Excom members weighed the advantages and disadvantages of invasion, bombing, quarantine, and diplomacy. The president gradually moved with a majority of ExCom advisers toward a quarantine or blockade of Cuba: incoming ships would be stopped and inspected for military cargo. McNamara persistently argued this alternative against the generals, Treasury Secretary Douglas Dillon, CIA director John McCone, and Dean Acheson, all of whom urged an air strike. When queried as to whether an air strike would knock out all of the known missiles, however, Taylor replied: "The best we can offer you is to destroy 90%." In other words, some missiles in Cuba would remain in place for firing against the United States. . . .

By October 22 the president had made two decisions. The first was to quarantine Cuba to prevent further military shipments and to impress the Soviets with U.S. resolve to force the missiles out. If the Soviets kept coming, more drastic measures would be taken. Second, Kennedy decided to inform the Soviets of U.S. policy through a television address rather than through diplomatic channels. ExCom advisers have dubiously argued that a surprise public speech became necessary to rally world opinion behind U.S. policy and to prevent Khrushchev himself from issuing a "blustering ultimatum." But some ExCom participants advised that negotiations be tried first. . . .

In his evening televised speech on October 22, Kennedy demanded that the Soviets dismantle the missiles in Cuba, and he announced the Caribbean quarantine as an "initial" step. The missile crisis soon became an international war of nerves. More than sixty American ships began patrols to enforce the blockade. The Strategic Air Command went on nuclear alert, moving upward to Defense Condition (DEFCON) 2 for the first time ever (the next level is deployment for combat). B-52 bombers, loaded with nuclear weapons, stood ready, while men and equipment moved to the southeastern United States to prepare for an invasion. The Soviets did not mobilize or redeploy their huge military, nor did they take measures to make their strategic forces less vulnerable. The Soviets also refrained from testing the quarantine: Their ships turned around and went home. But what next? On October 26 Kennedy and some ExCom members, thinking that the Soviets were stalling, soured on the quarantine. Sentiment for military action strengthened.

The "first real blink" in the crisis came in the afternoon of October 26. A Soviet embassy officer, Aleksander Fomin, met with ABC television correspondent John

Scali and urged him to carry a message to the State Department: The Soviet Union would withdraw the missiles if the United States would promise not to invade Cuba. Scali scurried to Rusk, who sent the emissary back to Fomin with the reply that American leaders were interested in discussing the proposal. In the meantime, a rambling private Khrushchev letter arrived with the same offer, claiming that the missiles had been deployed in Cuba only because the United States had been threatening the island.

In the morning of October 27, another Khrushchev message came, upping the stakes: Khrushchev would trade the missiles in Cuba for the American missiles in Turkey. Kennedy felt trapped, because "we are now in the position of risking war in Cuba and in Berlin over missiles in Turkey which are of little military value." . . .

In the afternoon of October 27 more bad news rocked the White House. An American U-2 plane overflew the eastern part of the Soviet Union, probably because its equipment malfunctioned. Soviet fighters scrambled to intercept it, and American jets from Alaska took flight to rescue the errant aircraft. Although the spy plane flew home without having sparked a dogfight, the incident carried the potential of sending the crisis to a more dangerous level. Worse still, a U-2 was shot down over Cuba by a surface-to-air missile (SAM). The shootdown constituted a serious escalation. A distressed McNamara now thought that "invasion had become almost inevitable." But Kennedy hesitated to retaliate, surely scared about taking a step toward a nuclear nightmare. The president decided to ignore Khrushchev's second letter and answer the first. And he dispatched his brother Robert to deliver an ultimatum to Soviet ambassador Anatoly Dobrynin: Start pulling out the missiles within forty-eight hours, or "we would remove them." . . . well invade Cuba with all its toil . . . when we could have gotten them out by making a deal on the same missiles in Turkey." But should the Soviets leak word of a "deal," Robert Kennedy told the Soviet ambassador, the United States would disavow the offer.

On October 28, faced with an ultimatum and a concession, and fearful that the Cubans might precipitate a greater Soviet-American conflagration, Khrushchev re-treated. Washington and Moscow struck an agreement. The Soviet Union promised to dismantle the SS-4s and SS-5s under United Nations supervision, and the United States pledged not to invade Cuba. The crisis had ended just when the nuclear giants seemed about to stumble over the brink. Although an embittered Castro thwarted a United Nations inspection system, U.S. reconnaissance planes monitored the missiles' departure. The Soviets also crated IL-28 bombers and shipped them back to the Soviet Union. In April 1963 the Jupiter missiles came down in Turkey. But Castro remained skeptical of the no-invasion pledge. As he once remarked to U Thant, it was difficult for Cubans to believe a simple American "promise not to commit a crime."

John F. Kennedy's handling of the Cuban missile crisis has received high grades as a stunning success and a model for crisis management. Secretary of State Dean Rusk applauded Kennedy for having "ice water in his veins." Arthur M. Schlesinger, Jr., has effusively written that Kennedy's crisis leadership constituted a "combination of toughness and restraint, of will, nerve, and wisdom, so brilliantly controlled, so matchlessly calibrated." Kennedy's handling of the crisis, as we know from declassified documents today, actually stands less as a supreme display of careful crisis management and more as a case of near misses, close calls, and narrow squeaks that scared officials on both sides into a settlement, because, in the words of McGeorge Bundy, the crisis was "so near to spinning out of control." "We were in luck," Ambassador John Kenneth Galbraith ruminated, "but success in a lottery is no argument for lotteries."

During the hair-trigger days of the crisis, much went wrong, the level of danger constantly rose, and weary and irritable decisionmakers sensed that they were losing their grip. "A high risk of uncontrollable escalation" dogged the crisis, as McNamara recalled. So much came apart; so much could not be reined in. The two U-2 incidents—the shootdown over Cuba and the straying over Soviet territory—rank high on the list. . . .

Not until October 27—to cite another misstep—did the administration think to inform the Soviets that the quarantine line was an arc measured at 500 nautical miles from Cape Maisi, Cuba. What if a Soviet captain inadvertently piloted his ship into the blockade zone? Danger lurked, too, in the way the commander of the Strategic Air Command issued DEFCON 2 alert instructions. He did so in the clear, instead of in code, because he wanted to impress the Soviets. Alerts serve to prepare American forces for war, but they may also provoke an adversary to think that the United States might launch a first strike. Under such circumstances, the adversary might be tempted to strike first. . . .

ExCom members represented considerable intellectual talent and experience, and the policy they urged on the president ultimately forced the Soviets to back down. But a mythology of grandeur, illusion of control, and embellishment of performance have obscured the history of the committee. ExCom debated alternatives under "intense strain," often in a "state of anxiety and emotional exhaustion." Two advisers may have suffered such stress that they became passive and unable to perform their responsibilities. An assistant to Adlai Stevenson recalled that he had had to become an ExCom "backup" for the ambassador because, "while he could speak clearly, his memory wasn't very clear." . . .

As for the Soviets, they, too, sensed a crisis spinning out of control. Khrushchev's letter of October 26 to Kennedy betrayed desperation, if not disarray, in the Kremlin. "You and I should not now pull on the ends of the rope in which you have tied a knot of war, because the harder you and I pull, the tighter the knot will become," the Soviet premier wrote. When the knot becomes too tight, Khrushchev observed, it will have to be cut, unleashing the "dread forces our two countries possess." Khrushchev also had to worry about *his* field commanders. We now know from Russian accounts that Soviet forces in Cuba possessed short-range nuclear missiles and that they had standing orders to use them if U.S. troops invaded the island—in short, the commander in Cuba, on his own, could have ordered their use. Given these circumstances and the downing of the U-2 over

Cuba, Khrushchev, too, faced a failure of control and the possible ascendancy of accident.

Add to these worries the Soviet premier's troubles with Fidel Castro, who demanded a bold Soviet response to U.S. actions and who might provoke an incident with the United States that could escalate the crisis. Castro pressed the Soviets to use nuclear weapons to save Cuba should the United States attack. "Such adventurists," remarked a Soviet decisionmaker. Khrushchev sternly told his advisers: "You see how far things can go. We've got to get those missiles out of there before a real fire starts." He sensed that time was running out, that events were outpacing the wits of leaders. The United States might strike Cuba from the air and invade, and then what? Like Kennedy, to head off disaster, he appealed for a settlement—and the two men and nations compromised. That Khrushchev had grown nervous and fearful about another dangerous twist in the crisis seems clear, because he took the unusual step of announcing the withdrawal of the missiles in a message on Radio Moscow. He did not want to waste the precious time that would have been required to encode, transmit, decode, and translate a diplomatic message. If the crisis had lasted more than thirteen days, remembered a U.S. adviser, "the whole thing would have begun to unravel."

President Kennedy helped to precipitate the missile crisis by harassing Cuba through his multitrack program. Then he reacted to the crisis by suspending diplomacy in favor of public confrontation. In the end, with the management of the crisis disintegrating, he frightened himself. In order to postpone doomsday, or at least to prevent a high-casualty invasion of Cuba, he moderated the American response and compromised. Khrushchev withdrew his missiles, while gaining what Ambassador Llewellyn Thompson thought was the "important thing" all along for the Soviet leader: being able to say "I saved Cuba. I stopped an invasion."

SUGGESTED READINGS

Vaughn D. Bornet, *The Presidency of Lyndon B. Johnson* (1983).

Carl Brauer, *John F. Kennedy and the Second Reconstruction* (1977).

Robert Caro, *Means of Ascent: The Years of Lyndon Johnson* (1990).

Robert Dallek, *Lone Star Rising: Lyndon Johnson and His Times* (1991).

John Lewis Gaddis, *Strategies of Containment: A Critical Appraisal of Postwar American National Security Policy* (1982).

Daniel Knapp and Kenneth Polk, *Scouting the War on Poverty: Social Reform Politics in the Kennedy Administration* (1971).

Allen Matusow, *The Unraveling of America: A History of Liberalism in the 1960s* (1984).

Walter A. McDougall, *The Heavens and the Earth: A Political History of the Space Age* (1985).

Herbert Parmet, *JFK: The Presidency of John F. Kennedy* (1983).

David Reimers, *Still the Golden Door: The Third World Comes to America*, 2nd ed. (1992).

FURTHER READINGS

Kennedy and the New Frontier

David Burner, *John F. Kennedy and a New Generation* (1988); James N. Giglio, *The Presidency of John F. Kennedy* (1991); Seymour Harris, *Economics of the Kennedy Years* (1964); Gerard T. Rice, *The Bold Experiment: JFK's Peace Corps* (1985); Arthur Schlesinger, Jr., *A Thousand Days* (1965); Garry Wills, *The Kennedy Imprisonment* (1982).

The Civil Rights Movement During the Kennedy Administration

Jack Bloom, *Class, Race, and the Civil Rights Movement* (1987); James Forman, *The Making of Black Revolutionaries* (1985); Ann Moody, *Coming of Age in Mississippi* (1970); Robert J. Norrell, *Reaping the Whirlwind: The Civil Rights Movement in Tuskegee* (1985); Harris Wofford, *Of Kennedys and Kings* (1980).

The Cold War During the Early 1960s

Graham Allison, *Essence of Decision* (1971); Michael Beschloss, *The Crisis Years: Kennedy and Khrushchev, 1961–1963* (1991); Trumbull Higgins, *The Perfect Failure: Kennedy, Eisenhower, and the CIA at the Bay of Pigs* (1987); Robert Kennedy, *Thirteen Days* (1969); Robert M. Slusser, *The Berlin Crisis of 1961* (1973).

QUESTIONS FOR DISCUSSION

1. Explain John F. Kennedy's election as president in 1960.
2. What was the New Frontier? How did it compare to other reform traditions in American history?
3. Were Kennedy's economic policies successful? Why or why not?
4. Analyze the Kennedy administration's record on civil rights.
5. Describe the policy of "flexible response" and assess the president's performance during the Berlin Crisis.
6. Explain American support for Diem during the Vietnam War. Was this a mistake?
7. According to Thomas G. Paterson, who was to blame for the Cuban Missile Crisis? What evidence does he cite?

CHAPTER TWENTY-SIX

THE TRAGEDY OF AMERICAN LIBERALISM:
Lyndon Johnson, the Great Society, and Vietnam

American liberalism seemed in full bloom in the mid-1960s. John F. Kennedy's successor in the White House guided through Congress the greatest reform program since the New Deal. The nation declared war on poverty and attempted to guarantee adequate medical care, nutrition, education, and housing to every citizen, regardless of color. In foreign affairs, the United States held the Soviet Union at bay with its huge military arsenal while confronting communist subversion in the developing world with economic and military aid. And then disaster struck—African Americans were bitterly disillusioned when the civil rights measures of the mid-1960s did not alleviate their poverty or eliminate their oppression and this coupled with a white backlash created a series of urban riots that left several inner-city ghettos smoldering ruins. Meanwhile, in its effort to defend the peoples of the Third World against the forces of international communism, the United States became bogged down in a war in Southeast Asia that was primarily civil in nature and that had more to do with indigenous nationalism than the conflict between communism and capitalism.

THE KENNEDY ASSASSINATION

John F. Kennedy might have won more impressively in 1964 than he had in 1960 and translated that into legislative victories during his second term, but fate intervened. On November 22, 1963, while on a campaign swing through Texas, the president was shot dead by a twenty-four-year-old ex-marine drifter

JFK's visit to Dallas in 1963 began on an upbeat note but ended in disaster. The president, Mrs. Kennedy, and Governor John Connally on their way past the Texas School Book Depository.

named Lee Harvey Oswald. Suddenly, Lyndon Baines Johnson was president of the United States. Prospects for passage of the Democratic reform program were brighter than if the incumbent had just won a landslide victory at the polls.

LYNDON JOHNSON'S VISION

Lyndon Johnson was born on August 27, 1908, in a farmhouse near the central Texas town of Stonewall. He was the eldest of the five children of Sam Ealy Johnson, Jr., a farmer and schoolteacher who served five terms in the lower house of the Texas legislature, and Rebekah Baines Johnson, also a schoolteacher. In high school in Johnson City, where his family moved when he was five, Lyndon proved to be an unwilling but rather successful student. After riding the rails in California for a time, he decided to attend Southwest Texas State Teacher's College in San Marcos. Upon graduation he taught secondary school for a year in Houston and then took a job as secretary to newly elected congressman Richard Kleberg, owner of the famous King Ranch. Within months he had mastered the system and ingratiated himself with veteran Capitol Hill operatives.

In 1937 Johnson decided to run for Congress himself and won. He quickly became a White House favorite, supporting a variety of New Deal programs which benefitted the nation as a whole and his home state in particular. Following a noncombat stint in the navy during World War II, Johnson ran successfully for the Senate in 1948 against former governor Coke Stevenson, a dyed-in-the-wool Texas conservative. Johnson's margin of victory was razor-thin; his enemies would charge thereafter that fraud had made the difference. In 1952 Johnson became Senate minority whip, at forty-four the youngest person to occupy a leadership position in the upper house. When the Democrats regained control of the Senate in 1955, he was elected majority leader. For the next five years he teamed with Eisenhower and Dulles to control the flow of foreign and domestic policy. His refusal to sign the Southern Manifesto and his support for the Civil Rights Acts of 1957 and 1960 spared Johnson the stigma of southern racism and made possible his nomination for the vice presidency in 1960.

Lyndon Johnson was a gigantic figure, a dynamo forever laboring to cajole or coerce legislators, interest groups, and the press into supporting his programs. A man of immense accomplishment and intense insecurity, Johnson was determined to prove to the eastern establishment that he was greater than any figure that it had produced. Personally, he was a man of paradox. Constantly working to accommodate his deeply rooted commitment to economic and social justice to political reality, he exuded cool confidence and iron determination one minute and gave in to fits of doubt and self-pity the next. Johnson was imbued with real concern for the poor and deprived, and he accepted the populist prescription of positive governmental action as a means of restoring opportunity. The Great Society, said Johnson, was to be "a place where the city of man serves not only the needs of the body and the demands of commerce but the desire for beauty and the hunger for community."

THE WARREN COMMISSION

The new president moved quickly to satisfy the lingering national curiosity and unease concerning Kennedy's assassination. Johnson asked the chief justice, Earl Warren, to head a blue-ribbon commission to investigate the killing. The report of the Warren Commission, released on September 27, 1964, ran to 296,000 words. To the enragement of conspiracy buffs, Warren observed that "the facts of the assassination itself are simple, so simple that many people believe it must be more complicated and conspiratorial to be true." Kennedy's death was the isolated act of a single individual, the commission concluded.

PRIMING THE ECONOMY

By the time Johnson took the oath of office, the tax bill that Walter Heller had persuaded Kennedy to sponsor had passed the House. Determined to placate businessmen and financial leaders who had considered Kennedy hostile and fiscally irresponsible, Johnson forced his departments and agencies to cut spending requests and submit a budget of $98 billion. With Senate conservatives such as Harry Byrd (D–West Virginia) satisfied, the tax-cut measure sailed through the Senate. Coming as it did during a period of almost no inflation, the tax cut generated a $52 billion increase in the gross national product during the year following its passage, and unemployment fell to an amazing 4.5 percent in 1965.

THE CIVIL RIGHTS ACT OF 1964

Lyndon Johnson's commitment to end discrimination and ensure equal opportunity for African Americans was both moral and political. He understood that Little Rock, Montgomery, and Oxford marked the death throes of an archaic system. The South, he believed, would have to rid itself of institutionalized racism and the brutality and demagoguery of the extreme segregationists if the national consensus that he so craved was to emerge. Consequently, he threw his full weight behind what would become known as the Civil Rights Act of 1964.

This landmark law prohibited discrimination in places of public accommodation; mandated a cutoff in funds to federal programs that discriminated; outlawed preference given in employment on the basis of race, color, religion, sex, or national origin; authorized the Justice Department to institute suits to facilitate school desegregation; created the Equal Employment Opportunity Commission; and provided technical and financial aid to communities desegregating their schools. Skillfully, Johnson and his congressional liaison staff put together a coalition comprised of liberal Democrats and moderate Republicans that was sufficient to impose cloture on the inevitable southern filibuster. The Senate passed the Civil Rights Act of 1964 in June by a vote of 73 to 27.

THE WAR ON POVERTY

The day following his predecessor's assassination, Johnson had told an aide: "I am a Roosevelt New Dealer. As a matter of fact . . . Kennedy was a little too conservative to suit my taste." In response to a genuine commitment to help the poor of all colors and ages as well as with an eye to the 1964 election, Johnson declared "unconditional war on poverty." The administration decided to retain Aid to Dependent Mothers and Children as the centerpiece of the welfare system, but it proposed a new mechanism, the Community Action program (CAP), as a means for breaking the cycle of poverty. In it, local welfare recipients as well as public officials would participate in planning for programs to stimulate local business, reduce unemployment, and provide for the basic needs of the community.

In his antipoverty message delivered to Congress on January 8, 1964, Johnson highlighted community action and recommended that it be funded initially with $500 million. In addition, the president created the Office of Economic Opportunity, an independent executive agency that was authorized to coordinate the war on poverty and direct programs not already supervised by existing cabinet departments. All in all, the Economic Opportunity Act created ten separate programs including the Head Start program to help preschoolers from disadvantaged backgrounds succeed in public school and Upward Bound to prepare impoverished teenagers for postsecondary education. Volunteers in Service to America (VISTA) was intended to function as a domestic peace corps working in behalf of the poor and undereducated.

TRIUMPH AND TRAGEDY

THE ELECTION OF 1964

At a commencement address delivered to the graduating class at the University of Michigan, Johnson simultaneously launched his 1964 presidential campaign and outlined his vision of the future. He and Congress would legislate a Great Society in which poverty, ignorance, and discrimination would disappear from the land. Like Franklin Roosevelt who used the Works Progress Administration and other programs to construct the New Deal voting coalition, Johnson envisioned the Great Society promises and programs as devices that would raise living standards, achieve social security and justice, and at the same time create a voting coalition that would ensure his triumph and that of the Democratic party. As luck would have it, the Republicans were busily abandoning the center the president was assiduously plotting to capture.

Contorted by internal bickering and frustrated by the Democratic resurgence of the late 1950s and early 1960s the GOP abandoned the moderate course it had been following since 1940 and succumbed to the sirens' song being sung by militant conservatives. John F. Kennedy's presidency corresponded to the emergence of a new radical right movement that *Time* magazine labeled the "Ultras." Drawn from all classes and walks of life but particularly numerous in the Southwest and California, the new right was ultra-patriotic and xenophobic. Intensely anticommunist, they came to equate liberalism with socialism and socialism with communism. The darling of the new right was Senator Barry M. Goldwater of Arizona, a department store tycoon and reserve air force general first elected to Congress in 1952. In his 1964 campaign tract, *Conscience of a Conservative*, Goldwater called for reduced government expenditures, elimination of federal bureaucracies, an end to forced integration, reassertion of states' rights, termination of farm subsidies and welfare payments, and additional curbs on labor unions. Above all, the Arizona conservative stood for "total victory" over communism. At the Republican convention in San Francisco held during the second week in July, the delegates chose Goldwater over the moderate candidate, New York Governor Nelson Rockefeller, and adopted a thoroughly conservative platform.

At the Democratic convention held in Atlantic City from August 24 to 27, Johnson was nominated by acclamation, and the delegates adopted a platform calling for enactment of the Great Society program and a foreign policy based on containment and competitive coexistence. The president selected the liberal senator from Minnesota, Hubert H. Humphrey, to be his running mate.

In the presidential campaign that followed, Lyndon Johnson maneuvered to occupy the political middle, aware that most Americans saw him as the only alternative to the radicalism of both right and left. Barry Goldwater played nicely into the Texan's hands. In foreign policy, the Republican candidate charged the Democrats with being soft on communism and pursuing a no-win policy. But he went further. When asked about the simmering war in Southeast Asia, Goldwater told reporters, "I'd drop a low-yield atomic bomb on the Chinese supply lines in North Vietnam or maybe shell 'em with the Seventh Fleet."

The GOP candidate was equally inept when it came to domestic policies. In Tennessee in the heart of the area rejuvenated by the TVA, he condemned public power. Goldwater also opposed Medicare for the aged, and Democratic campaigners reminded voters that the GOP nominee had once proposed making Social Security voluntary.

November brought a Democratic landslide of staggering proportions. Johnson and Humphrey garnered 43.1 million votes to 27.1 million for Goldwater and William E. Miller. The Democrats carried forty-four states and the District of Columbia which comprised 486 electoral votes, while Goldwater was able to claim only the Deep South and his native state of Arizona.

THE CIVIL RIGHTS MOVEMENT CONTINUES

Freedom Summer in Mississippi

In the spring of 1964 the focus of the "second reconstruction" shifted to Mississippi, racially and economically the most backward state in the Union. Although African Americans comprised 42 percent of the state's population, only 5 percent were registered to vote. The median income for black families was under $1,500 a year, less than one-third of that for white families. Like its economy, Mississippi's politics was dominated by a tiny planter class that for a century had manipulated white working-class prejudices to keep blacks "in their place."

Early in 1964 Robert Moses of SNCC and David Dennis of CORE came up with the concept of Freedom Summer. Black and white college students, carefully trained in the techniques of nonviolent resistance and political activism, would spread out across rural Mississippi registering African Americans to vote, teaching in "freedom schools," and organizing a "freedom party" to challenge the all-white Mississippi Democratic party.

The organizers of Freedom Summer anticipated violence, and they were right. On June 21 reports reached Moses and Dennis that three young project workers—Andrew Goodman, Michael Schwerner, and James Chaney—had disappeared in Neshoba County. Goodman and Schwerner were white, Chaney black. Six weeks later the three were discovered buried in an earthen dam. An FBI investigation subsequently uncovered a conspiracy involving local law enforcement officers and members of the Ku Klux Klan to murder them. Before the summer was out, three more civil rights workers died violently.

The March on Selma

The Freedom Summer project of 1964 drew national attention to the deplorable racism in Mississippi and to the fundamental importance to the civil rights movement of an unfettered franchise. Nevertheless, white resistance to black enfranchisement remained strong, and consequently, Martin Luther King decided in early 1965 to provoke Johnson and Congress into more dramatic action. Early in 1965 the head of the SCLC organized a series of demonstrations in Alabama to protest the continuing refusal of white authorities to grant black citizens the right to vote. After demonstrating at the courthouse in Selma throughout January 1965, civil rights workers decided to march from that city to Montgomery, fifty-four miles away, to present a petition to Governor George Wallace. At the Pettus Bridge outside of Selma two hundred local and state police set upon the demonstrators with tear gas, clubs, and cattle prods. Witnesses to the scene through taped television coverage, the American people recoiled at the sight of Alabama's finest beating defenseless men, women, and children. The president finally stepped in, federalizing the Alabama National Guard, and the walk was completed the third week in March.

The Voting Rights Act

Taking advantage of the groundswell of sympathy for African Americans generated by the march on Montgomery, the Johnson administration submitted a carefully crafted voting rights bill to Congress. By the end of July both houses had passed the Civil Rights Act of 1965, and the president signed the measure into law on August 6. This, the most important civil rights bill enacted to that date, authorized the attorney general to appoint federal election supervisors for states or districts which had literacy tests or other restrictive devices and in which fewer than 50 percent of eligible voters had cast their ballot in 1964. Those interfering with legitimate voters in their efforts to exercise the franchise were to be subject to fine or imprisonment or both.

Black Power

Less than a week after the president signed the 1965 Civil Rights Act, young, unemployed African Americans began looting, firebombing, and otherwise wrecking businesses in the Watts area of Los Angeles. Their objective, they announced to the media, was "to drive white 'exploiters' out of the ghetto." Firemen answering the alarm were attacked with rocks and bottles. Police and the National Guard moved in arresting looters and shooting those who resisted. When at long last the rioters had exhausted themselves, the ghetto lay in smoldering ruins.

The Watts uprising was, as King and members of the Johnson administration understood, symptomatic of a much larger problem. In Philadelphia, Chicago, Detroit, Memphis, and Houston African Americans lived in ghettos created not by law but by political and economic institutions controlled by whites and rooted in prejudice. As manufacturing moved to the suburbs or to smaller towns, inhabitants of the inner city were left stranded without transportation to reach suburban jobs or the means to relocate. In the face of unemployment and grinding poverty, families disintegrated, school dropout became epidemic, and those who did not succumb to crime and drugs were terrorized by those who did.

As one ghetto after another followed the Watts example in the searing summers of 1965 and 1966, black power advocates began to eclipse King, the SCLC, the NAACP, and the black churches in the struggle for the hearts and minds of the African-American masses. The leading prophet of regeneration through violence was Malcolm Little, the former convict who had succeeded Elijah Muhammed as leader of the Black Muslims. The Muslims, or Nation of Islam (NOI), were a puritanical association of African Americans that practiced a variation of the Islamic creed and that drew its converts primarily from the pimps, drug pushers, and generally down-and-out of the big city ghettos. Like other Black Muslims, Malcolm X (he had rejected his surname because it had been bestowed during slavery) preached black pride and self-reliance.

Meanwhile, Stokely Carmichael of SNCC and Floyd McKissick of CORE were invoking class action and violent confrontation. In their opinion, liberals, both black and white, were dangerously misguided. "We have to make integration irrelevant," Carmichael declared. When in 1967 the Detroit race riot left thirty-three black and ten white Americans dead, it seemed to many that the black power philosophy had come to fruition. Urban rioting and the white backlash that followed dramatically slowed the Johnson administration's civil rights campaign. The president was limited to appointing African Americans to high level posts in the federal government.

DOMESTIC PROGRAMS

The Drive for Universal Medical Care

Lyndon Johnson's commitment to the social justice movement, and more important, his ability to deliver on its promises, was nowhere better demonstrated than in the story of Medicare. The Medical Care Act of 1965 established for Americans sixty-five years of age and older a basic health care plan, generally referred to as Medicare, that was compulsory and financed by a payroll tax. This system, administered by the Social Security Administration, covered most hospital and some nursing home stays, diagnostic costs, and home health care visits. A proviso in the 1965 Medical Care Act, dubbed Medicaid, turned over federal funds to the states to help cover the medical expenses of the indigent.

Education

As was true of the New Deal, there was supposed to be something for everyone in the Great Society. Lyndon Johnson wanted to be known as "the education President," and he more than any other man who occupied the Oval Office deserved that label. Standing in the one-room schoolhouse near Stonewall, Texas, where he had begun his own education, Lyndon Johnson signed the Elementary and Secondary Education Act into law in April 1965.

This, the first federal aid to education measure in U.S. history, authorized the expenditure of 1 billion dollars to help local school districts pay for new facilities and additional staff that would equalize educational opportunity for poor children. It made funds available for textbooks, library facilities, adult education, and special education for the handicapped. The Johnson administration followed up its victory by persuading Congress to enact the Higher Education Act of 1965 which expanded basic aid to the nation's colleges and universities and established a program of low-interest student loans.

A Man on the Moon

Finally, Lyndon Johnson was an enthusiastic supporter of the space program. The state of the art Johnson Space Center in Houston was begun during his tenure. On July 16, 1969, *Apollo 11*, manned by Neil A. Armstrong, Edwin E. Aldrin, Jr., and Michael Collins, blasted off for the moon. On July 20 Armstrong and Aldrin entered the Lunar Excursion Module *Eagle* and began the descent to a landing site near the Sea of Tranquility. At 4:17 P.M. Armstrong radioed, "Houston, Tranquility Base here. The *Eagle* has landed." Several hours later Armstrong became the first person to walk on the moon. His exclamation— "That's one small step for man, one giant leap for mankind"—became one of the most famous quotes of the twentieth century.

JOHNSON, THE COLD WAR, AND VIETNAM

The new president, perceiving that he had little experience in foreign affairs, kept Kennedy's team—Bundy, Rostow, Rusk, McNamara—virtually intact. Yet he had had as much if not more experience than Jack Kennedy when he assumed office. Like his predecessor, Johnson was heavily influenced by history, particularly the events of the 1930s and 1940s as he interpreted them. Appeasement of the Axis powers had only encouraged further aggression and forced the United States to fight after many of its allies had already been defeated.

Johnson, like most other public figures of his time, fully accepted the domino theory and the notion of a monolithic communist threat. He was also acutely aware of the devastating impact the loss of China in the 1940s had had on the Democratic party. He repeatedly told his confidantes that he was not going to

American astronauts walking on the moon,1969.

open himself and his party to charges that he had sold South Vietnam out to the communists. A related consideration was Johnson's determination not to make a foreign policy misstep that would endanger his Great Society programs. As he perceived it, his ability to win acceptance of Medicare, VISTA, the Community Action program, Head Start, and other social welfare programs depended upon his ability to hold together a coalition of liberals and conservatives. When Johnson took the oath of office in November 1963, a majority in both camps were ardent Cold War warriors and believed that the United States ought to do all in its power to support an independent, noncommunist South Vietnam.

A Troubled South Vietnam

Quickly, Lyndon Johnson learned that South Vietnam was a creation of the Geneva accords and nothing more. Only one civilian was able to hold the presidency in the post-Diem period and he for only a matter of months. For a variety of reasons the military men who ruled from Saigon were unable to establish political and economic structures that the South Vietnamese people would support. They continually bypassed the legislature and subverted elections. Exposed to intense physical insecurity as the Viet Cong and government troops battled for the countryside and to exploitation by corrupt landowners and government officials, peasants and workers, students and Buddhists either joined the NLF or refused to support the government. Johnson and his advisors were aware of the deteriorating situation in Vietnam, but convinced themselves that they could build a viable noncommunist state that the South Vietnamese would ultimately be willing to fight and die for. As opposition to the war developed in the United States, Johnson found himself walking a tightrope at home and in Southeast Asia. The task as he saw it was to do enough in Vietnam to satisfy the hawks but not so much that he alienated the doves. Given the absolute determination of the North Vietnamese and National Liberation Front to expel the Americans and unify the country under their control, the result was a managed stalemate.

The Gulf of Tonkin Resolution

During the first months of his administration, Johnson resisted pressure from the Joint Chiefs of Staff for direct intervention, and continued Kennedy's policy of economic aid and advisors. He did authorize an expansion of U.S. support for covert raids against the North. On August 2, 1964, the U.S.S. *Maddox*, an American destroyer providing support for South Vietnamese raids against North Vietnamese–held islands, was attacked by communist torpedo boats in the Gulf of Tonkin. Two days later, the *Maddox* and a sister ship, the U.S.S. *C. Turner Joy*, fired on North Vietnamese patrol boats, claiming that they were under attack. Although subsequent investigations cast doubt on the American claim, Johnson authorized the U.S. Navy and Air Force to retaliate against communist bases on the coast of North Vietnam.

Immediately, the president went to Congress and requested a resolution authorizing him to take "all necessary measures to repel any armed attacks against the forces of the United States and to prevent further aggression." Told by Johnson that he had no intention of getting bogged down in a land war on the Asian mainland and that the resolution was needed to outflank Barry Goldwater, the Republican presidential nominee who had been urging a dramatic escalation of the war, Senate Foreign Relations Committee Chairman J. William Fulbright guided the resolution through the Senate, securing approval by a vote of 80 to 2. After brief deliberation, the House passed the resolution unanimously. From that time on, the executive branch would claim that in the Tonkin Gulf Resolution, the Congress had given the president permission to take whatever measures he deemed necessary to win the war in Vietnam.

The Decision to Escalate

With the political situation in Saigon deteriorating almost daily and the Viet Cong (VC) winning the war for control of the countryside, Johnson's military and civilian advisors came to the conclusion that an orchestrated bombing campaign against North Vietnam was absolutely essential. When North Vietnamese and VC troops attacked U.S. barracks at Pleiku and Qui Nhon during the first weeks of 1965, Johnson ordered aerial bombardment of selected North Vietnamese targets. The bombing was designed to buoy spirits in the South, demoralize the North, and interdict the flow of supplies and men coming down the Ho Chi Minh Trail. It did none of these things. In the spring, the Joint Chiefs and hard-line advisors like Walt Rostow argued for an all-out aerial assault and invasion of the North. Instead, the president authorized the introduction of eight thousand American combat troops.

At first, the marines and combat infantrymen were limited to action within a defensive perimeter around U.S. air bases. By the summer of 1965, however, Johnson had acceded to General William Westmoreland's request to use American troops in unlimited "search and destroy" missions. In July, he authorized the immediate dispatch of fifty thousand troops and agreed to put in fifty thousand more by the end of the year. Caught between his desire to avoid a nuclear Armageddon on the one hand and to deny the communists a victory in South Vietnam on the other, Lyndon Johnson had allowed himself to be drawn into a land war in Asia.

Stalemate

Americans fought well, won battles, provided massive economic aid and technical advice to thousands of Vietnamese but could not win the war. NVA troops occasionally fought company- and even brigade-level battles, but the brunt of the fighting was borne by small units and VC guerrillas who used hit-and-run tactics. Ho Chi Minh matched the Americans escalation for escalation; troops and supplies continued to pour down the complex of roads and trails named for him (see Figure 26–1).

With General Westmoreland and the U.S. Embassy assuring the American people that victory was just around the corner, the number of American troops increased steadily: 385,300 by the end of 1966 and 485,600 by the end of 1967. Two-and-a-half years following the introduction of combat troops, nearly ten thousand Americans had died in Vietnam. During this period, the bombing campaign gradually intensified. By the end of 1968, the United States had dropped 3.2 million tons of explosives on North Vietnam and areas of suspected enemy activity in the South. The conventional bombs and napalm gradually cratered, burned, and defoliated parts of the country beyond recognition. Free fire zones terrorized the rural population of the South and created huge numbers of refugees.

American escalation during the period from 1966 through 1968 was punctuated by periodic peace initiatives. Using formal and informal channels, the Johnson administration offered to negotiate an end to the war with Hanoi. American proposals always included the preservation of the Saigon regime and withdrawal of North Vietnamese forces from the South prior to American

FIGURE 26–1

The Vietnam War

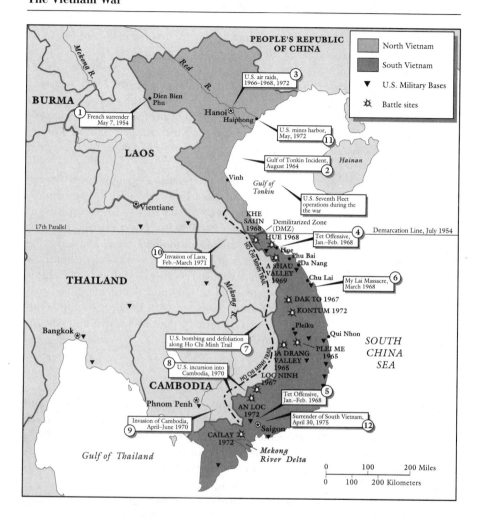

withdrawal. Hanoi and the NLF consistently rejected these terms as tantamount to defeat.

THE ANTIWAR MOVEMENT

By 1967 the war had spawned a bitter, divisive debate within the United States. On the political right were those who insisted that the administration was not doing enough. Comprised primarily of Goldwater Republicans and conservative Democrats, many of them from the South, the hawks, as the press dubbed them, were staunch Cold War warriors. Communism was an unmitigated evil, the regime in Hanoi was an extension of Sino-Soviet imperialism, and Vietnam was the keystone in a regional arch which would collapse if America lost its nerve.

Acting as a counterpoint to the hawks was a diverse collection of individuals and groups who opposed the war, viewing it as immoral, illogical, counterproductive, or all of these. The antiwar coalition included such establishment figures as Senator J. William Fulbright whose 1966 televised hearings on Vietnam stirred general unease throughout the country but was most visibly represented by individuals who were not professional politicians or policymakers—civil rights leader Martin Luther King, Jr., actress Jane Fonda, pediatrician and author Dr. Benjamin Spock, and heavyweight champion Muhammad Ali.

The antiwar movement included traditional pacifists—people for whom all wars were immoral— disillusioned liberals like Fulbright and former Undersecretary of State George Ball, who believed that in its obsessive anticommunism the United States was allying itself with governments fully as repressive as those in the Soviet Union and Communist China, and left-wing students and intellectuals who saw the war as an expression of an essentially corrupt political and economic system. Because this third strain, which became known as the New Left, grew out of established radical organizations, was related to the civil rights movement, and coincided with the burgeoning counterculture movement of the 1960s, it was initially the most active and controversial component of the antiwar coalition.

A Nation Divided

As American television displayed the horrors of Vietnam on a daily basis, and escalating American involvement produced a dramatic expansion of the draft, the student-driven antiwar movement gained momentum. In November 1965 some thirty thousand people convened in Washington to stage the largest demonstration against the war to that time. As the bombing and troop levels increased, so did protests and demonstrations.

Opposition to the war took many forms. Students against the war burned their draft cards, fled to Canada, or even mutilated themselves as part of a dual effort to protest the war and avoid serving in Vietnam. By war's end the draft resistance movement had produced 570,000 draft offenders and 563,000 less-than-honorable discharges from the military. But it was the mass demonstrations, carried inevitably by the major networks live or on the nightly news, that had the greatest impact on the public and White House. In the spring of 1967, five hundred thousand marchers of all ages converged on New York's Central Park chanting "Hey, hey, LBJ, how many kids did you kill today?" That October one hundred thousand antiwar activists gathered in Washington. For a time one-third of their number managed to block the entrance to the Pentagon, which protest leaders termed the "nerve center of American militarism."

Though most Americans were offended by antiwar protests and demonstrations, the countless acts of defiance kept popular attention on the war and created a sense of disunity that sapped the national will. Popular support for the war and particularly Johnson's handling of it dropped off sharply during 1967. In early August the president was forced to go to Congress and ask for a 10 percent surtax on incomes to help cover the skyrocketing deficit. Suddenly business leaders began to voice doubts about the war, and such formerly hawkish publications as *Time* magazine began to insist on a basic reconsideration of policy. As draft calls climbed to thirty thousand a month and the American death toll reached thirteen thousand, hawks as well as doves began to conclude that the war was a mistake. Johnson's approval rating plummeted to 13 percent.

THE TET OFFENSIVE

The last day of January 1968, the Viet Cong staged the Tet offensive, a massive, coordinated attack on virtually all of South Vietnam's populated areas. In all, they struck thirty-six of forty-four provincial capitals, five of six major cities, sixty-four district capitals, and fifty hamlets. Communist guerrillas managed to break into the U.S. embassy compound in Saigon, and VC and North Vietnamese troops succeeded in occupying and holding the imperial city of Hue for nearly three weeks. Though astounded by the breadth and audacity of the attacks, the U.S. and its South Vietnamese allies quickly seized the offensive. They retook every city and hamlet, inflicting forty thousand battle deaths on the enemy.

Westmoreland asked for an additional two hundred thousand troops to follow up the victory and break the military back of the communists once and for all. President Johnson refused. He had no choice. By 1968 the administration's failure to go all out to win the war had alienated hawks, while its incessant bombing and refusal to withdraw the five hundred thousand troops in South Vietnam continued to anger doves. More important, Westmoreland's constant predictions of victory appeared absurd in light of the Tet offensive. It widened a growing credibility gap into a yawning chasm.

THE ELECTION OF 1968

Vietnam and the Tet offensive induced first Senator Eugene McCarthy and then Robert Kennedy to announce for the Democratic nomination for president. Both ran as peace candidates. By the spring of 1968, Lyndon Johnson could not venture outside Washington without encountering large and hostile crowds. His new secretary of defense, Clark Clifford, recommended a sharp de-escalation of the war and ultimately U.S. withdrawal on the best terms Washington could negotiate. When McCarthy made a surprisingly strong showing in the New Hampshire primary, winning the support of hawks as well as doves, Johnson decided on a dramatic course of action. In a nationally televised address delivered on the evening of March 31, the president announced a partial bombing halt, invited Hanoi to engage in direct peace negotiations, and announced that he would not run for reelection.

Despite these startling pronouncements, Johnson and his successor, Richard Nixon, remained committed to the goal of an independent, noncommunist South Vietnam. Because the United States would not force its client government in Saigon to give way to a coalition arrangement that included the NLF and because it would not withdraw its military forces without a corresponding pullback by the North Vietnamese, the war in Southeast Asia would drag on for four more bloody years.

A GLOBALIST FOREIGN POLICY

All the while Lyndon Johnson was struggling with the complex issues of Southeast Asia, he had to deal with a host of other areas and problems: rioting in Panama; chaos in the Dominican Republic; a major outbreak of fighting in the Middle East; the ongoing campaign to achieve détente with the Soviet Union; and the dual effort to either oust or coopt Fidel Castro. Inevitably, these issues and events became intertwined with Vietnam and demonstrated the dangers of overcommitment.

THE DOMINICAN INTERVENTION

Lyndon Johnson was sensitive to the plight of the Latin masses but he was more sensitive to the continuing threat that Fidel Castro posed to his administration—in a political if not a strategic sense. When revolution erupted in the Dominican Republic in 1965 toppling the existing government and producing chaos in the capital city, Johnson and his stridently anticommunist assistant secretary of state for Latin American affairs, Thomas Mann, acted to ensure that the country did not evolve into another Cuba.

The causes of the Dominican Republic's many troubles were varied, but most were rooted in the thirty-year dictatorship of Rafael Leonidas Trujillo Molina. That worthy had brutally suppressed all opposition, turned the army into his personal palace guard, and ravaged his country's fragile economy. Then in the summer of 1961 assassins shot him through the head. His family tried to perpetuate his tyranny, but failed and fled into exile. In December 1962, the Dominicans elected the liberal intellectual, Juan Bosch, president. Seven months later a military coup overthrew him, its leaders charging that he was too tolerant of communists and communism.

In the spring of 1965 fighting erupted between officers loyal to Bosch, then in exile in Puerto Rico, and those who supported the military junta that had ousted him. With Santo Domingo in chaos President Johnson responded positively to a request from the anti-Bosch military faction for military intervention. Citing the need to protect American lives, the administration poured 20,000 marines and army troops into the tiny, impoverished country. Johnson and Mann's real motivation was to prevent the return of Bosch whom they perceived to be a potential Castro. "We don't intend to sit here in our rocking chair with our hands folded and let the Communists set up any governments in the Western Hemisphere," the president declared.

THE ARAB-ISRAELI CONFLICT

Relations between the Arab world, led by Egypt's Gamal Abdel Nasser, and Israel had grown increasingly tense in the years following the 1956 Suez crisis. In May 1967 Nasser persuaded the United Nations to withdraw the peace-keeping force that had been inserted between Egyptian and Israeli forces following the Suez imbroglio. The two adversaries faced each other directly across a huge demilitarized zone for the first time since 1956. Nasser moved quickly to fill the void. He ordered his army and air force to occupy the Sinai Peninsula, which it did, in the process seizing the strategically crucial town of Sharm el-Sheikh which overlooked the Gulf of Aqaba. At the same time, PLO fedayeen guerrillas launched attacks against Jewish settlements from their bases in the Sinai as well as from Jordan and Syria.

THE SIX-DAY WAR

Convinced that the frontline states and the PLO intended to attack, the Israelis decided to stage a preemptive strike. On June 6, the Israeli air force flew out across the Mediterranean to avoid Egyptian radar and then attacked from the north. Catching Egypt's planes on the ground, the Israelis virtually destroyed Nasser's air force. That scene was repeated in Jordan and Syria. For the next six days the Israeli army followed up on this initial success invading and occupying the Sinai, the old city of Jerusalem, the West Bank of the Jordan, and the strategic Golan Heights just inside Syria's border. With the capture of Sharm el-Sheikh, the Israelis once again controlled an outlet to the Arabian Gulf.

In November 1967, the United Nations approved Resolution 242, a measure designed to bring about a negotiated settlement to the ongoing Middle East crisis. It called for a multilateral guarantee of Israel's borders in exchange for a return of the territory seized in the Six-Day War. In addition, Israel would enjoy free access to "regional waterways" (Nasser had ordered the Suez Canal blocked with sunken ships shortly after Israel attacked) in the area, while Palestinians could look forward to "a just settlement of the refugee problem," a provision which they interpreted to mean the conversion of Palestine into a multinational state including both Jews and Palestinians.

The Jewish state insisted, however, that the Arab nations would have to extend formal recognition and give guarantees before the land seized in the Six-Day War was returned, and that they refused to do. Washington and various third parties attempted mediation but with no success. Fedayeen border raids and terrorist attacks mounted while Israel ruled the territories under its control with an iron hand. The region remained ripe for another explosion.

In the aftermath of World War II the United States had accepted the role of protector of the noncommunist world from Soviet and subsequently Chinese imperialism and from the scourge of Marxism-Leninism. The enormous task that the United States had defined for itself, then, was to protect the entire world from direct and indirect communist aggression. With the development of other global power centers and the growing importance of such non–Cold War issues as anticolonialism and the socioeconomic gap between countries of the northern and southern hemispheres, America's ability to act as arbiter of world affairs diminished sharply. The United States would have to pick and choose, intervening in those areas that bore directly on its national interest strategically and economically defined. Vietnam prevented such a rational course. Indeed, America's inability to prevent the outbreak of the Six Day War in the Middle East in 1967 and the polarization that followed indicated just how out of balance United States foreign policy was in the 1960s.

....

Historians of the Vietnam War who believe that American intervention constituted a tragic mistake have concentrated on the personalities, events, and forces surrounding the Johnson administration's decisions in late 1964 and early 1965 to bomb the North and introduce combat troops.

Writing while the war was still underway, a group of liberal historians argued that Johnson was a victim of circumstance. American leaders from Truman to Johnson had undertaken a series of incremental steps in Indochina which ended in disastrous U.S. involvement. Had the president known where it would lead, he would not have approved escalation. Others see Johnson as a prisoner of the containment policy, and the flawed assumptions—the myth of the monolithic communist threat and the domino theory—that underlay it. Still others argue that Johnson approved deepening U.S. involvement in Vietnam to ensure continued support for his Great Society programs from southern Democrats and some Republicans.

In the following selection from his acclaimed book Intervention, *Southeast Asia expert George Kahin faults not Johnson but the advisors whom he inherited from Kennedy. According to Kahin, Robert McNamara, McGeorge Bundy, Dean Rusk, and their lieutenants plunged the nation into an ill-conceived war in order to protect their positions and prestige, all the while dragging Lyndon Johnson with them.*

THE LOGIC OF ESCALATION
George McT. Kahin

Johnson's victory at the polls in November 1964 was so overwhelming that, in its wake, his scope for taking major new initiatives in Vietnam was much greater than either he or Kennedy had previously enjoyed. James Thomson saw this as providing the "last and most important opportunity that was lost" for disengaging the United States from Vietnam on acceptable terms. He concluded that, had Johnson been "more confident in foreign affairs, had he been more deeply informed on Vietnam and Southeast Asia, and had he raised some hard questions that unanimity [on the part of his advisers] had submerged, this President could have used the largest electoral mandate in history to deescalate in Vietnam, in the clear expectation that at the worst a neutralist government would come to power in Saigon and politely invite us out."

Although the strength of Johnson's position would have permitted him to take this course, it was ruled out by all of his senior advisers. Insofar as they did discuss with him the question of negotiations, they did so critically, admonishing that these were not to be considered for the present, and could not realistically even be explored until after the ratio of military power in South Vietnam had been drastically altered in favor of the Saigon government. Given the balance at the time, negotiations were regarded as tantamount to capitulation; even discussion of the matter was likely to be disastrous to the morale of the American protégés in Saigon. The advisers argued that any hint that the United States was disposed to move in such a direction would seriously risk collapse of the now tottering political edifice that it had built with such effort. In the wake of this, a neutralist, peace-oriented Saigon government would probably come to power and would insist upon negotiating a settlement on its own terms. As Paul Warnke, then a senior Pentagon legal specialist, later observed in critical vein: "For the United States to 'compromise' and permit the indigenous forces of Vietnam to work their own way would be to condone the demise of the anti-Communist regime we had supported in Saigon for twenty years."

By the early fall of 1964 George Ball—who as under secretary of state had earlier been largely absorbed by European matters—had become alarmed at the increasingly interventionist stance of the president's advisers and their constant

from George McT. Kahin, *Intervention: How America Became Involved in Vietnam* (New York: Knopf, 1986), 240–277.

denigration of negotiations. He believed that, as matters then stood with respect to negotiations, "the administration really didn't have anything to say to the Vietnamese communists except for the modalities of their capitulation." If it were serious about negotiations, the United States, he argued, would have to lower its sights and be prepared for a compromise solution. As for the proposition that negotiations would so shake the Saigon regime as to risk its collapse, he felt that this simply demonstrated the regime wasn't worth supporting. "My own position," Ball later recalled, "was that we should give it sixty days to shape up and if it didn't we should invoke Eisenhower's 1954 letter [with its clear conditionality of support] and get out. If it showed it wasn't worth our support, I didn't mind if it did collapse." He sought to warn Johnson of the danger and fruitlessness of an escalation in U.S. military involvement and alert him to possible courses and outcomes of negotiations.

To this end, Ball prepared an extensive memorandum for McGeorge Bundy, McNamara, and Rusk, assuming that after they had discussed it Bundy would pass it on to Johnson. (Though Ball himself had direct access to the president, he felt that in cases where he so strongly disagreed with these advisers, he should as a matter of courtesy first acquaint them with his ideas.) He recognized that these three were adamantly opposed to his ideas on negotiations, but he regarded the president as more open-minded than they on matters pertaining to Vietnam. He therefore hoped that the views contained in this October 5 memorandum would at least persuade Johnson that there were options to explore beyond the narrow range being presented by his senior advisers. Ball felt it especially important that the president be aware that there were possible negotiating processes and outcomes compatible with U.S. global prestige. Present policy, he pointed out, "has been justified primarily on political grounds . . . defended on the proposition that America cannot afford to promote a settlement in South Viet-Nam without first demonstrating the superiority of its own military power—or, in other words, giving the North Vietnamese a bloody nose." "What I am urging," he concluded, "is that our Southeast Asian policy be looked at in all its aspects and in the light of our total world situation. It is essential that this be done before we commit military forces to a line of action that could put events in the saddle and destroy our freedom to choose the policies that are at once the most effective and the most prudent."

Of several frameworks for achieving a negotiated settlement, Ball favored "a localized negotiation between a neutralist South Viet-Nam Government and the National Liberation Front." The United States would set the process in motion by emphatically reiterating to the South Vietnamese and to foreign governments [and presumably the American public] that it intended to remain in South Vietnam only so long as the South Vietnamese wished its help. At the same time, Washington could serve notice on the Saigon government that "we are determined to continue the struggle . . . *only* if they achieve a unity of purpose in Saigon, clearly express that unity, and create a government free from factionalism and capable of carrying on the affairs of the country." . . .

Though seeing an ultimate takeover by the communists as possible, Ball hoped that a solution more palatable to the United States might be achieved if other powers could be brought in to provide a guarantee of South Vietnam's continued neutralization—something for which he wanted the administration to begin planning immediately. But even if this had not been possible, the "diffused" and "postponed" takeover he postulated would undoubtedly have been preferable for the NLF, as well as for other elements in the South, to the abrupt and traumatic takeover by Hanoi that occurred in 1975, after animosities had been nourished and intensified by nearly a decade of the escalated American military intervention that Ball's colleagues soon induced Johnson to support.

There was, then, another important option that could have been presented to the president. But although McGeorge Bundy, McNamara, and Rusk all read Ball's brief, none chose to send it on to Johnson for the major review of policy he had requested for December 1. (It was only with the help of William Moyers of the White House staff that the memorandum finally reached the president, more than a month later.) Indeed, no negotiating option was prepared for the president, and his advisers continued to warn against consideration of one—at least until such time as the military balance had shifted decisively in favor of Saigon, a change they had already begun to conclude could not come about without the injection of additional U.S. fire power.

This was not the only instance when Johnson was denied the opportunity to consider possibilities for negotiations. U Thant [Secretary General of the U.N.] was convinced after his talks with Johnson and Rusk on August 6 that the president had encouraged him to arrange direct and secret bilateral discussions with Hanoi.

Within a month, via a senior Soviet U.N. official, U Thant had contacted Ho Chi Minh and obtained his approval for such talks. The weight of available evidence, however, indicates that Johnson was apprised of neither this nor U Thant's follow-up effort in December until after he made his decision to escalate in February 1965. James Thomson states, "In February 1965 McGeorge Bundy sent a note to me which indicated the President never knew about the Stevenson/U Thant negotiation effort." . . .

In early September 1964, the U.N. secretary general secured Hanoi's agreement to direct bilateral talks with the United States, stipulating that they be private—a major U.S. concern—and without Peking's knowledge (apparently a major Hanoi concern). He passed this word to U.N. Ambassador Adlai Stevenson but was advised that such talks should be postponed until after the election. On November 23–24 Rusk and Stevenson discussed U Thant's September initiative and "possible venues" for such a meeting. The next day Rusk asked Stevenson to ascertain "U Thant's thinking and what reaction he had had from Hanoi." Stevenson reported back to Rusk that U Thant had learned via the Soviets that Hanoi's response was "very affirmative." Two days later Stevenson reported to Rusk that U Thant was exploring the possibility of Rangoon as a place for talks between the American ambassador and North Vietnam's consul general, a Vietnamese of some stature. Soon afterward the secretary general reported to Rusk via Stevenson that General Ne Win, head of the Burmese government, had given his permission for such a meeting. But Rusk evidently authorized no reply. A month later U Thant contacted Stevenson again to inform him that Hanoi was "ready and willing" to enter into discussions with the United States and asked what the American position was. . . . Rusk was clearly not supportive of a follow-up, and McNamara was "flatly opposed" to U Thant's proposal, stating that the Saigon government would have to be told and that negotiations would have a devastating effect on it. On February 13, U Thant informed Stevenson's deputy, Charles Yost, that despite his "positive" response from Hanoi, he was still awaiting Washington's answer to what he regarded as "quite specific proposals."

Finally, alarmed by the resumption of U.S. reprisal bombings against North Vietnam, and feeling pressure from restive U.N. delegations worried over the course of events, U Thant publicly appealed on February 16 for negotiation via a reconvened Geneva Conference on Vietnam. But this attempt too, despite positive reactions from Moscow as well as Hanoi, Washington rebuffed. . . .

It was not until after the die had been cast—not until March 9, 1965, after the United States had mounted its sustained air war against the North and landed the first U.S. ground forces in Vietnam—that The New York Times reported U Thant's 1964 efforts. (The next day a U.N. spokesman publicly announced Washington's negative response.) And it was not until eight months after the Times's disclosure that the State Department's spokesman, Robert McCloskey, reversed repeated denials and acknowledged that the administration had indeed rejected U Thant's proposals. Deprecating the significance of this move, he stated that Dean Rusk's "antennae is [sic] sensitive" and that if Hanoi was "prepared for serious talks . . . the Secretary of State said that he would recognize it when it came." The New York Times later editorialized, "This comment reminds one of the ancient Roman practice of drawing auspices from the flight or the entrails of birds. It would be a shuddering thought that the fate of nations and thousands of young Americans depended on Dean Rusk's antenna. Yet this is what Mr. McCloskey indicated." Nor, of course, did he mention that the president's advisers failed to inform him of U Thant's pre-February peace efforts until after he had already committed himself to a major military escalation.

During the fall of 1964, as the political substance and military capacity of the South Vietnamese government eroded ever more rapidly, it had become starkly evident to Johnson's advisers that the policies they had been shaping ever since John F. Kennedy assumed the presidency had failed. However, since their own reputations were so closely bound up with these policies, it was difficult for them to call for a shift from a military to a political track. Even if more attuned to American interests, such a move would have exposed their own previous counsel and very possibly been costly to their tenure in the administration. On the other hand, moving to a policy of heavier and geographically expanded military intervention would be perceived by the American Congress and public as having consistency and continuity and would not—at least until after a failure of this further escalation—disclose the erroneous nature of the assumptions and perceptions upon which interventionism rested. Moreover, though only a few presidential advisers—largely among the military—believed that such an escalation would succeed, most, if not all, of the others apparently concluded that it had at least some chance of doing so. It was usually not difficult for these men to equate the U.S.

national interest with their own reputations. Or, as Robert Gallucci so aptly put it, "Using the phrase, 'protecting our commitment,' to explain American presence in Viet-Nam may be as pertinent in its application to individual actors as it is to the nation as a whole."

During the last months of 1964 these advisers became increasingly convinced that a major escalation of the U.S. military effort in Vietnam was necessary, and they believed that Johnson's newly established electoral strength gave him the authority to order this. James Thomson perceived that although the president had instructed his chief advisers to prepare as wide a range of Vietnam options as possible for him for postelection consideration and decision, explicitly requesting that "all options be laid out," in counseling him they presented such a narrow set of choices—"precluding any real Presidential choice among viable options"—that, whatever his own inclinations, he was virtually locked into a program for bombing the North.

The civilian advisers envisaged a bombing program less extreme than that advocated by the Joint Chiefs, but as extensive as seemed feasible without broadening the war enough to jeopardize U.S. global interests seriously. Most of them had become convinced that a bombing so intense and widespread as to destroy the North Vietnamese government would be certain to provoke a massive retaliation, in which Hanoi's units—which as yet had not appeared in the South—would flood across the seventeenth parallel in numbers that would quickly overwhelm Saigon's forces. They feared too that it could bring China into the war—a possibility that was taken very seriously throughout the course of the Johnson administration. Moreover, some argued that an unlimited bombing campaign would leave Hanoi with no further assets to protect, thus depriving the United States of any leverage to induce it to pressure the NLF to cease military opposition to Saigon. Or, in Taylor's vivid parlance, it was important not to "kill the hostage" by destroying North Vietnamese assets inside the "Hanoi do-nut." . . .

The penultimate revision of the NSC Working Group's position paper— "Courses of Action in Southeast Asia"—drafted on November 21 by William Bundy and Assistant Secretary of Defense for International Security Affairs John Mc-Naughton, constituted, together with a subsequent memorandum and oral presentation by Taylor, the fundamental basis for discussions by the president's advisers in arriving at their recommendations for him. The working group forwarded just three broad options.

Option A was "to continue present policies indefinitely," including intensifying existing covert forms of action against North Vietnam and in Laos, but with the additional element of U.S. reprisal actions against North Vietnam for any "spectacular attack by the VC within South Vietnam, particularly but not solely an attack involving U.S. forces or installations."

Option B called for the most dramatic escalation: "a systematic program of military pressures against the north, with increasing pressure actions to be continued at a fairly rapid pace and without interruption until we achieve our present stated objectives." It was evident that the working group preferred Option B, stating that it "probably stands a greater chance than either of the other two of attaining our objectives vis-à-vis Hanoi and a settlement in Vietnam"; the group acknowledged, however, that this course courted "considerably higher risks of major military conflict with Hanoi and possibly Communist China."

Option C stipulated slower-paced and more cautious, but still substantial, escalation. It provided for "graduated military moves against infiltration targets, first in Laos and then in the DRV [North Vietnam], and then against other targets in North Vietnam," giving the impression of "a steady deliberate approach . . . designed to give the US the option at any time to proceed or not, to escalate or not, and to quicken the pace or not." It hedged on the question of possible U.S. ground-force deployment in the South—reflecting the continuing lack of consensus among the president's advisers—stipulating that this would not be required unless Hanoi "threatened a ground move to the south." Certainly Option C was not presented as likely to produce any spectacular results. The working group assessed it as "more controlled and less risky of major military action than Option B . . . and more likely than Option A to achieve at least part of our objectives, and even if it ended in the loss of South Vietnam, our having taken strong measures would still leave us a good deal better off than under Option A with respect to the confidence and ability to stand firm of the nations in the next line of defense in Asia."

Essentially, then, these three options were variations of escalated military action; no option focused on a negotiated settlement. Any future possibility of negotiations was to be resisted, as the narrative in the *Pentagon Papers* assessed these recommendations, "until the North had agreed in advance" to U.S. conditions, and in effect negotiations were to be excluded in the short run under Options B and C because these preconditions were "entirely unrealistic," reflecting a "policy climate in Washington" that "simply was not receptive to any suggestion that U.S. goals might have to be compromised." Indeed, the favored Option B called for Washington to take "a totally inflexible position on negotiating." . . .

In this simplistic calculus presented by the president's advisers there was no trace of the genre of thinking that characterized Ball's sidetracked memorandum, nor was there any negotiating option. All negotiation was to be eschewed until the United States had won—that is, until Hanoi had brought the insurgency in the South to a halt and accepted a secure, noncommunist South Vietnamese state. As James Thomson later put it, "The advisers so effectively converged on one single option— juxtaposed against two other phony options (in effect blowing up the world, or scuttle-and-run)—the President was confronted with unanimity for bombing the North from all his trusted counsellors." This plan was presented to him as a means of raising the political morale and military aggressiveness of the Saigon regime, while decreasing those qualities among the Viet Cong, and inducing Hanoi not only to end its support of its southern comrades but to pressure them into laying down their arms. In looking back on this period, U. Alexis Johnson, who was then Taylor's deputy and a proponent of bombing, observed, "I don't feel that at this decision point we were able to present the President, in a clear cut fashion, the alternatives. . . . I don't think we served the President well." . . .

Johnson stipulated that he was prepared to endorse Phase I and Phase II only in principle, and that he would approve implementation of neither until certain strict conditions were met by the Saigon government. Consequently, his advisers, who were pressing for escalation, now found themselves up against a major obstacle. For

Lyndon Johnson insisted that a fundamental prerequisite be met before he would approve escalation to either level. This was spelled out clearly in his December 3 instruction to Taylor: "There are certain minimum criteria of performance in South Vietnam which must be met before new measures against North Vietnam would be either justified or practicable." He insisted that, "at a minimum, the government should be able to speak for and to its people. . . . It should be capable of maintaining law and order in the principal centers of population, make plans for the conduct of operations and insure their effective execution by military and police forces completely responsible to its authority." And, finally, the Saigon government "must have the means to cope with the enemy reactions which must be expected to result from any change in the pattern of our operations." . . .

The message that Taylor conveyed to Saigon's political and military leaders from President Johnson was very clear: there would be no U.S. military intervention against Hanoi until they demonstrated qualities they had thus far been unable to attain—political cohesion, governmental stability, and effectiveness in their own campaign against the Viet Cong. In particular, Taylor was requested "to bring home to all groups in South Vietnam the paramount importance of national unity," and to point out that "it is a matter of the greatest difficulty" for the administration "to require great sacrifices of American citizens when reports from Saigon repeatedly give evidence of heedless self interest and short sightedness among all major groups in South Vietnam."

Soon after Taylor's return to Saigon, however, his expectations of fostering order and stability among the various contending civilian and military factions were abruptly thwarted, and Johnson was given further justification for insisting that his conditions be met prior to any escalation. The first blow came from the politically organized Buddhists, who were now clearly out to topple the recently installed civilian Prime Minister Tran Van Huong, whom they regarded as opposed to their objectives and simply another in a series of American creations.*

Intensification of the Buddhist campaign to oust Huong led participants in a further top-level meeting in Washington to single out relations between the Buddhists and the GVN, and between the Buddhists and the United States, as "the problem of immediate priority." By December 16 Taylor was cabling Washington that the Buddhists were out to unseat Huong, "in full knowledge" that this was "contrary to [the] U.S. position." . . .

The second and most devastating blow to Taylor's hopes—and reputation—came from the still badly factionalized Saigon military. For, despite his briefing to Khanh and other senior officers on the new American inducements for political solidarity and better military performance, internecine warfare among the officer corps mounted and spilled over into Saigon's political life with a force that shattered what little coherence still existed. The precipitating factor in this denouement was the refusal of the largely powerless civilian legislative body, the High National

---

*Huong had not been Khanh's choice, but in any case Khanh remained de facto the major power in the government.

Council, to yield to the Young Turks' insistence that it pass a law requiring the immediate retirement of nine generals and thirty other officers with more than twenty-five years of service. . . . Exasperated by the council's show of independence, the Young Turks, Khanh, and most, if not all, of the rest of the Military Council (MRC) abolished the High National Council on December 20, arresting eight of its most influential members along with at least ten other civilian officials and political leaders. To consolidate their position, they replaced the MRC with a new Armed Forces Council (AFC)—a sort of revamped MRC in which they had greater representation. . . .

On December 22, Khanh issued an order of the day to the armed forces in which he pointedly warned against foreign intervention in Vietnamese affairs and, though pledging continued support of Huong and the chief of state, Suu, reserved the armed forces' right to change the government if they thought things were getting out of hand. The next day Khanh and most of the senior Vietnamese officers decided to have Huong and Suu declare Taylor *persona non grata* and officially request the U.S. government to withdraw him as its representative. If Huong refused to go along, these officers planned to hold a press conference the next day at which they would release a letter providing "detailed accounts of Ambassador Taylor's meetings with the four Vietnamese generals on 20 December as well as his 21 December ultimatum to General Khanh." But the embassy informed Huong and Khanh that Rusk had cabled that to declare the American ambassador *persona non grata* "would make it virtually impossible for the USG to continue [to] support [the] GVN effort." Khanh then persuaded the Young Turks to follow a more moderate course of action. The letter was not released, and although Khanh publicly charged the ambassador with abusing his power and insulting the generals, he stopped short of a *persona non grata* declaration. . . .

By the end of December 1964, then, it had become abundantly evident that the political situation in Saigon was continuing to deteriorate—moving further away from, rather than toward, the conditions that the president had posited as prerequisites for launching even a Phase I reprisal bombing. If there were doubts that Johnson was determined to stick to his conditions, they must have been dispelled with his denial of requests from both Taylor and the U.S. military that he order a bombing strike against the North. This was to be in retaliation for the Christmas Eve bombing, in the "very heart of [the] most heavily guarded section of Saigon," of the Brinks U.S. officers' billet, in which two Americans were killed and thirty-eight others plus thirteen Vietnamese injured. Military leaders and some civilian advisers (not including McNamara and Rusk) saw this as a flagrant example of the sort of provocation that was supposed to justify Phase I retaliatory air attacks. The president's refusal to bomb the North dramatically illustrated how far the political situation in Saigon fell short of the prerequisites he had set. Neither the American public nor international opinion, he concluded, was likely to believe that the NLF, rather than one of the Saigon factions, was actually responsible for the Brinks incident; indeed, it was several days before the administration itself concluded that the NLF was actually behind it. "In view of the overall confusion in Saigon," the State Department cabled Taylor, reprisal bombing against the North would be certain to elicit a "strong reaction in US opinion and internationally" that the administration was "trying to shoot its way out of an internal [Saigonese] political crisis."

To both the president and Taylor it was evident that the Saigon government could no longer be regarded as a satisfactory instrument of American policy, in either military or political terms. Moreover, the actions of Khanh, the Young Turks, and the Buddhists had revealed beyond a shadow of doubt that there was a glaring absence of either the political cohesion and stability or improved military effectiveness that Johnson continued to demand before any bombing campaign against North Vietnam could be launched. As long as the president held to this precondition, plans for such an escalation had to be shelved. Not for another six weeks, under mounting pressure by three of his most influential advisers—McGeorge Bundy, Robert McNamara, and Maxwell Taylor—did Lyndon Johnson abandon his position.

Suddenly, only ten days after the Brinks attack, the question was no longer one of improving the ARVN's military effectiveness, but simply trying to keep it from total collapse. The imminence of this possibility fueled the arguments of proponents of increased U.S. military intervention—whether they advocated an air war against the North, ground combat troops for the South, or both.

The precariousness of the ARVN's situation became progressively more evident during January and February 1965 as a consequence of a series of disastrous military engagements, a further decline in its morale, a mounting level of desertion, and exhaustion of the army's entire strategic reserve. This perception crystallized in the first week of January with the stunning defeat at Binh Gia, about forty miles southeast of Saigon, of two of the ARVN's best battalions, together with supporting armored and mechanized forces, by less numerous and relatively poorly armed Viet Cong forces—despite a major U.S. airlift of reinforcements and a swarm of armed American-piloted helicopters ordered into battle in support of the ARVN units. The magnitude and implications of this significant defeat were not fully divulged to the American public, though some diligent correspondents sensed its seriousness. A secret memorandum of January 5 to McGeorge Bundy from JCS chairman Earle G. Wheeler reported that in this battle there had been 445 Vietnamese and 16 American casualties, as against 132 Viet Cong (only 32 of which were confirmed by body count), and that 4 of the 124 U.S. helicopters engaged there had been shot down. . . .

Taylor saw the causes of this situation as "lack of stable government, inadequate security against the VC and nation-wide war-weariness." Among the basic factors responsible for the turmoil were "chronic factionalism . . . absence of national spirit and motivation," and "lack of cohesion in the social structure. . . ." Americans, he admonished, could not change these factors in any fundamental way and could only recognize their existence and adjust plans and expectations accordingly. In the existing governmental crisis, an American effort to salvage Prime Minister Huong would probably leave him "pretty much under military domination." If the government were still to be controlled by Khanh, "we will have to do hard soul-searching to decide whether to try to get along with him again after previous failures or to refuse to support him and take the consequences—which might entail ultimate withdrawal." If the United States was able to "mislay" Khanh and set up another officer as chief of state, it might have "a fresh option worth trying."

But whatever the outcome, "whether a jerry-built civilian government under military domination or a brand new military government, it will not get far," the ambassador said, "unless a new factor is added which will contribute to coalescing the political fashions around and within the government and thus bolster its position." As for that "new factor," the "only one which offers any chance of the needed success in the available time" that would help "pull the government together, stimulate pacification and raise the morale" was, he reiterated, a Phase II "program of graduated air attacks against the will of the DRV." Referring to the president's thesis that "this guerrilla war cannot be won from the air," Taylor assured him that he was in entire agreement "if we are thinking in terms of the physical destruction of the enemy," but that the bombing would be designed "to bring pressure on the will of the chiefs of the DRV. As practical men, they cannot wish to see the fruits of ten years of labor destroyed by slowly escalating air attacks." . . .

By threatening to withhold U.S. funds earmarked for a major expansion of Saigon's military budget, Taylor was able to pressure Khanh and the Young Turks to agree to a compromise. In order to secure release of the money, the generals undertook to free the jailed members of the High National Council, speed convening of a constitutional convention, continue backing Huong as prime minister, and increase military draft calls. In Taylor's opinion, the substantial military-aid funds would give him the leverage to prevent a government dominated by Khanh, and "for the immediate future" contain his ambitions "within the framework of increased military participation in the government." The ambassador thus prevailed upon Prime Minister Huong on January 19 to add four of the Young Turk officers to his Cabinet—General Nguyen Van Thieu as second deputy prime minister, General Nguyen Cao Ky as minister of youth and sports, General Linh Quang Vien as minister of psychological warfare, and General Tran Van Minh as minister of the armed forces, a portfolio previously held by Huong himself. With this Cabinet reshuffle achieved, Taylor agreed to release the funds required for increasing the total strength of the South Vietnamese armed forces from 560,000 to 660,000 men. . . .

Only some three weeks after the Armed Forces Council had entered into a covenant with Taylor to support Prime Minister Huong and his still predominantly civilian government, members of the embassy awoke on January 27 to find that the Saigon military had found it expedient to betray the agreement. With Buddhist backing and support from the Young Turks and the rest of the military council, Khanh presented the Americans with the *fait accompli* of Huong's ouster, and a mandate from Khanh's military colleagues for him to take charge of the government and resolve the crisis.

Khanh was, however, to savor increased authority for just twenty-three days, during which this astute opportunist sought to cling to power by straddling two incompatible positions—attempting to please both the Buddhists and the Americans. While discreetly demonstrating his support for the Buddhist-led peace movement—ultimately by covertly exploring possibilities for an accommodation with the NLF—he was privately assuring American officials that they could count upon him to support fundamental U.S. objectives, even assuring them that he favored American military escalation, which the Buddhists so strongly opposed. If U.S. officials, now increasingly panicked by the mounting popular demand for peace, had not ultimately gotten wind of Khanh's overture to the NLF, he might have managed to stay on longer: despite his role in ousting Huong, his acceptance of U.S. plans to bomb the North made him useful to proponents of this program. The president's national security adviser appears to have been Khanh's most ardent supporter. The day after Huong had been ousted from office, McGeorge Bundy cabled the outraged Taylor that, with respect to the president's goal of stable government, "we now wonder whether this requirement is either realistic or necessary." (His use of "we" is puzzling, for all available evidence points to Johnson's continued adherence to his original position.) Bundy further cabled on February 1, "If a Khanh-controlled government has some staying power and is reasonably effective, I think we're probably stuck with it."

With Bundy still supporting Khanh, Taylor was unable to get the green light he sought from Washington for mounting a coup. Thus, despite the ambassador's ongoing efforts to encourage various Saigon officers to take such an action, he still could not offer them the full assurances of Washington's support that might have given these men the necessary courage.

But Khanh was not the only or the biggest problem faced by the U.S. mission. There had now emerged what a CIA study for the U.S. Intelligence Board referred to as a "shift in the alignment of fundamental political forces" that was leading to "a social and political revolution," wherein power was now passing from "an elite of French-educated and predominantly Catholic mandarin types" to "a much more 'Vietnamese,' militantly nationalistic and potentially xenophobic group of which the political bonzes, the students and certain young generals are prime examples." This was marked by an upsurge of Buddhist power: they were now "strong enough to make unworkable any set of political arrangements their leaders care to oppose." The widely supported Buddhist movement was regarded as deriving its political strength "primarily from the fact that 'Buddhism' has become the rallying point for emotionally charged though inchoate revolutionary aspirations." It was to be expected that the now aroused "extreme nationalist sentiments" and their "xenophobic and anti-US overtones" would set "severe limits on the degree to which the US can influence Vietnamese actions." Moreover, the report concluded, "The chances have increased that nationalist sentiments, in combination with war weariness and frustrations will take a pro-neutralist turn which the Communists would certainly endeavor to fan and exploit. On the other hand, however, a vigorous nationalism identified with an indigenously devised government reflecting local political realities will be an essential ingredient for any dynamic and successful counterinsurgency effort."

The central problem was, of course, that such a Saigon government would not have followed policies compatible with Washington's. If it were indeed "indigenously devised" and actually reflected "local political realities" it would by definition be a government that would be independent of U.S. control and would respond to the broadly based popular desire for an end to the fighting and a peaceful settlement with the NLF.

Taylor acknowledged that the mass of South Vietnamese wanted peace, and it was the now enhanced capacity of the Buddhist monks to provide a channel for this sentiment that most alarmed U.S. officials. This concern dominated Taylor's cables during the last days of January. He warned Washington that the victory of the Buddhists and their dependent ally General Khanh had put the monks in a position of "increased prestige and influence in [the] country," whereby they "could create an atmosphere conducive to pressures for a negotiated settlement." The State Department responded by requesting Taylor's "estimate of possible actions we might take or approaches we might make to keep situation from moving towards atmosphere conducive to pressures for 'negotiated settlement.'" Taylor had a prescription, but in the face of the president's views, it required an altered rationale for American military intervention.

Following his inauguration, Lyndo0n Johnson still hung back from authorizing any bombing of the North—either retaliatory attacks or a sustained program. With nearly all of his senior advisers defecting to a pro-escalation position almost as ardent as that of the Joint Chiefs, Johnson was left with only Dean Rusk to support his stipulation that any such program remain conditional on the political improvement and stability of the Saigon regime; even Rusk soon came to abandon this position. Yet Khanh's ouster of Prime Minister Huong and the visibly rising influence and power of the Buddhists must have given the president additional pause.

Beyond the administration's embarrassment at the political chaos in Saigon, then, was its gathering alarm at the possibility that Buddhist leaders could channel the mounting tide of antiwar sentiment in South Vietnam into the creation of a government that would demand a cease-fire, a negotiated settlement with the NLF, and ultimately the departure of the Americans. This prospect seemed very real in early 1965. However awkward it was to request public support for an escalating U.S. intervention in behalf of the existing Saigon government, it would be patently absurd to expect such support for a peace-oriented, neutralist government that wanted the United States to leave....

Lyndon Johnson's key civilian advisers were almost all (with Rusk for a while remaining the exception) chipping away at his determination that Saigon must first demonstrate it had "cleaned up its own back yard." In pressing the president to change his position, the advisers abandoned their earlier argument that political cohesion in Saigon would be strengthened and its army's morale heightened by the mere promise of a future American bombing campaign. Since this was patently not the case, they now turned the old philosophy on its head, and what had been the rationale against bombing now became the rationale for it. Their earlier military-political equation was reversed so that no such improvement could be expected until after a sustained bombing campaign against the North had actually been launched. Without such a tangible earnest of American commitment—so their new argument ran—the United States would face the imminent prospect of a neutralist government in Saigon that would form a coalition with the NLF and ask the United States to leave....

Despite the arguments for bombing, Johnson was evidently still not convinced. According to James Thomson—and the accuracy of his recollection has been attested to by William Bundy—"The sense in the White House was that the President did not want to do this, and this was one reason for the McGeorge Bundy mission— his felt need for a final determination shows his reluctance." Chester Cooper, the

Bundy aide who accompanied him on this mission, later wrote that on the eve of their departure "the Administration seemed to be on dead center and the President was caught between McNamara's pleas for new initiatives and Rusk's reluctance to take any important new steps until the political situation in Saigon could be put in some semblance of order." Consequently, states Cooper, "The President agreed to send a high-level working group including members of his own staff to Saigon . . . for a fresh look. Out of such an examination, he felt, would come recommendations either to move ahead in new and more vigorous ways to gain the initiative against the Viet Cong or to proceed down a path of disengagement." Prior to the Bundy mission, Cooper concluded, "The option of disengagement, or at least the possibility of a serious consideration of disengagement or a scaling down, was a live one."

Annoyed by McGeorge Bundy's unstinting support of Khanh and apparently believing that if the national security adviser ever actually visited Vietnam he might develop a more realistic grasp of Saigon's politics, Taylor had earlier suggested to Johnson that it would be useful to send Bundy for a visit. The president had agreed to dispatch someone to look into "the enormous problem" of Saigon's "political unity." On January 27 he decided to send Bundy. Since the president accepted Taylor's advice that Bundy's trip be deferred until "the shape of [the] new [post–January-27-coup] government became more clear," the departure was delayed until February 3. Hours before Bundy boarded his plane, a cable from Taylor, presumably referring to his own support for a coup against Khanh, warned him, "You may be arriving just in time to witness some very important governmental developments. . . .We may give you an interesting time," and chided, "In any case you will find as a specific item high on our agenda: can the U.S. do business with a Khanh government? We shall expect you to defend the affirmative as we will be on the side of the negative."

When his plane left for Saigon, Bundy was hardly a detached, impartial referee. He had for many months clearly favored a major American military escalation in Vietnam. As early as May 25, 1964, he had recommended to the president that he "use selected and carefully graduated military force against North Vietnam," and his commitment was certainly evident three months later when, in the face of McNamara's reluctance to send in marines to guard U.S. installations, he had privately suggested to Johnson that he send in "a couple of brigade-size" U.S. ground forces for "operations against the Viet Cong." Moreover, the small group that accompanied Bundy to Saigon was made up of men, including John McNaughton, who shared the national security adviser's views on the need for a sustained bombing program.

At 2:00 A.M. on February 7, the fourth and last day of Bundy's stay in Vietnam, a company of Viet Cong soldiers launched an attack against a laxly guarded U.S. helicopter base and advisers' barracks at Pleiku in the Central Highlands. Eight Americans were killed, 126 wounded, ten U.S. planes destroyed, and numerous others damaged. This was one, and by no means the largest, of ten Viet Cong attacks launched that day, following the termination of a unilateral Viet Cong seven-day Tet (New Year) ceasefire. It did not produce as many military casualties as two battalion-sized attacks in an adjacent province, but it did result in by far the largest number of Americans killed and wounded of any incident in the conflict thus far. And, in contrast to the Brinks attack of December 24, this time there was no doubt that the Viet Cong were responsible. Bundy promptly joined other advocates of bombing in insisting that the Pleiku assault constituted the type of credible, clear-cut provocation cited by the president as a possible trigger for a one-shot American retaliatory air strike against the North. While checking intermittently by "secure phone" with Bundy in Saigon, Johnson then presided over a meeting of the National Security Council in Washington, attended by all the advisers save Rusk. Except for the Senate majority leader, Mike Mansfield, the entire group supported a retaliatory air strike by 132 carrier-based U.S. jets against four different barracks complexes inside North Vietnam. Less than fourteen hours after the Pleiku attack, U.S. planes were over North Vietnam. Phase I (code-named "Flaming Dart"), the retaliatory bombing campaign, had begun.

For some of the president's advisers, the Pleiku attack did not come as a great surprise—nor should it have, as McGeorge Bundy later implied in his remark "Pleikus are streetcars." In other words, you could expect one to come along presently, and you were ready to board it as soon as it did. But it was propitiously timed for him and others to persuade Johnson to adopt a policy of Tonkin Gulf–type reprisals. Bundy had good reason to expect one of these "streetcars" during his visit to Vietnam. Not only was it usual for the Viet Cong to launch heavy attacks just after the termination of Tet cease-fires, but U.S. intelligence reports had indicated one was to be expected against an American installation during Bundy's visit. The reason given by Allen S. Whiting, then the State Department's director of research and analysis for the Far East, for later referring to the post-Pleiku air raids against the North as "ostensibly" in response to the February 7 Viet Cong attack, bears directly on this question. "Actually," he states, "the raids were preplanned on the basis of the author's forecast that a Communist assault would be mounted against an American installation during the visit of McGeorge Bundy, special assistant for National Security Affairs." (Bundy, however, has recently said that he cannot recall being told this.) Also pertinent to this preplanning was the "unanswered" question reported by the *New York Times* White House correspondent Charles Mohr as to why all three of the normally widely dispersed attack carriers of the Seventh Fleet (from which the U.S. planes were launched) were concentrated near the coast of North Vietnam shortly before the reprisal bombing. The Pleiku pretext came on schedule; so did the reprisal bombing, or, as Whiting later observed, "The weekend events followed according to prediction and plan."

Suggested Readings

Larry Berman, *Planning a Tragedy* (1983).

Charles DeBenedetti and Charles Chatfield, *An American Ordeal: The Antiwar Movement of the Vietnam Era* (1990).

Todd Gitlin, *The Sixties* (1987).

George C. Herring, *America's Longest War*, 2nd ed. (1986).

Stanley Karnow, *Vietnam: A History* (1983).

Melvin Small, *Johnson, Nixon and the Doves* (1988).

Ronald Spector, *After Tet* (1992).

Harry Summers, Jr., *On Strategy: A Critical Analysis of the Vietnam War* (1981).

Kathleen J. Turner, *Lyndon Johnson's Dual War; Vietnam and the Press* (1985).

Marilyn B. Young, *The Vietnam War* (1990).

FURTHER READINGS

The Great Society Programs

Vaughn D. Bornet, *The Presidency of Lyndon B. Johnson* (1983); Greg J. Duncan, *Years of Poverty, Years of Plenty* (1984); Doris Kearns, *Lyndon Johnson and the American Dream* (1976); James T. Patterson, *America's Struggle Against Poverty* (1982); Bruce J. Schulman, *Lyndon B. Johnson and American Liberalism* (1995).

Civil Rights and the Emergence of the Black Power Movement

David J. Garrow, *Protest at Selma* (1978); Mary King, *Freedom Song* (1987); Bruce Perry, *Malcolm* (1991); Charles and Barbara Whalen, *The Longest Debate: A Legislative History of the 1964 Civil Rights Act* (1985).

The Johnson Administration's Approach to the Cold War

Desmond Ball, *Politics and Force Levels* (1980); Richard J. Barnet, *Intervention and Revolution: United States and the Third World* (1969); H.W. Brands, Jr., *The Wages of Globalism* (1994); Abraham Lowenthal, *The Dominican Intervention* (1972); John B. Martin, *Overtaken by Events* (1966); Jerome Slater, *Intervention and Negotiation* (1970).

Johnson, Vietnam, and the Vietnam Experience

Christian G. Appy, *Working-Class War: American Combat Soldiers in Vietnam* (1993); Larry Berman, *Lyndon Johnson's War* (1989); Robert Buzzanco, *Masters of War: Military Dissent and Politics in the Vietnam Era* (1996) Daniel C. Hallin, *The Uncensored War: The Media and Vietnam* (1986); Martha Hess, *Then the Americans Came: Voices from Vietnam* (1993); James Wirtz, *The Tet Offensive: Intelligence Failure in War* (1991).

QUESTIONS FOR DISCUSSION

1. Discuss the Civil Rights Act of 1964 and evaluate its impact on the Deep South. How did civil rights contribute to the emergence of black power?
2. Describe President Johnson's war on poverty. What progress, if any, did he make?
3. In what ways can the Great Society be compared to the New Deal?
4. What was Johnson trying to accomplish in Vietnam? Describe the effect of escalation on the American home front.
5. How can America's "victory" in the Tet offensive be viewed as a defeat?
6. Did American involvement in Vietnam affect its diplomacy toward Latin America and the Middle East? Explain.
7. George Kahin places blame for the disastrous war on Johnson's advisors. What evidence does he cite to support his claim?

CHAPTER TWENTY-SEVEN

CONTINUITY AND CONFLICT: American Society, 1960–1975

The war in Vietnam, racial polarization, and a rising inflation rate together with the ongoing arms race with the Soviet Union quickly dissipated the sense of purpose and cautious optimism that characterized America in the early 1960s. Focusing their frustration on the status quo, American college students rebelled against bureaucratized universities that treated them like cogs in a machine and a federal government that seemed determined to sacrifice them in a senseless war. Young people either clung to the conformity of the 1950s or attempted to create an alternative culture, one in which freedom of expression, economic equality, and social justice prevailed. Inspired by the civil rights movement, women organized, lobbied, and demonstrated to secure their economic and political rights. African Americans continued to agitate for full citizenship and became increasingly frustrated with the slow pace of the civil rights movement.

Protestants, Catholics, and, to an extent, Jews rallied either to traditional mores and institutions or embraced the activism that seemed determined to overturn those mores and institutions. Evangelicals, charismatics, and biblical literalists turned to the television to spread their ministry.

Education struggled to reflect changing social norms—integration rather than segregation; democracy rather than hierarchy in the classroom; and the inculcation of self-esteem rather that just literacy in the humanities, sciences, social sciences, and arts. Exhausted by the war, by economic insecurity, by the turmoil created by various social justice campaigns, America by the mid-1970s longed for the comparatively staid normality of the 1950s.

EDUCATION IN CRISIS

During the 1950s public schools became the object of widespread criticism by educators and social commentators. They charged that the system lacked intellectual vitality and discipline, that it encouraged mediocrity at the sacrifice of excellence, that it promoted athletics and social activities over academic endeavors. These attacks culminated with the publication of *The American High School Today* (1959) by James B. Conant, former president of Harvard University. He faulted the schools for neglecting the core curriculum of liberal education: literature, composition, foreign language, and philosophy. The educational system, he said, had become philosophically and institutionally incapable of caring either for its brightest or its dullest students.

Advocates of educational renewal were able to take advantage of the Soviet Union's spectacular success in putting two satellites into earth orbit in the fall of 1957. Sputnik dramatized the fact that Russia spent a far greater percentage of its budget on education than the United States and created the impression that America's Cold War adversary was far ahead of it in scientific expertise. For the first time, there seemed to be a broad national consensus linking the national interest with excellence in education. In 1958, Congress passed the National Defense Education Act which provided a system of generous loans and grants for college students. Federal aid under the act coupled with matching grants from the Fund for the Advancement of Education financed programs to improve teacher training, funded construction of new buildings, and provided incentives for the teaching of natural science and foreign language. Suddenly, it had become one's patriotic duty to learn calculus and Spanish (or Russian or Chinese if you were going into the CIA).

Despite the NDEA and other federal aid to education programs, public schooling continued to be characterized by crisis and reform. During the 1960s and 1970s elementary and secondary education had to cope with integration, affirmative action (legal rulings supported claims by African Americans and other minorities that because of current and historic discrimination, they were entitled to special consideration in hiring, college admissions, and other areas), and democratization. Increasingly, the public demanded that schools simultaneously educate and socialize the brilliant and affluent, the poor and the handicapped. Indeed, by 1970 the goal of American education seemed to have become that everyone emerge from the system with a minimum of education and a maximum of self-esteem. In 1975, the College Entrance Examination Board reported that scores on the Scholastic Aptitude Test taken each year by more than a million high school students had declined steadily from 1965 through 1975. That produced another massive outcry against "the rising tide of mediocrity." By the 1980s public education had become a major political issue; a number of state legislatures passed measures to encourage excellence, emphasize a core curriculum, and improve teacher performance.

While elementary and secondary education wallowed in self-doubt, higher education in America flourished. The post-1945 era witnessed nothing less than the democratization of American colleges and universities. College enrollment doubled between 1940 and 1960 and reached 12 million by 1980. With the expansion of higher education, a college degree became a prerequisite for a growing number of white-collar jobs. One study found that, whereas in 1942 only 30 percent of American business executives held college degrees, in 1952 60 percent had graduated from a four-year institution and that number continued to climb until by 1980 a college or university diploma was a prerequisite for employment in the corporate world. The expansion of the nation's colleges and universities was accompanied by the emergence of the United States as a leader in scientific and technological inquiry. Fueled first by World War II and then the Cold War, federal expenditures on universities and laboratories increased from $50 million in 1939 to $15 billion in the mid-1960s and helped create the "knowledge revolution." By that latter period, American scientists were leading the way in nuclear physics, medical research, aeronautical engineering, and computers.

RELIGION IN AMERICAN LIFE

Americans responded to the anxieties of the Cold War and the depersonalizing pressures of modern society by joining churches in droves. Church membership increased from 64.5 million in 1940 (49 percent of the population) to 125 million (64 percent) in 1965. Even with the cynicism spawned by Vietnam and Watergate and the cultural revolution of the 1960s, 140 million Americans (60 percent) attended worship services in 1982. Almost all denominations grew during this period with the Catholics, Baptists, and various Pentecostal groups showing the greatest rates of increase. Gallup polls taken in 1976 indicated that 34 percent of Americans had had a born-again charismatic experience.

By the 1960s mainstream denominations began turning outward, taking a more active part in the civil rights movement, participating in anti–Vietnam War demonstrations, and launching their own war on poverty. A New Theology rooted in the writings of Dietrich Bonhoeffer, a German theologian martyred by the Nazis, and Anglican Bishop John A.T. Robinson, suited to the social activism of the period, emerged. The New Theology emphasized the concept of *immanence*, the idea that God dwells in man, as opposed to *transcendence*, the notion of a remote God ruling from a distant heaven. It was therefore not only possible but necessary that human beings make God and the church relevant to new forces in society. Increasingly, moral absolutes and traditional forms of worship came under attack.

Many young people rebelled against the church while others sought to transform it. The stage musical (and later, film) *Jesus Christ Superstar* with its rock music and message of love and resistance to injustice had great appeal to the young. Populations of "Jesus freaks," who were Bible-oriented but adopted the language and lifestyle of the counterculture, began in California and spread to campuses across the country.

The 1970s was marked by a new surge of religious revivalism and fundamentalist fervor. Jesus movements developed not only on the periphery of Christianity, but within mainstream denominations as well, and the movement broadened its appeal and grew exponentially. Television preachers and faith healers such as Billy Graham, Oral Roberts, and Jimmy Swaggart drew millions of viewers and contributors.

Out of this upsurge of evangelical, pentecostal fervor came a political movement journalists tabbed the New Religious Right. Fiscally conservative, advocates of a states' rights constitutional philosophy, they paradoxically demanded that their moral and religious views be institutionalized as part of the civil order. The New Religious Right railed against the U.S. Supreme Court decision in *Engel v. Vitale* (1962) which held that compulsory prayer in schools was unconstitutional. They demanded that Congress outlaw abortion, denounced homosexuals as moral and biological perversions, and insisted that political candidates come out four-square in favor of "family values."

Leading this invasion of the secular by the religious was the Reverend Jerry Falwell, an independent Baptist evangelist and television personality from Virginia, who founded a political-religious movement called the Moral Majority. Traditional denominations generally rejected the Moral Majority's efforts to have the state enforce a conservative moral agenda, but the evangelical movement produced a much-needed spiritual invigoration within Protestant denominations.

EQUALITY OF OPPORTUNITY, DEMOCRACY, AND THE SUPREME COURT

One of the principal engines of social change in the 1960s and 1970s was the usually staid and traditional Supreme Court. Under the leadership of Earl Warren, a liberal California Republican with little experience in legal scholarship, the court ventured into new areas. The *Brown v. Board of Education* decision mandating integrated schools and *Yates v. U.S.*, (1956) in which the justices reversed the conviction of fourteen communists on the grounds that they had not actually organized a plot to overthrow the government, were merely hints of things to come. In 1962, Felix Frankfurter, an advocate of judicial restraint, retired to be replaced by the liberal Arthur Goldberg. After he became president in 1963, Lyndon Johnson filled a second vacancy on the court with NAACP lawyer Thurgood Marshall, the first African-American justice.

MAJOR RULINGS

With a clear majority of activists, the Warren Court issued a series of landmark decisions that extended to state and local jurisdictions the traditional rights afforded the accused in federal court. In *Gideon v. Wainwright* (1963), the justices decreed that indigent defendants were entitled to court-appointed counsel.

Perhaps the most famous civil liberties case of the post–World War II era was decided in 1966 when in *Miranda v. Arizona*, the Supreme Court ruled that those individuals arrested had to be informed of their constitutional rights or their arrests and succeeding judicial procedures against them were invalid. Other decisions stipulated that a suspect was entitled to have a lawyer present when being interrogated by police. In effect, the Warren Court said that the poor and ignorant were entitled to the same protections as the well-to-do and well-informed.

Throughout American history, the power of state legislatures to establish election districts for various representative bodies, including the national House of Representatives, had served as an obstacle to democracy. Voting areas were frequently created with an eye to reducing the power of minorities or urban areas, or to protecting vested interests. In 1962 in *Baker v. Carr* the court ruled that the Tennessee legislature had to redistribute its legislative seats to give the people of Memphis equal representation. In subsequent decisions, the justices extended the principle of one man–one vote to every political sphere. In effect, the court ruled that places in every legislative body be apportioned on the basis of people and not land.

BACKLASH AGAINST THE COURT

The activism of the Warren Court provoked a storm of criticism. The rulings that extended protection to criminals and those accused of subversive activities led some Americans to charge that the court had left the American people completely vulnerable to the twin evils of communism and crime. The John Birch Society, a fanatical anticommunist, proto-fascist organization founded in 1959, launched a campaign to impeach Earl Warren. When the chief justice and his colleagues outlawed prayer in the schools in the *Engel* case, conservatives charged that the court was also undermining the moral values of the country. "They've put the Negroes in the schools," complained one southern legislator, "and now they've driven God out." Legal scholars voiced fears that the high court's intervention into controversial social issues would politicize and therefore weaken it. But the members of the Warren Court were determined to heed Oliver Wendell Holmes' admonition that it was the duty of interpreters as well as makers of the law to reflect changing social conditions and protect the interests of *all* of the people.

THE WOMEN'S MOVEMENT

To an extent, the civil rights movement served as a catalyst for another important social movement of the 1960s and 1970s—feminism. Although the cult of the hearth that so dominated popular culture during the 1950s persisted into the next decade, the content of women's roles had changed since the end of World War II. By the 1960s employment for middle-class white and married women had become the norm rather than the exception; the two-income household had emerged as a prerequisite for the consumer culture. In 1970, for example, 60 percent of all families with an income of more than $10,000 boasted wives who worked. Yet most of these jobs were segregated by gender, there was little opportunity for professional advancement, and women did not receive equal pay for equal work. Old ideas persisted. Television programs, popular magazine articles, and motion pictures asserted in subtle ways that the wife who held a job was playing a supportive role rather than developing her own potential. The notion that the working wife was just helping out made possible the blending of old stereotypes with new conditions. In the world of women's rights there was no alternative ideology or critical mass of protestors to challenge traditional role models.

Nonetheless, powerful forces were at work eroding the cultural and social status quo. The working woman's experience simply did not square with conventional stereotypes. Segregated by sex and exploited though they were, women were exposed to and affected by the power and responsibilities of the workplace. Children of parents who both worked grew up with substantially different ideas of what was acceptable for men and women to do. Daughters of working women expressed the belief that women and men should share a variety of work, household, and recreational experiences.

THE STRUGGLE FOR ECONOMIC AND POLITICAL POWER

By the time John Kennedy and Richard Nixon squared off in the 1960 election, women's rights had become a compelling issue for the Democratic party. In 1961, Kennedy established the President's Commission on the Status of Women. Its report confirmed the existence of widespread discrimination in both the public and private sectors and urged passage of remedial legislation. In many ways, it was the *To Secure These Rights* of the women's movement. Title VII of the 1964 Civil Rights Act prohibited job discrimination because of race, color, religion, sex, or national origin. Meanwhile, a spate of feminist books and articles appeared which identified the roots of oppression, both external and internal. In 1963 Betty Friedan published *The Feminine Mystique*, questioning the value and satisfaction that middle-class women could derive from being housewives. She called the American home "a comfortable concentration camp." This book, along with Kate Millett's *Sexual Politics* (1970) and Germaine Greer's *The Female Eunuch* (1971), had an enormous impact on women.

In 1966, modern feminists founded the National Organization for Women (NOW) and elected Betty Friedan as its first president. This largest and most influential of women's organizations concentrated on legal challenges, allowed men to join, and functioned as an umbrella for many different agendas. NOW devoted much of its energy to passage of an equal rights amendment to the Constitution and to safeguarding a woman's right to abortion. In 1973, both chambers of Congress approved the Equal Rights Amendment, but it failed to gain the necessary ratification in three-fourths of the states. That same year in

The National Organization for Women had as its goal an increase in the political and economic power of women. A NOW march for gender equality "now."

Roe v. Wade the Supreme Court restricted the authority of states to prohibit abortion.

To direct the attention of the major political parties to women's issues, feminists founded the national Women's Political Caucus in 1971. Gradually, politicians, lawmakers, and bureaucrats became sensitized to the plight of battered women, the pressing need for state- and private-sector funded child care, and the existence of sexual harassment in the workplace.

A less structured, more extreme movement composed primarily of younger, unmarried women developed simultaneously with the more traditional feminist groups. These young activists shunned hierarchy, stressed group autonomy, and focused on informal consciousness raising sessions. Women in this branch of the movement wanted changes that went far beyond politics and economics. They worked to eliminate the traditional stereotypes relating to feminine behavior, educated their members in the use of contraceptives, and pointed out demeaning aspects of contemporary culture such as the use of sex to sell everything from beer to automobiles.

GAY LIBERATION

Gay and lesbian communities had existed since the founding of the republic, but not until the 1960s and 1970s did they begin to "come out of the closet" in significant numbers and to mobilize on behalf of political action to secure their constitutional rights. During the 1950s the Daughters of Bilitis and the Mattachine Society broke new ground in publicly agitating for an end to discrimination against gays in the military, in the workplace, in federal and state government, and in all areas of life. Then out of the gay communities in San Francisco and New York's Greenwich Village came the Society for Individual Rights and other organizations that simultaneously agitated for civil rights and supported gays and lesbians in their decisions to proclaim and defend their sexual identity.

But as was the case with the black civil rights movements, specific, dramatic acts of brutality and oppression proved more important to mobilizing gays and their supporters than institutions and organizations. Early in 1966 New York Mayor John Lindsay ordered his police department to crack down on homosexual activity in the area between Times Square and Washington Square. The American Civil Liberties Union chastised the mayor for confusing "deviant social behavior with criminal activity," but the authorities persisted. When in 1969 New York police raided a popular gay bar in Greenwich Village, the gay community rose up and staged an all-night protest. In the days that followed the "Stonewall Riot," as it was called, homosexual men and women formed the Gay Liberation Front. "We reject society's attempt to impose sexual roles and definitions of our nature," the group's manifesto read. "We are stepping outside these roles and simplistic myths. We are going to be who we are." Gay activists resorted to time-proven methods of protest, including street demonstrations and sit-ins and established connections with other protest movements by declaring their opposition to the war in Vietnam and their support of black liberation.

THE STUDENT MOVEMENT

The civil rights and feminist movements both stimulated and mirrored a rebellion by American college students against established institutions and authority in general. By the 1960s, the baby boomers, the generation born in the immediate aftermath of World War II, having experienced neither war nor depression and subjected to the homogenizing effects of television, were attending colleges and universities in unprecedented numbers. Many institutions of higher learning grew exponentially during this period, turning into bureaucratized, impersonal multiversities that increasingly stifled and alienated their student bodies. During 1960–1961 a small but significant number of white students joined the sit-in movement. Inspired by John F. Kennedy's idealism and appeals for sacrifice, others joined the Peace Corps or VISTA. As racism and poverty persisted, as American involvement in Vietnam deepened, and as evidence of the domination of American life by the military-industrial complex mounted, a full-fledged youth rebellion erupted on college campuses across the nation.

STUDENTS FOR A DEMOCRATIC SOCIETY

The student movement of the sixties manifested itself both politically and culturally. Inspired by the beat generation of the 1950s and by the natural rights philosophy of Jean-Jacques Rousseau, Tom Hayden, together with fellow University of Michigan student Al Haber, founded the Students for a Democratic Society (SDS) in 1960. Two years later Hayden promulgated what became known as the Port Huron Statement. The United States, he proclaimed, was dominated by giant organizations—corporations, universities, government bureaucracies—all of which by their nature oppressed and alienated the individual. Citing the civil rights movement as an example, Hayden proclaimed that students had the opportunity to restore participatory democracy to American life by seizing control of college campuses and the academic environment from faceless administrators. He and other student activists coined the term "New Left" to distinguish their brand of grassroots democracy from the Old Left of the 1930s which espoused traditional Marxism and held up Soviet communism as a worthy example.

THE FREE SPEECH MOVEMENT

It was Berkeley rather than Ann Arbor, however, that served as the first laboratory for New Left direct action. When, in October 1964, University of California Chancellor Clark Kerr announced that solicitations for political causes would no longer be allowed on campus, hundreds of student activists staged a sit-in. Over the next few days, the students' ranks swelled to more than two thousand. Even members of the ultraconservative Youth for Goldwater joined in. Eventually Kerr relented, but the students, having tasted victory, wanted more. Led by a dynamic philosophy student named Mario Savio, Berkeley students formed the Free Speech Movement (FSM). Initially the FSM was a protest in behalf of student rights, but it quickly escalated into a protest against the modern university.

By 1967, the focus of the SDS and the New Left had become the agonizingly stalemated war in Vietnam. Paradoxically, while college students proved most successful at avoiding service in Vietnam—only 2 percent of all inductees were college graduates—they took the lead in protesting the war. In the spring of 1967, five hundred thousand marchers of all ages gathered in Central Park in New York to demonstrate against the war. Dozens of young men ceremoniously burned their draft cards, and the so-called resistance phase of the antiwar movement was born. From then until 1971, when the antiwar movement broadened to include virtually all components of society, students constituted the cutting edge of opposition to the war.

Meanwhile, the SDS was becoming more militant and authoritarian. Like Stokely Carmichael, Tom Hayden allowed himself to be seduced by the radical rhetoric of black militants like Huey Newton. He abandoned his earlier commitment to participatory democracy and civil disobedience, condoning violence if necessary to overthrow the system. Lenin replaced Rousseau as the prophet of the SDS, and capitalist imperialism replaced the multiversity as the primary foe. In part due to activities by the newly militant SDS and in part to heightened tensions stemming from the war in Vietnam and urban rioting, confrontations between students and authorities on campuses across the country turned violent with greater frequency.

DAYS OF RAGE: THE 1968 DEMOCRATIC CONVENTION

The confrontation between America's discontented youth and its increasingly defensive establishment climaxed at the 1968 Democratic convention at Chicago. While inside the convention hall, Democratic delegates nominated Lyndon Johnson's pliable and pro-war vice president, Hubert Humphrey, outside, dissenters from the war prepared to square off with Mayor Richard Daley's policemen. Knowing that they were bound to receive exposure on national television, dissenters of every stripe from the SDS to idealistic supporters of Eugene McCarthy, to members of the nihilistic Youth International Party (Yippies), assembled on the streets bordering the convention hall and did everything in their power to provoke the police. They were successful. Before an appalled national television audience, Daley's officers rioted, clubbing and teargassing demonstrators as well as innocent bystanders. The Chicago riots helped elect Republican Richard Nixon and speeded up the disintegration of the youth movement.

THE COUNTERCULTURE

The student movement of the 1960s expressed itself culturally as well as politically. For many of the disaffected, long hair, bell-bottom pants, tie-dyed shirts, sandals, mind-altering drugs, rock music, and communal living were more important than revolutionary ideology or participatory democracy. The hippies, the direct descendents of the 1950s' beatniks, were, like their New Left counterparts, generally affluent, well educated young whites and were alienated by racism, war, materialism, conventional morality, and perceived institutional oppression. But they were also disillusioned with politics, considering "the system" so corrupt and corrupting that the only answer was, as their guru, Harvard Professor Timothy Leary, put it, to "turn on, tune in, and drop out."

The counterculture expressed itself in a variety of ways. Some members contented themselves with immersion in oriental mysticism, while others experimented with psychedelic drugs: LSD ("acid"), mescaline, peyote, or hallucinatory mushrooms. Perhaps the most universal hippie practice was the smoking of marijuana, "pot." America's alienated young people congregated in ever-expanding communes in San Francisco's Haight-Ashbury district or New York's East Village. Some fled urban areas to establish rural cooperatives where they could commune with nature and escape the grasp of Wall Street and Madison Avenue. Most found nature a bit less hospitable than they had anticipated and returned to suburbia within several months.

Woodstock, 1969, the ultimate counterculture happening.

Another pervasive aspect of the hippie phenomenon was the outdoor rock concert. In August 1969 more than four hundred thousand young people, more than twice the number anticipated, gathered on a six hundred–acre farm near Bethel, New York. Traffic backed up for twenty miles around and the revelers simply abandoned their vehicles to make the trek to the first annual Woodstock music festival—"three days of peace and music . . . and love." Festival-goers were drawn by a list of performers that read like a rock music Who's Who, including Richie Havens; Jefferson Airplane; Crosby, Stills, and Nash; and Jimi Hendrix. Aside from several bad LSD trips, inadequate sanitary facilities, and intermittent rain, the huge gathering was peaceful and upbeat, the ultimate "happening."

For the most part, leaders of the women's movement in America have defined success and achievement in political and economic terms. They have emphasized gender-free hiring practices, equal pay for equal work, penetration of the traditionally white male power structure, and democratization of the family. There are those, however, who have chosen to emphasize women's traditional roles as nurturers and defined success in terms of childbearing and homemaking. This emphasis on biological and psychological difference may be seen in the progressive movement's campaign for the passage of special laws limiting the number of hours women might spend in the workplace and other protective laws. In the ensuing essay, Lynn Y. Weiner traces the rise of the La Leche League, an organization committed to breastfeeding and hence to the nonseparation of mother and child. Its popularity, Weiner argues, demonstrates that many American women in the 1960s and 1970s remained committed to traditional gender roles and to motherhood, and were willing to organize to defend them.

RECONSTRUCTING MOTHERHOOD: THE LA LECHE LEAGUE IN POSTWAR AMERICA

Lynn Y. Weiner

In the 1950s: Formula was providing scientifically perfect food for babies. Anesthesia was saving mothers from the horrors of childbirth. Bottles were making it easy for anyone to care for the baby. Schedules and discipline from the moment of birth were preventing babies from ruling their parents' lives. . . . In 1956, seven women joined together in a movement that was to change the face of motherhood in America. They have devoted their lives to bringing mother and baby together again.

—KAYE LOWMAN, THE LLLOVE STORY, 1978

For almost four decades, the La Leche League—a voluntary association of women—has championed its cause of "good mothering through breastfeeding" in the United States and around the world. Although the league has been largely overlooked in scholarly discussions of women in the postwar era, it represents an important piece in the puzzle of twentieth-century social history. The league's publication, *The Womanly Art of Breastfeeding,* has sold some two million copies since 1958, and millions of women have attended league support groups, read league literature, or otherwise encountered league ideology. By the mid-1980s, the league claimed over four thousand support groups in forty-eight countries, and in the United States it had a reputation among many women as the primary source of expertise on motherhood—a position earlier held by the United States Children's Bureau.

from Lynn Y. Weiner, "Reconstructing Motherhood: The La Leche League in Postwar America," *The Journal of American History,* Vol. 80, No. 4 (March 1994), 1357–1381.

The La Leche League was organized during a turbulent period when the social roles of American women as mothers and as workers were contested in both ideology and practice. Nineteenth-century middle-class cultural definitions had promoted "the intense, essentially private nature of the mother-child bond and the primary responsibility of mothers for the well-being of their children." In the mid-twentieth century, those definitions were challenged by developments in fertility patterns, new scientific childbirth and infant-feeding techniques, feminism, and the rapid growth of the female labor force. Science had entered the nursery, which growing numbers of women would soon leave behind.

The La Leche League arose to defend traditional domesticity against the assaults of modern industrial life and to dignify the physical, biological side of motherhood in ways that proved to have surprising appeal to many Americans. Whereas the nineteenth-century version of middle-class "true womanhood" emphasized moral purity and piety in a secular and industrializing age, the league, in the scientific twentieth century, emphasized naturalism. Mother and baby were not so much icons of purity as symbols of nature and simplicity. But they were not just symbols. The founders of the league had a social outlook that can be called maternalist; that is, they implied that an empowered motherhood defined by "female" qualities would improve society. Their faith in this maternalist prescription enabled La Leche League women to focus their efforts. From the mid-1950s to the present, the La Leche League has pursued a steadfast mission: to "bring mother and baby together again" through the "womanly art of breastfeeding."

That mission attracted a variety of supporters. To those suspicious of the intrusion of experts into family life, the league presented a social role for mothers that restored a sense of autonomy to the private domestic realm. Health benefits to mother and child from breastfeeding, childbirth as a natural process, trust in one's own instincts—these notions found favor among women who questioned "scientific motherhood," an ideology initially developed during the late nineteenth and early twentieth centuries that promoted the authority of experts in the realm of child rearing. By the 1950s, "scientific motherhood" dominated mainstream approaches to family life. In addition, the social movements of the 1960s and 1970s welcomed the "natural" methods of the league and its challenge to the patriarchy of the medical establishment.

The league grew rapidly, especially in the 1960s and 1970s. From one meeting of twelve friends in the fall of 1956, the number of league groups multiplied to 43 in 1961, 430 in 1966, 1,260 in 1971, and to about 3,000 in 1976. By 1981, some 17,000 women had been trained as league leaders. While it is difficult to ascribe credit for the rise in breastfeeding in the United States from the mid-1950s through the mid-1980s, the incidence of breastfeeding by new mothers grew from about 20 to about 60 percent.

If some women saw the league's vision of motherhood as empowering and progressive, there was a catch. To meet league standards of on-demand breastfeeding, mother and infant must remain together. This was not too difficult in the 1950s, when fewer than one in five married mothers of young children under the age of six worked outside the home, but by 1980, that number had risen to almost one in two.

As maternal employment norms changed, a posture critical of working mothers made the La Leche League seem increasingly conservative. Like maternalist ideologies of past centuries, La Leche League motherhood gave public purpose to the private activities of domestic life; like advocates of those past ideologies, too, the league urged that women subsume their individualism for the greater good of the family and society. This essay will introduce the history of the league and explore the paradox embedded in the league's maternalist ideology—the way in which it simultaneously promoted women's autonomy and restricted women's roles.

At a picnic in the Chicago suburb of Elmhurst, Illinois, during the summer of 1956, two mothers—Mary White and Marian Tompson—sat under a tree nursing their babies. As other women approached them and admired what seemed a difficult and unusual task in an era when bottle-feeding was the norm, these mothers determined to help others learn the "womanly art" of breastfeeding. With five friends they formed the La Leche League, to give "mother to mother" help to women who wanted to nurse their infants. The "founding mothers" at first struggled to find a suitable name, for in those days, according to founder Edwina Froehlich, "you didn't mention 'breast' in print unless you were talking about Jean Harlow." The solution of "La Leche League" was offered by Mary White's husband, obstetrician Gregory White, who often gave his pregnant patients medals from a shrine in St. Augustine, Florida, dedicated to a Spanish madonna, Nuestra Señora de La Leche y Buen Parto, or, loosely translated, "Our Lady of Happy Delivery and Plentiful Milk."

The seven founders of the league were Roman Catholic, white, middle-class women who had become acquainted in two ways: through activism in the Christian Family Movement (CFM), an ecumenical Christian organization, and through a common interest in natural childbirth and breastfeeding. Like many white Americans in that era, all but one of the founders grew up in cities, but by the mid-1950s all but one lived in the suburbs. Three of the seven founders had college degrees; the husbands of most worked in professional occupations. Several of the founders were patients of Gregory White, who in his obstetrical practice favored natural childbirth procedures.

The Christian Family Movement, established nationally in 1949, was an important influence on the early league's organization and outlook. The CFM organized small discussion groups focused on family and such social justice issues as civil rights, based on an "action cell" format developed by Canon Joseph Cardijn, who held that "like ministers to like"—workers to workers, businessmen to businessmen, married couples to married couples. Typically, a CFM group consisted of five or six couples who followed a program of discussion about theology and social action centered on family life—their concern was not just with "the betterment of their own family situations but also with the life of families everywhere." Members were encouraged to share their thoughts while receiving the moral support of the group for their actions, including activities the member "could not or would not do alone." The Young Christian Workers, a social action group for single people, similarly influenced league founders before they married; Froehlich was the group's first national president.

Using a model similar to that of the Christian Family Movement, the first La Leche group meeting was held in Franklin Park, Illinois, on an October evening in 1956. That night, the seven founders and five of their pregnant friends discussed a *Reader's Digest* article advocating breastfeeding. Soon, with thirty and forty women crowding into living rooms, the meetings had grown so large that new groups formed to accommodate the demand. League founders quickly developed a series of five rotating sessions on pregnancy, birth, infant feeding, nutrition, and child rearing. Women gathered in members' houses and studied the material that eventually became the basis for *The Womanly Art of Breastfeeding,* first published in 1958. One meeting was held every three weeks, so that over the course of four months a participant attended all five; men were often invited to an additional "For Fathers Only" meeting as well. These small group sessions were facilitated at first by the founders and later by "league leaders," women who had successfully breastfed their babies at least a year and shared the league's maternalist philosophy. The groups provided information and emotional support for women wanting to breastfeed. Founder Mary Ann Cahill suggested, "we were considered . . . extremely radical . . . and this is why the [groups] were so important, because they gave you contact with other women who were also kind of thinking crazy."

The creation of small all-female groups of peers seems to have been an important source of the league's strength. The groups may have helped to break down the isolation of mothering in nuclear families—a growing problem during the era of rapid suburbanization and geographic mobility. In moving to the new postwar suburbs, many women moved farther away from relatives who in earlier times might have provided information and support for the task of mothering. . . .

The woman-to-woman approach of the groups was also evident in the league's hot-line telephone service and its publications. The league from the start received letters and telephone calls from women seeking advice about specific breastfeeding problems. The founders answered these queries "at home surrounded by . . . babies and children," and it was in response to the "never-ending stream of mail and the frantic phone calls" that the first version of *The Womanly Art of Breastfeeding* was put together, in loose-leaf folders sold as a "Course By Mail." The league newsletter first appeared in May of 1958 and was meant "to keep mothers in touch and give them somebody else to relate to or identify with . . . because at that time few mothers had anyone in their circle of friends who was breastfeeding," recalled founder Marian Tompson. The newsletter featured communications, poetry, photographs, and articles by league members. By 1960, four years after the founding of the organization, its headquarters averaged three hundred telephone calls and four hundred letters monthly. . . .

As membership in the league grew, it attracted a wider range of supporters who did not share the Catholic roots of the founders. Photographs and letters in league publications identified women who were African-American, Asian, and Hispanic as well as white, Jewish as well as Christian. In its writings the league itself maintained a nonsectarian posture. But women of color appear to have been in the minority of the membership. A 1970 survey by the psychologist Alice Kahn Ladas indicated that the majority of active league members were white, middle-class, native-born women, with those identifying themselves as either Catholic or of "no religious identity" present in larger numbers than in the general population. . . .

Although the league's founders had not initially planned for any kind of growth or set up a formal organizational structure beyond that of a local "club for nursing mothers," the league did grow, in part because of its complicated interactions with larger social trends. Though founded by women enmeshed in a distinctive Catholic subculture, the league clearly spoke to the enthusiasm felt by many Americans in the 1950s for nuclear family life. That the league emerged when it did was not surprising. The "baby boom" peaked in the mid-1950s in the United States as fertility rates, which had been steadily declining for nearly two centuries, sharply rose, as did the rate of marriage. Women coming of age during the 1950s gave birth to an average of 3.2 children, compared to an average of 2.4 children for women reaching adulthood during the 1930s. The founders of the league had many more children than was common even for the baby boom. The seven La Leche League founders claimed a total of fifty-three offspring (an average of more than 7 per mother); their families ranged from 3 to 11 children. While all seven founders were Roman Catholic, they have suggested it was not religious impulse but rather the desire to deal with the reality of households full of infants that motivated the league's beginning. Motherhood was clearly of central concern to these women who chose to shape a public meaning for their private lives.

The increased birth rate of the 1950s was accompanied by a pronatalist ideology, defined by the historian Elaine Tyler May as the "belief in the positive value of having several children." Many Americans in the postwar years believed that personal happiness for both men and women was to be found in an intensive family life focused on children, and that full-time motherhood was the ultimate fulfillment of femininity. The league gave formal expression to these pronatalist ideals, asserting that motherhood was "natural" and beneficial to women, children, and the social order.

The popularity of the league also reflected unease with approaches to motherhood and family life common among physicians and other experts in the 1950s. The kind of motherhood experts advocated was anything but "natural"—instead it was "scientific." Professional advice was to replace maternal instinct, and so child-rearing manuals, mothers' clubs, and physicians' counsel brought "modern" ideas about motherhood into the home. . . . Motherhood, in short, was to be controlled by experts rather than directed by instinct. Rationality and order, then important in such other arenas of industrial American culture as business, home economics, and education, informed proper mothering as well. Standards of efficiency, time, and measurement were to control a baby's day as well as a factory's routine.

Bottle-feeding was the preferred way to nourish a baby in 1956. The incidence of breastfeeding at one week of age had fallen to about 18 percent, a decline from about 38 percent in 1948 and from over 80 percent before 1920. Bottle-feeding first became popular in the United States in the late nineteenth century in part because of concerns about high infant mortality rates among the urban poor. Middle-class women soon adopted the new infant feeding method because of a desire to be fashionable and scientific. The historian Rima Apple suggests that the introduction of infant formula and the rise of pediatrics as a medical field led to the development of a mutually advantageous relationship between infant food companies and physicians. Taking another perspective, the historian Harvey Levenstein has argued that the male physicians who were replacing midwives by the turn of the century, "perhaps afflicted by . . . prudishness . . . tended to shy away from urging breastfeeding by mothers."

In the mid-twentieth century, bottle-feeding was a complicated and time-consuming affair. Mothers followed elaborate methods for preparing formula using evaporated, powdered, or whole milk, carefully calculated total milk volume spread over a certain number of bottles per day, and conscientiously sterilized bottles, rubber nipples, and bottle caps. Babies were often weighed before and after feedings. Advice books insisted that mothers consult their doctors about techniques and schedules; doctors were to "prescribe" breastfeeding or bottle-feeding and to mandate all aspects of mothering. . . .

Childbirth, like infant feeding, was defined as "scientific" in the 1950s. Advocates of scientific motherhood had by the 1920s and 1930s labeled childbirth a medical problem rather than a natural function, in part as a response to high infant and maternal mortality rates. As childbirth became medicalized, control of the birthing process fell away from women and their midwives and into the hands of physicians. By the mid-1950s, 95 percent of all births in the United States took place in hospitals—compared to about 50 percent in 1940 and fewer than 5 percent in 1900—and a high proportion of those births involved the use of pain-killing drugs, forceps, and other medical interventions. This medicalization of childbirth, begun earlier in the century in an attempt to secure safety and comfort for woman, now was seen by some as unpleasant, alienating, and manipulative. Further, medicated childbirth affected infant feeding because a mother who was drugged could not nurse her baby. And delivery in a hospital affected feeding because without flexible nursery policies, the baby could be brought to the mother only at certain times of the day, leading to tightly scheduled feedings.

Scientific motherhood was not uncontested. There was a "motherhood reform" community made up of people—health care providers as well as mothers and fathers—interested in returning mothering from the artificial or scientific to the "natural" sphere. By the mid-1950s there were throughout North America and Europe critics representing a variety of social perspectives who challenged invasive childbirth methods, artificial infant-feeding techniques, and rigid child-rearing practices. Some, for example, the British natural childbirth educator Grantly Dick Read, believed that motherhood embodied "essential femininity" and that childbirth was "woman's supreme triumph." Others presented arguments for woman-centered childbirth or more general critiques of modern industrial life. La Leche League founders communicated with many of these varied reformers, including the advocates of family-centered maternity care who in 1960 formed the International Childbirth Education Association. . . .

La Leche League leaders built strong ties with others in the international motherhood reform community of the postwar years, but they were especially influenced by two Chicago-area physicians critical of scientific motherhood: Gregory White, the husband of league founder Mary White, and White's former teacher, Herbert Ratner, a Chicago-area health commissioner. During the early 1950s, these doctors encouraged their patients to attempt home birth, natural childbirth, and breast-feeding, and they urged their patients to talk with each other about natural mothering techniques. . . .

Doctors Ratner and White urged league founders to broaden their interests from breastfeeding to the more general issue of mothering. Like many in the motherhood reform community, these men held an essentialist view of women that pre-supposed a natural and biologically based social role. To Ratner, breastfeeding symbolized woman's place in the social order. At the first league convention in 1964, his keynote address focused on the "art of mothering." He believed Americans had abandoned a family ideology that nurtured women and children. "Motherhood," he stated, "is an opportunity for growth. Three children nurture motherhood more than one. Each mothering experience enriches." He also suggested that women who bottle-fed their babies could too easily separate from them and "become vulnerable to other persuasions," and that a decision to bottle-feed "may be a sign of emotional difficulties in the mother." White also saw breastfeeding as a key to good motherhood. The mother who bottle-feeds, he stated, does not have high levels of pro-lactin, the hormone that contributes to milk production, and therefore she does not have the same physical feelings toward her baby. "She's handicapped," he said, "she may turn out to be a pretty good mother. But she could have been a lot better mother if she had breastfed." By 1958, league founders had begun to shape a mater-nalist philosophy centered on "good mothering through breastfeeding" that re-flected this essentialist model of womanhood.

At the heart of the La Leche League's philosophy was the notion that the needs of the infant—as interpreted by the mother rather than a doctor—should de-termine the practice and pace of mothering. . . .

Breastfeeding, as defined by the league, offered important advantages for the baby, the mother, and the social order. The first and most important beneficiary of breastfeeding was the child. According to the league, breast milk was the best infant food, fitted to the human digestive system; its use would lead to infant health, a gain in natural immunities, and the avoidance of allergies. A baby would also learn love and trust so that he or she might "go out and make a better world." The league ad-vocated prolonged breastfeeding because its founders believed that the emotional and physical health of an infant was strengthened by allowing the child, rather than a doctor's chart, to determine the duration of breastfeeding and the initiation of weaning. The idea that the child, her needs interpreted by the mother, should set the schedule for feedings and later for weaning distinguished the league from physicians who favored a breastfeeding regimen regulated by external norms of time. Many medical authorities approved nursing for a short period, from a few days to nine months, and they usually mandated feeding on a strict schedule of every three or four hours. For example, Frederic H. Bartlett wrote in the 1943 edition of his best-selling guide *Infants and Children*, "If you have plenty of milk you should nurse . . .

perhaps not longer than 7 months," and he recommended a regular feeding schedule of the "usual" hours of 6 A.M., 10 A.M., 2 P.M., 6 P.M., 10 P.M., and 2 A.M. But the league urged instead that mothers nurse their babies on demand for at least a year, and preferably longer. . . .

Second, the league promoted breastfeeding as beneficial to the mother. Breast-feeding would get women back into shape after pregnancy, help prevent breast cancer, and provide a natural form of birth control. Perhaps most important, breast-feeding would facilitate a woman's realization of her full potential as a person. In the first league statement of policy, circulated in 1964, the leaders suggested:

> a mother who chooses to mother through breastfeeding, finds it an excellent way to grow in mothering as her baby grows in years. And since the woman who grows in mothering thereby grows as a human being, any other role she may fill in her lifetime will be enriched and deepened by the insights and humanity she will bring to it from her experience as a mother.

The basic requirement for successful child rearing was a full-time, attentive mother who understood and accepted her "special vocation in life." As a corollary, league writers urged women to avoid such "mother substitutes" as pacifiers, high chairs, baby carriages, playpens, and, of course, bottles.

Finally, not only babies and women but also society would benefit from breast-feeding, because good mothering would foster trust and security in children who would become, as league founder Betty Wagner said, "secure, well-adjusted adults, healthy adults, who will make this world a better place to live." In this sense the La Leche League echoed earlier ideals of motherhood that directed women's energies into domestic activities and claimed a higher civic purpose in the raising of children. League leaders believed that breastfeeding "is the ideal way to initiate good parent-child relationships and to strengthen the family and hence the whole fabric of our society." League leaders also believed that their movement would promote social cohesion in another way. By emphasizing the common bond of gender, league leaders, like earlier maternalists, minimized class and racial distinctions between women. According to founder Marian Tompson, women who differed in other ways could meet on the "common ground" of breast-feeding. . . .

La Leche League leaders sometimes struck others as radical. Indeed, some of them welcomed the description. "Everything we did was radical," Cahill said, from supporting breastfeeding to advocating the later introduction of solid foods to "listening to the baby." They certainly offered a program radical in its challenge to basic assumptions of mid-twentieth-century American culture, whether patriarchal or feminist. In a society much taken with efficiency, the clock, and precision, league attitudes to time and nature can be described as preindustrial. The league encouraged women to let their babies, instead of the clock and the calendar, set the time for eating and the time for weaning, to orient themselves to a variable natural time pattern rather than a fixed schedule based on external authority. . . . This faith in "God's plan" focused on interpersonal relationships and "meaningful passiveness," rather than schedules and other externally mandated norms of behavior. The league urged women to "refuse to accept the attempted mechanization of human beings or to abandon their true, womanly role."

The league also questioned the pervasive glorification of individual achievement in American society. It is not surprising that the league showed more sympathy with mothers driven to work outside the home by financial need than with those who prized the possibility of achievement offered by a public career. In the league outlook, achievement in this sense meant less than did connection with people. Not only the league but many Americans assumed that women were by nature more attuned to people than were men. One author widely cited by league members, Arlene Rossen Cardozo, argued in her 1976 book, *Woman at Home,* that a "male model" of achievement and success had misled feminists, who "fled home in imitation of Man. And the man of the day was the Hollow Man, the Computerized Man" who placed a success ethic higher than human relationships. In this cherishing of personalism and emphasis on the claims of others, league advocates echoed earlier maternalist ideologies and appealed to many American women in the twentieth century. The essentialism of the league, moreover, prefigured aspects of a later strain of radical feminism that was committed to preserving and celebrating gender differences. . . .

Radical or conservative, the league's philosophy raised questions about American mores. The La Leche League's emphasis on intensive mothering led its leaders to criticize the consumerist "happy housewife" image of the 1950s that was first labeled in Betty Friedan's 1963 best seller, *The Feminine Mystique.* The happy housewife was concerned with appearances, of herself and of her house, and was above all a consumer of material goods. She was *not* first and foremost a mother. League leaders criticized this prescriptive image, urging mothers to attend to their children first. The league ran counter to American norms by implying that it was more important to build intense affectional ties between family members than to acquire and maintain the material trappings of a middle-class family. "What's important in your life," founder Mary White told a league convention in 1966, "is the people and not the things. And . . . especially while you have babies and small ones around, the most important people are your children." Time spent on housework, league leaders argued, was better spent with the family. . . .

If the league's maternalism codified a social role for women within a family defined less by consumerism than by personalism, it also prescribed a domestic role for men. The league argued that a father should, by supporting and encouraging the mother, enable her to nurture the baby more completely. Fathers should focus on family life rather than on professional success alone, spend more time with their children "because the joys of parenthood are meant to be shared," and participate fully in domestic tasks because the "authoritative, masculine man knows his dignity and stature are not in jeopardy when he performs a kitchen chore." The league newsletter on occasion published a June "Father's Day" issue that addressed such topics as how to offer support to a breastfeeding wife, and *The Womanly Art of Breast-feeding* discussed fatherhood in each edition. Just as the league helped shape a dimension of pronatalist womanhood, in its attention to fathers it helped shape notions of manhood in postwar American society.

Some women and men rejected the philosophy of the league because they disliked its moral fervor, complaining that the league used scare tactics and dogmatism to inflict feelings of guilt on women who failed to breastfeed or breastfed only a short time. Others argued that children who were breastfed too long might become infantilized and have difficulty separating from their mothers, who were overeager to conform to maternalist ideology. League policy makers, recognizing that reputation, warned leaders to avoid overzealousness. "League mothers need to be . . . noncritical with their non-breastfeeding friends, instead of militant and crusading about the subject," the newsletter editor cautioned in 1972. . . .

During the late 1960s and after, falling fertility rates, the rise of feminism, and an increase in maternal employment inspired a lively debate among league members about the meaning of motherhood in American society. While the basic message—that the ideal role for women was full-time motherhood focused on the natural needs of the baby—remained constant, the public reception of that message changed. The league initially challenged scientific motherhood and promised to empower women by helping them reclaim the arts of childbirth and infant feeding from the domain of experts. Now, the league was vocally challenging employed motherhood. To the league, both practices—health professionals intervening in the realm of motherhood and women working outside the home—represented a falling away from nature in a scientific age. In both cases, the prescription for social health was a return to "natural" behavior by women, where mother and child would form a "nursing couple" better to reflect traditionalist values. Thus an ideology of maternalism that in the mid-1950s sounded radical and empowering thirty years later impressed some as "extremely conservative." Tompson, one of the founders, wrote in 1970 that breastfeeding *was* conservative because it "ranks in status with traditional values of God, motherhood, and love of country."

The social context surrounding the league shifted dramatically from the time of its founding in 1956 through the 1980s. Fertility rates fell from a high in 1957 of 123 per thousand women between the ages of 15 and 44, to 96.6 in 1965, and to 66.7 in 1975. At the same time, economic pressures and opportunities for women outside the home increased. Maternal employment began a steady climb. In 1950, fewer than 12 percent of mothers with children under the age of six worked outside the home; by 1960, this had climbed to 19 percent, and by 1970, to 30 percent. By 1980, nearly 50 percent of mothers with children under six were in the labor force. These figures increasingly included the mothers of very young children. In 1978, the United States Census Bureau for the first time counted mothers of infants under the age of one year who were at work. That year, a startling 30 percent of mothers of infants were working, at least part time; 41 percent of all mothers with children under the age of two were employed. This "normalization" of maternal employment, combined with the growth of the feminist movement in the late 1960s and 1970s, put the league into sharpening conflict with women's lives and attitudes. The premise that a woman contributed to the world mainly by what she did within the home became anachronistic as family norms shifted to include maternal employment and less time-intensive child rearing. In response, league leaders and members increasingly addressed the issues of feminism and working mothers.

And yet the league flourished during these challenging years of social change. During the decade of the 1970s, the number of active La Leche League groups more than tripled, growing from 1,260 in 1971 to 4,327 ten years later. There were certainly many women claiming no allegiance to any philosophy other than traditional domesticity, and the league gave them a voice. But, in addition, the commonality between league practice and that of feminists and the counterculture may have overridden the ideological differences between them. League practice dovetailed, for example, with the "return to nature" ethos of the counterculture. Founder Lennon recalled that "by the time the '60s rolled around, people were beginning to accept certain things that were in 1956 really way out." League founders believed that the "hippie movement" aided in the popularization of the league "because they embraced all this natural stuff" and because their rebellion against the establishment included the medical establishment. . . .

The alliance of the counterculture with the league and, indeed, a general broadening of the league's constituency through the 1970s were not without tension. Many of the new members attempted to bring to the league agenda such issues as advocacy of natural foods, environmental politics, civil rights, home schooling, and family planning; others wanted the group to take a stand on abortion. But the league cautioned against "mixing causes," arguing in its 1973 "Statement of Policy" that, whatever the merit of other concerns, the message about mothering through breastfeeding must not be diluted. "People who support good mothering," the league stated, "may reject the League if it seems to be part of another movement." . . .

Another source of league growth was its increasing acceptance in the medical community. At first physicians who favored scientific motherhood considered the league marginal, believing that "breastfeeding fell into the medical domain, and that one nursing mother was not qualified to advise another." Gradually, however, the league gained respectability. Although the founders believed that "most of the questions and problems a nursing mother may encounter are not medical," they stressed that they did not "intend to invade the jurisdiction of the physician." From the beginning they consulted with physicians. They formed a "medical advisory board" for editorial approval of materials and advice on specific medical problems. By 1960, a physician in North Carolina cited the league's work favorably, saying that it advocated "a revival of the age-old conviction that nature is more reliable than science, that mother-love is more effective than aseptic precautions." In 1968 the *Journal of Pediatrics* published "A Salute to La Leche League International," cautioning the league against dogmatism but wishing them "continuing success." . . .

The founders of La Leche League have described themselves as early feminists, for they believed women should reclaim control of their bodies through natural childbirth and breastfeeding. An editorial in the league newsletter in 1966 stated that "feminism was with us long before Betty Friedan."

Elements of the maternalist ideology of the La Leche League had a natural appeal for some late twentieth-century feminists. Although many of the women who launched the women's liberation movement of the 1960s and 1970s attacked motherhood as a patriarchal construct reproducing traditional relationships within the family, others argued for a feminist version of maternalism. Both league maternalism and feminism questioned the control of childbirth and child rearing by the medical establishment, and both promoted a collective female consciousness reinforced by small group meetings. The league shared the feminist conviction stated by the philosopher Joyce Trebilcot in 1984 that "mothering must now be defined and controlled by women." . . .

By the late 1960s, league publications directly addressed feminism. Founder Mary White told the second international league convention in 1966 that most league women had wanted to "*be* somebody and get married too." And once women "accept—not just accept, but embrace wholeheartedly, the idea that mothering is a rewarding job, a job filled with all sorts of satisfactions, then we'll be able to see and enjoy all the benefits it has to offer." League members found satisfaction in embracing this active definition of motherhood. Beginning in the early 1970s, letters and articles in league publications debated the problem of woman's proper place. How should mothering be defined? What was a feminist? Could you be a feminist and a full-time mother? Readers thought so, the founding mothers thought so, and if their definition of feminism was dismissed by some, it nonetheless reflected the thinking of a significant number of American women. According to a 1972 survey, league members saw their organization as "traditionalistic in its advocacy of the family role of wife and mother [but] . . . liberating because it teaches members actively to define and achieve satisfying goals within this role." Members placed "their confidence in themselves and their sisters rather than passively following the advice of licensed professionals." Breastfeeding provided a link to other mothers and was therefore a sign of "womanly power." . . .

If league supporters often appropriated the language of feminism, most rejected feminist philosophy, especially the idea that women could work for wages and mother at the same time; they reacted to growing public acceptance of women workers with a strong reaffirmation of housewifery and motherhood. A woman's self-esteem and sense of worth, league representatives suggested, could be found at home as well as at work. The newsletter in the 1970s and 1980s printed reams of articles and correspondence about mothers who had planned to work or were working while their children were young but later decided to stay at home. . . .

League leaders strongly criticized the materialism and consumerism that, they believed, pushed women into the labor force. Many articles and letters from readers offered concrete ways in which families could survive on lower incomes by budgeting, bartering, and lowering living standards. But others recognized the economic need pulling many women into the work force and proposed maternalist public policies, such as mothers' pensions, to support women at home. In 1979, for example, founder Marian Tompson told a league conference that

> In our society where two income families are close to becoming an economic necessity, traditional mothering is being systematically stamped out. What we desperately need are policies that will allow women the choice of staying home to care for their babies without having to opt for poverty. Breastfeeding, once considered a medical problem, now becomes a political issue.

The league's service to working mothers was not consistent. Some La Leche League groups excluded working mothers, but others welcomed them. A 1984 survey found several groups in California, Connecticut, Florida, New Mexico, and New York that accepted or were oriented toward working mothers. The league has for over a decade been involved in peer-counseling programs for poor inner-city women, most of whom have to work for wages. League leaders estimated that by the 1980s, when membership began to slide after some twenty-five years of growth, up to half of the women attending meetings were employed outside the home. But if the league has in practice in some times and places been supportive and nonjudgmental about working mothers, ideologically it consistently valued full-time mothering for families. To be accredited as a group leader through the early 1980s, a woman "had to be pretty much at home" rather than at work.

League founder Mary White expressed the organization's general attitude toward working mothers when she stated at a league conference in 1981 that "any weakening in the link between the mother and her baby endangers the future health and security of the child." She added:

> We in La Leche have just as great an obligation to help [working mothers] . . . breastfeed their babies as we have any mother who comes to us for help . . . but, knowing what we know about mothering . . . shouldn't we want to do more? I think we must show all mothers how important full-time mothering is to their babies, to themselves, and to their whole families. How the needs of their babies are not only for mother's milk, or mother's breast, but for all of her.

Each successive edition of *The Womanly Art of Breastfeeding* offered more acknowledgment of working mothers. The most recent (1991) edition contains a chapter on breastfeeding tips for working mothers, followed by a chapter titled "Making a Choice" that urges mothers to consider staying at home while their children are young. The league's philosophy, then, while acknowledging the tremendous changes in women's lives, has remained steadfast in its vision of breastfeeding and full-time parenting of young children as the essence of "good mothering."

League maternalism, based on the notion of difference rather than equality between men and women, represented an important voice in the chorus of postwar interpretations of gender in the United States. The league embraced a biosocial understanding of women by defining female success and achievement through motherhood rather than through economics or politics. Because of the league's maternalism, which both asserted women's authority over the practice of motherhood and emphasized the importance of full-time motherhood, the group's history presents an interesting paradox. On the one hand, by the mid-1950s the league anticipated a strand of the feminist movement that was concerned with women's control over health care issues centered on childbirth and child rearing. On the other hand, by the early 1970s the league also challenged the emerging feminist ideology by questioning the consequences for children of the movement of women away from the home and into the workplace. In both cases, the league decried aspects of modern life that seemed to distance women from essentially natural behavior. The La Leche League reconstructed mothering in a way that was both liberating and constricting and so ironically offered both prologue and counterpoint to the emerging movement for women's liberation.

SUGGESTED READINGS

Terry H. Anderson, *The Movement and the Sixties: Protest in America from Greensboro to Wounded Knee* (1995).

William H. Chafe, *Women and Equality: Changing Patterns in American Culture* (1977).

Maurice Isserman, *If I Had a Hammer: The Death of the Old Left and the Birth of the New Left* (1987).

Kenneth Jackson, *Crabgrass Frontier: The Suburbanization of the United States* (1985).

Alfred Kazin, *Bright Book of Life: American Novelists and Storytellers from Hemingway to Mailer* (1973).

Nicholas Lemann, *The Promised Land: The Great Black Migration and How It Changed America* (1991).

Martin E. Marty, *Pilgrims in Their Own Land* (1984).

Elaine T. May, *Homeward Bound: American Families in the Cold War Era* (1988).

Charles Murray, *Losing Ground: American Social Policy, 1950–1980* (1986).

Diane Ravitch, *The Troubled Crusade: American Education, 1945–1980* (1983).

J. Harvie Wilkinson, *From Brown to Bakke: The Supreme Court and School Integration, 1954–1978* (1980).

FURTHER READINGS

Politics and Society During the 1960s

David Chalmers, *And the Crooked Places Made Straight: The Struggle for Social Change in the 1960s* (1991); David Farber, *Chicago '68* (1988); Lewis L. Gould, *1968: The Election That Changed America* (1993); Edward P. Morgan, *The 60s Experience* (1991); Charles R. Morris, *A Time of Passion: America, 1960–1980* (1984); Jon Wiener, *Come Together: John Lennon and His Time* (1984, 1991).

The Black Power Movement

Elaine Brown, *A Taste of Power* (1993); Clayborne Carson, *Malcolm X: The F.B.I. File* (1991); David Hilliard and Lewis Cole, *This Side of Glory: The Autobiography of David Hilliard and the Story of the Black Panther Party* (1993); Malcolm X and Alex Haley, *The Autobiography of Malcolm X* (1965, 1992); Manning Marable, *Race, Reform, and Rebellion* (1984).

The Counterculture and the Student Movement

Wini Breines, *Community and Organization in the New Left* (1982); Charles DeBenedetti, *An American Ordeal: The Antiwar Movement of the Vietnam Era* (1990); David T. Dellinger, *From Yale to Jail: A Memoir* (1993); Kenneth Heineman, *Campus Wars: The Peace Movement at American State Universities in the Vietnam Era* (1993); Timothy Miller, *The Hippies and American Values* (1991).

The Women's Movement and Gay Rights

Adam D. Barry, *The Rise of a Gay and Lesbian Movement* (1987); Martin Duberman, *Stonewall* (1993); Bell Hooks, *Ain't I a Woman: Black Women and Feminism* (1981); Blanche Linden-Ward, *Changing the Future: American Women in the 1960s* (1992); Kate Millett, *Sexual Politics* (1970, 1990).

QUESTIONS FOR DISCUSSION

1. Evaluate the effect of Sputnik on American education.
2. How did American religion change between 1960 and 1980?
3. What impact did Supreme Court rulings during this time period have on the nation's judicial system? In what ways did they contribute to social change?
4. The 1960s saw the reemergence of the women's rights movement. Trace its development and identify the various tactics its leaders employed.
5. Were the New Left and the counterculture of the 1960s always in agreement? Explain.
6. What effect did the youth movement have on the conduct of the war in Vietnam?
7. Compare and contrast the La Leche League, as described by Lynn Y. Weiner, with other social movements during the turbulent 1960s. Were these women feminists? Explain.

CHAPTER TWENTY-EIGHT

THE TRIUMPH OF CONSERVATISM

Throughout most of their history Americans have shared a common vision of the ideal society, one based on individual freedom, equal protection under the law, equal opportunity, and upward socioeconomic mobility through hard work and participation in the political process. Although the American dream has been just that for many disadvantaged citizens, its grip has been so strong that even those trapped by poverty, ignorance, or discrimination have continued to work within the system to make it a reality. In the face of persistent racism, the Vietnam War, sexism, and the pervasiveness of the impersonal, managerial society, however, many Americans in the 1960s began to question the validity of that shared vision. But in the end, the great majority reacted not by embracing new social experiments or putting in place radical political processes. Rather, they sought to resurrect the past, to escape into a new materialism; they abandoned reform at home and abroad, and focused their efforts instead on restoring and preserving traditional American values.

THE ELECTION OF 1968

HUMPHREY AND THE DEMOCRATIC NOMINATION

In the wake of Lyndon Johnson's announcement in March of 1968 that he would not run again, a three-way race for the Democratic presidential nomination developed. Eugene McCarthy continued to hammer away at the war in Vietnam, but he was increasingly eclipsed by the young, handsome Robert Kennedy who was able to attract not only the New Left and antiwar activists in general but also African Americans and liberal intellectuals. In April Vice President Hubert Humphrey announced his candidacy. A veteran of various liberal causes, Humphrey was both hurt and helped by his association with Johnson. The race narrowed down to a contest between Kennedy and Humphrey. But then on June 5, Kennedy, having just narrowly defeated Humphrey in the California primary, was gunned down by a deranged Jordanian immigrant named Sirhan B. Sirhan. McCarthy inherited many of Kennedy's delegates, but proved no match for Humphrey and Johnson at the Chicago nominating convention. Given the violent clashes between Chicago police and peace demonstrators on the streets and the rancorous debates in the convention hall, Humphrey's victory was pyrrhic.

THE RETURN OF RICHARD NIXON

The Democratic convention of 1968 enabled the Republicans to blame all of the tensions and divisions that plagued America on their adversaries and paved the way for the political comeback of one of the nation's most resilient figures— Richard Milhous Nixon. After his crushing defeat in the 1962 California gubernatorial campaign, Eisenhower's former vice president told reporters that they would never "have Richard Nixon to kick around again." But politics was his life, and he ingratiated himself with party regulars by working energetically for Barry Goldwater in 1964. With Nelson Rockefeller positioned on his political left and Ronald Reagan occupying the right, Nixon was able to claim the moderate center and with it the GOP nomination. For his running mate he chose former Rockefeller supporter Spiro Agnew. The opportunistic governor of Maryland had made something of a name for himself by taking a hard line against urban rioters.

During the ensuing campaign against Hubert Humphrey, Nixon abandoned the stridency of his early career. The picture of moderation and conciliation, he promised to "bring us together." All the while he denounced welfare cheats and government waste, Nixon made it clear that he had no intention of dismantling New Frontier and Great Society programs. Most tantalizing, he hinted that he had a "secret plan" for ending the war.

Hubert Humphrey was caught on the horns of a dilemma. He needed to avoid alienating Lyndon Johnson and Democratic power brokers who were determined to defend the previous administration's record on not only domestic reform but foreign policy as well. Despite his call for "unconditional" negotiations, Johnson would not abandon the government of Nguyen Van Thieu in Saigon, and sporadic bombing of North Vietnam continued. As it became clear that Humphrey could count on the support of union members and African Americans because of his long-standing and unflinching support of labor and civil rights, however, his campaign began to pick up steam. When in late September the Minnesotan broke with Johnson, announcing that, if elected, he would end the bombing of North Vietnam in an effort to achieve a breakthrough in the ongoing Paris peace talks, he closed the gap with Nixon to virtually nil.

GEORGE WALLACE AND THE AMERICAN INDEPENDENT PARTY

Since Franklin Roosevelt put together the famous New Deal coalition in 1936, the ability of Democrats to retain control of the White House depended upon their success in keeping the major elements of that political alliance intact. In 1968 a figure burst upon the national political scene who threatened to splinter the voting bloc that Democrats had depended on for a generation—George Corley Wallace. One of America's most accomplished political opportunists, Wallace had "stood in the schoolhouse door" and made a spectacular if unsuccessful attempt to prevent the integration of the University of Alabama.

Denouncing the NAACP, Martin Luther King, and "do-gooder" liberals, and promising to stamp out communism in Southeast Asia once and for all, Wallace made a brief run at the Democratic presidential nomination. Thwarted, Wallace then bolted and formed the American Independent party (AIP). Well financed by grassroots donations and prominent anticommunists, the AIP cut a wide swath in the South and in blue-collar neighborhoods in northern and midwestern cities.

Despite the challenge from Wallace, Humphrey continued to gain on Nixon throughout October; after Johnson caved in and agreed to suspend the bombing in Vietnam, pundits declared the election too close to call. Nonetheless, the Republican squeaked by with the smallest share of the popular vote of any candidate since 1916: 43 percent. Nixon carried a broad band of states from the Carolinas through the Midwest and the Sunbelt. Republican political strategist Kevin Phillips argued that it was that latter region that was and would continue to be crucial: "From space-center Florida across the booming Texas plains to the Los Angeles–San Diego suburban corridor," he wrote, "the nation's fastest-growing areas are strongly Republican and conservative." The combined popular vote for Nixon and Wallace—56.5 percent of the whole—indicated that a vast majority of Americans were sick of Vietnam, violent confrontation, social "permissiveness," and political extremism.

NIXON'S FIRST TERM

Richard Nixon was a man driven by his own insecurities. Despite the fact that in capturing the highest office in the land he had realized his lifelong dream, he still believed that the world was against him, filled with enemies determined to humiliate him and ruin his presidency. There was a streak of ruthlessness in his character, a tendency toward self-righteousness, and the self-made man's penchant for equating success with moral superiority. The new president was an intensely shy person who immediately set about isolating himself from Congress and the vast bureaucracy that operated the federal government. He assembled a powerful White House staff headed by John Ehrlichman and Robert Haldeman, giving them sweeping authority to run domestic affairs. For attorney general he selected John Mitchell, a hard-nosed partisan who tailored every decision to political considerations. Foreign policy was Nixon's great passion; he selected Harvard professor and international affairs specialist Henry Kissinger to be his partner in formulating grand strategy, and left Secretary of State William Rogers to keep the State Department busy on trivial matters.

DOMESTIC PROGRAMS

The Family Assistance Plan

Americans were hopeful as the new administration began its work. Nixon spoke the language of moderation, leading many to believe that his election signaled a return to the politics of accommodation that had characterized the Eisenhower era. Among Nixon's policy advisors were right-wing ideologues like Patrick Buchanan and William Safire, but there were liberals as well. Indeed, he assigned the task of welfare reform to Daniel Patrick Moynihan, a Democrat and one of the architects of the Great Society. Moynihan, Nixon's urban affairs advisor, proposed and the administration subsequently introduced into Congress the Family Assistance Plan (FAP). Instead of piecemeal payments, each family of four with no wage earner would receive an annual payment of $1600 plus $800 worth of food stamps. Democrats, many of whom had been pushing for a guaranteed annual income for the poor, criticized the plan for being too miserly and for requiring the head of household, usually an unmarried female, to register for employment. The FAP passed the House but failed to clear the Senate. As it turned out, the family assistance bill marked the outer limits of the Nixon administration's liberalism.

Nixon's Southern Strategy

With eyes continually on the 1970 mid-term elections and the 1972 presidential election, Nixon and his strategists were acutely aware that they would have to attract the lion's share of George Wallace's supporters to build a new Republican majority. By the time Nixon took office, desegregation, delayed for over a decade by judicial appeals, was getting ready to take effect in southern schools. With a view to segregationist sensibilities south of the Mason-Dixon line, Nixon and Attorney General Mitchell took steps to ensure that opponents of the *Brown* decision blamed the Supreme Court rather than the administration. In the summer of 1969 the Justice Department asked a federal judge to delay the integration of thirty-three school districts in Mississippi. The Supreme Court quickly rebuked the administration and ordered the state's elementary and secondary institutions "to terminate dual school systems at once." In March 1970 Nixon asked Congress for $1.5 billion to improve education and to help school districts meet problems caused by court-directed desegregation. But the president emphasized the distinction between *de jure* segregation based on discriminatory laws and *de facto* segregation based on residential patterns. He promised that transportation beyond "normal geographical school zones" to achieve integration would not be required.

After appointing the moderate and able Warren Burger to replace the retiring Earl Warren as chief justice of the Supreme Court, Nixon and Mitchell set about using subsequent appointments to implement their southern strategy. When the president nominated the conservative Clement Haynesworth of South Carolina to fill a vacancy on the Supreme Court, liberal Democrats, mindful that Haynesworth had done everything in his power to block that body's desegregation orders, came out against him in full force. Using conflict-of-interest charges, they succeeded in turning back his nomination. Furious, Nixon put forward the name of G. Harrold Carswell, a segregationist and Florida jurist whose record was so error-filled that Senator Russell Long defended him by declaring that the country needed a little mediocrity. "Brilliant . . . upside down thinkers" on the Supreme Court had been destroying the United States, the Louisiana legislator declared. When the senators narrowly rejected Carswell, Nixon denounced them for demeaning and insulting the South.

The Burger Court

With the white South reassured of his devotion to their interests, Nixon proceeded to nominate Harry Blackmun, a respected conservative from Minnesota, to the Supreme Court. Blackmun easily won confirmation as did Lewis Powell, a distinguished Virginia jurist and legal scholar. William Rehnquist, a rigid conservative who would eventually become chief justice, rounded out the Nixon Court. To the dismay of conservatives, however, there was no mass reversal of the Warren Court's decisions. The Burger Court ruled unanimously in *Swann v. Charlotte–Mecklenburg Board of Education* (1971) that cities had to bus students out of their neighborhoods if that was necessary to achieve integration. In other decisions the high court restricted the government's right to wiretap suspected subversives, overturned state laws prohibiting abortion, and insisted that the death penalty was "cruel and unusual punishment" and therefore unconstitutional except when state law made it mandatory in specific situations.

Nixonomics

Nixon would have preferred to concentrate on foreign affairs and limit his domestic activities to preparing for the next election, but the economy would not allow him that indulgence. Confronted with a staggering $25 billion deficit for fiscal 1968 and an inflation rate approaching 6 percent—the products of LBJ's determination to fight the war without raising taxes—Nixon rejected wage and price controls and opted instead for a tax cut and pressure on the Federal Reserve to raise interest rates. The White House got the business slowdown it wanted—the recession of 1969–1970—but the rate of inflation continued to rise. The stock market tumbled from an average of 900 to 600, the sharpest drop in thirty years.

Democrats ridiculed "Nixonomics" and "stagflation," the name given to the unusual combination of inflation and a stagnant economy. Adding to the administration's woes was a record 1971 trade deficit. In a dramatic reversal of policy, the president abandoned his conservative opposition to interventionist economic policies and authorized wage and price freezes. The new secretary of the treasury, John Connally, devalued the dollar and imposed a 10 percent surcharge on foreign imports. Partially as a result, America's trade position improved dramatically, and by the end of 1971 the recession was over.

Spiro Agnew and the Politics of Rhetoric

Unfortunately for the administration, the economic turnaround came too late to have much impact on the 1970 mid-term elections. But the Nixon administration did manage to control the reaction that American voters traditionally demonstrate against the party in power. The White House unleashed Vice President Agnew who blamed Democrats and liberals—he did his best to equate those two terms in the public mind—for everything from drug abuse to sexual permissiveness to crime in the streets. He blasted the media, denounced intellectuals, and pandered to middle America. The phrase-making Agnew—he damned the press in general as "nattering nabobs of negativism"—and Nixon's southern strategy kept Republican losses in the House to a minimum, and the GOP actually gained two seats in the Senate.

The New Federalism

When the new Congress convened in 1971, Nixon urged its members to prepare the way for "a New American Revolution." The philosophical heart of this melodramatic call to arms was the "new federalism." Nixon proposed to reverse the trend toward greater federal power that had been going on since the New Deal; he would remove decision making in economic and social matters from the hands of Washington bureaucrats, he promised, and restore it to states and localities. Specifically, the president proposed to eliminate a number of federal programs and substitute blanket grants to the states and cities to administer as they thought best. Revenue sharing was approved as the State and Local Fiscal Assistance Act of 1972. The measure turned back to the states $30.2 billion, but governors and mayors complained that because the Nixon administration simultaneously cut or abolished existing programs, the federal government was giving with one hand and taking away with the other.

NIXON AND THE VIETNAM WAR

Topping the administration's list of diplomatic priorities was an end to the war in Vietnam. Nixon believed that peace was essential if he were to capture a second term, and both he and Kissinger hoped to establish a new international order managed by the United States. A continuation of the conflict in Southeast Asia would interfere seriously with those plans. But Nixon perceived that he could not simply withdraw from Vietnam; the nation, he said, demanded "peace with honor." As it turned out, what that meant was victory for the United States and its ally in Saigon. The United States had given up on winning a purely military victory, Nixon told the American people shortly after his inauguration, but neither would his government accept a settlement in Paris that amounted to a "disguised defeat." He announced that the United States would set a timetable for withdrawal from South Vietnam if the DRV would do the same for South Vietnam, Cambodia, and Laos. Behind its rhetoric, the new administration was as committed to the preservation of an independent, noncommunist government in South Vietnam as Kennedy and Johnson had been.

Vietnamization

Unable to force Hanoi to make the slightest concession at the peace talks, Nixon decided to blast the enemy with a new bombing campaign and launch an amphibious assault across the seventeenth parallel. He was dissuaded by Kissinger and Secretary of Defense Melvin Laird who told him that such moves would have little or no impact on the communists and would be sure to rekindle the antiwar movement, largely dormant since the 1968 Democratic convention. In October of 1969 Nixon decided to fall back on a policy he had inherited from Lyndon Johnson—Vietnamization. In a major television address on November 3 the president declared that the Thieu regime was at last strong enough to defend itself; America was turning over the war to South Vietnam. As of April 1969 the United States had 543,000 troops in Vietnam. By the summer of 1972 that number had dwindled to fifty thousand. Vietnamization was a brilliant political stroke designed simultaneously to placate doves and hawks. The steady withdrawal of American troops cut the ground from beneath antiwar activists, while hawks were assured that the American-equipped and -trained South Vietnamese army could win a military victory over their communist opponents.

Cambodia and Kent State

For Vietnamization to work, however, the United States would have to do all in its power short of direct ground action to strengthen Nguyen Van Thieu's military position. To this end Nixon decided to take measures long advocated by the Joint Chiefs of Staff and rejected by Lyndon Johnson—air and ground attacks against communist sanctuaries in Cambodia and Laos. Portions of the Ho Chi Minh Trail ran through those countries and into South Vietnam, and the NVA had been using Cambodia as a staging ground for sallies into South Vietnam since the mid-1960s, despite the fact that the Cambodian government of Prince Norodom Sihanouk was officially neutral.

In the spring of 1969 Nixon ordered massive top secret bombings of Cambodia which continued for the next fifteen months. Then in March 1970 Sihanouk was overthrown in a coup headed by General Lon Nol, a staunchly anticommunist officer who wanted to drive the communists out of Cambodia. On April 29 South Vietnamese units with American air support attacked an

By 1970 the nation was deeply divided over Vietnam. Here National Guard troops caution antiwar demonstrators at Kent State.

enemy sanctuary in the Parrot's Beak, a strip of Cambodian territory thirty-three miles from Saigon. On April 30 American forces assaulted Fishook, a North Vietnamese base area fifty-five miles northwest of Saigon. That night Nixon went on national television and justified the invasion as a response to North Vietnamese aggression against Cambodia.

Within minutes of the president's televised address, antiwar activists took to the streets in New York and Philadelphia, and in the days that followed protests erupted across the country. The scores of marches and rallies that engulfed campuses from Maryland to Oregon—1.5 million students and half of America's twenty-five hundred campuses—were characterized by a sense of betrayal; the war was being expanded under the pretense of ending it. On May 4, 1970, four students were killed and ten wounded by National Guardsmen at Kent State University in Ohio. Nixon, who like Johnson believed that youthful protestors were either communists or cowards who wanted to avoid the draft, insensitively observed: "When dissent turns to violence, it invites tragedy." On May 14 police killed two black students and wounded twelve at Jackson State University in Mississippi.

Congress and the War

The Cambodian incursion also had the effect of crystallizing antiwar sentiment in Congress. Senator J. William Fulbright, chair of the Senate Foreign Relations Committee, and others had long been trying to attract conservatives to their cause by arguing that the conflict in Southeast Asia was unconstitutional. The expansion of the war into Cambodia frightened even staunch hawks like Sam Ervin (D–North Carolina) and John Stennis (D–Mississippi). Momentum began to build for a restoration of congressional prerogatives in foreign affairs. Hoping to reclaim lost powers, Congress repealed the Tonkin Gulf resolution which had authorized President Johnson to use the armed forces of the United States to protect themselves and South Vietnam, and debated a spate of resolutions cutting off funding for the war. Publication of the *Pentagon Papers*, a secret history of the war compiled during the 1960s at Secretary of Defense Robert McNamara's direction, further alienated congressional and public opinion by revealing a record of deliberate deception during the early stages of the war.

Despite the Cambodian incursion and continuing American bombing throughout Southeast Asia, the communists refused to give in. As U.S. troop withdrawals proceeded, Kissinger made thirteen trips to Paris to conduct secret negotiations with representatives of North Vietnam. All came to naught. Ho Chi Minh, who died in 1969, and his successors insisted that as a prerequisite for peace, the United States not only pull its personnel out of South Vietnam but that it withdraw support from the Thieu government as well. This Nixon refused to do.

The Military in Crisis

Vietnamization and mounting opposition to the war at home had a disastrous impact on the U.S. military in Vietnam. All parties involved in the war in Indochina engaged in random violence, but the disclosure that American soldiers had massacred more than one hundred unarmed Vietnamese civilians at the village of My Lai in March 1968 made war atrocities a national issue. The wanton slaughter of elderly men, women, and children orchestrated by Lt. William Calley caused many Americans to conclude that the war was brutalizing not only Vietnam but the United States as well. In addition, television continued to bring the war into the nation's living rooms on a nightly basis. In 1971 opinion polls reported that 65 percent of respondents believed it "morally wrong" for Americans to be fighting in Vietnam, though in 1972 almost the same percentage of those answering indicated support for Nixon's position that South Vietnam not fall under communist control. Veterans returning home from Vietnam were treated frequently with either indifference or hostility.

Confused and demoralized, some American soldiers in Vietnam began refusing patrol duty. Marijuana use was pervasive, and by 1970 an estimated 10 to 15 percent of military personnel were addicted to heroin. "Fragging" incidents—the use of hand grenades to get rid of unpopular officers—reached

In one of the most famous and disturbing scenes of the war, a young Vietnamese girl, her clothes burned off by napalm, runs away in terror.

nearly 2,000 by 1972. Demoralization of the military reinforced the mounting popular desire to get out of the war. In private, members of the Joint Chiefs of Staff and Secretary of Defense Melvin Laird urged withdrawal lest the honor of America's armed forces be permanently stained and its ability to fulfill its global strategic responsibilities severely impaired.

The Stalemate Continues

Still the war continued. Nixon relied increasingly on air and naval power to prop up the Thieu regime. By the end of 1971 the United States Navy and Air Force had dropped 3.3 million tons of bombs on the two Vietnams, Cambodia, and Laos. Still the communists refused to depart from their negotiating position. Desperate to win reelection in 1972, the president had Kissinger make a significant concession in his secret Paris discussions. The United States would agree to pull out of Vietnam in return for repatriation of all prisoners of war (POWs). Washington had abandoned its insistence on a simultaneous North Vietnamese withdrawal from the South. DRV negotiators in Paris countered by dropping their demand that there be a political settlement prior to a cease-fire and that the United States abandon Thieu. With Kissinger telling all who would listen that "peace is at hand," it appeared that the war would end just in time for the 1972 election. Thieu refused to go along, however. He could not see the wisdom of signing an accord that provided for a total U.S. evacuation while leaving 145,000 North Vietnamese troops in place in the South.

America Withdraws

Because the Democratic party continued to display the self-destructive tendencies that had produced the 1968 Democratic convention and because Americans were reluctant to change presidents in the middle of a war, Richard Nixon won in 1972 without a formal peace accord. After the Paris talks broke down in December, the president ordered B-52s to pound Hanoi and Haiphong, and authorized the navy to mine Haiphong Harbor. For twelve days American planes rained down destruction on the North Vietnamese cities. Though his critics denounced Nixon as a madman, there was method to his madness. The stated reason for the aerial assault was to force negotiating concessions from Hanoi, but in addition, Nixon wanted to demonstrate to Thieu that the United States still possessed massive firepower and had the will to use it against its enemies. A billion dollars worth of tanks, planes, and other equipment were rushed to South Vietnam. Though Thieu remained dubious, he finally agreed to sign a peace accord on January 23, 1973.

Under the terms of the Paris Peace Accords, the United States promised to remove its troops from Vietnam within sixty days in return for the release of all POWs. The political clauses allowed Thieu to stay in power, but they also legitimized the NLF and permitted North Vietnamese troops to remain in the South. Supporters of the war denounced the accords as nothing more than a cynical attempt to provide a decent interval between American withdrawal and Thieu's defeat. The last American troops departed in March 1973, and the "cease-fire war" began in earnest. More ARVN troops died in 1974 than in 1967. In March 1975 North Vietnam launched a major offensive, crossing the seventeenth parallel in force. Within weeks the communists had captured Saigon, renaming it Ho Chi Minh City. Thieu fled the country. The Vietnam War was over.

THE HERITAGE OF VIETNAM

For the people of Indochina the war meant 1.5 million dead, dislocation of a third of the population, and defoliation of one-third of the region's forest lands. For the United States it meant defeat after ten long years of war, the deaths of fifty-seven thousand young men, and years of inflation and deficits. More important, the war changed the way Americans thought about themselves and the world. The nation's vision of itself as benevolent, wise, and invincible was swallowed up in the jungles of Vietnam. To their consternation, Americans learned that the domino theory was fallacious—Cambodia fell to the Khmer Rouge, but Burma, Thailand, Malaysia, and other regional powers managed to resist communism—and that the communist threat was not monolithic. Communist China subsequently invaded Communist Vietnam after it had gone to war with Communist Cambodia. To an extent Vietnam pointed up the limits of U.S. power and caused some Americans to stop thinking in Cold War, bipolar terms. Those who reflected thoughtfully on the tragedy in Southeast Asia concluded that not everything that happened in the world was of equal concern to the United States and that Washington could not be the permanent guarantor of stability in a turbulent world.

KISSINGER'S WORLD ORDER

Ironically, Richard Nixon and Henry Kissinger sought extraction from the Vietnam quagmire so that the United States could play a greater rather than a lesser role in world affairs. The author of several books on international affairs, Kissinger viewed the world geopolitically rather than ideologically. He saw the United States at the center of a new international balance of power in which it negotiated from a position of strength but safeguarded its interests through diplomacy rather than force. Kissinger helped persuade Nixon that the world was no longer bipolar, that Soviet-American hegemony had given way to a system featuring a variety of new power centers, including the United States, the Soviet Union, Western Europe, China, and Japan. The task, as they defined it, was to establish and maintain a balance among the five and to ensure that regional conflicts such as that between Israel and the Arab states in the Middle East did not draw any of the great powers into a major war.

For such a plan to work, the United States would simultaneously have to establish a working relationship with Communist China and the Soviet Union, and widen the Sino-Soviet split that had begun in the 1960s. The first step in the Nixon-Kissinger grand design was to play "the China card." Following the Korean War, domestic anticommunism had made it necessary for successive American administrations to pursue a policy of hostile nonrecognition toward Beijing. The excesses of the Cultural Revolution of 1966–1968, in which radical Chinese youth loyal to Mao persecuted tens of thousands of middle-aged and allegedly middle-class Chinese, seemed to validate the notion that Maoism represented the ultimate in communist fanaticism. Nonetheless, when Russia stationed nearly fifty divisions along its Chinese frontier, Nixon decided that the world's most populous nation had become vulnerable and hence the time was ripe for a rapprochement.

Opening to China

In July 1971 Kissinger secretly journeyed to Beijing to arrange for a trip by Nixon the following year. Early in 1972 America's foremost anticommunist spent a week in China trading toasts with Zhou Enlai. On February 27 the president and his host signed a communiqué declaring that Taiwan, where Jiang Jieshi was still in power, was legally part of mainland China, that American forces would eventually withdraw from Taiwan, and that the island's future was to be settled by the Chinese themselves.

Détente with the Soviet Union

Fearful that their two bitterest enemies were making common cause against them and anxious to acquire American grain and technology, the Soviets immediately sought their own version of *détente*, that is, a relaxation of tensions. On May 12, 1972, Nixon traveled to Moscow where he and Soviet Premier Leonid Brezhnev signed a twelve-point document, the "Basic Principles" of détente. It provided for a Conference on European Security which was eventually held in Helsinki and which ratified Europe's post–World War II borders. Nixon undertook to seek most-favored-nation status (the extension of tariff concessions made to other countries) from Congress for the Soviet Union. Most important, the Soviet and American leaders signed a two-part arms limitation agreement, SALT. The first section limited the two superpowers to two hundred antiballistic missiles (ABMs) apiece; the second froze the number of offensive ballistic missiles for a five-year period.

POLITICAL DIRTY TRICKS

Nixon's foreign policy achievements would have allowed him to stage the 1972 election campaign as a triumphal procession, but in his insecurity, he was willing to leave nothing to chance. In 1971 Attorney General John Mitchell formed a Committee to Re-elect the President (CREEP). Specialists in political dirty tricks, notably Donald Segretti, harassed Democratic contenders, while G. Gordon Liddy of the White House "plumbers," a top secret group formed after publication of the *Pentagon Papers* to plug further leaks of government documents, developed an elaborate plan to spy on the opposition. Liddy's scheme included bugging the Democratic national headquarters in the Watergate apartment complex in Washington. In the early morning hours of June 17, police caught James McCord and four other men working under the direction of Liddy breaking into the Watergate offices.

NIXON'S SECOND TERM

THE 1972 ELECTION

The White House's political crime spree was quite unnecessary. The early leading contender for the Democratic nomination was Hubert Humphrey, but his association with the Vietnam War and the party's old guard doomed him from the outset. Another contender, Maine Senator Edmund Muskie, who was hounded unmercifully by the press and New England conservatives during the New Hampshire primary, broke down and cried on television. When George Wallace was shot and paralyzed from the waist down by Arthur Bremmer, a white Marylander, Nixon had conservative America all to himself.

Helped by party reforms which gave more representation at the national convention to women, blacks, and other minorities, George McGovern of South Dakota secured the Democratic nomination. He ran on a platform that advocated a negotiated settlement in Vietnam, a woman's right to abortion, and tolerance of different lifestyles. Party brokers such as Chicago Mayor Richard

Daley and leaders of the major unions were completely alienated and either stayed on the sidelines or supported Nixon. Using the slogan "Come Home, America," McGovern attempted to wage a crusade against the war and on behalf of reform, but to middle America he came off simply as antiestablishment and self-righteous.

Nixon shrewdly stood back and allowed McGovern's perceived extremism to become the dominating issue of the campaign. Memories of Nixonomics and of the GOP candidate's unsavory political past were swept away by the country's determination to repudiate radicalism and the politics of confrontation. Nixon's margin of victory, 60.4 percent of the vote, was eclipsed only by Lyndon Johnson's 1964 landslide. Although the Democrats retained control of both houses of Congress and Nixon continued to be viewed with distrust, the Republican victory gave substance to Kevin Phillips' prediction of an emerging Republican majority anchored in the Sunbelt.

WATERGATE

During the campaign George McGovern had complained bitterly about Republican "dirty tricks"—fake letters identifying Democratic candidates with unpopular or unsavory causes, planted hostile questioners or hecklers, and particularly the attempted break-in into Democratic National Committee headquarters in the Watergate building. Most dismissed his complaints as the whinings of a sore loser. A momentarily confident Nixon and his staff made plans for four more years in power.

In the spring of 1973 the Watergate case came before Federal Judge John J. Sirica, a jurist known for his toughness and long sentences. Under his relentless questioning, James W. McCord, security chief for CREEP and one of the burglars, broke. He revealed that he had received money from the White House and had been promised a pardon if convicted. During March and April, Nixon's White House team began to disintegrate. Counsel to the president John Dean refused to become a scapegoat and was forced out. Haldeman and Ehrlichman, both of whom were deeply involved in a cover-up attempt, resigned. So did Attorney General John Mitchell.

The Senate named North Carolina Democrat Sam Ervin to head a special committee to investigate the Watergate episode. No evidence surfaced that Nixon had ordered the break-in or that he had been aware of plans to burglarize the Democratic National Committee. But in a week of dramatic testimony carried on TV, Dean revealed that Nixon had been intimately involved in the cover-up. Indeed, less than a week after the break-in, he had ordered the CIA to keep the FBI off the case on the grounds that it involved national security. The president had even urged his aides to lie under oath if necessary. "I don't give a [expletive] what happens," the president told John Mitchell, "I want you to stonewall it, let them plead the Fifth Amendment, cover-up, or anything else. . . ." Perhaps most important, testimony at the Ervin hearings revealed that Watergate was just a small part of a larger pattern of criminality in which Nixon had ordered intelligence agencies to spy on his opponents and authorized the plumbers group to open their mail and burglarize their apartments to find incriminating evidence.

The White House Tapes

As the national trauma intensified, Nixon aide Alexander Butterfield revealed to the Ervin Committee that the White House had a secret taping system and that all of the president's most private conversations had been recorded. A yearlong battle for the Nixon tapes ensued. In October 1973 Harvard law professor Archibald Cox, whom Nixon had appointed special prosecutor to handle the case, took the president to court to force him to turn over the now-famous recordings. Thereupon Nixon ordered Cox fired, but in what became known as the Saturday night massacre, both Attorney General Elliot Richardson and his deputy resigned rather than follow the president's instructions. Eventually Cox gave way to Houston attorney Leon Jaworski, but Jaworski proved no more compliant. The new special prosecutor filed suit in due course, and on July 24, 1974, the Supreme Court ruled unanimously that the president must surrender the tapes.

NIXON'S RESIGNATION AND THE LEGACY OF WATERGATE

When Nixon balked, the House Judiciary Committee voted to recommend three articles of impeachment. The president deserved to be removed from office, the House indictment read, because he had obstructed justice through the payment of hush money to witnesses, because he was defying Congress and the courts by withholding the White House tapes, and because he had used federal agencies to deny American citizens their constitutional rights. Before the full House could meet to vote on impeachment, Nixon handed over the tapes. Fully aware that they implicated him in the cover-up, he resigned as president of the United States on August 9, 1974.

In one sense the Watergate scandal constituted America's darkest hour. Nixon was the first president in history to resign under fire. Twenty-five members of the administration, including four cabinet officers, were convicted. In short, Watergate confronted the nation with its gravest constitutional crisis since the Civil War. The burglary and revelations that followed produced a deep sense of disillusionment with what historian Arthur Schlesinger, Jr., would term the "imperial presidency." Following in the aftermath of Vietnam, the break-in and cover-up only deepened public cynicism toward a government that lied to its citizens and violated their constitutional rights.

At the same time, Watergate demonstrated the vitality of American democracy; the nation's institutions emerged from the crisis unscathed. Faced with a massive conspiracy by the executive branch, the press, the courts, and

A seemingly unperturbed President and Mrs. Nixon are escorted by the Fords across the White House lawn for their ignominious departure.

Congress had persisted and succeeded in uncovering wrongdoing that threatened the very foundations of the republic. Watergate prompted Congress to pass legislation to restore the balance of power within the three-branch federal system. The War Powers Act of 1973 required presidents to consult Congress before sending American troops into combat abroad and to withdraw U.S. forces within sixty days if Congress did not specifically approve their deployment. In reaction to the pervasive Nixon claim of "executive privilege," Congress strengthened the 1966 Freedom of Information Act to ensure that government agencies responded promptly to requests for information and placed the burden of proof on them for showing why documents should remain classified.

Because of his conservatism, his refusal to bring about an early end to the war in Vietnam, and Watergate, Richard Nixon has been one of the most harshly

criticized presidents in American history. Students of his presidency have por-
trayed him as a demagogue or a paranoid or both, a man whose blind am-
bition nearly destroyed constitutional democracy in America.

Nixon's death in 1994 caused some reassessment, with commentators
arguing that his moderately conservative domestic policies and pragmatic,
nonideological foreign policies accurately reflected the mood of the public. This
is the position taken by Alonzo Hamby in his essay on Nixon in Liberalism and
Its Challengers. *The president's anticommunism and distrust of the liberal,*
eastern elite accurately reflected the views of small town, working- and middle-
class America, Hamby argues. He recognized the flaws in liberal interna-
tionalism and attempted to return the country to a realistic foreign policy in
which it focused on its strategic and economic interests. Nixon was well on his
way to building a new political coalition, according to Hamby, until his
personal flaws brought him down.

THE FLAWED CHALLENGER: RICHARD M. NIXON
Alonzo L. Hamby

Richard Nixon reminds one of Clyde Griffiths, the antihero protagonist of Theodore Dreiser's *An American Tragedy.* Like Griffiths, he was born into poor but pietistic circumstances and indoctrinated with the American success ethic. Like Griffiths, he pursued wealth and recognition and was guilty of criminal behavior in the process. Griffiths was driven to murder and paid with his life; Nixon betrayed the trust that the American people had traditionally placed in their presidents and forfeited his political life, leaving the presidency in serious disrepair. Griffiths's short, unhappy life was of course a metaphor for the way in which the American Dream and the values connected with it could be perverted by the pressures of social reality. Nixon's career may tell us much the same thing; to the extent that it does, it tells us not simply about Nixon but about ourselves, and that perhaps as much as anything accounts for our national fascination with him.

Nixon's failure of character has obscured the fact that his presidency presented the contemporary American political tradition with its most coherent challenge yet.

from Alonzo L. Hamby, *Liberalism and Its Challengers: FDR to Reagan* (New York: Oxford University Press, 1985), 282–338.

In the main, this challenge, as opposed to the man who advanced it, enjoyed widespread popular support. During his years in the White House, Nixon sensed that the old internationalist liberalism had approached the point of exhaustion. He quite consciously adopted a set of "neoconservative" alternatives that contrasted sharply with traditional GOP right-wingism and sought to build a new majority in American politics. He was well along the road to success when forces within himself brought him down and aborted the effort.

Making It

It is difficult to read of Richard Nixon's childhood without experiencing feelings of considerable sympathy, even pity. Almost every feature of his youth conspired to deny him a sense of security and self-worth. He was born in 1913 in suburban Los Angeles, the second of five children, and grew to maturity in a family existing precariously at the margin of middle-class socioeconomic status. As a teenager, he managed the produce section of the family grocery store and filling station and made daily predawn drives into the city for fresh vegetables.

His father, Frank, must surely rank among the most difficult parents in the history of the presidency. A trolley conductor, farmer, carpenter, and finally the operator of a mom-and-pop general store, Frank Nixon spent his life struggling to make ends meet, never establishing an atmosphere of success or financial security for his children. Temperamental, quick to take offense, a stern disciplinarian, irritable, ulcer-ridden, he must have seemed at times a terrifying figure to a young child. As Richard Nixon has described it, his father was a classical totalitarian who expected instant obedience and did not flinch at the prospect of inflicting pain. "I learned early that the only way to deal with him was to abide by the rules he laid down. Otherwise, I would probably have felt the touch of a ruler or the strap as my brothers did."

The mother, Hannah Milhous Nixon, provided, it is true, an oasis of gentleness and stability in a hard, small world. Universally described as saintly and loved in the community, she was a source of reassurance and protection. Yet for some two years—crucial, formative years for a boy—she was away from home, having taken young Richard's tubercular older brother Harold to a nursing home in Arizona, where she did menial labor to pay the bills. A younger brother, Arthur, also fell prey to a degenerative disease, tubercular meningitis. Both necessarily received greater attention, and both died while Richard was in his teens. It is not surprising that the boy is widely remembered as quiet, introverted, studious, and hard-working.

In many respects, Richard Nixon grew up as a Horatio Alger type, a diligent poor boy aspiring to greater things. At home, he absorbed all the values of pietistic Protestantism and the petit bourgeoisie. At school, he was a grade grubber, a successful student politician, and a determined, if woefully inadequate, member of the football squad. Behind his model-child exterior, he seems to have harbored an intense, combative aggressiveness. This was possibly a reaction to all the frustrations that surrounded him, possibly an emulation of his father. Football, with its special blend of discipline and violence, always would hold a special attraction for him. It encouraged a tendency to envision combat as a metaphor for life. It gave to its heroes an acclaim and devotion that Nixon always would covet.

After graduating from little Whittier College, Nixon went off to Duke University Law School. Living on a scholarship in povertylike conditions, he was again an unsuccessful football player but a star student. His academic success he attributed, frankly and perhaps a bit too self-disparagingly, to his incessant study, characterizing himself as a young man with an "iron butt." He graduated second in his class.

He had practiced all the Horatio Alger values, but the world did not give him a Horatio Alger payoff. Along with a couple of friends, he traveled to New York to interview with some prestigious law firms. He did not receive a job offer. He sent a letter of application to the FBI, but nothing came of it. Instead, he wound up back in Whittier, practicing law with an older family friend. One has to wonder how hard he had tried. Perhaps like many an introvert, he found a return to a familiar, easily manageable environment preferable to the threats of a high-powered, uncertain world well beyond his experience.

As a young attorney handling routine cases, he worked tirelessly, occasionally sleeping overnight at the office. He earned a modest living and secured some community standing. Soon he was a trustee of Whittier College and an aspiring businessman. With some friends, he organized the Citra-Frost Company to produce frozen orange juice. Displaying his usual intense commitment, he was both president and sometime juice squeezer. The firm was thinly capitalized and it was unable to develop suitable packaging. After a year and half, it failed, leaving Nixon with a considerable financial and—no doubt—emotional loss. He could at least find a large measure of consolation in his marriage to Pat Ryan in 1940.

As it did with so many of the young men of his generation, World War II profoundly affected Nixon's future. He and his wife went to Washington and landed jobs with the Office of Price Administration. He later remembered the experience as distasteful and disillusioning. A conservative Republican who had grown up in a milieu of small-town individualism, he found himself working in a haven for New Deal Democrats, infamous for its miles of bureaucratic red tape. In August 1942, he obtained a commission in the U.S. Navy.

Eventually, Nixon wound up in the South Pacific as a supply officer, working on the edges of combat zones. He was an efficient, first-rate young commander who displayed considerable initiative in cutting rear supply areas and landing strips out of the bush; he took care of his men, and won rapid promotions. Along the way, he met and became a friend of the actor Jimmy Stewart. He also learned to play poker so skillfully that he came out of the service several thousand dollars richer. By 1945, he was back in Washington, working on the navy's legal staff, renegotiating procurement contracts. Several weeks after the surrender of Japan, he was discharged with the rank of lieutenant commander.

By now, Nixon had acquired a range of personal, administrative, and legal experience beyond anything he could have achieved in a lifetime of practice in Whittier. He felt ready to look for opportunities in Washington or New York. Then, unexpectedly, he received an offer that touched an ambition he had long harbored and brought him back home without hesitation.

A committee of Republican businessmen searching for a strong candidate to oppose Democratic congressman Jerry Voorhis paid Nixon's travel expenses for what amounted to an audition. The young veteran delivered a brief, forceful speech, contrasting the virtues of individual self-reliance with the evils of New Deal bureaucratic paternalism, then concluded with the somewhat incongruous assertion: "If the choice of this committee comes to me, I will be prepared to put on an aggressive and vigorous campaign on a platform of progressive liberalism designed to return our district to the Republican party." He won a top-heavy endorsement.

Voorhis was a respected four-term veteran of the House, widely admired in Washington and the author of a book on Congress that had won national attention. Still, he faced difficulties. The district belonged to neither party, and the year was a very bad one for any Democrat outside a safe district. Starting out as an underdog, Nixon aggressively rode the tide while his opponent was pulled under by it.

He personally put half his savings, $5,000, into the campaign. His supporters secured him the part-time help of a shrewd if rather unscrupulous campaign operative, Murray Chotiner, who had run Earl Warren's successful first bid for the governor's mansion and was devoting most of his time to William Knowland's race for the Senate. Chotiner's advice meshed well with the candidate's temperament: nothing was more important than hard work; always take the battle to the enemy; respond to an attack by going on the offensive; never play to the strengths of the opposition.

From January on, Nixon slugged away, his opponent in Washington most of the time. He faced Voorhis in a series of debates that fall and soon had him on the ropes, pounding at him on the two big national issues of the election—price controls and the spreading revulsion against Communism. Increasingly, he was prone to emphasize Communism, an easily manipulable vehicle for personal attack. Nixon never accused Voorhis of being a Communist as such, but he dredged up alleged radical statements from Voorhis's past and claimed he had accepted support from Communist-dominated labor organizations. Printed advertisements alluded to Voorhis's younger days as a registered Socialist. An anonymous telephone campaign, its extent uncertain and its relationship to the Nixon organization unknown, flatly labeled Voorhis a Communist. The same sort of tactics were used by many other Republican candidates across the country in 1946 and were frequently effective.

The challenger had more going for him than an instinct for the jugular. Like a good many returning servicemen who went into politics, he advertised his veteran status and was not shy about reminding his constituency that his opponent had spent the war in Washington. He occupied the middle of the road by pushing Voorhis over to the left and by evading a firm ideological stance of his own. He seemed an attractive young personality with his humble beginnings, his war record, his smooth yet sincere speaking style, and his attractive young wife and infant daughter.

On election day, he defeated Voorhis handily. The incumbent, an idealistic liberal deeply interested in the consumer cooperative movement, was of course neither a Communist nor a Communist sympathizer. Given the unfavorable political situation of 1946, he might well have lost on other issues. Nonetheless, many observers thought that the charges of Communism had been decisive, and Richard Nixon went to Washington believing that he had found a winning technique. He also had demonstrated that in the real world, the young man who constantly works and fights to get ahead cannot be overly fastidious. It was a lesson he accepted.

Nixon's two terms as a young congressman displayed his skill at the game of self-advancement. He made himself a leader among the Young Turk Republicans. He obtained coveted appointments to the House Education and Labor Committee (where one of his Democratic colleagues was John F. Kennedy) and the Un-American Activities Committee. He did his homework well, spoke effectively when he ventured into debate, and serviced his constituency faithfully. Ideologically, he remained hard to classify. On domestic issues, he usually voted as a Republican conservative. He was especially vehement in his criticisms of organized labor, which he tended to represent as an offshoot of the Communist conspiracy or a fraud against the American worker; he was a strong advocate of the Taft-Hartley Act.

In foreign policy, however, Nixon stood apart from the Taft "isolationist" bloc and reflected the experience of many young veterans of World War II. He supported most of the major Cold War initiatives of the Truman administration and was willing to incur some risks in the process. When informed in 1947 that his position in favor of the Marshall Plan was unpopular at home, he returned to his district, made some fifty speeches, and got his viewpoint across to the voters. Adopting the Cold War without reservations, he criticized the Truman administration only when he found its policies too soft.

He was always remarkably successful in identifying himself with the Communist issue. As a member of the Un-American Activities Committee, he avoided demagoguery and displayed some concern for the rights of witnesses. Nevertheless, he was anything but a civil libertarian. In 1948, with Sen. Karl Mundt of South Dakota, he sponsored legislation that would have required Communists to register with the government, denied them passports or the right to apply for federal employment, and made them subject to deportation if they were not U.S. citizens. The bill was pigeonholed after Thomas E. Dewey, the leading candidate for the Republican presidential nomination, denounced it as "nothing but the method of Hitler and Stalin." In 1950, it would be exhumed and incorporated into the McCarran Act.

The Alger Hiss controversy made Nixon a national figure. Among the Republican members of the Un-American Activities Committee, he most quickly overcame his doubts about Hiss's accuser, Whittaker Chambers, and emerged as the leader in the drive to obtain Hiss's eventual indictment for perjury. Whatever the truth about the Hiss case and whatever Nixon's own exaggeration of Hiss's importance as a Communist agent, there is no evidence to suggest that the young congressman engaged in any violation of Hiss's rights, made charges frivolously, or undertook in a frame-up. He simply felt that Hiss was guilty and stayed with the case; eventually, a jury agreed with him. In the process, he gained fame and positioned himself for a shot at a Senate seat. In 1950, he faced Congresswoman Helen Gahagan Douglas in one of the most notorious elections of the era.

A noted singer and actress before her move into the political world, and wife of the movie star Melvyn Douglas, Helen Douglas had spent three terms representing a liberal Los Angeles constituency. She was not especially popular among her House colleagues—Nixon recalls that Jack Kennedy delivered to him a $1,000 contribution from Joseph P. Kennedy and added his own best wishes—but the media attention that she orchestrated so naturally had made her one of the better-known figures in Congress. Glamorous, idealistically liberal, embodying the chic reformism of the Hollywood set, she was a perfect foil for Nixon. Although her political career had taken shape on the left wing of the Democratic party, Helen Douglas was in no way a Communist sympathizer. Like many liberals of the period, she was a reluctant cold warrior who had swung behind Truman's foreign policy only after being attracted by the idealism of the Marshall Plan. She had opposed the presidential candidacy of Henry Wallace, voted for the military aid to Western Europe, and supported the Korean War. Her husband was a leader of the California Americans for Democratic Action, the focus of anti-Communist liberalism in the state. (Another important figure in the state ADA was Ronald Reagan.)

Nixon and his managers chose to ignore these facts in a campaign that painted a mainstream liberal a virulent shade of hot pink. They distributed a highly selective list of congressional votes and quotations purporting to show that Mrs. Douglas's record was comparable to that of the notorious fellow-traveling New York congressman, Vito Marcantonio (who actually had supported Henry Wallace, voted against military aid to Western Europe, and opposed the Korean War). Shouting "pink" at every opportunity, Nixon and his supporters succeeded in making their opponent the issue.

On the defensive, the Democrats asserted that Nixon's negative voting record brought more comfort to the Communists than Douglas's. The tactic had no chance of success against the man who had gotten Alger Hiss. On election day, Nixon won by a wide margin. Apparently experiencing no twinges of regret about the crude innuendo that had helped bring him victory, he was capable of writing twenty-eight years later that the Douglas campaign, unequaled "for stridency, ineptness, [and] self-righteousness," had smeared *him* and that he had saved the state from being represented in the Senate by "one of the most left-wing members of Congress."

Twice Nixon had defeated well-known figures who at most might have been criticized for a liberal idealism a bit fuzzy around the edges. He had done so by implying that they were either subversives or dupes of subversives. As a senator, vice-presidential candidate, and at the beginning as vice-president, he frequently resorted to such methods. He was at most a half-step removed from the worst aspects of McCarthyism. A 1952 characterization of Adlai Stevenson epitomized the style: "Adlai the appeaser . . . who got a Ph.D. from Dean Acheson's College of Cowardly Communist Containment." Among Democrats, he became the most hated Republican, detested by many fellow congressmen, indelibly caricatured for the rank and file by the cartoonist "Herblock" as the dark-jowled compatriot of Joe McCarthy.

Nixon could plead with some justice that his use of the Communist issue was of a piece with the Republican rhetoric of the time, as employed by no less a figure than Robert A. Taft. After the conviction of Alger Hiss, Herbert Hoover had sent Nixon a telegram of congratulations that asserted: "AT LAST THE STREAM OF TREASON THAT HAS EXISTED IN OUR GOVERNMENT HAS BEEN EXPOSED IN A FASHION ALL MAY BELIEVE."

Even Thomas Dewey would from time to time lob charges of pinkness at the Democratic opposition. For Hoover or Taft or Dewey—and no doubt for Nixon—such declarations delivered a powerful emotional satisfaction that went beyond considerations of rationality. For a politician seeking a response from a partisan Republican audience, the Communist issue was the rhetorical equivalent of 101-proof bonded whiskey. It was not altogether surprising that a young up-and-coming GOP figure would seize on it.

But Nixon's anti-Communism was also imbedded deeply in his background and value structure. His Republicanism had not come from the study of economics; rather it was rooted in the assumptions and aspirations of the Protestant, entrepreneurial lower middle class with its belief in religion, patriotism, hard work, and traditional morality, its faith that the virtuous would get ahead in the world. The liberalism of the New and Fair Deals—most coherently expressed by secular intellectuals openly contemptuous of old absolutes, most visibly supported by the labor unions, most epitomized by the phrase *welfare state*—was an affront to the fundamental beliefs of Nixon and the many Republicans like him who constituted the most durable core of support for the party. From their perspective, Communism could seem just more of the same. Throughout his career, Nixon's appeal would be strongest not in the more sophisticated metropolitan areas of America but in the small towns and cities where the values of his youth remained strong.

Nothing in Nixon's career demonstrated the point more graphically than the "secret fund" crisis that nearly drove him from the Republican ticket in 1952. The charge itself was pressed hardest by sophisticated liberal intellectuals who tended to snicker at traditional ideals and who despised Nixon as a sanctimonious fraud. Nixon's famous television response, however cornpone it may have been, amounted to an instinctive reassertion of those ideals and a rallying of a vast constituency that still adhered to them. He talked of his modest background, his military service, his fight against Communism, his mortgages, his two-year-old car, and his family—the wife with the respectable Republican cloth coat, the two daughters, and the little dog they loved so much.

Whether or not he had depicted himself as he really was, he had put across the self-image he sincerely idealized. A groundswell of support kept him on the ticket. The defeat of Adlai Stevenson, denounced by Republican campaigners as an egghead sophisticate, provided a final confirmation of the way in which the GOP drive as a whole had been a "crusade" to reassert hallowed values. Nixon was not simply *in* this crusade; he was *of* it: "I felt instinctively negative toward Stevenson. I considered him to be far more veneer than substance, and I felt that beneath his glibness and mocking wit he was shallow, flippant, and indecisive."

Nixon had been chosen for the vice-presidential nomination largely because he appeared to embody the domestic world view of the Taft Republicans without sharing their isolationism. Based on the classic considerations of political balance, his selection occurred without Eisenhower's active participation. For the remainder of his career, his relationship with the Northeastern establishment would be distant. For the balance of the fifties, his relationship with Eisenhower would be ambiguous. . . .

Taking the nomination in 1960 was [for Nixon] in fact almost effortless. Nelson Rockefeller, the recently elected governor of New York, assayed a challenge, but he quickly discovered that all his considerable strengths as a campaigner, all his appeal to the independent voter, and all his vast wealth counted for little with the state and local functionaries who ultimately controlled the Republican convention. As a running mate, Nixon shrewdly chose Henry Cabot Lodge, Jr., ambassador to the United Nations, former senator from Massachusetts, widely popular for his tough retorts to the Russians in UN debates, and a leading figure among the Northeastern establishment Republican types who were still put off by Nixon.

It is difficult to ascribe Nixon's loss to any one or two factors. He was of course the candidate of the minority party, and he struggled against a soft economy. Nonetheless, two other important circumstances stand out even more—the debates and Nixon's relations with the working press.

Nixon's decision to meet Kennedy in a series of televised debates, foolish in retrospect, was understandable at the time. From his school days, he had been a polished debater. He had bested Voorhis in 1946 and had used television effectively in 1952. But in 1960, he was a quasi-incumbent with wider national recognition and a generally acknowledged lead in the presidential race. He forfeited an advantage when he agreed to meet Kennedy on equal terms and gave his opponent a special exposure. Nixon had forgotten, if he ever had understood, that television transmitted images and personalities; it was this function that had saved him in 1952, not his recitation of his fund's audit. In 1960, however, he was not alone in front of the camera, and pathos was not an acceptable tool for a presidential candidate. Kennedy was handsomer, and his style more in keeping with the expectations of American trend setters. Nixon's hot, impassioned demeanor and his uptight conventionality contrasted poorly with Kennedy's cool detachment and witty humor. He never had stood to gain much from the debates; he lost a great deal. . . .

Nixon's difficulty with the journalistic world exemplified certain personality problems that would forever haunt his political career. Absolutely central to his sense of identity was a self-image as a crusading underdog fighting against a host of privileged, unscrupulous enemies. He was incapable of admitting to himself that on occasion he had done wrong or had abandoned principle for opportunism. In his own mind, he never smeared his opponents; he just told the truth about them. It was he who suffered constant smears—from Helen Gahagan Douglas, from the Kennedys, from Pat Brown in 1962, and above all, from the press, which never had forgiven him for exposing Alger Hiss.

Having relieved a sense of guilt by transferring his own misdeeds to others, he could exhibit an indefatigable self-righteousness that was not simply a typical politician's hypocrisy. Feeling beset from all sides and mistreated by others, he could also lapse easily into a maudlin self-pity, reminding listeners of his humble origins, his hard work for the right causes, and the insufficient appreciation he received from the American people. He possessed an unhealthy suspicion of others and a lack of respect for the integrity of his opponents. . . .

The next four years played out with an almost inexorable logic. Nixon campaigned tirelessly for Republicans across the country in 1966. He stepped up his foreign travel. He prepared intelligent, thoughtful essays for journals of opinion. He even managed to establish friendly contacts with a few influential journalists such as Theodore H. White. In the meantime, the Johnson administration collapsed of its own weight, and the Democratic party suffered near-disintegration with the Wallace secession, the McCarthy revolt, the emotional insurgency and assassination of Bobby Kennedy, and the convention riots in Chicago. Easily nominated by the Republican convention, Nixon had somehow placed himself near the center of American politics with the liberal Humphrey on the left and the pseudo-populist, race-baiting Wallace on the right. He capitalized on the position by turning his television campaign over to shrewd media experts who packaged him as a reasonable, competent, relatively attractive statesman answering questions from groups of ordinary people seated around him.

On election day, Nixon squeezed out a narrow victory, running ahead of Humphrey by half a million votes. He polled 43.3 percent to 42.6 percent for the Democrat and 13.5 percent for Wallace. The election capped the most remarkable comeback in the history of American presidential politics. Moreover, it seemed to portend sharp shifts of direction both in foreign policy and in the trend toward liberal welfarism at home.

The Richard Nixon who won the presidency in 1968 was different from the candidate who had lost in 1960. He was more reflective, more inclined toward moderation, more pragmatic. He already had talked and written of the need to establish a relationship with mainland China, and he was pledged to pull the country out of Vietnam. His foreign policy would be "conservative"—not in the sense of being dogmatically anti-Communist but rather in the more authentic sense of being attuned to power relationships on a global scale with ideology a secondary consideration. At home, he would seek to control and limit the Great Society welfare state but not to destroy it. In a period of economic crisis, he would not hesitate to take strong federal action. To use a term that had not yet come into vogue, he had become something of a "neoconservative," alarmed at the excesses of the New Deal liberal tradition and determined to reconcile it with the classical values of conservatism. This objective was frustrated in the end less by any national doubts about its merits than by Nixon's considerable deficiencies of the spirit.

For all his immersion in the world of politics during most of his adult life, Nixon remained a distinctly unpolitical personality. He found little pleasure in the ritual camaraderie of handshaking and eager socializing so essential to the practice of American politics. A veteran political warrior who bore the psychological marks of years of nearly continuous, no-quarter combat, he was remarkably lacking in human warmth, uncomfortable meeting strangers, and inordinately fearful of their hostility or rejection. He was a self-conscious outsider who never ceased to resent a social and intellectual establishment that never had accepted him. Acutely conscious of the hatred of the liberals, he convinced himself that they were engaged in a constant conspiracy against him.

His behavior was that of a man who was markedly insecure and every bit as erratic as his predecessor. As president, he isolated himself from many of his cabinet members and congressional leaders and in fact, from all but a few trusted friends and advisers who for one reason or another did not threaten him. He surrounded himself with men who were second-rate (Spiro Agnew), or lacking strong substantive convictions (H. R. Haldeman and John Ehrlichman), or without an independent power base (Henry Kissinger, Daniel Moynihan). He was quick to engage in petty displays of displeasure with aides who seemed to get too much favorable press notice. Almost as if he felt too little to occupy the Oval Office, he frequently retreated to a smaller workplace in the Executive Office Building. At other times, as when he ordered the White House police dressed in European palace-guard–style uniforms, he seemed to take refuge in the imperial presidency. Plainly, he was uncomfortable with the position he had so arduously achieved.

Yet however insecure he felt, whatever the impulse to withdraw, he behaved as if he conceived of politics as a struggle for survival in a jungle. Having used spurious tactics against his opponents time and again, he was willing to employ almost any method that might bring victory. For all his service under Eisenhower, he somehow had failed to learn that presidents were not supposed to resemble alley fighters. His political Darwinism constituted a moral Achilles heel.

All the same, he was as much a moralist as any president in American history. Deeply attached to the values his parents had taught him, he perceived also that they constituted about the only politically useful common bond he had with many ordinary, working-class Americans who had tended to vote Democratic since FDR. Typically, he planned to rebuild the Republican party with a ruthless, no-holds-barred defense of the old morality.

In many respects, the neoconservatism he would adopt was simply the old liberalism of the 1940s and 1950s, as espoused by Truman or Kennedy at the working level and conceptualized by such thinkers as Reinhold Niebuhr at the intellectual level. Seen from the enthusiasm of the New Left or the expansiveness of the Great Society reformers, the old liberalism had come to look stodgy and dated. From the perspective of Vietnam, it appeared dangerously prone to Cold War military ventures. To a younger, more ambitious generation of liberals, unfettered by a sense of limits and anxious to distance itself from its elders, the old persuasion seemed unliberal.

The old liberalism had in fact moved in the direction of accepting some identifiably conservative values—the fragility of human nature, the futility of social engineering, the centrality of power in relationships between nations. To this, it had added a fervent conviction, developed by social thinkers who had witnessed and had sometimes personally experienced the parallel rise of German Nazism and Soviet Communism in the 1930s: totalitarian states were fundamentally alike beneath their different ideological masks; whether of the Left or the Right, they constituted abhorrent menaces to democracy.

Arthur Schlesinger, Jr., had codified these principles for the liberals in the 1940s as the "Vital Center." His work had become the point of departure for self-conscious efforts to square the liberal tradition with conservative principles in the 1950s, such as the New Conservatism and the New Republicanism. The neoconservatives who began to emerge in the late 1960s tended to have their intellectual roots in the old Vital Center liberalism more than in the New Conservatism. For the most part, they were one-time liberals who had occupied a position well to the left in American politics—many had been supporters and formulators of the Great Society. By the time Nixon was elected president, however, they had come to question both the assumptions and the techniques of liberalism as it had developed under Lyndon Johnson in the sixties. The Great Society, they believed, had become too ambitious, too wasteful, too redistributionist, too antimeritocratic.

They had, it is true, incorporated in their thinking some of the standard premises of American conservatism. Skeptical about extensive government intervention in the economy, they accepted the ethic of classical individualistic capitalism and argued in favor of greater leeway for free-market decision-making. Still, they fell well short of embracing laissez-faire or Social Darwinism. (The intellectual leader of the movement, Irving Kristol, found himself able to muster only *Two Cheers for Capitalism* in a volume published after Nixon left the presidency.) Reacting to the disorderly environment of the sixties and early seventies, they valued social stability. They emotionally supported the old-style liberal principle of equal opportunity and merit advancement as contrasted with the loose egalitarianism and advocacy of affirmative action of the newer liberals. Several of their leading figures—Daniel Bell, Irving Kristol, and Daniel Patrick Moynihan—had made their way up in society from unpromising beginnings and were disposed by experience to value effort, self-help, and opportunity even as they favored certain social reforms that might encourage those qualities.

They approached foreign policy in much the same spirit. Militant anti-Communists, they accepted the Cold War as a struggle of transcendent historical significance between liberal democracy and totalitarianism absolutism. Willing to concede in general terms the need for economic assistance and development in Third World nations, they nevertheless viewed the moral posturings and more extravagant material claims of the Third World as hypocritical. Almost always, they rejected the assertions that the difficulties of underdeveloped nations stemmed from Western imperialism, preferring instead to cite corruption, social disorganization, the absence of a liberal-democratic tradition, and ill-conceived efforts at socialism. Power, they believed, was in the last analysis the most important aspect of international diplomacy.

A final attitude underlay neoconservatism, one with which Nixon possessed a reflexive agreement. The neoconservatives were hostile toward the "New Class" of liberal and radical intellectuals who, it seemed, had come to dominate American culture in the sixties and whose beliefs clashed with theirs at every point. . . .

The World After Vietnam: Neoconservative Diplomacy and Its Limits

Richard Nixon had taken office as president with one clearly stated priority: to get the United States out of Vietnam. But he faced the equally difficult, if less emotional, problem of constructing a diplomacy that would take into account the emergence of a new world order in the 1960s. He had to deal with the rising visibility and influence of the Third World, the emergence of Japan and Western Europe as economic superpowers, the seeming diffusion of global power, and, as Vietnam appeared to have demonstrated, the limitations of American military strength. In this, as in no other area of his presidency, Nixon achieved considerable intellectual and emotional maturity. He possessed a strong grasp of world affairs, analyzed them with considerable dispassion, and was, above all, willing to recruit a strong figure to act as his aide.

His selection of Henry Kissinger as his chief foreign policy adviser was both surprising and inspired. While Kissinger came from and lived in worlds wholly removed from Nixon's, there also were personal similarities. Both men carried the scars of traumatic childhoods; both by nature were introverts; both saw themselves removed from an establishment that disdained Nixon and fell short of tendering Kissinger full acceptance. But most importantly, both had acquired as a result of their experiences a conservative view of human nature and, by extension, diplomacy.

Nixon's view of the world, an outlook that expressed the cynicism of a weary street fighter, had grown from the rhythms of victory and defeat in years of constant struggle. Kissinger's view, darker and more profound, stemmed from his childhood in Nazi Germany. He had witnessed brutal persecution first-hand and, with his family, had been fortunate to escape it. Like every Jew of European background, he found the slaughter of the vast majority of his people to be an inescapable presence in his mind. It imparted the certain knowledge that the human race harbored within itself a nearly inexhaustible capacity for inhumanity. Having once lived among Nazis, he naturally rejected the optimistic sentimentality that characterized so much of American liberalism. In a manner few Americans could comprehend, he had looked evil in the face and had measured its intractability.

Nixon and Kissinger both accepted the premise that power was the predominant factor in world politics and the balance of power the only reliable basis for relations among nations. These ideas were so alien to the American mind that it became necessary to conceal them. Depicting themselves as shapers of "détente" or "a generation of peace," they compromised their convictions to maintain their political support. Finally, they faced the handicap of having to lead a nation that was above all weary of power and its burdens, frustrated beyond measure by Vietnam, and increasingly attracted to the vision of withdrawal from an unpleasant world. Functioning in these difficult circumstances, they pursued the national interest much more effectively than would their immediate successors.

When Nixon took office, the American public demanded extrication from Vietnam. But where the opinion-shaping intelligentsia and its young followers expressed themselves in a style of moral indignation and quasi-pacifist outrage, Middle America tended more simply to be exhausted and disillusioned. To the opinion shapers, the war was immoral and should be terminated at once, even at the cost of delivering South Vietnam to the Communists. To Middle Americans, however, the war was a more ambiguous evil that needed to be brought to an end, but without national embarrassment. In adopting the objectives of Middle America, Nixon and Kissinger dealt themselves an extraordinarily difficult task. . . .

Nixon's objectives were at bottom the same as those of the Johnson administration. Both sought to preserve an independent South Vietnam and United States influence in Indochina. Nixon would carry on the war while winding down U.S.

participation and strengthening the South Vietnamese forces. To pursue victory while staging a withdrawal was a task so paradoxical that the most accomplished statesman would have found it difficult to explain. Nixon handled the job of gathering public support with particular ineffectiveness—indeed, with counterproductivity. Tactically, the job was well handled; it is possible to believe that had it not been for the destruction of his authority by Watergate, Nixon might have succeeded in maintaining South Vietnamese independence. Politically, it was managed in a way that displayed the president's inadequacies as a public leader.

To those most vehemently opposed to the war, Nixon was a hated, devious politician and a hard-line anti-Communist. He needed to conduct himself in a way that reached out to the antiwar intellectuals and neutralized at least some of them. Instead, he behaved in a way that inflamed the movement. He sent out contradictory signals, some of which could easily be taken as indications that the war was to be enlarged. He practiced confrontation instead of conciliation with the antiwar forces, and he displayed an emotionalism that no doubt reflected his own inner turmoil over having to orchestrate a policy of retreat so in conflict with his own combative instincts. The result was to lower the level of rationality in American politics, divide the country further, and bring antiwar sentiment to a point of near-hysteria. . . .

Amazingly, all the hostility between Nixon and his critics boiled down to little more on the rational level than an argument about the pace of withdrawal from Vietnam. Opponents might have argued compellingly in favor of a faster movement, questioned the feasibility of Vietnamization, or asserted that the continued expenditure of lives and treasure were not worth the gamble, but it is fair to observe that especially after Cambodia, the antiwar protestors were impelled by more than rational argument. . . .

It was ironic that in the process of finally achieving peace in Vietnam, Nixon was treated as if he were continuing the war full tilt. The blame for the venomous character of debate over the war could be spread generously. Yet much of the failure in the end was Nixon's. His character and reputation had preceded him, leaving many Americans with strong reservations about his intentions and trustworthiness. The tense, emotional style of his leadership served only to reinforce those doubts; and his irrepressible impulse to vilify and destroy his enemies created a bitter atmosphere. A major achievement of the Nixon presidency, the extrication from Vietnam also was a major example of Nixon's failure as a leader.

The rest of Nixon's diplomacy was in many respects attuned to the theme established by his Vietnam policy—that of an orderly retreat from an overextended position, an exercise made palatable by rhetoric extolling the goal of "a generation of peace." With the nation's sense of purpose and conviction of righteousness all but wiped out by Vietnam, American power, already barely useable, grew weaker in real terms as Congress cut military appropriations. There was an occasional surreptitious effort to wield power through Central Intelligence Agency operatives, as in Chile or Laos, but in the main Nixon and Kissinger attempted to conduct. . . .

At the time Nixon became president, the Cold War appeared on the wane. Intermittent disturbances—most serious among them the Soviet invasion of Czechoslovakia—had shaken but had not terminated the quest for mutual accommodation that had followed the Cuban missile crisis. Nixon understood full well that the old-style virulent anti-Communism no longer paid political dividends. Accepting the reality of the national mood, he attempted to defend American interests while cultivating friendship with the USSR.

Both in terms of public relations and even private conceptualization, the effort involved two diametrically opposed images of the Soviet Union: the rapacious aggressor and the benign, if somewhat backward, aspirant to full membership in the modernized, civilized community. Inconsistent conceptualization necessarily encouraged an inconsistent policy. Indeed, Nixon's approach to the Russians with its emphasis upon personal relations and manifestations of goodwill was not unlike Roosevelt's. As was the case with Roosevelt, it could boast of substantial accomplishments, but it encouraged illusions far grander than what it achieved.

On the surface, few nations appeared more receptive to a new diplomatic beginning than did the Soviet Union. Under Leonid Brezhnev, the USSR had taken on a bland, mediocre, nonthreatening appearance quite in contrast with its image under the evil Stalin or the blustering Khrushchev. The Brezhnev regime found itself more afflicted by open dissent than had any of its predecessors and gave the impression of having greater difficulty in dealing with a number of social and economic problems ranging from alcoholism to poor grain production. In fact, however, the Brezhnev government was the most adventurist in the history of the Soviet Union. As Nixon presided over a retreat of American power, Brezhnev oversaw a vigorous expansion of Soviet strength. . . .

The USSR thus presented two faces to the West. It was convenient to deal with the less threatening, and almost necessary to do so considering the lines of policy already established by Kennedy and Johnson and the way in which Vietnam had discredited the Cold War. Practically forced to proclaim a policy of "détente," Nixon and Kissinger were given neither the resources nor the time to engage in the sort of negotiations that might have produced real meaning for such a relationship. Thus, the character of détente was never definitively established. Neither the United States nor the Soviet Union really was prepared to abandon every opportunity for gain in international politics. Where then was the quest for influence permissible and where not? Was it all a matter of geography or of degree? . . .

Still, détente had a hard side, and nothing represented that better than Nixon's China policy. Writing in *Foreign Affairs* the year before he was elected president, Nixon had declared, "Any American policy toward Asia must come urgently to grips with the reality of China." The policy he advocated was sound, moderate, and remarkably un-Nixonian. The United States did not have to rush to give mainland China unreciprocated concessions, and it had to continue efforts to contain Chinese tendencies toward expansionism. But it also needed to make conciliatory gestures designed to bring China back into the international community and had to undertake a diplomacy that would *persuade* China to abandon foreign expansionism and turn to the solution of its domestic problems.

At once practical and idealistic, the argument was a remarkable departure from Nixon's early dogmatic anti-Communism. Behind it, moreover, there lay an unspoken but major assumption—China represented an important military counterpoise to

Soviet power in East Asia. The China card was a way of cementing the balance of power in a region that could not be stabilized by a militarily powerless, if economically prosperous, Japan. Nixon and Kissinger translated their design into reality with daring and opportunism.

The China policy was also good politics, and as was the case with U.S.–Soviet relations, political hype obscured both the hard intentions behind the opening to China and the limitations of the policy. Nixon visited China in February 1972, almost as the opening event of his presidential campaign. Television lent powerful immediacy to the event by transmitting one dramatic scene after another back to the United States.

The president proclaimed his efforts to be important steps in the building of a structure of peace. Understandably enough, neither he nor Kissinger dwelt on the limited character of what had been done. The reopening of diplomatic intercourse with China was all to the good, but as Kissinger himself would later write, the United States had not acquired a "China card" to play at will. What the China connection had done was to create a three-cornered relationship that with agile diplomacy the United States might use to its advantage. Nixon exaggerated his accomplishment, although his exaggeration was nothing compared to the euphoria that followed his trip among journalists and intellectuals. . . .

The Politics and Economics of Neoconservatism

During the 1960s, Richard Nixon had educated himself for the presidency primarily by acquiring a new expertise and sophistication in foreign policy. But he had inherited from Lyndon Johnson pressing socioeconomic problems, intensified no doubt by Vietnam but not likely to go away with the end of the war. Inflation was running at a then-frightening rate of about 5 percent. The sprawling jumble of Great Society programs, some of them functioning well, others a wasteful shambles, all had enormous potential for growth in their demands upon the federal treasury. The black revolution, embittered by the murder of Martin Luther King and exhilarated by the vocal rage of numerous militants, had become an angry force threatening to tear America into two societies. War-related dissent had been the catalyst for unusually acerbic political divisions and had created a large cadre of radicalized political activists disposed to continue their struggle against other aspects of the system once the war was over.

Nixon long had sensed that old-style orthodox Republicanism was not sufficient to deal with these challenges. He intended to continue leaning toward the Right, but he believed that the rigid Republican economics of the 1950s had severely damaged the party and sabotaged his 1960 bid for the presidency. As he took office in 1969, he was groping for an approach that would be both conservative and acceptable to the American people, one that would fit within the liberal tradition of Roosevelt and Truman yet maintain a critical attitude toward the Great Society. It would also have to mesh comfortably with his deeply felt personal belief in hard work and self-discipline.

The emergence of neoconservatism gave Richard Nixon a perspective that provided whatever coherence one can attribute to his policies and political strategies. Under the tutelage of Daniel Moynihan, a man of great charm and powers of persuasion, Nixon came to think of himself as a Tory reformer, an American Disraeli. Under the guidance of less likable men, he would become the spokesman of traditional Middle America leading a nasty crusade against the intellectuals.

In a general way, Nixon's domestic policies proceeded from certain assumptions largely held in common by thinkers who later would claim the neoconservative label. Moynihan had expressed some of these points of departure in an address, fittingly entitled "The Politics of Stability," to the National Board of the Americans for Democratic Action as early as 1967:

1. Liberals must see more clearly that their essential interest is in the stability of the social order; and, given the present threats to that stability, they must seek out and make much more effective alliances with political conservatives who share their interest and recognize that unyielding rigidity is just as great a threat to continuity of the social order as an anarchic desire for change.
2. Liberals must divest themselves of the notion that the nation—and especially the cities of the nation—can be run from agencies in Washington.
3. Liberals must somehow overcome the curious condescension that takes the form of defending and explaining away anything, however outrageous, which Negroes, individually or collectively, might do.

Speaking to the liberal establishment of the nation, Moynihan had delivered blunt challenges to the bulk of what had become the orthodoxy of reform in the sixties. Yet he had not abandoned the objective of reformist social change. Nixon found himself receptive to Moynihan's quest for alternative techniques that would combine conservatism and social activism; the most noted result of their collaboration was, of course, the Family Assistance Plan (FAP), destined to become the most significant failed initiative in the history of American social welfare politics since Truman's universal medical insurance proposal. Although orthodox GOP conservatives were aghast at its central concept of a guaranteed annual income for every American family, it appealed to many on the Right. It sought to bypass the bureaucracy as much as possible; by making direct payments to the poor according to nationwide standards, it would minimize casework surveillance and with it the demeaning psychological consequences of receiving welfare. "We hoped," Nixon has written, "to cut down on red tape, and before long to eliminate social services, social workers, and the stigma of welfare." The FAP intended to preserve family structures by removing the common prohibition against assistance to dependent children whose fathers were alive, well, and living at home. It would have encouraged work by requiring able-bodied recipients to accept jobs or vocational training and by providing benefits to those accepting low-paying employment.

Praised by a wide range of liberal and conservative observers who found its conceptual framework appealing, the FAP nevertheless was quickly ground to bits in the political process. Its projected cost alienated most Republican conservatives and divided Nixon's own administration; yet its rock-bottom benefits irritated many liberals. Moynihan put his finger on a large measure of the truth when he told Nixon that the Republicans, by and large, were not resisting efforts to kill the bill and that the Democrats wanted to deny the president an "epic victory" while blaming him for the defeat.

Understandably, however, Moynihan omitted one important factor—the president's own equivocal attitude about his creation. In retrospect, Nixon would defend the FAP mainly as a gamble worth taking in the hope of rehabilitating a discredited welfare system; his analogy suggests he felt considerable doubt. The president announced the plan, spoke out for it a few times, perhaps did a bit of serious lobbying for it, but failed to make it an urgent priority or an emotional cause. FAP might well have died in Congress anyway; by declining to give it the same sort of effort as, say, G. Harrold Carswell's appointment to the Supreme Court, Nixon ensured its demise.

Equally consistent with the mood of neoconservatism was the general concept of a "New Federalism" and its most specific incarnation, revenue-sharing. Republican moderates from the Eisenhower era on, Nelson Rockefeller among them, had sought a middle ground between the old conservative outlook and the centralizing tendencies of Democratic liberalism. Nixon and his brain trusters, William Safire and George Shultz among them, asserted the need for a New Federalism in which the national government would make broad policy and establish basic standards while leaving administration and determination of details to the states.

Revenue-sharing, the most visible embodiment of this approach, was attractive in its simplicity. The national government would remit to the states a portion of its revenue inflow with as few strings attached as possible. Along with the FAP, revenue-sharing was designed to deflate the growing power of the federal establishment. . . .

Race relations was another area in which neoconservatism sought an approach midway between the older conservatism and Great Society liberalism. Typically, the old conservatives had accepted segregation and all its consequences as a more or less justifiable, if occasionally unfortunate, exercise of personal choice, or matter of states' rights, or demonstration of black inferiority. Great Society liberals had developed an increasing obsession with racial injustice. They had been mightily impressed by the anger of black militance and had attempted to mobilize federal authority to put an end not simply to segregation but to every vestige of black inequality—social, political, economic.

Moynihan had exemplified the neoconservative reaction in his speech to the ADA. By 1970, he was advising Nixon that government had gone about as far as it could and that the issues of race had been "taken over by hysterics, paranoids, and boodlers on all sides." In a memorable sentence, soon leaked to the press and widely misunderstood, he declared, "The time may have come when the issue of race could benefit from a period of 'benign neglect,'" which he went on to define as one in which "Negro progress continues and racial rhetoric fades." Other influences were at work also, foremost among them the president's hope of making political gains in the South.

The Nixon approach to civil rights was far cooler than that of the Johnson administration, but it was well beyond anything Eisenhower could have envisioned and shocking to many old-style Republicans. The administration advocated a go-slow, voluntary approach to school integration, denounced the technique of busing children away from neighborhood schools, and at one point even sent Justice Department attorneys to file briefs in support of a Mississippi appeal for delay. Nevertheless, it did encourage the process of desegregation in the South, although it did so by employing financial incentives rather than pursuing adversary litigation. . . .

Moynihan has suggested persuasively that "Nixon and his opponents joined in a strange and almost sinister symbiosis." Liberal Democrats, who long had hated Nixon, were naturally inclined to see him as an enemy of the underprivileged and politically anxious to deny him any credit for advancing the goals of American liberalism. Their viewpoint may have been overly narrow-minded, but it was understandable, indeed quite normal. What was remarkable, as Moynihan has suggested, was that Nixon and those around him did not protest; instead, they seemed almost as anxious as the Democrats to conceal the liberal side of the administration. Nixon signed the Basic Grants bill into law with no official ceremony whatever; LBJ, Moynihan opines, would have staged a barbecue. The Republicans, Nixon included, found it hard to "internalize" the ethic of liberal government; they remained uncomfortable with it and had difficulty incorporating it into their rhetoric.

Finally, Nixon's natural political constituency—the heartland Republican middle class—and his potential following from the Democrats—the Southerners and the blue-collar workers—were profoundly alienated from those elements most identified with the Great Society. These were the "New Class" of intellectuals, professionals, and bureaucrats who formulated, administered, and legitimized American social welfare liberalism; and the client groups who received its benefits, especially blacks and other minorities. Nixon had great potential appeal to those Democrats who felt bypassed by their own party, but not if he were perceived as a trimmer making compromises with the forces they hated. His penchant for combat and confrontation sealed the situation; it would have been ludicrous to claim credit for advancing the goals of liberals whom he assailed bitterly in public. . . .

The results were disappointing by any standard. Nixon's "new economic policy" temporarily brought inflation to a crawl and cut into unemployment, but it provided little more than a scant respite. Unemployment remained higher than formerly had been considered acceptable; controls merely postponed wage and price increases, both of which took off as soon as Nixon initiated decontrol in early 1973. The administration had in fact done relatively little to attack the underlying causes of stagflation—low productivity, the "guns-and-butter" mentality that Lyndon Johnson had encouraged, and an out-of-control federal budget whose deficits invited increasingly severe Federal Reserve credit policies. The dollar devaluations amounted to a probably unavoidable recognition of international reality, but they also were inflationary.

In his memoirs, Nixon concludes that the new economic policy was largely a failure. It is unmistakable that when he left office, the economy, reeling from the oil shock that followed the Yom Kippur War, was in worse shape than when he had been inaugurated; and it seems relatively certain that even without the war and the Arab economic retaliation that followed it, he would have been lucky to return the nation to the uncomfortable economic situation in which Johnson left it. His best defense in the end was that the Democrats had no better ideas. His economic failures were to a great extent those of a nation unwilling to face up to more fundamental problems. Of course, his economic measures, like those of most politicians, were less a matter of ideological conviction than of a rational calculation of the best means of staying in power. On this account, they would be successful, laying as they did the economic basis for the president's reelection in 1972.

Although he had been elected with less than an absolute majority of the popular vote, Nixon took office with a distinct mandate from those groups in America who were in revolt against one aspect or another of the Great Society and the countercultural left-liberalism that had flourished alongside it. The George Wallace following added to Nixon's constituted a potentially unbeatable coalition of the disaffected—if Wallace were neutralized and if the administration's economic performance were satisfactory enough to allow blue-collar Middle America to vote its cultural prejudices. Republican political strategist Kevin Phillips optimistically proclaimed the emergence of a new Republican majority. No American political leader was better equipped by temperament and outlook than was Nixon to engage in a politics of cultural confrontation designed to build a new majority of the resentful.

Nixon and his political strategists were especially influenced by *The Real Majority,* a book written by Democrats Richard Scammon and Ben Wattenberg in an attempt to influence the course of their own party. Scammon and Wattenberg reminded their readers that the majority of Americans were unyoung, unpoor, and unblack. The Economic Issue that had loomed so large in partisan politics since the Depression was giving way, they contended, to the Social Issue, a web of doubts and concerns about all the cultural and political upheavals connected with the newer liberalism of the sixties. Much in the vein of Daniel Moynihan, they argued for a reconciliation between the new brand of liberalism and the older party constituencies—the blue-collar lower middle classes, the union workers, the ethnics, the old-style political organizations—openly regarded with scorn by the new liberals. They had little effect on the Democratic party; but to a large extent they defined the targets of Nixon's political strategy.

No part of that strategy had more visceral appeal for the president than its vocal opposition to the influence of what the neoconservatives called the New Class. The intellectuals, the media people, the bureaucrats, many nonentrepreneurial professionals, large portions of the college-educated public—all, according to the neoconservative diagnosis, had come to constitute a New Class in American life. Alienated from the traditional business ethic, the New Class leaned toward the politics of the Left, envisioning itself as the protector and leadership elite of the poor and the oppressed, the promoter of a more just society, the executor of a planned, welfarist economy. The New Class was the dominant force in governmental bureaucracies at all levels, in the educational establishment, in the print and electronic communications media. It had acquired a vested interest in welfarist government and in hostility to corporate enterprise. Daniel Moynihan greatly impressed Nixon with a memorandum attacking "the service dispensing groups in the society—teachers, welfare workers, urban planners, nutrition experts, etc.," many of whom he characterized as in the "resentment business":

They earn very good livings making the black poor feel put upon, when they are, which is often the case, and also when they are not. . . . On average, I would suppose, for example, that the white women who teach Head Start children earn about three times as much per hour as the black men who fathered the children. And for all this the results are really rather marginal so far as the children are concerned. In the meantime the black poor *seem* to be favored over the white near poor, the loud mouths get louder and temperatures rise.

Such an analysis touched almost every impulse in Nixon's personal and political experience, impugning as it did groups with whom he always had felt a reciprocal hostility and depicting the white lower middle class, a group with whom he identified, as ignored by an uncaring bureaucratic class. He also made caustic comments to his diary about what he called the "American leader class": "It's really sickening to have to receive them at the White House as I often do and to hear them whine and whimper and that's one of the reasons why I enjoy very much more receiving labor leaders and people from middle America who still have character and guts and a bit of patriotism." The political coalition he wanted to build—traditional Republicans plus Southerners, hard hats, and middle Americans—had as its common denominator a shared resentment against the New Class and the excesses of Great Society liberalism. Roosevelt had built a coalition with a politics of hope and benefits-dispensation; Eisenhower had established an unconquerable personal following with a politics of strength and warmth. Nixon characteristically would seek vindication and reelection through a politics of attack and resentment.

The leader of the offensive against the New Class was, of course, Vice-President Spiro T. Agnew. Agnew shared Nixon's values and personal experience to a remarkable degree. Like Nixon, he came from humble origins, having made his own way in the world. An inner-directed man who stopped just short of Social Darwinism, he exhibited open distaste for the welfare state and all but the neediest of those persons who made their livelihoods from it. He was ostentatiously traditional in his appearance and family life—a solid countersymbol to almost every cultural change that had made an impact on American life in the sixties. A stern law-and-order man, he had won his first modicum of national attention by delivering an angry lecture to Maryland black leaders in the wake of the Baltimore riots that followed the shooting of Martin Luther King, Jr. Agnew suddenly became the most visible Greek-American in the United States, and a prominent symbol to many of the scorned ethnics who still conceived of America in terms of the ethic of upward mobility and the morality of their parents. He would become the administration's most formidable rhetorical weapon.

With Nixon's encouragement and with the assistance of the Menckenesque speechwriter, Pat Buchanan, Agnew undertook a rhetorical offensive against the New Class that was entertaining and attention-grabbing in its use of alliterative phraseology ("nattering nabobs of negativism," "hysterical hypochondriacs of history") but also unsettling in its bitter, divisive character. He acidly portrayed the liberal intellectuals as the source of every ill in American life. They were effete, impudent snobs, presumably oblivious to the needs of the ordinary working

American. They were advocates of permissiveness, responsible, one might gather, for every manifestation of indiscipline and purposelessness in American life from disorder in the schools to the drug culture to crime in the streets. They were "radical liberals" lacking faith in their country and ultimately subversive of the American way of life. . . .

Nixon's 1972 victory demonstrated what the Social Issue could do when handled with restraint against an easy target. Self-described practitioner of the "New Politics," George McGovern was a living representation of the New Class. He was a certifiable egghead with a Ph.D. in history and experience as a college teacher. Long in the forefront of the antiwar movement, he verged on a commitment to pacifism and neoisolationism; one of his campaign slogans was "Come Home, America." He had no roots in the traditional Democratic party, which his campaign perceptibly bypassed. Ideologically, he was on the far left wing of the Democratic party in his concern for extended social welfare, women, and blacks. As chairman of a committee that established the procedures for representation at the 1972 Democratic convention, he had presided over the development of a quota system that outraged old-style white ethnic Democrats. Personally, he appeared irresolute when he withdrew a pledge of support to his chosen running mate, Senator Thomas Eagleton, after it was discovered that Eagleton once had undergone psychiatric shock therapy.

However much McGovern's nomination demonstrated the power of the liberal intelligentsia in the Democratic nominating decisions, his campaign displayed the isolation of that class in the broader arena of American politics. Scorned by the traditional Democrats, he had little chance of victory unless Nixon united the opposition himself. The president refused to do so and made certain that Agnew and other fire breathers were kept on a tight leash. His own campaign was a muted, barely visible affair that effectively utilized the tactical advantages and moral prestige of incumbency, leaving McGovern in the position of the wild-lunging attacker. Perhaps for the first time in his life, Nixon won a strong personal endorsement over his opponent. With nearly 61 percent of the ballots and forty-nine states, he could claim a solid vote of confidence, no matter how much of the total was based primarily on negative reaction to McGovern. He could even represent himself as a man above party, given the concurrent Democratic victories in Congress.

Nixon looked to his second term with ambitious objectives. He eliminated the system of economic controls that had kept prices down at the expense of disrupting important areas of the economy. He undertook a concerted effort to establish genuine presidential control throughout the executive branch by appointing trusted White House lieutenants to key managerial positions in one cabinet department after another. The Vietnam War finally over, he hoped to continue the delicate diplomatic processes he had set in motion involving détente and three-power diplomacy. Seemingly, he had established himself as a capable president who might achieve standing as a near-great chief executive. No one could imagine in January 1973, as he took the oath of office for the second time, that Richard Nixon would be destroyed by a third-rate burglary.

Breach of Faith

In June 1972, the District of Columbia police took into custody five burglars who had broken into the offices of the Democratic National Committee at the fashionable Watergate complex in Washington, apparently to plant a listening device. A trail of clues led incredibly from the perpetrators—three Cuban émigrés and two native-born Americans, all with CIA connections—to E. Howard Hunt, an administration consultant who a dozen years earlier had helped plan the Bay of Pigs invasion, and to G. Gordon Liddy, a Republican campaign official. All seven men were indicted; the head of the Nixon campaign committee, the president's close friend, former Attorney General John Mitchell, denied prior knowledge but resigned all the same.

As the Watergate Seven awaited trial that fall, the Democrats attempted unsuccessfully to make an issue of the episode. The American electorate, apparently unwilling to face the prospect of a McGovern presidency, behaved almost as a willing conspirator in the increasingly dubious pretense that the break-in had been the work of a few overzealous underlings. In fact, Nixon himself had secretly allowed his top domestic aid, H. R. Haldeman, to dissuade the FBI from a serious investigation that would have demonstrated otherwise.

Throughout 1973 and into 1974, the cover-up slowly came apart, partly because of pressure from a determined opposition, partly because Nixon and those around him displayed monumental ineptitude and inexplicable irresolution in dealing with a matter of political life and death. The events are well known: the conviction of the original Watergate burglars; the decision of their leader to implicate hitherto untouched administration figures; an investigation conducted by a special Senate committee headed by Sam Ervin of North Carolina; indictments of more administration figures; the resignations of FBI Director L. Patrick Gray and Attorney General Richard Kleindienst; the appointment of Archibald Cox as special prosecutor; the discovery that the president had taped most of his confidential conversations; the inexorable push to make the tapes public; the Saturday Night Massacre firing of Cox and others in October, 1973; the conviction of various administration officials on charges such as perjury and obstruction of justice; continued pressure from a new special prosecutor, Leon Jaworski; the issuance of some "sanitized" transcripts; court orders mandating full release of the tapes. Along the way, there also occurred the forced resignation of Vice-President Agnew under charges of taking illegal payoffs, an Internal Revenue Service assessment against the president for back taxes, and the revelation that some of the Watergate burglars had been part of a White House "plumbers" unit that had engaged in other illegal activities. During the last week of July 1974, the House Judiciary Committee recommended impeachment. A few days later, Nixon was forced by his own angry lawyers to release the "smoking gun" transcript of June 23, 1972, proving conclusively that the president long had known about cover-up efforts. On August 8, 1974, he became the first chief executive in American history to resign from office.

As with any series of events played out on the level of epic drama, Watergate was utterly fascinating in itself—for its human interest, its complexity, and its alteration of the course of American history. Beyond the public view of powerful men parading from the Senate committee rooms to the courtrooms and thence to public disgrace, however, there remain compelling questions. How could Watergate have happened in the first place? And how could a trivial surreptitious entry about which a president almost certainly had no advance knowledge be allowed to become a national obsession for nearly a year and a half? And how could this obsession bring down a leader who had been elected by overwhelming majorities? The answers appear to reside within Richard Nixon—in his own insecure, meanspirited personality and the responses it aroused.

Why did it happen in the first place? The break-in occurred on the evening of June 17, a week and a half after George McGovern had won the California primary, locked up the Democratic nomination, and thereby assured Nixon of an easy victory in November. Manifestly, it was not required by the exigencies of a close campaign. Nor was it particularly mitigated by the fact that other administrations had engaged in political bugging and other dirty tricks. At bottom it was yet another reflection of Nixon's reflex combativeness and anything-goes approach to politics. Nixon, Agnew, and Mitchell had passed down to the third and fourth echelons an attitude that the opposition was illegitimate and that the political contest with them might reasonably have a dimension of secret warfare not unlike that waged by the CIA against its Soviet counterparts.

Nixon's team not only reciprocated the hatred of the Democrats but also acquired the vindictiveness and ruthless amorality that always had characterized their chief's approach to politics. Nixon recalls of Charles Colson, one of the central figures of the cover-up, "I had always valued his hard-ball instincts." It followed naturally enough that Colson sensed his leader's priorities. So also did many of the other operatives close to the president: H. R. Haldeman, John Ehrlichman, John Dean, and John Mitchell all demonstrated no qualms about the destruction of evidence, perjury, and hush money payments. *Their* subordinates imbibed the mood also.

Thus, the Watergate break-in seemed a plausible enough course of action. It was simply another battle, however poor the tactical conception, in a continuing war. A stern denunciation and a sincere effort to hunt out the culprits probably never seriously entered the mind of the president and those around him. Instead they instinctively moved to control the damage by initiating a cover-up; rather than remove themselves from the problem, they made themselves part of it. . . .

Had Nixon acted more decisively at two critical points, he could have survived Watergate. His reputation would have been damaged, but he still could have functioned as chief executive. The first critical point came a few days after the break-in, when he could have come down against a cover-up and disowned any aide guilty of complicity in a shabby little crime. He might have done the same thing with more difficulty after the election. The second critical point came with the public discovery of the president's taping system. Only a group of audio tapes over which the president possessed full authority could confirm the charges brought against him. Their destruction would have made his removal from office almost impossible. Nixon's refusal to act doomed him. His inability to make the moves necessary to save himself strikes one as not simply the product of mistaken calculation but of deep-seated insecurity and self-destructiveness.

Why didn't he act? Nixon himself has faced this question with some openness, and much of what he says deserves to be taken at face value.

He probably was concerned, as he has claimed, with the fate of his close friends and associates, Mitchell, Haldeman, and Ehrlichman, whom he surely knew beyond a doubt to be involved in obstruction of justice. To let them down and face their rejection would have been an unpleasant prospect for a stronger man. To an individual of Nixon's insecurity, it was a nearly unendurable possibility. Characteristically, he attempted to transmute his reluctance to face the facts into a virtue, a nonpartisan virtue. "Whatever we say about old Harry Truman," he told John Ehrlichman at a point when Ehrlichman was desperately in need of reassurance, "while it hurt him, a lot of people admired the old bastard for standing by people who were guilty as hell, and, damn it, I am that kind of person. I am not one who is going to say, look, while this guy is under attack, I drop him."

Aside from exaggerating Truman's tolerance of criminal behavior, Nixon had also evaded the question of his responsibility as the nation's chief executive. As Henry Petersen, the federal prosecutor in charge of the Watergate investigation at that time, told Nixon, his reluctance to fire Haldeman and Ehrlichman might speak well for him as a man but poorly for him as a president. Two weeks later, events forced him to accept their resignations all the same, leaving them angry and disillusioned. Later, Nixon would recall the old British maxim that a successful prime minister had to be a good butcher. With self-pity and some hope of exculpation, he would declare that he had not been a good butcher. True enough; and, like most acts of bad butchery, his irresolute behavior had made a situation worse. Ultimately, what was at issue was the national interest, the duties of the presidency, and the preservation of the office itself; it was these Nixon butchered devastatingly.

Nixon also has addressed the problem of why he failed to destroy the tapes. Until very late in the game, the tapes were an unknown quantity, recorded, stored, and never reviewed. After their existence became known, after the Ervin Committee had subpoenaed them and the issue had become a matter for the courts, it became positively dangerous for White House staff members to listen to them. Knowledge of the tapes entangled one in a steadily growing web; it might entail embarrassing appearances before congressional committees or courts of law and expensive legal representation. Not knowing precisely what was on the tapes, Nixon probably did not realize how damaging they were. He has written that he believed they would exonerate him rather than convict him!

Still, it is hard to imagine that he ever really believed that they could be more helpful than harmful. It is equally difficult to assume that he thought that over the long haul he could withstand what was certain to be an intense public campaign for their release. One is driven to wonder whether Nixon preserved the tapes precisely because he knew he had done wrong and possessed some need to be punished.

Like many individuals who receive and internalize a set of rigid behavioral standards in their youth, Nixon had departed from values that had been deeply instilled in him in order to get ahead in the hard adult world; yet, far from abandoning those values, he proclaimed them at every opportunity and sought to make himself their personification. The contrast between his behavior and his rhetoric might appear a simple case of conscious hypocrisy, but in all probability it was a guilt-inducing situation that plagued him constantly.

Throughout Nixon's account of Watergate and many other episodes in his career, one finds a defensive, self-pitying tone that must indicate an attempt to cope with intimations of guilt. Envisioning his life as that of a man who moves from one extreme situation (crisis) to another, he places himself in settings that require more than ordinary morality. Constantly employing *tu quoque* argumentation, he asserts that his behavior is no different from that of others in the real world, that the indulgence of his opponents in various dirty tricks requires him to do the same sort of thing. Invariably depicting himself as a man set upon by implacable enemies, he attempts to shift the reader's attention from his motivation to that of those who are out to get him. The difficulty of managing this burden may well be the ultimate explanation of Nixon's politically suicidal behavior during the last year and a half of his administration. In his forced resignation from office, he at last experienced the judgment he probably had come to feel he deserved.

Tragically, that judgment extended not just to the man but to the political and diplomatic principles with which he had attempted to identify himself and, finally, to the office of the presidency as it had evolved by the end of the sixties. Nixon's major domestic and foreign policies were flawed, to be sure, and scarcely as successful as his defenders would have us believe. Nonetheless, they represented interesting, important efforts to adjust American life and American diplomacy to new realities. At his best, Nixon the domestic policy maker attempted to come to grips with problems that his liberal opponents had brought into being and had consistently dodged. Nixon the diplomatist engaged in an earnest and, for the most part, constructive effort to adjust U.S. foreign policy to an increasingly difficult world in which the nation no longer could assume either military or economic preeminence. A better man with fewer psychological burdens and more substantial qualities of leadership might have avoided many of the negative aspects of the Nixon presidency and won recognition as an above-average president. Nixon achieved only a personal disaster. Worse, he left the presidency itself an object of suspicion and scorn, awaiting a new Roosevelt or Eisenhower to restore its standing and provide a demoralized public with a sense of movement and purpose that could come only from the occupant of the White House.

Suggested Readings

Stephen E. Ambrose, *Nixon: The Triumph of a Politician* (1989).

John Morton Blum, *Years of Discord: American Politics and Society, 1961–1974* (1991).

Raymond L. Garthoff, *Détente and Confrontation: American-Soviet Relations from Nixon to Reagan* (1985).

William G. Hyland, *Mortal Rivals: Superpower Relations from Nixon to Reagan* (1987).

Stanley I. Kutler, *The Wars of Watergate* (1990).

Kim McQuaid, *The Anxious Years: America in the Vietnam and Watergate Era* (1989).

Herbert Parmet, *Richard Nixon and His America* (1990).

A. James Reichley, *Conservatives in an Age of Change* (1981).
William Safire, *Before the Fall: An Inside Look at the Pre-Watergate White House* (1975).

FURTHER READINGS

Nixon the Personality and Domestic Politics

Stephen Ambrose, *Nixon: The Education of a Politician* (1987); Fawn Brodie, *Richard Nixon* (1981); Jody Carlson, *George C. Wallace and the Politics of Powerlessness* (1981); Dan T. Carter, *The Politics of Rage: George Wallace, the Origins of the New Conservatism, and the Transformation of American Politics* (1995); Leonard Silk, *Nixonomics* (1972); Jules Witcover, *White Knight: The Rise of Spiro Agnew* (1972).

Nixon, Vietnam, and the Antiwar Movement

Walter H. Capps, *The Unfinished War*, 2d ed. (1990); Charles DeBenedetti with Charles Chatfield, *An American Ordeal: The Antiwar Movement of the Vietnam Era* (1990); Arnold R. Isaacs, *Without Honor: Defeat in Vietnam and Cambodia* (1983); William Shawcross, *Sideshow* (1979); Melvin Small, *Johnson, Nixon, and the Doves* (1988); Frank Snepp, *Decent Interval* (1977); Harry G. Summers, Jr., *On Strategy* (1982); Marilyn B. Young, *The Vietnam Wars, 1945–1990* (1991).

The Legacy of Vietnam

John Hellman, *American Myth and the Legacy of Vietnam* (1986); Ole R. Holsti and James N. Rosenau, *American Leadership in World Affairs: Vietnam and the Breakdown of Consensus* (1984); Susan Jeffords, *The Remasculinization of America: Gender and the Vietnam War* (1989); Myra MacPherson, *Long Time Passing* (1984); Norman Podhoretz, *Why We Were in Vietnam* (1982).

Kissinger's World Order and Détente

Virginia Brodine and Mark Seldon, eds., *Open Secret: The Nixon-Kissinger Doctrine in Asia* (1972); Seymour Hersh, *The Price of Power* (1983); Henry Kissinger, *Years of Power* (1982); Robert S. Litwak, *Détente and the Nixon Doctrine* (1984).

Watergate

Carl Bernstein and Bob Woodward, *All the President's Men* (1974); John Dean, *Blind Ambition* (1976); Jim Hougan, *Secret Agenda: Watergate, Deep Throat, and the CIA* (1984); Michael Schudson, *Watergate in American Memory* (1992); Theodore White, *Breach of Faith* (1975).

Questions for Discussion

1. Explain Richard Nixon's reversal of fortunes in the 1968 presidential election.
2. Describe and analyze Nixon's economic policies.
3. Did the policy of Vietnamization contribute to the ending of the war? Explain.
4. What effect did America's withdrawal from the war have on the global balance of power? Explain.
5. Describe the assumptions that underlay Henry Kissinger's foreign policy. Was he an effective statesman? Explain.
6. Discuss Watergate and its impact on the American people.
7. How does Alonzo Hamby assess Richard Nixon's strengths and weaknesses?

SEARCH FOR IDENTITY:
American Politics and Society from Ford to Reagan

Vietnam and Watergate left Americans dispirited and disillusioned. Frustrated by the country's inability to defeat communism abroad and solve the problems of poverty and racism at home, many citizens rejected the moderate-to-liberal political and social philosophy that had prevailed in America since World War II, and turned against not only liberalism but politics in general. Nixon's successors in the White House, Gerald Ford and Jimmy Carter, proved unable to reconnect the America people to politics and social issues. Then, in 1980 Ronald Reagan became president. For the next eight years he espoused the traditional American values of work, family, patriotism, and the right to unlimited self-aggrandizement. His seemingly benign conservatism and his apparently successful confrontations with the forces of international communism created a sense of well-being among the nation's middle and upper classes. Americans noted the burgeoning national debt, the continuation of executive abuses in foreign policy making, pollution of the environment, and other problems, but they escaped by immersing themselves in mass entertainment and the booming consumer economy. It was perhaps fitting that a movie actor was president during the 1980s.

GERALD R. FORD

Vice President Spiro Agnew could not succeed Richard Nixon because he himself had resigned in October 1973 when it was revealed that he had accepted bribes before and during his tenure as vice president. To replace him,

Nixon, with congressional approval, had selected House minority leader Gerald R. Ford. A man of limited intellect and a strict conservative philosophy, Ford presided over a lame duck administration which proved itself to be thoroughly undistinguished. After repeatedly assuring press and public that he had no intention of pardoning Nixon, he reversed himself, granting the former president a full pardon only a month after Nixon's resignation. Ford insisted that the move was necessary to end the national nightmare, but rumors of a deal persisted throughout his tenure in office.

As House minority leader, Ford had consistently led the fight against New Frontier and Great Society programs. Like his model, Robert Taft, he was a trenchant foe of the welfare state and an outspoken champion of business interests. Eisenhower's modern Republicanism seemed to have passed him by. During his fifteen months in office, Gerald Ford vetoed thirty-nine bills, thus eclipsing Herbert Hoover's record of negativism, and Hoover was in office more than twice as long. By resisting congressional pressure to cut taxes and increase federal spending, the president helped bring about the sharpest economic downturn since the Great Depression. Unemployment reached 9 percent in 1975, and largely due to declining tax revenues, the federal deficit climbed to $60 billion the next year. Inflation continued to rise as Ford refused to impose wage and price controls.

THE ENERGY CRISIS

A major factor contributing to inflation in the mid-1970s was soaring prices for Middle East oil. In 1967 in the Six Day War, Israel had devastated its Arab neighbors, taking possession of the Golan Heights from Syria, the Sinai peninsula from Egypt, and Jerusalem and the West Bank from Jordan. Instead of increasing Israeli security, however, these conquests only added to Middle East tensions. Determined to regain their lost territories and to force Israel to create a Palestinian state, Egypt and Syria launched a surprise attack on Israel on October 6, 1973. In this, the Yom Kippur War, the Arabs enjoyed initial success, but in mid-October the Israelis counterattacked, driving the Syrians back toward Damascus and trapping an entire Egyptian army near the Suez Canal. Kissinger, whom Nixon had made secretary of state in 1973, attempted to follow a neutral course, but the Arabs were infuriated that the United States chose to resupply Israel after its initial defeats.

On October 17 the Arab members of the Organization of Petroleum Exporting Countries (OPEC) announced a 5 percent cut in oil production with an additional 5 percent cut per month until Israel gave up the lands it had seized in 1967. When two days later Washington announced a $2.2 billion aid package for Israel, Saudi Arabia halted oil shipments to the United States. Other Arab producers followed suit. The ensuing production cuts, which led to a 10 percent drop in the global supply of oil, together with the embargo had a disastrous impact on the U.S. economy, which by 1973 was importing one-third of its daily petroleum needs. Increased imports from Iran, Libya, and Nigeria helped offset the Arab embargo, but American consumers began to

Automobiles lined up at gas stations following imposition of the Arab oil embargo.

panic. Long lines formed at gas stations as motorists kept topping off their tanks for fear of running out of fuel. The situation was worse in some parts of the country than others; in the Northeast gas was rationed.

In March 1974 Kissinger persuaded Israel to pull back from the Sinai, and the Arab embargo ended. OPEC production quotas remained in place, however, and oil prices began their steady, inexorable climb. In some areas of the United States gas prices rose some 600 percent (from \$.27 to \$1.50). Heating oil, which was of special importance to northern states, tripled in cost. Mounting prices for oil and natural gas, in turn, meant a steady increase in energy costs which fueled inflation in the United States. The revenues sent to OPEC members further weakened the economy, leading to periodic recessions, higher interest rates, and a slowing of economic growth.

JAMES EARL CARTER

THE ELECTION OF 1976

Fairly or unfairly, the American people blamed Gerald Ford for gas shortages, inflation, and unemployment. The Democrats, consequently, looked forward to the

1976 election with great anticipation. The 1972 McGovern debacle had left a void in Democratic politics, however. If the party was to recapture the White House it would have to bring the political bosses, organized labor, and farmers back into the fold without denying blacks, women, and Chicanos their hard-won victories. The man they chose to "bring us together" was James Earl Carter, a fifty-two-year-old peanut farmer from Plains, Georgia. Carter, who had served a stint in the Navy as a nuclear engineer and had enjoyed popularity and success as governor of his native state, promised that he was not like other politicians; he would not, he said, lie to the American people or succumb to the special interests and bureaucrats who predominated in Washington, DC. To attract organized labor, he named the popular liberal from Minnesota, Walter Mondale, to be his running mate.

Meanwhile, President Ford had beaten back a challenge from former Hollywood actor and governor of California, Ronald Reagan. Ford's desire to placate the conservative wing of the party, however, led him to jettison Nelson Rockefeller, who had served as his vice president, and select the abrasively partisan Robert Dole to be the GOP vice presidential candidate.

With both Carter and Ford running against "Washington insiders," the campaign was unenlightening and punchless. Carter argued that he was better suited than his GOP opponent to heal the wounds inflicted by Watergate and Vietnam. A prominent Baptist layperson, Carter was sometimes heavily moralistic if not judgmental. He pledged a government that was "as good and honest and decent . . . and as filled with love as are the American people." Fed up with politics and public affairs, voters turned out in record low numbers. Fewer than half of those eligible cast ballots. Carter won the popular vote by 40.3 million to 38.5 million and outscored Ford in the electoral college by 297 to 241.

CARTER'S DOMESTIC PROGRAM

The new president was an ambitious and intelligent man who sensed what people wanted at a basic, emotional level and knew how to make them think that he could give it to them. Liberals were certain that he would continue advances in civil rights, secure approval of the ERA amendment, put an end to industrial and consumer pollution of the environment, and make human rights the basis of American foreign policy. Conservatives were sure that as a southerner and successful businessman he would champion free enterprise, restrain the growth of the federal government, and protect overseas American interests—strategically and economically defined. Jimmy, as he was known to family and nation alike, encouraged everyone to think what they liked. He was especially adept at using Everyman symbols, carrying his own garment bag off the plane and walking hand-in-hand with wife Rosalynn and daughter Amy down Pennsylvania Avenue on inauguration day.

Unfortunately, President Carter proved better at campaigning than at governing. He had the vices of his virtues. There was no clear political philosophy underlying his rhetoric. He called himself a populist but that had little meaning in 1977. Many thought that a millionaire populist was a contradiction in terms.

In attempting to create balance in his administration he generated tension and conflict. In the White House he surrounded himself with fellow outsiders like presidential advisor Hamilton Jordan and press secretary Jody Powell. Yet top cabinet posts went to old-line Democrats: Cyrus Vance, a New York lawyer, as secretary of state; Michael Blumenthal, president of Bendix corporation, as secretary of the treasury; and Joseph Califano, a former Johnson aide, as secretary of HEW. Second-level positions in the agencies and departments, however, went to liberal reformers, followers of Senator Edward Kennedy, former presidential candidate George McGovern, and consumer advocate Ralph Nader. Increasingly, the bureaucracy which pushed radical reform worked at cross purposes with the White House staff which was determined at all costs to protect the president.

Combating Dependency on Foreign Oil

Carter's political and philosophical predicament became apparent during the debate over energy policy. Presenting a comprehensive energy bill to Congress, the president declared the forthcoming national campaign to achieve self-sufficiency was "the moral equivalent of war." The administration measure was broad based, creating a new cabinet-level Department of Energy, proposing tax incentives to promote conservation and stimulate new production, imposing penalties on enterprises that wasted and polluted, and offering subsidies to developers of solar and other alternative energy sources. Because the president and his staff had alienated much of the bureaucracy and had neglected to master the fine points of congressional politics, Congress gutted his energy bill. The measure that passed in August 1978 focused almost exclusively on new oil and gas production that would feed the country's seemingly insatiable thirst for energy.

Health and Welfare

Topping the Carter administration's list of social priorities were health care and welfare reform. But Joseph Califano's efforts to overhaul the nation's welfare system, which affected some 30 million Americans at a cost of $30 billion a year by 1977, received little support from the White House. President Carter proved unwilling to take the political heat that would result from cutting benefits and raising the retirement age. The HEW secretary failed in his effort to create a workable National Health Insurance plan when President Carter, who wanted to hold down costs and rely on the private sector, came into conflict with Senator Edward Kennedy, who favored a comprehensive system closely supervised by the federal government.

FOREIGN AFFAIRS

A New Panama Canal Treaty

In international affairs, Carter announced that defense of human rights would constitute "the soul of our foreign policy." But the president applied that dictum pragmatically, retreating from it when he perceived it to be in conflict with America's short-term strategic and economic interests. Carter, however, did prove more successful in dealing with nationalism in developing nations than any of his Cold War predecessors. Resentment in Panama over U.S. ownership and operation of the isthmian canal had reached the flashpoint during Lyndon Johnson's administration. Following anti-American riots in Panama City, Johnson had authorized the State Department to open negotiations with the government of General Omar Torrijos Herrera for the restoration of Panamanian sovereignty over the canal. The diplomatic process culminated in 1977 when President Carter signed two agreements; the first restored Panamanian sovereignty over the 500-square-mile canal zone and the second provided for the gradual transfer of ownership and operation of the canal to Panama. The United States reserved the right to intervene to defend the canal and to keep it running.

The Panama Canal Treaty immediately polarized Congress. Nationalists denounced the administration for giving away the nation's "strategic lifeline." In announcing his opposition to the treaty Senator S.I. Hayakawa told the Senate: "It's ours. We stole it fair and square." But the administration held firm. Carter's military advisors told him that defense of the canal without Panamanian help would require one hundred thousand troops, and if Panamanian guerrillas wanted to sabotage the waterway, the United States could not under any circumstance prevent them from doing so. With the help of influential Republicans such as Henry Kissinger and Gerald Ford, the treaty cleared Senate ratification by a bare one vote.

Crisis in Central America

In 1979 Marxist-led revolutions against repressive but pro-U.S. military governments broke out in Nicaragua and El Salvador. Appalled by the excesses of Anastasio Somoza who had exploited and brutalized the people of Nicaragua for a generation, the Carter administration expressed support for the Sandinista uprising. The new regime brought a modicum of social justice to Nicaragua but rejected democracy in favor of a Marxist collective dictatorship. Washington's efforts to moderate the revolution and keep the Sandinistas from developing ties with Castro's Cuba went for naught.

In neighboring El Salvador the growing conflict between the repressive military junta in control of the government and an insurgent movement that was clearly Marxist and Cuban-aided, threw Washington onto the horns of a dilemma. Carter's answer to the problem was to supply the military dictatorship simultaneously with arms and nonmilitary supplies which it used to battle the guerrillas while at the same time pressing the government unsuccessfully to institute democratic reforms. If the president and his advisors were able to distinguish successfully between Marxism and Sino-Soviet imperialism, they were unable to resist pressure from those anticommunists in the United States who were not.

Human Rights and Soviet-American Relations

The Carter administration's emphasis on human rights coupled with other factors dealt détente a severe blow. By the time the new administration took office, public opinion had set sharply against the Soviet Union. Under the autocratic leadership of Leonid Brezhnev, the Kremlin had stepped up its persecution of Soviet dissidents, led by physicist Andrei Sakharov and novelist Alexander Solzhenitsyn, and continued its harsh policy of denying Soviet Jews the right to emigrate to Israel. Moscow chose to view the Carter administration's emphasis on human rights as meddling in Soviet domestic affairs and was particularly affronted when the president chose to receive Soviet exiles at the White House.

As with other aspects of his program, Carter appointed two people with diametrically opposed views to preside over Soviet-American affairs. Secretary of State Cyrus Vance was committed to détente, while National Security Advisor Zbigniew Brzezinski was distrustful of the Soviets and wanted to protect America's strategic position and maintain its military superiority over the Soviets. In 1974 President Ford had met with Brezhnev in Vladivostok and signed a SALT II agreement which would limit each country to twenty-four hundred nuclear missile launchers each. The ceiling was so high as to be meaningless. Vance wanted far deeper cuts and proposed them in 1977. Encountering Soviet mistrust and resistance, the best he could get was a revised SALT II agreement which imposed limits of 2,250. Brzezinski, who declared that he was "the first Pole in 300 years in a position to really stick it to the Russians," wanted no limits at all. Though he could not by himself block ratification of SALT II, he persuaded President Carter to support two new weapons systems: a new MX missile to replace the existing Minuteman ICBMs and a fleet of nuclear missile–bearing Trident submarines. Regardless of SALT, the nuclear arms race would continue.

Brzezinski was also successful in playing the China card against the Soviets. Building on the opening made by Kissinger and Nixon in 1971, the United States restored full diplomatic relations with the People's Republic on January 1, 1979. The new Sino-American relationship presented the Soviet Union with the prospect of having to deal with two powerful enemies who just might begin coordinating their policies. Not coincidentally, in December 1979 Soviet tanks rolled into Afghanistan. The Soviet invasion, which touched off a long and bitter guerrilla war with Afghan mujahadeen rebels, was designed to prop up a pro-Russian, communist government. Brzezinski declared that it marked the beginning of a new thrust designed to spread Soviet domination to the Indian Ocean and Persian Gulf. With the invasion of Afghanistan, the Cold War revived in full force. Carter ordered a ban on the sale of high technology to Russia, embargoed the export of grain, persuaded Congress to reinstitute the draft, and even encouraged U.S. athletes to boycott the 1980 Olympic games held in Moscow. The invasion of Afghanistan and American retaliation set the stage for a massive escalation of the arms race in the 1980s.

A Road to Peace in the Middle East

The Middle East was the site of the Carter administration's most dazzling diplomatic triumph and its most disastrous defeat. During the three years following the Yom Kippur War, the region remained tense and absolutely polarized. For a variety of reasons the United States wanted to initiate a peace process that would allow Arabs and Jews to coexist and prosper. A peace settlement would blunt Soviet efforts to fish in troubled waters and secure American access to Middle Eastern oil. But the obstacles to Arab-Israeli détente remained formidable. The Arabs refused even to acknowledge Israel's existence until it returned the lands captured in the 1967 war. Moreover, they continued to back demands by the Palestine Liberation Organization that Israel be partitioned to create a permanent homeland for the Palestinian Arabs.

In the fall of 1977 a dramatic breakthrough occurred when President Anwar Sadat of Egypt announced that he was going to Tel Aviv for direct negotiations with Israeli Premier Menachem Begin. Bereft of oil, Egypt's economy was in the doldrums and its relationship with the Soviet Union had soured. Sadat decided that his country's interests could best be secured by rapprochement with Israel and closer ties with the West. Both Begin and Sadat were intense nationalists, which made their meeting all the more significant.

Begin and Sadat readily accepted Carter's invitation to meet at Camp David, the U.S. presidential retreat, in September 1978. For two weeks amid handshakes, toasts, and walks in the woods, Sadat and Begin negotiated. The international press provided the world with minute-by-minute coverage. Following several days of intensive discussion, the Egyptian and Israeli leaders signed an agreement promising that they would negotiate a bilateral peace treaty and launch a regional peace process that would lead to a comprehensive settlement. In the months that followed, talks between the two parties deadlocked. But after Carter made a dramatic trip to the Middle East in 1979 to spur negotiations, Sadat and Begin returned to Washington where they signed a formal treaty on March 26, 1979.

Under the terms of the accord Egypt extended diplomatic recognition to Israel in return for an Israeli withdrawal from the Sinai peninsula. Aside from calling for gradual self-government for the West Bank Palestinians, the treaty did not address the wider questions of return of the 1967 lands or the permanent fate of millions of Palestinian refugees. Nevertheless, the Israeli-Egyptian agreement constituted an important step in the peace process and was a signal diplomatic achievement for the Carter administration.

The Iran Hostage Crisis

Any sense of progress in the Middle East was soon cancelled, however, by the outbreak of the Iranian revolution. During the 1960s, ties between the United States and the shah of Iran, Mohammed Reza Pahlavi, had grown ever stronger. The shah combined a petroleum-financed campaign of modernization with brutal political repression. Despite rumors that his secret police tortured and

President Jimmy Carter with Egyptian President Anwar Sadat and Israeli Prime Minister Menachem Begin after the signing of the Middle East peace treaty in 1979.

killed dissidents, the United States sold billions of dollars of military equipment to Iran and relied on the shah to be the protector of American interests in the Middle East. All the while, Washington seemed to be completely unaware of the bitter discontent that the shah's rule was provoking all along the political spectrum from Iranian Marxists on the left to Muslim fundamentalists on the right.

To the consternation of the Carter administration and the surprise of the American people, the shah's government collapsed suddenly in January 1979 and was replaced with an Islamic republic headed by the aged and fanatical Muslim cleric, Ayatollah Ruhollah Khomeini. The new regime was bitterly anti-American; most Iranians were well aware that the CIA had trained SAVAK, the shah's universally detested secret police. The ayatollah continually railed against America as "the Great Satan," and burning of the stars and stripes became a prominent feature of Iranian patriotic celebrations. In the fall of 1979 the shah, suffering from incurable cancer, appealed to the Carter administration to be allowed to enter the United States for medical treatment. U.S. officials in Teheran warned that if Washington granted his request, reprisals against American diplomats would follow. President Carter, who could not bring himself to abandon a one-time ally and a man he had personally praised, granted entry to the shah and his entourage. In October 1979, as an irate Iranian mob paraded through the streets of Teheran, four hundred revolutionary guards disguised as students stormed the American Embassy and took fifty-eight marines and diplomats hostage.

Over the next year the Carter administration tried every tactic possible short of all-out war to gain the hostages' release. The United States first imposed an embargo and called upon its European and Far Eastern allies to join in. Dependent upon Middle Eastern oil and unwilling to jeopardize their prosperity, they refused. Whereupon, Washington attempted to intimidate the ayatollah by massing naval forces in the Persian Gulf. It was all bluff. Though the U.S. military was then working on the creation of a rapid deployment force, it would be several years before it was ready. In April 1980 the president authorized a desperate rescue attempt, but several U.S. helicopters broke down in the Iranian desert, and the mission had to be aborted. The long, agonizing hostage crisis became a symbol of American impotence and severely damaged Jimmy Carter's standing with the American people. Not until January 20, 1981, over one year after the crisis began and the day President Carter left office, did Iran release the hostages.

A FALTERING ECONOMY AND THE CONSERVATIVE TREND

Stagflation

If the hostage crisis were not enough, the nation was wracked by runaway inflation and mounting unemployment during the last months of Carter's tenure in office. A number of factors contributed to the new spiral of price increases. During the 1970s federal spending spun out of control. "Entitlements," as government payments to individuals under such programs as Social Security and Medicaid were called, increased exponentially. With the number of people over sixty-five growing 50 percent from 16.5 million in 1960 to 24.2 million in 1980 and with Social Security and other payments indexed to keep pace with inflation, entitlements consumed 80 percent of nonmilitary spending by 1980. There was, in addition, an unprecedented worldwide demand for commodities in the 1970s—oil and grain foremost among them. Population growth was outstripping production of fuel and foodstuffs. In the United States concentration in labor and industry—big unions and big business—led to price fixing and generous contracts which in turn stimulated increases in prices and wages. This at a time when worker productivity was declining from 3 percent per annum in the fifties and sixties to below 1 percent in the seventies. By 1980 the country was mired in recession with a 7.8 percent unemployment rate and inflation running at a 13.5 percent clip. All in all, inflation increased nearly 40 percent during Jimmy Carter's four years in office.

The Emerging Conservative Consensus

President Carter owed his election in 1976 to a widespread desire to return to traditional values, to abandon activism at home and abroad, and to rely on the private sector and the mechanics of the free market to restore prosperity to America. The president's perceived inability to realize these goals only whetted the country's desire for them. There was in particular rising middle-class

suburban resentment over high taxes, expanding welfare programs, and bureaucratic regulation. Californians staged a major tax revolt in 1978, passing
Proposition 13 which provided for a 57 percent reduction in taxes and a
dramatic cut in social services. The Sunbelt and the Far West, which enjoyed
a net gain of seventeen seats in Congress during the 1970s, became the political and demographic site of middle-class disaffection. The massive population shift from midwestern and northeastern cities to Florida, the Southwest,
and the West consisted mainly of skilled workers, young professionals, and
business executives who were attracted both by economic opportunity and by
a political climate that stressed individualism and laissez-faire government. In
the Sunbelt the young and successful could choose between the Republican
party and conservative, "boll weevil" Democrats who advocated stronger national defense abroad and less government intrusion at home.

Conservatism was, in addition, fueled by growing concern among Christian
evangelical and pentecostal groups at the growth of "secular humanism"—a
term that they used to describe everything from the theory of evolution to
sexual permissiveness—in American society. They and members of mainstream
religious denominations worried over the growing acceptance of homosexuals
in American society and burgeoning abortion and divorce rates. Jerry Falwell's
Moral Majority flourished both as a cultural and a political phenomenon. It
began holding seminars designed to teach members how to become active in
local politics. Among other activities, Falwell's organization published
"morality ratings" for congressmen and senators.

Another, related development that contributed to the conservative resurgence was a well-organized and well-financed backlash against the feminist
movement. Spearheading the effort was a right-wing Republican activist from
Illinois named Phyllis Schafly. It was she who orchestrated the movement to
defeat the Equal Rights Amendment and provided the inspiration for such
groups as "Women Who Want to Be Women" and "Females Opposed to
Equality." She characterized feminists as antifamily, "a bunch of bitter women
seeking a constitutional cure for their personal problems."

To an extent unknown in the post-depression era, conservatism became in-
tellectually respectable. Right-wing think tanks such as the American Enterprise
Institute sprang up in Washington and on the West Coast. Stanford University's
Hoover Institute managed to attract some of the nation's best minds and turned
out monographs touting the virtues of the free market and individualism. The
Heritage Foundation financed by conservative brewer Joseph Coors provided
many of the ideas that surfaced during the 1980s. On television William F.
Buckley used his stinging satirical wit to poke fun at "limousine liberals" and
"bleeding hearts" who were allegedly compromising the nation's principles to
satisfy the unsuccessful, unmotivated, and undisciplined. Former liberals such
as Daniel Patrick Moynihan blasted the Democrats for catering only to the
whims of minorities and those living on the cultural fringe. John Connally,
former Democratic governor of Texas and assistant secretary of the Navy under
John F. Kennedy, ostentatiously switched to the Republican party.

Republicans proved much more adept at mastering and manipulating information and media technology than the Democrats. They hired advertising executives and image managers to create pleasing public personae who came across well on television. GOP pollsters and campaign strategists were the best that money could buy. Republican telephone banks got out the vote on election day while direct mail campaigns elicited hundreds of thousands of dollars from small donors to complement the usual millions that came in from corporations and businesspeople. Ironically, reforms in campaign financing that were introduced following Watergate helped the Republicans more than the Democrats. A 1974 measure limited the amount of money that could be given by individuals but permitted the formation of PACs (political action committees) to which individuals could contribute and which then contributed without limitation to favored candidates.

RONALD REAGAN

By the end of the 1970s Ronald Reagan had taken charge of the Republican resurgence. The affable B-movie actor had first made a name for himself campaigning for Barry Goldwater in 1964. In contrast to the strident Goldwater, Reagan put the case for a return to individual freedom and reduced government activity in relaxed, confident, and persuasive terms. A year later, a group of wealthy Californians persuaded him to run for governor. Reagan proved to be a superb candidate. A master of television, he was able to present his strongly conservative message without appearing to be a rigid, right-wing ideologue. He displayed a surprising flexibility as governor. Forced to deal with a Democratic legislature, he made some concessions to their demands for increased taxation and spending. Reagan's specialty was the symbolic act. To appease critics of "academic permissiveness" he dismissed University of California president Clark Kerr; he then proceeded to increase spending sharply on higher education.

THE ELECTION OF 1980

In the spring and summer of 1980 Reagan easily beat back a challenge from former Texas congressman George Bush, a moderate, and captured the Republican nomination. Demonstrating the pragmatism that had carried him from Democratic head of the film actors union to Republican governor of California, he then named Bush to be his running mate. In his acceptance speech at the GOP convention in Detroit, Reagan enunciated the themes which had endeared him to those concerned with ideological purity—reliance on free market economics, a return to family values, less government and reduced taxes, and peace through military strength.

With his approval rating hovering around 30 percent, President Carter faced a stiff challenge from Senator Edward Kennedy. Once he became an official candidate, however, Kennedy too dropped in the polls. The fact that he had left the scene of an accident in 1969 when a car he was driving plunged off a bridge at Chappaquiddick, Massachusetts, killing a young woman who was riding with him, dismayed many voters. The Democrats renom-inated Carter and Mondale on the first vote and girded themselves for an uphill battle. With inflation and interest rates both running in double digits, the Russians in Afghanistan, and the hostages still holed up in the American Embassy in Teheran, there was no advantage to being an incumbent.

To no one's surprise, the Reagan-Bush ticket scored a resounding victory, capturing 51 percent of the popular vote to Carter-Mondale's 41 percent and outscoring the Democrats 489 to 49 in the electoral college. Independent can-didate John Anderson captured 8 percent of the popular vote but did not figure in the electoral contest. The Republicans also made impressive gains in Congress, capturing control of the Senate for the first time since 1952 and nar-rowing the Democratic margin in the House from 114 to 50. Journalist Theodore White argued that the Republican victory in 1980 marked nothing less than the climax of a gradual repudiation of New Deal liberalism that had been going on since World War II. The growing affluence of the average American, the population shift from the Rust Belt to the Sunbelt, the tur-bulence and uncertainty of the 1960s had produced a new Republican majority that had lost badly only once since 1952 and whose presidential candidates had polled 52.3 percent of the popular vote during that period compared to 47.7 percent for the Democrats.

At seventy the new president was the oldest man, the first actor, the first labor leader (he had been president of the Screen Actor's Guild), and the first divorced person to hold office. With his charm, eloquence, and genius for sim-plification, he was dubbed "the Great Communicator."

When he entered office, Ronald Reagan faced perhaps the gravest economic crisis since the Great Depression. Inflation had cost median income families $1,400 in annual purchasing power since 1970. With the prime interest rate hovering near 20 percent, home and auto sales had plummeted. The value of the dollar had dropped to 36 cents during the same period. The new president blamed the situation on excessive government spending and high taxation. "Government is not the solution to our problems," he told the American people in his inaugural address; "government *is* the problem."

DOMESTIC PROGRAMS

Reaganomics

More specifically, Reagan advanced the concept of "supply-side economics" as a means to put the nation back on the road to prosperity. He and his advisors attacked the theories of John Maynard Keynes which called for increased public spending in times of depression to put money in the hands of consumers who in turn would spend and stimulate the private sector. In contrast to this "demand side" approach Reagan proposed a massive 30 percent cut in income taxes and other tax breaks for the wealthy. Beneficiaries of this largesse would, he argued, give the rich increased incentive to work, save, and invest. The result would be a boom in the private sector and full employment. The resulting increase in gross income would swell the tax base to such an extent that loss in federal revenue from the tax cut would be more than made up. "Supply side," as David Stockman, Reagan's first budget director, said, "is 'trickle-down' theory," the theory that had prevailed during the Coolidge era, and held that, if you help the few at the top, benefits will trickle down to the rest.

The Reagan tax cut seemed a great gamble because the GOP candidate had promised during the 1980 campaign to balance the federal budget. And, in fact, the new administration did not intend to depend entirely on increased prosperity in the private sphere to swell the tax base. Reagan and Stockman, who dominated domestic policy during the first term, believed that they could best combat deficits by slashing social programs. Discerning politicians that they were, the president and his budget officer decided not to attack such popular middle-class entitlement programs as Social Security and Medicare. The only available targets for budget cutting in the view of the White House were programs requiring a "means test"—proof of need. Though such entitlements—school lunches, food stamps, aid to dependent mothers and children—accounted for only 18 percent of federal welfare payments, they were supported by the weakest lobbies and suffered almost $125 billion in cuts—60 percent—in 1981. Households earning under $10,000 suffered the greatest reductions. Reagan was committed to the notion of a social safety net—payments for those who because of age, disability, or illness were unemployable. Because he was opposed to income supplements, his social ax fell on the "working poor."

Deregulation

Not surprisingly, the new administration was committed to privatization and deregulation, a movement that had actually begun under President Carter. The administration sold Conrail, the government-owned freight railroad, to private investors on advantageous terms and then extended nearly $10 billion worth of federal loans to the new owners. The president wanted to sell Amtrak, the federally operated passenger line, and other agencies, but Congress balked. Reagan countered by rolling back the federal government in a number of nonlegislative ways—by cutting regulatory budgets, by diluting or abolishing regulations, by relaxing enforcement of environmental and other standards, and by staffing regulatory agencies with representatives of the businesses to be regulated.

Deregulation had a particularly important impact on the environment. James Watt, Reagan's first secretary of the interior, was a rancher and agribusinessman who believed it was the inalienable right of every American to exploit his or her environment without interference from the federal government. If America was going to continue to grow and prosper, Watt argued, its public property and resources would have to be restored to private control. Reversing conservationist policies started by Theodore Roosevelt, he attempted to sell nearly 35 million acres of public land, opened up the continental shelf to offshore oil and gas drilling, encouraged timber cutting in national forests, offered public land to coal companies, and facilitated the spread of strip-mining. Though Reagan steadfastly refused to abandon Watt, the interior secretary's insensitive remarks about environmentalists and his tasteless jokes about liberals, Indians, and Jews eventually forced him to resign.

The Sleaze Factor

Accusations of conflict of interest also contributed to Watt's downfall, but such charges made him typical rather than exceptional. Not since the Harding scandals had the nation witnessed as many public servants profiting personally from their office. Public outcry forced Ann Gorsuch Burford to resign as head of the Environmental Protection Agency for granting favors to industrial polluters. The president's deputy chief of staff, Michael Deaver, obtained an unsecured loan from a person who was later given a position in the government. After Deaver resigned, he set up a consulting firm to trade on his connections within the administration. Although some two hundred other Reagan appointees were also accused of unethical or illegal activities, the president himself remained untouched by any hint of impropriety. After he survived a 1981 assassination attempt with grace and courage, his popularity ratings soared. Reagan's personal charisma and facility as a television performer helped shield him from the political fallout generated by the scandals that riddled his administration. Congresswoman Patricia Schroeder tagged the Californian the "Teflon" president—the buck never stopped so the blame never stuck.

Conservative Backlash in Social Issues

Not surprisingly, organized labor, African Americans, and women did not fare well during the Reagan years. Presidential appointments to the National Labor Relations Board tended to favor management, and in 1981 Reagan fired members of the Professional Air Traffic Controllers (PATCO) who had participated in an illegal strike. Union membership dropped sharply in the 1980s reaching an all-time postwar low of 17 percent of the nation's full-time workforce in 1987. Catering to Schafly, Falwell, and the religious right, Reagan went to war against feminism. He opposed the ERA, abortion on request, and legislation guaranteeing equal pay for equal work. He did appoint Sandra Day O'Connor to the Supreme Court, the first woman to be so named, but critics noted her conservatism and denounced the move as tokenism. The president cut funds for enforcement of civil rights laws and initially opposed renewal of the Voting Rights Act of 1965. He was persuaded to change his mind about this, the most fundamental of civil rights bills, however, and with his acquiescence Congress extended the voting rights measure for another twenty years.

FOREIGN AFFAIRS

Heating Up the Cold War

Reagan had done his best to depict the United States under Jimmy Carter as the "pitiful, helpless giant" that Richard Nixon had predicted. Once in office he proved to be one of the twentieth century's most ideological presidents. The Cold War, Reagan insisted, was an uncompromising struggle between communism and capitalism, totalitarianism and freedom. To his mind there was no difference between Soviet imperialism and Marxism-Leninism; they were simply two sides of what he dubbed the "evil empire." Continuing the hard line that Carter had begun after the invasion of Afghanistan, Reagan proceeded with plans to place 572 ballistic and cruise missiles in Europe. The deployment was designed to offset Soviet medium-range missiles stationed in Eastern Europe and aimed at NATO countries.

The Pentagon and the industrial network that it supported flourished under Reagan. During the 1980s the military acquired the MX nuclear intercontinental ballistic missile, the B-1 bomber, and a six hundred–ship navy. By the end of Reagan's two terms in office the federal government had spent 2 trillion dollars, this at a time when spending on domestic programs was being sharply reduced. While expressing alarm about the burgeoning budget deficit, virtually all of the president's advisors agreed that the massive arms buildup would win the Cold War either by bankrupting a Soviet economy that was already faltering or giving the United States a massive military advantage.

At the same time it was building the most formidable arsenal the world had ever seen, the Reagan administration went through the motions of arms reduction negotiations. In response to pressure from nuclear freeze advocates in the United States and in the European nations which were under the gun from both Soviet and American short-range missiles, Washington put forth two new proposals in 1982. Both promised that the United States would not proceed with the development of new systems if the Soviets removed existing weapons from Eastern Europe, proposals which, not surprisingly, Moscow rejected. With the stalling of arms reduction talks, the nuclear race entered a new, more dangerous phase. The Reagan administration stepped up research and development on its Strategic Defense Initiative (SDI), a futuristic, space-based system of lasers and particle beams designed to destroy incoming missiles before they entered the atmosphere. Labeled "Star Wars" by the press and derided by experts as either unfeasible or too expensive, SDI nonetheless frightened the Russians into deploying larger and more accurate land-based ICBMs.

Containment in Nicaragua and El Salvador

Nowhere were the policies of Reagan, the anticommunist ideologue, more apparent than in Central America. Like many other Latin American republics,

Nicaragua and El Salvador were small nations with underdeveloped economies whose populations were divided between a wealthy landholding elite in league with a corrupt military and a mass of impoverished and disfranchised peasants. Carter had attempted a moderate course in both nations, providing support to the Sandinistas in Nicaragua in an effort to keep them from turning to Cuba and the Soviet Union, and using aid to the repressive regime in El Salvador as leverage for introducing reforms. Not so Reagan. If the communists succeeded in Central America, the president maintained, "Our credibility would collapse, our alliances would crumble, and the safety of our homeland would be in jeopardy." The State Department subsequently cut off all aid to Nicaragua in the spring of 1981, accusing the Sandinistas of persecuting the democratic opposition, embracing Marxism-Leninism, and serving as a conduit for Cuban arms into El Salvador. It was a self-fulfilling prophesy. Denied American aid, the government of Nicaragua became increasingly reliant on Havana and Moscow.

Reagan wanted to intervene directly to oust the Sandinistas, but when Congress, remembering Vietnam, balked, he turned to covert action. The CIA began recruiting, training, and arming anti-Sandinista Nicaraguans, called contras, in bases in neighboring Honduras and Costa Rica. This American-trained army, many members of which were linked to the former repressive Somoza government, wreaked havoc in their country, destroying power facilities, polluting water supplies, terrorizing the rural population, and even mining harbors. The principal impact of contra activity was to make the Sandinistas more repressive than they might otherwise have been and to turn Nicaragua into an armed camp. The Sandinistas placed the nation on a war footing and assembled an army of nearly sixty thousand men.

In El Salvador the Reagan administration stepped up support for a government headed by Christian Democrat Jose Napoleon Duarte. He was committed to moderate reform but had little control over his military whose right-wing death squads indiscriminately obliterated those suspected of aiding or even sympathizing with the leftist rebels. In 1984 Duarte won reelection by an overwhelming margin, and attempted once again to force reforms on the unwilling military and landowning clique.

Grenada

In the summer of 1983 American intelligence learned that Cuban engineers and soldiers were building an air strip on the tiny Caribbean island of Grenada. In October 1983, frustrated at the stalemate in Central America, Reagan ordered an invasion of the former British colony. His stated justification was protection of American medical students studying on the island from the Marxist dictatorship that had taken power. Despite evidence of ineptness and poor coordination by the American military, the massive U. S. assault on an island of 110,000 souls with no army or navy was, not surprisingly, successful. Most Grenadans and Americans hailed the invasion, but for many Latinos it brought up unpleasant memories of Theodore Roosevelt's gunboat diplomacy.

The arming of the contras and the invasion of Grenada were part of a larger policy which the press referred to as the Reagan Doctrine. "We must not break faith," the president declared in 1985, "with those who are risking their lives on every continent, from Afghanistan to Nicaragua, to defy Soviet-supported aggression." What Reagan had in mind, apparently, was a reversion to the early days of the Eisenhower administration when John Foster Dulles had promised to go beyond containment and "roll back" the Iron Curtain. The fortieth president wanted to do nothing less than facilitate a worldwide movement that would produce democratic regimes featuring "market-oriented" economies.

THE ELECTION OF 1984

Capitalizing on his personal charisma and an upswing in the economy, the president won a landslide victory over his Democratic opponent, Walter F. Mondale, in 1984. The election was notable principally for the fact that it featured the first woman vice presidential candidate. Mondale's running mate, congresswoman Geraldine Ferraro, added grace and intelligence to the ticket, but questions about her husband's financial dealings dogged her every step and made it difficult for the Democrats to take advantage of the "sleaze factor" that had plagued the Republican party since Watergate.

CLOUDS ON THE HORIZON

It seemed as 1986 opened that Reagan's popularity would continue unabated. On January 28 a horrified television audience watched as the space shuttle *Challenger* exploded shortly after liftoff, killing all on board. Despite subsequent revelations that NASA had not thoroughly researched the dangers of cold weather launchings, no one blamed the administration. When in April the president ordered air strikes against Muammar Qadaffi's Libya, the seat of much terrorist activity in the Middle East, the American public applauded. But then in November 1986 the first major cloud appeared on the Reagan horizon.

The Iran-Contra Affair

On November 3 a Beirut newspaper reported that the United States had secretly sold arms to the hated Ayatollah Khomeini. Despite its repeated declarations that it would never permit the transfer of, much less sell, munitions to Iran or negotiate with terrorists, the Reagan administration had apparently done just that in hopes of obtaining the release of Western hostages held in Lebanon by Hezbollah, an Islamic fundamentalist group linked to Iran. Then, on November 25 the nation learned that some of the funds from the sale of weapons had been "diverted" to the contras fighting in Nicaragua. Not only did such action constitute a policy blunder of major proportions, it was against the law. From 1984 to 1986 Representative Edward P. Boland of Massachusetts had attached a series of amendments to various appropriations bills making it illegal for any government agency to fund "directly or indirectly military or paramilitary operations" in Nicaragua.

Confronted with these revelations, Reagan and his circle of advisors at first denied everything. He had not, the president said, been bargaining for the release of hostages, only trying to create an opening to moderates in Iran—which was untrue. He flatly denied that there had been payoffs to the contras. In fact, the Great Communicator had repeatedly made it known to his subordinates that he wanted to find some way to aid the contras, Boland amendments or no Boland amendments. The president's oft-expressed wishes had opened the way for Lt. Colonel Oliver North, a much-decorated Marine and aide to the National Security Council specializing in counterterrorism. With the knowledge and approval of his superiors, National Security Advisors Robert McFarlane and Admiral John Poindexter, North worked through the Israelis to arrange for arms shipments to Iran and for subsequent payments to the contras.

During the spring and summer of 1987 a joint House-Senate investigating committee began holding televised hearings into the Iran-Contra matter. The sessions dominated public attention for months and revealed a tangled web of inept financial and diplomatic transactions, the shredding of incriminating government documents, personal profiteering by North, Poindexter, and others, and an administration awash with misguided patriotism. During four days of testimony the handsome, dynamic North won the hearts of anticommunist ideologues and super-patriots everywhere with his preachy self-righteousness. In the days that followed, more and more Americans came to the realization, however, that the decorated Marine had undermined the very Constitution he was pledged to uphold and that he had done so with the president's tacit approval.

Central America Again

Meanwhile, events were once again demonstrating the futility of U.S. intervention in Latin America. Alarmed by the growing involvement of the United States, the Soviet Union, and Cuba in Central America, those countries bordering Nicaragua took steps to end the fighting there. In 1987 Costa Rican President Oscar Arias put forward a regional peace plan which was intended to provide a framework for a cease-fire and negotiated settlement in Nicaragua. The Sandinistas balked at that format, but in 1988 President Daniel Ortega entered into direct negotiations with the contras; those talks produced a cease-fire by the end of the year. In El Salvador combat between government forces and Cuban-supplied rebels continued unabated. Not only did Duarte prove incapable of controlling the death squads, the Christian Democrats lost a general election to Alfredo Christiani's right-wing Arena party.

GLASNOST AND PERESTROIKA

The most positive note of Reagan's second term, ironically, was a thaw in relations with the Soviet Union. In 1985 a new secretary general of the Communist party of the Soviet Union came to power. Mikhail Gorbachev wanted to save communism and its governing apparatus by modernizing the Soviet economy and ending the Cold War. Campaigning under the banners of glasnost (openness) and perestroika (restructuring), he began harnessing the political, economic, and military bureaucracies to the interests of the general population. His need to transfer money, raw materials, and engineers from munitions production to the civilian sector opened up new possibilities for arms negotiations. Reagan and Secretary of State George Shultz were attracted by Gorbachev's urbanity and flexibility.

In November 1985 Reagan and Gorbachev held a genial summit meeting in Geneva where they discussed the possibility of a reduction in strategic forces and an interim agreement on Intermediate Nuclear Forces (INF). Following another dramatic but inconclusive summit in Reykjavik, Iceland, in 1986, Gorbachev came to Washington in December 1987, and he and Reagan signed a treaty eliminating medium- and short-range nuclear weapons. In addition to providing for short-notice, on-site inspection, the pact stipulated that the Soviet Union would destroy 1,752 missiles, and the United States 867. This amounted to only 4 percent of the total, but the INF treaty marked a significant beginning to nuclear arms reduction.

THE REAGAN DEFICIT

Like their forebears in the 1920s, Americans in the 1980s reveled in a prosperity that was rooted in self-delusion and irresponsibility, both social and fiscal. On the surface everything looked exceedingly rosy. The Federal Reserve Board's tight money policy along with the collapse of OPEC's high oil prices had brought the inflation rate down from 10.4 percent in 1981 to 3.7 percent in 1987. The tax cut of 1981 coupled with massive federal defense spending had turned the unemployment rate around, reducing it from 8.5 to 5.8 percent by the end of Reagan's first term. The dark side of this picture was that America was living well beyond its means by the end of the decade. The contention of supply-siders that increased economic activity would produce increased tax revenues proved to be an illusion. The tax cut, and especially tax breaks for the rich, huge defense budgets, and high interest rates which caused the federal government to have to pay more for the money it borrowed, meant unprecedented deficits. The gross federal debt which amounted to $935 billion in 1981 tripled during Reagan's two terms to $2.7 trillion.

As Reagan's second term neared its end, it became clear that the deficit was having disastrous consequences. More and more, America was living on other people's money. When Reagan was elected in 1980, the United States was the world's largest creditor to the tune of $150 billion. By 1988 the United States had become the world's largest debtor, owing other countries $400 billion. The Japanese in particular helped finance America's extravagance by buying U.S. Treasury bonds and subsequently American corporations, banks, and real estate. Because more and more of the federal government's revenues went to pay interest on the national debt, there was less and less money to invest in the infrastructure—the transportation system, energy exploration and production, scientific inquiry, and education in general.

Under the Reagan administration, the United States stubbornly refused to develop an industrial policy that would have targeted certain domestic industries for research and development subsidies to enable them to compete with German and Japanese firms. This, coupled with high wages and high interest rates, meant that American manufacturers became less and less able to compete with their foreign counterparts. Americans bought billions of dollars of foreign products, and the annual trade deficit ballooned. Economic self-sufficiency, the cornerstone of the nation's strength and independence, was rapidly eroding. For the first time since the early days of the republic, it appeared that America's fate was no longer in its own hands.

THE CULTURE OF GREED

Not coincidentally, the Reagan era was one of unparalleled greed and self-indulgence. "Greed is healthy," Wall Street speculator Ivan Boesky told a University of California commencement audience. "You can be greedy and still feel good about yourself." The administration set the tone through its policies and the personal conduct, or misconduct, of its members. The 1981 tax cut and the Tax Reform Act of 1986 were bonanzas for the upper and upper-middle classes. The latter measure certainly simplified the tax structure, reducing the number of categories from fifteen to two, but it also reduced the maximum rate on individuals from 50 to 28 percent. Federal revenues came to depend more and more on the regressive Social Security tax, a flat rate on all earned income up to $52,000. The lack of proper supervision over savings and loan institutions allowed them to make enormous loans for highly speculative real estate ventures. Reagan refused to police the industry, and as a result his successor inherited an economic problem of major proportions. Finally, the permissiveness of Reagan's appointees toward the Securities and Exchange Commission paved the way for a period of unparalleled greed and profit taking on Wall Street. Aided by inside information, misrepresentation, and computerized trading techniques, Boesky, Michael Milkin, and others made billions by looting corporations and engaging in profit taking. On October 19, 1987, the stock market suffered its worst collapse since the Great Depression. The average price dropped 22.6 percent costing investors $1 trillion. Only safeguards put in place during the New and Fair Deals kept the crash from touching off a general depression.

During the 1980s the rich in America got richer and the poor got poorer. The 10 percent of Americans at the bottom of the economic ladder paid 20 percent more in taxes in 1988 than they did in 1977 and the 10 percent at the top paid 20 percent less. Federal spending for the poor declined; jobs increased but mostly in the service sector, which paid less and provided fewer benefits. Two million manufacturing jobs disappeared. Real income declined for the

*Shocked onlookers following the October 19, 1987,
stock market crash. Because of safeguards put in place
during the New Deal, the economy was partially
insulated from the precipitous decline in prices.*

poorest 25 percent of the population while it increased for the richest quarter.
Most alarming was the dramatic growth of the American "underclass"—some
10 million Americans, living mostly in the inner city, whose lives were characterized by chronic poverty, single-parent households, drug addiction, crime,
and abuse of women and children. By 1990 one-fifth of all American children
lived in poverty. The United States, Daniel Patrick Moynihan noted sadly, had
become one of the few countries in which it was better to be old than young.

*The decade of the 1980s featured an intense public debate over environmental
matters. Partially as a result, the contemporary West became a major political
battlefield for those concerned about environmental issues and a focus for
western historians interested in the origins of contemporary problems. In the
article that follows, Richard White rejects the century-old frontier thesis of
Frederick Jackson Turner. Writing in the 1890s Turner argued that the frontier*

shaped the American character, economy, and political system in indelible ways. The openness, ruggedness, and egalitarian atmosphere that prevailed in this infant, fluid environment, Turner argued, reinforced the forces of democracy, pluralism, and tolerance that existed in older regions of the country. In his essay on the environment and the Northwest, White insists rather that man shapes nature to a much greater extent than nature shapes man. Those who moved west were utilitarian, exploitive, and fundamentally conservative as they strove desperately to recreate the politics and culture of the eastern or European communities from whence they came.

THE ALTERED LANDSCAPE OF THE PACIFIC NORTHWEST

Richard White

Any region of the United States, no matter how one defines regional criteria and boundaries, is a physical place with its own geography and climate, its own flora and fauna. Once this rather obvious statement was the heart of regionalism. During the early 20th century, geographical determinists argued that environment translated readily into culture, social structure, personality, and politics. In their crudest formulations, determinists argued, for instance, that rugged land regularly produced rugged individualists.

Even in the current intellectual climate, where the only things still being recycled are simplistic social theories, this kind of geographical determinism has so far failed to make a comeback. Still, reports of its demise may be premature. Geographical determinism, after all, seems no more unlikely than the currently fashionable assertions that laissez-faire economics and appeals to greed will create universal prosperity and social justice, and that militarism will prevent war. Nevertheless, geographical determinism remains momentarily dead, although its unfortunate legacy has been to turn attention away from regional studies of the relationship between the environment and the human societies which inhabit the land.

from Richard White, "The Altered Landscape: Social Change and the Land in the Pacific Northwest," in William G. Robbins et al., eds., *Regionalism and the Pacific Northwest* (Corvallis: Oregon State University Press, 1983), 109–124.

In a real sense, the determinists had gotten it all backwards. As George Perkins Marsh noticed more than a century ago, the land shaped societies decidedly less often than societies shaped the land. The implication of Marsh's insight is that a region is less likely to get men to match its mountains, than mountains to match its men (and women). This neat reversal is, however, too simple. Nature is not infinitely malleable. In the end the relationship between landscape and society, between environment and culture, is reciprocal. Human beings create landscapes, and these landscapes in turn have consequences for the society which created them.

The Northwest is, at least superficially, an apt place to examine the reciprocal influences of land and society. To Easterners, Northwesterners seem particularly tender in their concern for the land. This is an opinion maintained despite years of Hanford's nuclear wastes leaking into the Columbia River and eventually Dixie Lee Ray [governor of Washington, 1977–1980] leaking into the political system. It is an apt region, too, because, by defining the Pacific Northwest narrowly as everything between the Cascades and the Pacific and between British Columbia and California, it is possible to create a crudely homogeneous environmental region to study. Here vast changes have taken place in the land; a society has arisen, which claims (for vague and ill-defined reasons) to be regionally distinctive; and a vocal concern for the land has become a legitimate political issue.

In the Pacific Northwest, as in any region of the United States, there are diverse feelings and opinions about the land. Personal feelings and opinions, however, are not really at issue here; my concern is with how they develop, what power they exert, and with what results. These are basically historical questions even though they are often defined in excessively presentist and functional terms.

History matters a great deal in understanding the regional relationship to environment, but history cannot be confused with myth. What the American West spawns (for the good, I think) are the great myths of American culture which revolve around the clash of civilization and savagery and nature. These are, however, cultural divisions and must be understood as such; they are not useful historical divisions of the past. Untamed nature plays only a minor role in the history of the Northwest (or any part of the West). The high country of the Cascades and Olympics was (and still is) wilderness, but calling the land American settlers found "wilderness" only obscures the relationship between people and the land.

The first American settlers who penetrated into western Oregon and Washington entered a relatively stable and productive environment. For centuries Indian peoples had been burning forests and prairies, encouraging some species and discouraging others; more recently, they had adopted exotic plants and animals such as the potato and the horse. The species composition of both the forests and prairies were to a significant degree the result of Indian practices. The Northwest that American settlers found was an Indian-managed Northwest. This point is an important one. Any environment inhabited by human beings is, to varying degrees, a human-dominated ecosystem. The question is not domination per se, nor civilization versus wilderness, but rather how an environment is dominated and with what results. In the 1840s the environment west of the Cascades remained not only stable and productive, but also botanically distinctive. Indians manipulated native species, and few exotics were introduced; the managed ecosystem maintained itself without costly imports or serious deterioration.

White settlement destroyed the Indian Northwest. Indeed most whites failed to recognize that it even existed. Farmers simply mistook Indian handiwork for virgin nature. They sought out the prairies and openings to farm in preference to the massive fir forests, without realizing that Indian burning often created and maintained these prairies and shaped the species composition of both prairie and forest. Treating those Indians who survived the ravages of smallpox and influenza, murder and war, and displacement to reservations as so many primitive pyromaniacs, settlers banished the fires and in so doing began to change the forest composition and the balance between prairie and forest in ways they did not suspect. Settlers might think that they were putting the mark of human use on the land as they displaced the Indians and plowed and fenced and planted, but they were only reordering the land and imposing a different vision, one developed far from the place they settled.

Early settlers in the Pacific Northwest almost automatically sought familiar landscapes. They were newcomers in what remains a region of newcomers, and the familiar was not the native. Settlers, therefore, sought not so much to create as to recreate. A frontier in this sense was not the cutting edge of change, but rather the most conservative region of the country. As historians are increasingly emphasizing, settlement was not a process of individualists breaking ties and heading west, but instead the relocation of existing kinship groups and community groups. The connections between settlers in the Willamette Valley or the Puget Sound region created a web of kin and old neighbors. Settlers husbanded the familiar, and the new land became merely a foundation upon which to reestablish existing ways.

Settlers brought with them to the new land an idea of an ordered landscape—a cultural model, rather than a specific ecology. What was meaningful for the frontier farmer was the traditional sense of landscape reflected in the census categorization of land as either improved or unimproved. Improved land was essentially that from which native plants and animals had been eradicated; unimproved land was where they remained. In the traditional mixed farming of the Midwest and Border South (from which most migrants came), these categories implied different perceptions and uses of the land. Farmers invested great labor in improved land, fenced it, and limited its production to familiar useful species. They controlled it by means that went back centuries to other continents. . . .

Anglo-American influence on the Pacific Northwest, then, began simply as a result of attempts to impose old ways on a new place. As long as settlers remained subsistence farmers, domestic considerations shaped production decisions. These considerations seem to have been clearly utilitarian: farmers managed the land to feed and clothe their families. But arguments of simple utility are deceptive and deserve closer examination. To say something is useful explains little. It is not that people want only the useful, but rather that people define as useful and necessary whatever it is that they want. For instance, people have to eat, but why do they eat what they do? . . .

The logic of unreflective utility quickly established itself in the Northwest. The native landscape was neither sacred nor sentimental; it was merely an opportunity.

And opportunity quickly became the opportunity to make not just a living but a profit. This change was part of the larger transition to commercial farming in the United States. Its consequences appeared in the attitudes of northwestern farmers and through them in the landscape. As Walter Crockett, an early settler in Washington Territory, phrased it, his main object in settlement was

> to get the land subdued and wilde nature out of it. When that is accomplished we can increase our crops to a very large amount and the high prices of everything that is raised here will make the cultivation of the soil a very profitable business.(sic)

Crockett's ambitions and those of the settlers in the Willamette Valley for large profits in the commercial market were doomed to frustration for much of the 19th century. Farmers producing staple crops increasingly operated in a world market over which they could exert little influence. A farmer could accurately plan what his family would need, but he could not predict what the price of wheat would be or what specialty crop would sell. In relatively isolated, commercially marginal areas like the Pacific Northwest, what was profitable could change yearly. Some farms became a kaleidoscope of different crops and animals, while other farmers engaged in steady staple crop production could not compete and actually abandoned land. In both cases care of the land suffered, exotic weeds invaded the fields, and fertility declined. In the Willamette Valley there was actually an absolute decline in improved land between 1880 and 1900.

By the end of the 19th century, agricultural settlement had significantly contributed to a less distinctive northwestern landscape, one that was increasingly shaped by markets hundreds or even thousands of miles away. By introducing exotic species into the region and by trying to make it over in the image of other places, settlers had sparked an ecological invasion one botanist characterized as the most cataclysmic event in the natural history of the area since the Ice Age. In 1919 an examination of a seemingly native prairie landscape in the Willamette Valley revealed that one-half the species of grasses present were not indigenous.

In time, such introductions combined with surviving native species might have formed a new stable landscape. But the domination of the agricultural economy by large and impersonal markets insured that the only criterion of success in farming would be profit, and profit came only to those who quickly adjusted their fields to market demands. Thus commercial farming usually insured ecological instability. As the 20th century wore on, weeds and insects were only held at bay by increasingly costly applications of energy and poison to the land. There was little unique or regionally distinctive about successful farming in the Pacific Northwest. . . .

With the depletion of the forests of Michigan, Minnesota, and Wisconsin, accompanied by improvements in logging technology, changes in transportation and markets, and an influx of logging capital, the real assault on northwestern forests accelerated after the turn of the century. The donkey engine (a steampowered winch that could drag logs to a central place for shipment) and logging railroads allowed the logging of areas far removed from tidewater. The markets gradually expanded to include cedar and hemlock. Loggers took out immense amounts of timber cheaply and efficiently, but they left huge amounts of waste. Stumps, tops, branches, and trees shattered in the felling amounted to an average of 24,000 cubic feet of waste per acre. When this slash ignited, it burned at temperatures as high as 1,814 degrees and consumed not only the slash but 89 percent of the duff layer on the forest floor.

The seedlings that sprang up from fallen seeds in the wake of logging were often destroyed in these fires, which left unpromising conditions for any new trees that might follow them. By destroying the humus, fire lessened the moisture retention of the soil which was essential for the germination and survival of Douglas fir seedlings. It changed the nutrient balance of the soil and altered its ph. The sudden abundance of potassium, nitrogen, and calcium released from debris by burning encouraged those seedlings that survived to develop shallow root structures and large crowns and thus made them vulnerable to even short droughts. The black ash and charred debris also exacerbated drought by increasing heat retention in the soil on hot summer days by 25 degrees or more. Even to get a second crop of seedlings on the land following fires was difficult, since loggers no longer left an abundance of cull trees, and the logging of small tracts which could be reseeded by neighboring forests gave way to operations that covered huge areas.

Lumbermen cared little about all this. They realized the utility of protecting standing forests, but they ignored the fires that devastated cutover lands. Lumbermen claimed taxes prevented them from reforesting the lands they cut, but the evidence indicates such claims were specious. The real problem was that market prices did not justify restocking the forest. The logging companies cut and ran, and as a 1927 Forest Service report concluded, "whatever reproduction takes place, does so, for the most part, in spite of present methods, not as a result of them." . . .

By the early 20th century the new lumber industry, unlike farming, promised to provide a unique Northwestern landscape. It consisted of miles of huge shattered stumps surrounded by debris which, when accidentally ignited, burst into fires that burned for much of the summer. These devastated forests produced little but fire and bracken and filled the bays and rivers with eroded soil and logging debris, wiping out the spawning beds of the salmon. The ruin of the forest brought a generation of Northwesterners abruptly to the realization that ecology and society were connected; it became apparent that it is impossible to maintain human institutions, build roads, support schools, and meet public needs on a wasteland.

It is, however, naive to believe that the mere recognition of a problem insures its solution. The response to the logged-off lands took shape within the same cultural boundaries that produced the problem. The result was a back-to-the-land movement which was a complex brew of commercialism, class interest, and sincerely held agrarian beliefs.

The movement to settle the logged-off lands of the Pacific Northwest, like similar back-to-the-land movements in Michigan, Minnesota, Wisconsin, and the arid West, justified itself largely in regional terms. The northwestern back-to-the-land movement originated in the cities. City people promoted it, and ultimately the movement served urban interests. The West, and the Pacific Northwest in particular, have always been largely urban regions, but Westerners often manage to reconcile an urban reality with antiurban rhetoric. Proponents of the settlement of logged-off lands proceeded from the assumption that the cities were overpopulated while the rural districts were correspondingly underpopulated. From this fundamental imbalance flowed the myriad of social problems—unemployment, poverty, disease, moral decline—which they feared could destroy the Northwest and eventually the nation. This rhetoric was antiurban, but it paradoxically served urban interests. Blaming urban ills on too many poor people in the city not only avoided any serious analysis of the economic and social system, it proposed a simple solution to a pressing environmental problem. Urban poverty could be eliminated by shipping the poor to the logged-off lands, which they would then redeem with their labor. Ideally, the socially expendable poor of the cities would cultivate the surrounding land and alleviate the need to import millions of dollars worth of dairy products, pork, poultry, and vegetables from outside the Northwest. Not only would these new settlers retain needed capital in the area, they would also consume the products of urban industries and thus stimulate urban prosperity.

This vision was partly a response to the wasteland left behind by the loggers, but it was also a rejection of the forest itself. It represented an inability to come to terms with the realities of the ecology of the Northwest. Boosters of the movement denounced the Forest Service for its fledgling attempts to replant the forest on federal lands. When one enthusiast condemned the Forest Service for "trying to grow trees on land that should grow men," he was only underlining the logic of the whole movement.

Having denounced the city to serve the city's ends and having rejected the forest, the boosters of settlement offered all the venerable agrarian homilies. They argued that the attraction of people to the soil was instinctive, that urban life was unnatural, and that moral and civic virtue sprang directly from agriculture. They put these evocative and emotional appeals, however, firmly within a commercial context. Organizations from local chambers of commerce to the state government of Washington assured settlers that farming logged-off lands would surely make them comfortable and might very well make them rich. . . .

How many people were convinced by this propaganda is impossible to determine, but people did settle these lands. Western Washington alone gained 17,000 farms between 1900 and 1920, and 15,000 of them were under 50 acres, the farm size typical of the cutover region. By 1940 there were 36,370 such farms in western Washington. The ethnicity and social origins of these settlers shifted over time. Predominantly Scandinavian between 1900 and 1920, by the 1930s the flood of settlement was made up of drought-stricken migrants from the northern plains and urban workers who often sought little more than a small plot to grow food while they searched for work.

Settled on infertile lands and provided with little capital, these farmers were anachronisms in the commercial economy. Rural virtue didn't feed their families. Even boosters, while arguing that federal aid for settlement could fix matters, conceded that "isolation from markets, lack of roads, lack of neighbors, and lack of school facilities" often made farming logged-off lands a "life of dreary existence . . . without any practical rewards." State and federal surveys only verified such subjective impressions. The movement weakened in the 1920s, but quickened again in the 1930s as the cities disgorged their desperate poor, and environmental and economic disaster on the plains pushed people west. The cutover lands were hardly a haven. A survey in 1939 found that one-third of the farmers had been on relief sometime in the past two years, and among those who had settled in the 1930s, the figure was over 50 percent.

The damage the movement inflicted was not confined to the settlers. Their hilly infertile farms suffered with them. Depending on farming techniques and terrain, they eventually turned their fields into dense patches of bracken, watched them erode down hillsides, or abandoned them to the alder which thrived on the degraded land and replaced the original forests of Douglas fir. Even those rare areas (such as the floodplains of the Willamette) where logged-off farms eventually became productive benefited the original settlers little. This was a post–World War II development that demanded both flood control and a capital investment the original settlers could not muster.

The collapse of the back-to-the-land movement at the end of the Great Depression, while a blessing to both land and people, did nothing to check the commercial forces shaping the Northwest. Concern with the regional landscape now resided largely within the organized conservation movement, which had probably always been more powerful than the back-to-the-land movements. Conservation, like the market, provided a national context in which regional groups operated.

Conservation represented a reaction to the environmental disasters and waste brought by unrestrained entrepreneurial capitalism. The movement itself, however, was neither anticapitalist nor antidevelopment. As Samuel Hays has persuasively demonstrated, conservationists of the late 19th and early 20th centuries shared with corporate executives a strong belief in efficiency and planning as opposed to unrestrained competition. Their major goal was efficient production, with an emphasis on the renewal of resources whenever possible. In practice, conservation bureaucrats and corporate bureaucrats have always worked well together. . . .

On federal and state lands the landscape evolved within the framework of national development policy, instead of within the older arena of unrestrained use. At any given time this planned use pleased some groups and antagonized others, depending largely on whom the planning benefited. Quite often demands for states' rights or regional rights in such issues represented no more than the protests of those special interests who had lost out in the bureaucratic planning process, while pious support for conservation measures came from those groups who benefited from the same process. Economic interests remained decisive in shaping the public lands, but now an advantage went to those groups who could at least claim that the resources they used were renewable and that their activities were compatible with other uses. In practice, this meant that "guild organizations of lumbermen and stockmen" came to shape federal policy in much of the Northwest.

This description of early conservation policy in the Northwest seemingly neglects an important segment of the movement—the preservationists like John Muir, who sought to preserve land for scenery and recreation. Most of these people, however, also fit into the larger framework of planned land use for economic development. For a surprisingly long time, preservationists in Oregon concerned themselves largely with maintaining strips of scenic virgin timber along the highways for the tourists they zealously tried to attract. Scenery was but another engine for development. By such early 20th century standards, a recent governor of California who advocated sparing only enough redwoods to flank the highways might rank as a preservationist.

By the mid-20th century, planned development with an emphasis on renewable resources and a devotion to preserving scenery were all ensconced in northwestern land use. These basic tenets of conservation, however, were not always synonymous with a healthy environment. Nor were the conservationists who promoted them primarily concerned with the regional ecology. Conservation, too, reflected the needs of powerful economic groups within society. In the woods, conservation and economic rationalization produced managed forests, which grew ecologically simpler and simpler. At the extreme they have become genetically selected, chemically fertilized, aerially sprayed tree farms.

Like any radically simplified form of monoculture, these forests can become costly to maintain, and the poisoning of their predators and competitors can quickly shade over into the poisoning of human residents. The recent controversy over dioxins is a single example of this. The benefits of this policy largely accrue to the large timber companies. These forests are efficient, but efficiency is measured largely in terms of corporate profits and government revenues. The recent controversy over log exports shows that not everyone feels such measures reflect the larger economic well-being of the region, let alone the environmental health of the forest.

Similarly, local attempts to preserve scenery and wild resources often approached the land as a sort of environmental supermarket, in which one could choose to preserve certain natural populations while destroying others. As hunting and fishing became important to local and regional economies, both sportsmen and those who served their needs recognized that the wild populations they depended on were dangerously near elimination. The result was a flood of concern and regulation: hunting seasons enforced by local and state officials, laws to preserve shellfish beds, laws to ban fish traps and fish wheels, and the stocking of streams and lakes with hatchery-bred fish. Eventually such concerns encompassed attempts to preserve water quality, to protect the spawning beds of salmon, and to perpetuate endangered species. Most of this originally occurred, however, because a dollar value could be put on certain wild game populations.

Sportsmen became an economic interest group who secured members of a state bureaucracy (the fish and game agents) to serve their interests. The victories of sportsmen were victories over competing economic groups such as the canning companies who ran fish traps, the mill companies who polluted the rivers, or the Indian fishermen who competed for the catch. In many instances sportsmen's victories benefited the environment; in others, such as the Indian fishing controversy, conservation was a cynical mask. In virtually all cases, however, the aims of sportsmen remained quite selective. They could at once protect game animals and sponsor "predator days" to eliminate those species who competed with them for game. Until recently, the measures they sought had little sense of ecological balance and often rendered the regional ecology, if anything, less stable. Fish hatcheries, game farms, elaborate regulations, and a new bureaucracy are necessary to maintain the desired wild populations. These animals have often become mere commodities, valued not according to their place in the regional ecology, but rather according to their marketability. Like many state and local parks, they are maintained to attract visitors and further economic development.

Over the last decade many of the historical trends described here have been challenged and sometimes blunted. Ecology and ecosystem have entered common speech; environmentalists in the Northwest and elsewhere have searched for a language and a convincing rationale for creating a stable and ecologically distinctive environment. The results have been mixed. Wilderness areas have been preserved, the tendency to equate economic growth with wasteful consumption and environmental damage has been challenged, and the tendency of capitalism to reduce everything on the planet to a commodity has been questioned. Yet it would be premature to argue that the forces that have shaped the American landscape since settlement are no longer pertinent to its future.

In fact, environmentalism is currently receiving a vigorous counter-challenge. It can be forcefully attacked, in part, because it has too often been content with mystical or semireligious rationales for its efforts or else has taken the stance of a continuing protest against recurrent environmental catastrophes. The land ethic Aldo Leopold spoke of—a coherent vision of the human place in the ecosystem—has yet to be forcefully articulated. The real and vital connections between human societies and the natural world need to be stressed and understood. It is a dimension of human history too often oversimplified or neglected. The Northwest will certainly remain a center of environmental conflict, and it is a conflict to which the historical issues sketched here are pertinent.

Nearly a century and a half of American settlement has produced a regional landscape which has grown increasingly less distinctive and progressively less stable. That Northwesterners have not allowed natural systems to function without interference is neither surprising nor objectionable; all human societies shape their environment. What is more noteworthy is that alterations of the Northwest landscape have often proceeded with reckless disregard for the environmental limits of the area, as if ecosystems operated on a profit motive. Northwesterners have frequently acted as if the natural world exists largely as something to buy and sell and as if the regional ecology were infinitely malleable. The history of the region already shows that environmental destruction has social costs, but as long as these costs are borne by the powerless, this is an easy lesson to ignore.

The results of environmental destabilization and regional homogeneity may not be immediately catastrophic, but the costs are there, and they are incremental. The northwestern landscape, still a recent one, already grows increasingly costly to maintain and increasingly vulnerable to disruption. The costs of maintaining it are largely public; the profits of destroying it remain private. In an era which appears bent on repudiating public cost, this does not bode well for the land. Nor does it bode well for a distinctive regionalism in a section of the country which has repeatedly resorted to its mountains, woods, rivers, and oceans as symbols and sources of its distinctiveness. Northwesterners may still claim to be unique, but they will do so amid a landscape that reflects commercial homogeneity and ecological precariousness—a place where regional concerns and influence over the land have been thoroughly subordinated to national capitalist development. The mountains may then stand like skeletons, dead remains of an older and far more distinctive place.

SUGGESTED READINGS

James Bill, *The Eagle and the Lion: The Tragedy of American-Iranian Relations* (1987).
Peter N. Carroll, *It Seemed Like Nothing Happened* (1982).
Thomas Ferguson and Joel Rogers, *Right Turn: The Decline of the Democrats and the Future of American Politics* (1986).
Robert Hartmann, *Palace Politics: An Inside Account of the Ford Years* (1980).
William G. Hyland, ed., *The Reagan Foreign Policy* (1986).
Burton I. Kaufman, *The Presidency of James Earl Carter* (1993).
Harold Seidman and Robert Gilmour, *Politics, Position and Power* (1986).
Gaddis Smith, *Morality, Reason and Power: American Diplomacy in the Carter Years* (1986).
Winnifred D. Wandersee, *On the Move: American Women in the 1970s* (1988).

FURTHER READINGS

The Ford and Carter Presidencies

Carl Abbott, *The New Urban America: Growth and Politics in the Sunbelt Cities* (1981); Jimmy Carter, *Turning Point* (1992); George C. Edwards, III, *At the Margins: Presidential Leadership of Congress* (1989); Burton I. Kaufman, *The Presidency of James Earl Carter, Jr.* (1993); Mark J. Rozell, *The Press and the Carter Presidency* (1989) and *The Press and the Ford Presidency* (1992).

The Energy Crisis and the Economy

Barry Bluestone and Bennett Harrison, *The Deindustrialization of America* (1982); Sara M. Evans and Barbara J. Nelson, *Wage Justice: Comparable Worth and the Paradox of Technocratic Reform* (1989); Claudia Goldin, *Understanding the Gender Gap: An Economic History of American Women* (1990); Bruce J. Schulman, *From Cotton Belt to Sun Belt* (1990); Jon Teaford, *Cities of the Heartland: The Rise and Fall of the Industrial Midwest* (1993); Franklin Tugwell, *The Energy Crisis and the American Political Economy* (1988).

Carter, the Cold War, and Human Rights

Warren Christopher et al., *American Hostages in Iran* (1985); Walter LaFeber, *The Panama Canal* (1978, 1989); Anthony Lake, *Somoza Falling* (1989); Alexander

Moens, *Foreign Policy Under Carter* (1990); David Schoenbaum, *The United States and the State of Israel* (1993); Lars Schoultz, *Human Rights and U.S. Policy Toward Latin America* (1981).

Ronald Reagan and His America

Frank Ackerman, *Reaganomics* (1982); Sidney Blumenthal, *The Rise of the Counter-Establishment: From Conservative Ideology to Political Power* (1988); Lou Cannon, *President Reagan: The Role of a Lifetime* (1991); Rowland Evans and Robert Novak, *The Reagan Revolution* (1981); Roger E. Meiners and Bruce Yandle, *Regulation and the Reagan Era* (1989); C. Brant Short, *Ronald Reagan and the Public Lands* (1989); Garry Wills, *Reagan's America* (1987).

Reagan's Central American Policy and the End of the Cold War

Michael R. Beschloss and Strobe Talbott, *At the Highest Levels: The Inside Story of the End of the Cold War* (1994); Bradford Burns, *At War in Nicaragua* (1987); Thomas Carothers, *In the Name of Democracy: U.S. Foreign Policy Toward Latin America in the Reagan Years* (1991); Theodore Draper, *A Very Thin Line: The Iran-Contra Affairs* (1991); John Lewis Gaddis, *The United States and the End of the Cold War* (1992); Roy Gutman, *Banana Diplomacy* (1988); Walter LaFeber, *Inevitable Revolutions*, 2nd ed. (1984); Bob Woodward, *Veil: The Secret Wars of the CIA* (1987).

QUESTIONS FOR DISCUSSION

1. Explain the origins of the energy crisis and describe its effect on the American economy. How did the Carter administration respond to this challenge?
2. Discuss Carter's foreign policy successes and failures. How did the Iran hostage crisis contribute to his defeat in the election of 1980?
3. What factors contributed to Ronald Reagan's triumph in the 1980 presidential election?
4. Identify Reaganomics and explain how it changed American society.
5. Discuss Reagan's Latin American policies. Were they ideologically motivated? Explain.
6. Discuss the long-term implications of the Reagan deficit.
7. Compare and contrast the back-to-the-land and conservation movements of the late nineteenth and early twentieth centuries. What are the weaknesses, according to Richard White, of the current environmental movement?

A RAGE FOR CHANGE:
America in the 1990s

The early years of the twentieth century's last decade saw Americans deeply immersed in what journalists dubbed the culture wars and deeply disillusioned with a political system that appeared to be both insensitive and ineffective and a socioeconomic system that seemed geared only to the very rich and the very poor. Americans decided that they had had enough, were not going to take it any more, and were going to throw the rascals out. Unfortunately, there was no consensus as to what and who were to take their place. Social conservatives continued to agitate for prayer in the schools, an antiabortion amendment, and the freedom to bear and use arms. But opinion polls continued to indicate that a majority of Americans were pro-choice, in favor of gun control, and supportive of the principle of separation of church and state.

Conservatives advocated equal opportunity for women and minorities, but insisted that affirmative action was discriminatory and thus abhorrent. Liberals, although leery of hiring and admissions quotas, and of institutionally enforced political correctness, were still willing to bend over backwards to correct historic injustices. The only things that Americans could agree on was that the political system was too responsive to "special interests," the federal government was too big and inefficient, and taxes were too high and inequitably applied. A majority of the citizenry longed for a new leader, a cross between Harry Truman and John F. Kennedy, who would provide integrity, accountability, and inspiration to a country growing daily more cynical.

In 1989 the Berlin Wall came down. Two years later Moscow agreed to the dissolution of the Warsaw Pact alliance, and shortly thereafter the Soviet Union itself broke apart. The end of the Cold War revealed the existence of a multipolar world. America had to share the international stage, especially in the economic field, with a host of new power centers—Japan and Germany, of course, but the oil rich countries of the Middle East and the city-states of East Asia as well. Tribal and national rivalries touched off a series of famines, wars, coups, and migrations. The United States, deeply aware of the limits on its power but reluctant to relinquish the hegemony that it had exercised since the end of World War II, struggled to identify and defend its interests in the Balkans, the states of the former Soviet Union, the Pacific Rim, the Middle East, and Latin America. Aware that economics would dominate diplomacy in the post–Cold War era, Washington presided over the creation of a North American free trade zone, attempted to maintain civil relations with an increasingly nationalistic European Union and Japan, and participate in the economic development that was sweeping Southeast and East Asia.

GEORGE H. W. BUSH

THE ELECTION OF 1988

With Ronald Reagan prevented from running for a third term by the Twenty-second Amendment, Democrats looked to 1988 with cautious hope. When the Republicans nominated Vice President George Bush, a man long detested by hard-core conservatives, hope became anticipation. "If we can't beat George Bush," proclaimed one Democratic activist, "we'd better find another country." The early front-runner for the Democratic nomination was Senator Gary Hart of Colorado, an attractive, self-effacing individual and a favorite of the media. Richard Gephardt of Missouri centered his candidacy on an appeal to economic nationalism, a campaign directed none too subtly at the Japanese. Michael Dukakis, the serious, intelligent, "high-tech" governor of Massachusetts, promised to bring to the national scene the expertise that had turned his home state's economy around. The only Democratic aspirant who addressed the issues of racial discrimination, poverty, and war head-on was the Rev. Jesse Jackson, a black civil rights activist and ordained Baptist minister.

The media had delved into the private lives of presidential candidates before to make character a central campaign issue, but not to the extent that it did in 1988. When the *National Enquirer* and other tabloids revealed that Hart, married with children, was having an affair with model Donna Rice, his candidacy crashed. Several weeks later Delaware Senator Joseph Biden withdrew from the Democratic primaries when members of the media revealed that he had plagiarized part of a speech from a British politician. During the late 1980s investigative reporters discovered that Martin Luther King had plagiarized part of his Ph.D. dissertation and had had extra-marital sexual relationships. Public figures and some commentators declared that what individuals did with their private lives was irrelevant to their competence to hold public office. The media disagreed, criticized their predecessors for covering up for politicians who favored them, and insisted that dishonesty in one sphere was sure to produce dishonesty in others.

After Dukakis defeated Jackson in a majority of the Democratic primaries, he was duly nominated at the Democratic National Convention held in Atlanta. Taking Neil Diamond's "Coming to America" as its theme, Dukakis' acceptance speech emphasized his immigrant roots and his ability to govern an America which was becoming more self-consciously diverse. The Democratic nominee disappointed the liberal wing of the party when he shunned Jesse Jackson for the vice presidential nomination, selecting instead conservative Senator Lloyd Bentsen of Texas.

George Bush, who had fended off a challenge by the combative, partisan Senator Robert Dole of Kansas to capture the GOP nomination, disappointed virtually everyone by his choice of a running mate. Trailing Dukakis badly in the public opinion polls, Bush began the race by selecting the singularly undistinguished Dan Quayle of Indiana to be the vice presidential nominee. The son of a wealthy Indiana publisher, Quayle was something of a joke in the Senate, having once read a speech given him by an aide that had nothing to do with the topic being debated at the time.

While Dukakis and the Democrats focused on economic issues, blaming discredited Bush-Reagan policies for the deficit, GOP strategists decided to go for gut issues, ones that appealed to the nation's emotions and prejudices. To their delight, Republicans learned that the Democratic candidate while governor of Massachusetts had vetoed legislation requiring public school teachers to lead daily pledges of allegiance to the flag and had signed a weekend furlough bill for convicted criminals. Subsequent GOP ads linked the flag veto with Dukakis' membership in the American Civil Liberties Union, implying that Bush's opponent was not only unpatriotic but "permissive." The centerpiece of the GOP's negative public relations campaign, however, was the Willie Horton case. Horton was a Massachusetts inmate convicted of rape and assault. Freed on the furlough program, he fled the state to Maryland where he terrorized a couple and raped the wife. Ensuing Republican television spots showed a revolving door letting people out of prison and once again accusing Dukakis of permissiveness.

In fact, the 1988 election was a media-dominated event from first to last. Building on the Reagan heritage, both candidates concentrated on camera angles and a quote of the day that would be short and sensational enough to make the evening news. The average sound bite had declined from thirty seconds, to fifteen seconds, to nine seconds. In this sort of competition Dukakis (who remained ambivalent about running for president throughout) did not stand a chance. George Bush won 53 percent of the popular vote and carried forty states. The final tallies were 48,901,046 for Bush and 41,809,030 for Dukakis in the popular vote and 426 to 111 in the electoral college.

BUSH'S BACKGROUND

The son of Prescott Bush, an investment banker and U.S. senator, George Bush grew up in affluence in Connecticut, attending prep school and then Yale. After serving in World War II he moved to Texas where he made a fortune in the oil business. Before becoming vice president, Bush had been elected to office only once—as congressman from his Houston district. He ran unsuccessfully for the Senate and in 1980 for the Republican nomination for president. But Bush had held a number of responsible positions—chairman of the Republican National Committee, ambassador to China, and head of the CIA—in addition to the vice presidency. He was, moreover, no wimp, a term applied to him by *Newsweek* magazine. Bush had quit school to join the armed forces during World War II. He was the youngest fighter pilot in the Pacific theater and was shot down by enemy fire.

Bush proved to be a surprisingly popular president during his first year-and-a-half in office. Much of that had to do with the widespread sense of relief at the winding down of the Cold War, but in addition Bush, especially when compared to Reagan, seemed a man of compassion, a political leader who was willing to acknowledge that in the postindustrial age government still had certain obligations to its citizens. Reagan had replaced the picture of Harry Truman hanging in the White House with a portrait of Calvin Coolidge. Bush in turn substituted the likeness of Theodore Roosevelt. In many ways it was a symbolic move—an eastern, patrician president with a western patina. Moreover, like TR, the new chief executive would pursue an aggressive foreign policy.

DOMESTIC CONCERNS

Dealing with the Deficit

In his inaugural address Bush noted the corrosive effect the deficit was having on the economy and promised to cut the budget. Cleaning up after the thrifts put the new administration in a financial hole before it really got started, however. By 1989 hundreds of S&Ls had failed, and thousands of depositors were clamoring for their money. Congress expanded the role of the FDIC, which previously had taken care of banks only, so that it could bail out surviving savings and loans. The estimated cost to taxpayers over thirty years was $300 billion to $500 billion.

Perhaps George Bush's most concrete pledge during the campaign had been his "read my lips" promise not to raise taxes. Unfortunately, that stand did nothing to help the deficit which stood at $2.6 trillion at the end of the Reagan years, with an anticipated shortfall for 1991 of $260 billion. Reluctantly, on June 26, 1990, Bush announced that "both the size of the deficit . . . and the need for a package that can be enacted" required "tax revenue increases." That October Congress and the administration cooperated in passing a measure that raised rates on the top 2 percent of earners by eliminating certain deductions; that increased taxes on alcohol, gasoline, and expensive consumer goods; and that raised Medicare payroll taxes for workers. The budget office predicted savings of $40 billion for fiscal 1991 and $490 billion over the next five years. A sharp downturn in the economy sent tax collections tumbling, however, and the deficit for 1991 was $300 billion, the largest in history.

A Troubled Environment

Perversely, Bush, who had promised to be the "environment president," was confronted with one environmental disaster after another. The most visible and controversial involved the *Exxon Valdez*, a huge oil tanker that ran aground in Alaska's picturesque Prince William Sound, spilling millions of gallons of crude, spoiling a hundred miles of coastline including fisheries and animal habitats. The Coast Guard investigated and found that the captain of the tanker had been operating while under the influence of alcohol. Exxon was subsequently forced to pay $2 billion to clean the seashore and wash the fur and feathers of those birds and mammals which had managed to survive. The Bush administration condemned this and other spills and called for responsible corporations to clean up toxic waste dumps scattered across the country. But after voters in California and New York defeated tax initiatives to pay for costly cleanups, the administration proceeded warily.

Centrism and Controversy on the Supreme Court

Members of the new right anticipated that during the Bush administration they would begin to reap the judicial harvest that Ronald Reagan had sown by his appointments to the federal judiciary. And, in fact, in 1989, in *Webster v. Reproductive Services of Missouri*, the justices ruled in a five-to-four decision that states could deny access to public facilities to women seeking abortions. Writing for the majority, Chief Justice Rehnquist declared that "nothing in the Constitution requires states to enter or remain in the business of performing abortions." Though conservatives predicted a wave of laws prohibiting public hospitals and public employees from participating in abortions, that was not the case. Only Utah, Pennsylvania, and Louisiana enacted such measures. *Webster* did not overturn *Roe v. Wade*.

The president did his best to straddle the abortion issue. Early in his career he had seemed pro-choice, but during the presidential campaign he had declared "abortion is murder." Bush's first appointment to the Supreme Court was David Souter of New Hampshire. Souter's views on abortion were unknown, and he refused to discuss them during his confirmation hearings. When another vacancy appeared on the high court, however, Bush felt free to be more aggressive with his appointment because he had the opportunity to cloak a conservative social agenda in a black skin.

In mid-1991 the distinguished civil rights lawyer and Supreme Court justice Thurgood Marshall announced his retirement. To replace him Bush selected Clarence Thomas, a black federal court judge who had grown up impoverished in the segregated South. Two things made him attractive to the administration. First, Thomas' views were clearly conservative. In speeches, articles, and decisions, he had expressed reservations about a woman's right to abortion, criticized the concept of a minimum wage, questioned the efficacy of busing and affirmative action as mechanisms for achieving racial justice, and urged African Americans to rely on their own resources and intelligence to

Anita Hill taking the oath before testifying in Supreme
Court nominee Clarence Thomas' confirmation
hearings. Hill accused Thomas of sexual harassment.

advance in a multicultural world. Second, Thomas was black. Liberals opposed
to his conservative political and judicial philosophy and concerned about his
limited experience on the bench ran the risk of being labeled racists if they
opposed his nomination.

Thomas' confirmation hearings would have been controversial and inflammatory under any circumstances, but they escalated to the sensational when
Anita Hill, a University of Oklahoma law professor, testified that Thomas had
sexually harassed her when both worked for the Equal Employment Opportunity Commission (EEOC). The televised Judiciary Committee hearings attracted a national audience as Hill quietly but graphically detailed her
allegations. Thomas' appearance was a study in righteous indignation. He
denied all of Hill's charges and claimed that she had been put up to her assault
on his character by civil rights leaders whom he had previously written off as
habitual whiners and moaners. Following a stormy floor debate, the Senate
voted to confirm Thomas by a vote of 52 to 48.

Feminists and Sexual Harassment

Somewhat ironically, Thomas' nomination had the effect of galvanizing the temporarily moribund feminist movement. Anita Hill's ordeal before the Senate Judiciary Committee angered women of all political and sexual persuasions. A revived feminism rallied around the pervasive problem of sexual harassment. Republicans, Democrats, lesbians, heterosexuals, blacks, and whites supported laws and regulations, particularly on college campuses, that banned unwanted sexual approaches, abusive language, and even suggestive sounds and motions. Feminists, gay activists, and civil rights leaders thus placed themselves in uneasy alliance with social conservatives who had long pressed for restriction of the free speech amendment. But they argued that sexual harassment, like racial epithets, made life so uncomfortable for the harassed that the majority would have to accept some infringement on its rights. More significant, women's frustration with the male-dominated political power structure led to an unprecedented number of female candidates for local, state, and national office in 1992.

The Drug Problem

By the time of George Bush's inauguration, the American people were deeply concerned about the drug problem. In 1989 375,000 babies were born addicted to cocaine or heroin, and the drug traffic was serving as a massive capital formation mechanism for organized crime and inner-city street gangs. Shortly after his election, Bush named William Bennett, Reagan's controversial education secretary, to be his "drug czar." As such, Bennett would head the Office of National Drug Control Policy, a cabinet-level position without a department. The Bush-Bennett strategy was to emphasize law enforcement and interdiction rather than prevention and rehabilitation. Indeed, 70 percent of the $7.9 billion earmarked for the war on drugs went toward the construction of new prisons, additional DEA agents, and new prosecutors.

FOREIGN ISSUES

The Collapse of Communism

It was George Bush's great good fortune to be president when the Cold War finally came to an end. Like his hero Theodore Roosevelt, Bush was a pragmatic imperialist, determined to safeguard American interests, economically and strategically defined, short of armed conflict if possible but through force of arms if necessary. The president and his advisors were keenly aware of the limitations on American power, and they would resist calls for the United States to participate actively in the demise of the Warsaw Pact and the fall of communism in the Soviet Union. Their approach, one that would become familiar in the post–Cold War era, was one of watchful waiting.

Shortly after George Bush took the oath of office, the first democratic elections since 1917 were held in the Soviet Union. At the same time, encouraged by glasnost and perestroika, anticommunist, nationalist elements in the Baltic

FIGURE 30–1
Collapse of the Soviet Bloc

states of Estonia, Latvia, and Lithuania began challenging their communist puppet regimes and demanding the departure of Soviet occupation troops. And in Poland, Solidarity, under the leadership of Lech Walesa, pressured the communist dictatorship of General Voitech Jaruzelski into holding free elections. When in July Gorbachev announced to a meeting of Warsaw Pact leaders that his country would respect the national sovereignty of all nations and that in effect the Kremlin no longer cared how its neighbors conducted their internal affairs, the way was open for noncommunist, nationalist forces to seize control of the governments of Hungary, Romania, and Czechoslovakia. In Bulgaria the communist-dominated regime held on only by changing its name and promising to institute reforms (see Figure 30–1).

The most dramatic events of 1989 occurred in divided Germany, the overriding symbol of the Cold War and a polarized Europe. As thousands of East German citizens fled via Hungary and Austria, those who stayed behind demonstrated against the repressive government of longtime dictator and Kremlin puppet, Erich Honniker. Aware that Soviet troops would not be forthcoming, Honniker resisted the urge to use police and troops to crush the demonstrators. On November 9 the government announced that the border between East and West Germany was open. On November 15 wrecking crews moved in and began destroying the Berlin Wall, the twelve-foot-high concrete and barbed wire symbol of oppression in the GDR. Then on October 2, 1990, the East German Democratic Republic merged with the German Federal Republic into a single capitalist, multi-party state.

In the summer of 1991 Bush traveled to Moscow to sign a Strategic Arms Reduction Treaty with Gorbachev. The agreement committed both parties to a one-third reduction in their bombers and missiles, and to cuts in conventional forces as well. Shortly thereafter, on August 18 a group of hardliners representing the Red Army, the KGB, and the Communist party hierarchy attempted a coup. The group had Gorbachev placed under house arrest at the resort where he was vacationing and held incommunicado. Troops loyal to the plotters surrounded the Russian Parliament building in Moscow, but Boris Yeltsin, president of the Russian Republic, and a majority of the legislators refused to capitulate, declaring their support for Gorbachev.

When the leaders of the coup decided not to use force, the conspiracy collapsed. Eight were arrested and one committed suicide in captivity. Gorbachev rushed to the scene to take command, but Yeltsin had permanently upstaged him. The president of what used to be the Soviet Union belatedly resigned from the CPSU but to no avail. In December 1991 Yeltsin led the way in the creation of the Commonwealth of Independent States (CIS), which allied his Russian Federation with the Ukraine and Belarus (previously Byelorussia). Within a month eleven former Soviet republics had joined the CIS. All the while, the Bush administration maintained an official position of neutrality, although Washington quietly supported first Gorbachev and then Yeltsin. The United States promised economic aid to the Commonwealth but only if its leadership continued down the road toward democracy and free enterprise.

Tiananmen Square

The Bush administration was similarly circumspect in its dealings with Communist China. As the Chinese tasted the prosperity that trade with the West brought, and the World War II generation of leaders passed from the scene, China appeared to be following the path taken by the former Soviet Union. Unfortunately for Washington and Beijing, militant students in China were not willing to wait. In early May 1989 thousands of protestors gathered in Tiananmen Square before the mausoleum containing Mao's embalmed body. The young people erected a huge papier-mâché "Goddess of Liberty" and demanded democratic reform. As the month came to a close, Deng Xiaoping, Mao's successor, declared martial law, banned television crews from the square, and ordered the army to disperse the protestors. A number of reporters and photographers managed to remain on the scene, however, and beginning June 3 they recorded the Tiananmen "massacre" as government troops machine-gunned students and tanks rolled over defenseless protestors. Deng jailed the survivors and purged from his regime those who had sympathized with the pro-democracy movement.

The wave of outrage that swept the United States during the Tiananmen Square massacre proved to be relatively weak. The Bush administration con-demned Beijing for its repression and temporarily suspended sales of military and nonmilitary items. The following month, however, he dispatched National Security Advisor Brent Scowcroft to China to assure Deng and his associates that relations would return to normal as soon as the controversy died down.

The Panamanian Invasion

Though the Bush administration kept its distance from the ongoing civil con-flicts in Nicaragua and El Salvador it decided to send troops into Panama in late 1989. That small impoverished country had been ruled since the 1960s by the brutal and corrupt dictator, General Manuel Noriega. During the 1980s Noriega had angered the Reagan administration by simultaneously funneling aid to the contras and working undercover for Fidel Castro. Moreover, in 1988 two Florida grand juries indicted Noriega on charges that he participated di-rectly in the smuggling of drugs into the United States, that he accepted bribes for allowing Panamanian banks to launder drug money, and that he actually permitted Colombians to manufacture drugs in Panama. All the while, the Panamanian dictator had remained in the pay of the CIA.

Not long after George Bush took the oath of office as president, General Noriega cancelled the results of presidential elections that he failed to control and proclaimed himself "maximum leader." In mid-December President Bush approved "Operation Just Cause," and two weeks later twenty-seven thousand marines landed in Panama. Troops loyal to Noriega held off the marines for several days but then capitulated. The U.S. command installed Guillermo Endara as president and shipped Noriega back to Florida to stand trial for vio-lating American drug laws. Operation Just Cause had taken the lives of twenty-four U.S. soldiers, 139 Panamanian Defense Force troops, and at least three hundred Panamanian civilians.

Aggression in the Middle East: The Gulf War

Equally as popular with the American people and more justifiable on economic and strategic grounds than Panama was the Bush administration's decision to go to war with Iraq in early 1991. On August 2, 1990, Iraqi military strongman Saddam Hussein sent a large military force into tiny, oil-rich Kuwait. Hussein declared that Iraq was merely reclaiming what was its own. Kuwait, bordering

Iraq to the south, had been part of Iraq prior to the Paris Peace Conference of 1919. The real motivations behind the invasion were money and power, however. Hussein needed money to pay debts incurred during a long, bloody war with Iran; control of Kuwait's oil fields would satisfy that need and give Iraq a much larger say in the determination of world oil prices. Also, domination of Kuwait would provide easy access to the Persian Gulf.

The Bush administration responded to the invasion of Kuwait promptly and vigorously. Declaring that "this will not stand" and comparing Saddam Hussein to Adolf Hitler, President Bush began assembling a multinational coalition capable of driving Iraqi troops out of Kuwait. The factors that underlay that decision were several. Washington feared that Hussein would not stop with Kuwait, and in fact the Iraqi dictator began massing troops along the border with Saudi Arabia shortly after the takeover of Kuwait. In addition, a fully armed and oil-rich Iraq posed a potential threat to Israel, America's chief ally in the region. Rumors were already rampant that the Iraqi leader, an outspoken champion of the Palestinian cause, was building nuclear weapons, and it was well known that he had used poison gas against the Kurdish minority in his own country. But the real motivating force behind the war with Iraq was oil. If Hussein was allowed to keep Kuwait, he would control a quarter of the world's proven oil supplies; if he succeeded in overrunning Saudi Arabia, that figure would double. At that point he would be able to determine the price of oil, driving it through the ceiling if he wished, destroying the economies of America, Western Europe, and Japan.

Most members of the U.N. and all members of the Security Council favored military action. Britain, Saudi Arabia, and twenty-six other nations agreed to furnish troops while the Soviet Union and China quietly acquiesced in the decision to use force. With this wide-ranging support, the Bush administration launched "Operation Desert Shield" and within weeks had a seven hundred thousand-troop army, navy, and air force stationed in northern Saudi Arabia and the waters around Kuwait.

In November 1990 President Bush shifted the focus of the coalition's mission. The White House announced that "Operation Desert Storm" had as its goal nothing less than the liberation of Kuwait, and the U.N. Security Council set a date of January 15, 1991, for Hussein to evacuate his troops or face attack. When the deadline for an Iraqi pullout from Kuwait passed, Chairman of the Joint Chiefs of Staff Colin Powell authorized the commander of Desert Storm, General H. Norman Schwarzkopf, to initiate hostilities. For a month American, French, and British fighter-bombers attacked strategic targets within Kuwait and Iraq. On February 24 some 550,000 allied troops, 250,000 of them from the United States, crossed into Kuwait. Saddam promised the "Mother of All Battles," but the Iraqi Army and Air Force were no match for allied technology and firepower. After liberating Kuwait, Schwarzkopf drove ground troops into southern Iraq. In less than one hundred hours the battle was over. At a cost of 136 American lives, the coalition had smashed the Iraqi war machine, killing an estimated hundred thousand soldiers in the process (see Figure 30–2).

During the Gulf War Saddam Hussein rained Scud missiles down on Israel in an effort to draw that nation into war, thus destroying the U.S.-led coalition. Here a Scud explodes over Jerusalem.

FIGURE 30–2
The Persian Gulf War, 1991

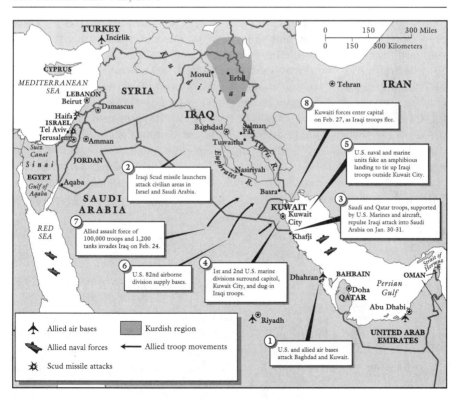

0   150   300 Miles
0   150   300 Kilometers

TURKEY
⚓ Incirlik

CYPRUS

MEDITERRANEAN
SEA   **LEBANON**   **SYRIA**
Beirut ⊗
Haifa ⚓ ⊗ Damascus
ISRAEL
Tel Aviv ⚓
Jerusalem ⊗ ⊗ Amman
Suez
Canal   **JORDAN**
Sinai
EGYPT ⚓ Aqaba
Gulf of
Aqaba   **SAUDI**
ARABIA
RED
SEA

Mosul ⊗ Erbil

Kurdistan

⊗ Tehran   **IRAN**

IRAQ
Baghdad ⊗ Salman
Pak
Tuwaitha ⊗
Nasiriyah

Basra ⊗

KUWAIT
⊗ Kuwait
City
Khafji

Dhahran ⚓   **BAHRAIN**
⊗ Doha   *Persian*
QATAR   *Gulf*
Abu Dhabi ⊗
UNITED ARAB
EMIRATES

OMAN

Strait of Hormuz

⚓ Riyadh

8 — Kuwaiti forces enter capital on Feb. 27, as Iraqi troops flee.

5 — U.S. naval and marine units fake an amphibious landing to tie up Iraqi troops outside Kuwait City.

2 — Iraqi Scud missile launchers attack civilian areas in Israel and Saudi Arabia.

3 — Saudi and Qatar troops, supported by U.S. Marines and aircraft, repulse Iraqi attack into Saudi Arabia on Jan. 30-31.

7 — Allied assault force of 100,000 troops and 1,200 tanks invades Iraq on Feb. 24.

6 — U.S. 82nd airborne division supply bases.

4 — 1st and 2nd U.S. marine divisions surround capitol, Kuwait City, and dug-in Iraqi troops.

1 — U.S. and allied air bases attack Baghdad and Kuwait.

✈ Allied air bases   ▨ Kurdish region
⚓ Allied naval forces   ← Allied troop movements
✻ Scud missile attacks

The Gulf War did much to restore America's shaky self-confidence. Despite deficits, lingering internal division, loss of power vis-à-vis Germany and Japan, the United States had been able to project its power quickly and decisively into an area vital to its strategic and economic interests. The nation seemed to have learned the lessons of Vietnam. The military insisted that the political objectives behind Desert Storm be clearly defined before they agreed to a military option. Once at war, the U.S.–led coalition applied maximum pressure and did not waver from the stated objectives of the operation—the liberation of Kuwait and the destruction of the Iraqi military forces threatening Saudi Arabia. The Bush administration formally consulted Congress, and then once hostilities began, kept a tight leash on the press.

WILLIAM J. CLINTON

THE ELECTION OF 1992

In the wake of the Gulf War George Bush basked in the national limelight, but his popularity proved fleeting. A prolonged economic recession began in July 1990, the sharpest if not the longest since the Great Depression. In December alone the nation's largest corporations—Xerox, General Motors, and IBM—cut their workforces by one hundred thousand. By 1992 the economy had lost more than 2 million jobs, and nineteen states were technically in a state of depression. The more the nation sank into the economic doldrums, the more confused the president seemed to become. At one point he acknowledged that "people are hurting" and then in the next breath declared that "this is a good time to buy a car." Commentators began to compare Bush with Herbert Hoover, a man still widely perceived to have been insensitive to or ignorant of the suffering caused by the Great Depression, but the president remained unperturbed. He believed that his victories in Panama and the Middle East would carry him to victory in 1992. Many commentators and most Republicans agreed with him. After fending off a challenge from former Nixon aide and right-wing ideologue, Patrick Buchanan, Bush was easily renominated by the GOP in the summer of 1992.

Bill Clinton

Democratic chances for recapturing the White House shrank when the only candidate of truly national stature, New York Governor Mario Cuomo, decided not to run. That left the door open for forty-five-year-old William Jefferson Clinton, the governor of Arkansas. Clinton hoped that his educational credentials, his intelligence, and his Kennedyesque good looks and capacity for self-effacement would offset the disadvantages of being from a rural, underdeveloped state. After graduating from Georgetown University in Washington, DC, where he supported himself by working in the mailroom of Senator J. William Fulbright, Clinton secured a Rhodes Scholarship to Oxford and then matriculated at Yale Law School. While there, he persuaded one of his brightest classmates, Hillary Rodham, to forsake the power corridors of the Northeast and return with him to Arkansas. At thirty-two years of age in 1979, Clinton became the youngest governor in the country, and he served continuously in that capacity with one two-year hiatus until his nomination for the presidency in 1992.

As his prospects for election or appointment to a national post increased, Clinton worked to position himself as a centrist. Beyond recommending a massive aid package for the former Soviet Union and anticipating cuts in the defense budget, the Arkansan neglected foreign policy and concentrated on domestic issues. He rejected the Reagan-Carter contention that government was the problem and argued that it simply had to be made more responsible to the needs of the people. Convinced that he would do anything to win—which was true—and that he could reattach lost constituencies such as the South and ethnic, working-class, middle Americans to the party—which was only partially true—Democrats gave him the nomination at their national convention in New York in August.

Clinton was an indefatigable campaigner; he immediately took the fight to Bush, homing in on pocketbook issues. Hillary Rodham Clinton, an independent, intelligent, and well-informed lawyer whose campaign specialties were health care and family abuse issues, was a definite plus. But there were negatives. For his efforts to be all things to all people and for his periodic lack of candor, the Democratic nominee became nicknamed "Slick Willie" by his enemies. Tales of his womanizing dogged him as governor and followed him on the presidential campaign trail. Clinton's forthright opposition to the Vietnam War probably won him more support than it lost, but evidence that he had dodged the draft damaged him with veterans' groups and conservatives in general.

H. Ross Perot

With Clinton's negatives and Bush's apparent unwillingness or inability to address the economic downturn, the way was open for the independent candidacy of H. Ross Perot. A millionaire data processing company executive and friend of Richard Nixon's, Perot criticized both political parties for not addressing real issues such as deficit reduction. His self-made image, his credentials as a political outsider, and his attacks on Congress and the president struck a responsive chord with a public tired of a government mired in perpetual gridlock. By July Perot had pulled even with the two major party candidates in the polls. But then, under attack from Republicans for his opposition to the Gulf War and his pro-choice views on abortion, Perot suddenly quit. Two months later, responding to appeals from his disillusioned supporters, he reentered the race, but his credibility had been irreparably damaged.

Demonstrating once again that except in time of war, pocketbook issues always take precedence over matters of foreign policy, American voters elected

Bill Clinton president. He captured 43 percent of the popular vote to Bush's 38 percent and won in the electoral college by a vote of 370 to 168. Perot failed to carry any states but tallied 19 percent of the popular vote, the best showing by a third-party candidate since 1912. In 1992 voters were worried about the future, about joblessness, about America's loss of competitiveness, about a government that was at the same time intrusive and irrelevant. Clinton won because he and his wife appeared to be smart, competent, and devoted to the public interest. With large Democratic majorities in both houses of Congress, the stage was set for the country to address social and economic issues that had gone begging for a quarter century.

A CALL FOR RECONCILIATION

In the midst of a gala inaugural celebration, Bill Clinton delivered his maiden address as president. Black poet and Arkansas native, Maya Angelou, preceded him and spoke of a new day. In his well-received speech, Clinton promised to end the deadlock and drift in government; he emphasized the need for change and called for "a new season of American renewal." The government, he declared, should be returned to "those to whom it belongs," that is, to those who lived outside the Washington, DC, beltway. "Today a new generation raised in the shadow of the Cold War assumes new responsibilities in a world warmed by the sunshine of freedom but threatened still by ancient hatreds and new plagues," he observed. The nation should act to redress social and economic grievances at home and protect its legitimate interests abroad, but it should move cautiously, carefully, wisely. Clinton would prove to be more cautious than anyone anticipated. Within two years political cartoonist Garry Trudeau, in his comic strip *Doonesbury*, would portray the president as a waffle.

DOMESTIC ISSUES

Environmentalism in the 1990s

The Bush-Quayle administration's insensitivity to environmental matters had played a role in the election. Even those who wanted to use the nation's natural resources for fun and profit feared the laissez-faire approach the Republican party had followed during the 1980s. Clinton's vice president, Albert Gore of Tennessee, was the author of the environmental manifesto *Earth in the Balance* and was named to head the administration's "green team." Gore and company promised to do nothing less than reverse federal policy and in the process boost energy efficiency, preserve wetlands, and reduce global warming.

Even before the election Congress had begun to assert itself. The Energy Policy Act of 1992 included incentives for renewable energy, established efficiency standards for appliances and experimented with nonpetroleum fuel in some of the government's vehicles. In the far Northwest environmentalists clashed with logging companies and local communities over the Endangered

Species Act. That measure gave the federal government power to protect habitats occupied by designated endangered species. In 1993 President Clinton named biologist Jack Ward Thomas to head the U.S. Forest Service, which regulated logging in national forests. Environmentalists were delighted because Thomas had once headed a scientific team which had called for banning timber cutting in some federal forests in the Northwest to protect the spotted owl.

Gays in the Military

During the campaign Clinton and his wife, Hillary, had made no effort to hide their liberalism on the major social issues of the day: gay rights, abortion, and equal rights for both women and African Americans. No issue was more emotional or controversial than that of gays in the military. On political if not moral and philosophical grounds the issue was a no-win affair. Gays and lesbians constituted less than 5 percent of the total population according to a 1994 study, and some of those who normally would support gay rights as a civil liberty were troubled by what they perceived to be an environment which subjected individuals to involuntary intimacy.

Instead of waiting until the end of his administration to take up the issue of gays in the military, Clinton led off with it. On January 21 the president instructed Secretary of Defense Les Aspin to draw up an executive order lifting the ban on homosexuals within the armed forces. The Joint Chiefs of Staff, supported by organizations such as the Veterans of Foreign Wars and the American Legion, protested vigorously. After President Clinton met with Senator Sam Nunn (D–Georgia), chairman of the Armed Services Committee, the administration announced what it termed "an honorable compromise." Under the "don't ask, don't tell" policy, recruiters were prohibited from inquiring about an individual's sexual orientation. Homosexuals could not be banned from the military for being homosexuals as long as they remained celibate while they were in the service. The honorable compromise was a political disaster, offending both liberals and conservatives.

A Pro-Choice President

Clinton was equally forthright and politically more astute in championing abortion rights. Two days after his inauguration, the president signed a series of executive orders reversing his predecessor's policies. No longer were doctors working in federally funded clinics forbidden to give advice on abortion; military hospitals were allowed to perform abortions; and funds for U.N. population programs which encompassed abortion were restored.

The election of a pro-choice president coupled with opinion polls showing that a majority of Americans were pro-choice if not pro-abortion seemed to galvanize radicals in the pro-life movement. On March 8, 1993, the Supreme Court declined to revive an invalidated Louisiana law which would have prohibited almost all abortions in the state. Following the firebombing in February of an abortion clinic in Texas, David Gunn, a gynecologist, was shot to death by a pro-life activist outside an abortion clinic in Pensacola, Florida. The director of Rescue America, Don Treshman, described the shooting as "unfortunate" but added: "The fact is that a number of mothers would have been put at risk by him and over a dozen babies would have died at his hands."

Health Care Reform

One of Clinton's first acts as president was to appoint his wife, Hillary, to head a task force charged with reform of the health care system. Following a period of intense study and debate, the administration unveiled its plan to the public in September 1993. In a televised address the president announced that universal health insurance was "the most urgent priority" facing the country.

At the center of the president's proposals was the formation of regional health alliances which would purchase high-quality health care at low cost. In the months that followed, an administration team headed by Mrs. Clinton lobbied the public and Congress in behalf of a system that promised federally guaranteed medical coverage for all citizens. The American Medical Association, insurance companies, and conservatives in general countered with a plan calling for a privately funded system to which all participants were required to contribute. By 1994 the debate, frequently confused, sometimes misleading, always complex had reached a crescendo.

In the end, Congress and the White House proved unable to reach a compromise, even though the Clintons agreed to a privately operated system if it involved universal coverage. Commentators spoke of the "failure" of the Clinton plan, and the perceived inability of the president to deliver on one of his primary campaign pledges helped drive down his popularity in the polls.

Gun Control

America in the 1990s seemed to be a nation enthralled with violence. Motion pictures and television made murder and mayhem seem commonplace. In the nation's inner cities, drug lords killed each other and innocent bystanders with abandon while gangs battled over turf and bragging rights. Middle-class youths in small towns began purchasing guns for protection and as status symbols. For years the issue of gun control had polarized the nation. Advocates pointed to the rising level of violent crime, the casual possession and use of every type of firearm by teens and even subteens, and to the emergence of a culture devoid of respect for human life. Opponents, citing the constitutional right of all citizens to bear arms, insisted that criminals rather than guns commit crimes. Law-abiding Americans had a right to defend themselves; the only thing the criminal underclass respected was the threat of retaliation.

The movement for gun control received an unwelcome boost from a series of violent acts that marred 1993. In September a British tourist was shot dead during an attempted robbery near Tallahassee, Florida, making him the ninth visitor to be murdered in the state that year. In February four agents of the federal Bureau of Alcohol, Tobacco, and Firearms (BATF) died during a raid on the Waco, Texas, headquarters of a religious sect called the Branch Davidians. Following a fifty-one-day siege federal authorities stormed the cult's complex; the inhabitants set their buildings and themselves on fire. In all seventy-two people died.

In the midst of the siege, President Clinton had taken the unprecedented step of speaking out against the National Rifle Association's opposition to gun control. Then on November 30 he signed the Brady Bill, named after James Brady, the former White House press secretary wounded in the assassination attempt on President Reagan in 1981. The legislation imposed a five-day waiting period to enable background checks to be made on would-be gun purchasers. The previous week, the Senate had approved a $22 billion anticrime program that prohibited the sale of handguns to juveniles, banned the sale of semiautomatic assault weapons, and provided for the recruitment of one hundred thousand additional police officers. Despite these breakthroughs, however, guns and violent crime continued to proliferate, threatening to turn America into an armed camp by the end of the century.

A Historic Budget Reversal

Responding to deep-seated public resentment toward bureaucracies and taxes, the Clinton administration moved to cut spending by slimming down the federal government and eliminating wasteful programs, and took advantage of the end of the Cold War by shifting funds from defense to essential social, educational, and anticrime programs. Shortly after taking office, Clinton announced a 25 percent reduction in the White House staff and called upon other agencies to follow suit. His 1994 budget promised to reduce the federal deficit $140 billion by 1997. This target was to be achieved by raising the tax rate on couples making $140,000 and more and single people earning $115,000 and up, and by raising the corporate income tax. The administration's economic program envisaged cuts in the defense budget of $123.9 billion between 1994 and 1998. Secretary of Defense Les Aspin announced the scrapping of Star Wars, and the administration began dismantling or scaling down ninety-two overseas military bases and 129 domestic installations.

FOREIGN AFFAIRS

Multilateralism Restored

In foreign affairs, Bill Clinton had promised, in rather vague terms, to address the problems of the post–Cold War era. The United States, he said, should provide aid to the former Soviet Union to help it down the road to democracy and free enterprise. Indeed, there were Wilsonian overtones to his foreign policy statements. Advancing democracy should be the object of "a long-term Western strategy," he said. At the same time, Clinton emphasized that the focus of future foreign policy would be the global economy. America would have to learn how to compete peacefully with Japan and the German-led European community. And, finally, Clinton seemed to echo former president Jimmy Carter in calling for an American-led campaign to ensure respect for human rights. Indeed, during the campaign he had simultaneously expressed support for the U.S.-U.N. peacekeeping force in Somalia and blasted the administration for not doing more to stop the sectarian conflict then raging in the former Yugoslavia.

Human Rights on Trial: Somalia

Despite its professed sympathy for human rights, the Clinton administration was afraid of becoming bogged down in another Vietnam-type conflict. The new regime inherited a situation, however, in which the United States was already deeply involved. Late in 1992 the Bush administration authorized a U.S.–led but U.N.–sanctioned military intervention into the east African state of Somalia. During the 1980s, first Moscow, then Washington poured weapons into this poor but strategically located nation of 5 million persons in an effort to win the support of dictator Mohammed Siad Barré. When the Cold War ended, he fled, but Somalia teemed with weapons.

What ensued was a civil war between rival clan leaders President Ali Mahdi Mohammed and General Mohammed Farah Aydid that impoverished the country, creating hundreds of thousands of refugees and mass starvation. Although a similar situation existed in Sudan, the American media focused on the swollen bellies and fly-covered corpses in Somalia. The Bush administration caved in to public pressure and on December 3 secured U.N. Security Council approval of military intervention. A week later twenty-eight thousand U.S. troops landed in Mogadishu. The expeditionary force set up a relief network but did not disarm the clansmen who withdrew to await events.

President Clinton was pledged to stay the course in Somalia, and he proved as good as his word. In June 1993 a price of $25,000 was placed on General Aydid's head, but the warlord remained at large. When a U.S. helicopter was shot down by Somali militiamen killing many of its occupants and a further eighteen Americans died in a firefight in October, the United States began to lose heart. During the spring of 1994 the last of the U.S. and U.N. troops withdrew. The military situation remained unresolved, but mass starvation had ended, and the semblance of a national economy had once again emerged in Somalia.

Democracy Returns to Haiti

Like most of its predecessors, the Clinton administration perceived Latin America and specifically the Caribbean basin as the area most vital to the U.S. national interest. The poorest republic in the Western Hemisphere, Haiti had suffered under one military strongman after another throughout the nineteenth and twentieth centuries. With the support of a tiny business and planting elite, these brutal dictators had exploited and oppressed the nation's peasantry. In 1991 the cycle appeared to be broken with the election of Jean-Bertrand

Aristide, a Catholic priest and social activist. Aristide, however, soon ran afoul of the military and the plutocracy. Late in the year he was driven into exile in the United States.

For three years the military regime of General Raul Cedras imposed a reign of terror on Haiti. Paramilitary thugs tortured and killed Aristide supporters and those suspected of opposition to the government. The United States imposed a blockade in an effort to bring down Cedras and restore Aristide to power, but the embargo only further impoverished rural peasants and the urban poor. Finally, President Clinton ordered military intervention. Before U.S. troops could land, however, former president Jimmy Carter persuaded Cedras to step down voluntarily. As a consequence, American troops occupied the country without resistance. Late in 1994 President Aristide returned to Haiti, and that unfortunate republic once again started down the path toward democracy and reform.

Bosnia

In 1991 the Yugoslav Republic had splintered along ethnic and religious lines. With the collapse of the communist regime, the federation, which included the states of Serbia, Montenegro, Croatia, Bosnia-Herzegovina, Slovenia, and Macedonia, broke apart. Slovenia and Croatia declared their independence. When Bosnia-Herzegovina attempted to break away, war erupted between the Serb and Croatian minorities in Bosnia on the one hand and the Bosnian government which was largely dominated by Muslims on the other.

For the next three years tens of thousands of people died as first the Croats and then the Serbs, aided by the army of the Serbian republic under the leadership of nationalist Slobodan Milosevic, secured control of large parts of Bosnia. During these campaigns the Serbs engaged in "ethnic cleansing" in which thousands of Muslims were raped, tortured, and killed. The Muslims and Croats conducted their own ethnic cleansing campaigns but on a much smaller scale. The United Nations inserted some twenty-four thousand peacekeeping troops into the combat zones and negotiated one cease-fire after another only to see all of them fall to the blood-and-soil nationalism of the Balkans. As President Clinton came into office the pressure on him to intervene militarily to relieve the Serbian siege of Sarajevo and to stop the bloodshed in general became intense. He insisted, however, that the Bosnian nightmare was a matter for NATO and the U.N. and that the members of those organizations in closest physical proximity to Bosnia, namely France and Germany, should take the lead.

Privately, the Clinton administration had decided that it would intervene in Bosnia only when and if the parties involved showed a willingness for peace. In 1995, after years of bloody fighting and ethnic cleansing and a crushing economic embargo imposed on Serbia by the U.N., the Serbs, Croats, and Muslims agreed to a cease-fire and to Bosnia-wide elections for a parliament and a three-person presidency. The Dayton Accords (named for the Ohio city where the negotiations took place) were to be backed by a fifty-thousand-person NATO force, including fifteen thousand American troops.

NAFTA

As far as international economics was concerned, Bill Clinton was as committed to free trade and American participation in a global economy as his Republican predecessors. With a great deal of effort he pushed through Congress the North American Free Trade Agreement (NAFTA) which gradually eliminated tariffs and other trade barriers between the United States on the one hand and Canada and Mexico on the other. In fact, the world became increasingly divided into three major economic blocs: the twelve-nation European Community (EC), the U.S.–Canada–Mexico free trade area, and a more fluid Asian development area powered by Japanese capital and featuring minieconomic superpowers such as South Korea, Singapore, and Taiwan. While Clinton facilitated creation of the North American bloc, he turned America increasingly away from Europe and toward the Pacific as American corporations positioned themselves to furnish economic infrastructure to such emerging giants as Communist China and Indonesia.

Thus did the end of the Cold War prove to be a mixed blessing. Though authoritarian and oppressive, communism and Sino-Soviet hegemony had imposed a kind of order on a large part of the world. The disintegration of this empire was replaced in only a very few cases with democracy and a free market system. Without a viable middle class, trained technocrats, capital, and an economic infrastructure, most former communist states found it impossible to move from socialism to capitalism. The attempted transition left huge voids filled by inflation and unemployment. Inevitably, the peoples of Eastern Europe and the former Soviet Union began to turn to nationalism and state socialism if not totalitarianism in a search for minimal security. The task that faced the Clinton administration during its remaining years was formidable: how to use shrinking American power and diminishing resources to combat totalitarianism, promote democracy, and foster human rights while protecting the nation's strategic and economic interests in an increasingly chaotic world.

REVOLT OF THE MIDDLE CLASS

Americans voted for Bill Clinton because they wanted change. But after two years in office, the president had failed to persuade the electorate that he had the will or the vision to change the status quo. That this was more a matter of public perception rather than reality made no difference. Voter turnout for the 1994 mid-term elections was among the lowest on record. Those American voters who did go to the polls were in an angry and defiant mood. The result was a Republican landslide. The GOP captured control of both houses of Congress for the first time in forty years. Speaker of the House Thomas Foley lost, the first holder of that office to go down to defeat since 1862. Not a single

Republican incumbent was ousted. Eleven Democratic governors suffered defeat, including Mario Cuomo of New York, arguably the nation's foremost liberal spokesperson.

Underlying the antigovernment sentiment that culminated in America in 1992 was the decline of the American middle class. During the period between 1945 and 1973 the rich got richer in America but so did the poor. During this period when worker productivity grew by an annual rate of 3 percent, incomes doubled for all working Americans—corporate executives, mail carriers, construction workers, and street cleaners. The vast American middle class could anticipate owning a modest home in the suburbs, complete with backyard and barbeque. Then stagnation set in.

Between 1979 and 1992 the person earning the exact median level income in America suffered a wage cut of about $100 a month. That is, after thirteen years of hard labor the typical member of the middle class in the United States made 4 percent less money. At the same time the rich grew richer. The typical full-time worker in the top third of income earners earned 7 percent more than he or she had in 1979 while the richest 5 percent enjoyed an increase of 29 percent. It was not that America was that much poorer, although productivity did decline during these years, but that income was being unevenly distributed. Inability to realize the American dream bred frustration among the American middle class and they vented their spleens at the polls.

THE REPUBLICAN CONTRACT WITH AMERICA

Leader of the new Republican majority was congressman Newt "Newtron" Gingrich from suburban Atlanta. With a Ph.D. in history and a penchant for futurism, Gingrich had made his way in the world as a partisan hatchetman. Gingrich, who was slated to be the next speaker of the House, Bob Dole, the Senate majority leader designate, and the rest of the GOP had campaigned on their Contract with America. That document, signed ostentatiously on the Capitol steps in September 1991, promised tax cuts for what they called the "middle class"—everyone making $200,000 or less—and a reduction in the capital gains tax. It called for an increase rather than a decrease in defense spending. All this was to be paid for by reductions in the federal bureaucracy and elimination of "nonessential" social programs. In this same vein, the GOP promised to propose an amendment to the Constitution requiring the federal government to present a balanced budget each year. The contract called for term limits, although after their landslide win, the victors announced that they had promised merely to bring the issue to a vote in Congress and not necessarily to support it. Public opinion polls subsequently revealed, however, that only a fraction of the public was familiar with the terms of the contract.

It took only weeks, moreover, for the electorate to sour on the abrasive Gingrich. A number of its supporters began to recoil from the Contract with America, moreover, when they realized that it was their programmatical ox that was to be gored and when they perceived that proposed GOP cuts would be only a monetary drop in the bucket compared to the costs of a tax cut and increased defense spending. There was, moreover, a fundamental philosophical and cultural cleavage in the new Republican majority pitting moralizers, who were concerned about family values and willing to countenance an intrusive government to safeguard them, against traditional conservatives who championed civil liberties, laissez-faire in a pluralistic society, and pragmatic problem solving. Bill Clinton, the most relentless and successful political campaigner since FDR, was down but not out.

THE ELECTION OF 1996

With Newt Gingrich and the Republicans riding high after their success in the 1994 mid-term elections, President Clinton wisely decided to occupy the political middle ground. Sensing that the American people in the end would tire of ideologues and extremists and that they desperately longed for bipartisan cooperation, he set about coopting the Republican program. Clinton pushed through Congress a crime bill which appropriated federal funds for the hiring of 100,000 additional police and shortened the appeals period for death-row inmates. The White House worked with Speaker Gingrich and Senate Majority Leader Bob Dole to hammer out a welfare reform bill that effectively ended AFDC, requiring welfare recipients to work after two years, and terminating all welfare payments after five years. Clinton reduced the federal workforce by 250,000, and partially as a result, the federal deficit fell by 60 percent. Though the president joined with Republicans in pledging to balance the budget by 2002, he locked horns with them over the fiscal 1996 budget which they attempted to use to reduce federal entitlement programs. The deadlock twice caused a temporary shutdown of the government, but in the end the administration won both substantively and politically. It protected Social Security, Medicare, and other benefits and succeeded in portraying the Republicans as insensitive to the needs of the poor and elderly.

There was no question about Clinton's renomination. After 1992 he and Al Gore had gone out of their way to conciliate various factions in the party and to appear to the public as humble listeners rather than as Boy Princes, to quote *Time* magazine. The Republicans struggled as usual with their right wing—the fundamentalists and states' righters who somewhat contradictorily pushed for an absolute ban on abortions and the right to die, prayer in public schools, funding for parochial schools, an absolute right to bear arms, and an end to affirmative action. Representing the GOP center, Senator Bob Dole of Kansas beat back a bid from the ultra-conservative Pat Buchanan. Dole, a decorated and wounded veteran of World War II, was an experienced Washington insider, a skilled negotiator, but a man with little charisma and no real distinctive program. During the campaign, Dole called for a massive tax cut and attempted to capitalize on the personal shortcomings of the president. The Republicans made some headway when it was revealed that Democratic National

Committee fundraiser John Huang had solicited millions from an Indonesian business consortium. The fact that the White House offered a night's lodging in the Lincoln Room to anyone contributing $100,000 or more to the campaign did not help Clinton either.

In the end, however, the public answered Bob Dole's constant campaign refrain, "Who Do You Trust?" by electing Clinton. The incumbent won with 50 percent of the popular vote and 379 electoral votes to Dole's 41 percent and 159 electoral votes. Ross Perot, heading his Reform party, captured only 9 percent and did not score in the electoral college. Clinton won because he appeared to be moderate, effective, and responsive, and because the economy was booming, with inflation, interest rates, and unemployment the lowest for any presidential administration since 1968. He also benefitted from the gender gap; women voted for the president 54 percent to 38 percent. Bill Clinton became the first two-term Democrat since FDR, but the Republicans retained control of both houses of Congress, the first time that had happened since 1930. The message that voters apparently sent in 1996 was that they wanted the bridge to the twenty-first century to be built on bipartisanship.

SUGGESTED READINGS

Peter Arno, *Against the Odds* (1992).
Rick Atkinson, *Crusade: The Untold Story of the Persian Gulf War* (1993).
Dallas A. Blanchard, *The Anti-Abortion Movement* (1994).
Michael Duffy, *Marching in Place: The Status Quo Presidency of George Bush* (1992).
Ken Gross, *Ross Perot: The Man Behind the Myth* (1992).
James Davidson Hunter, *Culture Wars: The Struggle to Define America* (1991).
David Maraniss, *First in His Class: A Biography of Bill Clinton* (1995).
Philip Shabecoff, *A Fierce Green Fire: The American Environment Movement* (1994).
James B. Stewart, *Blood Sport: The President and His Adversaries* (1996).
Gale Stokes, *The Walls Came Tumbling Down: The Collapse of Communism in Eastern Europe* (1993).

QUESTIONS FOR DISCUSSION

1. Discuss the importance of the "character issue" in the 1988 presidential campaign.
2. What was George Bush's approach to the problem of the national debt? How effective was it?
3. Describe the Bush administration's use of Supreme Court appointments to further the goals of the new right. What effect did the Clarence Thomas nomination have on the feminist movement?
4. Discuss the causes of the Gulf War and account for America's success in that conflict.

5. Assess Bill Clinton's qualifications for the presidency. Was his election in 1992 a watershed in American political history? Explain.
6. What were the principal domestic and international issues confronting Clinton after his election?
7. Identify the main features of the Contract with America and assess its influence on American politics.

COPYRIGHTS AND ACKNOWLEDGMENTS

Quarterly, 3d Ser., 38, no. 4 (October 1981), pp. 561–564, 570–600. Reprinted by permission of the Institute of Early American History and Culture.

Lloyd E. Ambrosius. From Lloyd E. Ambrosius, "Woodrow Wilson's Health and the Treaty Fight: 1919–1920," *International History Review* 9, no. 1 (February 1987), pp. 73–84. Reprinted by permission of the publisher.

John C. Burnham. From John C. Burnham, "The Progressive Era Revolution in American Attitudes Toward Sex," *Journal of American History* 59, no. 4 (March 1973), pp. 885–903. Reprinted by permission of the publisher.

Bruce Cumings. From *Child of Conflict: The Korean-American Relationship, 1943–1953*, by Bruce Cumings. Copyright © 1983. Reprinted by permission of the University of Washington Press.

Adam Fairclough. Excerpted from Adam Fairclough, "The Preachers and the People: The Origins and Early Years of the Southern Christian Leadership Conference, 1955–1959," *Journal of Southern History* 52, no. 3 (August 1986), pp. 403–440. Copyright © 1986 by the Southern Historical Association. Reprinted by permission of the Managing Editor.

James J. Flink. From *The Car Culture* by James J. Flink. Copyright © 1975 by The MIT Press. Reprinted by permission of the publisher.

Robert Griffith. Reprinted from *The Politics of Fear: Joseph R. McCarthy and the Senate*, 2nd edition, by Robert Griffith (Amherst: The University of Massachusetts Press, 1987). Copyright © 1970 by Robert Griffith, and Introduction to the Second Edition copyright © 1987 by Robert Griffith. Footnotes from the original were omitted in this reprinting.

Alonzo L. Hamby. Excerpted from *Liberalism and Its Challengers: From F. D. R. to Bush*, 2/e, by Alonzo L. Hamby. Copyright © 1992 by Oxford University Press, Inc. Reprinted by permission.

Waldo Heinrichs. Excerpted from *Threshold of War: Franklin D. Roosevelt and American Entry into World War II* by Waldo Heinrichs.

Copyright © 1988 by Waldo Heinrichs. Reprinted by permission of Oxford University Press, Inc.

George McT. Kahin. From *Intervention* by George McT. Kahin. Copyright © 1990 by George McT. Kahin. Reprinted by permission of Alfred A. Knopf, Inc.

Maury Klein. This article is reprinted from (9) pages of the October 1971 issue of *American History Illustrated*, with the permission of Cowles History Group, Inc. Copyright American History Illustrated magazine.

Leon F. Litwack. From *Been in the Storm So Long* by Leon F. Litwack. Copyright © 1979 by Leon F. Litwack. Reprinted by permission of Alfred A. Knopf, Inc.

John L. Offner. Reprinted from *An Unwanted War: The Diplomacy of the United States and Spain over Cuba, 1895–1898*, by John L. Offner. Copyright © 1992 by the University of North Carolina Press. Used by permission of the publisher.

Thomas G. Patterson. Excerpted from *Major Problems in American Foreign Relations*, Vol. 2, 4th edition, eds. Thomas G. Patterson and Dennis Merrill (Lexington, MA: D. C. Heath, 1995). Copyright © 1995. Reprinted by permission of the publisher.

Robert S. Salisbury. From Robert S. Salisbury, "The Republican Party and Positive Government: 1860–1890," *Mid-America: An Historical Review* 68 (January 1986), pp. 15–34. Reprinted by permission of Mid-America.

Lynn Y. Weiner. From Lynn Y. Weiner, "Reconstructing Motherhood: The La Leche League in Postwar America," *Journal of American History* 80, no. 4 (March 1994), pp. 1357–81. Reprinted by permission of the publisher.

Richard White. From "The Altered Landscape: Social Change and the Land in the Pacific Northwest," by Richard White, in *Regionalism and the Pacific Northwest*, ed. William G. Robbins et al. (Corvallis: Oregon State University Press, 1983). Reprinted by permission of the author.

INDEX

....

B